MAIN CURRENTS IN AMERICAN THOUGHT

D1539135

Main Currents in American Thought

AN INTERPRETATION OF AMERICAN LITERATURE

FROM THE BEGINNINGS TO 1920

Vernon Louis Parrington

VOLUME ONE · 1620-1800

The Colonial Mind

VOLUME TWO · 1800-1860

The Romantic Revolution in America

VOLUME THREE · 1860-1920

The Beginnings of Critical Realism
in America

HARCOURT, BRACE & WORLD, INC.

NEW YORK / CHICAGO / BURLINGAME

TO THE MEMORY

OF

J. ALLEN SMITH

SCHOLAR TEACHER DEMOCRAT GENTLEMAN

Omnium Amicus erat
qui
Justiciam ament.

FOREWORD

IT is with a certain feeling of temerity that I offer the present study of a field of American letters which has been pretty largely neglected. That feeling springs from no sense of the slightness of the materials treated of, or their remoteness from present-day interests. To one who has dwelt for any length of time amidst the polemics of colonial debate, a conviction of the greatness of the issues and the intellectual honesty and masculine vigor of the disputants, comes home with compelling force. The subjects with which they dealt are old-fashioned only in manner and dress; at heart they were much the same themes with which we are engaged, and with which our children will be engaged after us. The feeling springs rather from a sense of the complexity and many-sidedness of the materials, with their ramifications into theology and politics and economics, and with backgrounds that conduct to remote origins in European systems of thought; and it is quickened by the realization that the interpretation here offered, runs in many points counter to that frequently given. The point of view from which I have endeavored to evaluate the materials, is liberal rather than conservative, Jeffersonian rather than Federalistic; and very likely in my search I have found what I went forth to find, as others have discovered what they were seeking. Unfortunately the *mens aequa et clara* is the rarest of attributes, and dead partisanships have a disconcerting way of coming to life again in the pages of their historians. That the vigorous passions and prejudices of the times I have dealt with may have found an echo in my judgments is, perhaps, to be expected; whether they have distorted my interpretation and vitiated my analysis is not for me to determine.

Of the present volume portions of Book One have already appeared in a much abbreviated form in the *Cambridge History of American Literature*, and certain passages of Book Three have appeared in *Selections from the Connecticut Wits*, of the *American Authors Series;* and I am indebted to the courtesy of G. P. Putnam's Sons and of Harcourt, Brace and Company for the privilege of reprinting them here. My obligations

i

to many students are too great to be adequately acknowledged in
a few words; they appear at large in the footnotes. I find myself
especially indebted to the critical historians who for the past score
of years have been working with such fruitful results in the Revolutionary and Constitutional periods of our development. Without
the assistance of their searching investigations the difficulties in
the way of understanding those complex times would have proved
insuperable. To the sane and acute scholarship of my friend and
colleague, Prof. Edward McMahon, and to the generous counsel
and encouragement of the late Prof. J. Allen Smith, I am under
particular obligations; but in those instances in which I may
unwittingly have gone astray, the fault is mine. In a study dealing with so long a period of time and with such diverse and difficult
fields, I can scarcely hope to have escaped the many traps laid for
the unwary. Perhaps I should add that the seeming neglect, in
the present volume, of southern backgrounds, has resulted from
the desire to postpone the detailed consideration of the mind of
the South to a later volume.

V. L. P.

Seattle, January 1, 1926

INTRODUCTION

I HAVE undertaken to give some account of the genesis and development in American letters of certain germinal ideas that have come to be reckoned traditionally American—how they came into being here, how they were opposed, and what influence they have exerted in determining the form and scope of our characteristic ideals and institutions. In pursuing such a task, I have chosen to follow the broad path of our political, economic, and social development, rather than the narrower belletristic; and the main divisions of the study have been fixed by forces that are anterior to literary schools and movements, creating the body of ideas from which literary culture eventually springs. The present volume carries the account from early beginnings in Puritan New England to the triumph of Jefferson and back-country agrarianism. Volume II concerns itself with the creative influence in America of French romantic theories, the rise of capitalism, and the transition from an agricultural to an industrial order; and Volume III will concern itself with the beginnings of dissatisfaction with the regnant middle class, and the several movements of criticism inspired by its reputed shortcomings.

Such a study will necessarily deal much with intellectual backgrounds, and especially with those diverse systems of European thought that from generation to generation have domesticated themselves in America, and through cross-fertilization with native aspirations and indigenous growths, have resulted in a body of ideals that we reckon definitively American. In broad outline those germinal contributions were the bequests successively of English Independency, of French romantic theory, of the industrial revolution and *laissez faire*, of nineteenth-century science, and of Continental theories of collectivism. Transplanted to American soil, these vigorous seedlings from old-world nurseries took root and flourished in such spots as proved congenial, stimulating American thought, suggesting programs for fresh Utopian ventures, providing an intellectual sanction for new experiments in government. Profoundly liberalizing in their influence, they gave impulse and form to our native idealisms, and contributed largely to the outcome of our social experience. The child of two continents, America can be explained in its significant traits by neither alone.

In the present volume, I have examined with some care the bequests of seventeenth and eighteenth-century Europe to the colonial settlements, and in particular the transplanting to America of old-world liberalisms. In the main those liberalisms derived from two primary sources, English Independency and French romantic theory, supplemented by certain contributions from English Whiggery. From the first came the revolutionary doctrine of natural rights, clarified by a notable succession of thinkers from Roger Williams to John Locke, a doctrine that destroyed the philosophical sanction of divine right, substituted for the traditional absolutism the conception of a democratic church in a democratic state, and found exemplification in the commonwealths of Rhode Island and Connecticut. But unfortunately the liberal doctrine of natural rights was entangled in New England with an absolutist theology that conceived of human nature as inherently evil, that postulated a divine sovereignty absolute and arbitrary, and projected caste divisions into eternity—a body of dogmas that it needed two hundred years' experience in America to disintegrate. From this clash between a liberal political philosophy and a reactionary theology, between English Independency and English Presbyterianism, sprang the broad features of the struggle that largely determined the course of development in early New England, with which Book One is concerned.

Book Two deals with new beginnings from the raw materials of European immigrants, in other colonies than New England, who came hither singly and unorganized, and took immediate imprint from the new environment, creating during the eighteenth century the great body of yeomanry that was to determine in large measure the fate of America for a hundred years or more. It was to these scattered and undistinguished colonials that French romantic theory was brought by a group of intellectuals in the later years of the century, a philosophy so congenial to a decentralized society that it seemed to provide an authoritative sanction for the clarifying ideals of a republican order, based on the principle of local home rule, toward which colonial experience was driving. Exploring the equalitarian premises of the doctrine of natural rights, it amplified the emerging democratic theory by substituting for the Puritan conception of human nature as vicious, the conception of human nature as potentially excellent and capable of indefinite development. It asserted that the present evils of society are the consequence of vicious institutions rather than of depraved human nature; and that as free men and equals it is the right and duty of citizens to re-create social and political institutions to the end that they shall further social justice, encouraging the good in men rather than perverting them to evil. Romantic theory went further and provided a new economics and a new sociology. Since the great desideratum is man in a state of nature, it follows, according to the Physiocratic school, that the farmer is the ideal citizen, and agriculture the common and single source of wealth; and that in consequence the state should hold the tillers of the soil in special regard, shaping the public policy with a primary view to their interests. And since social custom is anterior to statutory laws, since the individual precedes the state, government must be circumscribed in its powers and scope by common agreement, and held strictly to its sole concern, the care of the social well-being. The political state, rightly conceived, must be reckoned no other than a great public-service corporation, with government as its responsible agent.

But while French romantic theory was spreading widely through the backwoods of America, providing an intellectual justification for the native agrarianism, another philosophy, derived from English liberalism of the later eighteenth century, was taking possession of the commercial towns. Realistic and material rather than romantic and Utopian, it was implicitly hostile to all the major premises and ideals of the French school. It conceived of human nature neither as good nor bad, but as acquisitive; and it proposed to erect a new social and political philosophy in accordance with the needs of a capitalistic order. It was concerned with exploitation and the rights of trade, rather than with justice and the rights of man. Its aspirations were expressed in the principle of *laissez faire*, and in elaborating this cardinal doctrine it reduced the citizen to the narrow dimensions of the economic man, concerned only with buying in the cheapest market and selling in the dearest. It would reduce the political state to the rôle of policeman, to keep the peace. With humanitarian and social interests, the state must not intermeddle—such functions lie outside its legitimate sphere. An expression of the aspirations of trading and

speculating classes, it professed to believe that economic law—
by which term it glorified the spontaneous play of the acquisitive
instinct—was competent to regulate men in society, and that if
freedom of trade were achieved, all lesser and secondary freedoms
would follow.

In the light of such over-seas bequests to the American venture,
the choice of materials for the present volume is predetermined.
The line of liberalism in colonial America runs through Roger
Williams, Benjamin Franklin, and Thomas Jefferson. The first
transported to the new world the plentiful liberalisms of a great
movement and a great century; the second gathered up the sum
of native liberalisms that had emerged spontaneously from a
decentralized society; and the third enriched these native liberalisms with borrowings from the late seventeenth-century natural-
rights school and from French romantic theory, engrafting them
upon the vigorous American stock. Over against these protago-
nists of liberalism must be set the complementary figures of John
Cotton, Jonathan Edwards, and Alexander Hamilton, men whose
grandiose dreams envisaged different ends for America and who
followed different paths. The Carolinian Seeker and the Jacobean
theocrat, the colonial democrat and the colonial Calvinist, the
Physiocratic republican and the capitalistic financier, embody
in concrete form the diverse tendencies of primitive America;
and around these major figures lesser ones will group themselves,
parties to the great struggle of those early years, the eventual
outcome of which was the rejection of the principles of monarchy
and aristocracy, and the venturing upon an experiment in republicanism continental in scope.

That our colonial literature seems to many readers meager and
uninteresting, that it is commonly squeezed into the skimpiest of
chapters in our handbooks of American literature, is due, I think,
to an exaggerated regard for esthetic values. Our literary historians have labored under too heavy a handicap of the genteel
tradition—to borrow Professor Santayana's happy phrase—to
enter sympathetically into a world of masculine intellects and
material struggles. They have sought daintier fare than polemics,
and in consequence mediocre verse has obscured political speculation, and poetasters have shouldered aside vigorous creative
thinkers. The colonial period is meager and lean only to those
whose "disedged appetites" find no savor in old-fashioned beef

and puddings. The seventeenth century in America as well as in England was a *saeculum theologicum,* and the eighteenth century was a *saeculum politicum.* No other path leads so directly and intimately into the heart of those old days as the thorny path of their theological and political controversies; and if one will resolutely pick his way amongst the thorns, he will have his reward in coming close to the men who debated earnestly over the plans and specifications of the Utopia that was to be erected in the free spaces of America, and who however wanting they may have been in the lesser arts, were no mean architects and craftsmen for the business at hand. The foundations of a later America were laid in vigorous polemics, and the rough stone was plentifully mortared with idealism. To enter once more into the spirit of those fine old idealisms, and to learn that the promise of the future has lain always in the keeping of liberal minds that were never discouraged from their dreams, is scarcely a profitless undertaking, nor without meaning to those who like Merlin pursue the light of their hopes where it flickers above the treacherous marshlands.

CONTENTS

CONTENTS

BOOK III: LIBERALISM AND THE CONSTITUTION

PART I

The Agrarian Defeat—1783–1787

BOOK ONE: LIBERALISM AND PURITANISM

LIBERALISM AND PURITANISM

COMMON report has long made out Puritan New England to have been the native seat and germinal source of such ideals and institutions as have come to be regarded as traditionally American. Any critical study of the American mind, therefore, may conveniently seek its beginnings in the colonies clustered about Massachusetts Bay, and will inquire into the causes of the pronounced singularity of temper and purpose that marked off the New England settlements from those to the south, creating a distinctive New England character, and disciplining it for later conquests that were to set a stamp on American life. The course of its somewhat singular development would seem from the first to have been determined by an interweaving of idealism and economics—by the substantial body of thought and customs and institutions brought from the old home, slowly modified by new ways of life developing under the silent pressure of a freer environment. Of these new ways, the first in creative influence was probably the freehold tenure of landholdings, put in effect at the beginning and retained unmodified for generations; and the second was the development of a mercantile spirit that resulted from the sterility of the Massachusetts soil, which encouraged the ambitious to seek wealth in more profitable ways than tilling barren acres. From these sources emerged the two chief classes of New England: the yeomanry, a body of democratic freeholders who constituted the rank and file of the people, and the gentry, a group of capable merchants who dominated the commonwealth from early days to the rise of industrialism. And it was the interweaving of the aims and purposes of these acquisitive yeomen and gentry—harmonious for the most part on the surface, yet driving in different directions—with the ideal of a theocracy and the inhibitions of Puritan dogma, that constitutes the pattern of life to be dealt with here. The Puritan and the Yankee were the two halves of the New England whole, and to overlook or underestimate

the contributions of either to the common life is grossly to mis-
interpret the spirit and character of primitive New England.
The Puritan was a contribution of the old world, created by
the rugged idealism of the English Reformation; the Yankee
was a product of native conditions, created by a practical
economics.

PART ONE: THE PURITAN HERITAGE
1620–1660

CHAPTER 1

ENGLISH BACKGROUNDS

I

THE body of thought brought to America by the immigrant Puritans, and which gave a special cast to the New England mind, may be summed in a phrase as Carolinian liberalism. It was the confused bequest of a hundred years of English idealism, struggling with the knotty problems of a complex society in transition from the old static feudal order to the modern capitalistic; and it took a particular form and received a narrow ideology from the current ecclesiastical disputes concerning the nature and governance of the true church. It was exclusively a product of the Reformation, unleavened by the spirit of the Renaissance. But though English Puritanism was wholly theological in its immediate origins, it gathered about it in the century and a half of its militant career all the forces of unrest fermenting in England. Economics and politics joined hands with theology; the center of gravity of the total movement tended to sink lower in the social scale; and in the end all England was involved in the great struggle.

In its deeper purpose Puritanism was a frank challenge of the traditional social solidarity of English institutional life by an emergent individualism, and far-reaching social readjustments followed inevitably in its train. If the evolution of modern society is conceived of as falling into two broad phases, the disintegration of a corporate feudal order into unregimented individual members of society, and the struggles of those free individuals to regroup themselves in new social commonwealths, the historical significance of English Puritanism may perhaps become clear: it was one of the disruptive forces that disintegrated the traditional solidarity of church and state by creating a revolutionary philosophy of individual rights that purposed to free the individual, both as Christian and subject, from subjection to a fixed corporate status.

5

The sixteenth century had announced the great doctrine of the priesthood of all believers, and the seventeenth century was engaged in adapting the forms of social and political institutions to that revolutionary principle. It was concerned to discover a new system of social organization that should adjust equitably the rights of the individual to the needs of the political state and to society. To that end the whole theory of the origin and functions of the political state must come in for review, and a new conception of the rights of the individual subject-citizen must be evolved.

This is the sufficient explanation of the close interweaving of theology and politics that marked the broadening movement of English Puritanism. Unless one keeps in mind the social forces that found it convenient to array themselves in Puritan garb, the clear meaning of it all will be lost in the fogs of Biblical disputation, and some of the ablest men the English race has ever bred will be reduced to crabbed theologians involved in tenuous subtleties and disputing endlessly over absurd dogmas. But tenacious disputants though they certainly were, pursuing their subtleties into the last refuge and cranny of logic, those Puritan dogmatists were very far from being vain practitioners of eccentricity. It is the manner and dress and not the matter of their argument that is strange; and if we will resolutely translate the old phrases into modern equivalents, if we will put aside the theology and fasten attention on the politics and the economics of the struggle, we shall have less difficulty in discovering that the new principle for which those old Puritans were groping was the later familiar doctrine of natural rights; and the final end and outcome of their concern for a more equitable relation of the individual to society, was the principle of a democratic commonwealth, established in the conception of political equalitarianism. Here are liberalisms in plenty to reward the search for the inner core of Puritanism. There was gunpowder packed away in Luther's doctrine of the priesthood of all believers, and the explosion that resulted made tremendous breaches in the walls of a seemingly impregnable feudalism. An intellectual like Roger Williams, who had thought his way resolutely to the logical outcome of the reforming principles, could not fail to be reckoned a firebrand by his generation. The doctrine of "thorough" was dangerously revolutionary.

If the economics of England had not been in a state of flux during the century following the accession of Elizabeth, the Puritan movement would not have moved forward by successive stages to the explosion of the Civil War. But because, as later in France, a rising economic order was restive under the restrictions of an outworn order, the Puritan protest found capable allies at hand, and supported by the money and arms of the commercial interests, it passed under the control of the latter and set about the great business of making England over in accordance with the new plans and specifications. On the whole it is no mistake to regard the Puritan revolution as primarily a rebellion of the capable middle class, whose growing trade interests demanded a larger measure of freedom than a paternal king and a landed aristocracy were willing to grant; and its significant contributions to the modern world were the two systems it did so much to further: the system of capitalism and the system of parliamentary government. From the Puritan conception of the stewardship of talents came a new ethic of work that provided a sanction for middle-class exploitation, by supplanting the medieval principle of production for consumption with the capitalistic principle of production for profit; and from the conception of the dignity of the individual came the sanction for the self-pride of the merchant that sustained him in his encounters with a domineering aristocracy. A prosperous merchant who accounted himself a son of God and who was persuaded that he was fighting for a freer England was no mean foe to be awed by the rustlings of a Cavalier. The London burgesses were the backbone of Puritanism in the days before the movement passed into the extremer form of Independency and was taken over by the sectarian radicals; and the Presbyterian middle-phase of Puritanism spread widely amongst the middle class throughout central and southern England. But in unloosing the traditional social bonds Puritanism awakened aspirations that in the end proved hostile to the middle-class program. It created bitter partisan divisions; it set the social underling and the aristocrat apart from the middle-class core, and created those major political parties that have since carried on the parliamentary struggle. Inevitably it sharpened class alignments, and the reactions of those alignments vitally affected the development of New England. The struggles in Massachusetts can scarcely be understood unless they are set against the greater struggles then going forward in England.

The three parties that emerged from the theological disputes, Anglican, Presbyterian, and Independent, followed, in the main, broad social cleavages and corresponded roughly to the later political divisions of Tory, Whig, and Democrat. The first stoutly upheld the absolutist principle in church and state. It stood for Bishop and King. Numbering probably a large majority of the English people, and led by the hereditary masters of England, it was dominated by the feudal spirit of corporate unity. It believed that social order, the loyal subjection of subject to ruler, was possible only through a coalescence of church and state. The subject-citizen was born into the one as he was born into the other, and owed allegiance both to his spiritual and temporal overlords. Authority, whether in church or state, was of divine origin, and Bishop and King were the Lord's anointed, answerable for their stewardship only to God. The second party was a compromise between aristocracy and democracy. It substituted the principle of elective stewardship for divine right. Rejecting the absolutism of the hierarchy, it turned to the system newly brought over from Geneva, a system that retained the principle of a state church, but which yielded control of the parish to the eldership, a select body of the best and wisest chosen by the laity, with final authority in doctrine and discipline vested in the synod. It drew its support largely from the London burgesses, but with a considerable following of country gentlemen. As the party developed it tended to merge with the nascent capitalism, restricted the doctrine of natural rights to property rights, and prepared the way for the later Whiggery of Pitt, or capitalistic imperialism. The third party was more or less consciously democratic in spirit and purpose, the expression of the newly-awakened aspirations of the social underling. Numbers of rebellious individualists appeared who wanted to be ruled neither by bishop nor elder, but who preferred to club with the like-minded and set up an independent church on a local, self-governing basis. They took literally the command of Paul, "Come out from among them, and be ye separate, saith the Lord, and touch not the unclean thing." That only was the true church, they asserted, which withdrew from all communion with sinners and rejected the authority of a sinful state; and so they called themselves Separatists.

Separatism, quite evidently, was the extreme left wing of the total Puritan movement, concerned to explore all the logical deductions from the revolutionary premise of the Reformation. It was the final expression of the disintegrating gospel of individualism implicit in the doctrine of the priesthood of all believers. Its unworldly sincerity was as uncompromising as its unworldly scripturism. Not finding sanction for them in the Bible, it rejected the established ecclesiastical authorities, and laid rude hands on the garments of Mother Church. Counsels of social expediency were accounted as dust in the balance against the explicit commandment of the Lord to separate from the sins of the world; and clinging to the text of the Scripture the Separatist was led straight to the conception of a Christian democracy. If the true church was a Congregation of the Saints, and if the Saints were equal in the sight of God, why should not the principle of equality prevail in the rule of the congregation? And if it were a brotherhood in Christ, owning allegiance to the King of Kings, by what Scriptural right did profane authorities exercise control over the tender consciences of the brethren? The autonomy of the congregation was a fruitful conception, certain to appeal to vigorous natures; and out of the loins of Separatism came a numerous and often ungainly progeny that greatly scandalized the conservative Carolinian: Anabaptist, Digger, Fifth-Monarchy man, Quaker, Seeker, Congregationalist—to name only a few—each following his particular path to his divinely sanctioned Utopia, regardless of social ties, denying the worth of social conformity. Imperious individualists, the Separatists were certain to prove an offense to all respectable folk, who demanded in the name of common sense that they be put down.

It was the doctrines of Separatism, quite as much as the principle of the independency of the congregation, that aroused the fierce antagonism of Presbyterians equally with Anglicans. In the main those doctrines did not derive from John Calvin; they go back rather to Wittenberg than to Geneva, to the principles of Luther and certain German sects. The Anabaptist and the Digger, clearly, were of German descent and of somewhat ancient lineage, offspring of late medieval communism and other primitive enthusiasms. The Quaker was a mystic, sprung from the New Testament, who denied the Scriptural validity of a Hebraized Calvinism and a hireling priesthood, and accepted the Holy Spirit as the sole guide to his feet. The Seeker, on the other hand, who may perhaps be regarded as the completest expression of Puritan radicalism, was an open-minded questioner who professed to have found no satisfactory answer to his inquiry concerning the nature of the true church, and was awaiting further light. The Seekers were individuals rather than a sect, few in numbers yet greatly influential, men like Roger Williams, Sir Harry Vane, Cromwell, and perhaps Milton, outstanding figures of a great age, who embodied the final results of Puritan idealism before it was submerged by the Restoration.

During the long years of rule by divine right under the first Stuarts, the Anglicans held the Puritan unrest in strict control. Nevertheless a hundred years of debate and changing economic conditions had rendered the attempt to erect in England a counterpart of the French centralized state, no better than an anachronism. The Presbyterian opposition grew rapidly in numbers and prestige, and the early years of the Long Parliament marked the culmination of Presbyterian power. The bishops were overthrown and the elders were in a fair way to seize control of England. But unfortunately for Presbyterian hopes, the radical sects thrown up out of the war clashed with the moderates and finally broke with them; whereupon followed the "root and branch" revolution that had been long preparing. The left-wing Independents secured control of the army and set about the work of erecting a government that should be a real commonwealth of free citizens. The voice of the underling, for the first time in English history, was listened to in the national councils, for the excellent reason that his sword was drawn to enforce his demands. But they were too small a minority to leaven the sodden mass of a people long subject to absolutist rule. The psychology of custom was against them. They could strike down their armed enemies in the field, but they could not liberate the minds of men unfit to be free. Militant Puritanism was overthrown and its idealisms became the jest of every drunken tapster in London. But fortunately, not before its political principles, long obscured by theology, were sufficiently clarified to be laid open to the common understanding of Englishmen. Out of the debates around the camp fires of the army had come a new philosophy that rested on the principle that the individual, both as Christian and citizen, derives from nature certain inalienable rights which every church and every state is bound to respect. This far-reaching doctrine of natural rights, to the formulation of which many thinkers had contributed and which received later its classic form from the pen of Locke, was the suggestive contribution of Puritanism to political theory, with the aid of which later liberals were to carry forward the struggle.

II

The far-reaching liberalisms implicit in the rejection of a hierarchical organization of the church were to discover no allies in the major premises of the system of theology accepted generally by the English Puritans, and by them transported to New England. Calvinism was no friend of equalitarianism. It was rooted too deeply in the Old Testament for that, was too rigidly aristocratic. It saw too little good in human nature to trust the multitude of the unregenerate; and this lack of faith was to entail grave consequences upon the development of New England. That the immigrant Puritans brought in their intellectual luggage the system of Calvin rather than of Luther must be reckoned a misfortune, out of which flowed many of the bickerings and much of the intolerance that left a stain on the pages of early New England history.

Two divergent systems of theology, it will be remembered, were spreading through northern Europe during the years of the Reformation, systems that inevitably differentiated in consequence of certain variations of emphasis in the teachings of Luther and Calvin. Both thinkers accepted the adequacy of the Scriptures to all temporal needs, but Luther was at once more mystical and more practical than Calvin, deriving his inspiration chiefly from the New Testament, discovering the creative source of the Christian life in the spiritual union of the soul with Christ, and inclining to tolerance of differences of opinion amongst believers; whereas Calvin was ardently Hebraic, exalting righteousness above love, seeking the law in the Old Testament and laying emphasis on an authoritarian system. The one was implicitly individualistic, the other hierarchical in creative influence. The teachings of Luther, erected on the major principle of justification by faith, conducted straight to political liberty, and he refused to compromise or turn away from pursuing the direct path. If one accepts the doctrine of the priesthood of all believers, one can scarcely refrain from following Luther in his conception of Christian liberty. If the mystical union of the soul with Christ has superseded all lesser loyalties by a higher and more sacred, the enjoyment of spiritual freedom must be reckoned the inalienable right of every child of God. Neither the political state nor the official hierarchy can justly coerce the individual conscience. "One thing and one thing only," said Luther in his *Treatise on Christian Liberty*, "is necessary for Christian life, righteousness and liberty." And from this he deduced the conclusion that "neither pope nor bishop nor any other man has the right to impose a single syllable of law upon a Christian man without his consent; and if he does, it is done in the spirit of tyranny." [1] Clearly, this is the spirit of uncompromising individualism that would eventually espouse the principle of democracy in church and state; and it was their native sympathy with such liberalism that led the radical Separatists to turn more naturally to Luther than to Calvin. Many of the differences that set Roger Williams so greatly apart from the New England brethren must be traced to the Lutheran origins of his thinking.

There was scant room in the rigid system of John Calvin for such Christian liberty. The Genevan thinker was a logician rather than a philosopher, a rigorous system-maker and dogmatist who knotted every argument and tied every strand securely into its fellow, till there was no escape from the net unless one broke through the mesh. To the formalist who demanded an exact system, and to the timid who feared free speculation, the logical consistency of Calvinism made irresistible appeal; and this perhaps suffices to explain its extraordinary hold on the rank and file of middle-class English Presbyterians. More original minds might break with it—men like Richard Hooker and Roger Williams and Vane and Milton—but academic thinkers and schoolmen, men whom the free spaces of thought frightened and who felt safe only behind secure fences, theologians like John Cotton and his fellows, made a virtue of necessity and fell to declaiming on the excellence of those chains wherewith they were bound. How narrow and cold was their prison they seem never to have realized; but that fact only aggravated the misfortunes that New England was to suffer from the spiritual guidance of such teachers. In seeking for an explanation of the unhappy union of a reactionary theology and a revolutionary political theory,

---

[1] See "The Babylonian Captivity," in *Works*, Vol. II, p. 233 (Philadelphia, 1915).

Harriet Beecher Stowe suggested in *Poganuc People* that the Puritan immigrants were the children of two different centuries; that from the sixteenth century they got their theology, and from the seventeenth their politics, with the result that an older absolutist dogma snuggled down side by side in their minds with a later democratic conception of the state and society. In England the potential hostility between Calvinist dogma and individual freedom was perceived by the more liberal Separatists, but in America it was not till the rise of the Revolutionary disputes of the next century that Calvinism was discovered to be the foe of democratic liberalism and was finally rejected. It is a fruitful suggestion, and in its major contention that the liberalisms implicit in the Puritan revolution were ill served by a reactionary theology, it is certainly in harmony with the facts.

That Calvinism in its primary assumptions was a composite of oriental despotism and sixteenth-century monarchism, modified by the medieval conception of a city-state, is clear enough today to anyone who will take the trouble to translate dogma into political terms. In recasting the framework of the old theology, Calvin accepted as a sovereign conception the idea of God as arbitrary and absolute will—an august *Rex regum* whose authority is universal and unconditioned; and this conception he invested with Hebraic borrowings from the Old Testament. The principle of absolutism, indeed, he could scarcely have escaped. It came down to him through the Roman Empire and the Roman Church, from the ancient oriental despotisms, and it was interwoven with all the institutions and social forms against which the Reformation was a protest. But unhappily, instead of questioning the principle, he provided a new sanction for it and broadened its sway, by investing it with divine authority and erecting upon it a whole cosmology. That the ancient Hebrew thinkers, in seeking to give concrete form to their speculations on the nature of Jehovah, should have made use of the political ideas of primitive Israel, that they should have used all the wealth of oriental imagery in describing the regal attributes of their God, was inevitable. They knew only oriental potentates, and so Jehovah became a greater Ptolemy, with Cherubim and Seraphim, Angels and Principalities and Powers, duly ranked about the heavenly throne. So saturated with monarchical and caste ideas is the Old Testament, that it is almost impossible today to put the old phrasing out of mind, and we talk as naturally of the Kingdom of God as did the men of that older world who knew no other political phraseology. Calvin rejected the individualism of Luther and followed in the footsteps of older thinkers like Duns Scotus. The monarchical principle was everywhere gaining ground in Europe. He had a lawyer's love of law, and law reposed in the absolute will of the prince. Hebraize this fact, erect a cosmology upon it, and we have the vital principle of Calvinism.

From this cosmic absolutism, that conceived of God as the stable Will sustaining the universe, binding together what otherwise would fly asunder, two important corollaries were derived: the universality of the moral law, and the necessity of divine judgment. From the former flowed that curious association of God's will with natural causes which induced Cotton Mather, when suffering from toothache, to inquire what sin he had committed with his teeth, and which left no free spaces or non-moral impulses in the lives of men. From the latter flowed the doctrine of theological determinism. If time is embedded in the eternity of God's mind, if to Him past and future are here and now, foreknowledge is an inevitable divine attribute, and predestination is only a finite way of expressing God's understanding of how human fate works itself out. Ally this doctrine of determinism with the Biblical account of the fall of man, and the doctrine of the elect becomes the theological complement of the class prejudices of the times. Bred up in the current aristocratic contempt for the sodden mass of the people, Calvinist theologians easily came to regard them as stupid, sensual, veritable children of Adam, born to sin and heirs of damnation. Only the elect shall be saved. That there was a remnant in Israel whom God had chosen, Isaiah had long before pointed out; and the doctrine of the remnant was confirmed for Calvinism by the sinful herd whose daily actions testified to their lost estate.

According to such a theology, the individual clearly is in no effective sense a free soul. There is no room for the conception of human perfectibility. The heritage of natural freedom was long since cast away by the common forefather; and because of the pre-natal sin which this act entailed on all mankind, the natural man is shut away eternally from communion with God. He is no better than an oriental serf at the mercy of a Sovereign Will that is implacable, inscrutable, the ruler of a universe predetermined in all its parts and members from the foundation of the earth. Except for the saving grace of divine election, which no human righteousness can purchase, all must go down to the everlasting damnation that awaits the sons of Adam. In the eyes of such a philosophy it is sheer impertinence to talk of the dignity and worth of the individual soul. Men are no other than the worms of the dust. The boon of eternal life is not included in God's enumeration of natural rights; it is a special grant from the Lord of the universe who is pleased to smile on whom he is pleased to smile. In the hard words of Paul, "Therefore hath he mercy on whom he will have mercy, and whom he will he hardeneth." And those on whom he hath had mercy are his Saints, and they are gathered into his church, as the free city-states had risen out of the muck of medieval despotism. They are the stewards of his righteousness and are called to the great work of rulership on earth that God's will may be done and righteousness may prevail over iniquity.

It was an ambitious program, and so long as the Presbyterian party maintained its ascendency in England it endeavored to thrust its Calvinism down every throat, no matter how unwelcome; but with the passing of power from its hands, and the growth of a common-sense spirit of toleration, Calvinistic dogma lost its authority and the minds of Englishmen turned to more humane philosophies. In New England, on the other hand, by virtue of a rigid suppression of free inquiry, Calvinism long lingered out a harsh existence, grotesque and illiberal to the last. In banishing the Antinomians and Separatists and Quakers, the Massachusetts magistrates cast out the spirit of liberalism from the household of the Saints.

CHAPTER II
THE TRANSPLANTING OF IDEAS

I

The Great Migration, it will be remembered, fell in the time of the Laudean reaction, when the Presbyterian Utopia seemed remote and the hopes of the Puritan dreamers were fallen low. The Boston leaders quitted England ten years before Charles summoned the Long Parliament, and twelve before the royal standard was unfurled at Nottingham. The armed struggle for supremacy was far below the horizon, and the outlandish philosophies that later sectaries were to propagate so diligently were as yet little known in the land. The generous grain of liberal thought was still in the milk, its fruitful doctrines unripened. The immigrant gentlemen who came to Massachusetts Bay were Puritan Anglicans who professed a hearty love for the mother church and were no friends to the principle of Separatism. They were potential Presbyterians who rejected alike the Arminianism of Laud and the autocracy of the bishops. It is reasonable to suppose that as strict Calvinists, trained in the ordinances as well as in the doctrine of the French theologian, they came hither with the conscious purpose of setting up the complete Genevan discipline in the new world. If such was their plan—and certainly before their coming over they seem not to have entertained any thoughts of Separatism—it received a check from the Plymouth influence and the Puritan experiment was turned aside from the path of its natural development.

It was a somewhat curious misadventure that was to entail unforeseen consequences. Except in matters of doctrine Pilgrim and Puritan consorted ill together. Their social antecedents were as unlike as their views on political and religious institutions. The intellectual leaders of Plymouth—whatever may be said of the London adventurers who joined the Holland group—had been nurtured in Elizabethan radicalism. They were Brownist-Separatists of plebeian origins, who had arrived at their conception of the true church from a close study of Biblical texts, with perhaps

16

some admixture of Anabaptist influence, nearly a generation before the Stuarts came with their divine-right theory. During their years on the continent they lived remote from the current of events in England, and under the guidance of the tolerant Robinson they had been disciplined in the theory and practice of primitive Congregationalism. On their removal to America they brought with them a consciously democratic church order, that met their simple needs and had taken shape from the experience of daily life. This democratic model of church government was spontaneously supplemented by the plantation covenant of civil government drawn up aboard ship, which was to serve as the organic law of the new commonwealth. Two cardinal principles— which at bottom were one—thus found their way to New England in the *Mayflower* the principle of a democratic church and the principle of a democratic state. When ten years later the Boston leaders were faced with the problem of erecting a social order, they accepted the Plymouth model of Congregationalism, but rejected the plantation covenant. They saw no need for the latter as they were already provided with an organic law. The charter which Winthrop was insistent upon bringing with them out of England was asserted to be the constitution of the commonwealth and, meticulously interpreted, was to determine largely the form and scope of the new political state. It was construed to grant a legal sanction to government; but as the charter of a Carolinian trading company it quite naturally restricted authority to the managing heads, and granted powers to its directors that were useful in managing trade ventures but might easily become intolerable if interpreted as the organic law of a commonwealth. With such enlargement of powers the directors of the corporation would constitute a political oligarchy. There was a striking difference, certainly, between the covenant of Plymouth and the charter-constitution of Massachusetts Bay, and a political philosopher could readily enough have foreseen the course that events would take in the Puritan commonwealth, given the men and the ideals in control.

II

THE PURITAN PRESBYTERIAN

To make clear what was involved in the attempt to adapt the Plymouth model of church government to the charter commonwealth, it is necessary to consider somewhat particularly the body of prejudice and principle brought to the new world aboard the *Lady Arbella*, as the Puritan contribution to New England. The capable leaders who created the early institutions of Massachusetts Bay colony were Jacobean Englishmen of middle station, half-way between the aristocrat and the burgess, with certain salient characteristics of both. Fashioned by a caste society, they transported to the little commonwealth an abundant heritage of class prejudice. They aspired to be reckoned gentlemen and to live in the new world as they had lived in the old, in a half feudal state, surrounded by many servants and with numerous dependents. They honored rank, were sticklers for precedence, respected class distinctions, demanded the hereditary rights of the gentry. They had been bred up in a static order where gentlemen ruled and the people obeyed, and they could not think in terms of the Plymouth plantation covenant, subscribed by all heads of families. To the modern reader of his journal there is something almost childish in Winthrop's insistence on public deference to his official position and his grief when the halberd-bearers refused to provide the usual formality to his little progresses. But if they aspired to be rated as gentlemen, there was much also of the burgess nature in them. They were potential capitalists, eager to accumulate ample landholdings, keen to drive a bargain, given to trade and with as sharp an eye to the main chance as any London merchant. The community of goods that marked the early days of Plymouth they disliked so greatly as to account it almost sinful. In the infancy of the settlement they entered upon an active mercantile life, building their ships for the West Indian trade, joining in the fisheries off the Newfoundland coast, venturing far in pursuit of gain. Active, capable men, excellent administrators rather than speculative thinkers, stewards of the public interests as well as their own, they would take it ill to have their matured plans interfered with by busybodies and incompetents. Their own counsel sufficed them and they wanted no help from outsiders.

Endow such men with religious zeal; let them regard themselves as particular repositories of righteousness; give them a free hand to work out their program unhampered by rival policies; provide them with a handbook elaborated in complete detail by a master system-maker; and the result was certain. Their Utopia must be a close-knit church-state, with authority reserved to the aristocracy of Christian talent. It is needless to inquire whether a definite conception of a theocracy was in their minds before their coming over; some such order was clearly implicit in their religious fervor, their Hebraic theology, their Genevan discipline, their aristocratic prejudices. They might nominally accept the Plymouth model of church-government, but they would meddle with democracy in church and state no more than necessity compelled. Circumstances, as well as their own promptings, would counsel quite an opposite course. They were engaged in a difficult and perilous undertaking, begirt by wilderness enemies, and fearful of hostile interference by the home authorities. If the venture were to survive, a drift towards centralization of power was as natural as it was inevitable. The common security would not suffer any dispersion of forces or domestic bickerings over authority. Dissatisfied members must be held in subjection and dangerous swarmings from the mother-hive must be prevented. The principle of Separatism was too disruptive to insure cohesive solidarity; the parts must be welded into a protective whole; and for such business what ideal was more efficient than a theocracy with Jehovah substituted for King Charles—not openly and seditiously, but quietly, in the hearts of the people. The historian need not wander far in search of the origin of the theocratic principle; it is to be found in the self-interest of the lay and clerical leaders. Ambitious men could not have devised a fitter means to weld together the two groups of magistrates and ministers, and endow their charter prerogatives with divine sanction. The Stuarts were bunglers at the business in comparison with Winthrop and Cotton. But if they worked the metal to such shape as they chose we must not forget that it had been well heated in the smithy of John Calvin. Overlook that fact and the theocracy becomes incredible.

There are perhaps sufficient grounds to assume that some plan of minority control was worked out before the migration took place. The preliminary discussions in England had been long and the terms of the charter were carefully seen to. By its provisions the right of franchise rested with the freemen of the corporation, in number about a hundred and ten. Of the total body of freemen it was known that only a small group would undertake the venture; probably fewer than a score came over with the emigrants, and through removals and death the number was speedily reduced to about a dozen. This handful of freemen constituted the court, and chose the governor, deputy governor, and the assistants or magistrates. These latter were to number eighteen according to the charter provision; but with more offices than eligible candidates, the number was necessarily reduced, and six assistants with the governor came to be reckoned a quorum of the court with sovereign powers.[1] It was a patriarchal undertaking, and to Carolinian gentlemen there was nothing unusual or unjust in a handful of leaders exercising plenary powers over the lives and fortunes of two thousand members of the commonwealth. If the charter could not have been construed as granting such powers, it is reasonable to assume that they would not have entered upon the business. The lay leaders were practical men. They had ventured their estates in the hope of bettering their condition, both spiritual and material, and with their personal fortunes at stake they were in no mind to intrust the fate of the undertaking to other hands than their own. They loved power quite as much as did the ungodly, and accounting themselves God's stewards they reckoned it sin not to use it in his name. As Puritans they would not keep a weather eye on the majority will. God did not speak in the Scriptures through majority votes; his chosen were a minority, the remnant in Israel.

A further sanction was at hand. If these Hebraized Englishmen created a close corporation and ruled magisterially, if the order in the new church-state was inquisitorial and stern, it was in strict conformity with the teachings and example of Calvin. Men deeply read in the *Institutes*, familiar with the Genevan Ordinances and the practices of the Consistory, were not likely to discover in them any lessons in democratic toleration. Righteousness may be fearfully relentless, and John Calvin had been a tyrant on principle. Iron-willed and masterful, he had risen to power in the turbulent city-state of Geneva in sixteenth-century fashion. A few splotches of blood on the white garments of the Church did not greatly trouble him. He was never squeamish about ways and means of furthering the Lord's work. He violated the right of refuge to bring to the stake the pantheistic Unitarian Servetus, and he thanked God when the bungling of the executioner prolonged the sufferings of certain others of his victims. The Genevan discipline was rigorous, and the clerical inquisitors were more relentless than the lay. The tyrannies that have been freely charged upon the New England oligarchy are easily explained in the light of the

[1] See James Truslow Adams, *The Founding of New England*, Chapter VI.

Calvinistic Ordinances. There were no whippings or banishments or hangings in early Pennsylvania where Quaker and Lutheran dwelt together in peace if not in fellowship. But they were New Testament men and not out of the Old, like the Saints in Massachusetts Bay. They worshiped a God of love rather than a God of wrath.

Granted the conception on which the theocratic experiment went forward, namely, that Jehovah was the sole lawgiver and the Bible the sufficient statute-book; granted also that these priests and magistrates were stewards of God's will; and the centralization of power in the commonwealth becomes invested with a higher sanction than the terms of the charter. It was an oligarchy of Christian grace. The minister was the trained and consecrated interpreter of the divine law, and the magistrate was its trained and consecrated administrator; and both were chosen by free election of the Saints. If unfortunately the Saints were few and the sinners many, was not that a special reason for safeguarding the Ark of the Covenant from the touch of profane hands? Hence all legislative experiments by annually elected deputies, no matter how exactly those experiments might fall in with the wishes of the majority, were sternly frowned upon or skillfully nullified. Not only were such popular enactments, it was held, too often prompted by the carnal desires of the natural man, but they were no better than an insult to God, as implying the insufficiency of the Scriptures to every temporal need. Unregenerate and sinful men must have no share in God's work. The Saints must not have their hands tied by majority votes. This explains, quite as much as mere love of power, the persistent hostility of the leaders to every democratic tendency. Such institutions as grew up spontaneously out of the necessities of the situation, were sharply hedged about by restrictions. The town meeting, which was extra-legal under the charter, was safeguarded by limiting the right of voting to freemen, except in a few trivial matters; and the more popular deputies, who inclined to become self-willed, were forced to accept the principle of magisterial veto on their actions. When a law was passed, it was purposely left vague as to penalties, in order to give a free hand to the judges to punish as they wished; and it was not till 1641, after much insistence from the representatives of the people, that Ward's Body of Liberties was finally adopted.

Later critics of Puritanism discover in the theocratic experiment of Massachusetts Bay a preposterous attempt to turn back the pages of history, and refashion Englishmen after an ungainly Hebraic pattern. But to the leaders of that experiment it seemed rather a Utopian venture to create in the new world a nobler social order than elsewhere existed. Whether such a society was either possible or desirable, has long since become only an academic question; what is more suggestive is the fact that in spite of some bitterness on the part of a small minority, the stewardship of an oligarchy remained the accepted principle of government in Massachusetts Bay until the vacating of the charter in 1684. That it lingered out so long a life is a testimony to the skillful opportunism of the leaders. They early adopted a strategic policy which the British ministry foolishly refused to adopt a hundred years later; they cautiously undermined any potential disaffection by admitting the wealthiest and most influential to the rights of freemen, thus allying the ambitious and capable members of society with the ruling group, and laying the foundations of a provincial aristocracy, which in the course of time would secularize the government and substitute an economic for a theocratic basis of authority. The loss of the charter only hastened what in the nature of things must have come about eventually.

III

CERTAIN MISTAKES

Skillful as were the theocratic rulers and logical as was their course, it seems plain in the light of later developments that they fell into certain grave mistakes at the very beginning of their work that were to hamper them seriously in after days. Those mistakes were the adoption of the covenant-principle of church organization borrowed from Plymouth, that started the new churches on the road to Congregationalism, and the granting of the land in fee-simple to non-freemen, that was to create an independent yeomanry. Of the two the second was far graver, for it threw the economics of the developing commonwealth on the side of local home rule and provided a substantial foundation for the erection of a democratic opposition to the oligarchy. If the plantation system of Virginia, or the Patroon system of New York, had been adopted, the covenanted church would naturally have followed the path of Genevan Presbyterianism in harmony with the desires of the leaders, and the democratic opposition both in church and state must have been starved into submission. But with the system of small holdings and the development of a vigorous yeomanry, the eventual development of Congregational-ism into a federated group of self-governing churches was pre-determined more rigidly than by any logic of John Calvin. The defeat of the Presbyterian program of the theocrats was implicit in a decentralized land system.

The decision of the Salem church in 1629 to adopt the Plymouth model, and the acceptance of that decision by later churches in Massachusetts Bay, has been abundantly commented upon, but the significance of it has been somewhat inadequately explored.[2] Very likely it was a deep hatred of episcopal rule that opened the mind of Endicott and his fellows to the reasoning of Dr. Fuller of Plymouth, and persuaded them to take this first step towards Separatism; nevertheless as disciples of Calvin, desirous of es-tablishing a Bible commonwealth, they must soon discover that a system centrifugal in tendency and decentralizing in spirit, unless closely restrained, was certain to lead them far from the Canaan of their hopes. Separatism was the negation of a state church, and the rule of the congregation was the negation of an official creed and ecclesiastical unity. If Congregationalism were suffered to develop its democratic potentialities, the leaders must even-tually find themselves in like position with Laud, with schismatics disturbing the orthodox harmony and rending the church from within. The authorities early began to feel, what the Anglican Lechford pointed out in 1641, that the system was dangerously democratic, and the principle of centralizing conformity was set to work. The spirit of Calvin's Consistory was invoked. Under the guise of brotherly counsel, or church fellowship, the principle of consociation was developed, a principle that opened a convenient door to official coercion. Brotherly counsel that comes armed with the weapon of excommunication, that points its argument with the threat of banishment or hanging, is certainly not the pure spirit of Christian fellowship that Congregational historians have chosen to see in the principle of consociation. The most ardent apologist has hard work in discovering the democratic

---

[2] See Williston Walker, *A History of the Congregational Churches in the United States*, Chapter IV.

principle of Congregationalism in the theocratic application of the methods of the Genevan Consistory. The early churches of the theocracy were Presbyterian in spirit and rule, in spite of the official promulgation of the covenant-principle in the Cambridge Platform. Certainly real Separatists like Roger Williams, who suffered from too much brotherly counsel and did not want a Christian fellowship imposed by magistrates, were under no illusions in regard to the coercive spirit that lay behind the principle of consociation.

More open and above board were the successive statutes that effectively nullified the principle of Separatism by erecting an official state church. The law of 1631, restricting the franchise to church members, and the law of 1635, making attendance at church compulsory on all, were followed in 1636 by a law requiring the approval of the magistrates and elders before a new church could be set up, and in 1638 by the institution of a system of state support for the ministry. The principle of the covenant was being pretty effectively whittled away. Equally Presbyterian was the movement for the establishment of a definitive state creed. In consequence of the Antinomian schism effected by the eloquent tongue of Mistress Anne Hutchinson, the first general synod was convened at Newtown in 1637, which sat for four and twenty days and drew up a list of eighty-two heretical opinions, "some blasphemous, others erroneous, and all unsafe," together with "nine unwholesome expressions," which were alleged to be disturbing the peace of the community. Whereupon the synod broke up, the members congratulating themselves "that matters had been carried on so peaceably and concluded so comfortably in all love." How much Christian love was awakened by such brotherly counsels in the heart of Mistress Hutchinson, who was banished and later slain by the Indians, is not revealed, but her sin was made of record as a warning to other schismatics. It was this: "He hath let me distinguish between the voice of my beloved and the voice of Moses," which being interpreted, meant an appeal from the Old Testament to the New, from Mosaic authority to the inner light.

With the promulgation of the Cambridge Platform by the synod of 1646–47, and the acceptance of the Westminster Confession of Faith, the work of creating the organism and creed of an authoritative state-church was completed. According to Williston Walker, the Cambridge Platform "pictures with great clearness the abiding principles of Congregationalism"—the covenant origin of the local church, the autonomy of the congregation, the sole authority of the Bible, and the fellowship of the churches.[3] But it needs the sharp eyes of an apologetic historian to discover the spirit of democratic Congregationalism in a discipline that sanctions the power of the state to intervene in ecclesiastical matters and requires the magistrate to enforce uniformity in creed and worship. "Idolatry, Blasphemy, Heresy, Venting corrupt and pernicious opinions, are to be restrayned and punished by civil authority," the Platform states. "If any church one or more shall grow schismaticall, rending it self from the communion of other churches, or shall walke incorrigibly or obstinately in any corrupt way of their own, contrary to the rule of the word; in such case, the Magistrate is to put forth his coercive power, as the matter shall require." If such be Congregationalism, how greatly have the later churches departed from the primitive faith! To the layman, wanting in insight, it would seem rather to be stark Calvinism, that reveals how completely the coercive spirit of the Ordinances and Consistory of the French theologian had come to dominate the theocratic mind of New England. The reluctant adoption of the Cambridge Platform by the suspicious deputies was the grim prelude to Baptist whippings and Quaker baitings, and the setting-in of the dark days of militant intolerance. "Yourselves pretend liberty of conscience," wrote Roger Williams in 1670, "but alas! it is but self, the great god self, only to yourselves."[4]

But while the covenant principle was thus being effectively whittled away by the theocratic leaders, another principle, likewise of Plymouth origin, was silently working to the overthrow of the theocratic power. Following the example of the Pilgrims the several towns apportioned their lands in fee to their members; and if so acute a political thinker as Daniel Webster is to be trusted, it was from the creative influence of freehold tenure that the political institutions of New England became later democratized. As a disciple of James Harrington, accepting the doctrine of economic determinism as it had been elaborated in the *Oceana*, Webster traced the spontaneous rise of republicanism in New England to the wide diffusion of property; and in the light of his economic interpretation the harsh intolerance of the Cambridge

[3] *Ibid.*, p. 162.
[4] *Narragansett Club Publications*, Vol. VI, p. 133.

Platform is seen to be only the aberration of a passing bigotry. In his anniversary speech at Plymouth he said:

Their situation demanded a parceling out and division of the lands, and it may be fairly said, that this necessary act *fixed the future frame and form of their government.* The character of their political institutions was determined by the fundamental laws respecting property. . . . The property was all freehold . . . alienation of the land was every way facilitated, even to the subjecting of it to every species of debt. The establishment of public registries, and the simplicity of our forms of conveyance, have greatly facilitated the change of real estate from one proprietor to another. The consequence of all these causes has been, a great subdivision of the soil, and a great equality of condition; the true basis, most certainly, of a popular government. "If the people," says Harrington, "hold three parts in four of the territory, it is plain there can neither be any single person nor nobility able to dispute the government with them; in this case, therefore, *except force be interposed,* they govern themselves." [5]

With such a clue it is easier to understand how the liberalisms implicit in Plymouth Congregationalism—its theory of compact in church and state—should find support from an independent yeomanry and eventually rise against the oligarchical rule. The new world would ultimately throw off the old-world repressions and explore the reaches of those generous idealisms that were the bequest of English Separatism. The fathers were engaged in an impossible undertaking. Sanctuaries were close at hand for all dissenters from the theocracy, in Connecticut for the Congregationalists, in Rhode Island for the Separatists, along the Maine frontier for the rebellious individualist. Seated securely in these regions beyond the reach of the Massachusetts magistrates, the diverse liberalisms that were being stifled by the oligarchy prospered and brought forth after their kind. Differentiation in the provinces was the natural counterpart of coercive conformity at the capital; and from very early days New England divided into three diverse groups journeying to their Utopias by different roads. Massachusetts Bay, Connecticut, and Rhode Island, were variant answers to the question of what might be expected to result from the domestication in a free environment of the inchoate idealisms of English Puritanism. How they differentiated themselves from the norm, and why, will perhaps become clearer from an examination of the diverse philosophies of their intellectual leaders.

[5] *Works,* Vol. I, pp. 35–36.

CHAPTER III
THE CHIEF STEWARDS OF THEOCRACY

I

MASTER JOHN COTTON

Priest

THE most authoritative representative in New England of the ideal of priestly stewardship was the excellent John Cotton, first teacher to the church at Boston. While pastor of the church of St. Botolph, in old Boston, he had dreamed of a Utopia of the Saints, unharassed by tyrannous prelates; and while sweetening his mouth with a morsel of Calvin, as he was fond of doing, no doubt he turned over in his mind the plans and specifications of that Utopia. "When God wrappes us in his ordinances," he said in his sermon to Winthrop's company on the eve of its departure from England, "and warmes us with the life and power of them as with wings, there is the land of Promise." Left behind by the departing brethren, he lingered for a while in an England that was every day becoming colder for such as dreamed of other Canaans than Laud's, until urged by many invitations, at the age of forty-six he followed overseas to devote his remaining life to the great work being done there. For more than a score of years he labored faithfully, and the New England which the emigrant generation bequeathed to its sons bore upon it the marks of John Cotton's shaping hand more clearly than those of any other minister.

It is not easy today to judge fairly the life and work of John Cotton. No adequate biography has been written, and his dreams and aspirations lie forgotten in the grave of lost causes and forsaken faiths. But to the Boston freemen of his own day, Master John Cotton was a very great man. Of excellent family and sound university training, he was both a notable theologian and a courteous gentleman. "Twelve hours in a day he commonly studied, and would call that a *scholar's* day," his grandson reported of him. From the hour when he entered Trinity College, Cambridge, at the age of thirteen, to his death in 1652, he was a bookman, and in sheer bulk of acquisition probably no man of his time outdid him.

In Cotton Mather's judgment he was "a most *universal scholar,* and a *living system* of the liberal arts, and a *walking library*." His intellectual equipment was so highly regarded that many excellent persons "believed that God would not suffer Mr. Cotton to err"; and that "if ever there be any considerable blow given to the Devil's kingdom," Master Cotton was the man for the business. No other New England champion was so renowned for "beating out the truth in controversie"; and when he turned to the work of answering Roger Williams, the latter exclaimed: "I rejoice it hath pleased [God] to appoint so able, and excellent, and conscionable an Instrument to bolt the Truth to the bran." But though he was bred in Elizabethan days and entered college in the year when Shakespeare's *Henry IV* and Jonson's *Every Man in his Humour* first appeared on the stage, there is no touch of Renaissance splendor in his crabbed style and ascetic reasoning. That was early washed out of him by the rising tide of Hebraism which was slowly submerging the England of poets and playwrights.

But however much he loved cloistered scholarship, the immediate source of his great influence was the spoken rather than the written word. By the universal testimony of his generation he was "a soul-melting preacher," whose reasoned eloquence swayed congregations trained to solid argumentative discourse. When he ascended the pulpit on Sundays and lecture days, he spoke as a prophet in Israel; and on occasions of public ceremonial, or when dissensions arose touching the polity of church or state, he was summoned by the magistrates to convince with his logic and persuade with his eloquence. The strong-minded Anne Hutchinson was but one of many who chose exile in New England rather than lose the edification of Mr. Cotton's preaching. Good men were drawn to him by his sweetness of temper, and evil men were overawed by his venerable aspect. He seems to have been an altogether lovable person, with white hair framing a face that must have been nobly chiseled, gentle-voiced, courteous, tactful, by nature "a tolerant man" who placidly bore with a dissentient and gladly discovered a friend in an antagonist. If his quiet yielding before opposition suggests that he may have been given to opportunism, or his fondness for intellectual subtleties drew from his grandson the comment "a most excellent casuist," we must not too hastily conclude that he served the cause of truth less devotedly than the cause of party.

For a score of years before his coming over, his position in the rising Puritan party had been honorable. Few among the dissenting ministers were better known, none more esteemed. He had shone as an intellectual light at the university, he had long been pastor of one of the loveliest churches in England, he counted among his friends some of the ablest contemporary Englishmen. To Cromwell he was one "whom I love and honour in the Lord"; to Lord Say and Sele, to the Earl of Warwick, the Earl of Lincoln, and a notable company of Puritan gentlemen, he was a trusted friend and lieutenant; to thousands of the substantial burgesses who were drawing together to form the new Puritan-Whig party, he was "a fixed and conscionable light." That such a leader should have been received with thanksgiving by the Boston congregation was to be expected; that he should have taken high place at once among the members of the Massachusetts oligarchy was equally to be expected. Thenceforth his busy career was no more than a reflection of the ambitions of the theocracy.

Unfortunately his daily contact with narrow-minded and intolerant men gave an unhappy bias to his later career. Cotton seems to have been something of a Puritan intellectual, with an open-minded curiosity that made him receptive to new ideas and tempted him to play with doctrines that were intolerable to his bigoted associates. It was possibly this native sympathy with free speculation that drew him into the camp of Mistress Hutchinson with her doctrine of the inner light. When the schism became serious, dividing the commonwealth into warring camps, Cotton seems to have become frightened and broke with the Boston Antinomians. In this matter he came near to being a shuffler. The Hutchinson trial with its resulting banishments was the turning point of his career in America as it was a crisis in the history of early New England. He was not a man to persecute and harry, nor was he one to stand in isolated opposition to associates whom he respected, and he allowed himself to be coerced by narrower-minded men like Endicott and Dudley. After 1637 the better nature of John Cotton was submerged by the rising intolerance, and "the most tolerant, as he was the ablest of the Massachusetts divines," was brought so low as to defend the meanest and cruelest acts of the oligarchy. He descended to disgraceful casuistry in defense of the first whippings of the Quakers, and he urged the death penalty upon King Philip's son and the enslavement of the remnant of

Philip's tribe, against the plea of John Eliot that "to sell soules for mony seemeth to me a dangerous merchandize." The sins of the oligarchy rest in large measure on the head of John Cotton, and the judgment of the most recent historian of New England must stand:

> With a broader mind and wider vision than any of the other clergy of the colony, he had not the courage to stand alone, beyond a certain point, against their unanimity in intolerance. The higher promptings of his nature were crushed by the united voice of the priesthood, as Winthrop's had been so short a time before, and the noblest of the colony's leaders, lay and clerical, from that time tended to sink to the lower level of their fellows.[1]

An apologist—and whoever has felt the charm of John Cotton's personality easily becomes an apologist—will perhaps find some grounds of excuse for his later conduct. He was in an unhappy position. He was ill at ease in his mind, and his frequent tacking in the face of adverse winds was characteristic of the intellectual who sees all sides of a question. He heartily approved of the theocratic ends that his associates were seeking, and his influential position made him the defender of acts which his better nature must have disapproved. The historian, however, will seek a more adequate explanation in the roots of his environment. The idealism of John Cotton was the fruit of his training, and his theocratic dreams were conditioned by the facts that he was both a Calvinist and a Carolinian gentleman. The fusion of these two influences resulted in the unique political theory of an ethical aristocracy, consecrated to moral stewardship in the state. A lifelong student of Calvin's *Institutes*, he found there a system of social organization that responded to every demand of the theologian and the aristocrat. The very texture and pattern of Cotton's political philosophy is exemplified in such a passage as this, over which he must have brooded much:

> When these three forms of government of which philosophers treat, are considered in themselves, I, for my part, am far from denying that the form which greatly surpasses the other is aristocracy, either pure or modified by popular government; not indeed in itself, but because it very rarely happens that kings so rule themselves as never to dissent from what is just and right, or are possessed of so much acuteness and prudence as always to see correctly. Owing therefore to the vices or defects of men, it is safer and more tolerable when several bear rule, that they may thus

1 James Truslow Adams, *The Founding of New England*, p. 170.

mutually assist, instruct, and admonish each other, and should any be disposed to go too far, the others are censors and masters to curb his excess. This has already been proved by experience, and confirmed also by the authority of the Lord himself, when he established an aristocracy bordering on popular government among the Israelites, keeping them under that as the best form, until He exhibited an image of the Messiah in David.[2]

As a Carolinian gentleman, this was as far as Cotton would go on the path of liberalism. The elders were responsible to God for the spiritual well-being of the people, and the state must aid and not hinder them in their leadership. The doctrine of unlimited popular sovereignty was for him no other than a thistle in the garden of the Lord. The desire for liberty he regarded as the sinful prompting of the natural man, a denial of the righteous authority of God's chosen rulers. If democracy were indeed the best form of government, was it not strange that divine wisdom should have failed to discover the fact? In the history of the chosen people nowhere does God approve the democratic as the best form, but the theocratic; was He now to be set right by sinful men who courted popularity by appealing to the selfishness of depraved hearts? To the scripturist the logic of his argument was convincing:

It is better that the commonwealth be fashioned to the setting forth of God's house, which is his church: than to accommodate the church frame to the civill state. Democracy, I do not conceyve that ever God did ordeyne as a fit government eyther for church or commonwealth. If the people be governors, who shall be governed? As for monarchy, and aristocracy, they are both of them clearly approoved, and directed in scripture, yet so as referreth the soveraigntie to himselfe, and setteth up Theocracy in both, as the best forme of government in the commonwealth, as well as in the church.[3]

If John Cotton, like other Carolinian gentlemen, was a confirmed aristocrat, he was at the same time a social revolutionary, who would substitute an aristocracy of the Saints for the landed aristocracy, and refashion society upon ethical rather than economic lines. At what time the ideal of a Presbyterian Bible commonwealth took shape in his mind, it is impossible to determine; but it was a natural outcome of his most cherished beliefs. A

[2] *Institutes*, Book IV, Chapter XX, Paragraph 8.
[3] "Letter to Lord Say and Sele," in Hutchinson, *History of Massachusetts Bay Colony*, Vol. I, p. 497.

devout scripturist, he accepted the Bible as a rule of universal application, perfect and final. The sufficiency of the Scriptures to all social needs was axiomatic with him; "the more any law smells of man the more unprofitable," he asserted in his draft of laws offered for acceptance by the commonwealth; and at another time he exclaimed, "*Scripturae plenitudinem adoro.*" He chose exile rather than yield to what he regarded as the unscriptural practices of Laud, and now that he was come to a new land where a fresh beginning was to be made, was it not his Christian duty to "endeavour after a *theocracy,* as near as might be, to that which was the glory of Israel, the 'peculiar people'"? The old Common Law must be superseded by the Mosaic dispensation; the citizen of the commonwealth must become the subject of Jehovah; the sovereignty of temporal authorities must serve the higher sovereignty of God.

Holding to such views the duty devolving upon him was plain: to assist the magistrates in checking the dangerous drift towards a democratic organization of church and state, which the new environment encouraged; and to defend the theocratic ideal against all critics. The first he sought to accomplish by creating a more perfect theocratic machinery. As we catch glimpses of him moving tactfully back and forth through the brisk little scenes, he seems always to have a finger in some magisterial affair. Three months after his arrival in Boston he preached a sermon, the purport of which Winthrop noted in his *Journal:*

After much deliberation and serious advice the Lord directed the teacher Mr. Cotton, to make clear by the scripture, that the minister's maintenance, as well as all other charges of the church, should be defrayed out of a stock, or treasury, which was to be raised out of the weekly contribution: which accordingly was agreed upon.[4]

In his first election sermon, preached in the May following, he joined issue with the democratic spirit of the deputies, by supporting a principle which was flagrantly oligarchical:

That a magistrate ought not to be turned into the condition of a private man without just cause, & to be publicly convict, no more than the magistrates may turn a private man out of his freehold, etc., without like public trial, etc.[4a]

Unrebuffed by the rejection of this curious doctrine of the freehold tenure of magistrates, Cotton made a more ambitious

[4] Vol. I, p. 116.   [4a] *Ibid.,* Vol. I, p. 125.

attempt to theocratize the state, when at the October court of 1636, in response to the persistent pressure for a fundamental law, he presented his code for adoption by the commonwealth, the scriptural origin of which is revealed in the title, "Model of Moses his Judicials." Cotton Mather tells of this venture in constitution making, in the following glowing but inaccurate words:

> On Mr. Cotton's arrival he found the whole country in a perplexed & a divided state, as to their *civill constitution*. . . . It was then requested of Mr. *Cotton* that he would, from the laws wherewith God governed his ancient people, form an *abstract* of such as were of a moral and a lasting equity; which he performed as acceptably as judiciously. But inasmuch as very much of an *Athenian democracy* was in the mould of the government, by the royal charter. . . . Mr. Cotton effectually recommended it unto them that none should be *electors*, nor *elected* therein, except such as were *visible subjects* of our Lord Jesus Christ, personally *confederated* in our churches. In these, and many other ways, he propounded unto them an endeavour after a theocracy, as near as might be, to that which was the glory of Israel, the "peculiar people." [5]

Cotton's code was rejected in favor of one, somewhat less Hebraic, prepared by Nathaniel Ward, but he continued to be the chief guide and mentor to the magistrates in political as well as theological matters, and his theocratic philosophy determined in large measure the policy of the oligarchy. To found an Hebraic state in which political rights should be subordinate to religious conformity, in which the magistrates should be chosen from a narrow group, with authority beyond the reach of the popular will, and with the ministers serving as court of last resort to interpret the divine law to the citizen-subjects of Jehovah—this was the great ambition of John Cotton; and the untiring zeal and learned scriptural authority which he dedicated to that ambition justify us in regarding him as the greatest of the New England theocrats. In the categories of the Puritan philosophy of ethical stewardship there was no recognition of the profane doctrine of natural rights. Freedom was the prerogative of righteousness; the well-being of society required that the sinner should remain subject to the Saint. Nowhere does he lay down this principle more unmistakably than in an important state paper:

[5] *Magnalia*, Vol. I, p. 265. Compare with this Cotton's own words: "The law, which your Lordship instanceth (in that none shall be chosen to magistracy amongst us, but a church member) was made and enacted before I came into the country; but I have hitherto wanted sufficient light to plead against it" (Hutchinson, *History of Massachusetts Bay Colony*, Vol. I, p. 498).

Now if it be a divine truth, that none are to be trusted with public permanent authority but godly men, who are fit materials for church membership, then from the same grounds it will appear, that none are so fit to be trusted with the liberties of the commonwealth as church members. For, the liberties of this commonwealth are such, as require men of faithful integrity to God and the state, to preserve the same. . . . Now . . . these liberties are such as carry along much power with them, either to establish or subvert the commonwealth, and therewith the church, which power, if it be committed to men according to their godliness . . . then, in case worldly men should prove the major part, as soon they might do, they would readily set over us magistrates like themselves, such as might . . . turn the edge of all authority and laws against the church and the members thereof, the maintenance of whose peace is the chief end which God aimed at in the institution of magistracy.[6]

This, quite evidently, is the negation of democracy, and it has been freely charged against his reputation by later critics. But in fairness it must be added, that it is equally the negation of the principle of hereditary aristocracy; and to reject the latter was a severer test of his integrity than to deny the former. He wanted neither a democracy nor an aristocracy to control the church-state. "Hereditary honors both nature and scripture doth acknowledge," he argued cautiously in reply to "Certain Proposals made by Lord Say, Lord Brooke, and other Persons of quality, as conditions of their removing to New-England." "Two distinct ranks we willingly acknowledge . . . the one of them called Princes, or Nobles, or Elders (amongst whom gentlemen have their place), the other the people." To the former he willingly accorded the right of rulership so long as they were of approved godliness, faithful to their stewardship. But "if God should not delight to furnish some of their posterity with gifts fit for magistracy, we should expose them rather to reproach and prejudice, and the commonwealth with them, than exalt them to honor, if we should call them forth, when God doth not, to public authority." It must be set down in John Cotton's accounts that he discouraged the transplanting of English aristocracy to the soil of Massachusetts.

There remains to consider how he conducted himself in another weighty matter that was laid upon his shoulders—the defense of the New England polity against old-world critics. Congregationalism had been somewhat caustically handled by the English

---

[6] Hutchinson, *History of Massachusetts Bay Colony*, Vol. I, Appendix 2.

Presbyterians, as smacking both of democracy and Separatism; and John Cotton was called to justify to them the apparent innovations. His most notable work in this field was his celebrated volume, *The Way of the Congregational Churches Cleared*, a treatise crammed, in the language of a contemporary admirer, with "most practical Soul-searching, Soul-saving, and Soul-solacing Divinitie"; "not Magisterially laid down, but friendly debated by Scripture, and argumentatively disputed out to the utmost inch of Ground." Into the subtleties of this learned work we need not enter; its main thesis alone need detain us, and that thesis was an implied denial of the democratic tendencies of the "New England way." Cotton was greatly concerned over the charge of Joseph Baillie, a vigorous Scotch Presbyterian, that Congregationalism was only a different form of lower-class Brownism, "a native branch of Anabaptism"; and that in resting ecclesiastical sovereignty upon "the particular, visible Church of the Congregation," it was Separatist in principle as well as in practice. The charge was true, but John Cotton was too thoroughly a Jacobean gentleman to concede it; dishonor would come upon the New England churches, he believed, if it were conceded. So he was driven to casuistry: "No marvall, if Independents take it ill to bee called Brownists. . . . He separated from Churches and Saints: we, onely from the world, and that which is of the world"; and then to a categorical denial, "for New England there is no such church of the Separation at all that I know of." [7] From this it was a natural step to a downright rejection of the democratic principle of Congregationalism:

Neither is it the Scope of my whole Book, to give the people a share in the Government of the Church. . . . Nay, further, there be that blame the Book for the other Extreme, That it placeth the Government of the Church not at all in the hands of the People, but of the Presbyterie. [8]

The same note of disingenuous casuistry runs through his well-known controversy with Roger Williams over the question of toleration. In seeking to parry the thrust that the Saints, after quitting England to escape persecution, had themselves turned persecutors, he argued: "There is a vast difference between men's inventions and God's institutions; we fled from men's inventions, to which we else should have been compelled; we compel none to men's inventions." From which it followed, that "if the worship

---

[7] See *Narragansett Club Publications*, Vol. II, p. 203.
[8] *Ibid.*, Part II, p. 15.

be lawful in itself, the magistrate compelling him to come to it, compelleth him not to sin, but the sin is in his own will that needs to be compelled to a Christian duty." [9]   The brethren of Massachusetts were not singular in believing that they were very near to God and privy to His will; nor were the dissenters to their policy singular in their skepticism concerning such infallibility; and when skepticism blows its cold breath upon it, the logic of John Cotton turns to ashes.   Not freedom to follow the ways of sin, but freedom to follow the law of God as he expounded that law—such was Cotton's restriction upon the "natural liberties" of the subject of Jehovah.   Let there be freedom of conscience if it be under no error, but not otherwise; for if freedom be permitted to sinful error, how shall the will of God and John Cotton prevail upon earth?

After the battle has been fought and lost it is easy to see the strategic mistakes; but it is not so easy to keep one's head in the thick of the struggle.   As John Cotton looked overseas at the social revolution then threatening to submerge, not only Presbyterianism, but the very social order in which he had been nurtured; as he considered the logical implications of the strange, heretical doctrines that were bandied about in pamphlet and sermon, he was put almost in a panic.   The solid foundations of church and state were threatened by mischievous men, not only in England but in the new Canaan which had cost so much in prayer and sacrifice; should he keep silent while, in the name of toleration, the gunpowder was being put in place for the work of destruction?   Even today we can feel the anxious concern of John Cotton's mind in such a vibrant passage as this:

I confess we . . . have cause to admire, and adore the wisdome, and dreadfull Justice of God herein, That seeing Mr. *Williams* hath been now as a branch cut off from the Church of *Salem* these many yeares, he should bring forth no spirituall good fruit: and that in such a season, when the Spirit of Error is let loose to deceive so many thousand soules of our English Nation: So that now their hearts are become as Tinder, ready to catch and kindle at every sparke of false light.   Even so, O Father, because thy good pleasure is such, to let loose this Spirit of Error in the mouth of this Backslider, in the very houre and power of darknesse: for these are the dayes of vengeance: when the Antinomians deny the whole law; the Anti-sabbatarians deny the Morality of the fourth Commandement; the Papists deny the Negative part of the second Commandement.   It is a

[9] See Hutchinson, *Papers*, Vol. II, pp. 131 ff.; quoted in Adams, *Founding of New England*, p. 261.

wofull opportunitie that God hath left Mr. *Williams* to, now to step in. . . . For, take away (as Mr. *Williams* doth) all instituted worship of God, as Churches, Pastors, Teachers, Elders, Deacons, Members, Publick Ministery of the Word, Covenant, Seales of the Covenant (Baptisme, and the Lords Supper), the Censures of the Church, and the like, what is then left of all the institutions, and Ordinances of God, which the Lord established in the second Commandement, against the Institutions, Images and Inventions of men in his worship.[10]

How easy it is for good men, in presence of the new and strange, to draw back in timid reaction; and failing to understand, or fearing for their prestige, to charge upon the new and strange a host of evils that exist only in their panic imaginations! In this great matter of toleration of conscience, it is quite clear today that the eyes of the troubled theocrat, "so *piercing* and *heavenly* (in other and precious Truths of God)"—as Roger Williams acknowledged—were for the moment sadly "over-clouded and bloud-shotten." For this the age was more to blame than the man. It was no fault of John Cotton's that he was the child of a generation reared under the shadow of absolutism, fearful of underling aggression, unable to comprehend the excellence inhering in the democratic faith. He reasoned according to his light; and if he rather too easily persuaded himself that the light which shined to him was the single divine light, he proved himself thereby an orthodox Puritan if not a catholic thinker. It is a pity that the priest in his later years overcame the intellectual, nevertheless the epitaph carved on his headstone does no violence to truth:

JOHANNES COTTONUS
Cujus Ultima Laus est,
Quod fuerit inter Nov-Anglos Primus.

To have been accounted by his fellows first among the notable company of Puritan emigrants was no slight testimony to the sterling qualities of Master John Cotton.

---

[10] "Master John Cottons Answer to Master Roger Williams," in *Narragansett Club Publications*, Vol. II, pp. 22–23.

II

JOHN WINTHROP

Magistrate

If John Cotton embodied the ideal and polity of the theocratic ministry, John Winthrop represented the ideal and polity of the theocratic magistracy. Rulership in the new church-state, while nominally the function of lay officers, in reality was quite as much ecclesiastical as political. The civil authorities were chosen by a narrow body of orthodox electors with a single view to theocratic ends. To the traditional conception of magistracy, in which the gentlemen of the Migration had been reared, was now added a special function, the care of the church, "the maintenance of whose peace," John Cotton asserted, "is the chief end which God aimed at in the institution of magistracy." The career of John Winthrop in Massachusetts must be judged, therefore, from this two-fold point of view. He was not exclusively, or chiefly, a civil governor, but a magistrate-elder; and his political conduct was determined by this dual character of his office. Unless one keeps in mind the theocratic framework of the early Massachusetts commonwealth, one cannot understand the limitations of his authority, or judge his conduct intelligently.

John Winthrop was a skillful executive upon whose shoulders largely rested the success or failure of the undertaking during the difficult early years. But he was very much more than that; he was a Puritan steward of temporal affairs, who accepted his stewardship as a sacred duty lying upon his conscience. A cultivated gentleman, "browghte Up amonge boockes & learned men," with a tender and sympathetic nature—inclining overmuch to mildness, as he confessed apologetically—by every right he belongs with that notable group of Puritans, with Eliot and Vane and Hutchinson and Milton, in whom the moral earnestness of Hebraism was tempered to humaner issues by a generous culture. There was in him not a little fruitful sap of Elizabethan poetry to quicken his thought, lifting him out of the petty world of Jacobean lawyer and landed gentleman, and opening his eyes to a vision of the future significance of the great venture to which he dedicated his later years. Grave and dignified, he looks out at us from his portrait with a certain stoic calm not untouched with sadness.

as if this life had proved a serious business, filled with responsibilities and weighty matters, and darkened by sorrow and disappointment. The pagan *joie de vivre* of Elizabethan times is gone, and in its stead is a serious intelligence that must grapple with realities and shape them to its will.

He had lived amply in England before his removal, with much that was feudal lingering in the habits of his patriarchal household; and in the little village of Boston he kept twenty male servants, some of them heads of families. A decay of fortune had come upon him during his last years on the family estate, and the hope of recouping his losses may have been an additional reason for venturing to remove to the new world. In his *Considerations for J. W.* he explains that "he cannot live in the same place and calling (as before) and so, if he should refuse this opportunity, *that talent which God hath bestowed upon him for publick service were like to be buried.*" Something to the same purpose is suggested in another passage, which touches upon the economic disturbances of the time, with the attendant extravagance and ostentation of the new rich:

This Land growes weary of her Inhabitants. . . . We are growne to that height of Intemperance in all excesse of Riott, as noe man's estate allmost will suffice to keepe saile with his æqualls. . . . The ffountains of Learning & Religion are soe corrupted as—men straine at knatts & swallowe camells, use all severity for mainetaynance of cappes & other accomplyments, but suffer all ruffianlike fashions & disorder to passe uncontrolled.[11]

Writing to his wife Margaret in 1629, he gave expression to apprehensions that were very likely quickened by his own failure to keep pace with his neighbors:

My dear wife, I am veryly persuaded, God will bringe some heavye Affliction upon this lande & that speedylye. . . . The Lorde hath admonished, threatened, corrected, & astonished us, yet we growe worse & worse, so as his Spirit will not always strive with us, we must needs give way to his furye at last.[12]

But material considerations alone scarcely suffice to explain the motives of one who wrote: "It were happy for many if their parents had left them only such a legacy as our modern spirit of poetry makes his motto, *Ut nec habeant, nec careant, nec curent.*"

[11] *Life and Letters of John Winthrop*, Vol. I, p. 310.
[12] *Ibid.*, Vol. I, p. 296.

Such consolation—that the Christian should possess nothing, desire nothing, trouble about nothing—may have been only the refuge of the stoic from the impending loss of material possessions; but the conscious discipline in ascetic Hebraism which was to change the Jacobean gentleman into a militant Puritan had already created a temper to which such stoic abnegation must appeal. Winthrop's diary, running from his fourteenth to his thirty-second year, is a homely record in self-discipline, not unlike Bunyan's *Grace Abounding*. It is introspective and tediously moralizing, but it reveals how long and arduous was the training before he felt confident that he was "improved in all the points of experimental Godliness."

But Winthrop was the child of a great age before he was born into the fellowship of the Saints; and when we come upon the natural man beneath the theological wrappings, we discover a many-sided, rich and sympathetic human nature. He had gone to school to the English Bible, and the noble Hebrew poetry stirred the poetic imagination that was his Elizabethan birthright. Like so many of his fellow Puritans he delighted in the Book of Canticles, and the rich oriental imagery flowed easily from his pen. In one of his last letters before he quitted the old home, he took leave of a friend in these words:

It is time to conclude, but I know not how to leave you, yet since I must, I will put my beloved into his arms, who loves him best, & is a faithful keeper of all that is committed to him. Now, Thou, the hope of Israel, and the sure help of all that come to thee, knit the hearts of thy servants to thyself in faith and purity. Draw us with the sweetness of thine odours, that we may run after thee—Allure us, and speak kindly to thy servants, that thou mayest possess us as thine own, in the kindness of youth, and the love of marriage—Seal us up, by that holy spirit of promise, that we may not fear to trust in thee—Carry us into thy garden, that we may eat and be filled with those pleasures, which the world knows not— Let us hear that sweet voice of thine, my love, my dove, my undefiled— Spread thy skirt over us, and cover our deformity—Make us sick with thy love—Let us sleep in thine arms, and awake in thy kingdom—The souls of thy servants, thus united to thee, make us one in the bonds of brotherly affection—let not distance weaken it, nor time waste it, nor changes dissolve it, nor self-love eat it out; but when all means of other communion shall fail, let us delight to pray for each other: and so let thy unworthy servant prosper in the love of his friends, as he truly loves thy good servants . . . and wishes true happiness to them and to all theirs— Amen.[13]

[13] *Life and Letters*, Vol. I, pp. 397–398.

When his heart was touched Winthrop's tenderness flowed out in a wealth of affectionate sympathy, that lends a rich and lovely cadence to his English prose. To a sister who had suffered the loss of her husband, he wrote:

Go on cheerfully (my good sister), let experience add more confidence still to your patience. Peace shall come. There will be a bed to rest in, large and easy enough for you both. It is preparing in the lodging appointed for you in your Father's house. He that vouchsafed to wipe the sweat from his disciple's feet, will not disdain to wipe the tears from those tender affectionate eyes. Because you have been one of his mourners in the house of tribulation, you shall drink of the cup of joy, and be clothed with the garment of gladness, in the kingdom of his glory. The former things, and evil, will soon be passed; but the good to come shall neither end nor change.[14]

At another time, writing to his son of the death of his father, Adam Winthrop, he said:

He hath finished his course; and is gathered to his people in peace, as the ripe corn into the barn. He thought long for the day of his dissolution and welcomed it most gladly. Thus is he gone before; and we must go after in our time: This advantage he hath of us—he shall not see the evil which we may meet with ere we go hence. Happy those who stand in good terms with God and their own conscience: they shall not fear evil tidings; and in all changes they shall be the same.[15]

A lovable man was John Winthrop, richly endowed and admirably disciplined, gracious in manner, persuasive in speech, generous in action—in all England there could scarcely have been found a leader better equipped for the work in hand, when at the age of forty-three he became head of the emigrant church-state, which by reason of its charter and the removal of the corporation to New England, was become effectively an independent commonwealth, free to shape its domestic polity as seemed best. During the score of years that remained to him, he was the guiding spirit of the Massachusetts settlements, impressing his will upon others by sheer force of character. It was inevitable that in so strange and unprecedented an experiment, undertaken in an environment so unfamiliar, serious and often bitter divisions would arise touching the fundamental principles of government. In the frequent discussions Winthrop bore a leading part; he marshaled his arguments with the skill of a lawyer; he separated the broad principle from the special circumstance; and in the end he usually carried the assent of his fellow counselors to his proposals. His social and political philosophy, in consequence, greatly influenced the development of Massachusetts Bay during the early years when its institutions and polity were taking shape, and throws much light on the spirit and purpose of that development.

Winthrop's political bias was unconsciously shaped by his experience, of which the determining fact was the principle and practice of Jacobean magistracy. As an English squire he had long served as magistrate, and this experience he brought to New England as a legacy from an autocratic past. In that old world the magistrate exercised a patriarchal police power well-nigh absolute, sanctioned by ancient custom, upheld by the church, and acquiesced in by subjects well trained in subordination. Transported to New England and adapted to theocratic ends, the principle of magistracy was both augmented in power and ennobled in conception. To the police power over things temporal was added a police power over things spiritual. In the Bible commonwealth the legislative function was regarded as of minor importance. The law being already set down in the Scriptures, the chief authority in the commonwealth naturally rested with the magistrates who were responsible for its strict fulfillment. As stewards intrusted with a divine stewardship, they exercised absolute legislative and judicial powers; in their councils the ministers were summoned to participate, but no others. It was the duty of the magistrates to debate and determine, and the duty of the people to obey.

To a modern this is no other than sheer absolutism, but it was deeply embedded in Calvinistic theory and practice, and was justified by the Puritan principle of special talents. God calls to the post of duty those best fitted to serve. As a devout follower of Calvin, Winthrop must have often pondered upon the passages in the *Institutes* which set forth the nature of magistracy and the duties of the magistrate, and in particular this: "If they remember that they are the vicegerents of God, it behooves them to watch with all care, diligence, and industry, that they may exhibit a kind of image of the Divine Providence, guardianship, goodness, benevolence, and justice." [16] To a devout Jacobean like Winthrop, this patriarchal conception of stewardship would appear as a

---

[16] Book IV, Chapter XX, Paragraph 6.

noble ideal, worthy of a Christian. The potential absolutism implied would scarcely trouble one who had grown up in a society where absolute authority was interwoven with everyday life. The Christian magistrate was still a magistrate, but with the great difference that his hands must be kept clean and his conscience clear. This nobler spirit of Calvinistic stewardship is revealed in Winthrop's *Modell of Christian Charity*, written on shipboard during the voyage out. A sense of profound responsibility devolving upon the leaders imparts dignity to the thought: they must bear and forbear, knitting themselves together in a common purpose, and seeing that "the care of the public" should "oversway all private interests." And this "care of the public," remained in theory if not always in practice, the guiding principle of Winthrop's official activities.

The bearing of this doctrine of magistracy upon the early movement of democracy in Massachusetts is not far to seek. If magistracy was a duty laid upon those of fit talents, they would serve God ill who should turn a willing ear to popular protests against magisterial policy. On this point Winthrop was adamant. He would have no meddling on the part of those who had not been called. When it was attempted to bring him to account before the congregation for an unpopular judicial decision, he denied the competency of the congregation in such matters, and then as he often did in cases of doubt, he made a "little book" in which he elaborated the thesis, "That a Church hath not Power to call any Civill Magistrate to give Account of his Juditiall proceedings in any Court of Civill Justice: and what the Church may doe in such Causes." [17] The shoemaker should stick to his last, Winthrop believed, and he would suffer no interference by the congregation with his duties as magistrate. On another occasion when difficulties had arisen in certain negotiations with the Connecticut settlements, he noted in his journal:

These and the like miscarriages in point of correspondency were conceived to arise from these two errors in their government: 1. They chose divers *scores* men, who had no learning nor judgment which might fit them for those affairs, though otherwise men holy and religious. 2. By occasion hereof, the main burden for managing of state business fell upon one or other of their ministers, (as the phrase and style of these letters will clearly discover), who, though they were men of singular wisdom and

[17] The heads of argument are given in *Life and Letters*, Vol. II, pp. 211–214.

godliness, yet stepping out of their course, their actions wanted that blessing which otherwise might have been expected.[18]

The political philosophy which underlay Winthrop's theory and practice of magistracy, was a Puritan modification of the commonly accepted English theory of a "mixt aristocratie." He had been trained in the law but was little given to speculative thought. There is evidence that he read somewhat in the fast accumulating political literature of the times, but little indication that his reading modified his theory or influenced his conduct. He was an administrator rather than a philosopher, and from the fragmentary records that have survived it is difficult to piece together a consistent political theory. As a magistrate under the dominance of the English Common Law, he seems to have accepted the constitutional theory of Coke, who sought to interpose the customary and ancient law of the land between the growing absolutism of the Crown, and the increasing importunity of the Commons, with sovereignty inhering in the judiciary. As a Puritan, however, he superimposed the law of Moses on the law of the land, and by ignoring the King on the one hand, and denying power to the representatives of the people on the other, he created the framework of a magisterial theocracy.

The two chief sources to which we must turn for his political views, in addition to his letters and journals, are: *A Replye to the Answ: Made to the Discourse about the Neg: Vote*, and *Arbitrary Governmt Described: & the Governmt of the Massachusetts Vindicated from that Aspersion*, both of which have been preserved in the form of heads of argument.[19] The principle that underlies these skeleton arguments is the theory of a state held static by exact constitutional arrangements. King and people represent the great supplementary functions of constitutional government, sovereignty and liberty; both are necessary in a well ordered society, and neither may encroach upon the other. This Winthrop regarded as the vital principle of the English constitution, which had been embodied in the government of Massachusetts.

The Government of the Massachusetts consists of Magistrates & Freemen: in the one is placed the Auth'ye, in the other the Lib'tye of the Com: W: either hath power to Acte, both alone, & both togither, yet by a distinct power, the one of Lib'tye, the other of Auth'ye: the Freemen

[18] *Ibid.*, Vol. II, p. 236.
[19] Both are given in the appendix to Vol. II of the *Life and Letters.*

Acte alone in all occurrences out of Court: & both Acte togither in the Gen'll Court: yet all limited by certaine Rules, bothe in the greater & smaller affaires: so as the Governm't is Regular in a mixt Aristocratie, & no wayes Arbitrary.[20]

In settled times and places this nice balance between sovereignty and liberty is maintained by use and wont; but in periods of disturbance, such as then existed in England, and in new experiments, such as marked the setting up of the commonwealth of Massachusetts, there was certain to be much pulling and straining between these antagonistic principles; and his refusal to accept this fact, and his stubborn insistence on transferring to New England the old English static order, brought on Winthrop's head many of the difficulties that greatly troubled his administration. Both in the old world and the new, the principle of liberty was encroaching on feudal authority. With the rise of the middle class, many Englishmen, and particularly the colonial New Englanders, were fast outgrowing the old paternalisms, and coming to regard them as no other than tyranny. The freemen of the Massachusetts towns were restive under the strict rule of the magistrate-elders, and a growing party of democratic deputies was eager to try its hand at government. All such democratic pretensions Winthrop held in contempt, although he was at pains to deny the arbitrary nature of magisterial rule.

Some of the deputies had seriously conceived, that the magistrates affected an arbitrary government. . . . For prevention whereof they judged it not unlawful to use even *extrema remedia*, as if *salus populi* had been now the transcendent rule to walk by, and that magistracy must be no other, in effect, than a ministerial office, and all authority, both legislative, consultative, and judicial, must be exercised by the people in their body representative.[21]

If government were regular it could not be arbitrary—this was Winthrop's brief reply to the deputies. In his arguments he deliberately avoided the difficult question of sovereignty; in part, no doubt, because of the delicate situation resulting from fear of royal interference, but chiefly because he was unwilling to bring into jeopardy the unlimited powers of magistracy. That he denied sovereignty to the people is abundantly clear from his actions, as well as from specific comment. By the law of the corporation, namely, the written terms of the charter, authority

[20] *Ibid.*, Vol. II, p. 454. [21] *Journal*, Vol. II, p. 240.

was vested in a limited body of freemen; and he saw no reason in expediency or otherwise to extend that authority. Thus he argued, "it is well proved & concluded by a late Juditious writer, in a booke newly come over, intituled an Answ: to Dr Ferne, that thoughe all Lawes, that are sup'structive, may be altered by the representative bodye of the Com:w: yet they have not power to alter anythinge w'ch is fundamental." [22] What delimitations were to be drawn between "superstructive" and "fundamental," he was not careful to make clear; but it is certain that he regarded as fundamental not only the charter terms and the British constitution but the will of God. Doubtful as this last may seem to students of political science, and difficult to determine, it was neither doubtful nor difficult to Winthrop and his fellow magistrates and ministers. The Mosaic law was specific. Back of the citizen-legislator was the subject of Jehovah, and he was politically free only to do the will of God. There must be divine sanction for all human law; lacking such sanction all majority votes and legislative enactments were null and void. Sovereignty inheres finally in God, and it is by his fundamental law that all superstructive laws and institutions must be judged.

In theocratic philosophy, therefore, the magistrate became no other than God's vicegerent, with authority beyond popular limitation or control. No English squire presumed to exercise the magisterial powers which Winthrop and his associates quietly usurped. Among other innovations they early claimed the right of veto on the acts of the deputies, and in reply to the dissatisfaction voiced at such arbitrary encroachment, Winthrop argued that the magisterial veto was no infringement on the liberties of the people, but was a means to "preserve them, if by any occasion they should be in danger: I cannot liken it better to anything than the brake of a windmill: w'ch hathe no power, to move the runninge worke: but it is of speciall use, to stoppe any violent motion, w'ch in some extraordinary tempest might endanger the wholl fabricke." [23] The convenient weapon of divine sanction Winthrop did not scruple to use at need. Thus when a petition was presented for the repeal of a law which arbitrarily decreased the number of deputies, he denied the lawfulness of the procedure:

---

[22] *Ibid.*, Vol. II, p. 438.
[23] *Discourse about the Neg: Vote, Life and Letters*, Vol. II, p. 434.

When the people have chosen men to be their rulers, now to combine together . . . in a public petition to have an order repealed . . . savors of resisting an ordinance of God. For the people, having deputed others, have no right to make or alter laws themselves, but are to be subject.[24]

The old English right of petition, in short, was not a right in theocratic Massachusetts, and any unauthorized joining together of citizens for political purposes was a conspiracy against the will of God. The practical result of this doctrine of magisterial vicegerency was that a small group of freemen set up an unlimited oligarchy over some four or five thousand of their fellow Englishmen, even going so far as to advance the novel doctrine of a freehold tenure of power.

Winthrop's extreme jealousy of popular power cannot be explained away by the doctrine of stewardship. Hooker of Hartford had no such distrust of the people, but he was not a gentleman, like Winthrop, and had not grown up with an aristocratic contempt for democracy. The preposterousness of democratic aspiration was a stock jest among English gentlemen, and in seeking to refute the arguments of the deputies for greater popular power Winthrop did little more than give a Hebraic twist to his aristocratic prejudices:

Where the chief Ordinary power & administration thereof is in the people, there is a Democratie . . . the Deputies are the Democraticall p'te of o'r Governm't. Now if we should change from a mixt Aristocratie to a meere Democratie: first we should have no warr'nt in scripture for it: there was no such Governm't in Israell. 2: we should heerby voluntaryly abase o'rselves, & deprive o'rselves of that dignitye, w'ch the providence of God hath putt upon us: w'ch is a manifest breach of the 5th Com't: for a Democratie is, among most Civill nations accounted the meanest & worst of all formes of Governm't: & therefore in writers, it is branded w'th Reproachfull Epithets as Bellua multorū capitū, a monster, &c: & Historyes doe recorde, that it hath been allwayes of least continuance & fullest of trouble.[25]

In an often quoted letter to Thomas Hooker, then engaged in erecting a democratic commonwealth in Connecticut, Winthrop diplomatically moderated his terms and put the aristocratic doctrine in more attractive form. "I expostulated about the unwarrantableness & unsafeness of referring all matter of counsel or judicature to the body of the people, *quia* the best is always the least, & of that best part the wiser part is always the lesser." [26]

[24] *Journal.*   [25] *Life and Letters*, Vol. II, p. 430.   [26] *Ibid.*, Vol. II, p. 237.

But he must have agreed heartily with another English gentleman, who writing to Winthrop under date of July 9, 1640, remarked pithily:

> I say agayne noe wise man shoud be soe folish as to live whear every man is master, & masters must not correct theyr servants: Where wise men propound & fooles determine, as it was sayde of the citties of Greece. [27]

As the responsible steward of God's plan for New England, Winthrop would not flatter the people by pretending to the doctrine of *vox populi, vox dei.* The multitude he regarded as factious, overswayed by expediency and self-interest, incapable of governing wisely. Law, by its nature, was ethical, the expression of God's absolute and just will; and this law, the magistrates were called of God to enforce.

From this conception of the absolute nature of law, came the famous discussion of liberty and authority, known as the "little speech," which is the most highly praised of Winthrop's utterances. In a certain police-court matter that had loosed the class prejudices of all parties, he had held against the popular feeling, and was impeached before the general court. Upon his acquittal he rose and addressed the court in words which he afterwards set down in his journal. No other episode in his varied career reveals so well the admirable poise of the man—the dignity, the self-control, the fair-mindedness, despite an attack that hurt him to the quick.

> For the other point concerning liberty, I observe a great mistake in the country about that. There is a twofold liberty, natural (I mean as our nature is now corrupt) and civil or federal. The first is common to man with beasts and other creatures. By this, man, as he stands in relation to man simply, hath liberty to do what he lists; it is a liberty to evil as well as to good. This liberty is incompatible and inconsistent with authority, and cannot endure the least restraint of the most just authority. The exercise and maintaining of this liberty makes men grow more evil, and in time to be worse than brute beasts: *omnes sumus licentia deteriores.* This is that great enemy of truth and peace, that wild beast, which all the ordinances of God are bent against, to restrain and subdue it. The other kind of liberty I call civil or federal; and it may also be termed moral, in reference to the covenant between God and man, in the moral law, and the politic covenants and constitutions amongst men themselves. This liberty is the proper end and object of authority, and cannot subsist without it; and it is a liberty to that only which is good, just, and honest. This liberty you are to stand for, with the hazard (not only of your goods,

but) of your lives, if need be. Whatsoever crosseth this, is not authority, but a distemper thereof. This liberty is maintained and exercised in a subjection to authority; it is of the same kind of liberty wherewith Christ hath made us free. . . . On the other side, ye know who they are that complain of this yoke and say, let us break their bands, etc., we will not have this man to rule over us. Even so, brethren, it will be between you and your magistrates. If you stand for your natural corrupt liberties, and will do what is good in your own eyes, you will not endure the least weight of authority, but will murmur, and oppose, and be always striving to shake off that yoke; and if you will be satisfied to enjoy such civil and lawful liberties, such as Christ allows you, then will you quietly and cheerfully submit unto that authority which is set over you, in all the administrations of it, for your good. Wherein, if we fail at any time, we hope we shall be willing (by God's assistance) to hearken to good advice from any of you, or in any other way of God; so shall your liberties be preserved, in upholding the honor and power of authority amongst you.[28]

The doctrine of aristocratic stewardship has never been more skillfully presented. It is John Cotton's reply to Roger Williams, translated into political terms; the philosophy of natural rights whittled down to a covenant between God and man. It rests on the assumption of an absolute law, superior to expediency. But may not honest men disagree as to what constitutes the good, just, and honest? and may not godly authority imperceptibly slide over into plain tyranny? Although the Saints may have professed themselves satisfied with Winthrop's doctrine, the pages of early Massachusetts history bear ample record of the dissatisfaction of the sinners. Most of the difficulties experienced by Winthrop in his administration of the commonwealth had their root in this assumption of arbitrary power, the immediate outcome of which was a spontaneous development of incipient democracy. How far such an assumption of divine custodianship may lead a generous man from the path of justice, appears in his summing up of the case against Mistress Anne Hutchinson, who because she insisted upon her own interpretation of the good, just, and honest, was adjudged "A woman not only difficult in her opinions, but also of an intemperate spirit." "The ground work of her revelations is the immediate revelation of the spirit, and not by the ministry of the Lord . . . and this hath been the ground of all these tumults and troubles; and I would that those were all cut off that trouble us." The kernel of the offense for which Mistress Hutchinson was banished, is then laid bare: "We see not that any should have

[28] *History of New England*, Vol. II, pp. 279–282.

authority to set up any other exercise beside what authority hath already set up." [29]

In this arbitrary judgment of Winthrop's—the natural fruit of the tree of theocratic stewardship—the "little speech" discovers its suitable commentary. Urged on by his bigoted associates, the kind-hearted governor descended to their level, and began the unhappy business of playing the tyrant under pretense of scourging God's enemies. The lords-brethren served notice upon all dissenters that henceforth there must be no dissent in New England. The admirable courage of Mistress Hutchinson availed no more against the magisterial interpretation of the good, just, and honest, than the boldness of Roger Williams before her; or later, the zeal of the Baptists who were sent away by Endicott; or later still, the piety of the Quakers, who were whipped at the cart-tail and hanged, men and women both. The policy of the political stewardship of the best and wisest never had fuller trial, with abler or more conscientious agents, than in Massachusetts Bay; and its failure was complete. Such progress as Massachusetts made towards freedom and tolerance was gained in the teeth of theocratic opposition; New England democracy owes no debt to her godly magistrates.

Bred up in a half-feudal world, the leaders of the Migration remained patriarchal in their social philosophy, unable to adapt old prejudices to new conditions. Human motives are curiously mixed, human actions rarely consistent; and if the shortcomings of John Winthrop show blacker by contrast with the excellence of the ideal which he professed, the fault must be charged against his time and associates and not against his manly, generous nature. Most English gentlemen of his day were steeped in a sodden Toryism, yet he earnestly desired to be a faithful steward of church and state. If as a gentleman he held firmly to the privilege of rulership, as a Christian he endeavored to rule honorably and in the fear of the Lord. If he followed the beaten path and tried to shape the great experiment by the traditional principles of his class; if his zeal at times led him into indisputable tyrannies; it was because he was led away from the light, not because he sought selfish ends. Godliness has its own special temptations, and it would be ungenerous to bear ill-will against so lovable a man.

[29] Hutchinson, *History of Massachusetts Bay Colony*, Vol. II, pp. 482–520.

CHAPTER IV

THE CONTRIBUTIONS OF INDEPENDENCY

I

OTHER ideals than those of Winthrop and Cotton, fruitful or feculent according to the special bias of whoever judges them, came out of England in the teeming days of the Puritan revolution to agitate the little settlements. A Hebraized theocracy could not satisfy the aspirations of advanced English liberals who were exploring all the avenues to freedom, and who, now that the old feudal bonds were loosening, were projecting a more generous basis for the reorganization of society. The democratic elements were beginning to make their voices heard in England; the doctrine of the priesthood of all believers was bearing fruit in the minds of obscure Independents; and the eventual outcome would be the shouldering aside of a snug Presbyterian order, and the clarification of a program for a democratic commonwealth. In those excellent words commonweal and commonwealth—words much on men's tongues in the creative later years of the Puritan revolution—was fittingly summed up the political ideal of Independency. English liberalism had come to believe that social conformity, established in the practice of coercion, with its monarchical state and hierarchical church, must give way to an order founded in good will, that conceived of the political state as a public-service corporation, concerned solely with the *res publica*, or public thing, careful of the well-being of all, allowing special rights or grants to none. The state, it was coming to be argued freely, rightly understood, was no other than society organized to further the great end of the commonweal; no longer must it remain a private preserve for gentlemen to hunt over.

But before that should come about a great battle must be fought, in New England as well as in old England. The principle of individual freedom must first be established securely in the public mind, and to that business the party of Independents devoted its energies. In the theory and practice of Independency two fundamental rights were implied: the right of the individual

51

to determine his own belief, uncoerced by external authority; and the right to join freely with his fellows in the institutional expression and spread of such belief. In order to realize the first, it was a necessary preliminary to establish the right of free inquiry on a firm constitutional basis—the principle that the state shall safeguard the citizen in the exercise of such right, and not hinder or thwart him; and in order to realize the second, it was necessary to establish in social practice a much more fiercely disputed principle, namely, the right to proselytize, to spread one's views freely, to endeavor to make them prevail over contrary views. Certainly neither right would be freely granted; they must be won in the teeth of supposedly divine sanctions to conformity. However intimately the two are related, it is over the second that the long fierce battle has been waged in modern history. Liberalism faces no severer test than in its attitude towards the right of unpopular minority propaganda. The broad principle of toleration of differences, so vital to a democratic society, searches out and lays bare every insincerity of liberal professions. The will to power is so universal in appeal, it is so quick to attack every threatening nonconformity, that no other social right has traveled so arduous a road, or lags so far in the rear of the liberal advance. The principle of religious toleration that was involved in the movement of Independency was the ecclesiastical form of a struggle, which, shifting later to the field of politics and then to economics, is still raging about us. The long battle is still far from being won. In few countries today do more than a small minority regard the principle of toleration otherwise than as a social luxury to be indulged in only when times are settled.

It was in the nature of things that a clash should soon come in Massachusetts Bay. There Independency would certainly be looked upon as no better than a weed from the devil's wilderness, and in the name of God and the theocracy it would be trampled under foot. Liberalism and the Cambridge Platform would no more mix than oil and water. But the more immediate and narrower question of religious toleration was only incidental to the broader divergencies that lay in antagonistic principles of church and state, and that brought on the clash. A general engagement was preparing between the principles of Presbyterianism and Independency, and the real issue at stake was the future form of society in New England—whether it was to be aristocratic or democratic. The free environment was a strong stimulus to idealists who looked upon the new field as a heaven-sent opportunity for their own special Utopias to take root, and who would bitterly resent any intrusion by a rival. Commonwealth building is a great adventure, and the Independents with their carefully elaborated plans would not sit quietly by and permit the Saints to preëmpt the land for their inhospitable theocracy without a struggle. In such a contest the more liberal party was fortunate in its leaders. Thomas Hooker and Roger Williams were men of creative ability, of inflexible purpose, of fine idealism, the ablest amongst the entire group of Puritan immigrants, in whom the great principles of Independency found worthy stewards; and the long struggle they carried on, each in his own way, with the theocratic leaders of Massachusetts was to affect profoundly the later development of New England. In the end the Presbyterianism of Boston was to surrender to the Congregationalism of Hartford. From Connecticut and Rhode Island, it must be recalled, rather than from the Bay colony, came those democratic principles and institutions that were to spread widely in later years, and create the New England that after generations have liked to remember.

II

THOMAS HOOKER

Puritan Liberal

Among the Englishmen who came to Massachusetts were some to whom the "New England way" seemed to promise a democratic organization of the church, and who looked with disapproval upon the Presbyterizing policy of the oligarchy. Of this number the congregations of Newtown, Dorchester, and Watertown were noteworthy for the quiet determination with which they seceded from the theocratic commonwealth, and set up for themselves in the Connecticut wilderness. Their leaders were liberals who believed that everything should be done decently and in order, but who were determined that the outcome of such decent orderliness should be a free church in a free state; and so while Roger Williams was engaged in erecting the democracy of Rhode Island, Thomas Hooker was as busily engaged in erecting the democracy of Hartford.

Concerning the "grave and judicious Hooker" surprisingly
little is known, in spite of the important work that he did and the
influence that he wielded during a masterful life. He was evidently
a man regardless of fame, who took small pains to publish his
virtues for the edification of posterity; what record he left behind
bears evidence of being the expression of a man to whom desire for
celebrity was nothing in comparison with the needs of his Master's
work. Unlike his fellow ministers he was not much given to making books. The works that bore the name of Thomas Hooker on
the title-page were put through the press usually by other hands
than his, and were taken from shorthand notes. His great contribution, *A Survey of the Summe of Church Discipline*, published
anonymously and in an imperfect form, was written against his
will in consequence of his having been drafted for the service by his
fellow ministers. In removing from Newtown he cut himself off
from the group of diarists who diligently recorded the happenings
of the day, and so failed of being portrayed and praised by divers
busy pens. Lacking exacter information, we are forced to rely
mainly upon such hearsay reports as have come down to us, pieced
out by Puritan tradition; and these reports make Thomas Hooker
to have been a strong and resourceful man, a better democrat than
his fellow ministers, the father of New England Congregationalism
as it later came to be when the Presbyterianizing tendency was
checked—a practical leader who rejected equally the reactionary
theocracy of John Cotton, and the leveling radicalism of Roger
Williams.

For the pronounced democratic sympathies of this "light of the
western churches"—a sympathy quite unusual in his day and
world—some grounds will be discovered in his commonplace
origin. Unlike John Cotton, who had a "descent from honourable
progenitors," Hooker was sprung from a plain yeoman family
that had made no stir in the world. His native hamlet, Marfield
in Leicestershire, numbered no more than six houses, tucked away
in a secluded countryside. His schooling was got by the aid of
scholarships: at Market-Bosworth and later at Cambridge, where
he entered as sizar, which meant among other things that he was
waiter on tables in the Hall. When he was settled in a forty-
pound living at Esher, in Surrey, he married a "waiting-woman"
to the wife of his patron; and when he died, after a laborious life
spent in the cause of righteousness, he left an estate appraised at

846 pounds, 15 shillings, exclusive of his books, more than half of which modest sum was represented by the Hartford homestead.[1] Which scanty information is sufficient to tell us that Thomas Hooker was a simple man in worldly ambitions as well as in origin, not given to climbing or feathering his own nest, with none of the great associates or aristocratic ties of Winthrop and Ward and Cotton, a churchman more inclined to the ways of Independency than to Presbyterianism.

In his professional work he was rather the pastor than the teacher, caring more for experimental religion than for theological disputation. He was an embodiment of the moral fervor of the Reformation that protested against the scandal of "dumb priests." He seems to have been the most stimulating preacher of early New England, and it was as a lecturer that he had made a name for himself before he was driven from his English charge by Laud. The lecturer was a characteristic Puritan innovation, much hated by the Anglicans. Translated into a modern equivalent, it meant an agitator who used the pulpit to spread the new gospel of free judgment in religious matters, and other gospels displeasing to absolutism. That such men were not liked by Charles and his Archbishop goes without saying; they were "the people's creatures" —a certain Tory churchman complained to the King—and "blew the bellows of their sedition." Such being the case it seemed but common prudence to muzzle them, and as early as 1622 James laid down an orthodox program, forbidding any of lesser rank than "a bishop or dean [to] presume to preach in any popular auditory on the deep points of predestination, election, reprobation, or of the universality, efficacy, irresistibility of God's grace," and restricting Sunday afternoon sermons to such innocuous themes as the "Catechism, Creed, or Ten Commandments."[2] It was an endeavor to stop men's thinking by putting the crown of martyrdom on the lovers of truth. To forbid the Puritan to talk of such things, to shut up the Word of God from him, was to blow the bellows of his sedition indeed.

That Thomas Hooker was not a man to be muzzled must have been clear to all who knew his stubborn English will. In his homely vigor he was not unlike Hugh Latimer, direct and vigorous in speech and action, not easily turned aside from the path of duty,

[1] See Walker, *Thomas Hooker, Preacher, Founder, Democrat.*
[2] *Ibid.*, pp. 40-44.

possessing much of the old bishop's courage in dealing with great men and their follies. He knew a fool and a tyrant in high places, and was bold to call them by their true names. "He was a person," said Cotton Mather, "who while doing his Master's work, would put a king in his pocket." He was the more dangerous because he had put his own temper under strict governance—"For though he were a man of cholerick disposition, and had a mighty vigour and fervour of spirit . . . yet he had ordinarily as much government of his choler as a man has of a mastiff dog in a chain; he 'could let out his dog, and pull in his dog, as he pleased.'"

So ardent a temperament, joined to remarkable powers of oratory, gave to Thomas Hooker very unusual popular influence, some measure of which is revealed in a letter of a certain sycophant of the court party, who wrote to Laud's tool, Chancellor Duck, under date of May 20, 1629, as follows:

All men's eares are now filled with ye obstreperous clamours of his followers against my Lord . . . as a man endeavouring to suppress good preaching and advance Popery. All would be here very calme and quiet if he [Hooker] might depart. . . . If he be suspended its the resolution of his friends and himselfe to settle his abode in Essex, and maintenance is promised him in plentifull manner for the fruition of his private conference, which hath already more impeached the peace of our church than his publique ministry. His genius will still haunte all the pulpits in ye country, where any of his scholers may be admitted to preach. . . . There be divers young ministers about us . . . that spend their time in conference with him; and return home and preach what he hath brewed. . . . Our people's pallats grow so out of tast yt noe food contents them but of Mr. Hooker's dressing. I have lived in Essex to see many changes, and have seene the people idolizing many new ministers and lecturers, but this man surpasses them all for learning and some other considerable partes and . . . gains more and far greater followers than all before him. . . . If my Lord tender his owne future peace . . . let him connive at Mr. Hooker's departure.[3]

Clearly the England of Laud with its pursuivants and tattling tongues of "dumb ministers"—who might well be jealous of his eloquence—was no fit place for the activities of Thomas Hooker. Even though he should be suspended, he would still be reckoned dangerous to prerogative with his private conferences and his following of young ministers. So he was driven overseas into Holland, whence after a few years' experience with the Archbishop's spies, and dislike of the Presbyterian system there practiced, he

3 *Ibid.*, pp. 45–46.

set forth for America where he arrived on the same boat with John Cotton and Samuel Stone, and was inducted as pastor of the church at Newtown which had been awaiting his coming over. Shortly thereafter began the open dissatisfaction of the Cambridge congregation with the policy of the oligarchy, which resulted three years later in the removal of Hooker and his church to Hartford. The causes of this removal—an event that profoundly agitated the colony—have been much discussed, but they have never been cleared of what may have been an intentional vagueness. Possibly, as Hubbard suggests, there were jealousies between Hooker and Cotton, Winthrop, and Haynes, which it would have been unseemly to expose in open court;[4] but the likelier explanation would seem to lie in the incompatibility of political views, which at bottom was a division on the question of aristocracy or democracy in church and state. The Cambridge men seem to have disliked the oligarchic rule of the magistrates; they doubtless sympathized with the popular party and may have encouraged the counter aggressions of the deputies, whose assertiveness fills so much space in Winthrop's journal and betokens his concern. It is likely that there was more dissatisfaction than got into journals, either private or official; and it is equally likely that Thomas Hooker was a prime force in quickening the democratic unrest. "After Mr. Hooker's coming over," said Hubbard in an often quoted passage, "it was observed that many of the freemen grew to be very jealous of their liberties." Nevertheless, Hooker was not a contentious person, to spread a clamor through the commonwealth and endanger the success of the plantation. He believed that "Time, Place, Outward Decency and Comelinesse" were desirable in the management of public affairs; and so instead of descending to sharp dispute with men whom he respected and loved even though he disagreed with them in political views, he chose to remove quietly out of their jurisdiction, making as little cause for embroilment as possible.

After all, the most illuminating commentary upon the causes of the removal is the spirit of the institutions set up in the new

---

[4] The testimony of Roger Williams seems to imply as much: "Mr. Haynes, Governor of Connecticut, though he pronounced sentence of my long banishment against me, at Cambridge, then Newtown, yet said to me . . . 'I think, Mr. Williams, I must now confess to you, that the most wise God hath provided and cut out this part of His world for a refuge and receptacle for all sorts of consciences. I am now under a cloud, and my brother Hooker, with the Bay, as you have been, we have removed from them thus far, and yet they are not satisfied.'" (*Letter to Major Mason* [1670], in *Narragansett Club Publications*, Vol. VI, p. 133 ff.)

settlement. While we need not go so far as to assert, with the historians of Connecticut, that "the birthplace of American democracy is Hartford," we must recognize in the Fundamental Orders adopted by the General Assembly, January 14, 1639, a plan of popular government so broadly democratic as to entitle it to be called "the first written constitution of modern democracy." [5] Concerning the important part played by Hooker in this work there can be no doubt. His influence was commanding, and the sneer of old Samuel Peters—"Hooker reigned twelve years high-priest over Hertford"—scarcely overstates the fact. And this great influence was thrown persistently in favor of democratic procedure in church and state. He definitely rejected the Boston practice of magisterial autocracy. In opposition to Winthrop, who asserted, "Whatsoever sentence the magistrate gives, the judgment is the Lord's, though he do it not by any rule prescribed by civil authority," Hooker argued:

That in the matter which is referred to the judge, the sentence should lie in his breast, or be left to his discretion, according to which he should go, I am afraid it is a course which wants both safety and warrant. I must confess, I ever looked at it as a way which leads directly to tyranny, and so to confusion, and must plainly profess, if it was in my liberty, I should choose neither to live nor leave my posterity under such a government.[6]

At another time, replying to Winthrop's justification of oligarchic rule on the ground that "the best part is always the least, and of that best part the wiser is always the lesser," Hooker frankly rested his case for democracy on the good sense of the people as a whole:

It is also a truth that counsel should be sought from counsellors; but the question yet is, who should those be. Reserving smaller matters which fall in occasionally in common course, to a lower counsel, in matters of greater importance which concerns the common good, a general counsel chosen by all, I conceive, under favour, most suitable to rule and most safe for relief of the whole.[7]

Before the General Court, on May 31, 1638, eight months before the Fundamental Orders were adopted, Hooker preached a remarkable sermon on popular sovereignty. Taking for his text

[5] Borgeaud, *The Rise of Modern Democracy*, p. 123.
[6] Quoted in J. T. Adams, *The Founding of New England*, p. 194.
[7] Walker, *Thomas Hooker, etc.*, p. 122.

Deut. 1:13—the passage on which John Eliot later erected his fantastic Utopia—he elaborated the thesis that "the foundation of authority is laid, firstly, in the free consent of the people," and therefore that "the choice of public magistrates belongs unto the people by God's own allowance," and "they who have the power to appoint officers and magistrates, it is in their power also, to set the bounds and limitations of the power and place unto which they call them." [8] This was Hooker's reply to the oligarchic policy of the Bay in limiting the number of freemen in order to maintain the supremacy of the magistrates; and it throws light on the comment written out of England in the spring of 1636, to John Wilson, that "there is great division of judgment in matters of religion amongst good ministers & people which moved Mr. Hoker to remove"; and that "you are so strict in admission of members to your church, that more than halfe are out of your church in all your congregations, & that Mr. Hoker befor he went away preached against yt (as one reports who hard him)." [9] In the new commonwealth there was neither a property qualification nor a religious test limiting the right of franchise; the admission of freemen was reckoned a political matter and left to the several township democracies. The reaction against the oligarchic policy of Massachusetts Bay carried far.

If we had Hooker's sermon in full we should know much more about his political theory; yet even from the meager and tantalizing notes that have been preserved, we can deduce fairly certainly the major principles of his philosophy. Three creative ideas seem to have determined his thinking: the compact theory of the state, the doctrine of popular sovereignty, and the conception of the state as a public-service corporation, strictly responsible to the will of the majority—ideas that Roger Williams elaborated in detail and during many years of service reduced to a working system in the commonwealth of Rhode Island. That Hooker should have grasped so firmly the essentials of the new democratic theory will surprise no one who is acquainted with the political speculations of English Independency. They were all implicit in the new theory of church and state that such thinkers as Williams and Vane and Milton were clarifying, and since the days of Robert Browne they had been familiar in one form or another to the young Puritan radicals at the universities. The compact idea, which held

[8] *Ibid.*, p. 125.　　[9] *Ibid.*, p. 88.

in solution the doctrine of natural rights, had established itself firmly in New England with the coming of the Pilgrims. The Mayflower compact and the church covenant provided the basis for the social organization of Plymouth; and the covenant idea had taken so strong a hold on the popular mind of Massachusetts Bay that the astute leaders of the oligarchy were quick to see the advantage of investing the charter, in the popular imagination, with the sanctity of the compact idea; and by a subtle process of idealizing, they transmuted the charter of a trading company into a fundamental organic law, that was reckoned an adequate written constitution to safeguard the rights of the people. It was a clever political move, but it seems not to have satisfied Thomas Hooker, who was too liberal in his views to accept the shadow for the substance. As a left-wing Independent he would have a real compact, and a popular fundamental law to safeguard the liberties of the people; and he saw to it that the new commonwealth was broadly based on the common will, rather than narrowly on the rule of the gentry. The democratic order of Connecticut was English Independency transplanted to the new world.

To Hooker New England Congregationalism owes as great a debt as does New England democracy. The last great work he undertook was a defense of the New England way against the criticism of the English Presbyterians. He was to prove a powerful advocate, for not only was he intellectually equipped to write a knotty book in answer to other knotty books, but unlike Cotton and Davenport and Mather, he was wholly in sympathy with Congregationalism, and had no mind to conceal or equivocate concerning its democratic tendencies. He would write no apology, but a frank and vigorous defense. His church polity, as elaborated in his *Survey of the Summe of Church Discipline*, is professedly Hebraic. "Ecclesiastical Policy," he asserts baldly, "is a skill of ordering the affairs of Christ's house, according to the pattern of his word," and he then proceeds to postulate the principle of absolutism by accepting a divine sovereign will. But this divine sovereignty was a blow struck at all temporal absolutisms, for it spoke through no vicegerent of pope, bishop, presbytery or magistrate, but only through the voice of the individual subject. It is the priesthood of all believers. "The *Supreme* and *Monarchicall* power resides onely in our Saviour, can onely be given and attributed to him, and to none other." There remained, then, the difficult business of determining how the sovereign will of Christ is to be wrought on earth, and into this Hooker delved with such convincing thoroughness that, in his own words, "no man that hath supped on Logick, hath a forehead to gainsay" his conclusions. He was bold in innovation—"a cause is not the lesse true, because of late discovered"; but after quieting "the stomachs of such, whose expectations are not answered in any opinion, unless it be moldy with age," he proceeds to explain the true nature of church organization thus:

But whether all Ecclesiasticall power be impaled, impropriated, and rightly taken in to the Presbytery alone: Or that the people of the Particular Churches should come in for a share, according to their places and proportions; This is left as the subject of the inquiry of this age, and that which occasions great thought of heart of all hands: Great thoughts of hearts in the Presbytery, as being very loth to part with that so chief privilege, and of which they have taken possession so many years. Great Thoughts of heart amongst the Churches, how they may clear their right, and claim it in such pious sobriety and moderation, as becomes the Saints: being unwilling to loose their cause and comfort, meerly upon a *nihil dicit:* or forever to be deprived of so precious a legacy, as they conceive this is, though it hath been withheld from them, by the tyranny of the Pope, and prescription of times. Nor can they conceive it lesse, then a heedlesse betraying of their speciall liberties, and not selling but casting away their inheritance, and right, by a careless silence, when the course of providence, as the juncture of times now present themselves, allows them a writt *Ad melius inquirendum. . . .* These are the times when people shall be fitted for such priviledges, fit I say to obtain them, and fit to use them. . . . And whereas it hath been charged upon the people, that through their ignorance and unskilfulnesse, they are not able to wield such priviledges, and therefore not fit to share in any such power, The Lord hath promised: To take away the vail from all faces in the mountain, the *weak* shall be as David, and David as an Angel of God.[10]

The church of Visible Saints confederating together to walk in the fellowship of the faith . . . is *Totum essentiale. . . .* Election of the People rightly ordered by the rule of Christ, gives the essentials to an Officer, or leaves the impression of a true outward Call, and so an Office-power upon a Pastor . . . *there is a communicating of Power* by Voluntary Subjection when, though there be *no Office-power, formaliter* in the people, yet they willingly yeelding themselves to be ruled by another, desiring and calling of him to take that rule; he accepting of what they yeeld, possessing that right which they put upon him, by free consent; *hence ariseth* this Relation and authority of Office-rule.[11]

[10] *Survey of the Summe of Church Discipline*, Introduction.
[11] *Ibid..* Part II, pp. 66, 72.

It is crabbed prose, not altogether worthy of a man who kept the thorns crackling under the pot when he stood face to face with his congregation, and though we may feel inclined to accept the challenge of a certain old Puritan, and "lay a *caveat* against the author's sweet and solid handling" of his matter, we shall be little inclined to lay a *caveat* against his doctrine. Here is no casuistry like John Cotton's, denying Congregationalism while ostensibly defending it; but a frank acceptance of the supreme power of the people. "The Lord hath promised to take away the veil from all faces"—in this faith Thomas Hooker walked all his days, and what he could himself do to remove the veil from the faces of the common people, he did heartily as unto the Lord, thereby proving his right to be remembered among the early stewards of our American democracy.

III

ROGER WILLIAMS

Seeker

The gods, it would seem, were pleased to have their jest with Roger Williams by sending him to earth before his time. In manner and speech a seventeenth-century Puritan controversialist, in intellectual interests he was contemporary with successive generations of prophets from his own days to ours. His hospitable mind anticipated a surprising number of the idealisms of the future. As a transcendental mystic he was a forerunner of Emerson and the Concord school, discovering an indwelling God of love in a world of material things; as a speculative Seeker he was a forerunner of Channing and the Unitarians, discovering the hope of a more liberal society in the practice of the open mind; as a political philosopher he was a forerunner of Paine and the French romantic school, discovering the end of government in concern for the *res publica*, and the cohesive social tie in the principle of good will. Democrat and Christian, the generation to which he belongs is not yet born, and all his life he remained a stranger amongst men. Things natural and right to John Cotton were no better than anachronisms to him. He lived and dreamed in a future he was not to see, impatient to bring to men a heaven they were unready for. And because they were unready they could not understand the grounds of his hope, and not understanding they were puzzled and angry and cast him out to dream his dreams in the wilderness. There was abundant reason for his banishment. A child of light, he came bringing not peace but the sword. A humane and liberal spirit, he was groping for a social order more generous than any theocracy—that should satisfy the aspirations of men for a catholic fellowship, greater than sect or church, village or nation, embracing all races and creeds, bringing together the sundered societies of men in a common spirit of good will.

Roger Williams was the most provocative figure thrown upon the Massachusetts shores by the upheaval in England, the one original thinker amongst a number of capable social architects. An intellectual barometer, fluctuating with every change in the rising storm of revolution, he came transporting hither the new and disturbant doctrines of the Leveler, loosing wild foxes with fire-brands to ravage the snug fields of the Presbyterian Utopia. He was the "*first rebel* against the divine *church-order* established in the wilderness," as Cotton Mather rightly reported. But he was very much more than that; he was a rebel against all the stupidities that interposed a barrier betwixt men and the fellowship of their dreams. Those who found such stupidities serviceable to their ends, naturally disliked Roger Williams and believed they were serving God by undoing his work. There is a naïve passage in the *Magnalia* that suggests how incomprehensible to the theocratic mind was this stormy petrel that came out of England to flutter and clamor about Boston and Salem, until he was driven forth to find such resting place as he might, there to bring forth after his kind.

In the year 1654, a certain windmill in the Low Countries, whirling round with extraordinary violence, by reason of a violent storm then blowing, the stone at length by its rapid motion became so intensely hot as to fire the mill, from whence the flames, being dispersed by the high winds, did set a whole Town on fire. But I can tell my reader that, above twenty years before this, there was a whole country in America like to be set on fire by the rapid motion of a Windmill in the head of one particular man. [12]

And John Cotton, worsted in his bout with his brilliant antagonist, and perhaps frightened at the latter's free speculation, found such satisfaction as he could in epithets. Roger Williams was an "evill-worker"; his "head runneth round"; "it would weary a sober

[12] *Magnalia*, Vol. II, p. 495.

minde to pursue such windy fancies," such "offensive and disturbant doctrines"; when "a man is delivered up to Satan . . .
no marvell if he cast forth fire-brands, and arrows, and mortall-
things"; "it is such a transcendent light, as putteth out all the
lights in the world besides."

The open facts of Roger Williams' life are known to everybody.
Born in the year 1603,[13] he became a protégé of the great Coke, was
educated at Cambridge, and destined for the law, but forsook it
for the ministry. He was well advanced in his studies and coming
to conclusions that must have disturbed his conservative friends,
at the time of the Great Migration. Beginning as an Anglican,
then turning Separatist, then Baptist, and finally Seeker,[14] he is
perhaps more adequately described as a Puritan intellectual who
became a Christian freethinker, more concerned with social commonwealths than with theological dogmas. He passed rapidly
through successive phases of current thought to end as a Leveler.
Before quitting England he had embraced the principle of Separatism, and on his first coming over he refused the teachership of the
Boston church—the position given to Cotton two years later—
because it had not broken wholly with Anglicanism. He went to
the more liberal Salem, where his inconvenient questioning of land
titles and his views on the charter brought him into conflict with
the Boston authorities. Refusing to be silenced he was banished
and made his way to Rhode Island—"sorely tossed for one fourteen
weeks, in a bitter winter season, not knowing what bread or bed
did mean"—there to found a commonwealth on democratic principles.

Yet how inadequately do such meager facts reveal the deeper
sources of his militancy! He lived in the realm of ideas, of inquiry
and discussion; and his actions were creatively determined by
principles the bases of which he examined with critical insight.
Instead of being a weather vane, blown about by every wind of
doctrine, he was an adventurous pioneer, surveying the new fields

---

[13] For the date, see *Rhode Island Historical Society*, Vol. VIII, p. 156; *Narragansett
Club Publications*, Vol. VI, p. 599.

[14] The Seekers were thus described by a contemporary English pen: "Many have
wrangled so long about the Church that at last they have quite lost it, and go
under the name of *Expecters* and *Seekers*, and do deny that there is any Church, or
any true minister, or any ordinances; some of them affirm the Church to be in the
wilderness, and they are seeking for it there; others say that it is in the smoke of the
Temple, and that they are groping for it there—where I leave them praying to
God." (Paget, *Heresiography;* quoted in Masson, *Life of Milton*, Vol. III, p. 153.)

of thought laid open by the Reformation, and marking out the several spheres of church and state in the ordering of a true commonwealth. He was the incarnation of Protestant individualism, seeking new social ties to take the place of those that were loosening; and as a child of a great age of political speculation his religion issued in political theory rather than in theological dogma. Like other Separatist-Levelers he had penetrated to the foundations of the New Testament and had taken to heart the revolutionary ideals that underlie its teachings. It was the spirit of love that served as teacher to him; love that exalted the meanest to equality with the highest in the divine republic of Jesus, and gave an exalted sanction to the conception of a Christian commonwealth. He regarded his fellow men literally as the children of God and brothers in Christ; and from this primary conception of the fatherhood of God and the brotherhood of man, he deduced his political philosophy. Like Channing two hundred years later, he sought to adjust his social program to the determining fact that human worth knows neither Jew nor Gentile, rank nor caste; and following the example of his Master he went forth into a hostile world, seeking to make it over.

With this spirit of Christian fellowship, warm and human and lovable, repudiating all coercion, there was joined an eager mysticism—a yearning for intimate personal union with Christ as symbolized in the parable of the vine and the branches, a union as close as that of the bride and her husband. Running through his writings is a recurrent echo of the Hebrew love-song that Puritan thought suffused with a glowing mysticism: "I am my beloved's and my beloved is mine: he feedeth among the lilies. . . . I will rise now, and go about the city in the streets, and in the broad ways I will seek him whom my soul loveth." But when he went out into the broad ways of Carolinian England, seeking the rose of Sharon and the lily of the valley, he discovered only abominations. The lover was tempted by false kisses; the Golden Image was set up in the high places, and the voice of authority commanded to bow down to it. And so as a Christian mystic Roger Williams became a Separatist, and set his mind upon the new world as a land where the lover might dwell with his bride. Yet upon his arrival there he found the churches still "implicitly National," and "yet asleep in respect of abundant ignorance and negligence, and consequently grosse abominations and pollutions of Worship, in which the choicest servants of God, and most faithfull Witnesses of many truths have lived in more or lesse, yea in maine and fundamental points, ever since the Apostasie." Which "abominations and pollutions of Worship," he now proposed to sweep away altogether.[15] It was not an easy program, nor one entered upon lightly. Better than most, Roger Williams understood how closely interwoven were the threads of church and state. Separatism, with its necessary corollary of toleration, could not be unraveled from Carolinian society without loosening the whole social fabric. It was a political question even more than ecclesiastical; and it could justify itself only in the light of a total political philosophy. No other man in New England comprehended so fully the difficulties involved in the problem, as Roger Williams, or examined them so thoroughly; and out of his long speculations emerged a theory of the commonwealth that must be reckoned the richest contribution of Puritanism to American political thought.

The just renown of Roger Williams has too long been obscured by ecclesiastical historians, who in emphasizing his defense of the principle of toleration have overlooked the fact that religious toleration was only a necessary deduction from the major principles of his political theory, and that he was concerned with matters far more fundamental than the negative virtue of non-interference in the domain of individual faith. He was primarily a political philosopher rather than a theologian—one of the acutest and most searching of his generation of Englishmen, the teacher of Vane and Cromwell and Milton, a forerunner of Locke and the natural-rights school, one of the notable democratic thinkers that the English race has produced. Much of his life was devoted to the problem of discovering a new basis for social reorganization, and his intellectual progress was marked by an abundant wreckage of

[15] The Biblical authority for Separatism Williams found in both general and specific injunctions. The former, in the second commandment, in the third chapter of Daniel, in the seventeenth and eighteenth chapters of Revelation—the "wine of her fornication" being the ceremonial and ordinances of the English church—and in the Song of Solomon. The latter were: Revelation, 18:4: "And I heard another voice from heaven, saying, Come out of her, my people, that ye be not partakers of her sins. . . ."; Isaiah, 53:11: "Depart ye, depart ye, go ye out from thence, touch not the unclean thing; go ye out in the midst of her; be ye clean, that bear the vessels of the Lord"; II Corinthians, 6:17: "Wherefore come out from among them, and be ye separate, saith the Lord, and touch not the unclean thing; and I will receive you." On these texts he based his argument with Cotton for the total separation of the New England churches. (See *Narragansett Club Publications*, Vol. I, p. 300.)

obsolete theory and hoary fiction that strewed his path. He was a social innovator on principle, and he left no system unchallenged; each must justify itself in reason and expediency or be put aside. Broadly the development of his thought falls into three stages: the substitution of the compact theory of the state for the divine-right theory; the rejection of the supposititious compact of the earlier school and the fictitious abstract state—still postulated by many thinkers—and the substitution of a realistic conception of the political state as the sovereign repository of the social will, and the government—or agent of the state—as the practical instrument of society to effect its desired ends; and finally, the difficult problem of creating the necessary machinery of a democratic common-wealth, as the exigencies of the Rhode Island experiment required. Throughout, the inspiration of his thinking was social rather than narrowly political or theological, and the creative source would seem to have been the middle ages with their fruitful principle of men in a given society enrolling themselves voluntarily as members of bodies corporate, finding in such corporate ties a sufficient and all-embracing social bond.[16]

In his substitution of the compact theory for divine right, Williams was brought face to face with the fundamental assumption of the Massachusetts theocracy, based on numerous passages of Scripture, that the political state is established and sanctioned by the God of the Hebrews—an assumption that was freely used to justify the engrossing of authority by the magistracy. As a theologian he critically examined the Scriptural authorities, and while conceding the divine source of government in general, he was careful to cut away all autocratic deductions from the Pauline assertion that "the powers that be are ordained of God." "Government and order in families, towns, etc., is an ordinance of the Most High, Rom. 13, for the peace and good of mankind" [17] he admitted; but he agreed with Richard Hooker in discovering this order of government to be no other than natural law. The state is divine in origin because it is natural, and what is natural is of God. The Hebraic commonwealth had been established imme-diately in an ordinance of Jehovah, but Christ and his disciples

[16] For much of the material made use of here, I am indebted to *The Political Theory of Roger Williams*, a dissertation by Dr. James E. Ernst of the University of Washington.

[17] "Letter to the Town Clerk of Providence," in *Narragansett Club Publications*, Vol. VI, p. 401.

regarded the state and God as distinct authorities, not to be
confused—"Render, therefore, unto Caesar the things which are
Caesar's; and unto God the things that are God's." The conclusion at which he arrived, then, from the merging of divine ordinances and natural law, was expressed in a doctrine that sets
apart the individual citizen in all his spiritual and intellectual
rights, from the subject of the commonwealth, and provides the
basis for his principle of toleration. "A Civill Government is an
ordinance of God, to conserve the Civill peace of the people, so
farre as concerns their Bodies and Goods," and no farther.[18] From
this position he never retreated.

> Every lawful Magistrate whether succeeding or elective, is not only the
> Minister of God, but the Minister or servant of the people also (what
> people or nation soever they be all the world over), and that Minister or
> Magistrate goes beyond his commission who intermeddles with that which
> cannot be given him in commission from the people. . . .[19]

Having thus reduced the divine-right field within narrow limits
and translated it into an abstraction, he preëmpts all the ground
of practical politics for his compact theory. In accord with a long
line of liberal thinkers running back through Richard Hooker to
Augustine and the earlier Roman school, he accepted the major
deductions from the compact theory of the state: that government
is a man-made institution, that it rests on consent, and that it is
founded on the assumed equality of the subjects. He had only to
translate these abstractions into concrete terms, and apply them
realistically, to create a new and vital theory. The covenant idea
of church organization had long been familiar to Separatists. To
this the Pilgrims had added the Mayflower compact and Thomas
Hooker had drawn up the Connecticut compact. Government
resting on consent and authorized by written agreement was then
no untried novelty when Roger Williams began his long speculations on the nature and functions of the political state. With
Hobbes he traced the origin of the state to social necessity. The
condition of nature is a condition of anarchy—a war of all against
all; and for mutual protection the state takes its rise. "The World
otherwise would be like a sea, wherein Men, like Fishes, would
hunt and devoure each other, and the greater devoure the lesse."[20]

[18]. "The Bloudy Tenent," in *Narragansett Club Publications*, Vol. III, p. 349.
[19] "The Bloudy Tenent Yet More Bloudy," in *Narragansett Club Publications*,
Vol. IV, p. 187.
[20] "The Bloudy Tenent," in *Narragansett Club Publications*, Vol. III. p. 398.

But unlike the fiction assumed by Hobbes and Locke, this was no supposititious contract between ruler and ruled in prehistoric times, but present and actual, entered into between the several members of a free community for their common governance; nor on the other hand, like Burke's irrevocable compact, was it an unyielding constitution or fundamental law; but flexible, responsive to changing conditions, continually modified to meet present needs. It is no other than a mutual agreement, arrived at frankly by discussion and compromise, to live together in a political union, organizing the life of the commonwealth in accordance with nature, reason, justice, and expediency.

From this conception of the flexible nature of compact law came the sharp delimitation between state and government that he was at pains to make clear, and that constitutes a significant phase of his theory. Having rejected in his thinking the fictitious abstract state, the repository of an equally fictitious abstract sovereignty, he located sovereignty in the total body of citizens embraced within the community consciousness, acting in a political capacity. The state is society organized, government is the state functioning—it is the political machinery devised by the sovereign people to effect definite ends. And since the single end and purpose for which the body of citizens erect the state is the furtherance of the communal well-being, the government becomes a convenient instrument to serve the common weal, responsible to the sovereign people and strictly limited by the terms of the social agreement. "The Sovereign power of all civill Authority," he asserted, "is founded in the consent of the People that every Commonwealth hath radically and fundamentally. The very Common-weales, Bodies of People . . . have fundamentally in themselves the Root of Power, to set up what Government and Governors they shall agree upon." [21] Since governments are but "Derivatives and Agents immediately derived and employed as eyes and hands and instruments," the state or sovereign people can make their "own severall Lawes and Agreements . . . according to their severall Natures, Dispositions and Constitutions, and their Common peace and wellfare." [22] Final appeal is to "the Bar of the People or Commonweal, where all may personally meet, as in some Commonweales of small number, or in greater by their Representatives"—a system that

[21] See *Narragansett Club Publications*, Vol. III, pp. 214, 355, 366.
[22] "The Bloudy Tenent Yet More Bloody," in *ibid.*, Vol. IV, p. 487.

suits with the "Nature, Conditions and circumstances of the People," according to the "Circumstances of time and place." [23] In a well-known passage he puts the matter more compactly, thus:

> From this *Grant* I infer . . . that the *Soveraigne, originall*, and *foundation of civill power* lies in the *People*. . . . And if so, that a People may erect and establish what *forme* of *Government* seemes to them most meete for their *civill condition:* It is evident that such *Governments* as are by them erected and established, have no more *power*, nor for no longer time, then the *civill power* or people consenting and agreeing shall betrust them with. This is cleere not only in *Reason*, but in the experience of all *commonweales*, where the people are not deprived of their naturall freedom by the power of Tyrants. [24]

The state, then, is society working consciously through experience and reason, to secure for the individual citizen the largest measure of freedom and well-being. It is armed with a potential power of coercion, but only to secure justice. In such a state government can subsist only by making proselytes to sound reason, by compromise and arbitration, and not by force. But if sovereignty inheres in the majority will, what securities remain for individual and minority rights? What fields lie apart from the inquisition of the majority, and by what agencies shall the engrossing of power be thwarted? The replies to such questions, so fundamental to every democratic program, he discovers in a variety of principles; to the former in an adaptation of the spirit of medieval society that restricted political functions by social usage, and to the latter by the application of local home rule, the initiative and the referendum, and the recall. In the large field he ascribes to social custom, he was a follower of Luther and a forerunner of French romantic thinkers. His creative conception was an adaptation of the medieval theory of the corporation, or group of persons voluntarily joining for specific purposes under the law; and this idea he applies to the vexed question of the relation of church and state. The legal status of the church, he argued, is identical with that of a trading company; it is a corporate body with corporate rights, and the several members enjoy all the freedoms and privileges that inhere in them by law and nature in their civil capacity. The character of its membership and the content of its creed are of no different concern to the civil magistrates than those of any

[23] "The Bloudy Tenent," in *ibid.*, Vol. III, p. 248.
[24] *Ibid.*, Vol. III, p. 248.

other corporation. "The state religion of the world," he asserted, "is a Politic invention of men to maintain the civil state." [25] Elaborated at greater length, his thesis is this:

The *Church* or company of *worshippers* (whether true or false) is like unto a . . . *Corporation, Society,* or *Company* . . . in *London;* which Companies may hold their *Courts,* keep their *Records,* hold *disputations;* and in matters concerning their *Societie,* may dissent, divide, breake into *Schismes* and *Factions,* sue and implead each other at the *Law,* yea wholly breake up and dissolve into pieces and nothing, and yet the *peace* of the *Citie* not be in the least measure impaired or disturbed; because the *essence* or being of the *Citie,* and so the *well-being* and *peace* thereof is essentially distinct from those particular *Societies;* the *Citie-Courts, Citie-Lawes, Citie-punishments* distinct from theirs. The *Citie* was before them, and stands absolute and intire, when such a *Corporation* or *Societie* is taken down.[26]

Having thus effectively secularized the church on its institutional side, he laid down twelve theses, of which these reach to the heart of the matter:

(1) *God* requireth not an *uniformity* of *Religion* to be *inacted* and *inforced* in any *civill state;* which inforced *uniformity* (sooner or later) is the greatest occasion of *civill Warre, ravishing* of *conscience, persecution* of *Christ Jesus* in his servants, and of the *hypocrisie* and destruction of millions of souls. (2) It is the will and command of *God,* that . . . a *permission* of the most *Paganish, Jewish, Turkish,* or *Antichristian consciences* and *worships,* bee granted to *all* men in all *Nations* and *Countries:* and they are onely to bee *fought* against with that *Sword* which is onely (in *Soule matters*) *able* to *conquer,* to wit, the *Sword* of *Gods Spirit,* the *Word* of *God.* (3) True *civility* and *Christianity* may both flourish in a *state* or *Kingdome,* notwithstanding the *permission* of divers and contrary *consciences,* either of *Jew* or *Gentile.*[27]

Abhorrent as such doctrine was to the Massachusetts theocrats, Roger Williams did not cease to press it home to their minds and consciences. "I know and am persuaded," he wrote Winthrop on July 21, 1637, "that your misguidings are great and lamentable, and the further you pass in your way, the further you wander, and the end of one vexation will be but the beginning of another, till conscience be permitted (though erroneous) to be free amongst you." [28] It was not toleration in the narrow sense of benevolent

[25] "The Bloudy Tenent Yet More Bloody," in *ibid.,* Vol. IV, p. 222.
[26] "The Bloudy Tenent," in *ibid.,* Vol. III, p. 76.
[27] Preface to "The Bloudy Tenent," in *ibid.,* Vol. III, p. 3.
[28] *Narragansett Club Publications,* Vol. VI, p. 51.

non-interference by an authority that refrained from exercising its reserved right, that Roger Williams was interested in; it was rather religious liberty as a fundamental right, that had never been surrendered to the civil power, that lay beyond its jurisdiction and was in no way answerable to it, that he upheld in his great work *The Bloudy Tenent of Persecution for Cause of Conscience;* and the long dispute with John Cotton was, in its deeper significance, a dispute between two schools of political theory and two experiments in commonwealth building. In that notable debate aristocracy and democracy joined issues, and the vital question of the rights and liberties of the individual citizen in the political state for the first time was critically examined in America.

From the foregoing analysis of his political theory it should be clear that Roger Williams was a confirmed individualist who carried to its logical conclusion the Reformation principle of the right of private inquiry. Only Vane and Milton of his generation of Englishmen went so far along that path. He had seen the liberalisms involved in Luther's premises submerged by the rising nationalism which ambitious princes found useful for selfish ends; and he had seen the policy of the Massachusetts magistrates driving boldly in the same direction. That Rhode Island should not repeat the old unhappy mistake of coercive absolutism, was a matter therefore of vital concern to him. A great experiment in democracy was to be tried, and to that experiment he devoted his life. Into the form and structure of the new commonwealth went the best thought of English Independency. It was founded on the principles of "liberty and equality, both in land and government," [29] and established in the sovereignty of the people. That government should not engross its powers, the compact entered into provided for frequent elections, a single-chambered legislature, joint and individual initiative of laws, compulsory referendum, the right of recall of all laws including the constitution, and appeal to arbitration. A rigid constitution, augmenting in authority with age and veneration, Roger Williams feared as acutely as did Paine or Jefferson. To vest sovereignty in the courts through the right of review and interpretation was repugnant to his whole political theory. The fundamental law could be interpreted only by the power that created it originally, namely,

[29] "Letter to the Town of Providence," in *Narragansett Club Publications*, Vol. VI, p. 263.

the sovereign people acting in a political capacity. Within the larger framework of the state the several towns retained the right of home rule in local matters. They were corporations, erected like the church in the spirit of medieval corporate law, competent to rule themselves, yet not infringing on the sovereignty that granted them their powers. In short, to adapt the words of a modern student, the state of Rhode Island as erected by Roger Williams in accordance with the principles of his political philosophy, was "nothing so much as a great public-service corporation." [30] Or, as another student has put it, "If democracy . . . in its ultimate meaning be held to imply not only a government in which the preponderant share of power resides in the hands of the people, but a society based on the principles of political and religious freedom, Rhode Island beyond any other of the American Colonies is entitled to be called democratic." [31]

It was a hazardous experiment to undertake in an age when the ark of the democratic covenant found few places of refuge. Its friends were only a handful and its enemies many and powerful, and had it not been for a group of defenders in Parliament, the Rhode Island venture would have been brought to a speedy end. English Independency saved for America what English Presbyterianism would have destroyed. To Sir Harry Vane Rhode Island owes a debt of gratitude second only to that due Roger Williams. But though its godly neighbors were not permitted to destroy Rhode Island, they were free to slander and spread evil reports, and so thoroughly did they do their work that for upwards of two hundred years the little commonwealth was commonly spoken of in such terms as Rogues Island and the State of Confusion; not indeed, till it left off following agrarian and Populistic gods, till it had ceased to be democratic, did it become wholly respectable. It was not so much the reputed turbulence of Rhode Island that was disapproved by the Boston magistrates; but rather the disturbing example of a colony at their very doors, which, in denying the right of the godly to police society, gave encouragement to evil-disposed persons in their own sober commonwealth. Every democracy, they believed, was so notoriously mad and lawless— as both sacred and profane authorities had sufficiently demonstrated—that the Boston oligarchy never forgave Parliament for

[30] Duguit, *Law in the Modern State*, p. 51.
[31] Gooch, *History of Democratic Ideas*, p. 80.

refusing them permission to establish a mandatory over their self-willed neighbors.

It was to prevent such meddling that Roger Williams had been at pains to secure a Parliamentary charter; and he saw to it that the charter terms should not restrict the democratic liberties. His faith in the sobriety and good sense of the people of Rhode Island was never shaken. In spite of many difficulties that grew out of the sharp individualism of vigorous characters, the colony proved to be a good place to dwell for those who were content to share the common rights and privileges. In a letter to Vane, written in 1654, the founder apologizes for some of the things reported of them, but the apology does not detract from the just pride with which he contemplated the solid achievements of the Rhode Island experiment:

Possibly a sweet cup hath rendered many of us wanton. We have long drunk of the cup of as great liberties as any people we can hear of under the whole heaven. We have not only been long free (together with all New England) from the iron yolk of wolfish bishops, and their popish ceremonies . . . but we have sitten quiet and dry from the streams of blood spilt by that war in our native Country. We have not felt the new chains of Presbyterian tyrants, nor in this colony have we been consumed with the over-zealous fire of the (so called) godly christian magistrates. Sir, we have not known what an excise means; we have almost forgotten what tithes are, yea, or taxes either, to church or commonwealth. We could name other special privileges, ingredients of our sweet cup, which your great wisdom knows to be very powerful (except more than ordinary watchfulness) to render the best of men wanton and forgetful.[32]

England gave her best when she sent us Roger Williams. A great thinker and a bold innovator, the repository of the generous liberalisms of a vigorous age, he brought with him the fine wheat of long years of English tillage to sow in the American wilderness. How much America owes to him is perhaps, after all the intervening years, not adequately realized; the shadow of Massachusetts Bay still too much obscures the large proportions of one who was certainly the most generous, most open-minded, most lovable, of the Puritan emigrants—the truest Christian amongst many who sincerely desired to be Christian. He believed in men and in their native justice, and he spent his life freely in the cause of humanity. Neither race nor creed sundered him from his fellows; the Indian was his brother equally with the Englishman. He was a Leveler because ne was convinced that society with its caste institutions dealt unjustly with the common man; he was a democrat because he believed that the end and object of the political state was the common well-being; he was an iconoclast because he was convinced that the time had come when a new social order must be erected on the decay of the old. *"Liberavi animam meam,"* he said with just pride; "I have not hid within my *breast* my *souls* belief." "It was more than forty years after his exile that he lived here," wrote Cotton Mather, "and in many thinges acquitted himself so laudably, that many juditious persons judged him to have the root of the matter in him, during the long winter of this retirement." Since those words were written increasing numbers of "juditious persons" have come to agree with the reluctant judgment of Cotton Mather, and are verily persuaded that Master Roger Williams "had the root of the matter in him." In his own day he was accounted an enemy of society, and the commonwealth of Massachusetts has never rescinded the decree of banishment issued against him; yet like so many unshackled thinkers, he was a seeker after a better order, friend to a nobler and more humane society. If he transported to America the democratic aspirations of English Independency, it is perhaps well to recall the price that was exacted of him for his service:

Let the reader fancy him in 1640, a man of thirty-four, of bold and stout jaws, but with the richest and softest eyes, gazing out over the Bay of his dwelling, a spiritual Crusoe, the excommunicated even of Hugh Peters, and the most extreme and outcast soul in all America.[33]

[33] Masson, *Life of Milton*, Vol. II, p. 563.

CHAPTER V

OTHER DREAMERS IN ISRAEL

I

NATHANIEL WARD

Elizabethan Puritan

THE most caustic pen of early New England was wielded by the lawyer-minister and wit, Nathaniel Ward of Ipswich, author of the crotchety little book, *The Simple Cobler of Aggawam*, and chief compiler of the celebrated *Body of Liberties*. He is a strange figure to encounter in the raw little settlements. To come into his presence is to feel oneself carried back to an earlier age, when the courtly wits were weaving their silken terms into gorgeous tapestries. Born about the year 1578, he was only five years younger than Ben Jonson. Highly educated and intimate with the best society of England and the continent, he was well advanced in middle life when he set foot in the new world, and in his late sixties when he wrote *The Simple Cobler*. Far more strikingly than any of his emigrant brethren he belonged in taste and temperament to the later Elizabethan world, which lingered on into the reigns of James and Charles, zealously cultivating its quaint garden of letters, playing with inkhorn terms, and easing its cares with clever conceits. Faithful disciple of Calvin though he was, he was something of a courtier as well, with a rich sap of intelligence, which, fermented by much thought and travel in many lands, made him the raciest of wits, and doubtless the most delightful of companions over a respectable Puritan bottle. "I have only Two comforts to Live upon," Increase Mather reported him as saying. "The one is in the Perfections of Christ; The other is in The Imperfections of all Christians."

The Simple Cobler of Aggawam is certainly the brightest bit of Renaissance English penned in America—an Elizabethan clipped garden set down in a wilderness of theology. It deserves to be far better known than it is, not only for its "convenient condiments" of speech that will tickle the palate of an epicure, but for its quaint exposition of the muddled state of England in the year 1645. Like a belated Euphuist, Nathaniel Ward delighted in fantastic words.

> If I affect termes [he confessed, by way of apology] it is my feeblenesse; my friends that know me, thinke I doe not: I confesse, I see I have here and there taken a few finish stitches, which may haply please a few Velvet eares; but I cannot now well pull them out, unlesse I should seame-rend all. It seems it is a fashion with you to sugar your papers with Carnation phrases, and spangle your speeches with new quodled words. . . . I honour them with my heart, that can express more than ordinary matter in ordinary words; it is a pleasing eloquence; them more, that study wisely and soberly to inhance their native language. . . . Affected termes are unaffecting things to solid hearers; yet I hold him prudent, that in these fastidious times, will helpe disedged appetites with convenient condiments, and bangled ears, with pretty quicke pluckes.[1]

The casual reader is chiefly impressed by the quaint satire of the book, with its caustic comment on women's fashions—the "foole-fangles" of "nugiperous Gentledames," who "transclout" themselves into "gant bar-geese, ill-shapen-shotten-shell-fish"; and it is such bits that are commonly picked out for reprinting in the anthologies. But the real significance of the work lies elsewhere. *The Simple Cobler* is an old man's plea for accommodation of differences. It is bitter with intolerance of toleration; it is torn between an old loyalty to King Charles whom Ward knew and loved—"my long Idolatry towards you," as he confesses sadly—and a new loyalty to Parliament; and it is sobered by a strong concern over the desperate condition of England, which required looking to speedily, he believed, if the realm were not to be torn past all mending. On both sides there was abundant "misprision of Treason," which properly considered, he held to be no other than a "misprision of Reason"; and it was in the hope of summoning reason back to the national councils that the Cobbler offered his humble suggestions for the consideration of Englishmen.

Ward had been a lawyer before he turned to the ministry, and he seems to have impressed himself upon his fellow emigrants chiefly as a "subtile statesman." In his own way he was a political philosopher, little given like Roger Williams to exploring theory and examining principles, but applying rather a shrewd common sense to the problems of the times. He was convinced that old ways no longer sufficed; that prerogative and liberty could not much longer strain and pull against each other without rending the

---

[1] *The Simple Cobler*, edition of 1843, pp. 89–90.

whole fabric of the commonwealth; and the kernel of the book lies
in a new theory of constitutional government for England which he
offers as a convenient way out of the difficulties. Ward recognized
that new interests were challenging the long sway of King and
Tories; and as the antagonisms of rival interests strengthened, the
insufficiency of the traditional use and wont to maintain a due
balance of power was daily becoming more apparent. Hence had
resulted confusion, and out of the confusion, civil war. From
these patent facts Ward had convinced himself that there must
be an overhauling of the fundamental law of England: the twilight
zones must be explored and charted; the several rights and privileges of King, Lords, and Commons, must be sharply delimited;
and thus every party in the government be brought to understand
the exact bounds of its sphere. Neither King nor Commons would
then encroach upon the other, and royal prerogative and popular
will no longer dwell at sword's point with each other. What was
needed, in short, was a written constitution, carefully arrived at
by common consent, the terms of which should be just to all.
Hitherto God "hath taken order, that ill prerogatives, gotten by
the Sword, should in time be fetched home by the Dagger, if
nothing else will doe it: Yet I trust there is both day and means
to intervent this bargaine."

To preserve a just balance between rival interests in the state,
and to hold all parties to their responsibility to God, were then the
two problems to which Nathaniel Ward addressed himself, and the
manner and terms of his argument are sufficiently revealed in the
following passages:

Authority must have power to make and keep people honest; People,
honesty to obey Authority; both a Joynt-Councell to keep both safe.
Morall Lawes, Royall Prerogatives, Popular Liberties, are not of Mans
making or giving, but Gods: Man is but to measure them out by Gods
Rule: which if mans wisdome cannot reach, Mans experience must mend:
And these Essentialls, must not be Ephorized or Tribuned by one or a few
Mens discretion, but lineally sanctioned by Supreame Councels. In
pro-re-nascent occurrences, which cannot be foreseen; Diets, Parliaments,
Senates, or accountable Commissions, must have power to consult and
execute against intersilient dangers and flagitious crimes prohibited by
the light of Nature: yet it were good if States would let People know so
much beforehand, by some safe woven *manifesto*, that grosse Delinquents
may tell no tales of Anchors and Buoyes, nor palliate their presumptions
with pretense of ignorance. I know no difference in these Essentialls,
between Monarchies, Aristocracies, or Democracies. . . . And in all, the

best Standard to measure Prerogatives, is the Ploughstaffe; to measure Liberties, the Scepter: if the tearms were a little altered into Loyall Prerogatives and Royall Liberties, then we should be sure to have Royall Kings and Loyall Subjects. . . .

He is a good King that undoes not his Subjects by any one of his unlimited Prerogatives: and they are a good People, that undoe not their Prince, by any one of their unbounded Liberties, be they the very least. I am sure either may, and I am sure neither would be trusted, how good soever. Stories tell us in effect, though nor in termes, that over-risen Kings, have been the next evills to the world, unto fallen Angels; and that over-franchised people, are devills with smooth snaffles in their mouthes. A King that lives by Law, lives by love: and he that lives above Law, shall live under hatred doe what he can. Slavery and knavery goe as seldome asunder, as Tyranny and Cruelty. I have a long while thought it very possible, in a time of Peace . . . for disert Statesmen, to cut an exquisite thred between Kings Prerogatives, and Subjects Liberties of all sorts, so as *Caesar* might have his due, and People their share, without such sharpe disputes. Good Casuists would case it, and case it, part it, and part it; now it, and then it, punctually.[2]

Nathaniel Ward was no democrat like Hooker and therefore no Congregationalist. "I am neither Presbyterian, nor plebsbyterian, but an Interpendent," he said of himself. But his "Interpendency" would seem to have been only an individualistic form of Presbyterianism. For the radical Sectaries who were rising out of the turmoil of revolution, he had the contempt of a thoroughbred Jacobean gentleman; and for their newfangled notion of religious toleration and their fetish of popular liberties—founded and nourished he believed in sentimentalism—he would substitute the solid reality of absolute truth, the faithful friend and coadjutor of which he professed himself to be. "Justice and Equity were before time, and will be after it"; and he regarded it as folly to try to circumvent them. He would have no great altering of the fundamental arrangements of society, such as Independents like Roger Williams were seeking. The solidarity of church and state was an anciently accepted principle, far safer to trust in, he believed, than the vagaries of unhistorical sects.

Experience will teach Churches and Christians, that it is farre better to live in a State united, though a little Corrupt, then in a State, whereof some Part is incorrupt, and all the rest divided. . . . The Scripture saith, there is nothing makes free but Truth, and Truth saith, there is no Truth but One. . . . He that is willing to tolerate any Religion, or discrepant way of Religion, besides his own, unless it be in matters

[2] *Ibid.*, pp. 54–55.

meerly indifferent, either doubts of his own, or is not sincere in it. . . .
He that is willing to tolerate any unsound opinion, that his own may also
be tolerated, though never so sound, will for a need hang Gods Bible at the
Devils girdle.[3]

As an honest Christian and a loyal subject he would honor both
the divine and temporal authorities; nevertheless, in order that
the law of God and the law of the land might be known of all and
march together, he would have the exact terms of the constitution
written out by "disert statesmen" in time of peace, and published
broadly, in Massachusetts as well as in England. And so when
he was commissioned to draw up a body of liberties for the new
commonwealth, he found the task congenial. As a lawyer he
seems to have been concerned at the non-legal methods of the
magistrates in dispensing judgment, so repugnant to the spirit
of the Common Law; and in the election sermon of 1641, that he
was invited to preach, he "advanced several things that savored
more of liberty, than some of the magistrates were prepared to
approve." [4] But it was the lawyer protesting against court
methods that spoke out, not the liberal concerned with broader
liberties. In a letter to Winthrop, December 22, 1639, dealing with
the body of laws, he questioned, "Whether it will not be of ill
consequence to send the Court business to the common consideration of the Freemen," adding:

I fear it will too much exauctorate the power of that Court to prostrate
matters in that manner, I suspect both Commonwealth and Churches
have discended to lowe already. I see the spirits of the people runne
high, and what they gett they hould. They may not be denied their
proper and lawfull liberties, but a question whether it be of God to interest
the inferiour sort in that which should be reserved *inter optimates penes
quos est sancire leges* [i. e. to the aristocracy with whom rests the power to
establish the law].[5]

The celebrated *Body of Liberties* was presented three years after
The Simple Cobler was written, and in spite of his frankly aristocratic bias, Nathaniel Ward did a real service to Massachusetts
by incorporating into the law of the commonwealth many of the
old English safeguards of person and property, in some instances
advancing beyond current English practice. Yet true to his
Hebraic leanings, and in harmony with the spirit of the theocracy,

---

[3] *Ibid.*, pp. 8, 10.   [4] *Ibid.*, Introduction.
[5] Dean, *Memoir of the Rev. Nathaniel Ward*, pp. 56–57

he added certain brutalities drawn from the Mosaic code that
were soon to drop away.

There is something refreshing in the extraordinary frankness of
this old Puritan of the days of Elizabeth. He was no demagogue,
but a stout upholder of authority, who accepted the rule of caste
and the law of an eye for an eye. The militant severity of his
judgments, and the caustic wit of his comments, suggest somewhat
startlingly how long and bitter would be the struggle in New
England before the spirit of liberalism should find wide acceptance there. Gentlemen of the immigrant generation were set in
their ways, and none more inflexibly than Nathaniel Ward. He was
too old to adjust himself to new conditions, a fact which he recognized by returning to England to die, leaving behind as a warning
certain pithy quatrains of which this is one:

> The upper world shall Rule,
>   While Stars will run their race:
> The nether world obey
>   While People keep their place.

II

JOHN ELIOT

A Theocratic Utopia

At the session of the General Court holden at Boston, May 22,
1661, it was ordered:

This Court taking notice of a booke entituled Christian Commonwealth,
written . . . by Mr. John Eliot of Roxbury in New England, which . . .
is justly offensive and in speciall relating to kingly Gouvernment in England, the which the said Mr. Eliot hath also freely and fully acknowledged
to this Court. It is therefore ordered by this Court and the Authority
thereof, that the said Booke be totally suppressed and the Authors ac-
knowledgement recorded; and that all persons whatsoever in this jurisdiction that have any of the said Bookes in theire Custody shall on theire
perrills within fowerteene dayes after publication hereof either cancel or
deface or deliver them unto the next Magistrate or to the Secretary,
whereby all farther divulment and improovement of the said offensive
Booke may be prevented.[6]

The little book over which such a pother was made by the New
England magistrates in the days when they were under the censorious eye of the newly restored Stuart government was the single

[6] *Massachusetts Historical Society Publications*, Vol. IX, Third Series, p. 128.

venture in the field of political speculation by the excellent John
Eliot, apostle to the Indians. It was a slender volume, written
about 1650, although not printed till 1659; but within the narrow
compass of twenty-one pages this dreamer in Israel has sketched
the outlines of an ideal Christian commonwealth. It was a day
and a world of idealists, and so John Eliot paused in the midst of
his missionary labors to fashion a brick for the building of that
temple which the Puritans of the Protectorate were dreaming of.
The idols had been broken by the hammer of Cromwell; the malevolent powers of this world were brought low; it remained now only
for the people of God to enter into a solemn covenant to establish a
commonwealth after the true divine model. That no mistake
should be made in so important a matter, John Eliot was moved
to send out of the American wilderness the plan of a Christian
Utopia, sanctioned by the Mosaic example and buttressed at
every point by chapter and verse, which he offered to the godly
Puritans of England as a suitable guide to their feet.

Naked theocracy is nowhere else so uncompromisingly de-
lineated as in the pages of *The Christian Commonwealth*. At the
basis of Eliot's political speculations were the two germinal conceptions which animated his theocratic brethren generally: the
conception that Christ is King of Kings before whom all earthly
authority must bow, and the conception that the Scripture alone
reveals the law of God. So long as the Stuarts were ruling at St.
James's speculative theocrats found it expedient to gloss their
principles with nice distinctions between temporal and spiritual
overlords; but with monarchy overthrown, they came out boldly
and urged the English people to put away all profane institutions.
"*Scripturae plentitudinem adoro*," John Cotton had exclaimed;
and to the same purpose John Eliot laid down the thesis:

There is undoubtedly a forme of civil Government instituted by God
himself in the holy Scriptures; whereby any Nation may enjoy all the
ends and effects of Government in the best manner, were they but per-
swaded to make trial of it. We should derogate from the sufficiency and
perfection of the Scriptures, if we should deny it.

The prayers, the expectation, and faith of the Saints in the Prophecies
and Promises of holy Scripture, are daily sounding in the ears of the Lord,
for the downfall of Anti-christ, and with him all humane Powers, Polities,
Dominions, and Governments; and in the room thereof, we wait for the
coming of the Kingdom of the Lord Jesus, who by his Divine Wisdom,
Power, Government and Laws, given us . . . in the holy Scriptures, will

reign over all the Nations of the earth in his due time: I mean the Lord Jesus will bring down all people, to be ruled by the Institutions, Laws, and Directions of the Word of God, not only in Church-Government and Administrations, but also in the Government and Administration of all affairs in the Common wealth.   And then Christ reigneth, when all things among men, are done by the direction of the word of his mouth: his Kingdom is then come amongst us, when his will is done on earth, as it is done in heaven, where no Humane or Angelical Policy or Wisdom doth guide anything, but all is done by Divine direction (Ps. 103:20); and so it shall be on earth, when and where Christ reigneth.

Much is spoken of the rightful Heir of the Crown of England, and of the unjustice of casting out the right Heir; but Christ is the onely right Heir of the Crown of England (Ps. 2:8) and of all other Nations also (Rev. 11:15).

That which the Lord now calleth England to attend is not to search humane Politics and Platformes of Government, contrived by the wisdom of man; but as the Lord hath carried on their works for them, so they ought to go unto the Lord, and enquire at the Word of his mouth, what Platforme of Government he hath therein commanded and prescribed.

From his Scriptural premises Eliot deduced a system of government that is altogether remarkable, not only for its rejection of the Separatist theory of natural rights, but for its naïve simplicity. Since the law has been declared once for all, perfect and final, there is no need for a legislative branch of government; and since Christ is sole ruler and king, there is no place for a profane head of the state; it remains only for the Christian theorist to provide a competent magisterial system to hear causes and adjudicate differences.   Society is concerned wholly with duties and not at all with rights; government, therefore, begins and ends with the magistrate.   In order to secure a suitable magistracy, Eliot proposed to divide society into groups of tens, fifties, hundreds and thousands, each of which should choose its rulers, who in turn should choose their representatives to the higher councils; and so there was evolved an ascending series of magistrates until the supreme council of the nation was reached, the decisions of which should be final.

The duties of all the Rulers of the civil part of the Kingdom of Christ, are as followeth: . . . to govern the people in the orderly and seasonable practice of all the Commanders of God, in actions liable to Political observations whether of piety and love to God, or of justice and love to man with peace.

Far removed as *The Christian Commonwealth* was from the democratic political theory of the Army radicals, or the practical

constitutionalism of Nathaniel Ward, it was the logical culmination of all theocratic programs. The ideal of social unity, of
relentless conformity, according to which the rebel is a social outcast to be silenced at any cost, dominates this godly Utopia as
mercilessly as it dominated the policy of Laud. In setting up King
Jesus for King Charles, there was to be no easing of the yoke upon
rebellious spirits; and in binding society upon the letter of the
Scripture there was to be no consideration for the aspirations of
the unregenerate. It is not pleasant to consider what the Saints
would have made of New England if their will had prevailed.
Curious as this little work is—testifying rather to the sincerity of
Eliot's Hebraism than to his political intelligence or his knowledge
of men—it is characteristic of the idealist who consecrated his life
to the Indian mission. How little disturbed he was by the per-
versities and limitations of everyday fact, is revealed in the policy
which he laid down for his Indian converts:

And this Vow I did solemnly make unto the Lord concerning them;
that they being a people without any forme of Government and now to
chuse; I would endeavour with all my might, to bring them to embrace
such Government, both civil and Ecclesiastical, as the Lord hath commanded in the holy Scriptures; and to deduce all their Lawes from the
holy Scriptures, that so they may be the Lord's people, ruled by him alone
in all things.

Which vow, considering the state of the Indian tribes to whom it
was to apply, may serve to throw light upon the reason for the
scant success of the Saints in their dealings with the red-men.

PART TWO: THE TWILIGHT OF THE OLIGARCHY
1660–1720

It is not pleasant to linger in the drab later years of a century that in its prime had known able men and accomplished notable things. A world that accepted Michael Wigglesworth for its poet, and accounted Cotton Mather its most distinguished man of letters, had certainly backslidden in the ways of culture. The final harvest of the theocracy must be reckoned somewhat scanty. English Independency had been the robust and rebellious child of a great age; New England Puritanism was the stunted offspring of a petty environment. With the passing of the emigrant generation, a narrow provincialism settled upon the commonwealth of Massachusetts Bay. Not a single notable book appeared; scarcely a single generous figure emerged from the primitive background. A thin soil and the law of Moses created a capable but ungainly race, prosaic and niggardly. Their very speech lost much of the native English beauty that had come down from medieval times. The clean and expressive idiom that Bunyan caught from the lips of English villagers, with its echoes of a more spontaneous life before the Puritan middle class had substituted asceticism for beauty, grew thinner and more meager, its bright homespun dyes subdued to a dun butternut. The town records which in the first years had been set down in dignified and adequate phrase became increasingly crabbed and illiterate, laboriously composed by plain men to whom spelling had become a lost art. The horizons of life in New England were contracting to a narrow round of chores and sermons. "When I first saw the Lieut. Governor," Sewall remarked of Stoughton, "He was Carting Ears of Corn from the Uper Barn." The picture suggests the pastoral note, but it suggests much else as well.

Against this incursion of the provincial the church was the single force to be counted on to do battle. The ministers did their best, but it needed abler men than were available to counteract the growing formalism of the times. They might lament that their admonitions fell on unheeding ears, that they preached in vain to a "sermon-proof, gospel-glutted generation"; but the blame must attach in part to the formalism of their appeals. The straw was over-threshed. The common provincialism infected the pulpit as well as the pew, and the creative vigor of the ministry steadily declined. The ground was being prepared for superstition and bigotry. As the belief spread through the New England villages that the end of the world would fall on the end of the century, men's thoughts naturally ran much on the demonology that is a logical consequence of the Hebraic dualism, and the most intelligent saw no reason to doubt that "the Evening Wolves will be much abroad, when we are near the Evening of the World." The psychology was being prepared for the witch-mania of Salem, and Cotton Mather was only echoing the common belief when he cried, "An Army of Devils is horribly broke in upon the place which is the *Centre*, and after a sort, the First-born of our *English Settlements*." [1] In this matter, as in so many others, the ministers were no better than their congregations; they were blind leaders of the blind, and they lent their sanction to the intolerance of the mass judgment. In an environment so stifling, with every unfamiliar idea likely to be seized upon as evidence of the devil's wiles, there was no room for free speculation. A generation under the terror of witchcraft was given over to stark reaction. The Salem outbreak was the logical outcome of the long policy of repression, that had hanged Quakers and destroyed independent thought, in its attempt to imprison the natural man in a straitjacket of Puritan righteousness. Emotions long repressed sometimes find sinister outlets, and the witchcraft madness was only a dramatic aftermath of a generation of repressions and inhibitions. [2]

It was during these unhappy years that power finally slipped from the hands of the oligarchy. With the charter gone, a Royal Governor presiding over the Council, and a property qualification instead of a religious test for suffrage, the old order was broken past mending. The members of the oligarchy still hoped against hope, and under the governorship of Phips they made heroic attempts to bolster up the cause; but the Quebec expedition was so badly muddled as to bring the commonwealth to the verge of ruin, and the Governor and Council wrote to England that God had "spit in our

[1] *Wonders of the Invisible World*, p. 14.
[2] See Lucien Price, "Witchcraft, Then and Now," in *The Nation*, Vol. CXV, No. 2987.

faces."[3] Whether or not that was a correct analysis of the divine reaction to the Quebec fiasco is of no importance today; a good many New Englanders, it would seem, doubted it, and under the pressure of high taxes, a depreciated currency and a great debt, they made their dissatisfaction heard at the royal court. When the English government at last "resolved to settle the Countrey," the end of the oligarchy was come. The cautious amongst them were for throwing the whole responsibility on the Lord: "the foundations being gone, what can the righteous do?" argued Judge Sewall with shrewd worldly-wisdom. But the ministers would make no compromise with Baal. The tongues of false prophets might seduce the people, but they stood for the old order, fighting a losing fight with righteous zeal. On June 1, 1702, Sewall noted in his diary that he had "much adoe to persuade Mr. Willard to dine with me," the pastor being in a sulk because the civil representatives had taken precedence over the ministers in the procession for proclaiming Queen Anne. But in the end even "good Mr. Willard" was forced to acknowledge that his loyalty was given to a lost cause.

[3] J. T. Adams, *The Founding of New England*, p. 442.

CHAPTER I

SAMUEL SEWALL

Yankee

BY good fortune an intimate record of daily life in old New England has been preserved in abundant detail. The diary of Samuel Sewall not only narrates the homely activities of Boston in the evening of the theocracy, *antiquis moribus, prisca fide*, but it unconsciously reveals the transformation of the English Puritan into the New England Yankee. The sober Boston citizens who on the Sabbath droned Windsor and York tunes, and took notes of long sermons, on week-days plied their gospel of thrift with notable success. They loved the meetinghouse as their fathers had loved it, but they were the sons and grandsons of tradesmen, and true to their English instincts they set about erecting a provincial mercantile society, dominated by the ideals of the little capitalist. Of this rising world of mercantilism, Samuel Sewall was a worthy representative. A Puritan magistrate and village capitalist, he made full use of his opportunities to worship God, to thrive and to rise. As the older ideal of theocratic stewardship is revealed in the career of John Winthrop, the newer practice of incipient capitalism is revealed in the life of Samuel Sewall.

The *Diary* is a fascinating book, with its petty gossip interwoven with matters of public concern, and its brisk activities set in a black border of innumerable funerals: the one among all the books of the time that is still quick with life after these two hundred years and more. In its meager entries we can trace the change that was coming to Massachusetts in the transition from a theocracy to a royal colony; and we can feel the strong emotions which that change aroused. The dry facts of history take on flesh and blood; forgotten names become living men walking the streets of Boston or arguing in the Council Chamber; Samuel Sewall himself becomes more real to us than our own contemporaries. He was the veritable embodiment of his serious, prudential Massachusetts, reflecting its changing fortunes with painstaking fidelity In that petty world of conventional piety and shrewd self-interest, the kind-hearted Judge bustled about, a sermon in one hand to soothe the doubts of the troubled, and a bit of chocolate in the other to comfort the bedridden—as honest and friendly and prosaic a soul as Massachusetts ever bred. If one wishes to understand the first native New England generation, one cannot do better than linger over the daily jottings of this lawyer-tradesman, who knew his Calvin far better than his Coke, and who while busily adding new acres to his holdings strove to keep the younger generation uncontaminated by wigs and revels and other godless things, by the sweet ravishment of the psalms, in the singing of which the voice of the Judge was lifted up with pathetic earnestness.

For many years after his death fame dealt more than generously with Samuel Sewall. The prosperity that came to him during his earthly pilgrimage long provided for his memory, and made of him a greater figure than either nature or good fortune created. Who does not know Whittier's tribute?

> Stately and slow, with thoughtful air,
> His black cap hiding his whitened hair,
> Walks the Judge of the Great Assise,
> Samuel Sewall, the good and wise.
> His face with lines of firmness wrought,
> He wears the look of a man unbought,
> Who swears to his hurt and changes not;
> Yet touched and softened nevertheless
> With the grace of Christian gentleness;
> The face that a child would climb to kiss;
> True and tender and brave and just,
> That man might honor and woman trust.

And a hundred and forty-eight years after the cold January day when all that was mortal of him was "honorably Inter'd" in the Sewall tomb whither so many of his family had gone before,[1] a brilliant student of early American letters gave fresh currency to the stately Sewall of tradition. "He was a man built, every way, after a large pattern. By his great wealth, his great offices, his learning, his strong sense, his wit, his warm human sympathy, his fearlessness, his magnanimity, he was a visible potentate among men in those days."[2]

That was before the diary was published and the lay figure of

---

[1] Two of his three wives and eleven of his fourteen children he had buried.
[2] Tyler, *History of American Literature during the Colonial Period*, Chapter XIII, Part IV.

tradition vanished in presence of the real man. We know Samuel
Sewall now and see him as he was. That he was a great man it is
impossible to make out; but that he was a small man by no means
follows. Behind the formal trappings of magistrate and councilor,
we discover a capable, middle-class soul, honest, simple-hearted,
serving himself yet not unmindful of his fellow townsmen, an
excellent neighbor and citizen, to whom the strongest appeal of
life was the economic. Like those kindred spirits, Defoe and
Franklin, the dominant inspiration of his life was prudential, as
befitted the descendant of generations of tradesmen. "Mr. Henry
Sewall, my great Grandfather," wrote the Judge in old age, "was
a Linen Draper in the City of Coventry in Great Britain. He
acquired a great Estate, was a prudent Man, and was more than
once chosen Mayor of the City." [3] In turning Puritan the English
burgess did not change his nature, and Samuel Sewall was true to
his breeding in fashioning his life upon that of his great grandfather. To acquire wealth and honors, to occupy a dignified position among his fellows, was the dominant ambition of his life.
With excellent thrift he fixed his young affections upon the only
child of a wealthy merchant, the richest heiress in the colony; no
penniless "waiting-woman," for Samuel Sewall, such as had contented the unworldly Thomas Hooker. He understood how desirable it is to put money in one's purse; so he made a great
alliance and proved himself a shrewd husbandman as well as a
kind husband. [4] From commerce and land speculation and money
lending and the perquisites of many offices, he accumulated
steadily until his wealth entitled him to be regarded as one of the
first citizens of Massachusetts. He did not forget his prudence
even in his generosities, but set down carefully in his diary what
his benefactions cost, that there might be no mistake when he
came to make his reckoning with the Lord. He knew his rights
and upheld them stoutly; and in the petty quarrels and litigations
in which he found himself involved, he stuck to the letter of the
law and usually won his point. He did not misuse his official
position to feather his own nest, but what might be got legally
from public office he took care to get.

   With abundant wealth the path of preferment was easy to him.

---

[3] *Diary*, in *Massachusetts Historical Society Collections*, Fifth Series, Vol. I, p. xi
[4] Compare his haggling over the terms of settlement upon a later proposed mar
riage; see *Diary*, Vol. III, p. 205.

From his election to the privileges of a freeman in 1678, at the age of twenty-six, to the end of a long life, he was continuously engaged in public affairs. He sought office and was not backward in pushing his claims upon a desirable post; [5] and by careful attention to business rather than by exceptional parts, he rose to a place of very great influence in the commonwealth. Like a competent man of affairs, he was prompt in meeting engagements—"am, I think, the most constant attender of Councils," he remarked of himself approvingly. He carried out to the letter the early advice given him: "Mr. Reyner . . . Advised me not to keep overmuch within, but goe among men, and that thereby I should advantage myself." [6] Capable, industrious, public-spirited, he led a busy and useful life that justified more than commonly the responsibilities which came to him. His qualities might be middle-class, but they were sterling and worthy of honor. It was a fortunate star that led him out of Tory England, where he would never have been more than a prosperous tradesman, to the new world where kindred spirits were erecting a commonwealth after his own heart.[7]

Nevertheless with all his excellent qualities Samuel Sewall was not a great or original nature. The evidence is convincing that he was a capable executive and administrator rather than a creative thinker or forceful leader; a Puritan embodiment of Defoe's merchant ideal; an example of the man who rises to civic honors by simple business virtues. He was at home in the narrow round of routine, but for bold speculation he reveals the incapacity of the practical soul. His intellectual interests were few; his ready curiosity was that of the uncreative mind, concerning itself with persons

[5] See *Diary*, Vol. III, p. 168.

[6] *Diary*, Vol. I, p. 32.

[7] The following is part of an obituary notice by his son:
In 1684, He was chosen a Magistrate of the *Massachusetts* Colony. . . . In 1692, He was appointed by King William and Queen Mary in their Royal Charter, one of the first Council for their Majesties in this Province, into which He was annually chosen and sat till 1725, when He resign'd his Election, having outlived all the others nominated in that Fundamental Constitution. In 1692 He was made one of the Judges, and in 1718, Chief Justice of our Superior Courts of Judicature thro' the Province, in which He sat till 1728, when his Infirmities growing on Him, He resign'd that Place also. In 1715, He was made Judge of Probates for this County of *Suffolk*, and continued in that Office till 1728, when He laid it down; it being the last Publick Post wherein He served and honoured his Country. *Diary*, Vol. III, pp. 409–410. In addition to the above, he was at times an overseer of Harvard College, censor of the press, and captain of the Ancient and Honourable Artillery Company; a frequent moderator of Boston town meeting, member of innumerable committees on church, parish and commonwealth matters, and adviser at large to whoever was in difficulties.

and happenings rather than with ideas. To say that Sewall possessed either an economic or political philosophy would be too generous an interpretation of his opinions. The views which he upheld vigorously were little more than prejudices. Of the several economic questions which engaged the attention of the Council during his years of service, the most insistent was the question of issuing bills of credit to supplement the scanty currency. There was the usual class alignment, the wealthy opposing the issues, and the poor generally favoring them. The position of Sewall was clear. He vigorously opposed every issue, from the conviction that the only honest money was hard money, even going so far as to prefer barter to bills.[8] Nowhere does he reveal any intelligent grasp of the economics of the problem, nor was he aware that his judgment might have been influenced by his private interests as a money lender.

In his political views he was equally unconcerned with broad principles. He seems to have been wholly unread in political theory, and like his fellow magistrates he never examined fundamentals. He accepted without question the right of the godly to police society, and he would have no meddling with affairs of state by tavern and fireside politicians. As a member of the oligarchy he naturally approved oligarchic rule. Although he would turn to the democracy for support against the Lords of Trade, when the latter were moving to overturn the theocracy, he put no trust in the political wisdom of the common people. He was as magisterial as John Winthrop in his belief in the principle of the stewardship of the elders. Stability of government was the prime essential; there must be no criticism of government by private individuals or by newspapers. On an occasion when Dudley's administration had been sharply attacked in a London paper, a copy of which had been brought over and talked about, there was a great pother in Council. Although Sewall was not willing to defend Dudley, he was troubled.

At last the Council voted, it tended to the disturbance of the Government. Lt. Govr. and Council order'd me to Reprimand Mr. Dummer. . . . I told him how intolerable it was for privat persons to print Reflections and Censures on the highest Acts of Government. . . . Twas ill done of them who printed it in London, and twas ill done by them that carried it on here.[9]

[8] See *Diary*, Vol. II, p. 366; Vol. III, pp. 87 and 345.
[9] *Diary*, Vol. III, pp. 84–85.

His characteristic attitude then comes out in the phrase: "I said . . . I was for upholding Government whether in or out of it." Samuel Sewall was no rebel against authority. But if he was firm in support of the *de facto* government, he was insistent that it should be honest. He protested to Governor Dudley against padding the muster pay-rolls [10] and he dissented strongly against introducing the current English practice of buying commissions in the army.[11] The scandalous corruption of English politics must not be permitted to sully the government of Massachusetts.

Sewall enjoyed in his lifetime the repute of a scholar. He was Latinist enough to justify his Harvard degree of Master of Arts; he read a good deal, and wrote and published books. But he seems to have cared nothing for pure literature, and was unacquainted with the English classics. His intellectual interest was in things either occult or inconsequential. Biblical prophecy was his favorite study, and his most ambitious work, *Phaenomena Quaedam Apocalyptica*, essayed to prove that America was to be the final "rendezvous of Gog and Magog." Although long a magistrate and judge of the highest court, he was not a lawyer. He received no preliminary training in the law, and there are few indications in the *Diary* that he read the literature of the profession. His indifference seems to have given concern to his friends, for on January 13, 1696, four years after he had been chosen judge, he noted:

When were there at first, Mr. Danforth bad me look on the Cupboard's head for a book; I told him I saw there a Law-book, Wingate on the Common Law. He said he would lend it me, I should speak to Amsden to call for it; and if he died, he would give it me. Again when took leave after prayer, He said he lent me that Book not to wrap up but to read, and if misliked it, should tell him of it.[12]

Primitive New England did not take kindly to lawyers, and in administering a patriarchal justice by rule of thumb, Sewall was like other New England magistrates. Neither did it take kindly to the spirit of free speculation, and in his potterings over occultisms he was confessing the sterility of intellectual interests.

If the kind-hearted Judge lacked capacity for bold and liberal thought, he lacked capacity as well for emotional fervor. He was quite without imagination. Despite his honest concern for his soul, and his sincere desire for the advancement of God's kingdom

[10] *Diary*, Vol. II, p. 228.   [11] *Ibid.*, p. 214   [12] *Diary*, Vol. I, p. 419.

in New England, Sewall did not possess a deeply religious nature. In his religious life he was the same prudent, plodding soul, that stowed away in his strong-box deeds to ample possessions during his pilgrimage through this vale of tears. The natural man was strong in his two hundred and odd pounds of flesh, and the religious mysticism that lurked in the heart of primitive Puritanism found no response in his phlegmatic soul. He was no Seeker, like Roger Williams, to be driven by a passionate fervor along untried paths; nor was he a philosopher, like John Wise, to concern himself with broad ecclesiastical principles. Instead, there is more than a hint of the tradesman's conception of religion—one has only to understand the profitableness of salvation to be led to invest in it. His religion must be orthodox; no untried methods or gambler's chances; a good business man will scrutinize title-deeds with due care, and the title-deeds to salvation are of the first importance. How characteristic are the following entries in the diary:

Sabbath, March 2d. I Pray'd in the Family, that might have an interest in God, Signed, Sealed and Delivered, and that all that tended to make it sure, might be perfected.

Febr. 6. [1718] This morning . . . I had a sweet and very affectionat Meditation Concerning the Lord Jesus; Nothing was to be objected against his Person, Parentage, Relations, Estate, House, Home! Why did I not resolutely, presently close with Him! And I cry'd mightily to God that He would help me so to doe!

23. 5. [1721] Mr. Prince preaches the Lecture, from Gen. 22. 18 . . . A very seasonable Discourse. One Fly was discovered in his Ointment: He asserted that the 1000. years Rev. 20. stood for Three Hundred and Sixty Thousand years; taking every day of the 1000. years for a year: as 365. days i.e. years. *Apage has nugas!* ["Away with this nonsense!"] [13]

No higher criticism for Samuel Sewall. If we quibble over the plain words of Scripture, how shall we be certain of the terms of the contract?

A man so cautious by nature, and with so large a stake in the existing order, could not fail to be a conservative, content with a world that justified itself by the prosperity which it brought him, and which it would bring to others, he doubted not, if they governed their conduct with equal prudence. He desired no innovations in church or state; established forms answered his needs and filled the measure of his ideal. The existing system was approved by all the respectable people of the community; there was every-

[13] *Diary*, Vol. I, p. 312; Vol. III, p. 165; Vol. III, pp. 281–282.

thing to gain in upholding it, and likelihood of loss in suffering power to pass into the hands of a royal governor or of the ignorant poor. And so, determined by complex motives, by habit, by class ties, by economic interest, and by honest liking, Samuel Sewall went with the stream of conventional orthodoxy, strong for the old theocratic principles, seeing no need for readjustments to meet changing conditions. The true principles of church and state had been laid down by the fathers, to which the common acceptance by the best people gave final sanction.

It is characteristic of the prosperous bourgeoisie, and the old Judge walked the streets of Boston, or sat in his pew, or took his place on the bench, as stubborn and unimaginative a conservative as any of his fellows. If his persistent opposition to change, whether in the matter of wigs, or Christmas keeping, or creed, or politics, was due in part to a phlegmatic love of use and wont, it was prompted also by an instinctive fear of innovation. The world doubtless is imperfect, but it answers to God's will and we understand its ways and can draw our contracts with open eyes. Whereas change, however desirable it may seem theoretically, entails too many disturbing uncertainties. Very likely it was this subconscious concern for his material interests that so often made the simple-minded Judge an unintelligent opponent of all popular movements looking to a freer and more liberal society. When his native kindliness was touched he spoke out frankly. His anti-slavery tract (*The Selling of Joseph*), slight in extent and somewhat overpraised by historians, was not only much in advance of his time, but it contains one sentence that should not be forgotten, "There is no proportion between twenty pieces of silver and liberty." Equally significant was his stand against capital punishment for counterfeiting.[14] Such acts as the following must also be set down to his credit: "I essay'd June 22 [1716], to prevent Indians and Negros being Rated with Horses and Hogs; but could not prevail." [15] His native sense of justice was as strong as his kindliness. Who does not know of his confession in regard to the witchcraft persecutions—an act that set all Boston tongues wagging. When he was convinced that he had made a grievous and sorrowful mistake, he rose in the congregation while the minister read his public acknowledgment of that mistake, and his repentance for his share in the unhappy business. Thereafter

[14] See *Diary*, Vol. III, p. 277.   [15] *Ibid.*, p. 87.

in commemoration he kept an annual day of prayer and fasting. We can forgive him much for that honest and manly act.

To the end of his life Sewall refused to go forward with the changing times, and his voluntary assumption of the office of *praefectura morum* laid him under a heavy responsibility to see that the primitive ways were upheld. He was magisterial in rebuke and few transgressors of the strict New England code escaped a censure. One would like to have James Franklin's private opinion of the sharp-eyed old Judge. To Franklin and other members of the Hell-fire Club—young fellows keenly interested in domesticating the new wit literature in homespun Boston, openly skeptical, inclining to Arianism and even to deism—he must have seemed a prosy old reactionary, upholding a decadent orthodoxy and an obsolete social order. No doubt many a sharp jibe was aimed at his back, for there were many to whom the older ways began to seem preposterous. It may very well have been that those who committed a certain prank which Sewall records may have had him in mind.

Aug. 3. [1717] . . . 'Tis sad it should be so, but a virulent Libel was starch'd on the Three Doors of the Meeting House, containing the following Words:

TO ALL TRUE-HEARTED CHRISTIANS

Good people, within this House, this very day,
A Canting Crew will meet to fast, and pray.
Just as a miser fasts with greedy mind to spare;
So the glutton fasts, to eat a greater share.
But the sower-headed Presbyterians fast to seem more holy,
And their Canting Ministers to punish sinfull foley.[16]

Happily there is another and pleasanter side to the character of Samuel Sewall, and one that looked forward to the future instead of backward to the past. Despite the harshness of the Puritan creed and the bigotry of Puritan rule, the fields and meadows of New England, that sent a breath of the countryside through the crooked streets of Boston, were a wholesome influence in the lives of men and women. Magistrate and money-lender though he was, Samuel Sewall was a countryman and farmer also, a judge of milch cows and fat porkers as well as criminals, a lover of robins and flowers and fruitful orchards, one who sat his horse well, and when on circuit often drew up at a rail-fence to discuss the crops

[16] *Diary,* Vol. III, pp. 116–117. Note the use of the word Presbyterian in these lines.

with some gossipy farmer. Above all, a lover of men, the most neighborly soul in the world, mingling freely with all classes, and although quite properly proud of a visit from the Governor or other great person, never above chatting with the carpenter, or doing a kindness to an old nurse. It was the friendly heart of the man that prompted so many little errands of helpfulness; and if sermons and tracts and good advice flowed from him like a spring freshet, if he was magisterial in petty rebuke, such little oddities of the man and the time did not detract from his sympathy or lessen his helpfulness. Men stood in awe of Cotton Mather, and children must have run from him, but neither awe nor fear threw their shadow across Sewall's path. We can make too much of the countless funerals that dot his pages, with their thrifty reckoning of gloves and scarfs and rings that were the queer perquisites of pallbearers. It was not an unwholesome world despite the smell of mortality that exudes from the old records, or the terrors of little children smitten with the fear of hell; and the homely round of Samuel Sewall's activities was very far from unwholesome.

It was his neighborliness that made him so representative of the leveling tendencies of a provincial village life—an easy comradeship with men of all conditions, unknown to the rigid class divisions of the old world. Going one day to visit the Jews' burial place at Mile-End, while on a visit to London, he invited the sexton to a pot of beer and a quiet chat, remarking in friendly fashion, "wisht might meet in Heaven: He answered, and drink a Glass of Beer together, which we were then doing." [17] His English friends would scarcely have understood that homely little scene, so natural to the colonial. Sewall is the first Yankee who reveals the native kindliness of the New England village. He was zealous to do good and to deal generously with others, because he had been generously dealt by. Growing more human with the ripening years, yet instinctively conservative, stubbornly intent on managing his own affairs in his own way and by his own agents, provincial to the core and strong in local pride, he reveals the special bent of the New England character, as it unconsciously differentiated itself from its English original. Not American as yet like Franklin, and no longer wholly English like Winthrop, far from democratic and yet no Tory, he was the progenitor of a practical race that was to spread the gospel of economic individualism across the continent.

[17] *Diary,* Vol. I, p. 301.

CHAPTER II

THE MATHER DYNASTY

I

FOR one who is not a loving student of the unamiable bickerings that clutter the records of early New England, and who does not read them by the gentle light of filial loyalty, it would seem presumptuous to venture into the thorny fields tilled by the Mathers. He is certain to get well scratched, and not at all certain to return with any fruit gathered. The rancors of dead partisanships beset him on every side, and the gossip of old wives' tales fills his ears. He will encounter many a slanderous hearsay, and the authentic documents to which he would naturally turn are often inaccessible, and always inhospitable. The countless tracts, for the most part inconsequential, that issued in an unbroken stream from the tireless Mather pens, consuming all the italics in the printer's case, constitute a veritable *cheval-de-frise* to protect their authors' literary reputations from any Philistine attack; and behind that bristling barricade they have long bidden defiance to casual invasion. Only a siege can reduce their stronghold and bring them forth into the clear light of day.

Two generations of Harvard scholarship have essayed the undertaking, but there is still wanting the detached critic who will set the Mathers against an adequate historical background, and appraise them objectively in relation to their times. The Harvard contributions are excellent in their way, but a consciousness of dealing with Harvard worthies would seem to have laid the writers under certain inhibitions. Exposition too easily slides into apologetics. The latest study [1] is a somewhat meticulous defense. It is an extraordinarily painstaking document, that has added to our knowledge of Increase Mather's life and work, but it was unhappily conceived in the dark of the moon, a season congenial to strange quirks of fancy. Some tangle it has cleared away, but fresh obstacles have been added by the intrusion of a thesis to be defended. In consequence, the interpretation of motives is

[1] Kenneth B. Murdock, *Increase Mather*, 1925.

colored by special pleading, and the very necessary inquiry into the sources of those virulent antagonisms that sprang up full-armed in the minister's every footprint is put aside as ungermane to a biography. It is an unfortunate assumption for it puts aside much that is crucial. The rehabilitation becomes too easy and complete. It proves too much. It would have us believe that in spite of all the smoke that gathered about Increase Mather's militant pilgrimage through life, there was never any fire of his kindling; that in spite of all the puddles through which the priestly politician splashed to reach his ends, no spot or stain ever smutched his gown. The contention may be sound, but it puts credulity to the strain, and unless one has something of a Mather stomach for marvels, one is likely to indulge in the luxury of doubt.

II

The Mathers were a singularly provocative family, capable, ambitious, certain to have a finger in every pie baking in the theocratic oven. From the emigrant Richard with the great voice, chief architect of the Cambridge Platform, to the provincial Cotton, the family combativeness and love of publicity put their marks on New England history. Of the three generations, certainly Increase Mather was the most generously endowed with capacity for leadership; an able man, practical and assertive, liking to be in the forefront of affairs, not wanting his light hidden under a bushel. An arch-conservative, he justified his ways to his conscience by the excellence of the heritage he strove to conserve. A formalist, he satisfied his intellectual curiosity by extolling the sufficiency of the creed of the fathers. He closed the windows of his mind against the winds of new doctrine, and bounded the fields of speculative inquiry by orthodox fences. He was of the succession of John Cotton rather than Thomas Hooker, a priestly theocrat, though never a shuffler like Cotton, less troubled by free inquiry, less by the intellectual. All his life he was inhibited from bold speculation by his personal loyalties and interests. As a beneficiary of things as they were, certain to lose in prestige and power with any relaxing of the theocracy, it would be asking too much of human nature to expect him to question the sufficiency of the established system of which he was the most distinguished representative. Not to have approved it would have been to repudiate his habitual way of thinking, his deepest prejudices, his strongest convictions. He had been molded and shaped by the theocracy; it was the very marrow of his bones; as well demand that pig iron turn molten again after it comes from the matrix. The ore of which he was fashioned was excellent, but once molded it was rigid; there would be no return to fluidity. And so determined by every impact of environment, by every appeal of loyalty, and by a very natural ambition, Increase Mather became a stout upholder of the traditional order, a staunch old Puritan Tory of the theocratic line. How could any promptings of liberalism find nourishment in such a mind?[2] Why should one expect to find in the works of such a man the seeds of new systems of thought or more generous institutions? He was the outstanding figure of the theocracy in the days of its overthrow, but intellectually he was not worthy to unloose the shoe-strings of Roger Williams.

In his professional capacity, Increase Mather was the priest rather than the theologian, a pastor of the flock, an expounder of the creed, rather than a seeker after new light. As a minister his mind was circumscribed by the thinking of John Calvin. He learned nothing from Luther, and was bitterly hostile to those phases of Independency that embodied the more generous Lutheran principles. No man was by temperament better fitted to embrace the coercive spirit of the Genevan discipline. Strong-willed and ascetic, he discovered in discipline the chief end for which the children of Adam are created. A profound admirer of the close-knit Genevan system, he was a Presbyterian in spirit, a man after Calvin's own heart, who clung to the old coercions in an age that was seeking to throw them off. If he counseled innovation it was in the way of strengthening ministerial authority, never in the way of liberalizing either creed or practice. It was the Congregationalism of the Cambridge Platform, and not that of early Plymouth, that he upheld; and to strengthen that order he turned earnestly to the practical work of Presbyterianizing. He was the prime mover in summoning the synod of 1679–80, requested by the Court to consider amongst other things what "may appear necessary for the preventing schisms, haeresies, prophaneness, & the establishment of the churches in one faith & order of the gospell,"[3] and the chief suggestions of the body, of which he was the conspicuous leader, were a return to a stricter discipline, and a strengthening

[2] Compare Murdock, *Increase Mather*, pp. 394–395.
[3] Quoted in W. Walker, *A History of Congregational Churches*, etc., p. 187.

of the passage in the Savoy Confession of faith—adopted by the synod—by borrowings from the Westminster Confession, which "more positively set forth the authority of the state in doctrinal questions." [4]

In 1691, while in London, Mather had been active in the work of uniting the Presbyterian and Congregational churches of England, under articles that would seem to have been more Presbyterian than Congregational; and in 1705, following the curiously spiteful controversy over the Brattle Street Church he joined vigorously in the proposed work of rejuvenating the New England system by engrafting further shoots from the Presbyterian stock. One of these grafts from the London agreement—the principle of licensing ministerial candidates by the association of ministers, thereby effectively preventing the intrusion of undesired members —established itself on the Congregational system; but another— the principle of associational control of the several churches—was blighted by the attack of John Wise.[5] What this desired consolidation of power in the hands of the ministers implied, is suggested by the terms of the Cambridge Platform, which asserted that "the work & duty of the people is expressed in the phrase of obeying their Elders," and that they may not "speak in church, before they have leave from the elders: nor continue so doing, when they require silence, nor may they oppose nor contradict the judgment or sentence of the Elders, without sufficient & weighty cause." [6] Recalling that the elders of a church had been reduced in number to the single minister, one may perhaps venture to suggest that a man ardently working to strengthen the hands of the ministerial oligarchy by further Presbyterianizing was no friend to Separatist-Congregationalism, nor one in whom the spirit of humility would work any lessening of the authority of the Lord's stewards.[7]

In his conception of toleration Mather followed naturally in the footsteps of John Cotton. He would tolerate all views that

[4] *Ibid.*, p. 190. His biographer has overlooked the significance of this. See Murdock, *Increase Mather*, p. 151.
[5] His biographer has somewhat slurred his account of the "Proposals." See p. 282. But his justification is worth noting: "If the original brand of Puritan piety was worth saving, and Mather believed it was, an oligarchic church government was the only means of securing it in an age when men were inclined to change their religious ideas as they changed their thought on other affairs."
[6] W. Walker, *A History of the Congregational Churches, etc.*, p. 205.
[7] Compare Murdock, *Increase Mather*, pp. 361–363.

were not in error, but his criteria of truth were so far from catholic
as to lead him into constant and vehement attack upon other
sects. As a responsible leader he was careful to clothe his attacks
with generous professions; but he never stepped forward to uphold
the right of free thought, or to dissuade his brethren from heresy-
baiting. His biographer is greatly impressed by the minister's
professions, and takes them at somewhat more than face value,
forgetting the ancient saying that by the fruits of men's lives they
shall be known. Casuistry is useful for purposes of defense, and a
skillful apologist can explain away much; but the spirit of toleration revealed in the following passages was certainly no child of
liberalism:

The "Anabaptists" had given trouble in New England. They had
installed as minister a man excommunicated from the Congregational
church, and, when their meeting-house was closed to them, they persisted in assembling publicly before its barred doors rather than worship
unmolested in a private house, To Mather these were attacks upon the
true faith, and manifest disturbances of the civil peace. Naturally there
is some acidity in his strictures on the " blasted Error" of "Antipedobap-
tism." . . . He denounces Baptists roundly enough, points to their
kinship with the turbulent Anabaptists in Europe, and writes: " Are they
not generally of a bad Spirit? Bitter enemies to the Lords most eminent
Servants? yea, to the faithfull Ambassadors, spitting the cruel venome of
Asps against them."

He then concludes: "Nor is the modern reader likely to disagree"
with the apology by President Oakes, who wrote in an introduction
to Mather's screed:

It is sufficiently known to those that know the Author, that he is none
of the Ishmaels of the times, that have their hand against every man
and love to be taking a Dog by the Ears . . . or to be dabling in the
waters of strife. . . . They that know his Doctrine and manner of life,
cannot but know that the life of his Spirit is in the things of practical
Divinity, and the great Design of his ministry is to promote the power and
practice of piety in the greatest instances. . . . I dare undertake . . . his
design . . . is not to traduce . . . those that are otherwise minded, or
expose them to severities & sufferings on the bare account of their
opinion.[8]

From these curious passages the unsympathetic realist is likely
to draw the conclusions that the spirit of mutual admiration came
to early birth in New England, and that it makes a vast difference

[8] Murdock, *Increase Mather*, pp. 138–139.

whose ox is gored. Something of the same casuistry is employed to explain away Increase Mather's unhappy part in the witch-craft mess.[9] The whole matter is involved and rendered difficult by guilty consciences and the need to save reputations, and per-haps the facts are not to be got at; yet it is only another instance to show how quickly candor flies out at the window when a Mather comes in at the door. One may make much or little of the son's statement that Increase grew more tolerant in his later years; it would seem at best to have been only the difference between black and dark gray. A dominating man does not take kindly to differ-ences of counsel. Increase Mather was a stout upholder of the law and order in the shaping of which he had a hand, but he looked with no friendly eye on the architects of a different order; and the bitterness of his later years was the natural consequence of a strong, proud, ambitious man, thwarted in his dearest projects.

If he contributed nothing to a more liberal theology or church organization, it is idle to expect him to have contributed to political speculation. As a leader of the theocracy he meddled much in practical politics, but it would seem that he was quite unread in the political philosophers and wholly ignorant of major principles. The great English liberals of Commonwealth times and later left him untouched. He bought and read many books, but almost none of a political nature.[10] Hobbes, Harrington, Sidney, Milton, Filmer, Locke, were as much out of his intellectual ken as were the speculations of Roger Williams. Interest in political theory had ceased in Massachusetts with the banishment of the great Independent, and the principles of liberal thinkers like Harrington and Milton would have awakened little sympathy in so stalwart a theocrat as Increase Mather. He was a practical man, an ad-ministrator and mentor, a stern *castigator morum* to the common-wealth, and as a college president he had been trained in a school little notable for its sympathetic consideration of the views of sub-ordinates. He got on ill with his Harvard tutors, and one of the unseemliest squabbles of his later years grew out of the bitterness sowed between a "strong" administrator and his teaching staff.[11] A man accounted less pious, concerned with ends more patently worldly, might well be reckoned dictatorial and domineering; but

[9] See pp. 294–295, where he seeks unsuccessfully to refute the position taken by J. T. Adams.
[10] See Murdock, *Increase Mather*, pp. 125–127.
[11] "The Brattle-Street Church Controversy," for which see *ibid.*, pp. 258 ff.

Puritan righteousness, perhaps, is not to be judged by profane standards, nor the same severity of judgment applied to politicians laboring in the theocratic vineyard, that is applied to the common breed.

Perhaps the happiest years of Increase Mather's arduous life were those spent in London as agent of the theocratic party to secure such terms as he could for the settlement of New England. It was a congenial task and a congenial field. His love of diplomacy and his fondness for England were both gratified. He mingled there on terms of equality with the intellectual leaders of English Nonconformity, and matched his wit with men high in station. He proved himself a skillful manager, but the threads were too tangled for any Puritan diplomat to smooth out, and he fell short of his hopes. The terms of the charter as finally drafted satisfied few of the Boston theocrats, and his nomination of Sir William Phipps for Governor was certainly ill-judged. Sir William had been converted to the true faith by Increase himself and was reckoned by him a chosen vessel of the Lord; but he turned out to be no better than a cracked pot, and with the coming of Dudley the political influence of Increase Mather was finally broken. He was maneuvered out of his position as president of Harvard and later suffered the mortification of seeing the post fall into the hands of Leverett, the old tutor now become an influential politician, with whom he had been bitterly at outs. "Doubtless there is not any government in the world," he wrote, "that has been laid under greater obligations by a greater man than this government has been by me. Nevertheless I have received more discouragement in the work of the Lord, by those in government, than by all the men in the world besides. Let not my children put too much confidence in men." [12] It is not pleasant to be ousted from one's position by politicians, and if one is certain that the slight intended for the servant falls on the Master, it is scarcely to be borne. If waves of black pessimism swept over him in those unhappy later years when his ambitions were hopelessly frustrated, there was provocation enough. He had outlived his age and the ablest of the native-born theocrats had become a byword and a mocking amongst the profane of Boston.

Not a great man, as the world reckons greatness, Increase Mather may scarcely be accounted a great Puritan. As a theo-

[12] *Ibid.*, pp. 373-4, note.

logian he was wanting in speculative vigor, and as a pastor he was wanting in self-denying love. It is not necessary to set him over against Roger Williams or Jonathan Edwards or William Ellery Channing, to reveal his intellectual and spiritual shortcomings. One has only to place him beside so rugged and honest a Puritan as Samuel Hopkins, who in true Christian humility, utterly regardless of his own fame, gave his life to theology and the care of the poor and the outcast, to realize how conventional a soul was Increase Mather, how incurious intellectually, how ambitious and self-seeking. Men loved Samuel Hopkins even though they might vigorously reject his doctrine, as they loved Roger Williams and Ellery Channing; but few seem to have loved Increase Mather. One might respect his abilities, but he was too austerely forbidding to like, too overbearing to awaken the spirit of good will. Ideas in the abstract held no interest for him. His biographer has happily recalled Mather's forgotten interest in scientific inquiry, and for this slight relief from the intolerable drab of his life-story one may be grateful. Yet one must not build too high on an insubstantial foundation. In the England that Mather loved, and toward which he was strongly drawn—hoping that opportunity would offer for a pulpit there—pottering over natural philosophy had become a mark of distinction, and a man so envious of repute would have wished to approve himself to those whom he admired. Though he lived in Boston he would not have it thought that he was provincial.

Of the miscellaneous literary output that flowed from his pen in an abundant stream, little need be said. It is of concern only to minute historians of the local. That he was master of an excellent prose style, clear and straightforward, is sufficiently evident; if his matter had been so good, his legitimate fame would have been far greater. The work on which his reputation largely rests is *An Essay for the Recording of Illustrious Providences*, printed at Boston and London in 1684, and twice reissued in the nineteenth century under the title *Remarkable Providences*. It is an amusing book of old wives' tales, not singular at all for the times, but characteristic rather; an expression of the naïveté that crops out in Winthrop's *History of New England*, and other writings of the emigrant generation, but now become a fashion amongst the lesser lights of the Royal Academy and English Nonconformists. It suited to a nicety the Mather love of marvels, and Increase

constituted himself a generous repository of all the chimney-
corner tales of the countryside. To call such a book "a scientific
and historical recording of phenomena observed in New England," as his biographer has done, is to gall the back of a thesis
with hard riding.[13] In one chapter only does Mather suggest
the spirit of scientific inquiry; four out of the twelve deal with
witchcraft and kindred topics; and the rest are made up of such
instances of divine providence as great fish jumping out of the sea
into the boats of starving sailors adrift, of the freaks played by
lightning and tornadoes, and of God's punishments on wicked
Quakers. At the time it was a harmless enough book, but in the
light of after developments it was scarcely so harmless. The
emphasis laid upon witchcraft was an unfortunate, if unconsidered,
influence in preparing the psychology of New England for the
Salem outbreak, and the minister later reaped a bitter harvest
from it.

"Not many years ago," he wrote in the preface to *Illustrious
Providences*, "I *lost* (and that's an afflictive *loss* indeed!) several
moneths from study by sickness. Let every God-fearing reader
joyn with me in prayer, that I may be enabled to redeem the time,
and (in all ways wherein I am capable) to serve my generation."
That Increase Mather sincerely desired to serve his generation
according to his lights, none may deny. His labors were appalling,
his reputation was great, and when he died the light of the old
churches went out. The spirit of Presbyterianism went to its
grave in New England, and not till a hundred years later did the
new light—which was no other than primitive English Independency—shine out in the life and work of William Ellery Channing. After two centuries Unitarianism recovered for the Massachusetts churches the spirit of early Separatism that had been
lost since the days of the Cambridge Platform. Channing finally
uprooted the vine that Increase Mather had so laboriously tended.

III

Of the unpopularity that gathered about the name of Mather
after the fall of the theocracy, the larger portion fell to the lot of
the son, the eccentricities of whose character made him peculiarly
vulnerable to attack. In his youth the spoiled child of Boston,
in middle life he was petulant and irritable, inclined to sulk when

---

[13] *Ibid.*, p. 170.

his will was crossed. In the career of no other New England Puritan is the inquisitorial pettiness of the Genevan system of theology and discipline revealed so disagreeably. The heroic qualities of an earlier age had atrophied in an atmosphere of formalism, and Boston Calvinism of the year 1690 had become a grotesque caricature of a system that in its vigor had defied the power of Rome and laid kingdoms at its feet. Embodied in Cotton Mather it was garrulous, meddlesome, scolding, an echo of dead voices, a shadow of forgotten realities. The common provincialism had laid its blight upon it. The horizons of the New England imagination grew narrow, and Puritan anthropomorphism unconsciously reduced the God of the Hebrew prophets to the compass of a village priest, clothed in stock and gown, and endowed with the intellect of a parish beadle. In the egocentric universe wherein Cotton Mather lived and labored the cosmos had shrunk to the narrow bounds of a Puritan commonwealth, whereof Boston was the capital and the prosperity of the North Church the special and particular object of divine concern. The mind of Increase Mather had been enlarged by contact with English life; the mind of the son was dwarfed by a village world.

Cotton Mather is an attractive subject for the psychoanalyst. Intensely emotional, high-strung and nervous, he was oversexed and overwrought, subject to ecstatic exaltations and, especially during his celibate years, given to seeing visions. In the carefully edited *Diary* which he left for the edification of his natural and spiritual children, at the beginning of his twenty-third year, is an apologetic entry—"*Cum Relego, Scripsisse Pudet!*"—that Professor Wendell has put into English thus:

A strange and memorable thing. After outpourings of prayer, with the utmost fervor and fasting, there appeared an Angel, whose face shone like the noonday sun. His features were as those of a man, and beardless; his head was encircled by a splendid tiara; on his shoulders were wings; his garments were white and shining; his robe reached to his ankles; and about his loins was a belt not unlike the girdles of the peoples of the East. And this Angel said that he was sent by the Lord Jesus to bear a clear answer to the prayers of a certain youth, and to bear back his words in reply. Many things this Angel said which it is not fit should be set down here. But among other things not to be forgotten he declared that the fate of this youth should be to find full expression for what in him was best; . . . And in particular this Angel spoke of the influence his branches should have, and of the books this youth should write and publish, not only in America but in Europe. And he added certain special prophecies of the great works this youth should do for the Church of Christ in the revolutions that are now at hand. Lord Jesus! What is the meaning of this marvel? From the wiles of the Devil, I beseech thee, deliver and defend Thy most unworthy servant.[14]

The passage throws a good deal of light on the psychology of Cotton Mather. Such visions were clearly the result of abnormal stimuli, acting on a neurotic temperament. From both sides of his family he inherited a tense nervous system that was aggravated by precocity and an unnatural regimen. The inevitable result was a hothouse plant of Puritan forcing. His religious exaltation flowered from the root of egoism. His vanity was cosmic. He esteemed himself a beacon set on a hill, a divine torch which the very hand of God had lighted. The success or failure of God's plan for New England, he believed, rested on his shoulders; and with such heavy responsibilities devolved upon him he was driven, hot-haste, by the prick of urgency. The king's business requireth haste. The work of the Lord cannot wait upon sluggards. "O then *To work* as fast as you can," he wrote in *The Magnalia*, "and of soul-work and church-work as much as ever you can. Say to all *Hindrances*. . . 'You'll excuse me if I ask you to be short with me, for my work is great and my time is but little.'" And so with an amazing activity that was little short of neurosis, he gave himself over to the great business of managing the affairs of New England in accordance with God's will.

In undertaking so difficult a job, he frequently came into conflict with other interpreters of God's plan for New England, and partisan venom gathered about him wherever he passed. Tact was never a Mather virtue, and Cotton made two enemies to his father's one. His quarrels trod on each other's heels, and a downright vindictiveness breathes through his private records of them. He railed at whoever disagreed with him, and imputed silly or malignant motives. The pages of his diary are filled with epithets that he flung privately at his enemies; one marvels that so many in the little town of Boston could be singled out as "strangely and fiercely possessed of the Devil." Robert Calef, whose *More Wonders of the Invisible World* was an inconvenient reply to his *Wonders of the Invisible World*, was set down as "a very wicked sort of a Sadducee in this Town, raking together a crue of Libels . . . an abominable Bundle of Lies, written on purpose, with a

[14] *Cotton Mather, Puritan Priest*, p. 64.

Quil under a special Energy and Management of Satan, to damnify my precious Opportunities of Glorifying my Lord Jesus Christ." [15] When an anti-Mather group of Cambridge men set up the Brattle Street Church, and invited Benjamin Colman, who had received Presbyterian ordination in England, by way of reply to the Mather group, to become their pastor, Cotton wrote in his diary:

A Company of Head-strong Men in the Town, the cheef of whom, are full of malignity to the Holy Waye of our Churches, have built in this Town, another Meeting-house. To delude many better-meaning Men in their own Company, and the Churches in the Neighbourhood, they past a Vote . . . that they would not vary from the Practice of these Churches, except in one little Particular. . . . But a young Man, born and bred here, and hence gone for England, is now returned hither, at their Invitation, equip'd with an *Ordination*, to qualify him, for all that is intended.

On his "returning and arriving here, these fallacious People" gave themselves over, in short, to "Their violent and impetuous Lusts, to carry on the Apostasy," and Cotton Mather prayed God to make him an instrument to defeat the "Designs that Satan may have in the Enterprise." [16] Similar passages of extravagant abuse of men so wicked as to disagree with him flowed from his pen in copious abundance. Although he constantly prayed that his daily life might be "a trembling walk with God," he was clearly a difficult fellow to get on with; and in the opinion of many he was justly described by a contemporary, as a "malecontent priest," consumed with an "Hereditary rancour" that made him "everlastingly opposite" to every will but his own.

The diary of Cotton Mather is a treasure-trove to the abnormal psychologist. The thing would be inconceivable if the record were not in print. What a crooked and diseased mind lay back of those eyes that were forever spying out occasions to magnify self! He grovels in proud self-abasement. He distorts the most obvious reality. His mind is clogged with the strangest miscellany of truth and marvel. He labors to acquire the possessions of a scholar, but he listens to old wives' tales with greedy avidity. In all his mental processes the solidest fact falls into fantastic perspective. He was earnest to do good, he labored to put into effect hundreds of "Good devices," but he walked always in his own shadow. His egoism blots out charity and even the divine mercy.

[15] *Diary*, Vol. I, p. 271.   [16] *Ibid.*, pp. 325–326.

Consider his account of an "execution sermon" preached to a name-less girl condemned for killing her natural child, and the light it throws on both minister and congregation:

The Execution of the miserable Malefactor, was ordered for to have been the last Week, upon the Lecture of another. I wondred then what would become of my *Particular* Faith, of her condition being so ordered in the Providence of God, that it should furnish me, with a *special Oppor-tunity* to glorify Him. While I was entirely resigning to the wisdome of Heaven all such Matters, the Judges, wholly without my seeking, altered and allow'd her Execution to fall on the Day of *my Lecture*. The *General Court* then sitting, ordered the Lecture to bee held in a larger and a stronger House, than that *old* one, where 'tis usually kept. For my own part, I was weak, and faint, and spent; but I humbly gave myself up to the *Spirit* of my Heavenly Lord and Hee assured mee, that Hee would send His good Angel to strengthen mee. The greatest Assembly, ever in this Countrey preach'd unto, was now come together; It may bee four or five thousand Souls. I could not gett unto the *Pulpit*, but by climbing over *Pues* and *Heads:* and there the Spirit of my dearest Lord came upon mee. I preached with a more than ordinary Assistance, and enlarged, and uttered the most awakening Things, for near two hours together. My Strength and Voice failed not; but when it was near failing, a silent Look to Heaven strangely renew'd it. In the whole I found Prayer answered and Hope exceeded, and Faith encouraged, and the Lord using *mee*, the vilest in all that great Assembly, to glorify Him. Oh! what shall I render to the Lord! [17]

Straightway thereafter, he rendered the Lord another character-istic service. No sooner was the girl hanged—for whose safe-keeping no good angel seems to have been available after the minister had bespoken his—than he hastened to the printer to arrange for printing the sermon, and "annexed thereunto, an History of Criminals executed in this Land, and effectually, an Account of their dying Speeches, and of my own Discourses with them in their last Hours. . . . I entitled the Book, PILLARS OF SALT." Clearly this was the time to peddle his wares, when all Boston was talking of the great event; and with a nose for publicity as keen as Defoe's, he flung together a jumble of material, and trusted to its timeliness to sell. Some such origin, no doubt, accounts for a good many of the small library of titles that bore his name, an output that seems to have justified the angelic prophecy of "the books this youth should write and publish." With a very lust for printer's ink, he padded his bibliography like

[17] *Diary*, Vol. I, p. 279.

a college professor seeking promotion; but in spite of all the prayers poured out in behalf of them, they would seem for the most part to have been little more than tuppenny tracts, stuffed with a sodden morality, that not even an angel could make literature of.

Holding so strong a conviction of apostleship, Cotton Mather would certainly play the politician, and quite as certainly blunder and go wrong. Far more than his father he was a bookman, who believed that all knowledge was shut up between pigskin covers. He was as lacking in worldly wisdom as a child, and in his ecstatic contemplation of the marvels wrought by God in primitive New England he never discovered that that older world had passed away. Another age was rising, with other ideals than ecclesiastical, which the three thousand books in his library told him nothing about. He was an anachronism in his own day. Living in an earlier age, when the hierarchy was in its prime, he would have been carried far on the tide of theocratic prestige; a generation later, when lay-power had definitely superseded clerical, he would have taken his place as a stout defender of Tory ways. But at the moment when a critical realignment of parties was under way in Massachusetts; when the villagers were becoming democratized and the gentry toryized; when even the clergy were dividing—Cotton Mather was a general without an army. He was a primitive Puritan in a Boston that was fast becoming Yankee, and his love for the theocracy grew stronger with every defeat.

The judgment of after times finds little in his political activities to approve and much to condemn. After all allowances are made the fact remains that he was a leader of reaction; and no protestations can obscure the motive of personal ambition. His own prestige was involved with that of the theocracy. It was due to the traditional authority of the ministry that he enjoyed the distinction of being a "Person, whom the Eye and the Talk of the People is very much upon," and any lessening of that authority would hurt him cruelly in his vanity. This remains the sufficient explanation of his varied political activities in the course of which he trimmed his sails to different winds. He first essayed a frontal attack on the secular power, but suffering a personal slight, he shifted and struck in the dark at an exposed flank; and finally, receiving only further mortification, he made overtures of peace and found his way back to the tables of the great. It was against the administration of the wily and unscrupulous Dudley that he waged his bitterest warfare. Failing to make headway by open hostility, he seized upon a current trade scandal, poured out his grievances in an anonymous pamphlet sent to London to be published, and awaited the result. It was a slashing attack, done in the tone of a lover of the ancient rights and privileges of New England, and it must have cut Dudley to the quick. A quotation or two will suffice to reveal the nature of the charges:

But, when the President [Dudley] was pleased, out of an Active and Passive Principle, to tell our Countreymen, in open Council, *That the People in* New-England *were all Slaves; and that the* only *Difference between Them and Slaves, was their not being* Bought *and* Sold: *And that they must not think the Privileges* of Englishmen *would follow them to the end of the World.* I say, when the People heard this, they lookt upon themselves in a manner Lost. . . .

All the People here are Bought and Sold, betwixt the Governour and his son Paul. . . .

This is the *Third Time* that he has been Trusted with Power from the *Crown* in *America,* and he has constantly Abus'd it, to the Dishonour of the Government, and almost Ruin of the People he was sent to Govern.[18]

There was enough truth in the charges to make them serious, but the spleen was quite too evident. The author was at once discovered and Cotton Mather suffered a vigorous counter-attack that damaged a reputation already undermined. Perhaps even worse was the social slight put upon him by those in government. What it cost him to be left out of the invitations of the great he reveals in the *Diary:*

2 d. 7m. [September] Friday. [1709] The other Ministers of the Neighbourhood, are this Day feasting with our wicked Governour; I have, by my provoking Plainness and Freedom, in telling this *Ahab* of his wickedness, procured myself to be left out of his Invitations. I rejoiced in my Liberty from the Temptations, with which they were encumbred, while they were *eating of his Dainties* and durst not reprove him. And, considering the Power and Malice of my Enemies, I thought it proper of me, to be this day Fasting, in Secret, before the Lord.

Ten years later there is a different story to tell. The minister has left the opposition bench and gone over to the government. A note in Sewall's diary tells the tale:

[18] *A Memorial of the Present Deplorable State of New-England . . . by the Male-Administration of their Present Governour, Joseph Dudley, Esq., and his Son Paul,* London, 1707, in *Massachusetts Historical Society Collections,* Fifth Series, Vol. VI.

March, 12. [1718/19] Dr. Cotton Mather prays again [in Council].
Preaches the Lecture from Prov. 29: 18. no Vision. [*Where there is no
vision, the people perish: but he that keepeth the law, happy is he.*] The
Govr., Lt. Govr., Mr. Dudley, Mr. Belcher press'd hard that there might
be an order of the Govr. and Council to print it. Col. Tailor, Clark,
Davenport, Sewall and others opposed it. For my part, the Dr. spake so
much of his visions of Convulsion and Mutiny, mentioning our being a
dependent Government, and the Danger of Parliamentary Resentments:
that I was afraid the printing of it might be an Invitation to the Parliament
to take away our Charter. Govr. would have it put to the vote: but when
he saw how hardly it went, caused the Secretary to break off in the midst.[19]

Here is a party alignment that tells its own story, and it needs no
very lively imagination to fill out the meager note and reënact the
little drama. The minister, eager to make overtures of peace,
falls into the Tory note, talks about mob-rule and the sinfulness
of popular unrest, calls upon authority to maintain law and order,
and hints at the expediency of preserving due colonial subservience
in view of possible resentments on the part of certain great men
in England. Sewall, as a "true New-England man," squirms
somewhat under the implications, but the little group of Tories
are loud in praise. Such a sermon, from so eminent a servant of
God, would aid wonderfully in strengthening the spirit of loyalty
to the crown, and it must be printed and circulated amongst the
people. But the opposition proved too spirited, and the manuscript was not dispatched to the printer, no doubt to Cotton
Mather's chagrin.

It was easy for so reactionary a nature to slide over into the
Tory. There was not a grain of liberalism in his make-up. His
antipathy to all popular movements was deep-rooted, for he knew
no other political philosophy than that of the obsolete theocracy
in which he had grown up. He was a bourgeois soul who loved
respectability and was jealous of his social position; no fraterniz-
ing with the poor and outcast for him, no profitless excursions into
the realms of Utopian justice. Though he might play to popular
prejudices to serve his political ends, he had scant regard for
popular rights. The highest privilege of the New England people,
he believed, was the privilege of being ruled by the godly. His
real attitude towards the plain people is revealed in a note by his
son, that refers to the days following the overturn of the Andros
government:

[19] Vol. II, p. 214.

Upon Discoursing with him of the Affairs he has told me that he always pressed *Peace* and *Love* and *Submission* unto a legal Government, tho' he suffered from some tumultuous People, by doing so; and upon the whole, has asserted unto me his *Innocency* and Freedom from all known Iniquity in that time, but declared his Resolution, from the View he had of the fickle Humors of the Populace, that he would chuse to be concern'd with them as little as possible for the future.[20]

As he grew older and the shadow of failure fell across his life, his bitterness towards a people that had rejected his admonitions is revealed on many a page of his diary. It was a "silly people," a "foolish people," "insignificant lice"—"The cursed clamour of a people strangely and fiercely possessed of the Devil"—"My aged father laies to heart the withdrawal of a vain, proud, foolish people from him in his age"—"It is the Hour of . . . Darkness on this Despicable Town." He could not easily forgive those who had wounded his love of power and lust of adulation, and he was too aloof from the daily life of men to understand the political and social movements of the times, too self-centered to understand his fellow villagers. He possessed none of the sympathetic friendliness that made Samuel Sewall a natural confidant to every one in trouble. He loved the people when they honored and obeyed him, but when they hearkened to other counsels he would fall to scolding like a fishwife. Doubtless he was sincere in thinking he would gladly die to save his people from their sins, but he had no mind to neighbor with them or humor their wicked love of power. He immured himself so closely within the walls of the old theocratic temple that he never took the trouble to examine the groundsills, and when the rotten timbers gave way and the structure came tumbling about his ears, he was caught unprepared and went down in its ruins.

Happily most of the printed output of Cotton Mather has fallen into the oblivion it deserved. It is barren of ideas, and marred by pedantic mannerisms that submerge the frequent felicities of phrase—old-fashioned on the day it came from the press. "In his *Style*, indeed," wrote his friend Thomas Prince, "he was something singular, and not so agreeable to the Gust of the Age. But like his *manner of speaking*, it was very *emphatical*." Yet he possessed very considerable gifts and under happier circumstances he might have had a notable literary career; but he

[20] Wendell, *Cotton Mather, etc.*, p. 82.

was the victim of a provincial environment. He was the most widely read man of his generation in America, and one of the few who followed sympathetically the current scientific movement in England. Like old Increase he dabbled in science; he was proud of his membership in the Royal Society, to which he forwarded his characteristic *Curiosa Americana*—a hodgepodge of those marvels in which his generation delighted. It was from an English source that he got the idea of inoculation for smallpox, which he urged upon Boston so insistently that a war of scurrilous pamphlets broke out. He made use of the method in his own family, incurring thereby much stupid abuse and at least one attack of violence. It was an intelligent and courageous experiment, that is not to be forgotten in casting up the accounts of Cotton Mather.

Of his major works two only call for brief consideration: the celebrated *Magnalia Christi Americana; or, The Ecclesiastical History of New England;* and the less known *Wonders of the Invisible World.* The latter is suggestive for the light it throws on the psychology of the witchcraft mania. The fantastic devil-fear, which bit so deeply into the imagination of Puritan New England, has already been commented on. In that common seventeenth-century delusion, Cotton Mather not only ran with the mob, but he came near to outdistancing the most credulous. His speech and writings dripped with devil-talk. The grotesqueries that marked the current marvel-tales crop out nakedly in his writings. "I have set myself," he wrote in the *Diary*, "to countermine the whole *Plot* of the Devil, against New-England, in every branch of it, as far as one of my *darkness* can comprehend such a *Work* of Darkness." His conviction of the malignant activities of Satan was so vivid, that in delivering a carefully prepared sermon on the *Wiles of the Divil*, he was fain, he tells us, to pause and lift up his eyes and cry "unto the Lord Jesus Christ, that he would rate off Satan," who "all the Time of my Prayer before the Lecture" had "horribly buffeted me"—by inflicting on the fasting priest certain qualms of the stomach. How tremendous he conceived to be the battle over a human soul, he describes thus:

The *Wilderness* through which we are passing to the Promised Land is all over fill'd with Fiery flying serpents. But, blessed be God, none of them have hitherto so fastned upon us as to confound us utterly! All our way to Heaven lies by *Dens of Lions* and the *Mounts of Leopards;* there are incredible Droves of Devils in our way. . . . We are poor travellers in a world which is as well the Devil's Field, as the Devil's *Gaol;* a world in which every Nook whereof, the Devil is encamped with *Bands of Robbers* to pester all that have their Faces looking Zionward.[21]

In the light of Mather's logic, "That there is a *Devil,* is a thing Doubted by none but such as are under the influence of the Devil," and "God indeed has the *Devil* in a *Chain,* but has horribly lengthened out the Chain," his private comment on the work—"that reviled book"—becomes comprehensible.

The *Magnalia* is a far more important work, the repository of a vast miscellany of information concerning early New England that his pious zeal saved from oblivion. It is the *magnum opus* of the Massachusetts theocracy, the best and sincerest work that Cotton Mather did. The theme with which it deals, and about which he accumulates marvels and special providences together with historical facts, was the thing which next to his own fame lay nearest his heart—the glory of that theocracy which men whom he accounted foolish and wicked were seeking to destroy. The purpose of the book has nowhere been better stated than by Professor Wendell:

Its true motive was to excite so enthusiastic a sympathy with the ideals of the Puritan fathers that, whatever fate might befall the civil government, their ancestral seminary of learning should remain true to its colours. . . . The time was come, Cotton Mather thought, when the history of these three generations might be critically examined; if this examination should result in showing that there had lived in New England an unprecedented proportion of men and women and children whose earthly existence had given signs that they were among the elect, then his book might go far to prove that the pristine policy of New England had been especially favoured of the Lord. For surely the Lord would choose His elect most eagerly in places where life was conducted most according to His will.[22]

When old Increase was near the end of his many years, a friend wrote to ask if he were still in the land of the living. "No, Tell him I am going to it," he said to his son; "this Poor World is the land of the Dying." The bitter words were sober truth. The New England of the dreams of Increase and Cotton Mather was sick to death from morbid introspection and ascetic inhibitions; no lancet or purge known to the Puritan pharmacopeia could save it.

[21] *Wonders of the Invisible World,* p. 63.
[22] *Literary History of America,* pp. 48–49.

Though father and son walked the streets of Boston at noonday, they were only twilight figures, communing with ghosts, building with shadows. They were not unlike a certain mad woman that Sewall tells of, who went crying about the town, " My child is dead within me." The child of Cotton Mather's hopes had long been dead within him, only he could not bring himself to acknowledge it. The fruit of the vine planted by the fathers was still sweet to him, and when other men complained of its bitterness, and fell to gathering from other vines, he could only rail at their perversity. He would not believe that the grapes were indeed bitter and the vine blighted; that the old vineyard must be replowed and planted to fresh stock. All his life he had set marvels above realities and in the end his wonder-working providence failed him. Prayers could not bring back a dead past; passionate conjurations could not strike the living waters from the cold granite of Puritan formalism. A New England flagellant, a Puritan Brother of the Cross, he sought comfort in fasts and vigils and spiritual castigations, and—it is pleasant to learn— in ways far more natural and wholesome. Incredible as it may seem, the following record is authentic, and it falls like a shaft of warm sunshine across the path of the morbid priest: "Augt, 15. [1716]. . . . Now about Dr. C. Mather Fishing in Spy-pond, falls into the Water, the boat being ticklish, but receives no hurt." [23] The restless minister who had fished overmuch in troubled waters, sometimes, it would appear, ventured for perch in Spy Pond.

[23] Sewall, *Diary*, Vol. III, p. 98.

CHAPTER III

STIRRINGS OF LIBERALISM

I

JOHN WISE

Village Democrat

IN the days when Sir Edmund Andros was seeking to fasten upon Massachusetts Bay the principles and practice of Stuart prerogative, an event occurred that greatly stirred New England. Taxes having been arbitrarily assessed in Council, the several towns were bidden appoint commissioners to collect them. When the order reached Ipswich, John Wise, minister of the second church, gathered the chief members of his flock together, and it was agreed by them to choose no such commissioner at the town meeting—"We have a good God, and a good king, and shall do well to stand for our privileges," the minister is reported to have argued. Soon thereafter John Wise was summoned before a star-chamber court on the charge of sedition. Upon his plea of colonial privilege, the president of the court, Dudley, is said to have retorted, "You shall have no more privileges left you than not to be sold for slaves." "Do you believe," demanded Andros, "Joe and Tom may tell the King what money he may have?" "Do not think," put in another judge, "the laws of England follow you to the ends of the earth." Thereupon with five others, John Wise was thrown into Boston jail, where he lay one and twenty days, and whence he was released only after payment of fifty pounds, giving bond in a thousand pounds for good behavior, and suffering suspension from the ministry. "The evidence in the case," he remarked afterward, "as to the substance of it, was that we too boldly endeavored to persuade ourselves we were Englishmen, and under privileges.[1] The year following, Andros having been driven out, John Wise brought suit against Dudley for having denied him a writ of *habeas corpus*.[2]

[1] A similar plea had failed Dr. Church when he offended the oligarchy twenty years before, who quite as arbitrarily had fined him six hundred pounds.
[2] See the account in Palfrey, *History of Massachusetts*, Vol. II, Book XII, p. 327;

Two years later Wise served as chaplain in the ill-managed Quebec expedition under Sir William Phipps. He bore himself well both in council and on the field; went ashore with the storming party; and if he had succeeded in his efforts to instil some of his own force into the leaders, the grand exploit might not have dwindled to such an unhappy ending. In a long account which he sent to Increase Mather, then in London, he did not mince matters, or attempt to throw on the Lord's shoulders blame that belonged elsewhere, but charged the fiasco to the cowardice of Major Walley, in command of the assaulting troops.[3] Clearly the Ipswich minister was a fighting as well as a praying parson, whom Cromwell would have delighted in.

Posterity has been too negligent of John Wise hitherto. Although possessed of the keenest mind and most trenchant pen of his generation of New Englanders, he was uninfected by the itch of publicity that attacked so many of his fellow ministers, and so failed to challenge the attention of later times. Called to serve in an outlying portion of the Master's vineyard he discovered little opportunity there and less inclination to magnify his own importance. He was too honest to persuade himself that God's fame was bound up with his own, and he was never forward to push his claims to priority in righteousness. Nevertheless what little we know of him is to his credit. An independent man, powerful of body, vigorous of intellect, direct and outspoken in debate, he seems to have understood the plain people whom he served, and he sympathized heartily with the democratic ideals then taking form in the New England villages. Such liberalism as emerged from the simplicity of village life found intelligent response in his sympathies, and he dedicated his keen mind and wide reading to the business of providing it with a philosophical justification. Some explanation of his democratic leanings may be discovered in his antecedents. His father was a self-made man who had come over to Roxbury as an indented servant—most menial of stations in that aristocratic old Boston world. He must have been of sound

and in Wise, *Vindication of the Government of the New England Churches, Introduction*. The current Tory interpretation of the common law of sedition was severe. "In 1679, at the trial of Henry Carr [Care], indicted for some passages in a weekly paper, the Lord Chief Justice Scroggs declared it criminal at Common Law to 'write on the subject of government, whether in terms of praise or censure, it is not material; for no man has a right to say anything of government'" (*State Trials*, VII, 929; quoted in Schuyler, *The Liberty of the Press in the American Colonies, etc.*)

[3] See *Massachusetts Historical Society Proceedings*, Second Series, Vol. XV, pp. 283–296.

and rugged stock, for in addition to a magnificent physique he endowed his son with manly independence and democratic self-respect, which stood the latter in good stead when, after having made his way through Harvard College, he came to speak for the people against the tax program of Andros, the reactionary ambitions of the Presbyterians, and the schemes of the hard-money men. In John Wise, Cotton Mather was to encounter an antagonist who was more than a match for him.

With the final overthrow of the theocracy and the lessening of the political power of the clergy, a critical period in the development of the church was reached, and with it a renewal of the old conflict between the Presbyterian and Congregational principles. In the year 1705, under the leadership of the Mathers, the Presbyterian party, which numbered among its adherents most of the ministers of the larger churches, put forth a series of "Proposals," looking to a closer union of the churches, and greater control of the separate congregations by the ministerial association. This was a challenge to the Congregationalists which John Wise could not overlook. The question touched the fundamentals of church organization, and when by way of preparation he turned to examine critically the work of the fathers, he found in it quite another meaning than Cotton Mather found. It was as a liberal that he went back to the past, seeking to recover the original Congregational principle, which, since the conservative triumph in the Cambridge Platform of 1648, had been obscured. When he was quite ready, he published in 1710, his *Churches Quarrel Espoused*, reissued five years later; and in 1717, his *Vindication of the Government of the New England Churches*, reissued together with the earlier work in 1772, and again in 1860. The two works were a democratic counterblast to the Presbyterian propaganda, and they stirred the mind of New England profoundly. What Edwards did later for the doctrinal side of Congregationalism, John Wise did for the institutional. His exposition of the Congregational principle was so luminous and convincing that it soon came to be regarded as authoritative, and more than a hundred years after the *Vindication* appeared the Chief Justice of Massachusetts cited it in support of a judicial decision.

The significance of John Wise in the history of democratic America lies in the fact that he followed "an unbeaten path," justifying the principle of Congregationalism by analogy from civil polity. Seemingly alone amongst the New England clergy of his day, he had grounded himself in political theory; and the doctrine upon which he erected his argument was the theory of natural rights, derived from a study of Pufendorf's *De Jure Naturae et Gentium*, published in 1672. Locke and the other writers of the English natural-rights school he seems not to have been acquainted with; but Pufendorf he had read closely, and he discharged the new theory against his opponents with telling effect. This was the first effective reply in America to the old theocratic sneer that if the democratic form of government were indeed divinely sanctioned, was it not strange that God had overlooked it in providing a government for his chosen people? Wise was the first New England minister to break with the literal Hebraism of the old school; like Roger Williams he was willing to make use of profane philosophies, basing his argument upon an appeal to history, a method which baffled the narrow Hebraists, putting them in a quandary.

After examining the three regular forms of civil government, and showing how each is related to "the many ennobling immunities" of the subject, Wise turned to the real business in hand, which was to inquire "whether any of the aforesaid species of regular, unmixed governments, can with any good show of reason be predicable of the church of Christ on earth"; whether the monarchical form as exhibited in papacy and episcopacy, the aristocratic form as exhibited in Presbyterianism, or the democratic form as exhibited in Congregationalism, is nearest the divine model as revealed in Scripture and the law of nature?

The gross inadequacy of the monarchical principle appears to him so certain that he concludes his argument with the comment "that God and wise nature were never propitious to the birth of this monster." The inadequacy of the aristocratic principle seems to him equally clear. The principle of stewardship, ideal though it may appear in theory, did not seem to work in practice, and he put his finger shrewdly upon the weakness of oligarchical rule in Massachusetts. Government by a "select company of choice persons" might be justified, if—

we could be assured they would make the Scripture, and not their private will the rule of their personal and ministerial actions; . . . but considering how great an interest is embarked, and how frail a bottom we trust, though we should rely upon the best of men, especially if we remember what is in the hearts of good men (namely, much ignorance, abundance of small ends, many times cloaked with a high pretense in religion; pride skulking and often breeding revenge upon a small affront, and blown up by a pretended zeal, yet really and truly by nothing more divine than interest or ill nature), and also considering how very uncertain we are of the real goodness of those we esteem good men . . . and . . . how Christianity, by the aforesaid principle, had been peeled, robbed and spoiled already, it cannot consist with the light of nature to venture again upon such perils, especially if we can find a safer way home. . . . In a word an aristocracy is a dangerous constitution in the church of Christ.[4]

This "safer way home," as he then proceeded to point out, lay in following the broad path of democracy:

But to abbreviate, it seems most agreeable with the light of nature, that if there be any of the regular forms of government settled in the church of God, it must needs be . . . a democracy. This is the form of government which the light of nature does highly value, and often directs to as most agreeable to the just and natural prerogatives of human beings. . . . It is certainly a great truth, namely, that man's original liberty after it is resigned . . . ought to be cherished in all wise governments; or otherwise a man in making himself a subject, he alters himself from a freeman into a slave, which to do is repugnant to the law of nature. Also the natural equality of men amongst men must be duly favoured; in that government was never established by God or nature, to give one man a prerogative to insult over another. . . . Honor all men. The end of all good government is to cultivate humanity, and promote the happiness of all, and the good of every man in his rights, his life, liberty, estate, honor, etc., without injury or abuse to any.[5]

From which he concludes that—

. . . a democracy in church or state, is a very honorable and regular government according to the dictates of right reason, And, therefore . . . That these churches of New England, in their ancient constitution of church order, it being a democracy, are manifestly justified and defended by the law and light of nature.[6]

A vigorous thinker was John Wise, with a shrewd knowledge of men and their selfishness. He would rule himself, well or ill, and would have others do likewise. Stewards in church and state, he would have none of. "Brethren," he exclaimed, "ye have been called unto liberty, therefore Hold your hold brethren! . . . pull up well upon the oars, you have a rich cargo, and I hope we shall escape shipwreck . . . daylight and good piloting will secure all."[7] "There is strong and sharp reasoning" in his pages, more

---

[4] *Vindication*, edition of 1860, pp. 50–53.   [5] *Ibid.*, pp. 54–55.
[6] *Ibid.*, p. 60.
[7] *The Churches Quarrel Espoused*, p. 116.

solid meat in his two volumes than in all Cotton Mather's muddled effusions. Like a good Englishman and a good Yankee he hated arbitrary power as he hated the devil. "The very name of an arbitrary government is ready to put an Englishman's blood into a fermentation; but when it comes and shakes its whip over their ears, and tells them it is their master, it makes them stark mad." [8]

Naturally so vigorous an advocate of democracy in the church was disliked by the gentlemen whose ambitions he thwarted. Such plebeian views were incomprehensible to Cotton Mather. When *The Churches Quarrel Espoused* was reprinted in 1713, prefaced with a commendatory letter signed by two well-known clergymen, the latter wrote to a friend:

> . . . A furious Man, called John Wise,[9] of whom, I could wish he had, *Cor bonum*, while we are all sensible, he wants, *Caput bene regulatum*, has lately published a foolish Libel, against some of us, for presbyterianizing too much in our Care to repair some Deficiencies in our Churches. And some of our People, who are not only tenacious of their Liberties, but also more suspicious than they have cause to be of a Design in their pastors to make abridgments of them; they are too much led into Temptation, by such Invectives. But the Impression is not so great as our grand Adversary doubtless hoped for.[10]

Two years later, when the *Vindication* was published, the sulky theocrat noted in his diary:

> 25 [May. 1717] G[ood] D[evice]. Should not I take into Consideration what may be done for the Service of the Ministry and Religion and the Churches, throughout the Land, that the Poison of Wise's cursed Libel may have an Antidote? [11]

Cotton Mather was unable to discover an antidote, and the poison of Wise's democratic philosophy was to prove of surprising vitality. As late as 1772, when his two works were reprinted on subscription, no fewer than 1133 copies were taken. That the argument of Wise was not without influence in the struggle then developing seems reasonable; but that it greatly influenced the thinking of the revolutionary leaders, as Professor Tyler supposes, is scarcely probable. The argument from natural rights was well known in 1772, and it was to Locke and not to Wise that men like Samuel Adams turned for help. Nevertheless, in denying to him

---

[8] *Ibid.*, p. 209.
[9] A gratuitous insult, as Wise was well known.
[10] "Letter to Robert Wodrow, September 17, 1715:" *Diary*, in *Massachusetts Historical Collections*, Seventh Series, Vol. VIII, p. 327.
[11] *Ibid.*, p. 450.

wide influence in the later period we are neither detracting from the honor that is rightly his as the first colonial to justify village democracy by an appeal to political philosophy, nor lessening the repute in which he should be held by Americans as the early defender of local self-rule.

The instinctive sympathy of John Wise with the plain people among whom he lived led him to stand with them in another matter that touched the interests of the farming class. The currency question had thrust its provocative demands into political councils, and sharply divided the electorate. City men like Samuel Sewall were jealous to maintain the English metallic currency, partly through custom and partly because its scarcity augmented its value; whereas the plain people of Ipswich, like so many country people, no doubt were impressed with the desirability of a landscript currency. Into this mighty controversy entered John Wise, who in the year 1721, under the pen name of *Amicus Patriae*, is reputed to have been the author of a book entitled, *A Word of Comfort to a Melancholy Country. Or the Bank of Credit . . . fairly defended by a Discovery of the Great Benefit, accruing by it to the whole Province, etc. Humbly dedicated to the Merchants in Boston.* It was "a well-managed and witty plea for paper money and 'inflation.'" With the economics of the problem that he was delving into, we are not concerned; many heads have wrestled with it since; we are concerned rather to point out that the democratic John Wise was on the same side with the democratic Franklin, in espousing paper currency.

After all, the significant thing that emerges from the life and work of John Wise, is the unerring directness with which he seized upon the core of primitive Congregationalism, and the breadth and vigor with which he defended it. After a spirited contest lasting three-quarters of a century, theocratic Puritanism yielded to ecclesiastical democracy. For two generations it had remained doubtful which way the church would incline. Dominated by gentlemen, it was warped towards Presbyterianism; but interpreted by commoners, it leaned towards Congregationalism. The son of a plebeian, Wise inclined to sympathize with the spirit of radical Separatism, bred of the democratic aspirations of Jacobean underlings; and this radical Separatism he found justified by the new political philosophy, as well as by facts of the New England village world. The struggle for ecclesiastical democracy was a forerunner of the struggle for political democracy which was to be the business of the next century; and in founding his ecclesiasticism upon the doctrine of natural rights, John Wise was an early witness to the new order of thought.

II

SOCIAL DRIFTS

Great changes, whether liberal or otherwise as the future might determine, were to come to Massachusetts from the new order with its Charter provision establishing a property qualification for suffrage. The venture in idealism was over and economic determinism reasserted its sway. New England was to swing back into the broad current of English political development. Following the Revolution of 1688 a new theory of the political state was rising in England—the theory that the state originated in private property and exists primarily for the protection of property; and this conception, thrust upon New England, was to cut sharply across the cleavages of the old order and create new ones. It substituted the dominance of wealth for the stewardship of righteousness; the stake-in-society principle for the Mosaic code. It set a premium upon acquisitiveness and subordinated the Puritan to the Yankee. It prepared the way for class alignments which must grow sharper with the increase of wealth, and would eventually produce a Tory group with natural longings for titles and a colonial aristocracy. How powerful this mercantile-Tory element was to become would depend upon the counter strength of the rising democratic group, with its freehold tenure of land, its town meeting, its Congregational church, and its distrust of aristocratic orders.

For the present, the world of John Wise was the real New England, thrifty, parsimonious, intensely local, driving straight towards a homespun democracy. The older fashioned New Englander, whatever his social position, did not take kindly to Toryism; and when it made its appearance in the train of the royal officials, swaggering somewhat and a bit insolent, it seemed to the colonial both alien and wicked. English Tory and Puritan Yankee frankly disliked each other; their ideals were incompatible, their manners unlike. A cloud of suspicion surrounded the English official as he walked the streets of Boston: suspicion of the hated church which he promptly set up, though not much given to worship;

suspicion of his political motives and the overseas authority which
he represented. In a vague way the New Englanders were convinced that he constituted a menace to their most cherished
rights and privileges; that he was secretly bent on undermining
the traditional liberties. And the English gentleman, with his
casual old-world arrogance, unwittingly aggravated the common
suspicion.

How great was the chasm that separated the two worlds is
sharply revealed by an episode in the career of Joseph Dudley,
son of the emigrant, who was made royal governor in 1702. Dudley
had lived much in England, had sat in Parliament, and had imbibed
prerogative notions of government. He little relished the homely
ways of New England and he bore himself somewhat haughtily.
One December day in 1705, as he was driving along a country road
with high snowdrifts on each side, he met with two loads of wood.
The chariot coming to a stop, Dudley thrust his head out of the
window and bade the carters turn aside and make way for him;
but they were inclined to argue the matter in view of the drifts.
Words were multiplied, and one of the carters cried—to quote
Sewall—"I am as good flesh and blood as you . . . you may goe
out of the way." In a rage the governor drew his sword and struck
at the fellow, who snatched the sword away and broke it. "You
lie, you dog; you lie, you devill!" cried Dudley, beside himself.
"Such words don't become a Christian," retorted the carter. "A
Christian, you dog!" cried Dudley; "a Christian, you devill! I
was a Christian before you were born!" and he snatched the
carter's whip and lashed him roundly. "Being in a great passion:
threatn'd to send those that affronted him to England." He arrested
both carters and threw them into jail, whence they were released
by the help of Sewall, who took their side though connected with
Dudley through marriage. They were of good yeoman families,
yet the matter hung on for nearly a year before they were discharged from their bonds.[12]

Village New England was becoming surprisingly independent
in spirit when plain countrymen stood upon their rights against
the Governor—"nor did they once in the Govrs . . . sight pull
of their hatts," as Dudley took pains to inform the Queen's justices.
Three generations in America were having their effect in the
creation of a homespun democracy. "Mr. Dudley's principles,

[12] The account with affidavits is given in Sewall, *Diary*, Vol. II, pp. 144-147.

in government, were too high for the Massachusetts people," commented a later Tory, whose own principles were high:

He found it difficult to maintain what appeared to him to be the just prerogative of the crown, and at the same time to recover and preserve the esteem of the country. The government had been so popular [i. e. democratic] under the old charter, that the exercise of the powers reserved to the crown by the new charter was submitted to with reluctance.[13]

If "the prejudices against him were great," some explanation is found in a letter written by his son, Attorney-General Paul Dudley, to an English friend, which came to the hands of Cotton Mather and was published by him:

I refer you to Mr. — for an Account of everything, especially about the Government, and the Colledge; both which, are Discoursed of here, in Chimney Corners, and Private Meetings, as confidently as can be. . . . This Country will never be worth Living in, for Lawyers and Gentlemen, till the *Charter* is *Taken Away*. My Father and I sometimes Talk of the Queen's Establishing a *Court of Chancery* in this Country; I have Writ about it, to Mr. Blathwayt: If the Matter should Succeed, you might get some Place worth your Return; of which I should be very Glad.[14]

If New England had grown restive under the theocratic oligarchy, it had no intention of being toryized by English placemen.

It was during these troubled years that a new force made its appearance in Massachusetts which Sewall noted: "Sept. 25 [1690]. A printed sheet entituled publick Occurrences comes out, which gives much distaste because not Licensed. . . ." A week later he added: "Print of the Governour and Council comes out shewing their disallowance of the Public Occurrences"; and the next day, "Mr. Mather writes a very sharp letter about it." This was Increase Mather, who would tolerate no such lawlessness of the press, which must be kept as a private preserve for the orthodox party. Against the Mather conservatism it was impossible to make headway, and the little sheet did not come to a second issue. Not till fourteen years later did Sewall set down a similar note: "April 24 [1704]. I went to Cambridge. . . . I gave Mr. Willard the first News-Letter that ever was carried over the River. He shew'd it to the Fellows." So began in America, at first unlawfully, and then with due propriety, the work of making and publishing newspapers. For seventy-two years thereafter, the

[13] Hutchinson, *History of Massachusetts Bay Colony*, Vol. II, p. 148.
[14] Sewall, *Diary*, Vol. II, Introduction, p. 109.

News-Letter was published continuously, justifying in all its utterances the confidence of Boston conservatism, espousing naturally
the Tory side in the pre-Revolutionary quarrels, and coming to a
sudden end on the evacuation of Boston by General Gage.

On December 14, 1719, the *Boston Gazette* entered the field as a
competitor for conservative readers, and two years later, August
17, 1721, the *New England Courant* appeared, the first organ of the
opposition.   It was edited by James Franklin, who possessed
much of the Franklin independence, untempered by the prudence
of Benjamin; and he set himself incautiously to the business of
assailing the strait-laced authorities of Boston.   He got together a
group of brisk young men, known as the Hell-fire Club, who flung
their vivacious satires at the Mathers with such effect as to
lead Cotton Mather to undertake the following "Good Device":

> Warnings are to be given unto the wicked Printer, and his Accomplices,
> who every week publish a vile Paper to lessen and blacken the Ministers
> of the Town, and render their Ministry ineffectual.   A Wickedness never
> parall'd any where upon the Face of the Earth.[15]

Although his prayers could not convert the wicked journalists,
his warnings availed with the magistrates, who took means to put
a stop to such disrespect.   Twice Franklin was arraigned for
contempt, and once he spent four weeks in the common jail.   By
way of counterblast to so disreputable a sheet, the *New England
Weekly Journal* appeared on March 20, 1727, an eminently respectable sheet, edited by Mather Byles and with such notable con-
tributors as the Reverend Thomas Prince.   But with the coming
of the *Journal* with its staff of writers who modeled their style
upon the Augustan wits, we are in the mid-current of the eighteenth
century, that was to enlarge the influence of the public press far
beyond what could have been foreseen from its small beginnings.
It was to penetrate the inland villages and slowly wear away their
insularity of temper and outlook, bringing fresh ideas to minds
that had long stagnated.   On the whole it was not a liberal press,
but its final effect was profoundly liberalizing.

[15] *Diary*, Vol. II, p. 663.

BOOK TWO: THE COLONIAL MIND

BOOK TWO

THE COLONIAL MIND

THE undistinguished years of the early and middle eighteenth century, rude and drab in their insularity, were the creative springtime of democratic America—plebeian years that sowed what after times were to reap. The forgotten men and women of those silent decades wrote little, debated little, very likely thought little; they were plain workmen with whom ideas counted for less than the day's work. The stir of achievement filled the land, daily penetrating farther into the backwoods and bringing new farmlands under the plow. The stern demands of necessity held men in their grip, narrowing the horizon of their minds, and obscuring the vision of their larger accomplishment. Along the Appalachian watershed a vast drama, magnificent in the breadth and sweep of its movement, was being enacted by players unconscious of their parts. Not until long after they had gone to their graves were the broad lines of that drama revealed. Today it is plain that those unremembered years were engaged in clearing away encumbrances more significant than the great oaks and maples of the virgin wilderness: they were uprooting ancient habits of thought, destroying social customs that had grown old and dignified in class-ridden Europe. A new psychology was being created by the wide spaces that was to be enormously significant when it came to self-consciousness. If this middle eighteenth century wrote little literature, it created and spread among a vigorous people something of far greater importance to America, the psychology of democratic individualism.

From this determining influence—too little recognized by later generations—the creative outlines of our history have taken shape. American ideals and institutions emerged in large part from the silent revolution which during the middle eighteenth century differentiated the American from the transplanted colonial; a change that resulted from an amalgam of the older English stock with other races, and the subjection of this new product on a great scale to the influence of diffused landholding. From these

131

two major facts of a new race and a free environment came the social and political philosophy of older America, to which we have traditionally applied the term democratic, and which unconsciously wove itself into our daily intercourse and ways of thinking.

PART ONE: THE MIND IN THE MAKING
1720–1763

CHAPTER I

COLONIAL BACKGROUNDS

I

NEW STOCK

IMMIGRATION in the eighteenth century was almost wholly economic in motive. The reports of free land and free opportunity in America penetrated to remote hamlets of Great Britain, and more slowly to the continent, and drew hither a rude influx of the dispossessed and disinherited of Europe. From the hopeless poverty of great masses of old-world laborers, increasing numbers sought escape through emigration, accepting the hardships and uncertainties of the migration in the hope of bettering themselves ultimately. A host of English nondescripts—broken men, bond servants, "gaol birds," the lees and settlings of the old world—came overseas, voluntarily or under duress, in numbers running into the hundred thousands, and shared with German peasants from the Palatine, or Scotch-Irish from Ulster, the back-breaking labor of subduing the wilderness. About these unfortunate men and women no romance has gathered; tradition and history have not remembered their names or glorified their deeds; yet their blood runs in the veins of most Americans today of the older stock, and their contribution to our common heritage was great and lasting.

Of the different racial strains that mingled their blood with the earlier English—Irish, Huguenot-French, German, Scotch-Irish—the last was by far the most important. Not since 1630, when the *Lady Arbella* and her companion vessels brought the Puritans to Massachusetts Bay, had there been an event so momentous to America as the arrival in 1718 of some four thousand Scotch-Irish from Ulster, the vanguard of an army which by the time of the Revolution had risen to approximately two hundred thousand, or more than twelve times the number of English who settled

Massachusetts. They were desperately poor; the available lands near the coast were already preëmpted; so armed with axes, their seed potatoes, and the newly invented rifle, they plunged into the backwoods to become our great pioneering race. Scattered thinly through a long frontier, they constituted the outposts and buffer settlements of civilization. A vigorous breed, hardy, assertive, individualistic, thrifty, trained in the democracy of the Scottish kirk, they were the material out of which later Jacksonian democracy was to be fashioned, the creators of that "western type which in politics and industry became ultimately the American type."[1]

Next to the Scotch-Irish, who for the most part were free peasants, the most important addition to eighteenth-century America were the indented servants. Mostly from England, Scotland, Ireland, and Germany, they represented all trades and some of the professions. The white slavers of the times were well organized and plied a brisk trade with satisfactory profits; and in consequence, a steady stream of indented servants poured into America to turn the wheels of colonial industry. In his history of the German redemptioners, Diffenderfer has printed a number of newspaper advertisements which throw a curious light upon the traffic: here are two:

From the *American Weekly Mercury*, February 18, 1729:
Lately arrived from London, a parcel of very likely English servants, men and women, several of the men Tradesmen; to be sold reasonable and Time allowed for payment. By Charles Read of Philadelphia, or Capt. John Ball, on board his ship, at *Anthony Millkinson's Wharf*.

From the same for May 22, 1729, announcements of two ships:
There is just arrived from Scotland, a parcel of choice *Scotch Servants*; Taylors, Weavers, Shoemakers and ploughmen, some for five and others for seven years; Imported by James Coults, etc.
Just arrived from London in the ship *Providence*, Capt. Jonathan Clarke, a parcel of very likely *servants*, most Tradesmen, to be sold on reasonable Terms.

The several nationalities were appraised and rated by careful merchants and the fittest import seasons considered.[2] The "best

---

[1] See Commons, *Races and Immigrants in America*, p. 37.
[2] Sometimes the profits were unexpectedly great, as is illustrated by the case of a certain George Martin, who contracted with a shipmaster to transport himself, his wife, and five children to America for fifty-four pounds. He paid down $16, but died on the passage. On the arrival of the vessel in port, the captain foreclosed on the contract, sold the widow for twenty-two pounds, the three eldest sons at thirty

time for Servants is about the month of May," one merchant wrote to his agent in Ireland; and another warned, "Irish servants will be very dull, such numbers have already arrived from Different parts & many more expected, that I believe it will be overdone, especially as several Dutch vessels are expected here, which will always command the Market." [3]

In the middle colonies, particularly Pennsylvania, the greater number of servants came from the Rhine country. Deceived by swindling agents, thousands of German peasants, eager to get away from their war-harried and plundered homes, sold themselves into servitude to pay their passage to America. For the better part of a century these German redemptioners thronged the ports of Philadelphia and Baltimore, as the following news items testify:

From *Der Hoch Deutsche Pennsylvanische Bericht*, August 16, 1750: Six ships with Irish servants have arrived at Philadelphia, and two ships with German Newcomers. Some say 18 more on their way here; others say 24 and still others 10,000 persons.

From the same, December 16, 1750: Capt. Hasselwood has arrived from Holland with the latest ship that brought Germans. It is the fourteenth that has come laden with Germans this year. 4,317 have registered in the Court House. . . . Besides these, 1,000 servants and passengers arrived from Ireland and England. [4]

Of the human side of this widespread traffic some little idea may be got from the diary of a certain John Harrower, a man of modest education who became an articled schoolmaster to a Virginia family in the year 1774. Following are some entries:

Wednesday, 26th. [January, 1774.] This day I being reduced to the last shilling was obliged to engage to go to Virginia for four years, as a schoolmaster for Bedd, Board, washing and five pounds during the whole time. I have also wrote my wife this day a particular Acct of everything that has happened to me since I left her until this date. . . .
Munday 31st . . . It is surprising to see the No. of good tradesmen cf all kinds, th't come on b'd every day . . . while the Clerk was filling up the Indentures the doctor search'd every serv't to see that they were sound . . . seventy-five were Intend [indented] to Capt Bowres for four Years. . . .

pounds each, and the two youngest, who were under five years of age, he sold for ten pounds, realizing one hundred and twenty-two pounds on a debt under fifty-one pounds. (Diffenderfer, *The German Immigrants into Pennsylvania*, p. 268).
[3] *Ibid.*, p. 229.
[4] *Ibid.*, Part II, "The Redemptioners," p. 209.

Munday 7th . . . at 4 pm put a servant ashore extreamly bade in a fever, and then got under saile for Virginia with seventy Servants on board all indented to serve four yeares there at their different Occupations. . . .

Munday, May 2nd. . . . At 2 pm the Capt carried five servts ashore to Hampton in order to sell their Indentures, But returned again at Midnight with[out] selling any more but one Boat Builder. . . .

Freiday, 6th . . . at Hobshole there was five Glasgow ships and an English Brigantine lying, at 2 pm we passed by Leedstown on our Star board hand where there was a ship from London lying with convicts. . . .

Wednesday, 11th. . . . At 10 A M Both Coopers and the Barber from our Mace [mess] went ashore upon tryall. At night one Daniel Turner a servt returned onb'd from Liberty so Drunk that he abused the Capt and Chief Mate and Boatswan to a verry high degree, which made him to be horse whipt, put in Irons and thumb screwed. on houre afterward he was unthumbscrewed, taken out of the Irons, but then he was hand cuffed, and gagged all night. . . .

Munday, 16th. This day severalls came on b'd to purchase servts Indentures and among them there was two soul drivers. they are Men who made it their business to go on b'd all ships who have in either Servants or Convicts and buy sometimes the whole and sometimes a parcell of them as they can agree, and then they drive them through the Country like a parcell of Sheep until they can sell them to advantage, but all went away without buying any. . . .

Munday, 23rd [May] . . . at same time all the rest of the servants were ordered ashore to a tent at Fredericksbg and several of their indentures were then sold. about 4 pm I was brought to Colonel Daingerfield, when we immediately agreed and my Indenture for four years was then delivered him and he was to send for me the next day.[5]

In some such fashion, year after year, thousands of immigrants were transported to America, there to mingle their blood with that of the earlier comers. They came as social derelicts, were greeted by the awaiting "soul-drivers," found masters, worked and got on, or lost heart and slipped away into the tempting back-country whither so many broken men went in search of refuge. They were a plebeian lot, and they endured the common fate of the underling. Very likely they transmitted to their children a bitter hostility to the ways of an aristocratic society, the residuum of old grievances, and this slowly accumulating animus was eventually to count heavily with lower-class colonials in favor of a more democratic order in the new world.

[5] For the entire diary, see *American Historical Review*, Vol. VI, pp. 65–107.

II

THE FRONTIER

Lubberland

The frontier, which exercised so creative an influence in shaping American character and institutions, was regarded in very different lights by the gentleman and the commoner. To the former it was no other than lubberland, the abode of rude leveling, the temptation to gross social laxity. It drew away servants who were needed, and kept the price of real estate low; and such very different persons as Cotton Mather and John Dickinson agreed in desiring to stop the constant drain into the backcountry, and keep settlers in the older portions. Descriptions of the frontier indited by aristocratic pens convey an idea very different from later democratic conceptions, and paint the ancestors of later Jacksonians in unlovely colors.

Among the earliest of these records is *The Private Journal kept by Madam Knight on a Journey from Boston to New York in the Year 1704*. Madam Knight was a sprightly and intelligent woman, keeper of a dame's school in Boston, who set down in the journal some of the odd things that came under her sharp eyes on her venturesome trip on horseback. As she drew away from the older settlements, signs of relaxing social convention multiplied with the worsening of the road. Connecticut, which had always been too democratic to suit the Boston taste, she found "a little too much Independant in their principalls." It was not careful to uphold proper social distinctions, but inclined to a free and easy leveling altogether offensive:

. . . They Generally lived very well and comfortable in their famelies. But too Indulgent (especially ye farmers) to their slaves: suffering too great familiarity from them, permitting ym to sit at Table and eat with them (as they say to save time), and into the dish goes the black hoof as freely as the white hand. They told me that there was a farmer lived nere the Town where I lodged who had some difference with his slave, concerning something the master had promised him and did not punctually perform; wch caused some hard words between them; But at length they put the matter to Arbitration and Bound themselves to stand to the award of such as they named—wch done, the Arbitrators Having heard the Allegations of both parties, Order the master to pay 40s to black face, and acknowledge his fault. And so the matter ended; the poor master very honestly standing to the award.[6]

---

[6] *The Private Journal, etc.,* p. 40.

In the unsettled country strange figures with rude decivilized ways made their appearance. Here is a description of one such product of the wilderness:

I had scarce done thinking, when an Indian-like Animal come to the door, on a creature very much like himselfe, in mien and feature, as well as Ragged cloathing; and having 'litt, makes an Awkerd Scratch with his Indian shoo, and a Nodd, sitts on ye block, fumbles out his black Junk [salt meat?], dipps it in ye ashes, and presents it piping hott to his muschee-to's (?), and fell to sucking like a calf, without speaking, for near a quarter of an hower. At length the old man said how do's Sarah do? who I understood was the wretches wife, and Daughter to ye old man.[7]

She thus describes a squatter's hut in the backwoods:

This little Hutt was one of the wretchedest I ever saw a habitation for human creatures. It was suported with shores enclosed with Clapboards, laid on Lengthways, and so much asunder, that the Light come throu' everywhere; the doore tyed on with a cord in ye place of hinges; The floor the bear earth; no windows but such as the thin covering afforded, nor any furniture but a Bedd with a glass Bottle hanging at ye head on't; an earthan cupp, a small pewter bason, A Bord with sticks to stand on, instead of a table, and a block or two in ye corner instead of chairs. The family were the old man, his wife and two children; all and every part being the picture of poverty. Notwithstanding both the Hutt and its Inhabitance were very clean and tydee.[8]

As Madam Knight meditated upon the causes of such poverty, she came to a characteristic Boston conclusion:

We may Observe here the great necessity and benefitt both of Educa-tion and Conversation: for these people have as Large a portion of mother witt, and sometimes Larger, than those who have bin brought up in Citties; but for want of emprovements, Render themselves almost Ridic-ulos, as above.[9]

It is in the chatty narrative of Colonel William Byrd of Virginia,[10] that we find the earliest detailed description of the fringe of squat-ter settlements. Colonel Byrd was the first gentleman of Virginia, a man of old-world education and some literary taste,[11] polished manners, and a vast number of acres of choice land which he had ac-quired and held largely tax-free, by means well understood among Vir-

[7] Ibid., pp. 29–30.   [8] Ibid., p. 28.   [9] Ibid., p. 45.
[10] "The History of the Dividing Line," in The Writings of Colonel William Byrd of Westover in Virginia, Esquire, New York, 1901.
[11] At his death his library contained some four thousand volumes, "the largest private library in the English-speaking colonies," according to his biographer.

ginia gentlemen.[12] Among the several capacities in which he served the commonwealth in return for his many acres, was to act as a member of a joint commission which in the year 1728 ran a boundary line between Virginia and North Carolina. As he sat his horse in the capacity of overseer, he observed many amusing things which he jotted down in his journal.

The backcountry, it would seem, had already developed the free and easy ways of a squatter world, shiftless, lubberly, independent, but animated by hostility towards the aristocratic Old Dominion, from which many of the settlers had come. North Carolina had long been a place of refuge for debtors, criminals, and runaway servants, who used their legs to even the score with a caste system; and Colonel Byrd regarded the lazy crew with amused contempt:

Surely there is no place in the World where the Inhabitants live with less Labour than in N Carolina. It approaches nearer to the Description of Lubberland than any other, by the great felicity of the Climate, the easiness of raising Provisions, and the Slothfulness of the People. Indian corn is of so great increase, that a little Pains will Subsist a very large Family with Bread, and then they may have meat without any Pains at all, by the Help of the Low Grounds, and the great Variety of Mast that grows on the High-land. The Men, for their parts, just like the Indians, impose all the Work upon the poor Women. They make their Wives rise out of their Beds early in the Morning, at the same time that they lye and Snore, till the Sun has run one third of his course, and disperst all the unwholesome Damps. Then, after Stretching and Yawning for half an Hour, they light their Pipes, and, under the Protection of a cloud of Smoak, venture out into the open Air; tho' if it happens to be never so little cold, they quickly return Shivering into the Chimney corner. When the weather is mild, they stand leaning with both their arms upon the corn-field fence, and gravely consider whether they had best go and take a Small Heat at the Hough; but generally find reasons to put off till another time. Thus they loiter away their Lives, like Solomon's Sluggard, with their Arms across, and at the Winding up of the Year Scarcely have Bread to Eat. To speak the Truth, tis a thorough Aversion to Labor that makes People file off to N Carolina, where Plenty and a Warm Sun confirm them in their Disposition to Laziness for their whole Lives.[13]

One thing Colonel Byrd noted everywhere: the lazy lubbers wanted chiefly to be let alone; they dreaded the possibility of falling within the Virginia line; they were content in their Eden,

[12] His father died possessed of 26,231 acres. He himself owned at his death "no less than 179,440 acres of the best land in Virginia."

[13] Op. cit., pp. 75–76.

and had no wish to exchange their freedom for the stricter rule of the Old Dominion:

> Wherever we passed we constantly found the Borderers laid it to Heart if their Land was taken into Virginia; they chose rather belong to Carolina, where they pay no Tribute, either to God or to Caesar. . . . Another reason was, that the Government there is so Loose, and the Laws so feebly executed, that, like those in the Neighbourhood of Sydon formerly, every one does just what seems good in his own Eyes. . . . Besides, there might have been some Danger, perhaps, in venturing to be so rigorous, for fear of undergoing the Fate of an honest Justice in Corotuck Precinct. This bold Magistrate, it seems, taking upon to order a fellow to the Stocks, for being disorderly in his Drink, was, for his intemperate zeal, carry'd thither himself, and narrowly escap'd being whipp't by the Rabble into the Bargain.[14]

> They are rarely guilty of Flattering or making any Court to their governours, but treat them with all the Excesses of Freedom and Familiarity. They are of Opinion their rulers woul'd be apt to grow insolent, if they grew Rich, and for that reason they take care to keep them poorer, and more dependent, if possible, than the Saints of New England used to do their Governours.[15]

To the student of colonial politics such glimpses are suggestive. They reveal how early was the popular distrust of magistrates and government; and they serve to explain the most striking characteristic of Revolutionary political practice—the movement to minimize the power of the judiciary and the executive, and magnify the power of the legislature; to keep authority within the control of the local democracies. "Every one does just what seems good in his own Eyes"—in this attitude of social *laissez faire* that throve on a diet of corn pone and salt pork was the origin of the coonskin democracy of Old Hickory that was to bring eventual disaster to the plans of gentlemen.

III

THE FRONTIER

Land of Promise

Quite another picture of the frontier was likely to be painted by the eighteenth-century democrat. In the well-known *Letters* of Crèvecœur, and in the recently published *More Letters from an American Farmer*,[16] is an analysis of frontier life and its creative

---

[14] *Ibid.*, p. 87. [15] *Ibid.*, p. 81.
[16] Published under the title of *Sketches of Eighteenth Century America* by the Yale University Press, 1925.

influence upon the emerging American character, far more sympathetic and thoughtful than the casual narratives of Madam Knight and Colonel Byrd. The author was a cultivated Norman-French gentleman, who about the year 1759 or 1760 entered the English colonies from Canada, was a surveyor for a time near Albany, a resident of Pennsylvania and of Ulster County in the province of New York, eventually acquired a farm of 120 acres in Orange County which he named "Pine Hill," married Mehetable Tippet of Yonkers, and became a competent tiller of the soil as well as a lover of country life. In disposition he was active and energetic, curious concerning the ways of nature and society. In Canada he had joined the army as lieutenant under Montcalm and was sent on a map-making expedition to the wilderness beyond the Great Lakes, and traveled from Detroit as far south as the Ohio River. After quitting Canada following the fall of Quebec, he traveled from Nova Scotia through the English colonies to the extreme south, and perhaps visited Bermuda and Jamaica, noting keenly the country and the manners of the people. Perhaps no other man before the Revolution was so intimately acquainted with the French and English colonies as a whole, with their near background of frontier and the great wilderness beyond, as this French American; and it was from long and intimate contact with the realities of colonial life that he wrote those comments that have preserved his name to the present.

The Revolution broke in upon his peaceful life with disastrous consequences. He took no part in the preliminary disputes, and was under grave suspicion by his neighbors in Orange County and by the British. He was thrown into prison in New York by his Majesty's officers, where his health was undermined and he was reduced to extreme straits. Finally permitted to sail for Europe without his family, he was shipwrecked off the coast of Ireland, but reached London where he disposed of his manuscripts, and eventually got over to France in August, 1781. After the peace he returned to America to find his wife dead, his children scattered, and his farmhouse burnt. For a time he was French consul at New York, where he interested himself in establishing a packet service between France and America, and in the improvement of agricultural methods, amongst other ways by the establishment of botanical gardens. He was a scientific farmer, introducing the system of cover crops into America and endeavoring to intro-

duce potato culture into France. He was a corresponding member
of the Académie des Sciences and the Royal Agricultural Society of
Paris, and a member of the Société d'Agriculture, Sciences, et Arts
de Meaux, and of the Société d'Agriculture de Caen. In 1790 he
returned to France where he died in 1813.

Underneath the discursive chat of his letters is the firm fabric of
economic fact. In the background of his thinking Crèvecœur was
quite definitely Physiocratic, in his warm humanitarianism as well
as in his agrarian bias. As the kindly Frenchman studied the ways
of colonial society and contemplated the future, he asked himself
the question, what was the American as he was perceptibly differentiating from his European ancestors? That a new race was
emerging in this new country, he was convinced; and that it was
not in consequence chiefly of a new mixture of blood—although
that was not without its influence—he likewise believed. A more
potent influence was at work and that influence was environment.
Crèvecœur was something of an economic determinist who sought
to explain laws, customs, institutions—the pattern of the social
web—by an inquiry into economic factors. *Mann ist was er isst.*
"Men are like plants; the goodness and flavor of the fruit proceeds
from the peculiar soil and exposition in which they grow. We are
nothing but what we derive from the air we breathe, the climate
we inhabit, the government we obey, the system of religion we
profess, and the mode of our employment." [17] Transplanted from
the meager opportunities of the old world to the rich soil and ample
spaces of America, the European undergoes a subtle transformation.

The rich stay in Europe, it is only the middling and the poor that
emigrate. In this great American asylum, the poor of Europe have by
some means met together, and in consequence of various causes; to what
purpose should they ask one another, what countrymen they are? Alas,
two thirds of them had no country. Can a wretch who wanders about,
who works and starves . . . can that man call England or any other
kingdom his country? A country that had no bread for him, whose fields
procured him no harvest, who met nothing but the frowns of the rich, the
severity of the laws, with jails and punishments; who owned not a single
foot of the extensive surface of this planet? No! urged by a variety of
motives, here they came. Every thing tended to regenerate them; new
laws, a new mode of living, a new social system; here they are become men:
in Europe they were as so many useless plants, wanting vegetable mould,

[17] *Letters . . .*, in edition of 1904, p. 56.

and refreshing showers; they withered and were mowed down by want, hunger, and war: but now by the power of transplantation, like all other plants, they have taken root and flourished! Formerly they were not numbered in any civil list of their country, except in those of the poor; here they rank as citizens. By what invisible power has this surprizing metamorphosis been performed? By that of the laws of their industry . . . his country is now that which gives him land, bread, protection, and consequence: *Ubi panis ibi patria,* is a motto of all emigrants. . . . Here the rewards of his industry follow with equal steps in the progress of his labor; his labor is founded on the basis of nature, *self-interest;* can it want a stronger allurement? [18]

From economic individualism in presence of unexploited natural resources, he deduces the natural emergence of a new American psychology that differentiates the colonial from the European peasant. If "from involuntary idleness, servile dependence, penury, and useless labor," the emigrant "has passed to toils of a very different nature, rewarded by ample subsistence"; if he has left off being a peasant and become a free-holder and citizen; will not this man "entertain new ideas, and form new opinions"? He possesses a stake in society; his horizons broaden, his ambitions quicken; this is his country.

An European, when he first arrives, seems limited in his intentions, as well as in his views; but he very suddenly alters his scale . . . he no sooner breathes our air than he forms new schemes, and embarks in designs he never would have thought of in his own country. There the plenitude of society confines many useful ideas, and often extinguishes the most laudable schemes which here ripen into maturity.[19]

He begins to feel the effects of a sort of resurrection; hitherto he had not lived, but simply vegetated; he now feels himself a man, because he is treated as such; the laws of his own country had overlooked him in his insignificancy; the laws of this cover him with their mantle. Judge what an alteration there must arise in the mind and thoughts of this man; he begins to forget his former servitude and dependence, his heart involuntarily swells and glows; this first swell inspires him with those new thoughts which constitute an American. . . . From nothing to start into being, to become a free man, invested with lands, to which every municipal blessing is annexed! What a change indeed! It is in consequence of that change that he becomes an American.[20]

He is an American, who leaving behind him all his ancient prejudices and manners, receives new ones from the mode of life he has embraced, the new government he obeys, and the new rank he holds. He becomes an American by being received in the broad lap of our great *Alma Mater*

[18] *Ibid.,* pp. 52–55.   [19] *Ibid.,* p. 76.   [20] *Ibid.,* pp. 77, 79.

Here individuals of all nations are melted into a new race of men, whose labors and posterity will one day cause great changes in the world.[21]

Having convinced himself that economic relaxation was the creative force in determining American institutions and psychology, he was led to examine the working of that force in diverse portions of America. It is neither in the older seacoast world, nor along the extreme frontier that he discovers his representative America; but in the broad stretches of clearings, the vigorous backcountry or "middle-settlements," where agriculture was followed soberly and effectively. "Some few towns excepted, we are all tillers of the soil," he pointed out; and it is the farmer of the middle region of New York and Pennsylvania, with his broad acres in prosperous cultivation, his economic independence, and his manly vigor, that he most delights to dwell upon:

Europe has no such class of men; the early knowledge they acquire, the early bargains they make, give them a great degree of sagacity. As freemen, they will be litigious; pride and obstinacy are often the cause of lawsuits; the nature of our laws and governments may be another. As citizens it is easy to imagine, that they will carefully read the newspapers, enter into every political disquisition, freely blame or censure governors and others. As farmers, they will be careful and anxious to get as much as they can, because what they get is theirs. . . . As Christians, religion curbs them not in their opinions; the laws inspect our actions; our thoughts are left to God. Industry, good living, selfishness, litigiousness, country politics, the pride of freemen, religious indifference, are their characteristics.[22]

The thinly settled backwoods with their restless squatter population, Crèvecœur regards as the rough vanguard of the westward-moving settlements. It is here, he points out, that the forces of leveling are strongest, that the last remnants of old-world distinctions and privileges are stript away, that the idea of individual freedom carries furthest, sometimes to social disaster. "He who would wish to see America in its proper light," he says, "and have a true idea of its feeble beginnings and barbarous rudiments, must visit our extended line of frontiers where the last settlers dwell."

Now we arrive near the great woods, near the last inhabited districts; there men seem to be placed . . . beyond the reach of government, which in some measure leaves them to themselves . . . as they were driven there by misfortune, necessity of beginnings, desire of acquiring large tracts of land, idleness, frequent want of economy, ancient debts; the re-

[21] *Ibid.*, pp. 54–55.   [22] *Ibid.*, pp. 57–58.

union of such people does not afford a very pleasing spectacle. . . . The few magistrates they have, are in general little better than the rest; they are often in a perfect state of war; that of man against man, sometimes decided by blows, sometimes by means of law . . . men are wholly left dependent upon their native tempers, and on the spur of uncertain industry, which often fails when not sanctified by the efficacy of a few moral rules. There, remote from the power of example, and check of shame, many families exhibit the most hideous parts of our society. They are a kind of forlorn hope, preceding by ten or twelve years the more respectable army of veterans which come after them. In that space, prosperity will polish some, vice and law will drive off the rest, who uniting with others like themselves will recede still farther; making room for more industrious people, who will finish their improvements, convert the loghouse into a convenient habitation, and rejoicing that the first heavy labors are finished, will change in a few years that hitherto barbarous country into a fine, fertile, well regulated district. Such is our progress, such is the march of the Europeans toward the interior parts of this continent. In all society there are off-casts; this impure part serves as our precursors or pioneers.[23]

Crèvecœur's chattiness and bucolic love of nature may easily obscure for the casual reader, the solid economic core of the *Letters*. The story of Andrew, the Hebridean, with its note of idyllic simplicity, reads like a tale out of the French romantics; yet in its broad outline it is the story of many an immigrant who penetrated to the hospitable backcountry, took land, and prospered. The strong coloring of the description is only partly French; in part it is a reflection of the spontaneous optimism that was working like leaven in colonial society. It is the old-fashioned phrasing rather than the matter that makes the *Letters* seem obsolete to modern readers. Change the wording, soften the bucolic enthusiasm, and the sober American of earlier generations, as he observed the arrival of the strong-armed peasant from the north of Europe, would have discovered nothing strange in such a sentiment as this:

After a foreigner from any part of Europe is arrived, and become a citizen; let him devoutly listen to the voice of our great parent, which says to him, "Welcome to my shores, distressed European; bless the hour in which thou didst see my verdant fields, my fair navigable rivers, and my green mountains!—If thou wilt work, I have bread for thee; if thou wilt be honest, sober, and industrious, I have greater rewards to bestow on thee—ease and independence. I will give thee fields to feed and clothe thee; a comfortable fire-side to sit by. . . . I shall endow thee besides with the immunities of a freeman. . . . Go thou, and work and till; thou shalt prosper, provided thou be just, grateful, and industrious.[24]

[23] *Ibid.*, pp. 58–60.   [24] *Ibid.*, pp. 90–91.

Andrew the Hebridean is a portrait painted by a Physiocratic humanitarian, but the idealism that would build peace and content on honest foundations, and would deny them to none, not even the poorest if they proved worthy, found frequent justification in the prosaic experience of colonial America. If many an immigrant found "soul-drivers" awaiting them, many others like Andrew found a more hospitable reception.

Across the peaceful scenes depicted in the *Letters* soon fell the dark shadow of civil war, and Crèvecœur's content was rudely broken in upon. As a French humanitarian he loathed war and all its works, and every instinct and argument counseled him to stand apart from the strife that seemed to him so meaningless. He liked peace and orderly ways and he could not work himself into a passion over the supposed wrongs of a people who seemed to him blessed above all others on this troubled earth. As a philosophical farmer he held the politician in contempt and refused to take seriously abstract theories of statecraft. The citizen who stuck to his plow was happier, he believed, than the citizen who talked noisily of his wrongs, and was eager to overset things. The rough leveling of the frontier he had found distasteful, and as he watched the development of the Revolutionary disputes, he seems to have discovered in the Whig program an irruption of the tumultuous frontier leveling that threatened to sweep away the common peace and well-being. The source of the unrest he traced to New England, the feculent wellspring of all the hypocrisies; it was inspired, he was convinced, by a selfish demagoguery and led by unprincipled mobsters. In so far as he held partisan sympathies, they inclined to the Loyalist side. His education in England and his breeding as a gentleman, drew him towards the Loyalist gentry with whom he associated in Orange County, and repelled him from the noisy ardor of the plebeian patriots. Yet in spirit he stood resolutely aloof, although his sympathies were cruelly hurt by the sufferings that fell under his observation. In certain letters only recently published (*Sketches of Eighteenth Century America*), he narrates the misfortunes that befell innocent men and women from the bitterness of civil strife,[25] and draws a picture of the lawlessness and greed of patriot committeemen, and the intolerance of the mob spirit, that is not pleasant to contem-

[25] See, e. g., "The Man of Sorrows," "The Wyoming Massacre," "The History of Mrs. B.," "The Frontier Woman."

plate.[26] Bitterness rarely exudes from his pen, but when he considers the ways of Whig politicians he now and then indulges in a passage that reveals his loathing of the mercenary spirit that he discovers in the new patriotism. In the conclusion of " The American Belisarius " he gives vent to his anger against those who outrage common morality; if it were not for the fact that this is a moral universe, he says ironically:

> I'd worship the demon of the times, trample on every law, break every duty, neglect every bond, overlook every obligation to which no punishment was annexed. I'd set myself calumniating my rich neighbors. I'd call all passive, inoffensive men by the name of inimical. I'd plunder or detain the entrusted deposits. I'd trade on public moneys, though contrary to my oath. Oath! Chaff for good Whigs, and only fit to bind a few conscientious Royalists! I'd build my new fortune on the depreciation of the money. I'd inform against every man who would make any difference betwixt it and silver, whilst I, secure from any discovery or suspicion by my good name, would privately exchange ten for one. I'd pocket the fines of poor militiamen extracted from their heart's blood. I'd become obdurate, merciless, and unjust. I'd grow rich, "fas vel nefas." I'd send others a-fighting, whilst I stayed at home to trade and to rule. I'd become a clamorous American, a modern Whig, and offer every night incense to the god Arimanes.[27]

A lover of peace and good will, a humanitarian concerned only with justice and the common well-being, seeking new ways to enlarge the returns of agriculture, devoid of petty ambition and local prejudice, a friend of man, Hector St. John de Crèvecœur was an embodiment of the generous spirit of French revolutionary thought, a man whom Jefferson would have liked for a neighbor. His sketchy and discursive writings may not be notable literature, but we could ill spare them from the library of eighteenth-century America.

[26] See, e. g., "The American Belisarius" and "Landscapes."
[27] *Sketches of Eighteenth Century America*, p. 249.

CHAPTER II

THE ANACHRONISM OF JONATHAN EDWARDS

I

BEFORE an adequate democratic philosophy could arise in this world of pragmatic individualism, the traditional system of New England theology must be put away, and a new conception of man and of his duty and destiny in the world must take its place. For the moment Calvinism was strengthened by the coming of the Scotch-Irish who spread the familiar dogmas along the frontier, remote from attack by old-world rationalism; nevertheless those dogmas carried within them the seeds of slow decay. The world that had created them lay in a forgotten past. The five points of Calvinism, postulated on a God of wrath, were no longer living principles answering to common experience; they were become no other than ghosts that walked on the Sabbath to terrify the timid. An intellectual *Aufklärung* was a necessary preliminary to the creation of a fruitful social philosophy. Theology must be made to square with actuality, or yield control of men's minds to more stimulating things.

But unfortunately there was no vigorous attack but only a tedious decay. The old was too deeply entrenched to be routed, and stricken with palsy it lingered out a morose old age. For years New England stewed in its petty provincialism, untouched by the brisk debates that stirred the old world. No vigorous disputant challenged its orthodoxy. In the year 1726 Cotton Mather wrote, "I cannot learn, That among all the Pastors of Two Hundred Churches, there is one Arminian; much less an Arian, or a Gentilist." [1] Nevertheless rationalism was in the air, and although it might be excluded from the minister's study, it spread its subtle infection through the mass of the people. The backwash of English deism reached the shores of New England, and by the decade of the forties a movement of liberalism seems to have got under way. The word Arminian sprinkles more freely

[1] Quoted in Walker, *History of the Congregational Churches in the United States,* p. 216.

the pages of controversial literature, indicating the nature of the attack being directed against Calvinism. Dogma was face to face with rationalism.

A critical movement had long been developing in England, undermining there the foundations of Calvinism; and in this work members of the Anglican clergy had aided. Hooker had been a rationalist and the influence of the *Ecclesiastical Polity* was thrown in favor of an appeal to reason and to history. He rejected a literal Hebraism for a more philosophical interpretation of the Scripture. "The Light of naturall understanding, wit and reason, is from God," he argued; "he it is which thereby doth illuminate every man entring into the World. He is the Author of all that we think or do by vertue of that light which himselfe hath given." [2] Because of this rationalizing tendency the Anglican clergy, before the middle of the seventeenth century, had passed from the Calvinistic to the Arminian position. The fundamental dogma of Arminianism was the doctrine of the freedom of the will—that the elect of God are not pre-chosen, but a righteous life and good works will bring men into the way of salvation. Destructive of the whole Calvinistic system as such doctrine was—striking at the taproot of determinism—Arminianism carried a social significance greater than its theological import: it was an expression of the ideal of individual responsibility that emerged from the decay of the feudal system. The first reformers had asserted the right to individual interpretation of the Scriptures; the Arminians threw upon the individual the whole responsibility, bidding him assert his will and achieve his own salvation.

English rationalism was carried further by a notable group of thinkers, including Milton and Locke, who rapidly passed from Arminianism to Arianism, and thence to Deism. By the beginning of the eighteenth century English Presbyterianism, which had clung to Calvinism long after the defection of the Anglicans, was undermined by the growing rationalism and finally passed over into Unitarianism. Calvinism had lost the battle in the old world and ceased to play an important part in the intellectual life of England. In the face of this steady drift away from the conception of a divine Will that dwarfed the human will and held it fixed in the mesh of the divine purpose, towards the conception of the responsibility of the individual and the significance of the moral

_____
[2] *Ecclesiasticall Politie*, sixth edition, Book III, p. 10.

code in the work of salvation, the New England Calvinists found their work cut out for them. A critical spirit was stirring, an incipient rationalism was beginning to ask questions; orthodoxy for the first time was on the defensive, and ill equipped for the pending battle.

But Calvinism had fallen into the clutch of forces greater and more revolutionary than either minister or congregation realized. To preach with convincing force one must appeal to the common experience; dogma must seem to square with the evident facts of life; it must appear to be the inevitable and sufficient explanation of the mysteries and perplexities that beset men in the world of reality. When it ceases to be a reasonable working hypothesis in the light of common experience, it is no longer a controlling influence in men's lives. And this was the unhappy predicament in which Calvinism now found itself. Take, for example, the doctrine of total depravity. In the corrupt worlds of Augustine and John Calvin such a doctrine must have seemed a reasonable explanation of the common brutality; an evil society must spring from the evil heart of man. But in the village world of New England the doctrine had lost its social sanction. When in moments of calm sense these provincial Calvinists asked themselves if the human heart were in truth utterly depraved, if they themselves and their neighbors were such vipers and worms as they professed to be, the conviction must have grown upon them that such professions were untrue. The everyday life of the New England village was animated by rugged virtues—by kindliness toward neighbors and faithfulness to a strict ethical code, rather than by hatred to God and man, or brutal wallowing in sin. In short, these villagers knew that they were very far from a bad lot; and when they pondered on this fact they must have discovered increasing difficulty in reconciling Sunday dogma and week-day experience. Although they repeated the familiar creed, the sanction for that creed was gone; it was the voice of dogma that spoke, and not the voice of reason and experience.[3]

Such is the explanation, as well, of the decay of another of the cardinal points of Calvinism—the dogma of special election. In an aristocratic society it is natural to believe that God has set men apart in classes; but as the leveling process tended to strip away social distinctions, the new individualism undermined the

[3] See Wendell, *Literary History of America*, p. 89.

older class psychology. When the common man has freed himself from political absolutism, he will become dissatisfied with theological absolutism. The right to achieve salvation is a natural corollary to the right to win social distinction; that one's future status lay wholly beyond the reach of one's will, that it rested in the hands of an arbitrary God who gave or withheld salvation at pleasure, was a conception that ill accorded with the nascent ideal of democracy. When that ideal should be sufficiently clarified, the dogma of the elect of God, like the aristocratic conception of the king's favorite, would be quietly put away in the potter's field.

As the century advanced, the growing dissatisfaction with Calvinism received fresh impetus from the new social philosophy of France. The teaching of Rousseau that in a state of nature men were good, that they are still sound at heart, and that the evils of civilization have resulted from a perversion of the social contract, would appeal to men whose experience was daily teaching them the falseness of the traditional dogmas; and the ideal of equality would come home with special meaning to men bred up in villages and on the frontier. Such doctrines were fundamentally hostile to the spirit of Calvinism: not only did Rousseau set the doctrine of human perfectibility over against the dogma of total depravity, but he quickened the passion of revolt against every form of arbitrary authority, theological as well as political and social. Although the provincial colonial might not come in immediate contact with such speculative philosophy, in the long run he could not escape being influenced by it, and that influence would count against a decadent theology that held men's minds in its tenacious *rigor mortis*.

The crux of the question, it came finally to be seen by the apologists of the old order, lay in the fundamental problem of determinism. Was the will of man effectively free, or was it held in strict subjection to the stable will of God? According as the decision went touching this question, would stand or fall the entire metaphysical structure of Calvinism. To this problem, therefore, the best minds among the ministers directed their thought; and the historical position of Jonathan Edwards, greatest of the defenders of Calvinism, is revealed in its true perspective when his labors are studied in the light of this vital question.

II

Never had the traditional theology been so sorely in need of a champion as at the beginning of the second quarter of the eighteenth century; and such a champion God raised up—many devout Calvinists believed—in the person of Jonathan Edwards. Armed at all points—a theologian equipped with the keenest dialectics, a metaphysician endowed with a brilliantly speculative mind, a psychologist competent to deal with the subtlest phenomena of the sick soul—here was a man who might be counted on to justify the ancient dogmas to the troubled churches of New England.

The offspring of four generations of religious enthusiasts, by every right of heredity and training the child of Puritanism, Jonathan Edwards was the last and greatest of the royal line of Puritan mystics. As a young man he felt himself to be living in the very presence of God; he was conscious of the divine life flowing through and around him, making him one with the Godhood; and he was filled with yearning for personal union with the divine love in Christ. His intellectual and spiritual life was molded by a God-consciousness as passionate as that of Spinoza; and it is this fact of a lifelong devotion to the God-idea that furnishes the clue to an understanding of his later development. Not content that God had marked him for His own, he must build a philosophical universe about the Godhood, justifying his mysticism by a metaphysical idealism. He must examine critically the foundations of his creed and establish his theology upon philosophy. No obscurity must remain unprobed, no link in the chain of reasoning escape challenge: he must base the five points of Calvinism upon a metaphysics that should relate them to a universal system of thought, giving them a cosmic as well as a Biblical sanction. It was a great ambition, likely to prove too difficult even for the remarkable powers of Edwards; and if in pursuit of new arguments for old doctrines, he found himself inclosed in a mesh of subtleties, if his theology and metaphysics were never quite reconciled, blame must be laid upon the difficulty of the undertaking rather than on the incapacity of the thinker. To one cardinal principle Edwards was faithful—the conception of the majesty and sufficiency of God; and this polar idea provides the clue to both his philosophical and theological systems.

Yet with this as a guide there is much that remains perplexing. There are inconsistencies in his thought as there were in his pastoral life; and we shall understand his position only when we recognize the contrary tendencies which confused him, as the inevitable consequences of a system of thought that was at once reactionary and progressive, the outcome of certain latent inconsistencies too antagonistic for any thinker to reconcile. As the defender of the traditional theology, setting his face against the developing experience of his generation, and as a rigid disciplinarian, reverting to the older Separatist conception of a church of the elect, and rejecting the "whole way covenant" of his grandfather Stoddard, he may perhaps appear in the light of a reactionary. But as the expounder of philosophic idealism he was looking forward to Emerson; and as the advocate of the new revivalistic methods, exalting the experience of conversion as the central fact of the Christian life, and assisting the forces that were drawing church and state apart, he was a pronounced revolutionist, the schismatic leader of the New Lights and the father of later Congregationalism. That Edwards was aware of certain inconsistencies is fairly evident; that he was puzzled, hesitated, and stopped halfway in his labors, is evident too, unless we believe, with Mrs. Stowe, that certain of his speculations were too daring to put into print. The chains that bound him were too strong to be broken; the contradictions that lay at the root of the Calvinistic system could be eradicated only by grubbing up the whole, and for that the time had not yet come.

In his early years, before his conversion turned him aside from his true path, setting the apologetics of the theologian above the speculations of the philosopher, Edwards gave promise of becoming a strikingly creative thinker. Following the native bent of his genius, he plunged into the study of metaphysics with such fruitful results that it seemed likely that New England Puritanism was at last to come to flower; that the mystical perception of the divine love, which had steeped the early Puritan thought in emotion and quickened it to poetry, was now to create a system of philosophy which, like transcendentalism in the next century, should adequately express the aspirations of the New England mind. There is no more interesting phase in the early history of Edwards than the transition from religious mysticism to philosophical idealism. The yearning for the knitting of the soul to Christ, as expressed

in the imagery of the Song of Songs, burgeoned into a larger idealism that translated the Rose of Sharon and the Lily of the Valley
into an all-pervasive spirit of divine life. In certain moods it is
the mystic who cries, "My soul breaketh for the longing it hath;
my soul waiteth for the Lord, more than they who watch for the
morning."

He was reading one day the words of Scripture [says Allen, paraphrasing
Edwards' diary], "Now unto the King eternal, immortal, invisible, the
only wise God, be honor and glory forever, Amen," when there came to
him for the first time a sort of inward, sweet delight in God and divine
things. A sense of the divine glory was, as it were, diffused through him.
He thought how happy he should be if he might be rapt up to God in
Heaven, swallowed up in him forever. He began to have an inward,
sweet sense of Christ and the work of redemption. The Book of Canticles
attracted him as a fit expression for his mood. It seemed to him as if he
were in a kind of vision, alone in the mountains or some solitary wilderness,
conversing sweetly with Christ and wrapt and swallowed up in God. . . .
God's Excellency, his wisdom, his purity and love, seemed to appear in
everything—in the sun, moon, and stars; in clouds and blue sky; in the
grass, flowers, trees; in the water and all nature, which used greatly to
fix my mind.[4]

In other moods the intellect gains ascendency over the emotions,
and it is the idealistic metaphysician who speaks. With a searching
curiosity that impelled him to ask what lies behind the outward
semblance of things, binding them into a coherent whole and
imparting to the world of experience a compelling unity, he came
early to an interpretation distinctly Berkeleyan. From what
source he derived it has been much debated and remains un-
answered; nevertheless it is clear that it is closely related to his
religious mysticism. When he inquired what lies back of the outward semblance, what is the thing in itself behind attributes and
qualities, the existence of which is implicit in our perception of
time and space, but which cannot be resolved into the things
perceived, it was natural that he should have interpreted this
Ding an sich in terms of God. "Men are wont to content themselves by saying merely that it is something; but that something
is He in whom all things consist."[5] The world of sensation thus
translates itself into a world of ideas; and this world of ideas, the
expression of the divine mind, is the only reality. The more
important of his early generalizations are given by Allen in some

[4] Jonathan Edwards, p. 25.   [5] Ibid., p. 13.

extracts from his notes on the "Mind": "Bodies have no existence of their own." "All existence is mental; the existence of all things is ideal." "The brain exists only mentally, or in idea." "Instead of matter being the only proper substance, and more substantial than anything else because it is hard and solid, yet it is truly nothing at all, strictly and in itself considered." "The universe exists nowhere but in the divine mind." "Space is necessary, eternal, infinite, and omnipresent. But I had as good speak plain. I have already said as much as that space is God." "And indeed the secret lies here,—that which truly is the substance of all bodies is the infinitely exact and precise and perfectly stable Idea in God's mind, together with His stable will that the same shall gradually be communicated to us, and to other minds, according to certain fixed and exact established methods and laws; or, in somewhat different language, the infinitely exact, precise, Divine Idea, together with the answerable, perfectly exact, precise, and stable will, with respect to correspondent communications to created minds and effects on their minds."[6]

Edwards had come to such conclusions before the normal unfolding of his mind was interrupted by his conversion. From the first a strong bias toward theology had tended to warp his interest in the purely metaphysical, and with the quickening of an active religious experience, he turned to examine the dogmas which expressed his faith. The call of the churches in distress came to him, and he made ready his logic to do battle with the enemy. Against the twin tendencies that were undermining the foundations of Calvinism—Arminianism with its humanistic emphasis and deism with its mechanistic—the deepest instincts of Edwards protested. The profound God-consciousness that filled him was stirred by what seemed an infidel attack upon the divine glory and sufficiency; the mystic and idealist was aroused to protest against a theology that conceived of religion as consisting of benevolence toward men rather than in union with God; and against a philosophy that in constructing a mechanical system was de-personalizing God into a vague First Cause, and bowing him politely out of the universe. In so great a crisis his duty seemed clear—to vindicate, not the ways of God, but God himself to men; to assert the glory

---

[6] For an examination of the philosophy of Edwards, see Adam Leroy Jones, "Early American Philosophers," in *Columbia University Contributions to Philosophy, Psychology and Education*, Vol. II, No. 4, Chapter 4.

and sufficiency of God even to the extent of minifying the capacities and potentialities of man.

The basis of his defense was already provided in his metaphysics, the conception of the divine idea existent in God's mind and expressed in His stable will. The needs of his polemics, however, thrust into relief the secondary rather than the primary element in his philosophy, exalting the doctrine of the divine will to the obscuring of the divine idea. How this came about is sufficiently clear in the light of the fact that in explaining the existence of evil, Calvinism fell back on determinism: the dogma of election could be fitted to the conception of a precise and stable will of God. The long feud between Arminianism and Calvinism resulted from emphasis laid upon different attributes of the Godhood. Shall God be interpreted in terms of will or love? If He is the sovereign ruler of the universe, He is also the common father; and that which broadly divides later theological systems from earlier is the shift from the former interpretation to the latter. The strategic weakness of Edwards's position lay in his assumption of the divine sovereignty as a cardinal postulate.

But in adhering to the doctrine of predetermined election by the sovereign will of God, Edwards did unconscious violence to the instincts of the mystic, that throughout his earlier speculations —and in much of his later, as well—impelled him to glorify the love of God the Father, and the sweetness of spiritual communion with Him. The practical necessities of the preacher, called upon to uphold the dogma of election in face of growing disbelief, seem to have forced him to such a position; but once having entered upon the train of speculation opened by the question of divine polity involved in "His having mercy on whom He will have mercy, while whom He will, He hardeneth," he came somewhat reluctantly to accept the doctrine of God's sovereignty as the cardinal principle of his theology, the creative source of his thinking. Thereafter he followed a path that led back to an absolutist past, rather than forward to a more liberal future. He had broken wholly with the social tendencies of his age and world.[7]

[7] For a statement of the doctrine, see Sermon XXXIV, "God's Sovereignty," in *Works*, New York, 1847, Vol. IV, p. 548.

Edwards unconsciously admits that the doctrine of sovereignty was reactionary. "From my childhood up, my mind had been full of objections against the doctrine of God's sovereignty, in choosing whom He would to eternal life, and rejecting whom He pleased, leaving them eternally to perish and be everlastingly tormented in hell." Later he came to regard such repugnance as the sinful expression of the

The philosophical conception of divine sovereignty was too abstract to concern the New England laity; it was rather against the dependent dogmas of election and total depravity that the revolt was rising. And in defense of these threatened dogmas Edwards put forth his best strength. The crux of the matter, obviously, lay in the difficult question of the power of will. The entire structure of Calvinistic theology had been erected upon the assumption of determinism; and it must stand or fall according as the argument should justify or fail to justify that hypothesis. If the human will is effectively free to choose between good and evil, the dogma of the elect must go down with the dogma of predestination; and the teachings of the Arminians—tending, as they seemed to the Calvinist, to abase the creator in exalting the creature, and minifying the sovereignty of God in magnifying the excellence of man—would be in a way to prevail. Around this crucial point the battle had long raged, and it was with full realization of the critical nature of the problem that Edwards resolved to penetrate to the root of the matter, and by subjecting the question of determinism to exact analysis, rout the enemies of Calvinism from the inmost keep of their stronghold. His celebrated work *On the Freedom of the Will*, written in 1754, not only was his most important contribution to theology, but it was the last great defense of the conservatism that was stifling the intellectual life of New England.

The argument of this knotty book rests on a psychological rather than a metaphysical basis. Compressed into the briefest terms it runs thus: will is subject to desire, and desire follows what seems to us good; hence the determining impulse is to be sought in the impulse to seek the apparent good. The ethical import of such an argument will turn, of course, upon the character of the good which the natural man may be expected to desire. To Rousseau with his benevolent interpretation of human nature nothing is to be feared from the subjection of will to desire. Nor to the younger Edwards, feeling his way along the path of tran-

natural man. As he saw further, his mind "apprehended the justice and reasonableness of . . . God's absolute sovereignty and justice with respect to salvation . . . as much as of anything that I see with my eyes; at least it is so at times. But I have often, since that first conviction, had quite another sense of God's sovereignty than I had then. I have often had not only a conviction, but a delightful conviction. The doctrine has very often appeared exceedingly pleasant, bright, and sweet. . . . But my first conviction was not so." Quoted in Allen, *Jonathan Edwards*, pp. 37–38.

scendentalism, rediscovering the doctrine of the inner light, was such subjection to be feared. In a remarkable sermon published in 1734, he had expounded the thesis, "That there is such a thing as a Spiritual and Divine Light, immediately imparted to the Soul by God, of a different nature from any that is obtained by natural means." [8] The divine splendor which the idealist had seen diffused through the material world the theologian was now merging with the regenerative life of the Holy Spirit which "acts in the mind of a saint as an in-dwelling vital principle." It is "a kind of emanation of God's beauty, and is related to God as the light is to the sun"; it is a new vision by means of which one may "see the beauty and loveliness of spiritual things." In such a reinterpretation of the Quaker doctrine—so harshly condemned by the earlier Puritans—Edwards entered upon a train of thought that threatened to disrupt the entire Calvinistic system. He was at the dividing of the ways; he must abandon transcendentalism or the dogma of total depravity.

Instead he sought refuge in compromise, endeavoring to reconcile what was incompatible. Herein lay the tragedy of Edwards's intellectual life; the theologian triumphed over the philosopher, circumscribing his powers to ignoble ends. The field of efficiency allotted by the later theologian to this "in-dwelling vital principle," was no longer coextensive with the universe, but was narrowed to the little world of the elect. In the primal state of man, Edwards argued, before the sin of Adam had destroyed the harmony between creature and creator, the light which flowed from God as from a sun shone freely upon His universe, filling its remotest parts with the divine plenitude; but with the fall the harmony was destroyed, the sun was hidden, and only stray beams broke through the rifts to shine upon those whom God willed them to shine upon; all else in creation was given over to eternal darkness. And if the natural man, thus cast into sudden darkness "as light ceases in a room when the candle is withdrawn," is a being whose will is impotent to his salvation, it follows that he will now be impelled as inevitably towards evil as before he was impelled towards good. Every instinct of a nature corrupt and compact of sin, and with no wish to exchange darkness for light—having no eyes for the divine glory—drives him to a blind and consuming hatred of God. He is become as a loathsome "viper, hissing and spitting poison

[8] Sermon XXVII, in *Works*, Vol. IV, p. 438.

at God," the outcast and pariah of the universe. There is no drawing back from the conclusion involved in the argument; the Edwardean logic moves forward by regular steps. The punishment meted out to sin is to be measured by the excellence of which the sin is a denial. God is of infinite excellence, and denial of His excellence is therefore infinitely sinful and merits infinite punishment. As a perfectly just judge God could not decree otherwise; because of the infinite heinousness of his sin, the natural man must receive the doom of eternal damnation.[9]

Under the rod of such logic—grotesque, abortive, unseasoned by any saving knowledge of human nature—Edwards preached that remarkable series of imprecatory sermons that sank deep into the memory of New England, and for which it has never forgiven him.[10] Unfortunate as those sermons were in darkening the fame of an acute thinker, disastrous as they were in providing a sanction for other men to terrify the imaginations of ill-balanced persons, we cannot regret that Edwards devoted his logic to an assiduous stoking of the fires of hell. The theology of Calvin lay like a heavy weight upon the soul of New England, and there could be no surer way to bring it into disrepute, than to thrust into naked relief the brutal grotesqueries of those dogmas that professed thus to explain the dark mysteries which lie upon the horizons of life. For a long while yet they were to harass the imagination of New England, but the end already could be foreseen. Once the horrors that lay in the background of Calvinism were disclosed to common view, the system was doomed. It might still wear the semblance of life; it might still remain as an evil genius to darken the conscience of men and women; but its authoritative appeal was gone. In this necessary work of freeing the spirit of New England, no

[9] See Sermon IX, in *Works*, Vol. IV, p. 226. The argument is unfolded in the following propositions: "Every crime or fault deserves a greater or less punishment, according as the crime is greater or less." "A crime is more or less heinous, according as we are under greater or less obligations to the contrary." "Our obligations to love, honor, and obey any being, is in proportion to its loveliness, honorableness, and authority." "But God is a being infinitely lovely, because he hath infinite excellence and beauty." "So that sin against God, being a violation of infinite obligations, must be a crime infinitely heinous, and so deserving of infinite punishment."

[10] See in particular Sermon XI, "The Eternity of Hell Torments"; Sermon XII, "When the Wicked shall have filled up the measure of their Sin, wrath will come upon them to the uttermost"; Sermon XIII, "The End of the Wicked contemplated by the Righteous; or, The Torments of the Wicked in Hell, no occasion of grief to the Saints in Heaven"; Sermon XV, "Sinners in the Hands of an Angry God," in *Works*, Vol. IV.

other thinker played so large or so unconscious a part as Jonathan Edwards; and it was the notorious minatory sermons—the translation into vivid images of the generalized dogmas—that awakened the popular mind to an understanding of the conclusions involved in the premises.

While Edwards was thus hastening the decay of Calvinism with his lurid painting of "the landscape of hell," in another phase of his work he was engaged in awakening an interest in religion among the slothful churches. He had long been interested in the phenomena of conversion, and as the great revival of the forties, led by Whitefield, spread from England to the colonies, he joined eagerly in the work. In consequence of an earlier revival in his parish of Northampton, his attention had been drawn to the little understood psychology of the awakening soul, and with the detachment of the scientist he set himself to study the problem. The terrors aroused by his minatory sermons provided his clinical laboratory with numerous cases of abnormal emotionalism. Day after day he probed and analyzed and compared, until as a result of his close studies in vivisection, he became a specialist in the theory of conversion, commanding the eager attention of a generation that had come to look upon this as the central fact of Christian experience. It is not easy today to be sympathetic with this phase of Edwards's work; it belongs equally with his dogmas to a world of thought that is no longer ours. The repulsive records as they are set down in his *Narrative of the Surprizing Works of God*, marked by evidence of pathological states of mind not far removed from insanity, no longer seem a testimony to God's beneficent presence; the spiritual writhings which this gentle-natured student watched with such fascination, appear rather to be cases for the alienist to prescribe for. But to Edwards the terrors of a five-year-old girl were not pathological; they were the soul-labors of the spiritual rebirth, the visible signs of the supreme miracle of the universe, filling him with wonder and awe at God's infinite mercy; and like a modern psychologist he was at enormous pains to chart the successive steps in the miraculous transformation.[11]

[11] According to Edwards there were four regular stages: (1) the first stirrings, when the sinner is brought under conviction that he is lost; (2) the realization of God's justice, that he merits damnation; (3) the breaking in of the light, the first "gracious discoveries" of God's mercies; (4) peace after the storm, the joy of assurance of salvation. For a fuller statement, see Allen, *Jonathan Edwards*, pp. 133–160.

Other and greater consequences were to flow from the new revivalism. The Great Awakening was the single movement that stirred the colonial heart deeply during three generations. It reveals, among other things, that America was still living in the world of the seventeenth century: that the upper class was not yet rationalized, nor the middle class commercialized. Theology was still of greater popular interest than politics. In its chief phenomena the Great Awakening was a return to an earlier age—to those unbalanced enthusiasms of the Puritan upheaval. It was essentially a mass movement. Its use of hypnotic suggestion, its lurid terrorism, its outcries and hysterical possessions, reveal like the Ranters of a hundred years before the phenomena of mob psychology, and it made appeal to the ill-educated, the isolated, the neurotic, to the many natural victims of hypnotic excitation bred by the monotony and austerity of village life. Its after effects were revolutionary, for the quickening of religious emotionalism marked the beginning of the end of Puritan formalism.

The bitter quarrel among the churches which followed as an aftermath was more than a theological dispute; it was a sign of the breaking up of the traditional parish system. The hierarchy had long before lost its authority, but in their several parishes the ministers still enjoyed patriarchal power. The tragic dismissal of Edwards from his parish was an unprecedented revolt against that authority. But greater changes were to follow. After the Great Awakening itinerant preachers made their appearance, who presumed to enter any parish without the consent of the minister, and preach such doctrines as they would. They were non-conforming free lances, hostile to the established church, whose stock-in-trade was the new emotionalism. Under their leadership, Separatist congregations were gathered that were not only an offense to the regular establishment but a challenge to its authority. Hundreds left the old congregations and flocked to the Baptists and Methodists, and naturally they would make trouble over paying taxes to support a church they had repudiated. In short, a little revolution was under way that was to end in the complete disintegration of the parish system.

By a curious irony of fate, Jonathan Edwards, reactionary Calvinist and philosophical recluse, became the intellectual leader of the revolutionaries. His insistence upon conversion as the sole ground of admission to communion was the final blow that de-

stroyed the old theocratic system which the Mathers had labored
to uphold. Church and state were effectively cut asunder by such
a test. There is no evidence that Edwards was concerned about
the political or social consequences that must result from the
abandonment of the traditional "Half-way Covenant." It was a
question of doctrine with him, involving only matters of church
discipline. Although he was accused of being a Separatist, and of
seeking to disintegrate the parish system, he had no thought of
attacking a parochial order that he held in high esteem. He was
unconcerned that his teachings led straight to the old Separatist
conclusion that it is the church mystical which Christ established,
and not the church visible. Nevertheless he became the creator
of the new Congregationalism, which in accepting the democratic
principles elaborated by John Wise and establishing the local
church as an autonomous unit, effectively nullified the Presbyterian
tendencies of the old order.

As one follows the laborious career of this great thinker, a sense
of the tragic failure of his life deepens. The burdens that he
assumed were beyond the strength of any man. Beginning as a
mystic, brooding on the all-pervasive spirit of sweetness and light
diffused through the universe, with its promise of spiritual emancipation; then turning to an archaic theology and giving over his
middle years to the work of minifying the excellence of man in
order to exalt the sovereignty of God; and finally settling back
upon the mystical doctrine of conversion—such a life leaves one
with a feeling of futility, a sense of great powers baffled and wasted,
a spiritual tragedy enacted within the narrow walls of a minister's
study. There was both pathos and irony in the fate of Jonathan
Edwards, removed from the familiar places where for twenty years
he had labored, the tie with his congregation broken, and sent to
the frontier mission at Stockbridge to preach to a band of Indians
and to speculate on the unfreedom of the human will. The greatest
mind of New England had become an anachronism in a world that
bred Benjamin Franklin. If he had been an Anglican like Bishop
Berkeley, if he had mingled with the leaders of thought in London
instead of remaining isolated in Massachusetts, he must have made
a name for himself not unworthy to be matched with that of the
great bishop whom he so much resembled. The intellectual powers
were his, but the inspiration was lacking; like Cotton Mather
before him, he was the unconscious victim of a decadent ideal and

a petty environment. Cut off from fruitful intercourse with other thinkers, drawn away from the stimulating field of philosophy into the arid realm of theology, it was his fate to devote his noble gifts to the thankless task of re-imprisoning the mind of New England within a system from which his nature and his powers summoned him to unshackle it. He was called to be a transcendental emancipator, but he remained a Calvinist.

CHAPTER III

BENJAMIN FRANKLIN

Our First Ambassador

THERE was a singularly dramatic fitness in the life and career of Benjamin Franklin. America has never been more worthily represented at old-world capitals than by this unpretentious commoner, drawn from the stock of the plain people. A plebeian in an aristocratic age, he was nevertheless, by common consent, first among colonial Americans in qualities of mind and heart. A wit and philosopher, rich in learning, charming in manners, ripe in the wisdom of this world, resourceful in dealing with men and events, he was one of the most delightful as he was one of the greatest men produced by the English race in the eighteenth century.

"Figure to yourself," he wrote in his seventy-second year, "an old man, with gray hair appearing under a marten fur cap, among the powdered heads of Paris. It is this odd figure that salutes you, with handfuls of blessings." An odd figure indeed in such a setting, but a figure that captured the imagination of Paris, as it has since captured the imagination of America; so novel as to seem romantic—a charming rustic philosopher who might have stepped out of the pages of Rousseau. And so the French aristocracy patronized *le bon homme*, and laughed with him at the affectations of this preposterous world, and made much of him for the zest that it discovered in a novel sensation. It was the same odd figure that had stood at the bar of the House of Commons and matched his intelligence against that of celebrated English lawyers; the same figure that had been called in council by the great Pitt—who thought himself too great to learn anything even from Franklin; that had been lashed by the scurrilous tongue of Wedderburn; that had seen a thousand bribes dangled before him by Lord Howe and other gentlemen—a figure that seems strangely out of place in that old-fashioned Tory world, with its narrow sympathies and narrower intelligence. And yet considered in the light of social revolutions, what other figure in eighteenth-century

Europe or America is so dramatically significant? The figure of the self-made democrat, with some three millions of his fellows at his back, and countless other millions to come, who was entering on a world-wide struggle for political mastery, the end of which no one can yet foresee? His presence in the councils of gentlemen was a tacit denial of their hitherto unquestioned right of supremacy. It was a rare personal triumph; but it was far more significant than that, it was the triumph of a rising class and a new social ideal.

Although Franklin's origins, whether Boston or Philadelphia, were narrowly provincial, his mind from early youth to extreme old age was curiously open and free, and to such a mind the intellectual wealth of the world lies open and free. From that wealth he helped himself generously, to such good effect that he early became an intellectual cosmopolitan, at ease with the best intellects and at home among the diverse speculative interests of the eighteenth century: the sane and witty embodiment of its rationalism, its emancipation from authority, its growing concern for social justice, its hopeful pursuit of new political and economic philosophies, its tempered optimism that trusted intelligence to set the world right. No other man in America and few in Europe had so completely freed themselves from the prejudice of custom. The Calvinism in which he was bred left not the slightest trace upon him; and the middle-class world from which he emerged did not narrow his mind to its petty horizons. He was a free man who went his own way with imperturbable good will and unbiased intelligence; our first social philosopher, the first ambassador of American democracy to the courts of Europe.

Fortune was kind to Franklin in many ways: kind in that it did not visit upon him the fate that befell his elder brother Ebenezer, of whom Sewall noted, "Ebenezer Franklin of the South Church, a male-Infant of 16 months old, was drowned in a Tub of Suds, Febr. 5, 1702/3"; kind also in that it set him in a land where opportunity waited upon enterprise, and where thousands of kindred spirits were erecting a society that honored such qualities as he possessed. In England he must have remained middle-class, shut in by a wall of prejudice; but in colonial America he found a congenial environment. Like Samuel Sewall, he swam easily in the main current of colonial life, won increasing honors, until—as he naïvely remarked—he came more than once to stand before kings. How fortunate he was is revealed by contrast with the career of his great English counterpart and fellow spirit, Daniel Defoe, whose *Essay on Projects*—a classic document of the rising middle class—might well have been Franklin's first textbook.

The earliest literary representative of the English middle class, Defoe preached the same gospel of social betterment. With his head full of projects for the advancement of trade and the material well-being of his fellows, he preached the new gospel of practical efficiency to a generation of wits, going so far as to assert that the ideal statesman should be sought, not among gentlemen but among merchants, whose training in business affairs had made them shrewd judges of men and capable in dealing with practical matters. But the London of Queen Anne was not a place in which to rise by preaching efficiency. Defoe's day had not yet come in England, and in spite of great abilities and arduous labors he remained a Grub Street hack, the servant and not the counselor of aristocratic politicians. Instead of coming to stand before kings—like the more fortunate Franklin—he stood often before constables; instead of cracking his joke and his bottle at Will's Coffee House, he was forced to study the ways of the unprosperous at Bridewell. But if he failed in his ambition to get on, he found a certain solace in the vicarious realization of his ideal. Robinson Crusoe, the practically efficient man making himself master of his environment, was the dream of Daniel Defoe; Franklin was the visible, new-world embodiment of that dream.

It was Franklin's supreme capacity for doing well the things which his fellow Americans held in esteem, that enabled him to rise out of obscurity to a position of leadership. Before he should be intrusted with the confidence of his fellow citizens, he must prove himself worthy of such confidence, and even in colonial America the task was far from easy. In the wealthier communities society was exclusive and select—nowhere more so than in Philadelphia— and it could not be expected to view with approval the advancement of a printer-tradesman, especially if he were a member of the plebeian anti-Proprietary party. It was an evidence of Franklin's discretion that he removed from Boston, where neither his father's chandlery shop, nor his brother's baiting of the ruling gentry, would serve his purpose. In Philadelphia, free from family entanglements, he bent himself to the task of securing a competence, understanding how easily the wheel turns on a well-greased axle;

and by the time he had come to his early forties he had kept his shop so well that henceforth it would keep him. He was ready to do his real work in the world; and in the choice of that work he revealed the curious *flair* for the timely that was so characteristic. His extraordinary successes in the field of civic betterments gained him the good will of the commonalty, and his experiments in natural philosophy won the approbation of the gentry. Interest in scientific inquiry, particularly in physics, had spread widely in England since the founding of the Royal Society, and to be an authority on magnetism was as evident a mark of breeding in Georgian England as discriminating judgment in the matter of manuscripts and mistresses had been a sign of culture among Florentine cinquecentists. In establishing a reputation as a natural philosopher, therefore, Franklin not only was acquiring dignity at home, but he was providing himself with a sure passport to European favor. And it was the seal of European approval that finally won for Franklin the grudging recognition of the first families of Philadelphia. A few held out against him and to the day of his death regarded him with disapproval; but in the end his personal charm prevailed with all but a handful of elderly Tory ladies. So delightful a wit and so useful a citizen could not be dismissed as a pushing tradesman.

Franklin first entered politics as a member of the popular party, then engaged in a bitter struggle with the Proprietors over tax matters, defense of the frontier, and other questions of acute popular concern. There was the usual colonial alignment between the backcountry yeomanry and the town gentry; between the agrarian and mercantile interests; and the dispute had reached a point where the yeomanry determined to appeal to the King to convert the commonwealth into a Crown Colony. As one of the leaders of the popular party, Franklin was singled out for attack. A bitter election went against him, and he lost his seat in the Assembly, only to be chosen Colonial Agent to England, there to begin his long diplomatic career. Probably no other attack which Franklin suffered was so coarse or vindictive as this assault by the Proprietary party, led by the first gentlemen of Philadelphia, John Dickinson among them. Unpleasant as the experience was, it proved of service to Franklin, for it taught him how quickly the hornets would be about the ears of anyone who disturbed the nest of official perquisites; and this was worth knowing to a colonial diplomat on his first mission to a court and parliament where yellow jackets were uncommonly abundant.[1]

He was nearly threescore when he set out on his diplomatic mission, which beginning modestly as temporary agent of the anti-Proprietary party of Pennsylvania, was to broaden immensely as the American difficulties increased, until he became in the eyes of all the world the spokesman of the colonial cause; first at London to King, Parliament, and people, and later at Paris to all Europe. It was a mission of discussion and argument, curiously illuminating to a colonial bred in a simple, decentralized world. Before he went abroad Franklin had been a democrat by temperament and environment; when he returned he was a democrat by conviction, confirmed in his preference for government immediately responsible to the majority will. Centralized Tory governments had taught him the excellence of town-meeting ways. At London he discovered widespread political corruption. It was a world flyblown with the vices of irresponsible power. The letters of Franklin are full of the scandal of bribe-taking and pension-mongering, of gross parliamentary jobbery. The elections of 1768 were a debauch, the brisk bidding of Indian nabobs sending the market price of parliamentary seats up to four thousand pounds. "It is thought," he wrote on March 13, "that near two millions will be spent on this election; but those, who understand figures and act by computation, say the crown has *two millions in places and pensions* to dispose of, and it is well worth while to engage in such a seven years lottery, though all that have tickets should not get prizes." [2] To expect such a government to be swayed by appeals to justice or abstract rights was plain folly, Franklin very quickly learned.

[1] "You know," wrote Franklin to his wife on the eve of his departure, "that I have many enemies . . . and very bitter ones; and you must expect their enmity will extend in some degree to you." He was forced to slip away and get secretly on board the vessel. His activities were reproved thus by a certain Tory lady:

> Oh! had he been wise to pursue
> The track for his talents designed,
> What a tribute of praise had been due
> To the teacher and friend of mankind.
>
> But to covet political fame
> Was in him a degrading ambition,
> The spark that from Lucifer came,
> And kindled the blaze of sedition.
>
> (In *Works*, Vol. VII, p. 267.)

In Sargent's *Loyal Verses of Joseph Stansbury and Doctor Jonathan Odell*, these verses are attributed to a less likely source.

[2] *Works*, Vol. VII, p. 398.

The colonial goose was there to be plucked, and gentlemen who gained their livelihood by skillful plucking would not easily be denied. "To get a larger field on which to fatten a herd of worthless parasites, is all that is regarded," wrote the celebrated London physician, Dr. Fothergill, to Franklin.[3] Even war with the colonies might not seem undesirable to some, for "an auditor of the exchequer has sixpence in the pound, or a fortieth part, of all the public money expended by the nation, so that, when a war costs forty millions, one million is paid to him."[4]

It was a bitter experience for one who had grown up in respect for England and veneration for English traditions. Franklin was not a man of divided loyalties, and his love of the old home was deep and sincere. He had many warm friends there, and the idea of American separation from the empire was profoundly repugnant to him. It was not till he was convinced beyond hope that America could expect from the English government nothing but ignoble dependence that he accepted the idea of independence. Again and again he complained bitterly of "the extreme corruption prevalent among all orders of men in this rotten old state."[5] "I wish all the friends of liberty and of man would quit that sink of corruption, and leave it to its fate." "I do not expect that your new Parliament will be either wiser or honester than the last. All projects to procure an honest one, by place bills, etc., appear to me vain and impracticable. The true cure, I imagine, is to be found in rendering all places unprofitable, and the King too poor to give bribes and pensions. Till this is done, which can only be by a revolution (and I think you have not virtue enough left to procure one), your nation will always be plundered, and obliged to pay by taxes the plunderers for plundering and ruining. Liberty

---

[3] *Ibid.*, Vol. V, p. 81.
[4] *Ibid.*, Vol. II, p. 428. A good deal of light is thrown upon the ways of the ministry in Franklin's account, *Negotiations in London*. See in particular pp. 37, 68, 76 of Vol. V, where Lord Hyde and Lord Howe exhibit special solicitude for his advancement. His letters tell of successive attempts to approach him, and among his works is a little skit in which he speaks of himself thus: "Your correspondent *Brittannicus* inveighs violently against Dr. Franklin, for his ingratitude to the ministry of this nation, who have conferred upon him so many favors. They gave him the post-office of America; they made his son a governor; and they offered him a post of five hundred a year in the salt-office, if he would relinquish the interests of his country; but he has had the wickedness to continue true to it, and is as much an American as ever. As it is a settled point in government here, that every man has his price, it is plain they are bunglers in their business, and have not given him enough." (*Works*, Vol. IV, pp. 534–535.)
[5] *Ibid.*, Vol. VIII, p. 146.

and virtue therefore join in the call, COME OUT OF HER, MY PEO-
PLE!"[6] "The people of England . . . are just and generous,"
wrote his friend David Hartley, member of Parliament, "and,
if it were put to the sense of the people of England, you would
not be left in any doubt whether it was *want of will*, or *want of power*,
to do you justice. You know the blot of our constitution, by
which, to our disgrace, and to your misfortune, a corrupt ministry,
sheltered by Parliamentary influence, are out of our immediate
control. A day of account may come, when the justice of the
nation may prevail; and if it comes not too late, it may prove a
day of reconciliation and cordial reunion between us and America."[7]
He is blind indeed who cannot see in such experience the explanation of Franklin's later efforts in Pennsylvania and in the constitutional convention to keep government in America responsive to
the will of the people.

During the long years of his ambassadorship, so rich in intellectual opportunity, Franklin was intimately concerned with economics
and politics, and he found in them subjects congenial to his talents.
By temperament he was what we should call today a sociologist.
He cared little for abstract reasoning, but much for social betterment; and this led him to examine critically current economic
theory in the light of present fact. All his life economics was a
major interest with him, and his several contributions entitle him
to be regarded as our first important economist, the only one
indeed before the nineteenth century. His chief guides in this
little explored field seem to have been Sir William Petty, the
statistician of the Restoration period, in his younger days, and the
French Physiocrats in later years. He was the first American to
abandon the traditional mercantile school—a generation before
other American thinkers had repudiated it; and he was the first to
ally himself with the rising school of *laissez faire*.

In the year 1729, when he was just turned twenty-three, Franklin
entered the field of economics with a pamphlet entitled *A Modest
Inquiry into the Nature and Necessity of a Paper Currency*. It is
a curiously suggestive work, not only for the light which it sheds
on his economic views, but on his social and political sympathies.
It marks his early alignment with the agrarian party, to which he
adhered to the end of his life. From the days when Samuel Sewall
first confronted the question of land-banks in the Massachusetts

legislature till the British government forbade all issues of bills of credit, the currency question was bitterly debated in the several colonies. It was primarily a class issue, in which the town merchants and money lenders found themselves outvoted by the agrarian debtors and small men. Little light had come from those debates on the nature of money and its social functions; but much heat had been engendered over the supposed question of honest versus dishonest money. With this cheap fallacy Franklin was not concerned; but he was greatly concerned in this and in later papers in expounding the quantitative theory of money, the nature of credit, and the important fact, overlooked by the hard-money men, that gold and silver are themselves commodities, fluctuating in value with supply and demand. This first pamphlet, Franklin afterward remarked, "was well received by the common people in general; but the rich men disliked it, for it increased and strengthened the clamor for more money; and, they happening to have no writers among them that were able to answer it, their opposition slackened, and the point was carried by a majority in the House." [8]

By much the most interesting idea in the pamphlet, however, is the elaboration of the labor theory of value. Commenting on this, McMaster says in his *Life of Franklin:*

> Bad as were his notions of political economy, his pamphlet contained one great truth,—the truth that labor is the measure of value. Whether he discovered, or, as is not unlikely, borrowed it, he was the first openly to assert it; and his it remained till, forty-seven years later, Adam Smith adopted it and reaffirmed it in "The Wealth of Nations." [9]

Unfortunately the biographer's knowledge of the history of economic thought was as faulty as, in his judgment, were Franklin's economic principles. In his *Treatise of Taxes*, written in 1662, Sir William Petty—whom Franklin in many ways greatly resembled—clearly elaborated the principle of labor-value; [10] it was restated by Vauban in 1707, in his *Projet d'une disme Royale*, by Hume in 1752, and later by the Physiocrats; and when Adam Smith wrote it was pretty widely known. There can be little doubt where Franklin got it. The similarity between his work and that of Sir William Petty is too evident to escape comment. But that does not lessen the significance of the fact that a self-

[8] *Works*, Vol. II, p. 254. [9] P. 64.
[10] See *Economic Writings of Sir W. Petty*, Cambridge Press, Vol. I, pp. 43–51.

trained provincial of three and twenty should have read Petty's work, seized upon the salient idea and turned it to effective use, years before economic students generally were acquainted with it. All his life Franklin took up ideas like a sponge, and what he took he incorporated with the solid results of his own observations.

During his stay in England Franklin came in close contact with the body of Physiocratic writings, which seem to have greatly stimulated his interest in economic thought. The school was at the height of its influence between the years 1763 and 1772, and had pretty well undermined the position of the mercantilists. They were the founders of modern social science and their teachings contained in germ the liberal doctrine of economics in its entirety. In their emphasis upon free trade and *laissez-faire* competition, on the police theory of the state, on property, security, liberty, on the natural laws of association and self-interest, and especially in their emphasis on land as the sole source of wealth, they presented a system of economics that fitted American conditions as Franklin understood those conditions. In one important point— their acceptance of an absolute prince—Franklin broke with them wholly; but their preference for agriculture over manufacturing and commerce accorded with his deepest convictions. America was notably happy and contented in comparison with Europe, and America would remain happy and contented, he believed, so long as land was abundant and her farmers remained freeholders. The new middle-class gospel of industrialism he profoundly distrusted. He shared Goldsmith's concern over the destruction of the English peasantry and the creation of a degraded proletariat. Manufacture and trade developed only where free land was inadequate or the peasants were dispossessed; industrialism sprang from the national poverty and was nourished by it. Writing in 1760 he said:

Unprejudiced men well know, that all the penal and prohibitory laws that were ever thought on will not be sufficient to prevent manufactures in a country, whose inhabitants surpass the number that can subsist by the husbandry of it. . . . Manufactures are founded in poverty. It is the number of poor without land in a country, and who must work for others at low wages or starve, that enables undertakers to carry on a manufacture, and afford it cheap enough to prevent the importation of the same kind from abroad, and to bear the expense of its own exportation. But no man, who can have a piece of land of his own, sufficient by his labor to subsist his family in plenty, is poor enough to be a manufacturer, and work for a master. Hence while there is land enough in America for our people, there can never be manufactures to any amount or value.[11]

Nine years later, in his *Positions to be Examined, concerning National Wealth*, he stated the Physiocratic theory thus:

There seem to be but three ways for a nation to acquire wealth. The first is by *war*, as the Romans did, in plundering their conquered neighbors. This is *robbery*. The second by *commerce*, which is generally *cheating*. The third by *agriculture*, the only *honest way*, wherein man receives a real increase of the seed thrown into the ground, in a kind of continual miracle, wrought by the hand of God in his favor.[12]

Franklin's prejudice against trade somewhat lessened in after years, as he considered the economic need of free exchange of commodities. In 1774, two years before the publication of *The Wealth of Nations*, he collaborated with George Whately in writing a pamphlet entitled *Principles of Trade*, that suggests Adam Smith. Franklin was acquainted with Smith, had visited him, and doubtless had discussed with him the theory of *laissez faire*, division of labor, use of machinery, and other principles of the new school, but no mention of him is made.[13] The central doctrine is thus elaborated:

Perhaps, in general, it would be better if government meddled no farther with trade, than to protect it, and let it take its course. Most of the statutes, or acts, edicts, *arrêts*, and placarts of parliaments, princes, and states, for regulating, directing, or restraining of trade, have, we think, been either political blunders, or jobs obtained by artful men for private advantage, under pretense of public good. When Colbert assembled some wise old merchants of France, and desired their advice and opinion, how he could best serve and promote commerce, their answer, after consultation, was, in three words only, *Laissez-nous faire:* "Let us alone." It is said by a very solid writer of the same nation, that he is well advanced in the science of politics, who knows the full force of that maxim, *Pas trop gouverner:* "Not to govern too much." Which, perhaps, would be of more use when applied to trade, than in any other public concern. It were therefore to be wished, that commerce was as free between all the nations of the world, as it is between the several counties of England; so would all, by mutual communication, obtain more enjoyments. Those counties do not ruin one another by trade; neither would the nations. No nation was ever ruined by trade, even seemingly the most disadvantageous.[14]

As a colonial, long familiar with the injustice of Navigation Laws, Boards of Trade, and other restrictions in favor of British tradesmen, Franklin agreed with Adam Smith on the principle

[11] *Works*, Vol. IV, p. 19.   [12] *Ibid.*, Vol. II, p. 376.
[13] *Ibid.*, Vol. II, p. 438.   [14] *Ibid.*, Vol. II, p. 401.

of free trade; but with later developments of the *laissez-faire*
school—its fetish of the economic man and its iron law of wages—
he would not have agreed. Plugson of Undershot was no hero
of his, and the social system which Plugson was creating would
have seemed to him as vicious as the old system with its "bad,
wasteful, plundering governments, and their mad destructive
wars." In his later speculations he was rather the social philosopher than the economist, puzzled at the irrationality of society
that chooses to make a pigsty of the world, instead of the garden
that it might be if men would but use the sense that God has given
them. "The happiness of individuals is evidently the ultimate
end of political society,"[15] he believed, and a starvation wage-
system was the surest way of destroying that happiness.[16] In
one of the most delightful letters that he ever wrote, Franklin
commented on the ways of men thus:

> It is wonderful how preposterously the affairs of this world are managed.
> Naturally one would imagine, that the interests of a few individuals should
> give way to general interest; but individuals manage their affairs with so
> much more application, industry, and address, than the public do theirs,
> that general interest most commonly gives way to particular. We assem-
> ble parliaments and councils, to have the benefit of their collected wisdom;
> but we necessarily have, at the same time, the inconvenience of their
> collected passions, prejudices, and private interests. By the help of these,
> artful men overpower their wisdom and dupe its possessors; and if we may
> judge by the acts, *arrêts*, and edicts, all the world over, for regulating com-
> merce, an assembly of great men is the greatest fool upon earth?. . . .
> What occasions then so much want and misery? It is the employment
> of men and women in works, that produce neither the necessaries nor
> conveniences of life, who, with those who do nothing, consume necessaries
> raised by the laborious. . . . Look round the world, and see the millions
> employed in doing nothing, or in something that amounts to nothing, when
> the necessaries and conveniences of life are in question. What is the bulk
> of commerce, for which we fight and destroy each other, but the toil of
> millions for superfluities, to the great hazard and loss of many lives? . . .
> It has been computed by some political arithmetician, that, if every man
> and woman would work for four hours each day on something useful, that
> labor would produce sufficient to procure all the necessaries and comforts of
> life, want and misery would be banished out of the world, and the rest of
> the twenty-four hours might be leisure and happiness.[17]

But the immediate problem of Franklin as representative of the
colonies at St. James's, was political—how to reconcile the antag-

[15] *Ibid.*, Vol. II, p. 323.
[16] See "Reflections on the Augmentation of Wages, etc.," in *Ibid.*, Vol. II, p. 436.
[17] "On Luxury, Idleness, and Industry," in *Ibid.*, Vol. II, pp. 448–451.

onistic ambitions of the sundered bodies of Englishmen; and the solution which he set forth with admirable clearness, bears the impress of a mind intent upon the reality behind parchment pretense. While lawyers were befogging the issue with legal quibble, and politicians were proving the unconstitutionality of the forces stirring in eighteenth-century America, Franklin was more concerned with adjusting imperial policy to existing fact. On one side were the colonies, in which the practice of local self-government had taken deep root; whether the practice was sanctioned by their charters or the British constitution was beside the question. On the other side was the British parliament, serving as a legislative body for its proper constituency, the people of the British Isles. Over both colonies and parliament, providing an effective but ungalling tie to bind the parts together, was the King, to whom both paid willing allegiance. So long as England was content to maintain the *status quo*, the colonies, Franklin believed, would remain loyal to the empire; but if the ministry persisted in its program of extending parliamentary sovereignty over the colonies, the outcome must be one of two things, federation or separation.

To the principle of federation Franklin was an early and faithful friend. The conception of a federal union of the several colonies was slowly spreading in America, and no other colonial had done so much to further it; in his well-known Plan of Union he had sketched the outlines of a federal constitution; what was more natural, therefore, than for him to think in terms of a Federated British Empire, as a statesmanlike solution of the present perplexities. The plan involved two problems: first, an inquiry into the nature and constitution of an imperial parliament, and second, provision for an equitable representation of the several divisions of the empire. The present difficulties had arisen out of the ambition of the British parliament to assume sovereignty over the colonial legislatures, thereby reducing them to a dependent status; those difficulties would be settled only by constitutional recognition of local rights and local sovereignties. "The British state," he argued, "is only the Island of Great Britain," and if by reason of familiarity with local needs, "the British legislature" is "the only proper judge of what concerns the welfare of that state," why does the principle not hold for the several colonial legislatures?

Here appears the excellency of the invention of colony government, by separate, independent legislatures. By this means, the remotest parts of a

great empire may be as well governed as the centre; misrule, oppressions of
proconsuls, and discontents and rebellions thence arising, prevented. By
this means, the power of a king may be extended without inconvenience
over territories of any dimensions, how great soever. America was thus
happily governed in all its different and remote settlements, by the crown
and their own Assemblies, till the new politics took place, of governing it
by one Parliament, which have not succeeded and never will.[18]

In this dream of a British Empire Franklin was far in advance
of his time. On both sides of the ocean selfish and unimaginative
men stood ready to thwart all such proposals; little Englanders
and little colonials in vast numbers were concerned with more
immediate and personal interests than those of the English race.
Nevertheless Franklin was convinced that the gods, if not the
Tories, were on the side of the colonies. The enormous increase
in material strength that the years were swiftly bringing to America
was an augury of good hope; the legitimate demands of America
would be granted when America had grown too strong to be
denied, which must be shortly. In the meantime it was the duty
of Englishmen, British and colonial alike, to endeavor "with unfeigned and unwearying zeal to preserve from breaking that fine
and noble China vase, the British empire." It was the traditional
policy of "protract and grow strong"—a wise and sane policy—
and Franklin clung to it until he was convinced of its utter futility.
One other choice remained—separation; and he made that choice
sadly, understanding better than most what it involved.

The years which followed were filled to the brim for Franklin
as well as for America. Ideals changed and principles clarified
swiftly; but his social philosophy was founded on too wide and
sobering an experience with men and governments, to sway with
every gusty passion of the times. He had been a democrat from
his youth up and in those critical first days of independence, when
the forces of agrarianism were taking possession of state governments, he threw in his lot with them, and joined heartily in the
stimulating work of providing a democratic constitution for
Pennsylvania. During the later years of reaction following the
peace, when so many Revolutionary leaders endeavored to stay
the agrarian movement and undo its work, he saw no cause to
lose faith in government immediately responsive to the majority
will. He was a forerunner of Jefferson, like him firm in the con-

[18] *Works*, Vol. IV, p. 282. For Franklin's views on American representation in
Parliament, see Vol. VII, pp. 315, 329.

viction that government was good in the measure that it remained close to the people. He sat in the Constitutional Convention as one of the few democrats, and although he was unable to make headway against the aristocratic majority, he was quite unconvinced by their rhetoric. For years he had been an advocate of unrestricted manhood suffrage, annual parliaments,[19] and a single-chamber legislature; and when he heard eloquent young lawyers argue that a single-chamber legislature, responsive to a democratic electorate, must lead to mob legislation, and that good government required a carefully calculated system of checks and balances, he remarked:

It appears to me . . . like putting one horse before a cart and the other behind it, and whipping them both. If the horses are of equal strength, the wheels of the cart, like the wheels of government, will stand still; and if the horses are strong enough the cart will be torn to pieces.[20]

When in 1790 it was proposed to substitute a bicameral system for the single-chamber in Pennsylvania, Franklin came to the defense of the simpler, more democratic form, with a vivacity little staled by years:

Has not the famous political fable of the snake, with two heads and one body, some useful instruction contained in it? She was going to a brook to drink, and in her way was to pass through a hedge, a twig of which opposed her direct course; one head chose to go on the right side of the twig, the other on the left; so that time was spent in the contest, and before the decision was completed, the poor snake died with thirst.[21]

Both his economic principles and his views on government have been condemned by Federalistic critics as tainted with populism. They both sprang from the same root of agrarian democracy. Whether Franklin or his critics more adequately represented the larger interests of eighteenth-century America is beside the present question; it is enough to note that all such criticism is leveled primarily at Franklin's democratic philosophy as a thing in itself undesirable, if not dangerous.

Franklin may often have been wrong, but he was never arrogant, never dogmatic. He was too wise and too generous for that. In the midst of prosperity he never forgot the unprosperous. All his

[19] See the pamphlet indorsed *Some Good Whig Principles*, of the probable date of 1768–69, in *Works*, Vol. II.
[20] *Works of Thomas Paine*, edited by Moncure D. Conway, Vol. IV, p. 465.
[21] In "Queries and Remarks Respecting Alterations in the Constitution of Pennsylvania," in *Works*, Vol. V, p. 167.

life his sympathy went out to whoever suffered in person or fortune from the injustice of society: to the debtor who found himself pinched by the shrinking supply of currency; to the black slave who suffered the most elementary of wrongs; to impressed seamen; to the weak and wretched of earth. He was a part of that emerging humanitarian movement which, during the last half of the eighteenth century, was creating a new sense of social responsibility. True to his Physiocratic convictions, Franklin was social-minded. He was concerned not with property or class interests, but with the common welfare; and in his quick sympathy for all sorts and conditions of men, in his conviction that he must use his talents to make this world better and not exploit it, he reveals the breadth and generosity of his nature. Reason and work, in his pragmatic philosophy, are the faithful handmaids of progress, of which war, whether public or private, is the utter negation. After long years of thought he rendered a judgment which later experience has not reversed,—"there is no good war and no bad peace."

It is to little purpose that certain shortcomings of Franklin are dwelt upon. "There is a flower of religion, a flower of honor, a flower of chivalry, that you must not require of Franklin," said Sainte-Beuve; a judgment that is quite true and quite obvious. A man who is less concerned with the golden pavements of the City of God than that the cobblestones on Chestnut Street in Philadelphia should be well and evenly laid, who troubles less to save his soul from burning hereafter than to protect his neighbors' houses by organizing an efficient fire-company, who is less regardful of the light that never was on sea or land than of a new-model street lamp to light the steps of the belated wayfarer—such a man, obviously, does not reveal the full measure of human aspiration. Franklin ended as he began, the child of a century marked by sharp spiritual limitations. What was best in that century he made his own. In his modesty, his willingness to compromise, his openmindedness, his clear and luminous understanding, his charity—above all, in his desire to subdue the ugly facts of society to some more rational scheme of things—he proved himself a great and useful man, one of the greatest and most useful whom America has produced.

PART TWO: THE AWAKENING OF THE AMERICAN MIND
1763–1783

CHAPTER I

IMPERIAL SOVEREIGNTY AND HOME RULE

I

BACKGROUND FACTS

THE American Revolution remains after a hundred and fifty years somewhat of a puzzle to historians. Much careful investigation has been done in the last two decades, but we still know too little to speak confidently or with a sense of finality. The appeal to arms would seem to have been brought about by a minority of the American people, directed by a small group of skillful leaders, who like Indian scouts, covered their tracks so cleverly that only the keenest trailers can now follow their course and understand their strategy. On the other hand, the philosophy of revolution is familiar to us. Revolutions are born of an abnormal state of mind, sensitized by an accumulated body of experience. They are psychological explosions, resulting from irritations commonly economic in origin, and they are conditioned in their programs by the stock of knowledge and aspiration peculiar to their time and place. Two determining facts, then, would seem to lie at the root of the American Revolution: the American psychology which shaped the colonial outlook, and the peculiar situation of the British Empire at the close of the French and Indian war.[1]

In old age John Adams "hazarded an opinion, that the true history of the American revolution could not be recovered," for "the revolution was effected before the war commenced. The revolution was in the minds and hearts of the people." [2] Accepting Adams's thesis of a change in American psychology, we may hazard a further opinion that the revolution resulted from the emergence

[1] An excellent short statement of the causes of the American Revolution is given by A. M. Schlesinger in *New Viewpoints in American History*, Chapter VII. Compare C. H. Van Tyne, *The Causes of the War of Independence*.

[2] Letter to Mr. Niles, January 14, 1818.

179

in the two countries of divergent interpretations of the theory and practice of sovereignty, which may be sufficiently distinguished by the terms local home rule and imperial centralization. In the beginning it was a clash of jurisdiction between colonial self-government and absentee paternalism; but later it developed into an open challenge of the monarchical principle. A popular will to self-rule had long been developing in America, and when the outbreak of hostilities clarified its latent objective, it speedily asserted a conscious republican purpose. To many of the early supporters of the colonial protest, this republican outcome was unforeseen and deeply regretted; but it was implicit in the whole history of colonial development, and must ultimately stand sharply revealed, once its aspirations were balked.

If the crisis was precipitated almost casually by the program of parliamentary regulation, the long drift towards alienation was far from casual. An American mind had been created by the silent pressure of environment. A large measure of economic freedom had developed an American liberalism, frankly and vigorously individualistic. It was not consciously democratic, or even republican. There were few avowed democrats in the stolid mass of colonial provincialism; a busy and commonplace routine offered little opportunity for revolutionary appeal to a people grown lethargic from economic abundance. Of social unrest, the common fuel of revolutionary fires, there was practically none; and but for a blundering ministerial imperialism that challenged this nascent liberalism, throwing over it the mantle of patriotism, the colonies would have written a very different history. Once the crisis was precipitated, however, and it became clear that imperial centralization was encroaching upon local rights, the liberal impulses in the background of the American mind assumed a militant form and purpose.

The existence of this native liberalism had been stupidly overlooked and ignored by responsible statesmen. With the exception of Franklin, colonial spokesmen were commonly members of the aristocratic group, among whom the Tory philosophy was spreading fast. Gentlemen in Boston, New York, Philadelphia, and Charleston fashioned their manners upon the polite world of St. James's and caught the Tory ways in politics as naturally as the London style in wigs. They associated with the royal officials, traveled in England, corresponded with members of Parliament, advised in all matters of colonial policy, and proved themselves the most shortsighted of counselors. Upon their heads rest in part the blunders of the ministry. In failing to understand the native liberalism of America, they not only shared responsibility for an unwise policy, but they hastened their own destruction. Samuel Adams could not have played so effectively upon the popular prejudices if the Hutchinsons and Olivers had not brought the Tory ways into wide disrepute by their arrogance.

Colonial liberalism, on the other hand, was not so simple and homogeneous as we long believed. It was rather a somewhat vague composite of the aspirations of three diverse geographical areas, with different economic interests, social ways, and political ideals. The middle and northern coast region, with its mercantile cities, was a distinct area; the tidewater region from Maryland to Georgia, with its plantation economy, constituted another; and the indefinite backcountry beyond the older settlements, stretching from Maine southward along the Alleghany watershed, constituted a third. The first was dominated by a merchant group— wholesale importers and exporters—wealthy and conservative, but with a great majority of the population—small tradesmen, mechanics and yeomen—far more democratic than the leaders. The second was controlled by the aristocratic planters, whose leadership during the crises of the dispute with England was rejected by an economically strong but socially inferior body of factors or alien middlemen. The third was composed of thousands of small freeholders, largely Scotch-Irish and German, who acknowledged no leadership, were unconsciously democratic in their ways, suspicious of the seacoast aristocracy, wedded to an agrarian philosophy. The merchant group was liberal only to the extent that liberalism meant profit: their commercial relations with England constituted them the closest tie between the two countries, and their timid love of established ways made them naturally conservative rather than revolutionary. The planter group possessed the traditional independence of English gentlemen: they would tolerate no outside dictation in matters concerning their own parishes, and their burdensome debts to English merchants cooled the ardor of their loyalty to Great Britain. The frontier agrarians, on the other hand, were pronounced liberals by environment and training to whom English ties were at the strongest only sentimental. They were republican in temper, and becoming class conscious during the ten years of debate, they grew rapidly in power and finally turned America against England. A recent historian has thus characterized the change of temper which brought these agrarians to the front as the fighting strength of the republicans:

A new class, formed within a decade, growing rapidly in numbers, was rising to power. In Pennsylvania, as in a number of other colonies, it consisted of small farmers in the back country, Scotch-Irish and German immigrants, reënforced by the voteless laborers and artisans of Philadelphia or other seaboard cities. . . . For over a decade this rising democracy had struggled for power against the little seaboard aristocracy of wealth and accepted social leadership. . . . The colonial masses could no longer be controlled by reverence for the high-born. The Quaker merchants of Philadelphia, the holders of manors on the Hudson, the tobacco and rice planters of Virginia and South Carolina, and even the great merchants, clergy, and professional men of New England, could no longer rule without question their social inferiors. . . . Thus, in 1774, came the climax in the struggle between rich and poor, East and West, those with a vote and those who were voteless, between privilege and the welfare of the common man. The two classes might work in harmony or might clash on the question of resistance to Great Britain, but they were pretty sure to be in opposition on the issue of individual rights. A merchant . . . might welcome the support of the mechanics and small shopkeepers against a grievous tax by the British Government, but the price, a right to vote and to hold office, he was sure to resent, and he grew more and more alarmed as the pressure became more insistent.[3]

From the imperial point of view there were the soundest reasons why, following the Treaty of Paris in 1763, Parliament should have desired to set about reorganizing the far-spread British Empire. Within a few years vast territories had been added to the crown, and if the scattered parts were to be gathered into a cohesive and powerful whole there was need of a definite policy of coördination and integration. The American colonies were only a small part of the total empire, and it was generally agreed among English statesmen that the old policy of "salutary neglect" could no longer serve imperial interests. If the Whig imperialists under the leadership of Pitt had been put in charge of imperial reconstruction, the outcome very likely would have been peaceful. But unfortunately for the empire the colonial problem became embroiled with English domestic politics. The purpose of the King was to set up a personal autocracy with Tory help, over-

[3] Van Tyne, *Causes of the War of Independence*, pp. 424-426.

throw the rule of the Whig families, eliminate from the ministry the more intelligent Old Whig leaders—Pitt, Camden, Barré, Burke, Shelburne—and bring in a narrow-minded group who held to the obsolete mercantilist theory of colonial dependency. The immediate outcome was the inauguration of a policy that ran counter to the economic interests of the three major colonial regions and aroused the hostility of important colonial groups. Every successive enactment was a greater blunder, until the crowning stupidity of the tea monopoly—which used colonial interests as a pawn in a game of the East India Company—threw the colonial fat into the fire.

The grievances of the merchants resulting from the regulatory trade acts were real and serious. However the ministry might justify those acts before Parliament, their effects were disastrous to substantial colonial interests, and to American eyes seemed designed to bring colonial trade into further subjection to English merchants. The attempt to suppress the widespread practice of smuggling was ill advised even though logical, for it aroused the consuming public as well as the middlemen, and gave popular backing to the protests of the merchants. The total political result was to align against Parliament the most influential groups in the trading towns—the wealthy importers and the professional classes—and provided opportunity to the radicals to spread their propaganda under cover of respectable leadership. The movement of resistance thus set on foot by the class-conscious merchants eventually slipped from their control and passed into the hands of the Sons of Liberty, who drove faster and farther than conservative business men would willingly follow; yet these latter soon found themselves coerced by tumultuous forces which they had unwittingly loosed. In consequence there came a time of divided counsels, and when independence was finally declared large numbers of the wealthiest and most dignified merchants turned Loyalist and threw in their lot with the King. More than two hundred quitted Boston on its evacuation by General Gage. Others stood apart as neutrals till the war was over, and then drew together in a compact organization to stem the tide of post-war agrarianism and assist in setting up a federal government after their liking.[4]

[4] For an admirable study, see A. M. Schlesinger, *The Colonial Merchants and the American Revolution: 1763-1776.*

The grievances of the plantation group were less obvious but none the less real. Probably more critical than taxation or the debts owed to English merchants, was the question of the western lands. The Quebec Act stirred the South as the tea monopoly stirred Boston and New York and Philadelphia. Involved in that act were certain long accepted colonial rights of domain, on the strength of which vast speculation in backcountry lands had been engaged in by English and colonial land companies and individuals.[5] The question was extraordinarily complicated, involving the rights of the Indians, the ambition of the Hudson Bay Company to retain the western wilderness as a vast fur preserve, the rights of Catholics in the French settlements, the rights of the imperial treasury to income from the sale of the lands, the rights of soldiers of the French wars to lands granted by colonial legislatures, the rights of frontiersmen to free settlement and exploitation, as well as specific grants to several colonies, in particular Massachusetts, Connecticut and Virginia. From this mass of conflicting interests, all eager to exploit an incalculably rich domain, little hope of satisfactory solution offered, and a wiser ministry would have kept hands off. But an ill-considered Parliamentary enactment cut the knot in a way to arouse the quick and keen resentment of America. Whatever may be said for the solution, one thing is clear; it set aside by arbitrary statute cherished rights which Virginian gentlemen, with their eyes on rich plantations to the West, deeply resented. It was a matter of vital concern to colonies like Virginia that they should control their wilderness frontier. The Quebec Act not only alienated thousands of western colonials, but it provided them with influential leaders like Washington and Robert Morris. It was more fuel to the radical bonfire.

In the end the fortunes of the revolutionary movement rested with the yeomanry, and this yeomanry with its agrarian outlook and republican sympathies, was in a mood to respond to radical appeal. That the farmer was induced to take down his squirrel rifle and fight King George was made possible by a number of irritations—his deep-rooted prejudice against aristocracy, his instinctive dislike of crown officials, his inveterate localism that

---

[5] This important subject has been examined by C. W. Alvord, *The Mississippi Valley in British Policies;* C. A. Beard, *An Economic Interpretation of the Constitution;* C. H. Van Tyne, *The Causes of the War of Independence.*

resented alien interference—as well as by substantial class interests. In every colony the party of incipient populism had been checked and thwarted by royal officials; and it was this mass of populistic discontent, seeing itself in danger of being totally crushed, and its interests ignored, that provided the rank and file of armed opposition to the King. Already Parliament had brought acute financial distress to the colonies by forbidding the emission of bills of credit; and other attacks on popular policies followed. The strength of the popular opposition to royal programs had lain heretofore in the legislative control of the purse; by threatening to withhold salaries, the democratic legislatures had been able to coerce the royal governor and the judges, and keep them somewhat responsive to the popular will. To the Tories such coercion was proof that the democratic claws needed cutting, and one of the purposes of the Stamp Act was the providing of a fund to pay the royal officials out of the royal chest. It was a skillful plan, but it overreached itself. Party alignment had become too sharp, agrarian suspicions had grown too sensitive, for the plan to succeed. The immediate, fatal result was the accession of a numerous body of fighting men to the other malcontents.

The American Revolution was one of the first fruits of a short-sighted imperialism. A generous policy of imperial federation would have returned incredible revenues to Great Britain; but the Tory ministry was not intelligent enough to let sleeping dogs lie. A sentimental attachment had kept America loyal. So long as his customary and traditional rights remained undisturbed, the colonial would throw up his cap for King George; but if he were driven to choose between loyalty and self-interest, between sentiment and profit, the choice was certain. If the heavy debts which the foolish wars of Pitt had bequeathed to the Empire had not seemed to offer a justification, the Tory blunderers would not have forced the issue; but once it was joined, vast numbers of Americans came to believe that the development of their country had reached a point where it would be hampered by further overseas regulation; that America must be free to exploit her resources to her exclusive advantage; and that such economic freedom would be possible only with political independence. It was the ill luck of the ministry to present the question so concretely that the colonial radicals were given an opportunity to awaken the latent forces of American liberalism and turn them against English sovereignty.

A militant nationalistic psychology resulted from a widespread propaganda, and the last ties with England were broken.

II

ARGUMENT AND PROPAGANDA

We understand the ways of propaganda today better than our fathers understood them, and the official pronouncements of diplomats and statesmen we have grown somewhat skeptical of. Historians of the American Revolution have paid rather too exclusive attention to formal speeches and state papers, forgetting that those speeches and papers too often served the purpose of obscuring and evading the real issues. The ten years of dreary debate preceding the clash of arms, during which theory and precedent were examined by partisan lawyers, did little more than serve party purposes on both sides of the Atlantic, investing immediate interests with nationalistic or imperialistic idealism. Honest men talked themselves into a passion, but they took good care that their cause should appear dressed to advantage.

On the American side the argument fell into two broad divisions: an attempt to justify the colonial position by appeal to the British constitution, and when that failed by an appeal to the extra-legal doctrine of natural right. To understand the obscure constitutional wrangle, it must be recalled that important changes in English constitutional practice had taken place since the colonies were founded. Parliamentary sovereignty had superseded royal sovereignty, or in other words, the sovereignty of property had superseded divine right autocracy; and this in turn was undergoing change in the second half of the eighteenth century—the sovereignty of landed property was challenged by the rising capitalism. The Revolution of 1688 had established the general principle that the state can take no property in the form of taxes or levies without the consent of the owner, given by himself or by his representative sitting in Parliament. But in current practice the system of representation had become so misshapen that a new theory had arisen to give constitutional sanction to existing methods. Refusal to reapportion representation had resulted in the notorious rotten-borough system, control of which boroughs was too valuable an asset to the ruling oligarchy to be surrendered. To justify the scandal a new theory of virtual representation was developed—a theory upon which turned much of the early revolutionary debate. In brief the theory asserted that as Parliament speaks for the total body of Englishmen, it makes no practical difference who elects them, where they live, who they are, or what interests they represent. Within the halls of Parliament they can be trusted to think and legislate for the nation as a whole. The essential constitutional principle requires only that there shall be a respectable body chosen from among the commons of England, in whose hands shall rest the custody of the purse, and who shall serve as a check upon the royal prerogative. Such was the parliamentary situation in 1763, and when appeal was made by the colonials to the principle of no taxation without representation, it was answered by appeal to the theory of virtual representation.

American constitutional practice, on the other hand, had developed in a contrary direction. Quite as consciously as Parliament, the several colonial legislatures rested on the principle of property rights, but a different system of representation had developed. By easy logic a geographical theory had emerged, by the terms of which a legislator must be a freeman of the district rather than of the realm, that he should hold power for a short period and frequently submit his conduct to the scrutiny of the electors, and that a district should bear a just per capita relation to the total population. The doctrine of virtual representation was alien to colonial theory, although in fact it might be applied to the large body of disfranchised non-property-holders. The broad difference, then, in the legislative practice of the two countries lay in the important distinction between local, numerical representation, and a grotesque system of borough jobbing. Both systems rested on a narrow suffrage, although the colonial basis was very much broader. The difference was without significance so long as the traditional relations between America and England continued; but when Parliament proposed to extend the theory of virtual representation to the colonies, and treat Massachusetts and Virginia as on a constitutional footing with Birmingham and Manchester, the difference became acute. No American colony was willing to become the pawn of parliamentary placemen, at the mercy of parliamentary jobbery.

The debate over this vital question was involved in obscurities by reason of the vagueness of the British constitution. If an

unwritten constitution be no other than established practice—
and it is true of the English constitution in spite of the body of
principles existing in such pronouncements as Magna Charta, the
settlement of 1689, and the Common Law—then the current
practice of Parliament must be accepted as constitutional. This
was the fatal weakness of the colonial argument, as it was the
weakness of Pitt and other defenders of America in Parliament.
When Pitt exclaimed with characteristic grandiloquence, "I come
not here armed at all points with law cases and acts of Parliament,
with the statute-book doubled down in dog-ears, to defend the
cause of liberty," he abandoned the legal ground to appeal to the
sense of justice and right of Englishmen. But the question could
not so easily be transferred from the domain of constitutional law.
For upwards of a hundred years Parliament had been sovereign,
and for the colonials now to deny its sovereignty meant one of
two things: either to go back to the obsolete principle of divine
right, or to postulate an extra-parliamentary body of constitutional law, unknown to English practice. A sovereignty inhering
neither in King nor Parliament, but in a super-constitution, was a
conception that had been played with by Coke in an endeavor to
exalt the Common Law, and hinted at by later Whig statesmen,
but which had never established itself in practice. The colonials
recognized the dilemma and made half-hearted attempts to evade
it. John Adams and Franklin endeavored to argue that as the
colonial charters were from the crown, and antedated the rise of
Parliament, Americans owed allegiance to the King and not to
Parliament, and hence parliamentary pretentions to sovereignty
over America were only a new form of unconstitutional prerogative. But the argument was taken seriously by neither side, and
was soon put away.[6]

It finally became clear to American leaders that if their cause
were to make headway, appeal must be made to broader principles.
Their case must rest on philosophical rather than on legal grounds.
This suffices to explain the shift from constitutionalism to abstract
rights, which marked the middle period of the debate. By 1773
it had become evident to thoughtful observers that the cause of
American liberalism must fail, or become revolutionary in purpose and intent, and to become such it must seek justification in

---

[6] For an excellent discussion of the constitutional questions involved, see C. H.
Van Tyne, *The Causes of the War of Independence*, Chapters VIII and IX.

extra-constitutional principles. And this justification it discovered in the writings of English liberals of the seventeenth century—in Sidney and Milton, and above all in Locke. The influence of Locke had long been paramount in English political speculation. He had been the apologist and defender of the settlement of 1689; the principles which he expounded lay at the base of the dynastic rights of the reigning house, and were nominally accepted by all the parliamentary leaders. The relations between natural rights and parliamentary sovereignty had not wholly clarified, and in the background of English constitutional thought still lingered a vague notion of certain natural rights above the constitution, and limiting parliamentary statutes. Thinkers as different as Blackstone and Camden subscribed to such doctrine, but it daily became more tenuous in the face of a growing acceptance of un-limited parliamentary sovereignty.[7]

In turning to Locke, therefore, the colonial debaters went back a century and picked up the argument of liberalism as it existed before it had been nullified by later English practice. They occupied a position similar to that defended by him a hundred years before; they were combating the same arbitrary rule that had brought on the Revolution of 1688. He had laid down the basic principle of revolution in the doctrine of certain natural rights of the subject which no state may subvert without peril to the original compact; he had asserted that taxation without representa-tion constituted such subversive tyranny; and he gave high sanction to the right and duty of resistance to an encroaching sovereignty. The noble words, "Chains are but an ill wearing how much soever we gild or polish them," uttered a note of defiance to arbitrary power which struck a responsive chord in the breast of the colonial liberal. In short, Locke's two *Treatises on Civil Government*, aimed at Sir Robert Filmer's absurd *Patriarcha*, were turned against Parliament and became the textbook of the American Revolution.

The ground had been well prepared. The argument of Locke went home with such convincing force to the colonial liberal be-cause it embodied conclusions towards which America had long been moving. It was an eloquent confirmation of native expe-rience, a sober justification of the psychology of individualism. The self-governing state had so long been an established fact in colonial life as to have assumed the complexion of a natural

[7] For this see Van Tyne, *ibid.*, pp. 234–238.

right. The political compact had taken form in American political thought, a generation before Locke gave currency to the theory, and Jefferson was expressing native conclusions drawn from American experience when he argued that "governments derive their just powers from the consent of the governed," and that "all men are created equal, that they are endowed by their Creator with certain unalienable Rights, that amongst these are Life, Liberty and the pursuit of Happiness." It is not true to assert that Jefferson was only reciting Locke, with modifications derived from the French humanitarians. It is nearer the truth to say that he made use of old-world philosophy to express and justify certain native tendencies then seeking adequate statement.

To such an experience, armed with such a philosophy, there must come eventually the conviction that both monarchy and aristocracy were irrational; that the ambitions of a coercive alien sovereignty were fraught with danger to the rights of the American citizen. The resurgent absolutism of Stuart times, with its doctrine of the omnicompetent state, which the King was reviving through the instrumentality of Parliament, was broken by the stubborn colonial resistance. Absolutism under whatever form was doomed in America, however slowly it might linger out its life. Jonathan Boucher might seek to revive Sir Robert Filmer, and preach to Americans the dogma of divine right through royal primogeniture from Adam, and other colonial Tories might applaud; but they were fast becoming anachronisms. The Revolution was to overthrow for Americans the principle of the absolutist state, and substitute a modified sovereignty, circumscribed by the utilitarian test of its relation to the common well-being of its citizens. For the first time in modern history it was discovered that "the true meaning of sovereignty," as a recent student has put it, is to be sought "not in the coercive power possessed by its instrument [the state,] but in the fused good-will for which it stands."[8]

III

CERTAIN SOCIAL CONSEQUENCES

The swift crystallization of colonial sentiment in favor of republicanism, as the crisis developed, produced the American revolution of which John Adams wrote. The long leveling process

[8] H. J. Laski, *The Problem of Sovereignty*, p. 12; see also Appendices A and B.

of a hundred and forty years, with its psychology of decentralization, fruited naturally in a new political philosophy fitted to new-world conditions. Monarchy, with its social appanage of aristocracy, was a caste institution wholly unsuited to an unregimented America. The war brought this revolutionary fact home to the consciousness of thousands of colonials; and the liberalism that before had been vaguely instinctive quickly became eager and militant. The old order was passing; the day of the Tory in America was over for the present; the republican was henceforth to be master of the new world. Out of this primary revolution were to come other revolutions, social and economic, made possible by the new republican freedom.

The swift rise of a political philosophy traditionally regarded as mean and traitorous was inexplicable to Tory gentlemen, and aroused a fierce retaliatory opposition. A social war of the classes, bitter, vindictive, followed upon hostilities against England. The arrogance of the gentry during those brisk days when the new spirit was rising is scarcely comprehensible to later Americans unused to such frankness. The republicans were scorned by the superior classes as unprincipled sedition-mongers, plotting treason against the King and society. If commoners flocked to town-meetings and outvoted the gentlemen, the latter were outraged at the presumption of the "mobsters" in flouting their betters. For the plain people to take things into their own hands was no other than anarchy. The familiar records of the day are filled with such aristocratic jests as this:

> Down at night a bricklayer or carpenter lies,
> Next sun a Lycurgus, a Solon doth rise.[9]

"The dirty mob was all about me as I drove into town," said Mistress Peggy Hutchinson, as she looked out on turbulent Boston from her father's chariot; and her feminine contempt for the common people was an echo of the universal Tory contempt for republican mechanics and farmers. It was the duty of the vulgar, as loyal subjects, to pay taxes and not lay them; to obey the law and not make it. By far the most important consequence of the Revolution was the striking down of this mounting aristocratic spirit that was making rapid headway with the increase of wealth. It sifted the American people as the migrations of the seventeenth

[9] Moore, *Diary of the Revolution*, Vol. II, p. 22.

century had sifted the English people, keeping the republicans at home and sending forth the Tories, weakening the influence of the conservatives and increasing the influence of the liberals. Few experiences in our history have proved so momentous in results as this shift of power and change in personnel that resulted from the great schism. A middle-class America was to rise on the ruins of the colonial aristocracy.

The unfortunate Loyalists were victims of their own blindness. They did not rightly estimate the driving power of the liberal forces released by the struggle, and failing to understand, they staked everything on the issue, and lost, and were driven rudely out of the land by the plebeian republicans whom they despised. The disruption of colonial society resulting from the expulsion of the Loyalists was far graver than we commonly assume. Shiploads of excellent gentlemen, and among them the most cultivated minds in America, were driven from their firesides and sent forth to seek new homes, whether in "Hell, Hull or Halifax" mattered little to the victors. Upward of forty thousand sought refuge in Canada; thousands more went to the Bahamas; and still other thousands returned to the old home. "There will scarcely be a village in England without some American dust in it, I believe, by the time we are all at rest," wrote the Loyalist Dutchman, Peter Van Schaak. Much suffering was endured and much bitterness engendered, and if for years the dominant temper in Canada was fiercely hostile to the United States, the mood is traceable to the expatriated gentlemen who transmitted to their children a grudge against the victorious republicans. It was an unhappy business, but it was scarcely avoidable once appeal was made to the sword. There was no longer place in America for the foolish dream of a colonial aristocracy.

The change of temper that came over American society with the loss of the Loyalists, was immense and far-reaching. For the first time the middle class was free to create a civilization after its own ideals. In rising to leadership it brought another spirit into every phase of life. Dignity and culture henceforth were to count for less and assertiveness for more. Ways became less leisurely, the social temper less urbane. The charm of the older aristocracy disappeared along with its indisputable evils. Although a few of the older wits like Mather Byles lingered on bitterly, and others like Gouverneur Morris accepted the situation philosophically, they belonged to the past. A franker evaluation of success in terms of money began to obscure the older personal and family distinction. New men brought new ways and a vulgar clamor of politics went hand in hand with business expansion. The demagogue and the speculator discovered a fruitful field for their activities. The new capitalism lay on the horizon of republican America, and the middle class was eager to hasten its development. But a new economic order required a new political state, and as a necessary preliminary, the spirit of nationalism began that slow encroachment upon local frontiers which was to modify profoundly the common psychology. Americanism superseded colonialism, and with the new loyalty there developed a conception of federal sovereignty, overriding all local authorities, checking the movement of particularism, binding the separate commonwealths in a consolidating union. This marked the turning point in American development; the checking of the long movement of decentralization and the beginning of a counter movement of centralization—the most revolutionary change in three hundred years of American experience. The history of the rise of the coercive state in America, with the ultimate arrest of all centrifugal tendencies, was implicit in that momentous counter movement.

CHAPTER II

THE MIND OF THE AMERICAN TORY

So nearly forgotten by later generations is the American Tory of Revolutionary times that it will be well to examine the genus with some care; for only by understanding the great authority inhering in his traditional leadership can we measure his power to thwart the ambitions of the republicans. In numbers the Tories were a very small minority; unendowed with wealth and position they would have been negligible; but as members of the local gentry they enjoyed great prestige which was highly serviceable to the royal cause. Although native born they aped the English aristocracy, and reproduced on a less magnificent scale the manners of the English landed families. Less arrogant than their old-world models, certainly much less corrupt in their politics, they exuded the same aristocratic prejudices and the same narrow sympathies. Their most cherished dream was the institution of an American nobility, with the seal of royal favor set upon their social pretensions. They were the embodiment of the aristocratic eighteenth century, in a world instinctively hostile to all aristocracies. Out of a numerous company of distinguished Tories, three will serve for consideration—Thomas Hutchinson, Royal Governor, Daniel Leonard, lawyer, and Jonathan Boucher, minister.

I

THOMAS HUTCHINSON

Royal Governor

The career of the last royal governor of Massachusetts affords a suggestive study in the relation of material prosperity to political principles. Descended in the fourth generation from the Antinomian enthusiast, Mistress Anne Hutchinson, whom all the authorities of Boston could neither terrify nor silence, but who suffered contumely and exile rather than submit her will to official censors, Thomas Hutchinson reveals in his stiff conservatism the common change that follows upon economic well-being. The House

194

of Hutchinson had long since abandoned all unprofitable radicalisms and had taken to the safer business of acquiring property
and respectability; in which work it had by God's blessing greatly
prospered, until it came to be reckoned the first house in the
province. With growing wealth political honors multiplied. The
grandfather of the governor had been the first Chief Justice of the
Common Pleas, Commander of the Forces, Assistant, and Councilor; and at his death in 1717 he was as eminent a citizen as Chief
Justice Sewall, the diarist. The governor's father, Thomas Hutchinson, Sr., devoted more attention to his calling of merchant
than to politics, nevertheless he sat in the Council for twenty-five
years, and was a colonel in the provincial militia. With the advent
of Thomas Hutchinson upon the scene, the respectability of the
house was assured, abundant wealth had been accumulated, and
the path of political preferment was open. The little colony was
eager to confer honors on so promising a son. He was ambitious
and thrifty, and he coveted the distinction and the material
rewards which officeholding brought. No Boston gentleman of
his day had a sharper eye for the main chance. He added office
to office, and at one and the same time he was Member of the
Council, Judge of Probate, Chief Justice, and Lieutenant Governor; and such other offices as he could not himself possess he
maneuvered to get into the hands of his sons, and brothers-in-law,
and dependents. One of those brothers-in-law, Samuel Mather,
son of Cotton Mather, who refused to follow his kinsman into the
Tory camp, called him "an avaritious man"; and avaricious of
power, even more than of money, he certainly was.

  With his abundant offices and honors, there was every temptation to conservatism. Unless there was hidden in him some lingering idealism, some seed of the ancestral radicalism to sprout and
grow into discontent, Thomas Hutchinson was marked for a
reactionary. And unhappily in his conventional soul there was
not the faintest spark of idealism. The enthusiasm of Mistress
Anne was washed clean out of the Hutchinson blood, leaving only
the native stubbornness; which stubbornness, dominating a
character cold, formal, arrogant, dogmatic, unimaginative, self-
righteous, was finally to play havoc with Thomas Hutchinson's
good fortune. The son of a merchant, he was a careful, methodical
soul, who studied how to save and invest; in a later generation he
would have been a great banker, but in his own he preferred to

invest in politics. How suggestive of Yankee thrift is such an entry as this:

> All the time he was at College he carried on a little trade by sending ventures in his father's vessels, & kept a little paper Journal & leger, & enterd in it every dinner, supper, breakfast, & every article of expense, even of a shilling; which practice soon became pleasant; & he found it of great use all his life. . . . Before he came of age, he had, by adventuring to sea from two or three quintalls [hundredweight] of fish, given him by his father, when about 12 years old, acquired four or five hundred pounds sterling.[1]

After a number of years in his father's countinghouse, learning the ways of eighteenth-century trade, he abandoned the mercantile career and entered politics at the age of six-and-twenty. From May 31, 1737, when he first took his place in the House of Deputies as one of the "Boston Seat," to June 1, 1774, when he quitted his country home at Milton to take ship for London and exile, he was a power in the political life of Massachusetts, reaching eventually the highest station. During that long period of thirty-seven years he was a spokesman of the New England gentry, always on the side of government, never in the opposition. That he ever critically examined the foundations of his political creed, there is nothing in the printed record to indicate. He had some of the tastes of the book-lover and scholar. He was deeply interested in the Puritan past, and his *History of Massachusetts Bay* was based on a wide knowledge of manuscript sources which he had been at great pains to collect. But in spite of a praiseworthy care for accuracy and impartiality, he lacked the creative imagination to reconstruct the past. He had pretty much freed his mind from religious bigotry, but he could not rid himself of a narrow partisanship, and his treatment of the agrarian movement was grossly unfair. His shortcomings as a political thinker were more striking. His knowledge of the political classics was of the slightest. When Samuel Adams made use of the natural-rights theory, Hutchinson's comment would indicate that he had no acquaintance with the theory and had not even read Locke.[2] He was little given to intellectual interests, and ill at ease in dealing with general principles. He possessed the mental qualities of a lawyer rather than a speculative thinker, and his long immersion in office contracted a mind naturally sterile to the routine habits of an administrator.

[1] *Diary and Letters*, Vol. I, pp. 46–48.
[2] See Hosmer, *Life of Samuel Adams*, p. 259.

He hardened early, and thereafter he was incapable of changing his views or liberalizing his sympathies. Consistency he erected into a fetish and once he had taken a position he would not budge from it. He did not understand the liberal America that was rising about him—neither the economic forces that were creating it nor the spokesmen who represented it; and he saw no reason for change. The House of Hutchinson had prospered under existing conditions, and other houses would prosper likewise, he believed, if they were equally honest and diligent. So he went his tactless, unintelligent way, barking his shins on every liberal tendency of the times, and hating the men who gave him trouble.

Hutchinson, in short, was a complete Tory, and if we would understand him and his class, we must first take into account the current Tory philosophy. Compressed into a sentence it was the expression of the will-to-power of the wealthy. Its motive was economic class interest, and its object the exploitation of society through the instrumentality of the state. Stated thus, the philosophy does not appear to advantage; it lays itself open to unpleasant criticism by those who are not its beneficiaries. In consequence, much ingenuity in tailoring was necessary to provide it with garments to cover its nakedness. Embroidered with patriotism, loyalty, law and order, it made a very respectable appearance; and when it put on the stately robe of the British Constitution, it was enormously impressive. The Tory theory of the British Constitution may well be regarded as a masterpiece of the gentle art of tailoring. Government by king, lords, and commons it asserted, approximated the ideal of a "mixt government," embracing the total wisdom of the realm, ruling in the interests of all, avoiding the evils of class domination, and chastising the refractory only for the common good. Gentlemen might well praise the "glorious British Constitution." It was their little jest at the expense of the English people, who were content to be exploited by them.

In this game of political pretense Hutchinson willingly shared. He knew that Parliament did not represent the English people; that it was controlled by a group of landed gentlemen with mercenaries in their pay; and yet in reply to repeated charges he revealed no hint of the truth, but reiterated the familiar Tory interpretation in the face of shrewd enemies who knew that he was insincere. In private among other gentlemen, Hutchinson

was frank enough.   He knew what was at stake in America—
whether political control should remain in the hands of "gentlemen
of principle and property," with the assistance of English Tories,
or whether it should pass into the hands of the majority.   And
so while declaiming against mobs, and preaching loyalty to the best
of kings, he secretly busied himself with influential persons in
devising methods to frustrate the Whig ambitions.   Moreover
in dealing with his enemies he was a thorough realist.   In his
comment on American Whigs and their political methods, he set
down many a shrewd and just estimate of their actions and motives.
But in defense of the English ministry he refused to face reality.
He quibbled and misrepresented and denied, stooping to dirty
politics to hold his party together and strengthen it.

At the moment when Hutchinson assumed the duties of governor the situation was tense.   Bernard had muddled things sadly,
and "the rage against him became, at length, so violent, that
it was judged necessary to recall him," [3] and he slipped off to
England to receive a baronetcy and a pension.   But he had brought
the commonwealth to the parting of the ways, and Hutchinson
found himself in a difficult position.   The roots of the trouble are
laid bare in the following affidavit of Bernard:

In the Province of Massachusetts Bay, when civil authority was reduced
so low as to have nothing left but the form of a government, and scarce
even that, an enquiry into the causes of so great a weakness in the governing power was unavoidable; and there was no entering upon such an
enquiry, without observing upon the ill effects of that part of the constitution of that government, whereby the appointment of the Council is left
to the people, to be made by annual election; and yet the Royal Governor,
in all Acts of prerogative, is subject to the controul of the Democraticall
Council.   This solecism in policy has been as hurtful in practice as it is
absurd in theory, and it is the true cause of the extreme imbecility of the
power of the crown in this government, at times when the exertion of it is
most wanted.   This is not an observation of a new date; it is of many years
standing; . . . ever since he has felt the effects which the popular constitution of the Council has had upon the Royalty of the government,
which is above three years ago; within which time, he has seen the King
deprived of the service of every man at the Council Board, who has
resolution enough to disapprove the opposition to the authority of the
King and the Parliament, and their supremacy over the *American* Colonies.
This, and this only, is the foundation of the charge of their endeavouring to
overthrow the charter; whereas his real desire has been, that the charter
should have a more durable stability, by means of a necessary alteration,

[3] Hutchinson, *History of Massachusetts Bay*, Vol. III, p. 255.

without which, he is persuaded it cannot have a much longer duration; as the abuse of the appointment of the Council now prevailing, must oblige the Parliament to interfere sooner or later.[4]

The more thoughtfully one considers this frank statement the more clearly it appears what grounds for party dissension lay in the "solecism" of a constitution whereby the "Royal Governor, in all Acts of prerogative," was "subject to the controul of the Democraticall Council." It would not be easy to patch up a working compromise between an absentee prerogative and the local democratic will; one or the other must be sovereign; and because the terms of the charter enabled the democracy to nullify the prerogative, Bernard concluded that the charter must be revised and the abuse corrected. In this Hutchinson agreed, and from the imperial point of view not without reason. "By an unfortunate mistake," he wrote in apology to Gage, "soon after the charter, a law passed which made every town in the Province a corporation perfectly democratic." With every passing year the mistake was becoming more unfortunate, and the vital problem before government, in the opinion of Hutchinson, was how to correct this unfortunate mistake, together with other like mistakes, with such happy skill as to check the democratic branch without arousing popular resentment. On this reef Hutchinson foundered.

As early as 1764 the meddlesome Bernard had proposed to the home government a complete remodeling of colonial governments on the English Tory plan; and by way of suggestion he forwarded some proposals looking to the eventual consolidation of the several colonies under a single royal government, the erection of a house of lords as a balance to the popular party and a comprehensive tax policy. It was one of numerous suggestions then being made for incorporating America into the British Empire, and extending the imperial power over the continent. Bernard's bias is sufficiently revealed in the following:

86. There is no government in America at present, whose powers are properly balanced; there not being in any of them, a real and distinct third legislative power mediating between the king and the people, which is the peculiar excellence of the British constitution.

87. The want of such a third legislative power, adds weight to the popular, and lightens the royal scale; so as to destroy the balance between the royal and popular powers.

[4] "Answer of Bernard to the Petition of the House of Representatives to the King," in *Works of Samuel Adams*, Vol. I, pp. 365-367.

88. Although America is not now . . . ripe enough for an hereditary nobility; yet it is now capable of a nobility for life.

89. A nobility appointed by the king for life, and made independent, would probably give strength and stability to the American governments, as effectually as an hereditary nobility does to that of Great Britain.[5]

It is not known to what extent Hutchinson indorsed so ambitious and comprehensive a plan. For years he had been Bernard's understudy, and supported him in all his policies; but being cautious by nature and attached to local custom, he probably would have rejected the plan of continental consolidation unless his personal ambition had been enlisted. Hosmer's attempt to clear his skirts[6] is not convincing. Recalling that Hutchinson yielded invariably to royal or ministerial suggestions, no matter how contrary to local custom, there is no reason to believe that he would have objected to any coercive program, which provided adequately for the colonial Tories.

In another matter that touched the political life of Massachusetts to the quick, Hutchinson was deeply engaged. The source of the power of the popular party lay in the democratic town meeting. In earlier days the Tories had made no objection to it, for it was amenable to control by the "better sort of people." But under the skillful politics of Samuel Adams and his fellows, it had become the chief instrument of opposition, and Hutchinson was determined to cut its claws. On so delicate a matter, however, it was only to the ministry that he could speak frankly; he must not appear to be laying a plot against an institution so long established as a part of the political machinery of the commonwealth. Under date of March 26, 1770, he wrote to the secretary of Lord Hillsboro:

There is a Town Meeting, no sort of regard being had to any qualification of voters, but all the inferior people meet together; and at a late meeting the inhabitants of other towns who happened to be in town, mixed with them. . . . It is in other words being under the government of the mob. This has given the lower part of the people such a sense of their importance that a gentleman does not meet with what used to be common civility, and we are sinking into perfect barbarism. . . . If this town could be separated from the rest of the Province, the infection has not taken such strong hold of the parts remote from it. The spirit of anarchy which prevails in Boston is more than I am able to cope with.[7]

---

[5] Quoted in John Adams, *Novanglus*, Second Letter.
[6] See his *Life of Thomas Hutchinson.*
[7] Quoted in *ibid.*, p. 180.

Writing to Hillsboro on April 19, 1771, he complained:

> In these votes and in most of the public proceedings of the town of Boston, persons of the best character and estate have little or no concern. They decline attending Town Meetings where they are sure to be out-voted by men of the lowest order.[8]

A month later, writing to his old crony, ex-Governor Bernard, he suggested a remedy which in one form or another he was constantly holding before the ministry, as an inducement to act:

> The town of Boston is the source from whence all the other parts of the Province derive more or less troubled water. When you consider what is called its constitution, your good sense will determine immediately that it never can be otherwise for a long time together, whilst the majority which conducts all affairs, if met together upon another occasion, would be properly called a mob, and are persons of such rank and circumstance as in all communities constitute a mob, there being no sort of regulation of voters in practice; and as these will always be most in number, men of weight and value, although they wish to suppress them, cannot be in-duced to attempt to do it for fear not only of being outvoted, but affronted and insulted. Call such an assembly what you will, it is really no sort of government, not even a democracy, at best a corruption of it. There is no hope of a cure by any legislative but among ourselves [*i.e.*, ministerial supporters] to compel the town to be a corporation.[9] The people will not seek it, because every one is sensible his importance will be lessened. If ever a remedy is found, it must be by compelling them to swallow it, and that by an exterior power,—the Parliament.[10]

In such advice—the destruction of the democratic machinery by an "exterior power" in order that control of government should lie beyond the reach of the popular will—we may discover ample grounds for democratic dissatisfaction with the governor. Hutchinson believed that when matters of state were settled by gentlemen over their wine, good government resulted; but when discussed by common people over their cider, the door was thrown wide open to anarchy. His particular *bête noire* was the mob, by which name he designated any gathering that had not received his gracious permission to assemble. It was his shortsighted will-ingness to arm himself with external authority against his fellow countrymen, that filled the years of his administration with so much bitterness. The more he lost ground, the more anxiously he

[8] *Ibid.*, p. 206.
[9] Hutchinson assumes the act of incorporation will lay restrictions upon the right of suffrage and the powers of the town meeting.
[10] *Ibid.*, pp. 206–207.

pleaded for help from the ministry. When certain of his private
letters came to the hands of Franklin and were sent home, Hutchinson was put in a rage. He had long been fearful of such a
diplomatic leak and urged secrecy, for if his private correspondence
should become public, he explained, "I have no security against
the rage of the people." [11] Much ink was used by his friends in
declaiming against the infamy of making public a gentleman's
private letters, and Hutchinson characterized it as an "affrontery"
such as "was never known before." That such private correspondence was in effect official correspondence, in that it aimed at
shaping parliamentary policy towards Massachusetts, was ignored
by these outraged gentlemen. Diplomats who plan privately
rarely like to be read publicly, especially when the public reads
how it is being bought and sold.

Very likely the Assembly overstated the case in declaring that
"there has been, for many years past, measures contemplated,
and a plan formed, by a set of men, born and educated among us,
to raise their own fortunes, and advance themselves to posts of
honor and profit, not only to the destruction of the charter and
constitution of this province, but at the expense of the rights and
liberties of the American colonies." [12] Hutchinson was too cautious
and too conservative to seek any revolutionary end; at the same
time he was too yielding to make a stand against any encroachment
that had legal sanction. From his narrow mind no help could
be expected touching the great matter of imperial federation. In
seeking a way out of the difficulties in which the British Empire
was daily becoming entangled, the royal governor could discover
no wiser plan than the abridgment of fundamental privileges which
a hundred and fifty years of slow growth had made the peculiar
possession of the colonies. The unhappy conclusion towards
which the American Tories were drifting he set forth in words which
were to become the most notorious he ever penned.

I never think of the measures necessary for the peace and good order of
the colonies without pain. There must be an abridgment of what are
called English liberties. I relieve myself by considering that in a remove
from a state of nature to the most perfect state of government, there must
be a great restraint of natural liberty. I doubt whether it is possible to
project a system of government in which a colony 3000 miles distant from
the parent state shall enjoy all the liberty of the parent state. I am cer-

---

[11] *Ibid.*, p. 199.
[12] *Resolves of the House of Representatives of Massachusetts Bay*, June 16, 1773.

tain I have never yet seen the projection. I wish the good of the colony
when I wish to see some further restraint of liberty rather than the con-
nexion with the parent state should be broken; for I am sure such a breach
must prove the ruin of the colony.[13]

Later writers, forgetful of Hutchinson's self-seeking record and of
his Tory philosophy, have inclined to leniency in judging him for
his stand on this crucial point. But in spite of his wig and scarlet
broadcloth robes he was only an unintelligent politician, who
served the hand that fed him. No better commentary could be
asked than is found in the caustic remark of the keenest Englishman of his day on the ministerial policy. In a letter of April, 1777,
Horace Walpole asked, "What politicians are those who have
preferred the empty name of *sovereignty* to that of *alliance*, and
forced subsidies to the golden ocean of commerce?" Hutchinson
was stubborn rather than wise. He would make no compromise
in the matter of sovereignty; there could be no lawful will but the
will of Parliament. "I know of no line that can be drawn between
the supreme authority of Parliament and the total independence
of the colonies," he replied to the Assembly, when it was struggling
with the idea of federation.[14] When the Council and House were
outlining a plan of imperial union, and seeking to demonstrate that
the "subordinate authorities" of the colonies were sovereign within
their fields, and "that, in fact, two such powers do subsist together,
and are not incompatible"; the governor with patient finality explained to them the true "nature of supreme power,"

. . . and urged, as an undeniable principle, that such a power is essential
in all governments, and that another power, with the name of subordinate,
and with a right to withstand or control the supreme in particulars, is
an absurdity—for it so far ceases to be subordinate, and becomes itself
supreme; that no sensible writer upon government ever denied what he
asserted; and whilst the council continued to hold, that two supreme
powers were compatible, it would be to no purpose to reason upon the other
parts of their message to him, or to deny what they adduced from a principle so contrary to reason.[15]

Hutchinson's position as the King's representative soon became
so difficult that a wiser man would have resigned. He was constrained to be the executive of a policy of government by ministerial

[13] *Ibid.*, p. 436. Compare the view of Van Tyne, *The Causes of the War of Independence*, p. 85.
[14] Speech of January 6, 1773.
[15] *History of Massachusetts Bay*, Vol. III, pp. 381–382.

instructions. Again and again he vetoed a measure, or dissolved the legislature, or took action contrary to the spirit of the charter; and the sole justification which he pleaded was a secret letter of instructions, the terms of which he refused to make public, and the object of which must be judged by his acts. "So long as he continued commander-in-chief," he replied to the House in one of their perennial wranglings, "he should think himself bound to conform to every signification of his majesty's pleasure." To the denunciations of the popular party he remained outwardly indifferent, strong in the supposed integrity of his official purpose. In time, he believed, the evil spoken of him by ambitious men would be forgotten, and his course would find vindication. The words of Bernard might well have been his:

He denies, that the opinion of the whole people of that Province can now be taken and ascertained, labouring as it does at present, under the baneful influence of a desperate faction, who by raising groundless fears and jealousies, by deluding one part of the people, and by intimidating the other part, has destroyed all real freedom, not only of action, but even of sentiment and opinion. But the Respondent doubts not but that his Administration has been approved by the generalty of the best and most respectable men of the Province.[16]

In spite of Hutchinson's endeavors to build up a prerogative party the drift of public opinion went steadily against him until he was convinced that he stood almost alone. "He was not sure of support from any one person in authority," he commented stoically, in telling of the tea troubles. The Council, the Assembly, the very constables were against him. Yet he went his way obstinately; he would fulfill to the last word the instructions of his superiors. The ministry might be unwise, but better the legal folly of Parliament than the madness of the democracy. To encroach upon the royal prerogative, Hutchinson believed was to endanger the nice balance of the constitution. He was convinced that "the present easy, happy model of government" was as near perfect as the ingenuity of Englishmen could devise; that the welfare of America was dependent upon a proper subordination of the colonies to the mother country; and that the popular party was plotting treason against their country and their king. The third volume of his history is a long argument to demonstrate the

[16] *Answer of Bernard to the Petition of the House of Representatives.*

wisdom of his own and Bernard's administrations. The liberal governor, Thomas Pownall, Hutchinson disliked, partly because of his easy familiar ways, but chiefly because he was not a prerogative man.[17] But if Pownall had been in Hutchinson's place, the history of the relations of Massachusetts and England would have run very differently.

It was his ingrained snobbery which, more than anything else, brought about his undoing. The aristocratic governor never differed with a lord, and rarely agreed with a commoner. It was intolerable to him that common fellows should dispute his reasoning or sit in judgment upon his official acts. It was their duty as loyal subjects to obey without question the mandates of the King's appointed spokesmen; and when town-meeting resolutions, put through by mechanics and petty tradesmen, criticised his conduct, or refused to accept the decision of the supreme court that the "Boston massacre" was not legally a "massacre," he saw in such acts only the madness of the mobocracy. That the people should suspect the probity of his majesty's judges was painful to him. As partisan bitterness increased, he became acutely suspicious of all who disagreed with him, and shut his mind against every argument. The debates and resolves in House and Council "abounded with duplicity and inconclusive reasonings." "The disingenuity and low craft, which appeared in so many of the messages, resolves, and other publick instruments," he commented, descended "to the level and vulgarity of a common newspaper essay." [18] To the leaders of the popular party, the group of keen debaters and parliamentarians who kept him constantly on the defense, he attributed an artful malignancy. The fathers of the Revolution do not appear to advantage in the pages of his history. The Otises had gone over to the opposition because the father had been disappointed on the occasion of Hutchinson's elevation to the coveted chief-justiceship. John Hancock's "ruling passion was a fondness for popular applause. . . . His natural powers were moderate, and had been very little improved by study." John Adams was a man whose "ambition was without bounds. . . . He could not look with complacency upon any man who was in possession of more wealth, more honours, or more knowledge than himself," and he went over to the opposition because of a slight

---

[17] For Hutchinson's statement of the Tory case, see Vol. III, pp. 352–355.
[18] *History of Massachusetts Bay*, Vol. III, p. 399.

upon him by refusal of a place on the bench. For Samuel Adams, his most relentless enemy, Hutchinson's hatred was boundless. He had defaulted as collector of taxes and for equivalent of his arrears of public money he had set up as defender of the public liberties, and he "made more converts by calumniating governors, and other servants of the crown, than by strength of reasoning." His main business in life was "robbing men of their characters."

It is unlikely that time will bring any vindication of the later career of Thomas Hutchinson. He was a stiff-necked official of scrupulous principle, whose principles were grossly reactionary. He was sincerely attached to the great ideal of imperial unity, but he conceived of that unity as embodied in the coercive sovereignty of the crown and parliament, with Tory gentlemen as exclusive administrators. Samuel Adams was not unjust in declaring, "It has been his principle from a boy that mankind are to be governed by the discerning few, and it has ever since been his ambition to be the hero of the few." Courteous and conscientious, with very considerable administrative ability, it was his misfortune to defend a social philosophy alien to the rough individualism of his fellow countrymen. He would think only in terms of imperial centralization, and they would think only in terms of local home rule. He conceived of the political state as a private preserve for gentlemen to hunt over, and they conceived of it as a free hunting-ground for all. He never understood the assertive, capitalistic America that was rising about him, and in joining issue with it he destroyed himself. "If we were not mad," he lamented, "I have no doubt we might enjoy all that liberty which can subsist with a state of government." It was the complaint of the Tory upon a democracy that preferred self-rule to the blessings of a trusteeship, which, like a lawyers' squabble, consumed the estate in fees. Quite evidently the "mobility," in the days of Thomas Hutchinson, was running into madness, for it demanded greater liberty than was compatible with a "state of government" sanctioned by crown officials—a fact which the royal governor grieved over but was helpless to restrain.

II

DANIEL LEONARD
Tory Lawyer

Probably the most finished prose writer, certainly one of the most cultivated minds, among the notable group of American Loyalists, was a young man of excellent family, who if events had turned out otherwise would have made a much greater name for himself. Daniel Leonard was a Harvard graduate and a member of the Boston bar, an effective speaker, of some weight in commonwealth politics, and aligned with Hutchinson, Sewall, and the crown party. In temperament and taste he seems to have been conspicuously aristocratic. He delighted in fine clothes and set up his coach and pair to drive from his countryseat to Boston— a gesture of opulence that excited the laughter of sober people, and led Mercy Warren to introduce him into her comedy, *The Group*, under the name of Beau Trumps. According to John Adams, who was a decided gossip, it was this cavalier love of display that led to his political undoing, overcoming his native sympathy with the party of revolution.

He wore a broad gold lace round the rim of his hat, he made his cloak glitter with laces still broader, he had set up his chariot and pair and constantly traveled in it from Taunton to Boston. This made the world stare— it was a novelty. Not another lawyer in the province, attorney or barrister, of whatever age, reputation, rank, or station, presumed to ride in a coach or chariot. The discerning ones soon perceived that wealth and power must have charms to a heart that delighted in so much finery, and indulged in such unusual expense. Such marks could not escape the vigilant eyes of the two arch-tempters, Hutchinson and Sewall, who had more art, insinuation, and address, than all the rest of their party.[19]

Under the pen name of "Massachusettensis," Leonard published a series of weekly letters addressed to "the Inhabitants of the Province of Massachusetts Bay," running from December 12, 1774, to April 3, 1775, a fortnight before the affair at Lexington. They were begun soon after the adjournment of the Continental Congress, and may be taken as the final statement of the Tory argument. They were exceedingly skillful partisan pamphlets, adapted with great adroitness to current prejudices and old loyalties. Their main appeal was to the psychology of the colonial,

[19] *Works*, Vol. X, pp. 194–195; quoted in Tyler, *Literary History of the American Revolution*, Vol. I, Chapter XVI.

and if the springs of that psychology had not been sapped by the rising liberalism, the appeal would have been extraordinarily persuasive. Probably the King's cause was never presented more convincingly, and the American Tories were delighted with the letters. "On my return from Congress," said John Adams, "I found the Massachusetts Gazette teeming with political specula- tions, and Massachusettensis shining like the moon among the lesser stars." [20] He at once replied to them under the pen name "Novanglus," beginning with a slashing attack in which the seventeenth-century republicans are called in to refute Leonard, and then reciting some plain facts about the British government and its American spokesman, which somewhat tarnished the latter's eulogies. But he soon strayed off into abstract disquisi- tion, and the controversy was brought to an abrupt end with the news from Lexington.

As in most Loyalist pamphlets, Leonard's appeal was primarily to the law and the constitution, and it is tagged with references to statutes like a proper lawyer's brief. But underlying the argument is a political philosophy which fairly represents the current Tory theory. The immediate purpose of the Letters was to make the rebellious spirit of the colonial Whigs toward their lawful sovereign appear both wicked and groundless, dangerous to the peace and well-being of society and inspired by the personal ambitions of demagogues. This major purpose involved him in two main arguments: first, on the heinousness of rebellion in general; and second, on the special heinousness of the Whig leaders. Leonard's political philosophy is implied rather than elaborated. With other American Loyalists he evaded broad principles; never- theless his total argument rests on a philosophical foundation too well known to be glossed over. He derived immediately from Hobbes, and he follows the *Leviathan* in his exaltation of the sovereign state. Men in a state of nature, he argued, live in a condition of anarchy, with the hand of all against all. Amid such chaos civilization is impossible, and the common need of security for person and property impelled men to erect the coercive state as an instrument of social protection. It first arose and has since been maintained from the necessity of holding in check the spirit of anarchy which continually threatens from the ambitions of designing men. This is the great danger that lies always in

[20] Preface to *Novanglus and Massachusettensis*, 1819.

wait, ready to destroy society. Government is a guarantee of the protection of the weak against the strong, and every friend of law and order must enlist his loyalty on the side of the lawful prince against all who would foment rebellion; for rebellion is the mischief-maker that unlooses all the evils of Pandora's box.

This was no more than the familiar stock-in-trade of the Tory, nevertheless Leonard becomes quite terrifying in describing the evils of sedition:

Rebellion is the most atrocious offence, that can be perpetrated by man, save those which are committed more immediately against the supreme Governor of the Universe, who is the avenger of his own cause. It dissolves the social band, annihilates the security resulting from law and government; introduces fraud, violence, rapine, murder, sacrilege, and the long train of evils, that riot, uncontrouled, in a state of nature. Allegiance and protection are reciprocal. The subject is bound by the compact to yield obedience to government, and in return, is entitled to protection from it; thus the poor are protected against the rich; the weak against the strong; the individual against the many; and this protection is guaranteed to each member, by the whole community. But when government is laid prostrate, a state of war, of all against all, commences; might overcomes right; innocence itself has no security, unless the individual sequesters himself from his fellowmen, inhabits his own cave, and seeks his own prey. This is what is called a state of nature.[21]

The "seeds of sedition" having been sown, they spring up and bring forth fruits of death; the "people are led to sacrifice real liberty to licentiousness, which gradually ripens into rebellion and civil war."

And what is still more to be lamented, the generality of the people, who are thus made the dupes of artifice, and the mere stilts of ambition, are sure to be losers in the end. The best they can expect, is to be thrown neglected by, when they are no longer wanted; but they are seldom so happy; if they are subdued, confiscation of estate and ignominious death are their portion; if they conquer, their own army is often turned upon them, to subjugate them to a more tyrannical government than that they rebelled against.[22]

Leonard then proceeds to supplement the Hobbesian argument by an elaborate appeal to the history of English law, and discovers ample sanction in a recital of a long list of statutory enactments and court decisions against the evil of sedition. As treason is the gravest social crime, so it has always been visited with the severest punishments. He states the history of legislation against treason,

[21] Letter of February 6, 1775, in *Novanglus and Massachusettensis*, pp. 187–188.
[22] *Ibid.*, pp. 152–153.

and points out how the statutes have been construed to reach so far as to embrace the gathering of private men in a warlike manner, with a design to redress public grievances or to better their economic condition. He makes a parade of the brutal laws of feudal times, and the decisions of Tudor and Stuart judges, justifying those pronouncements as a necessary defense of society against sedition-mongers and their subversive ambitions. By a natural transition he brings the argument home to his American readers. The aims and methods of the Whigs, he contends, constitute a clear violation of the law of treason. They are playing with the gallows, with their Committees of Correspondence—"the foulest, subtlest, and most venomous serpent that ever issued from the eggs of sedition," and the imperative need of the hour was to put a stop to all treasonable thought and action.

I saw the small seed of sedition, when it was implanted; it was, as a grain of mustard. I have watched the plant until it has become a great tree; the vilest reptiles that crawl upon the earth, are concealed at the root; the foulest birds of the air rest upon its branches. I now would induce you to go to work immediately with axes and hatchets, and cut it down, for a twofold reason; because it is a pest to society, and lest it be felled suddenly by a stronger arm and crush thousands in the fall.[23]

From the first major proposition, that all sedition is heinous, Leonard passed to his second, that the sedition of the American Whigs was peculiarly wicked, for it was grounded in no injustice on the part of England. If loyalty is the highest social virtue, that loyalty might justly be claimed by Great Britain as her due. "Has she not been a nursing mother to us, from the days of our infancy to this time? Has she not been indulgent almost to a fault?" The Whigs, he asserted broadly, have been patching together their supposed grievances out of cloth that never came from an English loom. It is the shoddiest of homespun, mean, and shameful.

We had always considered ourselves, as a part of the British empire, and the parliament, as the supreme legislature of the whole. Acts of parliament for regulating our internal policy were familiar. We had paid postage agreeable to act of parliament, . . . duties imposed for regulating trade, and even for raising a revenue to the crown without questioning the right, though we closely adverted to the rate or quantum. We knew that in all those acts of government, the good of the whole had been consulted, and whenever through want of information any thing grievous had been ordained, we were sure of obtaining redress by a proper representation of

[23] Letter of January 2, in *ibid.*, p. 159.

it. We were happy in our subordination; but in an evil hour, under the influence of a malignant planet, the design was formed of opposing the stamp-act, by a denial of the right of parliament to make it.[24]

Our patriots exclaim, "that humble and reasonable petitions from the representatives of the people have been frequently treated with contempt." This is as virulent a libel upon his majesty's government, as falsehood and ingenuity combined could fabricate. Our humble and reasonable petitions have not only been ever graciously received, when the established mode of exhibiting them has been observed, but generally granted. Applications of a different kind, have been treated with neglect, though not always with the contempt they deserved. These either originated in illegal assemblies, and could not be received without implicitly countenancing such enormities, or contained such matter, and were conceived in such terms, as to be at once an insult to his majesty, and a libel on his government. Instead of being decent remonstrances against real grievances, or prayers for their removal, they were insidious attempts to wrest from the crown, or the supreme legislature, their inherent, unalienable prerogatives or rights.[25]

The prerogative might not be argued, according to Leonard, nor the sovereignty of parliament discussed, for any such comment was "an insult to his majesty, and a libel on his government." The illegal Continental Congress had done both and thereby proved itself seditious.

The prince, or sovereign, as some writers call the supreme authority of a state, is sufficiently ample and extensive to provide a remedy for every wrong, in all possible emergencies and contingencies; and consequently a power, that is not derived from such authority, springing up in a state, must encroach upon it, and in proportion as the usurpation enlarges itself, the rightful prince must be diminished; indeed, they cannot long subsist together, but must continually militate, till one or the other be destroyed.[26]

The true animus of the Whig attack upon the nice balance of the British constitution Leonard professed to discover in a dangerous republican ambition. From the beginning there had been an excess of the democratic element in the charters and practice of many of the colonies; and this overbalance must in the end be rectified.

Our council boards are as destitute of the constitutional authority of the house of lords, as their several members are of the noble independence, and splendid appendages of peerage. The house of peers is the bulwark of the

[24] Letter of December 19, in *ibid.*, p. 147.
[25] Letter of March 27, in *ibid.*, pp. 217–218.
[26] *Ibid.*, p. 210.

British constitution, and through successive ages, has withstood the shocks of monarchy, and the sappings of democracy, and the constitution gained strength by the conflict.[27]

Lacking a peerage, which Leonard regrets, but which will come with time, American political practice is less stable than the English, more exposed to "the sappings of democracy"; but necessary steps have already been taken to stabilize it. The hands of the royal governor and judges have been strengthened against the democratic House, and "town meetings are restrained to prevent their passing traitorous resolves." The ideal towards which America must travel as fast as circumstance and the colonial temper will permit, is the wise balance of the English government, with local powers vested in colonial lords and commons, supervised by the King and the Imperial Parliament. In the midst of these present agitations, wickedly fomented by Whig smugglers—"a smuggler and a whig are cousin germans, the offspring of two sisters, avarice and ambition"—it should be remembered that "the terms whig and tory have been adopted according to the arbitrary use of them in this province, but they rather ought to be reversed; an American tory is a supporter of our excellent constitution, and an American whig a subverter of it." To bring these American subverters of the glorious British constitution to a sense of their obligations, Leonard refers them to the words of James Otis written ten years before:

It is a maxim, that the king can do no wrong; and every good subject is bound to believe his king is not inclined to do any. We are blessed with a prince who has given abundant demonstrations, that in all his actions, he studies the good of his people, and the true glory of his crown, which are inseparable. It would therefore be the highest degree of impudence and disloyalty, to imagine that the king, at the head of his parliament, could have any but the most pure and perfect intentions of justice, goodness and truth, that human nature is capable of. All this I say and believe of the king and parliament, in all their acts; even in that which so nearly affects the interests of the colonists; and that a most perfect and ready obedience is to be yielded to it while it remains in force. The power of parliament is uncontroulable but by themselves, and we must obey. They can only repeal their own acts. There would be an end of all government, if one or a number of subjects, or subordinate provinces should take upon them so far to judge of the justice of an act of parliament, as to refuse obedience to it. If there was nothing else to restrain such a step, prudence ought to do it, for forcibly resisting the parliament and the king's laws is high

[27] Letter of January 9, in *ibid.*, p. 171.

treason. Therefore let the parliament lay what burdens they please on us, we must, it is our duty to submit and patiently bear them, till they will be pleased to relieve us.[28]

The argument comes back finally to a threat; sovereignty rests not on good will but on coercion. The insincerity and unreality of the Tory appeal are only too patent. Those old pleaders were true to their breeding and their interests, for they regarded fact as little as a modern diplomat. They ignored or denied open and plain evidence. Nowhere, perhaps, does the weakness of Leonard's argument become more evident than in his refusal to admit the theoretical right of revolution. He professed allegiance to a king whose claim to the crown rested on revolution, and was justified by the apostle of Whiggery, Locke. But nowhere does he refer to Locke, and not until he was prodded by John Adams, who insisted that the Whig principles were "the principles of Aristotle and Plato, of Livy and Cicero, and Sydney, Harrington and Locke," did he concede that any other interpretation of revolution than the Hobbesian, was justifiable. In his last paper, of April 3, 1775, he replied to Adams thus:

I hold the rights of the people as sacred, and revere the principles, that have established the succession to the imperial crown of Great Britain, in the line of the illustrious house of Brunswick; but that the difficulty lies in applying them to the cause of the whigs . . . for admitting that the collective body of the people, that are subject to the British empire, have an inherent right to change their form of government, or race of kings, it does not follow, that the inhabitants of a single province, or of a number of provinces, or any given part under a majority of the whole empire, have such a right. By admitting that the less may rule or sequester themselves from the greater, we unhinge all government.[29]

By such logic does he whittle away the doctrine of the right of revolution. As a lawyer Daniel Leonard discovered a distinction between the Continental Congress of 1774 and the Revolutionary Convention of 1689, which rendered the former treasonable and the latter glorious. But the rising liberalism of America could see no such nice distinction, and a year later the brilliant young lawyer was forced to withdraw to Halifax. He was rewarded by a grateful King with the post of chief justice of Bermuda, lived to be nearly ninety, and died in London in 1829, one of the last of the exiled Loyalists.

[28] Letter of January 23, in *ibid.*, p. 181.   [29] *Ibid.*, p. 225.

JONATHAN BOUCHER

Tory Priest

The extremest expression of American Toryism came not un-
fittingly from an Anglican priest. The English church has always
been the mother of loyalty, and Jonathan Boucher of Virginia
and Maryland was the spiritual son of a notable line of bishops and
priests who upheld the royal prerogative through evil times and
good, throwing the august sanction of religion about the monarchical state. A fearless, capable, outspoken man was this English-
born southerner, taking counsel of his own thought, not over-
tolerant of those who differed with him, holding himself *in loco
parentis* to his parishioners, and exacting obedience from them.
He was another Increase Mather, with the same love of domination,
the same directness of purpose and strength of will. A man of
conspicuous parts and equally conspicuous position: not only a
clergyman, but a gentleman of affairs, owner of a large plantation
and many slaves, concerned with public business and a volunteer
statesman: a sort of unofficial adviser and secretary to draft provincial laws. Above all of independent mind. He would truckle
to no man, and he subjected the opinions of his neighbors to the
same scrutiny that he gave his own. For the popular orator and
the demagogue he had frank contempt, and mass prejudices and
mob power held no terrors for him.

There was both courage and futility in his free, outspoken career.
He refused to be intimidated or turned aside by popular disfavor.
"For more than six months I preached, when I did preach, with a
pair of loaded pistols lying on the cushions; having given notice
that if any one attempted, what had long been threatened, to drag
me out of the pulpit, I should think myself justified in repelling
violence by violence." One day he promptly knocked down a
burly blacksmith who had been set on him, but there came a time
when his church was filled with armed men, and his friends, fearing
for his life, held him back forcibly from mounting the pulpit. That
episode marked the end of his career in America. He had plainly
become obsolete, and he was driven home to his native England.
There as an old man, he published in 1797 thirteen sermons,
preached in America between 1763 and 1775, with an historical

preface, under the title, *A View of the Causes and Consequences of the American Revolution*, and dedicated to his old neighbor and friend, General Washington.

The political philosophy of Jonathan Boucher, as elaborated in these discourses, is frank and unequivocal. It is the voice of seventeenth-century Cavalier England, speaking to an alien people, bred up in another philosophy of government. Church and state, the Bible and the British constitution, the divine authority of God and the divine authority of the *status quo*, have got themselves curiously fused—and confused—in the mind of this disciple of Laud. It was the result not of ignorance but of conviction. When the revolutionary movement began to make a stir about him, the parish priest took the situation seriously and set about preparing himself to cope with it. Before then he had been no student of political theory, but now he turned to his books. "With sincerity in my heart, and my Bible in my hand," he said, "I sat down to explore the truth . . . to read and study what had been collected and laid down on the subject of government by writers . . . who got their materials . . . from the only pure sources of information, the law of God, and the law of the land." [30] The restriction in his choice of writers is suggestive of his bias; it eliminated at one stroke the main body of political speculation, not only the English thinkers of the preceding century, but the continental followers of the natural-rights school. Actually, however, Boucher did not limit himself so narrowly, for he refers frequently to Locke, and he was fairly familiar with the main doctrines of the revolutionary philosophy. But his most cherished discovery was Sir Robert Filmer's *Patriarcha*, and having digested Filmer's quaint theory, thenceforth he remained a confirmed patriarchist. The absurd jumble of Hebraic precedent and Tory prejudice which Filmer had laboriously put together and which Locke had knocked to pieces, was wholly convincing to this belated advocate of divine right, who proceeded to wipe the dust off the precious volume and expound its doctrines to an amazed congregation.

The single and sacred duty of the subject, Jonathan Boucher was convinced, is faithful obedience to the powers that are set over him. Those powers derive from God and are instituted for the subject's good. It follows, therefore, that the unpardonable sin is rebellion against lawfully constituted authority. "The doctrine

[30] *A View of the Causes*, etc., p. 591.

of *obedience for conscience sake*," he asserted, "is . . . the great *cornerstone* of all good government." [31] With Daniel Leonard he makes much of it, but he appeals rather to the sanctions of religion than to the law.

> Obedience to Government is every man's duty, because it is every man's interest; but it is particularly incumbent on Christians, because . . . it is enjoined by the positive commands of God. . . . If the form of government under which the good providence of God has been pleased to place us be mild and free, it is our duty to enjoy it with gratitude and with thankfulness. . . . If it be less indulgent and less liberal than in reason it ought to be, still it is our duty not to disturb the peace of the community, by becoming refractory and rebellious subjects, and *resisting the ordinances of God*.[32]

> Those great and good men, who, *like wise master-builders*, have from time to time so *fitly framed together* our glorious Constitution, well knew that *other sure foundation no man could lay* than . . . obedience, not only *for wrath*, but *for conscience sake*.[33]

Because this spirit of obedience was openly flouted in America, where every influence made for rough individual liberty, Jonathan Boucher feared for the future. Loose principles were abroad, notions of popular sovereignty under the majority will, that must give "rise to a low and unworthy opinion of government," unless the people were recalled to their duty. Particularly dangerous, he thought, was "that loose notion respecting government, which has long been disseminated among the people at large with incredible industry, namely, that all government is the mere creature of the people, and may therefore be tampered with, altered, newmodelled, set up or pulled down, just as tumultuous crowds of the most disorderly persons in the community (who on such occasions are always so forward to call themselves *the people*) may happen in some giddy moments of overheated ardour to determine." [34]

The unhappy results of such evil principles Boucher saw spread through America. With the insidious undermining of respect for law and government, the vicious conception of republicanism made its appearance. "Everything in America had a republican aspect," he commented in after years; and he agreed with Bernard that "the splitting America into many small governments weakened the governing power, and strengthened that of the people." [35] If Parliament had been wise enough to consolidate government in

---

31 *Ibid.*, p. 309.   32 *Ibid.*, pp. 507-508.   33 *Ibid.*, p. 306.
34 *Ibid.*, p. 313.   35 *Ibid.*, p. xliv.

America, drawing it to a single head, and investing it with dignity and authority, the country would not have become, like revolutionary France, "a mean and odious republic." As a minister and a loyal British subject, Jonathan Boucher would not seduce the American people "by any flowery panegyrics on liberty. Such panegyrics are the productions of ancient heathens and modern patriots: nothing of the kind is to be met with in the Bible, nor in the Statute Book. The word *liberty*, as meaning civil liberty, does not, I believe, occur in all the Scriptures." [36]

To respect the laws, is to respect liberty in the only rational sense in which the term can be used; for liberty consists in subserviency to law. "Where there is no law," says Mr. Locke, "there is no freedom." . . . True liberty, then, is a liberty to do everything that is right, and the being restrained from doing anything that is wrong.[37]

The evils which flow from disrespect for authority carry much further than the unsettling of the political *status quo;* they end by overturning the entire social order. If any group or class rejects the divine plan according to which God has set each in its due place, society as a whole is involved in strife that may lapse into anarchy. It was an unhappy scene, prophesying an unhappier future, that the minister beheld in contemporary America.

There never was a time when a whole people were so little governed by settled good principles. . . . Both employers and the employed, much to their mutual shame and inconvenience, no longer live together with anything like attachment and cordiality on either side; and the laboring classes, instead of regarding the rich as their guardians, patrons, and benefactors, now look on them as so many overgrown colossuses whom it is no demerit in them to wrong. A still more general . . . topic of complaint is, that the lower classes, instead of being industrious, frugal, and orderly (virtues so peculiarly becoming their station in life) are become idle, improvident, and dissolute.[38]

With social morality thus dangerously undermined, the Americans were a natural prey to demagogues, who filled the land with their clamor of patriotism and liberty. The situation in Virginia was peculiarly dangerous by reason of long-standing debts to English merchants which the planters were unable to pay; they found themselves in consequence, impaled on the horns of an unhappy dilemma, "to be loyal and be ruined, or to rebel and be damned." [39]

Instructed by the colonial troubles, Jonathan Boucher elaborated

[36] *Ibid.*, p. 504.
[38] *Ibid.*, p. 309.
[37] *Ibid.*, pp. 509 and 511.
[39] *Ibid.*, Preface, p. xlii.

a theory of the true origin and purpose of government, a theory taken straight out of Filmer, which he expands thus:

> As soon as there were some to be governed, there were also some to govern. . . . The first father was the first king: and . . . it was thus that all government originated, and monarchy is the most ancient form.[40]

> The glory of God is much concerned, that there should be good government in the world: it is, therefore, the uniform doctrine of the Scriptures, that it is under the deputation and authority of God alone that *kings reign and princes decree justice.* Kings and princes (which are only other words for supreme magistrates) were doubtless created and appointed, not so much for their own sakes, as for the sake of the people committed to their charge: yet they are not, therefore, the creatures of the people. So far from deriving their authority from any supposed consent or suffrage of men, they receive their commission from Heaven; they receive it from God, the source and original of all power.[41]

Instituted by God and functioning under divine sanction, government becomes, therefore, a divine instrument, for the security of which He is greatly concerned: "Everything our blessed Lord either said or did, pointedly tended to discourage the disturbing a settled government." "Unless we are good subjects, we cannot be good Christians." Jesus "thought it would be better, both for Judea in particular, and for the world in general, that . . . the people should not be distracted by a revolution, and . . . that there should be no precedent to which revolutionists might appeal." "The only very intolerable grievance in government is, when men allow themselves to disturb and destroy the peace of the world, by vain attempts to render that perfect, which the laws of our nature have ordained to be imperfect." "To suffer nobly indicates more greatness of mind than can be shown by acting valiantly."[42]

Jonathan Boucher was the high Tory of the Tory cause in America. He refused to strike his flag to the pirate craft of republicanism; he would not truckle to newfangled notions; but stood up stoutly to be counted for God and the King. In laying bare the heart of Toryism, he unwittingly gave aid and comfort to the detested cause of liberalism. It is reasonable to assume that such militant loyalty to the outworn doctrine of passive submission was a real disservice to the ministry, for it revealed the prerogative in a light peculiarly offensive to American prejudices. What a godsend to the liberals was such doctrine on the lips of so eminent a divine!

[40] *Ibid.*, p. 525.   [41] *Ibid.*, p. 534.   [42] *Ibid.*, pp. 535, 538, 542, 543.

CHAPTER III

JOHN DICKINSON

The Mind of the American Whig

For many colonials it was a hard and bitter choice that was thrust upon them by the political situation. They had no wish to choose between loyalty to the British Empire and love for their native land. So long as the quarrel remained a legal dispute over parliamentary encroachments, colonial sentiment was fairly united in opposition to the ministerial policy; differences of opinion arose over methods of defense, rather than the need of it. The threatened loss of home rule drew together radical and conservative. Although Governor Hutchinson asserted that the feeling against England ·was the work of a small populistic element—"in Massachusetts Bay the exception to the constitutional authority of Parliament was first taken, and principally supported, by men who were before discontented" [1]—it is clear that the active Tory party numbered at first few more than the royal officials and their beneficiaries. But when it came to the point of severing colonial relations with the mother country, comparatively few among the upper classes in the northern and middle colonies went with the party of independence. The moderate men, the conciliationists, were crushed between the two extremes, and the Tory party was greatly increased in numbers and influence.

Of this moderate party of conciliationists, the outstanding figure during the years of tedious debate was John Dickinson, of Philadelphia. His *Letters from a Pennsylvania Farmer*, published between December 2, 1767, and February 15, 1768, created considerable stir both in America and England, and if Hutchinson may be trusted, they "formed a temporary political creed for the colonies." Later he was chief draftsman of a notable series of state papers: the Declaration of Rights of the Stamp Act Congress; the two Petitions to the King and the Address to the Inhabitants of Quebec of the first Continental Congress; and finally the Articles

[1] *History of Massachusetts Bay*, Vol. III, p. 257.

of Confederation. Professor Tyler has fastened upon him the title of "penman of the Revolution"; but a juster title, and more in accord with the facts, would be "spokesman of the Colonial Whigs." From his first entrance into public life to the adoption of the Constitution, Dickinson was a consistent advocate of the political philosophy of which John Pym was the early representative, Locke the philosophical defender, and Pitt the parliamentary advocate—a philosophy which he accepted as the final embodiment of the long struggle for English freedom.

English Whiggery has been fortunate in its advocates. It has been expounded with great fervor and glossed with much eloquence. Its ends have been so persistently proclaimed as at one with the cause of human liberty, that in the mind of English-speaking people it early became synonymous with English liberalism. In so far as it represented a protest against divine right, such an interpretation was historically just. It was the expression of a rising class, and every rising class in its ostensible program professes to be liberal. But in the outcome Whiggery proved to be very different from generic liberalism. Examined critically the program of Whiggery is seen to have been compounded of substantial economic interests. Although the Whig party created the modern House of Commons and ministerial government, and wrote into the British constitution the principle of no taxation without representation, back of such revolutionary changes was a middle-class, property theory of society. It laid down as the first principle of political science the dogma that government is instituted for the protection of property; and it advanced by inevitable stages to the position that government should use its powers to extend the field of profitable operations and safeguard exploitation, the natural outcome of which was a policy of imperialism. On the pretense of furthering human liberty it carried the British flag and British goods to the ends of the earth. The great Pitt, grandson of the unscrupulous exploiter of India, completed the work begun by John Pym more than a century before; the American Revolution was the natural sequence of an imperialistic policy begun by Cromwell's Navigation Act, which, aimed immediately at the Dutch carriers, put the power of the government behind British shipping to the disadvantage of American competitors.

The philosophy of Whiggery had spread widely in America before the Revolution and numbered among its advocates probably the great majority of thoughtful Americans. Of these John Dickinson became the best known, although he was certainly not the ablest—less able, indeed, than his fellow Marylander, Daniel Dulany. Of Quaker extraction, Dickinson was a country gentleman who inherited broad acres, an honorable name, and high social position. His dignified standing was further assured by his marriage with the only surviving child of Isaac Norris, long Speaker of the Pennsylvania Assembly, and the most influential amongst a little group of wealthy merchants who had long ruled the commonwealth in patriarchal fashion. By his wife he came into possession of Fairhill, a country place of several hundred acres on the outskirts of Philadelphia, one of the show places of the city, of which the mansion with its stately façade, its waxed floors and red-cedar wainscoting, its books and paintings and statuary, its setting of gardens and fishponds and conservatories, was vastly impressive to a world that loved dignified display.

With such advantages of wealth and position he could hardly fail to get on in his profession, and within a short time after his return from the Inns of Court at London, where he had his training in the law, he became one of the leaders of the Philadelphia bar and was soon deep in commonwealth politics. He was a gentleman in a society of gentlemen and preferment came easily to him. His natural parts were respectable, he had improved himself by considerable reading in history and politics, he possessed a cultivated pen and some facility in debate. He understood commercial problems, could talk trade, was ready with statistics of imports and exports, and was an advocate of the paper money which Philadelphia merchants had discovered to be a stimulus to business. Among his intimate friends were Robert Morris, Thomas Willing, and George Clymer, representatives of the younger generation of Philadelphians, whose speculative enterprises were not approved by their conservative elders. And so by consequence he became the spokesman of the mercantile interests in their remonstrance against the ministerial policies.

But Dickinson was more than a legal adviser to clients who were in trade. As lawyer and statesman he was true to the best traditions of the English law and the British constitution, faithful to what he conceived to be the larger interests of the British Empire. In all his public acts he was animated by a scrupulous sense of duty, swerving no whit from the line of conduct marked out by his principles in spite of the clamor of opposition. From first to last he seems to have been guided by a fine sense of responsible stewardship that came to him from his English heritage. Certainly the dignity of John Dickinson and the integrity of his political career suffer little by contrast with certain popular representatives who governed their conduct by expediency rather than principle. The great ideal of imperial unity possessed him completely, and he would do nothing to bring it into jeopardy. He sacrificed his great influence with the radicals by his refusal to go with the majority for independence; he would not assist in disrupting the British Empire even though he could not preserve it. The refusal was difficult and it destroyed his popularity in a moment. He withdrew from active participation in political affairs, and for years afterwards, to the eyes of former associates, his conduct seemed to have been pusillanimous.

By temperament and breeding Dickinson was a conservative, and this native bias was emphasized by his English training in the law. The lawyers of the middle and southern colonies were far better trained than those of New England. Many were from the Inns of Court, where they had steeped themselves in the Common Law and had imbibed profound respect for the orderly processes of English legal procedure. They found intellectual satisfaction in tracing the evolution of constitutional practice, and their methods of thought were too strictly legal to suffer them to stray into the domain of extra-legal political speculation. Their appeal was to the law and the constitution; never to abstract principles. If, on the other hand, the revolutionary leaders of New England—and Virginians like Jefferson and Patrick Henry—were poorer lawyers they were better political scientists, for their legal training had been too casual and too scanty to contract their minds to statutes and precedents. Jefferson and John Adams were alike in this respect; their interests were speculative rather than legal; and they wrote more convincingly when defending the principles of Locke than in expounding Coke.

But John Dickinson remained always the lawyer. The English political thinkers of the seventeenth century scarcely touched the fringe of his mind. In consequence his writings are a long constitutional argument. He rarely refers to political authorities. The philosophy of Locke—whom he had read—is largely ignored, and Hume—"this great man whose political speculations are so much admired"—is quoted only in support of a constitutional interpretation. "The constitutional modes of relief are those I wish to see pursued on the present occasion," he insisted in reply to the natural-rights advocates, and the attitude is eloquent of the man. This scrupulous legalism he carried to such lengths that when the new constitution for Pennsylvania was adopted he refused to take office under it because he doubted the legality of the convention that framed it.

With such temperament and training Dickinson would seem to have had the making of an excellent Tory in him. What cause had he to quarrel with Great Britain, and why should he have risked his lot with the party of protest? It was not because he denied the ministerial theory of parliamentary sovereignty in America, for he acknowledged both the fact and the necessity for such sovereignty:

> He, who considers these provinces as states distinct from the *British Empire*, has very slender notions of *justice*, or of their *interests*. We are but parts of a *whole* and therefore there must exist a power somewhere to preside, and preserve the connection in due order. This power is lodged in the parliament; and we are as much dependent on *Great-Britain* as a perfectly free people can be on another. [2]

Nor was it because of old trade grievances—shipping restrictions, the spying of customs officers, prohibitions laid on manufactures, and the like. He accepted without challenge the English mercantile view of the economic relations of colonies to the mother country, and he professed to see in existing trade regulations only the incidental and necessary burdens of a system both salutary and just; he had no protest to urge against the principle of the Navigation Acts.

> Colonies have been settled by the nations of *Europe* for the purposes of trade. These purposes were to be attained, by the colonies raising for their mother country those things which she did not produce herself; and by supplying themselves from her with things they wanted. These were the *national objects*, in the commencement of our colonies, and have been uniformly so in their promotion. . . . The parent country, with undeviating prudence and virtue, attentive to the first principles of colonization, drew to herself the benefits she might reasonably expect, and preserved to her children the blessings, on which those benefits were founded. She made laws, obliging her colonies to carry to her all those products which she wanted for her own use; and all those raw materials

---

[2] "Farmer's Letters," in *Works*, Vol. I, p. 312.

which she chose herself to work up. Besides this restriction, she forbad them to procure *manufactures* from any other part of the globe, or even the *products* of *European* countries, which alone could rival her, without first being brought to her. In short, by a variety of laws, she regulated their trade in such a manner as she thought most conducive to their mutual advantage, and her own welfare.[3]

Not only did Dickinson concede to the mother country the right to regulate the entire system of colonial trade and industry to the primary advantage of British merchants, even going so far as to justify it by a false historical explanation of the rise of the colonies; not only did he profess to believe that such regulation had been exercised in a spirit of unselfish concern for the well-being of the empire; but he professed a faith in the King and the English people that suggests Hutchinson and Bernard. Consider such naïve adulation as the following:

We have an excellent prince, in whose good dispositions towards us we may confide. We have a generous, sensible and humane nation, to whom we may apply. They may be deceived. They may, by artful men, be provoked to anger against us. I cannot believe they will be cruel or unjust; or that their anger will be implacable. Let us behave like dutiful children, who have received unmerited blows from a beloved parent. Let us complain to our parent; but let our complaints speak at the same time the language of affliction and veneration.[4]

With so much conceded, what ground of serious quarrel remained? What was there to justify an American protest against the parliamentary program? Nothing less than the vital principle of taxation. In this matter the ministerial policy overrode the fundamental tenet of Whiggery. The situation was critical, for if the Tories denied the validity of the Whiggish principle in dealing with the colonies, they might deny it at home and the old battle of 1688 must be fought over. The right of control of the public purse by a chamber in which the property owners were represented, and which they would dominate, was a principle too vital to be yielded, and the English Whigs in Parliament, led by Pitt and Camden, took vigorous issue with the ministerial tax proposals. To American Whigs the proposed innovation was a calamity. To suffer control of the American purse to pass out of their hands into those of a group beyond their reach meant a return to a system of Tory spoliation; it meant that property and the rule of property

[3] *Ibid.*, p. 337.   [4] *Ibid.*, p. 327.

in America were threatened. To the colonial Whig the constitutional representative chamber could be no other than the assembly of the commonwealth of which he was a taxpayer. The English Parliament was alien if not hostile to his interests; and if the right of imposing taxes upon the colonies were held to lie in this overseas body, the colonials would find themselves in the identical position of their ancestors of the days of King Charles. No longer masters of their property, they would not be a free people.

All this John Dickinson understood perfectly, and as a large property owner he hastened to the defense of the principle of self-taxation. He proposed to show that the policy of the ministry, in advancing the new tax program, was a usurpation of power and a violation of the constitutional rights of American property owners; and that as such it should be resisted on constitutional grounds. This is the burden of the celebrated *Letters from a Pennsylvania Farmer*. In arguing their case the American debaters were embarrassed by a long series of precedents which seemed to prove that Parliament possessed sovereignty over the colonies; that such sovereignty had in fact been repeatedly acknowledged; and that a hundred years of fiscal legislation, unchallenged heretofore, had clearly established the parliamentary right of taxation. To this difficult point Dickinson directed his argument. The real point at issue, he contended, lay in the fundamental distinction between a tax and an imposition; Parliament possessed the constitutional right to impose the latter, but not the former. An imposition, he pointed out, is a fiscal arrangement made by the proper representatives, primarily "for the regulation of trade," and with a view to the general interests of the whole; whereas a tax is a "gift of the people to the crown, to be employed for public uses." The one is regulatory in intent, imposed in a paternal spirit; and though the result may lessen or increase the opportunity of the individual or the community to acquire property, it does not take away what has already been got; whereas a tax reaches into the pocket of the individual and takes from him what belongs to him alone. Unless the subject "give and grant of his own free will," such a tax had long been held unconstitutional. Of necessity, every tax must be internal, and since by their charter governments the colonies were granted the right to impose "internal taxes," Parliament has no right to impose them.

A "TAX" means an imposition to raise money. Such persons therefore as speak of *internal* and external "TAXES," I pray may pardon me, if I object to that expression, as applied to the privileges and interests of these colonies. There may be *internal* and *external* IMPOSITIONS, founded on *different principles*, and having *different tendencies*, every "tax" being an imposition, tho' every imposition is not a "tax." But *all taxes* are founded on the same *principles*; and have the *same tendency*. External impositions, for the regulation of our trade, do not "grant to his Majesty *the property of the colonies.*" They only *prevent the colonies acquiring property*, in things not necessary, in a manner judged to be injurious to the welfare of the whole empire. But the last statute respecting us, "grants to his Majesty *the property of the colonies,*" by laying duties on the manufactures of *Great-Britain* which they MUST take, and which she settled on them, on purpose that they SHOULD take. What *tax* can be more internal than this? Here is money drawn, *without their consent*, from a society, who have constantly enjoyed a constitutional mode of raising all money among themselves.[5]

This line of argument was not original with Dickinson. It had earlier been elaborated by Daniel Dulany of Maryland, in an able pamphlet,[6] which had provided argument to Pitt for his speech on the repeal of the Stamp Act.[7] Dickinson in turn quoted from Pitt's speech in support of his position.[8] How intimate was the connection between English and American Whigs, and how like was their reasoning, is made clear from a passage of a later speech by Pitt which Dickinson quoted in the preface to a collected edition of his works issued in 1801:

This universal opposition to your arbitrary system of taxation, might have been foreseen; it was obvious from the nature of things, and from the nature of man, and *above all* . . . from the spirit of WHIGGISM flourishing in *America*. The spirit which *now* pervades *America*, is *the same* which formerly opposed loans, benevolences, and ship-money in this country; is *the same spirit* which roused all *England* to action at the revolution, and which established at a remote era, your liberties, on the basis of that grand fundamental maxim of the constitution, that no subject of *England* shall be taxed, but by his own consent. To maintain this principle, is the *common cause* of the WHIGS, on the other side of the *Atlantic*, and on this. *It is liberty to liberty engaged.* In this great cause they are immoveably allied. It is the alliance of *God* and *nature*, immutable, eternal, fixed as the firmament of heaven. As an *Englishman*, I recognize to the *Americans*, their supreme unalterable right of property. As an *American*, I would

[5] *Ibid.*, pp. 332–333.
[6] *Considerations on the Propriety of Imposing Taxes in the British Colonies, for the Purpose of Raising a Revenue by Act of Parliament.*
[7] See Tyler, *Literary History of the American Revolution*, Vol. I, p. 111.
[8] *Works*, Vol. I, p. 320.

equally recognize to *England*, her supreme right of regulating commerce and navigation. This distinction is involved in the abstract nature of things; property is private, individual, absolute: the touch of another annihilates it. Trade is an extended and complicated consideration; it reaches as far as ships can sail, or winds can blow; it is a vast and various machine. To regulate the numberless movements of its several parts, and combine them into one harmonious effect, for the good of the whole, requires the superintending wisdom and energy of the supreme power of the empire. On this grand practical distinction, then, let us rest: taxation is theirs, commercial regulation is ours. As to metaphysical refinements, attempting to shew, that the *Americans* are equally free from legislative controul, and commercial restraint, as from taxation, for the purpose of revenue, I pronounce them futile, frivolous, and groundless.[9]

How characteristic of Pitt is the shrewd purpose, covered over with pretentious rhetoric, to seize the imperialistic substance of trade control for the London merchants, and graciously yield in the name of liberty, the shadow of taxation!

Discussion of abstract rights interested Dickinson no more than it did Pitt; but he cared greatly for English liberty, by which he meant the rights of propertied gentlemen recognized by the British constitution, for which his ancestors had struggled. He had no wish to enlarge those rights, for he believed they were adequate to the well-being of Englishmen. No thought of a republican form of government crossed his mind. He had no sympathy with democracy; he believed in a "mixed government" as exemplified in the British system; and while he was not an outspoken advocate of an American peerage, he would have approved of its institution. Like so many upper-class Americans, he was English as well as colonial; he could not conceive that the heritage of England to her sons was circumscribed by geographical lines, and he habitually thought and spoke in terms of the British Empire, and never in local terms. What he most feared was a misunderstanding that would widen into rupture. There is more than a hint of the doctrine of passive resistance in his counsel of moderation:

The cause of *liberty* is a cause of too much dignity to be sullied by turbulence and tumult. It ought to be maintained in a manner suitable to her nature. Those who engage in it, should breathe a sedate, yet fervent spirit, animating them to actions of prudence, justice, modesty, bravery, humanity, and magnanimity. . . . I hope, my dear countrymen, that you will, in every colony, be on your guard against those, who may at any time endeavour to stir you up, under pretense of patriotism, to any measures

[9] *Ibid.*, pp. xv-xvii.

disrespectful to our Sovereign and our mother country. Hot, rash, disorderly proceedings, injure the reputation of a people, as to wisdom, valour, and virtue, without procuring them the least benefit. I pray GOD, that he may be pleased to inspire you and your posterity, to the latest ages, with a spirit of which I have an idea, that I find a difficulty to express. To express it in the best manner I can, I mean a spirit, that shall so guide you, that it will be impossible to determine whether an *American's* character is most distinguishable, for its loyalty to his Sovereign, his duty to his mother country, his love of freedom, or his affection for his native soil [10]

In these earlier years of the controversy Dickinson seems to have remained placidly unaware of the sordid realities of parliamentary huckstering, the details of which Franklin was daily noting in his letters. He seems honestly to have believed in the justice and good intentions of the King and his ministers, and he felt little sympathy for the New England malcontents. But as the debate dragged on, and the English politicians in whose rectitude he had professed confidence, clearly were playing into the hands of British trading interests, going so far as to seek to bolster up the falling fortunes of the East India Company at the expense of colonial merchants, he was impelled to speak with plebeian warmth. His *Two Letters on the Tea Tax*, written in November, 1773, are as vigorous in denunciation as Samuel Adams could have penned.

Five Ships, loaded with TEA, on their Way to *America*, and this with a View not only to *enforce* the *Revenue Act*, but to *establish* a *Monopoly* for the *East-India Company*, who have espoused the Cause of the Ministry; and hope to repair their broken Fortunes by the Ruin of *American* freedom and Liberty! No Wonder the Minds of the People are exasperated . . . to a degree of Madness. . . . Pray have you heard, whether *they* and the *Ministers* have not *made a Property* of US, and whether WE, our WIVES and CHILDREN, together, with the HARD EARNED FRUITS OF OUR LABOUR, are not *made over* to this almost *bankrupt Company*, to augment their Stock, and to *repair* their *ruined Fortunes?* Justice seems to have forsaken the old World. . . . The Rights of free States and Cities are swallowed up in Power. Subjects are considered as Property. . . . Are we . . . to be given up to the Disposal of the *East-India Company?* . . . . Their conduct in Asia, for some Years past, has given ample Proof, how little they regard the Laws of Nations, the Rights, Liberties, or Lives of Men. They have levied War, excited Rebellions, dethroned lawful Princes, and sacrificed Millions for the Sake of Gain . . . hackneyed as they are in Murders, Rapine, and Cruelty, [they] would sacrifice the Lives of Thousands to preserve their Trash, and enforce their measures.[11]

[10] "Farmer's Letters," in *Works*, Vol. I, pp. 324-325.
[11] *Works*, Vol. I, pp. 459-461.

The ideal of a beneficent British Empire, extending English freedom through the world, appealed to the imagination of Dickinson; but the reality of British imperialism, "hackneyed in murders, rapine and cruelty," seeking to extend its exploitation to America, striking at the trade interests of Philadelphia and his merchant friends, was enough to disturb his legal calm. What fate awaited American rights and liberties if the London imperialists were permitted to prey upon them, he began to comprehend. The bones would be picked clean, and America would become another India. It was the deepening fear of such a possibility that sapped Dickinson's loyalty, and reconciled him to independence after the thing was done.

The later years of Dickinson were happier than those of the middle period. The conservative reaction that set in with the conclusion of peace carried the emerging party of nationalism back to the position of Whiggery, which Dickinson had tenaciously occupied. The leaders of that party were coming to agree on the necessity for a closer alignment in defense of property rule, and they gladly accepted Dickinson as an ally and co-worker. He was chosen a member of the Constitutional Convention, and there found a congenial audience for the exposition of his political principles. In the debates he spoke as a high Federalist who would like to go further toward the model of the British system than the state of the public mind rendered expedient. A strong and stable government, he believed, depended upon a just balance of king, lords, and commons.

A limited monarchy he considered as *one* of the best governments in the world. He was not certain that the same blessings were derivable from any other form. It was certain that equal blessings had never yet been derived from any of the republican forms. A limited monarchy, however, was out of the question. The spirit of the times, the state of our affairs, forbade the experiment, if it were desirable. Was it possible, moreover, in the nature of things, to introduce it, even if these objects were less insuperable? A house of nobles was essential to such a government. Could these be created by a breath, or by a stroke of the pen? No. They were the growth of ages, and could only arise under a complication of circumstances none of which existed in this country. But, though a form the most perfect, *perhaps*, in itself, be unattainable, we must not despair.[12]

Granted the necessity of a republican form of government, the question so vital to Whiggery remained, how could property secure

[12] *Elliot's Debates*, Vol. V, p. 148.

and maintain a commanding position in the government? The reply was obvious; it must be through limitation of suffrage rights. If the vote could be restricted to property holders, even though small freeholders were included, the common rights of property would be secure.

> Mr. Dickinson had a very different idea of the tendency of vesting the rights of suffrage in the freeholders of the Country. He considered them as the best guardians of liberty; And the restriction of the right to them as a necessary defence agst. the dangerous influence of those multitudes without property & without principle, with which our country like all others, will in time abound.[13]

A further safeguard offered in the proper constitution of the Senate. As a representative of a small state, Dickinson was concerned that the several states should enjoy a parity of power in the upper house, as he was concerned that the Senate should provide a safeguard for property interests. It must be rendered secure from factional unrest and democratic aggression. He was very likely at one with his friend George Clymer, in holding that "a representative of the people is appointed to think *for* and not *with* his constituents"; and to the end that the right persons should be chosen to do the national thinking, he laid down the principle that, "In the formation of the Senate, we ought to carry it through such a refining process as will assimilate it as nearly as may be to the House of Lords in England."[14]   Such expressions throw sufficient light upon Dickinson's opinions of democratic government, but they do not prepare us for a curious inconsistency that marked his last years, namely, his friendship for Jefferson and his sympathy with the Jeffersonian program. The reasons for this strange shift are not clear, but it is generally attributed to his fear of consolidation that might end in subordinating the small states to the greater ones. It certainly was not due to any sympathy with agrarianism.

Dickinson was in no sense a serious political thinker. He was a cultivated lawyer who defended with skill and grace a ready-made philosophy, unconcerned about the social significance of that philosophy. Scarcely anywhere else in his writings does he show to such poor advantage as in the nine *Letters of Fabius* written in defense of the Constitution during the great debate. There is

---

[13] *Ibid.*   [14] *Ibid.*, Vol. I, p. 163.

in them not a single illuminating comment. His most anxious
concern is shown in his reply to George Mason's direct charge, that
the "government will commence in a moderate aristocracy; it is
at present impossible to foresee whether it will, in its operation,
produce a monarchy, or a corrupt oppressive aristocracy." [15]
After searching the records of the past he concludes that "the
uniform tenor of history . . . holds up the *licentiousness* of the
people, and *turbulent temper* of some of the states, as *the only causes
to be dreaded*, not the conspiracies of federal officers." [16]   The
argument had been somewhat staled by Federalistic repetition,
but Dickinson soberly accepted it as sound historical interpretation.   His cleverest defense he found in an appeal to the analogy of
the British constitution, which has only one democratic branch,
and that "diseased" by inadequate representation, to withstand
the power and influence of king and lords; if English liberty has
been thus safeguarded, what danger can threaten America with
"a constitution and government, every branch of which is so
extremely popular"?[17]

However greatly the writings of Dickinson, from the Farmer's
Letters to the *Letters of Fabius*, may have appealed to Whiggish
lawyers, it is inconceivable that they should have appealed to the
rank and file of Americans.   As an eighteenth-century gentleman
he little understood the spirit of liberalism that was stirring in
many minds; he did not sympathize with the turbulent forces that
were driving towards a different social order; and in consequence
his technical arguments seem today curiously old-fashioned.
Franklin's common sense kept him a realist; but Dickinson's loyalty made him an idealist, incapable of understanding current economic forces either in England or America.   The colonial was so
ingrained in his habits of thought that it was hard for him to become an American.   So long as it was politic to profess loyalty to
England while remonstrating against ministerial policies, John
Dickinson was the man for the business.   But when it became
necessary to throw aside the mask of loyal professions, to stand
up and fight, he was thrust aside to make room for more vigorous
spokesmen.   No doubt there were desirable things which the radicals overlooked; no doubt the ideal of imperial unity, of a world-
wide federation of the several bodies of Englishmen, possessed a

[15] Quoted in Ford, *Pamphlets on the Constitution*, p. 332.
[16] *Ibid.*, p. 200.   [17] *Ibid.*, p. 212.

grandeur which ardent patriots held too cheap. But that ideal did not prevail, despite Dickinson's earnest endeavors; and in the new order which arose he probably never felt quite at home, or was free from a lingering regret. He belonged still in that older world in which he was bred.

CHAPTER IV

SAMUEL ADAMS

The Mind of the American Democrat

In the history of the rise of political democracy in America Samuel Adams occupies a distinguished place. He was by no means the first American to espouse the democratic cause, but he was the first to conceive the party machinery to establish it in practice. The single purpose of his life was the organization of the rank and file to take over control of the political state. He was the instrument of a changing world that was to transfer sovereignty from the aristocratic minority to the democratic majority. Political sovereignty inheres potentially in the mass will of the people; but if that will is restrained from exercising its strength by an undemocratic psychology, it remains powerless in presence of an organized minority. The America in which Samuel Adams labored was ripe to throw off the inhibitions of the popular will; and it was his perception of that fact, and the tenacity and skill with which he cajoled the mass to "make a push for perfect political liberty," that made him an outstanding figure in our history. In his hands the majority will became in reality the sovereign will. But before he could wield it he must create it; and before he could create it he must understand the mass mind. He must turn popular prejudice to his own purpose; he must guide the popular resentment at grievances into the way of revolution; he must urge the slow moving mass forward until it stood on the threshold of independence, beyond which lay the ultimate goal of his ambitions, the democratic state. And so, in pursuit of his life purpose, Samuel Adams became a master political strategist, the first of our great popular leaders.

The modern term, professional agitator, most adequately characterizes him. He was an intriguing rebel against every ambition of the regnant order. He hated every sort of aristocratic privilege, whether in the form of overseas prerogative or in the later guise of native Federalism; it must be swept away and a new, democratic order take its place. In the pursuit of this great end he daily counseled treason and made rebellion his business. Loyalty to the government *de facto* was no virtue in his political ethics; he was not frightened into conformity by the stigma attaching to the term rebel. America was founded in rebellion, he well knew, and it should continue in rebellion till every false loyalty was cast off and concern for the common well-being accepted as the single loyalty worthy of respect. "What has commonly been called rebellion in the people," he commented wisely, "has often been nothing else but a manly and glorious struggle in opposition to the lawless power of rebellious Kings and Princes." [1] He was the outstanding example in his day of the militant idealist to whom the dissemination of unrest was a matter of principle. No cause goes forward without its leaders, and democratic America owes Samuel Adams a debt which it has too grudgingly acknowledged.

He was born and grew up in an atmosphere of politics. His father was a prosperous, well-read gentleman who found politics a pleasant avocation; he established the Caucus Club for political discussion, and became one of the leaders of the popular party that opposed the Tory group, gathered about the royal officials. Its personnel can only be guessed at, but it was probably composed of small merchants, with a following of mechanics and other unimportant folk. It seems to have been greatly interested in currency reform, and the elder Adams was one of the principal organizers and stockholders of the Land Bank, a project for increasing the money of the commonwealth. The institution was roughly liquidated by government decree at the instigation of commercial rivals interested in "tight money"; the father lost heavily and the son was pretty much ruined by later attempts at arbitrary collection on his stock. It seems to have been a petty and altogether sordid move on the part of government, in which Hutchinson played an important part. With the loss of his money Samuel Adams, Jr., settled down to a meager, somewhat precarious existence, preferring politics to profits, and began that long, arduous career which resulted so momentously for America.

He had taken his two degrees at Harvard in the expectation of becoming a minister; but while an undergraduate he was more interested in the political classics than in theology, and he rejected the ministry for the law. But a brief experience with Coke sufficed, and he turned to more congenial fields. With a group of like-

[1] *Works*, Vol. II, p. 269.

minded young men he founded in 1748 *The Public Advertiser*, a weekly magazine of politics. In the essays which as a young man of twenty-six he wrote for that paper, he expounded a political creed frankly liberal. He began as he ended, anti-Tory and pro-democratic. From then till the beginning of the tax troubles he was a tireless contributor to the newspapers, and except during the administration of the liberal Pownall, always in the opposition. Hutchinson stated the exact truth when he said, "He was for near twenty years a writer against government in the public newspapers." The need was urgent, for during those years the government of Massachusetts was being subtly changed. With increasing prosperity, ways of thinking, like styles of dress, were becoming more like those of St. James's. Ambitious young men were drawn into the circle of the ruling group and caught with the bait of preferment. An aristocracy was emerging that wanted only titles to make ready to set up a House of Lords. Quite plainly it was time for the liberals to arouse the rank and file of the people to the danger, and this became the daily business of Samuel Adams.

The evidence available is insufficient to explain the motives which impelled him to take up and carry forward so difficult and thankless a work. The cost in personal ease and the good opinion of respectable people was great, the peril certain, and the reward dubious. Not lightly will a serious man compromise with treason; to talk republicanism was not profitable in Tory New England; and Samuel Adams, no more than another, was anxious to come to close acquaintance with the hangman. What secret motives inspired the heart of this ascetic Puritan—"he eats little, drinks little, sleeps little, thinks much," said the Loyalist Galloway, half sneeringly, half out of respect—we can only guess at. Very likely there was an old grudge at a government that had ruined him; very likely love of power stimulated his hatred of the ruling clique; very likely his close association with tradesmen colored his resentment at overseas regulation, for better than most, he knew that the American goose was reserved for English plucking. Nevertheless the more intimately one comes to know Samuel Adams the more inadequate seem all cynical and sordid interpretations of his strange career. He was no self-seeking politician, but a man of vision. He believed ardently in the principle of local home rule. Love of the New England town-meeting democracy was bred in his bones. More clearly than others he saw the danger of erecting a governing class irresponsive to the popular will. He was, in short, the embodiment of the rising spirit of the eighteenth century that found expression in individualism, that exalted liberty and hated tyranny—a spirit that had for its ultimate purpose the reduction of the powers of the political state.

His critical study of the methods of Tory politicians early stripped from government the last vestige of glamor so appealing to the ignorant. Adams understood too perfectly the secret springs and backstairs intrigues that determined governmental policies, to be taken in by appeal to his loyalty. English politics was a sordid business, conducted by professional traders, to whom loyalty and patriotism were no more than gestures to gull the simple. Quite as well as Franklin, Adams understood its ways. He had watched the steady unfolding of the ministerial program: how it was proposed to free the royal governor and judges from popular restraint by the payment of salaries from the royal chest; to change the charter in the interest of prerogative by vesting the nomination of the councilors in the governor; to disarm the democracy by destroying the town meeting as a political instrument; in short to substitute government by ministerial instructions for government by the people. As he watched the calculated encroachments upon the historical rights of the commonwealth— rights that were sanctioned by a hundred and forty years of exercise, and were now in danger from carelessness—he would have been faithless to his duty if he had not sought to arouse the people of Massachusetts to the danger. There was no idle rhetoric in the words, "No time can better be employed than in the preservation of the rights derived from the British constitution . . . . No treasure can be better expended, than in securing that true old English liberty, which gives a relish to every other enjoyment."[2]

In the fulfillment of this purpose to defend the democratic rights of Massachusetts, Adams became no mean master of political theory. In the works of no other writer is the total body of Revolutionary thought so adequately revealed. He was deeply read in the political classics, and all the great names—Hooker and Grotius, Pufendorf and Vattel, Coke and Blackstone, Locke and Milton and Sidney and Hume and Montesquieu—are spread largely through his pages to buttress his argument. In spite of the elusive

[2] *Works*, Vol. I, p. 348.

"meanders and windings" of his thought, veering and tacking as the winds blew, three broad lines of defense are clearly discernible. He rested his case on an appeal to the natural rights of man, to the particular rights and privileges of the British subject under the constitution, and to the express terms of the compact between the crown and its emigrant subjects laid down in the several colonial charters. Inasmuch as the American cause was to be argued before an old-world court, it was common prudence to seek to justify the seeming innovations of American institutional development, by old-world precedent and authority. If he could base the American grievance on the Whig doctrine of representation, he might rally the English Whigs to the American cause. This was sound constitutionalism, and Adams was too shrewd not to profess the highest respect for the glorious British constitution. "You know there is a charm in the word 'constitutional,'" he slyly suggested to a fellow colonial; and such respect, not to say veneration, he trumpeted to the world, until it may well have seemed that he did protest too much.

In his first line of defense Adams was on familiar ground, and he was supported by the authority of Locke, whose opinions were sacred in the eyes of English Whigs. What use he made of him is evident; "the immortal Locke," he calls him at one time, and at another, "one of the greatest men that ever wrote." He had been a disciple of Locke since his first interest in political theory, and he thought and spoke habitually in terms of the natural-rights school. It is sometimes asserted that the appeal to natural rights was made only after the breakdown of the colonial argument drawn from constitutional practice.[3] But as early as 1765 Adams based his argument on Locke in assuming the economic origin of government, and the inevitable connection between property and parliamentary representation.[4] How heavily he leaned on the natural-rights school appears again and again; particularly in a brilliant series of articles, signed "Candidus," written in 1771, where he paraphrases the *Second Treatise on Government*:

[3] Hutchinson seems to justify such a view from a passage written in 1770: "The leaders here seem to acknowledge that their cause is not to be defended on constitutional principles, and Adams now gives out that there is no need of it; they are upon better ground; all men have a natural right to change a bad constitution for a better, whenever they have it in their power." (Hosmer, *Life of Samuel Adams*, p. 259.)
[4] *Works*. Vol. I, p. 135.

Mr. Locke has often been quoted in the present dispute . . . and very much to our purpose. His reasoning is so forcible, that no one has ever attempted to confute it. He holds that "the preservation of property is the end of government, and that for which men enter into society. It therefore necessarily supposes and requires that the people should have property, without which they must be suppos'd to lose that by entering into society, which was the *end* for which they enter'd into it; too gross an absurdity for any man to own. Men therefore *in society having property*, they have such right to the goods, which by the law of the community are theirs, that no body hath the right to take *any part* of their subsistence from them without their consent: Without this, they could have no property at all. For I truly can have no property in that which another can by right take from me when he pleases, against my consent. Hence, says he, it is a mistake to think that the supreme power of any commonwealth can dispose of the estates of the subject arbitrarily, or *take any part* of them at pleasure. The prince or senate can never have a power to take to themselves the whole or any part of the subjects' property without *their own* consent; for this would be in effect to have no property at all."—This is the reasoning of that great and good man. And is not our own case exactly described by him? [5]

This was excellent doctrine in the eyes of the English Whigs, and it explains in part the support which Pitt and Camden lent to the colonial cause. But in his second line of defense, namely, that the English constitution was a fundamental charter of the natural rights of the subject, and that a statute which disregarded those natural rights was null and void, Adams was on less tenable ground. Every attempt to establish such a principle, whether that fundamental law be conceived of as the "law of God and nature," special compacts like the Magna Charta, or the Common Law, has met with failure in English constitutional practice. Nevertheless Adams made use of the argument, derived, very likely, from Coke.

Magna Charta itself is in substance but a constrained Declaration or proclamation, and promulgation in the name of King, Lords, and Commons, of the sense the latter had of their original, inherent, indefeazible natural Rights, as also those of free Citizens equally perdurable with the other. That great author, that great jurist, and even that Court writer Mr. Justice Blackstone holds that this recognition was justly obtained of King John sword in hand: and peradventure it must be one day sword in hand again rescued and preserved from total destruction. [6]

[Magna Charta] is affirm'd by Lord Coke to be declaratory of the principal grounds of the fundamental laws and liberties of England. "It is

5 *Works*, Vol. II, p. 299.
6 "The Rights of the Colonists," in *Works*, Vol. II, pp. 355-356.

called *Charta Libertatum Regni, the Charter of the Liberties of the kingdom,* upon great reason . . . because *liberos facit, it makes and preserves the people free.*" . . . If then according to Lord Coke, *Magna Charta* is declaratory of the principal grounds of the *fundamental* laws and liberties of the people, and Vatel is right in his opinion, that the supreme legislature cannot change the constitution, I think it follows, whether Lord Coke has expressly asserted it or not, that an act of parliament made against Magna Charta in violation of its essential parts, is void.[7]

Adams was probably fully aware of the weakness of the argument. The well known attempt of Coke to establish a body of super-parliamentary law that sanctioned the annulling of a statute had been a total failure. Parliament had refused to yield sovereignty to the lawyers. The Tories were on stronger ground in asserting Hume's doctrine that "the only rule of government is the established practice of the age, upon maxims universally assented to"; and the established practice was sufficient reply to the argument that "it is the glory of the British constitution that it hath its foundations in the law of God and nature." Moreover the doctrine of virtual representation was at hand to cover any discrepancy between natural rights and existing practice; the argument from Locke was met by a legal refinement which held that as the charter of Massachusetts was as of the manor of East Greenwich, the freemen of Boston were personally represented by the parliamentary member from that borough.

When Adams fell back upon his third line of defense, the appeal to the colonial charter, he broke with the English Whigs completely. The royal charters, by authority of which the colonies had been founded and governed hitherto, were exalted by him into a secondary fundamental law, subordinate to the English constitution, but with authority beyond an act of parliament. This organic law of the charter was "the only medium of their political connection with the Mother State," he argued, and as sacred to Americans "as Magna Charta is to the People of Britain, as it contains a Declaration of all their Rights founded in natural Justice." [8]

Thus we see that Whatever Governmt in general may be founded in, Ours was manifestly founded in Compact. . . . By this Charter, we have an exclusive Right to make Laws for our own internal Government & Taxation: And indeed if the Inhabitants here are British Subjects . . . it seems necessary that they should exercise this Power themselves; for

[7] "Candidus," in *Works*, Vol. II, pp. 325–326.   [8] *Works*, Vol. I, p. 28.

they are not represented in the British Parliamt & their great Distance renders it impracticable: It is very probable that all the subordinate legislative Powers in America, were constituted upon the Apprehension of this Impracticability.[9]

After all, the futility of argument as a colonial defense against Grenville or Townshend was evident to so shrewd a student of political realism as Samuel Adams. If the colonies were to preserve their traditional liberties, more effective means must be found than appeal to justice or colonial use and wont. Force must be used, and that force—short of armed rebellion—could be only an aroused public opinion. It was like to prove a difficult business, this arousing of an effective public opinion, and not wanting in danger; but neither difficulty nor danger would deter a calculating enthusiast like Adams from undertaking it. He was ready to devote his life to the work of creating and guiding a popular interest in political measures.

The means which he made use of were as novel as they were repugnant to the Tory statecraft. He was the first American to understand the power of publicity, and not the least of his services to democracy was his attack upon the principle of secret government. Affairs of state had always been guarded jealously from public knowledge, on the theory long before stated by Sir Robert Filmer that the subject must "have nothing to do to meddle with mysteries of state, such *arcana imperii*, or cabinet councils, the vulgar may not pry into." Adams now proposed to lay them open to common inspection. He insisted that questions of governmental policy be taken out of the exclusive jurisdiction of secret councils, and transferred to Faneuil Hall where the freemen of Boston might examine them, and where the "Cause of Liberty" might "be warmly espoused and ably vindicated." Here was a revolutionary proposal indeed, with its demand for public discussion and a popular referendum; and naturally it gave offense to the crown officials. It meant the vulgarization of government. It was a disturbing thought to such men that government might come to be regarded as the common concern of the tax-paying public; that the town meeting might fall under the control of the plebeian mass and crowd in with its demands upon the aristocratic Council. How could gentlemen deliberate freely and determine wisely, with demagogues sitting in judgment on every word and vote? So

[9] *Ibid.*, Vol. I, p. 29.

disturbing to gentlemen was any criticism that one of Hutchinson's followers went so far as to charge Adams with "Indecency in 'undertaking to answer a Governor's Message,'" to which he replied:

I know very well that it has been handed as a political Creed of late, that the Reasoning of the People without Doors is not to be regarded— But every ' transient Person" has a Right publickly to animadvert upon whatever is publickly advanc'd by any Man, and I am resolv'd to exercise that Right, when I please, without asking any Man's Leave.[10]

Effective organization of the rank and file of the people was the business at hand. It was a new problem and there was need of new methods. The Caucus Club, founded by his father, served as a training school for the leaders; there the policies were determined upon for the town meeting and the assembly, and there the plans for a continental union were laid in Non-Importation Agreements, organization of Committees of Correspondence, and the like. The program there agreed upon Adams made it his business to put through the town meeting, as the first step. When he faced his fellow Bostonians in Faneuil Hall he relied upon the influence which long years of familiar intercourse with all sorts and conditions of men had won for him, and many a Boston freeman went to the meeting ready to vote for "whatever the old man wanted." Behind the imposing figure of John Hancock, or the eloquence of John Adams, was certain to be the directing mind of the "master of the puppets," as Hutchinson sneeringly called Samuel Adams.

His hours of triumph in Boston town meeting or in the assembly were preceded by an incredible amount of labor with the pen as well as with the tongue, for this master politician was the journalist as well as the organizer of the New England revolution. The public opinion on which he depended was daily being made in chimney corners and tavern talk, and he proposed to mold it through the agency of a party press. No other pen in Boston was so busy as his. "There is Sam Adams writing against the Tories," his fellow townsmen are said to have remarked when they saw his familiar candle burning long into the night. When he was away in attendance on the Continental Congress he reproached his friends at home for neglecting the work of publicity. "Your presses have been too long silent. What were your Committees of Corre-

[10] "A Chatterer," in *Works*, Vol. II, pp. 45-46.

spondence about? I hear nothing of circular Letters—of joynt Committees &c. Such Methods have in times past raised the Spirits of the people—drawn off their Attention from picking up Pins, & directed their Views to great objects." [11]

With such neglect Samuel Adams could not be charged. As clerk of the inevitable Committee of Grievances appointed by the Boston town meeting in accordance with his prearranged plan, he wrote those plain-spoken papers that stirred the wrath of Tory gentlemen; as clerk of the assembly he was the chief author of successive state papers, which under guise of replying to the prerogative principles of Bernard and Hutchinson, set forth in masterly fashion the whole theory of colonial rights; and as Chairman of the Committee of Correspondence he appealed to his fellow Americans of every colony. Yet his official writings constitute only a minor part of his total work. His letters were innumerable and his newspaper articles crowded the desk of every friendly editor. The labors undergone and the energy consumed were enormous. It was no holiday task to create and guide a public opinion that was so constantly falling into apathy.

Running through the third volume of Hutchinson's *History of Massachusetts Bay* is a note of indignant protest at "the machinations of selfish and designing men" who at the precise time when the feeling between the two countries was friendliest, and an amicable settlement of differences seemed likeliest, were assiduous to breed fresh discord and frustrate the hopes of peace. That he had Adams chiefly in mind there can be little doubt. During the "calm interval" of the summer of '71, when, according to Hutchinson, "the province was more free from real evils" than for years, and when "to keep up a spirit of discontent, recourse was had, either to evils merely imaginary, or to such as were at a distance, and feared rather than felt," [12] Adams wrote the ablest of his many able newspaper articles. [13] In no other phase of his work is the craft of the man so evident as in these anonymous newspaper discussions. There was cunning as well as caution in his method. Changing his style with every fresh quill and every new pen name, putting forth an idea for the sake of denying it, then examining its merits cautiously, and finally advocating it boldly, he created

[11] *Works*, Vol. III, p. 289.
[12] *History of Massachusetts Bay*, Vol. III, p. 349.
[13] See in particular the "Candidus" articles in *Works*, Vol. II, in which he elabo rated his views on government by ministerial instructions.

like Falstaff a host of patriots out of a single Bostonian in brown homespun, making it appear that many were troubled over evils that were visible only to him. On occasion his style possesses the light touch, the leisurely detail, the easy pleasantry of a Spectator essay; [14] again, there is a note of biting irony and studied insult; [15] and again, there is dignified discussion in which Adams argues dispassionately with his countrymen, or pleads with them to stand together in defense of the common welfare. But in whatever vein or under whatever disguise he wrote, the conclusion of every argument was the implied suggestion, how much better it would be if the American people were to take into their own hands the management of their affairs.

But before the colonial could be induced to strike for governmental control, the old psychology of subserviency to the ruling class must be uprooted; and an effective means to that end was to lay bare the selfish motives of the aristocracy. To stimulate what we call today class consciousness was a necessary preliminary to a democratic psychology; and to this task Adams devoted every energy. The ways of the iconoclast are rarely lovely, and the breaking of idols is certain to wound sensitive souls. There was abundant justification for the charge of Hutchinson that "robbing men of their characters" was the "patriotic business" of Samuel Adams; but he missed the point in attributing to him the motive, *Gubernatorum vituperatio populo placet.* The respect that attached to Bernard and Hutchinson by virtue of their official positions was a powerful ally of ministerial authority; their words carried weight beyond the sanction of their logic; for the good of America their power must be destroyed. Doubtless Adams was ungenerous in attack; certainly he was vindictive in his hates; but the cold record as we read it today justifies one in the belief that the men whom he attacked were tools of the ministry, and must be struck down if the rights of Massachusetts were to be preserved. And it was due to the bitter denunciations of Adams that Thomas Hutchinson was driven from his native land and forced to take refuge in England, the best hated man in all the colonies.

But it was not enough to pull down the courtly Hutchinson, for behind the governor was a group of lawyers and judges, equally

---

[14] See "Puritan" articles, in *Works*, Vol. I, p. 201 *et seq.*
[15] See "Candidus," in Vol. II, p. 246; "Chatterer," in Vol. II, pp. 35, 39, 43; "Layman," in Vol. I, p. 322.

subservient to prerogative, adepts in the art of interpreting away rights by due process of law. It became part of the day's work, therefore, to lay open the sacred precincts of the courts to common inspection; to create a public opinion to review judicial decisions when those decisions were political rather than legal. It was a startling innovation for a private citizen to assert in the public press that "*state-lawyers*, attorneys and sollicitors general, & persons advanced to the highest stations in the courts of law, *prostitute* the honor of the profession, become *tools of ministers*, and employ their talents for *explaining away*, if possible, the Rights of a kingdom." Never before had the integrity of the colonial courts been openly attacked and the motives of the judiciary impugned. But it was far more startling for Adams to lay down the thesis, that in matters which concern the general welfare, the letter of the law is not to be considered final, and "the opinions . . . and determinations of the greatest Sages and Judges of the law in the Exchequer Chamber, ought not to be considered as decisive or binding . . . any further, than they are consonant to natural reason." [16] If Franklin was concerned to create a new economics in harmony with democratic needs, Samuel Adams was concerned to democratize the New England law. He was dissatisfied with a legal system created by a Tory past, and that had lately received a fresh Tory impress at the hands of Blackstone. Such a body of law could not answer the needs of a free people; it must be reshaped to conform to new needs. And the conclusion towards which his thinking pointed was the principle of a referendum of judicial decisions, for how otherwise could it be determined whether a given decision were "consonant to natural reason"?

Samuel Adams was little given to striking at the air, and he set himself to the work of cutting the claws of the more obnoxious judges with the same cool skill that marked his baiting of the governor. Certain of them who held plural offices he maneuvered out of the Council, on the ground that they ought not to exercise both legislative and judicial functions; and when Bernard protested that they had been members of the Council for years and by reason of "their knowledge of the public business, were almost necessary to the body," he replied that they were to be released "from the cares and perplexities of politics . . . to make further advances in the knowledge of the law"—which thrust, in view of

[16] *Works*, Vol. II, p. 436.

the notorious fact that few of them had been trained in the law, but had risen to the bench through political influence, must be reckoned a palpable hit.[17] Others beyond his immediate reach found their characters assailed and their motives aspersed, until popular respect for them was destroyed; and the unlucky judges who accepted payment from the royal chest found such a hue and cry raised against them that they were driven to make choice between the royal guineas or answering to the mob—a rude but effective way of stimulating their loyalty to the commonwealth. In short, this "master of the puppets," measuring the power of the judges and fearing their prerogative bias, did not scruple over ways and means of rendering them more responsive to the popular will, which in the eyes of the best people of Boston was no less than incendiary.

The work of Samuel Adams was largely done before the word democrat was given vogue by the French Revolution, and he cautiously refrained from using it; nevertheless he was probably the most thoroughgoing democrat of his generation of Americans. He was wholly persuaded that the sovereign people have a right to change their fundamental law, together with the interpretation and administration of it, whenever they desire; and that pending such change it was well to nullify an act of prerogative subversive of their interests. "We contend, that the People & their Representatives have a Right to withstand the abusive Exercise of a legal & constitutional Prerogative of the Crown," he argued in reply to Hutchinson; "whenever instructions cannot be complied with, without injuring the people, they cease to be binding."[18] From the necessary corollary, that the people are competent to judge of their own good and manage their own affairs, Adams did not shrink. Stated thus in general terms, the theory possessed no novelty. The sovereignty of the people had long been a staple of Whiggish theory; but Adams gave to the doctrine democratic significance. The people, in his philosophy, were something more than the wealthy and cultured minority to whom the Whigs appealed; they were the mass of men—the yeoman, the tradesman, the mechanic—all that multitude of homespun folk who had hitherto been mere pawns in the political game. Such a passage as this, written four years before Lexington, reads like Tom Paine and his doctrine of the *res publica:*

[17] *Works*, Vol. I, p 80.   [18] *Works*, Vol. II, pp. 22, 26.

The *multitude* I am speaking of, is the *body of the people*—no contemptible multitude—for whose sake government is instituted; or rather, who have themselves erected it, solely for their own good—to whom even kings and all in subordination to them, are strictly speaking, servants and not masters. . . . Philanthrop [Jonathan Sewall] I think, speaks somewhat unintelligently, when he tells us that the well being and happiness of the whole depends upon *subordination*; as if mankind submitted to government for the sake of being subordinate. . . . Mankind have entered into political societies, rather for the sake of restoring *equality*. . . . I am not of levelling principles: But I am apt to think, that constitution of civil government which admits equality in the most extensive degree, consistent with the true design of government, is the best.[19]

Accepting the sovereignty of the people, Adams was led to a pure democracy, based on the town meeting. He rejected every form of "mixt government," whether in the form of king, lords and commons, or in the form of constitutional checks and balances. That sober men should profess to prefer the dominion of the few to the rule of all, he could not understand. "I find everywhere some Men, who are afraid of a free Government," he said in 1776, "lest it be perverted, and made Use of as a Cloke for Licenciousness. The fear of the Peoples abusing their Liberty is made an Argument against their having the Enjoyment of it; as if anything were so much to be dreaded by Mankind as Slavery."[20] Democracy he believed was inevitable, for "in these times of Light and Liberty, every man chuses to see and judge for himself."[21] He was quite untroubled by any fear of the tyranny of the mass; he was a good enough historian to know that it is always the minority and not the mass that creates tyranny. Though Toryism might infect the government circles, and aristocracy appeal to the wealthy and ambitious, the great body of Massachusetts people were democratic, and he looked forward hopefully to a new political order, created by the popular mind. It came more quickly than he had expected, once the old inhibitions were removed. "New Govts are now erecting in the several American states under the Authority of the People," he wrote soon after Independence. "Monarchy seems to be generally exploded. And it is not a little surprising to me that the Aristocratick Spirit, which appeard to have taken deep Root in some of them, now gives place to that of Democracy." [22]

During the difficult after-years of reconstruction Adams re-

---

[19] *Works*, Vol. II, p. 150.   [20] *Works*, Vol. III, p. 244.
[21] *Ibid.*, Vol. II, p. 39.   [22] *Ibid.*, Vol. III, p. 305.

mained true to his democratic principles. As he had earlier resisted the encroachments of monarchical centralization, he later fought against Federalistic consolidation. He distrusted the Constitution as an undemocratic instrument, fearing a centralized authority removed from immediate control; and he joined heartily in the work of securing a Bill of Rights. He welcomed the French Revolution and followed closely the developing democratic philosophy which that great upheaval did so much to clarify and disseminate. He remained an unrepentant Jacobin during those acrimonious years when the Federalists were filling the air with their anti-Jacobin fustian. He had heard gentlemen rant before and was probably amused when, as Governor, he attended Harvard Commencement and listened to young Robert Treat Paine fulminate against the red atheism of France and its American spawn. Although a kinsman of John Adams and warm friend, he welcomed the election of Jefferson as a return to democratic principles after an unhappy period of "prejudice and passion," although he warned him, "you must depend upon being hated . . . because they hate your principles." The last letter in the collected edition of his works, addressed to his old friend Tom Paine, November 30, 1802, is an appeal for democratic unity; and the words with which it concludes—*felix qui cautus*—embody the principle of his amazing political strategy. In playing for great stakes it is well to be wary.

His anti-Federalism, aggravated by his frank advocacy of Jacobin principles, cost him heavily in after days, and like Philip Freneau his just fame was long obscured by partisan spleen. Although he retained his hold on the affections of the Massachusetts electorate, and was annually chosen Governor until the infirmities of age determined his withdrawal from public affairs, he was silently dropped from the roll of American patriots whose deeds were celebrated in current panegyrics. His manuscripts were scattered after his death, and he was in the way of being forgotten till Bancroft, in the next century, gave fresh currency to his earlier reputation. Since then the figure of Samuel Adams has grown steadily larger, although he still awaits a biographer who will set him in his due place in the history of American liberalism.

CHAPTER V

LITERARY ECHOES

The Revolutionary upheaval produced no polite literature in any respects comparable to its utilitarian prose. The expiring wit literature of England was an exotic that refused to be naturalized, and the times were unpropitious for the creation of a native poetry. An occasional dilettante like Mather Byles aspired to be a wit, but the reputation of the clever Bostonian owed more to his tongue than to his pen, and he is dimly remembered for the letter that he received from the great Mr. Pope, rather than for notable verse. Nevertheless in the early seventies pure literature was beginning to make a perceptible stir in New England. Clever young men in the colleges were turning moderns and making ready to wage a new battle of the books. They preferred the refinements of verse to the didacticism of sermons; they were discovering the charm of playful satire; and they found in the currently fashionable tetrameter a brisk vehicle for their attacks on academic dullness. They admired Churchill, then at the height of his brief fame, but they were restrained by a decent modesty and dared not go his length in brutal frankness. It was from these young men, amateurs in verse writing and amateurs likewise in politics, that the American cause mainly recruited its literary defenders. They might be flaming Whigs but they were also well-bred young gentlemen who studied the amenities and sought to unite patriotism with good form.

I

THE WHIG SATIRISTS

1. John Trumbull

There was the best of Yankee blood in the veins of John Trumbull. Among his kinsmen were the Reverend Benjamin Trumbull, historian of Connecticut, Governor Jonathan Trumbull—Washington's "Brother Jonathan"—and John Trumbull the painter. On his mother's side he was descended from the vigorous Solomon

Stoddard, grandfather of Jonathan Edwards. His father was a scholarly minister, long a trustee of Yale College, at which school the son spent seven years as undergraduate and tutor. He was a precocious youth with a strong love of polite letters, and a praiseworthy desire to achieve literary distinction. Greek and Latin had been the toys of his childhood and when he was seven years of age he passed the entrance examination to college. During the period of his tutorship he joined with Timothy Dwight and Joseph Howe in the work of overhauling the stale curriculum, supplementing Lilly's Grammar and Calvin's Institutes with Pope and Churchill. Like other aspiring youths of the day he dabbled in Spectator papers, practiced his couplets, and eventually produced *The Progress of Dulness*, the cleverest bit of academic verse till then produced in America. At heart Trumbull was thoroughly academic, and nothing would have suited his temperament better than the life of a Yale professor; but the prospects proving unfavorable, he began to mingle Blackstone with the poets in preparation for his future profession.

He was thus engaged during the middle years of the long dispute with England, the bitter wranglings of which seem to have disturbed him little in his quiet retreat. But in 1773 he resigned his tutorship to prepare himself further in the law. Removing to Boston he entered the office of John Adams, then rising to prominence as a spokesman of the popular party; and he took lodgings in the house of Caleb Cushing, Speaker of the Massachusetts Assembly. Placed thus at the storm center of provincial politics, he was soon infected with the Whig dissatisfactions and joined himself to the patriotic party. When Adams went to Philadelphia to sit in the Continental Congress, Trumbull withdrew to Hartford, where he established himself. Before quitting Boston he had published an *Elegy on the Times*, a political tract that seemed to Adams so useful to the cause that he marked the young poet for future service, and the year following he encouraged the writing of *M'Fingal*, the first part of which appeared in 1775. So great was the prestige it met with that Trumbull tinkered with it for seven years, publishing it finally in its completed form in 1782. The law seems to have been a jealous mistress then as now, and his dreams of further literary work were inadequately realized. He is believed to have had a hand in *The Anarchiad*, and he wrote some minor poems; but he soon drifted into politics, went on the bench,

finally removed to Detroit in 1825, and died there in 1831, at
the age of eighty-one. He had outlived his Revolutionary generation, long outlived his literary ambitions, and was pretty much
forgotten before he died. His collected works, published in 1820,
proved a losing venture for the printer. America in 1820 was
turning romantic, and few, it seems, cared to invest in two volumes
of echoes.

Trumbull's reputation rests exclusively on *M'Fingal*. It was so
popular in its time that more than thirty pirated editions were
issued. It was broadcasted by "news-papers, hawkers, pedlars,
and petty chapmen," and it served its partisan purpose. The
author was complimented by the Marquis de Chastellux on
fulfilling all the conditions of burlesque poetry as approved since
the days of Homer; but in spite of the indisputable cleverness of
some of the lines, it is not a great work. In its final form it is
spun out to extreme length, and pretty much swamped by the
elaborate machinery on which the poet visibly prided himself.
Even in the thick of attack Trumbull did not forget his academic
reading, but he explains his allusions with meticulous care. He
seems, indeed, rather more concerned about the laws of the mock
epic than the threatened rights of America. The Scotch Tory
hero is a figure so unlike the real Tory—the Olivers and Leonards
and Hutchinsons, with their love of power and dignified display—
that the caricature loses much in historical veracity. Trumbull's
patriotism was well bred and unmarked by fierce partisanship.
His refined tastes were an ill equipment for the turmoil of revolution. The ways of the radical were not lovely in his eyes; the Sons
of Liberty with their tar-pots and feather-beds were too often
rough fellows, and although they provided him with comic material
to set off the blunderings of the Squire, they probably seemed to
him little better than tools of demagogues. Very often this tousle-
headed democracy behaved like a mob, and Trumbull in his tie-
wig did not approve of mobs.

The more thoughtfully one reads *M'Fingal*, throwing upon it
the light of the total career of its author, the more clearly one
perceives that John Trumbull was not a rebellious soul. In the
year 1773, while projecting some fresh ventures in the Spectator
vein, "he congratulated himself on the fact 'that the ferment of
politics' was, as he supposed, 'pretty much subsided,' and that at
last the country was to enjoy a 'mild interval from the struggles

of patriotism and self-interest, from noise and confusion, Wilkes and liberty.'" He had then no wish for embroilment in civil war, no dreams of political independence. All his life he seems to have suffered from ill health, which probably sapped his militancy and lessened his pugnacity. From this temperamental calmness came a certain detachment that allowed his partisanship to remain cooler than the hot passions of the times commonly suffered. He could permit himself the luxury of a laugh at the current absurdities; and it is this light-heartedness that made *M'Fingal* so immediately effective. The rollicking burlesque of the Tory argument, the telling *reductio ad absurdum* of the Tory logic, must have tickled the ears of every Whig and provoked many a laugh in obscure chimney-seats. Laughter is a keen weapon, and Trumbull's gayety laid open weak spots in the Tory armor that were proof against Freneau's invective. It was a rare note in those acrimonious times, and one likes Trumbull the better for minding his manners and engaging in the duel like a gentleman. After all, this son of Yale had certain characteristics of the intellectual, and if his environment had been favorable and the law had not claimed him, very likely he would have given a better account of the talents that were certainly his. He wrote with ease if not with finish, and he possessed the requisite qualities of a man of letters. A lovable man he seems to have been, but somewhat easy-going, too lightly turned away from his purpose; and in consequence his later life failed to realize the expectations of his early years.

That he was not a Loyalist was probably due in large measure to environment and his family connections. Considering his temperament, it is not easy to discover any logical reason why he should have turned Whig. He had never suffered in his own fortune from existing arrangements; he was not a political idealist to throw the glamor of republicanism about the struggle; he had not subjected the colonial question to critical analysis. He was an academic dilettante, unconcerned with political principles, little more than an echo of the Connecticut gentry in such matters; and if he espoused the Whig cause it is a pretty good indication that Yale College was indoctrinated in Whig principles. An echo he remained throughout his life. When later he became a Federalist and enjoyed some of the emoluments of party victory, and when later still democracy lifted up its head in Connecticut, wearing the

French cockade, and bringing down upon it the wrath of all respectable people, he reflected faithfully the views of his class.
John Trumbull was a moderate liberal, but no leveler, no democrat,
no friend to Jeffersonian heresies. Democracy he detested heartily,
and he joined with the other Hartford Wits to draw its portrait in
unflattering terms. As a Connecticut gentleman he was insistent
on the supremacy of the tie-wig in government as well as in society;
he would scarcely have been a Connecticut gentleman had he
thought otherwise.

2. Francis Hopkinson, Esq.

If the career of Trumbull indicates that Whiggery existed among
the young collegians of Connecticut, the career of Francis Hopkinson suggests that the culture of Philadelphia, the great center
of fashion and wit, was Whiggish also. That it should have been
so is the more noteworthy, for the Quaker spirit of Philadelphia
was far less militant than the Puritan spirit of Boston; more
peaceful, if not more conservative. The city had long been dominated by a group of sober merchants who detested the leveling
tendencies of New England. But the domination of these older
men was passing; a younger generation, more aggressive in trade
and speculation, was rising to power; and that Philadelphia finally
went with the Whigs was due to the influence of these younger
merchants. When it became clear that the commercial interests
of men like Robert Morris and George Clymer were disadvantaged
by the connection with England, the ardor of patriotism grew
stronger, and talk of independence became common. No sooner
had business come out for independence than culture swung over;
the wit which would gladly have remained loyal applauded the
comments of the countinghouse, and the newspaper essay reflected
the new patriotic sentiments.

Chief among the Philadelphia wits was Francis Hopkinson,
Esq., a charmingly versatile dilettante, who to the vocation of
the law and the bench of admiralty, joined the polite avocations
of painting, music, natural philosophy, and literature. He was
indisputably clever, full of innumerable sprightly enthusiasms,
and master of cultivated speech and manners. Of his skill in
painting and music we cannot judge, but of his literary accomplishments the record has been preserved. Life seems to have
been an agreeable experience to him, and if his dainty enthusiasms

were a marvel to John Adams,[1] it would indicate that society in Philadelphia in 1775 was far more refined than in provincial Boston.

Hopkinson possessed ample means to gratify his polite tastes, and had long moved in the most exclusive circles. The son of an eminent lawyer, he had received the best education available in the colonies, after which he went abroad to acquire old-world polish. Some fourteen months were spent in England, where, as a near kinsman of the Bishop of Worcester, he frequented the best English society, made the acquaintance of eminent men, and even enjoyed the distinction of dining with my Lord North. On his return he prudently fell in love with an heiress of the Bordens, of Bordentown, and turned Jerseyman the better to administer his wife's estates. He entered the law, and doubtless at the solicitation of his kinsman the Bishop, he became a beneficiary of ministerial patronage: receiving appointment in 1772 to a sinecure post as collector of customs at Newcastle, and two years later being made mandamus councilor for New Jersey—a somewhat hazardous post, considering the nature of the office and the temper of the people. Already in Massachusetts certain gentlemen had learned that the compliment of royal recognition might cost too dear a price. That Hopkinson should have been tendered such an appointment as late as 1774, shows that he was regarded by the ministry as good Tory material.

During the anxious months of 1774, when intelligent Americans were trying to forecast the outcome of the growing radicalism of the colonial temper, Hopkinson must have done some serious thinking; with the result that when in September the Continental Congress assembled in Philadelphia, he offered to the members as his contribution to the discussion a clever little allegory wherein the whole question at issue between England and the colonies was sketched with a light touch that is an agreeable relief from the arguments of the official debaters. In *A Pretty Story* Hopkinson is frankly pro-colonial, and offers his wit to the service of his country. It is not a great work, but it shows that he had definitely put aside the ministerial temptation—probably to the disgust of the good Bishop—and had gone over to the Whigs. Two years later he took a seat in the Congress, and within a week voted for the Declaration of Independence, aligning himself against the conservative group led by his fellow townsman, John Dickinson.

[1] See *Familiar Letters of John and Abigail Adams*, p. 217.

What impelled Hopkinson to so momentous a shift in political opinion can be explained by no records that have been preserved, and must remain a matter of conjecture. Even less than Trumbull was he revolutionary in temper. His Whiggery was probably commercial in origin, a reflection of the economic interests of the merchant class with which he mingled. That he went so far as to attack the aristocratic spirit of the English government— its debauching of public servants and its sordid motives—may have been due quite as much to a refined integrity as to partisan advantage; but for an aristocrat to attack the aristocratic principle of government was unusual as it was dangerous for his class. But though he turned Whig he was no agrarian to substitute the majority will for the royal prerogative; and when the war was over and political re-alignment was under way, Hopkinson went with his group, became a stout Federalist, defended the Constitution, and enjoyed his share of the party emoluments. His wit was unembittered by the acrimonious disputes of Jacobin days, and his partisanship retained its note of casual sprightliness through the dogdays of the nineties.

His chief contributions to the debate over the Constitution were *The New Roof* and *Objections to the Proposed Plan of a Federal Government for the United States, on Genuine Principles.* They are delightfully clever, but the cleverness cannot conceal a good-natured contempt for the democratic underling and all his ways. The attitude of aristocratic superiority is the more striking for its easy bearing. The first is an implied eulogy of James Wilson, Scotch lawyer of Philadelphia, who as master-architect finds his plans for erecting a splendid roof over a "certain Mansion-house" violently opposed by Margery, a slattern midwife, for no better reason than that "in the construction of the new roof, her apartments would be considerably lessened." Margery, of course, is agrarian democracy, and to further her interests she incites three worthless servants to testify that the old leaky roof is better than the one proposed. Naturally their flimsy arguments are laughed out of court, and the wisdom of the architect is apparent to all except a "half-crazy fellow" [2] who filled the air with his "fustian," making himself a general nuisance to the disgust of all respectable people.

In the second of the two works, Hopkinson gives freer rein to

[2] "Philadelphiensis," one of the anti-Federalist pamphleteers.

his polite fancy, figuring the opposition to the Constitution under the form of a Wheelbarrow Society at the city gaol. Within those walled precincts, he suggests, the most advanced advocates of natural liberty may be found, and there the monstrous crime of the Constitution is most eloquently exposed. How foolish is this America that persists in believing what able lawyers and reputable gentlemen say of the merits of the document, and refuses to intrust the making of a fundamental law to such true liegemen of democracy as these knights of the chain-gang! It is all very witty, and provokes its laugh, and serves its purpose of heaping on the head of the opposition the class prejudice that was indignant at the insolence of plebeians in holding contrary views on a subject quite beyond their comprehension. But times change, and the sprightliest wit may lose its savor. Those old Federalist skits are as dead today as the marvelous pageant got up by Hopkinson to celebrate the adoption of the Constitution, an affair which greatly pleased the amiable little gentleman, a detailed account of which he prepared for the definitive edition of his works, where it may be read by the curious.

If Francis Hopkinson is no very important figure in our literary history, he is not without significance as a representative of our colonial culture that deliberately chose to be Whig rather than Tory. He risked much and he was amply rewarded. For years he sat on the bench of the Court of Admiralty, sparkled at dinners, and was a respected and influential member of a genteel society. If the recompense for his services during the perilous days was greater than fell to the lot of a democrat like Philip Freneau, who will wonder? Like rewards like, and the days of democratic rewards were not yet come in America.

II

THE TORY SATIRISTS

1. JONATHAN ODELL

Amongst the occasional writers who dedicated extemporized couplets to the defense of Toryism in America, there can be no doubt to whom belongs the primacy. Jonathan Odell was easily first as a purveyor of virulent Loyalist rhyme. Of the sternest Puritan ancestry, Odell was educated in medicine, and saw service in the West Indies as surgeon to his Majesty's forces. Turning

Anglican he was ordained priest in London, and came home to his native colonies as a missionary, to further the cause of episcopacy. Busily engaged with parochial duties, he chose to remain aloof from all political disputes, and during the early months of the war he refrained from taking sides. Unfortunately, however, he made acquaintances among some captive British officers, for whom he wrote a song in honor of the King's birthday, which was sung with much drinking of wine on June 4, 1776, the news of which getting abroad stirred the Whig partisans to anger. Soon thereafter matters grew too warm for Odell to remain longer neutral; he suffered certain humiliating personal experiences and was driven to seek refuge within the British lines. Thenceforth none was more ardent in the royal cause. He busied himself with innumerable intrigues to undermine the Whig strength, amongst others serving as a go-between in the unlucky André-Arnold affair. He remained implacable to the end, and not until the last Redcoat was withdrawn from the independent states, did he leave off urging reprisals. When it was all over he withdrew sullenly to Nova Scotia, was amply rewarded by his King, and sat down to nourish to the end of a long life the most virulent hatred of all Whigs and republicans. "Toryissimus," Professor Tyler calls him, borrowing Sir Walter's word; and the term hits to a nicety the bitter arrogant nature which so closely resembled in its essentials the "proud prelate Laud," from whom his ancestors had fled a hundred and fifty years before.

A vigorous man was Jonathan Odell, strong, capable, uncompromising, possessing a clear intellect and a heart little touched by Christian charity—a stern Hebraist who would sweep away with the besom of wrath all the enemies of his God and his King. He felt no hesitation in making out the list of the proscribed: the enemies of the King were *ipso facto* the enemies of God—rebels who were daily signing their own death warrants in overt acts of treason. Watching the seditious crew of "Congress men" seducing the colonials into unnatural rebellion against the best of kings and fathers, he took it to be his Christian duty to lay the rod of correction upon their shoulders. If they would not be warned they must be hanged. Not content with active intrigue, he pressed his pen into service, and during the year 1779 he wrote four pieces which for bitterness of satire outdid Freneau at his frankest. Freneau was bitter and brutal in all conscience, but he was never nasty; there were infamies of personal insult that he would not stoop to, vulgarities of innuendo that he was not guilty of. If he studied the art of Churchill, he stopped short of Churchill's grossness. But Odell the priest was unhampered by scruple; the meanest gossip found a place in his "acrid rhyme." No Christian charity spread its mantle over the shortcomings of his enemies, no Christian forgiveness found lodgment in his unforgiving heart. He was a son of the Old Testament and he girded up his righteousness with prayer.

> Ask I too much? then grant me for a time
> Some deleterious pow'rs of acrid rhyme:
> Some ars'nic verse, to poison with the pen
> These rats, who nestle in the Lion's den! [3]

The four satires which embody his holy wrath and which were little calculated to spread sweetness and light in a world sorely in need of them, are *The Word of Congress, The Congratulation, The Feu de Joie,* and *The American Times*—all written, probably, in the last months of the year 1779. Of these the first and the last are the most suggestive in their denunciation. The spirit which prompted him to turn to satire is given in the preface to the 1780 edition of *The American Times.*

The masters of Reason have decided, that when doctrines and practices have been fairly examined, and proved to be contrary to Truth, and injurious to Society, then and not before may Ridicule be lawfully employed in the Service of Virtue. This is exactly the case of the grand American Rebellion; it has been weighed in the balance, and found wanting: able writers have exposed its principles, its conduct, and its final aim. Reason has done her part, and therefore this is the legitimate moment for Satire. Accordingly the following Piece is offered to the Public. What it is found to want of Genius, the Author cannot supply; what it may want of Correction, he hopes the candor of the Public will excuse on account of the fugitive nature of the subject: next year the publication would be too late; for in all probability there will then be no Congress existing.

When we examine the work of Odell to discover the deeper springs of his thought, we come upon naked class prejudice, undiluted Toryism. His social philosophy is erected upon that unstable foundation; the actions of men are judged solely by that light. Of any valid or reasoned philosophy, social or political, he was as wanting as a child. Of any real understanding of his

[3] *Loyalist Poetry*, p. 55.

fellow Americans who had espoused the Whig cause, he was as lacking as General Clinton, whose "warfare," Odell asserted, "was the war of God." The colonial grievances which other Tories acknowledged to have some foundation, Odell casually ignored. There was no cause in heaven or earth for colonial disloyalty, he was convinced, except Whiggish perversity, and for such perversity there must be due punishment—the rope. In his mind's eye he sees the "impious crew," one after another silenced by the halter. There must be no ill-judged mercy; the best of the rebels must swing with the worst, for they are all sedition-mongers, all attainted traitors. From his vast ignorance Odell derived an equally vast confidence in the ultimate triumph of truth. There is a note of finality in his judgments that amazes, an infallibility that amuses. The Reverend Jonathan frankly acknowledges himself to be the boon companion of Reason, the favored suitor of Truth—from them only has he taken instruction and in their name he professes to speak. Whereas the Whigs are poor fellows who have held commerce with neither.

Odell is careful of his workmanship and organizes his materials with an eye to climax. *The American Times* is formally divided into three parts. The poem opens with a summoning of the infernal crew of sedition and the abuse of them severally, rising to a rhetorical conclusion in an address to Washington; then the leering portrait of the mother of all mischiefs, Democracy, is painted; finally comes a pure and lofty strain which summons Reason to decide in the great cause. Taxation, Independence, are haled before her august throne and there condemned, and the whole concludes with a vision of Britannia's guardian angel bearing a two-edged sword and proclaiming:

> At length the day of Vengeance is at hand:
> The exterminating Angel takes his stand:
> Hear the last summons, rebels, and relent:
> Yet but a moment is there to repent.
> Lo! the great Searcher ready at the door,
> Who means decisively to purge the floor:
> Yes, the wise Sifter now prepares the fan
> To separate the meal from useless bran.
> Down to the centre from his burning ire
> Ye foes of goodness and of truth, retire:
> And ye, who now lie humbled in the dust,
> Shall raise your heads, ye loyal and ye just;

Th' approving sentence of your Sov'reign gain.
And shine refulgent as the starry train.
Then, when eternal justice is appeas'd;
When with due vengeance heav'n and earth are pleas'd;
America, from dire pollution clear'd,
Shall flourish yet again, belov'd, rever'd:
In duty's lap her growing sons be nurs'd,
And her last days be happier than her first.[4]

Into this framework Odell has fitted a surprising number of
personal attacks. His ink blots out the good name of every Whig
on whom it drips. To the present generation it furnishes food for
wonder to see what a paltry appearance the fathers make in the
verse of this plain-speaking Tory. Jefferson, Paine, Morris, Adams,
Washington, and a host of others, are shallow creatures, in the
judgment of Odell, bereft of reason, void of honor, the very scum
of the revolutionary pot; whereas Clinton and Gage, Hutchinson
and Galloway, are holy instruments in the hand of God to cleanse
the land of pollution. The attack is rankly and grossly partisan,
with no saving grace of humor or humanity. The alpha and omega
of Odell's political faith was loyalty to the crown, and the bankruptcy of such a creed in revolutionary America is nowhere thrust
into harsher relief than in the bitter verses of this bitter heart.
Empty Jonathan Odell of prejudice, class interest, passion for
the prerogative, with their corollary of praise for an unmanly
truckling to the King, and nothing remains, the empty sack col-
lapses. It was a hardship that he should have been driven out of
his native country upon the failure of the King's cause, but what
could be done with a fellow who insisted that his empty sack was
stuffed with all the virtues? He was harshly intolerant in his
Toryism, and he encountered a victorious republican harshness.

2. SAMUEL PETERS

It is amusing to turn from the implacable Odell to the menda-
cious Peters, only to meet with another tale of abortive missionary
zeal. The Anglican clergy played a conspicuous part during the
Revolutionary troubles—a part that in many cases inspired small
regard for the establishment in the minds of a dissenting laity.
Not in vain did the church teach loyalty to authority, for while
the British Empire was breaking asunder, the Anglican ministers
were visible pillars of prerogative and with pen and voice lent

[4] *Loyalist Poetry*, p. 36.

effective aid to the royal cause. Sometimes their ardor outran their intelligence, their devotion betrayed their discretion; nevertheless their zeal contributed notably to the number and quality of the Loyalist writings.

For some inconceivable reason Samuel Peters was seized with a desire to plant the Anglican church in Congregational Connecticut—surely the strangest of desires and the strangest of men to undertake such a work. To uplift the banner of episcopacy in a commonwealth that for over a hundred years had been militantly Separatist, that did not want bishops and would not have them— here was missionary zeal that a plain man understands with difficulty. To have made headway at all there was need of apostolic fervor and an ingratiating tact; and Samuel Peters possessed neither. He was a gentleman who preened himself on his quality, exuding in speech and action a pride of caste that led him to speak of the American farmers as peasants—the only native Loyalist who thus aped the English. His abilities were far from mean, but his better qualities were corroded by overweening conceit. Possessed of all the arrogance of a lord and all the ostentation of a brewer, he was scarcely the man to serve the Connecticut laity with due Christian humility. He pointed out the truth authoritatively and then took it as a personal affront if his hearers failed to agree with him. And so, after explaining to the Congregationalists of Connecticut the infallible truth of the Anglican way, and being ready to minister to them according to that way, he fell into a pet when they refused to turn churchmen. The more he argued the more he got himself disliked, and when his tactless loyalism brought down the Sons of Liberty upon him and he was driven to Boston— whence he sailed for England where he survived for thirty-one years—he took a spirited revenge by writing his *History of Connecticut*, a work that solaced the early years of expatriation, and provided material for many an after argument.

It is an amazingly provocative book, over which the sons of Connecticut have disputed acrimoniously for a hundred years without coming to agreement. Fortunately those disputes are of far less concern today than the political philosophy tucked away in the pages of the *History;* the scandal is far less interesting than the shrewd comment on the causes of the American Revolution. Samuel Peters was a high Tory with the virtue of frankness, which defeat had made the more open. From his secure refuge in England he looked back upon the revolutionary upheaval, and his analysis of causes is the more suggestive from the fact that he had nothing to gain from truckling to popular opinion. His judgments are interesting even when he exaggerates. The colonial Tory is no longer serving immediate partisan ends, but after the battle has been fought and lost he takes a grim pleasure in pointing out to the English government its costly blunders. Affairs went ill in America, not because of too much Toryism on the part of government, but because of too little and too late applied. The explanation of the origin and spread of unrest in America, Peters regarded as very simple. The tap-root of the disaffection was republicanism, which through the criminal negligence of government was not severed in the days when the plant was small, but which was suffered to grow till the tree could not be pulled up or destroyed.

It appears to me, that the British government, in the last century, did not expect New-England to remain under their authority; nor did the New-Englanders consider themselves as subjects, but allies, of Great Britain. It seems that England's intent was to afford an asylum to the republicans who had been a scourge to the British constitution; and so, to encourage that restless party to emigrate, republican charters were granted, and privileges and promises given them far beyond what an Englishman in England is entitled to. The emigrants were empowered to make laws, in church and state, agreeable to their own will and pleasure, without the King's approbation.[5]

From the first they have uniformly declared, in church and state, that America is a new world, subject to the people residing in it; and that none but enemies to the country would appeal from their courts to the King in Council. They never have prayed for any earthly king by name. They always called themselves republicans and enemies to kingly government. . . . They hate the idea of a parliament. . . . They never have admitted one law of England to be in force among them, till passed by their assemblies. . . . They hold Jesus to be their only King, whom if they love and obey, they will not submit, because they have not submitted to the laws of the King of England.[6]

The natural fruits of this pernicious root of republicanism were the colonial hostility to the monarchical and aristocratic elements of the British constitution, together with all the domestic turbulence and lawlessness which have marked the history of New England from the first. If gentlemen wished an object lesson in republicanism, none better than Connecticut could be had; there

---

[5] *A General History of Connecticut*, Appendix, p. 374.   [6] *Ibid.*, p. 290.

from the earliest days, "republicanism, schisms, and persecutions," have gone hand in hand; and it was to make this clear to the world that Samuel Peters took the trouble to write his *History*.

> In the course of this work, my readers must necessarily have observed, in some degree, the ill effects of the democratical constitution of Connecticut. I would wish them to imagine, for I feel myself unable adequately to describe, the confusion, turbulence, and convulsion, arising in a province, where not only every civil officer, from the Governor to the constable, but also every minister, is appointed as well as paid by the people, and faction and superstition are established. The clergy, lawyers, and merchants or traders, are the three efficient parties which guide the helm of government. . . . *En rabies vulgi*—I must beg leave to refer my readers to their own reflections upon such a system of government as I have here sketched out.[7]

That such a people would respect the King's laws at a late day, when those laws lessened their profits, was foolish to expect. There had been much complaint from ministerial gentlemen in respect to colonial smuggling; but how idle was it to complain of the natural consequences of ministerial laxness chronic for a hundred years!

> Smuggling is rivetted in the constitutions and practice of the inhabitants of Connecticut . . . and their province is a storehouse for the smugglers of the neighboring colonies. They conscientiously study to cheat the King of those duties, which, they say, God and nature never intended should be paid. From the governor down to the tithing-man, who are sworn to support the laws, they will aid smugglers, resist collectors, and mob informers.[8]

In contemplating these open and notorious facts, which every member of government must have known, Samuel Peters came very near anger at the gross stupidity of the ministerial policy. The way to have met these difficulties was plain—the itch of democracy should have been cured with the salve of aristocracy. The natural leaders in the several colonies should have been taken care of by a judicious distribution of titles of nobility.

> The people of New-England are rightly stiled republicans: but a distinction should be made between the learned and unlearned, the rich and poor. The latter form a great majority; the minority, therefore, are obliged to wear the livery of the majority, in order to secure their election into office. Those very republican gentlemen are ambitious, fond of the power of governing, and grudge no money nor pains to obtain an annual office. What would they not give for a dignity depending not on the fickle will of a multitude, but on the steady reason and generosity of a King?[9]

[7] *Ibid.*, pp. 282–285.   [8] *Ibid.*, p. 320.   [9] *Ibid.*, p. 377.

There was shrewd, unclerical wisdom in the comment of Samuel Peters. If the gentlemen of England had founded their colonial policy on the principle of sharing the emoluments of rank and power with ambitious gentlemen in America, there might well have been quite another story to tell. But because they begrudged the small rewards, because they would have the shadow as well as the substance, they lost everything. An outcome so untoward and so stupid hurt Samuel Peters to the quick; but it was not his fault, and he doubtless found a crumb of malicious satisfaction in pointing out the ministerial stupidity after the mischief was done.

BOOK THREE: LIBERALISM AND THE CONSTITUTION
1783-1800

PART ONE: THE AGRARIAN DEFEAT
1783–1787

CHAPTER I
AGRARIANISM AND CAPITALISM

I

THE BACKGROUND OF IDEAS

English and French Contributions

WITH the close of the war the question of the times was the urgent problem of the form and control of the new political state to be erected: whether it should be the coercive sovereign of the whole, or should share its sovereignty with the several states. Although the problem was political, the forces that were driving to a solution were economic, and were commonly recognized as such. Agrarian and mercantile interests opposed each other openly and shaped their political programs in accordance with their special needs. Not until French romanticism popularized the doctrine of social equalitarianism was there any serious questioning of the principle of the economic basis of politics. The fact of property rule was challenged in America no more than in England, and the laws of suffrage in the several states were founded on that principle. The new state, therefore, took its shape from men who were political realists, deeply read in the republican literature of the seventeenth century, and inspired by the ideals of the rising English middle class. The opponents of the new state, on the other hand, were economic liberals who rejected English middle-class ideals, and inclined increasingly to the humanitarian theory of the French thinkers, though with an eye always upon American conditions. The struggle between these two schools of thought determined the final outcome of a long and acrimonious contest.

The English middle class had received its creative bent from seventeenth-century Puritanism. That vast movement survived political defeat and effected a silent revolution in English character that projected its ideals far into the future. It permeated the rising tradesman class, stimulated its ambition, and gave it an ethics precisely fitted to its needs. In inculcating the doctrine of a sacred calling to work, it substituted the modern attitude towards production for the medieval. It rejected the older conception of work for the sake of a livelihood, of production for consumption, and substituted the ideal of work for its own sake, of production for the sake of profit. It implicitly condemned the leisurely, play-loving and pleasure-taking activities of medieval England, and substituted a drab ideal of laborious gain, that measured life in terms of material prosperity and exalted the business of acquisition as the rational end of life. In the sanction of such an ethics, wealth became the first object of social desire; and this ideal, that answered the ambitions of the rising middle class, was preached under the authority of religion. To labor diligently in the vocation to which one is called of God, it was believed, was to labor under the great Taskmaster's eye, and in the confident hope of eternal reward.

No conceivable discipline was better calculated to breed a utilitarian race and create a nation of tradesmen. The immediate result was the emergence of a middle-class, unimaginative, laborious, prudential, who devoutly believed that the right to rise in the world, to pursue economic well-being in a competitive society, was the most sacred of human rights; that those who were faithful in little things, God would make rulers over great things. To scant one's service, whether to God or one's master, was the cardinal sin; work, thrift, self-denial, were the cardinal virtues. This amazing revolution in the ethics of work laid the basis upon which modern England was to rise; it carried in its loins the industrial revolution. The rise of the new ethics coincided historically with the final disintegration of the craft guilds, and the emergence of the great trading companies. It provided a desirable sanction for the modern principle of exploitation, and the development of the middleman system of distribution; and these conceptions the Puritanized English commercial class seized upon eagerly, and in capable fashion set about the work of creating the system of modern capitalism.

Every rising group is jealous of its interests and active in asserting them. It joins forces with whatever movements of current liberalism promise to further its purpose, but it will see to it that the wider movement shall serve its narrower ends. The commercial class gathered strength swiftly during the early seventeenth century, and with the gentry formed the backbone of discontent with the strong rule of Strafford. London was growing fast, "the abode of smoke, disease and democracy," as a contemporary gentleman phrased it; and the London burgesses supported Parliament heartily. The new money-economy wanted to be free from governmental restrictions and exactions, and the simplest way seemed to lie in asserting parliamentary sovereignty. That hope was frustrated after 1660 when control of Parliament passed into the hands of the landed gentry. The aristocracy was too strong for the middle class, and the latter was forced to buy its privileges in the open parliamentary market. Not until the intellectual liberalism of the later eighteenth century clarified its conception of the minimized state, did the money economy rise to fresh political consciousness, and then it joined heartily with the new liberalism in an attack upon the centralized powers of the political state.

The philosophy of this new liberalism was derived largely from two notable thinkers of the preceding century, Harrington and Locke, supplemented later by Adam Smith. The influence of the *Oceana* upon later thinkers was profound. In grasping and applying the principle of the economic interpretation of history Harrington laid the foundation of modern political theory. The true source of political power, he asserted, is economic power—"empire follows the balance of property." The form of government in a given country, whether monarchical, aristocratic, or democratic, according to the doctrine of economic determinism, depends upon the ownership of land, whether vested largely in one, in a minority, or in many. This primary economic power is modified, however, by the presence in every society of a natural aristocracy; the authority of character and ability imposes a natural leadership on those less capable, and disturbs the simple economics of the situation. Because of the resulting clash of interests, political stability can be secured only by a judiciously calculated system of checks; and the system which Harrington elaborated provided for a bicameral legislature—the aristocratic branch proposing and debating, and the democratic branch resolving—rotation in office, and the ballot, to the end that there should be a government of laws and not of men. His ideal was rulership by the best and wisest under well-considered laws, circumscribed by a written constitution.

Locke followed Harrington in founding his political theory upon economics, but he gave to it a characteristically middle-class interpretation. Harrington had been primarily concerned with a land economy; Locke was to become unconsciously a spokesman of a money economy. The persistent problem of that economy was the security of private property against sequestration, and the ultimate effect of Locke's teachings was to secure and strengthen the rights of property in the state. In basing his doctrine of property ownership upon labor, he prepared the way for a conception of economic power dissociated from land. In the universal communism which marks the state of nature, he argued, private property rights result from labor bestowed, and are ethically and socially valid. But in such a state of nature, the possession and enjoyment of property thus detached from the communal whole are at constant hazards. "The great and chief end, therefore, of men uniting into commonwealths and putting themselves under government, is the preservation of their property." [1] If such was the original purpose for which government was instituted among men, it follows that government must regard property rights with particular tenderness; for if the state prove untrustworthy, the original compact upon which it was erected is dissolved, and society returns to a state of nature. Locke therefore went far in asserting the inviolable rights of property, laying it down as a guiding principle that the sovereign in time of war may lawfully enforce conscription upon the bodies and lives of his subjects, but not upon their property. "The supreme power cannot take from any man any part of his property without his own consent," for "to invade the fundamental law of property" is to subvert "the end of government." [2] In thus asserting the sacredness of property, Locke laid the foundation of the new philosophy of capitalism.

As English capitalism grew stronger it began to envisage more critically the fundamental problem of the powers and functions of the political state. A state controlled by the landed interests, given to imposing vexatious restrictions upon trade, could not answer its needs; freedom rather than regulation was requisite to healthy development. From the Physiocratic teachings had come the new conception that economic well-being cannot be imposed from above by governmental paternalism, but results from un-

[1] *Second Treatise on Civil Government*, Chapter IX.   [2] *Ibid.*, Chapter XI.

trammeled individual enterprise. The great concern of government should be to assist and not hamper industry and trade; political policies should follow and serve commercial interests. Thus was provided the background from which emerged *The Wealth of Nations*, the declaration of independence of modern capitalism. Adam Smith completed the work of Locke, and gave definite form to the middle-class liberalism of eighteenth-century England, a liberalism that in the pursuit of commercial freedom found it desirable to limit the powers of the state. The Tory state had been centralized and paternal, the capitalistic state was to be reduced to the position of umpire between competitors. The net results, thus, of two hundred years of English middle-class struggle to free its economic ambitions from governmental restrictions was the conception of the social, political, and economic sufficiency of *laissez faire*. " Let alone " had been erected into a fetish.

In France, on the other hand, the economic interpretation of history dominated political thinking far less than in England, and the liberal movement owed more to a group of intellectuals than to the middle class. The French leaders were a remarkable group, far removed in temper from Harrington and Locke and Adam Smith. The Physiocrats were agrarians and the romantics were humanitarians. They followed the path of logic to broad principles. As leadership passed from Montesquieu to Rousseau, French liberalism abandoned the cautious historical appeal, and turned to generalization that carried far beyond liberalism. The Rousseau school became advanced radicals, aiming at the regeneration of society as a whole, seeking political justice by a universal appeal to reason. This explains the breadth and suggestiveness of their thinking, as well as the smallness of their immediate achievement. In seeking much they overreached accomplishment, for they had behind them no disciplined, class-conscious group, pursuing definite ends. But in outrunning their own time, they became leaders of later times; and the unfulfilled program of Rousseau carried over to become the inspiration of later humanitarianism.

The creative impulse of French romantic philosophy was a passionate social idealism. A disciple of Locke, Rousseau went further than his master and translated politics and economics into sociology. That a juster, more wholesome social order should take the place of the existing obsolete system; that reason and not interests should determine social institutions; that the ultimate ends to be sought were universal liberty, equality, and fraternity— such in brief were the main conceptions of his philosophy. "Regard for the general good" must be accepted as the sole test of laws and institutions. He attacked the problem by way of psychology, essaying a revaluation of human nature. Incalculable harm had been done, and grave mistakes made, Rousseau believed, by the old slanderous interpretation; to assume that every man is a knave, governed solely by self-interest, was an assumption contrary to fact. It was a generalization deduced from certain acquired characteristics. If in a competitive society men prove to be selfish, ambitious of power and distinction, brutal in seeking egoistic ends, the blame attaches to a vicious social system that has debased them from their natural state. In a state of nature men are kindly, rational, sociable; but in society the great rewards fall to the self-seeking. A ruthless social order is forever perverting the natural man; whereas if social rewards were bestowed on the social-minded, the innate sense of justice would speedily modify and control the impulse to egoism. The solution of the vexing social problem, Rousseau concluded, lay in a return to a state of nature, where under the determining influence of wholesome environment the individual should develop naturally, unperverted by false standards and unjust rewards.

French radicalism, then, was driving in the same direction with English liberalism, but it went much further. Both desired a loosening of the machinery of centralized power as represented by the political state; but whereas English liberalism protested against a paternalism that diminished its profits, French radicalism struck at the principle of centralization. Political institutions it regarded as artificial agencies for the purposes of exploitation—the state was little more than a tax machine; whereas the living source and wellspring of every true civilization is social custom, voluntary association, free exchange. The root of French radicalism was anarchistic, and its ideal was an agrarian society of free-holders. It would sweep away the long accumulated mass of prescriptive rights, the dead hand of the past, and encourage free men to create a new society that should have as its sole end and justification, the common well-being. A pronounced individualism characterized both movements, French and English; but in the one case it was humanitarian, appealing to reason and seeking social justice, in the other it was self-seeking, founded on the right of exploitation, and looking toward capitalism.

During the period with which we are concerned, American thought, become militantly self-conscious but still vague and inchoate touching any ultimate program, drew inspiration from both sources; but the deeper, controlling influence came finally to be English rather than French. The common doctrine of decentralization fitted American conditions, but to many Americans decentralization, whether social or political, had proved undesirable. The common doctrine of liberty accorded with the passions released by the Revolution, but the French humanitarian conceptions of equality and fraternity found little response in a middle-class, competitive world. On the contrary, the English doctrine of economic individualism made universal appeal. In presence of vast, unpreëmpted resources, the right of every man to preëmpt and exploit what he would, was synonymous with individual liberty. Any government which should endeavor to limit such exploitation would be bitterly assailed; and if the small man were free to enjoy his petty privilege, the greater interests might preëmpt unchallenged. The total influence of old-world liberalism upon the America of post-war days was, therefore, favorable to capitalistic development and hostile to social democracy. Until the early years of the nineties the democratic spirit of French radicalism was little understood in America, and the field remained free to the English middle-class philosophy, which appealed equally to the agrarian and the capitalistic groups.

II

THE POLITICAL SITUATION

Against this background of ideas, the political tactics of the year 1787 are sufficiently comprehensible. Two major problems had been settled by the war, namely, that henceforth the exploitation of America was to remain the prerogative of Americans, and that in the new country there was no place for a king or a titled aristocracy. But with these preliminaries settled, the problem remained to determine the form and powers of a national government. Should that government be entrusted with coercive sovereignty, or should it remain the titular head of confederated sovereign commonwealths? The latter solution had been accepted during the period of war, and in proposing abolition of the Articles of Confederation and the substitution of a new instrument, the burden of proof fell upon the advocates of the new. How the problem was met and the solution achieved by a skillful minority in face of a hostile majority is a suggestive lesson in political strategy. It is a classic example of the relation of economics to politics; of the struggle between greater property and smaller property for control of the state.

The strategic position of the large property interests in the year 1787 was favorable to a bold stroke. In the northern and middle states the controlling influence was wielded by a powerful money group that had been slowly rising during pre-Revolutionary days, and had greatly increased its resources and augmented its prestige as a result of war financing and speculation in currency and lands. They at once assumed the leadership which before had belonged to the gentry. Like all eighteenth-century realists they exhibited a frank property-consciousness that determined all their moves. With them affiliated such members of the older gentry as remained, the professional classes, ambitious Revolutionary officers who had set up the militant Order of the Cincinnati, together with a numerous body of the disappointed and the disaffected; the net result of which was a close working alliance of property and culture for the purpose of erecting a centralized state with coercive powers. They were powerfully aided by two outstanding characteristics of the eighteenth-century mind: an aristocratic psychology which was deeply ingrained in the colonial through the long unchallenged rule of the gentry; and the universal belief in the stake-in-society theory of government, evidenced by the general disfranchisement of non-property-holders. Property had always ruled in America, openly and without apology, and the money group could count on a spontaneous response to its demand that property should reorganize the feeble central government and set up one more to its liking. In the South this reorganization was unnecessary, for the planter aristocracy, in siding with the Revolution, remained masters of their society, and the money group had not risen to challenge their supremacy. It remained only for the northern interests to join forces with the planters to bring the great property interests of the country under one banner.

The status of the small property holders, on the other hand, was much less happy. They were in possession of many of the state governments, and were strongly wedded to the Articles of Confederation; but they were deep in populism and their agrarian measures offered rallying points for a powerful opposition. They lacked disciplined cohesion and were wanting in a broad program. The militant mood of Revolutionary days had given place to suspicion and disillusion, and their fighting strength was greatly weakened. They were suffering the fate of all post-war governments. The widespread depression was attributed to populist policies, and all the evils from which the country was suffering were laid at the doors of agrarian legislatures. Under such conditions the political strategy of the money group was predetermined. The issue was ready-made. Astute politicians like Hamilton seized the opportunity and crystallized the discontent by the ingenious argument that the trouble was too much agrarianism, that agrarianism resulted from too much democracy, and that the inevitable end of too much democracy was universal anarchy. The root of all the troubles, it was asserted, was the pernicious slackness of the Articles of Confederation which prevented a vigorous administration. There could be no prosperity until a competent national government was set up on a substantial basis.

The inevitable consequence was that the ideal of popular democratic rule received a sharp setback. The aristocratic prejudices of the colonial mind were given a more militant bias by skillful propaganda. Democracy was pictured as no other than mob rule, and its ultimate purpose the denial of all property rights. Populistic measures were fiercely denounced as the natural fruit of democratic control; all America was in danger of following the destructive example of New Hampshire and Rhode Island. "Look at the Legislature of Rhode Island," exclaimed a speaker in the New York Constitutional Convention, "what is it but the perfect picture of a mob!" The virus of democracy was a poison that destroyed the character of the people as well as government; was not the fate of Rhode Island a warning to the rest of the country? Here is a picture of that commonwealth, drawn by an English gentleman before agrarianism had done its worst.

The government of this province is entirely democratical, every officer, except the collector of the customs, being appointed . . . either immediately by the people, or by the general assembly. . . . The character of the Rhode Islanders is by no means engaging, or amiable, a circumstance principally owing to their form of government. Their men in power, from the highest to the lowest, are dependent upon the people, and frequently act without that strict regard to probity and honour, which ought invariably to influence and direct mankind. The private people are cunning, deceitful, and selfish: they live almost entirely by unfair and illicit trading. Their magistrates are partisan and corrupt: and it is folly to expect justice in their courts of judicature; for he who has the greatest purse is generally found to have the fairest cause. . . . It is needless, after this, to observe that it is in a very declining state.[3]

"Under the Articles of Confederation," comments a recent student, "populism had a free hand, for majorities in the state legislatures were omnipotent. Any one who reads the economic history of the time will see why the solid conservative interests of the country were weary of the talk about the 'rights of the people,' and were bent upon establishing firm guarantees for the rights of property." [4] The money-economy had made up its mind that such government as that of Rhode Island could not longer be tolerated. An example must be made of such hotbeds of anarchy; if reason would not be listened to, force must be used. An ardent Federalist, Judge Dana of Massachusetts, offered a possible solution:

This state [Rhode Island] will not choose delegates to the convention, nor order on their delegates to Congress. I hope they will not, as their neglect will give grounds to strike it out of the union, and divide its territory between their neighbors. . . . According to my best observation, such a division of this state would meet the best approbation of the commercial part of it, though they are afraid to take any open measures in the present state of things, to bring it about. Their interest must dictate such a measure; they never can be secure under the present form of government, but will always labor under the greatest mischief any people can suffer, that of being ruled by the most ignorant and unprincipled of their fellow citizens. This state is too insignificant to have a place on an equal footing with any of the others in the Union, unless it be Delaware. Therefore a bold politician would seize upon the occasion their abominable anti-federal conduct presents, for annihilating them as a separate member of the Union.[5]

"It is fortunate," wrote General Varnum to Washington, confirming Judge Dana's analysis of the economic divisions of Rhode

---

[3] Burnaby, *Travels through the Middle Settlements in North America in the Years 1759 and 1760.*
[4] Beard, *The Supreme Court and the Constitution.*
[5] Austin, *Life of Elbridge Gerry*, Vol. II, pp. 66–67.

Island, "that the wealth and resources of this state are chiefly in possession of the well affected, and they are entirely devoted to the public good."

It was Shays's Rebellion, that militant outbreak of populism that set all western Massachusetts in uproar, and spread to the very outskirts of Boston, which crystallized the anti-democratic sentiment, and aroused the commercial group to decisive action. With its armed attack upon lawyers and courts, its intimidation of legislators, its appeal for the repudiation of debts, it provided the object lesson in democratic anarchy which the "friends of law and order" greatly needed. The revolt was put down, but the fear of democracy remained and called aloud for stronger government. "We see the situation we are in," exclaimed a Boston member in the Massachusetts Constitutional Convention. "We are verging toward destruction, and every one must be sensible of it." Shays had failed, but with political power in the hands of agrarian legislatures, friendly to debtors, what dangers must not the future hold in store? Was it not the patriotic duty of the sober conservators of society to set up betimes a strong constitutional defense, before the rights of property were swept away by the fierce tide of democracy? Writing to Washington under date of October 23, 1786, General Knox argued:

On the very first impression of faction and licentiousness, the fine theoretic government of Massachusetts has given way, and its laws are trampled under foot. . . . Their creed is, that the property of the United States has been protected from the confiscation of Britain by the joint exertions of all, and therefore ought to be the common property of all. . . . This dreadful situation, for which our government have made no adequate provision, has alarmed every man of principle and property in New England. They start as from a dream, and ask what can have been the cause of this delusion? What is to give us security against the violence of lawless men? Our government must be braced, changed, or altered to secure our lives and property. We imagined that the mildness of our government and the wishes of the people were so correspondent that we were not as other nations, requiring brutal force to support the laws. But we find we are men—actual men, possessing all the turbulent passions belonging to that animal, and that we must have a government proper and adequate for him. The people of Massachusetts . . . are far advanced in this doctrine, and the men of property and the men of station and principle there, are determined to establish and protect them in their lawful pursuits. . . . Something is wanting and something must be done.[6]

⁶ Brooks, *Henry Knox*, pp. 194–195.

During these years of unrest the problem of a new fundamental law was carefully studied by the anti-agrarian leaders and solutions suggested. A remarkable change had come over their thinking. They discarded the revolutionary doctrines that had served their need in the debate with England. They were done with natural rights and romantic interpretations of politics and were turned realists. They parted company with English liberalism in its desire for a diminished state. Their economic interests were suffering from the lack of a strong centralized government, and they were in a mood to agree with earlier realists who held that men are animals with turbulent passions, and require a government "proper and adequate" for animals; and in view of local agrarian majorities, a proper and adequate government could not be had without a strong centralized state. The solution, they were convinced, lay in a return to some form of seventeenth-century republicanism, possibly modeled after Harrington, but with further checks upon the power of the democratic branch of the legislature, and a stronger executive. Hobbes with his leviathan monarchy had gone too far, but he had, at least, understood the need of a strong state; and a strong state, subservient to their interests, the business and landed groups were determined to set up as a barrier against a threatening agrarianism.

The great obstacle to such a program was the political power of the farmers, bred up in the traditional practice of home rule, jealous of local rights, and content with the Articles of Confederation. These home rulers would not take kindly to any suggestion of a centralized state, even though it should be republican in form. The thing must be done skillfully, if it were to succeed. To nullify where they could not override the political power of the agrarians, therefore, became the practical problem of the money-economy. The fear aroused by Shays's Rebellion provided the strategic opportunity, and the best brains of the country suggested the method. The struggle had begun which was to provide a new fundamental law for the United States.

CHAPTER II

THE GREAT DEBATE

WHEN one considers the bulk of commentary that has grown up about the Constitution, it is surprising how little abstract political speculation accompanied its making and adoption. It was the first response to the current liberal demand for written constitutions as a safeguard against tyranny, but it was aimed at the encroachments of agrarian majorities rather than at Tory minorities. It was the work of able lawyers and men of affairs confronting a definite situation, rather than of political philosophers; and it was accompanied by none of that searching examination of fundamental rights and principles which made the earlier Puritan and later French debate over constitutional principles so rich in creative speculation. Not a single political thinker comparable to the great English and French philosophers emerged from the struggle. The debate drew freely upon the materials supplied by those thinkers, but it added little that was new.

The Constitution was a venture in republicanism, on a scale and under conditions without historical precedent. It was inevitable, therefore, that the debate should concern itself greatly with the nature of republicanism and its adaptability to American conditions. As the argument developed, two major questions assumed critical importance: the question of the powers of the Federal state, and the question of the sovereign rights of the majority; and in dealing with both the debaters were on ground inadequately surveyed. Of definite republican theory little was available except the writings of a small group of seventeenth-century republicans. Of democratic theory, on the other hand, even less was available. American democratic aspiration had far outrun old-world liberalism, and had produced no independent speculation of its own. French democratic theory still awaited the rise of Jacobinism to clarify its principles. The party of Commonwealth Levelers, to be sure, with their doctrines of a "paramount law," manhood suffrage, and annual parliaments, offered much that might have proved suggestive; but the literature of the Levelers was buried too deep under Tory obloquy to be resurrected, and nowhere else was to be found any considerable body of democratic theory. It was inevitable, therefore, that the debaters should go back to the English liberals of the preceding century.

Consider for a moment the authorities bandied to and fro in the great debate. With such exceptions as Machiavelli, Vattel, Pufendorf, Montesquieu, they were the well-known English theorists, Hobbes, Harrington, Milton, Sidney, Halifax, Hume, and Blackstone. Unhappily for the democrats every one of these great names counted against their aspirations. Hobbes was a state absolutist whose *Leviathan* provided sharp weapons for those who wished to tone the government high; Hume was a Tory who accepted the traditional interpretation of human nature in the light of which democracy was the open door to anarchy; Blackstone was a Tory lawyer, who interpreted the British constitution by a narrow legalism that was obsolete before the *Commentaries* came from the press. Harrington, Milton, and perhaps Sidney, were republicans of strong aristocratic bias, and Halifax and Locke—the latter by much the most influential of all—were constitutional monarchists.[1] Every one of these great authorities either distrusted or violently condemned democracy, yet they provided the major body of theory made use of by the Federalists.

On the other hand, the slowly accumulating democratic theory was unknown to the members of the convention. In 1761 Robert Wallace had advanced an Owenite theory of property, attacking the principle of economic individualism as responsible for the current evils of government by landed property; but his book, *Various Prospects*, made no ripple on the placid waters of English liberalism.[2] In 1768 Joseph Priestley, a thinker who later was to exercise great influence in America, who lived here for a number of years and was intimate with Jefferson, published his essay, *First Principles of Government*, a work embodying the first English interpretation of the perfectibility of man, the rule of reason, the theory of the diminished state, and the Benthamite principle of utilitarianism or expediency in statecraft, which struck at the principle of coercive sovereignty. But the ideas of Priestley were probably little known in America in 1787, and his influence was

[1] These English liberals have been often regarded as democrats. Thus Merriam says of Locke, "He was the most famous of seventeenth century democratic thinkers." *American Political Theories*, p. 90.

[2] See Laski, *Political Thought from Locke to Bentham*, p. 188.

undermined further by a theological attack which sought to fasten upon him the stigma of atheism. In short, in this war of ideas the democrats were provided with little ammunition and fought at a great disadvantage. If the debate had taken place five years later, after the French Revolution had provided new democratic theory, the disparity of intellectual equipment would have been far less marked.

One other fact must be kept in mind, namely, that the great debate was in reality two debates, one carried on in the quiet of the convention hall, the other in the open. Each interprets the other, and taken together they reveal the conflict of forces and ideas that determined the form of the Constitution. In the privacy of the convention the speakers were free to express their views frankly, and in consequence a loose rein was given to the play of ideas; fundamental principles were examined critically and economic motives and class interests openly acknowledged. But in arguing the case before the generality of voters without doors a more cautious approach was necessary; arguments must be tempered to well-known prejudices, and circumspection must take the place of frankness. In the earlier debate, among innumerable lesser problems, two main questions dominated the argument: the question of the form of the centralized state—whether it should be aristocratic or republican; and if republican—as was inevitable—the question of what should be done about the majority will—how representation should be so refined as to guarantee stability to the government and security to the minority. In the second debate the appeal was to expediency rather than to principles, and turned on three chief points: the need of adoption in view of the desperate condition of the country; the adaptation of the proposed republican form to the vast extent of territory and diversity of interests; and the necessity of providing checks upon political parties if anarchy were to be avoided.

In the convention the need of a strong state, with powers beyond local legislatures, was not so much debated as assumed. By common consent it was agreed that the present lack of a centralized, coercive sovereignty, was the source of all current evils. How many members preferred monarchy to republicanism, in principle, it is impossible to determine; but they all realized the inexpediency of attempting to set it up; even Hamilton yielded to the logic of Colonel Mason's argument: "Notwithstanding the oppression

and injustice experienced among us from democracy, the genius
of the people is in favor of it, and the genius of the people must
be consulted." Accepting then the principle of republicanism as
a compromise between the extremes of monarchy and democracy,
the practical problem remained of erecting a system that should
secure the minority against the aggressions of political faction.
If the danger lay in an uncontrolled majority will, the way of
safety lay in imposing restraints upon that will. In elaborating a
system of checks and balances the members of the convention were
influenced by the practical considerations of economic determinism
more than by the theories of Montesquieu. They were realists
who followed the teachings of the greatest political thinkers from
Aristotle to Locke in asserting that the problem of government
lay in arranging a stable balance between the economic interests
of the major classes. The revolutionary conception of equalitarianism, that asserted the rights of man apart from property and
superior to property, did not enter into their thinking as a workable
hypothesis. The very conditions of the unsettled times were an
argument against it. Property, they argued, is the stabilizing
force in society; it is conservative and cautious; having everything
to lose by social upheavals, it is a restraining force upon factional
unrest. The propertyless, on the other hand, having nothing to
lose, easily become the victims of demagogues and embroil society
with foolish experiments. The republican experiment might work
in America because property was widely distributed, but in the
course of time a propertyless majority would arise, whose fickle
and subversive will must be held in check. The problem, therefore,
was to provide in time against such an eventuality. Certain
members of the convention did not go so far in their fear of the
propertyless, but relied upon the ability of property to protect
itself by extra-legal means. "Give the votes to people who have
no property," argued Gouverneur Morris, "and they will sell them
to the rich, who will be able to buy them." [3] But the more general
view was expressed by Madison:

> The landed interest, at present, is prevalent, but in process of time . . .
> when the number of landholders shall be comparatively small . . . will
> not the landed interests be overbalanced in future elections? and, unless
> wisely provided against, what will become of our government? In Eng-
> land, at this day, if elections were open to all classes of people, the property

[3] *Elliot's Debates*, Vol. I, p. 386.

of landed proprietors would be insecure. An agrarian law would take place. If these observations be just, our government ought to secure the permanent interests of the country against innovation. Landholders ought to have a share in the government, to support these invaluable interests, and to balance and check the other. They ought to be so constituted as to protect the minority of the opulent against the majority.[4]

This conception of the natural sovereignty of the landed interest with its stake-in-society theory of political rights, America inherited from England; and although the new Constitution professed to rest on the sovereignty of the people, the men who framed it refused to interpret the term, sovereignty of the people, in an equalitarian sense. They did not profess to be, in the words of John Quincy Adams, "slavish adorers of our sovereign lords the people." Every principle of their social and political philosophy taught them the desirability of limiting the majority will in order that the wiser minority will might rule. Paul Leicester Ford has asserted that "the Federal compact was the first deliberate attempt and assent of a majority to tie its own hands; to give to the minority guarantees of fair and equal treatment, without which democratic government is well-nigh impossible, save when developed along the lines of socialism." [5] Such partisan misinterpretation of plain historical fact is characteristic of our Federalist historians. If the hands of the disfranchised majority were tied by the voting minority, it is a bit absurd to attribute the resulting guarantees to an altruistic sense of justice, deliberately expressed by the former. Very possibly in a world so aristocratic as was America in 1787, no other course would have succeeded; but there is not a single historical fact to justify so naïve an interpretation, and the bitter partisan warfare which followed is sufficient to disprove it.

We are too prone to forget the wide popular disfavor with which the new Constitution was received. No sooner did the second debate open than it became evident that the majority opinion held quite a different conception of the sovereignty of the people than was expressed by the convention. It had no desire to tie its own hands; it did not take kindly to the proposal to transfer power from the several states to the Federal government. The villagers and small men were afraid of the new instrument; they asserted that it had been prepared by aristocrats and moneyed

[4] *Ibid.*, Vol. I, pp. 449-450.   [5] *The Federalist*, Introduction, p. viii.

men, and they repudiated the stake-in-society principle. "The Constitution," said General Thompson in the Massachusetts Convention, "and the reasons which induced gentlemen to frame it, ought to have been sent to the several towns to be considered by them. My town considered it seven hours, and after this there was not one in favor of it." In Rhode Island, where it was thus submitted, it was rejected "by a very great majority." The state of mind of the agrarian majority was thus expressed by Amos Singletary, of Sutton, Massachusetts:

These lawyers, and men of learning, and moneyed men, that talk so finely, and gloss over matters so smoothly, to make us, poor illiterate people, swallow down the pill, expect to get into Congress themselves; they expect to be the managers of this Constitution, and get all the power and all the money into their own hands, and then they will swallow up all us little folks, like the great leviathan.[6]

Among the host of pamphlets and newspaper articles that quickly appeared, *The Federalist* written by Hamilton and Madison with some help from Jay, and *Letters from the Federal Farmer to the Republican*, by Richard Henry Lee, fairly adequately present the opposing arguments. By common consent *The Federalist* was at once accepted by its party as an unanswerable defense of the Constitution; and its fame has grown greater with the passing years. No other work on political theory in the American library has been rated so high, or been more frequently cited. From the mass of contemporary pamphlets it emerges like a colossus. It "has been seriously and reverently called the Bible of Republicanism," says a legal historian, which "for comprehensiveness of design, strength, clearness, and simplicity . . . has no parallel among the writings of men, not even excepting or overlooking those of Montesquieu and Aristotle,"[7]; and a literary historian pronounces authoritatively, "it is so wisely thoughtful that one may almost declare it the permanent basis of sound thinking concerning American constitutional law."[8]

The Federalist was the work of able lawyers, with whom was joined a notable political thinker. In very large part it is of interest only to students of early constitutional theory and practice. It was designed as a frankly partisan argument to appeal to an

---

[6] Quoted in Harding, *The Federal Constitution in Massachusetts.*
[7] Carson, *History of the Supreme Court*, quoted by Ford, *The Federalist*, p. xxix.
[8] Wendell, *Literary History of America*, p. 118.

influential group in New York, many members of which had followed George Clinton and Robert Yates in opposition to the Constitution. On the political side it develops four main theses: the necessity for taking effective action in view of the self-confessed failure of the Articles of Confederation; the urgent need of a sovereign, unitary state, to avoid the horrors which must follow from "the political monster of an *imperium in imperio*"; the necessity of providing that justice shall prevail over the majority will; and the adaptability of the republican form to a great extent of territory and divergent interests. Of these the second and third lay bare the heart of Federalist political theory; and in the treatment of them there is no shrinking from the conclusions of the earlier debate, although the tone is conciliatory.

The argument for a unitary, sovereign state, developed by Hamilton, and the argument for justice, developed by Madison, rest upon the same basis and are regarded as the twin problems of government. The true sanction of government is found, not in good will, as Bentham and later democratic thinkers have urged, but in coercion; [9] and coercion is accepted as necessary because of universal selfishness. "Why has government been instituted at all? Because the passions of men will not conform to the dictates of reason and justice, without restraint." [10] Granted coercive sovereignty, government must guarantee justice to all; and justice demands that the majority shall suffer needful restraint equally with the minority. The great and insidious danger to good government has always been faction, the argument runs, and a chief merit of the Constitution lay in its provisions to lessen the disasters of factional ambition. "Complaints are everywhere heard from our most considerate and virtuous citizens, equally the friends of public and private faith, and of public and personal liberty, that our governments are too unstable, that the public good is disregarded in the conflict of rival parties, and that measures are too often decided, not according to the rules of justice and the rights of the minor party, but by the superior force of an interested and overbearing majority." [11]

No theory is more representative of the time than the theory of faction. It was a first line of defense thrown up against the advancing democratic movement. The term had long served conveniently to stigmatize any popular unrest, the "factious

[9] Number 15.   [10] *Ibid.*   [11] Number 10.

multitude" having been held synonymous in earlier usage with mob; but in the eighteenth century the word was applied generally to political parties. In a world moving inevitably towards manhood suffrage, a sharp alignment of parties with definite platforms was greatly feared by the minority, for the organization of the rank and file of voters must end in majority control. An honest appeal to the people was the last thing desired by the Federalists, and the democratic machinery of recalls and referendums and rotation in office, which had developed during the war, was stigmatized as factional devices which in the end must destroy good government. "As every appeal to the people would carry an implication of some defect in the government," argued Madison,[12] "frequent appeals would in a great measure deprive the government of that veneration which time bestows on everything, and without which the wisest and freest governments would not possess the requisite stability." "The danger of disturbing the public tranquillity by interesting too strongly the public passions is a still more serious objection against a frequent reference of constitutional questions to the decisions of the whole society."

In the remarkable tenth number, which compresses within a few pages pretty much the whole Federalist theory of political science, Madison has explained the Federalist objections to political parties and party government.

By a faction, I understand a number of citizens, whether amounting to a majority or minority of the whole, who are united and actuated by some common impulse of passion, or of interest, adverse to the rights of other citizens, or to the permanent and aggregate interests of the community. . . . If a faction consists of less than a majority, relief is supplied by the republican principle, which enables the majority to defeat its sinister views, by regular vote. . . . When a majority is included in a faction, the form of popular government, on the other hand, enables it to sacrifice to its ruling passion or interest, both the public good and the rights of other citizens. To secure the public good and private rights, against the danger of such a faction, is then the great object to which our inquiries are directed. . . . By what means is this great object attainable? Evidently by one of two only. Either the existence of the same passion or interest in a majority at the same time must be prevented; or the majority, having such coexistent passion or interest, must be rendered by their number and local situations, unable to concert and carry into effect schemes of oppression. If the impulse and the opportunity be suffered to

[12] Number 49.

coincide, we well know, that neither moral nor religious motives can be relied on as an adequate control.

In full agreement with the greater political thinkers of the past, Madison then traces political parties to economic sources. Since in every society the diversity of economic groups creates diversity of political programs, party divisions and party alignments are inevitable in the ordinary course of events. The unequal distribution of property is the realistic basis of all politics, and the "*sentiments* and *views* which arise from the possession of different degrees and kinds of property form the stuff of so-called 'political psychology.'" [13]

The diversity in the faculties of men, from which the rights of property originate, is . . . an insuperable obstacle to a uniformity of interests. The protection of these faculties is the first object of government. From the protection of different and unequal faculties of acquiring property, the possession of different degrees and kinds of property immediately results; and from the influence of these on the sentiments and views of the respective proprietors, ensues a division of the society into different interests and parties.

The latent causes of faction are thus sown in the nature of man; and we see them everywhere brought into different degrees of activity, according to the different circumstances of civil society. A zeal for different opinions . . . [has] divided mankind into parties, inflamed them with mutual animosity, and rendered them much more disposed to vex and oppress each other than to co-operate for their common good. . . . But the most common and durable source of factions has been the various and unequal distribution of property. Those who hold and those who are without property have ever formed distinct interests of society. Those who are creditors, and those who are debtors, fall under a like discrimination. A landed interest, a manufacturing interest, a mercantile interest, a moneyed interest, with many lesser interests, grow up of necessity in civilized nations, and divide them into different classes actuated by different sentiments and views. The regulation of these various and interfering interests, forms the principal task of modern legislation, and involves the spirit of party and faction in the necessary and ordinary operations of the government.

As a means of securing a necessary balance between rival interests, Madison approved a republican rather than a democratic form of government:

The two great points of difference, between a democracy and a republic, are, first, the delegation of the government, in the latter, to a small number of citizens elected by the rest; secondly, the greater number of citizens,

[13] Beard, *The Economic Basis of Politics*, pp. 29–32.

and greater sphere of country, over which the latter may be extended. The effect of the first difference is, on the one hand, to refine or enlarge the public views, by passing them through the medium of a chosen body of citizens, whose wisdom may best discern the true interests of their country, and whose patriotism and love of justice, will be least likely to sacrifice it to temporary or partial considerations.   Under such a regulation, it may well happen, that the public voice, pronounced by the representatives of the people, will be more consonant to the public good, than if pronounced by the people themselves, convened for the purpose. . . . The other point of difference is, the greater number of citizens, and extent of territory, which may be brought within the compass of republican, than of democratic government; and it is this circumstance principally which renders factious combinations less to be dreaded in the former, than in the latter. . . . Extend the sphere, and you take in a greater variety of parties and interests; you make it less probable that a majority of the whole will have a common motive to invade the rights of other citizens; or if such a common motive exists, it will be more difficult for all who feel it to discover their strength, and act in unison with each other.[14]

In such argument Madison was adapting to his purpose the views of Milton and other seventeenth-century republicans, to whom in the dangerous days when the Puritan Commonwealth was breaking up, the "noise and shouting of the rude multitude," the drunken ribaldry of the London rabble, was prophetic of "new injunctions to manacle the native libertie of mankinde." But it has long since become a commonplace of political observation that the minority and not the majority is the more dangerous to the common well-being, for it is the minority that most frequently uses government to its own ends.

    The contrast in temper and argument between *The Federalist* and Richard Henry Lee's *Letters from the Federal Farmer*,[15] is striking. The calmness and fair-mindedness of the work persuade one that it ill deserves the name partisan; it comes near to being a frank and disinterested examination of the proposed instrument of government. Its sharpest strictures are tempered by ready acknowledgment of excellent features. The burden of Lee's accusation is that the instrument is undemocratic; that it must result in placing the majority under control of the minority; and that it in no wise reflects the sober judgment of the body of the people. He is more restrained than Elbridge Gerry, who asserted that it

---

[14] Number 10.
[15] The full title is: *Observations leading to a fair examination of the system of government, proposed by the late Convention; and to several essential and necessary alterations in it.   In a number of Letters from the Federal Farmer to the Republican.*   Reprinted in Ford's pamphlets.

was the outcome of a conspiracy hatched in secret, a work of "such motley mixture, that its enemies cannot trace a feature of Democratic or Republican extract." But the Farmer's restraint adds weight to the serious charges which he brings against the instrument, and the unseemly haste of its advocates in urging its speedy adoption. It was not to destroy the work of the Convention that he pleaded for delay; but that it should receive full and fair consideration, and be disposed of as its merits or defects should warrant.

His first concern is that the Constitution should not be adopted with the inconsiderate haste for which *The Federalist* was pressing. "The first principal question that occurs, is, Whether, considering our situation, we ought to precipitate the adoption of the proposed Constitution?" Hamilton had made much of the desperate state of affairs that admitted of no delay; Lee replied by denying, with Franklin and other competent observers, that the present state was desperate. Matters were improving daily, peace was restoring the ravages of war.

I know uneasy men, who with very much to precipitate, do not admit all these facts; but they are facts well known to all men who are thoroughly informed in the affairs of this country. It must, however, be admitted, that our federal system is defective, and that some of the state governments are not well administered; but . . . we impute to the defects in our governments many evils and embarrassments which are most clearly the result of the late war. . . . When we want a man to change his condition, we describe it as wretched, miserable, and despised; and we draw a pleasing picture of that which we would have him assume. . . . It is too often the case in political concerns that men state facts not as they are, but as they wish them to be. . . . Men who feel easy in their circumstances, and such as are not sanguine in their expectations relative to the consequences of the proposed change, will remain quiet under the existing governments. Many commercial and monied men, who are uneasy, not without just cause, ought to be respected; and by no means, unreasonably disappointed in their expectations and hopes. . . . It is natural for men, who wish to hasten the adoption of a measure, to tell us, now is the crisis— now is the critical moment which must be seized or all will be lost; and to shut the door against free enquiry, whenever conscious the thing presented has defects in it, which time and investigation will probably discover. . . . If it is true, what has been so often said, that the people of this country cannot change their constitution for the worse, I presume it still behoves them to endeavor deliberately to change it for the better.

Granted that experience has demonstrated the need of revising the Articles of Confederation in certain essential points, Lee maintains that the enemies of democracy have been making undue capital out of the shortcomings of an emergency government, in the hope of subverting the democratic state governments and substituting a more aristocratic form.

The confederation was formed when great confidence was placed in the voluntary exertions of individuals, and of the respective states; and the framers of it, to guard against usurpation, so limited, and checked the powers, that, in many respects, they are inadequate to the exigencies of the union. . . . During the war, the general confusion, and the introduction of paper money, infused in the minds of people vague ideas respecting government and credit. We expected too much from the return of peace, and of course we have been disappointed. Our governments have been new and unsettled; and several legislatures, by making tender, suspension, and paper money laws, have given just cause of uneasiness to creditors. By these and other causes, several orders of men in the community have been prepared by degrees, for a change of government; and this very abuse of power in the legislatures, which in some cases has been charged upon the democratic part of the community, has furnished aristocratical men with those very weapons, and those very means, with which, in great measure, they are rapidly effecting their favourite object.

The methods by which the convention was brought together at a time when the "idea of destroying ultimately, the state government, and forming one consolidated system, could not have been admitted," is traced briefly with penetrating comment, and the unfortunate decision of some excellent republicans to take no part in the work is regretted:

Here the favorable moment for changing the government was evidently discerned by a few men, who seized it with address. . . . Tho' they chose men principally connected with commerce and the judicial departments, yet they appointed many good republican characters—had they all attended we should see, I am persuaded, a better system presented. The non-attendance of eight or nine men, who were appointed members of the convention, I shall ever consider as a very unfortunate event to the United States.—Had they attended, I am pretty clear that the results . . . would not have had that strong tendency to aristocracy now discernible in every part of the plan . . . the young visionary men, and the consolidating aristocracy, would have been more restrained than they have been.

Lee frankly concedes that the instrument possesses many excellent features, but he considers it greatly vitiated by the "want of that one important factor in a free government, a representation of the people." "Because we have sometimes abused democracy, I am not among those who think a democratic branch a nuisance."

"Every man of reflection must see, that the change now proposed, is a transfer of power from the many to the few." The present agitation may be traced to its source in "two very unprincipled parties," between whom stand the great mass of honest and substantial people:

One party is composed of little insurgents, men in debt, who want no law, and who want a share of the property of others; these are called levellers, Shaysites, &c. The other party is composed of a few, but more dangerous men, with their servile dependents; these avariciously grasp at all power and property; you may discover in all the actions of these men, an evident dislike to free and equal government, and they go systematically to work to change, essentially, the forms of government in this country; these are called aristocrats, m—ites, &c. Between these two parties is the weight of the community: the men of middling property, men not in debt on the one hand, and men, on the other, content with republican governments, and not aiming at immense fortunes, offices and power. In 1786, the little insurgents, the levellers, came forth, invaded the rights of others, and attempted to establish governments according to their wills. Their movements evidently gave encouragement to the other party, which, in 1787, has taken the political field, and with its fashionable dependents, and the tongue and the pen, is endeavouring to establish in a great haste, a politer kind of government. These two parties . . . are really insignificant, compared with the solid, free, and independent part of the community.

Calm voices such as Lee's were few in those strident days, and the Federalists fairly overwhelmed the silent majority with clamorous argument. Polite culture and professional learning joined forces to write down the agrarians. The Hartford Wits dedicated smart couplets to the cause; Francis Hopkinson made merry over their ways; Noah Webster confuted them with his economic interpretation of politics; lawyer-scholars like James Wilson and John Dickinson exposed their heresies; solid business men like Peletiah Webster contributed after the measure of their intelligence. In their ardor the Federalists went further. "What can be the views of those gentlemen in Boston," asked Lee pertinently, "who countenanced the printers in shutting up the press against a fair and free investigation?" From the strident debate emerged not only the Constitution, but political parties, no longer to be spoken of as factions, but eventually to be accepted as necessary agencies in republican government; and to understand their rival policies we must turn to examine the political philosophies of the outstanding leaders.

CHAPTER III

POLITICAL THINKERS

The English Group

OF this great age of American political thought, two important characteristics emerge: it was overwhelmingly English in its antecedents; and it was already differentiating its program from that of contemporary English liberalism. Nearly all the outstanding men—Jefferson, Adams, Washington, Wilson, Mason, Madison, Gouverneur Morris—were of the older liberal tradition, and with some notable exceptions, of the school of Pitt. Contemporary English liberals such as Priestley, Bentham, and Godwin numbered few adherents among the leaders of American thought. Economic conditions in America already were imposing conclusions that pointed in a direction other than that which English liberalism was traveling. The doctrine of the diminished state, which was making persistent headway among English liberals, could make no appeal to men who desired an augmented state; and liberalism as a policy was in ill repute at a time when men believed thay were suffering from too much liberalism. American political thought, therefore, followed an independent path, and in spite of its English origin came to conclusions that differentiated it broadly from the old-world theory.

I

ALEXANDER HAMILTON

The Leviathan State

Of the disciplined forces that put to rout the disorganized party of agrarianism, the intellectual leader was Alexander Hamilton, the brilliant Anglo-French West Indian, then just entered upon his thirties. A man of quite remarkable ability, a lucid thinker, a great lawyer, a skillful executive, a masterly organizer, a statesman of broad comprehension and inflexible purpose, he originated and directed the main policies of the Federalist group, and brought them to successful issue. For this work he was singularly well equipped, for in addition to great qualities of mind and persuasive ways he was free to work unhampered by the narrow localisms and sectional prejudices that hampered native Americans. He was rather English than American, with a certain detachment that refused to permit his large plans to be thwarted by minor, vexatious details, or the perversity of stupid men. He was like the elder Pitt in the magnificence of his imperial outlook.

Such a man would think in terms of the nation rather than of the state. He would agree with Paine that the continental belt must be more securely buckled. The jealousies and rivalries that obstructed the creation of a centralized Federal government found no sympathy with him. He was annoyed beyond all patience with the dissensions of local home rule. In his political philosophy there was no place for "the political monster of an *imperium in imperio*"; he would destroy all lesser sovereignties and reduce the several commonwealths to a parish status. For town-meeting democracies and agrarian legislatures he had frank contempt. The American villager and farmer he never knew and never understood; his America was the America of landed gentlemen and wealthy merchants and prosperous professional men, the classes that were most bitterly anti-agrarian. And it was in association with this group of conservative representatives of business and society that he took his place as directing head in the work of reorganizing the loose confederation into a strong and cohesive union. When that work was accomplished his influence was commanding, and for a dozen years he directed the major policies of the Federalist party. His strategic position as Secretary of the Treasury enabled him to stamp his principles so deeply upon the national economy that in all the intervening years since he quitted his post they have not been permanently altered. That we still follow the broad principles of Hamilton in our financial policy is a remarkable testimony to the perspicacity of his mind and his understanding of the economic forces that control modern society. And hence, because the Hamiltonian principles lie at the core of the problem which has proved so difficult of solution by modern liberalism, the life and work of Hamilton are of particular significance in our democratic development.

Hamilton was our first great master of modern finance, of that finespun web of credit which holds together our industrial life; and because his policies opened opportunities of profit to some and entailed loss upon others, they have been debated with an acrimony such as few programs have endured. About the figure of the brilliant Federalist the myth-makers have industriously woven their tales, distorting the man into either a demigod or a monster. The individual has been merged in the system which he created, and later interpretation has been shot through with partisan feeling; political and economic prejudice has proved too strong for disinterested estimate. Any rational judgment of Hamilton is dependent upon an interpretation of the historical background that determined his career, and in particular of the state of post-Revolutionary economics; and over such vexing questions partisans have wrangled interminably. Thus Sumner, in his life of Hamilton, asserts dogmatically that Federalism was no other than the forces of law and order at war with the turbulent, anarchistic forces unloosed by the Revolution, and that the putting down of the scheme of repudiation was the necessary preliminary to the establishment of a great nation. In the light of such an interpretation, Hamilton the far-seeing, courageous and honest master of finance, was the savior of nationality, the one supreme figure rising above an envious group of lesser men. But, as has been sufficiently pointed out in preceding chapters, the historical facts are susceptible of quite other interpretation; and as our knowledge of the economic struggle then going on becomes more adequate, the falsity of such an explanation becomes patent. If, on the other hand, we concede that the crux of the political problem in 1787 was economic—the struggle waging between farmer and business groups for control of government—then the position of Hamilton becomes clear; he was the spokesman of the business economy. He thought in terms of nationality and espoused the economics of capitalism, because he discovered in them potentialities congenial to his imperialistic mind.

The career of Hamilton followed logically from the determining facts of temperament and experience. He came to New York an alien, without position or influence, ambitious to make a name and stir in the world; and in the America of his day there could be little doubt what doors opened widest to preferment. He made friends easily, and with his aristocratic tastes he preferred the rich and distinguished to plebeians. Endowed with charming manners and brilliant parts, he fascinated all whom he met; before he was of age he was intimate with all the Whig leaders, civil and military, on Washington's staff and elsewhere, lending his brains to the solution of knotty problems, prodding stupider minds with illuminating suggestions, proving himself the clearest thinker in whatever group he found himself. It was by sheer force of intellect that he gained distinction. Singularly precocious, he matured early; before his twenty-fifth year he seems to have developed every main principle of his political and economic philosophy, and thereafter he never hesitated or swerved from his path. He was tireless in propaganda, urging on the proposed Constitutional convention, discussing with Robert Morris his favorite project of a national bank, outlining various systems of funding, advocating tariffs as an aid to domestic manufacture, and sketching the plan of a political and economic system under which native commercialism could go forward. His reputation as an acute and trustworthy financial adviser was well established with influential men north and south, when the new government was set up, and Washington turned to him naturally for the Treasury post, to guide financial policies during the difficult days immediately ahead. But so able a man could not be restricted within a single portfolio, and during the larger part of Washington's two administrations Hamilton's was the directing mind and chief influence. He regarded himself as Prime Minister and rode roughshod over his colleagues. Major policies such as that of no entangling alliances must receive his careful scrutiny and approval before they were announced; and in consequence more credit belongs to Hamilton for the success of those first administrations than is commonly recognized.

But when we turn from the administrator and statesman to the creative thinker, there is another story to tell. The quickness of his perceptions, the largeness of his plans and efficacy of his methods—his clear brilliancy of understanding and execution—are enormously impressive; but they cannot conceal certain intellectual shortcomings. There was a lack of subtlety in the swift working of his mind, of shades and *nuances* in the background of his thought, that implied a lack of depth and richness in his intellectual accumulation. Something hard, almost brutal lurks in his thought—a note of intellectual arrogance, of cynical contempt. He was utterly devoid of sentiment, and without a shred of idealism, unless a certain grandiose quality in his conceptions be accounted idealism. His absorbing interest in the rising system of credit and finance, his cool unconcern for the social consequences of his policies, reveal his weakness. In spite of his brilliancy Hamilton was circumscribed by the limitations of the practical man.

In consequence of such limitations Hamilton was not a political philosopher in the large meaning of the term. In knowledge of history he does not compare with John Adams; and as an open-minded student of politics he is immensely inferior to Jefferson. Outside the domain of the law, his knowledge does not always keep pace with his argument. He reasons adroitly from given premises, but he rarely pauses to examine the validity of those premises. The fundamentals of political theory he seems never to have questioned, and he lays down a major principle with the easy finality of a dogmatist. Compare his views on any important political principle with those of the greater thinkers of his time, and they are likely to prove factional if not reactionary. The two tests of eighteenth-century liberalism were the doctrine of individualism, and the doctrine of the minimized state; and Hamilton rejected both: the former in its larger social bearing, and the latter wholly. He was not even abreast of seventeenth-century liberalism, for that was strongly republican, and Hamilton detested republicanism only a little less than democracy. Harrington and Locke were no masters of his; much less were Bentham or Priestley or Godwin. He called the French revolutionary writers "fanatics in political science"; to what extent he read them does not appear. The thinkers to whom he owed most seem to have been Hume, from whom he may have derived his cynical psychology, and Hobbes whose absolute state was so congenial to his temperament. But political theory he subordinated to economic theory. He was much interested in economics. With the Physiocratic school and its agrarian and sociological bias he could have no sympathy, but with the rising English school that resulted from the development of the industrial revolution, he found himself in hearty accord. Capitalism with its credit system, its banks and debt-funding and money manipulation, was wholly congenial to his masterful temperament. He read Adam Smith with eagerness and *The Wealth of Nations* was a source book for many of his state papers. To create in America an English system of finance, and an English system of industrialism, seemed to him the surest means to the great end he had in view; a centralizing capitalism would be more than a match for a decentralizing agrarianism, and the power of the state would augment with the increase of liquid wealth.

But granted that he lacked the intellectual qualities of the philosopher, it does not follow that his significance diminishes. On the contrary his very independence of contemporary European theory enlarged his serviceableness to party. He was free to employ his intelligence on the practical difficulties of a new and unprecedented situation. English liberalism did not answer the needs of Federalism, if indeed it could answer the needs of the country at large. The time had come to decide whether the long movement of decentralization should go further, and confirm the future government as a loose confederacy of powerful states, or whether an attempt should be made to check that movement and establish a counter tendency towards centralized, organized control. If the former, it meant surrendering the country to a democratic *laissez faire*, and there was nothing in the history of political *laissez faire* as it had developed in America, that justified the principle to Hamilton. It had culminated in agrarianism with legislative majorities riding down all obstacles, denying the validity of any check upon its will, constitutional, legal or ethical. The property interests of the minority had been rendered insecure. There had been altogether too much *laissez faire*; what was needed was sharp control of legislative majorities; the will of the majority must be held within due metes and bounds. Even in the economic world the principle of *laissez faire* no longer satisfied the needs of the situation. Parliamentary enactments had aided British interests in their exploitation of America before the war; it was only common sense for an American government to assist American business. The new capitalism that was rising stood in need of governmental subsidies. Business was languishing; infant industries could not compete on even terms with the powerful British manufacturing interests, long established and with ample capital. From a realistic contemplation of these facts Hamilton deduced the guiding principle that has since been followed, namely, that governmental interference with economic laws is desirable when it aids business, but intolerable and unsound when it aims at business regulation or control, or when it assists agriculture or labor.

Throughout his career Hamilton was surprisingly consistent. His mind hardened early as it matured early, and he never saw cause to challenge the principles which he first espoused. He was what a friendly critic would call a political realist, and an enemy would pronounce a cynic. With the practical man's contempt for theorists and idealists, he took his stand on current fact. He looked to the past for guidance, trusting to the wisdom of experience; those principles which have worked satisfactorily heretofore may be expected to work satisfactorily in the future. Whoever aspires to become a sane political leader must remember that his business is not to construct Utopias, but to govern men; and if he would succeed in that difficult undertaking he must be wise in the knowledge of human nature. At the basis of Hamilton's political philosophy was the traditional Tory psychology. Failure to understand human nature, he believed, was the fatal weakness of all democratic theorists; they put into men's breeches altruistic beings fitted only for a Utopian existence. But when we consider men as they are, we discover that they are little other than beasts, who if unrestrained will turn every garden into a pigsty. Everywhere men are impelled by the primitive lust of aggression, and the political philosopher must adjust his system to this unhappy fact. He must not suffer the charge of cynicism to emasculate his philosophy; "the goodness of government consists in a vigorous execution," rather than in amiable intentions; it is the business of the practical man and not of the theorist.

It needs no very extensive reading in Hamilton to discover ample justification for such an interpretation of his political philosophy; the evidence lies scattered broadly through his pages. At the precocious age of seventeen he laid down the thesis, "A vast majority of mankind is entirely biassed by motives of self-interest"; and as political systems are determined by the raw material of the mass of the people, they must be conditioned by such egoism. A year later he discovered in Hume the central principle of his philosophy:

> Political writers, says a celebrated author, have established it as a maxim, that, in contriving any system of government, and fixing the several checks and controls of the constitution, *every man* ought to be supposed a *knave*; and to have no other end, in all his actions, but *private interest*. By this interest we must govern him; and, by means of it, *make him co-operate to public good*, notwithstanding his insatiable avarice and ambition. Without this, we shall in vain boast of the advantages of *any constitution*.[1]

At the age of twenty-seven he reiterated the doctrine, "The safest reliance of every government, is on men's interests. This is a principle of human nature, on which all political speculation, to

[1] *Works*, Vol. II, p. 51.

be just, must be founded." [2] Obviously this was not a pose of youthful cynicism, but a sober judgment confirmed by observation and experience.

Accepting self-interest as the mainspring of human ambition, Hamilton accepted equally the principle of class domination. From his reading of history he discovered that the strong overcome the weak, and as they grasp power they coalesce into a master group. This master group will dominate, he believed, not only to further its interests, but to prevent the spread of anarchy which threatens every society split into factions and at the mercy of rival ambitions. In early days the master group was a military order, later it became a landed aristocracy, in modern times it is commercial; but always its power rests on property. "That power which holds the purse-strings absolutely, must rule," he stated unequivocally. The economic masters of society of necessity become the political masters. It is unthinkable that government should not reflect the wishes of property, that it should be permanently hostile to the greater economic interests; such hostility must destroy it, for no man or group of men will be ruled by those whom they can buy and sell. And in destroying itself it will give place to another government, more wisely responsive to the master group; for even a democratic people soon learns that any government is better than a condition of anarchy, and a commercial people understands that a government which serves the interests of men of property, serves the interests of all, for if capital will not invest how shall labor find employment? And if the economic masters do not organize society efficiently, how shall the common people escape ruin?

Such are the fundamental principles which lie at the base of Hamilton's philosophy. He was in accord with John Adams and James Madison and Noah Webster, in asserting the economic basis of government, with its corollary of the class struggle. He not only accepted the rule of property as inevitable, but as desirable. As an aristocrat he deliberately allied himself with the wealthy. That men divide into the rich and the poor, the wise and the foolish, he regarded as a commonplace too evident to require argument. The explanation is to be sought in human nature and human capacities. For the common people, about whom Jefferson concerned himself with what seemed to Hamilton sheer

2 *Ibid.*, p. 298.

demagoguery, he felt only contempt. Their virtues and capacities he had no faith in. "I am not much attached to the *majesty of the multitude*," he said during the debate over the Constitution, "and waive all pretensions (founded on such conduct) to their countenance." His notorious comment—which the American democrat has never forgiven him, "The people!—the people is a great beast!"—was characteristically frank. Hamilton was no demagogue and nothing was plainer to his logic than the proposition that if the people possessed the capacity to rule, their weight of numbers would give them easy mastery; whereas their yielding to the domination of the gifted few proves their incapacity. A wise statesman, therefore, will consider the people no further than to determine how government may be least disturbed by their factional discontent, and kept free to pursue a logical program. Under a republican form good government is difficult to maintain, but not impossible. The people are easily deceived and turned aside from their purpose; like children they are diverted by toys; but if they become unruly they must be punished. Too much is at stake in government for them to be permitted to muddle policies.

It is sufficiently clear that in tastes and convictions Hamilton was a high Tory. The past to which he appealed was a Tory past, the psychology which he accepted was a Tory psychology, the law and order which he desired was a Tory law and order. His philosophy was not liked by republican America, and he knew that it was not liked. Practical business men accepted both his premises and conclusions, but republicans under the spell of revolutionary idealism, and agrarians suffering in their pocketbooks, would oppose them vigorously. He was at pains, therefore, as a practical statesman, to dress his views in a garb more seemly to plebeian prejudices, and like earlier Tories he paraded an ethical justification for his Toryism. The current Federalist dogma of the divine right of justice—*vox justiciae vox dei*—was at hand to serve his purpose and he made free use of it. But no ethical gilding could quite conceal a certain ruthlessness of purpose; in practice justice became synonymous with expediency, and expediency was curiously like sheer Tory will to power.

In certain of his principles Hamilton was a follower of Hobbes. His philosophy conducted logically to the leviathan state, highly centralized, coercive, efficient. But he was no idealist to exalt the state as the divine repository of authority, an enduring entity apart from the individual citizen and above him. He regarded the state as a highly useful instrument, which in the name of law and order would serve the interests of the powerful, and restrain the turbulence of the disinherited. For in every government founded on coercion rather than good will, the perennial unrest of those who are coerced is a grave menace; in the end the exploited will turn fiercely upon the exploiters. In such governments, therefore, self-interest requires that social unrest shall be covered with opprobium and put down by the police power; and the sufficient test of a strong state lies in its ability to protect the privileges of the minority against the anarchy of the majority. In his eloquent declamation against anarchy Hamilton was a conspicuous disciple of the law and order school. From the grave difficulties of post-Revolutionary times with their agrarian programs, he created a partisan argument for a leviathan state, which fell upon willing ears; and in the Constitutional convention, which, more than any other man, he was instrumental in assembling, he was the outstanding advocate of the coercive state.

In his plan of government presented to the Convention, the principle of centralized power was carried further than most would go, and his supporting speeches expressed doctrines that startled certain of his hearers. He was frankly a monarchist, and he urged the monarchical principle with Hobbesian logic. "The principle chiefly intended to be established is this—that there must be a permanent *will*." "There ought to be a principle in government capable of resisting the popular current."

Gentlemen say we need to be rescued from the democracy. But what [are] the means proposed? A democratic assembly is to be checked by a democratic senate, and both these by a democratic chief magistrate. The end will not be answered, the means will not be equal to the object. It will, therefore, be feeble and inefficient.[3]

The only effective way of keeping democratic factionalism within bounds, Hamilton was convinced, lay in the erection of a powerful chief magistrate, who "ought to be hereditary, and to have so much power, that it will not be his interest to risk much to acquire more," and who would therefore stand "above corruption." Failing to secure the acceptance of the monarchical principle, he devoted himself to the business of providing all possible checks upon the power of the democracy. He "acknowledged himself

[3] Brief of speech submitting his plan of Constitution, in *Works.* Vol. II, p. 415.

not to think favorably of republican government; but he addressed
his remarks to those who did think favorably of it, in order to
prevail on them to tone their government as high as possible." [4]
His argument was characteristic:

All communities divide themselves into the few and the many. The
first are the rich and well born, the other the mass of the people. The
voice of the people has been said to be the voice of God; and, however
generally this maxim has been quoted and believed, it is not true to fact.
The people are turbulent and changing; they seldom judge or determine
right. Give, therefore, to the first class a distinct, permanent share in the
government. They will check the unsteadiness of the second; and as they
cannot receive any advantage by a change, they therefore will ever maintain good government. Can a democratic assembly, who annually revolve
in the mass of the people, be supposed steadily to pursue the public good?
Nothing but a permanent body can check the imprudence of democracy.
Their turbulent and uncontrollable disposition requires checks. [5]

The argument scarcely needs refuting today, although curiously
enough, it was rarely questioned by eighteenth-century gentlemen.
It was the stock in trade of the Federalists, nevertheless Hamilton
was too acute a thinker not to see its fallacy. It denied the fundamental premise of his political philosophy. If men are actuated
by self-interest, how does it come about that this sovereign motive
abdicates its rule among the rich and well born? Is there a magic
in property that regenerates human nature? Do the wealthy
betray no desire for greater power? Do the strong and powerful
care more for good government than for class interests? Hamilton
was fond of appealing to the teaching of experience; but he had read
history to little purpose if he believed such notions. How mercilessly he would have exposed the fallacy in the mouth of Jefferson!
It was a class appeal, and he knew that it was a class appeal, just
as he knew that success knows no ethics. He was confronted by a
situation in practical politics, and in playing ignobly upon selfish
fears he was seeking to force the convention towards the English
model. He had no confidence in the Constitution as finally adopted,
and spoke in contemptuous terms of its weakness; whereas for
the British constitution he had only praise, going so far, according
to Jefferson, as to defend the notorious corruption of parliament
on the ground of expediency: "purge it of its corruption"—
Jefferson reports him as saying—"and give to its popular branch
equality of representation, and it would become an *impracticable*

[4] *Elliot's Debates*, Vol. V, p. 244.   [5] *Ibid.*, Vol. I, p. 422.

government; as it stands at present, with all its supposed defects, it is the most perfect government which ever existed." [6] The argument savors of cynicism, but it is in keeping with his philosophy; the British constitution owed its excellence to the fact that in the name of the people it yielded control of the state to the landed aristocracy.

It was as a statesman that the brilliant qualities of Hamilton showed to fullest advantage. In developing his policies as Secretary of the Treasury he applied his favorite principle, that government and property must join in a close working alliance. The new government would remain weak and ineffective so long as it was hostile to capital; but let it show itself friendly to capital, and capital would make haste to uphold the hands of government. Confidence was necessary to both, and it was a plant of slow growth, sensitive to cold winds. The key to the problem lay in the public finance, and the key to a strong system of finance lay in a great national bank. This, Hamilton's dearest project, was inspired by the example of the Bank of England. No other institution would so surely link the great merchants to government, he pointed out, for by being made partners in the undertaking they would share both the responsibility and the profits. It was notorious that during the Revolution men of wealth had forced down the continental currency for speculative purposes; was it not as certain that they would support an issue in which they were interested? The private resources of wealthy citizens would thus become an asset of government, for the bank would link "the interest of the State in an intimate connection with those of the rich individuals belonging to it." "The men of property in America are enlightened about their own interest, and would easily be brought to see the advantage of a good plan." Hence would arise stability and vigor of government.

Moreover, the bank would be of immense service in the pressing business of the public debt. In regard to this difficult matter Hamilton was early convinced that only one solution was possible: all outstanding obligations, state and national, must be assumed by the Federal government at face value, and funded. Anything short of that would amount to repudiation of a lawful contract, entered into in good faith by the purchaser; and such repudiation would destroy in the minds of the wealthy the confidence in the

[6] *Works of Jefferson*, Ford edition, Vol. I, p. 165.

integrity of the new government that was vital to its success. It was true that speculators would reap great and unearned profits; but the speculators for the most part were ʌhe principal men of property whose support was so essential that any terms were justifiable, and nothing would bind them so closely to the government as the knowledge that it would deal generously with them. It was true also that thousands of small men would lose by such a transaction; but under any existing social economy the small man was at a disadvantage, and the present state of affairs was not such as to justify Utopian measures. To alienate the rich and powerful in order to conciliate the poor and inconsequential seemed to him sheer folly. The argument of expediency must prevail over abstract justice; the government must make terms with those in whose hands lay the success or failure of the venture.

His report on the public credit, of January 14, 1790, is one of the significant documents in the history of American finance. It is the first elaboration by an American statesman of the new system of capitalization and credit developed in eighteenth-century England, and it laid a broad foundation for later capitalistic development. To less daring financiers of the time the public debt was no more than a heavy obligation to be met; but to Hamilton it offered an opportunity for revivifying the whole financial life of the nation. Let the debts be consolidated and capitalized by a proper system of funding, and the augmented credit would multiply capital, lower the rate of interest, increase land values, and extend its benefits through all lines of industry and commerce. It was a bold plan and it encountered bitter opposition, which was not lessened by the heavy taxation that it called for. In his tax proposals Hamilton revealed his political philosophy so nakedly as almost to prove his undoing. His doctrine of the blessing of a national debt smacked rather too strongly of English Toryism for the American stomach.

A national debt, if it be not excessive, will be to us a national blessing. It will be a powerful cement to our Union. It will also create a necessity for keeping up taxation to a degree which, without being oppressive, will be a spur to industry. . . . It were otherwise to be feared our popular maxims would incline us to too great parsimony and indulgence. We labor less now than any civilized nation of Europe; and a habit of labor in the people, is as essential to the health and vigor of their minds and bodies, as it is conducive to the welfare of the State.[7]

[7] *Works*, Vol. I, p. 257.

A further struggle was encountered over the proposals of an internal revenue and a tariff. In his advocacy of the former Hamilton encountered the vigorous opposition of the backcountry. The total lack of adequate means of transportation rendered the problem of a grain market a chronic difficulty to the frontier farmers. The most convenient solution lay in distilling, and so whisky had become the chief commodity of the farmer that was transportable and brought a cash price. In placing a tax upon distilled liquors, therefore, Hamilton struck so directly at the economic interests of thousands of backwoodsmen, as to bring a rebellion upon the new administration. He knew what he was doing, but he calculated that it was safer to incur the enmity of farmers than of financiers; nevertheless the fierceness of the opposition surprised him, and aroused all the ruthlessness that lay in the background of his nature. He called for the strong arm of the military and when the rising was put down, he was angered at Washington's leniency in refusing to hang the convicted leaders. In his advocacy of a tariff he was on safer ground, for he was proposing a solution of the difficult situation confronting the manufacturers. Something must be done to revive industry so long stagnant. The old colonial machinery had been destroyed and new machinery must be provided. Industrial independence must follow political independence; and the easiest way lay in providing a tariff barrier behind which the infant industries of America might grow and become sufficient for domestic needs.

In his notable report on manufactures, submitted on December 5, 1791, Hamilton showed his characteristic intelligence in his grasp of the principles of the industrial revolution. Certainly no other man in America saw so clearly the significance of the change that was taking place in English industrialism, and what tremendous reservoirs of wealth the new order laid open to the country that tapped them. The productive possibilities that lay in the division of labor, factory organization, the substitution of the machine for the tool, appealed to his materialistic imagination, and he threw himself heart and soul into the cause of industrial development in America. He accepted frankly the principle of exploitation. He was convinced that the interests of the manufacturers were one with the national interests, and he proposed to put the paternal power of the government behind them. With the larger social effects—the consequences to the working classes, congestion of population, the certainty of a labor problem—he concerned himself no more than did contemporary English states- men. He was contemptuous of Jefferson's concern over such things. He had no Physiocratic leanings towards agriculture; material greatness alone appealed to him; and he contemplated with satisfaction the increase in national wealth that would accrue from levying toll upon the weak and helpless.

Besides this advantage of occasional employment to classes having different occupations, there is another, of a nature allied to it, and of a similar tendency. This is the employment of persons who would other- wise be idle, and in many cases, a burthen on the community, either from bias of temper, habit, infirmity of body, or some other cause, indisposing or disqualifying them for the toils of the country. It is worthy of particular remark, that, in general, women and children are rendered more useful, and the latter more early useful, by manufacturing establishments, than they would otherwise be. Of the number of persons employed in the cotton manufactories of Great Britain, it is computed that four-sevenths, nearly, are women and children; of whom the greatest proportion are children, and many of them of a tender age.[8]

If the material power and splendor of the state be the great end of statesmanship—as Hamilton believed—no just complaint can be lodged against such a policy; but if the well-being of the individ- ual citizen be the chief end—as Jefferson maintained—a very different judgment must be returned.

Although the fame of Hamilton has been most closely associated with the principle of constitutional centralization, his truer sig- nificance is to be found in his relation to the early developments of our modern capitalistic order. In his understanding of credit finance and the factory economy, he grasped the meaning of the economic revolution which was to transform America from an agrarian to an industrial country; and in urging the government to further such development, he blazed the path that America has since followed. "A very great man," Woodrow Wilson has called him, "but not a great American." In the larger historical meaning of the term, in its democratic implications, that judgment is true; but in the light of our industrial history, with its corporate develop- ment and governmental subsidies, it does not seem so true. As the creative organizer of a political state answering the needs of a capitalistic order—a state destined to grow stronger as imperial- istic ambitions mount—he seems the most modern and the most

American of our eighteenth-century leaders, one to whom our industrialism owes a very great debt, but from whom our democratic liberalism has received nothing.

II

JOHN ADAMS

Realist

Midway between Hamilton and Jefferson stands John Adams, the most painstaking student of government and the most widely read in political history, of his generation of Americans. The noble art of government was a lifelong passion with him—the sublimest subject, in his opinion, which a free citizen could study. Solid, pragmatic, unimaginative, he was an admirable representative of the later eighteenth century with its vigorous understanding, its distrust of idealisms, its contempt for social theory. He was the political counterpart of Dr. Johnson. To a generation sniveling over the sorrows of life and seeking panaceas in Rousseau sentimentalisms, the English Tory proffered the consolation of the realist. Things are bad enough, heaven knows; poverty, injustice, disease, death, are evils which no optimism can shut its eyes to. But what can be done? The malady of human nature is a disease beyond the reach of romantic plasters. No quack remedies will cure ills that lie too deep for laws or kings—they only aggravate the trouble. Be sensible therefore. Endure like men what cannot be cured. Stop sniveling and make the best of things as they are.

The analogy between these two vigorous exponents of common sense is too obvious to miss. For years the chief business of John Adams was to bring home to Americans the lesson in realism which Samuel Johnson was urging upon his countrymen. The mischief of romantic idealisms was spreading widely in America, disseminated by propagandists like Tom Paine and theorists like Jefferson; there was high need that the people be brought back to sober reality. This duty he took upon himself. He was an uncompromising realist who refused to be duped by fine dreams or humanitarian panaceas; he was much given to throwing cold water on the hope of social regeneration through political agencies. And the reward which he gained for his voluntary labors was a personal unpopularity beyond that of any other statesman of the time. He was charged with apostacy from his earlier democratic faith, and the charge had sufficient foundation, unfortunately, to make it credible if one wished to believe it.

During the revolutionary struggle he had been a member of the left wing; during the early struggles under the Constitution he was a member of the right wing. The young man had been a stalwart defender of human rights, the old man was a stalwart defender of property rights; and this shift of position was fatal to his reputation with the rising democratic party. The French Revolution marked the critical turning point in his intellectual development. As a politician he was well-nigh ruined by it; but as a political thinker he owed it much. Before that vast upheaval came to challenge his somewhat conventional mind, he was a hard-working lawyer-politician, with a liking for legalistic constitutional theory; but as the Revolution went forward, he was forced into uncompromising reaction. While ardent young Americans were becoming pro-French, he became pro-British; while they were accepting the new leveling principles, he searched history to prove how inevitable are social distinctions and economic classes; while they looked hopefully forward to a democratic future, he gathered his materials for an interpretation of political forces that revealed aristocracy as the dominant factor in every society. Both Adams and his critics were products of the French upheaval, but facing in different directions; naturally, the antagonism between them became sharp and bitter.

The severest critic cannot deny to John Adams excellent qualities of mind and heart. A sound lawyer, a capable statesman, a vigorous thinker and courageous debater, he fought his way from obscurity to high position and many honors, and in every responsibility he acquitted himself in a fashion altogether worthy of the notable Adams posterity. A stubborn intellectual independence and a vigorous assertiveness were his distinguishing characteristics. He revealed to the full the Adams trait of going its own way and coming to its own conclusions. He was never the victim of mob psychology, and he was never careful of occasion or circumstance in speaking out his convictions. America has had too few independent minds, and much of Adams's unpopularity was the result of his refusal to hunt with the pack. Unfortunately his admirable qualities were offset by a blundering tactlessness and a colossal vanity that brought many troubles upon his head. He loved to be in the public eye and he studied the little arts of self-advertising. In his youthful diary he set down these characteristic words: "Reputation ought to be a perpetual subject of my thoughts, and aim of my behavior. How shall I spread an opinion of myself as a lawyer of distinguished genius, learning, and virtue?" Self-confident, domineering, and jealously suspicious—always on the lookout lest some honor due him should fall to another—he struggled through a career strewn with animosities and heartburnings that a nicer tact and a more generous nature would have avoided. He was his own worst enemy. He did not spare himself in public service, but he demanded strict payment and was inclined to haggle over the terms; in consequence his later days were embittered and his fame was less than he deserved.

Our present concern, however, is with the political scientist and not with the politician; with the theories of government that occupied so much of his thought, rather than with the policies of the statesman. He wrote voluminously, heavily, with no grace of style or savor of wit, and the long row of his collected writings may well appall the reader who proposes to make his acquaintance. Ponderous treatises are supplemented by lesser works and flanked by innumerable letters; his industry was prodigious and no one will wonder at his exclamation, "My hand is impatient of the pen and longs to throw it down." His important work divides broadly into two main divisions: his contribution to the colonial debate with England, and his elaborate system of government formulated during the years of French revolutionary debate. A brief consideration will suffice for the first, but the second requires more careful examination.

In his contributions to the colonial debate Adams concerned himself mainly with questions of constitutional law. He placed little reliance on the appeal to natural rights, and showed scant respect for "popular talk and those democratical principles which have done so much mischief in this country." [9] The American cause, he believed, should be based on constitutional principles, but those principles required restatement in the light of existing fact. They must be rescued from the narrow interpretation of little Englanders and adapted to meet the pressing needs of imperial federation. The English people were not all residents of the British Isles, and a constitutional practice suited to compact groups in a

[9] "Autobiography," in *Works*, Vol. II, p. 310.

common environment, was ill adapted to the needs of widely sundered bodies of British subjects. Into this difficult and momentous business of imperial federation, Adams plunged earnestly in an endeavor to chart the unexplored field. That the problem was the gravest then confronting Englishmen is abundantly evident today; that it received grossly inadequate consideration on both sides of the Atlantic is equally clear. In this field John Adams was a pioneer and his work possesses still some historical interest. This fact, too frequently overlooked, has been emphasized by a recent student, who has summarized the final results of Adams's thinking in the following theses: that the empire was an association of equals, each with independent legislative powers; that the British constitution was the fundamental law of the empire, defining the relationship of the constituent parts; and that it was the function of the judiciary to disallow a legislative act of any of the several legislatures which did not comport with the fundamental law, or which attempted to impose the will of one of the partners in violation of the fundamental understanding and its guarantee.[10]

Such, in compressed form, was Adams's elaboration and justification of the dogma of Otis, that an act against the constitution was void. In its relation to current English constitutional practice it was at once revolutionary and reactionary. It implied a double attack upon parliamentary sovereignty, first in limiting its powers by a super-parliamentary constitution, and then in subjecting its acts to judicial review. The final result would be the transfer of sovereignty from the legislature to the judiciary. The idea had been toyed with by English lawyers, but never seriously considered; it was alien to the whole theory and history of parliamentary development. English landed gentlemen have never been minded to grant the veto power to the judiciary, but have persistently retained sovereignty in the legislature. Nevertheless in such early speculation is found the germ of our later practice, as it finally developed through the decisions of Chief Justice Marshall.

In the works of his later period, such as *A Defence of the Constitution of Government of the United States of America* and *Discourses on Davila*, Adams emerged from the narrow field of constitutional law and elaborated a theory of government based on

---

[10] R. G. Adams, *Political Ideas of the American Revolution*, Trinity College Press, 1922, pp. 92–93.

wide reading and long observation. It was by way of reply to the French thinkers, and it contributed in large measure to the partisan passions of the time. Unfortunate circumstances attended the publication of the works. The *Defence of the Constitution* appeared at the moment when newspaper accounts of the absurd dress in which he appeared at the Court of St. James's were provoking republican jests; and the *Discourses on Davila* came out in the *Gazette of the United States*, when the country was buzzing about his childish fondness for titles and ceremonies. It was impolitic for Adams to publish in the *Gazette*, a virulently Federalistic sheet and anathema to all liberals. His unpopular theories could not fail to arouse republican antagonism when set over against such seeming commentary as this:

> *Take away thrones and crowns from among men and there will soon be an end of all dominion and justice.* There must be some adventitious properties infused into the government to give it energy and spirit, or the selfish, turbulent passions of men can never be controlled. This has occasioned that artificial splendor and dignity that are to be found in the courts of many nations. The people of the United States may probably be induced to regard and obey the laws without requiring the experiment of courts and titled monarchs. In proportion as we become populous and wealthy must the tone of the government be strengthened.[11]

The unfortunate effect of *Davila* upon a highly wrought public opinion Adams himself records: "the rage and fury of the Jacobinical journals against these discourses, increased as they proceeded, intimidated the printer, John Fenno, and convinced me, that to proceed would do more hurt than good. I therefore broke off abruptly."[12] But the mischief to his reputation had been done; henceforth Adams was popularly regarded as anti-republican. Debating the nature of aristocracy in the New York Constitutional Convention, one of the speakers said, "I would refer the gentleman for a definition of it to the Hon. John Adams, one of our natural aristocrats." Madison went so far as to charge that he was secretly a monarchist. The charge was absurd, as any examination of his political theory will convince. "It is a fixed principle with me," he wrote to Samuel Adams in 1790, "that all good government is and must be republican." But that he advocated a system of government hostile to agrarianism, that he was bitterly antagonistic

[11] *Gazette of the United States*, March, 1790; quoted in Forman, "The Political Activities of Philip Freneau," in *Johns Hopkins Studies in History and Political Science*, XX, Nos. 9–10.

[12] *Works*, Vol. VI, p. 272, note.

to French Jacobinism and all its works, is apparent to the most casual reader. He was a realist of the seventeenth-century school of English republicanism, attacking what he regarded as the delirium of democracy, appealing to experience in answer to abstract theory.

Adams erected his political system upon what he called "self-evident truths." He went to the root of the matter and directed his inquiry into the validity of the humanitarian psychology which asserted that men are good by nature, and may be trusted to deal justly with their fellows. He appealed to the whole unhappy record of past misrule to disprove the thesis. Instead of discovering in the average man a kindly, rational being—as Jefferson professed to discover—Adams found quite the contrary; and he summoned a host of historians and philosophers to witness that Machiavelli was right in his contention that "those who have written on civil government lay it down as a first principle . . . that whoever would found a state, and make proper laws for the government of it, must presume that all men are bad by nature; that they will not fail to show that natural depravity of heart whenever they have a fair opportunity."[13] In further substantiation of this fact he examined the history of governments past and present, and he found everywhere testimony to the truth that the mass of men are naturally indolent, selfish, given to luxury, shortsighted, jealous, tending to faction and all mischievous intrigue. Never does he find them given to virtue, choosing wisdom, seeking justice. They cannot endure that others should be superior in virtue, or rank, or power; but driven by ambition they strive to pull down their superiors in order themselves to rise. The men in any society who possess sufficient virtue to set justice above self-interest, are few and count for little in the scale against the selfish many.[14]

This Calvinistic doctrine that "human nature is not fit to be trusted," and that "men are never good but through necessity," being accepted—and John Adams was as clearly satisfied of its truth as "of any demonstration of Euclid"—he proceeded to translate it into political terms, and examine the bearing of it upon systems of government. At once a second fallacy of the humanitarian school emerged—men are impelled not by ideals

[13] *Works*, Vol. IV, p. 408.
[14] See "Defence of the Constitution, etc.," in *Works*, Vol. VI, pp. 9, 57, 97.

but by needs, not by reason, as Godwin argued, but by the desire for goods. In a social state the natural selfishness of human nature impels to economic aggression. Underneath the turbulent unrest which threatens every government is economic ambition. This is the rock on which all schemes of social justice founder—a rock which every sound political thinker will chart and recognize as a danger reef. Economics and biology provide the major social drives. "That the first want of every man is his dinner and the second want his girl were truths well known . . . long before the great philosopher Malthus arose to think he enlightened the world by his discovery."[15] The supposed liberty of a democratic state proves in practice to be no other than anarchy, running swiftly into license and ending in tyranny. All human societies are rooted in exploitation, the bitter fruit of which is domestic warfare.

The universal social state is one of ruthless class struggle, wherein the strong conquer the weak—this is the third deduction from the premises which Adams laid down. It cannot be otherwise, he argued, from the natural inequality of men. The rude mass being shiftless, ignorant, spendthrift, they are at the mercy of the strong, ambitious, and capable, who exploit them freely. Hence in every society emerges the division between patricians and plebeians, developing into caste as the social order grows complex. The self-interest of the patricians teaches them the need of class solidarity, and with intelligent solidarity the few easily seize control of the state and use it to their ends. Hence arises an aristocracy or oligarchy, which maintains its power through control of the economic resources of society. Control of property means control of men; for sovereignty inheres in economics. In presence of this historical fact it is foolish to declaim about natural rights; there are no rights except such as are won either by property or the sword.

That there should long exist a society without a property aristocracy Adams regarded as inconceivable. The French democrats with their talk of equality and fraternity were mischievous visionaries. "Every democracy . . . has an aristocracy in it as distinct as that of Rome, France, England." In older societies the aristocracy maintained supremacy through possession of the land. In America the vast extent of territory and the wide diffusion of land-

[15] Letter to John Taylor, in *Works*, Vol. VI, p. 516.

holding presented the most favorable opportunity in history for democratic development if such were possible; nevertheless the evidences of an aristocracy developing here were too patent to miss. The abundance of economic resources, Adams pointed out, was an invitation to gigantic exploitation, the logical outcome of which must be the emergence of a master group, richer and more powerful than the world has ever known. The power of economic appeal was nullified in America by no special providence.

Paper wealth has been a source of aristocracy in this country, as well as landed wealth, with a vengeance. Witness the immense fortunes made *per saltum* by aristocratical speculations, both in land and paper. . . . But, sir, land and paper are not the only source of aristocracy. There are master shipwrights, housewrights, masons, &c. &c., who have each of them from twenty to a hundred families in their employment, and can carry a posse to the polls when they will. These are not only aristocrats, but a species of feudal barons. . . .

Should a planter in Virginia sell his *clarissimum et illustrissimum et celeberricum locum* with his thousand negroes, to a merchant, would not the merchant gain the aristocratical influence which the planter lost by his transfer? Run down, sir, through all the ranks of society . . . from the first planter and the first merchant to the hog driver, the whiskey dram-seller, or the Scottish peddler, and consider, whether the alienation of lands, wharves, stores, pike stock, or even lottery tickets, does not transfer the aristocracy as well as the property.[16]

Believe—as John Adams believed regarding the funding operations—that "paper wealth is the madness of the many for the profit of the few,"[17] it is nevertheless a modern illustration of the old truth that the few do profit from the madness of the many, and by reason of such profit set themselves up as masters. If then the historian cannot escape the conclusion that political systems and social classes rest upon economic foundations, this fundamental fact must preside over the speculations of the political philosopher. Democracy is out of the question, even if it were desirable. The great and sole object of political science must be the preservation of liberty—the right of every individual to life, freedom, property, in an aristocratic society—and the frustration of the universal drive of self-interest which leads on the one hand to tyranny, and on the other to anarchy. Between these two poles of tyranny and anarchy, of oligarchy and democracy, every society oscillates; to prevent such oscillation and discover some mean between the extremes must be the business of the political philosopher. The

[16] *Ibid.*, pp. 508–509.   [17] *Ibid.*, p. 508.

pregnant fallacy of the French school, Adams insisted, lay in its doctrines of equality and fraternity. The meanest underling does not desire equality; men kiss the feet above them and trample on the fingers beneath. That the people love a lord is a sign of their abundant folly. Should the democrats abolish the principle of hereditary rank by law, it would still remain in fact; for the property basis on which it rests is transmitted legally from father to son, and each successive generation gains an adventitious advantage from its substantial heritage as well as from the historical splendor of the family name. On this rock every attempt at a democracy has foundered.

If these words are true, no well ordered commonwealth ever existed; for we read of none without a nobility, no, not one, that I can recollect, without a hereditary nobility; . . . It would be an improvement in the affairs of society, probably, if the hereditary legal descent could be avoided; and this experiment the Americans have tried. But in this case a nobility must and will exist, though without the name, as really as in countries where it is hereditary.[18]

The mortal weakness of democracy, Adams agreed with Madison and the Federalists generally, lay in faction, a disease which in the nature of the case he regarded as incurable. The use of party power other than justly was factional, and because the mass of men do not set justice above present interest, the unbridled rule of the majority drives straight towards mass tyranny. Despoiled by the superior ability of the aristocracy, the exploited plebeians fight back blindly; and where the constitution of government permits them to band together in a political party, they override the rights of the minority as ruthlessly as the latter before had denied the rights of the majority. Aristocratic exploitation leads to democratic leveling; and the resultant anarchy is but prelude to the rise of another aristocracy to repeat the unhappy process.

The passions and desires of the majority of the representatives being in their nature insatiable and unlimited by any thing within their own breasts, and having nothing to control them without, will crave more and more indulgence, and, as they have the power, they will have the gratification.[19]

If you give more than a share in the sovereignty to the democrats, that is, if you give them the command or preponderance in the sovereignty,

18 "Defence of the Constitution, etc.," in *Works*, Vol. VI, pp. 124-125.
19 *Ibid.*, p. 64.

that is, the legislature, they will vote all property out of the hands of you aristocrats, and if they let you escape with your lives, it will be more humanity, consideration, and generosity than any triumphant democracy ever displayed since the creation. And what will follow? The aristocracy among the democrats will take your places, and treat their fellows as severely and sternly as you have treated them.[20]

The end of every democratic experiment, Adams pointed out, has been the man on horseback. So inevitably does democracy culminate in despotism, that "in reality, the word democracy signifies nothing more nor less than a nation of people without any government at all, and before any constitution is instituted." [21] "Democracy never has been and never can be so desirable as aristocracy or monarchy, but while it lasts, is more bloody than either. Remember, democracy never lasts long. It soon wastes, exhausts, and murders itself. There never was a democracy that did not commit suicide." "The proposition that the people are the best keepers of their own liberties is not true. They are the worst conceivable, they are no keepers at all; they can neither judge, act, think, or will, as a political body. Individuals have conquered themselves; nations and large bodies never." [22]

Having thus examined the major doctrines of the French democratic school, namely, that men are good by nature, that the social end is liberty, equality, fraternity, and that social well-being will result from an appeal to reason, Adams had cleared the problem of what he regarded as misconceptions, and was ready to lay out a system of government which should demonstrate his skill in political architecture. The determining factor in laying down the main lines was sufficiently clear. Since property lies at the root of the problem of government, the business of devising a just and stable system of government resolves itself into the question, What shall be done about property? As an orthodox Whig Adams found part of his answer ready to hand. With Locke he believed that property rights are sacred, and that it is a chief business of government to protect private property against unjust expropriation. The security of property may be taken as the measure of the stability of government. "The moment the idea is admitted into society, that property is not as sacred as the laws of God, and that there is not a force of law and public justice to protect it,

---

[20] "Letter to John Taylor," in *Works*, Vol. VI, p. 516.
[21] *Works*, Vol. VI, p. 211.
[22] See "Defence of the Constitution, etc.," and in particular Vol. IV of *Works*

anarchy and tyranny commence."[23] "The very name of a republic implies, that the property of the people should be represented in the legislature, and decide the rule of justice," he argued, quoting Cicero.[24] Moreover, the futility of any other arrangement was axiomatic in his philosophy. If property is not granted representation, it will usurp it; if attacked, it will know how to defend itself; and the end will be the setting up of an oligarchy on the ruins of the republic. But if Adams agreed with Hamilton that the state should deal tenderly with the rights and interests of property, he refused to go with the latter in his sole concern for the wealthy. Greater property interests must be held in due balance with the smaller, for if unchecked the strong will drive on to ruthless exploitation of the weak, and society will be endangered from the top as in a democracy it is endangered from the bottom. It was this desire for a mean between oligarchy or monarchy on the one hand, and democracy on the other, that determined his choice of a republican form of government.

The difficult problem of property-power in the state, Adams was convinced, could be solved justly and permanently only by a judicious system of balanced interests. Subjected, as every government must be, to a persistent stress of rival interests, it must be constructed with calculated nicety, or the structure would fall of its own weight; and the sole principle, he believed, is that of the Gothic arch—the principle of thrust and counter-thrust. Provide in such manner that the selfishness of one group in society shall be neutralized by the counter selfishness of other groups, let the buttress support the arch at its weakest point, and upon such an equilibrium of counterforces great vaults and noble towers may be erected. It is the apotheosis of the system of checks and balances.

It is agreed that "the end of all government is the good and ease of the people, in a secure enjoyment of their rights, without oppression"; but it must be remembered, that the rich are *people* as well as the poor; that they have rights as well as others; that they have as clear and as sacred a right to their large property as others have to theirs which is smaller; that oppression to them is as possible and as wicked as to others. The rich, therefore, ought to have an effectual barrier in the constitution against being robbed, plundered, and murdered, as well as the poor; and this can never be without an independent senate. The poor should have a bulwark

[23] "Defence of the Constitution, etc.," in *Works*, Vol. VI, p. 9.
[24] *Works*, Vol. IV, p. 295.

against the same dangers and oppressions; and this can never be without a house of representatives of the people. But neither the rich nor the poor can be defended by their respective guardians in the constitution, without an executive power, vested with a negative, equal to either, to hold the balance even between them, and decide when they cannot agree.[25]

Such in brief was the master principle of that system of mixed government which John Adams advocated so persistently in the teeth of the popular demand for a simpler, more responsive form. It based itself frankly upon the dogma of the class struggle; it provided each class—as he recognized them in his simple social analysis—with a legislative arm with which to defend itself; and it set as arbiter between them an executive, carefully selected, who was supposed to represent that abstract *tertium quid*, the public. The keynote is struck in a line from Pope set on the title-page of the *Defence*—"All Nature's difference keeps all Nature's peace." That Adams greatly admired his handiwork is beyond doubt; that he was intellectually honest with himself is very likely true; but that there is a note of disingenuousness, a failure to take into account his pronounced bias towards property interest, is certain. There was ample ground for the popular dislike of his theory. This is not the place to enter upon an examination of the system of checks and balances, nor to insist that any such system becomes in practice an impossibility. It is more to the point to remark upon certain fallacies in his theory which Adams himself must have seen if his mind had been quite free from bias.

Adams's intelligent analysis of social forces should have saved him from the major fallacy of the doctrine of checks and balances. In imposing the doctrine of a separation of powers upon the doctrine of property power, he effectively denied the validity of the latter. Assuming for the sake of the argument that the Senate will represent property, what reason justified the assumption that the House would represent the small men, or that the President would speak for the whole? If property is sovereign, as Adams maintained—"Harrington has shown that power always follows property. This I believe to be as infallible a maxim in politics, as that action and reaction are equal, is in mechanics" [26]—will it not rule the House equally with the Senate? above all, will it not control so important an officer as the President? The theory

[25] "A Defence of the Constitution, etc.," in *Works*, Vol. VI, p. 65.
[26] *Works*, Vol. IX, p. 376.

that the President represents an abstract public is a disingenuous political fiction; in the light of Adams's theory of economic determinism it is a gross absurdity. Moreover, Adams invalidated his entire system by refusing to provide the necessary machinery by which the House could represent the small man. In denying manhood suffrage, he eliminated the proletarian and the renter from the political equation, and left them without political power; in his definition the small man was the freeholder, the representative of the middle class. The House, therefore, equally with the Senate, was the mouthpiece of property interests; the former more likely to be representative of land, the latter of capital.

Where did Adams get the major ideas of his political philosophy?[27] An omnivorous reader, he gathered from many sources, and his memory was a well-stocked storehouse of fact and theory. As a young man he was disciple of Locke and the natural-rights school, but as he grew older he abandoned the natural-rights theory. His interpretation of human nature he took over from Machiavelli, Hobbes and Hume, discovering in their psychology of self-interest and emulation—often mean but many times admirable—a conception in harmony with the Calvinism of his early training. He owed much to Bolingbroke, whom he read five times, but to James Harrington, the Commonwealth intellectual, he turned with a zest of discovery so great that he may not unjustly be called one of Harrington's disciples. From the *Oceana* he drew so abundantly that the most casual student of political theory must remark his indebtedness. Many of the major doctrines of Adams, which by dint of iteration have become associated with his name, were taken straight out of Harrington: such as the doctrine of a natural aristocracy; the economic basis of sovereignty, discovered in the close relation of property to power; the necessity of effecting a balance between rival interests, with the ideal state rendered static by a nice balance of governmental machinery; the conception of government by laws and not by men; and finally, the historical method of approach, the cautious appeal to past experience. Since Harrington's time many of these ideas had been restated: the defense of property rights by Locke; the principle of the separation of powers and the historical method by Montesquieu; the psychology of emulation by Hume and Robert Wallace, the latter

[27] For a detailed examination of the sources of his philosophy, see the excellent discussion in C. M. Walsh, *The Political Science of John Adams*, Chapters XV, XVI.

of whom is another Adams in his thesis, "Lust of power sets man against his neighbor to the profit of the rich." But in spite of these later reinterpretations and his own additions, John Adams remained essentially a seventeenth-century republican, preferring with Milton the rule of the aristocracy to that of plebeians, and hating all Jacobin radicalisms as the spawn of a dangerous romanticism that disregarded the plain teachings of history and the admonitions of common sense.

Though Adams was fiercely assailed as an advocate of class government, he was far less hostile to agrarianism than was Hamilton. He was no believer in unchecked government by wealth. His honest realism taught him the sophistry of Hamilton's assumption that gentlemen of property are equally gentlemen of principle, and that wealth voluntarily abdicates selfish interest. He feared the aggressions of the rich as much as the turbulence of the poor. The bulk of his property was in land, and his sympathies were enlisted on the side of a law-abiding agrarianism, rather than on the side of a speculative capitalism.[28] He would put down vigorously all such leveling as was implied in Shays's program, and the repudiations of Rhode Island; but he would not permit the powerful to exploit the poor through the instrumentality of government. This may explain in part his hostility to Hamilton and his partial sympathy with Jefferson. He stood between the two rival economies, arguing for a system of government that should be neither agrarian nor capitalistic, but should maintain a static mean; and in consequence he pleased nobody. His four years in the presidency disrupted the Federalist party, and prepared the way for the triumph of Jefferson. Though tactless and blundering in dealing with trimming politicians, he was an honest and courageous man, and his many sterling qualities merit a larger recognition than has been accorded them by a grudging posterity. In spite of his dogmatisms and inconsistencies he remains the most notable political thinker—with the possible exception of John C. Calhoun—among American statesmen.

[28] See Beard, *The Economic Origins of Jeffersonian Democracy*, p. 317.

PART TWO: POLITICAL DEMOCRACY GETS UNDER WAY
1787–1800

CHAPTER I

THE IMPACT OF THE FRENCH REVOLUTION

THE dramatic impact of the French Revolution upon a situation which for months had been overwrought entailed disturbing consequences. Within a week after the setting up of the new government there began that long series of events in France which carried far and gave birth to extraordinary hopes and fears; and throughout the remaining years of the century the French movement exercised a determining influence upon American parties and issues. In the words of Colonel Higginson, it "drew a red-hot ploughshare through the history of America as well as through that of France. It not merely divided parties, but molded them; gave them their demarcations, their watchwords and their bitterness. The home issues were for a time subordinate, collateral; the real party lines were established on the other side of the Atlantic." [1] The stirring of political passions afresh resulted in greatly clarifying political philosophies, and in rendering more exact, political alignments that before had been vague and inchoate.

The creative influence of the French Revolution upon the western world resulted from the enormous impetus which it gave to the movement to democratize American life and institutions. In no other country to which the sparks of revolution drifted was there such quantity of combustible material ready for the torch; and in setting afire this native material the French upheaval put a stop to the aristocratic reaction which had carried everything before it during the previous decade. It spread widely the spirit of leveling, and destroyed the last hope of the "monarchy men." But it did more—it gave a wide and popular currency to

[1] Quoted in Hazen, "Contemporary American Opinion of the French Revolution," in *Johns Hopkins University Studies in History and Political Science*, Extra Vol. XVI. The material in this excellent study has been used freely in the present chapter.

the ideal of democracy. Before the French Revolution the American mind had been curiously sensitive over the term democrat; even Samuel Adams had been driven by expediency to reject the word, and, amongst the radicals, few had the boldness to avow themselves democrats. By common consent the term had been covered with opprobrium; democracy was no other than a *bellua multorum capitum*, the hydra-headed monster of earlier Tories, licentious, irreligious, the very spawn of anarchy. But now the old conceptions were rapidly swept away, and democracy was accepted by liberals as the ultimate form of political organization, to which the American experiment was to be dedicated.

In thus imparting social idealism to political speculation, the Revolution not only elevated the democratic ideal, but it provided a body of philosophy, the lack of which had so seriously handicapped the democrats during the great debate. And this new philosophy gained extraordinarily wide currency in America under the stimulus of revolutionary enthusiasm. It made direct appeal to the vast majority who still remained among the political disinherited; it aroused them to political consciousness and intensified the class alignment that followed. The country divided sharply between left and right, and political discussion became more intense as the French movement developed. The English declaration of war upon France produced a crisis in America, and sharpened the party cleavage. The Federalists went with Great Britain and turned fiercely upon the democratic movement, assailing it with increasing venom. The democrats, on the other hand, became French partisans, and denounced all aristocrats with true republican fervor, becoming more radical as French Jacobinism developed. Never before had political passion risen to such heights in America, not even during the early days of the American Revolution; and never before had political ideas taken such hold upon the common people. Out of this increasing ferment emerged certain consequences of vast significance to the democratic movement: not only was an effective barrier erected against the further spread of aristocratic Federalism, but certain of its most characteristic doctrines disintegrated and disappeared. The current dogma of faction gave way to a more democratic interpretation of the majority will; the doctrine of the ethical absolute—the *vox justiciae, vox dei*—quietly yielded to the more practical conception of expediency; and the lately resurrected ideal of an augmented state received a temporary check, the majority preferring to intrust power to local bodies rather than to a central authority.

At the beginning the sympathy of America as a whole went heartily with the revolutionary movement in France. The adherence of Lafayette justified the cause to the most conservative. But with the advent of the Girondists to power a division in American sentiment appeared: Hamilton, John Adams, and other extreme Federalists drew back in disapproval; and with the rise of the Jacobins, party cleavage became sharp and bitter. All over America the liberals organized democratic clubs, instituted committees of correspondence, and actively forwarded the new leveling principles. The attack on ceremonial and titles of address in Congress, of which Maclay has left record in his *Journal*, was only a skirmish in the general war levied upon social distinctions.[2] It was to these democratic societies that Citizen Genêt made appeal; they rallied about him, toasted the French principles, and assured him of the warm support of the American people. The recall of Genêt was a blow to the American Jacobins, and they retaliated by direct appeals to the people to repudiate the act of the administration. Stung by their criticism of his policy of neutrality, Washington denounced them as "certain self-created societies" that offensively "assumed the tone of condemnation" of governmental policies; and went so far as to imply that such criticism was seditious. It was ill-advised for it was like a torch to dry leaves. The Federalists fell upon the democrats with gusto. They denounced the infidel French mobocracy and its American offspring. They declaimed against "secret organizations," imputing to them every evil known to Satan: the democratic clubs were called "demoniacal clubs," "nurseries of sedition," "hotbeds of atheism," "spawn of faction"; and common decency required that they be put down with a strong hand. In short the most eminent Federalists joined heartily in the silly work of turning the country into a bedlam.

A characteristic *odium theologicum* quickly gathered about the movement and extended to the whole democratic philosophy. Well-meaning but ignorant gentlemen saw in Jacobinism only atheism and immorality. John Adams professed not to know "what to make of a republic of thirty million atheists," and he attributed the unhappy result to the "encyclopedists and econo-

[2] For an amusing account see Hazen, *ibid.*, pp. 209-219.

mists, Diderot and D'Alembert, Voltaire and Rousseau," with their mad doctrines of the "equality of persons and property." But the more violently such men protested, the more insidiously "the infidel and irreligious spirit" spread through the land. It found its way into such strongholds of orthodoxy as Harvard College, to the scandal of the respectable; and as a counterblast to Paine's *Age of Reason*, a copy of Watson's *Apology for the Bible* was presented to every Harvard undergraduate, with what results in godliness no record remains to tell. On both sides there was more heat than light, more passion than reason, and in consequence such a tremendous hue and cry was worked up that the noise carried to the farthest outposts of settlement, and brought home to the most sluggish some realization of the significance of the world-wide movement of democracy then under way, and left few quite indifferent to the import of the tricolor cockade. It was the first great popularization of democratic ideals in America and when the hubbub finally subsided it was apparent to all that democracy had made a definite and stable advance, from which it must move forward to still other vantage points. Only a few unregenerate aristocrats shared with Gouverneur Morris his reasons for joy at the final overthrow of Napoleon: "'Tis done, the long agony is over. The Bourbons are restored. France reposes in the arms of her legitimate prince"; or who agreed with Robert Treat Paine in calling the democratic movement of the nineties "the melancholy record of our national degradation." The Federalists still hated Jefferson and his "revolution of 1800," but a triumphant agrarianism had broken them and their power for the time being.

So tremendous a movement naturally developed its literature of propaganda in America as elsewhere. In the main this was little more than an echo of the old-world debate, and, in particular, of the controversy between Burke and Paine which deeply stirred the entire English reading-public. Among the innumerable pamphlets, four works may be regarded as representative: Paine's *Rights of Man*, Barlow's *Advice to the Privileged Orders*, John Adams's *Discourses on Davila*, and John Quincy Adams's *Publicola;* and of these we need here concern ourselves only with *The Rights of Man* and *Publicola*, which clearly reveal the divergent political philosophies of the two parties. The chief point of difference is the familiar issue, so acrimoniously dealt with during the debate over the Constitution, the question of minority rights as opposed to the majority will. Paine had made wide appeal with his argument of social expediency against Burke's doctrine of pre-contract. His celebrated dictum, "That which a whole nation chuses to do, it has a right to do," if granted, must destroy the reasoning not of Burke alone, but of American Federalism, for it rested on an interpretation of sovereignty that was vital to the question. To Paine sovereignty was necessarily inherent in the present majority will; to assume that it rested elsewhere, whether in crown or judiciary or past generations, was to deny the fundamental tenet of democracy. There can be no trusteeship superior to the sovereign people, he asserted—no constitution beyond their rightful power to alter or destroy.

It was against this doctrine of the present sovereignty of the majority will that eleven articles signed *Publicola*, and appearing in the *Columbian Centinel* of Boston from June 8 to July 27, 1791, were directed. They were from the pen of John Quincy Adams, then in his early twenties and lately admitted to practice at the Boston bar. Written with considerable skill, they were at once accepted as the most effective reply offered to Paine's argument; but they have lost their appeal today and seem rather slight and tenuous essays in Federalistic legalism. The outstanding note is concern for minority rights. To permit the majority will to function unchecked seemed to this young lawyer to open wide the door to tyranny. It is justified by no political philosophy, he argued, certainly not by the doctrine of natural rights. If all men are endowed by their creator with certain inalienable rights, it follows that such rights must suffer abridgment from no power, whether monarchical or democratic. Power may override those rights temporarily, but power and rights are not synonymous terms. The gist of Adams's argument is thus set down:

This principle, that a whole nation has a right to do whatever it pleases, cannot in any sense whatever be admitted as true. The eternal and immutable laws of justice and of morality are paramount to all human legislation. The violation of those laws is certainly within the power, but it is not among the rights of nations. The power of a nation is the collected power of all the individuals which compose it. . . . If, therefore, a majority . . . are bound by no law human or divine, and have no other rule but their sovereign will and pleasure to direct them, what possible security can any citizen of the nation have for the protection of his unalienable rights? The principles of liberty must still be the sport of arbitrary power, and the hideous form of despotism must lay aside the diadem and the scepter, only to assume the party-colored garments of democracy.[3]

Concerning the repository of the "eternal and immutable laws of justice and morality," which are paramount to all human legislation, Adams is as vague as other Federalists; but he seems to imply that it is the body of English Common law, and that abstract justice is somehow interwoven with the British constitution. In other words, his argument conducts straight to the familiar doctrine of *vox justiciae, vox dei*, with its implied sovereignty of the judiciary. In this, with other thinkers of the abstract justice school, Adams was upholding the principle of judicial trusteeship in opposition to the democratic principle of the majority will. The distinction reveals exactly the different positions of the two parties: the democrats accepted the principle of utilitarian expediency; the Federalists espoused the doctrine of the ethical absolute as the final law. To a generation still strict in religious professions, the doctrine of the ethical absolute made strong appeal; but the democrats attacked it so sharply that it survived only by skillfully metamorphosing itself into judicial sanctions.

The final outcome of the long acrimonious discussion of fundamental principles was a curious reversal of positions: whereas the democrats were charged with being political and social romantics, appealing to a false psychology and following abstract theory, they were in fact idealists who pointed to the sordid facts of economic and social reality, in justification of new programs. No change could make things worse. The Federalists, on the other hand, finding the appeal to realism making against them, and fearful of the majority that was discontented with the *status quo*, took their stand upon abstract principle that was cousin german to a rigid legalism. It was a significant impasse to which they were brought by the exigencies of the political struggle.

---

[3] *The Writings of John Quincy Adams*, edited by W. C. Ford, Vol. I, pp. 70-71

CHAPTER II

POLITICAL THINKERS

The French Group

THE change which came over political thought in America in consequence of the rise of French Jacobin philosophy is not inadequately revealed in the writings of two men, quite dissimilar in antecedents and training, but alike in fundamental purpose— Thomas Paine and Thomas Jefferson. Both were speculative thinkers, profoundly in sympathy with French revolutionary ideals: but the former was detached from local patriotisms and national interests, a delegate at large in the cause of human rights, concerned with spreading the gospel of freedom in all lands; the latter remained wholly American, and while a keenly interested spectator of the French upheaval, he was primarily concerned to discover principles that would apply to native conditions and further the cause of American democracy. Paine therefore became the popular disseminator of the philosophy of republicanism, and Jefferson, the practical statesman embodying it in political programs. Warm friends, their influence became closely interwoven during the years when agrarian democracy was gathering its strength to strike down the rule of Federalism.

I

TOM PAINE

Republican Pamphleteer

No more striking figure emerges from the times than the figure of the Thetford Quaker. English in birth and rearing, in middle life Paine came to embody the republican spirit of the American revolution; and that spirit he made it his after business to carry overseas and spread among the discontented of all lands. He was the first modern internationalist, at home wherever rights were to be won or wrongs corrected. "My country is the world," he asserted proudly, "to do good, my religion." Throughout his later life he was a fearless skirmisher on the outposts of democracy

—another "Free born John" Lilburne, seeking to complete the great work begun and thwarted in an earlier century; and his career remains a stirring record of a time when revolution threatened to sweep away the power and privilege of all kings and aristocracies. Naturally his zeal cost him dear in reputation. The passions of all who feared the loss of sinecures gathered about his head, and he became the victim of an *odium theologicum et politicum*, without parallel in our history. The Tories hunted him in packs, and their execration and vituperation outran all decency. In London clubs it became the fashion for gentlemen to wear TP nails in their boot-heels to witness how they trampled on his base principles. He was proscribed and banished, and his books burnt by the hangman. He was regarded as worse than a common felon and outlaw, because more dangerous. In America gentlemen echoed the common detestation—to be a Paine-hater was a badge of respectability. "The filthy Tom Paine," John Adams called him, and the phrase stuck like a burr to his reputation. But "reason, like time," as Paine remarked "will make its own way," and the years are bringing a larger measure of justice to him.

Like Hamilton, Paine was an alien, but endowed with a heritage quite unlike that of the brilliant boy from the West Indies. When he landed in Philadelphia in the second week in December, 1774,[1] he was in his thirty-seventh year, and had seemingly made shipwreck of his life. He had been schooled in misfortune and was marked as a social inefficient. A broken staymaker and tobacconist, he had twice been removed from the office of petty exciseman for what today would be called unionizing activity. He had separated from his wife, and his mean and petty environment seemed to offer no hope of a decent living. One stroke of good fortune had come to him, when as a delegate from his union on some business with Parliament, he made the acquaintance of Franklin, who was taken with "those wonderful eyes of his," and advised America as a likely place for getting on. So provided with little more than Franklin's letter of introduction, he set sail for new worlds, cherishing the unmilitant plan of setting up in Philadelphia a seminary of polite learning for young ladies. But the times proved unpropitious for such a venture. He found himself in a world hesitating fearfully on the brink of revolution, the elec-

[1] For the date of his arrival, see *Massachusetts Historical Society Proceedings,* Vol. XLIII, p. 246.

tric atmosphere of which he found strangely congenial. He at once threw himself whole-heartedly into the colonial dispute, quickly seized the main points, mastered the arguments, and thirteen months after his arrival published *Common Sense*, a pamphlet that was to spread his name and fame throughout America.

The amazing influence of *Common Sense* on a public opinion long befogged by legal quibble flowed from its direct and skillful appeal to material interests. For the first time in a tedious, inconsequential debate, it was openly asserted that governmental policies rest on economic foundations; that the question of American independence was only a question of expediency, and must be determined in the light of economic advantage. Government is no more than a utility, and that policy which was most likely to secure freedom and security "with the least expense and greatest benefit," must be preferred. The point at issue before the American people, therefore, was whether a more useful arrangement would result from continuing the old connection with England, or from setting up for themselves; and it must be decided, not in the court room or council chambers, but in the countinghouse and market place, in the field and shop, wherever plain Americans were making a living. Let the common people consult their own needs, and determine the case without regard to legal or constitutional precedents. It was a simple matter to be judged in the light of common sense and their particular interests.

To further clear thinking on this fundamental matter Paine commented on the economic consequences to America of the English connection. Throughout colonial history, he asserted with some disregard to fact, dependence had resulted in disadvantage to America; England had systematically exploited the colonies and hampered development. Whatever prosperity had been won heretofore, had been won in spite of English hostility and interference; the peculiar economic position of the colonies had proved their best reliance in the past, and would prove still more advantageous in the future, if America were free from jealous, paternal restrictions. What reason was there to expect generous treatment from a power that had never shown generosity in past dealings? How skillful was the appeal to colonial self-interest is revealed in such passages as these:

We are already greater than the King wishes us to be, and will he not hereafter endeavour to make us less? To bring the matter to one point,

Is the power who is jealous of our prosperity, a proper power to govern us? Whoever says *No*, to this question, is an Independent, for independency means no more than this, whether we shall make our own laws, or, whether the King, the greatest enemy this continent hath, or can have, shall tell us *there shall be no laws but such as I like.*

America would have flourished as much, and probably much more, had no European power taken any notice of her. The commerce by which she hath enriched herself are the necessaries of life, and will always have a market while eating is the custom of Europe. As Europe is our market for trade we ought to form no partial connection with any part of it. It is the true interest of America to steer clear of European contentions, which she never can do while by her dependence on Britain she is made the makeweight in the scale of British politics.

Our corn will fetch its price in any market in Europe, and our imported goods must be paid for buy them where we will. . . . 'Tis as great folly to pay a Bunker-hill price for law as for land.

But Paine well knew that self-interest may be so clouded by prejudice as not to see the way its nose is pointing. Though the colonial talked of his grievances, he remained colonial in psychology, held in unconscious subjection to English traditions. He was in the clutch of outworn loyalties—loyalty to the crown and loyalty to the British constitution; and to this difficult problem Paine addressed himself with great skill. To a republican, as Paine seems to have been from his landing in America, the odium which George III had incurred was a heaven-sent opportunity. In order to strike at the monarchical principle, it was only necessary to point out that the folly of the King was the best commentary upon the foolishness of hereditary monarchy. The boldness and audacity of Paine's attack on the king-principle must have added greatly to the popularity of *Common Sense* along the frontier. It was the first clear, far-carrying appeal for republicanism addressed to American ears. How successful it was, how ruthlessly it stripped away the divinity that doth hedge a king, laying bare the stupidity of the king-cult, is suggested by the remarkable change in the American attitude towards monarchy that a few months brought about. After the appearance of *Common Sense*, middle and lower class Americans shed their colonial loyalties like a last year's garment, and thenceforth they regarded the pretentions of kings as little better than flummery. King George's disgraced exciseman had his revenge; he had thrust his royal master out of the colonial affection and destroyed the monarchical principle in America.

A more difficult task remained, that of instituting "an inquiry into the *constitutional errors* of the English form of government," in order to prove what gains would result if America took herself out of the English system. Here Paine faced, single-handed, a solid phalanx of lawyers. He was the first pamphleteer to question the excellence of a constitution that was proclaimed by American Tories as the wonder of the world and the envy of other nations. In the acrimonious disputes between 1765 and 1775, this was the single point on which all professed to agree. A vast deal of laudation had been uttered; innumerable legal pamphlets had been written; and no colonial had had the temerity to question the adequacy of the British constitution to colonial needs. And now came this republican, with penetrating comment on its origin and working, to disturb the common complacency by pointing out how ill fitted it was to answer the needs of America. It was a telling attack, made with skill and shrewd insight; and it had a great part in arousing a bitter antagonism to the English system in the minds of the American yeomanry.

Paine was not a constitutional historian, but he had a keen eye for realities. The fundamental fallacy of the English system, he asserted, lay in the so-called "mixt aristocracy," which was presumed to gather the wisdom of the realm in council with the king, but which was no more than a convenient arrangement for dividing the spoils. The House of Commons had grown out of the struggles of feudal barons against the king. It presumed to speak for the common people, but the rights of the people were thus recognized only to be thwarted by the old tyrannies. The "Republican materials, in the persons of the Commons, on whose virtue depends the freedom of England," were held in check by the "remains of aristocratical tyranny in the person of the Peers," and further restrained by the "remains of Monarchical tyranny in the person of the King." From the play of these elements arose the system of checks and balances which placed control in the hands of landed property. It was based on the assumption that "the King is not to be trusted without being looked after," and that "the Commons, by being appointed for that purpose, are either wiser or more worthy of confidence than the Crown." But in spite of the supposed balance "the provision is unequal to the task," for the Crown, as the dispenser of places and pensions, is more than a match for Commons in the game of politics.

The will of the king is as much the law of the land in Britain as in France, with this difference, that instead of proceeding directly from his mouth, it is handed to the people under the formidable shape of an act of parliament. For the fate of Charles the First hath only made kings more subtle—not more just.

This was but the beginning of a long assault on the British constitution which was to engage him much in after life. *Common Sense* was a pronouncement of the new philosophy of republicanism that was taking firm hold of the American mind, and which the French Revolution was to spread so widely. It was a notable contribution, of which Paine to the end of his life was justly proud.

As he came to America almost casually, with no conscious revolutionary intent, so in the critical year 1787 he returned to Europe with the peaceful intention of perfecting an iron bridge on which he was engaged. True to his Quaker breeding he was more interested in the arts of peace than of war, but again circumstance was too much for him. Before he had completed his bridge, delegates from France came to invite him to a seat in the National Assembly. A new day was rising there; the constitution of a freer order was being constructed, and so competent a workman could not be spared. In the thick of that eager world of constitution-making, Paine finally clarified his political philosophy and gave it wide currency. He became the pamphleteer of revolution to the English-speaking world, to Philadelphia and New York equally with London. Yet he was never an extremist; he was a Girondist rather than a Jacobin, and when the Girondists were overthrown and a dictatorship set up, he remained a constitutionalist. By the Jacobin radicals he came to be regarded as a reactionary from his willingness to retain monarchy in France; but Paine was a practical Englishman with a shrewd judgment of what was politically possible, and he refused to outrun reasonable expectations of accomplishment.

It was the simplicity and clarity of his political philosophy that made its appeal so widely effective. His thinking turned on the two fundamental questions, the source of government and the purpose for which it is instituted among men; and the major premise on which he reared his logic was the thesis that sovereignty inheres in the majority will. At the basis of his philosophy was the natural-rights theory, but given a fresh significance and vitality by the assertion of the doctrine of continuous reaffirmation of the social compact. Instead of deriving the sovereign state from a fictitious compact, presumably entered into in a remote past, he derived it—as Roger Williams had done a century and half before—from a continuous compact reaffirmed by each generation. With the birth of each individual appear fresh rights which no pre-contract can justly circumscribe or nullify; ancestral arrangements are valid only to the extent that they are acceptable to the living. Hence it follows, first, that the general body of the people may at any time remake the fundamental law, and bring it into accord with present desire; and second, that there can be no law superior to this popular will expressed through the majority. His most celebrated dictum—"That which a nation chuses to do it has a right to do"—a dictum that aroused a bitterer hostility than any other of his pronouncements—was the logical expression of his republicanism that differentiated between the sovereign people and their agency, the government; and this in turn he justified by a celebrated saying out of Swift, "Government is a plain thing, and fitted to the capacity of many heads." Like Jefferson, he would not have government kept from the people, the agent domineer over the principal.

The purpose of government Paine discovered in the Benthamite principle of expediency. If a diffused well-being results from the policies of government, such government is justified; but if the tax-levies are wasted in unsocial ways, if unjust impositions are levied, if exploitation or tyranny results, such government is not justified. The agent has cheated the principal, and must be called to account. The final test of every government Paine found in its concern for the "res publica, the public affairs, or the public good"; any government that "does not make the res publica its whole and sole object, is not a good government." In its most obvious phase, concern for the res publica means concern for the national economy, and this in turn conditions the taxes that shall be levied and the ends for which they shall be spent—whether upon the arts of peace or war. A beneficent government has no need of standing armies and navies, or an inquisitorial police; it is established in the hearts of the people and rests securely on the common good will. It is the injustice of government that creates armies to defend the earnings of injustice. But every wise government will respect its limitations. As a child of the eighteenth century, Paine hated the leviathan state as a monster created by a minority to serve the ends of tyranny. The political state he accepted as a present necessity, but he would not have its prestige magnified and the temptation to tyranny increased by the cult of nationalism. "Government is no farther necessary," he believed, "than to supply the few cases to which society and civilization are not conveniently competent." At best it is an artificial thing.

> Formal government makes but a small part of civilized life; and when even the best that human wisdom can devise is established, it is a thing more in name and idea than in fact. . . . The more perfect civilization is, the less occasion has it for government, because the more does it regulate its own affairs, and govern itself. . . . All the great laws of society are laws of nature.[2]

The maturest elaboration of Paine's political philosophy is found in *The Rights of Man*. This extraordinary work, the most influential English contribution to the revolutionary movement, was an examination of the English constitution in the light of what Paine held were the true source and ends of government. It is a brilliant reply to Burke, who rested his interpretation of the English constitution on the legal ground of the common law of contract. Following the Revolution of 1688, Burke had argued, the English people through their legal representatives, entered into a solemn contract, binding "themselves, their heirs, and posterities forever," to certain express terms; and neither in law nor in equity were they, of whatever generation, free to change those terms except by the consent of both parties to the contract. This was an elaboration of the theory of government tacitly held by the Old Whigs, which derived government from a perpetual civil contract as opposed to the radical doctrine of a revocable social contract; and in attacking it Paine allied himself with such thinkers as Price, Priestley, Franklin and Rousseau.[3] He pointed out the absurdity of carrying over the law of private property into the high realm of political principle—to seek to impose the dead past upon the living sovereignty. If sovereignty inhered in the English people in 1688, it must inhere in the English people in 1793, unless it had been violently wrested from them; no parchment terms of another age can bind that sovereignty other than voluntarily. Over against Burke's theory of a single, static contract, Paine set

---

[2] *Rights of Man*, Part II, pp. 407, 408.
[3] For an excellent discussion of this, see C. M. Walsh, *The Political Science of John Adams*, pp. 203–226.

the doctrine of the reaffirmation of natural rights. Any generation—as the generation of 1688—is competent to deal with its
affairs as it sees fit, but it cannot barter away the rights of those
unborn; such a contract on the face of it is null and void.

> Every age and generation must be free to act for itself *in all cases* as
> the ages and generations which preceded it. The vanity and presumption
> of governing beyond the grave is the most ridiculous and insolent of all
> tyrannies. . . . Every generation is, and must be, competent to all the
> purposes which its occasions require. It is the living, and not the dead,
> that are to be accommodated.[4]

Burke's defense fares even worse when the argument is examined
in the light of expediency. Illogical as the English system must
appear to the political philosopher, can it plead the justification
that it works; that it does well the things it is paid to do; that it
makes the *res publica* its main concern? The reply to such questions, Paine believed, should be sought in the condition of the
national economy; more particularly by an examination of the
account-books of the exchequer. The English people paid annually
seventeen millions sterling for the maintenance of government,
and what did they get in return? Nine millions of the total went
to pay interest on old wars, which in the budget was known as the
funded debt; of the remaining eight millions the larger part was
spent in new wars and sinecure pensions; whereas the real needs
of England—the true *res publica*—were shamefully neglected.
The English people got little for their money except new debts to
justify new taxes. The poor were even taxed for the benefit of the
great. Thus my Lord Onslow, who was particularly zealous in
the business of proscribing Paine as "the common enemy of us
all," drew four thousand pounds from the royal chest in sinecures,
which made him "the principal pauper of the neighbourhood, and
occasioning a greater expense than the poor, the aged, and the
infirm, for ten miles around." [5] Government on the hereditary
principle of Burke did not appear to advantage in the light of such
facts.

The injustice of aristocratic government, Paine believed, was
fast bringing it to its "rotting time" in England. "The opinions
of men with respect to government are changing fast in all countries; the enormous expense of governments has provoked the

[4] *The Rights of Man*, Part I, p. 278.
[5] "Letter to Lord Onslow," in *Works*, Vol. III, p. 36.

people to think, by making them feel." Englishmen must soon throw aside the outworn monarchical system and set up a republic. Economics was on the side of revolution. The great work of revising fundamental laws was the pressing business of the time. If this could be done peacefully, by means of a national convention, it were well; if not, it would come by means of an uprising of the people. It was no lawyer's business to be determined by the law of private property, but a practical matter of determining the real will of the nation and putting it into execution. The judgment of the people must be recorded, and the judgment of the people could be had only through an adequate system of representation based on free publicity. "I do not believe that the people of England have ever been fairly and candidly dealt by," Paine declared. Henceforth they must be taken into full confidence. There must be no more *arcana imperii*—"Nations can have no secrets; and the secrets of courts, like those of individuals, are always their defects."[6]

One of the great advantages of the American Revolution has been, that it has led to a discovery of the principles, and laid open the imposition of governments. All the revolutions till then had worked within the atmosphere of a court, and never on the grand floor of a nation. The parties were always of the class of courtiers. . . . In all cases they took care to represent government as a thing made up of mysteries, which only themselves understood; and they hid from the understanding of the nation the only thing that was beneficial to know, namely, *That government is nothing more than a national association acting on the principles of a society.*[7]

For the follies of government the people pay the bill—it was this elementary lesson in public economics that Paine sought to impress upon the popular mind; and they would still be cheated and plundered by gentlemen who prospered in cozening, until they took matters into their own hands. He had no fear of popular government. He believed in the essential fairness of men and their capacity to deal wisely with the problems of society if the necessary information were set before them. "As far as my experience in public life extends, I have ever observed that the great mass of people are always just, both in their intentions and their object; but the true method of attaining such purpose does not always appear at once," [8] he argued before the French Assembly; and the

6 *Rights of Man*, Part II, p. 428.
7 *Ibid.*, pp. 410–411.
8 Conway, *Life of Paine*, Vol. II, p. 4.

words express his settled conviction. Those who fear the people usually have very good reasons. Heretofore politics had been jealously guarded from free discussion; but now that the common people were coming to understand that government is justified only by its measure of service, the beginning of a new age was at hand.

The ripest product of Paine's speculations on the relation of government to the individual, is *Agrarian Justice*, a work too little known to modern readers. It is a slender tract, written in the winter of 1795-96, although not published till a year later; and it was an answer to a sermon by Watson, Bishop of Llandaff,[9] entitled *The Wisdom and Goodness of God in having made both Rich and Poor.* In this remarkable essay, Paine advanced from political to social theory, pushing his thought into the unexplored realm of economic justice. The prime impulse of his speculation is found in the contrast between the augmenting poverty of Europe and the ideal of equality; a contrast which in France had lately produced a proletarian revolt under Babeuf, and which in England was harshly aggravated by the brutal inclosure movement of the last forty years of the eighteenth century. The question which he considers lies at the heart of our social problem, namely, whether civilization is competent to cure the disease of poverty which everywhere it disseminates?

The question emerged naturally from the development of Paine's thinking. It was implied in his major principle of the *res publica*, and the solution must lie in the problem of the relation of government to social well-being. But in prescribing means to end, he parted company from Babeuf.[10] The latter was a Communist who approached the problem from the point of view of the proletarian who had been disappointed of the promised equality; whereas Paine, like Jefferson, was essentially a Physiocratic agrarian. His long residence in America had confirmed him in the belief that land monopoly was the root of economic inequality; and his observations of the evictions then going on in England, uprooting the peasants and sending them to industrial centers to become wage-workers, strengthened his conviction. The land problem must be solved if civilization were to be worth its cost,

[9] Author of *An Apology for the Bible* (a reply to Paine's *Age of Reason*), which was distributed among Harvard undergraduates. See above, page 324.

[10] For the program of Babeuf, see R. W. Postgate, *Revolution from 1789 to 1906*, pp. 24, 54-60.

and the technique of the solution, he believed, must be worked out by the state. With his usual directness Paine went to the heart of the problem:

> The first principle of civilization ought to have been, and ought still to be, that the condition of every person born into the world, after a state of civilization commences, ought not to be worse than if he had been born before that period. But the fact is, that the condition of millions, in every country in Europe, is far worse than if they had been born before civilization began, or had been born among the Indians of North-America at the present day.[11]

> It is not charity but a right, not bounty but justice, that I am pleading for. The present state of civilization is as odious as it is unjust. It is absolutely the opposite of what it should be.[12] . . . The contrast of affluence and wretchedness . . . is like dead and living bodies chained together.[13]

> It is the practice of what has unjustly obtained the name of civilization . . . to make some provision for persons becoming poor and wretched only at the time they become so. Would it not, even as a matter of economy, be far better to adopt means to prevent their becoming poor? [14]

The crux of the problem, Paine proceeds to point out, lies in the principle of private property; whether property rights are sacredly individual—as Locke had asserted—or are limited by social needs. In reply to this searching question Paine laid down the principle of social values, a theory curiously modern and profoundly suggestive, which makes *Agrarian Justice* read like a chapter out of *Progress and Poverty*. The principle is so broad, as Paine states it, that it applies equally to a capitalistic and an agrarian order.

> Personal property is the *effect of society;* and it is as impossible for an individual to acquire personal property without the aid of society, as it is for him to make land originally. . . . All accumulation, therefore, of personal property, beyond what a man's own hands produce, is derived to him by living in society; and he owes on every principle of justice, of gratitude, and of civilization, a part of that accumulation back again to society from whence the whole came . . . if we examine the case minutely it will be found that the accumulation of personal property is, in many instances, the effect of paying too little for the labor that produced it; and the consequence of which is, that the working hand perishes in old age, and the employer abounds in affluence. It is, perhaps, impossible to proportion exactly the price of labor to the profits it produces; and it

[11] *Works*, Vol. III, p. 329.
[12] This and the preceding sentence were expunged from all early editions by the censor.
[13] *Ibid.*, p. 337.   [14] *Ibid.*, p. 338.

will also be said, as an apology for the injustice, that were a workman to receive an increase of wages daily he would not save it against old age, nor be much better for it in the interim. Make, then, society the treasurer to guard it for him in a common fund; for it is no reason, that because he might not make a good use of it for himself, another should take it.[15]

It is the value of the improvement only, and not of the earth itself, that is individual property. Every proprietor, therefore, of cultivated land, owes to the community a *ground-rent* . . . for the land which he holds; and it is from this ground-rent that the fund proposed in this plan is to issue.[16]

Having thus pointed out an equitable source of social income—the returning to society what society has created—Paine proposed to deal with the problem of poverty by means of a ten per cent inheritance tax to provide a fund for the endowment of the young and the pensioning of the old. It was an early form of the state insurance idea. In his own thinking Paine doubtless went much farther than this, but the practical difficulty of separating the social moiety from the private right inclined him to favor an inheritance tax as the simplest and best plan; that it would lead to greater things as the social intelligence quickened, he very likely believed. To bring men to realize that society is responsible for poverty, and that its total eradication must be regarded as the first object of civilization, was his prime purpose. He was seeking to awaken the social conscience of his generation—a generation sorely in need of idealism to offset its love of profits. *Agrarian Justice* was a contribution to the slowly developing humanitarian sentiment, and it made appeal to minds already aroused by the revolutionary movement. The republican clubs that were springing up in England and America reflected the new social thought, and the most radical became the most humanitarian. As early as 1791, in an address signed by Horne Tooke, one of Paine's English lieutenants, it was declared:

We are oppressed with a heavy national debt, a burthen of taxes, an expensive administration of government, beyond those of any people in the world. We have also a very numerous poor; and we hold that the moral obligation of providing for old age, helpless infancy, and poverty, is far superior to that of supplying the invented wants of courtly extravagance, ambition, and intrigue.[17]

[15] *Ibid.*, p. 340.   [16] *Ibid.*, p. 329.
[17] *Address and Declaration of the Friends of Universal Peace and Liberty*, quoted in Conway, *Life of Paine*, Vol. I, p. 316.

The more critically one follows the thought of Paine the more evident it becomes that the master passion of his later years was concern for a new social economy. The well-being of society became an engrossing interest with him; and his zeal for political revolution was predicated on the belief that popular control of the political state was a necessary preliminary to a juster social economy. Nothing was to be expected from the old aristocratic order. His main attack, therefore, was directed against the monarchical system, but now and then he paused to level a thrust at the rising system of capitalism. If he hated King George and the Tories, he hated the younger Pitt and the imperialists even more. Over against *Agrarian Justice* should be set his pamphlet entitled *The Decline and Fall of the English System of Finance*, written in 1796, a skillful attack upon the new funding system. Paine could not foresee, of course, the enormous expansion of credit that was to accompany the industrial revolution, but in his commentary on the quantitative theory of money, and the social consequences of inflation, he unconsciously foretold later conditions. War he regarded as the great waster, the fruitful mother of social misery. With his Quaker training he was dedicated to pacifism, and he spent his life warring against war, and disease, and poverty, and injustice, and ignorance, and unreason; but no other war would he sanction. For those futile wars bred of the ambitions of courts and monarchs, and which for all their cost in blood and money served no social purpose, he would substitute arbitration. "War is the Pharo-table of governments, and nations the dupes of the game," he declared [18]—whereas arbitration is an appeal to reason which alone should adjudicate and determine between nations.

It would be idle to attempt to trace to their sources the major ideas of his philosophy. Probably Paine did not know where he got them. He was not a student like John Adams, familiar with all the political philosophers; rather he was an epitome of a world in revolution. He absorbed ideas like a sponge. He was so wholly a child of his age that the intellectual processes of the age were no other than his own. But he was very much more than an echo; he possessed that rarest of gifts, an original mind. He looked at the world through no eyes than his own. There is a curious remark in an early pamphlet which admirably expresses his method:

[18] *Rights of Man*, Part II, p. 413.

"When precedents fail to assist us, we must return to the first principles of things for information, and *think*, as if we were the *first men* that thought." [19] It was his remarkable ability to think from first principles that gave such freshness and vigor to his pen. He drew largely from French thought, but at bottom he remained English. If he was Gallic in his psychology of human nature and his passionate humanitarianism, he was English in his practical political sense and insistence on the economic sources of political action. In his political theory he was curiously like Roger Williams. A thoroughgoing idealist in aim, generous and unsparing in service to humanity, he was a confirmed realist in the handling of facts. He refused to be duped by imposing appearances or great reputations, but spoke out unpleasant truths which gentlemen wished to keep hidden. Clear and direct in expression, he seasoned his writings with homely figures and a frequent audacity of phrase that made wide appeal. He was probably the greatest pamphleteer that the English race has produced. and one of its great idealists.

During his residence abroad Paine habitually thought and spoke of himself as an American. He conceived it to be his mission to disseminate throughout Europe the beneficent principles of the American Revolution; yet nowhere was he hated more virulently than in America. To the animosity which his political principles excited among Federalists was added the detestation of the orthodox for the deism of the *Age of Reason*. The ministers outdid the politicians in virulent attack upon his reputation, until the generous Quaker, the friend of humanity and citizen of the world, was shrunk and distorted into "the infidel Tom Paine." It was a strange reward for a life spent in the service of mankind. Like all idealists he made the mistake of underestimating the defensive strength of vested interests, and their skill in arousing the mob prejudice. His thousands of followers among the disfranchised poor could not protect his reputation against the attacks of the rich and powerful. Although reason may "make its own way," it makes its way with wearisome slowness and at unreasonable cost. How tremendous were the obstacles that liberalism confronted in post-revolutionary America is revealed with sufficient clearness in the odium visited upon our great republican pamphleteer.

[19] *Works*, Vol. I, p. 155.

II
THOMAS JEFFERSON
Agrarian Democrat

The years following the great defeat were disastrous to the party of agrarian democracy. Under the brilliant leadership of Hamilton the Federalists went forward confidently, gaining daily a firmer grip on the machinery of government, and establishing their principles in far-reaching legislative enactments. Their appeal to the wealthy classes, to those who made themselves audible above the clamor, was electrical. Hamilton was the hero of the hour, and the effusive approval that augmented with every added profit to the money brokers, seemed to indicate that the country was enthusiastically behind the Federalist policy. To what despondency the democrats were reduced is revealed in Maclay's *Journal*, with its caustic comment on political measures and motives. But the tide was already at the turn. The ideas let loose by the French Revolution were running swiftly through America, awakening a militant spirit in the democracy. Antagonism to the aristocratic arrogance of Federalism, and disgust at its coercive measures, were mounting fast. If that inchoate discontent were organized and directed by a skillful leader, it might prove strong enough to thrust the Hamiltonian party from power. To that work Thomas Jefferson devoted himself with immense tact and untiring patience. A master of political strategy, he spun his webs far and wide, quietly awaiting the time when the bumbling Federalist bees should range too carelessly in search of their honey. Accepted at once as the leader of agrarian America, he was to prove in the course of a long life the most original and native of the political leaders of the time.

Despite the mass of comment that has gathered about Jefferson, the full reach and significance of his political philosophy remains too little understood. Uncritical praise and censure have obscured or distorted his purpose, and allied his principles with narrow and temporary ends. Detraction will not let him alone. The hostility of his enemies, as a recent biographer has remarked, has frequently taken "the peculiar form of editing his works or writing his life." [20] For this distortion there is, perhaps, more than usual excuse. Certainly Jefferson is the most elusive of our great political leaders.

[20] Francis W. Hirst, *Life and Letters of Thomas Jefferson*, p. 266.

Apparently inconsistent, changing his program with the changing times, he seemed to his enemies devoid of principle, a shallow demagogue who incited the mob in order to dupe the people. One of the most bitterly hated and greatly loved men in the day when love and hate were intense, he was the spokesman of the new order at a time of transition from a dependent monarchical state, to an independent republican state. Back of the figure of Jefferson, with his aristocratic head set on a plebeian frame, was the philosophy of a new age and a new people—an age and a people not yet come to the consistency of maturity, but feeling a way through experiment to solid achievement. Far more completely than any other American of his generation he embodied the idealisms of the great revolution—its faith in human nature, its economic individualism, its conviction that here in America, through the instrumentality of political democracy, the lot of the common man should somehow be made better.

From the distinguished group of contemporary political thinkers Jefferson emerges as the preëminent intellectual, widely read, familiar with ideas, at home in the field of speculation, a critical observer of men and manners. All his life he was a student, and his devotion to his books, running often to fifteen hours a day, recalls the heroic zeal of Puritan scholars. He was trained in the law, but he was too much the intellectual, too curious about all sorts of things, to remain a lawyer. For such a man the appeal of political speculation was irresistible, and early in life he began a wide reading in the political classics that far outweighed Coke and Blackstone in creative influence on his mind. He was equally at home with the English liberals of the seventeenth century and the French liberals of the eighteenth; and if he came eventually to set the French school above the English, it was because he found in the back-to-nature philosophy, with its corollary of an agrarian economics and its emphasis on social well-being, a philosophy more consonant with Virginian experience and his own temperament than Locke's philosophy of property. But he was very far from being a narrow French partisan, as has been often charged; rather he judged old-world theory in the light of its applicability to existing American conditions, and restrained his love of speculation by immediate practical considerations. The man of affairs kept a watchful eye on the philosopher in his study.

In the major doctrines of his political philosophy Jefferson was an amalgam of English and French liberalisms, supplemented by the conscious influence of the American frontier. That fusion early took place in his mind. The first bill that he introduced into the Virginia Assembly, at the age of twenty-six, was a bill to permit slave-owners to manumit their slaves; and his first published pamphlet, issued in 1774,[21] rejected the legal reasoning of John Dickinson and Daniel Dulaney—supporting the parliamentary right to impose external taxation—and took its stand on the doctrine of natural right to local self-government and freedom of trade. When two years later he drafted the Declaration of Independence the fusion was complete. The strong influence of French humanitarianism is revealed in the passage on slavery that was stricken out on the floor of Congress, and more significantly in the change in the familiar phrasing of the several natural rights. Samuel Adams and other followers of Locke had been content with the classical enumeration of life, liberty, and property; but in Jefferson's hands the English doctrine was given a revolutionary shift. The substitution of "pursuit of happiness" for "property" marks a complete break with the Whiggish doctrine of property rights that Locke had bequeathed to the English middle class, and the substitution of a broader sociological conception; and it was this substitution that gave to the document the note of idealism which was to make its appeal so perennially human and vital. The words were far more than a political gesture to draw popular support; they were an embodiment of Jefferson's deepest convictions, and his total life thenceforward was given over to the work of providing such political machinery for America as should guarantee for all the enjoyment of those inalienable rights. If the fact that he set the pursuit of happiness above abstract property rights is to be taken as proof that Jefferson was an impractical French theorist, the critic may take what comfort he can from his deduction.

That Jefferson was an idealist was singularly fortunate for America; there was need of idealism to leaven the materialistic realism of the times. It was a critical period and he came at the turn of a long running tide. He watched the beginnings of the political shift in America from isolated colonial commonwealths to a unitary sovereign state; and his wide reading and close observation had convinced him that the impending change was fraught

[21] *A Summary View of the Rights of British America*, Williamsburg.

with momentous issues for the common man. He had meditated much on the social results of the slow oscillations in western civilization between social decentralization and centralization, with their contrasting political and economic structures; and he understood how the movement from simplicity to complexity—from freedom to regimentation—creates a psychology and an institutionalism that conducts straight to the leviathan state, controlled by a ruling caste, serving the demands of exploitation, heedless of the well-being of the regimented mass. This great lesson in social drifts he brought home to America. There had been created here the psychology and institutions of a decentralized society, with a corresponding exaltation of the individual and the breakdown of caste. In the broad spaces of America the old-world coercive state had dwindled to a mere police arrangement for parochial duties; the free citizen refused to be regimented; the several communities insisted on managing their affairs by their own agents. Such was the natural consequence of free economics; but with the turning of the tide would not the drift towards centralization nullify the results of earlier American experience and repeat here the unhappy history of European peoples?

To the philosophic mind of Jefferson, such a question was not academic, but urgent and vital. He had been bred in that older world, he believed passionately in the excellence of its virtues, and his political and social philosophy was determined by that experience. He sprang from a society deep-rooted in an agrarian economy, and he wished to preserve that society. Born on the Virginia frontier, he had never seen a hamlet so large as twenty houses before his eighteenth year; his neighbors and associates were capable and vigorous frontier democrats, who managed the affairs of local government with the same homespun skill that went to their farming. "It is not difficult," remarks an acute critic, "to see how the great principle of Jefferson's life—absolute faith in democracy—came to him. He was the product of the first West in American history; he grew up with men who ruled their country well, who fought the Indians valiantly . . . . Jefferson loved his backwoods neighbors, and he, in turn, was loved by them." [22] This early conviction of the excellence of a freehold order was confirmed by later experience; wide observation and much travel convinced him that no other people was so favored

[22] Dodd, *Statesmen of the Old South*, p. 23.

by circumstance as the American, or so vigorously self-reliant. That such well-being resulted from a plastic economics, he regarded as self-evident; and from this economic freedom came political freedom. In his European travels he saw everywhere want and wretchedness dwelling in the shadow of the aristocratic state, and he could not dissociate the two. Political tyranny was the outward and visible sign of greater tyrannies that ran down to the very roots of society; the leviathan state was the convenient instrument through which those tyrannies took their heavy toll of the common well-being. America was a land of free men; it was exploited neither by an aristocracy nor a plutocracy. Surely there could be no greater or nobler ambition for an American than to assist in preserving his country from the misery that must attend a change from the present happy condition of democratic industry, to the serfdom of the European wage-taker and peasant.

To a mind imbued with such conceptions the appeal of the Physiocratic theory of social economics would be irresistible. The ground was prepared for the sowing of the seeds of the liberal French thought. With its emphasis laid upon agriculture, its doctrine of the *produit net*, its principle of *laissez faire*, and its social concern, the Physiocratic theory accorded exactly with his familiar experience, and it must have seemed to Jefferson that it was little other than a deduction from the open facts of American life. He had read much in the works of the Physiocratic group, and was intimately acquainted with DuPont de Nemours; and the major principles of the school sank deep into his mind and creatively determined his thinking, with the result that Jeffersonian democracy as it spread through Virginia and west along the frontier assumed a pronounced Physiocratic bias. The sharp struggle between Jefferson and Hamilton must be reckoned, in part at least, a conflict between the rival principles of Quesnay and Adam Smith, between an agrarian and a capitalistic economy. Much as Jefferson feared the ambitions of an aristocracy, he feared quite as much the creation of a proletariat. As he looked into the future he saw great cities rising to breed their Roman mobs, duped and exploited by demagogues, the convenient tools of autocracy; and counting the cost in social well-being, he set his face like flint against the rising capitalism. A free yeomanry he regarded as the backbone of every great people, the producers of the real wealth, the guardians of manly independence; and the number of factory workers measured for him the extent of social disease. It is this Physiocratic conception that explains his bitter hostility to protective tariffs, national banks, funding manipulations, the machinery of credit, and all the agencies of capitalism which Hamilton was skillfully erecting in America. Not to have hated such things Jefferson must first have emptied his mind of the teachings of experience and the lessons of the social philosophers.

In the *Notes on Virginia* there is a well-known passage that amplifies his favorite thesis that a sound American economy was an agrarian economy:

The political economists of Europe have established it as a principle, that every State should endeavor to manufacture for itself; and this principle, like many others, we transfer to America. . . . But we have an immensity of land courting the industry of the husbandman. Is it best then that all our citizens should be employed in its improvement, or that one half should be called off from that to exercise manufactures and handicraft arts for the other? Those who labor in the earth are the chosen people of God, if ever he had a chosen people, whose breasts he has made his peculiar deposit for substantial and genuine virtue. It is the focus in which he keeps alive that sacred fire, which otherwise might escape from the face of the earth. Corruption of morals in the mass of cultivators is a phenomenon of which no age nor nation has furnished an example. It is the mark set on those, who not looking up to heaven, to their own soil and industry, as does the husbandman, for their subsistence, depend for it on casualties and caprice of customers. Dependence begets subservience and venality, suffocates the germ of virtue, and prepares fit tools for the designs of ambition. . . . Generally speaking the proportion which the aggregate of the other classes of citizens bears in any state to that of its husbandmen, is the proportion of its unsound to its healthy parts, and is a good enough barometer whereby to measure its degree of corruption. While we have land to labor then, let us never wish to see our citizens occupied at a work-bench, or twirling a distaff . . . for the general operations of manufacture, let our work-shops remain in Europe. It is better to carry provisions and materials to work-men there, than bring them to the provisions and materials, and with them their manners and principles. . . . The mobs of great cities add just so much to the support of pure government, as sores do to the strength of the human body. It is the manners and spirit of a people which preserve a republic in vigor. A degeneracy in these is a canker which soon eats to the heart of its laws and constitution.[23]

Such was his attitude in 1782, an attitude identical with Franklin's. Thirty-four years later he had modified his views of industrialism. The bitter experience of the Napoleonic wars, with the

[23] *Writings*, Vol. III, pp. 268–269.

hardships and losses visited upon neutral shipping, had convinced him of the need of domestic manufactures, and he was then deeply interested in improved machinery, new methods, original ventures. "We must now place the manufacturer by the side of the agriculturist," he conceded, or remain in economic dependence. But how much further the country should be industrialized, whether it "shall be proposed to go beyond our own supply" to compete in foreign markets, was not yet clear to him; the problem remained still to be determined whether "the *surplus* labor" would be "most beneficially employed in the culture of the earth, or in the fabrications of art." [24] In such commentary Jefferson failed to measure the thrust of economic determinism that drives every people to go through with the industrial revolution, once it is begun; but if we recall the primary principle of his political philosophy, that the "care of human life and happiness, and not their destruction, is the first and only legitimate object of good government," we may perhaps judge what would have been his attitude towards a centralized industrialism. He would have judged its desirability, not by the balance sheet of corporate business, but by the social ledger. As a social economist he could not think in terms of the economic man, nor simplify human beings to labor commodity, nor reduce the social tie to the cash nexus. It is inconceivable that he should have shared Hamilton's satisfaction at the contemplation of women and children—and many of the latter "of tender age"—wasting away in the mills; he was too social-minded for that, too much an idealist, too human in short. Though necessity might force him away from a simple agrarian economy, it does not follow that he would become partisan to a centralizing industrialism, with control vested in banking credit.

It is a common charge that Jefferson was consumed with suspicion, and it is set down against him as the mark of a mean and ungenerous nature. That in later years he was suspicious of fair-spoken advocates and plausible programs was as true of Jefferson as of Sam Adams; he had learned like the Boston democrat the virtue of the saying, *felix qui cautus*, and with so much at stake he would practice caution. He feared many things, for he was acutely aware of the incapacity of the heedless majority to defend itself against an able and instructed minority. As a child of an aristocratic age he fell into the mistake of visualizing that minority

[24] *Ibid.*, Vol. X, p. 8.

in the guise of a landed gentry, rather than in the guise of plutocracy; but in his quick fear of a minority he had all history as counselor. When he took his seat in Washington's cabinet his suspicions of the Hamiltonian program were quickly aroused. He believed that a monarchy was aimed at, and if that proved unattainable, then a highly centralized state designed to hold in check the democratic tendencies. His line of reasoning may be summarized thus: In consequence of the republican enthusiasm of the early years of the Revolution, democratic reorganization of the several state governments had been successfully achieved. Very great progress towards democracy had been made. Certain legislative acts of agrarian assemblies were now being turned against democracy, to invalidate it as a working system of government. But if agrarian majorities had used their power to enact laws beneficial to their interests, they were only applying a lesson learned from long experience with aristocratic legislatures. Such acts were no serious indictment of the democratic principle, and to make partisan use of them to justify curtailing the powers of the majority, was a betrayal of popular rights. And this, Jefferson believed, was the deliberate purpose of the Federalist leaders. Unable to stem the popular tide in the several commonwealths, the wealthy minority had devised a plan to superimpose upon the sovereign commonwealths a centralized federal government, so hedged about as to lie beyond the reach of local majorities, and hence able to override and nullify the democratic will. Once safely established, this federal government would gather fresh powers into its hands, until there emerged a rigorous machine, modeled after the British system, and as little regardful of the common interests. If this were not the Federalist purpose, why all the praise of the British system as the ripe product of experience, exactly adapted to the political genius of the English race?

In the matter of appeal to past experience, which provided the staple of Federalist argument, Jefferson discovered fresh grounds of fear. The past he looked upon as evil, and the record of experience was a tale of injustice and bitter wrong. He would not have America follow the trodden paths, for whither they led he knew too well. He would countenance no entangling alliances with old-world upper-class systems of statecraft, for such systems would reproduce in America the evils it should be the chief business of America to prevent. There must be erected here no counterpart of the European state; there must be no king, no aristocracy, no plutocracy; but a new democratic organization of government, in which the welfare of the whole people should be the sole concern.

When I left Congress in '76 [he wrote as an old man] it was in the persuasion that our whole code must be revised, adapted to our republican form of government, and now that we had no negatives of Councils, Governors and Kings to restrain us from doing right, that it should be corrected in all its parts with a single eye to reason and the good of those for whose government it was planned.[25]

Not past experience but present need should instruct America in drawing the plans of a new system of government and a new code of law. In analyzing the evils of European systems Jefferson came to certain conclusions that dominated all his later thinking, and that may be phrased thus: The political state tends inevitably to self-aggrandizement, the logical outcome of which is a political leviathan, too big and too complex for popular control. With sovereign powers vested in the hands of governmental agents, those agents lie under a constant temptation to corruption and tyranny, and in the end they align the powers of the state on the side of the most ambitious and capable. The greater the power of government, the ampler its revenues, the more energetic its administration, the more dangerous it may become to the rights of men; for where the prize is greatest, men struggle most ruthlessly, and what prize could be greater than the privilege of exploiting society in the name of the state? History knows no objective more tempting to the will to power, than the control of the absolute state. A government adequately socialized, intent solely upon furthering the common well-being, Jefferson would have been unanxious about. But such governments existed only in the dreams of Sir Thomas More and the Utopians; he could discover none such either in the past or present. Everywhere strong governments were little more than efficient tax-machines to support armies and provide subsidies and places for the minority. Against such forces of corruption the people struggle in vain.

If such was the common testimony of old-world experience—and no man who knew the inner workings of government there would deny it—what reason was there to expect that like causes would work unlike results in America? To what purpose was the talk of strong government encouraged amongst the holders of the public

[25] "Autobiography," in *Writings*, Vol. I, p. 57.

debt? To what end had lobbyists for the funding bill invaded the floor of Congress? It was idle to expect in America a nullification of the law, that where power sits within, corruption waits without. The love of power is universal. Most men are potential autocrats, the strong and capable may become actual autocrats. No man is good enough, no group of men, to be trusted with unrestrained powers—in America any more than in Europe. A centralized government in control of the tax-machine, and secure from popular restraint, would undo the results of the Revolutionary War. The movement to consolidate power, Jefferson asserted, was "but Toryism in disguise." "The generalizing and concentrating all cares and powers into one body . . . has destroyed the liberty and the rights of men in every government which has ever existed under the sun."

Our country is too large to have all its affairs directed by a single government. Public servants at such a distance, and from under the eye of their constituents, must, from the circumstance of distance, be unable to administer and overlook all the details necessary for the good government of the citizens; and the same circumstance, by rendering detection impossible to their constituents, will invite the public agents to corruption, plunder and waste.[26]

The practice of local home rule had grown up in America in response to native conditions; it had resulted from democratic needs; and Jefferson was too thoroughly American, too instinctively democratic, to overlook the significance of local sovereignties in a democratic philosophy. From the sharp contrast between American and European practice he deduced a cardinal principle, namely, that good government springs from a common interest in public affairs, and that such common interest is possible only when the field of activities is circumscribed. Set government apart from the people, or above them, and public interest is lost in a sense of futility. The danger of an encroaching tyranny by a superimposed sovereignty, is made easy by the public lethargy in respect to distant and unfamiliar things, and establishes itself through the psychology of custom. Jefferson was never greatly concerned about stable government; he was very much more concerned about responsive government—that it should faithfully serve the majority will. He made no god of the political state. He had no conventional reverence for established law and or-

[26] *Writings*, Vol. VII, p. 451.

der; he inquired rather what sort of law and order he was asked
to accept, was it just or unjust. Changing conditions make ancient good uncouth, and established institutions tend to fall
into dry-rot, or to become tyrannical. Men are more important than constitutions, and the public well-being is more sacred
than statutes. An occasional revolution, he commented grimly
apropos of the hue and cry over Shays's Rebellion, is salutary; if it
does not come of itself it might well be brought about. Progress
in government results from experiment; and it is easier and safer
to experiment on a small scale than on a great. Inertia increases
with size, and the more consolidated the government, the more
unyielding it becomes. The longest delayed revolutions are the
gravest.

In asserting the principle of the majority will, Jefferson like
other democratic thinkers of the time, found himself countered
by the argument of abstract justice. Vehement denunciation had
greeted Paine's doctrine that what a nation chooses to do, it has
a right to do. There can be no rights, it was confidently asserted,
superior to the right. The people may legislate, but it remains to
determine the validity of statutes in the light of justice; that which
is unjust is *ipso facto* null and void. It was Coke's doctrine of
judicial review, set up in America after its repudiation in England,
and Jefferson's hostility to it was bitter. As an intellectual he had
none of the lawyer's complacency with legal principles, or conceit
of the law's sufficiency; and as a democrat he would not yield
sovereignty into the hands of the judiciary. He had no veneration
for the Common Law of England: it had grown up by slow accre-
tions during centuries of absolutism; how should it be expected to
answer the needs of a freer age? It must be purged of outworn
elements, imbued with democratic sympathies. The Revolution
had been fought in defense of rights that are broader and more
human than legal principles; and to hand over those rights to be
interpreted away by lawyers, seemed to him moonstruck madness.
It was the law of Blackstone rather than of Coke that he feared
most—that "elegant" canonization of the malign influences of
Tory reaction, and that was so cried up by the smatterers and
"ephemeral insects of the law" in America; whereas Coke "was as
good a Whig as ever wrote":

  Blackstone and Hume have made tories of all England, and are making
tories of those young Americans whose native feelings of independence do

not place them above the wily sophistries of a Hume or a Blackstone. These two books, and especially the former [Blackstone], have done more towards the suppression of the liberties of man, than all the million of men in arms of Bonaparte, and the millions of human lives with the sacrifice of which he will stand loaded before the judgment seat of his Maker.[27]

As Jefferson grew older his fear of judicial encroachment on the popular will became acute, but it shifted from distrust of the Common Law to concern over the Supreme Court. A strong and outspoken hatred of the Federal judiciary runs through all his later writings, and he lost no opportunity to popularize the thesis—"It is a misnomer to call a government republican, in which a branch of the supreme power is independent of the nation."

The great object of my fear is the Federal Judiciary. That body, like gravity, ever acting, with noiseless foot, and unalarming advance, gaining ground step by step, and holding what it gains, is engulfing insidiously the special governments into the jaws of that which feeds them.[28]

It is a very dangerous doctrine to consider the judges as the ultimate arbiters of all constitutional questions. It is one which would place us under the despotism of an oligarchy. . . . The Constitution has erected no such single tribunal, knowing that to whatever hands confided, with the corruptions of time and party, its members would become despots.[29]

As Jefferson watched Chief Justice John Marshall gathering all things within the purview of the Federal judiciary, preparing future strongholds by the skillful use of *obiter dicta*, legislating by means of judicial interpretation, nullifying the will of the majority, and with the power of repeal made nugatory by the complexity of the process, he saw clearly what the outcome would be. Surely that was no democracy where judge-made laws were enforced by bench warrants, and where the sovereign power lay beyond the immediate reach of the popular will. The government that he desired would not rest on the legal fiction of an abstract justice above statutes and constitutions, whereof a group of judicial gentlemen were the repositories and guardians. It would be like Paine's, "a plain thing, and fitted to the capacity of many heads"; for "where the law of the majority ceases to be acknowledged, there government ends; the law of the strongest takes its place."

Granted the truth of Jefferson's premises that power tends to contract to the hands of a few, and that all government of the few

[27] *Ibid.*, Vol. VI, p. 335.   [28] *Ibid.*, Vol. X, p. 189.   [29] *Ibid.*, Vol. X, p. 160.

is vicious, then democracy is the only form of government under which an approximation to justice can be realized. A class will serve class interests. Government by an aristocracy is government in the interest of the aristocracy. For the staple argument of the Federalists, that gentlemen of principle and property alone may be intrusted with affairs of state, Jefferson had a quiet contempt. "I have never observed men's honesty to increase with their riches," he remarked. On the contrary, he regarded the "better sort of people" as a chief hindrance to the spread of social justice. The past had been evil because the past had been exploited by gentlemen of principle and property. They had kept government away from the people, and with their secret councils and secret diplomacy they had plundered the taxpayers and drenched nations in blood. Their selfish rivalries everywhere exacted a heavy toll of society and left behind a trail of poverty and wretchedness. The future would be better in the degree that mastery passed into common hands.

From the conclusions of his democratic premise he did not shrink. If it were indeed true that the people were beasts, then the democratic government of the future would be a bestial government—and even that might be better than the old arrangement of masters and slaves. But the American people whom Jefferson trusted were very far from beasts; he was convinced that they were honest and well-meaning; and if government were brought close to them, kept responsive to their will, a new and beneficent chapter in human history would open. The populistic laws passed by the legislatures of Rhode Island and New Hampshire, about which such an uproar was raised by fearful creditors, and which were urged as an argument against popular government, gave him no concern. He understood the ways of propaganda, and he never accepted judgment of the American people from the mouths of their enemies. The cure for the evils of democracy, he believed, was more democracy. The whole are far less likely to be unjust than the few; and if sovereignty does not rest in the majority will, where shall it lodge?

Hume, the great apostle of toryism, says "the Commons established a principle, which is noble in itself, and seems specious [i. e. pleasing], but is belied by all history and experience, *that the people are the origin of all just power.*" And where else will this degenerate son of science, this traitor to his fellow men, find the origin of *just* power, if not in the majority of the society? Will it be in the minority? Or in the individual of that minority? [30]

The America of Jefferson's day was a simple world, with a simple domestic economy. More than ninety per cent were plain country folk, farmers and villagers, largely freeholders, managing their local affairs in the traditional way. There were no great extremes of poverty and wealth, no closely organized class groups. With its sharp restrictions on suffrage and the prestige accorded the gentry, it was still far from a political democracy; but it was hastening towards a more democratic order. Remote from the cesspools of European diplomacy, and not yet acquainted with imperialism, it had no need for a leviathan state. Economic conditions sanctioned a *laissez-faire* government, simple and unambitious. In such a world the well-known words of Jefferson's first inaugural address, justified themselves to all who did not seek to use the state for personal advantage.

A wise and frugal government, which shall restrain men from injuring one another, which shall leave them otherwise free to regulate their own pursuits of industry and improvement, and shall not take from the mouth of labor the bread it has earned. This is the sum of good government, and this is necessary to close the circle of our felicities.

In one significant direction he would extend the scope of government—the encouragement of education. An intelligent people is necessary to a democracy; free schools are a sign of a free society. Tyranny thrives on ignorance and superstition, and every exploiting group fears popular education. Free himself in thought and action, believing in the unshackled commerce of ideas, hating all censorships, Jefferson accounted the founding of the University of Virginia his largest contribution to the well-being of his native commonwealth.

To all who profess faith in the democratic ideal Jefferson is a perennial inspiration. A free soul, he loved freedom enough to deny it to none; an idealist, he believed that the welfare of the whole, and not the prosperity of any group, is the single end of government. He was our first great leader to erect a political philosophy native to the economics and experience of America, as he was the first to break consciously with the past. His life was dedicated to the service of freedom, and later generations may well recall his words, "I have sworn upon the altar of God eternal

[30] *Ibid.*, Vol. VII, p. 356.

hostility against every form of tyranny over the mind of man." Europe made Jefferson wholly American. From his studies in France he came to see that where men enjoy free access to the sources of subsistence, government is likely to be simple and honest, and society free and content; but where a policy of preëmption has run its course, the function of government is seduced from its social purpose to perpetuate the inequalities which spring from the progressive monopolization of natural resources, with augmenting corruption and injustice. To preserve government in America from such degradation, to keep the natural resources open to all, were the prime desire and object of his life. That such an effort was foredoomed to failure, in presence of imperious forces that shape society beyond the capacity of political means to change or prevent, cannot detract from the nobility of his ideal, or the inspiration of his life. Among the greater thinkers of the constitutional period Jefferson remains by far the most vital and suggestive, the one to whom later generations may return most hopefully.

CHAPTER III

THE WAR OF BELLES LETTRES

To turn from the field of political theory to the realm of polite literature is not to quit the partisan battle-ground. The long struggle between Federalist and Democrat was too bitter and absorbing, too sharp in its alignment, not to conscript gentlemen of culture equally with politicians. Every available quill was called to the colors, and a civil war of *belles lettres* broke out, that exceeded in animosity any other known to our literary history. Attack and counter-attack were slashing and acrimonious. Gentlemen forgot their manners and indulged fiercely in tall language. Satire ran about the streets seeking new victims to impale; slander lay in wait for every passer-by. The crudest lies found willing listeners and sober ministers turned from writing sermons to enshrine pothouse tales in heroic couplets. In this virulent battle the Federalists, on the whole, had the better of it, for they were greater masters of invective and flayed their victims less clumsily; but the Democrats made up in ardor what they lacked in skill, and the blows that fell on carefully tied wigs must have hurt cruelly. As poetry those old satires may seem to us feeble enough, but as historical documents they are eloquent. The passion of a world in revolution, the hopes and fears of our forefathers as they watched the great fires consuming the world in which they had grown up, still survive in those stinging lines, as a reminder to later generations of the rough and inhospitable way that democratic America has traveled in its onward course.

I

THE FEDERALIST GROUP

1. THE HARTFORD WITS

What Federalism was capable of in the way of polite letters is sufficiently revealed in the work of a coterie of poetasters who are known in our literary histories as the Hartford Wits. The title of the group suggests their literary antecedents. They were the representatives of a literary mode that had slowly percolated through the crust of Puritan provincialism and imparted a certain sprightliness to a dour temper. They were the literary old-guard of the expiring eighteenth century, suspicious of all innovation, contemptuous of every idealistic program. They stood stoutly by the customary and familiar. The nineteenth century was knocking at their door, but they would not open to it. And as they saw that new century coming in the guise of revolution, exciting to unheard-of innovations in the fields of politics and economics and religion and letters, giving rise to Jacobin Clubs and Jeffersonian democracy, they set themselves seriously to the work of barring its progress through their own little world. They conveniently associated the economic unrest of post-war days, that gave birth to a strange progeny in Rhode Island and New Hampshire and Massachusetts, with the contamination of French atheism, charged all unrest to the account of democracy, and hastened to put it down in the name of law and righteousness. They hated new ways with the virtuous hatred of the well-to-do, and dreamed of a future America as like the past as one generation of oysters is like another.

There is a certain historical fitness in the fact that the Wits should have arisen in Connecticut and been the intellectual children of Yale. For generations the snug little commonwealth had been the home of a tenacious conservatism, that clung to old ways and guarded the institutions of the fathers with pious zeal. Nowhere else in New England did the ruling hierarchy maintain so glacial a grip on society. The Revolution of '76 had only ruffled the surface on Connecticut life; it left the social structure quite unchanged. The church retained its unquestioned control of the machinery of the commonwealth; and the church was dominated by a clerical aristocracy, hand in glove with a mercantile aristocracy. Fresh currents of thought that were stirring the pulpits of eastern Massachusetts—suggestions of an Arianism that was to lead to the Unitarian schism—did not reach so far as New Haven, and Yale was content to remain the bulwark of an obsolete Calvinism. In such a soil Federalism would flourish like Jonah's gourd; and it exuded a special odor of sanctity from the Calvinism in which it was rooted. To stout Federalists like Timothy Dwight, the current dogma of total depravity sufficed to disprove the validity of all democratic aspiration. It was a presumption little short of blasphemous to assert that sinners are competent to manage the temporal affairs of society. The doctrine of equalitarianism was a particular stench in the nostrils of the aristocratic clergy, who disliked all leveling. The Irish immigrants seem to have been the most offensive equalitarians. A New England gentleman, traveling in Pennsylvania in the nineties, wrote home: "I have seen many, very many Irishmen, and with a few exceptions, they are . . . the most God-provoking Democrats on this side of Hell." And in 1798 Harrison Gray Otis wrote: "If some means are not adopted to prevent the indiscriminate admission of wild Irishmen and others to the right of suffrage, there will soon be an end to liberty & property." [1] To prevent, if possible, such an unhappy outcome, the upper classes of New England fell to organizing and drilling all the elements of conservatism for a vigorous defense. They wrote and spoke and preached, till the mind of respectable New England was saturated with prejudice. The democratic principle was converted into a bogey to frighten the simple. Such a hideous misshapen imp of darkness, such a vile hag of anarchy had never before been painted for the imagination of honest Yankees to shudder at; and if democracy seemed to them a wild and fearsome thing making ready to destroy their venerated social order, they only believed what the minister preached on the Sabbath and the squire asserted on week days. The plebeian democrat, very likely in debt, was quite overwhelmed by the organized forces of village respectability.

In this great work of saving the commonwealth of Connecticut from the pollutions of democracy the Hartford Wits were competent laborers. The more important members of the group were John Trumbull, Timothy Dwight, Joel Barlow, Lemuel Hopkins, David Humphreys, Richard Alsop, and Theodore Dwight. To these may be added the names of Dr. Elihu Hubbard Smith and Dr. Mason F. Cogswell, who were friends and occasional collaborators. Nearly all were Yale men with a pronounced Yale predilection for Calvinism and Federalism, admirable representatives of the oligarchical upper class of the provincial Connecticut society. Timothy Dwight, grandson of Jonathan Edwards, was a minister and president of Yale; Hopkins, Smith and Cogswell were physicians of high professional standing; Trumbull and Theodore Dwight were lawyers; Barlow and Humphreys found

[1] Quoted by Samuel Eliot Morison in *Harrison Gray Otis*, Vol. I, p. 107.

their way into the diplomatic field, and Alsop was a merchant.
They were all comfortably well off and several were wealthy.
Alsop was one of the few millionaires of the time; Barlow acquired
a fortune in France; and Humphreys late in life established a
textile industry incorporated for half a million. Hot Federalists,
they found in Washington, Governor Trumbull, and Fisher Ames,
their political mentors and guides. The most active of the group
politically, was Theodore Dwight, who with his cousin Timothy
was a director of the Eagle Bank, a Federalist institution, and
bitterly opposed to the chartering of Republican banks. When
one of the latter applied to the legislature for a charter he denounced
it as a "child of intrigue and the mother of Discord." He was deep
in the Hartford Convention, serving as its secretary and later as
its historian. He denounced Jeffersonian republicanism as seeking
to "discredit the ministry, decry religion, and destroy public
worship," and as he saw it spreading through New England he
attributed to it the certain decay of morality and the impending
break-up of family ties, exclaiming with somewhat extreme vivacity: "The outlaws of Europe, the fugitives from the pillory and
the gallows, have undertaken to assist our own abandoned citizens, in the pleasing work of destroying Connecticut. . . . Can
imagination paint anything more dreadful on this side of hell!"

Later generations remember best the massive character of
Timothy Dwight, a man endowed with all the Connecticut virtues
and walking amongst his fellows with magnificent confidence in
his powers. A great preacher, an authoritative theologian, a
distinguished administrator—"every inch a college president"—
a ready counselor on any knotty point be it in law or politics or
finance or agriculture or *belles lettres*, a born leader of men, and
by way of recreation an inditer of Hebraic epics and huge didactic
poems and ample Connecticut pastorals, a confirmed traveler
observing the manner of life in many commonwealths and preserving his observations in solid volumes—he was a man to compel
the admiration of his fellows and put his stamp upon his age. So
vast was the contemporary reputation of Timothy Dwight, and so
many-sided, it may seem ironical that time should have shrunk him
to the narrow compass of a paragraph in our literary history. And
yet the more curiously one considers the work of the great president
of Yale, the more insistent become one's doubts concerning the
fineness of this nugget of Connecticut gold. It shows very sus-

picious signs of tarnish. His commanding presence and authoritative manner, his sonorous eloquence, his forwardness in defense of what few doubted, his vehement threshing of straw long since reduced to chaff, his prodigious labors, his abundant printing, no longer seem so authentic a seal of greatness as they seemed to his open-mouthed contemporaries; and one suspects that he impressed his fellow citizens by the completeness with which he measured up to every Connecticut ideal, rather than by the creative vigor of his mind. The great Timothy, in short, seems to a later generation to have been little more than a walking repository of the venerable Connecticut *status quo*.

The intellectual inquisitiveness that gave birth to disintegrating theory in the mind of his grandfather Jonathan Edwards, and made him a profoundly revolutionary influence in his time, was wholly lacking in the grandson. The latter refused to follow the questioning intellect into unsurveyed fields. He would not meddle with change. His mind was closed as tight as his study windows in January. He read widely in the fields of rationalism, but he read only to refute. Now and then to be sure, certain generous promptings visited him: he spoke out against slavery; he encouraged the higher education of women. But from such temptations to become a living voice he turned away to follow the main-traveled road of Connecticut prejudice. His eyes were fixed lovingly upon the past, and his fondest dreams for his native commonwealth hovered about the ideal of a church-state which John Cotton had labored to establish and Increase Mather to preserve. It is with those capable theocrats of Massachusetts Bay, rather than with Thomas Hooker of Hartford, that he is to be associated. Two men could scarcely be more alike than Timothy Dwight and Increase Mather; their careers ran in similar lines; each was the unmitered pope of his generation, and each owed his extraordinary influence to the same sterling qualities. As ecclesiastical politicians they drew no line between religious and secular affairs, but were prompt with a hand in every affair of the commonwealth. They spoke and wrote with unquestioned authority. They regarded the minister as the responsible leader of society who must not suffer his flock to be led astray. The church was the guardian of morality, and the state was its secular arm. The true faith must not be put in jeopardy by unfaith. To Timothy Dwight infidelity and democracy went hand in hand, and to suffer the commonwealth to fall under the control of the godless meant the end of all morality and religion. To uphold the established order—of which he was a distinguished member—was for him the first of Christian duties. A stalwart Federalist, he was a good hater of all Jacobins. His detestation of Jefferson was virulent and he swallowed the nastiest tales about the great Virginian without a qualm, never doubting their authenticity. It was sometimes hinted that he was too much the aristocrat to feel the warmest sympathy for the unprosperous, and there seems to have been ground for the suspicion. The unprosperous were likely to be infected with Jeffersonian heresies, and as he watched them being drawn off to the York-state frontier, he rejoiced that their voting power was no longer to be feared. Such restless spirits, he pointed out, "are impatient of the re-straints of law, religion, and morality; grumble about the taxes, by which Rulers, Ministers, and Schoolmasters are supported. . . . We have many troubles even now; but we should have many more, if this body of foresters had remained at home." [2] If the dis-affected did not like the way the Congregational-Federalist party managed the good state of Connecticut, it were a godsend if they should remove beyond its boundaries.

But it is with the literary work of Timothy Dwight that we are more immediately concerned, and in all his abundant output, totaling fourteen volumes and perhaps as much more in manu-script, the same solid qualities are revealed. It is the occasional work of a man wanting humor, playfulness, grace, lacking subtlety and creative suggestiveness, but with a shrewd common sense, a great vigor, and a certain grandiose imagination. A sonorous declaimer, he dearly loved combat and the shock of marshaled argument. He went out of his way to invite majestic effects. In *The Conquest of Canaan* he described so many thunderstorms that Trumbull suggested he ought to furnish a lightning rod with the poem. Such a man could not move easily in narrow spaces. An epic was none too slight to contain his exuberant rhetoric. His ready versification, one often feels, runs like a water pipe with the faucet off; the words flow in an unbroken stream with never a pause to pick or choose. Yet even in his amazing copiousness there is vigor; a well-stocked mind is pouring out the gatherings of years. When he pauses to give advice—as he was fond of doing— his abundant sense is worth listening to; the homely wisdom of

[2] *Travels*, Vol. II, p. 458.

his talk to the farmers in the sixth part of *Greenfield Hill* is not unlike Franklin. As a satirist he belongs to the Churchill school; he is downright, abusive, often violent, quite lacking the lightness of touch and the easy gayety that runs so pleasantly through *M'Fingal*. His *Triumph of Infidelity* is solid old-fashioned pulpit-thumping. The spirit of toleration was withheld from him by his fairy godmother, and he knew no other way of dealing with those who persisted in disagreement after their mistakes had been pointed out, than the cudgel. In this tremendous poem he lays about him vigorously. On Hume and Voltaire and Priestley, and all their followers, his blows fall smartly. Bloody crowns ought to be plentiful, but—though he does not seem to know it—the blows fall on straw men and none proves mortal. On the whole one prefers him in the pastoral mood when he lays aside his minis-terial gown, and *Greenfield Hill*, unless one excepts the *Travels in New England and New York*, remains his most attractive work. Yet even that is sadly in need of winnowing. A great college president Timothy Dwight may very well have been; he was worshiped by his admirers only this side idolatry; but a great thinker, a steadfast friend of truth in whatever garb it might appear, a generous kindly soul loving even publicans and sinners, regardful of others and forgetful of self, he assuredly was not.

2. "The Anarchiad"

Most of the political satire of the Wits was done in collaboration, and consists of occasional sketches contributed to newspapers—with explanatory comments and notes—dealing with matters of current interest. Of the major works thus produced, *The Anarchiad*, *The Echo*, and *The Political Greenhouse*, the first will suffice to reveal the political sympathies of the Hartford group. *The Anar-chiad* is a mock epic designed to counteract the populistic tenden-cies of post-war times. It was published in *The New Haven Gazette* between October 26, 1786, and September 13, 1787. In 1861 it was resurrected from a long sleep by Luther G. Riggs, and re-issued with an introduction and notes. "This fearless satire," according to the editor, "is supposed to have exerted great and beneficial influence upon the public mind, and to have tended in no small degree to check the leaders of insubordination and infidel philosophy"; and it must be regarded as " a *national Poem*, battling nobly for the right universal, for the majesty of law, and for the

Federal government." The idea was got from a contemporary English screed entitled *The Rolliad*, one of the numerous political satires of which the late eighteenth century was so fond. Probably most of the members of the group had a hand in it, but the acrid quality of its comment owes more to Hopkins than to the others.

For such work the angular Connecticut physician was admirably fitted. The son of a Waterbury farmer, Dr. Lemuel Hopkins was the most picturesque member of the Hartford Wits, the most characteristically Yankee. Brought up at the plow-tail, he received nevertheless an excellent education, and because of a hereditary predisposition to consumption turned to the medical profession. After serving his apprenticeship at Wallingford he entered upon his practice at Litchfield in 1776. During the Revolution he served for a short time as a volunteer, but soon returned to his lancet and medicine case. In 1784 he removed to Hartford where he spent the remainder of his life. In person he was tall, lean, stooping, rawboned, with coarse features and large brilliant eyes. His uncouth appearance and eccentricity of manner made him a striking figure, and his caustic wit rendered him a redoubtable antagonist. As a physician he stood at the head of the Connecticut profession. He was one of the founders of the Medical Society of Connecticut, and as a frequent contributor to professional literature he exerted a wide influence on the current practice.

The eccentric doctor seems to have been as honest as he was outspoken. He was uncompromising in his warfare on all quacks, both medical and political. For a time as a young man he was a disciple of French infidel philosophy, but he cured his mental indisposition by a severe Biblical regimen, and having restored himself to the robust health of Calvinistic Christianity, he devoted himself to the work of curing others. He became in consequence a specialist in the treatment of the ravages caused by the *bacillus gallicus*. For every sort of humbug he had a hearty contempt, and any political nostrum not listed in the Federalistic materia medica he regarded as arrant quackery. He thought no better of old wives' remedies in government than in medicine, and when the Rhode Island legislature passed its paper-money act in 1785, and six months later Shays's Rebellion broke out, and mobs were besieging the legislature of New Hampshire, he proposed to speak plainly to the good people of Connecticut on the follies of popular delusions. This would seem to have been the origin of *The Anar-chiad*. It sprang from the indignation of Dr. Hopkins, when, to quote from the poem,

> In visions fair, the scenes of fate unroll,
> And Massachusetts opens on my soul.
> There Chaos, Anarch old, asserts his sway,
> And mobs in myriads blacken all the way.

The sardonic temper of Dr. Hopkins fitted him for virulent satire, and in this bitterest of the productions of the Wits, the reins were on the neck of the muse. Scarcely another New England satire reflects so sharply the class consciousness that underlay the bitter struggle between agrarianism and capitalism. It is a slashing attack upon agrarian economics and democratic liberalism, a versified echo of the anger of creditors who were fighting the measures of populistic legislatures. The staple of the satire is the wickedness of all paper-money issues, with the State of Rhode Island as the chief of agrarian sinners. About this main theme is gathered a miscellany of Federalist shibboleths—the godlessness of Shays and his crew, the seditious spirit of all who oppose the new Constitution, the demagoguery of democratic politicians—and the satire rises to a patriotic crescendo in declaiming against the folly of the democratic ideal. So tremendous a work, however, cannot be adequately described; the lines must speak for themselves. The following bits may serve in lieu of the whole, the first of which is a comment on Rhode Island, the pariah of States:

> Hail! realm of rogues, renown'd for fraud and guile,
> All hail! ye knav'ries of yon little isle.
> There prowls the rascal, cloth'd with legal pow'r,
> To snare the orphan, and the poor devour;
> The crafty knave his creditor besets
> And advertising paper pays his debts;
> Bankrupts their creditors with rage pursue,
> No stop, no mercy from the debtor crew.
> Arm'd with new tests, the licens'd villain bold,
> Presents his bills, and robs them of their gold;
> Their ears, though rogues and counterfeiters lose,
> No legal robber fears the gallows noose.
> Look through the State, the unhallow'd ground appears
> A pen of dragons, and a cave of bears;
> A nest of vipers, mix'd with adders foul;
> The screeching night-bird, and the greater owl:
> For now, unrighteousness, a deluge wide,

Pours round the land an overwhelming tide;
And dark injustice, wrapp'd in paper sheets,
Rolls a dread torrent through the wasted streets;
While net of law th' unwary fry draws in
To damning deeds, and scarce they know they sin.
New paper struck, new tests, new tenders made,
Insult mankind, and help the thriving trade.
Each weekly print new lists of cheats proclaims,
Proud to enroll their knav'ries and their names;
The wiser race, the snares of law to shun,
Like Lot from Sodom, from Rhode Island run. . . .[3]

Nor less abhorr'd, the certain woe that waits
The giddy rage of democratic States,
Whose pop'lar breath, high-blown in restless tide,
No laws can temper, and no reason guide:
An equal sway, their mind indignant spurns;
To wanton sway, the bliss of freedom turns;
Led by wild demagogues, the factious crowd,
Mean, fierce, imperious, insolent and loud,
Nor fame, nor wealth, nor power, nor system draws—
They see no object, and perceive no cause;
But feel, by turns, in one disastrous hour,
Th' extremes of license, and th' extremes of power. . . .

Will this vain scheme bid restless factions cease,
Check foreign wars, or fix internal peace?
Call public credit from her grave to rise,
Or gain in grandeur what they lose in size? . . .
But know, ye favor'd race, one potent head
Must rule your States, and strike your foes with dread.
The finance regulate, the trade control,
Live through the empire, and accord the whole.
Ere death invades, the night's deep curtain falls,
Through ruin'd realms the voice of UNION calls; . . .
On you she calls! attend the warning cry;
YE LIVE UNITED, OR DIVIDED DIE! [4]

But chief the race allured by fleeting fame,
Who seek on earth the politicians name;
Auspicious race! whom folly joys to bless,
And wealth and honor crown with glad success;
Formed, like balloons, by emptiness to rise
On pop'lar gales, to waft them through the skies . . .
See, from the shades, on tiny pinions swell
And rise, the young DEMOCRACY of *hell!*
Before their face the *powers of Congress* fade,
And *public credit* sinks, an empty shade;

[3] Number III.   [4] Number X.

Wild severance rages, wars intestine spread,
Their boasted UNION hides her dying head;
The forms of government in ruin hurl'd,
Reluctant empire quits the western world.[5]

Amid such democratic welter and mortal confusion the sole
hope of safety lies in Federalism, and the sapient leader who
shall bring order out of the wild misrule is thus greeted:

Ardent and bold, the smiling land to save,
In council sapient as in action brave,
I fear'd young Hamilton's unshaken soul,
And saw his arm our wayward host control; . . .
Fire in his eye, and thunder on his tongue.[6]

Other work the Hartford Wits did, but none which need detain
us. Soon changes and removals broke up the coterie, and they
went diverse ways to diverse rewards: Timothy Dwight to safeguard Yale undergraduates in New Haven, Humphreys to the
American legation at Paris, Trumbull to the Michigan frontier,
and Barlow to his notable career in Europe. But happily not
before they had contributed their portion of sweetness and light
to the great debate. The Wits were no skulkers in presence of
"insubordination and infidel philosophy," when their economic
interests were touched.

II

THE FRENCH GROUP

The Wits were not devoid of cleverness, but they were wanting
in ideas. They were partisans rather than intellectuals. In the
rôle of self-appointed custodians of Federalist moralities they
were rather tedious fellows, who substituted fustian for creative
thought, and blew up their verses with flatulent rhetoric. They
sealed the windows of their minds against the disturbing winds
of doctrine that were blowing briskly; they inspected the family
tree of every new idea to determine its respectability. An occasional fresh idea is necessary to keep one from falling into staleness
and mediocrity; but the Wits chose to remain too ignorant to be
interesting, and it is a relief to turn from them to the more stimulating company of the French partisans. Here at least there was
intellectual sincerity: a genuine desire to understand what was

[5] Number XI.   [6] Number IX.

going on in the larger world of thought; to use what brains God had given them to better the lot of the American people. Philip Freneau, Joel Barlow, and Hugh Henry Brackenridge were not intellectual giants, but they represent the best intelligence then being devoted to literature in America, and their work retains a suggestiveness today far beyond that of the Hartford Wits.

1. PHILIP FRENEAU

Poet of Two Revolutions

It is fitting that our first outstanding poet should have been a liberal. The idealist has always seen deeper into the spirit of America than the realist, and been less complacent with halfway achievement. And it is equally fitting that his idealism should have got him into trouble with the dominant group of his generation. Philip Freneau was a volunteer in two revolutions, a color-sergeant carrying the newly unfurled flag of democracy in the thick of civil strife. He was a lifelong rebel, whose rebellions turned out to be patriotic or seditious as they went with or against the purpose of the victorious party. In the Revolution of '76 he fought shoulder to shoulder with John Adams and Hamilton and Washington, and his services were accorded high praise. His poems inspired patriotic enthusiasm, greatly aided the national cause, and won wide approval. But in the Revolution of '93 he parted company with Adams and Hamilton and Washington. When the old leaders turned back in fear at the unloosing of democratic aspirations, he went forward to new battles. He served the cause of '93 with the same ardor that had inspired his pen in '76. It was not a new cause in his eyes, but the old; not a different war, as Federalists asserted, but other battles of the same war—the never ceasing struggle for human freedom.

In thus breaking with the party of Federalism and casting his lot with the democratic Jacobins, Freneau contracted a serious *mesalliance* that destroyed his good name. Thereafter he was marked as a vulgar democrat, a disseminator of insubordination and infidelity, an evil influence among a respectable, God-fearing people. The further he went in his new crusade, the lower he sank in decent opinion, until the poet of the American Revolution came to be regarded as the hireling mouthpiece of Jefferson, a writer of wretched and insolent doggerel, an incendiary journalist—a mean and paltry figure beside the stately forms of the Fathers of the Constitution. Gentlemen exhausted the resources of ample vocabularies to express their detestation of his leveling ways. To Timothy Dwight he was "A mere incendiary, or rather . . . a despicable tool of bigger incendiaries, and his paper . . . a public nuisance." To the gentle-natured Irving he was "A barking cur," and to Washington, whose words were accorded a quasi-royal respect, he was "That rascal Freneau": rather loose expressions, certainly, for cultivated gentlemen to apply to another cultivated gentleman, the friend of Madison and Brackenridge. It is evident that Freneau and the great Federalist leaders disagreed somewhat violently in their interpretations of the purpose and scope of the new venture in republicanism.

The source of their disagreement lay in divergencies of social philosophy too great to be bridged. In his republicanism Freneau had gone far in advance of the Federalists. He was a democrat while they remained aristocrats. He had rid himself of a host of outworn prejudices, the heritage of an obsolete past, which held them in bondage. He had read more clearly the meaning of the great movement of decentralization that was shaping a new psychology, and must lead eventually to democratic individualism. He had no wish to stay or thwart that development; he accepted it wholly with all its implications. He had freed his mind from the thralldom of caste; he was impelled by no egoistic desire to impose his will upon others; he was wholly free from the lust of economic aggression, either for himself or for his class. He was an idealist who cared only for the *res publica*, the common well-being, and he desired chiefly that the new American government should serve the needs of a free people. There was no envy in the soul of Freneau, and no self-seeking. He was the friend of civilization rather than the advocate of particular forms of government. He put his trust in local self-rule rather than in a coercive state. Like Paine he distrusted all centralizing power. Like Franklin he regarded the every-day world of business and politics as a preposterous arrangement, unconcerned with justice; and he took it on himself to do what he could to make it over. All his life he was an unmuzzled advocate of whatever new movements gave promise of lessening the old tyrannies. In championing the cause of democracy, he championed a score of lesser causes: Unitarianism, deism, antislavery, Americanism in education: thereby bringing down on his head the resentment of all the conservatisms, religious, political, economic, social, then prospering in America. Nevertheless he went his way through a sordid world of politicians and speculators, feeding upon whatever shreds of beauty he met with, a dreamer and an idealist sneered at by exploiters, a spirit touched to finer issues than his generation cared for.

The chief desire of Freneau's life was to be a poet, and if the country had not been turmoiled by revolution, doubtless he would have been content to "live unpromoted and write poems." But revolution and not poetry was the serious business of the age, and he chose to have a hand in that business. Many later critics have lamented his choice. They regret that he did not turn aside from the battle-ground to wander in pastoral fields; that he was not content with the *noctes coenaeque deum* where the minstrel's song is sufficient passport to hospitality. It is a nice question of literary ethics. The raw material of poetry was in Philip Freneau; there was need only of calm years to master his art and clarify the vague romanticism of his nature. He had only to stand apart from the turmoil, refusing to soil his hands with politics, and cultivate his faculty for verse, to have made himself the indisputable founder of American poetry. He was endowed with a romantic imagination and love of natural beauty, a generation before the romantic revival, and he might well have become a notable contributor to that revival.

But he refused to stand apart. He would not hire a substitute to defend the cause of freedom. There was rough work to be done, and the democrats were too few to spare so competent a workman. So when poetry proved unequal to the task he turned journalist, and set to work in a field unclaimed by the muses. It was an immense sacrifice, bringing disaster to all hope of contemporary fame, and tarnishing his reputation in after years. His place in American letters was fixed by a Federalist verdict, and he has since remained obscure and neglected by all, save an occasional historian who dips into a few poems, regrets that the smell of revolution is so rank, and dismisses him with the comment that Campbell and Scott did him the honor to appropriate a figure of speech without acknowledgment. Only within recent years has a collected edition of his poems been accessible, and his prose writings still remain buried in newspaper files. In consequence the literary critics have echoed the political critics, and given new life to the old partisanship. Thus Professor Wendell remarks that "a considerable part of his poetry . . . consists of rather reckless satire, not conspicuously better or worse than much other satire of the period." [7] Even Professor Tyler, usually so generous in sympathy for our early writers, dismisses Freneau with these words:

> The poor old man, thus found dead on the lonely New Jersey moor, had undoubtedly some sweetness in his heart; but he permitted very little of it to work its way down to the tip of his pen. With that pitiless pen of his he had fought many a fierce fight in his day. . . . He was the poet of hatred, rather than of love. . . . Among all his verses, the reader finds scarcely one lyric of patriotic enthusiasm, nor many lines to thrill the hearts of the Revolutionists by any touch of loving devotion to their cause, but everywhere lines hot and rank with sarcasm and invective against the enemy. . . . Like Odell, Freneau was a good hater; his was the wrathful muse; his chosen warfare was grim, unsparing, deadly. He was the satirical gladiator on behalf of the Revolution, even as Odell was the satirical gladiator in opposition to it.[8]

Such commentary is neither discriminating nor just. That the ways of Freneau were often ruthless it needs only a casual reading of his satire to perceive; that he was a good hater is quite as apparent; but that the deeper springs of his nature were bitter is not true. He was no satirist like Churchill to love filth and delight in venom. It was an age of partisan ruthlessness, and if Freneau was a fierce partisan it was because the new hope then whispering to liberals was in danger of being stifled by selfish men who feared it. The vision of a free republic arising on the ruins of colonial monarchy had taken possession of his imagination; a republic admirable in justice and righteous in all its ways. That vision, he believed, might be realized if the republicans stood firm in its defense. A thousand perils beset it. The lingering colonial traditions—the ties of old custom—were powerful advocates of the old inequality; the greed of profit and power—the ambitions of a monied aristocracy—were equally powerful advocates of new tyrannies. Not only must George III and his Tory supporters be driven from the land, but the work thus begun must be carried through. An army of domestic enemies must be dealt with—a formidable aristocracy of wealth and family. Naturally it would be no holiday task. The King had no mind to be driven out of his American dominions, and the Federalists had no mind to surrender control of the new American state. And so no choice

[7] *Literary History of America*, p. 300.
[8] *Literary History of the American Revolution*, Vol. I, p. 172.

remained to the republicans but to make the advocates of monarchy and aristocracy appear so hateful in the eyes of the people that they would rise and destroy them.

In times of profound upheaval the demands of partisanship are stern and exacting. The gray-goose quill may serve the cause of peace, but the porcupine quill stings and rankles more; and if Freneau was given to using the latter it was because he cared greatly for the ends to be achieved. "How oft has rugged nature charged my pen with gall," he lamented late in life as he contemplated the enemies he had made. Sensitive and proud, he had a Gallic impetuosity of onset. If he plundered the broadsides of their store of abuse and ransacked the dictionaries of their wealth of scurrility, it was not because he loved abuse and scurrilities. If like Sam Adams, he was given to robbing men of their characters, it was due to no personal or selfish motives; those great ones whom he lampooned so fiercely, he believed were enemies of the new order. If "his chosen warfare was grim, unsparing, deadly," as Professor Tyler asserts, it was because he was fighting for a great ideal against men who were equally grim, unsparing, deadly. Unembittered laughter had little opportunity to try its sanative qualities in that long warfare of bushwhackers.

During the last quarter of the century the writings of Freneau in verse and prose constitute an abstract and brief chronicle of the times. If they seem old-fashioned to us today, they were quite new-fashioned to the men who first read them. The early satires, printed in 1775 must have fallen upon American ears with almost startling effect. A revolutionary change had come over Freneau; he had broken wholly with the colonial temper and turned nationalist a year before the Declaration of Independence. When he graduated from Princeton College in the summer of 1771, he wrote in collaboration with Hugh Henry Brackenridge a commencement poem entitled *The Rising Glory of America*, in which the youthful collegians, bred up in a hotbed of Whiggery, were as British as Pitt himself. The new English imperialism fairly rioted in the swelling couplets. The poem is a prophecy of the time when the British flag should wave from the Atlantic to the Pacific over a contented people, who "warm in liberty and freedom's cause," gloried in the name of Briton. Agriculture and commerce are duly celebrated as the twin pillars of American prosperity, and the pages of colonial history are combed for great names and heroic deeds. On the roll of American heroes Braddock, Sir William Johnson, and Whitefield are the most conspicuous. Oddly enough Washington's valor at the time of Braddock's defeat was unknown to these collegians in 1771, but was afterwards discovered and inserted in later editions. Following independence Freneau revised the poem and the changed circumstances played havoc with the colonial text. Braddock was silently expunged together with "Britannia's warlike troops, Choice spirits of her isle." "False Gallia's sons" becomes "Gallia's hostile sons." A notable tribute to English generosity seemed incongruous to Freneau after his experience on the prison ship and was deleted. He no longer felt that

> The British epithet is merciful,
> And we the sons of Britain learn like them
> To conquer and to spare.

What happened to Freneau during the years following his graduation is uncertain, but in July, 1775, he appeared in New York City with his pockets stuffed with another sort of verse, which he scattered among the print-shops, the rebellious spirit of which may be judged from the prayer,

Libera Nos, Domine.—Deliver us, O Lord, not only from British dependence, but

> From the scoundrel, Lord North, who would bind us in chains,
> From a royal king Log, with his tooth-full of brains,
> Who dreams, and is certain (when taking a nap)
> He has conquered our lands, as they lay on his map.

> From a kingdom that bullies, and hectors, and swears,
> We send up to heaven our wishes and prayers
> That we, disunited, may freemen be still,
> And Britain go on—to be damned if she will.[9]

The colonial slipped easily from Freneau and left him wholly American. And with the colonial psychology there slipped from him also the useless impedimenta of old-world social and political philosophies. How far he advanced towards the democratic conception of society, during those first rebellious years, is not clear; but he had set his foot on a path that must conduct him far if he did not turn back. And it is certain that he never turned back. His declaration of independence from King George was the first of many such declarations of independence—for himself

[9] *Poems*, Pattee edition, Vol. I, p. 141.

and his fellow Americans. Thereafter his serious business was the work of stripping from the colonial every loyalty which still bound him to England. He supplemented the work of Paine in teaching men whose fathers were English that they were of another nation; that they could no longer remain both English and American, but must make choice between the two allegiances. Year after year he stirred the troubled waters, arousing the spirit of nationalism by attacking everything pro-British. His attacks on the English generals, the Tories, the royalist printers, were but means to the great end of uprooting the traditional dependence on England and quickening the new national psychology.

The second stimulus to Freneau's revolutionary ardor came from the French uprising. Later in the summer of 1775 he had quitted New York and sailed for the West Indies. He spent two years on the Island of Santa Cruz, then and later engaging in sea voyages about the islands and along the American coast. They were creative years, when removed equally from the distractions of war and the utilitarianism of America, he was free to cultivate the romantic strain of poetry that was strong in him. Then followed unhappier days. A period of stagnation had come to him during the years of post-war reaction; and if fresh fuel had not been brought from overseas to kindle anew his social enthusiasms, it is likely that he would have drifted into a stale and unprofitable old age. The spirit of romantic poetry was deadened by an unsympathetic environment, but with the democratic hope rising in France came a fresh call to arms. He discovered a larger and nobler interpretation of his republican creed, that was to transform it into French Jacobinism and arm it for a new leveling crusade. If he could not be a poet to America he would enlist in the army of democracy. Not only must the new government be made French-democratic instead of English-Whig, but all distinctions of rank must be swept away, together with every tyrannical dogma of church and state. In short there must be a social house-cleaning, the limits of which were to be determined only by reason and the common democratic good. So Freneau enthusiastically joined with Paine and Jefferson in the partisan labor of spreading the new faith.

His literary activity during this second period was remarkable. Songs and odes and satires came from his ready pen in unending stream, eager, cutting, vibrant with feeling. It requires an intimate knowledge of the times to make out the identity of every figure at which he shoots his arrows, but it needs no very intimate knowledge to measure the intensity of his partisanship. The democratic hopes and fears of those vibrant days find reflection in many an acrid verse. He was at one with Jefferson in his concern at the monarchical reaction.

> In ten short years, of freedom weary grown
> The State, Republic, sickens for a throne.

The man who attached to the pen name of Peter Slender the letters O. S. M.—One of the Swinish Multitude—would not fail to take the part of the private soldier neglected by the state:

> Sold are those arms which once on Britons blazed,
> When, flushed with conquest, to the charge they came;
> That power repelled, and Freedom's fabrick raised,
> She leaves her soldier—famine and a name! [10]

Nor would he fail to capitalize the aristocratic contempt of the Federalists for that same swinish multitude.

> Lodge where you must, drink small-beer where you can,
> But eat no roast pig, if no Federal man. . . .

> Your mouth was made for rye or barley bread;
> What claims have you to halls of state,
> Whose business is to stand and wait,
>   Subservient to command?
> What right have you to white-bread, superfine,
> Who were by nature destin'd for "a swine"—
>   As said good Edmund Burke,
>   The drudge of Britain's dirty work,
> Whose mighty pamphlets rous'd the royal band! [11]

During the tumultuous year of '93 Freneau issued a series of *Probationary Odes by Jonathan Pindar, Esq.*, which reflect sharply the partisan passions aroused by the French Revolution. They were lampoons directed at members of government who were in the democratic black-book, chiefly John Adams, Knox, and Hamilton. The introductory poem was addressed *To all the Great Folks in a Lump;* the second, *To Atlas,* was an attack on Hamilton; the third, *To A Select Body of Great Men,* was a lampoon of the Senate; and the fourth, *To a Would Be Great Man,* was addressed to Freneau's particular *bête noire,* John Adams. This last, apropos

[10] *The American Soldier.*   [11] *To Duncan Doolittle.*

of *Davila*, will serve to show the popular reception which that unfortunate work received.

> Daddy Vice, Daddy Vice,
> One may see in a trice
> The drift of your fine publication.
>   As sure as a gun
>   The thing was just done
> To secure you a PRETTY HIGH station.

> When you tell us of *kings*
> And such pretty things
> Good mercy! how brilliant your page is!
>   So bright is each line
>   I vow you'll shine
> Like—a glow worm to all future ages.

> On Davila's page
> Your discourses so sage
> Democratical numskulls bepuzzle,
>   With arguments tough
>   As white leather or buff,
> The republican Bull Dogs to muzzle.

> 'Tis labor in vain,
> Your senses to strain,
> Our brains any longer to muddle;
>   Like Colossus you stride
>   O'er our noddles so wide
> We look up like frogs in a puddle.

If Freneau's hatred of the men who opposed the democratic movement was immeasurable, his enthusiasm for the new age of reason that he believed was rising was as boundless. His pages during those years of Jacobin radicalism are dotted thick with odes to liberty and addresses to republicans; probably more fully than any other pages they reflect the spirit that in England and America was forming Tom Paine clubs, and projecting innumerable programs of social reform. A new social conscience was stirring in Freneau, broadening immensely the horizon of his thought; and if he counted rather too confidently on the appeal to reason to bring the golden age, he proved himself thereby a true child of his generation. In such lines as these one discovers the spirit that moved Godwin to write *Political Justice*.

> How can we call those systems just
> Which bid the few, the proud, the first,
>   Possess all earthly good;

While millions robbed of all that's dear
In silence shed the ceaseless tear,
  And leaches suck their blood. . . .

Let laws revive, by heaven designed,
To tame the tiger in the mind
  And drive from human hearts
That love of wealth, that love of sway,
Which leads the world too much astray,
  Which points envenomed darts:

And men will rise from what they are;
Sublimer, and superior, far,
  Than Solon guessed, or Plato saw;
All will be just, all will be good—
That harmony, "not understood,"
  Will reign the general law.

For, in our race, deranged, bereft,
The parting god some vestige left
  Of worth before possessed;
Which full, which fair, which perfect shone,
When love and peace, in concord sown,
  Ruled, and inspired each breast.[12]

In quite another vein, that reveals Freneau's unusual mastery
of colloquial prose, is the following passage, impersonating Robert
Slender, the country philosopher.

Mr. Editor,
  Having heard that there was a tavern at about the distance of a mile or
so from my favorite country spot, where now and then a few neighbors
meet to spit, smoke segars, drink apple whiskey, cider or cider-royal, and
read the news—a few evenings ago, I put on my best coat, combed out
my wig, put my spectacles in my pocket, and a quarter dollar—This
I thought was right; for although Mrs. Slender told me eleven-pence was
enough, says I, I'll e'en take the quarter dollar, for a man always feels
himself of more consequence when he has got good money in his pocket—
so out I walks with a good stout stick in my hand, which I always make a
point to carry with me, lest the dogs should make rather freer with my
legs than I could wish. But I had not gone more than half the way, when,
by making a false step, I splash'd my stocking from the knee to the ancle.
Odds my heart, said I, see what a hand I have made of my stocking; I'll
be bail, added I, I'll hear of this in both sides of my head—but it can't
now be helped—this, and a thousand worse accidents, which daily happen,
are all occasioned by public neglect, and the misapplication of the public's
money—Had I, said I, (talking to myself all the while) the disposal of
but half the income of the United States, I could at least so order matters,

<hr />

[12] *On False Systems of Government.*

that a man might walk to his next neighbor's without splashing his stockings or being in danger of breaking his legs in ruts, holes, gutts, and gullies. I do not know, says I to myself, as I moralized on my splash'd stocking, but money might with more profit be laid out in repairing the roads, than in marine establishments, supporting a standing army, useless embassies, exorbitant salaries, given to many flashy fellows that are no honor to us, or to themselves, and chartering whole ships to carry a single man to another nation—Odds my life, continued I, what a number of difficulties a man labors under, who has never read further than Lilly's grammar, and has but a poor brain—had I been favored with a good education, I could no doubt readily see the *great usefulness* of all these measures of government, that now appear to me so unaccountable—I could then, said I, still talking to myself, see the reason why the old patriots, whose blood flowed so freely in purchasing our independence, are cast aside, like a broken pitcher, (as the Scripture says) and why the old tories and active refugees are advanced to places of power, honor and trust.[13]

In another writer so whimsical a note would have no other purpose than to fill a Spectator paper. But the garrulous Robert Slender is Freneau in quieter vein, pursuing his old purpose. As a social philosopher his opinions are oddly like those of Tom Paine. In commenting on the government's use of the people's money he was seeking to awaken interest in the social possibilities of government: that government would better serve the *res publica* through internal improvements, than by creating armies and navies and providing posts and pensions for great men. This was a fashion of thought which Paine had done much to spread, and in the midst of a pompous Federalism, when gentlemen professed to believe that government could acquire reverence in the people's eyes only by being hedged about with ceremonial, Robert Slender's cogitations were very much to the point. If government were truly democratized, if it concerned itself with realities, serving the people in the homely affairs and common needs of everyday life, there would be no need of aristocratic ceremonial. Like Paine, Freneau was an idealist, with his head full of ideas which to practical men were only silly French notions; and yet the idealist, in this matter of the *res publica*, was the true realist.

For all his Jacobinism Freneau might have been spared some of the odium that gathered about his head if he had not turned partisan journalist and put himself in the thick of the fight. In the eighteenth century the newspaper editor had not yet wholly risen

---

[13] *Letters on Various Interesting and Important Subjects, etc.*, by Robert Slender, 1799; quoted by Pattee, Introduction to *Poems of Philip Freneau*.

from the rank of mechanic; he was still a master-printer, with hands much too ink-stained to pass himself off as a gentleman, and with financial resources too limited to be intellectually independent. If his paper were largely literary he made no powerful enemies, but let him enter politics or seek to mold public opinion on important matters, and he was likely to meet the fate of John Mein, outspoken editor of the *Boston Chronicle*, who was destroyed for exposing the weakness of the merchants' non-importation policy.[14] Freneau had had considerable experience in newspaper work at times when his sea life had grown irksome, but he took no active part in politics until the fall of 1791, when he set up the *National Gazette* in Philadelphia, and began that tumultuous career lasting two years which brought so much abuse upon him.

The detailed story of his connection with the *Gazette* is given in an admirable study,[15] and need not be recounted further than to bring into relief the bare essentials. Soon after the formation of the new government Hamilton had provided himself with a newspaper, *The United States Gazette*, that was an effective advocate of all Hamiltonian policies. The editor, John Fenno, seems to have been a vigorous fellow, into whose hands Hamilton threw much of the public printing, and whose debts he paid when they became pressing. Alarmed at the influence wielded by the newspaper, Jefferson and Madison approached Freneau, who had been contemplating a new venture, with the suggestion that he set up a rival democratic paper. To encourage him Jefferson gave Freneau a small post as translator in the State Department, worth $250 a year. The *National Gazette* was thereupon established, and for two years a war between the hostile papers went on fiercely. If the *United States Gazette* lauded the virtues of the English government, extolled the wisdom of Hamilton and abhorred all Jacobins, the *National Gazette* retorted in kind, attacking the Secretary of the Treasury and applauding the growing Jacobite spirit that struck at every form of aristocracy. It became the common clearing house for democratic propaganda, and Freneau's influence spread so widely that he may justly be regarded as "the leading editor in America" during those critical years.

It is quite evident today that "the chief business of the *Gazette*

[14] See A. M. Schlesinger, *The Colonial Merchants and the American Revolution*, Chapter IV.

[15] Forman, "The Political Activities of Philip Freneau," in *Johns Hopkins Studies in History and Political Science*, Vol. XX.

was to destroy Hamilton." Probably more largely than any other writer, Freneau awakened a popular distrust of Federalist men and measures, which a few years later was to break the party. Jefferson's often-quoted remark, "His paper has saved our Constitution *which was fast galloping into monarchy*, and has been checked by no one means so powerfully as by that paper," is somewhat extravagant; nevertheless the universal detestation in which Freneau was held by all Federalists is sufficient testimony to his influence. Washington was greatly ruffled and wanted to remove him from his petty post in the State Department, but Jefferson would not consent. It seems that Washington felt no ill-will toward John Fenno, who drew six times the sum from the public treasury that Freneau received. But Fenno was no democrat, "hostile to garter, ribbon, crown, and star;" Fenno was no unsparing critic who would attack even Washington if he lent himself to undemocratic ends; whereas Freneau was plain-spoken, and no gentleman likes plain speaking from subordinates.

All this was a hundred years ago and more. The inditers of those partisan scurrilities, Democrat and Federalist alike, have long since ceased their bickerings. Words which once stung like a whiplash have become only echoes of dead passions. As the struggles of those tumultuous years fall into truer perspective, the figure of Philip Freneau takes on larger and nobler proportions. The cloud of calumny that long obscured his virtues is dissipating, and we discover in him an eager child of an age of democratic aspiration, the friend and advocate of social justice. Like Paine and Jefferson and Franklin, he was a notable American, who gave himself unselfishly to the work of furthering the common well-being. "It was a long and stormy life," says Forman, "and it was lived for human rights and human freedom"—

> Still on the people's, still on Freedom's side;
> Still in the cause of man severely true.

After all, the poet in Freneau was deeper than the partisan. Despite his conviction that a sordid America cared nothing for poetry—that "an age employed in edging steel can no poetic raptures feel"—his love of beauty was never killed nor the spring of poetic creation dried up. In moments of release from cares he found solace in the poetry that welled up from the unembittered depths of a rich and generous nature. The portrait drawn by

Professor Tyler depicts one side of Freneau; the following lines,
from a very late poem, reveal another:

> The world has wrangled half an age,
> And we again in war engage,
> While this sweet, sequestr'd rill
> Murmurs through the valley still. . . .
>
> But, with all your quiet flow,
> Do you not some quarrels know!
> Lately, angry, how you ran!
> All at war—and much like man.
>
> When the shower of waters fell,
> How you raged, and what a swell!
> All your banks you overflow'd,
> Scarcely knew your own abode!
>
> How you battled with the rock!
> Gave my willows such a shock
> As to menace, by its fall,
> Underwood and bushes, all:
>
> Now you are again at peace:
> Time will come when that will cease;
> Such the human passions are;
> —You again will war declare.
>
> Emblem, thou, of restless man;
> What a sketch of nature's plan!
> Now at peace, and now at war,
> Now you murmur, now you roar;
>
> Muddy now, and limpid next,
> Now with icy shackles vext—
> What a likeness here we find!
> What a picture of mankind! [16]

This was the valedictory of Philip Freneau. His life was bitter
and turbulent, cast in a bitter and turbulent age; yet he found
some grains of comfort in the contemplation of nature and the
exercise of the poet's craft. Through it all his heart remained
clean and his hands unstained. If he was not a great poet whom
all the critics praise, he loved beauty and served it in a careless
world among an indifferent people, and it ill becomes America to
forget his contribution or deny him some portion of the honor
that has fallen generously to others no more deserving.

[16] *The Brook of the Valley.*

2. JOEL BARLOW

Jacobin

That he should have long associated with the Hartford Wits and collaborated with them in defense of Connecticut Federalism must have seemed to Joel Barlow in after years the choicest bit of comedy in his varied career. His subsequent adventures led him far from the strait path of Yale orthodoxy. In those ripe later years life had pretty well emptied him of all dogmatisms and taught him the virtue of catholic sympathies. He had become acquainted with diverse philosophies and had observed the ways of alien societies, and from such contacts the horizons of his mind had broadened and his character mellowed. It was a long road that he traveled from New Haven to his Washington salon. Born a Connecticut Yankee, he accepted in his youth all the Connecticut conventions, and graduated from Yale with as complete a stock of respectable opinions as his classmate Noah Webster. An energetic capable fellow, he wanted to get on in life. He wanted to be rich and famous, and he tried many roads that promised to lead to that desirable goal—law, politics, journalism, poetry, psalmody, speculation. Needing a job he volunteered soon after graduation as chaplain in the army. He had not prepared for the ministry and while preaching somewhat indifferently to ragged soldiers he dreamed of poetic fame, and devoted more time to his couplets than to pious meditation. His abilities discovering no more profitable field for exercise than writing verse, he was pretty much at a stand till chance sent him abroad as agent for one of the speculative land-companies that were springing up like mushrooms in post-war America. There he found his opportunity. In France, where he established his headquarters, he entered a world of thought vastly different from that of prim little Hartford. It was an extraordinarily stimulating experience into which he threw himself with zest. Seventeen years, from 1788 to 1805, he spent abroad on that first visit, and those years changed the provincial Yankee into one of the most cosmopolitan Americans of his generation. From a member of the Hartford Wits, ardent in defense of the traditional Connecticut order, he had become a citizen of the world, outspoken in defense of the rights of man.

It was this later Barlow, completely new-outfitted by French romantic tailors, that after years remember and that early friends could not forgive. In adopting the Jacobin mode and setting himself to the serious business of political thinking, he invited the caustic criticism of his former associates; yet nothing in his life was more creditable or marks him more definitely as an openminded, intelligent man. He was as receptive to new ideas as Timothy Dwight was impervious. He plunged boldly into the maelstrom of speculation then boiling in Europe. He moved in the society of the intellectuals, inquired into the latest political and social theories, turned humanitarian, reëxamined his Calvinistic theology in the light of current deism, and became one of the free democratic thinkers swarming in every European capital. He was equally at home in London and Paris, passing long periods of time in both cities. An active member of the Constitutional Society of London, he was intimate with Joseph Priestley, Horne Tooke, and Tom Paine, sympathized with every liberal movement, and offered his pen to the cause of a freer England. His *Advice to the Privileged Orders* was eulogized by Fox on the floor of Commons, and the Pitt ministry was moved to suppress the work and proscribe the author. Thereupon Barlow went into hiding. There seems to have been considerable provocation for the government's action. "It is safe to say," remarks his biographer, "that no political work of the day created so wide an interest or was so extensively read." With Paine and Barlow both loose in England there was need of the government looking to its fences.

In 1793 he was made a citizen of France. His French career was not unlike Paine's, whom he resembled in many ways. He had much of the latter's genius for publicity and skill in propaganda, and his career was a great stimulus to radicals at home. He was not too busy to serve his country in a diplomatic way. He risked his life to aid American prisoners in Africa and by his skill and address eventually freed them—an achievement that few men could have gone through with successfully. In the meantime he had not neglected his private affairs. He made a fortune in the French funds, which he increased by able merchandising. He had come to his goal by distant roads, and on his return to America in 1805 he took up his abode at Washington, creating a delightful countryseat on the outskirts of the raw little capital where he maintained a salon for American liberals. He seems to have felt no inclinations towards Connecticut; the old ties were broken now for good, the French Jacobin could not fit into the rigid grooves of Hartford Federalism. Six years later he was impressed a second time into the diplomatic service, was sent to France on a difficult mission, followed Napoleon, then on the Russian campaign, was caught in the break-up of the grand army, suffered exposure, contracted pneumonia, and died in a village near Cracow in Poland—a fate which many honest Federalists regarded as amply merited by his vicious principles.

The later reputation of Barlow has been far less than his services warranted or his solid merits deserved. His admirable prose writings have been forgotten and the *Columbiad* returns always to plague him. The common detraction of all Jacobins and democrats fell heavily on so conspicuous a head. "It is simply impossible," says his biographer, "for the historian of Federal proclivities and environment to do justice to the great leaders of Republicanism in America." Barlow was forced to pay a heavy price for his intellectual independence. Detraction was always lying in wait for him. John Adams, who had suffered many a sharp thrust from him, wrote to Washington, "Tom Paine is not a more worthless fellow." Of the Yale dislike Barlow was well aware, for he once confessed that he would have presented the school with some needed chemical apparatus but he "supposed that, coming from him, the college authorities would make a bonfire of them in the college yard." [17] Yet it is hard for a later generation to discover wherein lay the viciousness of his life or principles. A warmhearted humanitarian, he was concerned always for the common well-being. The two major passions of his life were freedom and education. During the last years at Washington he was ardently promoting a plan for a great national university at the seat of government, and had he lived ten years longer his wide influence would probably have accomplished it. His sins would seem to have been no other than an open break with the Calvinism and Federalism of the Connecticut oligarchy—somewhat slender grounds on which to pillory him as an infidel and a scalawag.

The social foundation of Barlow's political philosophy is lucidly presented in the *Advice to the Privileged Orders*, a work that deserves a place beside Paine's *Rights of Man* as a great document of the times. It does too much credit to American letters to be suffered

[17] Purcell, *Connecticut in Transition*, p. 27.

to lie buried with a dead partisanship. It is warm with the humanitarian enthusiasm that had come down as a rich heritage from the Physiocratic school of social thinkers. Two suggestive ideas lie at the base of his speculations: the doctrine of the *res publica*, and the doctrine of social responsibility for individual well-being. The former, given wide currency by the *Rights of Man*, resulted from the imposition of social conscience on abstract political theory, out of which was derived a new conception of the duties and functions of the political state—the conception that the state must be the responsible agent of society as a whole rather than the tool of a class, and that its true concern is the *public thing*, safeguarding the social heritage as a common asset held in trust for succeeding generations; the latter resulted from the inquiry into the relations of the political state to the individual citizen—its responsibility as the social agent, for the social waste of wrecked lives and thwarted happiness, a waste that a rational social order would greatly lessen if not eradicate. Barlow flatly denied that the primary function of the state is the protection of property interests; its true end lies in securing justice. But justice without equal opportunity is a mockery; and equal opportunity is impossible unless the individual citizen shall be equipped to live on equal terms with his fellows. Hence the fine flower of political justice is discovered in education; in that generous provision for the young and the weak that shall equip them to become free members of the commonwealth. Like Paine's *Agrarian Justice*, the *Advice to the Privileged Orders* is an extraordinarily modern work, far more comprehensible today than when it was written. That the "State has no right to punish a man, to whom it has given no previous instruction," and that "She ought not only to instruct him in the artificial laws by which property is secured, but in the artificial industry by which it is obtained," are doctrines that seem far less preposterous to us than they seemed to Timothy Dwight. The president of Yale College was greatly troubled over Calvinistic sin; Joel Barlow was greatly troubled over social injustice; in that difference is measured the distance the latter had traveled in company with the French Jacobins.

The root of his political thinking is the doctrine of equalitarianism. "Only admit," he says, "the original, unalterable truth, *that all men are equal in their rights, and the foundation of everything is laid.*" Accepting the romantic doctrine that human nature is excellent in its plastic state, and capable of infinite development, he is untroubled by the fact of human selfishness. He sees no bogey in democracy to frighten timid souls, no specter of anarchy in the rule of the people.

They say mankind are wicked and rapacious, and "it must be that offences will come." This reason applies to individuals; but not to nations deliberately speaking a national voice. I hope I shall not be understood to mean, that the nature of man is totally changed by living in a free republic. I allow that it is still *interested* men and *passionate* men, that direct the affairs of the world. But in national assemblies, passion is lost in deliberation, and interest balances interest; till the good of the whole community combines the general will.

If government be founded on the vices of mankind, its business is to restrain those vices in all, rather than to foster them in a few.[18]

It was his sensitive social conscience that brought him to revolt against all class government. He had seen the naked sordidness of such governments in Europe, and he watched with concern the beginnings of like government in America. The significance of the Hamiltonian program could not escape so shrewd an observer as Barlow; he was too much a realist to take political professions at face value. "I see," he wrote, "immense fortunes made by our funding legislators out of the public funds which they funded for themselves." Politics for profit was a sorry spectacle to him, and he occupied his mind much with the problem of erecting the machinery of an adequate democratic state that should be faithful to its stewardship as agent of the whole.

It was this difficult problem with which he dealt in his *Letter to the National Convention of France.* In this suggestive work two ideas determined his thinking: the doctrine of the sovereignty of the majority will, and the doctrine of government as a social agent. In both he returned to the position of Roger Williams a hundred and fifty years before. The sovereignty of the majority will he conceives to be continuous and immediately effective; it cannot be held in check by a rigid constitutionalism, for as Paine had pointed out, such constitutionalism is no other than government from the grave. He proposed therefore, that the fundamental law be amendable by legislative enactment, one legislative body proposing and the next determining, under full publicity. As a guarantee that such action should express the popular will, that

---

[18] *Advice to the Privileged Orders*, pp. 66, 70.

love of power on the part of the agent should not defeat the purpose of society, he held that there must be annual elections. Representatives should be periodically excluded from candidacy, and other representatives fresh from the people sent up, for "power always was and always must be a dangerous thing." The principle of recall he regarded as indispensable in a democratic government, for it "will tend to maintain a proper relation between the representatives and the people, and a due dependence of the former upon the latter. Besides, when a man has lost the confidence of his fellow citizens . . . he is no longer their representative; and when he ceases to be their's, he cannot in any sense be the representative of the nation." The fundamental principle of state-craft Barlow states thus: "Every individual ought to be rendered as independent of every other individual as possible; and at the same time as dependent as possible on the whole community." The familiar romantic doctrine of the diminished state is implicit in all his reasoning. Like Paine he would do away utterly with the old mystery of government under which ambitious men cloak their will to power; "for whatever there is in the art of government, whether legislative or executive, above the capacities of the ordinary class of what are called well-informed men, is superfluous and destructive and ought to be laid aside."

A thoroughgoing radical in economics and politics, Barlow was no innovator in polite literature. He had pulled himself out of many a Connecticut provincialism, but he stuck fast in the bog of provincial poetry. It has long been the fashion to make merry over *The Columbiad*, and there is only too patent a reason for it. To criticize it is a work of supererogation. The appeal of "the grand style" seems to have been too much for him. Some explanation doubtless is to be found in the fact that he was working over an earlier poem done in the days of an ebullient patriotism. It was a mistake to return to it, for the heroic note in the vein of a political pamphleteer must play havoc with it. What he now attempted, in the light of his long European experience, was to embody in the narrative suitable political ideas, transforming *The Vision of Columbus* into an epic glorifying the great republican experiment. His purpose is set forth in the preface.

[The] real object of the poem is to inculcate the love of national liberty, and to discountenance the deleterious passion for violence and war; to show that on the basis of republican principle all good morals, as well as good government and hopes of permanent peace, must be founded; and to convince the student in political science, that the theoretical question of the future advancement of human society, till states as well as individuals arrive at universal civilization, is held in dispute and still unsettled only because we have had too little experience of organized liberty in the government of nations, to have well considered its effects.

The humanitarian note is strong. War, slavery, monarchy, injustice, the tyranny resulting from political inequality, and a host of other evils, social and political, are assailed in vigorous declamation. It may not be good poetry but the sentiments are those of an enlightened and generous man. The conclusion rises to a vision of a golden age of international commerce and universal peace, when "earth, garden'd all, a tenfold burden brings," and the sundered nations shall draw together, and—

> . . . cloth'd majestic in the robes of state,
> Moved by one voice, in general congress meet
> The legates of all empires.

In that future time science will have learned "with her own glance to ken the total God," and philosophy will "expand the selfish to the social flame." Of the political ideas incorporated in the massive work some suggestion may be got from the following lines:

> Ah, would you not be slaves, with lords and kings,
> Then be not Masters; there the danger springs.
> The whole crude system that torments this earth,
> Of rank, privation, privilege of birth,
> False honor, fraud, corruption, civil jars,
> The rage of conquest and the curse of wars,
> Pandora's total shower, all ills combined
> That erst o'erwhelmed and still distress mankind,
> Boxt up secure in your deliberate hand,
> Wait your behest to fix or fly this land.

> Equality of right is nature's plan;
> And following nature is the march of man.
> Whene'er he deviates in the least degree,
> When, free himself, he would be more than free,
> The baseless column, rear'd to bear his trust,
> Falls as he mounts and whelms him in the dust. . . .

> Too much of Europe, here transplanted o'er,
> Nursed feudal feelings on your tented shore,
> Brought sable sires from Afric, call'd it gain,
> And urged your sires to forge the fatal chain. . . .

Restore their souls to men, give earth repose,
And save your sons from slavery, wars and woes

    Based on its rock of right your empire lies,
On walls of wisdom let the fabric rise;
Preserve your principles, their force unfold,
Let nations prove them and let kings behold.
EQUALITY, your first firm-grounded stand;
Then FREE ELECTION; then your FEDERAL BAND:
This holy Triad should forever shine
The great compendium of all rights divine,
Creed of all schools, whence youths by millions draw
Their themes of right, their decalogues of law;
Till men shall wonder (in these codes inured)
How wars were made, how tyrants were endured.[19]

Diverse politics incline to diverse literary judgments, and the critics are not yet done with Joel Barlow. If he was not a great poet or a great political thinker, he was at least capable, open-minded, generous, with a sensitive social conscience—certainly the most stimulating and original of the literary group that foregathered in Hartford. Injustice has long been done him by overlooking his picturesque career, and his services to America, and restricting his introduction to posterity to a few lines from *Hasty Pudding*. To make a mush of so honest a thinker, to ignore his very considerable contributions to the cause of democracy, is to impose too heavy a penalty for his defection from Connecticut respectability. He suffered quite enough in his lifetime. In the thick of his revolutionary struggles abroad his wife begged him "to go home and be respectable"; but it was not in the ardent nature of Joel Barlow to listen to such counsel of timidity. He was in too deep to go back, and so while Timothy Dwight was gathering laurels from every bush in Connecticut, this apostle of humanitarianism, this apostate from Calvinistic Federalism, was content to remain a byword and a shaking of the head in the villages of his native commonwealth. For all which, perhaps, the Washington salon and the intimate association with Jefferson may have served as recompense. Better society could not be found even in Hartford.

[19] *Book VIII.*

3. Hugh Henry Brackenridge

Free-Lance Democrat

In taking leave of this disturbant time when new social theories were bringing confusion to weak understandings, one cannot do better than to dip into the wittiest and most readable sketch produced by that vigorous generation, as well as one of the sanest. *Modern Chivalry* was the single noteworthy contribution to American letters by Hugh Henry Brackenridge, a western Pennsylvanian of Scotch birth, and a graduate of Princeton in the class with Freneau and Madison. With the former he had practised his couplets, collaborating in writing the commencement poem, *The Rising Glory of America*. After leaving college he tried his hand at the usual things open to young graduates, was tutor in the college, taught in an academy, studied divinity, served as chaplain in the Revolutionary army, and later read law. He removed eventually to the frontier town of Pittsburgh, was active in Republican politics, became an ardent pro-French sympathizer, and finally went upon the supreme bench of Pennsylvania. He wrote for his own amusement and tried his hand at various kinds of polite literature, producing a masque, a poetic drama on Bunker Hill, prose essays, some sermons, and turned at last to satire. For this he was admirably equipped; he possessed a keen, well-balanced mind, a prose style delightfully colloquial and a wit pleasantly caustic.

Brackenridge is a refreshing person to come upon after one is satiated with the heroic. A free-lance critic, independent in thought and act, he was no vociferous party or class advocate given to enlisting God on his side. Federalist and Republican alike might lose their heads and indulge in unseemly clamor, but Brackenridge with good Scotch judgment refused to howl with the pack. A stout and unrepentant democrat, he was no visionary to shut his eyes to unpleasant facts lest they disturb his faith. As he considered the turbulent confusions of an America in rough process of democratization, he saw the evils as clearly as the hope, and it amused him to satirize those evils after the manner of Don Quixote. *Modern Chivalry* has proved somewhat of a puzzle to later critics who have not cleared their minds of the old cobwebs of Federalist criticism. Thus a literary historian has suggested that it is "a half-hidden satire on democracy"[20] and he inclines to number it among the literary ram's horns that were blown against the walls of the democratic Jericho. But such an interpretation certainly misses the point. Brackenridge had become a thorough Westerner with a fresh point of view. Among the stump fields of his Pennsylvania circuit he was equally removed from the cynicism of Hamilton and the romanticism of Barlow. He saw all about him a rough and tumble democracy, living a vigorous and capable if not lovely life. As a democrat he accepted the fact of political equality and approved of it; the thing was there and needed no justification or defense. Some of its ways were foolish, many of its purposes were shortsighted; it amused him therefore to sharpen his pen against certain of its absurdities and essay the remedial effects of unembittered laughter. He was a realist concerned with realities.

Modern Chivalry is our first backcountry book. It is redolent of stump-lands and their rude leveling ways, and for years it was immensely popular along the western frontier. It is a satire aimed primarily at backwoods shortcomings, but with an eye that kept turning towards the older settlements to scrutinize their equal shortcomings. Its main theme is concerned with certain weaknesses of popular sovereignty already unpleasantly evident as a result of the extension of suffrage; and in particular with the unseemly office-hunting zeal of coonskin candidates. The preposterous spectacle of a pushing fellow with no qualifications setting himself up for high office was to become more frequent with the later rise of Jacksonian democracy; but already there was abundant justification for the satire of Brackenridge. The records of the time are loud in criticism of the demagoguery that resulted from the sudden shift of leadership in consequence of the social upheaval following the Revolutionary War. The old leaders of the aristocratic tradition had fled or had fallen into disfavor, and new men, too often of small capacity and less breeding, had pushed into the seats of authority. With the triumph of Jefferson this transfer of power went forward briskly to the scandal of all aristocrats. The lust of office spread like the plague, and demagogues caught the popular ear, none too nice to distinguish between sense and fustian. Irving brushed against the democratic weakness in his brief venture into politics, and vented his spleen in *Rip Van Winkle.*

[20] Cairns, *History of American Literature*, p. 147.

It is this which Brackenridge deals with primarily in *Modern Chivalry*, the first part of which was published in 1792 and the second in 1805. The general leveling of offices, he pointed out, was not democracy, but the abuse and ruin of democracy. America was engaged in a great and noble experiment; the success of that experiment depended upon an honest and intelligent electorate; it must not be brought to failure by demagogues through the incapacity of the voter.

Brackenridge had come in later years to be a pacifist. He had had his fill of revolutions and armed revolts. As a principal arbitrator during the tumult of the Whisky Insurrection, he had come to fear popular lawlessness; and as a friend of the French Revolution he was concerned at the methods of the Jacobin leaders. Commenting on the Whisky Insurrection he said in later years:

> I saw before me anarchy, a shock to the government, a revolution impregnated with the Jacobin principles of France. . . . Let no man suppose I coveted a revolution; I had seen the evils of one already in the American; and I had read the evils of another, the French. My imagination presented the evils of the last strongly to my view, and brought them so close to a possible experience at home, that during the whole period of the insurrection, I could scarcely bear to cast my eye on a paragraph of French news.[21]

A reasonable and intelligent democracy, holding steadily to the purpose of the common good, was his cherished ideal. He was not a political philosopher interested in general principles. His purpose was to satirize manners, not to speculate on causes; and in the days of triumphant republicanism the most conspicuous target was offered by the tousled head of the demagogue, "the courtier of democracy." In the preface to the 1846 edition, the editor thus summarizes the political views of Brackenridge:

> An enlightened democracy was looked upon by him as the true nobility. He considered the true democrat as the true gentleman, who *ought* to feel a stain on his fair reputation, "as a wound." He maintained "that democracy is not in its nature coarse, and vulgar, or destitute of high integrity and honor." The aim and end of his writings was to raise the standard of democracy, and to elevate "the noble of nature" to the same level with any other noble, in those qualities which constitute true nobility. The noble of nature, in his opinion, ought not to yield to the noble of aristocracy or monarchy, in strict integrity, in liberal and benevolent feelings, in propriety of manners and general intelligence.

[21] *Modern Chivalry*, edition of 1846, p. 170.

The work is a string of adventures, interspersed with miscellaneous discussion, of Captain John Farrago—who is evidently Brackenridge himself—and his bog-trotting servant Teague O'Regan. The Captain is an intelligent person, well read in the literature of the times, and "a good deal disposed to subscribe to the elementary principles" of Paine's *Rights of Man*. He can summarize neatly the arguments on both sides of the political questions of the day, but he retains the open mind and cautious judgment of the independent. He is a free-lance critic, democratic in sympathies but unsparing in exposure of absurdity. His hits fall right and left, on the country yokel, the city speculator, members of Congress, the institution of slavery. He is greatly concerned to preserve his servant from the temptations of ambition which assail him in the backwoods as well as in Philadelphia. The career of Teague O'Regan is a broad satire on the mounting ambition of old-world peasants to push their way up. That the underling should rise in a democratic country was well; but that he should be in unseemly haste to scramble into positions beyond his capacities, that in pushing his private fortunes he should bring ridicule upon the democratic experiment, was not well. Teague O'Regan's desire to scramble discovered quite too fertile a field for his own or the country's good. He is nearly sent to Congress by a backwoods constituency, listens to other seductive appeals, and in the end is sent by President Washington to the West as a revenue officer, where he falls into the untender hands of the whisky rioters, and finds his Irish beauty marred by a coat of tar and feathers.

It is in his burlesque of electorate methods that Brackenridge hits most sharply at the current tendencies of republicanism. The ways of the backwoods he caricatures by describing a contest between an honest deacon and an ignorant Scotch-Irishman, which he came upon in his peregrinations.

When they looked upon the one, they felt an inclination to promote him. But when, again, on the other hand, they saw two kegs which they knew to be replenished with a very cheering liquor, they seemed to be inclined in favor of the other. The candidates were called upon to address the people, and the grave person mounted the stump of a tree, many of them standing round, as the place was a new clearing. His harangue was listened to by some of the older and more sedate, and one man, hard of hearing, seemed to make great effort to catch the sounds. As soon as the man of the two kegs took a stump, he was surrounded by an eager crowd.—
"Frinds," said he, in the native Scotch-Irish, "I'm a good dimicrat, and

hates the Brattish—I'm an elder of the meetin', forby, and has been overseer of the roads for three years:—An' ye all know, that my mammy was kilt o' the Ingens—now all ye that's in my favor, come forit an' drenk." Appetite, or rather thirst, prevailed, and the voters gave their votes to the man with the two kegs.[22]

If whisky decided elections in the backcountry, business controlled them in the city. The following is almost modern in its caricature:

The candidates were all remarkably pot-bellied; and waddled in their gait. The captain inquiring what were the pretensions of these men to be elected; he was told, that they had all stock in the funds, and lived in brick buildings; and some of them entertained fifty people at a time, and ate and drank abundantly; and living an easy life, and pampering their appetites, they had swollen to this size.

"It is a strange thing," said the captain, "that in the country, in my route, they would elect no one but a weaver or a whisky-distiller; and here none but fat squabs, that guzzle wine, and smoke segars." . . . "No, faith" (said his friend), "there is na danger of Teague here, unless he had his scores o' shares in the bank, and was in league with the brokers, and had a brick house at his hurdies, or a ship or twa on the stocks . . . all is now lost in substantial interest, and the funds command everything."[23]

That there might be no mistake as to the meaning of his satire Brackenridge set down at the end an explicit statement of his purpose.

As already hinted by some things put into the mouth of the captain, I could make it a principal matter to form the heart of a *republican government*. And in order to this, keep out all that nourishes *ambition*, the poison of public virtue. . . . In the American republics, we retain yet a great deal of the spirit of monarchy. The people are not aware of the phraseology itself, in some instances. . . . The first lesson I would give to a son of mine would be to have nothing to do with public business, but as a duty to his country. To consider service in civil life, no more to be desired than service in the military. . . . Those who say to them, *vox populi vox dei*, offer up an incense to flattery, as impious as the worshippers of the Cæsars. They should be warned to beware of flatterers, whose object is not to serve them, but themselves. The demagogue in a democracy, and the courtier in a monarchy, are identical. They are the same, plying the same arts in different situations. . . . I shall have accomplished something by this book, if it shall keep some honest man from lessening his respectability by pushing himself into public trusts for which he is not qualified; or when pushed into public station, if it shall contribute to keep him honest by teaching him the folly of ambition, and farther advancement. . . . This is in great part, the moral of this book; if it should be at all necessary to give a hint of it.

[22] *Ibid.*, p. 105.   [23] *Ibid.*, pp. 127–128.

One may do a worse service to democracy than to point out its faults. Brackenridge was no truckler either to King George or to his neighbors. Living in the midst of a coonskin democracy, he refused to believe that there was any particular virtue in coonskin. It is not the cap but what is under it that signifies. He was a vigorous individualist, a confirmed democrat, a friend of all honest liberalisms, a man who honored his own counsels and went his own way. We could better spare more pretentious books from the library of our early literature than these clever satires that preserve for us some of the homely ways of a time when American institutions were still in the making.

CONCLUSION

With the triumph of Jefferson in the great struggle of 1800, the first democratic battle had been won at the polls, but victory remained still in doubt. The new liberalism was in the saddle, but how long it would keep its seat, or whither it would drive, no one could foresee. The aristocratic eighteenth century was still in secure possession of all the vantage points of polite culture. It still held the positions of honor and emolument and dictated the ways of society. The tie-wig and smallclothes had not yet been put to rout by homespun and coonskin, and were laying plans to make good the first defeat. Polite letters were still content with the old wit ideal, still enamored of the couplet, still in love with caustic satire, still transfixing democracy with its sharp quills. The nineteenth century with its cargo of romanticisms had not yet crossed the Atlantic, and while Napoleon was strewing Europe with the wrecks of old empires, America was still dwelling in the twilight of a century that was loath to be gone.

The account in the American ledger was complex and not easily cast up, yet Jefferson might well have regarded with satisfaction the results of two hundred years of new-world experience. The drift was all in the direction he was facing. The age of theology was gone, the age of political speculation was passing, the age of constitution building was over. Disintegration had come upon every system of caste brought hither from the old world; the free economics of a decentralized society had proved a sufficient solvent to destroy the principle of monarchy and of aristocracy, and prepare the American mind for a venture in republicanism. Overseas liberalisms had flourished in the soil that proved inhospitable to overseas conservatisms; and it was these European liberalisms that provided the mold into which ran the fluid experience of America to assume substantial form. That the venture in republicanism would inure to the benefit of agrarian America—to the producers on their scattered farms—Jefferson seems never to have doubted; and the ready naturalization of the philosophy of equalitarianism in the backwoods settlements might well have seemed to justify his hopes. Nevertheless new forces were preparing that were to bring about momentous changes in nineteenth-century America. Capitalism with its banks and credit and elastic currency and its psychology of speculation, and industrialism with its technique of factory production, were already at work preparing a different pattern of life for America, a pattern wholly unlike that of the simpler agrarianism with its domestic economy, which Jefferson represented. A new romanticism of the middle class was eventually to shoulder aside the aspirations of gentleman and farmer alike, and refashion America after its own ideal. What was implied in that momentous change provides the theme for another study, and cannot be entered upon here.

BIBLIOGRAPHY

Only the more important titles dealt with in the present study are listed hereunder, together with selected biographical and critical material. The invaluable bibliographies in the *Cambridge History of American Literature*, four vols., New York, 1917-22, cover most of the writers considered, and the reader is referred to them for detailed material.

BOOK I: PART I

I. ENGLISH BACKGROUNDS: For the broader European movements, see Preserved Smith, *The Age of the Reformation* (New York, 1920). For English movements, see David Masson, *Life of Milton* (6 vols., London, 1859-80). The important ideas of Luther will be found in *An Open Letter to the Christian Nobility of the German Nation Concerning the Reform of the Christian State* (1520); *The Babylonian Captivity of the Church* (1520); *A Treatise on Christian Liberty* (1520). For discussion, see L. H. Waring, *The Political Theories of Martin Luther* (New York and London, 1910). For Calvin, see Williston Walker, *John Calvin, The Organiser of Reformed Protestantism* (New York and London, 1906; with bibliographical note).

II. THE TRANSPLANTING OF IDEAS: For political history see James Truslow Adams, *The Founding of New England* (Boston, 1921). For literary history consult the invaluable work of Moses Coit Tyler, *A History of American Literature, 1607-1765* (2 vols., New York, 1878). Histories of Congregationalism will be found in Henry M. Dexter, *The Congregationalism of the Last Three Hundred Years as Seen in Its Literature* (New York, 1880; with full bibliography); Williston Walker, *A History of the Congregational Churches in the United States* (New York, 1900); also W. Walker, *Creeds and Platforms of Congregationalism* (New York, 1893).

III. JOHN COTTON: Little of Cotton's work has been reprinted. *A Reply to Mr. Williams His Examination* was reissued in *Narragansett Club Pub.*, Vol. II, pp. 1-240. His most important work is *The Way of the Congregational Churches Cleared* (London, 1648).

No life has been written. See Cotton Mather's *Magnalia;* W. Walker's *Ten New England Leaders* (New York, 1901); A. Young, *John Cotton's Life and Letters. Chronicles of the First Planters, etc.* (Boston, 1846).

JOHN WINTHROP: *Journal* . . . (Hartford, 1790); as *The History of New England* . . . edited by J. Savage (2 vols., Boston, 1825-26, 1853); edited by J. K. Hosmer (2 vols., New York, 1908).

See R. C. Winthrop, *Life and Letters of John Winthrop* (2 vols., Boston, 1863, 1866, 1869, 1895). J. Twitchell, *John Winthrop, First Governor of Massachusetts* (New York, 1892).

IV. THOMAS HOOKER: His works have not been reprinted. The *Survey of the Summe of Church-Discipline* . . . was published in London in 1648. Contemporary notes of his *Sermon before the General Court on May 31, 1638,* were printed with comment by J. Hammond Trumbull, in *Conn. Hist. Soc. Col.;* Vol. I, No. 19.

For his life, see G. L. Walker, *Thomas Hooker, Preacher, Founder, Democrat* (New York, 1891; with bibliography by J. H. Trumbull).

ROGER WILLIAMS: *The Works of Roger Williams. Edited by members of the Narragansett Club* (6 vols., Providence, 1866-1874).
No satisfactory life has been written. The best is Oscar S. Straus, *Roger Williams, the Pioneer of Religious Liberty* (New York, 1894). See also Edmund J. Carpenter, *Roger Williams; A Study of the Life, Times and Character of a Political Pioneer* (New York, 1909; Grafton Hist. Series).

BOOK I: PART II

I.   SAMUEL SEWALL: *Diary* (printed in *Mass. Hist. Soc. Col.*, Series 5, Vols. 5-7).
No life has been written.

II.   INCREASE MATHER: The extensive bibliography is confused, and a definitive list is being prepared by T. J. Holmes and G. P. Winship. Few works have been reprinted, and about the only available title is *Illustrious Providences* (Boston and London, 1684; London, 1687); under title of *Remarkable Providences* (London, 1856, 1890).
The authoritative life is by Kenneth B. Murdock, *Increase Mather, The Foremost American Puritan* (Harvard University Press. 1925; with bibliography). See also Williston Walker, *Ten New England Leaders* (New York, 1901).

       COTTON MATHER: The bibliography is enormous, but few titles are available. *The Wonders of the Invisible World* (Boston, 1693) has been twice reprinted: with title, *Salem Witchcraft* . . . and notes by S. P. Fowler (Cambridge, 1861); and with I. Mather's *Account of the Tryals of the New-England Witches* (Library of Old Authors, London, 1862). *The Bostonian Ebenezer*, Boston, 1698, was reprinted in Old South Leaflets, Boston, 1896. The *Magnalia Christi Americana*, London, 1702, was reissued (2 vols., Hartford and New Haven, 1820); and the same with notes by T. Robbins, and translations of foreign quotations by L. F. Robinson, and a life by S. G. Drake (Hartford, 1853). The *Essays to Do Good* has been reprinted ten times, the latest editions London, 1842, and Boston, 1845. The most available text is *Selections from Cotton Mather*, edited with introduction, by K. B. Murdock (New York, 1926; American Authors Series).
The best life is by Barrett Wendell, *Cotton Mather, Puritan Priest* (New York, 1891; Harvard University Press, 1925). See also A. P. Marvin, *The Life and Times of Cotton Mather* (Boston, 1892).

III.   JOHN WISE: *The Churches Quarrel Espoused* . . . (Boston, 1710, 1715, 1745, 1772); reissued with the *Vindication*, with introduction by J. S. Clark (Boston, 1860). *A Vindication of the Government of the New-England Churches. Drawn from Antiquity; the Light of Nature; Holy Scripture* . . . (Boston, 1717, 1772); reissued with the preceding title (Boston, 1860).
No life of Wise has been written.

BOOK II: PART I

I.   COLONIAL BACKGROUNDS: See Herbert L. Osgood, *The American Colonies in the Eighteenth Century* (2 vols., New York, 1924).

       NEW STOCK: See John R. Commons, *Races and Immigrants in America* (New York, 1902, 1920). F. R. Diffenderfer, *The German Immigrants into Pennsylvania* . . . (New York, 1900). *The Diary of John Harrower* (*Amer. Hist. Review*, Vol. VI, p. 65).

       THE FRONTIER—Lubberland: *The Journal of Sarah Kemble Knight* (New York, 1825; Albany, 1865; Norwich, Conn., 1901).

       WILLIAM BYRD: *Westover Manuscripts: containing the History of the Dividing*

Line . . . *A Journey to the Land of Eden* . . . (Petersburg, Va., 1841); reissued under title, *The History of the Dividing Line* (edited by T. H. Wynne; 2 vols., Richmond, 1866). Also *The Writings of "Colonel William Byrd of Westover in Virginia, Esq."* Edited by J. S. Bassett (New York, 1901).

THE FRONTIER—Land of Promise: *Letters from an American Farmer* . . . (London, 1782; with note by W. P. Trent and introduction by Ludwig Lewisohn, New York, 1904). *More "Letters from an American Farmer,"* edited with introductions by H. L. Bourdin, R. G. Gabriel, and S. T. Williams, and issued under the title, *Sketches of Eighteenth Century America* (New Haven, 1925).

For the life of Crèvecœur, see Julia Post Mitchell, *St. Jean de Crèvecœur (Col. Univ. Studies in English and Comp. Lit.,* New York, 1916).

II. JONATHAN EDWARDS: *Works* (8 vols., Leeds, 1806-11). *Works*, edited by S. E. Dwight (10 vols., New York, 1829, 1830). *Works* (10 vols., Edinburgh, 1847). Numerous other editions and many reprints.
The best life is by V. G. Allen, *Jonathan Edwards* (Boston, 1889, 1890; with bibliography). See also Woodbridge Riley, *American Thought* (New York, 1915).

III. BENJAMIN FRANKLIN: The best edition of his works is that edited by J. Bigelow (10 vols., New York, 1889). The *Autobiography* was first printed complete by J. Bigelow, New York, 1874. The latest reprint is in the American Authors Series, edited with introduction by Percy H. Boynton (New York, 1926).
Of the several lives, see James Parton, *Life and Times of Benjamin Franklin* (2 vols., New York, 1864), J. B. McMaster, *Benjamin Franklin as a Man of Letters* (Boston, 1887); J. T. Morse, *Benjamin Franklin* (American Statesmen Series, Boston, 1889). See also W. A. Wetzel, *Benjamin Franklin as an Economist (Johns Hopkins Studies in Hist. and Pol. Science,* Thirteenth Series, Vol. IX, pp. 421-476). A recent life: Phillips Russell, *Benjamin Franklin: The First Civilized American* (New York, 1926).

BOOK II: PART II

I. IMPERIAL SOVEREIGNTY AND HOME RULE: For the literature of the Revolutionary period, see the invaluable *Literary History of the American Revolution,* by Moses Coit Tyler (2 vols., New York, 1897; with annotated bibliography). For the political phases, see C. H. Van Tyne, *The Causes of the War of Independence* . . . (Boston and New York, 1922); A. M. Schlesinger, *The Colonial Merchants and the American Revolution, 1763-1776* (New York, 1918); J. T. Adams, *Revolutionary New England, 1691-1776* (Boston, 1923).

II. THOMAS HUTCHINSON: *The History of Massachusetts* (3 vols., Boston and London, 1764-1767-1828; Vols. I and II, Boston, 1795). *Diary and Letters of Thomas Hutchinson* . . ., edited by P. O. Hutchinson (2 vols., Boston, 1884-1886). J. K. Hosmer, *Life of Thomas Hutchinson* (Boston, 1896).
DANIEL LEONARD: *Massachusettensis* (London, 1776); reissued with *Novanglus* by John Adams, and ascribed on the title page to Jonathan Sewall (Boston, 1819).

JONATHAN BOUCHER: *A View of the Causes and Consequences of the American Revolution* (London, 1797).

III. JOHN DICKINSON: *Political Writings* (2 vols., Wilmington, 1801). *Writings,* edited by P. L. Ford (3 vols., Philadelphia, 1895).

See C. J. Stillé, *The Life and Times of John Dickinson* (Philadelphia, 1891).

IV.   SAMUEL ADAMS: *Writings*, edited by H. A. Cushing (4 vols., New York, 1904–08).

See J. K. Hosmer, *Samuel Adams* (Boston, 1884); revised edition (1898, American Statesmen Series). W. V. Wells, *The Life and Public Services of Samuel Adams* (3 vols., Boston, 1865).

V.   JOHN TRUMBULL: *Poetical Works* (2 vols., Hartford, 1820). *The Progress of Dulness* (New Haven, 1772–73). *An Elegy on the Times* (Boston, 1774; New Haven, 1775). *M'Fingal* (printed in parts from 1775 to 1782, and much revised; first published entire, Hartford, 1782; numerous contemporary editions). *The Progress of Dulness* and *M'Fingal* are reprinted in *The Connecticut Wits*, edited with introduction and bibliography by Vernon L. Parrington (New York, 1926, American Authors Series).

No life of Trumbull has been written.

FRANCIS HOPKINSON: *Miscellaneous Essays and Occasional Writings* (2 vols., Philadelphia, 1792). George Hastings, *Life and Works of Francis Hopkinson* (University of Chicago Press, 1926).

JONATHAN ODELL: *The Loyal Verses of Joseph Stansbury and Doctor Jonathan Odell*, edited by Winthrop Sargent (Albany, 1860).

SAMUEL PETERS: *A General History of Connecticut . . . to which is added an Appendix, wherein New and True Sources of the Present Rebellion are pointed out . . . By a Gentleman of the Province* (London, 1781; New Haven, 1829; New York, 1877).

BOOK III: PART I

I.   AGRARIANISM AND CAPITALISM: A vivid account of the party struggles of the time is given in Claude G. Bowers, *Jefferson and Hamilton* (Boston, 1925, with full bibliography). For political theory, see Harold J. Laski, *Political Thought in England from Locke to Bentham* (New York, 1920). Charles E. Merriam, *A History of American Political Theories* (New York, 1903). A dramatic account of Shays's Rebellion is given in Edward Bellamy, *The Duke of Stockbridge* (New York, 1901).

II.   THE GREAT DEBATE: The bibliography is extensive. See J. Elliot, *Debates in the Several State Conventions on the Adoption of the Federal Constitution . . .* (4 vols., Washington, 1827, 1836; 5 vols., Philadelphia, 1906). Max Farrand, *Records of the Federal Convention of 1787* (3 vols., New Haven, 1911). S. B. Harding, *The Contest over the Ratification of the Federal Constitution in the State of Massachusetts* (New York, 1896). Charles A. Beard, *An Economic Interpretation of the Constitution of the United States* (New York, 1913). *The Federalist*, numerous editions; the best are those edited by H. C. Lodge (New York, 1886) and by P. L. Ford (New York, 1898). Richard Henry Lee, *Observations leading to a fair examination of the system of government . . . In a number of Letters from the Federal Farmer to the Republican* (reprinted in *Pamphlets on the Constitution of the United States, 1787–1788*, edited by P. L. Ford, Brooklyn, 1888).

III.   ALEXANDER HAMILTON: *Works, Comprising his Correspondence*, edited by J. C. Hamilton (7 vols., New York, 1850–51). *Works*, edited by H. C. Lodge (10 vols., New York, 1885).

There are numerous lives. See J. C. Hamilton, *The Life of Alexander Hamilton* (2 vols., New York, 1834). H. C. Lodge, *Alexander Hamilton* (Boston, 1882, 1898). J. T. Morse, *The Life of Alexander Hamilton* (2 vols., Boston, 1876). See also Gertrude Atherton, *The Conqueror* (New York and London,

1902). A. H. Vanderberg, *The Greatest American, Alexander Hamilton . . . with a Symposium of Opinions by Distinguished Americans* (New York and London, 1922). F. S. Oliver, *Alexander Hamilton: An Essay on the American Union* (New York, 1907)—an English view.

JOHN ADAMS: *Works . . . with a Life of the Author,* edited by C. F. Adams (10 vols., Boston, 1850–56).

See J. Q. Adams and C. F. Adams, *The Life of John Adams* (2 vols., Philadelphia, 1871). J. T. Morse, Jr., *John Adams* (Boston, 1884, 1898). *Letters of Mrs. Adams, the Wife of John Adams,* edited by C. F. Adams (2 vols., Boston, 1840). C. M. Walsh, *The Political Science of John Adams* (New York, 1915).

BOOK III: PART II

I. THE IMPACT OF THE FRENCH REVOLUTION: Abundant material will be found in Charles D. Hazen, *Contemporary American Opinion of the French Revolution* (Baltimore, 1897, *Johns Hopkins Studies in Hist. and Pol. Science,* Extra Vol. 16). See also *The Journal of William Maclay,* edited by E. S. Maclay (New York, 1890). For *Publicola,* see John Q. Adams, *Writings . . .,* edited by Worthington C. Ford (7 vols., New York, 1913–17).

II. TOM PAINE: *Writings . . .,* edited by Moncure D. Conway (4 vols., New York, 1894–99). Moncure D. Conway, *Life of Thomas Paine . . . To which is added a Sketch of Paine by William Cobbett . . .* (2 vols., New York and London, 1892).

THOMAS JEFFERSON: *Writings,* edited by H. A. Washington (9 vols., Washington, 1853–54). *The Works of Thomas Jefferson* (with *Anas* and *Autobiography*), edited by P. L. Ford (12 vols., New York, 1904–05).

Numerous lives, many of which are wholly unreliable. The official biography was written by Henry S. Randall, *The Life of Thomas Jefferson* (3 vols., Philadelphia, 1858, 1871). Of later studies the following are excellent: David S. Muzzey, *Thomas Jefferson* (New York, 1919); Francis W. Hirst, *Life and Letters of Thomas Jefferson* (New York, 1926)—an English view; and Albert Jay Nock, *Jefferson* (New York, 1926). See also Sarah N. Randolph, *The Domestic Life of Thomas Jefferson* (New York, 1871) and Thomas E. Watson, *The Life and Times of Thomas Jefferson* (New York, 1903).

III. THE FEDERALIST GROUP: For backgrounds of the Hartford wits, see Richard J. Purcell, *Connecticut in Transition: 1775–1818* (Washington, 1918). William A. Robinson, *Jeffersonian Democracy in New England* (New Haven 1916). Samuel E. Morison, *Life and Letters of Harrison Gray Otis* (2 vols. Boston, 1913). For criticism, see F. Sheldon, "Pleiades of Connecticut" (*Atlantic Monthly,* Vol. XV). Mrs. Annie R. Marble, *Heralds of American Literature* (Chicago, 1907). Moses Coit Tyler, *Three Men of Letters* (New York, 1895)—Dwight and Barlow. The writings of the Wits have long been out of print. The most available text is *The Connecticut Wits,* edited with introduction and bibliographies, by Vernon L. Parrington (New York, 1926, American Authors Series), which reprints large portions of Trumbull, Timothy Dwight, Barlow, Humphreys, *The Anarchiad,* and portions of *The Echo.*

TIMOTHY DWIGHT: The most important titles are *The Conquest of Canaan . . .* (Hartford, 1785). *The Triumph of Infidelity . . .* (1788). *Greenfield Hill . . .* (1794). *Travels in New England and New York: 1796–1815* (4 vols., New Haven, 1821–22; London, 1823).

See W. B. Sprague, *Life of Timothy Dwight* (Sparks *Lib. Amer. Biog.*, Second Series, Vol. IV, Boston, 1845).

THE FRENCH GROUP: PHILIP FRENEAU: *Poems*, edited for the Princeton Hist. Assoc. by Fred L. Pattee (3 vols., Princeton, 1902–07). Victor H. Paltsits, *A Bibliography of the Separate and Collected Works of Philip Freneau, together with an Account of his Newspapers* (New York, 1903). Mary S. Austin, *Philip Freneau, Poet of the Revolution* (New York, 1901). S. E. Forman, *The Political Activities of Philip Freneau* (Baltimore, 1902, Johns Hopkins Studies in Hist. and Pol. Science, Series XX, No. 9-10). Mrs. Annie R. Marble, *Heralds of American Literature* (Chicago, 1907).

JOEL BARLOW: His works are out of print, but portions will be found in *The Connecticut Wits* (New York, 1926). The important titles are: *The Vision of Columbus* . . . (Hartford, 1787; London, 1787). *A Letter to the National Convention of France* . . . (London, 1792). *Advice to the Privileged Orders in the Several States of Europe* . . . (London, 1792, 1796). *The Conspiracy of Kings* . . . (London, 1792). *The Hasty Pudding* . . . (New York, 1796; Salem, 1799; Stockbridge, 1799). *The Columbiad* (Philadelphia, 1807; London, 1809).

Charles Burr Todd, *Life and Letters of Joel Barlow* (New York, 1886). See also Tyler, *Three Men of Letters* (New York, 1895), and Marble, *Heralds of American Literature* (Chicago, 1907).

HUGH HENRY BRACKENRIDGE: *Modern Chivalry: Containing the Adventures of Captain John Farrago, and Teague O'Regan, his servant* . . . (2 vols., Philadelphia, 1792; Vol. 3, Pittsburgh, 1793; Vol. 4, Philadelphia, 1797). These four volumes constitute Part I. Part II was issued in two volumes, Philadelphia, 1804–05. Many revisions and changes of the text followed. The complete work was issued in four volumes (Philadelphia, 1815), the fourth volume containing new material. Another complete edition was issued in two volumes (Pittsburgh, 1819). For detailed information see *Cambridge History of American Literature* (Vol. I, p. 526).

An account of Brackenridge and in particular of his experience during the Whiskey Rebellion, in a memoir by H. M. Brackenridge, prefaces the edition of 1846 and later editions. No life of Brackenridge has been written. His fugitive writings in verse, drama, and prose are numerous but inaccessible. Some comment on Brackenridge is given in Henry Adams, *Life of Albert Gallatin* (Philadelphia, 1879).

INDEX

THE ROMANTIC REVOLUTION
IN AMERICA

FOREWORD

IN justification of the choice of writers and allotment of space in the following pages, let it be said frankly that I have been guided by what I conceived to be the historical significance of the several documents. With aesthetic judgments I have not been greatly concerned. I have not wished to evaluate reputations or weigh literary merits, but rather to understand what our fathers thought, and why they wrote as they did. This will serve to explain the considerable number of pages devoted to southern letters, as well as to certain well-nigh forgotten figures. For the purpose I had in view such a method was inevitable. Lost causes have a way of shrinking in importance in the memory of later generations, and the historian must go back to the days before their overthrow, and view them in the light of their hopes. Time is not always a just winnower; it is partial to success and its verdict too often inclines to the side of the biggest cannon or the noisiest *claque*. The exhuming of buried reputations and the revivifying of dead causes is the familiar business of the historian, in whose eyes forgotten men may assume as great significance as others with whom posterity has dealt more generously. Communing with ghosts is not unprofitable to one who listens to their tales. To our fathers John Taylor and Beverley Tucker and Fisher Ames were living figures; they spoke for their generation, and they may have something still to say to a later generation. For dealing at length with such men as Hugh Legaré and Gilmore Simms and John P. Kennedy and Herman Melville, no apologies need be offered. They have too long been slighted. Walt Whitman I have chosen to regard as the forerunner of a later school, and have reserved the consideration of his work for another study. Certain other men I have omitted regretfully out of regard to space—diverse figures such as Orestes Brownson, Albert Brisbane, and John Esten Cooke, together with a group of poets and essayists, who though they have long been reckoned ghosts are nevertheless well worth knowing. Even echoes imply substance somewhere.

V. L. P.

Seattle, February 22, 1926.

i

INTRODUCTION

THE present volume is the second in a proposed study of the main tendencies of American thought as expressed in our literature. In the preceding volume I have considered the incoming into America of certain old-world ideals and institutions, and the subjection of those ideals and institutions to the pressure of a new environment, from which resulted the overthrow of the principles of monarchy and aristocracy, and the setting up of the principle of republicanism. In the present study I purpose considering certain new growths that sprang up in the land thus cleared—what particular forms they assumed and why they assumed such forms. The delimitations of the period to be treated of are fixed by two wars that disturbed the normal unfolding of national experience: the War of 1812 that hastened the development of nineteenth-century ideals, and the Civil War that uprooted certain of the crasser growths of those vigorous years. The half century that lay between these dramatic episodes was a period of extravagant youth, given over to a cult of romanticism that wrought as many marvels as Aaron's rod. In the South, in New England, and on the western frontier, it laid hold of men's minds, consuming the stubble of eighteenth-century harvests, sweeping away the drab realisms of a cautious past, and offering in their stead more alluring ideals. Revolutions, greater and lesser, trod on each other's heels; the common adventure led into unexplored paths; and the final outcome for which it was all preparing was the emergence of a new middle class that in the succeeding half century was to subdue America to middle-class ends.

Such drastic overturnings of the customary and familiar, such swift ruptures with the past, quite evidently do not come from trivial causes. Men do not put off the old before the new is ready; and if in those credulous years they turned romantic and refused to heed the counsels of experience, it was because the soil had been new-plowed for the growing of such crops as their fathers had not known. The grapes from which the wine of romance is vinted, it must not be forgotten, are rooted in the common earth. The

iii

loveliest romantic dreams spring from a parentage that is humbly prosaic. There is no more fruitful source of romantic hope than a fluid economics that overflows all narrow preëmptions and sweeps away the restrictions that hamper free endeavor. With fresh economic realms to conquer, the dullest plodder discovers a stimulus in anticipation that sets him upon creating a Utopia. The breaking up of the static, the bold adventuring upon new worlds, is the fertile soil in which romance springs most luxuriantly. It needs no uncommon eyes, surely, to discover in the swift changes that came to America in the wake of the second English war, the seed-bed of those ebullient romanticisms which in politics and economics, in theology and literature, turned away so contemptuously from the homespun past. Of a sudden America was becoming a new world with potentialities before undreamed of; and this new America was no longer content with the narrow ways of a more cautious generation. The older America of colonial days had been static, rationalistic, inclined to pessimism, fearful of innovation, tenacious of the customary. It conceived of human nature as evil, and accounting men incurably wicked, it opened no doors to Utopian dreams of a golden future. The round of daily life was confined within a narrow domestic economy, with few and rare changes in social status. Growth in population came mainly from natural increase. Exploitation was laborious, and such wealth as was laid by was gained in shop and field, in fisheries and shipping. With its expectations cramped by a drab agrarianism, it was content to remain primitively self-sufficient, not given to seeking riches by speculative short-cuts, clinging to the habitual, distrustful of change.

During the thirty-odd years between the Peace of Paris and the end of the War of 1812 that older America was dying. The America that succeeded was a shifting, restless world, youthfully optimistic, eager to better itself, bent on finding easier roads to wealth than the plodding path of natural increase. It conceived of human nature as acquisitive, and accounting acquisitiveness a cardinal virtue, it set out to inquire what opportunities awaited it in the unexploited resources of the continent. The cautious ways of earlier generations were become as much out of date as last year's almanac. New commonwealths were rising in the wilderness; immigration from war-torn Europe was pouring in; wild lands were daily coming on the market. Money was to be made by the enterprising, and the multitude of the enterprising was augmenting with the expansion of the settlements. The ideal of a static society having been put away, progress was assumed to be the first law of nature, and innovation was accepted as the sign and seal of progress. It was our first great period of exploitation, and from it emerged, as naturally as the cock from the mother egg, the spirit of romance, gross and tawdry in vulgar minds, dainty and refined in the more cultivated. But always romance. The days of realism were past, and it was quietly laid away with the wig and smallclothes of an outgrown generation.

Unfortunately economic romance is more imperious in its demands than literary romance. Its dreams follow objective desires, and in America of those days of new beginnings the desires of diverse economic groups conducted straight to antagonistic imperialisms. The major interests of the three great sections of the country differentiated more and more sharply. The East was discovering its Utopia in an industrial capitalistic order. With the flocking of immigrants to the factories began the extraordinary expansion of the cities and the movement of centralization that was eventually to transform America from a rural to an urban society, supplanting the farmer by the business man and disintegrating the traditional psychology. The new manufacturing and the new finance were subjecting an agrarian people to the dislocations and readjustments implied in the industrial revolution, the outcome of which no man could foresee. The reaction of this new industrialism upon the South was immediate. With the improvements in textile manufacturing came greater demands upon the new southern staple, and an agriculture that had long been static with its traditional crops of indigo, rice, and tobacco, began to look forward confidently to a Utopia founded on cotton, and conceived an imperialistic dream of expanding fields of white bolls and black slaves, reaching into Mexico and embracing the West Indies. The new South left off apologizing for slavery and hoping for its ultimate extinction. Slavery had become enormously profitable and it proposed to exploit the negro as frankly as New England was exploiting the Irish immigrant, but more humanely if possible, in something of the patriarchal spirit.

Meanwhile in the Inland Empire was arising an economics that looked with little favor on the imperialisms of eastern capitalism or southern slavery; an economics equalitarian in temper, decentralizing in impulse; nourished on the idealism of the Declaration of Independence, but interpreting it to mean the natural right of every free citizen to satisfy his acquisitive instinct by exploiting the national resources in the measure of his shrewdness. Democratic in professions, it was middle-class in spirit and purpose. Discovering the inflowing tide of immigration to be favorable to speculation, it sought its Utopia in county-seat towns where land holdings mounted in value with every new wave. No narrow horizons bounded a realm that stretched to the Pacific and into the remote Northwest, and no stodgy ways of money-getting could satisfy men whose imaginations ranged through such spaces. This country was theirs to do with as they chose, and if eastern capitalism or southern slavery interfered with their inalienable rights, their Sharp's rifles were at hand for defense. In the vast territory drained by the Mississippi—the "Valley of Democracy," a recent writer has chosen to call it—was conceived what may be accounted the most romantic dream that ever visited the native mind of America. It impressed de Tocqueville, who discovered the poetry of America in this romance of a moving frontier, in the vision that led the pioneer on his conquering way westward, hewing at an interminable wilderness that was matched only by his ambitions.

Such swift expansions, such mounting romanticisms of temper, must inevitably provide themselves with correspondent philosophies to phrase the new aspirations. The nineteenth century was not content to think in the narrower terms of the eighteenth, but must refashion its thought to suit the romantic style. The modes which it came to accept were for the most part of European origin, adapted to new-world needs. From France and England, and later from Germany, came variant schools of romantic theory that at bottom were a common glorification of the ideal of individualism; and this very diversity of interpretation made possible in America an appeal to different classes and diverse interests, the sum total of which was a many-sided contribution to social theory, but a contribution which carried within it the seeds of later conflict.

The first stage in the romanticization of American thought resulted from the naturalization of French revolutionary theory. Its devious progress through the country can be traced fairly accurately. Landing first in Virginia in the early seventeen-seventies, it met with a hospitable reception from the generous planter society and spread widely there the fashion of Physiocratic agrarianism. Traveling thence westward into the Inland Empire it domesticated itself in frontier log cabins under the guise of an assertive individualism, to issue later as the coon-skin democracy of the Jacksonian revolution. Eventually reaching New England, the last haven and refuge of eighteenth-century realism, it disarmed Yankee antagonism by assuming the dress of Unitarianism and preached the doctrine of human perfectibility with such conviction as to arouse the conscience of New England to an extraordinary enthusiasm for reforming man and society. And coming finally to New York it inoculated the mind of the emerging proletariat with its doctrine of the rights of man, with Fourieristic and other Utopias, and turmoiled contemporary politics with equalitarian Locofoco programs. No other philosophy assumed so many and such attractive disguises, or wrought such changes in American ideals, as this French romanticism with its generous humanitarian impulses. The ground was ready for the seed it was to sow, and if in the judgment of a hostile philosophy the crop turned out to be tares, increasing thousands believed it to be excellent wheat, to the growing of which America was to be dedicated henceforth.

The rival philosophy, which came to view with increasing dislike the doctrines of French romanticism, was of English middle class origin and sprang from the long struggle of that class to loose the hands of the landed gentry from control of the state. Phrased persuasively by Adam Smith, it embodied the principle of liberalism as that principle was understood by men of affairs. It conceived of a social Utopia that must result if economic forces were given free play; if governmental restrictions on trade were done away with and individual enterprise were free to buy and sell in the open market. Springing from the same root of individualism that brought forth French romanticism, it flowered in an economics that denied the aspirations of the French school. Assuming as its determining principle the common instinct of acquisitiveness, it set up the economic man as the criterion of conduct and proposed to reorder society to the single end of trade. Thus sanctioned and given free rein, the principle of acquisitiveness set forth on its triumphant march through western civilization. Accepted by the English middle class as the ultimate social philosophy sufficient to all needs, it presented to willing eyes the ideal of exploitation as the goal of social progress.

But transported to America, the new philosophy soon discovered unforeseen obstacles in its path. The acquisitive instinct was here enormously strengthened by the vast unpreëmpted resources lying all about, but unfortunately those resources were too great or too speculative to be exploited by individual effort. Capital was wanting, and unless collective funds were available, exploitation must be slow and inadequate. There was need of the state to further the opening up of western lands and to throw its guardianship about an infant industrialism. Roads and canals could not wait on individual enterprise; tariffs and subsidies could flow only from the government. Hence arose a modification of *laissez faire*, from which resulted the theory that a democratic state stands *in loco parentis* to the economic interests of its citizens, and should guarantee the progressive well-being of strategic groups on whose prosperity depended the common well-being. It was this modification of the English philosophy that the Whig party came to embody in its platform, and which by pooling the interests of western speculators, eastern financiers and New England industrialists, sponsored the "American Plan," a curiously ingenious scheme to milk the cow and divide the milk among those who superintended the milking.

Meanwhile in the imperialistic South was arising a distinctive philosophy, native to the special conditions imposed by slavery, that was to set it apart from both eastern and western economics and draw it inevitably into a narrowing isolation. Frankly defensive in purpose, rejecting alike French equalitarianism and English individualism, it sought to justify the institution of slavery by an appeal to realism and square it to the theory of democracy by analogy with northern industrialism. The conception of a Greek democracy, which was the last citadel of the southern mind, was a skillful compromise between the antagonistic principles of aristocracy and democracy, the most romantic ideal brought forth by our golden age of romance. Assuming the middle-class principle of exploitation as the creative source of every civilization, it proposed to erect a free state on the basis of a slave proletariat after the model of ancient Athens. A democracy, it argued, is possible only among equals. In every society hitherto the inevitable inequality between economic classes has nullified every democratic program. Master and man, exploiter and exploited, are necessarily opposed in vital economic interests; and this potential clash, this fundamental antagonism of classes, has been intensified by the rise of industrialism. Exploitation has been brutalized by the impersonal wage-system, and the proletariat has been reduced to sodden and embittered beasts. If now as honest realists we recognize frankly that equality cannot exist between inferior and superior races, if we accept the inevitable proletarian status of the negro, if finally we concede the truism that the lifelong relations between master and slave are more humane than the temporary relations between wage-giver and wage-earner, we shall concern ourselves less with a romantic equalitarianism and more with a rational conception of a democracy of equals that may conceivably erect a civilization worthy of the name.

It was an ingenious theory, but unfortunately it left out of account the ambitions of the middle class, and it was this class that in the end destroyed it. Whether they will it or not, imperialisms have a way of clashing with rival imperialisms. Reality persists though romance may deny it, and in their several programs the three diverse sections of America were driving blindly to a collision. In that bitter collision the dream of the South was destroyed. With the overthrow of the aristocratic principle in its final refuge the ground was cleared of the last vestiges of the eighteenth century. Thenceforth America was to become wholly middle class, and such romance as it might bring forth was to be of another sort.

The literature of this extraordinarily vigorous period we are now to deal with, not in the narrow field of *belles lettres* alone but in the outlying fields of social and political philosophies. The difficulties in the way are many. To endeavor to penetrate critically to the intellectual core of a period, to weigh this romance in realistic scales, to take off the outer wrappings and lay bare the inner truth, is no May-day undertaking. The critic finds himself at every turn confronted by reputations distorted by contemporary praise or censure. In the formal biographies written in that golden age of myth-making, criticism too often gave way to eulogy. Our fathers wrote like gentlemen, but unfortunately too often they believed that in preparing a biography a gentleman was under obligation to speak well of the dead. No blemishes were to be recognized, no disagreeable truths to find a place in their immaculate pages. In consequence scarcely a single commentary of the times is to be trusted, and the critic is reduced to patching together his account out of scanty odds and ends, or else settling down to do a series of full-length portraits, in which work, quite evidently, he will not get far. The inadequacies of the present study I am painfully conscious of: its omissions, its doubtful interpretations, its hasty generalizations, its downright guesses; but in the present lack of exact knowledge of the history of American letters, I do not see how such inadequacies can be avoided.

CONTENTS

BOOK I: THE MIND OF THE SOUTH

PART I

The Virginia Renaissance

PART II

The Renaissance of Slavery

CONTENTS

BOOK III: THE MIND OF NEW ENGLAND

PART I

The Twilight of Federalism

BOOK ONE: THE MIND OF THE SOUTH

THE MIND OF THE SOUTH

To those who follow the main-traveled road of American experience, as we know it today, the mind of the old South seems curiously remote. It is so archaic, so wholly apart from all present-day ambitions, as to appear singular. Yet the continental highways we now travel so familiarly, it must be remembered, were not the highways of an earlier America. It is the North that has changed, and not the South, and the nationality that sits so easily upon us would have seemed ominous to the simpler world that determined the ideals of the Old Dominion. The southern mind has grown old-fashioned, but it is native and of long and honorable descent. It derived its singularity from the eighteenth century in which it took shape; and it retained the clear impress of its origins long after the eighteenth century had become an anachronism in America. It was primarily political, of the French rather than the English school; but it was economic also, out of Quesnay and Du Pont de Nemours rather than Adam Smith, with a frank bias towards the Physiocratic agrarianism that was so congenial to the needs and temper of a plantation society; and this political agrarianism, parochial in its outlook rather than national, suffices to explain the singularity of the southern mind in the eyes of a later industrialized America.

Simple and homogeneous in the early years of the nineteenth century, it nevertheless carried the seeds of disruption within it. Beneath the surface of this common political agrarianism disintegrating forces were at work, that were to produce broad cleavages of thought and lead to sharp differences of outlook and polity. An old South and a new South dwelt side by side, and to the West lay a frontier that took particular form as it came under the determining influence of one or the other. Virginia and South Carolina were the germinal centers of southern culture, from which issued the creative ideas that gave special forms to the brood of frontier states. Kentucky and Tennessee were the intellectual heirs of Virginia; Alabama and Mississippi were the intellectual heirs of South Carolina. Of these two schools of thought that looked in different directions and sought different ends, Jefferson and Calhoun were the intellectual leaders; and the contrasts in their philosophies—the rejection by the latter of equalitarian idealism, and the substitution of economic realism—mark the diverse tendencies which in the end disrupted the South. Jackson and Lincoln were followers of the Jeffersonian school; Jefferson Davis finally went with Calhoun; and Henry Clay, lacking an adequate philosophy, wavered between them. The differences between these men were open and patent, and any analysis of the mind of the South, any attempt to understand the conflict of tendencies that marked the development of southern thought between 1800 and 1860, must give due weight to such differences. The problem, therefore, instead of being single is threefold, and involves an examination of the mind of Virginia, the mind of South Carolina, and the mind of the new West from the Ohio River to the Gulf.

PART ONE: THE VIRGINIA RENAISSANCE

CHAPTER I

THE OLD DOMINION

THE history of the Old Dominion is an easy chapter in the textbook of economic determinism. It is a modern instance that exemplifies the law of land distribution and political control as laid down by James Harrington; it is another Oceana seated by the James River, that would not suffer a king to rule because gentlemen held the land and acknowledged no feudal dues or royal prerogatives. On the surface its history seems little more than a bundle of paradoxes. From the raw materials of English middle-class stock it created a distinguished and capable aristocracy, that was restrained from feudal tyranny by a vigorous yeomanry that held its land in fee simple and stoutly maintained its rights. Established on a slave economy, it adopted an agrarian economy, espoused a republic, and accepted the doctrine of democratic equalitarianism. It was generous, humanitarian, independent; parochial in its jealousies, yet farsighted in outlook; tenacious of its authority and quick to defend it, yet never mean or grasping. During the noonday of its power its influence was always on the side of local democratic freedom and the common well-being. It opposed the encroachments of the centralizing state and the spirit of capitalistic exploitation; yet its domestic economy rested on the most primitive of all exploitation.

But these paradoxes disappear when the history of Virginia is interpreted in the light of its land economy. By force of circumstances the Old Dominion became broadly American in its social philosophy, the interpreter of America to herself. Native conditions created there a native psychology, and this native psychology spread widely through the frontier states where a like economics provided suitable breeding places. Virginia was the mother of the agrarian West, as New York, Philadelphia, and Boston were the progenitors of the mercantile and industrial

East; and in the frequent clashes between country and town, between agrarianism and capitalism, the ideas of Virginia have commonly opposed the ideas of the northern cities. Between the older colonial America and later industrial America, stand the ideals of the Old Dominion, more humane and generous than either, disseminating the principles of French romantic philosophy, and instilling into the provincial American mind, static and stagnant in the grip of English colonialism, the ideal of democratic equalitarianism and the hope of humane progress. The nineteenth century first entered America by way of the James River.

The renaissance in Virginia began with the transition from middle-class to plantation ideals that marked the last half of the eighteenth century; and it was given intellectual stimulus by the libertarian natural-rights philosophy that in England and France was undermining the old order. There were no cities either mercantile or social, in the Old Dominion, and no industrialism. Life everywhere centered in the plantation. The navigable rivers of the tide-water region were favorable to the development of a decentralized economics, and in spite of royal commands to create adequate seaports, and heavy taxes by the commonwealth, trading towns did not prosper. For two hundred years Virginia refused to create a native middleman group to handle its staples, but preferred to deal through British factors and ship directly, preferably in Dutch bottoms. Each planter insisted on putting his hogsheads of tobacco aboard ship at his own wharf, and receiving his merchandise direct from London. The system was wasteful, and Madison was active in an attempt to limit by law the ports of entry to two, in order to build up a middleman machinery; but the plan broke on the fixed prejudices of plantation masters who had come to share the old English dislike of tradesmen. Virginia stubbornly refused to adopt middle-class methods, even though refusal cost her dear. She preferred to be exploited by British factors rather than create a domestic class to devour her resources.

The system had grown up in earlier times when the merchant spirit was strong in Virginia. It is often assumed that the Virginia aristocracy was descended from emigrant Cavaliers who fled from England during the commonwealth period; but the facts of history do not bear out such a theory. It was descended largely from vigorous middle-class stock—from men who had been merchants in England and in turning planters brought to the business qualities that had been developed in mercantile pursuits. In the seventeenth century Virginia society exhibited few of the usual characteristics of the Cavalier. It was frankly *bourgeois*, pushing, avaricious, keen in driving hard bargains, with no high sense of honor, canny rather than impulsive, preferring the law to the duel, hating war and only half-hearted in defense against the Indians—a little world of London burgesses new seated on the banks of the James and the Rappahannock. "Beyond doubt," concludes a recent student, "the most numerous section of the Virginia aristocracy was derived from the English merchant class" (Thomas J. Wertenbaker, *Patrician and Plebeian in Virginia*, p. 28), pretty much the same class that settled Boston and Philadelphia. For a hundred and fifty years these merchant ideals characterized Virginia society. Speculation in land was universal; exploitation was open and shameless; the highest officials took advantage of their positions to loot the public domain, resorting to divers sharp practices from tax dodging to outright theft. One gentleman added a cipher to a grant for two thousand acres, and although the fraud was commonly known, so great was his influence that no one disputed his title to twenty thousand acres. While governor, Alexander Spotswood issued patents for sixty thousand acres to dummy holders, who deeded the land to him after he had retired from office.[1]

In the third quarter of the eighteenth century such practices came to an end. The merchant spirit died out among the Virginia planters, and the Cavalier spirit took its place. A high sense of personal and civic honor became the hall-mark of the landed aristocracy, and for upwards of a hundred years this common code gave to Virginia an enviable distinction. Both in national and commonwealth politics her representatives were clean-handed and jealous to deserve the public faith reposed in them. Among the planters were good business men, of course, notably Washington, who under his stately manners concealed a capable mind for speculative affairs. He engaged in various enterprises; speculated heavily in western lands; was president of the Potomac Company, organized to improve navigation and connect his holdings with salt water; and at his death was one of the wealthiest men in America. But such a career was very unusual in Virginia after

[1] For these and other facts, see Wertenbaker's book (mentioned above), pp. 95-99.

the Revolutionary War. Washington, indeed, may properly be regarded as the last of the eighteenth-century gentlemen, who like Colonel William Byrd was interested in accumulating vast holdings as well as cultivating his plantation. Even more characteristic of an earlier day was John Marshall, the last of the great Virginia Federalists, who was nearer akin to Robert Morris, with whom he had business dealings, than with Jefferson or John Randolph of Roanoke.

The opportunity for such careers in Virginia was passing. Population was draining off into the West and few immigrants came to settle. With no rapidly growing cities the incentive to speculate in unearned increment was lacking and liquid capital was inadequate. The economics of plantation life developed agrarian rather than capitalistic interests. In the midst of a rapidly changing America, a world given over to exploitation, increasingly middle class and contemptuous of the older aristocratic order, the Old Dominion remained static and unchanging. The plantation aristocracy was marooned by the rising tide. It repudiated the ways of trade and industry and sharply criticised the North for its plebeian spirit. "Commerce is certainly beneficial to society in a secondary degree," said Governor Tyler in 1810, addressing the Virginia legislature, "but it produces also what is called citizens of the world—the worst citizens in the world" (quoted in Wertenbaker, *Patrician and Plebeian in Virginia*, p. 102). Enterprising young men who a generation before would have been strong Federalists and supported the new capitalism, found such an atmosphere stifling and migrated to the new South—to Kentucky, Tennessee, Mississippi, or farther West still, where greater opportunity awaited them. Virginia produced no more Washingtons or Marshalls, but turned whole-heartedly to the school of Jefferson, providing the leaders of states-rights agrarianism. She broke off all intellectual alliances with the mercantile and industrial North, and withdrew within her own plantation world.

Purged thus of its Federalist remnant Virginia became increasingly libertarian in its social and political philosophy. Its mind had taken form at the time when French humanitarianism was in the air, and it discovered much in the new philosophy that appealed to its romantic spirit. A quick and jealous concern for personal liberty and the rights of man was a common passion. The gentlemen of the Old Dominion were bound together by caste solidarity, but they remained strikingly individual, never amenable to group coercion, expressing their convictions freely and ready to uphold their views by the code of the duel. "No people ever lived," said Alexander H. Stephens in 1867, "more devoted to the principles of liberty, secured by free democratic institutions, than the people of the South" (*Constitutional View*, etc., Vol. I, p. 539). The right of dissent from majority opinion was the imprescriptible right of every gentleman. In no other part of America could the career of John Randolph be paralleled—a free-lance critic of politicians and political measures, who turned his caustic wit against whom he would, an arch individualist in opinions as other Americans were in acquisitiveness. Politics was an absorbing game in Virginia. Debarred from commercial pursuits, ambitious young Virginians went in for law and politics, with an eye upon a congenial career at Washington. This serves to explain the long predominance of southern leadership in the national government. For two generations the South provided a surprising number of first-class men whose influence was commanding. Until the problem of slavery became acute, and leadership passed from moderate Virginians to Fire Eaters from further south, the influence of Virginia at Washington was thrown on the side of republican simplicity, low taxes and the decentralization of power. The armed clash over slavery very probably might have been averted if the spirit of the Old Dominion had prevailed.

CHAPTER II

THE HERITAGE OF JEFFERSONIANISM

I

To the young Virginia Republicans of the year 1800, Jeffersonianism seemed to be a comprehensive social philosophy peculiarly adapted to their needs. It offered a practical and humane program of national development in harmony with existing fact and native genius. It had not yet been distorted by the caprice of circumstance into a somewhat nebulous idealism, nor confined within the narrower limits of political equalitarianism and states-rights theory. By later generations Jefferson has been interpreted too exclusively in terms of the Declaration of Independence, the glowing idealism of which has proved curiously elastic and has been stretched by later libertarian movements to meet their special and particular ends: by the Jacksonian democracy in their struggle for manhood suffrage; by the Abolitionists in their attack upon a slave-sanctioning Constitution; by other idealists in their various crusades. The great name of Jefferson, in consequence, has come to be commonly associated with the conception of democracy and the ideal of social justice. But to his young Virginia followers in the morning of the Republican movement, the perennial suggestiveness of their leader lay in the fact that he embodied for them the many-sided liberalism of French revolutionary thought, its economic and social idealisms equally with political. They interpreted him more adequately, for they understood, as later interpreters frequently have not, how deeply the roots of his natural-rights philosophy went down into current economics. Of the different French writers who gave shape and substance to his thinking, the strongest creative influence on the mature Jefferson came from the Physiocratic group, from Quesnay, Condorcet, Mirabeau, Du Pont de Nemours, the brilliant founders of an economy that was primarily social rather than narrowly industrial or financial. Historically the Physiocratic school is as sharply aligned with idealistic agrarianism as the Manchester school is aligned with capitalistic industrialism. The conception that agriculture is the single productive form of labor, that from it alone comes the *produit net* or ultimate net labor increment, and that bankers, manufacturers and middlemen belong to the class of sterile workers, profoundly impressed the Virginia mind, bred up in a plantation economy and concerned for the welfare and dignity of agriculture.

Franklin had first given currency to the Physiocratic theory in America a generation earlier, but it was Jefferson who spread it widely among the Virginia planters. He did more; he provided the new agrarianism with a politics and a sociology. From the wealth of French writers he formulated a complete libertarian philosophy. His receptive mind was saturated with romantic idealism which assumed native, congenial form in precipitation. From Rousseau, Godwin and Paine, as well as from Quesnay and Condorcet, came the idea of political justice and the conception of a minimized political state, assuming slightly different forms from filtering through different minds. The early doctrine of *laissez faire, laissez passer*—a phrase given currency by Gournay, the godfather of the Physiocratic school—proved to be curiously fruitful in the field of political speculation, as in economic. From it issued a sanction for natural rights, the theory of progress, the law of justice, and the principle of freedom. The right of coercion was restricted by it to the narrowest limits, and the political state was shorn of all arbitrary power. "Authority," the Physiocratic thinkers concluded, "should only employ the force of the community to compel madmen and depraved men to make their conduct conform to the principles of justice."

So far Jefferson went gladly with the Physiocrats, but in their acceptance of a benevolent despotism he discovered a denial of their first principles, and turned to the more congenial democratic group. With the political principles of Godwin and Paine he was in hearty accord. With them he accepted as an historical fact the principle that government is everywhere and always at war with natural freedom, and from this he deduced the characteristic doctrine that the lover of freedom will be jealous of delegated power, and will seek to hold the political state to strict account. From this same principle, following Paine, he deduced the doctrine of the terminable nature of compact, which he set over against the legal doctrine of inviolability. In this matter French liberalism and English legalism were at opposite poles. Replying

to Burke's doctrine of irrevocable compact, Paine had written
The Rights of Man, which Jefferson did much to popularize in
America, and with the broad principles of which he was in complete
accord. "The earth belongs in usufruct to the living," Paine
had argued, and the dead possess no rights over it. Government
from the grave is a negation of the inalienable rights of the new-
born; hence social justice demands that a time limit should automatically revoke all compacts. Since no generation can rightly
deed away the heritage of the unborn, the natural limit of every
compact is the lifetime of the generation ratifying it. "No society," Jefferson said, "can make a perpetual Constitution, or
even a perpetual law."

In this suggestive theory of the terminable nature of compact
is to be found the philosophical origin of the later doctrine of states
rights. However deeply it might be covered over by constitutional
lawyers and historians who defended the right of secession, the
doctrine was there implicitly, and the southern cause would have
been more effectively served if legal refinements had been subordinated to philosophical justification of this fundamental doctrine.
With a frank contempt for all legalists Jefferson believed that
social well-being was not to be bounded by constitutional limitations or statutory enactments; that political action should be
governed by reason rather than by historical precedent. He had
discovered that the political state does not remain static, but gathers power by the law of physical attraction; with increasing power
it becomes increasingly dangerous to natural freedom; hence a
long-established and venerable constitution may become, by reason of its hold upon the popular affection, the most useful of agencies to cloak aggressions on the rights of the people. The love of
profits is always seeking to overthrow the rule of justice. Human
selfishness persistently distorts civic conduct, warping it from
ideal ends. But the shortcomings of existing political states
cannot abrogate the law of justice or destroy the love of freedom.
To safeguard freedom from encroachment by the political state, and
to establish the rule of justice, were always the great and difficult
ends that Jefferson aimed at, and as a follower of the Physiocratic
school and a Virginia planter he turned naturally to a *laissez faire*
agrarianism in opposition to a centralizing capitalism.

But he was much too sound a political thinker and too sagacious
a party leader to rest his case upon abstract theory. In all his later

writings and counsels he kept his mind close to economic fact, and the Jeffersonian movement was a long and effective training school in the economic basis of politics. It habituated the motley rank and file of the electorate to think in economic terms and to regard political parties as the instruments of economic groups. This was in keeping with the soundest eighteenth-century tradition, before romantic dogma had divorced politics and realism; and in so far Jefferson agreed with his Federalist opponents, Hamilton and John Adams. A decade of acrimonious debate had made it plain to the common voter that the real struggle in America lay between the rival capitalist and agrarian interests, of which the Federalist and Republican parties were the political instruments. The Congressional enactments of the first twelve years had further clarified the issue. The funding plan had visibly increased the number and wealth of the rising capitalist group. The first banks were being erected and the complex machinery of modern credit—the hated "paper system" that had driven out the traditional metallic currency—was being rapidly built up. A small financial group in the northern cities was growing powerful from discounting and money-brokerage. The truth was slowly coming home to the farmers and small men that war is profitable to the few at the cost of the many; that from the egg of war-financing was hatched a brood of middlemen who exploited the post-war hardships and grew rich from the debts that impoverished the producing farmers. This ambitious class, hitherto negligible in America, was provided with the means to make a vigorous fight; it invoked the political state as an ally, and under Hamilton's leadership used the administration to serve its financial interests. It looked with open hostility upon every agrarian program, was cynical towards French romantic theories, and was restrained by no scruples. To loose the hands of this capable class from the helm of government, to keep America agricultural, and the Federal state secondary in all but necessary police powers to the several commonwealths, was the avowed and logical purpose of the Jeffersonian Republicans.[1]

The leaders of the movement were men who in capacity and training were worthy opponents of the capable Federalists. In surprising number they were from the Old Dominion, gentlemen of the best Virginia stock, who in the last decades of the eighteenth

---

[1] See Charles A. Beard, *The Economic Origins of Jeffersonian Democracy*, Chapter XIII.

century engrafted upon a generous plantation tradition the Physiocratic doctrines of France. A finer race of gentlemen America has never produced, and it was fortunate for the Jacksonian movement, which produced no notable thinkers and contributed little to political and economic theory, that the preceding generation had given adequate form to the philosophy of agrarianism. That theory took definite shape between 1800 and 1820. In the days of Hamilton's control of the Treasury Department, the agrarian opposition was weakened by the lack of such a theory; but the necessities of the situation were a prod to the young Republicans, and the philosophy of agrarianism rapidly crystallized. In its final form it was an extraordinarily interesting and native expression of two hundred years' experience of a society founded on agriculture—a reasoned defense of an older America against the ambitions of a younger and more vigorous.

II

JOHN TAYLOR
An Agrarian Economist

The intellectual leader of the young Republicans in the great attack on the economics of Federalism was a thinker too little recognized by later Americans. His just fame has been obscured with the cause for which he labored, and his reputation lies buried with the old agrarian *régime*. Nevertheless John Taylor of Caroline County, Virginia, "the philosopher and statesman of agrarianism," was the most penetrating critic of Hamiltonian finance and the most original economist of his generation. Unambitious, simple, honest, calm and dignified in bearing, he embodied the heroic virtues of the great age of Virginia. In his *Thirty Years' View*, Thomas H. Benton describes him thus:

I can hardly figure to myself the ideal of a republican statesman more perfect and complete than he was in reality:—plain and solid, a wise counsellor, a ready and vigorous debater, acute and comprehensive, ripe in all historical and political knowledge, innately republican—modest, courteous, benevolent, hospitable,—a skilful, practical farmer, giving his time to his farm and his books, when not called by an emergency to the public service—and returning to his books and his farm when the emergency was over. . . . He belonged to that constellation of great men which shone so brightly in Virginia in his day, and the light of which was not limited to Virginia, or our America, but spread through the bounds of the civilized world. (Chapter XVIII.)

Taylor was a member of Congress at the time of the funding operations and contributed two notable pamphlets to the public discussion: the first, issued in 1793, entitled *An Examination of the Late Proceedings in Congress Respecting the Official Conduct of the Secretary of the Treasury;* the second, issued the following year, entitled *An Inquiry into the Principles and Tendencies of Certain Public Measures.* Twenty years later, in 1814, he embodied his matured convictions in a stout volume, printed at Fredericksburg, entitled *An Inquiry into the Principles and Policy of the Government of the United States.* The work is tediously prolix—dressed, according to Benton, "in a quaint Sir Edward Coke style"—even more tediously moralistic; but in spite of very evident stylistic shortcomings, it deserves, in the opinion of Professor Beard, "to rank among the two or three really historic contributions to political science which have been produced in the United States" (*Economic Origins of Jeffersonian Democracy*, p. 323). It was the last of the eighteenth-century works, solidly reasoned, keeping a main eye upon economics and refusing to wander off into the bog of constitutionalism, concerned rather with the springs and sources of political action and the objectives of political parties. It summed up adequately the agrarian argument against capitalism, analyzed the current tendencies, and provided a convenient handbook for the Jacksonian movement, from which the latter drew freely in the dispute over the Bank.

Like Jefferson's, the agrarianism of Taylor was founded in the Physiocratic economy. He was convinced that the tiller of the soil was the only true economist, and that if republican America were to retain its republican virtues it must guard against every system of exploitation, for in exploitation lay the origin of social caste. America had rid itself of the feudal principle of a landed aristocracy, which in the past had provided the machinery of exploitation, by the abolition of the law of primogeniture and entail, only to be confronted by a graver danger, the new aristocracy of liquid wealth. His main purpose, therefore, was an examination of the sources of power of the capitalistic order, and the successive steps by which it had risen to power. His analysis is acute and reveals a mind concerned with the realities that lie beneath outward appearances. It is the economics of history that concern him most, for as fully as John Adams he was convinced that economics determine the form of the political state. In his analysis of the origins of government, he discovers in every society a master class that becomes the beneficiary of sovereign power: the political state is first erected and thereafter used to safeguard the past acquisitions and to further the present ambitions of a dominant economic group which calls itself an aristocracy; and such an aristocracy imposes its will upon the exploited mass, crudely by the sword and purse, and subtly by the skillful use of psychology. Once in control of the political state it intrenches itself behind certain fictions which profess to carry moral sanction. This political jugglery plays many tricks to catch the gullible; arrayed in the garb of patriotism, loyalty, obedience to authority, law and order, divine right, it carries a weighty appeal. When these moral fictions fail, the fictions of the law step in, and such doctrines as the sacredness of contract translate the stealings of the master class into vested interests which the state is bound to protect. There is a fine irony in Taylor's implied references to Burke's doctrine of a changeless constitution based on a non-revocable compact, and Hamilton's doctrine of the public faith, which, he argues, were clearly designed to sacrifice the common good to the interests of a class:

Law enacted for the benefit of a nation, is repealable; but law enacted for the benefit of individuals, though oppressive to a nation, is a charter, and irrepealable. . . . Posterity, being bound by the contracts of its ancestry, in every case which diminishes its rights, man is daily growing less free by a doctrine which never increases them. A government intrusted with the administration of publick affairs for the good of a nation, has a right to deed away that nation for the good of itself or its partisans, by law charters for monopolies or sinecures; and posterity is bound by these deeds. But although an existing generation can never reassume the liberty or property held by its ancestors, it may recompense itself by abridging, or abolishing the right of its descendants. (Page 61.)

The two theories to which he devotes chief attention are the natural aristocracy theory of John Adams, and the capitalistic aristocracy theory of Hamilton. The first of these takes its bias from stressing the inequality inherent in the nature of men; individuals are biologically unequal; and from this fact Adams deduces that the thrifty rise to opulence and the thriftless sink into poverty by reason of individual qualities. Society can neither keep a strong man down nor thrust a weak man up. Between the rich and the poor, the capable and incapable, a state of war exists, held in check by the strong hand in feudal and monarchical societies, but necessarily open and bitter in a democracy. Hence the inevitable failure of democracy wherever it is tried, and the necessity of nicely calculated checks in a republic to prevent the equal tyranny of an aristocracy and a mob. The second theory, the Hamiltonian, justifies itself by the same theory of human nature. It accepts the fact of social inequality as inherent in men, but it sees no reason to pursue Utopian dreams. Recognizing the universal fact of economic control, it erects the state upon exploitation as preferable to anarchy. This capitalistic state it defends before a gullible public by eloquent appeals to the national faith, the security of property, the fear of lawlessness.

Having thus analyzed the two theories Taylor seeks to cut the ground from under both by arguing that social classes cannot be historically explained by the fact of biological inequality amongst individuals, but rather by accidental opportunity, unscrupulousness, and brute force. All aristocracies, whether feudal, natural, or capitalistic, take their origin and uphold their dominion, not from superior excellence or capacity, but from exploitation, that beginning in a small way grows by what it feeds on till it assumes the proportions of a colossus. Exploitation breeds a continually augmenting exploitation that conducts inevitably to caste regimentation. All aristocracies are founded in social theft. They are not established in the morality of nature, but exist as parasites on the social wealth; they levy upon the producer; and the only preventive is to destroy the foundations on which they rest by taking from them the means of exploitation.

In conjuring up phantom dangers of feudal aristocracies, Taylor pointed out, John Adams was fighting dead issues. No feudal aristocracy could arise in America; land was too plentiful and the quick jealousy of the people would strike it down. The danger to republican institutions was closer at hand; it was the poison of the new capitalism that was spreading its virus through all the veins of the national life. And in order that the American people might know something of the history of this innovating force which they must reckon with, John Taylor proceeded to open to them a page in the economics of capitalism. The aristocracy of credit, founded on "monopoly and incorporation," he pointed out, had arisen first in England with the growing power of the middle class; it had gone forward swiftly in consequence of the Napoleonic wars, and through the agencies of the Bank of England and the Consolidated Debt, it had secured control of the public credit. It had arisen first in America in consequence of the financial disturbance resulting from the Revolutionary War, and had further strengthened its position by the War of 1812. Ambitious men had taken advantage of the national necessities to create an artificial paper system identical with that of England. They had profited immensely from the funding operations and the National Bank; they were setting up their private banks in every city and town, and through the manipulation of credit were taking heavy toll of the national production. A money monopoly was the most dangerous of all monopolies, and the master of all.

Taylor had grown up under the traditional domestic economy. He was habituated to think of production in terms of consumption, and of money as a stable measure of exchange. He could not adjust his mind to the theory of production for profit, of middle-man speculation, as socially legitimate; and when that speculation extended to the national currency, and exacted its profits from the medium of exchange, he took alarm. Gold and silver are fairly stable commodities that allow of no sudden increase or diminution, and in consequence a specie currency does not readily lend itself to speculative juggling. But a paper system has no natural limitations. Expanded and contracted at the will of speculators, it subjects the business of the country to the exploitation of money brokers. Vast sums had thus been taken from the people by the funding operations. Gold and silver had been driven out of circulation, and with their disappearance a riot of speculation had begun by which only the brokers had profited. Such was the origin of the new money aristocracy that had already taken possession of the state and was using it for the sole end of exploitation. America must make choice between agrarianism and capitalism; the two were incompatible, John Taylor was convinced, and unless the ambitions of the paper-money aristocracy were held in check, the American producer would come under the heel of middle-class exploitation.

So suggestive was the reasoning of Taylor, so interesting for the light it throws on the agrarian mind of the Virginia Republicans, that it will be well to set down his theses in compact form. As summarized admirably by Professor Beard, his argument runs thus:

1. The masses have always been exploited by ruling classes, royal, ecclesiastical, or feudal, which have been genuine economic castes sustaining their power by psychological devices such as "loyalty to the throne and altar."

2. Within recent times a new class, capitalistic in character, has sprung up, based on exploitation through inflated public paper, bank stock, and a protective tariff, likewise with its psychological devices, "public faith, national integrity, and sacred credit."

3. In the United States, this class was built up by Hamilton's fiscal system, the bank, and protective tariff, all of which are schemes designed to filch wealth from productive labor, particularly labor upon the land.

4. Thus was created a fundamental conflict between the capitalistic and agrarian interests which was the origin of parties in the United States.

5. Having no political principles, capitalism could fraternize with any party that promised protection, and in fact after the victory of the Republicans successfully entrenched itself in power under the new cover.

6. The only remedy is to follow the confiscatory examples of other classes and destroy special privilege without compensation. (*Economic Origins of Jeffersonian Democracy*, p. 351.)

In the great battle of ideas that followed the conflict of interests, the Virginia agrarians armed themselves with trenchant weapons. In intellectual equipment they were a match for the ablest of the Federalists; in social idealism, in generous concern for the *res publica*, or common public business, in sober and practical humanitarianism, they were far superior. Between John Taylor of Virginia, spokesman of planter agrarianism, and Fisher Ames of Massachusetts, spokesman of Boston Federalism, the contrast could scarcely be greater. It is a contrast in social culture, in humane ideals, in interpretations of the native genius of America; and in the comparison it is not the Virginia Republican who suffers.

CHAPTER III

JOHN MARSHALL

Last of the Virginia Federalists

UNLIKE John Taylor of Caroline, whose fame lies buried with his cause, the reputation of John Marshall has taken on immense proportions with the later triumph of his principles. There is abundant reason for the veneration in which he has come to be held by present-day disciples of Hamilton. More than any other man he saved the future for Federalism. During the critical years of the Jeffersonian and Jacksonian assaults upon the outworks of nationalism, he held the inner keep of the law, and prepared for the larger victories that came long after he was in his grave. His strategic judicial decisions served as a causeway over which passed the eighteenth-century doctrine of the sovereignty of the law, to unite with the new philosophy of capitalistic exploitation. The turbid waters of frontier leveling and states-rights democracy washed fiercely about him, but he went on quietly with his self-appointed work. He was one man who would not bow his neck to the majority yoke, would not worship the democratic Baal. He profoundly distrusted the principle of confederation. Convinced that the "continental belt" must be buckled tightly, he gave unstinted service to the cause of consolidation. The imperative need of a sovereign political state to curb the disintegrating forces of America was axiomatic in his thinking. Looking upon all democratic aspirations as calculated to destroy federal sovereignty, and convinced that the principle of equalitarianism was a bow strung to wield against society, he stoutly upheld the principle of minority rule as the only practical agency of stable and orderly government. Holding such views it was a matter of high and patriotic duty with Marshall to use his official position to prevent the majority will from endangering interests which were far more sacred in his eyes than any natural rights propagated in the hothouse of French philosophy. He was the last of the old school of Federalists and the first of the new.

That John Marshall should have come out of Virginia is perhaps the most ironical fact in the political history of the Old Dominion. Quite unrepresentative of the dominant planter group that had gone over to Jefferson, bitterly hostile to the agrarian interests that spoke through John Taylor, he was the leader of a small remnant of Virginians who followed Washington through the fierce extremes of party conflict. He was the last and ablest representative of that older middle-class Virginia, given to speculation and intent on money-making, that was being superseded by a cavalier Virginia concerned about quite other things than financial interests. He belonged rather to Boston than to Richmond. His intense prejudices were primarily property prejudices. He was the Fisher Ames of the South, embodying every principle of the dogmatic tie-wig school of New England Federalists. Profoundly influenced by Hamilton and Robert Morris, he seems to have found the Boston group more congenial in temper and outlook. The explanation of his strong property-consciousness is to be discovered both in his material ambitions and his professional interests. He was a business man rather than a planter. He was heavily involved in land speculation and held stock in numerous corporations launched to exploit the resources of the state. Robert Morris, whose daughter married Marshall's younger brother, was his financial adviser and advanced money with which to purchase the Fairfax estate, an investment that cost the buyers the very considerable sum of fourteen thousand pounds and numerous lawsuits. He was a director in banks and a legal adviser in important cases involving property rights. His financial interests overran state boundaries and his political principles followed easily in their train, washing away all local and sectional loyalties.

Like his kinsman Jefferson, Marshall was bred on the Virginia frontier, and to the end of his life he retained the easy and careless democracy of dress and manners that marked his early environment. In his deportment he was far removed from the prim respectability of the Boston Federalists. A friendly, likable man, fond of pitching horseshoes and sitting in a game of cards, he was outwardly a genial member of the crude little Richmond world where politics and law and speculation engrossed the common attention. An easy-going nature, he was wholly wanting in intellectual interests. Strangely ill-read in the law, he was even more ignorant of history and economics and political theory. His mind took an early set, and hardened into rigidity during the

reactionary years that lay between Shays's Rebellion and the rise
of Napoleon. Of social and humanitarian interests he was utterly
devoid. One might as well look for the sap of idealism in a last
year's stump as in John Marshall. French romantic philosophy
he regarded as the mother of all vicious leveling. There is no
indication that he had ever heard of the Physiocratic school of
economics, or had looked into the writings of Rousseau or Godwin
or Paine. The blind sides of his mind were many; his intellectual
contacts were few; yet what he saw and understood he grasped
firmly. The narrowness of his outlook intensified the rigidity with
which he held to his fixed opinions; and his extraordinary courage
coupled with a dominant personality clothed his strategic position
as Chief Justice with fateful influence on the later institutional
development of America.

Although Marshall's later fame is the fame of a lawyer, he was
in reality a politician whom fate in the person of John Adams
placed on the Supreme Court bench at a critical moment, where his
political opinions translated themselves into the organic law of the
land, and shaped the constitution to special and particular ends.
Masterful, tenacious, manipulating his fellow judges like putty,
he was a judicial sovereign who for thirty-five years molded the
plastic constitution to such form as pleased him, and when he died
the work was so thoroughly done that later generations have not
been able to undo it. His political opinions, therefore, become a
matter of very great importance to the historian, for they help
to explain the peculiar direction taken by our constitutional
development. Materials for a just estimate of his remarkable
career were long wanting, but with the appearance of Beveridge's
able and explicit *Life of John Marshall* it is now possible to view
him in exact historical perspective. Carefully documented, the
work is a genial and readable interpretation that will go far to
revivify the fame of the great Federalist. And yet in spite of its
abundant documentation—drawn perhaps somewhat overmuch
from Federalist sources—it is essentially a *biographie à thèse* that
is careful to magnify the nationalism of its hero and to minify the
property consciousness. It provides a picturesque setting, but
it is a bit careless in its evaluation of the rival philosophies then
struggling for supremacy. Concerning the economics of the great
contest between Federalism and Republicanism it offers very
inadequate information, with the result that Jefferson is reduced

to the status of a master politician set over against the constructive statesman. The intellectual limitations of the lawyer have reacted in these pages upon his political enemy. Certain of the old Federalist prejudices have come to life again in these entertaining pages.

The two fixed conceptions which dominated Marshall throughout his long career on the bench were the sovereignty of the federal state and the sanctity of private property; and these found their justification in the virulence of his hatred of democracy. No man in America was less democratic in his political convictions. Underneath the free and easy exterior of the Chief Justice was as stalwart a reactionary as ever sat on the Supreme Court bench. He was utterly indifferent to popular views, and he calmly overturned the electoral verdicts of his fellow Americans with the deliberateness of a born autocrat. Not only were his important decisions political opinions, but they were Federalist opinions. America had made definite choice between the Federalist and Republican theories of government. It had repudiated the rule of "gentlemen of principle and property" and set up a very different rule. But to this mandate of the supposedly sovereign people Marshall declined to yield. Defeated at the polls, no longer in control of the executive and legislative branches of the government, Federalism found itself reintrenched in the prejudices of John Marshall. He boldly threw down the gage to the majority will, and when the long fierce struggle was over, he had effectively written into the fundamental law of the land the major tenets of the repudiated philosophy. "Judicial statesmanship," Mr. Beveridge calls these political decisions, and bids us admire statesmanship on the bench; yet the phrase runs so far as to merge the judge in the politician—an honest but somewhat indiscreet admission that the law may be twisted to partisan ends. The frankly political nature of Marshall's decisions was universally recognized at the time, and this explains the intense partisanship they evoked, the fury of the Republicans and the extravagant praise of the Federalists. The so-called Jeffersonian assault on the judiciary, of which so much has been made by the orthodox historians, and which came near to wrecking the system, was not primarily an attack upon the courts but upon political judges who used their places to serve party ends. It is a dangerous thing for the bench to twist the law to partisan or class purposes, yet to this very thing John Marshall was notoriously given.

As a judicial statesman, then, rather than a lawyer, Marshall is to be judged, and to such a business the political historian is more competent than the legalist. His important decisions fall into two main groups: those like Marbury *vs.* Madison that assert the supremacy of the judiciary over the legislature—that is, the power of the Supreme Court to nullify an act of Congress; and those like the Yazoo Fraud case and the Dartmouth College case, that assert the irrevocable nature of contracts. The first was an official pronouncement of the principle that Hamilton had elaborated in *The Federalist*, namely, that the constitution is a law and as such lies within the field of judicial interpretation. This was sound Federalist doctrine, and Marshall welcomed the opportunity to engraft it upon the fundamental law of the land, going far out of his way to bring it within the judicial purview.[1] It was a bold and skillful move, and as Beveridge remarks, it announced a principle that "is wholly and exclusively American. It is America's contribution to the science of the law" (Beveridge, *Life of John Marshall*, p. 142). A contribution, it should be added, which with the multiplying of republican constitutions in the later nineteenth century was pretty generally rejected.

Even more partisanly Federalist were the decisions touching the nature of contract. These reached to the heart of the bitter opposition of the commercial and financial interests to the legislative acts of populistic majorities. Suffering heavily from the post-war confusions, those majorities had struck blindly at the profiteers whose well-feathered nests were securely protected by the law. The revolt was natural and human; a rough sense of social justice lay behind it; but because it struck at the most prosperous and capable members of society, who held the professional classes in retainer and dominated the agencies of publicity, it aroused an extraordinarily vindictive opposition. Dip into the literature of the seventeen-eighties and nineties anywhere, in the *Anarchiad* and the *Echo* of the Hartford Wits, or the private letters of indignant gentlemen, and the animus of the respectable classes is clamorously revealed. At bottom it was no other than this, that the law of business must be made the law of the land, and that any populistic tampering with such law was wicked and anarchistic. How determining was this spirit in the matter of the Constitutional

---

[1] For an excellent discussion see Beveridge, *Life of John Marshall*, Vol. III, Chap. III.

Convention is sufficiently well known. In the new constitution certain practices of populistic majorities were estopped—the emission of bills of credit and paper money, and laws impairing the obligation of contracts; but such provisions, strictly interpreted, did not reach to all cases. There were still gaps in the law of business through which populistic majorities might force their bills. To stop those gaps and complete the great work of rendering business secure was the problem to which Marshall addressed himself; and in the Yazoo Fraud case and the Dartmouth College case, he brought the long Federalistic struggle to a triumphant issue.

An examination of the first of these two celebrated cases will suffice to reveal the spirit of his judicial statesmanship. The state of Georgia, through its Legislature, had contracted to sell thirty-five million acres of land—the great part of the territory now comprising the states of Alabama and Mississippi—to certain speculative companies "at less than one and one-half cents an acre." The passage of the bill was marked by more than the usual jobbery, so common with a generation fond of looting the public domain. The fraud was so gross that the state of Georgia was thrown into a fury that visited itself upon the corrupt legislators. A new legislature repealed the law and rescinded the contract; but some of the land had already been resold to investors in Boston and Philadelphia, who brought their claims before the Supreme Court. The state of mind in which the chief justice heard the argument is thus suggested by Beveridge: "Marshall was profoundly interested in the stability of contractual obligations. The repudiation of these by the legislature of Virginia had powerfully and permanently influenced his views upon this subject. Also Marshall's own title to part of the Fairfax estate had more than once been in jeopardy. At that very moment a suit affecting the title of his brother's to certain Fairfax lands was pending in Virginia courts" (Vol. III, p. 584). To suggest that a nicer judicial honor would have inhibited Marshall from sitting in the case is perhaps going too far if one accepts the principle of judicial statesmanship. Certainly Marshall discovered none of the scruples that must have troubled George Wythe. In awarding claims for compensation to the investors he held that the act of the Georgia legislature was a contract and as such was inviolable. The crux of the decision, however, lay in the pronouncement that the courts cannot examine the motives that induce legislators to enact a law, that the people are bound by their agents and must suffer the penalties of choosing unwise or corrupt agents. The upshot of the verdict, in plain language, was that a legislative contract is sacred no matter how corruptly got. A curious decision, surely, for one who professed to venerate the common law. A Virginian of the type of John Randolph would never have reasoned thus to a conclusion that laid open the public domain to the deals of clever lobbyists and encouraged the betrayal of official stewardship. He would scarcely have sacrificed the public interests to the law of business.

The bitter hostility which Marshall's decisions aroused in his native commonwealth reveals how far the Virginia of Jefferson had traveled from the Federalism of the commercial North. The states-rights philosophy and the philosophy of consolidation were at swords' points; the agrarian and capitalistic economies were engaged in a mortal duel; that it should have been a Virginian who saved the day for the Hamiltonians, erecting the old Federalism into the law of the land, and conducting by his decisions straight to an augmented, consolidated state, under the shadow of whose power the development of corporate finance might go forward without agrarian let or hindrance, was a bitter brew for the Jeffersonian planters to drink. As Marshall grew old he drew farther away from his fellow Virginians. In his last years he was perhaps the most reactionary man in America. "Should Jackson be elected," he wrote in 1828, "I shall look upon the government as virtually dissolved" (Beveridge, Vol. IV, p. 463). His last hatreds he divided between Old Hickory and the rising democratic movement. He bitterly resisted the spread of manhood suffrage; he would make no change even in the antiquated judicial system of Virginia; he would have no overturning of anything established. A stubborn autocrat he remained to the end, and there was a certain ironic fitness in his last encounter with the executive power. The autocratic lawyer met his match in the autocratic soldier who grimly remarked, "John Marshall has made his decision, now let him enforce it."

Nearly a century has passed since these happenings [concludes Beveridge] and Marshall's attitude now appears to have been that of cold reaction; but he was as honest as he was outspoken in his resistance to democratic reforms. He wanted good government, safe government.

He was not in the least concerned in the rule of the people as such. Indeed, he believed that the more they directly controlled public affairs the worse the business of government would be conducted. He feared that sheer majorities would be unjust, intolerant, tyrannical, and he was certain that they would be untrustworthy and freakishly changeable. (Vol. IV, p. 507.)

A strong, resourceful, honest, capable man was John Marshall. In so far there is pretty common agreement. Beyond this, comes in the sundering blade of political theory. Concerning the wisdom of his judicial statesmanship it is idle to expect Federalist and Democrat to agree.

CHAPTER IV

THE OLDER PLANTATION MIND

I

PLANTATION BACKGROUNDS

THE literary renaissance of Virginia began in the late twenties when the English romantic movement reached the quiet plantations. Till then the Virginia mind had lingered pleasantly in the twilight of the liberal eighteenth century, following ways of thought it had learned of revolutionary France, and writing with a leisurely finish it had learned of Augustan England. In that older Virginia dignified sentiment was accepted as the hall-mark of breeding— a sentiment somewhat ornate and consciously elegant, that recognized its obligations to a strict morality, and laid its nosegay at the feet of the pure and beautiful and good. When the Virginian essayed somewhat infrequently to commit his thoughts to paper, he wrote as an old-fashioned gentleman, conscious of his social responsibility, consulting classic standards of taste, and embellishing his sentences with bits of choice Latin. But after the year 1830 sentiment gave place to romance, and dignity to exuberance of fancy. A new generation, trained in the school of Sir Walter Scott, fell to the pleasant task of portraying the familiar plantation life in glowing colors and investing it with romantic charm.

The plantation tradition, it will be remembered, first took shape in the Old Dominion and assumed its salient features at the hands of Virginia romantics. Its development was contemporary with the New England transcendental movement, and in origin and spirit it was as native to Virginia as the philosophy of idealism was native to Massachusetts. Inspired by an over-seas romanticism, it accepted the materials it found at hand and transmuted the easy-going plantation life into enduring romance. The work was begun by Kennedy in his idyllic *Swallow Barn*. The picture thus slightly sketched was given stronger colors by Caruthers, and received completer form from John Esten Cooke. From their hands Thomas Nelson Page took his materials to refashion to

28

suit the taste of a later day. No realism added its sobering touches to the romantic picture thus early drawn, and none has since been added. A golden light still lingers upon the old plantation. Memories are still too dear to the Virginian to suffer any lessening of the reputed splendors of *ante bellum* days. The tragedy of a lost cause has woven itself into the older romance and endowed the tradition with an added sanction. It has long since spread beyond the confines of Virginia and become a national possession. North as well as South is so firmly convinced of its authenticity that realism has never had the temerity to meddle with it.[1]

It was a romanticizing age, and in Virginia congenial materials were ready to hand. The distinction of a plantation aristocracy set in the midst of a bucolic republican society, with its genial hospitality, its individuality, its sharp contrasts of whites and blacks, its clutter of cabins for background to the pillared mansion, its wide neighborhood interests, its outdoor life, its patriarchal spirit, was a distinction that no romantic could overlook, the most individual and native picturesque in all America. Life on the plantation was uncramped by the drab routine and skimpy meanness of the New England farm; it was unsoiled by the coarseness and vulgarity of the frontier; it had none of the sordidness of the middle-class town. It might be wasteful, but it was good material for literature; and hence the Virginia romantic had no need to seek the picturesque in England and Spain, as Irving had done. He had only to pick and choose from the familiar stuff lying all about him, emphasizing the agreeable, overlooking the unpleasant, fashioning his figures and action to suit the ideal of a golden age of plantation society. Yet the result, it must be confessed, is not wholly adequate. Virginia has suffered gravely from the want of a sober realism. It is not so much that the worst did not get into the romantic tradition—shortcomings in Virginia life which even Wirt hints at—as that the best did not get in. The plantation master of the romantics falls grossly short of the reality that Virginia provided. The simple dignity of John Taylor, the ingrained Puritanism of Lee and Jackson, the catholic culture and fine integrity of George Wythe, have been left out of the tradition. The Virginian created by the romantics is absurdly inferior to such men, who by any standard were as admirable a group of

[1] For an excellent study, see Francis Pendleton Gaines, *The Southern Plantation,* 1925.

gentlemen as America has ever bred. A little honest realism would have corrected the picture, to the advantage of the Old Dominion.

At the time when the romantics were beginning their work of constructing the plantation tradition the intellectual renaissance of Virginia was passing. With the fading of the French influence after 1820 came increasing isolation and a conscious sectionalism. Intellectual discipline and catholic tastes became rarer. Virginia had no share in the revolutionary enthusiasms of the Utopian thirties and forties, when New England expected the Promised Land to appear at the next turn in the road; it received no stimulus from the expansive systems of thought that were setting all Europe in ferment. The new Germany seems to have made no impression on the Virginia mind, neither its philosophical idealism nor its provocative higher criticism. The new interest in social speculation and experiment that arose in Massachusetts with the beginnings of industrialism awakened no response in Virginia. Plantation society was static, and social speculation was unwelcome. The theories of Comte, of Fourier, of Owen were unknown; Utopian experiments were untried. If Virginia escaped the curse of industrialism it lacked the intellectual stimulus that came to New England with the rise of the textile mills. Social unrest bred no protests against the plantation order. The revolutionary mood was gone, and after 1820 the stimulus to intellectual life grew weaker. English romanticism as exemplified in the work of Scott and Tom Moore was the single foreign influence that spread amongst the plantations, and the new literature accepted the cult of the picturesque romantic. With the passing of the great age of Virginia the tradition of her greatness remained to be gathered up and preserved.

II

WILLIAM WIRT

To Virginia gentlemen of the old school it must have seemed a bit ironical that William Wirt should have come to be accepted as the literary representative of the Old Dominion in the days of John Randolph of Roanoke. Born in Maryland in 1772 of Swiss parentage, Wirt belonged to Virginia only by adoption, and although on terms of intimacy with the plantation gentry he embodied few of the traits that went to the making of the plantation tradition. In temperament he was far removed from the easy-going planter. A certain canny thrift marked him, a pronounced desire to rise in the world and cut a distinguished figure. He was careful to make a good investment of his talents, attentive to profitable undertakings, whether in law or eloquence or speculation. His mature life ran a singularly prosperous and dignified course. He gathered property and reputation and office, and in every position he acquitted himself honorably. To do less than well in any undertaking he would have accounted a stain upon his reputation. In every company he made himself liked. There was none of the aggressive individualism of John Randolph, in wait for an opportunity to send home a shaft of rankling wit, but always a studious concern to please. He was troubled that anyone should think his criticism severe in *The British Spy,* and he hesitated long before publishing his *Patrick Henry* for fear offense would be taken at the few blemishes he discovered in his hero. An honest man and a capable, sterling after his kind but not notably intellectual, not creative, he owed his advancement to very practical qualities: an engaging personality and genial wit, a knack at formal oratory, a graceful pen, a persevering pursuit of his profession, the cultivation of desirable friendships. An excellent lawyer, he never turned aside from the law to meddle with politics; yet he was on good terms with the politicians, and he reached the top of his ambition by appointment to the Attorney-Generalship of the United States, a post which he held for upwards of twelve years.

In training and culture Wirt was of the sound eighteenth-century tradition. He was bred in the classics, English literature, and the common law. When he set up in his profession his library consisted of Blackstone, *Don Quixote,* and *Tristram Shandy.* His literary taste was formed by the later writers of the eighteenth century, by Gray, Hervey, Young, Ossian, Burke, Sterne, rather than by Pope and Dryden. In *The British Spy* he praises Bacon highly and lavishes commendation upon Addison, regretting that the *Spectator* "should be thrown by, and almost entirely forgotten, while the gilded blasphemies of infidels, and the 'noontide trances' of pernicious theorists, are hailed with rapture, and echoed around the world" (*Letter X*). Yet the determining influence in his own writings, it is clear, came from the sentimentalists and from Burke. From the former he caught the note of polite emotion. and from the latter the strain of sonorous eloquence. His well-bred sensibilities were constantly in the service of his pen or tongue, to lend pathos to an affecting bit of description or to transport his hearers by a melting appeal. A look, a gesture, a pose, was nicely calculated to bring sympathetic tears to the eyes of his auditors. To touch the emotions he considered the triumph of art, and to conduct through the emotions to a sound morality, its sole justification.

As a member of the Virginia bar Wirt took pride in the tradition of sober culture that had grown up amongst its distinguished practitioners. The members of that bar were gentlemen as well as lawyers, who would rather go wrong in their legal authorities than in their classical embellishments; they were orators as well, careful of their diction and meticulous in rounding a period. In these excellent qualities Wirt early distinguished himself. He had read more than most, and apposite quotations from the classics came easily to his pen to grace the pellucid flow of his English. One of the signal triumphs of his life was when in an elaborate legal argument before the Supreme Court at Washington, he retorted a passage of the *Aeneid* upon his opponent, to provide a text for a burst of the exuberant rhetoric that so delighted his generation (*The British Spy*, 1855, pp. 88–90). His love of ornate speech seems to us curiously old-fashioned, yet it was the manner of the times, and he gave himself to it with enthusiasm—*vivo gurgite exundans*, as he would have chosen to say. The chief interest of his life was oratory, and how skillful a practitioner he was adjudged by his own generation is revealed in the comment of a contemporary who often admired "the blaze of his reasoning and declamation":

The march of his mind is direct to its object, the evolutions by which he attains it, are so new and beautiful, and apparently necessary to the occasion, that your admiration is kept alive, your fancy delighted, and your judgment convinced, through every stage of the process. . . . There is no weak point in his array, no chink in the whole line of his extended works. Then the sweet melody of voice, the beautiful decorations of fancy, the easy play of a powerful reason, by which all this is accomplished, amaze and delight. His pathos is natural and impressive; there is a pastoral simplicity and tenderness in his pictures of distress, when he describes female innocence, helplessness, and beauty, which the husband on whom she smiled should have guarded from even the winds of heaven which might visit it too roughly, "shivering at midnight on the winter banks of the Ohio, and mingling her tears with the torrent, which froze as they fell;" it is not a theatrical trick, to move a fleeting pity, but a deep and impressive appeal to the dignified charities of our nature. (*Ibid.*, pp. 84–85.)

Wirt's literary reputation rests chiefly upon *The British Spy* and *Sketches of the Life and Character of Patrick Henry*, both of which may be characterized in the admirable phrase above quoted, as studies in "the dignified charities of our nature." The former was done hastily at the age of thirty, the latter was toiled over for years and appeared when he was forty-five. They were received with vast approval and set him quite in the front rank of American literary fame. Yet the contemporary popularity of *The British Spy* is inexplicable to us today. It is astonishing that so slight a thing should have achieved so great a reputation, and it suggests the depths of literary poverty in which the Virginia of 1803 was sunk. The work is a miscellany—hodgepodge perhaps is a juster term— of character sketches, geology, description, rhapsody, moralizing, with the faintest suggestion of criticism. The sketch which achieved the greatest celebrity, the description of the blind preacher (*Letter VII*, pp. 195–202), is elaborately artificial and sentimental, done from Sterne. The sketches of contemporary politicians, and in particular that of Jefferson, contributed much to current appeal, and the casual criticism aroused a mild remonstrance. There is a certain grace of style after the late eighteenth-century manner, abundant sentiment and little wit. Perhaps the happiest touch is the title; only a British spy could discover material for criticism in the excellent life and ideal institutions of Virginia, or insinuate that the commonwealth was lacking in public spirit— that its roads were as bad as its schools, and that the "one object throughout the state" was "to grow rich." But it was a very moral spy who was troubled that "the noxious weed of infidelity had struck a deep, a fatal root, and spread its pestilential branches far around"; and who lamented that "our eccentric and fanciful countryman, Godwin, had contributed not a little to water and cherish this pernicious exotic" (*Letter VII*, p. 203).

The demands made upon the dignified charities of our nature Wirt found more insistent when he came to write the life of Patrick Henry. He was troubled by his materials, as well as by the want of them. He complains repeatedly in his letters of the difficulties of the task. There were blemishes in the character of his god, spots that marred his divinity; yet how to clean them away and not spoil the natural appearance was a problem. He could not tell Virginians that Patrick Henry in his old age was grasping and vain, that he changed his politics as he grew rich. The idea was too repugnant to his own good nature, and to the taste of the times. The age was sentimental and romantic even in its eulogy. It took seriously the motto, *de mortuis nil nisi bonum;* it was patriotically engaged in making a myth out of the figures and events of the Revolution; and sober truth is not to be expected from the stately biographies that emerged from this period of excessive patriotism. The writers were too much in awe of their subjects, too much concerned to present them in full dress with wig and cloak and sword, and see to it that they acted a proper part. It was in this attitude that Wirt first approached his theme, but failing to achieve the desired result, he turned the work into eulogy of Henry's oratory. This was the most congenial of tasks to one so deeply interested in the art of the orator. The fragmentary records that had come down were a challenge to his inventiveness, and he set himself to recreate the lost speeches, from scanty notes. How admirably he succeeded is shown in the celebrated "give me liberty, or give me death" speech, that became at once an American classic. One could forgive him much for such a masterpiece.

The leaders of that older Virginia society were lawyers rather than planters, and Wirt's excursions into the field of *belles lettres* were only pleasant outings from the court-room. His intellectual interests were narrow. Though bred in an atmosphere of politics, he cared nothing for political theory, was wholly unread in the political classics, and untouched by the flood of social speculation that came with the French Revolution. He drifted politically with the stream of his generation, taking color from the changing waters. Brought up a Jeffersonian Republican, he remained curiously ignorant of the economic and political philosophy of agrarianism. He was little given to abstract speculation on the rights of man, and was never partisan to a cause. He was a genial embodiment of those colorless times when the enthusiasms of eighteenth-century liberalism were dead and the romanticisms of nineteenth-century exploitation were not yet risen, known in the history books as the era of good feeling. Fundamentally conservative and somewhat conventional, he would not look with approval upon the new men and new ways that came in with the western democracy. Upon the accession of Jackson he went over to the Whig party. He supported Clay, yet for some reason, perhaps a harmless vanity, he accepted a nomination for the presidency by the Anti-Masons in 1832 and went down before the hosts of the Jacksonians. Two years later his blameless life was brought to a close. A kindly and honorable gentleman of old-fashioned tastes, with a culture founded in Blackstone, embellished by Addison and Sterne, and given a classic dignity by Livy, he filled the measure of the excellencies as they were understood in the Old Dominion in the days before romance had created the plantation tradition.

III

NATHANIEL BEVERLEY TUCKER
A Virginia Fire Eater

In striking contrast to the amiable Attorney-General was another Virginia lawyer and judge who ventured into literature and whose one important novel created a mighty stir in its day. Beverley Tucker was twelve years younger than Wirt. Half brother of John Randolph of Roanoke, for some years on the bench in Missouri, and long professor of law at William and Mary College, he was a well-known figure in the Old Dominion, and his vigorous speech was much applauded at conventions where southern gentlemen met to talk over their grievances. In him were richly embodied all the picturesque parochialisms that plantation life encouraged. He was so completely and exclusively Virginian as to deserve the epithet " Virginianissimus." He never traveled, never compared diverse civilizations, never questioned the excellence of that in which he had been bred. His loyalty to his native commonwealth was a consuming jealousy for its honor, and he tucked the horizons of Virginia about him like a Hudson's Bay blanket and defied the cold winds of the North. Beyond Mason and Dixon's line lay a foreign country, and he judged all foreign countries by their size and color on his wall map. He was the arch-romantic of his generation and his *Partisan Leader* is the repository of the curious political and economic romanticisms of the ardent southern mind.

Over his after-dinner bottle of Madeira, Beverley Tucker may well have been the raciest and most delightful of companions. Like Samuel Johnson, he found his pleasure in a mind well stocked with robust prejudices and a wit to phrase them tellingly. He never spared his epithets nor hesitated to damn an opponent.

Like Fisher Ames, he coddled an aggravated case of political spleen and luxuriated in a picturesque pessimism. The clouds hung low over his mind, and the future of Virginia appeared as black to him as the future of Massachusetts appeared desperate to the Boston Federalist. His pessimism no doubt was a solace to his old age and provided a sauce for his dinner. Temperamently he was curiously like the New England Jeremiah. He followed Calhoun with the unreasoning and passionate conviction with which Fisher Ames followed Hamilton. He foresaw a future laid waste by the ravenings of democracy, and like Ames he took pleasure in sketching the dark picture. It would be no fault of his if the easy-going planters remained indifferent to the political monster that in the guise of Jacksonian democracy had made his den at Washington and was preparing to devour the liberties of sovereign commonwealths. He would make haste, while the shadows of those liberties remained, to arouse Virginia to its peril before the jaws closed upon it.

It was to this end that he wrote *The Partisan Leader*, an obvious attempt to dramatize the political philosophy of Calhoun and breathe into it a war psychology. Its single purpose was to popularize the doctrine of secession and encourage Virginia to act upon it. The book was printed at Washington by the notorious Duff Green, who had quitted Jackson and gone over to Calhoun, and appeared under the pen name of Edward William Sidney. Written in the last years of Jackson's second term, it prophesied Van Buren's succession and his setting up a dictatorship. The beginning of the action is projected thirteen years into the future. Van Buren is assumed to be in his third term and is seeking election a fourth time. He is in secure and insolent possession of "the presidential throne." He has surrounded himself with a horde of democratic sycophants; his political machine is well oiled and the army and navy are at his bidding. Virginia has been split asunder by factions. Mercenaries in Van Buren's pay occupy the public stations, and supported by Federal bayonets they carry things with a high hand. The lower South, under the leadership of South Carolina, has already seceded, and freed from the exploitation of northern tariffs is economically rejuvenated. The Virginia patriots are biding their time, working under cover and making detailed plans to carry the commonwealth over to the new Confederacy when the hour shall strike. The hand of fate is no other than economic pressure. The free South has provided an eloquent object lesson to Virginia planters. By reason of a trade treaty with England, by the terms of which each country exports to the other its natural wares unvexed by artificial restrictions—an industrial economy and an agricultural mutually benefiting by the exchange —the cotton and tobacco growers to the south of Virginia are enjoying a prosperity unshared by the exploited planters of the Old Dominion. When economic depression shall have finally opened the eyes of Virginians to the folly of a federal union that sacrifices southern interests to fatten northern manufacturers, the commonwealth must drop into the lap of the Confederacy like a ripe persimmon. In the meantime a mysterious Mr. B.—presumably Calhoun—moves adroitly behind the scenes, shaping matters for the great event—a super-statesman, a man of godlike sagacity and divine benevolence, a heroic embodiment of all the magnanimous southern virtues, compared with whom Webster and Clay are common political mercenaries and Jackson a paltry charlatan.

It is a romantically extravagant book, quite the absurdest in the library of the old South. It possesses no savor of humor or pleasantry of satire. Tucker was too deadly in earnest to play with his theme. He had so long and bitterly brooded over the supposed wrongs of Virginia that he had lost all sense of proportion. He lacks a cool skill in dissection; he has not learned the gentlemanly art of flaying his victim; he defends Virginia with a matchlock instead of a rapier. Gilmore Simms credited him with one of the most finished prose styles of the day, and a very recent critic remarks that "no other American of the time wrote with such classical restraint and pride as Tucker" (*Cambridge History of American Literature*, Vol. I, p. 312). But there is little evidence of such mastery in *The Partisan Leader*. It is the work of an unpracticed writer, with a command of rhetoric to furnish forth a southern stump-speaker, but quite inadequate to the needs of a competent novelist. Compared with Simms or Kennedy he is a mere bungler. His characters are as wooden as Cooper's females, and his plot is grossly distorted by his polemics. The drama sags under the weight of the sacred cause. There is inadvertent comedy in the picture of Van Buren as the man on horseback—the sleek, well-groomed politician of history rises somewhat inadequately to the rôle. In comparison with Kennedy's *Quodlibet* his attack upon Jackson is only caricature. Beverley Tucker was a patriotic

Virginian whose craftsmanship proved inadequate to the serious business in hand.

The backgrounds of his thought are clearly Jeffersonian. His prejudices run strongly for eighteenth-century *laissez faire*. He is a confirmed agrarian and his hatred of industrialism amounts to an obsession. He will have nothing to do with protective tariffs that lay a tax upon the planter to aid the manufacturer. In his advocacy of political decentralization he is a disciple of Calhoun, but more pessimistic than his master. Southern interests can be adequately protected, he is convinced, only by a jealous insistence on the sovereign powers of Virginia, and so long as Virginia remains within the centralizing federal Union those sovereign powers will suffer a subtle diminution. The simple-minded and magnanimous southern planter was no match in the political game with unscrupulous and ambitious Northerners. But in certain significant aspects of his political philosophy, Beverley Tucker broke with the Jeffersonian tradition. Two current developments had quite destroyed his faith in the democracy of Jefferson. The rise of Jacksonianism had seated the rabble in power, and the spread of Abolitionism was threatening to infect that triumphant rabble with its poison. The very life of Virginia was at the mercy of a hostile democracy, and to protect themselves and their slaves from the encroachments of a democratized federal government seemed to him the urgent business of the southern planters. Unless a move were made speedily it would be too late, for the power of the northern democracy was fast outstripping the confederate power of the South.

Tucker's intense prejudices color every judgment, and in consequence his misunderstanding of the North was colossal. He imagined a profit-mongering clown whom he dubbed Yankee, and solemnly assured himself that it was an authentic likeness. The Abolitionist was a Yankee with an added Puritan malignancy. In his defense of slavery Tucker has corrected the sentimental mistake of Jefferson in assuming the extinction of slavery to be desirable, but he professes an equally humanitarian spirit. His benevolence toward the negro is so warmly generous that one is ready to weep at the sad fate of the faithful slave who is in danger of being turned out into the cold world by the wicked Abolitionists. The loyal attachment between master and servant, he argues, is too finely generous to be understood by the mercenary North. The Yankees "have not the qualities which would enable them to comprehend the negro character. Their calculating selfishness can never understand his disinterested devotion. Their artificial benevolence is no interpreter of the unsophisticated heart. . . . They know no more of the feelings of our slaves, than their fathers could comprehend of the loyalty of the gallant cavaliers from whom we spring; and for the same reason. The generous and self-renouncing must ever be a riddle to the selfish" (p. 205, edition of 1861). Hence it is the clear duty of the magnanimous planter to keep his generous and self-renouncing slaves out of the clutches of the selfish Abolitionists.

Something of the ardency of Beverley Tucker's convictions is revealed in certain fragments of his letters to Gilmore Simms, to whom he poured out his heart in uncensored words, and whose magazine, *The Southern Quarterly Review*, he made use of to further the cause. In those letters he writes himself down a frank and whole-hearted Tory. There is an inveterate and ingrained aristocracy of temperament that will not mince words when it comes to dealing with democracy. In his comment on the growing democratic spirit he is virulent. He has lost all hope for Virginia in the year of grace 1851. "She is sunk in the slough of democracy, which has no sense of honor, no foresight, and is never valiant but against its own instruments" (W. P. Trent, *William Gilmore Simms*, p. 186). Georgia is in an even worse way. His spleen at the commonwealth of Stephens and Toombs—"filled as that State is with Yankee traders"—spits out venom: "She has been bought, and her price is in the pockets of those she trusted." He quotes sardonically the comment of a Georgia senator: "The State of Georgia is a damned rascal. I bought and sold her, and will buy her and sell her again when I please" (*ibid.*, p. 182). His only hope is in South Carolina, and he pleads with Simms for decisive action. Calhoun's kingdom is singularly blessed, for no base democracy there sullies the purity of manly councils. As early as 1820 Tucker had come to realize that the Union was a curse to the South. "I vowed then, and I have repeated the vow, *de die in diem*, that I will never give rest to my eyes nor slumber to my eyelids until it is shattered into fragments. . . . Time was when I might have been less desperate, because I could have sought refuge under some emperor or king. But all such refuges are broken up, and there is now no escape from the many-headed despotism of numbers, but by a strong and bold stand on the banks of the Potomac. . . . If we will not *have* slaves, we must *be* slaves." He then makes his great appeal:

And what are our democracies but mobs? South Carolina alone can act, because she is the only State in which the gentleman retains his place and influence, and in which the statesman has not been degraded from his post. You are fast coming to that hopeless and irreclaimable condition; and then all hope of action is gone. Work now. . . . The twilight is already upon you, and hence I fear you will not act even *now*. And if not now—never, never, never! (*Ibid.*, p. 187.)

It was not granted to Beverley Tucker to know what harvests were to be gathered from his sowings. He did not live to see the fields of his beloved commonwealth drenched in the blood that he had done more than his share to let. In that bitter struggle it is certain that he would have borne his part valiantly. He had sown to the wind, and he would have welcomed the whirlwind. But the outcome must have broken his proud heart, and it is well that he was not spared to see his hopes turn to ashes in his mouth.

CHAPTER V
ADVENTURES IN ROMANCE

I

WILLIAM ALEXANDER CARUTHERS

A Virginia Liberal

In the early thirties came the transition in Virginia from the essay-sketch that had prevailed since the appearance of *The British Spy*, to the full blown romance of love and adventure. The older type had been a blend of nature description, social observation, character sketches, with somewhat injudicious portions of sentiment and moralizing, and with frequent resort to the old letter-form of fiction that lingered out a surprising old age. Not only is the transition revealed in the work of John P. Kennedy, whose *Swallow Barn*, written in 1832, was followed in 1835 by *Horseshoe Robinson*, but quite as strikingly in the work of Dr. William Alexander Caruthers, whose *Kentuckian in New York, or, the Adventures of Three Southerns*, published in 1834, was followed at once by *The Cavaliers of Virginia*, 1834–35.

Dr. Caruthers was a genial and cultivated Virginian from the Piedmont region, with a ready wit and a clever pen, who had pretty well rid himself of the intense and narrow parochialisms that restricted the sympathies of Beverley Tucker. He was a Virginia liberal of the older school, before the renaissance of the slave cause transferred southern leadership to the South Carolina group, and he shared none of Tucker's partisanship for Calhoun. He had traveled widely both south and north, and had discovered that human nature was much the same on both sides of Mason and Dixon's line. This experience qualified him to become a shrewd and kindly interpreter of both sections of the country, and his *Kentuckian in New York* was an excellent contribution to the cause of intersectional good-will. He sends two young South Carolinians just out of college on a trip north, who fall in with a Kentuckian on the way, and together they enjoy life in New York City, lose their hearts and meet with divers romantic and amusing adventures. A fourth character, a young Virginian, he sends to South Carolina,

41

likewise to lose his heart and encounter adventures; and the copious letters that travel between them are filled with intelligent comment on unfamiliar ways. The writers are generous-minded young liberals with keen eyes, and their observations still make excellent reading after nearly a hundred years.

The South Carolinian who falls romantically in love with a New York girl is far from a Calhoun Fire Eater. He can see good even in the Yankee, whom he defends against the common southern prejudice by arguing that Yankee chicanery has resulted from a niggardly environment and the competition that comes with over-population, a competition that Virginia has been spared by the draining off of her population west; and as for the Yankee "canting and sniveling," "tell me," he remarks, "if you have not, in the very bosom of your great valley, as genuine Presbyterians and Round-heads as ever graced the Rump Parliament, or sung a psalm on horseback? And to give the devil his due, these same Presbyterians are no bad citizens of a popular government" (Vol. I, p. 72). Virginia has judged the North out of her prejudices rather than knowledge, and the advice Caruthers gives his Virginia neighbors, as an antidote to the suspicions of Beverley Tucker, is to travel beyond the boundaries of the Old Dominion.

Every southern should visit New-York. It would allay provincial prejudices, and calm his excitement against his northern countrymen. The people here are warm-hearted, generous, and enthusiastic, in a degree scarcely inferior to our own southerns. . . . Many of these Yorkers are above local prejudices, and truly consider this as the commercial metrop-olis of the Union, and all the people of the land as their customers, friends, patrons, and countrymen. Nor is trade the only thing that flourishes. The arts of polished and refined life, refined literature, and the profounder studies of the schoolmen, all have here their distinguished votaries,—I say distinguished, with reference to the standard of science in our country. (Vol. I, p. 181.)

The material prosperity of the North contrasts painfully in his mind with the condition of his native Carolina, and there is a note of apprehension in his comment:

The more I see of these northern states, the more I am convinced that some great revolution awaits our own cherished communities. Revolu-tions, whether sudden or gradual, are fearful things; we learn to feel at-tachments to those things which they tear up, as a poor cripple feels at-tached to the mortified limb, that must be amputated to save his life. A line of demarkation in such a case is distinctly drawn between the dis-eased and the healthy flesh. Such a line is now drawing between the

slave and free states, I fear. God send that the disease may be cured
without amputation, and before mortification takes place. I know that
this latter is your own belief. What think you now, since you have seen
the greater extent of the disease? (Vol. I, p. 165.)

The question is addressed to another young man on his travels,
a young Virginian who has gone south, and who is even more
troubled at what he finds. He cannot bring himself to think well
of the sacred institution as he sees it in South Carolina. There it
is laid bare in all its naked exploitation. The humaner relations
between the races that he has known in Virginia have been destroyed by the absentee system with its drivers and overseers—
"to these animals," he says, "I have always had an utter aversion."
The evils of the large-scale system have carried farther; slavery in
the Carolinas has destroyed the middle class of yeomen, unduly
exalted the aristocracy and utterly debased the poor white. The
single spot he heartily approves in the two commonwealths is
Salem, a Moravian settlement where no slavery exists, where all
work, and where education is thought so well of that the daughters
of the first southern families go there for their schooling. In Salem
he found an answer to the southern problem far more competent
than Nullification.

Here, then, is a triumphant answer—an answer in deeds, instead of
words—in the happiness, and the substantial wealth of these simple and
primitive Moravians. Here . . . is an industrious, intelligent, and
healthy community, in the very heart of all the misery I have described.
Let us then improve by the lesson, seek out the sources of their prosperity,
find the point where their plans diverge from ours, and, my word for it
. . . we become a great, a flourishing, and a happy people. (Vol. I, p. 80.)

To the problem of slavery he returns constantly, and his views
may perhaps be sufficiently understood from the following passages:

The poor of a slave-country are the most miserable and the most
wretched of all the human family. The grades of society in this state are
even farther apart than in Virginia. Here, there is one immense chasm
from the rich to the abject poor. In the valley of Virginia, or in the
country where you are, there are regular gradations. The very happiest,
most useful, and most industrious class of a well-regulated community, is
here wanting. Their place is filled up by negroes; in consequence of which,
your aristocrats are more aristocratic, and your poor still poorer. The
slaves create an immeasurable distance between these two classes, which
can never be brought together until this separating cause be removed.
You know I am no *abolitionist*, in the incendiary meaning of the term;

yet I cannot deny from you and myself, that they are an incubus upon our prosperity. This we would boldly deny, if a Yankee uttered it in our hearing; but to ourselves, we must e'en confess it. If I am, therefore, an abolitionist, it is not for conscience-sake, but from policy and patriotism. (Vol. I, pp. 76–77.)

With us [in Virginia] slavery is tolerable, and has something soothing about it to the heart of the philanthropist; the slaves are more in the condition of tenants to their landlords—they are viewed as rational creatures, and with more kindly feelings. . . . *Here* slavery is intolerable; a single individual owning a hundred or more, and often not knowing them when he sees them. . . . The slaves here are plantation live-stock; not domestic and attached family servants, who have served around the person of the master from the childhood of both. . . . Here, besides your white overseers, you have your black *drivers;*—an odious animal, almost peculiar to the far south. It is horrible to see one slave following another at his work, with a cow-skin dangling at his arm, and occasionally tying him up and flogging him when he does not get through his two tasks a day. . . . I do not observe much difference between the North and South Carolinians, except in the case of those who inhabit the most southern portions of the latter state. There your rich are more princely and aristocratic, and your poor more wretched and degraded; but to tell you the plain truth, many of your little slaveholders are miserably poor and ignorant; and what must be the condition of that negro who is a slave to one of these miserable wretches? (Vol. II, pp. 115–119.)

To the solution of the difficult problem Caruthers offers no easy plan. He cannot go with the northern "enthusiasts" who propose immediate emancipation. They do not comprehend the complexity of the problem. "We cannot set slaves free among us. Such a course would dissolve the social compact. It would set at defiance all laws for the protection of life, liberty, and property, either among them or the whites." He foresaw clearly what happened during the unhappy days of reconstruction. "Would it be any reparation of an hereditary wrong, to plunge the subjects of that wrong, with ourselves, into irretrievable ruin, to attain nominal justice?" The free negroes would constitute a menace more serious than the northern city mobs, which latter Caruthers had no liking for. "These city mobocracies, composed as they are, principally of wild Irish, are terrible things"; how much worse would be a negro mobocracy? A confirmed agrarian, he finds his chief hope in a vigorous yeomanry, and until the South shall develop that, matters must go ill with it. In the midst of the Carolina system his thoughts return fondly to his native state. He is under no illusion in regard to the tide-water region of Virginia. It has lived a generous life, but spendthrift and wasteful, and has come to evil days. But in the West, beyond the mountains, a newer and more vigorous age is rising that "will sweep away the melancholy vestiges of a former and more chivalrous and generous age."

Poor, exhausted eastern Virginia! she is in her dotage. Her impassable roads protect her alike from the pity and contempt of foreign travellers; but with all her weakness, with all the imbecilities of premature age upon her, I love her still. (Vol. II, p. 194.)

Of this more vigorous age the prototype is the title-hero of the volume, the stalwart Kentuckian whose native intelligence and racy speech delight the Carolinian. This free son of the untamed West is portrayed with bold strokes, and if his talk leans somewhat heavily on the current convention of frontier humor, if Montgomery Damon in his picturesque exaggerations suggests Davy Crockett, the result is none the less salty. Caruthers does not descend to caricature, but writes with gusto, and the Kentuckian's single letter is a little masterpiece in the vein of the free frontier humor that was competing with the cavalier romantic for popular approval. His whimsicalities, Caruthers tells us, he hopes will encourage "a smile of good-humor" so that this maiden product of the author's pen may find its way into the good graces of the reader—a course reckoned "the more necessary by a southern aspirant, as there is evidently a current in American literature, the fountainhead of which lies north of the Potomac, and in which a southern is compelled to navigate up the stream if he jumps in too far south" (Vol. II, p. 218.)

The Cavaliers of Virginia, or the Recluse of Jamestown, announced in the postscript to the *Kentuckian in New York*, and published soon afterwards, is a full-fledged historical romance, with Bacon's Rebellion for a background and a somewhat melodramatic figure of a recluse warrior for its romantic hero. There is brisk action, dramatic Indian fights, much ruffling of young cavaliers, and a fine aristocratic swagger, but Caruthers' sympathies seem to incline to the more democratic elements and in the end his rebellious hero proves himself a match for the brisk young blades. There is excellent reading in it, as there is in his last work, *The Knights of the Horse-Shoe; a Traditionary Tale of the Cocked Hat Gentry in the Old Dominion*, published in 1845, and reissued as late as 1909; a genial story of Governor Spotswood's time. Caruthers deserved a better fate than fell to his lot. In spite of his excellent work surprisingly little is known about him; even the spelling of his name and the date of his death are matters about which there is disagreement. From a slight sketch contributed to *The Knicker-bocker Magazine* for July, 1838, *Climbing the Natural Bridge*, it is known that he was a student at Washington College, now Washington and Lee, at Lexington, Virginia, in the year 1818, and the signature affixed carries only one "r." He seems to have removed later to Savannah, Georgia, an enthusiastic description of which he gives in the *Kentuckian in New York*. No doubt he there practiced medicine and died in his prime, perhaps in the year 1846. Virginia historians have inconsiderately neglected a cultivated and open-minded writer who embodied the finer spirit of the Old Dominion and whose stories have contributed their portion to the plantation tradition.

II

JOHN PENDLETON KENNEDY
A Southern Whig

A far more prosperous course was run by John P. Kennedy, whose sympathies drew him north rather than south, and who early learned that it is better to serve a rising than a decaying order. Very like Caruthers in temperament and gifts, a liberal in all his sympathies, he found the ties that bound him to the Old Dominion more fragile, and the drift of circumstance carrying him with the stronger current. It was a kindly fate that took him in charge, bringing him abundant prosperity and contemporary fame.

One of the most attractive figures of his generation was this son of a Maryland father and a Virginia mother. A gentleman of much personal distinction, high-minded and of wide culture, endowed with a pleasant wit, easy manners and generous nature, he is an agreeable representative of the *ante bellum* Southerns, an American Victorian of the Cobden-Bright school, standing midway between the northern radical and the southern Fire Eater. Like Henry Clay, he was a Whig engrafted on a Jeffersonian root. Born and educated in Baltimore, he was a son of the borderland, with strong ties of kinship and love that drew him to the Old Dominion, and even stronger ties of intellectual, social and financial interests that drew him towards Philadelphia and New York,

Saratoga and Newport. As a young man he found his inspiration in the life of William Wirt, whose biography he afterwards wrote. Like Wirt, he dreamed of combining law and letters and adopting the life of a southern gentleman; but he discovered little that was congenial in the exactions of the law, and in spite of considerable success as attorney for certain Baltimore interests, he largely abandoned the profession. He loved his Chaucer and Shakespeare more than his Coke and Blackstone: he was more interested in Dickens and Thackeray and Carlyle and Irving and Scott than in John Marshall's decisions, and he followed the more congenial path. He tried his hand likewise at politics. He was a member of Congress for six years, was Secretary of the Navy during the last months of President Fillmore's administration, and was of service to the Whig party as spokesman on dignified occasions. But he was never a practical politician, and the rough and tumble of political life he found utterly distasteful. As he grew older he unconsciously drew further away from his southern antecedents. In his later years there was little to distinguish him from Irving and Robert C. Winthrop and other northern friends. He had left the world of Beverley Tucker far behind him. He had severed all ties with Virginia and South Carolina, and during the Civil War he was a militant Unionist, though it cost him much grief and the loss of old friendships.

Kennedy's life ran an usually placid and prosperous course, greatly unlike that of Gilmore Simms. His father was a Scotch-Irish merchant of Baltimore who married Nancy Pendleton, daughter of an excellent Virginia family with many honorable connections. His early years were not unlike Irving's—a little Latin and Greek and much outdoor life, with a desultory education got from vagrant books. The course of study at the local college afforded far less intellectual stimulus than *Tristram Shandy*, over which he pored of evenings, dissecting the prose style to discover the secret of its charm, and filling his notebooks with elaborately colloquial sentences, highly seasoned with dashes and exclamation points. Graduating at eighteen, he enlisted in a Baltimore regiment to fight the British, who were preparing their raid on Washington. He went through the campaign as a summer lark, emerging unscathed from the single skirmish. The field was lost, but whether the honor of the crack Fifth was left on the battle ground may be judged from Kennedy's humorous

comment. "Soon we had the famous 'trial of souls'—the battle
of Bladensburg. The drafted militia ran away at the first fire, and
the Fifth Regiment was driven off the field with the bayonet. We
made a fine scamper of it. I lost my musket in the mêlée while
bearing off a comrade" (Tuckerman, *Life of Kennedy*, p. 79).

Throughout his twenties Kennedy was a studious dilettante in
letters and politics and law. He married but lost his wife and son
within the year; with his friend Peter Hoffman Cruse he published
a series of Baltimore sketches in two volumes entitled *The Red
Book;* and at the age of thirty-four married again. His second
wife was the daughter of Edward Gray, a wealthy Baltimore
cotton-spinner who at the age of eighteen had emigrated from
northern Ireland to Philadelphia, became a bank clerk and a
Federalist simultaneously, adopted Washington and Hamilton—
whom he occasionally met in a professional way—as his particular
heroes, prospered greatly, purchased the Ellicott Mills a few miles
out of Baltimore, and set up a half feudal estate vastly attractive
to discriminating visitors like Irving.

Kennedy's marriage to Elizabeth Gray in 1829 seems to have
been the turning-point of his life. Before this he had been a
disinterested liberal in his views, concerning himself in a political
way with such humanitarian issues as the repeal of the brutal
debtor laws. He had never been an avowed Jeffersonian like
William Wirt and many of his Virginia connections, but the Jeffersonian idealism must have appealed to the generous sympathies
of the young man. Immediately upon being taken into the Gray
family he adopted its ample scale of living, its genial hospitality,
its social and political philosophy. The influence of the masterful
Edward Gray was thenceforth a dominant creative factor in
Kennedy's life, and he followed faithfully in the footsteps of his
father-in-law. The profits of the Ellicott Mills had been greatly
increased by the tariff act of 1824. Naturally Edward Gray was
an ardent protectionist, and Kennedy frankly espoused the same
policy. He accepted Henry Clay as his political leader, was sent
to Congress on a protectionist platform, lectured before Workingmen's Institutes on the advantages of industrial development, and
gained a very considerable reputation as an expounder of the
American Plan. After the war he became a Republican, voted
for Grant, and adopted extreme nationalist views. That the
family income was dependent on tariff favors is a detail which

only a more realistic generation would suggest in explanation of his political course; the fact remains, nevertheless, that the youthful disciple of William Wirt adopted the new philosophy of prosperity, became president of the board of directors of the Baltimore and Ohio Railway, invested in West Virginia coal lands, and was by way of becoming a captain of industry. The break with his southern antecedents was complete and final; he went with his native city in preferring the industrial to the plantation economy.

Baltimore in Kennedy's day was a thriving port with a growing trade to the West Indies and Europe. It had long been a convenient market for the tobacco of Virginia, and with the development of the clipper service its over-sea commerce expanded greatly. Unlike Charleston, the mercantile interests predominated over the planter. Middle-class ideals, to be sure, were still tempered by the dignified decorum that lingered on from the eighteenth century. Merchants still emulated the gentry and strove for personal distinction. They professed benevolent ideals and their talk was much of public spirit and the progress of the town. They adopted the romantic faith of their class in the beneficent processes of trade and industry in furthering social well-being, and they endowed Mechanics Institutes and founded public libraries and museums with all the ardor of converts. In this agreeable work of expounding the gospel of progress, Kennedy joined heartily. It satisfied the latent idealism of his nature and recompensed him for the loss of his Virginia heritage. Intellectually he was too honest to pervert the gospel of progress to selfish class interest and seek to hide the perversion behind sonorous platitudes, as his friend Robert C. Winthrop of Boston was guilty of doing. He had too much love for the English language to misuse it even in defense of the family income. He could not contract his mind to the compass of a Whig politician's. His defense of industrialism, in consequence, embodies the spirit of the best English liberalism as that liberalism was interpreted by Victorian Englishmen. He seems to have been honestly convinced that the future well-being of America was dependent upon the development of an industrialism to provide an economic balance between manufactures and agriculture.

Like his friend Irving, Kennedy was a devout romantic, with a love of the old-time picturesque; but as a consistent Whig he would spin and weave his romance out of domestic materials, refusing to import. He was a child of the effervescent days following 1812, when the static eighteenth century was breaking up and an ebullient romanticism was permeating the land. Of this youthful period his thought reveals the clear impress. Washington Irving from long pottering over the old-world picturesque had become English romantic, with an inveterate dislike of all innovation. The vulgar nineteenth century was destroying for him the charm of the eighteenth; he would have had the world remain as it was before the American and French revolutions had despoiled life of picturesque feudal ways. Whereas Kennedy, sharing in a romanticism that was economic and social—that was creating a wonderful America of the future out of the raw materials of life—was content to remain native, at home in the land of his birth. He might turn to the past for the figures and scenes of his stories, but he discovered in the activities of the present materials for romance quite as fascinating. He was wholly Victorian in his genial optimism. He was receptive to new ideas and promising ventures. He listened sympathetically to inventors and scientists and promoters. He was instrumental in securing Congressional aid to erect Morse's telegraph line between Washington and his native city. As Secretary of the Navy he provided for Commodore Perry's expedition to Japan, and the expedition to search for Dr. Kane in the Arctic regions. But unfortunately his economic romanticism gradually undermined his literary romanticism; he outgrew his earlier literary ambitions, and the romances of his later life never got written. In the end the gospel of progress was his undoing.

That the generous comfort in which he lived afforded him leisure, means of travel, contact with distinguished people, goes without saying; but that it was favorable to letters is far from clear. Divided interests consumed his energies and kept him an amateur to the last. His literary development was an evolution from a sketchy and humorous Addisonian, with its echoes of the eighteenth century, to the full Victorian romantic. The foreign elements from an earlier time slowly settled to the bottom of the vat and left the pure wine of romance. But it took time. Like other amateurs he was influenced by current literary successes, and was much given to following the changing fashions. His three best-known books, written between the ages of thirty-six and forty-five, are unlike enough to have been written by different men. *Swallow Barn,*

like the youthful sketches of *The Red Book*, is Irvingesque, and
the Irving influence crops out again in a late book *Quodlibet;*
but *Horseshoe Robinson* is substantial Revolutionary romance,
done in sober narrative with touches of realism; and *Rob of the
Bowl* is light and whimsical cavalier romance, all atmosphere and
small talk, utterly unlike Irving.   It is in this latter book, perhaps,
written in 1838 at the age of forty-two, that Kennedy really found
himself; he seems to move through the scenes more easily and with
greater delight than in any other of his pages.

That the leisurely sketches of *Swallow Barn* belong to the school
of Irving is a fact as obvious as Kennedy's love for the idling
plantation life.   Quite too much, however, has been made of this
imitativeness—it is an imitativeness rather of method than of
theme or style.   If it was not quite a pioneer work in the field of
local description, it was amongst the earliest.   Paulding had
dealt with Dutch colonial life, and Timothy Flint and James Hall
had begun the descriptive literature of the West; but little else
had been done at the time *Swallow Barn* appeared.   Longstreet's
Georgia Scenes came out two years later.   Intrinsically as well as
historically the work is curiously suggestive.   Nowhere else does
the plantation life of the Old Dominion in the days before its decline appear so vividly as in these discursive pages: "the mellow,
bland, and sunny luxuriance of her old-time society—its good fellowship, its hearty and constitutional *companionableness*, the thriftless gaiety of the people, their dogged but amiable invincibility of
opinion, and that overflowing hospitality which knows no ebb."

Like Irving, Kennedy went back to the old home, but that old
home was Virginia and not England; and there he found still
lingering on the great plantations charmingly romantic anachronisms that had disappeared elsewhere—a spontaneous romanticism of temperament that gave color and zest to the daily routine.
The aloofness of plantation life had bred in the Virginia gentry a
piquant individuality, a distinction as of old morocco or calfskin.
Philly Wart, the shrewdly humorous fox-hunting lawyer; old Mr.
Tracy of The Brakes, "turning a little sour with age" and resem-
bling "that waterish, gravelly soil that you see sometimes around
a spring, where nothing grows but sheep-sorrel," who cherishes
a hereditary boundary dispute, pursuing his hypothetical rights
through all the law courts and discovering, when the matter has
been amicably settled by arbitration, that much of the zest has

gone out of his life; the heroine Bel Tracy, a frank wholesome girl
with a dash of Di Vernon in her romantic affectations that lead
her to play at hawking: such figures fit as naturally into the background as the pampered house servants, the horseback riding, the
constant visiting, the abundant dinners. Especially the dinners,
when the neighborhood is invited in. The table spread with
opulent hospitality and careless profusion—the baked ham at
one end and the saddle of roast mutton at the other, with fried
chicken, oysters, crabs, sweet potatoes, jellies, custards—a prodigal feast that only outdoor stomachs could manage, and all by
way of preliminary to the dusty wine-bottles and easy stories
that hold the men long after the ladies have withdrawn. Surely
the romance of Old Virginia, preserved in these light-hearted
discursive pages, is worth remembering by later generations who
have forgotten how to live so genially.

In 1832 when *Swallow Barn* was written, the southern mind was
just at the turn in its attitude towards slavery, and Frank Meriwether, a Virginian Sir Roger de Coverley, bred in the humanitarianism of the older liberals, accepts the institution as a present
evil that is in a way of natural extinction. Slavery in *Swallow
Barn* is kept in the background. There are slaves, of course, on
the plantation, many of them; but they are in the tobacco fields
or the quarters, far from the mansion; and not till near the end of
the book does Kennedy's curiosity induce him to visit the cabins
and draw out Frank Meriwether in talk on slavery. The result is
what one could have foreseen. The plantation master was the
victim of a benevolent romanticism that vaguely looks for a solution to colonization schemes that will return the negro to Africa;
but like other southern gentlemen he is somewhat testy at the suggestion of outside interference. Slavery he regards as an exclusive
southern problem, to be solved by those who understand its complex domestic implications. It would be better for everybody if
Abolition busybodies would mind their own affairs and cease
stirring up feelings where no good can come of it. To prove that
Virginia gentlemen are aware of their responsibility, Meriwether
offers a half humorous suggestion that negro emancipation might
well follow the example of English villeinage, with a slow break-up
of the system, the emancipated negro to remain in a protective
feudal relation to his master. It was an amiable notion to play
with, and it fitted the feudal psychology of the plantation.

In these early sketches Kennedy revealed an easy knack at writing that gave promise of excellent work later. He has lightness, grace, refinement, an eye sensitive to picturesque effects, delight in line and texture and color, an agreeable wit and playful sentiment, a relish for English idiom and the literary colloquial. In *Horseshoe Robinson*, written three years later, he abandoned the essay-sketch and turned to the school of historical romance then in full swing. The story is done in the orthodox manner of the thirties; it is compounded of equal parts gentry and commoners, the former providing respectability and the latter dramatic interest, the whole garnished with a few historical figures. There is quite obvious concern for authentic reality. The title-hero, a shrewd homespun scout, is carefully drawn from life; the background of bushwhackings and forays and onsets, and the numerous company of blackguards and honest folk, are painted in skillfully; and the whole conducts to a dramatic finale in the battle of King's Mountain. It is an excellent tale, quite worth reading today, but scarcely comparable in vividness and brisk action—in picaresque realism which any true war story must embody—with *The Partisan* of Gilmore Simms, written in the same year of 1835. Realism was not Kennedy's forte and after *Horseshoe Robinson* he abandoned the field of the Revolution which offered so rich an opportunity for the robuster genius of the Charleston romancer.

In *Rob of the Bowl* Kennedy opened a promising vein that he never adequately explored—the vein of the cavalier romantic. Temperamentally he was ill fitted to deal with rollicking action or picaresque adventure; he preferred the leisurely, discursive romantic, subdued to gentle raillery or humorous tenderness. One trembles to think what Simms would have made of the materials that Kennedy brought together in this tale of old St. Mary's in the days of Charles II. Here is the raw stuff of a true bloody-bones thriller: a gentlemanly blackguard with the stumps of his legs bound in a huge rocking trencher and moving about with the help of crutches, who is deep in the contraband trade; a swaggering young pirate, a Brother of the Bloody Coast, who falls in love with the daughter of the Collector of the Port and kidnaps her from her father's house; a romantic lover, slender and clerkly, but skillful with the rapier, who turns out to be the son of Rob; a haunted house that covers the smuggling operations of Rob and Captain Cocklescraft; and all this set against a background of partisan struggle between Roundhead and Cavalier, Protestant and Catholic, in the early days of the Maryland settlement.

But in the handling the story is far removed from a bloody-bones tale. The action is deliberately subdued to the humoresque; atmosphere is studiously created; adventure is held in strict subjection to the whimsical; and a mellow old-time flavor is imprisoned in the leisurely pages. Kennedy had an appreciative eye for picturesque characters, and in *Rob of the Bowl* he has gathered a choice group, limned—as he would choose to say—with a partial hand. Garret Weasel, the garrulous pot-valiant innkeeper, and Dorothy his termagant spouse; Captain Jasper Dauntless, the cogging, wheedling swordsman who twists Dame Dorothy about his fingers and inveigles his host into undue commerce with his cups—these to be sure are stock characters, but they are done with excellent vivacity. Their abundant talk is well seasoned, and if the action sometimes drags, the company is good and the drinking is a sufficient end in itself. All the while he is writing Kennedy keeps half an eye on Elizabethan literature to assure himself of the exact turn of phrase. His vocabulary is saturated with the homely old speech, and his characters talk as if they had culled all the simples of English cottage gardens to garnish the staple of their wit. He has a keener delight than Simms in the picturesque archaic. He far surpasses Irving in easy mastery of the old-fashioned colloquial, as indeed he surpasses all our early novelists. He delights in the courtly wit of the Cavalier equally with the humors of Dogberry and Falstaff and Captain Bobadil, and he quite evidently is seeking to cross the sparkle of Congreve with the robustness of the Elizabethans. The result may sometimes appear a bit self-conscious; his phrases too often seem to be on dress parade; but he can plead his precedents in justification. In its fondness for the literary colloquial his prose style almost suggests Thackeray, and it is this suggestion, perhaps, that gave rise to the tradition that Kennedy wrote for the former a certain chapter of *The Virginians*. That he supplied Thackeray with materials for his Virginia backgrounds may be accepted as true, but the indebtedness probably went no further.

Rob of the Bowl is certainly Kennedy's best work, as it is one of the most finished and delightful of our earlier romances. Although it ran to six editions, the latest in 1907, it has scarcely received the recognition its lightness of touch deserves. But instead of opening the vein further he turned away to venture in new fields. *Quodlibet*, written in 1840,[1] is a surprising successor to *Rob*—a satire on Jacksonian democracy, done with a light touch and great good humor. In those acrimonious days when Old Hickory's attack on the Bank so embittered its Whig partisans, Kennedy kept his temper, tipped his shafts with laughter and sent them neatly between the joints of the Democratic armor. Against such amusing satire fustian is helpless. The book is keen, vivacious, sparkling. The supposed follies of Jacksonianism—its deification of the majority vote, its cant of the sovereign people, its hatred of all aristocrats, its demagoguery and bluster and sheer buncombe—are hit off with exuberant raillery. The story professes to be an account of the rise to prosperity of the Borough of Quodlibet, under the beneficent smile of Democratic finance. Mean and insignificant before the coming of Jackson, with the removal of the "Deposites," "like Jeshurun, it waxed fat," with its rows of brick shops built on speculation and its Patriotic Copper-Plate Bank that issued an unlimited supply of beautifully engraved notes as a stimulus to enterprise. To be sure the bank broke and the cashier absconded with his family to Europe, but its untoward end was attributed by all Jacksonian New Lights to the vile machinations of the Whigs. It was certainly Nick Biddle and the Barings, with their hatred of Old Bullion Benton's democratic gold coinage, that were the devil in the pot to spill the people's porridge.

Yet even in its laughter Kennedy's political bias is sharply and narrowly partisan. The satire is a capitalistic counter to the agrarian attack on the rising money power, and it is colored by the chagrin of gentlemen who find themselves displaced by plebeians. Something of the old aristocratic contempt for the plain man functioning as a political animal lingers in its pages, which the bubbling humor does not wholly conceal. In Jackson's onslaught on the Bank, Kennedy discovers only an impudent demagoguery; it is selfish and stupid, turmoiling the country for partisan ends and seeking to cover its petty spite with the mantle of patriotism. The Old Hero cuts a sorry figure in these brisk pages, and Van Buren a

---

[1] The characteristic title is *Quodlibet: Containing some Annals thereof, with an Authentic Account of the Origin and Growth of the Borough and the Sayings and Doings of Sundry Townspeople: Interspersed with Sketches of the Most Remarkable and Distinguished Characters of that Place and its Vicinity. Edited by Solomon Secondthoughts, Schoolmaster, from original MSS. Indited by him, and now made Public at the Request and under the Patronage of the Great New Light Democratic Central Committee of Quodlibet.*

still sorrier one. The satire sparkles amusingly, but it is drawn from the old Federalist vintage and it preserves the flavor of a time when gentlemen frankly resented the rule of the unwashed majority. For that very reason *Quodlibet* is an unusually interesting document. It is the most vivacious criticism of Jacksonianism in our political library, one of our few distinguished political satires, and it deserves a better fate than to gather dust on old shelves.

After *Quodlibet* Kennedy did little else. The last twenty years of his life were largely wasted. His dignified life of William Wirt, published in 1849, seems to have met with approval, for it ran to six editions. Our grandfathers liked stately narrative that portrayed their subjects in full dress; and Kennedy gave them an impeccably respectable work in which all the rugosities of character were ironed out neatly and a fine starchy effect achieved. It is hard to understand how a writer so keen to detect the whimsical should have drawn so lifeless a picture of the genial Attorney-General. Perhaps the memory of Wirt's reputed greatness rested too heavily upon him; or it may have been that a lawyer in old Virginia lived as colorless a life as the narrative suggests; at any rate the novelist who never had failed to breathe life into the characters of his fiction, somehow failed in depicting this excellent gentleman of the old school. During the Civil War Kennedy contributed to the northern cause his *Letters of Mr. Paul Ambrose on the Great Rebellion in the United States*, in which he again showed that he could keep his temper and argue calmly. It was a difficult theme for which he was inadequately equipped. His constitutional argument is not impressive and it makes an ill showing when set over against Alexander H. Stephens' *Constitutional View of the War between the States*. He was a man of letters rather than a lawyer, and if he had eschewed politics and law and stuck to his pen our literature would have been greatly in his debt. Few Americans of his day were so generously gifted; none possessed a lighter touch. He has been somewhat carelessly forgotten even by our literary historians who can plead no excuse for so grave a blunder.

III

EDGAR ALLAN POE
Romantic

It is from this slovenly background of aristocratic Virginia, with its liberalisms and conservatisms running at cross purposes, that the enigmatical figure of Poe emerged to vex the northern critics. In so far as any particular environment determined his highly individual and creative nature, it was the indolent life of the planter gentry, shot through with a pugnacious pride of locality, with a strong dislike of alien ways, with haughtiness, dissipation, wastefulness, chivalry. In his proud, irascible individualism that went out of its way to pick a quarrel, there is something of the spirit of John Randolph of Roanoke, but pied and streaked with unfortunate qualities that to many observers seemed the marks of the mere charlatan. As a southern gentleman he imbibed the common dislike of New England, and this dislike was aggravated by its diverse conception of the functions of art, and by the misfortunes that attended his literary career. An aesthete and a craftsman, the first American writer to be concerned with beauty alone, his ideals ran counter to every major interest of the New England renaissance: the mystical, optimistic element in transcendentalism; the social conscience that would make the world over in accordance with French idealism, and that meddled with its neighbor's affairs in applying its equalitarianism to the negro; the pervasive moralism that would accept no other criteria by which to judge life and letters—these things could not fail to irritate a nature too easily ruffled. The Yankee parochialisms rubbed across his Virginia parochialisms; and when to these was added a Yankee preëmption of the field of literary criticism, when a little clique engaged in the business of mutual admiration puffed New England mediocrities at his expense, the provocation was enough to arouse in a sensitive southern mind an antagonism that rivaled Beverley Tucker's. In his unhappy pilgrimage through life Poe was his own worst enemy, but he took comfort in charging his ill fortune upon the malignancy of others.

Southern though he was in the deep prejudices of a suspicious nature, his aloofness from his own Virginia world was complete. Aside from his art he had no philosophy and no programs and no causes. He got from Virginia what was bad rather than good, and his alienation from the more generous southern ideals did him harm. It was perhaps harder to be an artist in that slack southern society than in New England—harder to be a romantic concerned only with twilight melancholy. It would have been hard enough anywhere in Jacksonian America. His romanticisms were of quite another kind than those his countrymen were pursuing; and the planter sympathized with them no more than did the New York literati, or the western men of letters. In a world given over to bumptious middle-class enthusiasms, there would be scant sympathy for the craftsman and dreamer. There was no unearned increment to be got from investments in "the misty mid-region of Weir," which Poe threw on the market. The technician concerned with the values of long and short syllables would find few congenial spirits in a world of more substantial things; and the purveyors of shoddy tales would not take it kindly if their shortcomings were pointed out and a more competent craftsmanship insisted upon. And so, like Herman Melville, Poe came to shipwreck on the reef of American materialisms. The day of the artist had not dawned in America.

So much only need be said. The problem of Poe, fascinating as it is, lies quite outside the main current of American thought, and it may be left with the psychologist and the belletrist with whom it belongs. It is for abnormal psychology to explain his "neural instability amounting almost to a dissociated or split personality," his irritable pride, his quarrelsomeness, his unhappy persecution complex, his absurd pretentions to a learning he did not possess, his deliberate fabrications about his life and methods of work, his oscillations between abstinence and dissipation, between the morbidly grotesque and the lucidly rational, his haunting fear of insanity that drove him to demonstrate his sanity by pursuing complex problems of ratiocination. Such problems are personal to Poe and do not concern us here. And it is for the belletrist to evaluate his theory and practice of art: his debt to Coleridge and Schlegel; the influence of the contemporary magazine on his conception of the length of a work of the imagination; the value of his theory of the tyrannizing unity of mood in the poem and short story; the provocation to the craftsman of the pretentiousness of contemporary American literature, joined to a flabby and crude technique; the grossness of the popular taste and the validity of his critical judgments. Whatever may be the final verdict it is clear that as an aesthete and a craftsman he made a stir in the world that has not lessened in the years since his death, but has steadily widened. Others of greater repute in his day have fared less prosperously in later reputation. He was the first of our artists and the first of our critics; and the surprising thing is that such a man should have made his appearance in an America given over to hostile ideals. He suffered much from his aloofness, but he gained much also. In the midst of gross and tawdry romanticisms he refused to be swallowed up, but went his own way, a rebel in the cause of beauty, discovering in consequence a finer romanticism than was before known in America.

PART TWO: THE RENAISSANCE OF SLAVERY

CHAPTER I

SOUTHERN IMPERIALISM

I

By the year 1824 a change was becoming evident in the South that was to affect profoundly the course of southern thought in regard to her peculiar institution. The passing of the long Virginia hegemony was a sign that southern opinion was undergoing a revolutionary overturn, and that leadership henceforth would rest with men of a different philosophy. The humanitarian spirit that marked the thought of the preceding generation was dying out, to be replaced by a frank recognition of local economic interests. Expectation that slavery was on the way to natural extinction was yielding to the conviction that the system was too profitable to the South to permit its extinction, and this in turn bred an imperious desire to spread it westward to the Pacific. With this significant shift from apology to imperialism, it became clear to ardent pro-slavery men that lukewarm Virginians of the old tradition were not the spokesmen to entrust with the fortunes of the South, and leadership passed to the South Carolina school. In that momentous shift much was implied. It was more than a shift from Jefferson to Calhoun, from humanitarian idealism to economic realism. It marked the complete ascendancy of a small minority of gentleman planters over the inarticulate mass of southern yeomanry, and the assertion of the aristocratic ideal as the goal of southern society. It denied the principle of democracy as that principle was understood in the North and West, and it rejected the new humanitarian spirit of western civilization. It abandoned the Jeffersonian equalitarianism that was so deeply rooted in the southern mind from Kentucky to Georgia; it cast aside the agrarianism of John Taylor and the older Virginians; and it set up in place of these congenial conceptions the alien ideal of a Greek democracy. More momentous still, it threw down the gauntlet to the ideals of the middle class, then in the first flush of a triumphant career, and in the armed clash that eventually resulted, it was destroyed by that class.

The intellectual capital of southern imperialism was Charleston, but its numerical strength lay in the Black Belt, with South Carolina to the east and Texas to the west, a compact territory the heart of which was Georgia, Alabama, Mississippi and Louisiana. In this new South that was rapidly passing through its frontier development, the patriarchal system of Virginia gave way to a system of negro exploitation, more naked as it passed further westward. It was here that the proportion of slaves to whites was greatest; it was here that slave labor was most profitable; and it was here in consequence that the slave economy was most militant. The Black Belt became the native habitat of the southern Fire Eater. In the late twenties and early thirties South Carolina provided the outstanding leaders of the new school; but the philosophy of imperialism spread rapidly and western men came more and more to the front. George McDuffie and Bob Toombs, perhaps the boldest of the loquacious tribe of Fire Eaters, came from Georgia; Alexander H. Stephens was bred in the same turbulent state; L. Q. C. Lamar and Jefferson Davis were from Mississippi. For the most part self-made, products of a frontier environment, these western extremists had got from Jefferson little more than an assertive individualism that easily espoused the states-rights philosophy and prompted them to defend their immediate interests. It was this vigorous group that largely created the new southern psychology and prodded the southern mind along the path marked out for it to travel. Democratic in their attitude towards the white voter, middle class in their love of exploitation, they retained little of the spirit of the Virginia school.

The expansion of the South to the Gulf region came a generation later than the settlement of the Ohio valley. The Creek Indians who clung tenaciously to the rich lands of Mississippi were long an obstacle to the white advance, and the settlers filtered in slowly. Moreover the slave economy was ill fitted to the business of pioneering. It was difficult to transport negroes and establish great plantations in a wilderness; there was too little security in a region that offered every temptation to the slave to run away. The plantation system could prosper only after a considerable degree of development had been effected and sufficient negroes provided. On the other hand, the rich soil, virgin and productive, offered every inducement for large-scale production of cotton, tobacco and sugar. Here the economics of slavery could be fairly tested, and if the system were found to be profitable it would spread of its own impulse beyond the Mississippi, becoming more imperialistic with every extension, ambitious to seize Texas with its filibusters, looking as far as California and the Oregon territory for future expansion. But while planning for such expansion it must secure its strategic front at Washington, making certain that no rival economy should control the central government to its disadvantage. It was an ambitious program, but it was all implicit in the evident fact that slavery in the Black Belt proved to be profitable.

The explanation of this sudden prosperity of the Black Belt is a matter of familiar knowledge. Coincident with the first westward expansion of slavery came a revolution in the technique of the English cotton industry that brought about corresponding changes in southern agriculture. The production of cotton textiles in England had long been held back by the difficulty of spinning a fine and even thread. When this problem was solved at the beginning of the century by the invention of new machines, the cotton industry at once developed amazingly, making heavy demands upon the supply of American raw materials. This supply in turn was greatly increased by the invention of the cotton gin, and the combined result of these inventions was an upheaval in southern agriculture. In the eighteenth century the southern staples were tobacco, rice and indigo; by 1825 the staples had become cotton, tobacco and sugar. Almost in a decade cotton had become king. In 1791, three years after Andrew Jackson settled in Nashville, the total export of cotton was only 200,000 pounds. In 1803 it had risen to 40,000,000 pounds, and by 1860 the export for the year was of the value of nearly two hundred millions of dollars. Such figures provide a sufficient explanation of the militant spirit of the slave economy after 1820. Here was an enormous vested interest, the economic life of the South, that could not suffer its present or future profits to be put in jeopardy by any political party on any pretext. Its well-being and its prestige were both at stake. The peculiar institution, which a generation before was commonly believed to be in the way of natural extinction, had the South by the throat.

It was the strategic weakness of the South that the spirit of exploitation, which following the peace of 1783 had spread through America like the itch, should there have assumed its most hateful form, far more revolting to the humanitarian sense and far less justifiable to uneasy consciences than wage slavery. With every extension the system became necessarily more brutal in exploitation. As new plantations were opened the natural increase of negroes was inadequate to meet the pressing demands for slaves. Since the abolition of the traffic with Africa the occasional smuggling by venturesome runners—many of whom were respectable New England church members—had provided a totally inadequate supply of raw material; the price of slaves rose steadily, and this in turn led to increasing speculation in negroes. Buying and selling by middlemen went on briskly, to the horror of northern humanitarians and the concern of southern. So brutal and open was the exploitation that Alexander H. Stephens—the kindest-hearted of men—went so far as to advocate the reopening of the slave trade with Africa, as the lesser of the two evils. The better South hated what it could not help. Although the slave trader remained a social pariah with whom no gentleman would associate, his business was a necessary evil of the system and could not be eradicated.

The reaction of the slave system upon the southern people, both plantation masters and poor whites, was wholly evil. The generous culture of Virginia failed to take root in the Black Belt. The development of the plantation system under hired overseers infected the masters, few in numbers and absolute in power, with an exaggerated sense of their own greatness. The aristocratic spirit of the Old Dominion had been tempered by a feeling of patriarchal responsibility that humanized the relations between master and slave, and more generous social contacts had created an admirable republican squirearchy. But in the frontier Gulf states the rapid expansion of the plantation system created an aristocracy given to swaggering, *bourgeois* in spirit, arrogant in manners. Republican simplicity was losing vogue and there was much loose talk about the superiority of the classes. It is said that when Alexander H. Stephens was appointed a delegate to the Confederate Convention at Montgomery, he refused to attend till he was assured that the jingoes would make no attempt to set up a monarchy. Gideon Welles is authority for the story that when news came to Washington of the secession of South Carolina, Mrs. Jefferson Davis was all aflutter: "She said she wanted to get rid of the old government; that they would have a monarchy South, and gentlemen to fill official positions" (*Diary*, Vol. II, p. 256). Such stories were probably the result of war hysteria; nevertheless they suggest a bias in the southern temper that reveals how far the new South had drifted from its Jeffersonian moorings.

Of this new South with its grandiose dreams of slave imperialism, fate selected Jefferson Davis to be the political leader and spokesman. The choice may have proved unfortunate, but it was logical. Much calumny has been heaped upon his name, but that is the common fate of partisans of lost causes. The real Jefferson Davis is to be sought in some mean between the extravagant adulation of his friends and the slanders of his enemies. Not a great man certainly; in no sense comparable to Lee or Stonewall Jackson or Alexander H. Stephens; he was very far from a petty or time-serving nature. As time softens the old animosities it reveals the features of a high-minded southern gentleman who possessed the virtues and the weaknesses of his race. Simple and austere in tastes, he was the product of a crossing of the southern Puritan with the aristocratic tradition of the Old Dominion. If he was not of the old cavalier stock he was a gentleman by instinct and training. His father was half Welsh, half English; his mother Scotch-Irish. He came of Revolutionary stock. After the war his father settled in Georgia and later removed to Kentucky, where the son was born in Todd County in 1808. While still a small child he was taken to Wilkinson County, Mississippi, where he was brought up on a plantation. Educated at Lexington, Kentucky, and at West Point, he proved a serious, capable student, who loved reading but possessed little intellectual curiosity. His ideas were few, but those he embraced he clung to with the tenacity of a strong nature. Resigning from the army after a few years of honorable service, he settled down as a plantation master. He was summoned from his isolation by the call for troops to serve in the Mexican campaign, went through several battles with unusual distinction, and proved himself an extremely able officer. With his military fame the path to political preferment was open and he demonstrated his ability in Congress. At the outbreak of the secession movement he was eager to receive the appointment as commander of the southern armies, but fate called him to the presidency of the Confederacy and he devoted his best strength unselfishly to the cause, only to find the accumulated bitterness of the North heaped upon his single head. It was an unhappy lot, but there was iron in him, and he bore it like a man.

Jefferson Davis was cut out of the same tough oak that fashioned John C. Calhoun. Hard and unyielding, tenacious of opinion, dictatorial, somewhat inclined to arrogance, he might break, but he would not bend. The Scotch-Irish stock was rarely genial or tolerant, and Davis possessed none of the seeming pliability of Lincoln that yielded the non-essentials to secure the essentials. Utterly lacking in humor and easy-going good nature, he offended by his very virtues. Profoundly Puritan, he was narrow and rigid, a legalist in temperament, proud and jealous of authority. Meticulously honest, he could not get on well with men; he quarreled with his generals and wore himself out trying to do everything himself. Politically he was a strict constructionist of the most rigid views. He refused to follow Calhoun into the camp of Nullification. His patriotism was extreme, and only a greater loyalty to his state made him an advocate of secession. At bottom he was a Jeffersonian and to the end of his life he was faithful to the principles of his party. Kindly and humane, he treated his dependents with singular consideration. He set up a curious little democracy amongst the slaves of his plantation, and his negroes were devoted to him with rare loyalty. There was in his nature not the slightest trace of the exploiter; he was a patriarchal master after the old Virginia ideal, with no hint of the speculator or middleman. The background of his thought was agrarian and he shared with Jefferson a dislike for capitalistic industrialism. The President of the Confederacy may have been an unfortunate civil leader, but the slanders that so long clung to his name are only worthy of the gutter. The sin that he was led into was not counted a sin in his southern decalogue; it was the sin, not of secession, but of imperialism—a sin common to all America in those drunken times when the great West invited exploitation.

CHAPTER II

WINDS OF POLITICAL DOCTRINE

I

An economic revolution so widespread and profound could not fail to impress its ideals on current political thought. In the year 1825 three streams of tendency were flowing through the southern mind, rising from different sources, incompatible in spirit and purpose, strong in their diverse appeals; and in the end the major current was certain to engulf the lesser. The humanitarianism of Virginia, the individualism of the new West, and the imperialism of the Black Belt might seem to mingle their waters for a time, but there would be confusions of thought and diversity of counsels until one or another had worn a deeper channel through which the dominant opinion might run. There could be no more fascinating study in the economics of political theory than the changing mind of the South during the critical decades from 1820 to 1850, as it followed the course determined by its peculiar institution. Political thought passed under the jurisdiction of slavery, and every southern writer took his daily bearings from that polar fact. It is unintelligent to charge upon southern politicians a lack of consistency—to point out that after 1820 Calhoun reversed himself on every major political principle. It was true of Calhoun, as it was true of Webster and true of Clay. In a rapidly changing America, with economics in a state of flux, men were no longer free political agents, guiding themselves by the fixed stars of accepted theory; they were borne like corks on the current of the times, and their inconsistency is the surest evidence that they spoke for their constituents. The North and the South were at the parting of the ways, and if southern imperialism created for its needs a philosophy of particularism, it was met by a counter philosophy of nationalism created for its needs by northern capitalism, which likewise was following the path of its manifest destiny. The charge of innovation, indeed, lies more justly against northern theory than southern; it was Webster rather than Calhoun who ignored the teachings of the fathers.

Of these three streams of tendency it was the new imperialism

67

of the Black Belt that wore the deepest channel, gathering its tributaries till it was swollen to an overwhelming flood that drew in every lesser current. Every other interest was eventually sacrificed to slavery, every ambition was laid upon that consuming altar. Southern political thought, in consequence, came to be an ingenious study in the strategy of defense. From the somewhat vague doctrine of states rights as struck off by the Virginia school was elaborated a complete philosophy of particularism with its principle of a protective state veto. Tremendous as was the stir created by the doctrine of Nullification, that doctrine was little more than a warning gesture, a militant expression of the southern temper. The time was not ripe for the critical issue, the philosophy of the new South was not yet clarified; the objective was clearly seen, but the defenses were incomplete, the line of campaign not yet laid down. That great work was in the skillful hands of Calhoun, and much was yet to be done. The deeper purpose that lay behind the gesture of Nullification was the purpose of erecting in the slave states a civilization founded on a landed aristocracy that should serve as a sufficient counterweight to the mercantile and industrial civilization of the North; and in the event that the institution of slavery were not assured of peaceful extension through the new West, to secede and establish a southern Confederacy wherein a generous civilization might develop, modeled after the Greek democracy. Such at least was the dream of the noblest minds of the South.

Thrown early upon the defensive, southern political thought found too little time to examine fundamental principles. The necessities of the situation entailed a meticulous constitutional debate, in which the terms of the Constitution were examined with microscopic care, and interpreted in the light of their historical origin. Something of the sterility of the lawyer's mind marked the long debate; and little of the suggestiveness of the philosopher's. Acute as was Calhoun's reasoning, it reveals the weakness of contemporary political thought, northern as well as southern. It concerned itself too exclusively with government under the Constitution—its origin, the just interpretation of the terms of the fundamental law, the potentialities of consolidation inherent in the principle of loose construction. To the broader problems of the nature and functions of the political state—questions that had so deeply interested the speculative minds of the French school—quite inadequate consideration was given. The drift of circumstance was in the way of creating a leviathan state. Southern orators railed at consolidation in abundant and florid language, but they concerned themselves little with the deeper problem of the relation of the political state to the well-being of the citizen. This common weakness is strikingly evident in the work of Calhoun's successor, Alexander H. Stephens, whose interest was so exclusively historical and constitutional as almost to exclude him from a place among political philosophers.

II

JOHN C. CALHOUN

· Realist

The greatest figure in that long controversy was certainly John C. Calhoun, a man who set his face like flint against every northern middle-class ambition, and with his dream of a Greek democracy steered his beloved South upon the rocks. A truly notable figure was this ascetic Carolinian. In the passionate debates over slavery he daily matched powers with Webster and Clay and proved himself intellectually the greatest of the three. He is the one outstanding political thinker in a period singularly barren and uncreative. His influence was commanding. Tall, lean, eager, with no humor, no playfulness, lacking the magnetic personality of Clay and the ornate rhetoric of Webster, speaking plainly and following his logic tenaciously, this gaunt Scotch-Irishman became by virtue of intellect and character, driven by an apostolic zeal, the master political mind of the South, an uncrowned king who carried his native Carolina in his pocket like a rotten borough. Long before his death he had expanded a political philosophy into a school of thought. What he planned a hundred disciples hastened to execute. Like Jefferson he was a pervasive influence in shaping men's opinions. It was impossible to ignore him or to escape the admonitory finger that pointed at every weak and shuffling compromiser.

Whatever road one travels one comes at last upon the austere figure of Calhoun, commanding every highway of the southern mind. He subjected the philosophy of the fathers to critical analysis; pointed out wherein he conceived it to be faulty; cast aside some of its most sacred doctrines; provided another founda-

tion for the democratic faith which he professed. And when he had
finished the great work of reconstruction, the old Jeffersonianism
that had satisfied the mind of Virginia was reduced to a thing of
shreds and patches, acknowledged by his followers to have been
a mistaken philosophy, blinded by romantic idealism and led
astray by French humanitarianism. To substitute realism for
idealism, to set class economics above abstract humanitarianism,
was the mission to which Calhoun devoted himself. He undid for
the plantation South the work of his old master. Speaking in the
name of democracy, he attacked the foundations on which the
democratic movement in America had rested, substituting for
its libertarian and equalitarian doctrines conceptions wholly alien
and antagonistic to western democracy, wholly Greek in their
underlying spirit.

Calhoun's career was linked indissolubly with slavery. He was
the advocate and philosopher of southern imperialism, and in
defense of that imperialism he elaborated those particularist
theories which prepared the way for the movement of secession.
Born and bred in South Carolina, he was enveloped from infancy
in the mesh of southern provincialisms. Except for two years at
Yale, where he graduated in the class of 1804, and eighteen months
reading law in Connecticut, his life was spent between Washington
and his plantation. He was in temperament a Puritan, of that
Scotch-Irish strain which, scattered along the wide American
frontier, greatly modified the American character and gave to the
South such different leaders as Stonewall Jackson and Jefferson
Davis. It was a hard, stern race—that Scotch-Irish—little responsive to humanitarian appeal; and Calhoun was harder and
sterner than most. He held his emotions in strict subjection to
his reason. Intent on thinking every problem through from
premise to conclusion, concerned always with fundamental principles, he would have become, in an environment congenial to
humanistic thought, a distinguished intellectual. His mind would
have lost its rigidity and become pliable from contact with diverse
streams of theory, and his speculations would have found new
horizons from more generous intellectual acquisitions. But unhappily there was nothing either at Washington or in South Carolina
that tended to liberalize his thinking. He had not gone to school,
as Jefferson had done, to the great thinkers of Europe; he had not
found an intellectual stimulus in revolutionary systems of philos-

ophy. He dwelt all his life in the arid world of politicians. His two years at Yale may even be accounted a calamity. Timothy Dwight and Calhoun were cut out of the same cloth. The South Carolina Puritan would only be confirmed in his dogmatisms by the most dogmatic of Yankee Puritans; and in consequence his career, like Jonathan Edwards', suffered from a narrow, ingrowing intellectualism. He was a potential intellectual whose mind was unfertilized by contact with a generous social culture.

Calhoun's public life covered the forty years from 1810 to 1850, from the first administration of Madison to that of Zachary Taylor. For nearly half of the total period, up to the year 1828, he was a politician of ability but without distinction. He entered Congress at a time when the young men from the South and West were becoming impatient with the cautious policy of the old Republicans led by Jefferson and Madison. The war psychology was mounting under British pin-pricks, and the young nationalists, forgetful that bayonets and cannon and ships are not easily defeated by rhetoric, were eager to teach the Mistress of the Seas some much-needed international manners. In those early years Calhoun joined with Clay in driving through Congress a war policy. In this he seems to have represented his constituents, whose patriotism was always somewhat bellicose. During the shameful war experience, the cool analytical Calhoun came near to exhibiting the tawdry marks of the jingo; and thereafter for years there was little to distinguish him from a Hamiltonian Federalist. He was a throughgoing nationalist of the school of loose construction. He advocated a protective tariff on the ground that "it would form a new and most powerful cement, far outweighing any political objections that might be urged against the system" (Gaillard Hunt, *John C. Calhoun*, p. 29). As yet he had discovered no constitutional scruples against the exercise of this or other implied powers. He was, he said, "no advocate for refined arguments on the Constitution. The instrument is not intended as a thesis for the logician to exercise his ingenuity on. It ought to be construed with plain, good sense; and what can be more express than the Constitution on this point?" (*ibid.*, p. 30). As Secretary for War in Monroe's cabinet he was an advocate of internal improvements, and he submitted to Congress an elaborate report on a proposed system of roads and canals. Until the critical year 1828 there was little in Calhoun's career to distinguish him from Clay. The tide of national expansion was running strong; the growth of exploitation was creating a middle-class psychology; and Calhoun in these earlier years was as unconsciously middle class as afterwards he became consciously aristocratic. He sprang from an acquisitive race, and to the end of his life some remnants of the old instincts clung to him despite his repudiation of the middle-class political philosophy.

The year 1828, marked by a fierce discussion in South Carolina of the Tariff of Abominations, proved the turning-point of his career. As Vice President he had been little more than a spectator of the growing discontent in his native state at the contrast between the industrial prosperity of New England and the agricultural depression of the South. But he could no longer remain an idle spectator. Pamphlets and newspaper articles were appearing that sharply challenged his position. Capitalistic Federalism and democratic equalitarianism were equally under fire. The celebrated Dr. Cooper, an Englishman long resident in South Carolina, who had suffered under the Alien and Sedition law, had vigorously attacked the natural-rights dogma, and was active in arousing the public mind against Calhoun's consolidationist tendencies.[1] The publication in 1821 of Yates's *Minutes of Debates of the Constitutional Convention* had awakened widespread interest in an historical interpretation of the Constitution, and the time was ripe for a new period of constitutional debate. The tariff act of 1828 provided the immediate occasion. It opened the flood gates, and the waters of states-rights doctrine that had long been gathering rushed forth in a torrent. Calhoun hesitated no longer. The problem and the solution had both clarified themselves in his mind, and he at once took the lead in directing the unrest to achieve a definite end.

Calhoun's contribution to political theory—a contribution that elevates him to a distinguished place among American political thinkers—was the child of necessity, and received its particularist bias from the exigencies of sectional partisanship. With the rapid expansion of the nation westward, and the consequent augmenting of a potentially hostile free-soil power, the South was doomed to become increasingly a minority voice in the councils of government; and if it were to preserve its peculiar institution it must find more adequate means of self-protection than it had enjoyed hitherto.

---

[1] See Merriam, *American Political Theories*, p. 231; Gaillard Hunt, *John C. Calhoun*, p. 64.

The tendencies most to be feared, in his judgment, were the spontaneous drift towards consolidation, and an uncritical faith in numerical majorities. He was convinced that America had too thoughtlessly accepted the principle of political democracy as a sufficient safeguard against the danger of arbitrary government. Soon or late it must discover, what the South already was discovering, that numerical democracy, unrestrained by constitutional limitations on its will, is no friend to political justice. The critical test of every government is the measure of protection afforded its weakest citizen; and judged by this test a democratic state, when power has come to be centralized in few hands, may prove to be no other than a tyrant. Irresponsible in its unrestraint, the majority vote may easily outdo an Oriental despot in arbitrary rule, and the more power it wields the more ruthless will be its disregard of minority opinion. The political philosopher who proposes to formulate an ideal democratic system of government, therefore, must deal critically with this fundamental problem of political justice, for upon the solution will turn the excellence and permanence of every democracy. It was to this baffling problem that Calhoun addressed himself.

In seeking a constitutional defense for the threatened southern interests, he drew from the two great reservoirs of American constitutional theory. From the Jeffersonian Republicans he derived his familiar doctrine of states rights in opposition to the consolidating principle; from the Federalists of the Montesquieu school he drew his theory of static government, resulting from exactly balanced powers; and from the amalgamation of these diverse theories he formulated a new principle. Both schools of earlier thought, he had come to believe, had been sound in their major premises, but both had gone astray in certain important deductions. The experience of forty years, with the democracy constantly augmenting its powers, had demonstrated to Calhoun's satisfaction both the grave danger that lay in the principle of consolidation, and the insufficiency of existing checks on the Federal government. The prime mistake of the Jeffersonians, he conceived, was their belief that the democratic majority will necessarily serve the cause of political justice; and the miscalculation of the Federalists resulted from the belief that the division of powers provided in the Constitution was adequate to prevent arbitrary government. He now proposed to correct these two mistakes by providing an additional check through the simple expedient—as logical as it was efficacious, granted his premises—of recognizing the veto power of the individual commonwealth upon an act of the Federal government. Stripped of its states-rights limitation, this was in germ the principle of the referendum, modified, however, by certain suggestive provisions.

The veto-power as a protective principle Calhoun regarded as the hallmark of constitutional government. Granted that sovereignty under the Constitution inheres in the people, and that all authority is delegated, it follows that government is no more than an agent with strictly defined fiduciary powers, all the acts of which are subject to review by the principal. Whether such review shall be immediate and plenary, or at more or less remove and limited, becomes therefore a fundamental question of constitutional polity. Unfortunately much confusion has resulted from an intentional vagueness, contributed by interested groups to further particular ends, in the common understanding of the terms, the people and government. The former is rarely, as is usually assumed, a homogeneous body with common interests, but a congeries of individuals and groups and classes with diverse and often antagonistic interests; and the latter—in a republic— is never a sacred entity, the residuary legatee of sovereignty, to criticize which is to commit the crime of *lèse-majesté*, but a group of officials invested with temporary authority and actuated by motives common to all men. A necessary preliminary, therefore, to an intelligent understanding of the principle of veto is a critical analysis of these much misunderstood terms.

Calhoun was far too honest a realist to be under any hallucinations in regard to political government. He estimated at its full significance "the never-ending audacity of elected persons." Power he knew to be the most insidious of poisons; every government is liable to the disease of auto-intoxication. Seated securely in office the agent assumes all the prerogatives of the principal and clothes his acts with the sanctity of sovereignty. Armed with the taxing power, he distributes penalties and benefits with partial hand, and unless an adequate defense protects the weaker interests they will suffer a legal exploitation. Every government justly rests under suspicion, and only the most critical scrutiny of its conduct can keep it decently honest. Popular government, from which the Republicans hoped too much, changes only the outward form of the selfish struggle for power by substituting party rule for class rule. With its disciplined party machine the lure of political spoil encourages the most shameless exploitation of the weaker groups, who have no recourse.[2] Hence, the more popular the government, the more ruthless becomes the majority rule; and any system of checks and balances that does not adequately restrain this inherent tendency of party rule must prove a failure. However carefully the political philosopher may provide for a division of powers among executive, legislature and judiciary, he must fail of his object, for a regnant majority will control all three branches of government, and thus intrenched will defy the protests of the minority. The Montesquieu theory had proved a failure in practice.

An even greater danger, in Calhoun's judgment, lay in the current misinterpretation of the term " the people," the result of which was the obscuring of the economic basis of society and the befuddling of the whole problem of government. To this disastrous result, he believed, both schools of political thought had contributed. The early Republicans had oversimplified the political problem by assuming a clear division between ruler and subject. The conception was a heritage from European experience, where it had taken form as a strategic move to align the unthinking mass against a despotic monarchy. The Jeffersonians had used it to like purpose in their struggle against consolidation, appealing to a common democracy against the aristocracy. The early Federalists were even more blameworthy, for, understanding clearly the economic origins of political power and the economic ends served by the political state, they made their knowledge serve their interests and concealed their designs by deceptive appeals to patriotism. Every realist knows that "the people" is a political fiction. Society is made up of individuals, each with his particular interest. The total interests of the subject-citizens are necessarily complex. Group and classify them as he may, the political philosopher can never merge the parts in a coalescing whole, but must recognize that the problem remains one of adjustments and compromises. It follows therefore that any facile assumption that government represents the people or rests on the will of the people is a disastrous fallacy. Popular government rests on the will of the majority; aristocratic government rests on the will of the aristocracy; and

[2] See "A Disquisition on Government" in Calhoun's *Works*, Vol. I, pp. 41-42.

despotic government rests on the will of the despot. It is an axiom that the political state is partisan to those who administer it. The stakes of rulership are high; the game of politics never lacks its devotees; the business of deceiving the people in order to pluck the goose has long been one of the respectable professions.

The perennial problem of constitutional government, then, in Calhoun's philosophy, remains what it was seen to be by the Federalist followers of Montesquieu—the problem of restraining government by constitutional checks to the end that it be kept just. Existing machinery having demonstrated its inadequacy, it remained to provide more effective. Freedom Calhoun regarded as the crown jewel of civilization, hardly won, easily lost. But freedom was not to be measured by *habeas corpus* acts and similar legal restraints on tyranny; it was freedom from legal exploitation and statutory dictatorship. "The abuse of delegated power, and the tyranny of the stronger over the weaker interests, are the two dangers, and the only two to be guarded against; and if this be done effectually, liberty must be eternal. Of the two, the latter is the greater and most difficult to resist" (*Works*, Vol. VI, p. 32). In more definite terms the problem is thus stated:

Two powers are necessary to the existence and preservation of free States: a power on the part of the ruled to prevent rulers from abusing their authority, by compelling them to be faithful to their constituents, and which is effected through the right of suffrage; and a power to compel the parts of society to be just to one another, by compelling them to consult the interest of each other—which can only be effected . . . by requiring the concurring assent of all the great and distinct interests of the community to the measures of the Government. This result is the sum-total of all the contrivances adopted by free States to preserve their liberty, by preventing the conflicts between the several classes or parts of the community. (*Ibid.*, Vol. VI, pp. 189–190.)

In elaboration of the second phase of the problem Calhoun contributed the principle on which his reputation as a political thinker must rest—the doctrine of a concurrent majority. He found his solution in an expansion of the principle of democracy— recovering the true principle, he was fond of insisting—by superimposing upon the consolidated, indiscriminate numerical majority the will of a geographical majority; or in other words, by a special form of sectional referendum.

It results, from what has been said, that there are two different modes in which the sense of the community may be taken: one, simply, by the right of suffrage, unaided; the other, by the right through a proper organism. Each collects the sense of the majority. But one regards numbers only, and considers the whole community one unit, having but one common interest throughout; and collects the sense of the greater number of the whole, as that of the community. The other, on the contrary, regards interests as well as numbers;—considering the community as made up of different and conflicting interests as far as the action of the government is concerned; and takes the sense of each, through its majority or appropriate organ, and the united sense of all, as the sense of the entire community. The former of these I call the numerical, or absolute majority; and the latter, the concurrent, or constitutional majority. ("A Disquisition on Government," in *Works*, Vol. I, p. 28.)

In such speculation on the possibility of achieving political justice by the machinery of representation, Calhoun was face to face with a revolutionary conception—the conception of proportional economic representation. The idea was implicit in his assumption of an existing economic sectionalism that must find adequate expression through political agencies. He had come to understand the futility of a miscellaneous numerical majority; he had only to go back to eighteenth-century philosophy and substitute economic classes for economic sectionalism, finding his social cleavages in economic groups instead of geographical divisions, to have recast the whole theory of representation. Clearly, he had made enormous strides in his thinking. He had long since put behind him the philosophy of Jefferson. He had subjected the principle of democracy to critical scrutiny. But instead of rejecting it as an unworkable hypothesis, as the Hamiltonian Federalists had done, he proposed to establish it on a sound and permanent basis. The ideal of democracy he conceived to be the noblest in the whole field of political thought, but misunderstood and misapplied as it had been in America, it had become the mother of every mischief. This betrayal of democracy he laid at the door of the Jeffersonians. They had accepted too carelessly the romantic dogmas of the French school, and had come to believe that democracy was synonymous with political equalitarianism.

It was this false notion that had debased the noble ideal, and delivered it over to the hands of the mob. To assert that men are created free and equal is to fly in the face of every biological and social fact. The first business of the true democrat, therefore, was to reëxamine the nature of democracy and strip away the false assumptions and vicious conclusions that had done it incalculable injury. The Greeks, he pointed out, understood its essential nature better than the moderns. Democracy assumes a co-partnership among equals. Its only rational foundation is good will, and it can function only through compromise. From this it follows that in a society composed of high and low, capable and weak, worthy and unworthy—as every historical society has been composed—a universal democracy is impractical. The numerous body of social incompetents will suffer one of two fates: they will be exploited by the capable minority under the guise of free labor, or they will be accepted as the wards of society and protected by the free citizens—they must inevitably become either wage slaves or bond slaves, in either case incapable of maintaining the rights of free members of the commonwealth. Democracy is possible only in a society that recognizes inequality as a law of nature, but in which the virtuous and capable enter into a voluntary co-part-nership for the common good, accepting wardship of the incompe-tent in the interests of society. This was the Greek ideal and this ideal had created Greek civilization.

Calhoun was thus brought face to face with the natural-rights theory, which the glowing rhetoric of the Declaration of Independ-ence had disseminated throughout America, and which lay as a virus at the heart of Jacksonianism. To destroy that theory, he believed, was a necessary preliminary to any rational theory of democracy, and he turned to the business with characteristic frankness. Upon the venerable dogmas he threw the light of his realism, subjecting them to critical analysis. The origin of govern-ment in compact was only a myth. The amiable being known as man in a state of nature, whose portrait had been drawn by the French romantics, he discovered in neither social nor biological history. The true origin of government, he asserted in common with John Adams, is to be found in practical necessity; government arises, as Hobbes had pointed out, from the universal fact of human selfishness. It has always been found necessary to lodge coercive powers in certain hands as a social protection against individual aggression; and since all men are impelled by self-interest, political systems are determined in form and scope by this universal in-stinct. Without government there is anarchy; with government there is potential tyranny. The crucial problem to be solved by the political philosopher, hence, is to determine the just delimitation between sovereign power and individual liberty; the one protecting the rights of the whole, the other keeping open fresh opportunity to advance.

Having thus established government on the firm basis of social necessity, he proceeded to examine the romantic dogmas of liberty and equality.

It follows, from what has been stated, that it is a great and dangerous error to suppose that all people are equally entitled to liberty. It is a reward to be earned, not a blessing to be gratuitously lavished on all alike;—a reward reserved for the intelligent, the patriotic, the virtuous and deserving;—and not a boon to be bestowed on a people too ignorant, degraded and vicious, to be capable either of appreciating or of enjoying it. Nor is it any disparagement to liberty, that such is, and ought to be the case. On the contrary its greatest praise,—its proudest distinction is, that an all-wise Providence has reserved it, as the noblest and highest reward for the development of our faculties, moral and intellectual. A reward more appropriate than liberty could not be conferred on the deserving;—nor a punishment inflicted on the undeserving more just, than to be subject to lawless and despotic rule. This dispensation seems to be the result of some fixed law;—and every effort to disturb or defeat it, by attempting to elevate a people in the scale of liberty, above the point to which they are entitled to rise, must ever prove abortive, and end in disappointment. . . .

There is another error, not less great and dangerous, usually associated with the one which has just been considered. I refer to the opinion, that liberty and equality are so intimately united, that liberty cannot be perfect without perfect equality. That they are united to a certain extent,— and that equality of citizens, in the eyes of the law, is essential to liberty in a popular government, is conceded. But to go further, and make equality of *condition* essential to liberty, would be to destroy both liberty and progress. The reason is, that inequality of condition, while it is a necessary consequence of liberty, is, at the same time, indispensable to progress. . . . It is, indeed, this inequality of condition between the front and rear ranks, in the march of progress, which gives so strong an impulse to the former to maintain their position, and to the latter to press forward into their files. This gives to progress its greatest impulse. To force the front rank back to the rear, or attempt to push forward the rear into line with the front, by the interposition of the government, would put an end to the impulse, and effectually arrest the march of progress. ("A Disquisition on Government," in *Works*, Vol. I, pp. 55–56.)

It was the persuasive ideal of a Greek democracy in the plantation states that lay back of Calhoun's defense of slavery—a defense that thrusts into sharp relief the change of southern attitude in the decade of the thirties. The earlier Jeffersonian attitude had been fairly expressed by a Georgia representative in the debate on the Missouri question:

Believe me, sir, I am not a panegyrist of slavery. It is an unnatural state; a dark cloud which obscures half the lustre of our free institutions! . . . Would it be fair; would it be manly; would it be generous; would it be just, to offer contumely and contempt to the unfortunate man who wears a cancer in his bosom, because he will not submit to cautery at the hazard of his existence? (Quoted in Hunt, *John C. Calhoun*, p. 53.)

But with slavery put upon its defense, the southern spokesmen passed from apology to praise. From the first, Calhoun accepted the system implicitly, but now he subjected it to critical analysis in the light of his theory of a Greek democracy. Over against it he set the northern system of wage labor, and he came to the conclusion that the latter was more brutal and inhumane than the former. He was convinced that heretofore the South had made a serious mistake in apologizing for its peculiar institution, and in expecting its eventual extinction. In this matter the fathers had been wrong. No serious-minded Southerner any longer believed that slavery was on the way to natural extinction. It was spreading daily and must be permitted to spread. The hopes of southern civilization were bound up with it. The North must be brought to recognize it as a beneficent institution, necessary to a free, cultivated democracy, the only alternative to those fierce conflicts between wage labor and capital which already in the manufacturing states were threatening the permanence of American institutions. In a speech delivered in 1838, Calhoun thus sketched the new southern conception:

Many in the South once believed that it [slavery] was a moral and political evil. That folly and delusion are gone. We see it now in its true light, and regard it as the most safe and stable basis for free institutions in the world. It is impossible with us that the conflict can take place between labor and capital, which makes it so difficult to establish and maintain free institutions in all wealthy and highly civilized nations where such institutions as ours do not exist. The Southern States are an aggregate, in fact, of communities, not of individuals. Every plantation is a little community, with the master at its head, who concentrates in himself the united interests of capital and labor, of which he is the common representative. These small communities aggregated make the State in all, whose action, labor, and capital is equally represented and perfectly harmonized. Hence the harmony, the union, the stability of that section which is rarely disturbed, except through the action of this Government. The blessing of this state of things extends beyond the limits of the South. It makes that section the balance of the system; the great conservative power, which prevents other portions, less fortunately constituted, from rushing into conflict. . . . Such are the institutions which these deluded madmen are stirring heaven and earth to destroy, and which we are called on to defend by the highest and most solemn obligations that can be imposed on us as men and patriots. ("Remarks on the State Rights Resolutions in Regard to Abolition. January 12, 1838," in *Works*, Vol. III, p. 180.)

Thus in the end the political philosopher turns partisan to a cause. His fruitful speculations on the theory of representation, his inquiry into the economic basis of politics, remained incomplete, the larger reaches only half explored. Espousing the ideal of democracy, he yielded to the seductions of a Greek republic. Beginning as a Jeffersonian, he ended as the philosopher of a slave aristocracy, from whose principles men like Governor McDuffie of South Carolina deduced the dictum that "the laboring population of no nation on earth are entitled to liberty, or capable of enjoying it." It was a curious dream, yet no more curious than his faith in an obsolete article in the Constitution to withstand the advance of a hostile economy. There is something almost tragic in the self-deception of this clear-minded realist in his appeal to a paper defense against economic forces. "The Constitution—no interference—no discrimination," he cried passionately in repudiating the right of Abolition petition. "These are the grounds on which the battle may be safely fought. . . . You must tell these deluded fanatics, you have no right to intermeddle in any form or shape. . . . Expediency, justice, plighted faith, and the Constitution: these, and these only, can be relied on to avert conflict" (*Works*, Vol. III, p. 190).

Lost faiths and repudiated prophets go down to a common grave. The living have little inclination to learn from the dead. The political principles of Calhoun have had scant justice done them by later generations who incline to accept the easy opinion that the cause which triumphs is altogether the better cause. What Calhoun so greatly feared has since come about. He erected a last barrier against the progress of middle-class ideals—consolidation in politics and standardization in society; against a universal cash-register evaluation of life: and the barrier was blown to pieces by the guns of the Civil War. Historically he was the last spokesman of the great school of the eighteenth century, the intellectual descendant of John Adams. The two men were much alike in the broad principles of their political philosophy, and identical necessities brought them to identical conclusions. They agreed in the fundamental principle that property will rule by reason of its inherent power, and that political justice is attainable only by a nicely calculated system of checks and balances, which provides each important group with a defensive veto. But in the social experience on which Adams founded his doctrine, political antagonism was potential in rival classes, and justified a division of powers on the model of the British constitution. In the intervening years, however, the economic alignment had become sectional, the rise of party government had created a new problem, and the earlier division of powers seemed to demand a supplementary veto if the nice balance contemplated in the Constitution were to be maintained. This was the kernel of the states-rights doctrine which Calhoun elaborated with such skill. That he should have associated the principle with a cause that was doomed was disastrous to the just fame of Calhoun. More, it was disastrous to the vital democratic principle of decentralized powers. In championing a Greek democracy Calhoun affronted the latent idealism of America, and the harm he did to agrarian democracy was incalculable.

III

ALEXANDER H. STEPHENS

Constitutionalist

Southern scholars are pretty well agreed that the ablest defender of the doctrine of secession was Alexander H. Stephens, the Georgia commoner. He was sprung from the plain people. Brought up in severe poverty, self-taught, the friend of the poor, he was no child of an exclusive planter aristocracy, and was never quite trusted by them. The victim of a slight, ramshackly physique, never weighing a hundred pounds, never knowing a well day, fearfully handicapped in the everyday matter of living, it is amazing that soul and body held together for seventy-one years and more amazing that he accomplished what he did. "Throughout life," says one of his biographers, "he was practically a brain without a body." Temperamentally despondent, he was driven into restless activity to forget self. His will was fine-tempered steel and ill health never broke his courage even when it laid him on his back. He feared nothing, but took a position and argued a cause without regard to personal consequences. He never flinched from the personal encounters which the lawless code of Georgia politics invited. A morbid consciousness of his feeble physique sometimes drove him into truculence, and on one occasion he was stabbed eighteen times by a certain ornament of the Georgia bench, and saved his life only by grasping the blade that was driven at his throat. But such encounters can be explained on the ground of overcorrection; the real Stephens was gentle, peace-loving, hating all swaggerers military or civilian, "a man of generous sympathies, of broad humanity, a democrat of democrats, a friend of all the world" (Pendleton, *Alexander H. Stephens*, p. 253). The words *Non sibi sed aliis*, cut in his tombstone at Crawfordville, come nearer the truth than epitaphs usually do. He was never selfishly ambitious and he could justly say after the fall of the Confederacy, "I am old and weak in bodily infirmity, but I have done my duty to God and my country, and I am ready for whatever fate may be assigned me" (*ibid.*, p. 393).

Stephens was a lifelong student of politics, regarding it as "one of the most intricate, as well as interesting subjects that can engage the attention of reflecting minds." He was not a political philosopher like Calhoun, concerned with principle and theory, but a constitutional historian concerned to trace the genesis and development of the fundamental law of the land. He was probably more widely read in the early literature of the Constitution than any other man of his generation. He had thumbed and dog-eared Elliot's *Debates*, and could cite dates and explain circumstances for the elucidation of doubtful points or the correcting of an unhistorical interpretation. He knew the genesis of every article, of almost every word in the Constitution, and the reasons which determined the special form which each assumed; and this exact knowledge equipped him for the task of critical commentator on earlier commentators. Unfortunate was the theorizer who fell into his hands. Federalist expositors like Story and Motley, given to rash generalization from inadequate data, suffered disaster under his critical inspection. With his fund of historical knowledge he was amply prepared for the labor of love to which he turned after the war, and in his *Constitutional View of the War between the*

States he produced one of the most notable studies in the origin of the Constitution that we have.

Certain deep personal needs, taking form in passionate conviction, determined the bias of Stephens' political philosophy, which was quite simple, consistent and inflexible, from his first entry into public life until his death. There was no subtlety in his intellectual processes, no balancing uncertainly between diverse appeals, but a clear faith which he expounded to the common voter in confident expectation that it would awaken sympathetic response. His extensive reading was not so much a disinterested search for light on the ideal relations of men in society, as for confirmation of certain prepossessions. That those prepossessions were shared by his fellow Georgians, that they were the natural product of existing social conditions, gave to them an added sanction. The creative source of his philosophy was a passionate love of freedom; and his meditations convinced him that the only freedom worth a tuppence is civil liberty under civil law—that the test of any civilization is the concern it manifests for the safeguarding of such liberty by exact and adequate constitutional provisions. His reverence for law was a religion with him, and his love of the Constitution as the fostering mother of the law was only this side idolatry. "No stronger or more ardent Union man ever lived than I was," he asserted late in life. Intense loyalty was almost commonplace amongst the people from whom he sprang. Love of the Union, and of the Constitution as a guarantee of that Union, was far stronger in the South before the Civil War than in the North. But it was the Constitution of the fathers, not a newfangled consolidating instrument that drew all power to Washington, that they loved. Pride of locality—naïve though it might be and provincial—the spontaneous pride of a simple untraveled people—was rooted in the southern heart. It was nourished by a deep love of homestead and neighborhood, natural to an agrarian society; and it came to political expression in the doctrine that the commonwealth must be free to manage its own affairs in its own way. The theory of states rights, amongst such a people, was not an abstract principle but an expression of the psychology of localism created by everyday habit. This explains the intensity of conviction which colors the thought of Stephens. The principle of local sovereignty was inbred. He rarely deigns to argue the question. He never concerned himself with abstract argument—as Jefferson had done

—to prove the superior excellence of local home rule. This failure, indeed, may perhaps be accounted his greatest weakness as a political thinker. Rather he was concerned to prove that state sovereignty existed prior to the Union, that it was jealously guarded at the making of the Constitution, that it had never been surrendered, and hence was the constitutional order until destroyed by the Civil War. But if he refrained from abstract argument touching the desirability of localizing political power, he exhibited a Jeffersonian fear of unregulated power which consolidation makes possible.

This passionate love of freedom he exemplified in his own career. He followed his convictions and spoke his own mind, regardless of occasion or circumstance. He was no man's tool. He hated a demagogue and never curried favor with his constituents or calculated popular response. In his public life he considered himself a representative of the people of Georgia, and the one object of his labors was the preservation of that constitutional liberty in which they had grown up. In furtherance of this policy he found himself not infrequently at odds with other southern leaders. He vigorously opposed his party in its Mexican war policy, looking upon it as no other than imperialistic vandalism aimed at a weaker neighbor for the purpose of extending slave territory. There was no glamor for him in military victories; he would not concede that a republic might plead manifest destiny in extenuation of armed aggression, or that the ends of civilization may be furthered by war. In a speech opposing the policy of his fellow Whigs, he thus expressed his conception of national progress:

I am no enemy to the extension of our domain, or the enlargement of the boundaries of the republic. I trust the day is coming, and not far distant, when the whole continent will be ours; when our institutions shall be diffused and cherished, and republican government enjoyed, throughout the length and breadth of this land. . . . That this is our ultimate destiny, if wise counsels prevail, I confidently believe. But it is not to be accomplished by the sword. . . . Republics never spread by arms. We can properly enlarge only by voluntary accessions. . . .

There is much said in this country of the party of progress. I profess to be of that party; but I am far from advocating that kind of progress which many of those who seem anxious to appropriate the term exclusively to themselves are using their exertions to push forward. Theirs, in my opinion, is a downward progress. It is a progress of party, of excitement, of lust of power; a spirit of war, aggression, violence and licentiousness. It is a progress which, if indulged in, would soon sweep over all law, all order, and the Constitution itself. . . . It is to progress in *these* essential attributes of national greatness that I would look: the improvement of mind, the "increase and diffusion of knowledge among men," the erection of schools, colleges and temples of learning; the progress of intellect over matter; the triumph of mind over the animal propensities; the advancement of kind feeling and good will among the nations of the earth; the cultivation of virtue and the pursuits of industry; the bringing into subjection and subservience to the use of man of all the elements of nature around us; in a word, the progress of civilization, and everything that elevates and ennobles man. This . . . is not to be done by wars, whether foreign or domestic. Fields of blood and carnage may make men brave and heroic, but seldom tend to make nations either virtuous or great. (Quoted in Pendleton, *Alexander H. Stephens*, pp. 79–80.)

A man of peace, Stephens was greatly agitated over the movement of secession. He fought the Fire Eaters to the bitter end in his native state, but like other high-minded Southerners he went out with his commonwealth. Loyalty to Georgia was stronger than loyalty to the nation. But in the new order he preserved his old principles. The Jeffersonian democrat could not forget his teachings. When the Confederacy was discussing its proposed Constitution, he took alarm at some loose talk about the desirability of setting up a monarchy. His old friend Bob Toombs, one of the ablest of the southern leaders, quite frankly preferred the English system to the American.[3] There seems to have been considerable comment to like effect amongst the Tory hot-heads; but the wind was not blowing in that direction and such straws were only the stirrings of vagrant eddies. The Constitution as adopted was more democratic than the older instrument—an outcome to which Stephens contributed greatly.

As Vice President of the Confederacy he constituted himself the special guardian of constitutional liberty, and his jealous concern at what he regarded as administrative usurpations of power brought on grave differences with President Davis. Even in the urgent crises of war he would not sanction the use of extra-constitutional powers. He knew better than most that power grows by what it feeds on, that too often war destroys the liberty it professes to be serving. To win the war and lose the peace, to secede in defense of constitutional rights and then tamely yield them up, seemed to him a pitiful ending, and when President Davis suspended the right of *habeas corpus* and his generals

---

[3] See Pendleton, *Alexander H. Stephens*, p. 231, note.

proclaimed martial law, he took alarm. "All such orders," he said, "are palpable and dangerous usurpations, and if permitted to continue will end in military despotism. . . . Better in my judgment that Richmond should fall, and that the enemy's armies should sweep our whole country from the Potomac to the Gulf than that our people should submissively yield obedience to one of these edicts of our own generals" (Pendleton, *Alexander H. Stephens*, p. 292). Freedom of speech he would not have interfered with under any excuse. The suspension of civil law he considered a threat aimed at every citizen of the South. He had heard, he said, that one purpose of the act was "to control certain elections and certain expected assemblages in North Carolina"—where there was a good deal of disaffection—"to put a muzzle upon certain presses, and a bit in the mouth of certain speakers of that State. If this be so, I regard it as the more dangerous to public liberty" (*ibid.*, p. 313). To the question, "Can you not trust the President?" he replied in words that deserve to be remembered:

To the question of whether I would not or cannot trust him with these high powers not conferred by the Constitution, my answer is: I am utterly opposed to everything looking to or tending toward dictatorship in this country. There is no man living and not one of the illustrious dead, whom, if now living, I would so trust. . . . I would not turn on my heel to choose between masters. I was not born to acknowledge a master from either the North or the South. I shall never choose between candidates for that office. I have no wish or desire to live after the degradation of my country, and have no intention to survive its liberties, if life be the necessary sacrifice of their maintenance to the utmost of my abilities. (*Ibid.*, pp. 313–314.)

No argument of expediency, no appeal to military necessity ever moved him from the belief that the sole justification of government is the maintenance of liberty, and that the sole guarantee of such liberty is the orderly process of civil law. He was harassed by the encroachment upon individual freedom demanded by war, north as well as south. "The North to-day," he said, "presents the spectacle of a free people having gone to war to make freemen of slaves, while all they have as yet attained is to make slaves of themselves" (*ibid.*, p. 293). Perhaps no other public man in America kept his head amidst the passions of the time so completely as Stephens. He was utterly beyond reach of jingo appeal, and he suffered what the individual must expect to suffer who pits his single conscience against the mass will. He was branded as a traitor, and only his extraordinary hold on the affections of the plain people of Georgia saved him from the bitterest experience.

During the black period following the southern collapse, when he was disfranchised, broken in health past mending, and hated by the followers of President Davis, Stephens sought distraction in writing American history. Three and a half years, from 1867 to 1870, he devoted to his *Constitutional View of the Late War between the States.* The case for states rights has never been more convincingly put than in this monumental study. The first volume in particular, which deals with the history of the Constitution, is an acute and able work. The thesis on which it rests is the doctrine which Paine and Jefferson derived from the French school, namely, that a constitutional compact is terminable. Elaborated by Stephens and applied to the case in question, the doctrine becomes this: that the right of secession is a civil as well as a revolutionary right; that it is implied in the compact originally entered into by the several states; that any state may rightfully take back what it had peacefully granted, when such action shall seem to it desirable. The sovereign commonwealth has never abrogated its sovereignty; the Constitution is a Federal compact amongst equals; the United States is a federated Union, not an organic nation. To conceive of the organic law as a consolidating instrument binding the individual citizen immediately to the central government, as Webster and Judge Story had done, was not only unhistorical but contrary to every fact and every tradition. To arrive at the principle of consolidation, and hold that the right of secession is only a revolutionary right, one must deliberately shut one's eyes to the early history of the Constitution.

Not content to prove the original compact nature of the Constitution—an argument that runs through fourteen hundred pages, buttressed by a mass of citations from all sources and wholly convincing in its evidence—Stephens undertakes to prove the wisdom of the fathers in establishing the federal union in compact. In respecting existing loyalties to the several commonwealths, they not only preserved the local democracies—which, as a Jeffersonian, Stephens believed were the foundation of good government—but they established the federal state on a strong and enduring foundation. The Hamiltonian consolidationists had asserted that a strong state must rest on the principle of coercive sovereignty, that it can be held together only through the exercise of

authority. Stephens replied by laying down the counter principle
that the secret of a strong and enduring state is to be discovered
in the spontaneous loyalty of its citizens, and that in consequence
a democracy which rests on the good will of the people as a whole
is the most enduring of all forms.

A Government, to be worth anything, . . . must be strong. Its parts
and members must be held together by force of some sort. This I cordially
admit. We do not differ as to the force or its extent; we differ only as to
its nature and character. Should it be a physical or moral force? In my
judgment, the strongest force that can hold the parts or constituent
elements of any Government together is the affection of the people towards it. (*Constitutional View, etc.*, Vol. I, p. 526.)

Affection, he reasoned, cannot be coerced. It must spring
spontaneously from the recognition that government is useful,
that it is just, that it treats all its parts and members equally,
that it is an agency erected by a free people to serve the ends of
freedom. Allegiance is an individual compact between the citizen
and government. Destroy the principle of voluntary allegiance,
seek to coerce the citizen, impose upon minorities the ruthless will
of majorities, subjugate individual commonwealths, and the federal Union which Jefferson believed to be "the strongest Government on Earth," would indeed become what Hamilton in
his blindness to the secret of power believed that it was—"a
frail and worthless fabric." "But the indissoluble union between
the several states of this Confederated Nation is, after all, not in
the *right*, but in the *heart*" (*ibid.*, Vol. I, p. 527). So long as the
rights of all are respected, the common interest and common
loyalty will preserve the union. Injustice alone is to be feared, for
no political bonds can long resist the action of this most potent
of social dissolvents.

Modern as Stephens was in the assertion of the principle of good
will as the source of sovereignty in democratic government, he
belonged to his own generation in his blindness to economic
motives. He thought exclusively in legal and constitutional terms;
he remained wholly a lawyer. It is hard to understand how one
so profoundly read in our political history should have failed to
discover the workings of economic forces beneath the surface of
politics. Calhoun, bred in the same Jeffersonian school, had found
his way through the mist of equalitarianism to the solid realism
of an earlier day; but to the last of his fourteen hundred pages of

exposition Stephens retained the illusion that the political state is something apart from economics and superior to it. He conceived of government as an end in itself, and this lends an air of unreality to his thinking. An ardent Jeffersonian, he reduced the philosophy of his master to the compact theory of government. The economic basis of Jefferson's philosophy, his love of an agrarian order and hatred of capitalistic exploitation—motives which serve to explain and justify his theory of local self government— Stephens wholly ignores. The result is a grotesque perversion of a philosophy which John Taylor had elaborated clearly. Jefferson was a much greater political thinker than Stephens conceived, although he called him the "greatest philosophical statesman" America has produced. In his estimate of Andrew Jackson he falls into the same mistake. He attempts to reduce the confused career of Jackson—half middle-class in his earlier years and later returning to agrarian principles—to the same narrow compass of the compact theory. Even Webster, for whom he entertained "the highest esteem and admiration," and in praise of whose moral qualities he is almost fulsome,[4] he quite failed to understand. Webster's theory of the Constitution, he clearly demonstrated, was utterly unhistorical; but Webster's economic alliances he ignored. What havoc was wrought in current politics by suffering political theory to obscure economic reality is suggested by the fact that Stephens, a Jeffersonian in every instinct, turned Whig and voted for Webster in 1852—after the latter's death. Politics makes strange bedfellows, yet it must have been an ample bed that could sleep the spokesman of an agrarian economy and the spokesman of capitalism side by side.

In his attitude towards slavery Stephens was a product of his Georgia environment. His views were ready-made, out of the common southern storehouse. The economic determinism which he ignored in politics had its revenge, and the man who often differed with his constituents on political issues fell victim to the subtle power of economics. As the South Carolina philosophy took form, issuing finally in the romantic conception of a Greek democracy, it imposed itself imperiously on the southern mind, on the commoner equally with the aristocrat. It was impossible to escape, unless, like Moncure Conway, one were of an idealistic temper far different from the common run. For Stephens it

---

[4] See *A Constitutional View*, etc., Vol. I, pp. 406–408.

proved impossible. In this matter of slavery he had no individual opinion; his mind was molded by the common psychology and became a repository of the common prejudice. He followed his fire-eating friend Bob Toombs into the camp of Calhoun, and talked about a Greek democracy in true Charleston style. In a speech delivered on March 21, 1861, shortly after he was chosen Vice President of the Confederacy, he gave expression to the new philosophy in these words:

The prevailing ideas entertained by . . . most of the leading statesmen at the time of the formation of the old Constitution were that the enslavement of the African was in violation of the laws of nature; that it was wrong in principle, socially, morally, and politically. It was an evil they knew not well how to deal with, but the general opinion of the men of that day was that, somehow or other in the order of Providence, the institution would be evanescent and pass away. . . . Those ideas, however, were fundamentally wrong. They rested upon the assumption of the equality of races. This was an error. Our new government is founded upon exactly the opposite idea; its foundations are laid, its corner-stone rests upon the great truth that the negro is not equal to the white man; that slavery—subordination to the superior race—is his natural and normal condition . . . in conformity with the ordinance of the Creator. . . . Our Confederacy is founded upon principles in strict conformity with these [Divine] laws. This stone which was rejected by the first builders "is become the chief of the corner"—the real "corner-stone" in our new edifice. (Pendleton, *Alexander H. Stephens*, pp. 251–254.)

To the end of his life Stephens saw no reason to change his opinion on negro slavery. He regarded it as more humane than wage slavery because of the patriarchal responsibility devolving upon the master. The institution was not founded, he said, on "the erroneous dogma of the greatest good to the greatest number," but on the broader principle of securing "the greatest good possible, morally, intellectually, and politically, to all classes of persons . . . without necessary wrong or detriment to any" (*Constitutional View, etc.*, Vol. I, pp. 539–542). In his relations with his own slaves he followed the best traditions of the South. His kindness won their loyalty and affection. "Ef he ain't in heaven," said a house servant after his death, "'tain't no use for anybody else to try to git dere" (Pendleton, *Alexander H. Stephens*, p. 100). To the argument of Hinton Helper that the system was economically ruinous to the poor white, he seems to have given no consideration; but to the argument of the Abolitionist that it was immoral, he replied with deep conviction. On that point he would not yield an inch. After quoting a miscellany of Biblical texts from the earliest Hebraic times down to Paul, he comments naïvely:

> To maintain that Slavery is *in itself sinful*, in the face of all that is said and written in the Bible upon the subject, with so many sanctions of the relation by the Deity himself, does seem to me to be little short of blasphemous! It is a direct imputation upon the wisdom and justice, as well as the declared ordinances of God, as they are written in the inspired oracles, to say nothing of their manifestation in the universe around us. (*Ibid.*, Vol. II, p. 83.)

It is doubtful wisdom for the layman to meddle with Scripture. Stephens was a sounder interpreter of the writings of the constitutional fathers than of the will of God.

A careful historian devoted to a single idea rather than a creative political thinker; a thorough democrat of the Jeffersonian school, humanitarian, liberty-loving, courageous; a man who devoted his life to the preservation of constitutional liberty as it had taken shape before the industrial revolution unsettled the basis of modern life, Alexander H. Stephens was an honest gentleman who bravely defended the traditions of the South in the face of a new order. He was of an earlier generation, instinctively hostile to all consolidation, which, under the impulse of economic evolution, was obliterating state lines, gathering financial power in great reservoirs, and creating a new alignment between labor and capital. With such evolution it was axiomatic that political practice should follow economic fact; that a consolidating wealth should create a consolidated political state. Great enterprises with ramifications in every section would not long tolerate a multitude of state sovereignties; sovereignty must be centralized at Washington where it could be guided and controlled. The war only hastened what in the nature of things was inevitable. Stephens rightly insisted that slavery was only the immediate *casus belli*. The deeper cause was the antagonistic conceptions of the theory and functions of the political state that emerged from antagonistic economic systems. That the principle of local self-government should have been committed to the cause of slavery, that it was loaded with an incubus certain to alienate the liberalism of the North, may be accounted one of the tragedies of American history. It was disastrous to American democracy, for it removed the last brake on the movement of consolidation, submerging the democratic individualism of the South in an unwieldy mass will, and

surrendering the country to the principle of capitalistic exploitation. Stephens never seems to have realized this grave mistake in
strategy. He never realized that the principle of democracy, in
the cause of which he believed that he was faithful to the end,
received a staggering blow from the enlistment of northern
liberalism under the banners of a consolidating nationalism.
He remained to the last an unreconstructed Jeffersonian, convinced
that the lost cause was the cause of liberal democracy.

IV

FRANCIS LIEBER
A New-Modeled Federalism

To turn from Calhoun and Stephens to Francis Lieber is to pass
from the South to the North, from an obsolescent political theory
to a prophetic conception, from the doctrine of states rights to
the principle of an evolving state that draws all lesser sovereignties into its orbit by the law of attraction. Joseph Story had
educed the legal conception of the organic nature of the federal
union from the terms of the Constitution; Francis Lieber provided
a philosophical background that justified the same conclusion;
and under the combined legal and philosophical attack the compact theory found its philosophical breastworks leveled, its natural-
rights theory undermined, and its commanding position effectively
turned.

The figure of our first academic political philosopher appears
oddly out of place in the midst of South Carolina politicians, yet
fate set the studious German in the thick of the Fire Eaters, to
cogitate a philosophy of freedom in the land of slavery, and to justify the spirit of nationalism amongst the advocates of particularism. For twenty-one years he lived quietly in his southern classroom and study, disregarding the passions that buzzed about him,
elaborating ideas that in later years came to exercise a determining influence upon our academic political thinkers, and publishing ponderous volumes that marked the beginning of the swing
away from the natural-rights philosophy and towards the conception of an engrossing political state. Applying German liberalism
to American constitutionalism, he succeeded in new-modeling the
Federalism of Hamilton and sending it forth to meet the needs of
an imperializing generation. He agreed with Calhoun in the

latter's attack on French romantic theories; he agreed with Webster in the conception of the organic nature of the federal compact; but he went further and elaborated a theory of the state as an historical development that receives its form and spirit from the impress of social needs. Building on a foundation provided by Montesquieu and Burke, guided by Hamilton and Marshall, he set about erecting a structure that in the hands of Theodore Woolsey and John W. Burgess came to overtop all local and state sovereignties—an imperial authority that, in the words of Burgess, must become "the organ of interpretation in last instance of the order of life for its subjects" (Merriam, *American Political Theories*, p. 299). In that subtle shift of vocabulary from citizen to subject appears the final result of the speculations begun by Lieber, which in rejecting the natural-rights philosophy overthrew the defenses erected by the eighteenth century against an engrossing political state, and set the individual citizen at the mercy of a new divine-right sovereignty. "Really the state cannot be conceived," according to Burgess, "without sovereignty, *i. e.* without unlimited power over its subjects; that is its very essence" (Merriam, *American Political Ideas: 1865–1917*, p. 380).

Between the democratic Stephens and the imperializing Burgess stands the work of Francis Lieber. Born in Germany in the year 1800, son of a well-to-do Berlin family, Lieber's youth and young manhood fell in stirring times. When only fifteen he served in the Waterloo campaign under Blücher, was wounded, stricken with typhus, and nearly lost his life. From those perilous experiences he emerged a pronounced liberal. During the Metternich reaction he fell under suspicion, served a prison term for his political opinions, graduated from the University of Jena, and in 1822 went to Greece with a group of young German idealists to serve the cause of revolution. Disgusted with the Greek character he made his way to Italy, fell in with the historian Niebuhr, became tutor to the latter's son for a year, continued his university studies, was a second time imprisoned, and finally in 1826 quitted a hopelessly reactionary Germany, spent a year in England, and then emigrated to America, following the example of Prof. Charles Follen. In Boston he taught gymnastics for a time, edited the *Encyclopedia Americana,* and in 1835 was appointed to the professorship of history and political economy in South Carolina College. Here he remained till 1856, teaching, writing, and acquiring academic fame. In 1855 he aspired to the presidency of the college, a post then vacant, but his political theories were in disrepute with the legislature, and his views on slavery were under general suspicion. Becoming embroiled with the politicians, he lost the post, resigned his professorship, and went to New York City, and in 1857 he was called to the new chair of history and political science at Columbia, where he remained till his death in 1872.

The two books on which rests his reputation, *Political Ethics* (1838–1839) and *Civil Liberty and Self-Government* (1853), are substantial volumes quite lacking the genial note that marks his *Stranger in America* (1834), a series of sketchy letters that among other things contains an extraordinarily vivid account of his experiences at Waterloo (*Letters VI, VII*). To a casual reader these excursions into the philosophy of politics are as soberly respectable as a judge's wig, as studiously conventional as a professor's gown. He went about the business of blowing up the accepted Jeffersonian philosophy decently, in the name of the law and under the high sanction of liberty. There can be no doubt that this German liberal was a passionate lover of liberty, and no doubt of his conviction that freedom is possible only in a society under the reign of law. Like Hamilton, he had no local ties or state loyalties to circumscribe his political allegiance. It was natural for him to think in terms of nationality. His bitter experience in Germany had laid open to him the fatal weakness of petty states, and he was loath to see repeated in America the history of warring antagonisms that disrupted the German people. He was a profound admirer of the British constitution, more English than German in his conception of liberty.

The nationalism of Lieber was identical with that of John Adams. It was, in a phrase, government by law. But this government by law was both political and legal. The former, he believed, was admirably provided for by the federal Constitution; the latter was equally provided for by the body of the Common Law; with these twin safeguards, he was convinced, the liberty of the citizen was assured. In his interpretation of the Constitution Lieber added little that was new. He followed the older Federalists back to Montesquieu, and accepted the existing system of constitutional checks as the final word of political wisdom. In *Civil Liberty and Self-Government* he glorifies the federal system as the apotheosis of representative republicanism, quite unconcerned at its undemocratic features. The sufficiency of the Common Law to all social needs and the implicit sovereignty of the judiciary, he regards as equally axiomatic. "The law," he says, "must be the lord and our 'earthly god,' and not a man, a set of men, or the multitude" (*Civil Liberty and Self-Government*, p. 208). Yet with the common blindness of the legalist, he proceeds to erect a profession above society, and exalts a group of judges, appointive and not elective, preferably holding office for life, as the embodiment of impartial justice. That it is a presumption contrary to fact seems not to have entered his mind. That judicial interpretation implies judicial legislation, and that judicial legislation implies the sovereignty of lawyers, are logical deductions of which his philosophy made no account. Unfriendly to a democracy, he was content to yield authority into the hands of the judiciary.

But if in his exaltation of the Common Law he was as extreme a legalist as Hugh Legaré, in his doctrine of historical evolution he discovered the seeds of freedom in what he calls institutions. By these he means the organic expressions of daily life, or the customs of society which take spontaneous form from its needs. It is no other than the social fabric that Tom Paine was fond of contrasting, in its pervasive and beneficent coöperation, with the repressive tyrannies of the political state. Where liberty reposes thus in the social fabric, Lieber argues, the sovereign power is held in check; and where institutional freedom has not taken root, the political state will run into absolutism.

"Liberty," he argues, "is a thing that grows, and institutions are its very garden beds. There is no liberty which as a national blessing has leaped into existence in full armor like Minerva from the head of Jove. Liberty is crescive in its nature. It takes time, and is difficult, like all noble things. . . . It must be defended, developed, conquered, and bled for. It can never be added, like a mere capital on a column; it must pervade the whole body" (*Civil Liberty and Self-Government*, pp. 334–335, third edition). "Liberty stands in need of character," and this character is received from social institutions. He then proceeds:

. . . An institution is a system or body of usages, laws, or regulations of extensive and recurring operation, containing within itself an organism by which it effects its own independent action, continuance, and generally its own farther development. Its object is to generate, effect, regulate, or sanction a succession of acts, transactions, or productions of a peculiar class or kind. The idea of an institution implies a degree of self-government. Laws act through human agents, and these are, in the case of institutions, their officers or members. (*Ibid.*, p. 300.)

It was the deep-rooted *civisme anglais*, he believed, that had developed the orderly liberty of the English race; and it is this same institutional spirit that provides the surest check upon the augmenting power of the political state. There can be no tyranny where society is trained and disciplined in liberty.

The creative source and origin of this excellent *civisme anglais* Lieber discovered in the principle of local self-government; in the exercise of local control of local interests; the enjoyment of innumerable lesser sovereignties within the larger national organism. These lesser sovereignties are both civil and social, and the amount of liberty enjoyed in a given society is measured by the independent vigor with which they function. The exercise of definite rights by the several states is clearly one of the important institutional functions of self-government, but it is only one. The New England town-meeting, county and city governments, are even more important, while outside these civil organisms are innumerable social organisms, exercising their common right of establishing by-laws for their own governance, and spreading the spirit of liberty through all the practices of society.

According to the Anglican view, institutional self-government consists in the fact that all the elementary parts of the government, as well as the highest and most powerful branches, consist in real institutions . . . [but it] consists, farther, in the unstinted freedom and fair protection which are granted to institutions of all sorts, commercial, religious, cultural, scientific, charitable, and industrial, to germinate and to grow—provided they are moral and do not invade the equal rights of others. It receives its aliment from a pervading spirit of self-reliance and self-respect—the real afflatus of liberty. (*Ibid.*, p. 320.)

This, quite evidently, is the spirit of *laissez faire* applied to political philosophy. A people thus used to order their social affairs, as the English people have long done, will prove competent to manage their political affairs; and the widespread spirit of individual independence will prevent the drift towards unregulated centralism with its corollary of tyrannical power. The conception of institutional liberty embodies much of the spirit of Jeffersonianism, and it goes back in its origins as far as Roger Williams.

The states-rights advocates, Lieber implies, were mistaken in seeking the principle of liberty through particularism. In magnifying the individual commonwealth they overlooked the more vital units of self-government. To erect the state above the nation was no lasting solution of the most difficult problem in political philosophy, namely, the coördination of sovereign power with individual liberty; it was only to substitute one sovereignty for another, whereas to encourage the spread of self-governing bodies through society was to provide the necessary countercheck to centralizing power and coördinate liberty and sovereignty under the reign of law.

A stimulating thinker was this German liberal with his historical method and his conception of an evolutionary freedom rooted in the institutions of the English people. He gave a new turn to speculation on the origin and nature of the political state, the immediate consequence of which was the repudiation of the compact theory and natural-rights philosophy by our academic political scientists. The organic conception of the political state fell in with the centralizing movement that followed the Civil War, a movement which the forces of institutional self-government have been powerless to prevent. On the whole the influence of Lieber has been rather against than for that liberty which was so dear to him, and the explanation is to be found in the tragic divorce, in his thinking, of politics and economics. His inveterate legalism and his failure to investigate the economics of politics proved in the end the undoing of his liberalism.

CHAPTER III

THE DREAM OF A GREEK DEMOCRACY

I

THE pronounced drift of southern thought, in the years immediately preceding the Civil War, towards the ideal of the Greek democracy, has been too carelessly forgotten by later times. It was no vagrant eddy but a broadening current of tendency. In its blend of romanticism and realism it fitted exactly the temper of the plantation mind, imparting a fine idealism to shiftless realities and setting a generous goal to be achieved by somewhat inadequate agencies. A humane and cultivated democracy, set free from the narrow exactions of economics to engage in the higher work of civilization, was a conception worthy of the generous southern mind, a conception that does not suffer by contrast with the northern dream of an exploitative industrialism. That it was an impossible dream does not lessen its significance as an expression of the best southern aspiration in the days when slavery was on the defensive.

It is plain enough now that this drift of thought resulted from the need of clarifying the logic of the situation, by bringing into harmony two seemingly irreconcilable facts, the system of negro slavery and the rising spirit of white democracy. The feudal principle, which lurks in the background of all slave systems and which was peculiarly congenial to the plantation temper, was confronted on every side by the stubborn democracy of the yeomanry. A hundred miles beyond Charleston the feudal spirit encountered the leveling individualism of the frontier; and this passion for equality, that grew fiercer with every remove westward, was a stumbling-block in the way of the planter aristocracy. Caught thus between the two forces of a Jeffersonian democracy and a slave economy, southern thought found in the Greek ideal the most natural compromise. Since manual labor was black, a white skin was a guarantee against serfdom, and the common race prejudice was accounted sufficient to draw even the poor whites to the support of slavery. The sharp cleavage between the races provided the basis for the conception of a common white democracy of the

99

master class, every member of which shared in the supremacy of the race and was free to enjoy the profits of negro exploitation. The enterprising small farmer might rise to be a gentlemanly planter, providing his children with leisure to fit themselves for citizenship in the commonwealth and assist in the great work of creating a southern civilization. The Greek ideal, in short, met the double need of southern economics and southern prejudices, and made its appeal even to the frontier spirit of equalitarianism.

A native growth and rooted deep in southern realities, the new conception emerged in response to the changing times. It may be considered the plantation counterpart of northern industrialism, marking the reaction of the southern mind to the economic revolution in western civilization. With their diverse economics, North and South were facing in different directions, and the Greek ideal was as natural in Charleston as industrial feudalism was natural in Lowell. Created in part as an ingenious measure of defense, it provided an excellent counter offensive against alien critics by turning the light of inquiry upon the bases of capitalism and thrusting upon the attention of godly Puritans the dependence of culture upon exploitation. The new industrialism was creating a new philosophy of labor, and this philosophy the southern apologists seized upon and turned to their special ends. They accepted certain of the capitalistic premises, but they interpreted those premises in a spirit of drastic realism, deducing conclusions disconcerting to the apologists of industrialism. In defending the plantation system they attacked the factory system; in upholding black slavery they attacked wage slavery; and in this game of the pot and the kettle the exploitative root of both systems was nakedly exposed.

The major premise of the new southern philosophy was identical with that of northern capitalism, namely, that every civilization rests on labor exploitation. However quaintly they might embroider this fact with romantic patterns, they saw it clearly and deduced from it the conclusion that the North was indulging in a vicious fallacy in confusing wage labor with free labor. In every industrialized society, they pointed out, free labor is an anachronism; where it exists it is a hold-over from a simpler social order. The development of industrialism tends to draw all labor into its capacious maw, and the labor surplus that results from evicting the peasant from the land creates a competitive labor market that speedily reduces the laborer to the status of a wage-slave. Since slavery, then, in some form is the inevitable counterpart of modern civilization, the question that presses on the conscience of every enlightened and generous observer is the question of the relative well-being of the slave under the different systems. Upon this question the southern apologists turned their shrewdest analysis. They examined the condition of the proletariat in the English mill towns; they commented on the callous exploitation of the textile workers in Massachusetts; they assessed the waste in the labor turnover under the factory system; they considered the seeds of class war sown by industrialism and pointed out the insecurity of society under a system of capitalistic irresponsibility. In their estimate of the social evils of industrialism they concurred in the findings of Carlyle and antedated much of the criticism of Ruskin. The huge mass of unpalatable fact which they uncovered was the same mass that inspired George Ripley and Albert Brisbane and Horace Greeley to seek a way out by the path of coöperative commonwealths.

But in the hands of these apologists the argument was turned to the narrower end of proving that the southern field-hand fared better than the northern mill-hand. They recognized both systems as capitalistic, established in labor exploitation; but they proved to their own satisfaction that the southern was far humaner, more truly social. In the South, they pointed out, there was no waste in the labor turnover, no ugly labor scrap-heap, no ruthless efficiency in using up the human material. The master was responsible to society for the treatment and conduct of his slaves, and the southern conscience was far tenderer in the matter than the northern. The workers were never troubled by uncertain means of subsistence. The young were free from care, the old and infirm were adequately provided for. Living conditions were commonly pleasant, and the personal relations between master and slave kindly and loyal. When every argument against slavery had been urged it still remained true that the patriarchal tie that existed on the plantation was more humane than the cash-nexus of capitalism. In this fundamental matter Carlyle was right; and right also in his insistence on the need of capable masters. The South was fortunate in its system. On the self-sufficient plantations there was many an Abbot Sampson directing his little world wisely and humanely; collectively these Abbot Sampsons formed a capable and socially

responsible ruling class worthy of their trust. The economic returns of a wage-slave industrialism might be greater, but the returns in civilization were far less.[1]

Such, in brief, was the reaction of the southern mind in the early
fifties to the challenge of an industrializing generation. It was not
till the publication of *Uncle Tom's Cabin* in 1851 that southern
apologists were fully aroused to the need of counter propaganda.
They had been moving slowly towards the conception of a Greek
democracy under the leadership of Calhoun, but now under the
sharp prod of Abolitionism they turned militant. Facts were
collected and arguments clarified, and the war was carried home to
New England. In three years following *Uncle Tom*, according to a
recent student, fourteen pro-slavery novels appeared together with
other matter.[2] Much of the material made use of in these stories
was conveniently assembled in a work entitled *Pro-Slavery Argument*, published in 1852, a collaboration by Professor Dew of
William and Mary College, Chancellor Harper of the Supreme
Court of South Carolina, Governor Hammond of South Carolina, and Gilmore Simms. The first reviewed the Scriptural
authority for slavery; Chancellor Harper drew from Hobbes
the familiar argument that "a state of nature is a state of war";
Simms elaborated the patriarchal theory; but Governor Hammond developed the more significant argument of the degradation of the wage-slave, an argument elaborated at considerable
length in another work entitled *Letters on Slavery*, in which he
presented the results of his investigation of English factory conditions. The novels that Miss Tandy comments upon have been
pretty much forgotten, but the titles of some of them sufficiently
reveal the lines of attack. L. B. Chase's *English Serfdom and
American Slavery* (1854), J. W. Page's *Uncle Robin in His Cabin
in Virginia and Tom without One in Boston* (1855), and S. H.
Elliott's *New England Chattels* (1858) quite evidently reflect the

---

[1] The same argument was made use of by northern supporters of slavery.
Gordon Bennett's *New York Herald*, for example, "printed a description of slum
life in Liverpool, remarking that compared with the English laborer, 'the slave
lived like a prince.' He had his cabin, neat, clean, and weather-proof: he had his
own garden patch, over which he was lord paramount; he was well fed, well lodged,
well clothed, and rarely over-worked; sleek, happy, contented, enjoying his many
holidays with gusto, he lived to a great age" (quoted in Allan Nevins, *The Evening
Post: A Century of Journalism*, p. 271).

[2] See Jeannette Reid Tandy, "Pro-Slavery Propaganda in American Fiction in the
Fifties," *South Atlantic Quarterly*, January–March, 1922. See also Francis Pendleton Gaines, *The Southern Plantation*, Chapter III.

new southern philosophy. If the South were attacked, it was not without weapons to defend itself.

II

WILLIAM J. GRAYSON

Of this very considerable literature of defense, *The Hireling and the Slave* presents in convenient compass the most telling southern arguments, and reveals in its sharp contrast of realism and romanticism the common southern temper. Its author, William J. Grayson, was a cultivated South Carolinian who had served two terms in Congress and for years was collector of the Port of Charleston. He was widely read, was familiar with contemporary English writers on economics, and possessed a fluent pen. He had published "an elaborate heroic poem entitled *The Country*," in which he had sung "the praises of rural life and agricultural pursuits" (Introduction to Grayson's *Life of James L. Petigru*), and a volume entitled *Chicora and other Poems*, the title work of which was a romantic poem celebrating the primitive virtues of the Indian. Politically he was affiliated with the anti-Calhoun party of Unionists. His closest friend was James L. Petigru, a sketch of whose life he wrote as a last labor of love, during the unhappy days of the Charleston siege. He did not go so far as Petigru in refusing to have any part in a war that he opposed, but the tragedy of it cut him to the quick. He was no Fire Eater, but a southern moderate—a gentleman of old-fashioned tastes whose views may be taken as those of the cultivated Charleston group to which he belonged, of Petigru, of Legaré, of Alfred Huger.

The Hireling and the Slave, published in 1856 when Grayson was sixty-eight and dedicated to Petigru, is a poem in heroic couplets of approximately 1600 lines, divided into two parts. The first part draws a realistic picture of the life of the wage-slave, the second paints an idyllic picture of the life of the bond-slave. In this second part the spirit of romance holds high carnival; the descriptions are done with gusto and the rural pleasures that fall to the lot of the negro provide a striking contrast to the mean environment of the factory worker. About this contrast are grouped the lesser arguments: the hypocrisy of the Yankee Abolitionist, the sentimentalism of English humanitarians, the wisdom of providence in providing masters to protect the negro from destruction by a superior race and train him through apprenticeship in slavery to carry the blessings of civilization to Africa.   The heroic couplet was deliberately adopted to offer "some variety to the poetic forms that are almost universally prevalent."   "The poetry of the day is, for the most part," Grayson remarked, "subtile and transcendental in its character"; yet "the school of Dryden and Pope is not entirely forgotten," and "the most fastidious appetite may tolerate an occasional change of diet, and exchange dainties now and then for plainer fare" (*The Hireling and the Slave*, Preface, pp. xiv–xv).   The poem seems to have been popular in the South, and a southern reviewer declared that "it ought to be on every man's mantel" (*Life of James L. Petigru*, p. vii).

   In the preface Grayson discusses the subject of slavery with a candor somewhat unusual, acknowledging its evils, yet discovering compensations.   As an expression of intelligent southern opinion on a question in which the passions of the country were becoming deeply engaged, his views deserve quotation.   Slavery, he says,

. . . is that system of labor which exchanges subsistence for work, which secures a life-maintenance from the master to the slave, and gives a life-labor from the slave to the master.   The slave is an apprentice for life, and owes his labor to his master; the master owes support, during life, to the slave.   Slavery is the Negro system of work.   He is lazy and improvident.   Slavery makes all work, and it insures homes, food, and clothing for all.   It permits no idleness, and it provides for sickness, infancy, and old age.   It allows no tramping or skulking, and it knows no pauperism.

This is the whole system substantially.   All cruelty is an abuse; does not belong to the institution; is now punished, and may be in time prevented.   The abuses of slavery are as open to all reforming influences as those of any civil, social, or political condition.   The improvement in the treatment of the slave is as marked as in that of any other laboring class in the world. . . .   If slavery is subject to abuses, it has its advantages also.   It establishes more permanent, and, therefore, kinder relations between capital and labor.   It removes what Stuart Mill calls 'the widening and imbittering feud between the class of labor and the class of capital.' It draws the relation closer between master and servant.   It is not an engagement for days or weeks, but for life.   There is no such thing with slavery as a laborer for whom nobody cares or provides.   The most wretched feature in hireling labor is the isolated, miserable creature who has no home, no food, and in whom no one is particularly interested. *This is seen among hirelings only.* (*Ibid.*, Preface, pp. vii–viii.)

   The principle on which Grayson bases his argument is the principle that civilization rests on labor exploitation, but as a good churchman he attributes the evil to God and discovers the children of Adam to be suffering from the primeval curse—"Slave, hireling, help—the curse pursues him still." More specifically the thesis which he defends is this, "The state of the hireling and the slave [is] the same substantially—the condition hard labor, the reward subsistence;" and the conclusion which he draws is that the slave obtains a larger return for his labor than the factory hand. The picture he paints of the condition of the wage slave of England is Hogarthian in its details:

> There, unconcerned, the philanthropic eye
> Beholds each phase of human misery;
> Sees the worn child compelled in mines to slave
> Through narrow seams of coal, a living grave,
> Driven from the breezy hill, the sunny glade,
> By ruthless hearts, the drudge of labor made,
> Unknown the boyish sport, the hours of play,
> Stripped of the common boon, the light of day,
> Harnessed like brutes, like brutes to tug, and strain,
> And drag, on hands and knees, the loaded wain:
> There crammed in huts, in reeking masses thrown,
> All moral sense and decency unknown,
> With no restraint but what the felon knows,
> With the sole joy that beer or gin bestows,
> To gross excess and brutalizing strife,
> The drunken hireling dedicates his life:
> Starved else, by infamy's sad wages fed,
> There women prostitute themselves for bread,
> And mothers, rioting with savage glee,
> For murder'd infants spend the funeral fee;
> Childhood bestows no childish sports or toys,
> Age neither reverence nor repose enjoys,
> Labor with hunger wages ceaseless strife,
> And want and suffering only end with life;
> In crowded huts contagious ills prevail,
> Dull typhus lurks, and deadlier plagues assail,
> Gaunt Famine prowls around his pauper prey,
> And daily sweeps his ghastly hosts away;
> Unburied corses taint the summer air,
> And crime and outrage revel with despair. (*Ibid.*, pp. 24–25.)

Grayson does not stint his facts but traces the wretchedness of the wage-slave through all the phases of his misery to provide a background for the happier lot of the bond-slave. It is an unlovely picture, done with considerable vigor, from which one turns gladly to contemplate life on the southern plantation.

And yet the life, so unassailed by care,
So blessed with moderate work, with ample fare,
With all the good the starving pauper needs,
The happier slave on each plantation leads;
Safe from harassing doubts and annual fears,
He dreads no famine in unfruitful years;
If harvests fail from inauspicious skies,
The master's providence his food supplies;
No paupers perish here for want of bread,
Or lingering live, by foreign bounty fed;
No exiled trains of homeless peasants go,
In distant climes, to tell their tales of woe:
Far other fortune, free from care and strife,
For work, or bread, attends the Negro's life,
And Christian slaves may challenge as their own,
The blessings claimed in fabled states alone—
The cabin home, not comfortless, though rude,
Light daily labor, and abundant food,
The sturdy health that temperate habits yield,
The cheerful song that rings in every field,
The long, loud laugh, that freemen seldom share,
Heaven's boon to bosoms unapproached by care,
And boisterous jest and humor unrefined,
That leave, though rough, no painful sting behind;
While, nestling near, to bless their humble lot,
Warm social joys surround the Negro's cot,
The evening dance its merriment imparts,
Love, with its rapture, fills their youthful hearts,
And placid age, the task of labor done,
Enjoys the summer shade, the winter sun,
And, as through life no pauper want he knows,
Laments no poor-house penance at its close.   (*Ibid.*, pp. 50–51.)

Convinced of the righteousness and humanity of slavery Grayson
turns with scorn upon the Abolitionists and their meddlesome interference with the beneficent ways of Providence. With a few dexter-
ous turns of the spit he browns each one nicely like a roasted goose.
His descriptions strip off the gay plumage and reveal the naked
fowl. He makes a good job of it, as witness these bits:

There supple Sumner, with the Negro cause,
Plays the sly game for office and applause;
What boots it if the Negro sink or swim?
He wins the Senate—'tis enough for him. . . .
He heeds nor court's decree nor Gospel light,
What Sumner thinks is right alone is right. . . .

There Greeley, grieving at a brother's woe,
Spits with impartial spite on friend and foe. . . .
To each fanatical delusion prone,
He damns all creeds and parties but his own,
Brawls, with hot zeal, for every fool and knave,
The foreign felon and the skulking slave; . . .
And faction's fiercest rabble always find
A kindred nature in the Tribune's mind;
Ready each furious impulse to obey,
He raves and ravens like a beast of prey. . . .

There Seward smiles the sweet perennial smile,
Skilled in the tricks of subtlety and guile;
The slyest schemer that the world e'er saw;
Peddler of sentiment and patent law;
Ready for fee or faction to display
His skill in either, if the practice pay. . . . (*Ibid.*, pp. 38–40.)

As he contemplates Mrs. Stowe his full wrath is stirred. He does not spare her sex. Southern chivalry serves the pure and good in lovely woman, not the malignant and selfish. An unsexed woman is hateful to it, and after extolling the true womanliness of Florence Nightingale, angel of mercy, Grayson pays his compliments to the Yankee propagandist thus:

Not such with Stowe, the wish or power to please,
She finds no joy in gentle deeds like these;
A moral scavenger, with greedy eye,
In social ills her coarser labors lie;
On fields where vice eludes the light of day,
She hunts up crimes as beagles hunt their prey;
Gleans every dirty nook—the felon's jail,
And hangman's mem'ry, for detraction's tale,
Snuffs up pollution with a pious air,
Collects a rumor here, a slander there;
With hatred's ardor gathers Newgate spoils,
And trades for gold the garbage of her toils.

In sink and sewer thus, with searching eye,
Through mud and slime unhappy wretches pry;
In fetid puddles dabble with delight,
Search every filthy gathering of the night;
Fish from its depths, and to the spacious bag
Convey with care the black, polluted rag;
With reeking waifs secure the nightly bed,
And turn their noisome stores to daily bread.

(*Ibid.*, pp. 42–43.)

The Hireling and the Slave, is vigorous propaganda, carefully documented and pointed with modern instances, the work of an intelligent and humane writer who might be blind to certain evils in slavery but whose eyes were open to the social ills that grew rankly in the muck of industrialism. Outside of the South few in America had as yet come to understand so much—a handful of New England idealists, Parker and William Henry Channing and Emerson and Wendell Phillips, and Orestes Brownson, and a handful of Utopians, Albert Brisbane and George Ripley and Horace Greeley. The inadequacy of southern thought was identical with that of northern: blinded by sectional economic interests, they saw only half the truth. They beheld the mote in a brother's eye, but considered not the beam that was in their own.

CHAPTER IV
ADVENTURES IN BELLES LETTRES

I

OLD CHARLESTON

IN the year 1825 the little city of Charleston, with its fourteen thousand whites and more than fourteen thousand blacks, was perhaps the most delightful spot in America. The Mecca of plantation fashion and the capital of plantation politics, it prided itself on its genial and distinguished society. It was the last stronghold in America of the older pride of aristocracy. The tone of society still remained pretty much what it had been before the schism of '76. Social lines were rigid and an old-fashioned conservatism of temper marked the upper class. Despite the large admixture of French Huguenot blood the manners and prejudices of the aristocracy retained the pronounced British cast that came down from pre-Revolutionary times, and if Dr. Johnson could have stepped from the Fleet Street of 1780 to the Charleston of 1825 he would have felt almost at home. "We are decidedly more English than any other city of the United States," said Hugh Legaré," whose love of the English character was second only to his love of Charleston. It was a gay world with its country squires and their horses and racing, its Madeira drinking, its promenades and dancing and assemblies; one to win the affection of all who liked lighthearted ways.

But underneath this gay life was a more serious Charleston, which in certain of its aspects was not unlike Boston. From both the Huguenot and Scotch-Irish strains came a sobering Puritanism that gave a serious cast to thoughtful natures and disciplined them in a strict morality. Calhoun was far more Puritan than Fisher Ames, and Hugh Legaré than Edward Everett. Life was likely to be a serious business to these southern Puritans, filled with weighty responsibilities, to be lived, like Milton's, as ever in the great Taskmaster's eye. Aristocrat though he was, young Hugh Legaré was no gay cavalier treading the primrose path, but as serious-minded as any Roundhead. Victorian in manners, he would have found the bluff speech of the old revolutionary, General Charles Cotesworth Pinckney—"more pregnant with meaning than prudish in dress"—somewhat too "salt" for refined ears. It was this note of Puritanism that marked the finest characters in Charleston and gave its tone to society; but it was a Puritanism of conduct rather than dogma. Charleston gentlemen were of the English church, and their Puritanism, unwarped by Calvinism, assumed a moral rather than a theological cast.

The lawyer came to assume the position of intellectual leadership taken by the minister in New England. A profound respect for law dominated the Charleston mind. Blackstone was the Charleston Bible, and the lawyer who was master of dignified oratory was looked upon with high regard. The aristocracy opened its doors to young James Louis Petigru, an Irish-Huguenot lawyer with his own way to make, but it closed them tightly against young Gilmore Simms, apprentice to an apothecary and unread in the classics. Ambitious youths therefore turned to the law as a congenial career, for there reputations lay, and political influence. A pronounced cult of the law, and regard for orderly procedure, went hand in hand with the old English respect for individual rights. Charleston gentlemen could not be coerced, even by their own politicians, and Legaré was bitter against the Nullifiers because the spirit of dictation was "alien to our old habitudes, to the gentle courage, the courteous hostility, the mild and merciful justice, the proud submission to *law* and respect for right, which once distinguished our low country society from and above all other American society" (*Writings*, Vol. I, p. 211).

Politically Charleston was of the old Federalist tradition, as that Federalism was embodied in the picturesque figure of General Pinckney. Outside the narrow circle of the aristocracy, Federalism had long since given way to a democratic faith with its background of states-rights Jeffersonianism; but it lingered amongst the gentry and provided the nucleus of the later Union party. Grayson tells a story of Petigru that suggests the bitterness of the back-country democracy towards the old Federalism. The latter one day was being abused by a swamp-sucker "who lavished on him all the foul epithets and appellations he could remember or invent, of which rogue and scoundrel were among the most moderate." At last he hit upon a term of reproach "which at that day comprised everything hateful—he called him a 'damned Federal,'" and was promptly knocked down for the insult (William J. Grayson, *James Louis Petigru*, pp. 83–84). But the Charleston vintage of Federalism was little more than a stout conservatism that idealized the Union and preached the sufficiency and sacredness of the law. It was social rather than political or economic—the assertion of the prescriptive right of gentlemen to govern the state. Jeffersonianism never took possession of the first circles of Charleston as it did in Virginia, and French revolutionary philosophy found there an uncongenial soil. The profound conservatism of the aristocracy is sufficiently expressed in a comment of Hugh Legaré—"The politics of the immortal Jefferson! Pish!" (*Writings*, Vol. I, p. 207.) Physiocratic agrarianism found few advocates amongst Carolina gentlemen. The Charleston mind was political and legal rather than economic in its interests, and as a commercial port Charleston was more sympathetic with capitalism than with agrarianism. Its politics, in which it found much diversion, it preferred highly seasoned, and when Nullification divided the state into hostile camps, the Nullifiers and Unionists brought Charleston to the verge of civil war. Respect for law and the amenities vanished before the hot demands of partisanship.

The culture of Charleston was as conservatively old-fashioned as its politics. Such a renaissance as it enjoyed before the Civil War wrought its destruction was delayed by its rejection of French romantic thought until the beginning of the thirties, and synchronized with the renaissance of New England. When the romantic spirit appeared about 1825, it was primarily English, of the school of Tom Moore. There had never been any literature in Charleston worthy of the name, except such as had come from London, bound in calfskin and tooled morocco. Those who affected a love of letters were still enamored of the heroic couplet and the Addisonian essay. Not until he went to Brussels in 1832 did Legaré, the most brilliant southern linguist, take up the study of German. The classics still dominated education, and literary taste inclined to a mingling of wit and sentiment. Young and Ossian and Mrs. Radcliffe held honored places on Charleston bookshelves. The young poets were deep in Byron, and Sir Walter was in high repute. But Wordsworth and Shelley and Keats were scarcely mentioned, and Carlyle could not hope to gain a hearing. Nevertheless by the year 1828 the example of the *North American Review* proved so stimulating an incentive that the scholarship of Charleston collaborated to establish the *Southern Review*, which ran a sober course for four years, providing a medium for learned articles on law, letters and politics. It was a serious venture that concerned itself little with *belles lettres*, but the intellectual resources were inadequate, and on Legaré's departure for Europe *The Review* came to an end. Later, Gilmore Simms labored to the same purpose, but even his enormous energy was insufficient to sustain a magazine esteemed worthy of southern genius, and the work languished. Facile writers were fewer in Charleston than in Boston.

But despite any shortcomings in the way of letters, to members of its polite circles Charleston was the most delightful of American cities, and its society the most distinguished. "I have never, since I could form an opinion on such matters," wrote Legaré from Brussels, where he mingled with the most cultivated society, "doubted of the immense superiority of Carolina society over all others on that continent, and now feel it more than ever" (*Writings*, Vol. I, p. 218). It was a common opinion of southern gentlemen, who, with their English notions of a landed aristocracy, believed that "fixed landed property is of the essence of civil society, properly so called." It embodied the planter ideal of a social capital, uncorrupted by a vulgar plutocracy. Its highways ran out to the plantations; the free citizen of the Greek democracy drew his wealth from the soil; the slave labored while the master rode to and fro from the city. Law and politics were regarded as respectable vocations for sons of gentlemen, but the ideal life was acknowledged to be that of the planter, with his three thousand acres, his three hundred negroes, his ricks of rice and bales of tobacco and cotton. The profits that came from the law were certain to be invested in land, and the young attorney dreamed of retiring in middle life to a well-stocked plantation. To become a member of the ruling squirarchy was an ambition that filled and satisfied the Charleston imagination.

II

WILLIAM CRAFTS
Charleston Wit

The slightness of literary achievement in the Charleston of 1825 is sufficiently attested by the considerable local fame that rewarded the efforts of the volatile William Crafts. Born in Charleston in

1789, the son of a well-to-do Yankee father and a southern mother, he was sent to Harvard to complete his education, distinguished himself in the classics and in declamation, achieved a gownsman's fame for the brisk informality of a Latin oration, and carried back to Charleston a great reputation as a wit and scholar. He went into the law but burnt too few candles at the shrine of Blackstone; was seized with political ambition and proposed to make a great name for himself as a statesman, but his politics were not agreeable to his constituents and his career failed to arrive. He was a graceful orator in the florid southern style, an agreeable fellow with a pleasant wit, who loved society, dabbled in prose and verse, but proved to be unstable. He spread too much canvas to the uncertain winds and his unballasted bark came to grief. He died at the age of thirty-seven, leaving his writings to be gathered up and published by his family—a miscellany that brought down upon it the severe judgment of Hugh Legaré.

William Crafts was a transplanted Bostonian who essayed to domesticate Harvard culture among the polite circles of Charleston. As an undergraduate he admired the graceful preaching of Buckminster and the acrid eloquence of Fisher Ames. The latter he seems to have adopted as his political godfather, and from him he accepted a decadent Federalism that got him into trouble when later he entered politics. But the chief model on whom he shaped his life seems to have been Robert Treat Paine, in the declining sun of whose fame the young Harvard undergraduate warmed himself. With a less pregnant wit, a less trenchant prose style, a less masculine oratory, he succeeded in becoming a smaller edition of a petty master. The parallelism in the lives of the two apostles of wit is striking. They were both dabblers, but Crafts possessed less skill and dabbled less felicitously. They both broke with the rigid decorum of their circles, but Paine achieved a more tragic shipwreck. They both marked the last ebbing of the eighteenth century before the wit ideal was submerged by the incoming tide of romanticism, and the reputations of both have been forgotten.

In Crafts' case, certainly, no injustice has been done. Such literary wealth as he displayed would seem notable only in an indigent society. His prose is vapid and feeble in the essay, and stilted and artificial in the oration. His verse is insignificant in quantity—two formal poems and a handful of occasional pieces—

and wanting in distinction of phrase or imagery. It is the work of a graceful imitator of doubtful models. He wrote at the moment when the long supremacy of Pope was yielding to the popularity of Moore, and his verse wavered between the old loyalty and the new love. *Sullivan's Island*, a carefully elaborated descriptive poem, applies the structure and method of *Windsor Forest* to a local theme, following the original so closely as to imitate the detail. His skill in the grand manner may be judged by a single passage that phrases feebly what Pope had done vigorously:

> When cooler gales foretell departing day,
> The plaintive curlew homeward wings his way—
> Now stoops, then soars, and fearing danger nigh,
> To guardian heaven pours forth its piteous cry.
> Alas! in vain. The fowler's fond reply,
> Still deemed its own, but tells it where to die.

The Raciad is less crudely imitative. It is a brisk and rather amusing account of the outpouring of Charleston society to the races, the great event of the year in the gay southern capital. It is done with some sprightliness, it is an amiable historical document, but it is not important. When Crafts died in 1826 Charleston had done little in the way of creative literature, but the stirring of the waters was beginning. The following year a young apothecary just admitted to the bar published a volume entitled *Lyrical and Other Poems*, first fruits of the colossal labors of Gilmore Simms. In 1828 Hugh Legaré got *The Southern Review* on its feet, a substantial magazine that aspired to be the mouthpiece of southern culture. With the beginning of the thirties the Charleston renaissance was under way.

III

HUGH SWINTON LEGARÉ

Charleston Intellectual

A far solider nature than the ebullient Crafts was Hugh Swinton Legaré. Of distinguished social position, the most cultivated mind in the South before the Civil War, and one of the most cultivated in America, he was an embodiment of the serious Charleston that served as counterweight to the gayer. In Legaré the moral earnestness of the South came to its most attractive expression. The repository of two streams of ethical idealism, he was as Puritan as Calhoun. Natively aristocratic, with a high sense of personal integrity and civic responsibility, a profound student of law and letters, with the Charleston parochialism brushed away by wide travel and intimate acquaintance with old-world civilizations and classical cultures, he represented the excellent seriousness that came to flower on the Carolina plantation as well as in the New England meetinghouse. Southern Puritanism might be less ungainly than that of Massachusetts, but it was equally introspective, given to melancholy; and Hugh Legaré found his life as serious an affair, and as laborious, as any New England Calvinist discovered his to be. It is no holiday business to serve righteousness; wisdom does not flower in the primrose path of dalliance; and this Charleston gentleman emerged from a prolonged and arduous self-discipline as complete a Puritan as Theodore Parker.

Descended in the fifth generation from a Huguenot ancestor who settled in Charleston about 1695, he was French in name and by cherished family tradition, but in little else. Through successive intermarriages, the original French strain was pretty much diluted by the Scotch and English, and few Gallic traits came down to him. In temperament and sympathies he was the child of his mother, Mary Swinton, of Scotch Covenanter blood. The native seriousness that came to him by right of inheritance was intensified by fate. Inoculated for the smallpox in his fourth year, the poison lingered in his system, keeping him sickly for years and permanently stunting the lower half of his body. Thus set apart from active life, he turned to books and entered upon the career of a scholar. At the time of his death in 1842, at the age of forty-five, he was perhaps the best linguist and the most widely read man in America. A mature student of the classics, he was intimately acquainted with French, Spanish, Italian and German, and had added Romaic as a help to his Greek. This may seem a meager list in comparison with Theodore Parker's nineteen languages, but the substantial acquisitions he gathered from the several bodies of literature were far from meager.

Yet immense as were those acquisitions they were only supplementary to his professional studies. The Charleston Puritan gave to the study of law the same intensity that the Boston Puritan gave to theology. Not content with a three years' reading course in a law office, he went to Europe to pursue his studies more comprehensively. At the University of Edinburgh he plunged into an investigation of the Roman and Civil Law, which henceforth was to be his major intellectual interest. He found in the continental systems, he believed, a body of legal principles more comprehensive and philosophical than the English Common Law, and the ambition grew upon him to ingraft certain features of the Civil Law upon American practice. After two years' intense study he came home, engaged in active practice of his profession, and ten years later, at the age of thirty-five, was appointed *chargé d'affaires* at Brussels, where he spent four rich years. His diplomatic and social life was subordinated to his studies, into which he threw himself with the keenest zest, enlarging his knowledge of modern letters and adding to his encyclopedic knowledge of legal systems. In 1841 he was appointed Attorney-General of the United States in the cabinet of President Tyler, and upon Webster's retirement was given the additional portfolio of Secretary of State *ad interim*. While on a visit to Boston with President Tyler to assist in the Bunker Hill Monument celebration, he was taken suddenly ill and died at the home of his friend Professor Ticknor. The man thus prematurely cut down was a nature of vast solidity. Profoundly serious, inclined to the blackest melancholy, as pessimistic as Fisher Ames, with no leaven of humor, no romance, no careless idling, he was a hard taskmaster to his days. He toiled prodigiously at his self-appointed tasks. His standards were severe, whether in letters or law or politics or morals. As a critic he dealt with substantial subjects: *The Constitutional History of Greece; The Origin, History and Influence of Roman Legislation; Early Spanish Ballads; Jeremy Bentham and the Utilitarians; Lord Byron's Character and Writings*—solid dissertations done with German thoroughness—reviews of huge compass that provided opportunity for independent treatises. As a lawyer he was rather a philosophical historian than a special pleader. He was far more given to exploring the labyrinths of ancient codes than to arguing cases. His legal erudition appalls the layman. He had sat at the feet of black-letter philosophers; he had been instructed by sages long since forgotten. His mind was an ample storehouse of archaic legal maxims. He delighted in the crabbed law Latin—its sententious phrases worn to the quick, the residuum and repository of the wisdom bequeathed by past generations. Richer in poetry than any verses of Byron were the

Latin words *habeas corpus* to one who, like this scholar, understood
how packed they were with English history, how rich in suggestion
to all who love English freedom. From this immense erudition
came his love for old books and venerable authorities. Blackstone
he looked upon as a modern—"a gentleman's law book, clear, but
not deep"; and the wisdom of my Lord Coke seemed to him not so
mellow as that drawn from the more capacious vats of earlier days.
He quoted Grotius and Vattel and Pufendorf and Bourlamaqui
more readily than the South Carolina Digest, and the names of
Papinian and Ulpian and Modestinus and Voet and Cujacius,
of the *Corpus Alaricianum*, of the Justinian, Gregorian, Hermoge-
nian, and Theodosian codes, slipped familiarly from his pen. How
many outlandish authorities were contained in the huge inkwell
on his desk it is idle to conjecture. Probably not three men in
America comprehended the significance of half the references that
he offered for the consideration of his fellow lawyers, or were
competent to question his deductions. Even the learned Judge
Story and Chancellor Kent seem mere dabblers in comparison
with this philosophical historian.

Such learning must inevitably mold one's thinking in kindred
fields, and he came naturally to espouse what for want of an exacter
term may be called the Common Law theory of politics. It is a
conception of law as an organic growth, the result of man's laborious search for a rational freedom in the social body, the single
and avowed end of which is justice. It has taken form not by the
decrees of legislatures, but by decisions of the judiciary, tested
and reëxamined and reargued generation after generation; built
up code by code through slow evolution, the wisdom of the past
serving as counselor to the present; continuously expanding its
jurisdiction from the community to the nation, and from the
nation to a world society; the one guarantee of a sober and rational progress. Theorists and philosophers come and go; revolutions succeed and fail; foolish statutes and temporary constitutions
have their day; but the organic body of the law survives all surface
change, building into the fabric of society what experience proves
to be good, sloughing off what experience has outgrown—the
tempered rule of social justice; the exact measure of every civilization compared with which the majority will is a crude and inadequate makeshift.

From such a conception it follows that government is little more

than ancillary to the law, and political principles are sound in the
measure that they are founded on legal principles. Thus by following the musty path of jurisprudence Legaré arrived at the same
goal that John Cotton had reached two hundred years before—
the apotheosis of magistracy. With the older Puritan he could
assert, *Scripturae plenitudinem adoro.* The sufficiency of the law
to social justice was axiomatic in his thinking. But the scriptures
which he adored were the words of the judges, whose decisions
were above the authority of legislator or governor and little
concerned with a transient majority will. The old theocrat had
set up his theocracy; the modern lexolater would set up his lex-
ocracy; but the end was pretty much the same. Very likely Legaré,
like the present-day lexolater, would deny the conclusion, yet
it was implicit in his premises, and his scorn of political theory
was sufficient proof. Practical politics he regarded as rather a
trumpery business that achieves no solid results.[1] The political
philosopher he was profoundly suspicious of. The flood of speculation let loose upon the world by the revolutions of the
seventeenth and eighteenth centuries seemed to him to have
invited disaster, and the political classics of those revolutions
he cared little for. He distrusted the "era of illumination"
that sacrificed use and wont to abstract theory. "We have not
too much faith in the 'march of intellect,'" he remarked dryly,
"and would not . . . pitch our anticipations in too high a key"
(*ibid.*, Vol. II, p. 264). But his greatest contempt he reserved for
the intellectual revolutionaries—"hair-brained metaphysicians
and empirical demagogues" (*ibid.*, Vol. I, p. 216), who would upset the nice balance of the law. To this matter he returned again
and again, with the scorn of the legal mind for ambitious political
systems. "Innovators or Revolutionists, who go only for an
imaginary abstract rectitude and symmetry of government," he
said, "are always dangerous, and sometimes the greatest curse
with which heaven in its wrath can visit an offending people"(*ibid.*,
Vol. II, p. 286).

I have no faith at all in speculative politics. A theorist in government
is as dangerous as a theorist in medicine, or in agriculture, and for precisely the same reasons—the subjects are too complicated and too obscure
for simple and decisive experiments. I go for undisputed results in the
long run. (*Ibid.*, Vol. I, p. 303.)

_____
[1] See *Writings*, Vol. II, p. 104.

Man begins a revolution, but its issues are with God alone. The voluntary revolutions of man have always been abrupt, violent and for the worse: so that the wisdom of antiquity laid it down, as a maxim, that every fundamental change in the State must needs be bloody and deadly. (*Ibid.*, Vol. II, p. 297.)

This inherent conservatism of the legal mind explains Legaré's intellectual sympathy with Federalism and his contempt for Jefferson. The latter to him was the prince of demagogues, and his ink was vitriol when he wrote of him, as thus in one of his letters: "The immortal sayings and doings of the holy father in democracy—the servant of the servants of Demos (whose nose of wax he knew better than anybody how to shape to his own convenience,)—the infallible, though ever-changing, St. Thomas of *Canting*-bury. And here, you may be sure, I *cross* myself devoutly and cry out, with an all-fervent benediction to that canonized worthy, *pax tecum* (pronounced, you know, *Scottice*, *pox tacum*)" (*Writings*, Vol. I, p. 208). Modern political theories seemed to him mere upstart doctrines compared with the venerable principles of the law, and he came to look with suspicion on all political liberalism not sponsored by lawyers and supported by briefs. A passionate lover of liberty, he was as distrustful of democracy as John Adams, and his condemnation was as frank— "that scene of wild impulse, and tyrannical misrule—a pure democracy" (*ibid.*, Vol. II, p. 271). No state, Beverley Tucker pointed out, was so little democratic as South Carolina, and Legaré shared the common Charleston distrust of it. As he watched England and France during the tumultuous thirties, and saw the struggle over Nullification at home, his concern for the future became acute and his pessimism as black as Fisher Ames'. In a letter from Brussels, in the year 1833, shortly after the passage of the English Reform Bill, he wrote:

Mankind have too little sense to maintain, for any length of time, a well-tempered democracy, and a great deal too much to bear an unlimited one—the most dreadful form of " State sovereignty," beyond all doubt, in which the descendants of the father of the first murderer have ever given loose to their ruffian instinct of violence and oppression. If they have a moderate policy of the kind, which happens (as all complicated machines will) to be occasionally a little out of order, their only idea of a remedy is to pull it down, and along with it every thing that makes a civil society worthy of its name. Who could ever have dreamed that the law of brute

force which now crushes Europe . . . should be deliberately adopted in
America, instead of the really sublime institutions of a federal jurisdiction,
(fallible, of course, but generally right) and that this relapse into downright barbarism should be vaunted, by the most enlightened men in the
Southern States, as a *grand* improvement and the only thing wanting to
make our government as perfect as we have been swearing it was all along.
(*Ibid.*, Vol. I, p. 210.)

Back of this ingrained conservatism was a tender Puritan conscience that must twist his legal studies to ideal ends. After all it
was no other than a juridical romanticism that Hugh Legaré discovered in the bottom of his scholar's cup. As medieval as Sir
Walter, he sought his romance in old law-courts rather than in
feudal castles, in black-robed advocates rather than in knights and
ladies; and he persuaded himself that those old litigations, preserved in scraps of Latin and law French, were dramatic episodes in
the ceaseless battle for human rights, whereof the single objective
was justice. Slowly, stone upon stone, the lawyers were erecting
an impregnable citadel, within which justice kept her inviolable
court. It is a pleasant fiction still believed in by lawyers of the old
school, and to Legaré in his study it bore the very semblance of
truth. He had read too many law books; he had speculated too
little on politics; immersed in his codes, he had forgotten to inquire
into the hidden springs of sovereignty. In his contempt for practical politics he had neglected to study even the primer of economic
determinism. To the economic historian, Legaré's boundless faith
in the sufficiency of legal processes is incomprehensible. A few
lessons from the wiser Jefferson would have taught him much that
he needed to know concerning the economic sources of power. In
his attitude towards the law Jefferson was a suspicious realist.
He had no faith in legal codes that had grown up under monarchical
and aristocratic systems, and he put no trust in government by
lawyers. He could not understand how the Common Law, interpreted by the Tory Blackstone, and applied by Federalist lawyers,
should serve the needs of a democracy. Democratic America, he
was convinced, must create a new democratic law, and hold its
judiciary in strict subjection to its will; to surrender sovereignty
to an aristocracy of the bench would mean the abdication of democracy. But Legaré refused to go to school to Jefferson. He
clung to his romantic conception of the law with the same passionate conviction that Calhoun clung to his romantic dream of a

Greek democracy; and with the ebbing of the romantic tide they were both left stranded.

But if Legaré was unsympathetic towards the new political theory that came from the French intellectuals, and frankly hostile to the new political practice that came in with the Jacksonians, he warmly approved the new economics that came with the Industrial Revolution. In his whole-hearted acceptance of Adam Smith he seems not a Carolinian at all, but an English liberal of the Cobden-Bright school. He adopted the principle of *laissez faire*, the gospel of progress, the attitude of optimism. He accepted the theory of the beneficence of commerce as a universal civilizing agency, and he looked forward confidently to an eventual parliament of man, a future federation of the world. Commerce in the end must outlaw war, and peace with freedom would spread the blessings of civilization to the ends of the earth.[2]

A convincing object-lesson in the sufficiency of the principle of *laissez faire*, he discovered in the amazing progress of America. The mainspring of that progress he found in economic freedom— freedom "from those undue restraints and that impertinent interference of government in the interests properly belonging to individuals." "I know," he said, "that the cardinal spring and source of our success is freedom—freedom of thought, freedom of speech, freedom of action, freedom of commerce" (*Writings*, Vol. I, p. 306). The greatest of these was free trade between the states. His travels in England and the contrast between English progress and continental backwardness confirmed him in this belief. "The doctrine of Free Trade," he asserted, "is a great fundamental doctrine of civilization. The world must come to it at last, if the visions of improvement in which we love to indulge are ever to be realized" (*ibid.*, Vol. I, p. 272). He went further and accepted the Industrial Revolution with its division of labor as a necessary agency of social amelioration. "It is evidently in the order of nature, and we must take it with all its good and all its evils together." In forecasting the effect of that revolution he was troubled by no fears.

Sir, it is a favorite phrase of those who boast of what is called "the march of intellect," that things are thus changed because the "schoolmaster is abroad." But I tell you that something far more effective than the schoolmaster, a mightier than Solomon, is abroad. It is the STEAM-ENGINE—in

2 See "The Arbitrament of National Disputes," in *Writings*, Vol. I, pp. 355-357.

its twofold capacity of a means of production and a means of transport—
the most powerful instrument by far of pacification and commerce, and
therefore of improvement and happiness that the world has ever seen;
which, while it increases capital, and multiplies beyond all imagination
the products of industry, brings the most distant people into contact with
one another . . . effaces all peculiarities of national character, and
promises, at no distant period, to make the whole Christian world, at
least, one great family. . . .

A people well clad and well housed will be sure to provide themselves
with all the other comforts of life; and it is the diffusion of these comforts,
and the growing taste for them, among all classes of society in Europe—
it is the desire of riches as it is commonly called, that is gradually putting
an end to the destructive and bloody game of war, and reserving all the
resources hitherto wasted by it, for enterprises of industry and commerce,
prosecuted with the fiery spirit which once vented itself in scenes of peril
and carnage. (*Ibid.*, Vol. I, pp. 285–286.)

Remembering how dependent were southern cotton interests on
English industrialism and commerce, one can understand Legaré's
acceptance of *laissez faire* economics. His idealism, his local pride,
his romanticism, were all enlisted in its behalf, and he painted in
glowing colors. But his frank advocacy of capitalism is harder to
understand, except perhaps on the ground that Charleston was a
considerable shipping port and his clients were engaged in commerce. In the bitter dispute with Jackson over the Bank, Legaré
adopted northern views on national finance. Although nominally
a Democrat, he had never been an agrarian, and he went with
Webster and Clay against the subtreasury scheme and a metallic
currency. His thoughtful speech on *The Spirit of the Sub-Treasury*,
delivered in 1837, was thoroughgoing Whig doctrine, asserting
the excellence of the modern banking system and extolling the
economic fruitfulness of credit. He repudiated every principle
of John Taylor; denied every dogma of agrarian economics; and
eulogized the English financial system as the germinal source of
English greatness. Applying the principle of credit to American
conditions, he discovered the secret of American expansion in the
principle of speculative borrowing, and expanded his doctrine of
economic freedom by asserting that freedom to borrow was a
necessary preliminary to freedom to work. "A people have been
enriched by debt," he argued, overlooking the possible fallacy
of a *post hoc ergo propter hoc*, "and 'by owing, owe not.' " As
he contemplated the amazing progress of the nation, his lyric
enthusiasm becomes prologue to a somewhat lame conclusion

that enthrones the banker as the fairy godmother of the hardy pioneer.

There is a grandeur and a majesty in this irresistible onward march of a race, created, as I believe, and elected to possess and people a continent. . . . We may become so much accustomed to such things that they shall make as little impression upon our minds as the glories of the Heavens above us; but, looking on them, lately, as with the eyes of the stranger, I felt, what a recent English traveller is said to have remarked, that far from being without poetry, as some have vainly alleged, our whole country is one great poem. Sir, it is so; and if there be a man that can think of what is doing, in all parts of this most blessed of all lands, to embellish and advance it, who can contemplate that living mass of intelligence, activity and improvement as it rolls on, in its sure and steady progress, to the uttermost extremities of the west; who can see scenes of savage desolation transformed, almost with the suddenness of enchantment, into those of fruitfulness and beauty; crowned with flourishing cities, filled with the noblest of all populations; if there be a man, I say, that can witness all this passing under his very eyes, without feeling his heart beat high, and his imagination warmed and transported by it, be sure, sir, that the raptures of song exist not for him. . . .

But of this rational, diffusive liberty, among a people so intelligent as ours, the credit system is the natural fruit, the inseparable companion, the necessary means and instrument. It is part and parcel of our existence. Who ever heard of CREDIT in a despotism, or an anarchy? It implies *confidence*—confidence in yourself, confidence in your neighbor, confidence in your government, confidence in the administration of the laws, confidence, in a word, in your destiny, and your fortune, in the destinies and the fortunes of the country to which you belong; as, for instance, in the case of a great national debt. It is the fruit, I say, of all that is most precious in civilized life, and to quarrel with it is to be ungrateful to God for some of the greatest blessings he has vouchsafed to man. (*Writings*, Vol. I, pp. 306-307.)

Such ebullient rhetoric fits the mouth of the politician rather than the scholar, and such careless logic comes oddly from a southern intellectual. In his ignorance of the economics of John Taylor, Legaré was unprovided with principles to reply to his own arguments, and unaware of the lameness of his confident conclusions. But though he might glow with optimism as he contemplated the westward expansion, for the future of the South and of his own beloved state he was deep in pessimism. From the first he had dissented vigorously from the program of Nullification. An ardent Union man, he believed with his friend James Petigru that secession meant ruin for South Carolina. Calhoun seemed to him a monomaniac, consumed by a single idea. He feared the hot

passion of the states-rights party and he was troubled over slavery.
His travels abroad had acquainted him with European views on
the subject; he watched the spread of English humanitarianism
and he had come to recognize the institution as an anachronism.
It seemed to him impossible for the South to withstand much longer
the augmenting pressure of civilized opinion.   He could justify
slavery in his own eyes both by ancient law—*servitus est constitutio
juris gentium*—and by comparison of the condition of the negro
with that of the English wage worker.   The ideal of a Greek democracy was vastly congenial to his aristocratic temperament, but
he knew that it was a romantic dream, and he was oppressed by the
shadow of impending ruin.   Writing from Brussels on April 8,
1833, he concluded an anxious letter thus:

It ends in my not knowing what to think, except that dangers are
around and above and below and within our poor little State,—which
may God preserve us from! I ask of heaven only that the little circle I
am intimate with in Charleston should be kept together while I live,—
in health, harmony and competence; and that, on my return, I may myself be enabled to enjoy the same happiness, in my intercourse with it,
with which I have been hitherto blessed. *We* are (I am quite sure) the
last of the *race* of South-Carolina; I see nothing before us but decay and
downfall,—but on that very account, I cherish its precious relics the
more. . . . Yet my heart sinks within me often when I think of what
may too soon be, and I say, in those touching words, "Why should not my
countenance be sad, when the city, the place of my fathers' sepulchres,
lieth waste, and her gates are burnt with fire." (*Writings*, Vol. I, p. 215.)

Thus like old John Winthrop two hundred years before, this
descendant of southern Pilgrims, this Charleston lawyer and
intellectual, found the words of the Hebrew Scriptures rising to his
lips in moments of deep emotion.   In spite of travel and many
books and ripe culture and catholic sympathies, Hugh Legaré
remained Puritan at heart, sorely puzzled with life, the burden of
his days heavy upon him, walking soberly in the way of duty.
North or south, the Puritan was still Puritan, whether he were
Theodore Parker, the Boston radical, or Hugh Swinton Legaré,
the Charleston conservative.

IV

WILLIAM GILMORE SIMMS

Charleston Romancer

From the background of old Charleston emerged, about the year 1825, the figure of Gilmore Simms, lately a drug clerk but now come to the dignity of admission to the bar; a tall, vigorous young fellow, with little formal schooling, no Latin or Greek, without land or slaves, but heavily involved in Byronic odes and like unprofitable investments; a social nobody soon to be married at the age of twenty to a girl of no better station than his own, who offered himself as candidate for the poet laureateship of the South. A somewhat presumptuous proceeding on the part of a plebeian quite outside the cultivated circle of the Petigrus and Grimkés and Hugers and Legarés, who were the accepted custodians of Charleston culture and who did not take kindly to ambitious newcomers. They regarded literature as a polite art that could flourish only in polite circles, and they turned a cold shoulder upon a young man whose ways suggested the Carolina buckra.

After all these years one may well cherish a grudge against the amiable little city for its shabby treatment of Gilmore Simms. The most richly endowed of any son she ever gave birth to, he was snubbed for years by the social oligarchy and suffered keenly from the ostracism. His extreme parochialism made him the more sensitive to the slight. An ardent Southerner, loyal to all the Carolinian totems and taboos, he accepted the Charleston judgment in literature and politics as the very law and the prophets. He loved the soil of South Carolina, he loved the people and the way of life, and he was steeped as no other Carolinian in local history and tradition. He could perceive no shortcomings in a society he warmly admired, and he accepted the Charleston provincialisms as the lover accepts the mole on his mistress' cheek. The more Charleston snubbed him, the more admirable he professed to believe was an aristocracy that so jealously guarded its fine exclusiveness. His lifelong ambition was to receive recognition from his native city, and when after the death of his first wife and his marriage to the daughter of a prosperous planter, he gained admission into the ranks of the lesser gentry, he eagerly made common cause with them. He accepted the Carolinian standards and conventions; he advocated social caste: he honored the southern gentleman as God's best handiwork; he unconsciously reflected an aristocratic arrogance towards all social inferiors. He abandoned the Jeffersonian philosophy of his youth and adopted the revised gospel of Calhoun. He became, in short, a Carolina Fire Eater. He set up as a militant defender of slavery and collaborated with other eminent Carolinians to develop the proslavery argument.[3] He could have escaped the subtle compulsions of the southern system only by emptying his mind of his dearest prejudices, and this he had neither the will nor the wish to do. And so in spite of the fact that his every instinct was democratic, and every natural impulse generous and manly, he fought the battles of the peculiar institution as stoutly as if he had been born to his three hundred slaves; and he suffered in consequence the loss of pretty nearly everything, including his art. After his death, his friend Paul Hayne wrote of him: "Simms's genius *never had fair play!* Circumstances hampered him!" The judgment is just. Parochial Charleston brought about his literary undoing.

In taste and temperament Simms was a pronounced realist, but his career took shape from a generation given to every romantic excess. His genius, in consequence, was always at cross purposes with the popular taste. His realism turned naturally to low-life adventure; his upper-class romance became stilted and posturing, and his love of action degenerated into swashbuckling. That he survived such mishaps at all, suggests the enormous vitality of the man. If there had only been a little more of the intellectual in him, if he could have detached himself as an artist from the immediate and present, he might have risen superior to his unfortunate environment. But he was constitutionally incapable of aloofness, and hence incapable of criticism. To analyze, compare and judge was impossible to so ardent a nature. He must be partisan to a people and a cause, rather than to his art. The South that he loved was romantic, and he would appeal to the world as a Southerner. He wore his sectional prejudices as the southern politician wears his rumpled Prince Albert coat, broad-brimmed hat and black string tie. He never realized what a clutter of useless luggage he carried into his study. It is a pity that he constricted himself to the shell of an outworn order, instead of realizing that social orders and institutions are significant to the novelist

[3] See above, page 102

only as he stands apart from them, observing their ways and considering their interplay in the lives of men and women. It was a major loss to American letters that he should not have striven to be an artist first, and a southern romantic only at a later and more convenient season. If he had served his art more jealously, if he had learned from Poe to refuse the demands of inconsequential things, he would have viewed his beloved Charleston with keener eyes and portrayed it more adequately.

But he would not serve his art alone. Unhappily he conceived that he owed an imperative duty to his native commonwealth, and in fulfillment of that duty he frittered away his enormous vitality in delivering patriotic orations and occasional addresses, serving in the Legislature, pottering over politics, lecturing upon literature, founding and editing magazines and essaying to bring culture to Charleston by fiery impetuosity of appeal. He struggled as few other Americans have done to further the cause of letters in a desperate environment; but creative literature could neither be cajoled nor coerced to take up an abode in the indolent little city, and Simms wore himself out in a fruitless undertaking. Our literature has suffered few greater losses than this wasting of the genius of Gilmore Simms in trumpery fields that belong to the literary dray horse. It was the inevitable outcome of the conflict between the creative artist and the citizen of South Carolina.

Little as he is known to later readers Simms is by far the most virile and interesting figure of the Old South. He was built on a generous plan. He was endowed with a rich and prodigal nature, vigorous, spontaneous, creative. There was in him much of Whitman's largeness and coarseness, much of his delight in the good things of earth. He wrote with extraordinary gusto, and his fine strong face suggests that he lived with equal gusto. As a professional man of letters he turned out an incredible amount of work, by ordinary two tales a year—solid works of five hundred pages each—together with poems and plays and pot-boiling stuff to tax the capacity of two or three hack writers. He poured out his material copiously, lavishly, with overrunning measure. His stories flow as generously as his Jamaica rum. He is a veritable geyser of invention, an abundant sea of salty speech. He has no sense of restraint; he does not stop to prune the tangle of his imagination; he refuses to strip the plot of extraneous incident to hasten its action. He is as episodic as Dickens at his worst, piling up action and multiplying threads till the story bogs down. The major plot is always struggling from hummock to hummock in the endless swamp where his characters slip in and out, rarely getting to firm ground, yet never quite submerged. Prodigal of adventure and loving action, clumsy as the natural man when confronted with sentiment, he is an American Fielding with a dash of Smollett. He is at ease only out of doors, in the fields and swamps and highways; there his speech becomes racy, and there the rich poetry of his nature, which somehow rarely got into his verse, comes to abundant and spontaneous expression. When he enters the drawing-room his stilted language betrays his lack of ease. He writes with his pen and not with his heart. The plantation tradition has him in its grip and his fine ladies and gentlemen are done up with much literary starch. But let him come upon a happy-go-lucky blackguard and he loves him as Fielding would have loved him. The amusing scene in which Lieutenant Porgy heaves a pot of hot hominy in the face of a Scotch dragoon is quite evidently reminiscent of Parson Adams' recourse to a dish of hog's blood in a certain tavern brawl.[4] Like Fielding also is his criterion of morality. A frank and generous nature is his infallible test of worth, and if his patriotism led him to bestow a large share of generosity on the patriots, and a correspondingly meager share on the Loyalists and British, he was but exercising an ancient prerogative of the romancer.

Contemporary romanticism engrafted on a nature fundamentally realistic developed a pronounced strain in his work which, for lack of an exacter word, we may call picaresque. This comes out at its worst in the crude border tales of *Richard Hurdis* and *Border Beagles*, stories marked by the coarseness of the eighteenth century, backwoods versions of *Jonathan Wild*. At its best it created a goodly company of blackguards that are an asset to American literature. Simms dearly loved a rogue, and the more picturesque the latter's knavery the more he loved him. A gentleman villain turns to a thing of wood in his hands, but a low-born rascal he creates out of living flesh and blood. A surprising number of low figures, both rogues and honest men, enliven his cluttered pages, individual, racy, often poetic. Realistic in speech and action, they are men of special gifts, nimble of wit and rich in imagination, sometimes fallen to base uses and sometimes ennobled

[4] See *Katherine Walton*, Chapter XLI.

by affection for their superiors. Thumbscrew, Supple Jack Bannister, and Joe Ballou, the partisan scouts; Isaac Muggs, mine host
of the Black Riders; Goggle the half-breed; Hell Fire Dick of To-
phet, the blackguard converted by *Pilgrim's Progress;* Sam Bost-
wick the Squatter—these are admirable figures, done with inimitable spirit, the choicest collection of homespun in American
literature. They impart life and drama to Simms's tales. Remove
them, and his romances are only a welter of stilted language and
starchy situations. The scene, for example, between Jack Bannister and Isaac Muggs, in which the latter is converted to true republican principles by appeal to a backwoods ordeal by battle,
is magnificent in its broad humor, and it is a pity that Simms did
not give freer rein to his genius for such work. It is incomprehensible that a man who could put into the mouth of Thumbscrew such
language as the following could have stooped to scribble the love
scenes between Ernest Mellichampe and Janet Berkeley:

When it so happens that the things a man's got to love gits fewer and
smaller, they gits more valuable, Airnest, in his sight; for he knows mighty
well, if he loses them, that he's jist like an old bird that comes back to the
tree when the blossoms and the flowers have all dropped off, and are
rotting under it. It's mighty nigh to winter in his heart then, Airnest—
mighty nigh—and the sooner he begins to look out a place to sleep in, the
wiser man you may take him to be. (*Mellichampe*, Chapter IX.)

But Simms was too inveterately episodical to construct a pretty
plot, and too careless in his generous southern hospitality to dis-
criminate between guests at his board. He throws a huge miscellany on the table from which each may choose what pleases his
taste.

Here again romanticism did him an evil turn. Southern taste
was too aristocratic to like coarse fare. Gentlemen must dine like
gentlemen even though black rascals served as waiters. Common
fellows were well enough in the background, but they must not
presume to crowd their betters from the table. In such matters
Simms was constrained to follow the orthodox literary tradition.
From Shakespeare to Scott the notion prevailed that legitimate
romance must be conceived of as a flitch of bacon, the lean of vulgarity alternating with the fat of gentility. Hence Simms was
forced to keep a weather eye on the popular taste lest it be offended
by too free an offering of the low. His negroes, such as Scipio and
Bram and Benny Bowlegs, are more worth while than their mas-

ters, and his swamp-suckers are done with more gusto than the officers; but when the plot demands the appearance of the gentry he sends his black-bottle rapscallions about their business. Except in occasional instances, as in the case of old Colonel Sinclair, the Carolinian baron—a testy old gentleman done in the best gouty manner—Simms does the "quality" badly and the canny reader soon learns to skip the genteel passages in order to visit with Lieutenant Porgy or follow the adventures of Hell Fire Dick or Supple Jack Bannister. There is ample fare at his generous board, but one must pick and choose.

The critics have made quite too much of the Gothic extravagancies that mar so many of his pages. It is true that Simms was a generous purveyor of "blood-pudding" romance with its gory exploitation of crime and mystery. Nothing can excuse or extenuate such folly in the abstract; but it is easily comprehensible. It was a part of the price which the professional man of letters had to pay as caterer to a provincial reading public. After the surprising success of *Guy Rivers*, Simms deliberately tested the taste of his readers by sending forth *Richard Hurdis* under a pen name; and the equal success of the latter convinced him that American readers liked such fare. He had a living to make; the market was limited, and he resolved to give the public what it wanted. This accounts for his major sins. An enormous number of chapters, together with whole volumes such as *Charlemont* and *Beauchampe*—preposterous accounts of a notorious murder case in Kentucky—deserve no better fate than the rubbish heap. They are in no sense literature; yet unfortunately the very great powers of Simms are too commonly measured by such trash, instead of by his Revolutionary tales.

Simms was a loving student of older English literature and drew much of his water from excellent wells. A happy instinct led him back to the robust time of Elizabeth and those masculine playwrights whose ample natures were so like his own. Shakespeare may be reckoned his particular master—especially the prose of Shakespeare with its Cheapside colloquialisms and racy idiomatic rhythms. No better training school could be desired, and his loving apprenticeship to the older vernacular serves to explain the source of Simms's greatest literary virtue. From long familiarity with the Elizabethans he derived his mastery of English idiom that sets him widely apart from most other contemporary Americans. In easy

outpouring of picturesque speech, of the lithe and muscular idiom
of the older literature, he was without a rival in his generation.
Many an old Elizabethan phrase lingered in the southern backwoods, and many an indigenous turn of speech had sprung from
homely new-world experience. All such Simms seized upon with
the relish of a gourmand, stirring them into the great pot from
which he ladled such generous spoonfuls. Later critics have been
singularly obtuse in their failure to do justice to his rich linguistic
equipment. Quite too much comment has been devoted to his
careless slips in rhetorical construction, and quite too little to his
command of masculine English prose. It is absurd to couple him
with Cooper in sinning against good writing. They are as unlike as
two men could well be. Simms is incomparably the greater master
of racy prose, as he is much the richer nature. The only contemporary indeed who approaches him is Melville in *Moby Dick*.
He is careless and slovenly enough in all conscience; when he goes
on a rampage he mouths his lines like any town crier. But though
he keeps a sharp eye on the groundlings, though he is often preposterous, he is rarely wooden, never feeble.

The Elizabethan influence comes out strikingly in the character of Lieutenant Porgy, the spoilt child of his imagination,
who runs through the Revolutionary romances as a sort of comic
chorus. Despite Professor Trent's opinion to the contrary, Porgy
is a South Carolinian Falstaff, quite evidently done with a close
eye to the original. He is a very mountain of a fellow, with huge
paunch and spindling shanks from too much sitting at the table
and in the saddle—the most amusing and substantial comic
character in our early fiction. As a South Carolina gentleman,
Porgy of course was no liar or coward or woman cheater. In battle
he is an avalanche of patriotic valor, and in his deference to the
weak and dependent, in his free-handed generosity that encum-
bers him with penniless hangers-on, he is model of southern chivalry. But in the far greater matters of the belly, he is strikingly
Falstaffian. He is not so much a valiant trencherman, as an artist in food and drink. He lived to eat and he ate to speculate on
the virtues of a good dinner. "He took philosophy with him to
the table, and grew wise over his wine" (*Woodcraft*, Chapter
XVIII). He is an epicure in words, a gourmand of wit. The
copious stream of his speech runs on in an endless flow, sometimes
roily but never stagnant. A pat aphorism or a picturesque phrase

is as succulent to him as Carolina terrapin. When philosophy fails he stoops to horseplay, but his practical jokes are carried off with theatrical splendor, with colossal assurance. Like Falstaff he is fond of practicing his wit on his followers. His Bardolph is a certain Geordie Dennison, the swamp poet of the troop; and Porgy honors him as one artist honors the craft of another.

But the most satisfying comradeship lies between Porgy and Black Tom, fellow practitioners of the gentle art of cookery, sworn liegemen to roasts and soups and stews. Together they make the swamp commissariat bloom like a Covent Garden market. They are master foragers untroubled by an overnice conscience. "Do as much stealing in an honest way as you can," the lieutenant remarks to Tom. "D—n the patriotism that can't eat stolen fruit!" At a pinch the native resources of the swamp are boldly commandeered The creative masterpiece of the valiant Porgy was a notable banquet which he proffered General Greene and his staff in their swamp quarters. His infinite resourcefulness in this great affair, his huge inventiveness, elevate the dinner to the rank of a culinary epic. The swamp frogs that he speared by moonlight, and the young alligators that he took by subtle stratagem, were transmogrified into delectable dishes served to his guests under the alluring names of *alerta* and *lagarta*.[5] The scene is done with a gusto that only the worshiper of fleshpots could achieve. Simms delighted in Porgy because he was himself something of a Porgy. There is good fare for those who sit at table with the fat humorist of *The Forayers;* the ready talk does not lack the salt of wit. The later Porgy of *Woodcraft* scarcely comes up to the earlier. His debts weigh too heavily on his spirits for the easy play of his fancy; he is less redoubtable as a wooer than as a warrior; nevertheless there is excellent humor to be enjoyed at Glen Eberle, and some extraordinary pranks.

The two major themes with which his romances deal, as has been often pointed out, are the frontier and the Revolution; but the intimate connection between them has not been so commonly remarked. In much of his better work the two themes blend into one. The conditions of civil war in the South thrust into sharp relief the cultural and psychological frontier that clung to the outskirts of the plantations—the ragged edges of a society that kept the

5 See *The Forayers*, Chapters XLIII–XLVI.

poor whites submerged and bred a numerous progeny of coarse and primitive creatures, little better than social outcasts. Not the least of the curses of slavery—as Helper pointed out—was its blighting effect on the less prosperous whites who environed every plantation with its special frontier. With his strong bias towards realism Simms refused to romanticize what was inherently unlovely. Like Baldwin in his *Flush Times of Mississippi and Alabama*, he discovered an ample supply of blackguards and sharpers in the no man's land beyond the settlements. The log cabins of the swamp country harbored their motley crew in no wise different from their fellows of the farther frontier along the Mississippi; and these precious rascals he drags from their lurking-places to exhibit in the light of day. The frontier in consequence is rarely absent from his stories, and it is this picaresque interpretation that sets him so sharply off from Cooper. A recent student, in commenting on the contrast between the frontier of Cooper and Simms, suggests that "perhaps the earlier frontier had been intrinsically more dignified than that which Simms had observed; perhaps the difference is that Cooper's had lain deeper under the softening shadow of the past" (Van Doren, *The American Novel*, p. 65). But this is quite to miss the point, both of Cooper and Simms. The real explanation is to be sought in the different interpretations of the romantic and the realist. Cooper's frontier existed only in his imagination. When he came face to face with the reality, as in the case of old Aaron Thousandacres and his lawless brood, he hated it too frankly to portray it justly. The stern Puritan squatter and his fiercer wife are magnificent caricatures, drawn to serve a partisan purpose. They provide a romantic contrast to the honest Chainbearer, spokesman of the psychology of the settlements; but set beside Simon Suggs, master of the frontier technic of easy money, as depicted by Joseph Baldwin, they are as romantic as Cooper's Indians.

The picaresque note is frankly emphasized in Simms' Revolutionary tales. All the swamp-suckers and rapscallions found their heaven-sent opportunity in the disorders of civil war. No realist could write about the Revolution in South Carolina without noting the flocks of buzzards gathering to fall upon the carrion. War is not a heroic thing in these stirring pages. It invites debauchery and encourages brutality. Blackguards put a black stain on military glory. In the preface to *The Scout*, Simms remarks:

To burn and slay were not the simple performances of this reckless period and ravaged country. To burn in wantonness and to murder in cold blood, and by the cruellest tortures, were the familiar achievements of the time: . . . The face of the country was overrun by outlaws. Detached bands of ruffians, formed upon the frontiers of Georgia, and in the wilds of Florida—refugees from all the colonies—availed themselves of the absence of civil authority to effect a lodgment in the swamps, the forests, and the mountains. These, mounted on swift horses, traversed the state with the wind; now here, now there; one moment operating on the Savannah, the next on the Peedee; sometimes descending within sight of the smokes of the metropolis; and anon, building their own fires on the lofty summits of the Appalachian ridge.

Now and then in his pages war flashes out in romantic or heroic episodes, but for the most part it is mean and degrading, a thing to be hated. Simms loved action too keenly not to make the most of the countless onsets and forays, the ambushing of Hessians and the cutting off of wagon trains; he found in them material for many a brisk page and stirring adventure; but in the end it is the brutality of it all, the unhappy loosing of evil passions, that gives him most concern. It was a hard world, and the soft-hearted Jack Bannister, speaking with the tongue of Simms, could find comfort only in stoicism. "A man ought not to be too soft about the heart, in a world like this, so full of rascals that need the knockings of a hard and heavy hand."

It is this strong seasoning of the picaresque, perhaps, that accounts for the neglect that has befallen the work of Simms. Many blackguards and generous potations of Jamaica rum consorted ill with the genteel tradition in letters that grew up in the days following the Civil War; and romantic memories of a lost cause threw an idyllic haze over earlier times. The Revolutionary War lay too far in the past for a generation suffering from a great tragedy to concern itself with, and the vivid and vital work of Simms scarcely outlived its creator. The Revolutionary tales have been largely forgotten, and from his abundant work only The Yemassee has survived in popular affection, and this partly from the vogue of Cooper. The winnowing has been severe and scarcely just. The best of Simms is not in The Yemassee, but in those stirring tales of Marion's men who carried on a bushwhacking campaign under the hot sun of the dog days. The Partisan and The Forayers and Woodcraft deserve a better fate than has befallen them. The ghost of Cooper does not haunt the pages to challenge comparison, as it does *The Yemassee*, and bring into question their relative merits. There Simms is at home, in the swamps and fields and villages, with men whose ways he knew and loved, and his generous nature followed its own impulses.

But in dealing with the Indians he entered a domain preëmpted by the romantic, and his picaresque realism suffered a disastrous rivalry. Like Robert Montgomery Bird's *Nick of the Woods*, *The Yemassee* is heavily marked by the frontier psychology. It was unfortunate, perhaps, that Simms did not follow Cooper's example and plunge into the wilderness, leaving behind him the squatter and settler with their sordid prose. Instead, his Indians are encompassed by a dark background of civilization, and their tragic destiny is poignantly dramatized in the fate of young Occonestoga, besotted with the white man's rum, and doomed to a destruction far less poetic than befalls Uncas fighting his hereditary foes. Nevertheless a wealth of romantic material is crowded into the volume, enough to serve Cooper for half a dozen tales. In simplifying his plots to the uncomplicated problem of flight and pursuit, the latter gains in dramatic swiftness of movement, but he loses in abundance of accompanying action—the sense of cross purposes and many-sided activities, which *The Yemassee* so richly suggests. The latter is an elaborately carved and heavily freighted Spanish bark that is left far astern by the trim Yankee clipper ship; yet its cargo of the gold of the Indies is far richer. It is the familiar story of southern prodigality and wastefulness— an exuberant nature pouring out its wealth in spendthrift fashion, and failing to achieve the greater results attained by a simpler nature held in closer restraint. After all it is idle to compare Cooper and Simms, and even more futile to catalogue the latter as a disciple of the Cooper school. Simms was far too rich in his own right to live as a dependent on anyone, and certainly far too original to be an imitator. Nature was lavish in her gifts to him, and as if his fame as a story-teller is less than Cooper's, the debit must be charged against his unfortunate environment.

The later years of Simms were utterly devastated by the unhappy war, in which, as was to be expected, he was a stalwart and uncompromising partisan. His native commonwealth that had long treated him shabbily, sacrificed him in the end to her folly. It was his own fault of course, but how could one warped by the pervasive southern provincialism hope to escape? Scratch a Carolinian of the Calhoun school and you find a Fire Eater. In this respect Simms was not different from the McDuffies and Hamiltons from whom he took his cue—gentlemen whom, because they were politically prominent, he regarded as socially intelligent. That a man of such native powers as Simms should have taken seriously the Charleston politicians—blown up like a pig's bladder after butchering; that he should himself have aspired to become another such bladder—these are sobering facts to remind us that the man of letters is very likely to be a child outside his study walls. What was wrong with Simms that he read the signs of the times so badly? This, that he lived in a world of unreality, of social and economic romanticism, that was forever benumbing his strong instinct for reality. His father-in-law owned seventy slaves; his neighbors and acquaintances owned slaves; all South Carolina gentlemen owned slaves; and in judging this matter of slavery Gilmore Simms went unquestioningly with his little world. He who had drunk of the rich wine of Elizabethan culture came at last to drink himself under the table with his drafts of Charleston Jamaica. The dream of a Greek civilization based on black slavery was discovered in the bottom of the cup of southern romanticism. And Simms emptied his bottle with the rest. Charleston, no doubt, has paid a sufficiently heavy price for her too copious potations, but she can never atone for the undoing of her greatest son—for the foolish intoxication that befuddled the generous mind of Gilmore Simms. The loss is not Charleston's alone; it is a loss to our common American literature. There is food for thought in the words of the epitaph which he composed for himself: "Here lies one who, after a reasonably long life, distinguished chiefly by unceasing labors, has left all his better works undone." Juster words could not have been written, nor more tragic.

CHAPTER I

NEW WORLDS

I

WHILE Calhoun was instructing the South in the theory of a Greek democracy, other sons of the South were learning, in the new world to which they had removed, the ways of a very different democracy—a democracy native to the frontier and quite unconcerned with Greek ideals. In the Ohio valley was gathering a multitude of rough libertarians who had exchanged the restrictions of the old settlements for the freedom of the new. To these bumptious levelers rulership by established authorities made no appeal. They attached no respect to broadcloth, but preferred to manage their affairs in their own way by appeal to the majority. Taught by experience the worth of certain Jeffersonian principles, they took seriously the doctrine of equality and proposed to put it into practice. They were coonskin apostles of liberty and equality—if not of fraternity—backwoods democrats who by virtue of numbers established in common practice the principle of the sovereignty of the popular will. Springing up naturally on the frontier, the practice of democracy received from it a new validity and became the determining factor in the nationalism that America was creating in the early years of the nineteenth century. That it was a crude and often shoddy democracy, that it never justified its pretentions in the eyes of a critical realism, did not lessen the zeal with which men clung to it or weaken their loyalty. Democracy became the common faith of the West, and in becoming the common faith of the West it was put in the way of becoming the common faith of America.

If the romantic temper is a spontaneous by-product of social change, that temper found in the upheaval attending the western migration a plentiful aliment that had been wanting in the static eighteenth century. In that older world men had been held fast in the grip of the customary and familiar; but in the free West all was new and strange. The crossing of the Appalachian barrier that had long held back the settlements was an adventurous undertaking that fired the imagination. Romantic in spirit and scope, it was meanly picaresque in a thousand unlovely details. Plain men engaged in it, provident and improvident, hard-working and shiftless; heroes had a share in it, but blackguards and outlaws and broken men—the lees and settlings thrown off from the older communities—had a share as well. The world that provided a stage for the courage of Daniel Boone and the fighting qualities of George Rogers Clark bred also the Davy Crocketts and Mike Finks and Col. William Suggses, who discovered there opportunities for the development of less admirable qualities; and it engulfed in its depths a host of nameless adventurers who drifted into the wilderness settlements, drank and quarreled and begot children, suffered from the chills and ague, spread a drab poverty along the frontier, and were put away under ground and forgotten by the more fortunate who salvaged prosperity from the abundant wreckage.

From this crude society emerged the new states with governments designed to serve simple ends. Jealousy for his sovereign right to do as he pleased was the chief concern of the free western voter; as a sovereign citizen he refused to be subject to the creature commonwealth. If governors and legislators and judges got uppish he would throw them out of office and put in others who better understood the rights of free Americans. It was this rude equalitarianism that marked the early stage of western commonwealth building. Naïve Jeffersonians, these frontier citizens had not learned from Hamilton how useful the political state may become to those who know how to control its policies to their particular ends; but that lesson they were soon to learn. The citizens of Georgia received excellent instruction from no less a man than Chief Justice Marshall in the matter of the Yazoo frauds; and as such lessons sank into their minds their political philosophy underwent a silent change. The coonskin individualism that created Jacksonian democracy was gradually undermined by a middle-class individualism that inclined to the Whiggery of Henry Clay. The former was a spontaneous expression of the frontier spirit, the latter a calculating expression of the maturing settlement. The one discovered its native habitat on the backwoods farm, the other in the county seat town. The one was agrarian *laissez faire*, the other was exploitative paternalistic. The followers of Jackson wanted the state kept simple and frugal, the followers of Clay wanted it to engage in ambitious programs of internal improvement; and from these antagonistic principles emerged a bitter feud between Democracy and Whiggery that in western townships revived the old alignment of agrarian and Federalist of earlier times.

In such a contest the principle of Whiggery must eventually triumph. It was an expression of "the genius of the times." Economics and psychology were daily arguing in its behalf. From the first early settlements of the Ohio valley, it must be remembered, circumstances were creating a new middle class that was to stamp itself indelibly on western life and institutions. The spirit of speculation had entered the wilderness with the early surveyors. With its vast resources the Inland Empire offered the first opportunity to exercise the newly won right to exploit the western hinterland, and it was seized upon greedily. Agriculture was still the common business and land hunger the common passion. The irruption of the land-hungry hordes upon the fertile Ohio valley, it will be recalled, synchronized with the speculative debauch that followed the conclusion of the peace of 1783, and this in turn was a by-product of the sudden expansion of the new capitalistic finance. Speculation had suddenly become every man's business, and wild lands and wild-cat banks, joining fortunes for better or worse, brought forth a characteristic progeny. The new gospel of progress found more willing hearers than the old gospel of righteousness. Every adventurer into the Ohio valley was a potential speculator, and every settler was eager to sell out to a later comer at an advance. The real estate agent followed close on the footsteps of Daniel Boone, quick to profit from the explorations. Land was the staple commodity and such a turnover had never before been known in America. Every clearing in the woods was speedily capitalized, and every townsite was reckoned rich in potential values. The new cities were founded in unearned increment and prospered with its increase. With European peasants flocking to the West from their poverty-stricken countries, and the exploited of the East seeking new openings there, it was an unlucky speculator who could not exchange his paper values for substantial equivalents. Law, religion, education, culture, were pressed into the service of speculation. How widely the spirit permeated the West is suggested in the experience of Timothy Flint, frontier missionary. Writing from Saint Charles, Missouri, in 1818, he commented somewhat bitterly:

> Religion, when I came here was considered contemptible. The phalanx of opposition was in array from one end of the street to the other. Why did they invite me here? On speculation. A minister—a church—a school—are words to flourish in an advertisement to sell lots. (John Ervin Kirkpatrick, *Timothy Flint, etc.*, Appendix B, p. 293.)

From the determining factors, then, of abundant wild lands, rapid increase in population, and an elastic credit, operating on a vast scale, came the optimistic, speculative psychology of the new West. It is the common disease of every period of unstable economics. It had traveled west with every extension of the frontier; and it became acute in the Ohio valley in the romantic days following the War of 1812. In colonial times before the upheaval of the Revolution, prices of land and commodities had been stable. The basic silver currency varied little in quantity or value; coin was scarce, but the occasional emission of paper money produced little disturbance, for the reason that the farmer habitually reckoned his income in the produce of his farm and fireside. But with the unsettling of exchange values by the wide use of bank notes, prices at once shifted to a speculative basis. The familiar commodities ceased to have a fixed use value, and a cash psychology superseded the traditional commodity value. The old stability was gone. The familiar domestic economy that functioned primarily in terms of consumption rather than profit disintegrated under the workings of a paper system and gave place to a speculative economy.

It was this revolution that set apart the new West from the older traditional America and made it the special repository of the new middle-class spirit of progress. The change had been long preparing. Writing from Boonesborough in January, 1776, the agent of the Transylvania Land Company pointed out that the western country "abounded with land mongers," and that his company had already issued nine hundred patents.[1] These adventurous spirits were only pioneers pointing the way for later hordes that after 1815 pushed eagerly onward. "Old America seems to be breaking up, and moving westward," commented a traveler in 1817 as he watched the long line of Conestoga wagons moving towards Pitts-

[1] See James Hall, *Romance of American History*, Appendix.

burgh; and in the fall of the same year Timothy Flint said of Saint Charles, Missouri, that "there was an average of one hundred people every day coming to the town, or passing to near-by points. Nearly all were poor and not one family in fifty had a Bible " (Kirkpatrick, *Timothy Flint, etc.*, p. 102). "This western fever has seized old and young," remarks a character in Cooper's *Home as Found*, "and it has carried off many active families from our parts of the world. . . . Most of the counties adjoining our own have lost a considerable portion of their population." One reason for this vast exodus from the East is suggested by a recent student who remarks: "A considerable part of the significance of the frontier lies behind the frontier. In one sense, the westward expansion of the American people was a flight from the new industrialism" (Norman Ware, *The Industrial Worker*, p. xx). To these adventurers from the East was added an increasing immigration. During the period from the close of the Revolution to the War of 1812, the annual immigration averaged no more than four or five thousand. In the year 1817 it rose to 22,000, and thereafter an augmenting stream poured into America and filtered westward. They were natural prey to shrewd promoters, and in *Martin Chuzzlewit* Dickens has drawn a picture—not wholly caricature— of what befell some of them. But whatever might be their individual fate, they provided fuel to the fire that was consuming the old agrarianism and clearing the ground for the western middle class.

II

With land as its staple commodity the West naturally interpreted progress in terms of increasing land values; and these in turn were dependent on better markets, better roads, and a freely flowing tide of immigration. In a country of such vast distances internal improvements were an everyday necessity. With every mile that a turnpike was driven into the wilderness new opportunities were opened up. Monies paid for wild land went into the Federal treasury; it was only just, according to the western view, that such monies should return to the West in the form of public improvements, for with such improvements tax values were increased, prices of all commodities rose, and progress was furthered. The Federal government could not fairly leave its offspring to shift for themselves, but must consider itself *in loco parentis* to the rising commonwealths. It was a persuasive argument, appealing alike to farmer and speculator, to town and country, but it played havoc with the older Jeffersonianism. Jefferson thought always in terms of the agrarian producer functioning in a stable economic world; speculation was not in his philosophy; unearned increment was a crop he never calculated on; and in sympathy with an older liberalism he would reduce the state to the narrow rôle of policeman. But the new West, thinking in terms of its immediate needs, desired a broad and benevolent paternalism. It wanted the Federal government to butter its bread regardless of the ultimate cost of the butter.

The complete embodiment of this spirit of paternalistic progress was the master politician of the times, whose dramatic career, beginning as a Jeffersonian and ending as a Hamiltonian, suggests the confusions of a world in transition. Henry Clay was the hero of the new West, the spokesman of the new ambitions. A man of great personal charm, engaging manners, buoyant temperament, exuberant patriotism, and persuasive tongue, he migrated in 1797 at the age of twenty-one from Richmond, Virginia, to Lexington, Kentucky, then a booming county-seat town only twenty-two years removed from the building of its first blockhouse. The population of the state had more than doubled in seven years, and by 1797 it had risen above 180,000. Of this aggressive little world Clay soon became the accredited representative at Washington. He had been brought up under the old domestic economy and carefully tutored in the Jeffersonian philosophy. For four years he had been private secretary to George Wythe, a distinguished Virginian of the older generation, a profound lawyer and teacher, a scholarly political thinker, a humanitarian, and a confirmed agrarian. When Clay left Virginia he carried with him the Jeffersonianism of Wythe; but he was wanting in the trained intellect of his preceptor and his views were inadequately grounded. His subsequent career revealed him as an impressionable nature modifying his convictions with his environment. In Kentucky the spirit of speculative expansion seized him and inoculated his mind with the new gospel of progress. He early convinced himself that government was not doing its full duty unless it helped its citizens to make money, and he persistently pressed on Congress the need of federal aid to develop the West. In 1812 he fell victim to the war psychology, turned jingo, and substituted an ardent patriotism for sober reason. Thereafter he became increasingly nationalistic, demanding a strong army and navy, pleading for a loose construction of the constitution, arguing for paternalism. His Jeffersonianism was quietly put away like a garment out of style. Grossly ignorant of the schools of economic thought, he was an opportunist who shifted from the older domestic economy to the later capitalistic, without comprehending the significance of the change. Unread in history and political theory, he trusted his fluency to get him out of any inconsistencies he might blunder into. In the course of his long career he found himself at different times on both sides of every important question; yet gravitating to the middle-class position, the exponent of exploitation in the name of progress, spokesman of the commercial, financial and manufacturing interests, a new-model Federalist passionately defending the new money economy—a curious ending for one who began as a pupil of George Wythe.

And yet not curious when one considers the ambitions of the world that molded him. Clay was a born politician who rarely came to grips with reality. Devoted to the principles of republican liberty as he found them in the Constitution, he professed to believe that government could be trusted to distribute favors with impartial hand. Personally honest, he never realized how often he allowed himself to become the unconscious tool of powerful economic interests. With his desire to please everybody he was an easy prey for skillful lobbyists. He had been at one time attorney for the Bank, yet he denied vehemently that his defense of the institution had been influenced by such connection. He had become a Hamiltonian without gaining Hamilton's clear understanding of the economic basis of politics. A brilliant opportunist, he was guided by no fixed political principles but tacked with the shifting winds. A brilliant romantic, he was the persuasive prophet of an age that was dreaming of a prosperity that should gather in certain favored reservoirs through the agency of subsidies and taxes, and trickle thence through all the land to water the roots of industry. It was fitting that such a man should be the father of Whiggery, and fitting also that he should stand as the embodiment of the spirit of compromise. One great lesson, at least, he had learned, that greater men too often do not learn, the lesson that republican government rests on good will and that such good will demands a policy of give and take among rival interests. Compromise may be displeasing to earnest souls, but it is implied in any workable system of democratic rule.

Like Calhoun and Webster, Clay was a victim of changing times. If he had lived a generation later, when the middle-class revolution had been accomplished and the principle of capitalism was in undisputed control, he would have achieved a far greater personal success. But capitalism was not yet strong enough to uphold him against rival economies, and he failed of his lifelong ambition to be President. He was broken by the Jacksonian revolution, in spite of the fact that no other American politician has been so loved by a hero-worshiping electorate—and it should be added, has been so lovable.

CHAPTER II
TWO SPOKESMEN OF THE WEST

I

ANDREW JACKSON
Agrarian Liberal

CLAY's pleasant dream of a paternalistic prosperity for America got its first rude awakening from General Jackson and his motley following of western equalitarians and eastern proletarians. Gentlemen were suddenly reminded that the plain people had been overlooked in the distribution of benefits. The waters of prosperity, it would seem, had been trickling somewhat too scantily to them from the great reservoirs where they were impounded; and as they saw the wealth pouring into private ponds through governmental pipe lines, a natural human envy took possession of them. In theory the pipe lines belonged to them, and the impounded waters were to be used for common irrigation; but in practice the mains seemed to conduct only to Lowell industrialists and Philadelphia and New York capitalists, and the waters turned out to be privately owned. As the recognition of this fact came home to the producing mass it provided a rallying point for an anti-monopolist movement and determined the great objective of the Jacksonian attack, the assault on the Bank.

The driving force of the new Democracy was the same class-feeling that had done service a generation before, the will to destroy the aristocratic principle in government. This conscious class-feeling had been strengthened by the spread of the dogma of equalitarianism through the frontier, and this in turn had brought about an extension of manhood suffrage which enfranchised a numerous body of voters who turned against an aristocracy that had long resisted their demands for the vote. The spirit of 1798 was rising afresh, and the re-alignment assumed the form of a democratic-aristocratic struggle, which for the moment obscured the more significant fact of an emerging middle class. The battle seemed to lie between homespun and broadcloth for control of government, and this serves to explain the odium that quickly

145

attached to Jacksonian Democracy in polite circles. In drawing together mechanics and frontiersmen, the new party inevitably became a lower-class instrument, offensive to gentlemen of the old school of politics. The records of the times carry abundant evidence, often amusing, of this aristocratic contempt. In the early forties a girl of seventeen living on a Mississippi plantation, describing Jefferson Davis—whose wife she afterwards became—was surprised at the contrast between his politics and his manners. "Would you believe it," she wrote, "he is refined and cultivated, and yet he is a Democrat!" (*Jefferson Davis, A Memoir by his Wife*, Vol. I, p. 192.)

There were quite evident reasons for this aristocratic contempt. The new Democracy was heavily weighted with what gentlemen were pleased to call the rabble. Fresh Democratic recruits had been gathering since Jefferson molded the first party of protest. Industrialism was creating a city proletariat, and the frontier was producing the coonskin voter; neither as yet possessed any adequate political philosophy, but they needed no philosophy to enlist against the traditional privileges and perquisites of broadcloth. They had had their fill of such rule. The stake-in-society theory was worn threadbare, and other philosophies were preparing. Meanwhile in the person of Old Hickory they saw the visible embodiment of their vague aspirations, and they turned to him with an unquestioning loyalty that nothing could weaken. He was our first great popular leader, our first man of the people. If he aroused a wild enthusiasm in breasts covered by linsey-woolsey, it was because he believed that linsey-woolsey had its stake-in-society equally with broadcloth. He was one of our few Presidents whose heart and sympathy were with the plain people, and who clung to the simple faith that government must deal as justly with the poor as with the rich. Believing so, he could not be turned aside from his course by paid clamor, but with a courage rare in the White House he dared make a frontal attack on the citadel of exploitation in the face of an army of mercenaries.

The dramatic career of Andrew Jackson, so unlike that of Jefferson, which was determined by a speculative temperament and founded on a critical examination of diverse systems of society and politics, was shaped in large measure by prejudice and circumstance. A man of iron will and inflexible purpose, he was almost wholly lacking in political and social philosophy. His conclusions were the reactions of a simple nature of complete integrity, in contact with plain fact. Fundamentally realistic, he cherished few romanticisms. There was no subtlety in his mental processes and this lack kept him free from the temptation to follow devious paths beloved of politicians. He must take the shortest way to his objective, crashing through such obstacles as lay in his path. He was never a bookish man. He was surprisingly ill read, and his grammar and spelling were those of the plain people. He loved horse racing and was a master of profanity; yet in spite of characteristics that link him with Davy Crockett, he possessed an innate dignity and chivalry that set him far above the wag of the canebrakes. He was a born leader whose headlong onslaughts and rash mistakes might imperil the cause but could not shake the confidence of his followers. All who knew a man when they saw one respected Andrew Jackson. Imperious and dictatorial, he knew how to command but not to obey; he took orders from no one, not even his superiors, unless such orders fell in with his own plans. In short General Jackson represented the best which the new West could breed in the way of capable and self-reliant individualism, and the backwoodsmen loved him for the enemies he made, and backed him loudly in his fight against the aristocratic East.

When Jackson settled in Nashville in 1788, at the age of twenty-one, the Cumberland valley had somewhat under five thousand inhabitants scattered a distance of eighty-five miles along the river. The first settlements had been made only nine years before, and Nashville was a frontier post with frontier manners. Into this rough society the young Scotch-Irishman fitted easily. His smattering of the law sufficed to gain him clients and he soon became a local political leader. When he was only twenty-nine he was sent to Philadelphia as the first Congressman from the state of Tennessee, where he came in contact with the "aristocratic Neebobs" of the government and heartily disliked them. The next year he was sent to the Senate, but a single session satisfied him and he resigned to accept a judgeship in the state Supreme Court, which post he held for six years. During these early years he was unconsciously following the path that conducted straight to a middle-class philosophy. He threw himself into speculation, bought and sold land in great blocks, traded in horses and slaves, set up a general store, and was well on the road to wealth when the panic of 1795 caught him unprepared. He lost most of his extensive holdings, including his homestead and many of his slaves, and removed to a six hundred and forty acre tract eight miles from Nashville—the Hermitage—which was to become one of the famous places of America. With this removal his middle-class ambitions fell away and he became a planter with a simple agrarian point of view; and this old-fashioned agrarianism became in later years the determining force in all his political thinking.

He was fifty-eight when he emerged as a potential candidate for the Presidency in 1822, and for years his sole interests, other than those of his plantation, had been military. He was singularly wanting in any formulated political philosophy, and his reëlection to the Senate two years later did little to supply the lack. He had picked up some shreds of the protectionist theory and in a letter written in 1824 he went so far as to declare for a "judicious" protective tariff, basing his view on the grounds of the country's economic unpreparedness at the time of the War of 1812, on the lack of markets for the produce of western farms, and on the desirability of drawing labor from the farm to the factory. But he added a significant passage that reveals the agrarian bias of his mind. To the end of his life he insisted that he was an old Republican of 1798, and this comment of 1824 suffices to connect his later attack on the Bank with Jefferson's attack on Hamilton's fiscal policy.

> Beyond this, I look at the Tariff with an eye to the proper distribution of labor and revenue; and with a view to discharge our national debt. I am one of those who do not believe that a national debt is a national blessing, but rather a curse to a republic; inasmuch as it is calculated to raise around the administration a moneyed aristocracy dangerous to the liberties of the country. (Quoted in Bassett, *Life of Andrew Jackson*, Vol. I, p. 346.)

The tariff was the only question on which he was receptive to Whiggish arguments, and although he never openly repudiated a protectionist policy he soon grew lukewarm in its support. Such other fragments of Whiggery as found accidental lodgment in his mind were swept away in the fierce struggles that marked his years in the White House. During those eight years Jackson found himself, and the man who emerged from the struggle was an agrarian of the old Virginian school. As he came to understand the significance of the principle of exploitation he learned to interpret social classes in terms of economics. He instinctively hated all aristocrats, extending his dislike to the circle that pretended to social preëminence in Tennessee, speaking of them contemptuously as the "aristocrats of Nashville." But in these later years a change in his vocabulary appeared; his favorite phrases became "the monied capitalists" and the "hydra of corruption." He had come to associate aristocracy with the control of the economics of society. He was learning how aristocracies are built up through the instrumentality of the state; and as that lesson sank into his mind his opposition to such class favoritism hardened into adamant. He would put a stop to such practices, cost what it might. His attack on the Bank was perhaps the most courageous act in our political history; he knew how fiercely it would be defended; yet he was amazed at the number of hornets that issued from the shaken nest. "Such has been the scenes of corruption in our last congress," he wrote in 1833, "that I loath the corruption of human nature and long for retirement, and repose on the Hermitage. But until I can strangle this hydra of corruption, the Bank, I will not shrink from my duty." And a little later, "I want relaxation from business and rest, but where can I get rest; I fear not on this earth" (Bassett, *Life of Andrew Jackson*, Vol. II, pp. 635, 637).

As his policy unfolded it became clear that Jackson had not changed with the changing times. He remained to the last the product of an earlier domestic economy, with an old-fashioned horror of debt. He was too generous to be frugal, too kind-hearted to be thrifty, too honest to live above his means. He desired a simple independence for himself and for his country. He believed that the government should pay its debt, reduce its revenues, and live simply. In his austere personal rectitude he exhibited a Puritan conviction of the sacredness of stewardship; he must return to the common people, who had put their trust in him, an honest reckoning of that trust. It was not in his nature to betray their faith. He would have nothing to do with the new theory that government is an agency to help business. To take profits from an instrument erected supposedly for the common good was abhorrent to his old-fashioned views; it was impossible for him to lend the sanction of his office to particular or special interests; and when circumstances made the Bank the central vexing problem of his administration, his position was predetermined by every conviction of his mind. While he was President he would not allow the government to be used for business ends; he would not permit its funds or credit to be turned to private profits; he would not tolerate a money monopoly, no matter how conventionally correct its operations might be proved to be, that challenged the sovereignty of the national government. The twin powers of the purse and sword—to recall Clay's famous phrase that every Whig orator used on the stump—were in Jackson's opinion the ultimate tests of sovereignty; and to turn over the money of the government to private hands for private use, he believed, was as grave an abrogation of sovereign rights as would be the use of the army and navy by private interests for private ends.

In the judgment of many critics Jackson, in his ignorance of the intricacies of capitalistic finance, wantonly destroyed a necessary credit system, thereby bringing a devastating panic on the country. Whether or not that judgment is true is of little importance today. More interesting historically is the fact that in his attitude towards the Bank, as in his attitude towards internal improvements, Jackson returned to the agrarian position of Jefferson and John Taylor, nullifying for a time the victories gained by the middle class during the boom period of nationalism. The more he learned about the methods of capitalistic finance, the more he distrusted it. His prejudices were his strength. He disliked speculation and he could see nothing permanently wise or sound in a speculative economy that put American industry at the mercy of bankers to expand or contract credit. With an old-fashioned love of a stable currency he gave his warm support to the project to return the country to a specie basis. "The great desideratum, in modern times," he said in his message to the twenty-fourth Congress, "is an efficient check upon the power of banks, preventing that excessive issue of paper whence arise those fluctuations in the standard of value which render uncertain the rewards of labor." The establishment of additional mints to provide an adequate coinage of gold or silver became therefore a natural corollary of his attack upon bank currency. It was John Taylor's economics written into the law of the land.

In his attitude towards the state Jackson followed the nationalistic tendencies of the West. He was as patriotic as Clay, and in spite of strong states-rights sympathies he contemptuously rejected Calhoun's theory of nullification. But he had no love for an omnicompetent state. More and more he drifted back to the Jeffersonian position in his conception of the powers and duties of the federal government. Replying to the vote of censure of 1834, he stated his ideal of government in words that would have become Jefferson's first inaugural speech. He had been charged with being ambitious, to which he replied:

> The ambition which leads me on, is an anxious desire and a fixed determination, to return to the people, unimpaired, the sacred trust they have confided to my charge—to heal the wounds of the constitution and preserve it from further violation; to persuade my countrymen, so far as I may, that it is not in a splendid government, supported by powerful monopolies and aristocratical establishments, that they will find happiness, or their liberties protected, but in a plain system, void of pomp—protecting all, and granting favors to none—dispensing its blessings like the dews of heaven, unseen and unfelt, save in the freshness and beauty they contribute to produce. It is such a government that the genius of our people requires—such a one only under which our States may remain for ages to come, united, prosperous, and free. (Benton, *Thirty Years' View*, Vol. I, p. 427.)

The evils entailed on America by the Jacksonian revolution were many, but they cannot properly be charged against Andrew Jackson. They came in spite of him, and they came as a result of the great object lesson in the manipulation of the majority will that his popularity had laid bare. His instincts and the main outline of his policy were Jeffersonian; but neither he nor any other man was strong enough to stop the current of middle-class individualism then running. The American people were wanting in an adequate democratic program suited to the changing times, as they were wanting in desire for a social democracy. And when his capable hands fell from the machine he had created, it was seized by the politicians and used for narrow partisan ends. Yet one far-reaching result survived the movement, the popularization of the name of democracy and the naïve acceptance of the belief that the genius of America was democratic. In choosing a party name the Jacksonians were shrewder politicians and better prophets than the Whigs. For better or worse the American masses, and in particular the nationalistic West, had espoused the principle of democracy, and interpreted it in terms of political equalitarianism —a principle that had inspired a fanatical hatred in the breasts of old Federalists. To gentlemen of that earlier school democracy had meant the right of the propertyless majority to plunder the minority in the name of the law. The later Whigs did not make so blundering a mistake. Instead of proclaiming democracy the mother of all mischiefs, they welcomed it as an effective aid in vote-getting. Learning their lesson from Jackson, the Whig politicians outdid him in democratic professions. They had discovered that business has little to fear from a skillfully guided electorate; that quite the safest way, indeed, to reach into the public purse is to do it in the sacred name of the majority will. Perhaps the rarest bit of irony in American history is the later custodianship of democracy by the middle class, who while perfecting their tariffs and subsidies, legislating from the bench, exploiting the state and outlawing all political theories but their own, denounce all class consciousness as unpatriotic and all agrarian or proletarian programs as undemocratic. But it was no fault of Andrew Jackson if the final outcome of the great movement of Jacksonian democracy was so untoward; it was rather the fault of the times that were not ripe for democracy.

II

LINCOLN

Free-Soil Liberal

The equalitarian West that bred Andrew Jackson bred Lincoln also, a man with the same homespun mind, the same sterling integrity of nature, the same instinctive democracy, but shaped by an environment in which the new philosophy of progress had displaced the older agrarianism. The road of middle-class ideals he traveled further than Jackson, but in the end he also turned back to pick up once more the democratic faith then being repudiated by the proponents of slavery, north as well as south. Long an ardent Whig of the Clay school, and thoroughly indoctrinated in a paternalistic nationalism, he was brought, as every thoughtful American of the times was brought, to weigh the program of slave imperialism in the scales with the Declaration of Independence. The doctrines of that great document lay before every man's feet in those uncertain days, to get over as one could. They could not easily be evaded or got round; they must be dealt with. Rufus Choate, representing Boston Toryism, had come upon them and dismissed them as "glittering and sounding generalities." Calhoun, representing southern imperialism, had come upon them and essayed to destroy them by a critical realism. Lincoln, embodying the spontaneous liberalism of the West, came upon them and paused to take his bearings afresh. He could neither wave them aside nor destroy them. The deep-rooted equalitarianism of his simple social philosophy found in them an eloquent pronouncement of its democratic faith, that set him upon considering how such doctrine might be squared with the reality of slavery. The agrarianism of John Taylor and the Whiggery of Henry Clay could tell him nothing about that; he must seek elsewhere; and the solution he found in an amalgamation of equalitarianism and free-soilism, in an adaptation of western Whiggery to Jeffersonian principles.

Whatever party name he might call himself by, in his love of justice and his warm humanity Lincoln was essentially Jeffersonian. He respected property rights, but other rights he believed more sacred. And as he watched the emergence in the South of the ideal of a Greek democracy, as he considered how the party of Jackson had become the party of Calhoun and Douglas, bent solely on strengthening and spreading the institution of slavery, his equalitarianism took alarm. He could not sit quiet while the principles of the Declaration of Independence were being openly flouted; he must speak out; he must arouse the idealism of the people to deal with the iconoclasts. In an important pronouncement written in 1859, he set the problem before them thus:

Remembering . . . that the Jefferson party was formed upon its supposed superior devotion to the personal rights of men, holding the rights of property to be secondary only, and greatly inferior . . . it will be . . . interesting to note how completely the two [parties] have changed hands as to the principles upon which they were originally supposed to be divided. The Democracy of today hold the liberty of one man to be absolutely nothing, when in conflict with another's right of property; Republicans, on the contrary, are for both the man and the dollar, but in case of conflict the man before the dollar. . . . But, soberly, it is now no child's play to save the principles of Jefferson from total overthrow in this nation. . . . The principles of Jefferson are the principles and axioms of free society. And yet they are denied and evaded, with no small show of success. One dashingly calls them "glittering generalities." Another bluntly calls them "self-evident lies!" And others insidiously argue that they apply to "superior races." These expressions, differing in form, are identical in object and effect—the supplanting the principles of free government, and restoring those of classification, caste, and legitimacy. . . . They are the vanguard, the miners and sappers of returning despotism. We must repulse them, or they will subjugate us. (Letter to H. L. Prince and Others, April 6, 1859, in *Works*, Vol. V, pp. 125–126.)

Two conceptions were here competing in Lincoln's mind, the older equalitarianism that sprang from French humanitarianism and the newer economics that came from English *laissez faire;* and the attempt to reconcile them suggests how far he had traveled along the path of western Whiggery. With the spirit of enterprise he had no complaint; the ideal of progress was associated in his mind with a fluid economics that permitted the capable to rise through skillful exploitation. He had no love for the stable economics of the eighteenth century that Jackson preferred; the profit motive, functioning freely, he regarded as the legitimate driving force of society; but he was concerned that competition should be open to all on equal terms. As he watched the transition from an agrarian to an industrial order, he found himself more in sympathy with the new than the old. Accepting the principle of exploitation he came to the position of the little capitalist who believed that in America capitalism could be democratized by the simple method of keeping the opportunities for exploitation open to every citizen. It was common view of western Whiggery, and in so far Lincoln remained a Whig, content with a system which he accepted as peculiarly suited to the genius of the American people. In a late speech he summed it up thus:

What is the true condition of the laborer? I take it that it is best to leave each man free to acquire property as fast as he can. Some will get wealthy. I don't believe in a law to prevent a man from getting rich; it would do more harm than good. So while we don't propose any war upon capital, we do wish to allow the humblest man an equal chance to get rich with anybody else. When one starts poor, as most do in the race of life, free society is such that he knows he can better his condition; he knows that there is no fixed condition of labor for his whole life. . . . I want every man to have a chance—and I believe a black man is entitled to it— in which he can better his condition—when he may look forward and hope to be a hired laborer this year and the next, work for himself afterwards, and finally to hire men to work for him. That is the true system. (Speech at New Haven, March 6, 1860, in *Works*, Vol. V, pp. 360–361.)

But as a western man Lincoln was far more concerned over the application of *laissez faire* to the problem of western lands, and as he contemplated the practical workings of "squatter sovereignty" he learned how the free functioning of *laissez faire* may be interfered with by economic imperialisms. That lesson determined his final stand. The virgin prairies beyond the Mississippi were coveted equally by northern and southern exploiters; and who should finally possess them, whether the small freeholder or the slave-master, was a question that could not be put off forever. None knew this better than the small farmers who were already staking out homesteads there. If Congress yielded to the pro-slavery demands their economic future would be endangered. It was the free-soil West that sent the first anti-slavery men to Washington and provided the backbone of the new party. Not the respectable West, but the plain people, Whig as well as Democrat. "Much of the plain old Democracy is with us," said Lincoln in 1858, "while nearly all the old exclusive silk-stocking Whiggery is against us. I don't mean nearly all the old Whig party, but nearly all of the nice exclusive sort" (Letter to A. C. Henry, in *Works*, Vol. V, p. 95). It was no humanitarian regard for the rights of the negro that welded them into a militant party. Racially and economically the free-soiler was hostile to the black, whether slave or free. The Topeka constitution adopted by the Kansas free-soilers barred all negroes from the new state; Kansas was to be a white man's country. The free labor of the West wanted no competition with an alien race, and was prepared to fight both the white master and free black for exclusive possession of the national domain. There were few John Browns among these western homesteaders—uncompromising idealists who rebelled at the injustice done the negro. The free-soiler hated slavery because it threatened his immediate interests; nevertheless as the great struggle developed, the moral injustice of slavery was thrust to the fore and imparted a humanitarian motive to the free-soil argument. This humanitarian motive Lincoln seized upon, wedded it to the ideal of national union, and thus doubly armed went forth to the fight.

To amalgamate idealism and economics is no easy task. "Public opinion," he said in a speech at Hartford, "is founded, to a great extent, on a property basis." But it is not the sole basis. The ideal of justice comes in to upset all purely economic calculations. "The property basis will have its weight. The love of property and a consciousness of right and wrong have conflicting places in our organization, which often make a man's course seem crooked, his conduct a riddle" (*Works*, Vol. V, p. 330). Beyond question it was this recognition of the perennial conflict between economics and justice, between realism and idealism, that explains the hesitancies and harassing doubts that marked Lincoln's development. To reconcile the principle of exploitation with the Declaration of Independence it was necessary to stick like a flea to *laissez faire*— to eliminate slave labor and accept only free labor. Lincoln was a slow man and cautious, and he pulled himself forward to such a position by main force. He was not a rare intellect like Thoreau, to think swiftly to a conclusion and abide the consequences. He was a political leader rather than an intellectual, and he could advance only a little ahead of the slow-moving mass he sought to draw after him. A hundred invisible ties held him back—his belief in the rights of local democracies, his respect for law and order, his devotion to the Constitution, his recognition of property interests in the slave, his understanding of the complexity of the problem, with the entire economy of the South resting on a slave basis. Here were difficulties enough to trouble an honest mind. His practical sense, which is only another name for political realism, restrained his idealism and made him of necessity an opportunist, willing to yield much if he might save the Union. A simple, tolerant, easy-going man, he was at bottom a realist who had come to understand what may be considered the greatest truth in political science, namely, that an enduring state must rest on willing allegiance. Force cannot compel loyalty; authority may put down revolt but it cannot destroy the seeds of discontent; for that only the sovereignty of good will is competent, and in free states the sovereignty of good will must rest upon compromise. Lincoln was a better democrat than Jackson, for he would rather persuade than drive. If Hamilton embodied the aristocratic principle of coercive government, Lincoln embodied the democratic principle of give and take, that prefers compromise to bayonets. With a cause resting on the common good will it might safely be trusted to muddle through.

Slowly pushed forward by his cautious realism, Lincoln was forty-nine before he reached the "divided house" position of the Douglas debates, that was to entail such consequences. It was a bold pronouncement to address to a generation desperately engaged in erecting sham defenses against reality, in fleeing from the truth that cried aloud to be heard. But he would not let men stop their ears longer; the truth must be spoken to their understanding.

In my opinion [he said] agitation will not cease until a crisis shall have been reached and passed. "A house divided against itself cannot stand."

I believe this government cannot endure permanently half slave and half free. I do not expect the Union to be dissolved—I do not expect the house to fall—but I do expect it will cease to be divided. It will become all one thing, or all the other. Either the opponents of slavery will arrest the further spread of it, and place it where the public mind shall rest in the belief that it is in the course of ultimate extinction; or its advocates will push it forward till it shall become alike lawful in all the States, old as well as new, North as well as South. (Speech at Springfield, June 16, 1858.)

The situation could not have been put more neatly. It was an appeal of honest realism to put away all shoddy romanticisms, all mean evasions, and to face the situation fairly; and it cut across the murky clouds like a flash of lightning. Thenceforth there could be no longer a conspiracy of silence; the problem of slavery had been brought home to the common mind and common conscience, the question of its relation to our national unity and national well-being had been brought out into the realm of homely discussion. It is the democratic way, and as an honest democrat, Lincoln stripped away all the protective coloring of lies that politicians use and appealed to the honesty of plain men. The same method he applied to the Dred Scott decision. He proposed to bring to the bar of the majority opinion the stale legal romanticisms of the Supreme Court. He refused to accept the divine right of the courts to rulership, he denied the sovereignty of the judiciary, and proposed to make a political issue of the matter. He would have it settled in town-meetings and at the polls, by the plain people, and not by lawyers and judges. It was a reversion to Jeffersonian principles, to the simple democratic creed that fundamentals of public policy must be determined by the people themselves.

Lincoln had thought his way slowly to the "divided house" position, but he could not pause there. Those were hurrying times, and the liberalism of yesterday was inadequate for the liberalism of today. A weak man or a time-server would have gone upon the rocks, and a man of unyielding policy must have broken; to be certain of one's conclusions was possible only to one who saw less than the whole. Patience and an open mind alone could be relied on, an intelligent opportunism alone would serve during the months the country was fiercely debating with itself; and the heart-breaking hesitation of Lincoln, the troublesome doubts and perplexed questionings, reveal as nothing else could the simple integrity of his nature. He must go forward, but he must carry the people with him, the North as a whole, the border states if possible, even the rebellious South if charity might suffice. Though in arms, they were Americans, and their hearts must be brought to willing allegiance; how otherwise could a democratic people emerge from the bitterness of civil war? He was not made for a dictator, and blood and iron he accounted poor cement to mend the sundered democracies. He trusted the better impulses of men to prevail in the end, because with Jefferson he believed in the essential justice of the plain people. In this faith he exemplified his democracy. Not a great political thinker, he was a great leader because he never forgot that he was one with those he led.

The slow unfolding of Lincoln's mind is sufficiently revealed in the changing quality of his speeches. He was rarely eloquent—never after the ornate fashion of the time; and the bits of Hebraic poetry that have come to be associated with his name are singularly few and belong to the last years of his life. His usual style was plain homespun, clear and convincing, but bare of imagery and lacking distinction of phrase. The thought seems to break into speech hesitatingly, in the way of a man visibly seeking to adapt his words to his meaning. Matter he judged to be of greater significance than manner. Few men who have risen to enduring eloquence have been so little indebted to rhetoric. Very likely his plainness of style was the result of deliberate restraint, in keeping with the simplicity of his nature. When he let himself go he discovered a well of poetry in his heart. When he chose he could even play the rhetorician. In those rare moments when he put caution behind him, his words fell into a stately rhythm that suggests the orator. Witness such a passage as this:

In those days our Declaration of Independence was held sacred by all, and thought to include all; but now, to aid in making the bondage of the negro universal and eternal, it is assailed and sneered at and construed, and hawked at and torn, till, if its framers could rise from their graves, they could not at all recognize it. All the powers of earth seem rapidly combining against him. Mammon is after him, ambition follows, philosophy follows, and the theology of the day is fast joining the cry. They have him in his prison-house; they have searched his person, and left no prying instrument with him. One after another they have closed the heavy iron doors upon him; and now they have him, as it were, bolted in with a lock of a hundred keys, which can never be unlocked without the concurrence of every key—the keys in the hands of a hundred different men, and they scattered to a hundred different and distant places; and they stand musing as to what invention, in all the dominions of mind and matter, can be produced to make the impossibility of his escape more complete than it is. (Speech at Springfield, June 27, 1857, in *Works*, Vol. II, pp. 327–328.)

But he did not often let himself go. As one reads his speeches one feels that an English diffidence held him back—this and the strong prose of his environment. Like a true Anglo-Saxon he was reluctant to speak out, afraid to let his emotions seize upon his speech. Only at the last did that diffidence yield to complete unconsciousness. The Gettysburg speech and the Second Inaugural are marked by the sincerity and self-effacement that ennobled the words of John Brown in the Virginia court-room—it is the eloquence which rises from the heart when life has been felt in its tragic reality, an eloquence that Webster could not rise to. Such words come only to those who have been purified by fire; they are the distillation of bitter experience. But the mass of his speeches are in quite another manner—that of the simple, everyday world that bred him. He had none of the itch of publicity that afflicts the second-rate mind. Webster was a magnificent poseur; Edward Everett repeated the same academic oration a hundred times; but Lincoln was too modest to pose and too honest to turn parrot and speak by rote. He was a man who loved to talk with his neighbors in homely metaphor, and it was then that his thought clothed itself in whimsical humor. He did not wear his heart on his sleeve, but like Mark Twain he let it slip out in a witticism.

Even more than Washington has Lincoln suffered at the hands of the myth makers. Of late years he has come to be looked upon too often as the invaluable asset of the political party that he honored in its founding, and too rarely as the embodiment of the kindly, liberal soul of our native democracy in the simpler days of a fluid economics and an unsophisticated equalitarianism. With his instinctive kindliness, his abiding faith in the good will of men, his dislike of coercion, his readiness to compromise, he may seem old-fashioned to a generation that has grown intolerant—but that is a reflection on our own times rather than on Lincoln. The real Lincoln can grow old-fashioned no more than Jefferson. As he went back in a day of sordid imperialisms to the earlier liberalism of the great Virginian, seeking to rescue the idealism of the Declaration of Independence from the desecration of the market place where it was openly flouted, so in a day of vaster imperialisms and greater complexity we may take counsel of his humanitarianism, his open-mindedness, his trust in tolerance and good will, his democratic faith that held firm in spite of disappointment. The market place is mighty now as it was then, and liberalism finds as few friends there; but when did its gods become immortal?

CHAPTER III

THE FRONTIER IN LETTERS

WHEN the West began to appear in literature in the late twenties and early thirties, it was the Ohio valley that became the beneficiary of the new interest, and over the vast region through which flowed the Beautiful River—as far as the Mississippi and beyond—was thrown the romance of the settlement. It was a beguiling theme with its background of dark forests and bloody Indian fights, with its venturesome flatboats that drifted with the current, its picturesque rivermen, "half horse, half alligator," who towed their heavy crafts upstream, its rude miscellany of settlers who intrusted their families and goods and cattle to great rafts and set forth hopefully on waters that were to bear them presumably to the Promised Land—a theme to appeal to imaginations easily stirred to romance. There was a darker side to be sure; wrecks in plenty littered the shores, wrecks of fortune and character and life; outlaws and blackguards thronged the river and preyed on the adventurers; but in spite of such misadventures the great movement was invested with dramatic interest, and the Ohio valley became the particular repository of the romance of the frontier, a monopoly which later times never despoiled it of and which only the Golden Coast of California ever remotely rivaled. It was fortunate in that its early history was recorded by a romanticizing generation that wove its myths about the wilderness scouts, that delighted in the picturesque talk of river boatmen and discovered themes for epics in the founding of new commonwealths.

From the first, therefore, the literature of the new West fell naturally into the romantic note. The early writers who essayed to deal with frontier materials were eastern men who proposed to exploit the romance of the Inland Empire as frankly as their fellow adventurers were exploiting the material resources. Gradually in their work two main conceptions crystallized, which came to overshadow all lesser themes: one localized itself in Kentucky and took form in the poetic conception of the Dark and Bloody ground; the other associated itself first with the rivermen but quickly diffused its spirit through the backwoods and took form in the conception of western humor. The first was a heritage from the early days when the Indian tribes fought for their ancient hunting grounds and fell upon the isolated stations with knife and tomahawk; the second grew up with a later generation that had penetrated far into the wilderness, where, stimulated by much whisky, its rough vigor found issue in exaggerated boasting. Each created its legendary hero about whom popular imagination wove its myths: the figure of Daniel Boone came to symbolize the heroic qualities of a race of scouts and backwoodsmen who matched their wits in woodcraft with the Indians and proved the quality of their Kentucky rifles in many a brush with the warriors; and the figure of Davy Crockett came to embody in the popular mind the loquacious eccentricities and exaggerated wit that were already passing into a literary tradition. Many hands contributed to the common work: writers as different as James Kirke Paulding with his *Westward Ho!*, Robert Montgomery Bird with his *Nick of the Woods*, Nathaniel Beverley Tucker with his *George Balcomb*, Albert Pike with his *Prose Sketches and Poems*, Augustus Longstreet with his *Georgia Scenes*, and Joseph G. Baldwin with his *Flush Times of Alabama and Mississippi*—to name only a few. From such diverse elements was created the new literature of the West that was contemporary with the rise of Jacksonian democracy and that gave wide currency to certain romantic conceptions.

I

THE ROMANTIC FRONTIER

Of this very considerable group of writers the two who earliest wrote from immediate first-hand knowledge of frontier life were Timothy Flint, Harvard graduate and missionary, and Judge James Hall, Pennsylvania lawyer, both of whom spent a considerable portion of their mature lives in the West. Of Timothy Flint's restless wanderings and periodic settlements, at Saint Charles, Missouri, at New Orleans, at Alexandria on the Red River in Louisiana, at Cincinnati, with frequent returns to his native Massachusetts and a short editorial experience in New York City, it is impossible to speak in detail; they suggest, however, the breadth and intimacy of his knowledge of the West got from twenty-five years' experience there from 1815 to his death in 1840. Few men traveled so widely through the frontier, or carried with them such keenly observant eyes. He wrote much, conducted for several years a literary magazine in Cincinnati, was for a short time editor of *The Knickerbocker Magazine* on the withdrawal of Charles Fenno Hoffman, and established a considerable reputation as a representative of western letters. Much of his work was frankly casual, but his *Recollections of the Last Ten Years, Passed in Occasional Residencies and Journeyings in the Valley of the Mississippi*, published in 1826, and his four novels published between 1826 and 1830, make up the first important contribution to the new literature of the West.

In temperament Timothy Flint seems to have been something of a realist. In his daily life he was frankly outspoken and critical, often to his own hurt, and some of the many troubles he met with in his honest preaching to frontier heathen, resulted from this plain speaking. He refused to measure life and conduct by the crude western standards, and the enmities resulting from such refusal brought about a rupture with the home society that had supported his missionary undertaking. It was this intellectual honesty that filled his *Recollections* with an invaluable body of observation and criticism, and constituted it an important source-book for later historians. Paulding early made use of it writing his *Westward Ho!*—published in 1832—and in his introduction, after paying tribute to Flint's "picturesque description," he went on to say that the work "has not met its deserts, and he should be highly gratified if this passing notice served in any way to call public attention to its interesting details." Unfortunately the occasional realism of the *Recollections* gave place in his novels to romance saturated with sentiment and heavily coated with moralizing. With a fund of exact information at his disposal he chose to turn away from reality and project his stories into regions he had visited only in imagination. *Francis Berrian, or the Mexican Patriot*, deals with a Southwest far beyond his extremest journeyings; *The Life and Adventures of Arthur Clenning* is a romanticized version of Robinson Crusoe; and *The Shoshonee Valley* is a romance conceived out of tales told him by far western travelers, woven into an extravagantly romantic plot. The only one of his tales that makes use of familiar settings is *George Mason, the Young Backwoodsman; or "Don't Give up the Ship,"* in which he put some of the materials gathered in his journeyings up and down the Mississippi, but sentimentalized and moralized out of all realism. It is a pity that Flint should have fallen in with the extremest mode of the times, for in many essential respects he was the best qualified man of the West to write an honest account of a world just taking form.

The literary reputation of Timothy Flint soon came to be over-shadowed by that of Judge Hall. "Among writers of short nar-ratives, the most characteristically Western fiction of the time," remarks a recent student, "James Hall was clearly preëminent; and he became the central figure in a kind of school of experiment-ers in the materials of frontier life" (Ralph Leslie Rusk, *The Literature of the Middle Western Frontier*, Vol. I, p. 274). In the early twenties he had ridden the circuit in Illinois as a very young lawyer, when the settlements were scattered thinly through the southern portion of the state. At Vandalia he started the *Illinois Monthly Magazine*, which survived for two years, when he removed to Cincinnati and established *The Western Monthly Magazine*, which in the four years from 1832 to 1836 became one of the "most important of the pioneer period." "The purpose," says the student above quoted, "was not so much to introduce the East to the West as to make the West conscious of itself" (Rusk, *ibid.*, Vol. I, p. 173). To this end Hall was writing and publishing short tales and descriptions, and he had already collected a miscellany of prose and verse by several hands which he issued as an annual, *The Western Souvenir, a Christmas and New Year's Gift for 1829*. Thus launched on a literary career, he wrote in the next twenty years a very con-siderable amount, including tales, sketches of manners, history and casual comment.

His best-known story is probably *Harpe's Head*, which he later incorporated with other tales in a volume entitled *Legends of the West: Sketches Illustrative of the Habits, Occupations, Privations, Adventures and Sports of the Pioneers of the West*, and published in 1832. The work proved popular and passed through half a dozen editions. Sketchy and loose in construction, it belongs to the school that hovered between the essay and the romance, delight-ing in the picturesque, exuding sentiment, and going out of its way to exploit the pleasantly horrible. It is a mingling of Virginia chivalry and frontier bravery, woven about a central plot of a daughter of a Virginia house who removes to Kentucky under tragic circumstances, is abducted by a roving band of Indians, and subsequently rescued. Additional romantic interest is sought in

the melodramatic deeds of the title hero—a well-known border
ruffian with an insatiable blood-lust who murders his unsuspecting
victims wherever he comes upon them—and in the curious exploits
in rattlesnake killing of Hark Short, a waif from the Carolina
swamps who lives like a fox in his den. The interest of the story
today lies in the pleasantly idealized descriptions of such scenes as
the barbecue and the camp meeting, rather than in the portrayal
of backwoods characters. Although Hall frequently professed his
devotion to realism, there is little evidence of it; occasional figures like Pete Featherton, whose rifle had been bewitched, and
occasional indulgence in a conventionalized backwoods dialect,
serve only to heighten the somewhat gaudy romance of the whole.
Yet even such timid ventures brought on his head criticism from
a Cincinnati editor "for tiring the reader with vulgar backwoods
expressions" (Rusk, *ibid.*, Vol. I, p. 282).

That Hall's interest in backwoods eccentricities of speech and
manner suffered a heavy handicap from the romantic taste of his
readers may easily be believed. Matter excluded from his tales he
sometimes put into his introductions. Thus in the third edition of
Harpe's Head he analyzed at some length certain characteristics of
the crude pioneers who were creating the psychology of the West—
their fondness for drinking, betting, horse-trading, stump-speaking,
swearing. Particularly it is the exuberance of their picturesque
language that he emphasized, an exuberance that was already becoming a literary tradition and that flowered in the cento of western
folk ways that were gathered into the Davy Crockett myth. A
single passage will suffice to suggest some of the elements from
which Davy was created:

> Though usually taciturn in the presence of strangers, [the frontiersman]
> is communicative to his friend or guest, has often strong colloquial powers,
> with quaint, singular, figurative, and even eloquent forms of expression.
> His language, which is commonly brief, sententious, and abrupt, becomes,
> when excited by the interest of the subject or by passion, highly expletive,
> and redundant with exaggerated forms and figures of comparison. When
> he swears—and he is probably not more given to this exceedingly vulgar
> vice than other men—but when he does swear in earnest, his philology
> becomes concentrated, and explodes with an appalling energy, which
> would have astonished even the celebrated army in Flanders. (*Ibid.*,
> Introduction, p. xii.)

In his last collection, *The Wilderness and the War Path*, published
in 1846 and including some earlier tales, Hall contributed little that

was new. There is the same heavy romance with touches of realism, and by way of reply to Bird's interpretation of the Indian character he exploits the romantic qualities of the red man; but his failures are commoner than his successes, and his work as a whole must be regarded as a sacrifice to the bad taste of his generation. From this judgment, perhaps, should be excepted his *Romance of American History*, which is still pleasantly readable.

II

THE REALISTIC FRONTIER

Far more vital than these literary tales with their heavy coating of romance are the few realistic sketches—only too rare in those exuberant days of the high-flown—that preserve the authentic ways of backwoods life in their rude vernacular. Of such sketches those that most faithfully reveal the impress of the frontier, preserving down to the present the note of verisimilitude, are *Georgia Scenes* by Augustus B. Longstreet, and the *Autobiography of Davy Crockett*, to which may be added, perhaps, Joseph G. Baldwin's *Flush Times of Alabama and Mississippi*.

1

AUGUSTUS LONGSTREET
The Georgia Frontier

For some reason no glamour has ever gathered about the Georgia frontier. It may be that fate conspired against it in bestowing no idealizing historian to throw a romantic haze over life in the pine woods. Or perhaps it was the Georgians themselves who did the commonwealth an evil turn. As a matter of sober fact what could even romance do with the raw materials that went to the making of this crude southern Yankee state? How could the most confirmed romantic discover rare graces in the indigenous Cracker, or weave poetry about the ubiquitous peddler with his pack of Yankee notions? Any honest historian could hardly avoid taking into account the ungainly throng that attended a gander pulling, or depict Ransy Sniffle as other than a pallid, pot-bellied, clay-eating grotesque. Crude, uncouth, drab, with primitive passions and unlovely manners, Georgia offered scanty materials for the most ardent eulogist. Frontier life there ran a petty round between fist fights and horse races, between politics and religion. These were the staples of everyday existence, as necessary to the natural man as whisky and salt pork; and the honest Georgian preferred his whisky straight and his politics and religion red-hot. The Jeffersonian hated the Federalist vindictively; and Presbyterian, Baptist, and Methodist regarded each other malignantly, convinced that the devil was stoking his fires for the lost neighbor who persisted in sitting under the wrong preaching. Denominationalism on the Georgia frontier was as harsh and unforgiving as political partisanship. Alexander H. Stephens believed that the plain people of Georgia were the most democratic on the face of the earth, and the kindliest; yet the pugnacious little democrat was himself nearly butchered by a democratic neighbor. In depicting such a society realism was the only honest method; but to make it palatable it must be well seasoned with humor. If it were garnished with moralizing, so much the better. There must be no subtleties in the treatment, no literary touches. The humor must be in the backwoods vernacular, and the preaching open and aboveboard—frank pulpit-thumping lessons to awaken the surliest sinner.

For such business Gus Longstreet was ideally fitted. A true child of the Georgia border, he never quite outgrew his early environment. Born in Augusta in 1790 of New Jersey parents, Holland Dutch but with a large admixture of English blood,[1] he came of plain stock. A driving, robust, energetic fellow, never squeamish, with a ready wit, he was at home amongst the plain people, the greatest wag in every gathering. He could knock a man down or shoot out a squirrel's eye with any champion of them all; he could enter into a dance or a revival meeting with equal ardor, or take the stump against a seasoned campaigner. A fellow must be simple-minded who would expect to get the best of him in swapping horses, or in the way of a practical joke. It came hard for so vigorous a plebeian to settle down as a substantial citizen, and the dignified titles that he gathered in the course of a long and prosperous career—judge, doctor of laws, doctor of divinity— fitted him somewhat incongruously. On the whole one prefers the plain Gus Longstreet to Judge Longstreet, but his neighbors, who thought they knew a man when they saw one, thrust his titles upon him. Besides he had gone to college and was thereby lifted to a place of distinction which he could not avoid. The process of

[1] The family name of Langestraet was given an English form by his grandfather.

scraping off the bark of the frontier followed orthodox southern lines. A few years' schooling at Dr. Moses Waddell's celebrated Academy, where at different times Calhoun, Crawford, McDuffie, Petigru and Legaré prepared for college, and two years at Yale, provided him with a stock of rusty Latin to suffice a college president; and a winter or two at the law school in Litchfield, Connecticut, following Calhoun's high example, furnished him with enough Blackstone to meet the demands of Georgia law courts. Thus provided intellectually, he went forth boldly to cope with the Georgia world as he found it.

It was a plebeian world that approved his plebeian qualities. There was nothing of the southern patrician in Gus Longstreet, nothing of the ascetic Puritan that marked so deeply men like Calhoun, Legaré, and the Grimkés. In his strong instinct of acquisitiveness, his canny thrift that never failed to seize advantage by the forelock, his desire to get on in the world while serving God, he was a Georgia Yankee, with an emotional religion that took comfort in discovering that God was always on his side of any controversy. Yankee also was his knack of doing many things well enough to impress his less capable neighbors. He was a frontier jack-of-all-trades, passing easily from one profession to another, lawyer, newspaper editor, writer, minister, politician, teacher, and between times busying himself with all sorts of odd jobs, doing everything readily and nothing thoroughly well. A good talker, his chief interests were politics, religion, and money-making. He wrote much in careless haste, apologizing always for the lack of finish; but except for the sketches which were gathered under the title of *Georgia Scenes*, he produced nothing that needs to be remembered. At the age of forty-eight he quitted the law for the Methodist ministry, proved to be a mediocre preacher, and was soon given the berth of president of Emory College, a denominational school then recently established at Oxford, for which his literary reputation and his reputed scholarship seemed to fit him. Later he was president for a few months of Centenary College, Louisiana, but found the place uncongenial, resigned, and was chosen president of the University of Mississippi, where he served seven years and made full use of the opportunity to speculate in real estate. At the age of sixty-six he was made president of the University of South Carolina, where he ruled patriarchally till the school was closed by the war.

How great a man he was judged to be by his fellow Georgians is hard for us to realize today. Throughout his later years he was regarded by his friends as the brightest ornament of Georgia society, a Christian gentleman who was a model to southern youth, a scholar who had brought honor to the commonwealth, an author who had silenced the reproach that the state had produced no literature. Yet it must be confessed that the Judge shrinks in compass when taken out of his native environment. Beside John P. Kennedy or Hugh Legaré, he lacks distinction either of mind or manner; compared with Gilmore Simms he is only an amateur in letters. His latest biographer [2] has sifted a mass of material to prove the solid and eminent worth of the man; yet no impression of intellectual vigor emerges from the analysis; one must take it on the authority of somewhat incompetent witnesses. The figure that emerges from the clutter of contemporary estimate is that of a capable, expansive, middle-class soul, disputatious in the lordly southern manner, genially domineering, magnificently superior to logic, given to erecting an imposing structure of convictions on the slightest of foundations, impatient of contradiction and inclined to lose his temper when the argument went against him— a witty, agreeable gentleman, at home amongst mediocre preachers, and an oracle to admiring friends. He was on terms of intimacy with not a single first-class mind. He had no intellectual curiosity and was incapable of rigorous intellectual processes. Yet good fortune had marked him for her own. A small investment in letters, made at odd moments between law cases and farming operations, returned him such dividends in the way of contemporary fame that for forty years thereafter he lived in the sunshine of a literary reputation. No other American, unless it were William Wirt, ever drew such ample revenues of popular praise from a casual investment, and certainly none ever expanded with greater self-satisfaction. To the end of his life he was the much-sought-after author of *Georgia Scenes*, and the most ambitious southern magazines were glad to publish his frequent effusions; in all of which the Judge delighted, for he was a simple soul and accounted himself an apostle of southern culture, a mentor of southern taste, and he loved to see his name in print.

As a man close to the people Longstreet reflected the current Georgia views on politics. He was an idolatrous admirer of

[2] John Donald Wade, *Augustus Baldwin Longstreet.*

Calhoun and George McDuffie. The former he rated "above William Pitt, or any other premier who ever lived before or since his day" (Wade, *Augustus Baldwin Longstreet*, p. 124) and the latter he regarded as "hardly inferior to him in anything." Calhoun's innate Hebraisms, so deeply imbued with a patriarchal spirit, fitted to a nicety his own Hebraized conception of a Jeffersonian order. Writing of Calhoun, in after years, Longstreet remarked with evident approval:

I believe that he regarded the government of the children of Israel in the wilderness, the most perfect that ever existed on earth. Be that as it may, he called my attention to it more than once as exactly the government ours ought to be, or was intended to be. "There," said he, "each tribe had its place on the march and in the camp, each managed its own concerns in its own way, neither interfered in the slightest degree, with the private affairs of another, nor did their common head interfere with any of them in any matters, save such as were of equal interest to all, but unmanageable by them as separate and distinct communities." (*Ibid.*, p. 60.)

The background of his political thought was Jeffersonian agrarian. He was always a countryman at heart, and his dearest interests were agricultural. But he seems to have been quite unread in political theory, and probably had never heard of John Taylor's economic principles. Suffering from an incurable political itch, he was one of the earliest and most ardent of states-rights advocates. He went for Nullification before either Calhoun or McDuffie had espoused it; and he followed his premises through to the logical end of secession. But with the growth of northern Abolitionism his Jeffersonianism began to disintegrate. Garrison's appeal to equalitarianism and the rights of man aroused all his southern prejudices. A philosophy that could be turned against the sacred institution was no philosophy for a southern gentleman, and like Calhoun he repudiated the whole French liberal philosophy that he had imbibed in his youth. He even went so far as to play with Calhoun's doctrine of economic representation. Writing to President Lamar, of Texas, in the late thirties, he said, "A government should have a legislative assemblage to represent each of its large economic interests, one, say, agricultural, one manufacturing, one commercial. No bill not acceptable to all three of these assemblages should become a law" (*ibid.*, p. 138). But in defense of slavery he argued as a minister rather than an economist. He declined to consider it an economic question;

he would not discuss it as a social question; political theories, he believed, had nothing to do with it. The right to hold slaves he regarded as a moral question to be determined exclusively by the authority of the Bible, and on such a question he professed to speak with assurance. He was vastly annoyed at the Abolitionists' unchristian appeal to the old doctrine of equalitarianism, and in 1845 he wrote angrily, "Will not some of you accept my ideas and then argue through the question on that basis, without taking recourse to the Declaration of Independence or throwing up a breastwork out of the long-forsaken rubbish of the Social Contract, or bewildering your pursuers in the mazes of metaphysical subtlety?" (*ibid.*, p. 282). His religion was deeply involved in the institution of slavery, and it seemed to him uncharitable for an intellectual like Theodore Parker to question the sufficiency of a southern minister's texts, or to drag him beyond his intellectual depths. So exasperated did he grow that finally he would have no fellowship with northern Methodists, and was a prime mover in the great schism that rent the church into sectional branches. Abolitionism seemed to him hypocrisy and blasphemy and as a minister of Christ he could not hold fellowship with those who rejected the Master's word. After the war, in reviewing the long controversy, his Christian pugnacity flared up anew, and he flung at the northern churches the accusation that they had been "the most man-astounding, God-offending foes that we had" (*ibid.*, p. 367).

There could be no more telling commentary on the literary poverty of *ante-bellum* Georgia than the extraordinary popularity of Longstreet's sketches. Written for the most part between the years 1832 and 1836, while he was publishing the *State Rights Sentinel*, they profess to be authentic documents of frontier life in Georgia in the early years of the century, and the deliberate note of realism contributes to the impression of authenticity. The love of the romantic that spread like the plague among southern men of letters during the long reign of Sir Walter, fortunately did not infect the robust nature of Longstreet. The best of the sketches are spun out of the vernacular; they are as objective as Longstreet could make them—conscious studies in the local, done with obvious delight in butternut ways and frontier dialect. The quality of the work improves as he draws nearer the backwoods, and comes upon the unregenerate Cracker in his native habitat.

There his humor has free play, exuding in practical jokes and ready repartee, in boyish pranks and homely idiom. And there he finds characters to his liking and bits of realistic drama. If one were to single out the sketch that is most indigenous to the Georgia frontier, the truest local document, the choice might well fall on *The Fight*, an account of a bloody meeting between back-woods gladiators brought on by skillful diplomacy of Ransy Sniffle, a grotesque clay-eater and Longstreet's favorite character. Other excellent sketches are *The Gander Pulling, The Shooting Match, Georgia Theatrics, The Horse Swap, The Militia Company Drill*—stories that throw an unromantic light on the ways of the Georgia Cracker. Longstreet was as uncritical as his readers and his frequent failures are glaring in their badness. Perhaps the worst of the sketches are the absurd *The "Charming Creature" as a Wife*, a crude sermon on the folly of marrying a lazy woman; *The Song*, an overdone burlesque, and the puerile *The Debating Society*, a heavy practical joke which for some inexplicable reason Poe thought the best of the whole.

Slight though the sketches in *Georgia Scenes* are, they embody solid merits; they are not literary and they are quite unaffected by Irving and the exploitation of the picturesque. Realism was only too rare in those days of high-flown romance, and how honestly realistic was Longstreet's work is revealed by a comparison with James Hall's contemporary stories of the West, such as *Harpe's Head*, or even with Kennedy's *Swallow Barn*. After all Gus Longstreet was an original, and he set the style that was followed in a long series of frontier sketches, and established the tradition of frontier humor that flowered at last in Mark Twain.

2

THE DAVY CROCKETT MYTH

The Narrative of the Life of David Crockett of the State of Tennessee was woven from the same stuff that Longstreet made use of, but the fabric is of far better texture. It is the great classic of the southern frontier, far more significant than *Georgia Scenes*, far more human and vital. Realistic in method, it is romantic in spirit. In its backwoods vernacular it purveys the authentic atmosphere of the cabin and the canebrake; it exhibits the honesty, the wit, the resourcefulness, the manly independence of a coonskin hero; it reveals, in short, under the rough exterior of a shiftless squatter and bear-hunter, qualities that are sterling in every society where manhood is held in repute. It is an extraordinary document, done so skillfully from life that homespun becomes a noble fabric and the crudest materials achieve the dignity of an epic.

The thing had long been waiting to be done. The literary romantics had tried their hand at the frontier materials and had failed, and then came a realist of the Georgia school who used the stuff as he found it and created a lasting document. A practiced writer collaborated with a picturesque talker, and the fame of the Tennessee Congressman was made. Romantic America found a new hero and Davy Crockett reaped a surprising reward. He had the good fortune to preëmpt the romance of the backwoods, to file on an unsurveyed tract of western life, and when the lines were run it was found that his claim embraced all that was native and picturesque along the Mississippi frontier. Popular imagination seized upon him and endowed the mighty hunter of the canebrakes with the fugitive romance that had been gathering for years. He was erected into a mythical figure that drew to itself the unappropriated picturesque that sprang spontaneously from the crude western life. How this astonishing result came about, how good fortune came to single out Davy Crockett for her smiles, offers a somewhat amusing commentary on the ways of an unsophisticated generation.

That in its later development, if not in the beginning, the Davy Crockett myth was a deliberate fabrication scarcely admits of doubt, nor that its immediate purpose was frankly partisan. It did not spring from the soil of the Tennessee canebrakes; it was created at Washington. It was not the spontaneous product of popular imagination; it was the clever work of politicians. The successive stages through which it passed in its triumphant progress can be traced fairly accurately with the aid of a little historical imagination. Roughly they were three; the exploitation of Davy's canebrake waggery, the exploitation of his anti-Jackson spleen, and the exploitation of his dramatic death at the Alamo. The first phase is embodied in the *Sketches and Eccentricities of Col. David Crockett, of West Tennessee* (1833); the second, in *An Account of Col. Crockett's Tour to the North and Down East* (1835), and *The Life of Martin Van Buren* (1835); and the last, in *Col. Crockett's Exploits and Adventures in Texas* (1836).

Midway between the first and second stages stands *A Narrative of the Life of David Crockett, of the State of Tennessee* (1834), which may be accepted in the main as authentic autobiography. None of the five was written by Crockett. He probably had a hand in the first in spite of his repudiation of the work, for most of the important facts of his life and the language of many of the picturesque episodes were taken from its pages to be reproduced in the *Narrative*. The *Tour* and *Martin Van Buren* were claimed by him and were certainly done under his eye and with his help, but the *Exploits* is quite as certainly sheer fabrication, done by a hack writer after Davy's death. It was the politicians who contributed most to the success of the myth. They exploited Davy as a convenient weapon against Jackson, saw their work prosper beyond all expectation, get out of their hands, enlarge itself to a cento of backwoods romance and pass into folklore. It was an unforeseen outcome that must have been vastly amusing to those who set the thing going.

The early thirties, it will be remembered, were robustious times when broadcloth in politics had suddenly gone out of style and homespun had come in. The new coonskin democracy had descended upon Washington, and picturesque figures provided with ample plugs of tobacco were making themselves free with Congressional perquisites. Nothing like it had been seen before in the city of dignified politicians, and the spectacle must have delighted the wags of the capital. But to the members of the overthrown dynasty the Jacksonian votes which these picturesque backwoodsmen represented were very far from amusing. The loss of desirable offices was a hard lesson that taught them the need of catering to this new element of the great American democracy. In their remunerative occupation as representatives of the prosperous and genteel constituencies of the East, the old-school politicians had too long overlooked the power of the plain voter which the progress of manhood suffrage was daily increasing. Hence began a desperate campaign to counteract the Jacksonian appeal. The coonskin vote could no longer be ignored and shrewd plans were laid to capture the backwoods for the new Whig party. The program of internal improvements was well enough in its way, and the old Revolutionary cry of the sword and the purse might prove useful; but the party needed a picturesque figure to draw the coonskin democracy to its standard. Men rather than principles appealed to the West, self-made men, speaking the western vernacular, imbibing western views with their whisky, uncorrupted by broadcloth. This explains the tremendous Whig hurrah over log cabins and hard cider that marked a later campaign; and this explains likewise the singular fate that overtook Davy Crockett, the bear-hunter from the canebrakes.

Davy had first come to Washington during Adams' administration, and in four years' loafing and boasting at the Congressional bar had achieved some distinction as a picturesque original with the tongue of a wag. He spoke rarely in the House and the few records in the *Congressional Debates* are sadly commonplace. Until after he broke with Jackson his political influence at Washington was negligible. But that fortunate break was the beginning of his fame. He had unwittingly made himself. He had become a valuable asset to the Whig party. To find a native Tennesseean, a real coonskin democrat, one who had served under Jackson and been sent to Congress as a Jacksonian, as authentic a Westerner as the General himself, at bitter personal odds with Old Hickory, ready to talk out in meeting and eager to repudiate the latter's attack upon the Bank, was a find indeed to the hard-pressed Whigs; and they would have been no politicians if they had not used what God sent. In consequence Davy soon found himself talked about. His picturesque eccentricities began to be exploited. His rugged western honesty was applauded; his shrewd backwoods intelligence was praised; his frontier humor was skillfully touched up; his characteristic motto, "go ahead," was seized upon as an expression of the progressive spirit of the lusty young Whig party. In short he was speedily turned into a myth by ways not unknown in our time, and sent forth as useful campaign material in the fight for political righteousness. Davy was vastly surprised at his sudden rise to fame. He had never realized how great a man he was; but he accepted it as an agreeable fact and went ahead.

The work had already begun with the publication of the *Sketches and Eccentricities of Col. David Crockett*, that came from the clever pen of some journalist with a liking for the new vein of backwoods humor. A Whig bias runs through the pages, but the book is more a character sketch than a political document. The first embroiderings raid upon the original homespun are seen in an extravagance of picturesque language—an extravagance quite lacking in the more realistic *Narrative*. A well-known passage

professing to relate an occurrence on Davy's first trip to Washington will serve to reveal an early stage of the myth-making process—the fathering upon Davy of a type of humor then being
exploited by clever young writers:

> I was *rooting* my way to the fire, not in a good humour, when some
> fellow staggered towards me, and cried out, "Hurrah for Adams!" Said
> I, "Stranger, you had better hurrah for hell, and praise your own country."
> Said he, "And who are you?"
>
> "I'm that same David Crockett, fresh from the backwoods, half-horse,
> half-alligator, a little touched with the snapping-turtle; can wade the
> Mississippi, leap the Ohio, ride upon a streak of lightning, and slip without
> a scratch down a honey locust; can whip my weight in wild-cats—and
> if any gentleman pleases, for a ten-dollar bill, he may throw in a panther—
> hug a bear too close for comfort, and eat any man opposed to Jackson."
> (*Ibid.*, Chapter XIII.)

The touching up of the picturesque in the *Sketches* seems to
have been a little too much for Davy, who resented the note of
clownishness; but he was not the man to permit undue modesty
to blight so agreeable a myth in its tender stage. He loved to swagger in the public eye too much for that, and he joined heartily
with his new political friends to clothe it in more dignified dress.
His incredible egotism was aroused and he swallowed the Whig
bait, hook, line and sinker. He began to take himself seriously
and set about the business of propagating the myth. He conceived the plan of issuing in his own name books which he humorously claimed to have written in the same way that the President
wrote his state papers. Some wag having suggested his name for
the presidency to succeed Jackson, Davy was at great pains to
advertise the fact to the world. To link himself with Jackson in
the public eye and to contrast his own rugged honesty with the
latter's reputed abandonment of democratic principles, was the
single purpose of these Whig documents. The autobiography was
quickly followed by the *Tour*, and this by the *Life of Martin Van
Buren*, each more obvious propaganda than the last, and frankly
designed to undermine the popularity of the President and his
advisers with the coonskin democracy. Who the writer was that
lent his pen to the work has never been determined. A recent
student has adduced testimony to prove that it was Augustin S.
Clayton, a Georgia Congressman, a ready talker and writer, a man
of sound culture, a close friend of Longstreet and fond of the
backwoods vernacular. The argument is plausible, but the case is

not established.[3] In the *Life of Martin Van Buren* the mask is dropped and all the malicious gossip of the Congressional lobby is poured out on "little Van," the "heir-apparent to the 'government.'" The backwoods character is retained only in an occasional coarseness or deliberate lapse of grammar inserted in a text that is written with vigor and skill. The book is far less amusing than Kennedy's *Quodlibet*. Davy is pretty much lost out of its pages and its contribution to the myth was probably slight.

It is in the *Tour*, on the title page of which Davy formally accepts the brevet dignity of Colonel conferred upon him by the writer of the *Sketches*, that the myth expands more genially. A clever and amusing campaign document, it is a masterpiece of Whig strategy to gull the simple. The loquacious Davy joined heartily with his managers to cash in on his reputation. His egotism was played upon at every turn and he was quite unconscious that he had become a mere cat's-paw to pull Whig chestnuts out of the coals. He was paraded at meetings with Daniel Webster, given great dinners, applauded for his rustic wit and homespun honesty, presented with a fine rifle; and he seems never to have realized how grossly he was being exploited. His self-esteem was proof against dillusionment and he accepted the applause greedily. Wherever he went he was taken in charge by the young Whigs. Everything was carefully arranged beforehand. News was sent forward that he was coming; crowds were gathered to greet him; publicity was attended to; morning, noon, and night he was invited to speak, and the speeches were carefully reprinted—not the authentic speeches, probably, but good campaign material nevertheless. It was a gratifying experience and Davy swelled up like a turkey cock.

As a result of his tour he was immensely strengthened in his new political faith and became a staunch nationalist. When he first went to Congress he was anti-tariff and had won his seat on that issue; but he was invited to Lowell, shown an idyllic picture of contented and prosperous mill-hands, dined, given a prepared table of statistics proving how industrialism "is calculated not only to give individual happiness and prosperity, but to add to our national wealth and prosperity," and bidden Godspeed in the work of spreading the true gospel among the honest, simple-minded and patriotic frontiersmen. After having been presented

[3] See John Donald Wade, "The Authorship of David Crockett's *Autobiography*," *Georgia Historical Quarterly*, September, 1922.

by Mr. Lawrence with a fine suit of domestic broadcloth, Davy
would have been an ingrate not to vote for a protective tariff.
But alas! the opportunity never came. A backwoods constituency
that had never been dined by Lowell capitalists and had little use
for fine broadcloth, a constituency that persisted in throwing up
coonskin caps for Old Hickory in spite of Lowell statistics, resented his apostasy from the Democratic faith and at the next
election invited him to stay in the canebrakes. The gorgeous
bubble was pricked. Davy had expanded under prosperity
and could not now endure adversity. In a fit of anger he quitted
his family and the state of Tennessee, went off on the mad chase
to Texas and in March of the next year fell at the Alamo. Vain,
ignorant Davy Crockett! A simple-minded frontiersman, he
went down to Jericho and fell among thieves, and when they
were done with him they left him despoiled politically but invested
with a fame that has grown to this day. After his death other
hands took up the work, wove around his name the humor and
romance of the frontier, and made of him a legendary figure. It
would have pleased Davy to know how the myth had prospered.[4]

Yet from this crude romanticism, this picturesque propaganda
of coonskin days, one solid contribution remains—the autobiography. It is a striking bit of realism, done after the manner of the
Longstreet school. There is politics in it, of course. Written just
after Davy had gone through a bitter campaign from which he had
emerged triumphant, it is a bold pronouncement that he wears no
collar marked "My dog—Andrew Jackson." In the campaign of
1830 he had been defeated by the Jacksonians, but two years later
he "made a mash" of his opponents, and the elation of that victory
adds a certain cockiness to his habitual swagger. But it is much
more than a political tract; it is a vital frontier document. The
main facts of his biography, as set down there, may be accepted as
true, and the general picture of backwoods existence in Tennessee;
but the humor has been elaborated and the effect of the picturesque
heightened by his collaborator. Such added touches were only
natural. The real Davy was very far from romantic. An honest
picture of the Tennessee democracy in its native habitat would
reveal few idyllic features. It was a slovenly world and Davy was

---

[4] Among the miscellaneous material gathered together in the *Exploits and
Adventures in Texas* and attributed to Davy is Longstreet's *Georgia Theatrics*,
lifted verbatim from *Georgia Scenes*.

pretty much of a sloven. Crude and unlovely in its familiar details, with its primitive courtships and shiftless removals, its brutal Indian campaign and fierce hunting sprees, its rough equality, its unscrupulous politics, its elections carried by sheer impudence and whisky, the autobiography reveals the backwoods Anglo-Irishman as an uncivilized animal, responding to simple stimuli, yet with a certain rough vigor of character. Wastefulness was in the frontier blood, and Davy was a true frontier wastrel. In the course of successive removals he traversed the length of Tennessee, drinking, hunting, talking, speculating, begetting children, scratching a few acres of land to "make his crap," yet living for the most part off the country; and his last squatting place on the Obion River, seven miles from the nearest neighbor, was as primitive as the first. Willing to endure almost incredible hardships to obtain a keg of gunpowder to celebrate Christmas, risking his skin to kill a bear with a butcher knife, he was never much given to mending fences or enlarging his plow lands. He was a hunter rather than a farmer, and the lust of killing was in his blood. With his pack of hounds he slaughtered with amazing efficiency. A later generation would call him a game-hog. His family must have had Gargantuan appetites to have consumed one-tenth of the meat that fell before his beloved Betsy; the rest went to the dogs and hogs and buzzards. His hundred and five bears in a single season, his six deer shot in one day while pursuing other game—two of which were left hanging in the woods—serve to explain why the rich hunting grounds of the Indians were swept so quickly bare of game by the white invaders. Davy was but one of thousands who were wasting the resources of the Inland Empire, destroying forests, skinning the land, slaughtering the deer and bear, the swarms of pigeons and turkey, the vast buffalo herds. Davy the politician is a huge western joke, but Davy the wastrel was a hard, unlovely fact.

Strip away the shoddy romance that has covered up the real man and the figure that emerges is one familiar to every backwoods gathering, an assertive, opinionated, likable fellow, ready to fight, drink, dance, shoot or brag, the biggest frog in a very small puddle, first among the Smart Alecks of the canebrakes. Davy was a good deal of a wag, and the best joke he ever played he played upon posterity that has swallowed the myth whole and persists in setting a romantic halo on his coonskin cap. Yet in spite of the romantic machinery the play turns out to be broad farce.

BOOK TWO: THE MIND OF THE MIDDLE EAST

BOOK TWO

THE MIND OF THE MIDDLE EAST

THE literature of the Middle East during the years of the romantic revolution, unlike contemporary letters north and south, revealed no coalescing unity of spirit and purpose; it was rather the
casual and somewhat fortuitous expression of two cities, both of
which were divided by language and custom into fairly equal
groups, and neither of which had developed a homogeneous native
culture.   There were no intellectual hinterlands to Philadelphia
and New York, as there were to Boston and Charleston and Richmond; no common ideals spread over broad areas, no dominant
schools of thought, no branching roots by which a common literature might be nourished.   In consequence it may, perhaps, be
reckoned a misuse of terms to speak of the mind of the Middle
East, as one may speak of the mind of New England or of the Old
Dominion, where in spite of pronounced variations of individual
temperament a common culture had set its mark on the literature.
There were few common ties and few intellectual sympathies to
bind together the men of letters of New York or Philadelphia.
Certainly Irving and Paulding and Cooper and Melville and
Whitman reveal none of that strong community of taste and purpose that marks the Concord group, or the Boston-Cambridge
group, or even the Charleston group.   They expressed no common
culture, they had been disciplined in no common faith, and they
were held together by no common economic or political or intellectual interests; as a result their writing is a frank expression of
individual temperament and taste, unfettered by schools, drawing
its nourishment from no common soil.   They stand on their own
feet, and to understand them requires no critical examination of a
complex cultural background.   And yet this very diversity may
prove to be symptomatic of the hurrying changes that the rise of
the middle class was bringing to America—to the city perhaps even
more dramatically than to the country.   The confusions and

diversity of thought that mark the literature of Philadelphia and New York may, perhaps, most adequately suggest the mercurial temper of the revolutionary transition from the eighteenth century to the nineteenth, of which the romantic spirit was the natural expression.

CHAPTER I

THE OLD CAPITAL

I

In the year 1800 one might well have expected Philadelphia to retain indefinitely its proud ascendency as the cultural capital of America. For decades no other colonial city had come near to rivaling it as a pleasant center of wealth and refinement. Its society was accounted the politest and most agreeable in America, and during the Revolutionary War young British officers had found its hospitable drawing-rooms an agreeable substitute for London clubs. It had long prided itself on its culture and it was on chatty terms with the fine arts, with books and music and painting, with actors and plays and playhouses. It was the recognized center of the publishing business, and its busy presses turned out books and magazines and newspapers for remote colonial readers. Ambitious young men were drawn to it as by a magnet, and Matthew Carey from Ireland and William Cobbett from England were outstanding figures amongst the many who found Philadelphia as attractive as Franklin had earlier found it. Certainly it was the least provincial spot in America in 1800, managing to keep abreast of the latest English fashions in letters as well as smallclothes; and when the supercilious Tom Moore favored the city with his presence in the summer of 1804, he found there the companionship which in some measure compensated for the meanness of the rest of America, where he professed to see:

> One dull chaos, one unfertile strife,
> Betwixt half-polish'd and half-barbarous life,
> Where every ill the ancient world can brew
> Is mixed with every grossness of the new.[1]

The pronounced intellectual stir expressed itself not only in *belles lettres*, and in the scientific experiments of Franklin and Rittenhouse, but more adequately still in politics. Political disputation would seem, indeed, to have been the common Philadelphia passion. Party forces were more equally divided than in

[1] Quoted in Oberholtzer, *Literary History of Philadelphia*, p. 178.

Boston. From the beginnings of the Revolutionary disputes Philadelphia had produced notable disputants on both sides— pamphleteers like Joseph Galloway and John Dickinson, and satirists like Joseph Stansbury and Francis Hopkinson. In the succeeding decades partisan pens had augmented rather than abated their vigor. During Washington's administration the French Revolution shook Philadelphia as it shook no other American city, and the fierce battle between Federalist and Jacobin was waged with amazing fury and limitless invective. The deadly journalistic duel between Freneau and Fenno in their two *Gazettes* was reflected in the equally bitter duel of couplets between Matthew Carey and William Cobbett. If Philadelphia was not more catholic than Boston, it was at least better informed on party questions, for clever writers were daily flinging their arguments at its head. So long as the political capital of the nation remained in Philadelphia the city was clearly the place for the young American to sharpen his wits, inform his mind, and quicken his literary enthusiasm.

Economically the future of the city seemed equally bright. A younger generation of speculative merchants had taken the place of the older conservatives, and great fortunes were being made with a rapidity before unknown. When title to the western lands passed from the crown to the new republic, Philadelphia merchants took the lead in land speculation, and Robert Morris entered upon a spectacular career that profoundly impressed his generation. The city became the chief center of land speculation to which western and southern investors looked. Economic opportunities increased with the setting up of the new government, and the stir of national politics increased the general activity. With the establishment of the Bank, Philadelphia became the financial capital of the country, receiving and disbursing the monies of the government and attracting outside funds for investment. The decade of the nineties was its golden age. Then came the removal of the seat of the Federal government to Washington, and the gay little city underwent a swift eclipse. It was an unwilling victim to the topography of the North American continent. Between it and the Inland Empire, on which rested its future economic expansion, lay the Appalachian mountain range. To be sure, the opening of the Pittsburgh turnpike seemed to promise that Philadelphia should become the shipping port for the Ohio valley; but the law of gravity sent the produce of the back-country downstream to New Orleans, rather than upstream to the East. Mountains were a serious barrier then to cheap transportation, and in consequence the contributory hinterland to Philadelphia was narrowly restricted, and with the rise of the more fortunately situated New York her economic ascendency was lost past recovery.

A like unforeseen fate overtook the cultural aspirations of the ambitious little city. In the year 1799 Timothy Pickering, Secretary of State in Adams' cabinet, invited to Philadelphia as his secretary Joseph Dennie, a young Boston lawyer who had achieved a wide reputation as a writer of Addisonian essays; and with his coming the literary vigor of Philadelphia flared up in a last brilliant blaze. He established *The Port Folio*, gathered a club of congenial spirits, and gained an extraordinary reputation throughout the country at large. Dennie was a fierce Federalist who hated French Jacobinism with more than the ardor of his party, and he was encouraged by Tom Moore, who wrote,

> Long may you hate the Gallic dross that runs
> O'er your fair country and corrupts its sons.

But with the swift decay of Federalism Dennie's own fortunes fell into a like decay, and with the suspension of *The Port Folio* in 1809 the golden age of Philadelphia came to a definite end. Though it long retained its primacy as a publishing center, and though later *Godey's Lady's Book* became almost a national institution, its intellectual vigor lessened, and its literary leadership passed to other cities. It succumbed to the tastes of Victorianism and became the acknowledged home of "female genius" that for years fed the American reading public on cambric tea. It enjoyed no such renaissance as came to Boston and Charleston, and ambitious young writers abandoned it for more promising fields. While other cities were caught up in the swirl of romantic expansion that followed the War of 1812, Philadelphia remained content with the ways of the eighteenth century, immersed in an old-fashioned culture. With its geographical position disqualifying it to reap the harvest of the westward movement, and with no Merrimac falls to invite industrial development on a great scale, its fate was sealed. It had been a delightful capital for an older America, but it was too narrowly environed, too straitened in potential resources for exploitation, to become the capital of a more expansive and ambitious generation.

II

Yet it enjoyed a brief moment of literary creativeness before the hand of fate finally settled upon it. In the twilight of the eighteenth century the new liberalisms that were turmoiling Europe found their way to Philadelphia, and for the moment it seemed as if the city were to lead the thought of America in its venture into new fields. It was a convenient port for the unloading of foreign romanticisms, and under the stimulus of national politics the demand for such commodities was greatly increased. Certainly in no other American city did the French upheaval quicken so sympathetic a ferment, and with this ferment came a more romantic spirit in letters. The English pre-romantics found there responsive readers. In the verse of young Philadelphians began to appear a note of the vague, the mysterious, the melancholy, echoes of Gray and Cowper and Ossian, as a pleasant relief from vigorous satire as practiced by the Hartford Wits. But it was in the field of fiction that the new spirit most adequately revealed itself, and particularly in the work of a young Philadelphian who had broken wholly with the Federalism that immured the sympathies of young poets like William Cliffton, and welcomed the romantic philosophies then being formulated by radical thinkers in France and England.

Brockden Brown was fortunately spared the fate that might well have been his if circumstances had not determined otherwise. As a boy he had meditated epics on romantic historical figures, inspired perhaps by Dwight and Barlow; but from so profitless a career he was saved by an early introduction to overseas fashions. By William Godwin and Mary Wollstonecraft he was influenced as profoundly as was young William Ellery Channing a few years afterward, and with like results. Later generations have too carelessly forgotten how persuasive to young intellectuals, a century or more ago, was the philosophy of Godwin. To generous minds there was something vastly attractive in his confident appeal to reason and justice; and to a new world and a new venture in government it came with double appeal. How could the republican experiment better justify itself than by establishing justice in the new social order—justice for men and justice for women who had too long suffered under narrow handicaps? It was certainly an ideal worth serious consideration—particularly since the French school had suggested that the germinal source of social injustice must be sought in institutions rather than in the nature of man. It was natural enough for gentlemen who profited by social wrong to charge that injustice was inherent in human nature—that man's innate selfishness was to blame for the ills of society. But the new thinkers were of an inquiring turn of mind, and under their critical scrutiny the old conception was seen to rest on a perversion of fact. Gentlemen had got the cart before the horse. The crying evils of civilization, when analyzed, were traceable to vicious environment, to social and political maladjustments; not to human nature. The mind of the infant is plastic. Very well. If it is molded by social environment, why is it so often misshapen and perverted to base purposes, if institutions are not at fault? why may it not be molded to nobler ends under more beneficent institutions? Reason is a common possession; the ideal of justice is a common ideal. The evil genius that has hitherto thwarted their benevolent work is the overgrown political state, debased to selfish ends. Once let the beneficent sway of social instincts supersede the exploiting machinery of the political state, and reason must conduct to justice. The heart of man is sound. Let it be free to follow its natural promptings and war must give way to peace, the selfish struggle of classes disappear in a common brotherhood.

To an ardent young American like Brockden Brown, with the Hamiltonian struggle for power before his eyes, such a philosophy must have come with immense appeal. America confronted a future unmortgaged to the past; why should it repeat the old follies and mistakes that had reduced Europe to its present level? Here the pressure of vicious institutions was light as yet. Here the appeal to reason and justice was less hampered by selfish preëmptions. Let social commendation be bestowed on the uncorrupted heart, on generous impulses, on native integrity of character. Let education be a natural unfolding of humane instincts, not a sharpening of wits to overreach one's fellows. Let rewards go to frank, outspoken truth, rather than to chicanery and deceit. Inspired by such sentiments, Brockden Brown proposed to make fiction serve social ends. He would spread the gospel of Mary Wollstonecraft and Godwin by means of popular tales. The views of the former he elaborated in *Alcuin; A Dialogue*, which in the year 1798 presented for the consideration of the American people the Wollstonecraft feminism in such passages as this:

Marriage is an union founded on free and mutual consent. It cannot exist without friendship. It cannot exist without personal fidelity. As soon as the union ceases to be spontaneous, it ceases to be just. This is the sum. If I were to talk for months I could add nothing to the completeness of the definition.

But it is in *Arthur Mervyn* that he gives his fullest pronouncement of what he conceives must be done in America. He takes his hero fresh from the plowtail, one of nature's noblemen, and traces his triumphant course through the thick of sordid intrigue to a happy end. Generous in instincts, impulsive in sociability, responsive to suffering, hating injustice, loving the pure and disinterested, Arthur Mervyn is a Godwinian figure drawn to captivate the imagination with the social ideal. It is not so much the plot of the story that reveals the enormous influence of Godwin—patent as the likeness is to *Caleb Williams,* but rather the expansive nature of the title hero, whose instincts bid him espouse justice, and whose life is an implied criticism of all that is sordid and mean.

With the political romanticism of his work was joined a literary romanticism that likewise came from England, where it was muddying the stream of English fiction and turning it aside from the vigorous realism of the middle eighteenth century. The movement that Paulding dubbed the "blood-pudding school" was one of the by-products of the romantic development that ran a far more disastrous course in America than in England, distorting the growth of native fiction for half a century. It was perhaps unfortunate for the American novel that *Wieland* should have been Brockden Brown's most finished work, for it contributed in consequence more powerfully to the spread of the melodramatic. Lacking his strain of rationalism, other writers reveled increasingly in the luridly picaresque, till the popular taste was so debauched that Gilmore Simms found it well-nigh impossible to struggle against it. For this of course Brown was not to blame; yet his gross romanticisms of manner persisted long after his Godwinian romanticisms had faded out of the popular mind, if indeed they ever found lodgment there.

III

Brockden Brown's career was in a sense symbolic of the fate of his native city—a few brilliant years and then a swift decline. Death cut him down before he fulfilled his promise. Something

of a like fate befell his most brilliant successor, Robert Montgomery Bird, probably the ablest man of letters that Philadelphia
produced. Caught up by the romantic movement at the beginning
of his precocious career, he plunged into dramatic writing and from
1830 to 1834, between the ages of twenty-four and twenty-eight,
he wrote four plays for Edwin Forrest, one of which, *The Gladiator*,
met with extraordinary success, both in this country and in England; and another, *The Broker of Bogota*, kept the stage for years.
At the age of thirty he gave over the writing of plays and turned
to other fields. The explanation of so unusual a course, according
to a recent historian, is not far to seek. He had been overreached
by Forrest, and after parting with his manuscripts to the actor,
the playwright found himself in the condition of the farmer who
after shipping his potatoes to market discovers himself to be in
debt to the commission merchant.[2] That he determined to try
a different crop was natural enough, but unfortunate for the
American drama.

Of his subsequent ventures into the field of romantic fiction, one
at least was an extraordinary success, rivaling if not surpassing
The Gladiator in popular favor. *Nick of the Woods, or the Jib-
benainosay* still remains one of the few outstanding tales of the
Kentucky settlement. Published in Philadelphia in 1837, it has
been reissued in successive editions, more than twenty in all
down to the present. It was translated into German in 1838,
into Dutch in 1877, and into Polish in 1905. There is abundant
reason for its popularity. It is a story of calculating revenge, done
with extraordinary vividness and set against a romantic background. A frontier Quaker, trusting in the spirit of good will,
finds his non-resistance futile; he is set upon by Indians, his family
murdered before his eyes, and himself scalped and left for dead
beside his burnt cabin. Recovering, he sets forth on a fierce career.
Under the mask of a non-resistant, so effectively worn as to awaken
the contempt of the frontier Indian-haters, he became a hunter of
men, and his secret passages through the wilderness leave no other
trail than the marked bodies of slaughtered warriors. The Jib-
benainosay is an uncanny figure who strikes with appalling
suddenness, a Nemesis that fills the hearts of border Indians with
terror and turns their dreams to nightmares—one of the most
striking and fearful figures in our early fiction. The Indians whom

[2] See A. H. Quinn, *A History of the American Drama*, etc., pp. 244–248.

he pursues so remorselessly are depicted as thorough savages. In describing them Bird has put all his romanticisms aside. There is no sentimentalizing of the noble red man in the brisk pages of *Nick of the Woods;* the warriors are dirty drunken louts, filled with an unquenchable blood-lust, whom the frontiersman kills with as little compunction as he would kill a rattlesnake. The ugly feud that so long soiled the Border is depicted with almost startling frankness, and through its worst phases moves the figure of Bloody Nathan, professing to be a man of peace whilst cutting an appalling lot of notches in his gun, an epileptic who perhaps deceives even himself.

If one likes stirring action that is certain to end in blood-letting, there is good foraging in *Nick of the Woods*, despite its excesses of conventional romance. And there is much else as well. Bird had evidently studied his western materials with some care, and he did his part to popularize certain conceptions that literature had come to associate with the Ohio valley. The character of Ralph Stackpole is clearly suggestive of the wild antics supposed to be common to the river boatmen. "The history of this wild scape-gallows," says Bird, "his prowess in the pin-fold and the battle-field, his adventure on the beech-tree, and his escape from the meshes of the law, with other characteristic events not included in our relation, are recollections still cherished in some parts of Kentucky, and made the theme of many a gleesome story." But what seems more suggestive today is Bird's conscious attempt to reproduce the new type of western humor that found its expression in the Davy Crockett myth. Perhaps the wild extravagance of Ralph Stackpole's vocabulary goes back to Mike Fink, perhaps it derives from Davy himself; at any rate the mode had spread so widely by 1837 that this Philadelphia man of letters had come to believe that such was the indigenous form of humor in the new West of the Ohio valley, and he took particular pains to draw the irrepressible Ralph with vigorous touches. A pronounced romantic, Bird unconsciously contributed his mite to the myth of western humor.

CHAPTER II

THE NEW CAPITAL

I

VERY different from the gay and cultivated Quaker City was the commercial port of Manhattan, with its Yankee energy ingrafted on the stolid Dutch stock, which fate seized upon and transformed into the greatest of our new cities, the favorite home of the genius of American enterprise. Never a cultural capital as Philadelphia had been, and as Charleston was becoming—a fact which Fenimore Cooper untactfully announced to the world—it was ambitious to acquire commercial and financial ascendency; and this ascendency of the economic over the cultural, this frank evaluation of progress in terms of exploitation, marks the definite transition from the eighteenth century to the nineteenth, the triumph of an aggressive middle class over the leisurely ways of an older landed aristocracy. The romance of expansion was creating there a new psychology, and this new psychology was preparing the city for leadership in the new age that was rising. Its strategic position brought to it the produce of the new settlements that were pushing west to the great lakes and beyond; its aggressive traders were reaching out for a share in the markets of the world; the plodding methods of money-getting that had satisfied an earlier generation no longer satisfied men who had discovered the richer possibilities of capitalistic manipulation. The potentialities that lay in the capitalistic system were shrewdly explored, and the necessary machinery of the new finance was devised. The acquisitive spirit of the city found itself in a position to profit from the rage of speculation that was running through the country, and it quickly outdistanced its rivals in the race for financial supremacy.

The changes that came to New York in the last years of the old century were enough to muddle a head stronger than Rip Van Winkle's. The quiet ways of colonial times were gone, and in their stead was a restless activity that had no leisure for its pipe and mug in the sleepy tavern. Business and politics could not wait on men who like Wouter Van Twiller pickled their dreams in tobacco smoke. The bewilderment of old Rip on his return from the hills was the bewilderment of the colonial mind in the presence of a new order. When Washington came to New York to assume the presidency, the town contained approximately 29,000 inhabitants, some two thousand of whom were slaves. Fifty years later the census of 1840 set down its population as 312,710. In 1789 Albany was a Dutch village of four or five thousand, and a few miles to the West lay an unbroken wilderness. Within the narrow zone of the quiet settlements old and new dwelt in close proximity. The most feudal of American aristocracies fringed the banks of the Hudson from Albany to Manhattan; and reaching out through the Mohawk valley that aristocracy was laying a network of speculative land-holdings through which a flood of Yankee pioneers was making its way from the long-settled lands of Connecticut and Massachusetts. The frontier was close at hand; the leveling spirit was near neighbor to the feudal; potential economic rivalries were becoming actual, and the days of a static, power-proud Dutch aristocracy were numbered. The spirit that had dominated the commonwealth from its founding was tenacious of life, but on January 26, 1839, died Stephen Van Rensselaer, last of the Patroons, courteous, dignified, a worthy embodiment of the old patriarchal virtues, who had outlived his age; and hard upon his death came the final break-up of the traditional order. The small men got the land they had long tilled and the influence of the Dutch gentry slowly disintegrated. A new order was rising that had discovered shorter roads to wealth than feudal rents. While the more energetic of the old order, men like Gouverneur Morris and Judge William Cooper, were deep in land speculation, in Manhattan a new aristocracy of capitalism was rising. Wall Street was losing the distinction of housing the most exclusive of the landed gentry, to gain a greater distinction as the home of the new aristocracy of credit. By 1825 the rise of industrialism, the development of banking, the completion of the Erie Canal, the influx of proletarian immigrants, and the drift of population to the towns had fixed the destiny of the city. In becoming the chief repository of the new capitalism New York had become the first and greatest of our middle-class capitals.

Of this new Manhattan the representative citizen was a man whose aggressive ambitions differentiated him sharply from Stephen Van Rensselaer, and whose dramatic career of exploitation seemed to Washington Irving to embody the romantic potentialities of America. John Jacob Astor was to the New York of 1825 what Robert Morris had been to Philadelphia a generation before—an evidence of the wealth that was to be got by those who would boldly exploit the vast resources of America. A German immigrant who landed in America with small funds, immediately following the Peace of Paris, Astor embarked in the fur trade, acquired a fortune which he invested in Manhattan land, and then laid his plans to engage in a great venture in imperialism. Stirred by the Lewis and Clarke expedition, he proposed to explore the virgin resources of the far Pacific Northwest. With the tacit approval of the government he undertook the hazardous project of the Astoria settlement, sent his agent to the Russian posts of Alaska, and by subsidizing an army of trappers proposed to gather the peltries of the entire Northwest for the rich Canton market. It was a grandiose conception worthy of a feudal baron of commerce. It was knit up with dreams of conquest; it necessarily entailed open warfare with the English companies whose ambitions were equally grandiose; it was certain to be attended by bitter hardships on the part of the venturesome agents to whom it was intrusted; and the outcome was uncertain as a gambler's chance. Irving has thrown over his narrative of the great venture a glamour of patriotism; to him it appeared as a plan of empire building; but whether patriotism or profit was the determining impulse in the mind of John Jacob Astor, the settlement of Astoria suggests the romantic aspirations that were making over the lethargic world of Dutch Manhattan, in the venturesome days of the new capitalism. Stephen Van Rensselaer and John Jacob Astor would have had difficulty in understanding each other.

II

In sharp contrast with Boston, New York was wanting in intellectual background and intellectual stimulus. It had never gone to school to dogmatic theology and neither clergy nor laity had been disciplined by a severe Puritan regimen. Gentlemen were little given to metaphysical speculation and the subtleties of creed never provided the staple of talk in the farmer's kitchen. The terrors of hell rarely troubled the sluggish imagination of the Dutch, and the extraordinary stimulus that came to the serious-minded New Englander from long contemplation of the ways of God, was lacking amongst a more prosaic people. No other stimulus supplied the want and in consequence ideas and books were held in low esteem and the things of the mind suffered. The English gentry commonly sent their sons to the English universities, but the Dutch by common report seem to have been indifferent to schooling and opportunities for education were sadly inadequate. The result was a low plane of intellectual life, which even in Cooper's time was remarked by him. There were brilliant and cultivated intellects, wits like Gouverneur Morris and statesmen like John Jay; yet even under the stimulus of Revolutionary and Constitutional controversy the contribution of New York to political theory was far slighter than that of New England or Virginia. *The Federalist* was its single notable production, and even in that the papers of Madison were no inconsiderable part. As a commercial port it attracted young men ambitious to rise in the world of affairs rather than in the world of letters. Unlike Philadelphia it had never been a cosmopolitan meeting ground for aspiring young intellectuals and purveyors of polite culture, nor an important center of printers, publishers and book dealers. Aside from Philip Freneau, who had long since established himself in New Jersey when he was not at sea, it had contributed little to pure literature, or even to the political satire that deluged Philadelphia. As a creative center it ranked far below Hartford, Connecticut, where in the seventeen-eighties and nineties wit had become a staple commodity for export. And yet despite its intellectual lethargy it was a pleasant little town, with a note of cosmopolitanism that rendered life amongst the upper classes genial and urbane. The spirit of aristocracy was as yet little weakened by alien newcomers from the more republican New England, and city and commonwealth were ruled by a little group of old-fashioned gentlemen who upheld the rigid Federalism of the tie-wig school.

In the year 1800 the political leaders of the state were men of long established reputations, Hamilton, Jay, Gouverneur Morris, Rufus King, with whom was closely associated the brilliant lawyer James Kent, afterward Chancellor. Only two of the five were of the older New York stock: Rufus King was from Maine, Hamilton from the West Indies, and Kent was of Yankee Presbyterian ancestry. Politics were already becoming turmoiled by faction, with bitter cleavages and vindictive struggles for the spoils of office that sadly confused the logic of the earlier alignment. The old Federalist party was led by the distinguished gentlemen named above; the Democratic party was led by the Livingstons and Clintons; and outside both was the ambitious Aaron Burr who played a lone hand against the field. After the death of Hamilton the disintegration of the old parties went forward rapidly. The Livingstons and Clintons broke, and a fierce political feud arose between them. The former were accounted the true Jeffersonians, but under the name of Lewisites they drifted towards the Federalist remnant; the Burrites went to pieces after the disgrace of their leader; and the Clintonians remained masters of the field, with a motley support drawn from Tammany Hall Irish, Wall Street bankers, and odds and ends of all factions. From this sordid situation, rendered conspicuous by the extension of suffrage under the new constitution, emerged two master politicians, adepts in all the arts of party manipulation, who exploited the prejudices of the voting masses in a way to justify the gloomy fear of demagoguery that haunted the minds of the old Federalists. Martin Van Buren and Thurlow Weed, Democrat and Whig, were finished products of the new school of practical politicians who held that office-holding was the great end of partisan struggle, and that principles must not stand in the way of success.

III

Through this fierce scramble of rival politicians moved a scholarly figure who preserved to the last the dignity and distinction of an earlier age. James Kent, whose long life and ripe legal learning were devoted to upholding what he conceived to be the ultimate principles of law and politics, was the chief political thinker of the transition days of New York. A disciple of Locke and Blackstone, remodeling seventeenth-century liberalism into eighteenth-century conservatism, he was concerned to erect the barriers of the Common Law about the unsurveyed frontiers of the American experiment, assigning exact metes and bounds beyond which it should not go. Like John Marshall and Joseph Story he was expert in devising legal springes to catch unwary democrats, and while the Jeffersonians were shouting over their victories at the polls, he was engaged in the strategic work of placing the Constitution under the narrow custodianship of the English law. An ardent Federalist and later an equally ardent Whig, he reveals in his precise thinking the intimate relations that everywhere exist between economics, politics, and legal principles. With John Adams he accepted the dictum of Locke that "the great and chief end . . . of men's uniting into commonwealths, and putting themselves under government, is the preservation of their property"; and believing that the English Common Law was the securest of all agencies devised to safeguard the subject in the enjoyment of his property rights, he made no difficulty in imposing that law upon the Constitution, circumscribing the written document by Common Law fences. Government he conceived to be a patriarchal institution erected for the single purpose of coercing the vicious, and as such it must remain in the hands of the good, the wise and the wealthy. It did not need the authoritative pronouncement of his great master to convince him that the wealthy included the good and wise. Observation of the "barbarian Jackson" and his rude followers was enough to convince him of the truth of the fact. "All theories of government that suppose the mass of the people virtuous," he wrote to Webster, "and able and willing to act virtuously, are plainly utopian, and will remain so until the Saturnian age" (William Kent, *Memoirs and Letters of James Kent*, p. 207). Profoundly distrustful of democracy, he brought all his wide reading in the history of ancient and medieval republics to demonstrate the favorite Federalist conviction— a conviction that Paulding in his *Letters from the South* paid his respects to [1]—that democracy is only a euphemism for mob-rule and that it must speedily conduct to anarchy and despotism. All leveling principles he repudiated without waiting to hear cause. Until necessity counseled otherwise he looked with suspicion on the holders of liquid wealth, as likely to prove wanting in the wisdom and goodness that came naturally to the landed proprietor. He would have the many ruled by the few, but those few he would have owners of great estates.

After all, the learned Chancellor was only a transplanted Yankee of the Fisher Ames school, with something of the austerity and intellectual vigor of his two Puritan grandfathers. An ardent admirer of Hamilton, he early broke with the more liberal faith of his family and joined himself to the extreme Federalists. He was advanced rapidly by Governor Jay, enjoyed for years both office

[1] See *Letters*, etc., Vol. I, p. 207.

and distinction, and ably defended the party of his choice. Fearful
of agrarian laws and the sequestration of property by the enfranchised poor, he fought stubbornly every proposal for an extension
of suffrage or a larger measure of self-government for the cities.
Defeated in the great constitutional convention of 1821 he soon
after lost his office and retired to write his *Commentaries on American Law*, a work that was to exercise a creative influence on the
later development of our jurisprudence. That American law came
to be deeply colored by Federalist political theory, that it upheld
from the bench principles that had been repudiated at the polls,
was due in no little measure to the legal scholarship of this last of
the New York Federalists. What a recent historian has borrowed
to describe another applies with equal felicity to Chancellor
Kent—"his pigmy hope that life would some day become somewhat
better, punily shivered by the side of his gigantic conviction that
it might be infinitely worse" (Fox, *Decline of Aristocracy in New
York Politics*, p. 243). As he contemplated the ways of the triumphant Jacksonians, he found such consolation as he could in
turning back to an older century with its narrow outlook and sober
culture. Writing to his brother in 1835, he said:

There never was such misrule. Our Tory rich men are becoming startled
and alarmed at our downhill course. My opinion is that the admission
of universal suffrage and a licentious press are incompatible with government and security to property, and that the government and character
of this country are going to ruin. This suffrage is too great an excitement
for any political machine. It racks it to pieces, and morals go with it. It
is probable England is going the same way. We are becoming selfish,
profligate, crazy. . . . Give me the writings of Addison and Locke, and
the Presbyterianism of Dr. Ripley, Dr. Stiles, and old Dr. Rogers. (Kent,
Memoirs and Letters of James Kent, pp. 218-219.)

IV

With the extraordinary upheaval in economics and politics
New York unfortunately underwent no corresponding intellectual revolution. The renaissance that a generation earlier had
created a new Virginia, and that was awakening in Massachusetts
a many-sided intellectual activity, touched the mind of New York
only lightly. The ground was unprepared for the new philosophies.
To Virginia, French romantic theory had come with the appeal
of a new gospel for the reason that plantation economics fell in
with the major premises of Physiocratic liberalism, and the old-

world dogmas seemed to find new-world justification. To New England, German idealism had come likewise with the appeal of a new gospel, after Unitarianism had broken the fetters of Calvinism and set free its traditional idealism. But among the young men of New York in 1825 neither France nor Germany was a determining influence. With an inadequate cultural background and no responsive economics, they were attracted only casually to the current European liberalisms. They were wanting in idealism and in consequence the major intellectual and social movements of the times influenced the form and content of the new Knickerbocker literature far less profoundly than was the case in New England. New York was as insular as Charleston. That the growing economic unrest would ultimately find expression in a controversial or Utopian literature, was a matter of course; and that the cosmopolitanism of the city should make for vigorous discussion, was equally a matter of course. Nevertheless Albert Brisbane, William Leggett, Parke Godwin and Horace Greeley were far less representative of the dominant literary spirit than Irving and Halleck and Willis of the earlier group, or Stedman and Stoddard later.

The Knickerbocker movement was inaugurated by four young men whose clever sketches caught the provincial ear of polite society and set the new fashion in prose and verse. Irving and Paulding in *Salmagundi*, and Halleck and Drake in the *Croaker Papers*, were lucky adventurers whose slight crafts made the most prosperous of voyages. Bright young fellows with a charming literary swagger, they aspired to be wits and exploit the amusing foibles of Broadway. Twelve years separated the two ventures, and in the interval Byron and Scott had been supplanting Moore and Campbell in the esteem of the Town, and the literary mode of New York was changing. From their gay provincialism, happily Irving and Paulding later freed themselves; Drake died at the age of twenty-five; but Halleck retained to the end of a leisurely life the mannerisms of the Croaker period—a crochety wit who affected persiflage, a brisk young buck who gently slid into a *blasé* old buck, a free lance in verse who lived in state on the income of a small literary investment made in his twenties.

The very considerable reputation of Fitz-Greene Halleck resulted in part from the literary sterility of New York in his early days, and in part from the personal popularity of the man. A Connecticut Yankee, descended on his mother's side from old

John Eliot, he was drawn to the city as a promising field for an accountant, and eventually found his way into the office of John Jacob Astor by whom he was later pensioned. He accepted the views and shared the antipathies of his Wall Street associates, but with a certain affectation of individuality that took delight in shocking them by whimsical pronouncements in favor of the Catholic church and the monarchical system. There is perhaps a suggestion of seriousness in the remark that Bryant has preserved: "The ship of state," so he reports Halleck as saying, "must be governed and navigated like any other ship, without consulting the crew. What would become of the stanchest bark in a gale, if the captain were obliged to call all hands together and say: 'All you who are in favor of taking in sail, will please to say ay'" (*Orations and Addresses*, p. 186). His political affiliations were Federalist-Whig, and his satire exudes much of the old prejudice against the democratic mass. The pompous long-winded DeWitt Clinton was a fair mark for his shafts; [2] the demagoguery of office-seeking politicians was a fruitful theme for his wit; [3] and Halleck's satire plays upon them with good-natured raillery. But his gayety cannot hide a certain animus in dealing with the tousled-headed democracy. When the labor movement was painfully getting under way in New York Halleck contemplated the curious phenomenon with a tolerant contempt—in something of the spirit of a wit of pre-Revolutionary times who amused the Town with his couplet:

> Down at night a bricklayer or carpenter lies,
> Next sun a Lycurgus or Solon doth rise.

As an illustration of the attitude of polite society in New York a hundred years ago towards the aspirations of the proletariat, Halleck's forgotten *Epistle to Robert Hogbin, Esq., Chairman of the Committee of Working-Men, etc.*, deserves quotation:

> Mr. Hogbin,—I work as a weaver—of rhyme—
>   And therefore presume with a working-man's grace,
> To address you as one I have liked for some time,
>   Though I know not (no doubt it's a fine one) your face.
>
> There is much in a name, and I'll lay you a wager
>   (Two ale-jugs from Reynolds), that Nature designed,
> When she formed you, that you should become the drum-major
>   In that choice piece of music, the Grand March of Mind.

2 See *Governor Clinton's Speech*.   3 See *The Recorder*.

A Hogbin! a Hogbin! how cheering the shout
  Of all that keep step to that beautiful air,
Which leads, like the treadmill, about and about,
  And leaves us exactly, at last, where we were!

Yes, there's much in a name, and a Hogbin's so fit is
  For that great moral purpose whose impulse divine
Bids men leave their own workshops to work in committees,
  And their own wedded wives to protect yours and mine! . . .

When the moment arrives that we've won the good fight,
  And broken the chains of laws, churches, and marriages,
When no infants are born under six feet in height,
  And our chimney-sweeps mount up a flue in their carriages—

That glorious time when our daughters and sons
  Enjoy a *blue Monday* each day of the week,
And a clean shirt is classed with the mastodon's bones,
  Or a mummy from Thebes, an undoubted antique—

Then, then, my dear Hogbin, your statue in straw,
  By some modern *Pig*malion delightfully wrought,
Shall embellish the Park, and our youths' only law
  Shall be to be Hogbins in feeling and thought.

In Halleck's better work there is sometimes evident a certain
critical detachment that permitted him to see both sides of his
theme. In the lines to his native Connecticut he has taken pretty
accurately the measure of the Puritan and the Yankee. He rests
under no awe in presence of the old worthies, and he throws overboard the pious fairy-tales of Cotton Mather—"that slanderer
of the memory of our fathers"—only to forgive the preacher who
scolded his friends "up from earth to heaven" because of the
"sour grapejuice in his disposition." Unfortunately little of his
work possesses the virility of *Connecticut*. His most ambitious
poem, *Fanny*, is a feeble and discursive satire on the social climber. It was a great favorite at the time and passed through several editions, but the sparkle is gone out of its affected jauntiness
and little has been lost in its being forgotten. Halleck's casual
literary activity continued only for the brief period between the
years 1819 and 1828; thereafter for close on forty years he was
content to turn out an occasional *jeu d'esprit*, enjoy the deepening
twilight of his reputation, and watch his fellow Yankee, Willis,
invest his talents in the ephemeral. The day of the wit was past
in New York.

CHAPTER III

TWO KNICKERBOCKER ROMANTICS

I

WASHINGTON IRVING

FORTUNATELY the stolid New York of earlier days was not to pass away without bequeathing to posterity some fragments of its chronicles. In the midst of a pleasant society of smallclothes and tie-wigs, of feudalism and Federalism, appeared young Washington Irving at the precise moment when Sansculottism was beginning to make a stir in the land, and gentlemen were putting away their knee-breeches to don a republican dress—a decline in taste to which he would not easily reconcile himself. A boyish wit from the eighteenth century, a genial loiterer in the twilight of the old, he found himself out of humor with the ambitions that were making over the little city he loved. The present seemed to him not so amusing as the past, nor so picturesque. That he had any business with the world of trade and speculation he could not believe. Its concerns were not his. Its new Wall Street counted for less in his eyes than the pipe of old Diedrich Knickerbocker. Its decadent Federalism that was clinging to the wreck of its hopes, and its roistering Democracy that wore greasy clothes, spoke with an Irish accent, and was marshaled to the polls by Tammany Hall, were of less consequence to him than the black bottle that brought such curious adventures to Rip Van Winkle. The wit and romance he took pleasure in were of another sort than the kind his generation was getting drunk on—more insubstantial, less heady, picturesque rather than profitable. So Irving gently detached himself from contemporary America, and detached he remained to the end of a loitering life, untroubled by material ambitions, enjoying the abundance of good things that fell in his way, mingling with prosperous folk and liking everybody—men as diverse as John Jacob Astor and Martin Van Buren and John P. Kennedy—and unconsciously taking the color of his environment, careful to turn into limpid prose such romantic tales as he came upon and achieving thereby both reputation and profit—a pleasant blame-

203

less way of living, certainly, yet curiously unrepresentative of the America in which chance had set him and which was to claim him as its first man of letters.

An incorrgible *flâneur*, Irving's business in life was to loaf and invite the picturesque. A confirmed rambler in pleasant places, in the many lands he visited he was a lover of the past rather than the present, seeking to recreate the golden days of the Alhambra or live over the adventurous mood of the fur trader. The immediate and the actual was an unsatisfying diet for his dreams. There was in him nothing of the calm aloofness of the intellectual that stands apart to clarify its critical estimate, and none of the reforming zeal of the Puritan that is at peace only in the thick of a moral crusade. The duty of saving the world was not laid on his untroubled soul. No man of his generation was less of a rebel than Irving, and he went his way unconcerned at things that quite upset Fenimore Cooper's peace of mind. In his early days, to be sure, he broke with the ambitious middle class—if gently drawing away can be called breaking—because he could not bring himself to like its ways and the devastation those ways were entailing on the leisurely world he loved. Revolutions seemed to him somewhat vulgar affairs. The French Revolution had brought destruction on too many lovely things, and the industrial revolution was taking too heavy a toll of the picturesque, to please him. He thought it a pity that steam should drive the clipper ship from the seas and put an end to snug posting in the tally-ho. Progress might be bought at too dear a price. The bluff squire with his hounds, the great hall with its ancient yuletide customs, the patriarchal relations between master and man, seemed to him more worth while than the things progress was substituting for them; so he turned away from the new and gently ingratiated himself into the past in order to gather up such fragments of the picturesque as progress had not yet destroyed.

But only for a time. His dislike of capitalism rested on no more substantial basis than its substitution of vulgar trousers for gentlemanly smallclothes. It was too new to have achieved dignity or the charm of assured position. When that time should come and masters of finance should stand before the world as generous dispensers of patronage, when the development of business should have produced its new barons, Irving's dislike would lessen and he would associate with the new capitalism on the same easy terms that he associated with the old feudalism. In the meantime he stood apart, unconcerned with praise or blame. The industrial revolution might work itself out as it would. The seventeen years he spent abroad on his great pilgrimage were black years for England. Wretchedness and poverty were all about him if he chose to see. The "condition of England" question was rising out of the factory smoke to challenge the conscience of England. But he did not choose to see and his conscience was untroubled. As he idled about the countryside or visited the hospitable manor houses, his eye was caught by the grace of medieval spires rising from parish churches rather than by the condition of the proletariat. He saw no children working in the coalpits, for he did not choose to visit the collieries. He sympathized vaguely with the new social movements then getting under way, but it was not in his nature to be partisan to a cause. He may not have been a Tory but he had lived so long with Tories and enjoyed so frankly the charm of upper-class society, that his outlook was unconsciously determined by such intimate contacts. While Secretary to the Legation at London in the reform years from 1829 to 1831, he was aware of the tremendous stir all about him, but his infrequent references to the Reform Bill in his letters turned usually on its disastrous effects on the publishing business. Only once during his long residence abroad does he seem to have felt deeply the significance of the current revolutionary unrest, and the mood that swept him away from his habitual indifference bears the marks of a sudden awakening. Writing from London on March 1, 1831, he said:

We are in the beginning of an eventful week. . . . However, *the great cause of all the world* will go on. What a stirring moment it is to live in. I never took such intense interest in the newspapers. It seems to me as if life were breaking out anew with me, or that I were entering upon quite a new and almost unknown career of existence, and I rejoice to find my sensibilities, which were waning as to many objects of past interest, reviving with all their freshness and vivacity at the scenes and prospects opening around me. I trust, my dear Brevoort, we shall both be spared to see a great part of this grand though terrible drama that is about to be acted. There will doubtless be scenes of horror and suffering, but what splendid triumphs must take place over these vile systems of falsehood in every relation of human affairs, that have been woven over the human mind, and for so long a time have held it down in despicable thraldom. (Pierre M. Irving, *Life and Letters of Washington Irving*, Vol. II, p. 199.)

Irving lacked a month of being forty-nine when he wrote this confession of interest in matters political. It marks the first appearance of liberalism in his thinking, and the last—somewhat vague to be sure, unduly bottomed on romantic expectations, yet significant in so placid a life and explanatory of his course, when a year later he returned to America to knit up once more the raveled threads of his interests. It was as an incipient liberal that he came back to a land then in the first flush of the Jacksonian victory, eager to discover a romantic charm in the vast changes that had come during the seventeen years he had been abroad. He plunged into the business of re-discovery with enthusiasm. He was in want of new literary materials, and as he took his bearings, his creative interest was stirred to write on American themes. He went to Washington and for three months listened to the great debate on Nullification. He talked with business men and politicians, with those who were prosperous and prominent, and he drifted easily with the tide of liberalism. To be sure he could scarcely be called a Jacksonian. Parties and causes did not greatly interest him even then. An intelligent man, indeed, could hardly be less concerned about political principles. Thirty years before, as a clever young man about town, he had gone with the dominant Federalism of the times, and had amused himself with political ambitions. His brother Peter was editor of the Lewisite paper the *Chronicle*, but Josiah Ogden Hoffman, with whose firm Irving was connected during his desultory incursion into the law and to whose daughter Matilda he was betrothed, was an old Loyalist and ardent Hamiltonian. His wife, to whom Irving was warmly attached, was a daughter of John Fenno, Hamilton's editor. Under such tutelage it was natural for Irving to poke good-natured fun at President Jefferson's red velvet breeches in *Salmagundi;* but his venture into practical politics proving little to his taste, he quickly gave over such ambitions. In a letter to a clever young lady of Republican sympathies, he thus announced his abandonment of political hopes:

I am as deep in mud and politics as ever a modern gentleman would wish to be; and I drank beer with the multitude; and I talked hand-bill fashion with the demagogues; and I shook hands with the mob, whom my heart abhorreth. . . . Truly this saving one's country is a nauseous piece of business, and if patriotism is such a dirty virtue,—prythee, no more of it. (*Life and Letters*, Vol. I, Chap. XI.)

Years now separated him from that youthful experience. His long absence from his native land had completely alienated him from the fierce partisanship of contemporary America and he could view matters political with calm detachment. Inclined to make the best of any government *de facto*, he found it easy on his return to accept Jacksonianism, and he soon discovered a genuine liking for Old Hickory. "The more I see of this old cock of the woods," he wrote from Washington, "the more I relish his game qualities" (*ibid.*, Vol. II, p. 255). No doubt his early friend Paulding had much to do with his ready acceptance of the new order, although he had come in close contact with Martin Van Buren at the London legation and was drawn to him. "He is one of the gentlest and most amiable men I have ever met with," he wrote to his brother, "with an affectionate disposition that attaches itself to those around him, and wins their kindness in return" (*ibid.*, Vol. II, p. 220). Although distrustful of some of the "elbow counsellors" of the Democracy he found little cause for criticism and soon came to be regarded as one with them. The Jacksonians were eager to make political capital out of his literary reputation, and he was urged by Tammany Hall to stand for Congress and later to accept a mayoralty candidacy. In 1837, probably through the intervention of Paulding, he was offered a post in Van Buren's cabinet. These partisan offers he had the good sense to decline, but when in 1842 he was tendered the post of Minister to Spain he gladly seized the opportunity to revisit a land he loved. His nephew is explicit in his statement that the offer came wholly unsolicited, but Fenimore Cooper was of another opinion.[1] Very likely Cooper was misinformed, but whatever the truth the appointment was a godsend to Irving. His affairs were in a bad way. The popularity of his writings was on the wane, the panic had caught him with much of his capital invested in unprofitable land speculations, and the "Roost" at Tarrytown was a heavy drain, although he wrote whimsically, "I beat all the gentlemen farmers in my neighborhood, for I can manage to raise my vegetables and fruits at very little more than twice the market price" (*Life and Letters*,

---

[1] Writing to his wife a month afterwards, Cooper said: "By the way, Mrs. Willing has let out the secret of Irving's appointment. He wrote to Webster to remember him *if any good thing offered*. So that instead of not asking for the office, he asked for anything that was good. There has been more humbug practised concerning this man than concerning any other now living" (Cooper, *Correspondence of James Fenimore-Cooper*, Vol. II, p. 469).

Vol. II, p. 320). Only a severe nature like Cooper, sorely wounded by the angry reception of his own honest criticism, would cavil at an appointment so honorable to the government.

A friendly nature, Irving discovered friendliness wherever he went. His own generosity appealed to the generosity of others, and he found it easy in consequence to take a kindly view of men and parties. He was harassed by none of Cooper's quick suspicions and rigid principles, and it must be added he had none of Cooper's intuitive penetration into the secret springs of human action that made the latter so acute a critic of contemporary America. The sharp contrast in moods in which the two men returned to America from their travels, the one harshly critical of middle-class economics and frontier leveling, the other responding naïvely to the enthusiasm for speculative expansion and eager to exploit the romance of the westward movement, sufficiently reveals the difference between them. The one was a dogmatic Puritan with the dictatorial ways of the quarter-deck, the other was a play-boy of letters temperamentally incapable of critical analysis. There was not a grain of realism in Irving's nature. His cheerful optimism was little more than the optimism of the prosperous. Wholly ignorant of economics, he never comprehended the significance of the revolutions in process all about him, and this naïveté blinded him to the motive of John Jacob Astor in financing Astoria, as it blinded him to all the major forces of the times. He was easily brought to see the romance of the great struggle between rival companies for mastery of the fur trade, but he did not comprehend how the glamour he threw about the venture must inevitably strengthen his patron's investment in imperialism. Gullible as a child, he discovered nothing more significant in the great struggle between agrarianism and capitalism for control of government than the ungenerous suspicions and novel theories it bred. For the outstanding liberals of New York he had scant sympathy. William Leggett, Horace Greeley, Albert Brisbane, William Cullen Bryant, influenced his views far less than did the masters of Wall Street; and from the courageous movement of Locofocoism he drew back in distrust. The one letter in which he elaborated such political convictions as he had come to hold, is an interesting document that deserves quotation.

As far as I know my own mind, I am thoroughly a republican, and attached, from complete conviction, to the institutions of my country; but

I am a republican without gall, and have no bitterness in my creed. I have no relish for puritans either in religion or politics, who are for pushing principles to an extreme, and for overturning everything that stands in the way of their own zealous career. I have, therefore, felt a strong distaste for some of those locofoco luminaries who of late have been urging strong and sweeping measures, subversive of the interests of great classes of the community. Their doctrines may be excellent in theory, but, if enforced in violent and uncompromising opposition to all our habitudes, may produce the most distressing effects. The best of remedies must be cautiously applied, and suited to the taste and constitution of the patient. . . . Ours is a government of compromise. We have several great and distinct interests bound up together, which, if not separately consulted and severally accommodated, may harass and impair each other. . . . I always distrust the soundness of political councils that are accompanied by acrimonious and disparaging attacks upon any great class of our fellow-citizens. Such are those urged to the disadvantage of the great trading and financial classes of our country. You yourself know. . . how important these classes are to the prosperous conduct of the complicated affairs of this immense empire. You yourself know, in spite of all the common-place cant and obloquy that has been cast upon them by political spouters and scribblers, what general good faith and fair dealing prevails throughout these classes. Knaves and swindlers there are doubtless among them, as there are among all great classes of men; but I declare that I looked with admiration at the manner in which the great body of our commercial and financial men have struggled on through the tremendous trials which have of late overwhelmed them, and have endeavored, at every pecuniary sacrifice, to fulfill their engagements. (*Life and Letters*, Vol. II, pp. 312–313.)

This persuasive presentation of the philosophy of compromise, with its implicit defense of capitalism, marks Irving's drift back to the middle class with which he had long before broken. In the six years since his return he had watched the country react to the great panic, and he went with it in its veering towards the Whiggery of Henry Clay. The fragile bonds of his attachment to the Democracy were becoming tenuous; other attachments were insensibly drawing him towards the more congenial representatives of wealth. He had all his life associated with the Tory classes and it was easy for him to transfer his loyalty to the American Tories. Under such influences began a slow *rapprochement cordial* towards the new philosophy of progress. He was seized with the common mania of speculation and made some unfortunate investments in wild lands and railways that seriously hampered him later, and he commercialized his literary reputation by such money-making ventures as *Astoria* and the *Adventures of Captain Bonne-*

ville. He discovered a new romance in the great business of exploitation, and found the hand of God in the profits of unearned increment. In the letter above quoted from, he justified the ways of speculation thus:

There are moral as well as physical phenomena incident to every state of things, which may at first appear evils, but which are devised by an all-seeing Providence for some beneficent purpose. Such is the spirit of speculative enterprise which now and then rises to an extravagant height, and sweeps throughout the land. . . . The late land speculations, so much deprecated, though ruinous to many engaged in them, have forced agriculture and civilization into the depths of the wilderness; have laid open the recesses of primeval forests; made us acquainted with the most available points of our immense interior; have cast the germs of future towns and cities and busy marts in the heart of savage solitudes, and studded our vast rivers and internal seas with ports that will soon give activity to a vast internal commerce. Millions of acres which might otherwise have remained idle and impracticable wastes, have been brought under the dominion of the plough, and hundreds of thousands of industrious yeomen have been carried into the rich but remote depths of our immense empire, to multiply and spread out in every direction, and give solidity and strength to our confederacy. All this has in a great measure been effected by the extravagant schemes of land speculators. I am, therefore, inclined to look upon them with a more indulgent eye than they are considered by those violent politicians who are prescribing violent checks and counter measures, and seem to have something vindictive in their policy. (*Life and Letters*, Vol. II, p. 314.)

Thus did Irving become completely domesticated in the new world that Rip Van Winkle had found so disconcerting when he came upon it out of the quiet colonial past. The rediscovery of America proved to be an agreeable business, and profitable in a professional way. His enthusiasms, which in 1831 he felt were "waning as to many objects of past interest," were stimulated by the vast stir of the country, and the spirit of romance once more ran briskly in his veins. The better part of a year he rambled widely about the country, in order, as he said, to get at home "upon American themes." He visited Boston and the White Mountains, then West to Ohio and St. Louis, then with an Indian commissioner he penetrated the southwest prairies as far as the wild Pawnee country beyond the South Canadian River, then to New Orleans and Charleston, finally settling down in Washington to immerse himself in politics. From there he passed over the Potomac for an extended trip through the Old Dominion, returning to New York where he spent some time with Astor at Hell Gate, finally in 1835 settling at Tarrytown which was to be his home to the last. He had definitely determined on his new field of work. His imagination had been stirred by his visit to the prairies; the romance of the westward expansion was beginning to find expression in the works of Timothy Flint and James Hall; the public interest was ripe and John Jacob Astor was at hand to encourage him. Thus stimulated Irving proposed to make the field of western romance his own, with the result that he published in quick succession *A Tour of the Prairies*, *Astoria*, and *The Adventures of Captain Bonneville*.

On the whole the new venture did not prosper. The spirit of the West was not to be captured by one whose heart was in Spain. In *A Tour of the Prairies* there is a certain homely simplicity and straightforwardness that spring from a plain recital of undramatic experience; and in *Astoria* there is an unembellished narrative of appalling hardship and heroic endurance, with none of the tawdry romantics that mar the work of Flint and Hall. Yet neither is creatively imaginative, neither stirs one with a sense of high drama. The atmosphere of Snake River could not be created in the quiet study at the "Roost"; it needed the pen of a realist to capture the romance of those bitter wanderings in mountain and sagebrush. It is journeyman work, and on every page one is conscious of the professional man of letters faithfully doing this day's allotment. It is much the same with his *Life of Washington*. In this last great undertaking Irving no longer writes with gusto. The golden days of Diedrich Knickerbocker and Rip Van Winkle are long since gone; the magic is departed from his pen; and a somewhat tired old gentleman is struggling to fulfill his contract with his publisher. It was a mistake to venture on the work, despite the fact that he had long been planning it. His historical equipment was inadequate. He might make a pretty story out of Washington's early life and his days with the army, but he was far too ignorant of politics, too credulous in judging his materials, to interpret justly the fierce party struggles that seethed about the President. Quite unconsciously in this last work he returned to the political prejudices of his youth, and wrote an account of Washington's administrations deeply colored by his Federalist sources.

The most distinguished of our early romantics, Irving in the end was immolated on the altar of romanticism. The pursuit of the picturesque lured him away into sterile wastes, and when the will o'-the-wisp was gone he was left empty. A born humorist, the gayety of whose spirits overflowed the brim, he was lacking in a brooding intellectuality, and instead of coming upon irony at the bottom of the cup—as the greater humorists have come upon it after life has had its way with them—he found there only sentiment and the dreamy poetic. As the purple haze on the horizon of his mind was dissipated by a sobering experience, he tried to substitute an adventitious glamour; as romance faded, sentiment supplied its place. So long as youth and high spirits endured, his inkwell was a never-failing source of gayety, but as the sparkle subsided he over-sweetened his wine. This suffices to account for the fact that all his better work was done early; and this explains why the Knickerbocker *History* remains the most genial and vital of his volumes. The gayety of youth bubbles and effervesces in those magic pages, defying time to do its worst. The critic may charge the later Irving with many and heavy shortcomings, but the romantic smoke-clouds that ascend from Wouter Van Twiller's pipe cannot be dissipated by the winds of criticism.

II
JAMES KIRKE PAULDING

Far more native to the limitations and hardships of American life and far more loyal to its homely aspirations was James Kirke Paulding, whose literary reputation came to be so deeply overshadowed by that of his early friend. Sprung from plain stock—whether English or Dutch his son remained in doubt, although inclining to believe the former—and cradled in the fierce partisanship of the Revolutionary struggle, he never abandoned his inherited liberalism or found his love of country growing less. To the end of his life he remained a primitive American of an earlier generation, somewhat puzzled by the ways of another age that speculated in prosperity by running in debt, and measured a man's wealth by the amount he owed. His father had been an active Whig in a Tory neighborhood who did not stint his service to the Revolutionary cause. He was a member of the local Committee of Safety, and acted as State Commissary to the Revolutionary forces, a post which in the end brought him to ruin. In the dark days of the struggle he pledged his private credit for supplies, and was never reimbursed by a negligent commonwealth. The outcome was financial disaster. The father was imprisoned for debt and his courage broken, and the family long suffered from want. "We were not only poor," the son wrote later, "but steeped in poverty." But there was excellent stuff in the awkward, dreamy country boy. He was "built of stubborn oak," he remarked whimsically, "seasoned in the school of poverty, like an old chimney-piece in a log cabin." When at the age of nineteen he was suddenly plunged into the world of New York City, he was shy, uncouth, self-educated, and felt himself an alien in Wall Street and Broadway. For the Federalist upper class he seems to have felt the instinctive hostility of the outsider; but through the agency of the Irvings—an elder sister having married William Irving—he was brought into the companionship of a group of clever young men, and under the stimulus of high talk and exuberant pranks, the latent idealism of his nature expanded freely. This was his university, and while it left something to be desired in the way of discipline, suffering too free a rein to his discursive fancy, it quickened his native wit, awakened his creative imagination, and put him to school to the pleasant craft of writing. The *Salmagundi Papers* were the first fruits of the literary apprenticeship of the group, and although Irving has come to receive the chief credit for them, the wit of Paulding seems quite as sprightly, and his gayety as fresh.

That his later career in letters was less notable resulted in part from the fact that he was an inveterate rambler by nature, and partly from the fact that writing with him was occasional, a pleasant relief from humdrum duties, and he did not choose to lay a curb on his vagrant ways. In letters as in life he was always discursive, forgetful of his objective in his delight at the beauty of the countryside, loading his pages down with nature descriptions and clogging the action of his tales with somewhat tedious homilies. After forty years of writing he remained still an amateur, incapable of pruning the wilful tangle of his fancy—an essayist of the leisurely school who ventured incautiously into the realms of verse and fiction without mastering the technic of the business. There was perhaps too much of the homespun in him to permit him to become an artist. The experience of his youth marked him too deeply, and all his life he remained as conscious a son of the people as Hamlin Garland was later, delighting to chronicle the ways of the obscure, somewhat militant in proclaiming the excellence of homely virtues. Formed in an environment that bred a spontaneous democracy, he was a confirmed equalitarian, untroubled by the itch to rise in the world or exploit his fellows. Alone among the Knicker-bocker group, he was a Jeffersonian in the fundamentals of his social creed; not in the lesser matters of Kentucky Resolutions and the like, but in his Physiocratic leanings, in his profound distrust of all middle-class programs and his preference for the simple country ways over the city economy; and it was this deep-rooted agrarianism that set him against capitalism and made him a later Jacksonian. In him there spoke out the authentic New York, not of Broadway merchants or Wall Street bankers, but of the plain rank and file of the people. Untouched by foreign travel but widely acquainted with his native America, he was fashioned out of the wool from the fireside loom and domestic dye-pot.

A writer so consciously and completely American would find abundant occasion to put his pen to the service of his country at a time when every English traveler turned critic and on his return home published a volume of truculent disparagement of ways and things American. For the most part those volumes were a defense of Toryism by the easy method of attacking democracy, and they annoyed Paulding beyond measure. He would not let them go un-answered, and from *The Diverting History of John Bull and Brother Jonathan* (1812) to *John Bull in America* (1825), he published five different replies, varying his attack from argument to burlesque. Something more than loyalty to his country seems to have spurred him on. His dislike of England was inveterate, partly because of the old Revolutionary feud, partly because of later antagonisms. Almost at the hour of his birth the Paulding family had been forced to quit their home for fear of the British and Tories who daily threatened them; and a deep hatred of the British Tory he drew in with his mother's milk. To him England was a Tory country, reeking with social injustice, the home of ancient abuses, and necessarily the implacable enemy of democratic America. He was convinced that want and tyranny and subserviency dogged the daily life of the English common people; and the English Reviews that attacked the ways of democracy with caustic British superior-ity, filled his honest republican heart with wrath, and he jabbed his quill into the tough skin of John Bull with patriotic vigor. The shame of the burning of the capitol rankled in the American heart, and Paulding discovered fresh grievances in remembering that from England had come the banking system and the "shin-plaster dynasty" that would breed in the new country the evils of the old if they were not looked to. He was convinced that the mother country wished ill to her offspring, and he thanked God in successive volumes that democratic America was not what Tory England was.

For despite the English travelers—Weld, Parkinson, Ashe, Bradbury, Hall, Trollope, and all the rest of the loquacious tribe— Paulding was persuaded that America constituted the hope of the future. Here in this land he believed that men should eventually achieve a measure of well-being undreamed of in the old world; already the old tyrannies had been destroyed, the ancient poverty abated. From this stubborn idealism nothing could turn him aside. It finds expression in an early poem, and it provides the theme for his last novel. *The Backwoodsman*, published in 1818, is a rambling and somewhat plethoric idyll of the West, the hero of which is an archetype of the oppressed and exploited, who finds a generous asylum in the free land beyond the Alleghenies, and like Crèvecœur's Andrew the Hebridean, expands the horizons of his mind under the beneficent touch of freedom. *The Puritan and His Daughter*, written over thirty years later, deals with a different phase of the same general theme. It is a vivid picture of the strife engendered in America by immigrant families who bring hither their old-world feuds and animosities, and the curative influence of the free environment that, in discovering the good rather than the bad in neighbors, draws together the younger generation despite the jealous parental authority that would keep them apart. The bigoted fathers make trouble enough—the fanatical Puritan who fought with Cromwell and the headstrong Cavalier who defended divine right—wilful men whom even the common frontier perils cannot reconcile or make tolerant; but they are powerless to thwart the ways of nature. The son of the Cavalier discovers an attractive woman in the daughter of the Puritan, and when love walks in the twilight what matters theology or politics. Youth has its own notions of divine right; in its creed the dogmas of John Calvin and Robert Filmer have no place; and if the lovers are more tolerant than the fathers it only proves that a freer environment will manage to soften the traditional animosities and beget a kindlier race from the merging of classes. Such at least is the characteristic thesis that Paulding elaborates through two volumes of discursive narrative interspersed with bits of vigorous action.

Of this kindly melting pot Paulding himself was a product. He had rid himself wholly of all ties that would bind him to Europe. He was partisan to no cause or party, literary or political, of the old world. He was content to be American and suffer his native land to bound his loyalties. In his own literary practice he refused to imitate the current English fashions and he spoke his mind freely to the American reading public for its greedy swallowing of cheap imported food. He did not take kindly to the English romantic writers, and went often out of his way to have a dig at his two pet aversions, Scott and Byron.[2] His amusing tale of *Koningsmarke, the Long Finne*, is a good-natured burlesque of certain romantic mannerisms of the Waverley novels, and a defense of Cooper's *Pioneers* for its homely realism. Paulding's dislike of the "blood-pudding" fiction that had come over from England, and that proved so disastrous to the genius of Gilmore Simms, was inveterate, and in his whimsical dedication of *The Puritan and His Daughter* to the sovereign people he comments on the public taste thus:

I am not ignorant of your preference for high-seasoned dishes of foreign cookery, most especially blood-puddings, plentifully spiced and sauced with adultery, seduction, poisoning, stabbing, suicide, and all other sublime excesses of genius. I am aware also that Your Majesty, being yourself able to perform impossibilities, believed nothing impossible. Possessing this clew to Your Majesty's royal approbation, I solemnly assure you I have gone as far as I could to secure it, with a safe conscience. I have laid about me pretty handsomely, and sprinkled a good number of pages with blood enough, I hope, to make a pudding. If I have any apology to make to Your Majesty, it is for permitting some of my people to die a natural death, a thing so unnatural that it has been banished from all works of fiction aiming at the least semblance to truth. . . . But, may it please Your Majesty, I am troubled with weak nerves, and my great grandfather was a Quaker. I am, therefore, naturally averse to bloodshed, and have more than once nearly fallen into convulsions over the pages of Monsieur Alexandre Dumas, whom I consider a perfect Guillotine among authors. In short, may it please Your Majesty, I abjure poisoning, or smothering with charcoal, and confess myself deplorably behind the spirit of this luminous age, which is as much in advance of all others, as the forewheel of a wagon is ahead of the hind ones.

In his politics—and as a good American of the times he took his politics seriously—Paulding found in the popular drift towards Jacksonian democracy an expression of his deepest convictions.

---

[2] See *Letters from the South*, Vol. I, *Letter XXII*.

It was moving in the direction he had long faced, and he went with it whole-heartedly, enjoyed some of the emoluments of office, and eventually served as Secretary to the Navy in the cabinet of Van Buren. With Jackson's attack on the Bank he must have been in deep sympathy, for his dislike of the new financial system was of long standing. His father had suffered heavily from a depreciated Continental currency, and he early came to distrust all banks and banking. His political views, indeed, were pretty much determined by the Physiocratic convictions that underlay his thinking. He had been a Jeffersonian long before the rise of Jacksonianism. Portions of his *Letters from the South*, published in 1817, seem like excerpts from the agrarian writings of John Taylor of Caroline. There is the same contemptuous analysis of the "shin-plaster dynasty," the same concern at the growth of trading towns, the same conviction that cities and poverty and low morals go hand in hand, the same trust in the perennial wholesomeness of country life. Such a passage as this will suffice to reveal his leanings towards a Physiocratic economy:

I was saying, that we have too many people living in cities, in proportion to our farmers, who, after all, are the backbone of every country, whence originates its riches and its solid strength. . . . Yet our people cling to the towns and cities, attracted by the hope of sudden wealth, and despising the slow, yet sure, rewards of agriculture, which, without leading a man to inordinate riches, secure him for ever from the chances of sinking into beggary or want. The race of paupers receives no recruits from them; for in all my sojournings, I may say with truth, that I never saw an industrious farmer forsaken, "or his seed begging bread." One great cause of the disproportion of numbers . . . between the agricultural and other classes of the community, is the great system of paper money, which has struck at the root of regular, persevering industry, whose rewards, though slow, are always certain. For some years back, hardly a tradesman in our cities, and of late in our little towns (each of which, however insignificant, has now its snug little bank) thinks of growing rich by his industry. No; he must get accommodations at some bank, and plunge into speculations: nor can you now go into a cobbler's stall without seeing a bank notice, or perhaps two or three, stuck up with an awl at the chimney-piece, to remind the honest gentleman that he owes a great deal more than he can pay. Thus is the axe laid to the very root of national morals, and consequently national prosperity, and the whole American people, farmers excepted, sunk into an abject subjection to banks and their directors. (*Letters from the South*, Vol. I, pp. 100–102.)

So confirmed an agrarian would easily arrive at agrarian conclusions in his meditations on the nature and functions of the political state. Unlike Irving, who, having no political convictions, was equally pleased with Whig or Democrat if he happened to be a gentleman, Paulding was something of a political philosopher with clear-cut doctrines. He was too shrewd an observer of ways political to be caught by party cries, or to ignore the class selfishness that would make government a party to its ends. As a Jeffersonian he retained an old-fashioned distrust of the political state. As an eighteenth-century liberal he would keep the state within narrow bounds. Jealous for a freedom worthy of free citizens, he wanted government to keep hands off what did not concern it. He would not have the state used as a cat's-paw to pull anybody's chestnuts out of the fire, whether in the form of Clay's American System, or what not. For protective tariffs and internal improvements—those grandiose schemes for hastening prosperity—he felt an old-fashioned repugnance that found issue in amusing caricature. In *Westward Ho!* he introduces a French publican of a Mississippi River village who does not care for Yankee improvements and describes them thus:

Diable! monsieur, another improvement; last year they assess me for one grand public improvement! one road to go somewhere, I don't know. Eh bien! I pay the money. Well, this year they assess me for one other grand public improvement—very grand—voilà, monsieur, one other road, right alongside the other, both going to the same place. Diable! I no want to travel on two turnpike roads. Ah! monsieur le colonel, I shall be very rich, O! very rich indeed, by these grand improvements. They take away all my land to make room for the grand improvement; they take away all my money to pay for him, and then they tell me my land worth four, six time so much as before. Peste! what that to me when my land all gone to the dem public improvement, hey? I shall be very rich then. Diable! I wish myself gone to some country where every thing was go backwards—what you call tail foremost, instead of forwards, for the dem march of improvement shall ruin me at last. (Vol. II, Chapter XVI.)

Satire aimed at the new gospel of progress is not infrequent in Paulding. In *Koningsmarke* he drew the picture of a politician that was perhaps intended for a burlesque of Henry Clay. The worthy Wolfgang Langfanger, member of the council of Elsingburgh, having "brought his private affairs into great confusion, by devoting too much time to the public good," began "to think it high time the public good should repay some part of its weighty obligations. He had accordingly invented, and persuaded the Heer Piper to put into practice, a system of internal improvement, which has been imitated, from time to time, in this country ever since with great success. The essence of his plan consisted in running in debt for the present, and living afterwards upon the anticipation of future wealth" (Book Second, Chapter VI). Big with his wonderful idea the busy councilor projected great docks and wharves for the commerce that was to be invited to come, a fine canal that would cut off a full six miles for barges that were not yet on the stocks, and a magnificent plan of new streets that led through houses that must be pulled down and fields that must forego their usual harvests. Such goodly improvements naturally cost money, and to maintain the public credit taxes were levied, and still more taxes, until, like the French tavern-keeper, the good people of Elsingburgh were brought to doubt the wisdom of investing in future prosperity at so high a present cost.

But the masterpiece of Langfanger's policy was that of pulling down an old market, and building a new one in another part of the village, in the management of which business he is supposed to have laid down the first principles of the great and thriving science of political economy, or picking people's pockets on a grand scale. He caused the people living near the old market to pay roundly for its removal as a nuisance; and then he caused the people that lived about where the new one was to be built, to pay roundly for the vast pleasure and advantage of its neighbourhood. Thus he pinched them through both ears, and got the reputation of a great financier. (Book Seventh, Chapter III.)

Koningsmarke is Paulding's most interesting work, and the utter neglect that has overtaken it is far from deserved. It is native and original, full of shrewd comment and sly satire, and it embodies most of Paulding's pet theories and aversions. Few books of the time are more amusing than this tale of the Long Finne who moves in a dark cloud of mystery woven by Bombie of the Frizzled Head, barks his sturdy shins on many a blood-curdling adventure, proves a true knight to his lady, and in the end turns out to be a very ordinary fellow who has been blown up to heroic size by the black art of romance. Paulding must have had great fun writing it, for his wit still preserves its freshness after a hundred years. It is a whimsical satire on the ways of the hour, literary and other, set against the background of an old Swedish settlement on the banks of the Delaware; but the chief purpose of its quizzical pages is the pouring of a broadside into the picturesque hull of contemporary fiction. It is an attack on the abundant extravagance of current romance that had been inflated by "Monk" Lewis and Sir Walter. Paulding cleverly hits off the high-flown and ghostly, the love of blood pudding, the snobbish contempt for the homely and native. Written in 1823, the year of Cooper's *Pioneers*, it defends the realism of characters and setting in that work against the charge of vulgarity and commonplace, but it takes pains to satirize Cooper's noble red man of the forest. Paulding's Indians are more like Bird's than Cooper's, material for burlesque rather than romance, but as he runs over the names of the warriors—"the Big Buffalo, the Little Duck-Legs, the Sharp-Faced Bear, the Walking Shadow, the Iron Cloud, the Jumping Sturgeon, the Belly Ache, and the Doctor, all legitimate sovereigns, with copper rings in their noses, blanket robes of state, and painted faces"—amusement at their childishness is tempered by the recognition that they have been overreached and dispossessed by the grasping white men.

In some of his later work the line between burlesque and serious is not so clearly marked, and one hesitates to pronounce whether *Westward Ho!* is a sober attempt at popular romance or a *reductio ad absurdum* of the current romantic flummery. Certainly it is a preposterous story with its melancholy hero driven mad by fear of madness and indulging in gibberish that comes straight out of Shakespeare, and with its ample crop of stock characters—Master Zeno Paddock and Mrs. Judith Paddock with their prying inquisitiveness, Colonel Dangerfield the easy-going Virginia gentleman who in staking his estate on a horse race embodies the plantation tradition, and Bushfield the backwoodsman who cannot live in a world that has left off its moccasins, and removes to a place where there are no laws and no lawyers and where constables do not visit a man who has thrashed his neighbor. *Westward Ho!* is not an amusing book; it is quite lacking in local color, and its casual bits of realism and occasional satire are too inconsequential to signify. *The Dutchman's Fireside*, written at about the same time, is far more successful. It purports to be an account of the Knickerbocker society in the days of the Old French war, and it contains some lovely pictures of old times that one reads with pleasure; but it indulges somewhat freely in adventure amongst the Indians and in the war, and its love story is needlessly romantic. Although Paulding still protests against a blood-pudding diet, he indulges occasionally in the high-flown, to the detriment of the idyllic note. Romance was all about him and he could not wholly escape its compulsions. Too casual in his work, too undisciplined in the craft of writing, he remained to the end an amusing amateur, a homespun man of letters who never took the trouble to master his technic. There was excellent stuff in him, solider perhaps than in Irving, but his failure suggests the difference between the journeyman and the artist.

CHAPTER IV

JAMES FENIMORE COOPER
Critic

FENIMORE COOPER is one of the puzzling figures of his generation. In his substantial character was embodied what may well appear no more than a bundle of contradictions. Romancer and social critic, feudal-minded yet espousing a republican faith, he pretty much baffled his own generation in its testy attempts to understand him, as he has pretty much baffled later times. No other major writer, unless it be Whitman, has been so misunderstood, and no other offers a knottier problem to the student of American letters. The stubborn clay of his nature was molded to a pattern unlike that of his fellows, and the difference was long accounted to him as a grave shortcoming. His outspoken individualism was a constant irritant to a sensitive majority, and his aloofness from the common enthusiasms was reckoned no better than treason to his native land. The right of the individual to question the herd pronouncements was a right not acknowledged by the herd, and the more it tried to silence Cooper's tongue the more caustic and loquacious it became. He refused to be silenced though it should come to open warfare. His later years in consequence were rendered unhappy by a thousand petty vexations, and his creative work was brought only this side of shipwreck.

How and why so great a misadventure befell him are questions of prime importance to which little attention has been given. That his tactlessness was at fault is commonly believed—his tactlessness and a certain pugnacious virtue that would inculcate righteousness by means of a broken head. But such an explanation, true enough so far as it goes, does not go far enough. The trouble lay deeper than that; it lay in the mind of Cooper himself, in the doubts and uncertainties that dwelt side by side with stubborn dogmatisms, troubling his speculations and perplexing his plainest counsels. And that trouble must be traced to an underlying conflict between the man and his age, between the ideal and the real, between high loyalties and petty fact. Fenimore Cooper was the barometer of a gusty generation, sensitive to every storm on the far horizon. No other observer of that changing generation suffered so keenly in mind and conscience from the loosening of ancient ties, and none labored so hard to keep his countrymen to the strait path of an old-fashioned rectitude. His busy life covered the middle years of the great shift from an aristocratic order to a capitalistic order, and this revolutionary change provided him ample materials for brooding speculation. At every turn in the road fresh doubts assailed him. The perplexities and dogmatisms that clutter so many of his later pages, playing havoc with his romantic art, are a testimony to the confusions of a generation in the midst of epic changes. As honest a man as ever spoke his mind frankly, he endeavored to reconcile the irreconcilable, and establish sure standards amid the wreck of all standards. He could not drift. He must discover some working agreement between the old America and the new, between the reputed excellencies of the traditional aristocratic order, and the reputed justice of the democratic ideal. But unfortunately for this difficult business he was temperamentally ill-equipped. He was always at war with himself. His loyalties and his conscience ran at cross-purposes. His mind was packed with prejudices as an egg with meat. He was too partisan to compromise, and too honest to be content with the shoddy. His instinctive romanticisms were always being buffeted by fact, and his troubled mind in consequence was forever constructing laborious defense-mechanisms.

For those deep confusions that marred his later work and brought such bitter misunderstanding upon him, his heritage was much to blame. A romantic at heart, he was out of sympathy with the dominant romanticisms of his generation. Certain hold-overs from the past held him back from hearty participation in the present. He loved the world that was falling into decay too much to put away its virtues with its smallclothes; he would preserve what was excellent in the old to enrich and dignify what was excellent in the new; he would have the young democracy learn the decorum of a staid aristocracy. It is this fond lingering between worlds that sets Cooper apart from his fellows. He was an English squire of the old school turned republican, who did not quite like the company he found himself in. He was equally puzzled at the bumptious leveling of the coonskin democracy, and the exploitative spirit of Wall Street Whiggery. But though he railed at the newfangled ways with the testiness of a squire, he was too confirmed a republican, too deeply concerned that the great venture in republicanism should demonstrate its wisdom, to overlook its shortcomings. He would have it be so true to its ideal that the world would acknowledge its excellence. He could not circumscribe his duties to election-day hurrahs; he must ferret out treason in the market place; he must be faithful in counsel though he utter unwelcome truths. It was the very faithfulness of Cooper to his conception of an ideal republic that brought him into collision with his fellows and filled his later days with bitterness.

It is easy to see where Cooper got those stubborn notions that marked him as the last of our eighteenth-century squires and left him obsolete after the adoption of the Constitution of 1821. From his father, from the Tory rector of St. Peter's, Albany, who first schooled him, from the Loyalist family of De Lancey into which he married, from Governor Jay and the old gentry with whom he was brought up, he imbibed certain stalwart conservatisms—political, religious, social, economic—that mingled in his blood and nourished the tissues of caste prejudice from which his maturer social philosophy struggled in vain to escape. In spite of his deliberate acceptance of the democratic principle, as he understood that principle, he remained at heart as sturdily eighteenth-century as any fox-hunting master of English acres. He had early been bred in the old traditions at Otsego Hall where he spent his boyhood. His father, Judge William Cooper, "a testy and choleric gentleman easily wrought into passion,"—whom he idealized as Judge Temple in *The Pioneers*—was an old-school politician of high Federalist persuasion, a vigorous, not to say truculent, embodiment of the stake-in-society principle of statecraft. Smitten with the common itch for large land holdings, he had got his hands on a huge virgin tract which he managed in the old baronial fashion. He was a real lord of the manor and late in life he recalled that "there were 40,000 souls holding land, directly or indirectly, under me"; and in the year 1800 "he set up a claim to having placed the plough upon more acres than any other man in America" (quoted in D. R. Fox, *The Decline of Aristocracy in the Politics of New York*, p. 136). Otsego Hall in Cooperstown was a frontier citadel of Federalism defending the western marches against Jeffersonian democracy, and Judge

Cooper used his economic power over tenants with telling effect. He "rode far and wide in the cause of Jay and later Aaron Burr, always preaching the musty doctrine that government had better be left to gentlemen, and that simple folk should vote as they were told" (*ibid.*, pp. 136–137). When persuasion failed he resorted to threats, and in 1792 he was before the legislature on impeachment charges. From the testimony it appears that the patriarchal Judge used direct methods with tenants in arrears; he "had been round to the people and told them that they owed him, and that unless they voted for Mr. Jay, he would ruin them" (*ibid.*, p. 140). By such arguments it was thought some seven hundred votes had been brought into the Federalist column by this exemplar of the old virtues.

But Cooper had drifted with his age far from such old-fashioned methods of class domination. In spite of his great love for his father he seems never to have espoused the latter's political creed. With the disintegration of Federalism the young man went with the country in its turning towards French romanticism. When and why he adopted the democratic faith is not apparent, but until middle life it would seem that he concerned himself little with political theory. He remained a provincial American with an intense pride of patriotism. But his long stay in Europe, lasting from June, 1826, to November, 1833, and the Jacksonian revolution that took place during his absence, put him upon an anxious examination of first principles, and thereafter to the end of his life the social and political problems of America were a burden on his conscience. He arrived late at a reasoned political faith, as he arrived late at his literary art, and it is impossible to trace the steps of his intellectual development; yet confused though his thinking was, and shot through with narrowing prejudices, he persistently sought for the light; and the germinal source of his dissatisfactions was the deepening conviction that, in Franklin's phrase, the affairs of this world are preposterously managed. From this conviction Cooper never swerved. The contrast everywhere between the real and the ideal took hold of his mind as an obsession, and put an end to his contentment. His romantic art suffered from the intrusion of realism; the romancer was constantly impelled to turn critic. It was his travels more than anything else that destroyed his provincial contentment. The perturbing influence of that experience abroad has never perhaps been adequately considered by his critics. No other American was so unsettled by contact with European civilization. It was a Europe in the throes of revolution and Cooper threw himself with enthusiasm into French politics, hoping for a wise republican issue from the overturn. But it was a Europe also of dignified and generous culture that was a challenge to his Americanism. It made a critic of him and turned his mind to political and social problems. Europe appealed to his native aristocratic prejudices, but repelled his democratic; Jacksonian America appealed to his democratic prejudices, but rode roughshod over his aristocratic. He found himself nowhere at home. Puzzled and perturbed, he leveled his shafts at both worlds and sought a haven of refuge in vicarious existence, at times in the wilderness beyond the soil and smutch of the Jacksonian frontier, at times in the Utopian world of *The Crater* where an honest man could find free play for his creative energy, until the trouble makers came upon him.

In temperament and outlook this later Cooper was another John Adams modified by changing times. A realist in his long brooding over social and political evils, he was at heart an idealist greatly concerned with justice amongst men, with a romantic fondness for dwelling on the virtues of earlier days. Like Adams he understood very well that equality is a Utopian dream; that social classes exist in every society that has accumulated property, and that sovereignty in the long run will fall into the hands that control the social economics.[1] The problem he set himself to consider was the problem of reconciling this universal fact with his own predilection in favor of democracy. That he regarded himself as a democrat his emphatic assertions suffice to prove; but no more than Emerson was he deceived by the spurious democracy of the times. "The writer believes himself to be as good a democrat as there is in America," he said in the Introduction to *The American Democrat*. "But his democracy is not of the impracticable school. He prefers a democracy to any other system, on account of its comparative advantages, but not on account of its perfection. He knows it has evils; great and increasing evils, and evils peculiar to itself; but he believes that monarchy and aristocracy have more. It will be very apparent to all who read this book, that he is not a believer in the scheme of raising men very far above their natural propensities." He would lift his voice in no hurrah for the ma-

[1] See the Preface to *The Redskins*.

jority, for he knew that the majority was very likely to be the tool
of the demagogue. He saw no peculiar virtue or special intelligence
in a coonskin cap, and he discovered no advantage in log cabins
and hard cider as a training school for statesmen. He had watched
the disgraceful campaign of 1840 with concern that gentlemen
should stoop to the demagoguery that marked that electoral
debauch; and it confirmed him in the conviction that "old-
fashioned, high principled gentlemen" of an earlier age would
never have been guilty of such traffic in votes—men like Chancellor
Livingston who devoted his later years to raising Merino sheep,
or John Jay who after filling with dignity many high offices retired
to his estate to concern himself with new varieties of melons.

Hating all humbug, Cooper made it his business to free his mind
from the several varieties of cant that were overrunning America
like pigweed. "Had a suitable compound offered," he said of
The American Democrat, "the title of this book would have been
something like 'Anti-cant.' " Roughly, the history of his essays in
criticism falls into two broad phases: the struggle to pull himself
out of the bog of eighteenth-century caste philosophy—from that
stake-in-society theory which his father upheld; and the struggle
to escape the fallacies of the nineteenth-century philosophy rising
about him—from the rude equalitarianism of Jacksonian democracy, and the materialism of capitalistic exploitation. His abandonment of the principle of gentleman-rule marks his definite break
with the philosophy of Federalism and the substitution of democracy. It cost him a prolonged struggle, for the social-stake theory
ran with many of his oldest predilections, and the evidence of that
struggle is scattered broadly through the pages written in the late
thirties; but having convinced himself of the social wrong involved
in the principle, he was tireless in refutation. In *The American
Democrat* he laid down the principle that "A government founded
on the representation of property, however direct or indirect, is
radically vicious. . . . It is the proper business of government to
resist the corruptions of money, and not to depend on them" (*On
Property*, p. 141). But it is *The Monikins*, a strange book much
laughed at by the critics, rarely read and little understood, that
concerns itself most largely with the theory. Sadly bungled though
the satire quite obviously is, it is nevertheless a spirited attack on the social-stake principle that reveals how far Cooper
had traveled from the doctrines of Hamilton and Webster, of

Federalist and Whig. Both England and America—Leaphigh and Leaplow—show meanly under his caustic analysis, the former perhaps more meanly than the latter; their institutions, societies, politics, manners, are an unlovely compound of cant and hypocrisy; and the root of the common meanness he discovers in human selfishness. He conceives of man as a queer mixture of good and evil from whom much is not to be expected; something nearer to Swift's conception than William Ellery Channing's; with too much of the Monikin in him to pass for a child of God; prone to error even under a republican system; insolent, tyrannical, loving fetishes, given to brag, too poor-spirited to be free, gilding his fetters and belying Locke's saying that chains are an ill wearing. There are depths of bitterness in *The Monikins* that startle the reader. It is a tale of doubt and disillusion, Gulliver-like in its fierceness of attack, that strikes through all the shoddy romanticisms of the times and reduces the current democracy to humbug. Subjected to such analysis the old Federalist shibboleth of men of principle and property is no more than the East wind in empty bellies. The possession of money does not change human nature; rich as well as poor are driven by selfish interest, and to give a loose to property power is to invite political disaster.

Your social-stake system supposes that he who has what is termed a distinct and prominent interest in society, will be the most likely to conduct its affairs wisely, justly, and disinterestedly. This would be true, if those great principles which lie at the root of all happiness were respected; but unluckily, the stake in question, instead of being a stake in justice and virtue, is usually reduced to be merely a stake in property. . . . Now, all experience shows that the great property-incentives are to increase property, to protect property, and to buy with property those advantages which ought to be independent of property, viz., honors, dignities, power and immunities. I cannot say how it is with men, but our [Monikin] histories are eloquent on this head. We have had the property-principle carried out thoroughly in our practice, and the result has shown that its chief operation is to render property as intact as possible, and the bones, and sinews, and marrow of all who do not possess it, its slaves." (*The Monikins*, Chapter XXVII.)

But though Cooper might deny the validity of the eighteenth-century social-stake theory, he saw no valid reason to abandon his eighteenth-century economics. In his preference for a social order founded on agriculture he was as confirmed a Physiocrat as Franklin or Jefferson; and this preference determined his judgment on the economic revolution under way in America. A people living close to the soil was living more wholesomely, he believed, than a city people immersed in trade and manufacture. For the capitalistic expansion that followed the new fiscal system of the seventeen-nineties, he felt an instinctive repugnance. Banking and the manipulation of credit seemed to him mean and sordid, and the spirit of speculation that was overrunning the land he believed was destructive of common morality. The activities of Wall Street he looked upon with the eyes of an English squire. To expect any sane progress from such worship of money, to assume that a high and excellent civilization could result from such worship, seemed to him plain madness. "God protect the country that has nothing but commercial towns for capitals," he wrote his wife in 1839 (Cooper, *Correspondence of James Fenimore Cooper*, Vol. II, p. 404), and the comment found amplification in many a caustic passage in his novels of criticism. A materialistic middle class with its gospel of progress interpreted in terms of wasteful exploitation seemed to him the hateful progeny of a period of "moral occultation"; and against this "Yankee" philosophy he waged an unrelenting warfare. In *The Monikins* he drew a gloomy picture of the America of the thirties when the land had come under a great moral eclipse; and in *Home as Found* and *The Redskins* he commented bitterly on the universal restlessness that was driving thousands to the new West to seek their fortunes. The settlement of the Inland Empire was no romance for him. The Great Migration seemed to imply the break-up of the older America he loved; and the impact of the frontier spirit upon the country seemed likely to destroy the last excellence of an earlier age. It marked for Cooper the final triumph of the acquisitive Yankee spirit, grasping and lawless in its crude leveling.

From these germinal sources—his love of the dignified ways of the old manorial families, his contempt for the middle class, his dislike of a bumptious leveling, his hatred of brag and cant and enterprise—came those sharp contrasts in his pictures that set the vulgar present over against the dignified past. His criticism was in no small part the reaction of a romantic to the unlovely works of an economic revolution. From his loyalty to the old came that subtle romanticizing of the eighteenth century that lends a charm to his tales, and from it came also that vindictive hatred of the frontier that spurred him to ill-balanced criticism. He could not like the new that was destroying the old. Like Emerson he was a man without a party, but unlike him he sought consolation in the past rather than the future. The excellence he yearned for he found in that older world whose stable ways were as yet unsettled by the romantic revolution, and from the meanness of the present he stole away to find consolation in the dignity and worth of honester times. The late eighteenth century became, therefore, his romantic haven and City of Refuge to which he returned gladly. He was always seeking to revitalize the old in an environment where, as he lamented, "the eighteenth century may be set down as a very dark antiquity."

That Cooper unconsciously romanticized the past is only too evident. Too often he accepted its self-proclaimed virtues as sober fact and created a race of squires that never existed outside his pages. Realist though he was in certain moods, he abandoned his realism in the presence of the tie-wig gentry. His father was as graspingly eighteenth century as Gouverneur Morris and saw to it that his own nest was well feathered; yet the son failed to perceive that the dignified professions of those old gentlemen were little more than splendid gestures. He made the mistake of taking them at their face value. Honest himself, he attributed an equal honesty to the older generation, and he watched with unfeigned regret the disintegration of an order that seemed to him the repository of much that was excellent. Fragments of its ideals he clung to; its dignity, its concern for breeding and manners, its fine distinction. Fragments also of its political convictions: its concern for law and order, its belief that all just law is founded in morality, its insistence that American government is one of principles and not of men. He put his finger shrewdly on certain fallacies of eighteenth-century theory, but he took too many of its values at par. The twilight is a mighty sorcerer and Cooper was bewitched by the half light that lingered softly on the familiar past.

This suffices to explain the grounds of the charge of aristocratic leanings that Cooper was persistently brought under. His bold defense of the landed gentry gave mortal enmity to the Jacksonians, and the tactlessness with which he pointed out the crude provincialisms of America—the bumptious plebeians he set over against the priggish gentlemen—was rubbing salt on open sores. *Home as Found* and *The Redskins* were onslaughts on the ways of the sacred majority that America could not forgive him for. Yet no counter criticism ever moved Cooper from his conviction that gentlemen of an earlier generation possessed dignity, principles, character, far beyond the speculators and politicians and "small-potato lawyers" of the present time of "moral occultation"; and the difference in favor of the old he traced to the economic basis of the tie-wig gentry. Believing with John Adams that an aristocracy is implicit in every established society, he frankly preferred a landed to a capitalistic aristocracy. Gentlemen of the old school were neighborhood patriarchs. Secure in position and possessions they disdained to keep an ear to the ground or court a silly popularity. They were squires with a high sense of responsibility to themselves and society. Their stake in the land was a stabilizing influence in their lives; and their ample way of living, their well-bred leisure, their courteous bearing learned from a cosmopolitan experience, seemed to Cooper a desirable influence in a society lacking refinement and exact standards. To supplant them with the new gentry of Wall Street seemed to him plain folly, and he watched the decay of the old families with a pathetic concern. The Anti-Rent novels are a long defense of a thesis that comes to final expression in such a passage as this from *The Redskins:*

I say that, in a country like this, in which land is so abundant as to render the evils of a general monopoly impossible, a landed gentry is precisely what is most needed for the higher order of civilization, including manners, tastes, and the minor principles, and is the very class which, if reasonably maintained and properly regarded, would do the most good at the least risk of any social caste known. (Chapter XXVI.)

It is not hard, indeed, to understand Cooper's preference for Stephen Van Rensselaer the Patroon, to John Jacob Astor the fur trader, or Commodore Vanderbilt the ferryman; yet such preference was charged against him as un-American.

It was this revulsion from the meanness of the present that sent Cooper into the wilderness or out on the high seas, to seek adventure in the company of nature's noblemen, and forget the sordidness of the real. Here again the French school prompted his thinking, if only to supplement the romance of his boyish recollections. Natty Bumppo is quite evidently man as he came from the hand of nature, uncorrupted by the vices of the settlements; indeed one might question whether the back-to-nature literature can show another figure so enduringly vital as the Leatherstocking. From this same material is fashioned Uncas and the younger Chingachgook and still other lovable figures of his romances. They belong to the free wilderness beyond the settlements, where the dramatic flight and pursuit go on unchecked by impertinent fences. Here their native virtues expand and their generous gifts find ample play. They shunned the settlements as Cooper shunned them. On the frontier, the middle ground between nature and civilization, Cooper's spirits flagged. He had no love for the stumpy clearings, the slovenly cabins, the shiftless squatters; the raw devastation of the ax grieved him and he breathes contentedly only after he has left the last scars behind and is in the deep woods beyond the smell of rum. Such a man obviously was unfitted to write a just account of the frontier as it straggled westward. He hated its ways too fiercely to do justice to it, and when he comes upon it in his tales, when he introduces a frontier figure such as Ishmael Bush in *The Prairie* or old Aaron Thousandacres in *The Chainbearer*, it is to depict the unhappy state of society where the virtues of nature are gone and the refinements of civilization not yet come. No writer has set down a more sweeping indictment of the frontier than Cooper, and he set it down because the frontier seemed to him the muddy source of the vulgar leveling he hated so heartily. A gentleman, whether Indian or squire or scout, Cooper loved to be with; but a vulgarian he could not endure, and a rascal stirred his Puritan wrath. In consequence there runs through his work little of the amusing picaresque strain that the heartier nature of Gilmore Simms delighted in, and that made him a truer chronicler of frontier ways.

Democrat though he professed to be, Cooper shrank from the logical application of the democratic principle. The adoption of manhood suffrage in New York brought in its train a sorry scramble of demagogues to sway the popular will, a debasement of the press, and a vulgarizing of political life that proved a sore trial to Cooper's faith. He was too severely moralist to enjoy the little weaknesses of human nature, but must set himself up as custodian of public morals. Affronted by a bumptious vulgarity, he became the assailant rather than the critic of Jacksonian ways. The land to which he returned in 1833 was a broad target for his shafts and he sent them into the white. The America of log cabins and hard cider seemed to him to have repudiated the traditional standards, moral as well as cultural, and he attributed the disintegration to the corruption that came from the extension of the suffrage to

classes unprepared to use it wisely. It was this that embittered
his criticism in the caustic pages of *Homeward Bound* and *Home
as Found*. He was startled and resentful at the changes. "You
have been dreaming abroad," remarked one of the characters in
the former, "while your country has retrograded, in all that is
respectable and good, a century in a dozen years" (*Homeward
Bound*, Chapter XVII). The colossal brag, the meaningless unrest, the abysmal provincialism, he marked as the natural by-
products of the mob mind. In throwing off its old restraints
America was coming to deny all standards of decency and excellence. "What then do you deem our greatest error—our weakest
point?" asks one of his characters, and the reply is explicit:

> Provincialisms, with their train of narrow prejudices, and a disposition
> to set up mediocrity as perfection, under the double influence of an ig-
> norance that unavoidably arises from a want of models, and of the irre-
> sistible tendency to mediocrity in a nation where the common mind so
> imperiously rules. (*Home as Found*, Chapter XXV.)

It was during the bustling decade of the forties, when the agrarian unrest in York State was putting in jeopardy the old
manorial system, that Cooper's antagonism to the spirit of leveling became bitterest; and it was in defense of the old system that
he wrote the Anti-Rent trilogy that should always be set over
against the Leatherstocking tales. Taken together the two series
contain pretty much the whole of Cooper, his sea tales excepted;
either alone gives an inadequate and partial view. The one is a
social study, the other a romantic epic. The one gives a picture of
the changes the years have brought to a given region, the other
follows the retreating wilderness as the frontier moved westward.
The Anti-Rent novels present the reverse of the romantic picture
of the Leatherstocking tales. Their central figure is Aaron Thousandacres the squatter, who has come out of Connecticut to
possess what pleases him, regardless of legal rights. Offspring
of generations of covetous, psalm-singing Puritans, he has no
difficulty in justifying his lawlessness by Yankee logic. The
devil can quote Scripture, and in this respect old Thousandacres
is the devil's own son. When Scripture fails the easy gospel of
natural rights comes to his aid; the written law may be on the
side of the title-holder, but natural law is on the side of the
squatter.

"There's two rights to all the land on 'arth, and the whull world over," the squatter replied to Chainbearer's legal argument. "One of these rights is what I call a king's right, or that which depends on writin's, and laws, and sich like contrivances; and the other depends on possession. It stands to reason, that fact is better than any writin' about it can be." (*The Chainbearer*, Chapter XXV.)

Such lax doctrine, to Cooper, was the evil fruit of the spirit of lawlessness that was laying a blight upon America. A retributive bullet ends the fierce career of old Thousandacres, but his tigress wife, his rough sons and slattern daughters are driven from their home to plunge deeper into the wilderness, there to beget other generations of squatters whose vicious doctrines return to plague society. No romance blends with the tale of their lives; no sympathy softens the picture of the stern old Yankee. He has set himself against law and order and must yield or be destroyed. It is the old story of the struggle for land, a struggle that went on for generations between speculator and squatter, between rich and poor, with much wrong and much right on both sides; yet Cooper's sympathies are cold to the squatter's plea and he enlists God, morality, and the law, in defense of a title to forty thousand acres wheedled from the Indians for ninety-six pounds, York currency, spent in trinkets. Righteousness without a sense of humor is not easy to live with.

In much of his later work Cooper's romantic impulses are held in check by a growing tendency towards realism. It was there from the first but as he grew more critical it spread over more of his pages. He tried to hold the scales of his judgment even, but his realism was marred and distorted by his vehement nature. A mind exuding prejudice is ill equipped to deal objectively with material, and Cooper was too inveterate a moralist to accept the principle of impersonal detachment. He prided himself on facing fact, but he loved to preach; and having pointed out the wrongfulness of vicious morals he must follow it with a vigorous homily on right conduct. And yet despite his gross shortcomings there is a deal of realism scattered through his volumes. He consciously tried to be a chronicler of manners, to depict America truly, to recreate fairly present and past, red man and white, Dutch and Yankee. His prejudices certainly got the better of him in dealing with New England, and his romance certainly got the better of him in describing the Mohicans. Yet though he might roman-

ticize Uncas he did not romanticize Saucy Nick in *Wyandotté*,
but drew an excellent picture of the struggle between the drunkard
and the warrior in the heart of the Tuscarora that reveals much of
the Indian nature—an analysis that holds the scales more evenly
than they are held in *The Last of the Mohicans* or in Bird's *Nick
of the Woods*. The book as a whole, indeed, is an excellent example
of Cooper's desire to substitute a critical for a romantic treatment
of materials. In his discriminating analysis of the motives separating families in the Revolutionary war, there is no glorification
of partisanship, no prejudiced espousal of a sacred cause, no division of sheep and goats. Cooper will have none of the cheap romance of patriotism, but probes skillfully into the motives and
impulses that divided honest men amid the difficulties of civil war.
More than that, he makes his villain one of the patriot party who
uses the unsettlement of the times to cover his dirty tracks. It is
a characteristic document that deserves to stand beside *Satans-
toe* as an example of his later work.

Politics was all about Cooper while he was writing these tales,
and his sporadic incursions into criticism led him into the field of
political theory. So doughty a warrior must break a lance when
all America was engaged in a great political tourney. While Whig
and Democrat were loudly professing allegiance to the new doctrine of majority rule, Cooper was making his way back to the
principles of the eighteenth century and discovering the essence of
good government in self-restraint. The mistake of the new school,
he was convinced, lay in confusing the present will of the majority
with the rule of the people; the mistake of the old school lay in
confusing the will of the minority with the rule of the people.
Above and beyond both majority and minority is the eternal
principle of justice, and any government that flouts that principle
is bad government, no matter how sanctioned. In a republic
which foolishly believes that the voice of the people is the sole
criterion of right, the problem of justice is peculiarly difficult, for
what remedies are available in cases "in which the people themselves
happen to go astray, *en masse*"? It is the problem that attends
every ethical interpretation of sovereignty, and it awakened acute
concern in Cooper's mind. He could find no solution except in the
good sense of the people, and with a vicious press and persuasive
demagogues doing their best to befuddle the public mind, the outlook seemed dark. It was not the people he distrusted, but the

self-seekers who set up to be leaders of the people. All the noise was made by demagogues who proclaimed their own mouthings to be authentic public opinion. How ineffectively Cooper struggled with the problem is written down in many a passage in his critical novels.

God help the nation [he said in *The Redskins*] where self-government, in its literal sense, exists. . . . When a people that has been properly educated by experience calmly selects its agents, and coolly sets to work to adopt a set of principles to form its fundamental law or constitution, the machine is on the right track, and will work well enough so long as it is kept there; but this running off and altering the fundamental principles every time a political faction has need of recruits, is introducing tyranny in its worst form—a tyranny that is just as dangerous to real liberty as hypocrisy is to religion. (Chapter XIII.)

Some observers pretend that . . . respect for law is gradually decreasing among us [he argued in *The Chainbearer*] and that in its place is sensibly growing up a disposition to substitute the opinions, wishes, and interests of local majorities, making the country subject to men instead of principles. The last are eternal and immutable; and coming of God, men, however unanimous in sentiment, have no more right to attempt to change them, than to blaspheme His holy name. All that the most exalted and largest political liberty can ever beneficially effect is to apply these principles to the good of the human race, in the management of their daily affairs; but when they attempt to substitute for these pure and just rules of right, laws conceived in selfishness and executed by the power of numbers, they merely exhibit tyranny in its popular form, instead of in its old aspect of kingly and aristocratic abuses. It is a fatal mistake to fancy that freedom is gained by the mere achievement of a right to govern, unless the manner in which that right is to be both understood and practised is closely incorporated with all popular notions of what has been obtained. The right to govern means no more than the right of the people to avail themselves of the power thus acquired to apply the great principles of justice to their own benefit, and from the possession of which they had hitherto been excluded. It confers no power to do that which is inherently wrong, under any pretense whatever. (Chapter XXVIII.)

Like Hugh Henry Brackenridge before him, Cooper was a democrat who criticized the ways of a reputed democracy because of his love for an ideal republic. Too few of his kind have arisen in America; too few who dare to speak their minds unterrified by public opinion. An individualist of the old English breed, he could not be intimidated or coerced in the matter of his rights by any clamor, whether of newspapers or mobs. He had his shortcomings in plenty, both as romancer and critic. Testy, opinionated, tactless, forever lugging in disagreeable truths by the ears, he said many wise things so blunderingly as to make truth doubly offensive, and he hewed at his art so awkwardly as well-nigh to destroy the beauty of his romance. Yet the more intimately one comes to know him, the more one comes to respect his honest, manly nature that loved justice and decency more than popularity. His daily life became a long warfare with his fellows, who exacted of him a great price for his idealism; but later generations should love him none the less for the battles he fought. That America has been so tardy in coming to know him as a man and a democrat, as well as a romancer, is a reflection upon its critical acumen.

CHAPTER V

SOME CONTRIBUTIONS OF NEW ENGLAND

IT was the good fortune of New York to draw to the bustling city some of the best and most vigorous minds of New England. If the sons of Yankees flocked thither, the sons of Puritans came likewise, and the contributions of these latter to the idealism of a society rather too fond of material progress must not be overlooked. The literature of New York in particular was heavily indebted to New England. One need only run over a list of writers who came from New England to realize how great was its total contribution to the production of the New York group. Bryant and Halleck and Willis and Greeley and Beecher and Curtis and Tuckerman and Parke Benjamin and Stedman and Stoddard and even, in a sense, Melville, were products of that more serious-minded world that was to create transcendentalism and issue in strange projects of social reform; they were men who would easily share the ethical enthusiasm of their Puritan fellows, and create a literature concerned with other than aesthetic values. Not all of them were Puritan in ideals; Halleck and Willis quite evidently not; nevertheless the severe idealism of their work sets it apart from the productions of the Knickerbocker school. Perhaps not above, but certainly apart; and this unlikeness calls for some special consideration. Over against Irving and Paulding and Cooper may be set Bryant and Greeley and Melville, and the sharp contrast between them will serve to differentiate the native mind of New York from that of New England.

I

WILLIAM CULLEN BRYANT
Puritan Liberal

For upwards of half a century now too much of Bryant has been obscured by the brightness of his early fame. Since his death a serious injustice has been done him by the critics, who have dwelt too exclusively on his work in the field of verse to the neglect of other work in fields perhaps quite as significant. The journalist has been forgotten in the poet, the later democrat who spcke for American liberalism has been displaced by the youthful versifier who described American scenery. For this our bellettristic historians, who are impatient of any incursions into matter of fact, are to blame. Yet to ignore so much of Bryant results in underestimating him, and this serves to explain the thin and shadowy quality of his present reputation. He was a much larger man and more significant than the critics have made him out to be. His active and many-sided life is very inadequately expressed in the slender volume of his verse, excellent as much of that is. The journalist and critic who for fifty years sat in judgment on matters political and economic as well as cultural, who reflected in the *Evening Post* a refinement of taste and dignity of character before unequaled in American journalism, was of service to America quite apart from his contribution to our incipient poetry. He was the father of nineteenth-century American journalism as well as the father of nineteenth-century American poetry. In the columns of the *Evening Post* the best liberalism of the times found a place, inspired and guided by Bryant's clear intelligence. The lucidity of his comment and the keenness of his humanitarian criticism set the editor apart from shriller contemporaries, and made him a power for sanity in a scurrilous generation. But with his death the evanescent character of even the highest journalism asserted itself, and with the fading of his journalistic reputation the earlier Bryant of *Thanatopsis* shouldered aside the Bryant of the *Evening Post*, and an unconscious distortion of his career began, a distortion made easier by the fact that no outstanding work of the later period remained to restore the balance. In this he is like Jefferson. He is scattered piecemeal through his occasional writings as the latter through his letters, and the task of piecing him together and visualizing his work as a whole has not yet been done.

It will not prove an easy task. The narrow but real genius of Bryant is peculiarly elusive. His was essentially a self-pollenizing nature that needed few contacts with other minds. He lived within himself, little swayed by modes of thought, slowly maturing the native fruit of his speculation. The very tenacity and persistence of his intellectual life, the rigid integrity of his thinking, suggest the confidence of one who drew his nourishment from within, whose life was an organic growth. It is impossible to mistake his origins. The roots go down to deep substrata of Puritan seriousness and Puritan austerity, and the fruits which they nourish —somewhat scanty it may be but of firm texture and good keeping qualities—possess the slightly acrid flavor of old Puritan orchards where the care of the husbandman is pitted against harsh seasons and a meager soil. There is no pagan luxuriance, no riot of color or scent. The ethical idealism of New England is given stately form if not rendered altogether lovely; the passion for righteousness is held in restraint but it retains much of its tempered acidity. Happily there was little of the schools in Bryant, and nothing of the intellectual play-boy. His early life in the Berkshire hills, on his father's farm, as student at Williams College for a few months, and as a country lawyer, threw him upon his own intellectual resources and made possible a normal unfolding of his mind. He was fortunately spared a much-coveted life at Yale, where the narrow classicism and ungenerous dogmatisms could have done him little good. From Timothy Dwight the young Bryant could have got little to enrich his mind, and he might have got some disastrous checks. Left to himself he appropriated such nourishment as fell in his way and went forward on the path of a sober liberalism.

That he went forward at all is sufficient testimony to his native integrity of character. In 1825 when he removed to New York, the intellectual renaissance of Boston was just at the beginning, and in his new environment he never quite kept pace with the transcendental enthusiasms that so stimulated the New England radicals. At Great Barrington where he had been growing more discontented with his "shabby" profession of the law, he discovered little to encourage an independent liberalism. Bred up in an environment of intolerant Federalism and an equally intolerant Calvinism, he had much to outgrow and little to feed on. Few innovating ideas penetrated to the Berkshire hills where he was brooding on life and poetry, and the training of his youth was strong upon him. As a mere boy he had expostulated with President Jefferson in shrill heroic couplets, declaiming on the latter's reputed moral lapses and inviting him to resign his high office. He had summoned Napoleon to the bar of Cummington respectability and adjudged him guilty of high crimes against humanity; but such rhetorical outbursts were only echoes of a narrow world he was soon to outgrow. The blight of the tie-wig school of Fisher Ames did not fasten itself deeply on him, and by the time he had reached his twenties he was moving towards the twin goals towards which liberal New England was moving—the Unitarianism of Channing and the democracy of Jefferson. It was far more difficult for a Berkshire man to think his way through to such revolutionary goals than for a Concord; yet the unschooled Bryant who had never visited Boston till he went there in his twenty-seventh year to read a poem before the Phi Beta Kappa society at Harvard had already outstripped the Cambridge scholastics in the great work of setting his mind free. The stages through which he passed cannot easily be traced, but the fact of his decisive break with the dogmas of his youthful world is plain enough. During the last years at Great Barrington he put himself upon a course of reading and thinking, and from that provocative experience emerged the Bryant that we know. Calvinism and Federalism he put away, and he went up to New York completely new-outfitted in a fashion he never afterwards saw reason to change. In politics and religion, as in poetry, he was a man of few ideas, but those ideas were creative, and determined all his thinking.

For this change that was unconsciously preparing him for his later work on the *Evening Post*, Bryant owed something to his father, who had turned moderate Unitarian, but very much more to the Berkshire family of Sedgwicks, one of whom, Catherine M. Sedgwick, was just beginning her modest career as a "lady novelist;" another, Henry M. Sedgwick, was at the head of the New York bar, wealthy and liberal-minded; and a third, Theodore Sedgwick, Jr., was a trusted adviser on legal and economic matters, on whose pen Bryant came to rely in a difficult situation. Theodore Sedgwick seems to have been a liberal of the English school of Bright and Cobden, a confirmed free trader, and he induced Bryant to undertake a course of reading in political economy. During the years 1822 to 1824 the young man turned away from poetry and law to study Adam Smith, Thornton, and Ricardo, together with a number of pamphlets that issued from the Parliamentary debates over free trade in 1820. The adventure proved stimulating and definitely determined his attitude towards men and measures at a moment when American ideas were in a state of flux. It was therefore as an English liberal that he judged Jackson and

Clay and Webster, and as an English liberal that he weighed the Utopian programs of Greeley and Brisbane and Ripley. There is no evidence that he read the works of the French romantics, although the major ideas of Rousseau came to him in the guise of Unitarianism; and this aloofness from the social enthusiasm of French thought, this failure to sympathize with the idealism of the new sociology, may perhaps be accounted his greatest intellectual shortcoming. Rousseau and Godwin and Mary Wollstonecraft could have taught him much that he needed to know, could have warmed his cool blood and awakened his Puritan sense of justice to the wrongs of an exploitative order. A dash of Utopian enthusiasm would have made him a better poet and a better editor; but lacking that he found himself sometimes out of sympathy with men and women whom he should have understood better. A liberal might smile at the measureless zeal of Fanny Wright and Robert D. Owen; might dislike the militancy of the Abolitionists; he might well counsel moderation; but he should not add his shaft to the flight sent against them. But unfortunately Bryant too often distrusted those who outran him, and would rather attack than restrain them.[1]

As an English liberal it was inevitable that Bryant should turn Democrat and support Jackson against Clay and Adams; and an ardent Democrat he remained till the re-alignment over the slavery question turned him into a free-soiler. He early supported Lincoln for the Republican nomination—the more easily because members of his family had removed to Illinois and there followed the career of Lincoln sympathetically—and he accepted the Republican faith till the open alliance of the party with post-war capitalism aroused his opposition and weakened his allegiance. Democrat though he was in conviction and sympathy, Bryant was never a Jeffersonian, perhaps not even a Jacksonian, but rather an anti-Whig, who measured the new America of the industrial revolution and capitalistic finance by the yardstick of eighteenth-century liberalism. As a disciple of Adam Smith, believing in the sufficiency of *laissez faire*, he looked askance at an engrossing political state that enlisted its sovereign powers on the side of the longest purses, and he viewed with scorn the mercenaries of the bench and Senate who defended the new citadels

[1] See his satire on Fanny Wright in *The Evening Post*, January 29, 1829, quoted by Allan Nevins, *The Evening Post*, etc., pp. 126–127.

of capitalism. In spite of his augmenting wealth he remained a simple countryman at heart, never a city man, never liking the ways of Wall Street, concerned with other things than money-making. If he had supplemented Adam Smith with Du Pont de Nemours he might easily have followed Jefferson into a Physio-cratic agrarianism; if he had been bred in the frontier West he might have discovered more sympathy for a coonskin equalitarianism with its engrossing majority will. As it was, he occupied a middle ground between Jefferson and Jackson, an economic individualist who refused to conceive of the political state as a fat cow to be milked by whoever could lay hands on her. He wanted no share of the milk for himself and he saw no reason why others should have any. He turned his back on all middle-class temptations, refusing to speculate, not grasping at unearned increment, be-lieving that America had a nobler destiny in store than could be measured by exploitation. An old-fashioned liberal, he set himself resolutely against the exploitative spirit that was clamor-ing for internal improvements, a protective tariff, speculative prof-its. The bitter struggle over the Bank and the American System, in which he was drawn to Jackson by principle as well as by admira-tion for his courage, laid the emphasis in his mind on financial and industrial problems and made him the outstanding journalistic op-ponent of Henry Clay. From first to last Bryant was anti-Whig.

There were times, to be sure, when he went further than that; times when his ingrained liberalism threw off its cool restraint and flamed up in dangerously disturbing fashion. In the depths of his Puritan nature was a quick sense of justice that might un-cover strange potentialities; and associated as he was in the inti-macies of daily work with two of the most radical spirits in New York, William Leggett and Parke Godwin, he could not remain untouched by their social enthusiasms. The former was a man of immense vitality and boundless sympathies, to whom social justice was a religion. A left-wing equalitarian democrat, Leggett hated all tariffs, subsidies, monopolies, credit manipulation, everything that the new capitalism represented. His sympathies were enlisted on the side of the new proletarian movement, and with the zeal of a knight-errant he greeted every opportunity to do battle for the cause. A home-made radical, created out of the native economics of the industrial revolution, he has been called by a late historical writer "one of the most sincere and brilliant apostles of democracy that America has ever known." His political leaders in the *Evening Post* aroused the admiration of such different men as Whittier and Walt Whitman, and were "perhaps the most potent force in shaping the ideas of democracy" held by the latter (Allan Nevins, *The Evening Post, etc.*, p. 141). His son-in-law, Godwin, on the other hand, was a radical of the imported school, an ardent disciple of Fourier, deeply concerned with communistic experiments at Brook Farm and elsewhere, and an assistant editor of *The Harbinger*, the mouthpiece of Brook Farm after it passed from transcendental to Fourierist control. His *Democracy, Pacific and Constructive*, was accounted by Horace Greeley the best of the contemporary studies of collectivism. Less militant than Leggett, his radicalism ebbed with the years and growing prosperity, but it sufficed to instruct Bryant in the elements of the current Utopian philosophies.

With such associates the older man was led somewhat unwillingly into the thick of social struggle and his mind shifted unconsciously to the left. The movement of Locofocoism in particular absorbed Leggett and drew Bryant after him. Set on foot by a combination of reforming economists opposed to banks, paper money, and monopolies, and the rising proletarian movement then beginning its long struggle to unionize the city workers, Locofocoism represented the extreme left wing of democratic equalitarianism, the avowed objective of which was to take government out of the hands of bankers and lodge it in the hands of the producers. It was one of the first native attempts at conscious class alignment between capital and labor. "What distinguishes the present from every other struggle in which the human race has been engaged," wrote Fanny Wright, "is that the present is evidently, openly and acknowledgedly a war of class. . . . It is the ridden people of the earth who are struggling to overthrow the 'booted and spurred riders' whose legitimate title to work and starve will no longer pass current" (quoted by Fox, *Aristocracy in the Politics of New York*, p. 396). How the democratic radicalism of Leggett was received by conservative New York is thus described by the historian of the *Evening Post:*

He was charged [says Nevins] with Utopianism, agrarianism, Fanny-Wrightism, Jacobinism, and Jack Cade-ism. His writings were said to set class against class, and to threaten the nation with anarchy. Gov. William M. Marcy called Leggett a "knave." The advance of the Locofoco movement was likened to the great fire and the great cholera plague of these years. When Chief Justice Marshall died in the summer of 1835, Leggett unsparingly assailed him and Hamilton as men who had tried "to change the character of the government from popular to monarchical," and to destroy "the great principle of human liberty." . . . Ex-Mayor Philip Hone was handed that editorial on the Albany steamboat by Charles King, and dropped the journal with the vehement ejaculation, "Infamous!" "This is absolutely a species of impiety for which I want words to express my abhorrence," he entered in his diary. (Allan Nevins, *The Evening Post, etc.*, p. 152.)

The enthusiasm of Leggett sometimes carried further than the more tempered liberalism of Bryant could follow. He shared Leggett's distrust of Marshall and Hamilton, but he seems to have been only a moderate supporter of Locofoco principles. The paper had been brought close upon financial breakers by its attack on the money-interests. The working classes read it eagerly, but their indorsement could not make good the loss of advertising and patronage by the wealthy; yet even in such straits Bryant remained true to his liberalism and joined his associates in upholding the proletarian cause. The labor union movement had aroused the wrath of the employers and the courts were appealed to to suppress it. In May, 1836, "twenty-one journeymen tailors who had formed a union were indicted for a conspiracy injurious to trade and commerce," and after a trial the presiding judge charged the jury to bring in a verdict of guilty. Bryant at once attacked the judge in the *Evening Post:*

We do not admit, until we have further examined the question, that the law is as laid down by the Judge; but if it be, the sooner such a tyrannical and wicked law is abrogated the better. . . . The idea that arrangements and combinations for certain rates of wages are injurious to trade and commerce, is as absurd as the idea that the current prices of the markets, which are always the result of understandings and combinations, are injurious. (*Ibid.*, pp. 164-165.)

When the tailors were heavily fined by the court Bryant returned to the attack. He again pointed out the fatuousness of the legal logic by showing how the very price current was a similar evidence of conspiracy, and then appealed to a sense of common fairness:

Can anything be imagined more abhorrent to every sentiment of generosity and justice, than the law which arms the rich with the legal right to fix, by assize, the wages of the poor? If this is not slavery, we have forgotten its definition. Strike the right of associating for the sale of labor from the privileges of a freeman, and you may as well bind him to a master, or ascribe him to the soil. (*Ibid.*, p. 165.)

From defending the rights of free labor to defending the rights of free speech, was an easy step. When James G. Birney's Abolitionist press was suppressed by a Cincinnati mob, Bryant spoke out vigorously. "So far as we are concerned, we are resolved that this despotism shall neither be submitted to nor encouraged. . . . We are resolved that the subject of slavery shall be, as it ever has been, as free a subject for discussion, and argument, and declamation, as the difference between whiggism and democracy, or the difference between Arminians and Calvinists" (*ibid.*, p. 171). And when Elijah P. Lovejoy was murdered and his press thrown into the river, Bryant replied to those who believed that the Abolitionists had got their deserts: "Whether they erred or not in their opinions, they did not err in the conviction of their right, as citizens of a democratic State, to express them; nor did they err in defending their rights with an obstinacy that yielded only to death" (*ibid.*, pp. 171–172). From the defense of free speech Bryant went forward to the defense of free soil, and in 1848 he bolted Lewis Cass, the Democratic nominee, and joined the "Barnburner" movement that nominated Martin Van Buren. The terse pronouncement of the convention, indeed, might well be taken as an epitome and summary of Bryant's lifelong liberalism—"We inscribe on our banner Free Soil, Free Speech, Free Labor, and Free Men."

A trenchant critic of the rising capitalism, delighting in exposing the fallacies of the new economics and in pricking the bladders of political reputations—suggesting, for example, that it was scarcely god-like of the great Webster to accept a purse of $65,000 from his high tariff friends—Bryant was perhaps the most distinguished of the liberals created by the revolutions that were enthroning the middle class in power. The simplicity of his *laissez-faire* philosophy, like his admiration for "Old Bullion" Benton—whom he rated one of the greatest statesmen of the times—may seem somewhat old-fashioned today; but his ingrained democracy, his sturdy defense of the rights of free men, his championship of unpopular causes, his tolerance and fairness and keen sense of justice, ought not to seem old-fashioned. He may not have been a great poet, but he was a great American.

II

HORACE GREELEY

Yankee Radical

Horace Greeley has suffered far more disastrously than Bryant the common fate of journalists, yet his place in nineteenth-century America was too important and his influence on current democratic ideals too great, to be carelessly ignored. A Yankee radical transported to New York, he was the spokesman of the common sense and practical intelligence of the plain people of the North, seeking to understand the revolutionary upheaval then going forward, and bring it if possible to some issue in elementary justice. Far from being the visionary he was so often accounted, he was the most practical of men, accepting fact and seeking to square theory with reality; as ready to adopt new social machinery as the mill-owner to adopt a new invention. If there were social maladjustments, why should they not be set right? The patent confusions of the times seemed to him a challenge to the common intelligence. If civilization meant anything it ought to mean a generous life for the producing mass, and with the abundant resources of America the common well-being would never lie in jeopardy if simple justice prevailed. America had not yet fulfilled its promise; it had not yet become the haven for the poor and outcast its potential means allowed; nor with its growing cities where poverty found a congenial home, and its patrimony of raw lands flung to speculators, was it likely to become so unless greater ingenuity were applied to the problem. The industrial revolution was driving western civilization into uncharted seas; clearly, it was only common sense to take bearings and lay as fair a course as possible. To accomplish this Greeley was ready to entertain any promising suggestion. Intellectually curious, he had the wit to understand that the older agrarian America was being destroyed by forces that could not be stopped; they could only be guided. His eyes were wide open to what was taking place. He foresaw certain consequences implicit in the industrial revolution that his fellows were blind to. If it brought material advancement and the multiplication of conveniences—things excellent in themselves —it brought as well a sinister exploitation of the producers, as England with her Manchester slums had learned to her sorrow. If America were driving straight toward such dead-seas of wretch·

edness, surely only a conscienceless fool would refuse to help trim the sails.

No more admirable Yankee than Horace Greeley ever went West to make his fortune. With his Yankee capacity for hard work, his daring enterprise, his vigorous independence, he embodied an extremely sensitive social conscience, keen sympathy for those who do the work of the world, and a transparent honesty of mind and purpose. Bred up in the narrow poverty of the Vermont hills, remote from the culture of Boston and Cambridge, he retained the angularities that marked his frontier origin. His ungainly and shabby exterior was the outward, visible sign of a niggardly youth; yet underneath the uncouth exterior was as warm a heart as ever beat in Yankee bosom. His early life was a bitter struggle, aggravated by the succession of economic depressions that from 1819 to 1838 repeatedly brought hardship upon the country. Cradled thus in the anxieties attending the transition from an agrarian to a capitalistic order, nurtured in the harassing uncertainties that followed the break-up of the old static economy, he longed for a more rational social system, unsoiled by the heart-breaking wreckages that drifted into the new slums, unembittered by the lonely tragedies that laid a blight on the frontier. He believed that the honest worker, whether in the factory or on the farm, deserved a better fate than commonly fell to his lot. It was a scandal that poverty should dog his footsteps in a land potentially so rich as America; that those who did the necessary work of society should find themselves reduced to the status of the slave, whether black or white; and he early determined to explore the reasons why the workingman received so small an increment of the augmenting wealth of the industrial revolution. His struggles to gain a foothold in New York set him upon thinking, and before he was thirty he began those speculations on ways and means of returning to the producer a fair reward for his work, that were to occupy his mind to the last. The farmer and the wage-earner he took to his heart, and the furtherance of their well-being—despite the persistent and vindictive opposition he encountered—became a major objective of *The Tribune*.

Greeley's mind was as homespun as his clothes, and he never quite outgrew certain Vermont parochialisms that retarded his intellectual development. The environment in which he was bred was staunchly Federalist-Whig, marked by the exuberantly nationalistic spirit that sprang from the War of 1812; and the seeds of his national economy were sown in those years when to become nationally self-sufficient was the great ideal of America. It was natural for him to accept the leadership of Clay, whom he idolized, and to look to the Federal government for an adequate policy of internal improvements and national development. "We Vermonters were all Protectionists," he said in his *Recollections*. In 1828 the village of Poultney, where he was serving his apprenticeship, gave 334 votes for John Quincy Adams and only four for Jackson. Starting with this back-country faith in a benevolent paternalism, Greeley early began his speculations on an ideal national economy; and the conclusion to which he came, and which he never saw reason to question later, was that government must impose an intelligent wardship upon economic forces, that, left to themselves, tend always to the anarchy of individualism. He had suffered in his own person from the inadequacy and uncertainty of the financial and industrial machinery of the times; he was impatient of all purposeless floundering; the more he read the more rational it seemed that statesmanship must be judged by its intelligent concern to lessen the social waste and reduce the social friction. *Laissez faire* he pronounced a "suicidal" policy; it was an invitation to anarchy; it had impoverished India, and must impoverish America. From a critical study of the teachings of the Manchester school he came to two major conclusions: that agriculture and manufacturing are complementary industries, and the closer they are drawn together the better for the nation; and that a wide national economy can result only from investing the state with adequate regulatory powers. Hence his approval of Clay's American System. The judicious intervention of government by means of a protective tariff to foster the "infant industries," would secure them a domestic market that would—he allowed himself to hope—be regulated by domestic competition, would do away with the waste represented by transportation charges, and would return to the farmer an increase in price represented by those charges. In his opinion, however, protection was a temporary expedient, necessary only until American industries should get on their legs. "Protection is the shortest way to get free trade," he said in 1851 (*The Tribune*, January 23).

Greeley was never the tool of capitalistic interests that such an argument might seem to imply. All his mature life he persistently fought the aggressions of capitalism; yet in this crucial matter of protection his influence was thrown powerfully on its side, and the ingenious argument he expounded was at once taken over by the industrialists and used with telling effect. What particular turn he gave to the older Whig statement, adapting it to the prejudices of a more democratic electorate, a present-day economist has thus summarized:

The protective tariff, favored by the Whigs, was something different in his hands. The tariff arguments of his boyhood had been capitalistic arguments. Protect capital, their spokesman said, because wages are too high in this country. Eventually wages will come towards the European level and we shall not need protection. Greeley revised this plea; protect the wage earner, he said, in order that he may rise from this present condition of slavery. The only way to protect him against the foreign pauper is to protect the price of his product. But since capital owns and sells his product, we must needs protect capital. We know right well, he says, that a protective tariff cannot redress all wrongs. . . . The extent of its power to benefit the laborer is limited by the force and pressure of domestic competition, for which Political Economy has as yet devised no remedy. (John R. Commons, "Horace Greeley and the Working Class Origins of the Republican Party," *Political Science Quarterly*, Vol. XXIV, pp. 468–488.)

The argument for protection has been little improved since it came from Greeley's hands in the late forties and early fifties.[2] Nor, it must be added, has political economy devised the remedy for the evils of competition, that Greeley was concerned about, unless monopolistic control be regarded as such. Considering his extraordinary influence with the mass of farmers north and west, it must be accounted a calamity to agrarian prospects that *The Tribune*—a paper that Professor Commons characterized as "the first and only great vehicle this country has known for the ideas and experiments of constructive democracy"—should have thrown its influence on the side of artificial industrial expansion. That the mind of the northern farmer became so deeply inoculated with protectionist views, and has since persistently remained so, was due to Horace Greeley far more than to any other man.

The irony of it becomes apparent when the deeper spirit of Greeley's life is probed. Though he called himself a Whig, he was in all fundamental interests and conceptions a Jeffersonian, seeking in the spirit of the great Virginian to fashion a new philosophy to suit

[2] For his statement, see "Labor's Political Economy," in *Hints toward Reforms*.

the new times, more like him in free speculation than any other northern thinker of the day. It needed years for him to throw off the Federalist-Whig prepossessions of his youth, and work back to Jeffersonian fundamentals; but in the end he did work back, and in the end—always excepting this one matter of protection with its corollary of state paternalism—he came by his own path to the major conclusions Jefferson had reached a half century before. He was a spokesman of the older America seeking a way out of the confusions the middle class was bringing on the later America. In his social-mindedness that set justice above exploitation; in his readiness to change existing institutions in order to achieve justice; in his strong preference for an agrarian order as more wholesome than an industrial; in his trust in the good will of the plain people and faith in the local democracies; in his acceptance of the principle of states rights that during the struggle over slavery led him to advocate that the South be suffered to depart in peace:—in such conceptions he was a Neo-Jeffersonian, seeking to adapt the old principles to the needs of a different order. Greeley had never read the works of the French Physiocrats; he was unacquainted with their doctrine of the *produit net;* very likely he would not have accepted their teachings to the extent that Jefferson did. Nevertheless from his own experience he had come to agree with them in the exaltation of agriculture over other forms of labor, as he had come to agree with them in their social-mindedness. Greeley may be accounted a stepson, at least, of the old French school.

That for so long a time he should have turned aside from the path of Jeffersonianism to immerse himself in Utopian speculations and adventures may appear strange; and yet for so eager and hopeful a temperament it was the most natural thing in the world. It marked a step in the speculations through which he passed in pursuit of that remedy for domestic competition which the political economists had not provided. He was twenty-nine when Albert Brisbane's *The Social Destiny of Mankind* appeared in 1840, and on October 21, 1841, the first comment on Fourier socialism was printed in *The Tribune*, then only six months old. Thereafter for years *The Tribune* was the chief organ for the spread of collectivistic principles in the United States, Brisbane expounding Fourierism in the fifties, and Karl Marx contributing a weekly letter on European movements in the sixties, while lesser men contributed freely according to their special Utopian lights. With all this Greeley was in profound sympathy. Much of the theory he did not agree with; many of the plans and specifications seemed to him ill conceived; but convinced of the gross evils of civilization he welcomed free speculation as promising the only hope for their cure. Like Jefferson and William Ellery Channing, he put his trust in the unshackled mind, for like them he believed in the essential excellence of human nature when unperverted by vicious institutions.

It was this romantic faith that induced him to invest heavily in time, thought and money, in the Fourieristic foundations of the forties, the North American Phalanx in particular offering an opportunity for experiment on a considerable scale. In his deep concern over the selfishness of the competitive struggle, he was willing to turn from the bankrupt political economists to consider the plans of the "social architects." From Plato down those architects had been engaged on plans of ideal commonwealths, wherein the principle of brotherhood should supersede the principle of competition, and he believed the time had come when the great experiment might be tried with some reasonable hope of success. If the principle of collectivism could be successfully substituted for a chaotic individualism, the solution of the ancient problem of social injustice might be in a way to be achieved. This in itself, he believed, "would do for domestic competition what protection would do for foreign competition" (John R. Commons, *Horace Greeley, etc.*). When associationism failed, Greeley turned his thoughts eagerly to coöperation as a promising means of eliminating the waste of the middleman and destroying the wage system.[3] Somehow the middleman must be got rid of, he believed, if labor were to reap an adequate reward from its work. If one method did not achieve the result, another must be tried. To leave off seeking a solution was to acknowledge that society must remain a pigsty, with the strongest hogs appropriating the swill.

Such persistent venturing into Utopian experiment made Greeley the laughing-stock of more practical men who accepted the acquisitive instinct as the voice of God and were busily engaged in exploitation for their individual advantage; more important, it reveals how tenuous were the ties that held him to the Whiggery he still professed. Stalwart Whigs of the Webster

[3] See "The Organization of Labor," in *Hints toward Reforms.*

school, middle-class bankers and industrialists, grew impatient with such pestilent heresies as exuded from *The Tribune*, and denied that Greeley was a Whig. In 1847 *The Courier and Enquirer* angrily protested:

> There can be no peace in the Whig ranks while the old New York Tribune is continued to be called Whig. . . . The *principles* of the Whig party are well defined; they are *conservative* and inculcate a regard for the laws and support of all established institutions of the country. They eschew *radicalism* in every form; they sustain the constitution and the laws; they foster a spirit of *patriotism*. . . . The better way for the Tribune would be at once to admit that it is only Whig on the subject of the Tariff . . . and then devote itself to the advocacy of Anti-Rent, Abolition, Fourierite, and Vote Yourself a Farm doctrines. (*The Weekly Tribune,* August 21, 1847; quoted in Commons, *Horace Greeley, etc.,* p. 473.)

The real animus of the middle-class dislike of Greeley is to be sought in his active championship of the great exploited classes, the farmer and wage-earner. He was always sowing the seeds of discontent amongst them. The betterment of their condition, he believed, was fundamental to any sound social progress. He was convinced that their well-being was interrelated; that whatever affected the one must affect the other. If the city proletariat were prosperous, the farmer's produce sold at better prices; and if the farmers were prosperous, the country would draw off the surplus labor from the towns and thereby sustain the wage scale. The key to the situation, he came to believe, lay in the land situation. The application of science to farm processes was a necessary preliminary to agrarian improvement, and he put the great influence of *The Tribune* behind the movement for scientific instruction in crop handling. But far more fundamental and immediate was the need of a drastic change in the Federal laws governing land sales. Believing that the wild lands of the West were a natural refuge for those who fled from the exploitation of the factory, he was concerned that those lands should be made available to the poorest settler. Greeley very well knew that the ruthless exploitation of the English proletariat was an inevitable consequence of the enclosure movement. Dispossessed of their land and lacking means to emigrate, the peasant had been thrown like sheep to the industrial wolves. Sunk in a hopeless wage-slavery, the Manchester factory-hand was an object-lesson in the fate that awaits the landless, too striking for a shrewd observer like Greeley to miss; and his agrarian program was proof that he had taken Goldsmith's warning to heart:

> Ill fares the land, to hastening ills a prey,
> Where wealth accumulates and men decay.

The freeholder, whatever the hardships of his lot, was still a free man and a free citizen, no fodder to fling to a huge-bellied industrialism.

To keep him thus free and independent, Greeley put himself vigorously into the great agrarian movement of the forties and fifties—the movement to democratize the national land policy that eventuated in the Homestead Act of 1862. The conception of the strategic usefulness of the western lands as a refuge for the city proletariat he derived from George Henry Evans, who in 1828 had established *The Working Man's Advocate*, was active in organization work with the mechanics of New York City, and contributed to the cause numerous pamphlets, one of which, issued in 1844, was entitled *Vote Yourself a Farm*. The pioneer work had been well done when, in 1845, Greeley joined the movement, accepted the arguments, and thenceforth was tireless in spreading the doctrine. The principle on which he should work he laid down in *The Tribune:*

> The freedom of the public lands to actual settlers and the limitation of future acquisitions of land to some reasonable amount, are . . . measures which seem to us vitally necessary to the ultimate emancipation from thraldom and misery. What is mainly wanted is that each man should have an assured chance to earn and then an assurance of the just fruits of his labors. (Quoted in Commons, *Horace Greeley*, etc., p. 482.)

To accomplish this result Greeley introduced into Congress the first Homestead bill, according to the proposed terms of which any *bona fide* settler might file on one hundred and sixty acres of public land, to be paid for within seven years at the rate of $1.25 an acre; all public lands not thus filed on by actual settlers were to be listed at $5.00 an acre.[4] Greeley's bill was aimed directly at the old scandal of favoring wealthy speculators at the expense of the small man, a scandal that ran far back into the past. The traditional argument had been that the government could not go into the retail land business, but should sell in great blocks to responsible men who should in turn put settlers on the land. The

---

[4] See Charles Sotheran, *Horace Greeley*, p. 255.

policy had bred huge corruption, it had aroused bitter opposition, and had roiled the politics of more than one state holding western lands. In the early years of the century the province of Maine had repudiated Massachusetts Federalism and turned to the Republican party by reason of discontent with the old system [5] and the fierce Anti-Rent riots in New York State were of recent occurrence. It was against this policy of favoritism that Greeley protested, thereby bringing on his head sharp criticism from the respectable class, who declaimed bitterly against the demagoguery of a man who openly advocated a "vote yourself a farm" policy. To pay a middleman's price for public land, after that land had been wheedled from Congress in the dark of the moon, seemed to many gentlemen the only honest and patriotic way; but Greeley was unconvinced by such reasoning, and his concern over the problem became acute when the railroads began to appropriate huge tracts of the public domain. The policy of subsidizing them thus seemed to him wasteful and vicious; it ran directly counter to his fundamental principle of limitation of land holdings; it was repeating on a vast scale the ominous landlordism of the past.

Man has a *natural right* to produce and acquire property [he wrote], and therefore, I condemn a system of Land Monopoly, which robs the producer of one-half to seven-eighths of the fruits of his toil; and often dooms him to absolute starvation on the soil which he has faithfully and effectively tilled! The right of owning land is one thing: the right to own thousands and even millions of acres of land is another. The problem is learning to distinguish the one from the other. (*The Tribune*, April 24, 1849.)

"Settle the lands compactly and railroads will be constructed through them rapidly and abundantly," he said later. "The grants do essentially interfere with the true policy of granting lands in limited allotment to actual settlers" (*ibid.*, March 16, 1852). His proposed policy was far-sighted and socially just, but it was repudiated by a speculative middle class that would not have its unearned increment curtailed by visionaries.

Thoughtful as was Greeley's concern for the farmer, his concern for the city worker was even greater. The wretchedness of the New York slums was daily under his eye, and his honest heart was troubled at what he saw. That he should have sympathized with the emerging labor movement was inevitable; his conscience dic-

[5] See William A. Robinson, *Jeffersonian Democracy in New England.* pp. 43-45.

tated his stand, but his eager mind drove him to intelligent inquiry and vigorous support. He was the first American of wide reputation and influence to give serious consideration to the effects on the working class of the industrial revolution with its gospel of exploitation. The exploitation of natural resources was well enough; but the exploitation of human life was a different matter. A material prosperity based on social injustice, a civilization founded on slavery, he would have none of. That this great matter of slavery was inadequately understood and too narrowly interpreted by the Abolitionists, he was early convinced. He agreed with William Grayson and the southern apologists, that slavery existed in New York as well as in Charleston. "The worker of the Nineteenth Century," he said in *The Emancipation of Labor*, "stands a sad and care-worn man"; in America as well as in Europe he is falling into "that train of thought which is beginning to encircle the globe, and of which the burden may be freely rendered thus—'*Why should those by whose toil ALL comforts and luxuries are produced or made available enjoy so scanty a share of them?*'" If Theodore Parker could have lived a few years longer he must have shared Greeley's concern; but amongst the Abolitionists only Wendell Phillips joined with him in espousing the cause of the working class. Others held aloof. When appealed to in the middle-seventies to aid the labor movement, William Lloyd Garrison denied the existence of wage-slavery in America, and indignantly declined to take part in the proletarian agitation.[6]

Greeley's views would be reckoned advanced even today; before the Civil War they were regarded as incendiary, calculated to awaken class prejudice in a country where, as all patriotic Americans knew, classes did not exist. What, for example, could simple-minded Abolitionists make of a letter he wrote declining to attend an anti-slavery convention in Cincinnati in 1845?

You will readily understand that, if I regard your enterprise with less absorbing interest than you do, it is not that I deem Slavery a less but a greater evil. If I am less troubled concerning the Slavery prevalent in Charleston and New-Orleans, it is because I see so much Slavery in New-York, which appears to claim my first efforts. . . . [I would not] undertake to say that the Slavery of the South is not more hideous in kind and degree than that which prevails at the North. The fact that it is more flagrant and palpable renders opposition to it comparatively easy and its speedy downfall certain. But how can I devote myself to a crusade

6 Garrison, *Life of Garrison*, Vol. IV, p. 248.

against distant servitude, when I discern its essence pervading my immediate community and neighborhood?

I understand by Slavery, that condition in which one human being exists mainly as a convenience for other human beings—in which the time, the exertions, the faculties of a part of the Human Family are made to subserve, not their own development, physical, intellectual, and moral, but the comfort, advantage, or caprices of others. . . . In short, wherever service is rendered from one human being to another . . . where the relation . . . is one not of affection and reciprocal good offices, but of authority, social ascendency and power over subsistence on the one hand, and of necessity, servility, and degradation on the other—there, in my view, is Slavery. ("Slavery at Home," in *Hints toward Reforms*.)

Here is a definition that may well be considered Utopian; but however transcendental his general conception, Greeley was far too practical to pursue abstractions. Having diagnosed the common disease that infects all modern civilization, he was willing to use remedies that came to hand. Before 1845 he opposed labor legislation, on the ground that the evil was social; but later he supported the movement to limit the legal working day by statute. More and more, however, he came to believe that any lasting betterment must come from effective organization of the workers; that the salvation of labor lay in its own hands; and the great end towards which he looked was coöperation. The stumbling-block that stood in the way of coöperative effort was the common distrust and suspicion that poisoned the minds of working men; until they emptied their hearts of that evil, the path that labor must follow would be flinty and its life meager and hard.

An incorrigible idealist, clearly, was this Yankee plebeian whom Cooper believed a vulgarian, Godkin held in contempt, and Bryant turned his back on and would not speak to—a strange, child-like figure, with his round moon-face, eyes blinking through spectacles and a fringe of whiskers that invited the pencil of the cartoonist—yet carrying the sorrows of the world in his heart and vexing his soul with all the problems of society; an idealist who in the most sordid place in America, and after years of fruitless experiment, could still stand before his fellow Americans and thus sum up his social philosophy—"the avocations of Life, and the usages and structure of Society, the relations of Power to Humility, of Wealth to Poverty, of served to servant, must all be fused in the crucible of Human Brotherhood, and whatever abides not the test, rejected" (*Hints toward Reforms*, p. 400).

In this faith—foolish it may be accounted by practical men, and
futile, but certainly not mean, not ignoble—Horace Greeley lived
and worked; to it he gave such strength and powers as were his,
and he died at sixty-one of a broken heart.   He foolishly wished
to be President, but the American electorate that read his paper
refused its votes, and his hopes were destroyed by the careless
many who were untroubled about industrial pigstys.

III

HERMAN MELVILLE

Pessimist

Set down beside the austere Bryant and the plebeian Greeley,
Herman Melville seems grotesquely out of company; and yet such
proximities may suggest, better perhaps than words, an explanation of the futility of his dreams and the irony of the bitter penance
of his days.   Lifelong he was lacerated by the coldly moral in
his environment, and harassed by the crudely practical; and without forcing the comparison, one may feel that Bryant and Greeley
embodied in nobler form the twin forces that seized upon his bold
and rich nature, and bound it to the rocks to be fed on by eagles.
Like Jacob he wrestled all night with an angel, yet got no blessing
from the touched thigh.   Instead, his free spirit was tormented and
his adventurous heart seared with fire.   Far more truly than of
De Quincey might one say of Melville: *Eccovi*, this little child has
been in hell!   All the powers of darkness fought over him, all the
devils plagued him.   They drove him down into the gloom of his
tormented soul, and if they did not conquer, they left him maimed
and stricken.   The golden dreams of transcendental faith, that
buoyed up Emerson and gave hope to Thoreau, turned to ashes
in his mouth; the white gleams of mysticism that now and then
lighted up his path died out and left him in darkness.   Life
could not meet the demands he made on it, certainly not life in
America in the eighteen-fifties; the malady lay deeper than Greeley thought—it lay in the futility of life itself; and so after
pursuing his vain dreams to the ends of the seas, the rebellious
transcendentalist withdrew within himself while awaiting annihilation.   There is no other tragedy in American letters comparable
to the tragedy of Herman Melville.   Bryant's melancholy is only
the gentle pensiveness of twilight compared to the midnight of

his pessimism. Hawthorne's gloom is no more than the skeptical questioning of life by a nature that knew no fierce storms; Poe's is only the atrabilious wretchedness of a dipsomaniac.

In the presence of a nature so tempestuous and fiercely honest, it is a rash critic who will dogmatize. There is no simple clue to his mystery, no common pass-key to unlock his mind. Raymond Weaver in his brilliantly creative study has perhaps done all that the critic can to light up the darkness, and later commentators can only follow in his footsteps. In so far as a simple explanation may suffice, the biographer finds it in certain frustrations that curdled the milk of his romance and turned it sour. Like Mark Twain in later years, he recoiled savagely from the smug conventions of society; but when he spoke out his views—instead of discreetly locking them up in his safe—and found himself fiercely assailed for unorthodoxy, he bade the world go to the devil and would have nothing more to do with its praise or blame. A proud sensitive nature, he took the world's contumely *au tragique*, and suffered it to mortify him. Or perhaps he was more like James Branch Cabell than Mark Twain. An arch romantic, he vainly sought to erect his romantic dreams as a defense against reality, and suffered disaster. In love with the ideal, and pursuing it in a wild adventure into the South Seas—his magic realm of Poictesme—yet "not so much bound to any haven ahead as rushing from all havens astern," he found there only disenchantment. Seeking his satisfactions in love of mother and wife, he came upon utter disillusion. The austerely prim and coldly correct Maria Gansevoort, to whom his boyish heart yielded itself passionately, was clearly no woman to satisfy his need of intelligent sympathy, and he fled moodily from the pale negations of a stifling environment. Even the finely loyal Elizabeth Shaw whom he married seems only to have completed his disillusion, and he withdrew into his study, and falling into "Plato's honied head," like Tashtego into the whale's head, "sweetly," or wretchedly, "perished there." It is the plague of the idealizing mind that is forever comparing a wife in her morning kimono with the Helen of his dreams. It is the curse of possession that plays havoc with romance; and because Melville's dreams were passionately beautiful, because he made heavy demands on life, his disillusion was bitter. And so like Felix Kennaston in Cabell's *Cream of the Jest*, and like Shelley in *Epipsychidion*, Melville fashioned his dream-figure to love. The elusive figure of Yillah in *Mardi*, whom he loves and loses and seeks, in a madly grotesque and satirical pursuit through all the civilizations of his land of Poictesme, is so suggestive of Cabell's *Domnei*, that it perhaps may be accounted the latter's prototype.

Remembering the mingled strains of Melville's ancestry, the critic is tempted to discover in his New England blood the source of his transcendental visions. Yet the influence is not easy to trace. Half Dutch and half Yankee, he certainly got his vigorous physique and hot temper from the former. His maternal grandfather, Major General Peter Gansevoort, was a huge bulk of a man who achieved high distinction in the Revolutionary War, and whose traditional prowess filled the boy's heart with pride. His mother, Maria Gansevoort, whom the son closely resembled in physique, was crossed in blood with that of the Van Rensselaers, the Ten Broecks, the Van Schaicks—the proudest families of the old Dutch *régime*—and was deeply imbued with the distinction of her patroon ancestry—"a cold, proud woman, arrogant in the sense of her name, her blood, and the affluence of her forebears" (Weaver, *Herman Melville*, p. 34). His debt to the New England strain is not so easily appraised. His paternal grandfather, Major Thomas Melville of Boston, a graduate of Princeton and wealthy in his own name and through his wife Priscilla Scollay, was not without his flashes of enthusiasm in early life, taking part with Joseph Story's father in the Boston Tea Party. But his incipient radicalism was soon washed out of him; he turned rigidly conservative, and to his death in 1832 he lingered in the twilight of the eighteenth century. As Federal naval officer of the port of Boston, he was a familiar figure in his cocked hat and knee breeches; and it was of him that Holmes wrote the verses, *The Last Leaf*.

He was of Scotch descent, and Melville's father traced the family line back to the thirteenth century, Herman Melville being twentieth in direct descent from Sir Richard Melvill, who in 1296 was forced to swear allegiance to Edward I of England. The blood seems to have run somewhat thin in Allan Melville, a conventional, pragmatic soul, who after making five trips to Europe, at the age of thirty-two, having carefully weighed the advantages, fixed his affections on Maria Gansevoort whom he met at Albany, and wooed with more propriety than passion. He entered business in New York city as an importer of French goods;

but hard times descended on "the greatest universal mart in the world," and in 1832, when Herman was thirteen, Allan Melville died leaving Maria Gansevoort and her eight children pretty nearly penniless. The struggle with poverty set its mark on the cold, proud woman whose ambitions centered about the success of affluence; and it left a mark of quite another sort on the son who was soon to measure her ideals with devastatingly critical eyes. The ways of mother and son were at the parting.

The volcanic passions pent up in Herman Melville's heart, the ardent imagination that sent him forth on long quests and brought him home empty-handed, can scarcely be traced to any source in Maria Gansevoort or Allan Melville. A strange, incomprehensible child he seemed to his mother, and strange and incomprehensible he remained in the eyes of the family—an ugly duckling of another breed than theirs. A bitter sense of aloofness and alienation from the intimacies of family sympathy seems early to have taken possession of him, and he felt himself quietly thrust out of the circle of respectable contacts. Melville's writings are filled with thinly veiled autobiography, and it is a careless reader who does not see in *Pierre* and *Moby Dick* confessions as frank as Rousseau's. "Call me Ishmael," is the opening injunction of the latter, and the book closes with a glimpse of "the devious cruising *Rachel*, that in retracing search after her missing children, only found another orphan" (Weaver, *Herman Melville*, p. 62). An Ishmael Melville unhappily conceived himself to be, an outcast and wanderer on the earth because man is an outcast and wanderer, to whom Nirvana is the only comfort and hope; and when he returned disillusioned from the South Seas, when he found no home by his own fireside, when he discovered his transcendental craftsmanship driving on the rocks of economic necessity, when the public rejected his mystical dreams and he was inexorably "damned by dollars," he perforce turned in upon his own broodings and sought solace in Plato. Driven by need from his hill farm in the Berkshires, he buried himself in the "Babylonish brick-kiln of New York," to pass long years pottering about the customhouse. It was the vast futility of life as he experienced it, that sent him to his study to find there such compensation as he might.

The stages in Melville's progress towards Nirvana are sufficiently marked by the four books, *Typee*, *Mardi*, *Moby Dick*, and *Pierre*. The first is his answer to the French romantic Utopia of man in a state of nature. That the rankling wounds in man's heart are poisoned, if not originally inflicted, by social institutions, he was partly convinced, and he felt a lively concern lest western civilization should bring its futile restlessness to the simple island people. The kindliness and simplicity of life in the valley of Typee, the compensating virtues of the unsophisticated primitive, he found lovable; but as the unhappy heir of centuries of Christian conscience, as a child of Hebraic ideals of righteousness, he could not eradicate the deep roots of ethical unrest. With Fayaway it was different. "Civilization had given her no veils; Christianity had given her no compunctions. She was neither a mystery nor a sin" (*ibid.*, p. 260). But he could not become a simple child of nature had he wanted to. He could never find his Nirvana in mere sensuousness; he could not sink into the mud of animal existence. Even while he bathed in the languorous calm of Typee, floating idly with Fayaway on the stream of being, his heart was beyond the narrow hills, and a cosmic nostalgia seized upon him. That chapter of his life ended in futility, and so he made his way back once more to the familiar places, with expectation still undaunted. Certain of his experiences on that return journey he has recorded in *White Jacket*, the story of his cruise on a man-of-war; and how near it brought him to oblivion is told in the episode of the threatened flogging before the mast, when fate intervened to save Melville from flinging himself overboard, carrying with him the brutal captain of the *Neversink*.

Amidst the constrictions of the old world to which he had come back, a fresh vision of happiness opened to him in his love for Elizabeth Shaw, and he made a desperate plunge into marriage. The post-thalamion of that thwarted romance was *Mardi*—a far-ranging "pilgrimage for a lost glamour," "a quest after some total and undivined possession of that holy and mysterious joy that touched Melville during the period of his courtship" (*ibid.*, p. 279). *Mardi* is a vast welter of satire and idealism, formless and wild, which in turn was no more than prologue to *Moby Dick*. This colossal book, fierce as *Gulliver*, broad as Rabelais, with its *saeva indignatio* that laughs as it rends life, is the great confession of his defeat. "It is good to laugh," he says in *Mardi*, "though the laugh be hollow. Women sob, and are rid of their grief; men laugh and retain it. Ha! ha! how demoniacs shout; how all skeletons grin; we all die with a rattle. Humor, thy laugh is divine."

And the conclusion to which the philosopher comes is this: "Beatitude there is none. And your only Mardian happiness is but exemption from great woes—no more. Great Love is sad; and heaven is Love. Sadness makes the silence throughout the realms of space; sadness is universal and eternal" (*ibid.*, p. 279).

After *Moby Dick*, what remained but to put the external world of experience aside and turn in upon his own thwarted hopes to analyze them? *Pierre, or the Ambiguities* is his spiritual autobiography, the confession of a stricken soul. In the inconsequential matter of plot, a story of incest and murder and suicide, in its deeper purpose, it is a wild fierce tale of mortal passions, that traces the *élan* of mystical idealism to the buried depths of procreative instinct. It is the last bewildering attempt to understand the sources of the dream that had ridden him, and it is discovered in the passionate struggles of Enceladus, titanic offspring of the incestuous union between Heaven and Earth, to regain the kingdom from which he has been thrust. In *Mardi* the search for Yillah had been carried on under the watchful eye of Hautia, the temptress, whom "his whole heart abhorred," yet to whom at last he went in her bower of Flozella-a-Nina—"The-Last-Verse-of-the-Song"; for in "some mysterious way seemed Hautia and Yillah connected." In *Pierre* Hautia reappears as Isabel, likewise a child of Heaven and Earth, who is set over against Lucy—the pure daughter of Heaven alone; and this dark Isabel robed in the midnight of her hair, by appealing unconsciously to Pierre's noblest impulses, draws him from the safe orbit of the Gansevoort moralities, and makes of him "the fool of Truth, the fool of Virtue, the fool of Fate." Isabel is wild, unquestioning, mysterious passion, untouched by any Hebraisms; and this half-sister of his blood, this lovely embodiment of his star-crossed dreams, drives him unwittingly to destruction. Pierre learns at last that the vision brings poison in its kisses, for the divine in the heart of Enceladus is mingled with the clay of earth. The dream is man's final ironical curse; Yillah and Hautia and Lucy and Isabel—changing embodiments of the same mystical idealism—bring death to their lovers—this is the conclusion of *Pierre*, a conclusion that Mr. Cabell would not take kindly to. It was a black and bitter book, like *Moby Dick* "broiled in hell-fire," to fling at an easy-going public that cherished its Gansevoort conventions. With its fierce disillusions *Pierre* is the apogee and Nirvana of the spiritual romanticisms of the day.

That Melville was the spiritual child of Jean Jacques, that the consuming nostalgia he suffered from was mortal, the most casual acquaintance with his passionate rebellions should make clear; and that his pessimism was a natural end and outcome of his transcendental speculations, once those speculations had come to intimate contact with life, is perhaps equally clear. Transcendentalism in Concord village and at Walden pond, was one thing. Emerson's infrequent anger at the folly of men was soothed by the perfect art with which he phrased it, and never seriously ruffled his temperamental placidity. Thoreau's mystical communings were with the young god Pan; he was too wise to seek to domesticate a woodland nymph, and he was fortunate in escaping the dun twilight that gathers about the slow years of physical decay. But transcendentalism in the forecastle of the whaler *Acushnet*, transcendentalism that drove fiercely into the blood-red sunsets of dwarfing seas, transcendentalism in the hot and passionate heart of a man whose vast dreams outran his feet— this was something very different from the gentle mysticism of cooler natures and unembittered hearts where no Promethean fires were raging.

For Herman Melville, amidst the nameless obscenities of an alien environment, to keep his faith in the goodness of life strong and sweet, would have needed the boundless charity and simple paganism of Walt Whitman. But unfortunately for his peace of mind, though he might immerse himself in Plato, Melville was no Greek; he was Hebraic rather, out of Ecclesiastes, and Solomon and Jesus. "Away," he cries in *Pierre*, "ye chattering apes of a sophomorean Spinoza and Plato, who once did all but delude me that the night was day, and pain only a tickle. Explain this darkness, exorcise this devil, ye cannot. Tell me not, thou inconceivable coxcomb of a Goethe, that the universe cannot spare thee and thy immortality. . . . Already the universe gets on without thee. . . . Thou wert but the pretentious, heartless part of a man. Lo! I hold thee in this hand, and thou art crushed in it like an egg from which the meat hath been sucked" (Chapter XXII—3). From the lips of the ancient Preacher he had learned that all is vanity—even Pan. "The truest of men was the Man of Sorrows," he says, "and the truest of all books is Solomon's, and Ecclesiastes is the fine hammered steel of woe. All is vanity. ALL. . . . He who . . . calls Cowper, Young, Pascal, Rousseau,

poor devils all of sick men; and throughout a care-free lifetime
swears by Rabelais as passing wise, and therefore jolly;—not that
man is fitted to sit down on tombstones, and break the green damp
mould with unfathomably wondrous Solomon" (Weaver, *Herman
Melville*, pp. 151–152). After *Pierre* came *Clarel*—years later—
in which the theological doubts and religious unrest that mark
the poetry of Arnold and Clough in England came to expression
in a world that was untouched by them.[7] The abyss that lay
between Melville and America had become deeper and wider.

Like all the transcendentalists Melville was a democrat, but
his democracy sprang rather from his sympathies than from his
philosophy. It was a democracy learned rather from Ecclesiastes
than from Emerson; it sprang from his pessimism rather than
from any transcendental faith in the divinity of man. He knew
only too well how weak and foolish are the children of Adam; but
in presence of the common fate to which the indifferent years
hurry us, how stupid and callous are the social distinctions that
society erects! Why should not life be a leveler, as well as death?
His experience before the mast had taught him sympathy for the
common man; he regarded quizzically the ways of the exploiting
few and the sufferings of the exploited many; and he smiled ironically at the neat little classification that divides the human animal
into sinners and saints. He was as comprehensive a democrat as
Whitman, of the same all-embracing school that denied the
common social and ethical categories of excellence; but alienated
from his fellows, not drawn to them as Whitman was. It was not
a sense of social aloofness that held him apart, but the isolation of
loneliness. "When you see or hear of my ruthless democracy on
all sides," he wrote to Hawthorne, "you may possibly feel a
touch of a shrink, or something of that sort. It is but nature to be
shy of a mortal who boldly declares that a thief in jail is as honorable a personage as Gen. George Washington. . . . It seems an
inconsistency to assert unconditioned democracy in all things,
and yet confess a dislike to all mankind—in the mass. But not
so"(*ibid.*, pp. 320–321). He then goes on: "But truth is the
silliest thing under the sun," and does not deign to explain. "Believe me," he says of *Pierre*, "you will pronounce Pierre a thoroughgoing Democrat in time; perhaps a little too Radical altogether
to your fancy" (*ibid.*, p. 37).

[7] See Weaver, p. 365.

Such a man would not so much turn critic as embody criticism. His life—even more than Emerson's—laid upon America, was a yardstick to measure the shortcomings of a professed civilization. Cooper was a critic whom America could understand, and America hated him for his unpleasant frankness. Melville it could not understand, and it turned away and ignored him. Perhaps it was well enough that his generation could not comprehend his devastating speculations, and called him mad; or it would have cried out to crucify this maligner of all the tribal fetishes. He would level every barrier against the unpleasant that his age was erecting. He outran Thoreau in contempt for current material ideals. To turn scornfully away from the triumphs of his fellows—from the fruits of the industrial revolution and the romantic gospel of progress—this was incomprehensible blasphemy! Yet what had Herman Melville in common with middle-class America? Its hopes and fears were not his. He was troubled about life, and not about things. He was not concerned about politics or the political state. He was not concerned with trade, or money-getting, or romantic imperialisms. He was not even greatly concerned with political democracy, although in his time he had been as hot a republican as the best of them. The shoddy democracy of his time made his gorge rise; and to this shoddy democracy that shrilly proclaimed its excellence he paid his respects in words that suggest Lowell's *Cathedral*, but with a depth of significance that Lowell was incapable of. In the poem *Clarel*, into which Melville crowded so much of his later speculations, he comments thus:

> This world clean fails me: still I yearn. . . .
>
> This side the dark and hollow bound
> Lies there no unexplored rich ground?
> *Some other world:* well, there's the New—
> Ah, joyless and ironic too!
>
> Ay, Democracy
> Lops, lops; and where's her planted bed?
> The future, what is that to her
> Who vaunts she's no inheritor?
> 'Tis in her mouth, not in her heart.
> The past she spurns, though 'tis the past
> From which she gets her saving part—
> That Good which lets her evil last.
>
> Behold her whom the panders crown,
> Harlot on horseback, riding down

The very Ephesians who acclaim
This great Diana of ill fame!
Arch strumpet of an impious age,
Upstart from ranker villeinage:
Asia shall stop her at the least
That old inertness of the East. . . .

But in the New World things make haste:
Not only things, the *state* lives fast—
Fast breed the pregnant eggs and shells,
The slumberous combustibles,
Sure to explode. 'Twill come, 'twill come!
One demagogue can trouble much:
How of a hundred thousand such? . . .

Indeed, those germs one now may view:
Myriads playing pigmy parts—
Debased into equality:
Dead level of rank commonplace:
An Anglo-Saxon China, see,
May on your vast plains shame the race
In the Dark Ages of Democracy. . . .

Your arts advance in faith's decay:
You are but drilling the new Hun
Whose growl even now can some dismay;
Vindictive in his heart of hearts.
He schools him in your mines and marts
A skilled destroyer. . . .

Old ballads sing
Fair Christian children crucified
By impious Jews: you've heard the thing:
Yes, fable; but there's truth hard by:
How many Hughs of Lincoln, say,
Does Mammon, in his mills, to-day,
Crook, if he does not crucify?

The impieties of 'Progress' speak;
What say *these*, in effect to God?
'How profits it? And who art Thou
That we should serve Thee? Of Thy ways
No knowledge we desire; *new* ways
We have found out, and better. Go—
Depart from us!' And if He do?
Is aught betwixt us and the hells? . . .

For Herman Melville, at least, the barriers betwixt him and the
hells had long been gone, and only Nirvana awaited him.

BOOK THREE: THE MIND OF NEW ENGLAND

BOOK THREE

THE MIND OF NEW ENGLAND

The New England renaissance was tardy in appearing and of brief duration, yet in the few years of its extraordinary vigor it imparted a stimulus to American life that its historians have not greatly exaggerated. We are now far enough from it to see that it was the last flowering of a tree that was dying at the roots, but in the tumultuous thirties it seemed to be a new birth of the native New England mind, opening on new worlds and great adventures. Though its prophecies might be little heeded at its own fireside, and unheard in the vast stretches of the West where men were clearing and building after quite different plans than the Concord architects were drawing, its significance in the development of American idealism—the ethical imprint it stamped on American culture—endured long after it had spent its force. It was the last and in certain aspects the most brilliant of the several attempts to domesticate in America the romantic thought of revolutionary Europe; and with its passing, civilization in this western world fell into the hands of another breed of men to fashion as they saw fit.

The revolutions in thought that lie between the eighteenth century with its aristocratic rationalism that conceived of human nature as evil, and the nineteenth century with its middle-class economics that conceived of human nature as acquisitive, are more clearly defined in New England and more sharply differentiated, than elsewhere in America. The flood of romantic speculation with its humanitarian emphasis on the potential excellence of man and the equality of human rights, that in Europe had diffused itself widely, in Massachusetts flowed into narrow channels prepared by Puritan discipline, and swept away habits of thought that had dominated New England for two hundred years. The intensity of the Puritan nature, once it embraced the new conceptions, imparted to them an intellectual and emotional unity that serves to explain the creativeness of the New England renaissance, as it serves to explain its failure to spread widely

271

beyond the confines of Massachusetts. Appearing a generation
later than in Virginia, it drew its inspiration more largely from Germany than from France; it was intellectual and ethical rather than
political and economic; and in consequence it held little in common
with the Physiocratic agrarianism of Jefferson. The latter was
sufficiently native to American economics to appeal to the common
man from Maine to Georgia; the former was native only to New
England Puritanism. Its idealism appealed only to rare souls,
disciplined by speculation and trained in ethical values, men of
strong character and fine distinction who counted for much more
than numbers.

After all it is the ethical note that marks the Puritan. That
New England has run so different a course from other parts of
America has been due chiefly to its desire to serve God even though
it might be serving self. Its material life has always been plentifully seasoned with the salt of religion. It sat under the teachings
of an austere ethics, as it lived under the compulsions of a narrow economics; and the result was the development of a middle
class distinct from that of the West where the desire to get on was
less hampered by the desire to get to heaven. The outstanding
social figures in early New England were the minister and the
merchant; and these twin authorities—joined after the Revolution
by the rising profession of the law—ruled in patriarchal fashion
the inarticulate mass of the yeomanry. From these traditional
leaders the policy of New England received a twofold bent: a bent
to the ethical and a bent to the practical. The two have rarely
fused in a harmonious and fruitful life, but for the most part have
dwelt side by side under a covenant of noninterference, the character of current social ideals taking its impress from one or the
other as it gained a temporary ascendency. In the three hundred
years of New England history the minister has enjoyed two periods
of intellectual ascendency: the first during the early days of the
theocracy, when the commonwealth was ruled by the laws of God
and John Calvin; and the second, between the years 1830 and
1850, when John Calvin was finally put aside and New England
was in the way of being remodeled in accordance with the plans
of God alone. Between these brief periods of ethical enthusiasm
lies the main history of New England, a history that counts for
little in our intellectual and aesthetic development, but that meant
much and ill to the cramped minds of her sons.

This long stretch, arid and unlovely, was dominated wholly by the merchant. Its parsimonious thrift, relieved by few generous impulses, was hostile to all change and to the romance that is bred of change. There was no rapid inflow of settlers to bring fresh energy and expansion. The exuberant growth of other parts of America was never shared by rural New England, and in consequence the harvest of unearned increment was rarely reaped from her sterile acres. Except in the shipping towns there was little economic development. On its secluded little farms New England was living a narrow parochial life, cooping up its mind in a rigid theological system and disciplining its character by a self-denying ordinance. Public affairs were managed by the squire, for the minister was too busy defending John Calvin against the Arminians to have a care for much except morality and dogma. The renaissance became of necessity, therefore, a movement of liberalism—a vehement protest against the torpor of the dogmatist whose mind was shut up in a dead system. It was a sudden reawakening of the ethical passion of Puritanism that had slept for two centuries; a vision of a new heaven and a new earth that it proposed to take by storm. It proposed to rid the mind of New England of its decadent loyalties—the nightmare dreams of Calvinism that debased human nature, and the counting-house dreams of Federalism that conceived of man as an exploitative animal. It had discovered anew the beauty of righteousness, and in the name of righteousness it proposed to throw off the old tyrannies and create a society wherein the mind should be free and the soul enjoy its religion. The battle against Calvinism was only preliminary to greater battles which constituted the intellectual revolution that marked the renaissance.

It was the New England minister, and the spiritual heirs of the minister—a group of intellectuals and reformers more notable than New England had before bred—that gave to the movement its pronounced ethical quality. It was freedom for individual righteousness that they sought; not freedom for intellectual epicureanism, for romance, for aesthetic or pagan beauty. The transcendentalists and reformers had little time to amuse themselves with such things. They were too eager for the coming of the kingdom to dawdle over fiction or patronize the playhouse. They had been bred from their youth up on printer's ink; they came of a race that had long respected the printed page. Literary men by inheritance, they esteemed themselves stewards of a great cause. In rejecting their fathers' hell they became the more zealous to make a heaven of this world; and although the more practical Yankee was skeptical of their plans and would not suffer them to turn Boston into a transcendental Utopia, they succeeded in making such a stir as New England had never before known. For a brief time, at least, liberal ideas found a welcome in homes where they had hitherto been strangers; for a brief time the intellectual and not the merchant dominated New England.

PART ONE: THE TWILIGHT OF FEDERALISM

CHAPTER I

THE PASSING OF THE TIE-WIG SCHOOL

I

OLD BOSTON

THE year 1815, that brought to a close the unfortunate American venture into the maelstrom of the Napoleonic wars, may be conveniently taken to mark for New England the transition to the nineteenth century. With the rise of Unitarianism and the development of the new industrialism, a ruder and more vigorous age entered Boston. It met with a somewhat chilly reception. The patriarchal eighteenth century still clung to its warm chimney corner, not liking to be dispossessed by heirs of whom it testily disapproved. The old order stood on its dignity, tenacious of its habitual authority. It lived quietly in an aristocratic past, unregardful of the vigorous commonwealths rising beyond the Appalachian mountains, and contemptuous of the new political philosophy that preached the rights of man. A persistent continuity of temper marked the ruling class, a continuity little disturbed by the tumultuous revolutions of the past two generations. Although nearly half the voters of Massachusetts, in the year 1800, were Jeffersonian republicans, the knowledge of that fact only stiffened the backbones of the regnant caste. It colored their minds with a virtuous pessimism, but it edged their temper with the zeal of righteousness. The Boston mobsters, it would appear, were republican, and when the present custodians of the ark of decency were gathered to their fathers, very likely evil days would come upon the land; but while the righteous lived they would be faithful to their stewardship. Their own households, at least, they would keep clean of all democratic pollution; and so Boston and New Haven and Hartford—the capitals of New England culture—drew about them the garments of Federalist righteousness. Since the Revolution of '76 a new authority had risen on the ruins of the old Tory authority, but in spite of the change of

personnel and outward political forms, the spirit of respectable
New England remained pretty much what it had always been.
John Quincy Adams and Fisher Ames and Josiah Quincy were
little different in character and aims from Thomas Hutchinson
and Joseph Sewall and Daniel Leonard—they were common
chips from the tough old New England oak. High-minded yet
narrow; devout yet not emotionally religious; thrifty yet generous
in approved causes; engaged in overseas commerce yet oddly
parochial—they were men fashioned by a rugged environment into
vigorous stock, that would hold tenaciously to what they had got
and would tolerate no insubordination on the part of their social
inferiors.

With its twenty-five thousand inhabitants Boston ranked fourth
in size among American cities. Philadelphia, the social capital
of America, was nearly three times as large; New York nearly
two and a half times; and even Baltimore had lately come to ex-
ceed her in population. The economic forces that make for liberalism had become largely impotent. Free land had long since
been exhausted in Massachusetts and social lines were fixed. The
northern frontier of Maine and New Hampshire was rugged and
uninviting, and York State lay to the West. Except in the Connecticut valley the soil was thin and farming unproductive, and
in consequence the more ambitious turned to commerce and manufacture which the physical conditions of the country invited.
The dominant interest of Boston was commercial, and the ruling
coterie of merchants and lawyers was narrowly Whiggish. They
had modified their pre-Revolutionary political philosophy no further than to substitute the word republican for monarchical. The
aristocratic temper dominated the town meetings, and the principle of property rule was commonly accepted as the essence of
political wisdom. In substituting Federalism for Toryism there
was no easing of the restrictions on rebellious plebeians. Quite
repudiated were the rude leveling ways of the great Revolutionary adventure. Boston gentlemen had come to understand
too well the danger of encouraging the mob, for as Fisher Ames
pointed out in 1787, "The people have turned against their
teachers the doctrines, which were inculcated to effect the late
revolution" (*Works*, p. 11). Boston had had enough of revolutions
since Daniel Shays had got up one of his own aimed at the Boston
purse, and French Jacobins had let loose their devastating

ideas upon a gullible world. Revolutions that were not made in Boston, by Boston gentlemen, were quite certain to be wicked and seditious; and Boston had definitely gone out of the revolution business. It wanted above all things to undo the mischief that had already been done, and take back into safe hands the political power which in the days of revolutionary enthusiasm had been seized by the agrarian democracy.

In the last decade of the eighteenth century the intellectual isolation of New England was sharply accentuated and the consequent intellectual stagnation became more disastrous. In other portions of America French revolutionary theories of man and society were spreading widely and shouldering aside the outworn past. A romantic equalitarianism, based on the doctrine of human perfectibility, was displacing the traditional economic realism, established on the dogma of total depravity. The leveling movement, in consequence, was provided with a persuasive idealism that awakened troublesome aspirations in the disfranchised majority and gave a strong impetus to the democratic movement. But New England leaders stood resolutely apart, accounting all equalitarianism sheer romantic folly. The old stubborn realism held its ground, interpreting political principles in terms of economics, and dogmatically maintaining the sacred rights of property. Boston Federalism refused to have anything to do with "atheistic France," the fruitful mother of Jacobin follies. Pollution, it was convinced, must result from any commerce with infidel and innovating ideas. Gunpowder that was played with might explode, and New England wanted no blowing up of her excellent society. Virginia had lent credulous ears to the voice of France, and the result was the atheist Jefferson and the rabble of his licentious followers. Massachusetts was not gullible and it would tolerate no Jeffersonian atheisms. And so instead of adapting French romantic philosophy to new world needs, seizing upon its social idealism to leaven the crude American lump— as Jefferson and Colonel Mason and John Taylor and many another Virginia gentleman had done—Boston Federalism rejected French ideas in the mass, dubbed French idealism Jacobinism, and turned back upon a stubborn reaction.

The disastrous consequences of that rejection upon the mind of New England cannot easily be measured. It is clear enough, nevertheless, that the renaissance was delayed a full generation, and when it came it assumed certain provincialisms that greatly lessened its permanent influence upon the rest of America. The impress of its contribution upon our national thought has been far less permanent than that of Virginia, that came a generation earlier and was primarily economic and political. It is a suggestive fact that in the work of adapting the new Federal Constitution to democratic ends, New England contributed no creative leader, none in any way comparable to Jefferson; but on the contrary her most representative leaders—and in particular Webster—followed the eighteenth-century tradition in combating the equalitarian advance in the interest of economic groups. Some explanation of this fact may be found, perhaps, in the selfish isolation of New England Federalism, that closed the door on the liberal thought of France.

In consequence of such isolation Boston became the recognized home of the philosophy of a stake-in-society. If it clung tenaciously to an old-fashioned Federalism after it had been abandoned elsewhere, it was because Boston was more middle-class than Charleston, and had not learned from experience with Jacksonianism how easily the majority will may be shaped and controlled to particular ends. It inherited the old Tory contempt for democracy and relied on the old stock arguments to combat it. Its habitual tone was one of virtuous arrogance. The one great and ever-present fear that haunted the pillows of worthy Boston merchants and turned their dreams to nightmares, was fear of the mob getting out of hand; and democracy, for them, was only a euphemism for the mob—the ever-present menace to sober and decent government. In the judgment of Theodore Dwight, brother of Timothy, "there could be nothing more dreadful this side of hell." Nowhere else in America did the reaction against the democratic ideal carry so far as in Boston. The church and the merchant associations joined with polite society to cry it down, and upon the head of the democrat fell the most extravagant vituperation. For a generation few respectable New Englanders raised their voices in defense of democracy; but gentlemen of principle and property followed the lead of the little clique that was driving straight towards the Hartford Convention—blind sailors navigating the Dead Sea of Federalist pessimism.

All this was before the reputed time of plain living and high thinking. Intellectual Boston was as parochial as political Boston.

The lights whom Bostonians regarded as the torch-bearers of New England culture have long since been extinguished and their names forgotten even in Beacon Street. Amongst the literati of the little Boston of 1800 the historian need concern himself with no more than two or three: Fisher Ames (1758–1808), the Federalist lawyer-wit, and Robert Treat Paine (1773–1811), esteemed the ninth wonder of the Boston world. Other figures there were, of course, in addition to the literati: Harrison Gray Otis, the eloquent voice of Faneuil Hall, and Josiah Quincy, whom Lowell likened to an old Roman of the elder virtuous days, and who during a long life of ninety-two years was an example of stalwart and antiquated Federalism. Old Boston bred dignified figures in plenty, men admirably equipped to be college presidents, ambassadors, orators on formal occasions, purveyors of cultivated inutilities and polished commonplace—men like Edward Everett, whom all Boston praised while they lived and forgot when they were dead; but it bred no thinkers or men of letters who count in the larger history of America. Boston was still parochial, content with little things.

II

FISHER AMES

The Oracle of the Tie-Wig School

Of this testy little world that clung to its smallclothes and tie-wig, refusing to adopt the Jacobin innovation in dress and manners and politics, declining to temper its prejudices to the gusty whims of a leveling age, Fisher Ames was the universal counselor and oracle. A vivacious little gentleman to whom politics was the breath of life, he achieved so tremendous a reputation in his short lifetime that all New England looked to him for leadership and Harvard College wanted to make him its president. He came of vigorous stock, prone to consult its own will and speak its opinions with no squeamish concern for a neighbor's views. His brother, Dr. Nathaniel Ames, was as violent a Republican as Fisher was a Federalist, a hater of all lawyers whom he accounted the "pettifogging interest"; and when the two members of the family came together at dinner the talk must have been worth hearing. Diverse worlds and hostile philosophies faced each other over the roast, and the sauce no doubt was well spiced. Dr.

Nathaniel had a pretty gift himself in the way of pungent speech, and Fisher's wit was the admiration of all New England. When Gouverneur Morris—reputed the greatest wit in America—visited Massachusetts, Fisher Ames was pitted against him, and Boston believed that the honor of the Bay State was worthily upheld. His pet hobby was the inherent tyranny of all democracies, and when he once got astride his wooden horse and dug in the spurs, the onset was tremendous. The letters that have come down to us are a gold mine of picturesque vituperation, from which one may dig a wallet of choice nuggets. The vivacity of his anathemas is delightful, and one would give much to have heard Dr. Nathaniel's retort militant.

There are the solidest grounds for regarding Fisher Ames as the representative citizen of Boston in the year 1800. He was the cleverest and most intelligent spokesman of a social and political circle quite untouched by the new French liberalisms, content with the habitual and familiar, and mightily concerned that the future should be as like the past as one generation of oysters is like another. A lawyer who shared the strong property consciousness of the Boston merchant, and a churchman who accepted the moral leadership of the Calvinist clergy, he offered stout and uncompromising resistance to innovation. "A change, though for the better, is always to be deplored by the generation in which it is effected," he said. "Much is lost and more is hazarded" (*Works*, p. 15, edition of 1809). The new gospel of progress that came in with French romanticisms, he would have none of. In the face of a noisy Jacobinism that threatened to carry all before it, he fought a spirited fight, turning pamphleteer when his broken health removed him from Congress, counseling and scolding his fellow Federalists with his last breath. Others might truckle and compromise, but not Fisher Ames. His faith was founded on the solid granite of Yankee prejudice.

The very solidity of that prejudice made him the trenchant spokesman of the older Boston conservatisms—that and the vivacity of his prose style which is approved Augustan, uncorrupted by what he dubbed "pompous Johnsonian affectation." His contemporary reputation was enormous. Accounted a great orator, he was accounted an even greater political philosopher, and his pamphlets were appraised by President Kirkland of Harvard as "the light of genius and wisdom darted athwart the gloom of our political chaos." "In the character of Mr. Ames," said the Harvard president, "the circle of the virtues seemed to be complete, and each virtue in its proper place" (*Works*, Introduction, p. xxviii). Yet in spite of so authoritative a pronouncement, Fisher Ames does not seem today so great a man as he seemed to his own generation. From the data collected in a stout volume published soon after his death as "a voice of instruction and warning to his country," and from the letters published by his son in 1854, it is plain enough that this "powerful and original genius" was a retailer of somewhat shopworn goods, a complete Federalist Tory after the current Boston fashion. To Fisher Ames Federalism, as understood in New England, was a religion. He defended it with the ardor of the moralist, convinced that it included all the political virtues, and that whoever rejected it was a child of the devil. Whenever he considered the unpromising state of the country—which luxury he often indulged—whether in the midst of Shays's Rebellion or of the Jeffersonian revolution, he fell into black pessimism. He grew hot from fires of his own kindling, and the gloomier he became the more vigorously he blew the bellows.

To the sinful publican self-conscious virtue is peculiarly irritating, and since Fisher Ames accounted most of his generation political publicans, he was at odds with all but a scant remnant of Federalist saints. From this isolation, from the defeat that overwhelmed his party in the great election of 1800, and from aggravating ill health, which beginning when he was thirty-seven incapacitated him three years later for public life, he fell into a state of chronic political despondency that extracted a grim pleasure from the contemplation of democratic follies and the anarchy towards which the country was hastening. During his last years his wit became acid; his letters are filled with caustic comment to sharpen the temper of those on the fighting line. Of these racy comments, so characteristic of Federalist spleen, a few examples must serve to convey the spirit: "Our country is too big for union, too sordid for patriotism, too democratic for liberty." "We are in the hands of the philosophers of Lilliput." "I have as loyal and respectful an opinion as possible of the sincerity in folly of our rulers." "As to liberty, we are to have none—democracy will kindle its own hell, and consume in it." "Democracy is a troubled spirit, fated never to rest, and whose dreams, if it sleeps, present only visions of hell." In his last years Fisher Ames had become a shrill Jeremiah crying in the gates of an Israel that mocked the old prophets.

His political philosophy was simple, yet so native to Calvin-ist-Yankee New England, and historically so characteristic, that it provides a useful candle to throw light into the old New England garrets. In certain aspects it is close kin to the Whiggery of Locke and Pitt, particularly in its concern for the sacred right of prop-erty rule—a principle that he casually recognizes in his frequent assertion that "the mass of the federalists are the owners of the commercial and monied wealth of the nation" (*Works*, p. 426). But in post-Revolutionary Boston, suffering from the acute fright inflicted by Daniel Shays, this English Whiggery had come to as-sume a particular native form that differentiated it from its orig-inal. In the primitive Calvinist-Yankee world political theory had been shaped by the theocratic conception of stewardship, by which was meant an authoritative leadership reposing in the best and wisest, yet subject to the will of God as revealed in the Bible. Minister and magistrate, therefore, professed to justify their acts, not by expediency or interest, but by absolute ethical standards. From this early practice developed the pronounced ethical temper of New England political thought that set it apart from the Virginia school, a temper that persisted after the transfer of authority from Puritan minister and magistrate to Tory mer-chant and lawyer. With the growth of the aristocratic spirit in the middle eighteenth century, the squirearchy assumed unchal-lenged political leadership, and it was from the remnant of the old gentry remaining after the expulsion of the Loyalists, strengthened by a new generation of merchants and lawyers, that Boston Fed-eralism drew its personnel. It professed republicanism, but it was instinctively aristocratic. It was true to its Puritan origins in expounding its political philosophy in terms of an absolute moral-ity, and true to its aristocratic origins in assuming to be the special custodians of law and order. It no more questioned its special right to rulership in the state than it questioned its social position; and in both politics and society it professed the ancient doctrine of stewardship.

The kinship between the political philosophy of Fisher Ames and John Adams is quite evident. They are cut out of the same Puri-tan-Yankee cloth, but the former is a more careless tailor. Founded on less adequate analysis and lacking the wide historical appeal of Adams, assuming rather than proving the fact of a universal property aristocracy, and the economic origins of political power, the philosophy of Ames postulates the same ideal of justice as the end of government, discovers in faction the dragon to be slain, and concludes that only a static division of powers can insure political stability. Nevertheless the difference between the two men is enormous. John Adams was a philosopher, and Fisher Ames was only a lawyer-politician. The ideal of justice which the former postulated was fundamentally noble, whereas the ideal of justice which the latter assumed was narrowly legal. Both accepted the Puritan doctrine of human wickedness—a doctrine derived from medieval Toryism—and from it deduced the necessity of a coercive sovereignty; but Fisher Ames went further and assumed that the Puritan doctrine of the elect and the Yankee doctrine of the successful were one and the same, and that God's remnant in Israel was no other than the prosperous merchants and lawyers of Boston. All the great multitude of the unprosperous, by the same doctrine, were the mass of the unregenerate, condemned for the good of society to be ruled by a rod of iron.

The noble doctrine of justice, therefore, became for Fisher Ames little more than the divine right of the minority to coerce the majority, in the name and through the agency of laws and statutes. In his view justice was little more than a drab realist in a lawyer's wig, adjudicating title deeds, and delivering its findings out of law books. Its one concern was to safeguard what had been got, rather than to secure just and equal rights. It dreaded all rude and tumultuary innovation, and would tolerate no change that was not implicit in legal principles. Its golden rule was due process of law. Love of one's neighbors was, no doubt, an excellent private virtue, but it was impractical, if not immoral, in the state. Concern for the improvident sinners must not influence government to impair the rights of the thrifty saints; for government was instituted and exists to safeguard established things. "The chief duty and care of all governments," he argued, "is to protect the rights of property and the tranquillity of society" (*Works*, p. 125). Hence to Fisher Ames government was the common policeman and judge, whose function was to arrest the turbulent and bring them to the bar of the Common Law. Its beginning and end was the Tory principle of coercion. Its sovereignty was arrogant and domineering, taking no account of the democratic

principle of good will. "The motives to refuse obedience to govern‑
ment are many and strong," he explained; "impunity will multi‑
ply and enforce them. Many men would rebel, rather than be
ruined; but they would rather not rebel, than be hanged" (*Works*,
"Lucius Junius Brutus"). With government thus conceived of,
naturally he desired that it should be strong; that it should im‑
pose its will ruthlessly upon the rebellious. Naturally also he
regarded every idealist, the Rousseaus and Paines and Jeffersons—
all the mischievous hosts of "democratick babblers"—as a dan‑
gerous enemy of law and order, desperately bent on overturning
the rights of vested interests and the tranquillity of society. This
is sufficient to explain the vindictiveness of his assault upon Shays
and his followers, as "bankrupts and sots, who have gambled or
slept away their estates"—while in the Revolutionary army—and
were now engaged in the business of treason against the common‑
wealth, and the characteristic conclusion that he draws—"the
certainty of punishment is the truest security against crimes"
(*Works*, "Lucius Junius Brutus," p. 3). To Fisher Ames and
Daniel Shays, justice seems to have had very different aspects.

To the uncritical there is a certain persuasive dignity in the
philosophy of Boston Federalism. Gentlemen like Fisher Ames
were careful to appear well in public; they liked to be regarded
as faithful stewards of the common weal. Concern for the *res
publica* they professed so heartily that it seems ungracious to
question their motives. How excellently they could make out a
case for themselves will appear from the following exposition of
Fisher Ames' philosophy, as it was understood by a Harvard presi‑
dent:

Mr. Ames was emphatically a republican. He saw that many persons
confounded a republick with a democracy. He considered them as essen‑
tially distinct and really opposite. According to his creed, a republick is
that structure of an elective government, in which the administration
necessarily prescribe to themselves the general good as the object of all
their measures; a democracy is that, in which the present popular passions,
independent of the publick good, become a guide to the rulers. In the
first, the reason and interests of the society govern; in the second, their
prejudices and passions. The frame of the American constitution supposes
the dangers of democracy. . . . [The constitutional checks] are contri‑
vances and devices voluntarily adopted by the people to restrain them‑
selves from obstructing, by their own mistakes or perversity, the attain‑
ment of the publick welfare. They are professed means of insuring to the
nation rulers, who will prefer the durable good of the whole to the transient

advantage of the whole or a part. When these provisions become in-
effectual, and the legislator, the executive magistrate, and the judge become the instruments of the passions of a people, or of the governing majority, the government, whatever may be its form, is a democracy, and
the public liberty is no longer safe. True republican rulers are bound to
act, not simply as those who appoint them *would*, but, as they *ought;*
democratick leaders will act in subordination to those very passions which
it is the object of government to control. . . . Then it is, that men, not
laws, govern. (*Works*, Introduction, pp. xxiv–xxv.)

"The durable good of the whole" is an excellent phrase; but
when the skeptical critic asks for more exact plans and specifications,
the only answer is a request for a vote of confidence. The representative is presumed to be wiser and more patriotic than his
constituents—quite above passion or interest—and may safely
be intrusted with "the publick good." "The love of country,"
Fisher Ames was fond of insisting, "is the morality of politics,"
and the Federal Constitution he believed to be so happily balanced
that partisan selfishness must transmute itself into patriotism.
But when we dismiss these amiable generalities—which reveal to
what straits gentlemen were reduced in their contest with democracy—and examine the political principles that lie behind them,
they do not appear so amiable. They imply as necessary corollaries a continuous aggrandizement of the political state, the principle of coercion, and the psychology of fear. It is no other than
the old Tory arrogance, new-modeled to suit republican taste.
Fisher Ames seems to have had no faith in the principle of good
will or the expediency of compromise; his contempt for the opposition was as frank as Hamilton's.

Government does not subsist by making proselytes to sound reasons
or by compromise and arbitration with its members; but by the power of
the community compelling the obedience of individuals. If that is not
done, who will seek its protection, or fear its vengeance. ("Lucius Junius
Brutus," *Works*, p. 5.)

For let it be remarked, that a feeble government produces more factions
than an oppressive one; the want of power first makes individuals legislators, and then rebels. Where parents want authority, children are wanting in duty. It is not possible to advance further in the same path; the
one will conduct us first to anarchy, and next to foreign or domestick
tyranny; the other, by the wise and vigorous exertion of lawful authority,
will lead to permanent power, and general prosperity. I am no advocate
for despotism; but I believe the probability to be much less of its being

introduced by the corruption of our rulers, than by the delusion of the people. ("Camillus," *Works*, p. 17.)

A weak government, Ames argues insistently, is no other than a hotbed of faction, and faction is the fruitful mother of democratic anarchy. Again and again he returns to an exposition of the familiar eighteenth-century dogma that found its classic exposition in the tenth number of *The Federalist;* and his argument takes on darker colors from the Calvinist background of his mind. To those who have been reared on the sour doctrines of reprobation and election, the children of Adam become a major political concern. If God has cast off and denied the mass of the unregenerate, how shall the political philosopher hope to redeem them? If divine wisdom has granted them no part in the congregation of the righteous, what rights have they in the republic of the patriotic? To Fisher Ames town and village and farm showed plentiful examples of those whom the devil had marked for his own, and if they were gathered into a numerical democracy with the saints, how should the minority of the latter safeguard the Ark of the Sanctuary? How should the durable good of the whole be provided for? Thrift and godliness were not exactly synonymous terms to the Calvinist-Yankee, but it was clear that the godly will practice thrift, and those who have thriven, have *ipso facto* made out a case for their godliness. In this uncertain world two things seemed reasonably clear: that the poor are in a more doubtful state than the rich; and that in a moral world only the elect may be expected to serve the cause of morality. The wicked incline to democratic faction, but the prosperous serve the durable good of the whole.

To one cradled in such prejudices, the current phrase, "gentlemen of principle and property"—a phrase that provides the chorus to his thought—lacked the savor of cynicism that it suggests to modern ears. It was compounded of the ideals of Puritan and Yankee, and Fisher Ames seems never to have questioned its adequacy, or doubted its finality. To gentlemen of principle and property he looked to provide a bulwark against the immoral multitude; they were the stewards of society, on whom devolved the duty of protecting the whole from democratic faction. They had erected the Federal Constitution, which Jacobins were seeking to destroy; and in defense of that Constitution he brought forth his heaviest artillery. He contributed nothing new to the discussion;

but he repeated the familiar arguments with the gusto of a dog-matist. "Simple governments," he asserted, "are despotisms; and of all despotisms, a democracy, though the least durable, is the most violent" (*Works*, "American Liberty," p. 382). The mortal weakness of all democracies he discovered in their immorality. A democracy will make every people "thoroughly licentious and corrupt." "The known propensity of a democracy is to licentiousness, which the ambitious call, and the ignorant believe to be liberty."

> The great object, then, of political wisdom in framing our constitution, was to guard against licentiousness, that inbred malady of democracies, that deforms their infancy with grey hairs and decrepitude. (*Ibid.*, p. 384.)

> There is universally a presumption in democracy that promises everything; and at the same time an imbecility that can accomplish nothing, not even preserve itself. (*Works*, "Falkland," p. 151.)

"Politics should have no passions," this caustic old Federalist professed to believe, yet his bitterness against the Jeffersonians who threatened to overturn the funding law, the national bank, the midnight judicial appointments, and other measures of the best Federalist minds, was almost unseemly. It would appear that "the durable good of the whole" flew out at the window, when danger to commercial interests came in at the door. To erect a strong government and then lose control of it was a disaster indeed. With the political state in the hands of atheistic democrats, Fisher Ames was prepared to welcome the coming of anarchy, and his pessimism throve on the prospect. But that no warning might be lacking he laid down the whole theory of government in plain terms, that even Jefferson might understand:

> But the essence, and almost the quintessence, of good government is, to protect property and its rights. When these are protected, there is scarcely any booty left for oppression to seize; the objects and the motives to usurpation and tyranny are removed. By securing property, life and liberty can scarcely fail of being secured: where property is safe by rules and principles, there is liberty. (*Works*, "Phocion," p. 181.)

This is pure Federalism, stripped of all cant, speaking out frankly. It is the philosophy of John Locke brought in to serve the rising capitalism of New England, threatened by a Physiocratic agrarianism. The dogma of political morality has yielded to economic realism. The stake-in-society principle is the reply of the Puritan‹ Yankee to the democratic romanticism of Jefferson and Madison —a principle which, fortunately, "these apostles from the race-ground and the cock-pit" paid little heed to.

To a sophisticated generation, long familiar with the political ways of gentlemen of principle and property, Fisher Ames appears as a caustic little gentleman, vivacious and intolerant, who nodded his tie-wig dogmatically, and spoke his opinions oracularly. He quite evidently relished his ample store of old-fashioned prejudices, cherished them carefully, and prided himself on the wit with which he set them forth.   If he was not the repository of all political wisdom that he believed himself to be, he was at least no demagogue, and in honoring him the Boston of the year 1800 was but painting its own portrait. It would be ungracious, perhaps, to add that Fisher Ames and Boston Federalism, defeated in their cherished projects, were both suffering from an extraordinarily aggravated case of the political spleen.

III

ROBERT TREAT PAINE, JR.
Wit

Young Tom Paine, who took his brother's and his father's name— partly because a certain other Tom Paine had achieved a fame that Boston did not regard as enviable—shared with Fisher Ames the literary renown of the New England capital, a renown so great that Boston paid him quite astonishing sums for such couplets as his indolence suffered him to turn off. The popularity of his wares was a notable instance of the working of the law of supply and demand. The patriotism of Boston preferred domestic to imported goods, and he offered his verses to a public not very critical of quality. Boston had never had a poet of her own, while Connecticut with her Hartford Wits was the envy of all New England. Certain poetesses to be sure, had tried with "hallowed hands" to "attune Columbia's lyre"—to quote Paine's eulogy of Mrs. Sarah Wentworth Morton, "blest Philenia, noblest of the choir" (*Works*, "Menander to Philenia," p. 129)—but their sentimentality was a bit cloying, and when genius appeared in the person of a Harvard graduate, graced with wit and adorned with all the learning of the schools, Boston was quick to acclaim him as her own.

The young man thus seized upon, and as it were raped by fame, was the last of the eighteenth-century wits, the most dashing product of a generation that patched its verse with tags of the classics and called it lisping in numbers. In temper and manners he belonged wholly to the tie-wig school that swaggered till the War of 1812 and then became obsolete overnight. As a young man about town he displayed the latest London clothes and set himself up as the very glass of fashion. Although he wore his own hair, he clung to smallclothes and like an honest Federalist refused to adopt Jacobin trousers. He was indisputably clever and he cultivated a pretty wit as assiduously as any Augustan. He talked in epigrams, and a convivial evening—of which he was quite too fond for his own good—was a failure that did not produce a *bon mot* to run through the town. His biographer has preserved a number of such for the amusement of posterity, and one at least deserves to be remembered by our younger critics. When the prohibition against the theater was repealed in 1793, he remarked, "The Vandal spirit of puritanism is prostrate in New-England." In cleaving to wit and abandoning Puritanism, Paine broke with sober Boston convention, and soon all respectable folk began to shake their heads. A thriftless fellow, he played with the devil openly in the eyes of all Boston. He drank too much, he gambled, he haunted the theater and was a favorite of the greenroom, he became the first dramatic critic born and bred in New England, and when he married the daughter of an English actor, his father disowned him. Quite naturally he came to poverty, dissipated his strength, suffered many a humiliation, and died at the age of thirty-seven, leaving his widow and young children to be provided for by a public benefit at his beloved Federal Street theater.

Little of his wit, unfortunately, found its way into his verse, which, modeled ostensibly on Dryden and Pope, lacks their vigorous common sense, and laboring to be sublime succeeds in being heavy. His couplets swell sonorously, but his thought does not keep pace with his rhetoric. He follows his recipe carefully; adjectives duly support the nouns; the caesuras are justly spaced and the balance of the parts is as nice as if weighed in an apothecary's scales. He seasons the whole with the staples of personification and poetic diction; everything has been provided for, and yet the cake is fallen that he takes from the oven. Something is lacking to lighten the sodden mass. A contemporary critic, viewing the finished product, expressed his judgment thus:

Of Mr. Paine, as an author, we cannot speak in terms of unmingled praise. His verse, indeed, seldom loiters into prose; but it must be confessed, that his prose is here and there "tricked and frounced, till it outmantles all the pride of verse." His numbers are, perhaps, never feeble or faultering, but a wild and frolic imagination, occasionally, wantons through his periods, and sometimes displays itself in contemning the chaster elegancies, and sometimes in neglecting the severer decencies of thought and diction. (*Works*, Introduction, p. lxxviii.)

It is certainly a partial eye that discovers a wild and frolic imagination in these lumbering imitations of Pope, or in the occasional excursions into the languorous fields of Della Cruscan sentiment. When Paine ceases to be a wit he becomes an offense. To his admiring contemporaries his poetry seemed to be pure metal, but to later generations it is only plate, with the brass showing through the worn spots. *The Ruling Passion*, delivered before the Phi Beta Kappa Society in 1797, is perhaps the first poem of Paine's that is much more than vacuous and turgid rhetoric; and this is redeemed, in spite of liberal helpings from Pope, by a certain vivacity of satire, phrased with Augustan smartness. Such couplets as these still preserve a jaunty literary swagger for later ears; how they tickled the more susceptible ears of our grandfathers must be imagined:

> Where you send genius, send a fortune too;
> Dunces by instinct thrive, as oysters woo!
> For ne'er were veins of ore by chymist found,
> Except, like Hebrew roots, in barren ground!

Paine early grew old, and before he had reached his thirties his mind had taken a rigid conservative bent. His affections were fixed upon a past that was visibly falling into decay, and its ways were endeared to him in the measure that they decayed. It was a matter of personal pride with him to embody in his own manners the aristocratic bearing of pre-Revolutionary times.

Mr. Paine [says his biographer] attached great consequence to *manners*. . . . He was modelled upon the *old school*. Without being familiar, he was easy among friends, and courtly to strangers. In colloquial discussions, he rigidly adhered to the law of politeness; and in mixed society, he neither courted the *high*, nor avoided the *low*. . . . He frequently deplored a supposed decay of *manners*. With concern, he used to inquire

"In manners, where is the successor of Gen. Knox to be found?" It was with him a constant topick of complaint, that *"The old, genteel, town families, had been elbowed out of house and home, by newcomers:"* that *"instead of the polished manners of a city, we should soon exhibit that growth of gentility, which is produced by ingrafting dollars upon village habits and low employments."* (*Works*, Introduction, p. lxix.)

Affecting an aristocratic bearing, Paine was as complete a Tory as the republican environment permitted. If he despised the new, pushing middle class that had risen since the Revolution, he held in contempt the numerous company of those he dubbed the yokel, the peasant, the hind, or the plow-tail. Under the circumstances the best that he could do politically was to turn Federalist, and he embraced the principles of Fisher Ames with genteel conviction. "In politics," says his biographer, "Mr. Paine was a disciple of the old federal school. He understood the constitution, as Washington administered, and as Hamilton had expounded it" (*ibid.*, p. lxxvii). During his undergraduate days he had dabbled in French revolutionary philosophy, and "the fanatic Atheism of France, decorated in all the meretricious charms of eloquence and philosophy, took a transient possession of his mind" (*ibid.*, p. lxxviii). At graduation in 1792, he read a poem entitled *The Nature and Progress of Liberty*, in which he eulogized "liberal thought," proposed to follow "Reason," declared that "the rights of man" are a gift from heaven, proffered the hand of fellowship to France—

> May struggling France her ancient freedom gain,
> May Europe's sword oppose her rights in vain—

and launched a devastating couplet at the great English opponent of the Revolution—

> The fame of Burke, in dark oblivion rust,
> His pen a meteor—and his page the dust.

Three years later, on proceeding Master of Arts, he presented a poem in very different vein. Three years were a generation in those stirring times, and by 1795 the penetrating vision of this genius of twenty-two had discovered the atheist poison in the cup of French democracy. *The Invention of Letters* rises to a climax in a satirical elaboration of a line from the poem of 1792—"Licentious morals breed disease of state." Having learned his lesson from Fisher Ames, the sapient young Federalist announces that democracy is the mother of faction, and faction leads on to anarchy. In this poem for the first time Paine's wit runs freely, and certain lines are as jaunty as he ever penned.

> For place or power, while demagogues contend,
> Whirled in their vortex, sinks each humbler friend.
> See Crispin quit his stall, in Faction's cause,
> To cobble government, and soal the laws!
> See Frisseur scent his dust, his razor set,
> To shave the treaty, or to puff Genet!
> In doubtful mood, see Mulciber debate,
> To mend a horse-shoe, or to weld the state!
> The whip's bold knight, in barn, his truck is laid,
> To spout in favour of the carrying trade!
> While Staytape runs, from hissing goose, too hot,
> To measure Congress for another coat;
> And still, by rule of shop, intent on pelf,
> Eyes the spare cloth, to cabbage for himself!
>
> Envy, that fiend, who haunts the great and good,
> Not Cato shunned, nor Hercules subdued.
> On Fame's wide field, where'er a covert lies,
> The rustling serpent to the thicket flies;
> The foe of Glory, Merit is her prey;
> The dunce she leaves, to plod his drowsy way.
> Of birth amphibious, and of Protean skill,
> This green-eyed monster changes shape at will;
> Like snakes of smaller breed, she sheds her skin;
> Strips off the serpent, and turns—Jacobin.

In view of the fact that Governor Samuel Adams, chief of the New England Jacobins, was to occupy the stage, President Willard had diplomatically struck from the manuscript the ten lines last quoted; but Paine had the audacity to re-insert them in speaking, and the tumultuous applause was sufficient proof that it was not from a Harvard audience that Sam Adams got the votes that annually returned him governor.

Verse imposed some slight restraint on Paine's rhetoric, but in prose when he was in full career—as in the grotesque eulogy of Washington which stirred the patriotism of Boston Federalists—the reins are on the neck of his eloquence, and he takes all barriers with fiery abandon. Fact troubles his wild and frolic imagination not at all, but like any plebeian demagogue—whose factional appeals he so furiously condemned—he blew the bellows of Federalist partisanship with extraordinary vigor, stoking his fire with rumor and misrepresentation and party spleen. No slander was too gross, no lie too palpable to serve his end. He baited the democrats quite shamelessly, and aroused the mob of Boston gentlemen like a true Tory. One of his political orations has been preserved by his editor in the collected edition of his works, for the enlightenment of posterity—an oration delivered in 1799, "at the request of the young men of Boston," on the theme of France and democracy. In this extraordinary composition Paine seems to have been quite ravished by his own rhetoric, that flashes in many a feint and parry before it impales its victim. It is a Federalist philippic, designed to destroy the good name of all who have quitted the sacred Federalist tribe. Words could hardly go further; disregard for truth could scarcely be more brazen. Paine's delight in clever antitheses overweighs any scruples in regard to just statement. "The French Republick," he asserted, "has exhibited all the vices of civilization, without one of the virtues of barbarism." One or two bits from this tremendous oration, that in "the glow of feeling, the swell of language, and the brilliancy of sentiments" has "very seldom been surpassed," and that was "received with rapturous and enthusiastic applause," must suffice to illustrate the justice of the Federalist claim to the custodianship of political good manners. "Politics should have no passions," Fisher Ames asserted—which excellent principle young Robert Treat Paine exemplified thus:

Political Empiricism has never attained, in any age or nation, so universal an ascendency, as at the present day in the "Illuminated Republick." Unfettered by the fear of innovation, and unshackled by the prejudice of ages, the modern Frenchman is educated in a system of moral and religious chimeras, which dazzle by their novelty those volatile intellects, which prescriptive wisdom could never impress with veneration. Every Frenchman, who has read a little is a pedant; and the whole race of these hornbook Philosophers is content with the atheism of Mirabeau . . . the absurd philanthropy of Condorcet, and the visionary politics of Rousseau. These are the boundaries of their literary ambition, of their political science. Hence it is, that they pretend to be too enlightened for belief, too virtuous for government.

The feculence of party is not yet drained of its rankest sediment. The worshippers of democracy, though their altars are thrown down, are not yet converted from their devotions. The frozen snake has still some sparks of animation; and, if placed by compassion near your hospitable fires, he will revive with exasperated venom, and sting the hardy fool that fostered him. Deal therefore with these ferocious demoralizers, as our crafty mariners trade with the savages of the Indian ocean—with your men at their posts, your guns loaded, and your slow matches burning. (*Works*, p. 319.)

For all democrats Paine had the hearty contempt of an honest man for a rogue, but for the intellectuals who expounded the new romantic philosophy his indignation was measureless. "The legitimate plebeian democrat," he asserted, is "an enemy to all government, under which he holds no office"; but fling him a bone from the public table and "he becomes the very scavenger of administration." The "Illuminated Jacobin," on the other hand, "never changes his principles."

His whole science is directed to unhinge society, his whole ambition to plunder it. He is too ravenous to be content with a system of order himself; and too selfish to permit its enjoyment by others. Like a hog in a flower-garden, he sets no value on the variegated foliage he destroys, and seems only desirous to root out every twig of vegetation, that can satiate his voracity. (*Ibid.*, p. 321.)

To such fustian was he reduced when his wit left him. That a gentleman could talk like that, and other gentlemen applaud, is a sad commentary on the intellectual honesty of partisanship, even amongst decent Federalists. Fustian was the order of the day, and Paine was merely baying with his pack. If only he had not professed such virtues his extravagance might be forgiven; but extravagance ill becomes a distinguished repository of political wisdom. Once, indeed, his vivacity got him into a nasty mess. While editor of *The Federal Orrery*, he accepted in 1795 a political poem entitled *The Jacobiniad*, the satire of which Paine "new-pointed and new-edged" before printing. The democrats, at whom it was directed, were vastly incensed, and a mob gathered before his lodging but was dispersed. Later the son of one of the victims challenged him to a duel. Paine declined but armed himself with an unloaded pistol. Accidentally meeting his challenger in the street, he drew his weapon, but the young fellow, standing in no awe of a favorite of the muses, struck the pistol down and proceeded to give Paine a sound drubbing. To such base treatment may genius come, when wit forgets that a sally of the tongue may invite a counter sally of the fists. And so we leave him in the dust of the street, ignobly laid low by the strength of that vulgar democracy which was to bring down so many things held dear by Boston Tories. His was, very largely, a wasted life—wasted by sheer indolence and feeble will. He was a fellow of some parts, and a sentence from one of his dramatic criticisms may not inaptly apply to him: "The character is not a sot, but his humor has a mellower tilth for having been husbanded and manured by 'the excellent endeavor of drinking.'"

CHAPTER II

WINDS OF POLITICAL DOCTRINE

I

INTO the complacent little Boston of Fisher Ames and Robert Treat Paine came the Embargo, the War of 1812, and the industrial revolution to upset its static order and destroy its snug provincialism. The old Federalism with its Hartford Convention and plans for New England secession went the way of mortality, carrying with it to the grave the old pessimism and the old spleen. The jealous isolationist policy was quietly forgotten in Boston; the gospel of secession was preached no more; George Cabot and Timothy Pickering gave way to other leaders; and provincial Boston joined with Kentucky and Tennessee in extolling a romantic nationalism. It sent to Washington a new spokesman, who joined with Henry Clay in a paternalistic program of national expansion, and took command of the forces combating the rising separatism of the South Carolina school. By the year 1830 Boston had traveled far from the times of the Hartford Convention.

The sufficient explanation of so striking a change is to be found, of course, in the changing economics of Massachusetts. The Embargo had proved a major disaster to New England shipping; and the Boston merchants, counting their losses from idle and dismasted ships, water-logging at the wharves, found just cause for hating the policy of the administration. But if the shipping business was brought face to face with tragedy, the manufacturing interests stumbled upon unexpected prosperity. With British imports cut off, the home market offered a tempting opportunity to Yankee enterprise. The familiar story of the swift rise of New England industrialism need not be recounted here. It is enough to remark that with the growth of domestic manufactures a new group of economic leaders appeared, and the policy of New England shifted from pro-mercantilism to pro-industrialism. It was a difficult choice at first between the antagonistic claims of the Boston merchant and the Lowell manufacturer; between the carriers of foreign goods who demanded free trade, and the makers of domestic goods who demanded a protective tariff. The traditional view of

New England was strongly for free trade. In 1807 a Federalist lawyer asserted it to be "an unalienable right," and in 1820 Judge Story asked, "Why should the laboring classes be taxed for the necessaries of life?"[1] The tariff bill of 1824 got only one vote from Massachusetts; but in the four years between the passage of that act and the "Tariff of Abominations" of 1828, Massachusetts went over definitely to industrialism. Thenceforth she was to be the leader in the movement looking to governmental paternalism, substituting the expansive Federalism of Hamilton for the restrictive Federalism of Fisher Ames, and becoming in consequence whole-heartedly nationalistic.

Equally significant, though less observed, was the changed attitude of Massachusetts towards the great republican experiment. Gone was the older generation, with its face turned to the past and its heart bound up with the patriarchal ideals of a decadent squirearchy. Gone also were the disturbant fears of democracy. The menace of Daniel Shays, that had put the old Federalists in a rage at democracy, was long since forgotten; and the nervous panic over French Jacobinism, that had upset New England for a decade, had subsided. In the light of longer experience with its ways democracy was seen to be far from terrifying. The hobgoblin of faction that had benightmared the dreams of Fisher Ames was discovered to be only a bogey to frighten naughty boys. Massachusetts had kept off the agrarian reef, despite war and economic unrest, and with her new constitution of 1820 property interests were as secure as any old Federalist could have wished. Gentlemen of principle and property were still in control of the state; and if less emphasis was laid on principle and more on property—if less regard seemed to be paid to gentlemen of breeding and manners, and more to assertive self-seeking—business was no less secure than in the good old days, and its profits were greater. And so, master of its looms and a growing home market, New England industrialism regarded genially the great western movement, fostered by a benevolent paternalism, confident of extending its markets with every mile of westward expansion. To encourage the development of the West and South by a Federal policy of internal improvement became, therefore, common business foresight, provided of course that the Constitution should follow pop-

[1] Quoted in Theodore Parker, *Daniel Webster: Additional Speeches*, Vol. I, p. 195. Considerable information will be found in this excellent study.

ulation and safeguard business interests against local agrarianism and the menace of particularism.

By the year 1830 both dangers lay black against the political horizon. The triumph of Jackson had enthroned the agrarian menace at Washington and produced such a scrambling of frightened interests—such a rattling among the old bones of Federalism and scurrying among the young limbs of industrialism—as the country had not seen for many a year. Henry Clay appealed to his followers in the West, and Webster marshaled his adherents of the East, and from the coalescing of these incongruous elements emerged the Whig party to do battle with Old Hickory. It was a patchwork army at best. In the hour of peril, principles go by the board. The Whig party was lineal heir of the old Federalism, but it denied its philosophical patrimony. It substituted expediency for the old economic realism, and began and ended intellectually bankrupt. Its bitter and unseemly squabbles over the Bank and tariff, its platitudes of patriotism and its pose of disinterestedness, the venom of its personal attack upon Jackson, were the earmarks of a policy of shallow opportunism that failed to make use of such victories as fell to its lot, for the simple reason that it could never agree on what to do. Such cohesive power as held it together—aside from petty antagonism to Jackson—was the vague assumption that the well-being of the American people was dependent on governmental patronage; the belief that each economic group and section must receive its special favor, and that through tariffs and bonuses and internal improvements the country as a whole must prosper. Of this principle of special favors—a return to the seventeenth century from which eighteenth-century liberalism was a reaction—the American System of Henry Clay was the chief expression, and it remains the most significant bequest of the Whig party to our political history.

The Whig party was the first attempt of our rising middle class to erect a political platform in accordance with middle-class ideals, and its failure was due to the fact that the time was not ripe for undisputed middle-class control. The merchant aristocracy of the North was overthrown, but the planter aristocracy of the South was still to be reckoned with; and its particularistic ambitions in the end wrecked the Whig coalition of the West and East. By 1820 a revolutionary change had taken place in the political philosophy of the plantation school. From an ardent nationalism

Calhoun was leading his followers back to the earlier doctrine of states rights; and New England industrialism found itself confronted with the doctrine which the Hartford junto had played with, but now with far more drive behind it. The slave economy was entertaining imperialistic dreams, and to effect its ends was building up a new constitutional philosophy. Southern writers had long been at work, and the weight of their authority was behind the new particularism. *Rawle on the Constitution*, a states-rights exposition, was the official textbook on civics at the United States Military Academy, and from it, while a student at West Point, Jefferson Davis declared that he first imbibed states-rights principles. Other authoritative southern works that were widely read were John Taylor's two studies: *Construction Construed and Constitutions Vindicated* (1820), and *New Views of the Constitution of the United States* (1823); some years later came Henry St. George Tucker's *Lectures on Constitutional Law* (1843); and these were only preliminary to Calhoun's searching exposition in his *Disquisition on Government* and *An Inquiry into the Nature of the Constitution of the United States*.

To meet this theory of particularism there was need of a resurgent Federalism, with a new nationalistic interpretation of the Constitution. The compact theory of the Federal state must be refuted by the organic theory; the conception of federated commonwealths must yield to the conception of a coalescing sovereignty. The old battle must be fought over again with fresh arguments. The sanctity of the Constitution must be asserted, but that sanctity must be thrown over a nationalistic rather than a particularistic interpretation. It must be shown that despite the vehement protestations of southern loyalty, a particularistic Constitution was a denial of loyalty and must end in the destruction of the national union. For this difficult business New England was as yet unprepared. The old Federalist arguments were obsolete, and many of those Federalists had been deep in the Hartford Convention. The new industrialism must provide its own theory, and it was fortunate in discovering two men whose combined learning and eloquence proved equal to the task.

II

The name of Webster has been so closely associated with the movement of constitutional nationalism as to overshadow the just fame of one who has many claims to be regarded as the intellectual leader of the school.   Joseph Story was a Salem lawyer whose reputation, considerable as it is, is scarcely commensurate with his influence on our later constitutional development.   Of the same Harvard class with William Ellery Channing, he dabbled in polite letters as a young man, but went into the law, entered politics, became Associate Justice of the Supreme Court, and for a time was Dane professor of law at Harvard.   He came of radical stock.   His father, a physician at Boston till he removed to Marblehead, was a militant Revolutionary Whig, one of the score or so of Indians who made up the Boston Tea Party, and a leader amongst the group of Sons of Liberty who seized and gagged the sentinels and carried off two brass fieldpieces from the Common where the British commander had posted them to overawe the town.   The son grew up an ardent republican.   As a very young man he became an outstanding leader of the unfashionable party, then in the minority, and suffered certain humiliations on account of his political opinions; on one occasion, according to Theodore Parker, being "knocked down in the street, beaten, and forced to take shelter in the house of a friend, whither he fled, bleeding, and covered with the mud of the street" (*Additional Speeches*, Vol. I, p. 178).   Of these youthful heresies few indications appeared in his later life.   Republican though he might be, he was utterly devoid of any radical tendencies, and when he took his seat on the Supreme Court bench he was speedily drawn into the powerful orbit of John Marshall, shared the latter's views on all major constitutional questions, and turned Whig.   He became a close friend of Webster and from 1816 to 1842 he was his chief adviser on knotty legal, constitutional, and international questions.   "From that deep and copious well of legal knowledge," Parker asserts, Webster drew freely "whenever his own bucket was dry" (*ibid.*, p. 170).

This shift from Republican to Whig came about quite naturally. New England liberalism, it must be remembered, produced no intellectual leaders till late, and no clear-cut political philosophy. Though it nominally accepted the leadership of Jefferson it never was won over to the Physiocratic economics or states-rights principles of the Virginia school.   Story was at no time a Jeffersonian, but rather an eager and avowed disciple of Washington, "little infected with Virginia notions, as to men or measures."   In his *Autobiography* he wrote:

The republican party then and at all other times embraced men of very different views on many subjects. Nay, a Virginia republican of that day, was very different from a Massachusetts republican, and the anti-federal doctrines of the former state then had and still have very little support or influence in the latter state, notwithstanding a concurrence in political action upon general subjects. I was at all times a firm believer in the doctrines of General Washington, and an admirer of his conduct, measures and principles. . . . I read and examined his principles, and have made them in a great measure the rule and guide of my life. I was and always have been a lover, devoted lover, of the constitution of the United States, and a friend to the union of the states. I never wished to bring the government to a mere confederacy of states; but to preserve the power of the general government given by all the states, in full exercise and sovereignty for the protection and preservation of all the states. (Story, *Life and Letters of Joseph Story*, Vol. I, p. 128.)

That he had as little sympathy with the Physiocratic economics of Jefferson is apparent from his early activities in furthering the new paper system. While a member of the Massachusetts legislature, as a young man, he was active in pressing for bank franchises, and upon the establishment of the Merchants' Bank of Salem he became its president. Like Washington and Marshall he espoused the new gospel of capitalism, with none of the agrarian prejudices of the landed gentry to hold him back. He was the political twin of the great Chief Justice, and a Whig in spirit long before Webster. "I seem to myself," he remarked late in life, "simply to have stood still in my political belief, while parties revolved about me; so that, although of the same opinions now as ever, I find my name changed from Democrat to Whig, but I know not how or why" (*ibid.*, Vol. I, p. 546). Though somewhat naïve the comment is just. Anti-federalism in Massachusetts would seem to have been largely a capitalistic protest against the narrow tie-wig Federalism; and while Joseph Story sat upon the Supreme Court bench, adapting legal principles to the new needs of business, the country was moving forward to the middle-class philosophy that he had early come to hold.

In the year 1833 he published his *Commentaries on the Constitution*, the fruit of long labors, which was at once accepted throughout the North as a classical authority, and which has held its ground pretty well since. In method and temper, as well as objective, the exposition of Story stands in sharp contrast to that of the southern school. In its particularism the latter appealed to the history of the Constitution in the making, and to French romantic philosophy; whereas the former followed English constitutional theories to nationalistic ends. Story was steeped in the Common Law and his thinking reveals the strong influence of Blackstone. In passing through the mind of the great Tory commentator, English constitutional theory had received a pronounced Tory bias, and something of this remains after filtering through the mind of Story. The ideal of a strong and efficient political state, with its corollaries of a coercive sovereignty, of the duties of a subject rather than the rights of a citizen, of loyalty to government rather than concern for political justice, derives immediately from English theory and practice. Much likewise he took from the older Federalists: their fear of an encroaching legislative power; their concern at faction; their faith in checks and balances to restrain the majority will. But his chief inspiration came from the spirit of the Common Law—that subtle influence that Jefferson so greatly feared. His legalism was inveterate; the final, authoritative answer to all questions he discovered in the decision of the courts. Against such a mind, deeply read in the law and with scanty knowledge of economics and political theory, the waves of liberal and romantic thought broke impotently. His reasoning may be convincing to a lawyer, but to the historian his exposition is often weak, his data inadequate, and his conclusions not infrequently contrary to fact.

In building his argument Story drew his materials freely from *The Federalist*, from the writings and decisions of Marshall, and from Blackstone. The backbone of the work is Hamilton and Marshall, from whom he quotes constantly, supplemented by a host of decisions by Federalist judges. With its pronounced bias *The Commentaries* must be regarded as a partisan document, which like *The Federalist* has grown in authoritativeness with the triumph of its party principles. Its surprising weakness on the historical side has come to be overlooked since the downfall of southern particularism, but during the debates that preceded the Civil War the work was sharply handled by southern historians, and in his *Constitutional View of the War between the States* Stephens quite demolished Story's feeble attempt at an historical justification of the anti-compact theory. The weight of historical evidence, to present-day students, would seem to be on the side of the states-rights argument, although in certain aspects both sides were innovators: Story in overleaping the period of French ascendency when the Constitution took shape, and going back to the older English tradition; and the compact school in reasserting the compact theory at a time when the spirit of nationalism was undermining it. Story seems to have been conscious of his weakness, for he expressly repudiates the method of interpreting the work in the light of contemporary testimony at the time of its formulation. In so doing he not only violates the principle that a document is to be construed in the light of the common understanding when it was drawn; but with naïve inconsistency, he constantly appeals to *The Federalist*, pretty much ignoring the opposition pamphlets, and interprets the Constitution in accord with its commentary. But for the most part he clings to the strict letter of the document. He lightly brushes aside the whole compact argument by asserting dogmatically that the phrase, "We the people of the United States," must be understood in its simple literal sense, and that thus interpreted, the Constitution is seen to derive immediately from the individual citizens acting in their sovereign capacity without the intermediation of the state governments. The dispute long waged furiously about this point and Story's analysis touches only the fringe of the argument.

Very likely it is presumptuous for one who is not a lawyer to express an opinion, yet these celebrated *Commentaries* seem today very little more than a new-modeled Federalism, adapted to changing conditions. Underneath the somewhat crabbed and narrow legalism is a common-sense realistic political philosophy, an embodiment of English constitutional tradition as it grew up under a Tory régime, that reveals scant sympathy with French romantic theories. The work is an unconscious testimony to the tenacious hold of the English Common Law on the legal mind of America, as well as to the rising spirit of nationalism. It did much to strengthen both. It was a triumph of the lawyer over the historian and political philosopher, and it marks the beginning of the lawyer's custodianship of the fundamental law. In spite of its somewhat petty legalism and prosaic common sense, a note of veneration for the great document runs through the tedious pages, constituting the work at once both a commentary and a eulogy.

DANIEL WEBSTER

Realist and Constitutionalist

A far solider mind, strongly realistic and broadly philosophical, acute in analysis and with great powers of imagination, was the mind of the distinguished leader of the New England Whigs. Not the equal of Story as a lawyer, he was far superior as a political thinker. No man more richly endowed in mind and person has played a part on the stage of our public life, and in spite of gross shortcomings in character and the betrayal of his own promise, Webster retains an aura of the heroic about him. He was a great man, built on a great pattern, who never quite achieved a great life.

In Emerson and Webster were completely embodied the diverse New England tendencies that derived from the Puritan and the Yankee: the idealistic and the practical; the ethical and the rationalistic; the intellectual revolutionary, ready to turn the world upside down in theory, planting at the base of the established order the dynamite of ideas, and the soberly conservative, understanding the economic springs of political action, inclined to pessimism, neither wishing for Utopian change nor expecting it. The physical contrast was as striking as the mental. The child of the Puritan was slender, nervous, with a lambent energy that played freely in a rarefied atmosphere; the child of the Yankee was massive, solid, somnolently heavy till an idea awakened his faculties, a lover of the fleshpots, careless of conventional morals, rankly physical, and yet with an assured stateliness of manner, a slow imagination that expanded majestically and a rich eloquence that moved forward by regular stages to a great objective. Emerson was the child of a long line of ministers, and ministerial in his unworldliness; Webster was a Yankee squire, the descendant of some fox-hunting master of broad English acres, who by a freak of fortune had got born into the family of a New Hampshire yeoman. No Englishman was ever more English than he. He loved the substantial things of life: his Marshfield farm; his cattle and horses and crops; his rides afield and the return to good dinners and rich wines. Nothing is more characteristic or more likable—more redolent of the natural Webster—than his concern for agricultural improvements. His homely talk on *The Agricul-*

ture of England, filled with facts that had come under his observant eye, reveals a side that is too little known. It is an English country squire talking to his neighbors about the homely things they all care for; and when after long years and disappointed ambition and utter weariness, he returned to his Marshfield farm to die, it was his cattle and his fields that offered a last solace to the broken man.

Webster's intellectual development falls into distinct and rather sharply defined periods. Before 1825 his mental processes were still under the dominion of the solid, rationalist eighteenth century, with its realistic politics and its *laissez faire* economics. With the emergence of the constitutional disputes at the end of the twenties, when the lawyers and historians were busy at their commentaries, he came increasingly to take a legalistic view of government. During the acrimonious forties, with slavery dividing the country into hostile camps, he was bitten deeply by presidential ambitions, and thenceforth to the end of his life he was little more than a politician—a rôle for which he was singularly ill-fitted, and which brought bitterness and disillusion to his last days. Since his death both earlier and later phases of his career have fallen into the background, and the middle period of constitutional interpretation has stamped itself indelibly upon his fame. Yet in many respects the solid reasoning of the political philosopher is more valuable than the stately but somewhat ill-grounded declamation of the defender of the Constitution; and his just fame is increased rather than lessened by recalling his earlier contribution to our institutional development.

Webster was a sound political scholar, if not an outstanding creative thinker. He was of the distinguished line of political realists, from Harrington through Locke and Burke, to Hamilton, Madison and John Adams. He derived equally from seventeenth-century liberalism and eighteenth-century Federalism. He was widely read in the political classics, and his vigorous mind laid hold upon major principles and examined them closely. His intellectual master was the acute thinker of the English Commonwealth period, James Harrington, whom he pronounces "one of the most ingenious of political writers," and to whose suggestive doctrine of economic determinism he returns persistently. That Harrington was not the originator of the doctrine he was well enough read to have discovered; but he pays him high tribute as the

thinker who gave the doctrine form and currency. It is the substantial realism of the *Oceana* that appealed to a mind thoroughly
indoctrinated with political realism, before the rise of manhood
suffrage and the spread of equalitarianism had brought a change
in American political theory. Both his major premises and his
mode of reasoning bear the impress of the classic English school.
In the year 1820, within a single week, he made two speeches,
which as expositions of his political philosophy are the most illuminating he ever uttered, and which should stand side by side:
the *Basis of the Senate*, delivered before the Massachusetts Constitutional Convention, and the Plymouth speech on *The First Settlement of New England*. They supplement each other and together
give an admirable elucidation of the stake-in-society principle
that embodied a conviction he never abandoned. They are compact
of Harrington, Montesquieu and John Adams—the last authentic
expression of the old Federalism, before the democratic storms had
driven it into new roadsteads and whipped its flag from the hal-
yards where it had long waved.

In his admirable argument Webster accepts as axiomatic the
theory of division of powers, with the attendant machinery of
checks and balances. He accepts equally the familiar view of
eighteenth-century liberalism, that the legislature as the self-conscious custodian of the popular will is certain to prove the engrossing member of government whose ambition is most to be feared.
To expect a stable balance between Senate and House when their
characters are undifferentiated by diverse modes of selection—
a result that must follow from choosing both on the numerical
majority principle—seems to him the judgment of political inexperience. The wiser method, he believed, was to seek counsel
of the philosophers and the clear teachings of history. The first,
Webster insisted, have rightly laid down the principle of a stake-
in-society as the true measure of political justice:

I take the *principle* to be well established, by writers of the greatest
authority. In the first place, those who have treated of natural law have
maintained, as a principle of law, that, as far as the object of society
is the protection of something in which the members possess unequal
shares, it is just that the weight of each person in the common councils should bear a relation and proportion to his interest. Such is the
sentiment of Grotius, and he refers, in support of it, to several institutions
among the lesser states. ("The Basis of the Senate," in *Works*, Vol. III,
pp. 13–14.)

At the basis of the stake-in-society principle is the doctrine of economic power as the controlling factor in determining the form and scope of the political state. In support of this doctrine of determinism Webster appeals to Harrington:

It is his leading object, in his *Oceana*, to prove, that power *naturally* and *necessarily* follows property. He maintains that a government founded on property is legitimately founded; and that a government founded on the disregard of property is founded in injustice, and can only be maintained by military force. "If one man," says he, "be sole landlord, like the Grand Seignior, his empire is absolute. If a few possess the land, this makes the Gothic or feudal constitution. If the *whole people* be landlords, then it is a commonwealth." "It is strange," says an ingenious person in the last century, "that Harrington should be the first man to find out so evident and demonstrable a truth as that property being the true basis and *measure* of power." In truth, he was not the first. The idea is as old as political science itself. It may be found in Aristotle, Lord Bacon, Sir Walter Raleigh, and other writers. Harrington seems, however, to be the first writer who has illustrated and expanded the principle, and given to it the effect and prominence which justly belong to it. To this sentiment, Sir, I entirely agree. It seems to me to be plain, that, in the absence of military force, political power naturally and necessarily goes into the hands which hold the property. In my judgment, therefore, a republican form of government rests, not more on political constitutions, than on those laws which regulate the descent and transmission of property. . . .

The English Revolution of 1688 was a revolution in favor of property, as well as of other rights. It was brought about by men of property for their security; and our own immortal Revolution was undertaken, not to shake or plunder property, but to protect it. The acts which the country complained of were such as violated the rights of property. An immense majority of all those who had an interest in the soil were in favor of the Revolution; and they carried it through, looking to its results for the security of their possessions. ("The Basis of the Senate," in *Works*, Vol. III, pp. 14–16.)

Harrington's principle that "if the *whole people* be landlords, then it is a commonwealth," Webster justified by appeal to American history. The spontaneous birth of republican institutions out of colonial experience he attributed to the wide diffusion of property. The land tenure of primitive New England was the creative source of her popular government.

Their situation demanded a parcelling out and division of the lands, and it may be fairly said, that this necessary act *fixed the future frame and form of their government.* The character of their political institutions was determined by the fundamental laws respecting property. . . . The property was all freehold . . . alienation of the land was every way facilitated, even to the subjecting of it to every species of debt. The establishment of public registries, and the simplicity of our forms of conveyance, have greatly facilitated the change of real estate from one proprietor to another. The consequence of all these causes has been, a great subdivision of the soil, and a great equality of condition; the true basis, most certainly, of a popular government. "If the people," says Harrington, "hold three parts in four of the territory, it is plain there can neither be any single person nor nobility able to dispute the government with them; in this case, therefore, *except force be interposed*, they govern themselves." ("The First Settlement of New England," in *Works*, Vol. I, pp. 35–36.)

Wholly English then, after the soundest English liberal tradition, was Webster's political philosophy in the year 1820, compact of sober eighteenth-century realism, quite unaffected by French romantic equalitarianism. The great principle to which he adhered was the principle that government to be stable must be founded in men's interests; thus founded no cause is given for revolutionary upheavals. "The disastrous revolutions which the world has witnessed, those political thunder-storms and earthquakes which have shaken the pillars of society to their very deepest foundations, have been revolutions against property." Such were Webster's convictions on the eve of those two great upheavals, the rise of Jacksonian democracy and the rejuvenation of the slave economy, that unseated the authority of the old school of political realism, and turned him aside from the plain path to lose himself in a tangle of constitutional legalism.

English also was his economic theory, to which, like Franklin before him, he gave close thought. In the year 1820 he was a frank disciple of Adam Smith and the *laissez faire* school. Mercantilism he derided as exploded;[2] and Physiocratic agrarianism seemed to him unduly hostile to commerce. He never concerned himself, like Franklin, with humanitarian ends. His sympathies went strongly for free trade, individual initiative, and a competitive order—sympathies which to the end of his life he never wholly outgrew. In those early days the mercantile interests commanded his loyalty far more readily than the manufacturing interests. Next to his Marshfield farm he loved a full-rigged ship, and the thought of Yankee skippers plowing the seven seas in well-freighted bottoms fired his imagination and kindled his patriotism.

[2] See "The Tariff," in *Works*, Vol. III, pp. 118–122.

But if in the background of his thought he remained *laissez faire*, with the necessary implications of a diminished political state and reliance upon the law of supply and demand above tariffs, bounties, and political regulations, unfortunately in the foreground of expediency were the loud demands of his constituents for protective tariffs, internal improvements, and a policy of governmental paternalism. His economics came into collision with politics, and under the drive of necessity he went reluctantly along the path which Hamilton had marked out a generation before.

The change came between the years 1824 and 1825. In the earlier year he aroused himself to a strong defense of *laissez faire* economics in opposition to Clay's clever campaign cry, the American System; in the later year he endeavored half-heartedly to defend New England interests in the game of subsidies. He was honestly ashamed of the whole mess; to Webster any tariff was a "tariff of abominations"; but his mouth was stopped by the clamor of the Lowell textile masters.[3] But having chosen his side, thereafter he defended his course vigorously, and joined forces with Clay in extolling the principle of protection. The same dubious shift is revealed in his changing attitude towards public finance. In 1815 he was an old-fashioned Federalist in his preference for a metallic currency and his belief that the public credit must rest on the public income; bank paper, stocks, bonds, and other agencies of the new finance he distrusted as likely to encourage speculation.[4] Twenty years later he was the outstanding champion of the Bank in its mortal quarrel with Jackson. In defending his public career before his constituents in Faneuil Hall in 1842, he said: "The subject of currency has been the study of my life, in preference to all other public topics"; and the result of those studies had made him a confirmed bullionist. Nevertheless when "Old Bullion Benton" proposed to restore a metallic currency, Webster derided the plan on the ground that bank money was necessary; and when the subtreasury system was established he denounced it bitterly.[5] He was a partisan to the cause of the Bank, and as its attorney he defended its case before the American public, as he defended its cases before the Supreme Court. He was no longer a free man but was deep in the subsidies of financial interests; nevertheless his old

[3] See his "Apology and Defense," in *Works*, Vol. V, pp. 146, 240.
[4] See "The Bank of the United States," *Works*, Vol. III, p. 35.
[5] See "Speech in Wall Street," in *Works*, Vol. II, p. 55.

realism convinced him—as it had convinced Hamilton—of the necessity of shaping the public policy to the desires of the bankers. He justified it not only on the grounds of economic determinism, but by professing to discover in business the strong friend of national unity. The planters and farmers were local and sectional in outlook, but the "mercantile classes, the great commercial masses of the country, whose affairs connect them strongly with every State in the Union and with all the nations of the earth, whose business and profession give a sort of nationality to their character"—these men, he argued, gave solidity and stability to government—they were the cohesive force that bound the whole together.[6] In serving such clients he was but serving a greater cause.

After 1824 the earlier Webster with his solid understanding, his frank realism, his honest exposition of fundamental principles, slowly gave way to the lawyer, the politician, the opportunist of the unhappy later years. With the change the last authentic voice of the eighteenth century was silenced; the break with the old English tradition was complete. Immediate, domestic issues muddied his thought, and Webster and America plunged into a bitter partisanship produced by the new alignments of an equalitarian agrarianism, a capitalistic industrialism, and a feudal slavocracy. Federalism was dead and in its stead was the Whig party, patched together of odds and ends, devoid of principles, seeking only expediency; and of this party Webster became an outstanding spokesman. It was an ignoble time, and his great abilities were not substantial enough to save him from the common meanness. Whoever wishes to understand how great was his fall need only compare the speech of 1820 on "The Basis of the Senate" with the "Declaration of Whig Principles and Purposes" of 1840 (*Works*, Vol. II, p. 41).

To his contemporaries, however, his position was secure. His reputation was extraordinary, and he seemed as fixed and brilliant as the north star. After the reply to Hayne, his fame as the defender of the Constitution was in every mouth. That celebrated speech, perhaps the most celebrated in our congressional history, was delivered on the January 26, 1830, and awakened an amazing response. Men were moved to tears by its eloquence, and its circulation in pamphlet form exceeded that of any other pamphlet

---

[6] See "The Landing at Plymouth," in *Works*, Vol. II, pp. 204-205.

since the founding of the government. It is not a great constitutional argument, but it better served the purpose of inspiring in the public a grandiose conception of national unity under the organic law, than any reasoned statement could have done. For political purposes rhetoric was more effective than historical argument, and its sonorous sentences, and in particular the stately conclusion, vastly appealed to the taste of the generation. Three years later Webster applied himself more closely to the subtleties of the question. Calhoun's masterly argument with its exposition of the theory of concurrent majorities could not be answered by rhetoric, and on February 16, 1833, Webster spoke on "The Constitution not a Compact between Sovereign States" (*Works*, Vol. III, p. 449). His argument is strictly legal and rests on four theses: that sovereignty inheres in the people; that as individuals acting collectively in their sovereign capacity, they ordained and established the Constitution; that the Constitution thus established is the supreme law of the land, acting immediately upon the individual citizen and recognizing no intermediary sovereign state; and that as an "executed contract" it is irrevocable and final, with the necessary functions to construe its powers and execute its will.

Of these four theses, two may be regarded as Webster's chief contribution to the great debate: the doctrine of immediacy, and the doctrine of an executed contract. The latter, quite obviously, is no more than Burke's theory of the British constitution as founded on a compact entered into following the Revolution of 1688, and as such, by analogy from the Common Law, inviolable without the consent of both parties to the instrument. As developed by Burke the theory is somewhat tenuous, but as applied by Webster to the interpretation of a written document it is extraordinarily plausible to the legal mind. The doctrine of immediacy, on the other hand, would seem to have been derived from Judge Story. The argument of Webster in expounding the principle of immediate contact between the individual citizen and the Constitution follows the argument of Story's *Commentaries* too closely to escape comment. Theodore Parker explicitly states that Webster got his argument from Story, and circumstances bear out his assertion. The two men had long been close friends. Webster's speech was delivered a month after the *Commentaries* was finished. In his earlier speeches such principle found no place, and it is reasonable to suppose that, confronted by the Calhoun resolutions

Webster should have turned to the materials gathered by his learned friend and frequent adviser. Here was his reply ready to hand, a mass of legal fact and constitutional exposition, together with a clear and simple theory. Nearly a month elapsed before Webster rose to speak, and then he threw *Story on the Constitution* at Calhoun's theory of compact. Whether such an interpretation is reasonable or not, the speech added greatly to Webster's reputation as an expounder of the Constitution.

In 1833 he stood at the meridian of his renown; thereafter the westering sun of his fame went slowly down. He had come to evil times when opportunism and compromise—so imperative if the country were to hold together at all—seemed immoral to men who insisted that righteousness be legislated upon America, and weakness to men who demanded their pound of flesh. The black shadow of slavery fell across his path, and despite his wish to avoid all controversy on the subject, he could not evade the issue. It drove him into a corner, and the sword of the Constitution that he sought to defend himself with was turned in the end against him. Webster's antipathy to slavery was of long standing and he gave frank expression to it in his speeches. The position which he finally came to assume, in face of the growing abolition sentiment in Massachusetts, was taken deliberately and was worthy of a lawyer. He would oppose the extension of slave territory, but he would not interfere with slavery in the old slave states. The Constitution, he argued, recognized slavery as existing in certain commonwealths by virtue of state laws, but those laws did not run beyond the confines of the state. The territories were under Federal law, and no injunction was laid upon Congress to extend the laws or institutions of any state or group of states over the territorial domain. In his speech on "Exclusion of Slavery from the Territories," on August 12, 1848, he stated his position thus:

It will not be contended that this sort of slavery exists by general law. It exists only by local law. I do not mean to deny the validity of that local law where it is established; but I say it is, after all, local law. It is nothing more. And wherever that local law does not extend, property in persons does not exist. Well, Sir, what is now the demand on the part of our Southern friends? They say, "We will carry our local laws with us wherever we go. We insist that Congress does us injustice unless it establishes in the territory in which we wish to go our own local law." This demand I for one resist, and shall resist. It goes upon the idea that there is an inequality, unless persons under this local law, and holding property by authority of that law, can go into new territory and there establish that local law, to the exclusion of the general law. (*Works,* Vol. V, p. 309.)

It was the unfortunate Seventh of March Speech that proved Webster's undoing—this and the Fugitive Slave Bill in which he was deeply implicated. The situation was desperately critical, Webster was pessimistic, and this was a last gesture of reconciliation with the South. Presidential ambitions and runaway slaves were stewing in a common political pot with Abolition societies and northern mercantile interests. Webster was puzzled, hesitated, emptied another glass of the wine of the Constitution, and went for the Fugitive Slave Bill. It was a tragic political mistake. To be sure a tremendous address was presented to him, signed by the most respectable persons in Boston and Cambridge, but it was an empty honor. Webster's influence was gone, never to be regained. There is something pathetic in his futile attempt to stifle the New England conscience by ramming the Constitution down its throat:

Sir, the principle of the restitution of runaway slaves is not objectionable, unless the Constitution is objectionable. If the Constitution is right in that respect, the principle is right, and the law providing for carrying it into effect is right. If that be so, and if there is no abuse of the right under any law of Congress, or any other law, then what is there to complain of? ("Speech on the Compromise Measures," in *Works,* Vol. V, p. 433.)

And there is something pathetic also in the hurt vanity of the old man that his judgment should be questioned. His self-pride was offended when the Abolitionists rejected his legal dogmatisms, and set up their own dogmatisms. He regarded them as mischief-makers. "I am against agitators, north and south," he exclaimed petulantly. He recognized no higher law than the Constitution and Blackstone, and he would suffer no popular interference with Congress.

Then, Sir, there are the Abolition societies, of which I am unwilling to speak, but in regard to which I have very clear notions and opinions. I do not think them useful. I think their operations for the last twenty years have produced nothing good or valuable. . . . They have excited feelings. . . . I cannot but see what mischiefs their interference with the South has produced . . . everything that these agitating people have done has been, not to enlarge, but to restrain, not to set free, but to bind faster, the slave population of the South. (" Seventh of March Speech," in *Works*, Vol. V, p. 357.)

I desire to call the attention of all sober-minded men at the North, of all conscientious men, of all men who are not carried away by some fanatical idea or some false impression, to their constitutional obligations. I put it to all the sober and sound minds at the North as a question of morals and a question of conscience. What right have they, in their legislative capacity or any other capacity, to endeavour to get around this Constitution, or to embarrass the free exercise of the rights secured by the Constitution to the persons whose slaves escape from them? None at all; none at all. Neither in the forum of conscience, nor before the face of the Constitution, are they, in my opinion, justified in such attempt. (*Ibid.*, p. 355.)

If the later Webster had no message for the conscience of New England, neither had he any for the intelligence of New England. The realistic Federalism that had listened to him in 1820 was gone, submerged by the flood waters of the renaissance; and the current transcendentalism seemed to him insubstantial and dangerous. The rising liberalism of the forties left him wholly untouched; it could not leaven the heavy materialism of his nature. He was quite unacquainted with the new Massachusetts that was coming to expression; he had lived too long with "the lawyers, the politicians, and rich merchants and manufacturers," to understand the greater world of Concord. While he had been living on the subsidies of State Street, and contracting his mind to the compass of a banker's, the intellect of Massachusetts had become liberal. And in becoming liberal it aroused him from indifference to hostility. Writing to a friend in explanation of his refusal to visit Concord in his later years, he said:

Many of those whom I so highly regarded in your beautiful and quiet village have become a good deal estranged, to my great grief, by abolitionism, free-soilism, transcendentalism, and other notions which I cannot but regard as so many vagaries of the imagination. (Quoted in Sanborn, *Life of Thoreau*.)

But if he was scarcely acquainted with the little group of thinkers and liberals—Emerson, Thoreau, Channing, Parker, Garrison, Phillips, Edmund Quincy, Whittier, Lowell, Higginson, Harriet Beecher Stowe, Margaret Fuller—they were well acquainted with him and took his measure exactly. The intellect of Massachusetts —so long ignored by Webster—had its revenge. Its voice carried

farther than his, and it painted his portrait in no flattering strokes.
The fierce storm that suddenly beat upon him broke the old man's
spirit. He had fed too long on adulation to endure censure. No
doubt that censure was severe, but it was far juster than the
earlier adulation had been. Whittier's *Ichabod* is familiar to every
American schoolboy. Lowell, then in his liberal mood, characterized him as "a statesman who had communicated no impulse
to any of the great ideas of the century, as a statesman whose
soul had been absorbed in tariff, banks, and the Constitution,
instead of devoting himself to the freedom of the future." Emerson, who had long studied him critically, gave an extraordinarily
just analysis of his character:

Mr. Webster is a man who lives by his memory, a man of the past, not
a man of faith or of hope. He obeys his powerful animal nature;—and
his finely developed understanding only works freely and with all its
force, when it stands for animal good; that is, for property. He believes,
in so many words, that government exists for the protection of property.
He looks to the Union as an estate, a large farm, and is excellent in the
completeness of his defence of it so far. He adheres to the letter. . . .
What he finds already written, he will defend. Lucky that so much had
got well written when he came. For he has no faith in the power of self-
government. Not the smallest municipal provision, if it were new, would
receive his sanction. In Massachusetts, in 1776, he would, beyond all
question, have been a refugee. He praises Adams and Jefferson, but it
is a past Adams and Jefferson, that his mind can entertain. A present
Adams and Jefferson he would denounce. So with the eulogies of liberty
in his writings,—they are sentimentalism and youthful rhetoric. He can
celebrate it, but it means as much from him as from Metternich or Talley-
rand. This is all inevitable from his constitution. All the drops of his
blood have eyes that look downward. ("The Fugitive Slave Law.")

To the transcendental mind Webster's economic realism was
peculiarly repugnant, and it was this which inspired Theodore
Parker's critical analysis of Webster's career—the most scathing
and explicit of all contemporary estimates. What Parker discovers most hateful in Webster's career was his adherence to the
principles of Federalism, from the "Basis of the Senate" speech in
1820, to the New York speech on November 18, 1850. The
persistence of his economic realism was an affront to the liberals
of the humanitarian school that had moved far from the position
of Fisher Ames. Webster might do lip service to humanitarian
ideals, Parker asserted, but always he came back in the end to his
polar conception—"The great object of government is the protec-

tion of property at home, and respect and renown abroad" (*Works:
Additional Speeches*, Vol. I, p. 220).

It was this same persistent realism that made Webster so useful
to the rising capitalism. His work in the Senate was supplemented
by his work in the court room. He was the greatest corporation
lawyer of the day, certain to be found defending vested interests,
never on the side of the leaner purse. Probably more than any
other man except John Marshall, he contributed to the work of
bringing the Constitution under the sovereignty of the judiciary.
His most significant contribution, certainly, was his argument in
the celebrated Dartmouth College case, delivered before the
Supreme Court in 1818, which resulted in one of the foundation
decisions on which later has been erected the solid structure of our
corporation law.[7] By engrafting upon the Constitution the
principle that a contract lies beyond the reach of legislative power
to annul, the decision assured greater security for private property
than exists under any other judicial system in the world. Alexander Hamilton could not have asked for more.

It was the singular ill fortune of Webster to have been born too
late to profit from the old mercantile Federalism to which his
affections were always attached, and too early to profit by the
industrial Federalism that came to greatness after the Civil War.
If fate had been kinder to him, and he had appeared on the political
horizon a generation earlier or a generation later, he would have
reaped in far greater abundance those high civic honors he so
foolishly coveted. The economic groups whom he served would
have been in position to reward a servant so conspicuously able
and useful. As a contemporary of John Adams he might have
become a notable political philosopher—provided always that he
had not turned Tory as Emerson suggested. But unhappily for his
fame he was launched between tides on a stormy sea and his
stately bark foundered in the squall of Abolitionism.

---

[7] Theodore Parker denied Webster credit for the argument, pointing out that
"the facts, the law, the precedents, the ideas, and the conclusions of that argument,
had almost all of them been presented by Messrs. Mason and Smith in the previous
trial of the case" (*Additional Speeches*, Vol. I, p. 171). The statement is confirmed
by Beveridge.

PART TWO: THE RISE OF LIBERALISM

CHAPTER I

THE RENAISSANCE

To write a history of Massachusetts, I confess, is not inviting to an expansive thinker. . . . From 1790 to 1820 there was not a book, a speech, a conversation, or a thought in the State. About 1820, the Channing, Webster, and Everett era begun, and we have been bookish and poetical and cogitative since. (Emerson, *Journals*, Vol. VIII, p. 339.)

In such summary fashion in the year 1852, Emerson recorded his judgment on half a century of intellectual life in Massachusetts. It was the comment of an exacting critic. In its characterization of the extraordinary ferment of thought that marked the decades of the thirties and forties, it is quite inadequate; but in its contemptuous dismissal of the age of Fisher Ames and Robert Treat Paine it was scarcely unjust. The utter sterility of those old times Emerson understood only too well. It was the world of his own youth, whose pale negations he had come to hate. The creative impulse was stifled, the mind had grown stale from tedious iteration. But at last the old barriers gave way, and into this narrow illiberal world, that had long fed on the crusts of English rationalism and Edwardean dogmatism—dry as remainder biscuit after voyage—broke the floods that had been gathering in Europe for years, the waters of all the streams of revolution that were running there bank-full. Before this inundation the old provincialisms were swept away, and for the first time in its history, and the last, the mind of New England gave itself over to a great adventure in liberalism.

Quite evidently the renaissance resulted from the impact of the romantic revolution upon the Puritan mind, and it issued in a form native to New England experience. Animated by the common spirit of Utopianism, its dreams were unlike those of Virginia or the West, founded on a different economics and seeking different ends. Massachusetts had discovered a particular road leading to Utopia by way of the industrial revolution, and the textile mills on the Merrimac began weaving a new pattern of life for New

England. The old static agricultural order was broken in upon, and with the social disruption came naturally an intellectual disruption. The mind of that older New England had been held in the close keeping of the church, and the movement of intellectual emancipation became therefore at the outset a movement leveled at theological conservatism; it was concerned first to rid New England of the incubus of Calvinistic dogma. The Calvinists were of tough fiber and tenacious of opinion, and to turn their flank was no summer campaign. The result was a long battle of ideas, a fierce struggle between the old deterministic theology and the new romantic philosophy, with victory slowly inclining to the latter. This major struggle gave to the renaissance its profoundly ethical spirit that set it off sharply from the earlier renaissance of Virginia; and not the least important of the results of the movement was the liberation of the New England conscience from its long bondage to dogma, setting it free to engage in a larger work in the world. What that conscience accomplished in the brief period of its freedom; what causes it espoused and what reforms it carried through—how it quickened a humanitarian zeal in New England and imparted a militant spirit to its culture—these are phases of the total movement not to be neglected by the historian.

In the realm of ideas the renaissance was largely dominated by old-world thought. From the abundant stores of European revolutionary doctrine the New England liberals drew freely— more freely perhaps from German idealism than from French Utopianism. Germany meant much to the awakening mind of New England, by reason of its spiritual and intellectual kinship. Plato was their common father, a transcendental mysticism their common experience. Philosophical idealism with its indwelling Godhood that exalted man to the divine and transformed a mechanical universe into the dwelling place of divine love—this was a dynamic faith, appealing to men long nurtured in faith, more seductive to the children of Puritanism than any political or economic romanticisms. It opened to them new heavens when the old were closed and encouraged them to go forth on great ventures.

But the renaissance was very much more than a transplanting of German idealism. France had a shaping hand in it, and England. Jean Jacques came before Hegel, and Unitarianism before transcendentalism. It was social and literary as well as philosophical. In so far as that which was essentially one may be divided, the

movement involved three major strands: the social Utopianism
that came from revolutionary France; the idealistic metaphysics
that emerged from revolutionary Germany; and the new culture
that spread with the development of literary romanticism. To
distinguish these three strands is one thing; to endeavor to separate
them is quite another. They interweave and blend in varying
patterns; they are but different, new-world phases of a comprehensive European movement that runs far back into the
preceding century—a movement that in transferring economic
and political mastery from the aristocracy to the middle class, in
destroying the worm-eaten feudal order and clearing the way for
the new capitalistic order, laid open a broad path into the nineteenth century. The extraordinary appeal of this vast movement
to the liberal mind of America resulted from the fact that an
identical revolution was under way here. In New England,
perhaps more dramatically than elsewhere in America, the day of
the middle class was dawning, aristocratic ideals were disintegrating, and the hopes of men were running high. To humanize
this emerging society, to awaken it to a nobler faith in human
destiny, to further the cause of social justice, to create a democracy of the spirit—this was the deeper romantic purpose, however
vaguely comprehended, that was fermenting in the New England
renaissance, and it was this that gave to it a spirit so warmly
ethical.

Now quite evidently a movement so extraordinarily complex
would appeal diversely to different minds, and in its development it drew to itself a singularly various following. To the sons
of respectable Federalism it was the new romantic culture that
appealed; to the militant conscience of Puritanism it was the
inspiration of social Utopianism; to the emancipated intellectuals
it was the metaphysical idealism. Its many-sidedness was both
confusing and stimulating. How shall we explain a movement
that embraced such different men as Everett and Channing and
Parker and Garrison and Whittier and Emerson and Longfellow
and Holmes; men often mutually repellent, sometimes sharply
critical of each other? No single mind sums up the whole—the
theological, humanitarian, mystical, critical, and cultural aspirations of the awakening—as perhaps Goethe may be said to have
done for Germany. Emerson, Thoreau and Parker possibly
embodied it most adequately; they were transcendental individ-

ualists, intellectual revolutionaries, contemptuous of all meanly material standards. But quite evidently Everett would not travel far along the transcendental path they pointed out, nor Holmes, nor Longfellow. These latter expected no romantic Utopias, wanted no such Utopias. Cambridge and Boston satisfied their hopes; they found the world not such a bad place for those who knew how to meet it on its own terms. Yet they too were children of the awakening, and in following their individual paths they contributed in their own way to the disintegration of the old authoritarian order that had long held the mind of New England in subjection. Each in some measure and after his own fashion was a rebel, and their total rebellions made up the sum of New England's bequest to a more liberal America. Yet in this eager and somewhat vague liberalism to which the renaissance was dedicated in spirit, the note that runs through the several programs is a note of reaction from the aspirations of the middle class. It was an ethical protest against the harsh and unjust realities of the industrial revolution that was so ruthlessly transforming the old order of life in New England; and it took the form of a return to a simpler life. To struggle free from the chains of the eighteenth century, only to be bound in new chains, was an ignoble ending to the emancipation that free men could not envisage with satisfaction.

CHAPTER II

LIBERALISM AND CALVINISM

THE first stirrings of new life were felt within the church, the repository of such learning as Harvard College disseminated through
the Massachusetts villages. For two hundred years the dogmas of Calvin had lain as a heavy weight on the mind of New England. Revolutions had taken place in English and continental
theology, but New England Calvinism had kept closely within the
narrow confines of its creed, annually turning over the exhausted
soil and reaping an ever scantier harvest. Since the days of Edwards there had been abundant speculation and much exercise in
syllogisms, but no scrutiny of major premises. Such an examination was long overdue, with the romantic revolution under way
in France, and new theories of human nature and the relation of
man to society and the state, spreading widely. But unfortunately
the odium which New England conservatism quickly fastened
upon the French school frightened the orthodox. The stigma
of atheism was put upon every harmless bantling of the numerous
French brood, and in the terror of reaction the pulpit, following
the lead of the reactionary pew, aroused itself to cleanse the church
of every innovation. English Arianism, even worse things, it
was discovered, had stolen into Congregational pulpits during the
relaxed period of the Revolution; a dangerous spirit of liberalism had spread silently through the tidewater churches, capturing
the strongholds of Boston orthodoxy.

By the year 1800 it was high time for the old Congregationalism of Jonathan Edwards to take counsel with itself. "Let us
guard against the insidious encroachments of *innovation*—that evil
and beguiling spirit which is now stalking to and fro in the earth,
seeking whom it may devour," exclaimed Jedidiah Morse, the
arch reactionary, in the days when French ideas were knocking
at the doors of New England. And by innovation the doughty
Jedidiah meant any idea that had been stumbled on, new since the
days of the great Edwards. To go back to the pure Edwardean
doctrine, to purge the church of incipient Arminianism and Arian-

321

ism and Socinianism—together with such other innovations as
might show their faces anywhere—became thenceforth the chief
business of the devout New England of 1800. To timid souls the
ideas of their grandfathers seemed far safer than the ideas of their
fathers; and so theology followed politics in turning its back upon
the freer, more generous world that beckoned.

Nevertheless French liberalism slowly won its victories. It
needs high walls to keep out ideas. Excluded from the drawing-
rooms and counting-houses, ostracized in society and politics,
romantic philosophy slipped quietly into Boston by the door of
theology, and took lodgings in the homes of the first families. To
those who enjoy the little ironies of history, the easy subjugation
of respectable Boston by that very Jacobinical heresy against
which Boston was so bitter is too amusing to be overlooked.
Changing its name and arraying itself in garments cut after the
best Yankee fashion, the gospel of Jean Jacques presently walked
the streets of Boston and spoke from its most respectable pulpits,
under the guise of Unitarianism. The heretical doctrines of the
excellence of human nature and the perfectibility of man were
preached to Federalist congregations so persuasively that instead
of repudiating them and asserting the total depravity of their
neighbors, simple-minded merchants approved the doctrines and
cheerfully paid their pew-rent. It was a respectable and bloodless
revolution. Under its discreet disguise Unitarianism accomplished
for New England what Jeffersonianism had accomplished for the
South and West—the wide dissemination of eighteenth-century
French liberalism. It opened the New England mind to fresh
ideas. Out of Unitarianism was to come the intellectual renaissance, with its transcendental philosophies and social reforms, its
enlarged conception of democracy and its Utopian dreams, which
made New England count so effectively in the developments of
the half century.

The twenty-five years between 1790 and 1815 were the nascent
period of Unitarianism, when it was reëxamining the old Calvinist
dogmas in the light of the new liberalism, weighing the doctrines
of election and reprobation in the scale with the doctrines of God's
beneficence and man's excellence, and coming definitely to reject
them as blasphemy against God and defamation of human nature.
And it was during these critical years that the upholders of the
traditional orthodoxy were most actively concerned to provide

a defense for the sacred dogmas of their grandfathers. The liberal advance produced a conservative reaction, and the lines of battle were sharply drawn. The capture of Harvard College by the Unitarians in 1805, and the founding of Andover Theological Seminary by the Calvinists in 1808, were dramatic events in a long intellectual and legal struggle that aroused much bitterness and bequeathed to the churches a rich legacy of unchristian animosities. Good men on both sides—to recall a contemporary witticism—were quite too ready "to fight for the glory of God as if the very devil were in them."

The traditional Calvinism defended itself with spirit, asserting so vehemently that it was still a living faith, that the corpse was not yet an authentic corpse, that it succeeded at least in postponing its own burial. It was deeply entrenched in the inertia of custom, but intellectually it was in really desperate straits. It was slowly disintegrating from dry-rot with which both minister and theology were stricken. With its major premises tacitly denied by Yankee experience, it was unfortunate in being defended by as humorless and ungainly a breed of theologians as ever quarreled over the loving-kindness of God. Clinging to the defenses which Jonathan Edwards had erected against the incursion of old-world ideas, it declaimed its dogmas and damned the human race with tedious iteration. Over-threshed straw makes poor fodder, and after a two-hour battle with potential infidelities, many a good minister descended from his pulpit lamenting that his exhortations had been wasted on "a sermon-proof, gospel-glutted generation." Yet he went faithfully back to his study to consume the day in argument with a supposititious Arminian, and in spinning cobweb systems between the worm-eaten rafters, quite oblivious to the common-sense world without his walls. The difficulties in which those old Calvinists found themselves very likely seemed tragic to them; but to later generations, endowed with some saving grace of humor, the situation was not without its spice. The good men were undeniably caught in a distressing dilemma. They were laboring prodigiously both to sit tight in the old dogma of determinism and yet wriggle out; to maintain election and reprobation and yet insert somehow the thin edge of personal responsibility; to prove to the satisfaction of the pew that man is both bound and free. It was a hard necessity to be under, to damn man by predestination, and "yet worry out enough freedom for him

to be decently damned on," as a late critic has remarked;[1] to
send him to hell by divine decree, yet prove that he went of his
own accord. Yet they must do that impossible thing if they were
to justify their theology to common-sense congregations that were
drifting into indifference.

The whole thing was monstrously unreal and it resulted in
hatching such a brood of tenuous subtleties as we have difficulty
in comprehending today. Theological fame in Massachusetts
came to be measured by the skill with which the logician made
out to stand on both sides of the fence at the same time. Had it
not been for Jonathan Edwards New England Congregationalism
would have drifted comfortably with the tide of liberalism; but
his uncompromising spirit held it anchored. This masterly spinner
of theological systems bequeathed to his successors an unfinished
work; but he had clearly envisaged the problem and suggested a
line of attack. In his great inquiry into the nature of will he had
hoped to provide an infallible means of reconciling the irreconcilable by arguing that the will is dependent on desire. The natural
man, according to the Edwardean logic, is free to serve God as
the highest good if he desires, but he lacks the desire unless God
reveals himself as that highest good, and such revelation rests
with God's pleasure. "Moral responsibility lies in the choice, not
in the cause of the choice." [2] With this distinction suggested between natural and moral freedom, Calvinistic speculation went on
hopefully till it attained its culminating triumph in Nathaniel
Walker's ingenious doctrine of certainty with power to the contrary. Walker was a pupil of Timothy Dwight's, and one of the
foundation professors of the new Yale Divinity School, established
to combat Unitarian heresies. A tremendous rattling of the bones
of the Connecticut churches followed his pronouncement that
man's acts are not necessitated by a rigid law of cause and effect,
but that his choices are so connected with antecedent conditions
of soul and environment, that to God's perception it is certain
what they will be, although he possesses full power of contrary
choice.[3]

As we contemplate those old theological abstractions, dead now
as Lot's wife, the universe of our fathers shrinks to a petty compass,

[1] See Fenn, *Religious History of New England: King's Chapel Lectures*, p. 130.
[2] See Williston Walker, *A History of the Congregational Churches in the United States*, p. 283.
[3] *Ibid.*, p. 356.

not much larger than the snug little state of Connecticut, curiously egocentric, curiously anthropomorphic. Obviously such grotesqueries could not endure indefinitely. Presently there must appear the common-sense housewife with her broom, and the dusty cobwebs would disappear. English Arianism, emerging out of English Presbyterianism, and long under suspicion of the New England fathers, first opened the windows and let a little fresh air into the New England churches. But back of Arianism was the total body of eighteenth-century rationalism, with its theology rooted in new political and social philosophies, and its doctrines derived from conceptions of God and man hostile to Calvinistic determinism. There could be no reconciling them. Calvinism must extirpate English rationalism or be disintegrated by it.

But rationalism refused to be extirpated. Here and there in Massachusetts pulpits appeared a new order of preachers, young men who had broken with the old dogmas and were plainly bitten with the English distemper. Of these the most notable was Jonathan Mayhew, from 1747 to 1766 pastor of the West Church, and the freest-spoken minister in Boston. Mayhew was a thoroughgoing liberal, not to say radical, an intimate friend of Otis and John Adams, and chief clerical leader of the opposition to the English ministry. He had broken through the narrow parochialism of Boston; he corresponded with the intellectual leaders of English dissent, and while still a young man was on the highroad to Arianism. He seems to have been a brilliant fellow, bold and frank in speech, with great and popular powers as a preacher, and his early death alone prevented him from anticipating some of the work of Channing.[4] A like fate abruptly terminated the work of another able young man, Lemuel Briant, pastor of the Braintree church from 1745 to his death in 1753. Briant was John Adams's pastor and, like Mayhew, an Arian, with a ready wit that his adversaries must have found disconcerting. "I have always tho't," he remarked apropos of the familiar dilemma, "that so far as any Man is pure (let it be in a greater or lesser Degree) he is not filthy." [5] But the coming on of the Revolutionary disputes and the disturbance of war put a stop to the normal development of the movement; and the general reaction following the treaty of peace gave encouragement to the Calvinistic reaction and temporarily strengthened the Edwardean

[4] *Ibid.*, pp. 276–277.   [5] *Ibid.*, p. 272.

school. Nevertheless the liberal doctrines of Mayhew and Briant, falling in with the French philosophy, prepared the way for the conscious Unitarian revolt at the end of the century.

That revolt was fundamentally ethical rather than theological, and the name Unitarian, which the liberal movement accepted somewhat reluctantly from its opponents, very inadequately describes its special genius. The term derives from the middle eighteenth century, before religious thought had come under the influence of the new social philosophy; and it suggests a primary theological bias in a movement that was far more significantly ethical and social. The early liberals, forerunners of Unitarianism, were theologians given to probing in rationalistic spirit, the mystery of the Godhood. Now, denial of the Trinity has been common to all Unitarians, although individually they might profess an Arian or a Socinian interpretation of the nature and rôle of Jesus; but what is more important, they have been from the first close Scripturists, disliking exact theological systems and setting biblical authority above human. By the time the name had come to be generally accepted—about the year 1815—it had already lost much of its earlier significance, for emphasis had shifted from the mystery of the Godhood to the problem of the relations existing between the children and the Father. On the one hand supernaturalism tended to disappear in morality, and on the other religion tended to seek an authoritative basis in idealistic philosophy and justify itself by intuitionism. "The soul," argued Channing, in his exposition of a later Unitarian theology, "is the spring of our knowledge of God." "Here is our primitive teacher and light." "The only God, whom our thoughts can rest on, and our hearts can cling to, is the God whose image dwells in our own Souls" (*Works*, Vol. VI, Introductory Remarks, p. 21). Unitarianism, in other words, reversed the thought process of Calvinism. Instead of debasing man to a mean creature, subject to a God of wrath, it professed to discover a loving Father in the human heart of love. Here was a revolution indeed, a revolution in which were the seeds of transcendentalism, of social Utopias, of pretty much the entire intellectual awakening of New England. The old Calvinism had no weapons to meet such an attack; the new creed lay outside its realm of thought. What that creed finally came to be, under Channing's influence, is thus stated by a recent historian:

Man is God's child, made in His image and object of His love; his reason and conscience are divine witnesses to truth and light, and when governed by them he walks in the ways of God, safe in his Father's love and care. The God in whom their opponents believed—a God of election and reprobation, capable of dooming an entire race because its ancestors disobeyed a God of arbitrary will and discriminating grace—seemed to them simply an immoral being and they frankly said so. (Fenn, *Religious History of New England, etc.*, p. 125.)

In its noblest expression Unitarianism became essentially a humanistic religion, rational, ethical, individual, yet with deep and warm social sympathies. In Channing's excellent phrase, it discovered the apotheosis of religion in "the adoration of goodness." It issued in conduct because it developed character. The highest testimony to the excellence of the faith is the noble company of men and women who subscribed to its creed. And yet after all, Unitarianism was rather an attitude of mind than a creed. It was the recovery of the original principle of New England Separatism, lost during the long years of orthodox conformity—the principle of the open mind and free inquiry. Let each devout soul, each group of fellow believers, Unitarianism announced, seek the truth where it may be found; let each give to it such outward form as best reveals its divine nature; not seeking to impose a particular interpretation upon others, but each taking upon himself full responsibility for his spiritual welfare. Authority it regarded as the prop of the weak; dogma, as the body of a faith that is dead. As free souls, mature and self-reliant, the Unitarians would be their own authority, would fashion their own creed. The Scriptures lie open and the heedful eye will discover God's revelation in their pages. The deeper spirit of Unitarianism is not inadequately embodied in the text, "Search the Scriptures, for they are they which testify of me." No abler or more devout Scripturists ever preached in America than the Unitarian ministers, and if bolder souls like Theodore Parker went further than others, if their free handling of old interpretations gave offense to the timid, that fact provided no sanction to coerce or stifle free inquiry. Toleration of differences, respect for devout free thought—this return to the position of Roger Williams two centuries before was the vital principle of Unitarianism. Like him, the Unitarian was a seeker, open-minded and free. Others might be intolerant, others might regard themselves as the sole custodians of truth, but not he.

But if the Unitarians who followed Channing were liberals

in religion, they were conservatives in well-nigh everything else. Amongst the laity the adoration of goodness was sufficiently tempered by Yankee thrift to keep it from interfering seriously with the practical business of getting on in the world; and in consequence the new faith gathered its supporters from amongst the prosperous rather than the needy, from Federalists rather than Democrats. The commercial dominated the intellectual and emotional in their prim and somewhat cold congregations. "The Unitarians," it was commonly said, "were the cult of the arrived." As successful men, these Boston merchants and manufacturers did not believe that they were the sons of Adam, children of iniquity. They thought better of themselves and of God than Calvinism permitted them to think; "one who was born in Boston," the current jest put it, "had no need to be born again." Generous in all approved philanthropies these Unitarian laymen might be, but emotionally religious they were temperamentally incapable of being. Until the infusion of the rich sap of transcendentalism, that gave it new life and brought it to bloom, Unitarianism was in grave danger of dying at the root. But with the spread of the philosophy of intuitionalism, the negative individualism of Unitarianism became positive, broke with the respectable conservatism of commercial congregations, and overflowed in a rich and generous faith. Authority, dogma, creed, were swept away by this new faith in an indwelling divinity, with its intuitive sanctions, and Unitarianism merged in the larger movement of the renaissance.

II

WILLIAM ELLERY CHANNING

To the austerely spiritual Channing the guiding principle of Unitarianism was identical with the spirit of primitive New England separatism—the principle of freedom in religious matters, the individual speaking his mind frankly, shepherd and flock feeding as they would, without fear and without coercion. The soul is responsible to itself and its own conscience; there are no orthodoxies and no heterodoxies, but a duty is laid upon the individual to seek truth with an open mind and be steadfast in its service. It was this spirit of open-minded liberalism that led him along the path of unmilitant individualism, seeking freedom only to the end of righteousness, and counting righteousness the fine flower of freedom; desiring peace and universal fellowship; loath to found a sect; yet driven by those who denied freedom to themselves as well as others to become the champion and leader of a great schism that sundered the traditional unity of Congregationalism, and erected a new faith on the altars of the old.

Channing's heritage was drawn from the deepest wells of New England idealism; and filtered through his finely ethical mind it emerged pure and limpid, the living waters of the new faith. His noble preëminence was due to the simple spirituality of his nature. Intellectually, he was neither great nor original. In scholarship he was distinctly inferior to academic theologians like Andrews Norton and to omnivorous students like Theodore Parker. Almost wholly introspective he was influenced slowly by world-currents of thought, and such alien ideas as found lodgment in his mind took on a native form and color from his own convictions. Nevertheless though his meditations revolved about the pole-star of his own experience, his theology cautiously took shape under the pressure of two ideas that came to him from the latter years of the eighteenth century—the ideas of God's beneficence and of man's excellence. Once lodged in his mind, those ideas led to quite revolutionary consequences, not only in their disintegrating effect upon the Calvinistic dogmas in which he had been reared, but in the generous romanticism which they bequeathed to Unitarian theology. His intellectual development was late and halting, yet that he liberated himself at all was remarkable considering the world that bred him—Newport, frequented by wealthy planters and enriched by the slave trade, Cambridge and Boston then in the stagnancy of Federalist complacency. Of the same generation with Robert Treat Paine and Josiah Quincy, only a few years older than Rufus Choate and Edward Everett, as a boy sitting under the preaching of Samuel Hopkins—the rugged expounder of the Hopkinsian doctrine of willing to be damned for the glory of God, a doctrine so repugnant to the major tenets of Channing's theology—he belonged by temperament and training to the parochial world that accounted Fisher Ames a great orator, and looked with suspicion on the new century that was crowding in on its comfortable preserves.

From the deep New England ruts Channing pulled himself with incredible difficulty. His frequent reactions almost kept pace with his progress. For years he oscillated between freedom and dogma, now dominated by the Hopkinsian influence and thrown back

upon a morbid Calvinism by ill health; then resolutely casting off
the evil spell; until the year 1815, when the conservative wing
declaring war upon the liberals, he was drawn into the controversy
and took upon himself the burden of defending the liberal cause.
He was then thirty-five, but it was not till four years later, in the
celebrated Baltimore sermon at the ordination of Jared Sparks,
that he offered a definitive statement of the new theology.   The
sermon brought him wide fame and fastened upon him the leadership of the Unitarian movement.   Comment upon the new doctrines was widespread, and the circulation of the sermon in pamphlet form, according to a late biographer, "was not exceeded by
any American publication until in 1830 Webster made his memorable reply to Hayne" (John White Chadwick, *William Ellery
Channing*, p. 147).   The creative influence of that sermon in clarifying certain doctrines of Unitarianism and integrating the society
should not blind us to the fact that it embodies only a portion of
Channing's theology—the idea of God's beneficence.   It is a
reasoned attack upon Trinitarian Calvinism, upon those dogmas
which reveal—in Channing's expressive phrase—"how mournfully
the human mind may misrepresent the Deity"; but it takes no
account of the idea which later he came to place first—the idea of
man's excellence.

Finer than the Baltimore sermon in its restrained eloquence—
an eloquence that burns with an intensity rare in Channing—and
in its dramatic exposition of the doctrine of the atonement, is the
sermon entitled *Unitarian Christianity most Favourable to Piety*,
delivered in 1826 at the dedication of the second Unitarian church
in New York City.   In this sermon Channing made use of a daring
comparison which startled his friends and gave mortal offense to
orthodox Calvinists.   It is probably the most dramatic passage
to be found in his writings, and it so well exemplifies the temper of
the controversy that it deserves quotation.   After discussing the
Edwardean philosophy of infinite punishment and the nature of
atonement, he proceeded:

Let me, then, set it before you, in new terms, and by a new illustration;
and if in so doing, I may wound the feelings of some who hear me, I beg
them to believe, that I do it with pain, and from no impulse but a desire
to serve the cause of truth.—Suppose, then, that a teacher should come
among you, and should tell you, that the Creator, in order to pardon his
own children, had erected a gallows in the centre of the universe, and had

publicly executed upon it, in room of the offenders, an Infinite Being, the partaker of his own Supreme Divinity; suppose him to declare, that this execution was appointed, as a most conspicuous and terrible manifestation of God's justice, and of the infinite woe denounced by his law; and suppose him to add, that all beings in heaven and earth are required to fix their eyes on this fearful sight, as the most powerful enforcement of obedience and virtue. Would you not tell him, that he calumniated his Maker? Would you not say to him, that this central gallows threw gloom over the universe; that the spirit of a government, whose very acts of pardon were written in such blood, was terror, not paternal love; and that the obedience which needed to be upheld by this horrid spectacle, was nothing worth? Would you not say to him, that even you, in this infancy and imperfection of your being, were capable of being wrought upon by nobler motives, and of hating sin through more generous views; and that much more the angels, those pure flames of love, need not the gallows and an executed God to confirm their loyalty? You would all so feel, at such teaching as I have supposed; and yet how does this differ from the popular doctrine of atonement? (*Works*, Vol. III, pp. 197–198.)

In seeking an explanation of Channing's break with New England orthodoxy—a breach that widened greatly with years, coming to embrace politics and economics as well as theology, alienating many of his own congregation and bringing acute grief to him— one can scarcely over-emphasize the influence of his Virginia experience. During the twenty-one months that he spent on the southern plantation, painfully isolated and lonely, he grappled seriously with a body of thought from which the environment of his youth had pretty much shut him away. Virginia in 1798 was ardently Jeffersonian, and French romantic philosophy was a commonplace in Virginia libraries. While Channing never went over wholly to Jeffersonianism, but retained certain Federalist prejudices after the old foundations had turned to quicksand under his feet, he there began a long process of speculative brooding that was to carry him far from the political principles of Boston. French revolutionary thought provided his chief intellectual stimulus during the critical Virginia period. Rousseau he read with profound interest, together with Godwin's *Political Justice* and Mary Wollstonecraft's *Rights of Woman*. The Physiocratic economics that sanctioned the agrarian bias of Jeffersonian democracy seems to have made no appeal to a mind primarily ethical in outlook, yet he went so far as to dabble in communistic theory, and for a time contemplated joining a communistic community. From France, moreover, he derived the idea of the excellence of human nature and the perfectibility of man, ideas which became the mainspring of his later thinking, creatively determining both his theology and his social philosophy, and transforming his whole intellectual world.

In July, 1800, eight months before it took formal possession of the White House, "French infidel philosophy" made its appearance in New England in the person of a slight, health-broken youth, who returned to his quiet theological studies, quite unmindful of the gunpowder he had brought back in his intellectual luggage. It was long before a spark was to strike home, but the powder was there and would do its work eventually. In passing through Channing's mind, the contributions of French romanticism merged with the native heritage of New England idealism, and supplemented by contributions from English Arian thought, slowly assumed definite form that came to issue in three dominating ideas, namely: God is love, man is potentially noble, religion is an excellent life. Enveloping these master ideas, in which they were carried as in a medium, was a pervasive ethical spirit that colored all his thinking and eventually took form in that striking phrase into which all of Channing is compressed, "the adoration of goodness—this is religion." This constituted his reply to the Edwardean theology that debased man to the sole end of exalting a monstrous God— the doctrine of "sweetness and light" was set over against the dogmas of reprobation and election.

With his profound sense of justice, Channing could not follow "the adoration of goodness" into an aloof and mystical pietism. The temptation was strong, for his finely aristocratic and hesitant nature prompted him to stand apart from all turmoil and partisan struggle. He disliked controversy and distrusted all dogmatists. The world of economics and politics was exceedingly distasteful to him; he would gladly stop his ears against the clamor of organized groups and strident parties. The Abolitionists, with whose purpose he deeply sympathized, seemed to him intolerant and their tactics vulgar. There is a measure of justice in Garrison's comment after Channing's death: "His nerves were delicately strung. The sound of a ram's horn was painfully distressing to him. He was firmly persuaded that nothing but a silver trumpet was needed to cause the walls of Jericho to fall; and he did his best upon his own." [6] And yet, however unwillingly, he was drawn in-

---

[6] Compare a fuller estimate in Garrison, *William Lloyd Garrison*, Vol. III, pp. 239–242.

evitably into an agitation that touched both his religion and his humanity; and between 1835 and 1837 he issued three notable contributions to the controversy: *Slavery*, a reply to the Southern apologists; *The Abolitionists*, an open letter to James Birney, whose Abolition press had been wrecked by an Ohio mob; and a noble appeal to Henry Clay against the annexation of Texas. In the latter year he spoke in Faneuil Hall at a turbulent meeting called to protest against the murder of Lovejoy, the meeting at which Wendell Phillips made his dramatic first appearance on the Abolition platform.

The point of view from which Channing approached the problem of slavery is clearly set forth in his *Introductory Remarks*, written in 1841 for a collected edition of his works, and which constitutes his *apologia pro vita sua*.[7] In this extraordinarily lucid and just statement he reduces the master passions of his life to two—respect for human nature, and reverence for human liberty—passions which were inseparable in all his thinking. Of the first he says, "The following writings will be found to be distinguished by nothing more than by the high estimate which they express of human nature. A respect for the human soul breathes through them." This attitude he elaborates at length:

An enlightened, disinterested human being, morally strong, and exerting a wide influence by the power of virtue, is the clearest reflection of the divine splendour on earth. . . . The glory of the Maker lies in his work. . . . Those men glorify God most, who look with keen eye and loving heart on his works, who catch in all some glimpses of beauty and power, who have a spiritual sense for good in its dimmest manifestations, and who can so interpret the world, that it becomes a bright witness to the Divinity.

I have also felt and continually insisted, that a new reverence for man was essential to the cause of social reform. . . . There can be no spirit of brotherhood, no true peace, any farther than men come to understand their affinity with and relation to God and the infinite purpose for which he gave them life. As yet these ideas are treated as a kind of spiritual romance. . . . The reception of this plainest truth of Christianity would revolutionize society, and create relations among men not dreamed of at the present day. . . . Men would know the import of the word Brother, as yet nothing but a word to multitudes. None of us can conceive the change of manners, the new courtesy and sweetness, the mutual kindness, deference and sympathy, the life and efforts for social melioration, which

[7] In the Glasgow edition of 1844 it prefaces the sixth volume.

are to spring up, in proportion as man shall penetrate beneath the body to the spirit, and shall learn what the lowest human being is.

Out of this reverence for human nature flowed his "reverence for Liberty, for human rights; a sentiment which has grown with my growth, which is striking deeper root in my age, which seems to me a chief element of true love for mankind, and which alone fits a man for intercourse with his fellow-creatures."

It is because I have learned the essential equality of men before the common Father, that I cannot endure to see one man establishing his arbitrary will over another by fraud, or force, or wealth, or rank, or super-stitious claims. It is because the human being has moral powers, be-cause he carries a law in his own breast and was made to govern himself, that I cannot endure to see him taken out of his own hands and fashioned into a tool by another's avarice or pride. It is because I see in him a great nature, the divine image, and vast capacities, that I demand for him means of self-development, spheres for free action—that I call society not to fetter, but to aid his growth.

In such humanitarian idealism did French romantic philosophy come to flower in the generous mind of this son of New England. He was no longer narrowly Unitarian; he had become a social revolutionary with Utopian dreams. The minister's wealthy parishioners might worship the common Father complacently under the shadow of slavery, black or white, but the minister could not; he had caught a glimpse of the Promised Land and would lead his flock towards it. Unhappily, the vast abyss of negro slavery lay between, and Channing considered it with grow-ing concern. In his examination of the problem he was broadly philosophical rather than narrowly partisan. He rested his case against slavery on an ethical adaptation of the natural-rights theory.[8] Since man is both rational and moral, he argued, he cannot be deprived by law or custom of the essential preroga-tives of personality. The inalienable rights of man are in es-sence no other than the rights of personality—the right to exercise his reason, to seek light of his conscience, to enjoy the fruits of his labor, to enter into domestic relations, in short to be free to live as a man in a state of civilization. To treat man as property is the grossest denial and violation of that which by its nature is inviolable and inalienable. Channing pushed his argument further and asserted that the institution of slavery was not only irrational

[8] For a brief discussion, see Merriam, *American Political Theories*, pp. 217-221.

and immoral, but a fundamental denial of democracy. It must end in perverting the political state to its own evil. The southern conception of a Greek democracy resting on black slavery he looked upon as the final prostitution of the democratic ideal. "Those who tell us that slavery is a necessary condition of a republic, do not justify the former, but pronounce a sentence of reprobation on the latter." For those text-mongerers who professed to justify slavery by Scripture, he had only scorn. By such methods polygamy might as readily be justified.

Inquiry into the nature and scope of individual rights brought Channing face to face with the problem of the political state and the duties of citizenship. Here his break with Boston Federalism was final and complete. He judged men and institutions by ethical standards; State Street judged them by economic standards. By his own path he went back to the eighteenth century, and interpreting the functions and province of government in the light of Godwin's *Political Justice*, he arrived at the conception of a constantly diminishing political state that should eventually disappear. The dogma of political sovereignty he denied: "The state is equally restrained with individuals by the Moral Law" ("Slavery," in *Works*, Vol. II, p. 37). The expediency of some restraint upon individual action he accepted, but with the proviso that it be exercised only to the end of the common well-being. "The authority of the state to impose laws on its members I cheerfully allow; but this has limits, which are found to be more and more narrow in proportion to the progress of moral science" (*ibid.*, p. 38). "That government is most perfect, in which Policy is most entirely subjected to Justice, or in which the supreme and constant aim is to secure the rights of every human being" (*ibid.*, p. 38). To such a government loyalty will be given gladly; but in the event that expediency should prevail over justice, and the state should prostitute its power by exploiting one class for the benefit of another, then must loyalty be transferred from the state to the higher law. "Justice is a greater good than property, not greater in degree, but in kind." "The good of the individual is more important than the outward prosperity of the State" (*ibid.*, pp. 40, 44). In such doctrines Channing paid his respects to the political philosophy of Webster.

The final outcome of his political thinking was a close approximation to the position of Jefferson. His distrust of power grew more apprehensive as he reflected on the common abuse of power, and the cheap and paltry appeals by which the unthinking are swayed. Before the organized power of the mass, the individual is helpless. In the *Introductory Remarks* he went further than he had done in earlier writings in analysis of the state, and such a passage as this might have been penned by John Taylor of Caroline County. It is pure Jeffersonianism.

So fearful is the principle of which I have spoken, that I have thought it right to recommend restrictions on power and a simplicity in government beyond what most approve. Power, I apprehend, should not be suffered to run into great masses. No more of it should be confided to rulers than is absolutely necessary to repress crime and preserve public order. A purer age may warrant larger trusts; but the less of government now the better, if society be kept in peace. There should exist, if possible, no office to madden ambition. . . . One of the tremendous evils of the world, is the monstrous accumulation of power in a few hands. . . . Is any man pure enough to be trusted with it? Ought such a prize as this to be held out to ambition? Can we wonder at the shameless profligacy, intrigue, and the base sacrifices of public interests by which it is sought, and, when gained, held fast? Undoubtedly, great social changes are required to heal this evil, to diminish this accumulation of power. National spirit, which is virtual hostility to all countries but our own, must yield to a growing humanity, to a new knowledge of the spirit of Christ. Another important step is, a better comprehension by communities that government is at best a rude machinery, which can accomplish but very limited good, and which, when strained to accomplish what individuals should do for themselves, is sure to be perverted by selfishness to narrow purposes, or to defeat through ignorance its own ends. Man is too ignorant to govern much, to form vast plans for states and empires. Human policy has almost always been in conflict with the great laws of social well-being, and the less we rely on it the better. The less of power given to man over man the better. (*Works*, Vol. VI, pp. 26–27.)

Channing had evidently read his *Political Justice* to good effect, for the spirit of eighteenth-century liberalism had passed into his thought and given shape to his political philosophy. In his hatred of war, his pacifism, his humanitarian concern, his social-mindedness, his repudiation of all coercive centralizing power, he proved himself a child of Godwin. He would have no tyranny, whether by the organized state or by the unorganized mass. He extended to all men the right of free thought and free speech. In no other cause did he speak more vehemently than in defense of this democratic right. When the Abolitionists were mobbed and their presses broken he rejoiced in their refusal to be silenced.

"From my heart I thank them," he wrote. "I am myself their debtor. I am not sure, that I should this moment write in safety, had they shrunk from the conflict, had they shut their lips, imposed silence on their presses, and hid themselves before their ferocious assailants. . . . I thank the Abolitionists, that in this evil day, they were true to the rights which the multitude were ready to betray." Then follows a passage that is perennially true, considering how hardly won and easily lost is the right of free speech:

Of all powers, the last to be entrusted to the multitude of men, is that of determining what questions shall be discussed. The greatest truths are often the most unpopular and exasperating; and were they to be denied discussion, till the many should be ready to accept them, they would never establish themselves in the general mind. The progress of society depends on nothing more, than on the exposure of time-honored abuses, which cannot be touched without offending multitudes, than on the promulgation of principles, which are in advance of public sentiment and practice, and which are constantly at war with the habits, prejudices, and immediate interests of large classes of the community. Of consequence, the multitude, if once allowed to dictate or proscribe subjects of discussion, would strike society with spiritual blindness, and death. The world is to be carried forward by truth, which at first offends, which wins its way by degrees, which the many hate and would rejoice to crush. The right of free discussion is therefore to be guarded by the friends of mankind, with peculiar jealousy. It is at once the most sacred, and the most endangered of all our rights. He who would rob his neighbor of it, should have a mark set on him as the worst enemy of freedom. ("The Abolitionists," in *Works*, Vol. II, p. 161.)

High-minded and generous was this child of Puritan idealism who had gone to school to French infidel philosophy—never untrue to the principle of free inquiry which in demanding for himself he willingly granted others. He calmly accepted the fact of disintegration which is implicit in all liberalism—the denial of traditional authority and ancient custom—partly because he believed the old ways were bad, but in part also because he held strongly to his faith in human nature. Despite failure and discouragement he clung to his cardinal belief—"My one sublime idea, which has given me unity of mind, the greatness, the divinity of the soul." He broke the more willingly with an ungenerous past because he envisaged a nobler future. An intuitive individualist, he was a forerunner of transcendental individualism, and he found himself in hearty accord with Emerson's doctrines in the Divinity School address. With the later rationalistic phase of

Unitarianism which began with Theodore Parker's memorable
South Boston sermon *On the Transient and Permanent in Christianity*, in May, 1841, he found himself only partly in intellectual
sympathy. He remained a supernaturalist after the younger
generation had rejected supernaturalism; but his sturdy adherence
to the principle of liberalism would not suffer him to join in the
Unitarian hue and cry raised against the young radical. Unitarianism turned orthodox, and bent on erecting new dogmas,
seemed to him treasonable to every liberal hope. "As to Mr.
Parker," he wrote, "I wish him to preach what he thoroughly
believes and feels. I trust the account you received of attempts
to *put him down* was in the main a fiction. Let the full heart pour
itself forth!" (John White Chadwick, *William Ellery Channing*,
p. 357.) Sixteen months after he penned those words Channing
was dead, but the spirit of his life was embodied in the great ferment that was rising about him when he died. "Let the full
heart pour itself forth"—to many sober Bostonians it seemed that
New England had taken that injunction quite too literally and
was pouring forth disturbant and gusty heresies, but Channing
would scarcely have disapproved.

CHAPTER III
LIBERALISM AND THE SOCIAL CONSCIENCE

I

THE SOCIAL MIND

UNITARIANISM was generous in its bequests to New England, and amongst its contributions to a nobler life not the least valuable was its warm social sympathy. Channing's tender social conscience sprang directly from his humanitarian religion. Not from the hard old Calvinism did he get this fine flower of a humane life, but from the new French philosophy. Not from bounding his ethics by the Decalogue, or hating sin more than he loved generosity, did he break the hard shell of Puritan righteousness; but by metamorphosing the sinner into a child of God and sharing with him the divine promise. Other-mindedness came naturally to a religion established in a God of love. The social conscience could not remain indifferent to injustice visited upon the children of a common Father. Yet other-mindedness was a virtue practiced too little in Calvinist New England. That old world had been more concerned with hopes of individual salvation, with propitiating an angry God, than with its present obligations to its neighbors. Hard doctrine—which the old Puritan loved—was likely to make hard characters, and an ascetic society was likely to breed close-fisted natures. The conscience was tender in New England, but it was tender chiefly as the guardian and monitor of the Ten Commandments; it gave itself too little concern about the new commandment which Jesus laid upon his disciples. It disciplined men and women in personal righteousness, it created self-reliant characters, it scrutinized narrowly the neighborhood conduct; but its social issues were likely to be mean and petty. The righteousness of which it professed to be guardian and monitor too often fell far short of generous manly stature.

From this hardness of the old religion came the hardness of the social conscience. When the Yankee was driven by brutal fact to admit that he was his brother's keeper, he usually took care to get a few honest pennies out of his brother's board and lodging.

The village poor were provided for by farming out, as the taxes were farmed out. The town meeting haggled narrowly over the terms, and substantial deacons underbid each other. Though the price might be low, some profit might still be got from the pauper's keep. It was a cold, hard, unsympathetic world for the social unfortunate, whether pauper, debtor, or idiot; and it was harsh as well to the children of all but the wealthy. The hours of toil were long, and the public schools about which the historians have bragged rather too loudly, were poor affairs, starved by the common niggardliness, ill taught and ill provided. The academies and colleges that professed to keep the torch of learning aflame were largely perquisites of the gentry. It is beside the point to assert that public schools existed in New England long before Virginia had any, and that poor boys stinted and starved their way through Harvard and Yale. Well known as such facts are, they do not testify to a high social sense in a people supposed to have been tender of conscience. The Calvinist was taught to fear God rather than to love him. It was a strong man's business to save one's soul and make a decent living; and in the social code of New England the weakling must take his chance.

There was helpful neighborliness of course in old New England, and much honest kindliness. Some of the hardest of dogmatic Calvinists were the most considerate and gentlest of men. Old Samuel Hopkins of slave-running Newport was a generous soul who preached the gospel of love to one's fellows, and practiced the virtues of apostleship to the poor and outcast. He denounced the slave trade to parishioners who knew all the inlets of the West African coast, and got himself well disliked. His congregation preferred his hard theology to his inconvenient humanitarianism, and kept him poor all his days. The dogmatic Timothy Dwight scathingly attacked slavery in his *Greenfield Hill*, denounced the injustice done the negro, and even protested against the extension of capital punishment. Yet for all such protests the common conscience was untouched. The Yankee was always standing in the way of the Puritan's righteousness. Respectability was founded on property, and respectability was mightier in New England than even John Calvin. It was the brutal debtor laws that brought on Shays's Rebellion, which Federalist church members put down and denied the grievances. It was no tender conscience that ex-tinguished slavery in Massachusetts, for long after it became unprofitable there the Yankee skipper was still in the slave trade. Dignified Tory Row on what is now Brattle Street, Cambridge, was built by gentlemen who drew their wealth from West Indian slave plantations.[1] William Lloyd Garrison's offense in Baltimore, for which he was thrown into jail, lay in publishing the name of a Massachusetts shipmaster from Newburyport—Garrison's native town—who was engaged in the coastwise slave traffic.[2] In the year 1830 there were somewhat more than a hundred Abolition Societies in the United States, not one of which was in New England; and in the first number of the *Liberator* Garrison wrote, probably without exaggeration, that he found "contempt more bitter, opposition more active, detraction more relentless, prejudice more stubborn, and apathy more frozen," in New England, "than among slave owners themselves." [3] The old Puritan conscience might be tender, but it refused pretty steadily to take on any larger job than Sabbath-keeping and dogma-saving. It was inquisitorial rather than humanitarian, and the sins which it hunted down were theological rather than social.

The bridge between this older world and the later was thrown across by Unitarianism. With its shift of emphasis from a God of wrath to a God of love came the entering wedge that was to split away the egoism of the old theology—its thralldom to the conception of personal sin—and lay bare an inner core of altruism. It was another sort of conscience that Unitarianism discovered, a conscience that welcomed the new social thought of romantic Europe, and applying it to the facts of life in America created the new humanitarianism which bit so deeply into the New England of the forties. From this movement the intractable nature of the Yankee held him back, but the Puritan speedily transformed the hard theological conscience into a tender social conscience, that bewildered the conventional morality with its sweeping program of reform.

The awakening of the new spirit may perhaps be held to date from the growing opposition to war that was an aftermath of the Napoleonic period with its huge debts and vast social suffering. The inhumanity of war profoundly impressed thoughtful minds that had come under the influence of the sociological movement,

---

[1] See T. W. Higginson, *Old Cambridge*, p. 149.
[2] See Garrison, *William Lloyd Garrison*, Vol. I, Chapter VI. The court held that it was libelous to seek to bring into disrepute an action that was legal.
[3] Quoted by S. E. Morison in *Harrison Grey Otis*, Vol. II, p. 263.

and when Channing in 1812 preached his first anti-war sermon
the new humanitarian spirit found expression. In his espousal
of pacifism Channing was following in the footsteps of the social
revolutionaries of the preceding century. He fell short of Tom
Paine in analysis of the economic and dynastic sources of war,
and in appreciation of its social consequences; nevertheless his
denunciation was significant of a changing social attitude. From
this early attack to the rise of the Garrisonian Non-Resistance
Society of the late thirties and early forties, the spread of the pacifist movement was rapid. Transcendentalism was eloquently
anti-militaristic, and Emerson, Alcott and Parker were outspoken
in denunciation of the war spirit. To the war against war soon
was added the war against drink, and with the establishment in
Boston in 1826 of the *National Philanthropist,* under the patronage
of the "Massachusetts Society for the Suppression of Intemperance"—a paper of which Garrison was editor for a few months—
began the long agitation for the suppression of the liquor traffic.
From such feeble beginnings the ardor of reform grew and spread
swiftly, enlarging its program to embrace anti-slavery, woman's
rights, [4] prison reform, repeal of the harsh debtor laws, vegetarian-
ism, associationism, until it caught the contagion of the perfectionist and transcendental movements and issued in a comprehensive
program of universal reform. The golden age of New England
was quite as much the golden age of the New England conscience
as of the New England mind.

II

The fame of transcendentalism has too much obscured the contemporary movement of perfectionism, a movement which marked
the extreme expression of the new conscience, the most revolutionary of its aspirations, the apotheosis of ethical radicalism. Its
want of literary skill narrowed its appeal and the archaic quality
of its enthusiasm lessened its following; yet in spirit it was native
to Puritan idealism, and it enlisted the active sympathy of many
of the finer souls of New England. How greatly reform was furthered by the movement of perfectionism is not easily determined,

---

[4] This was an outgrowth of the anti-slavery movement and emerged from the
conservative opposition to women's appearing on the abolition platform. The
reply of the Quakeress, Angelina Grimké, to Elizabeth Beecher's *Essay on Slavery
and Abolitionism, with reference to the Duty of American Females,* in 1837, marks the
definite beginning of the movement. See Garrison, *William Lloyd Garrison,* Vol. II,
pp. 133–134.

but it is clear that its influence permeated much of the revolutionary activity of the times. Scratch an ardent Abolitionist and you were likely to find a potential perfectionist.

The doctrine was first elaborated by John Humphrey Noyes, a young Vermont mystic, who, under the influence of the revivalist excitement of the early thirties, elaborated a social creed that re-embodied much of the teaching of the extreme left wing of English Commonwealth thought. Noyes was a primitive religious nature, with the tenderest of consciences, vastly troubled over current materialisms; and his speculations reveal a curious throw-back to early English Puritanism. He was a Yankee Fifth Monarchy man. Two hundred years of Yankee experience slipped from his mind, and he walked and talked with the old millennial spirits, the Diggers and Levelers of Commonwealth times. A devout Scripturist, he took literally the injunction of Matthew, "Be ye therefore perfect, even as your Father which is in Heaven is perfect." A primitive Christian, he proposed to re-order society with the naïve simplicity of the apostle Eliot. In his mystical speculations, social, political, and religious radicalisms were stirred in a common pot and simmered down to what may be called spiritual anarchism. Noyes was a Yankee "root and branch" man, a single-minded apostle of "thorough." He would not strain at gnats and swallow camels, but he rejected the camels first and then proposed to get rid of the gnats. In 1834 he established a small monthly paper called the *Perfectionist*, which was very probably as revolutionary a sheet as was ever printed in America. He made converts, including Garrison, Edmund Quincy, son of Josiah Quincy, the Grimké sisters, Henry C. Wright and other Abolitionists, and made an increasing stir in the world, to the great concern of respectable folk who swallowed their camels without a grimace.

Some notion of the main doctrines of this seventeenth-century creed may be gained from a letter of Noyes to Garrison, written in 1837, from which the following is taken:

I have subscribed my name to an instrument similar to the Declaration of '76, renouncing all allegiance to the government of the United States, and asserting the title of Jesus Christ to the throne of the World. . . . When I wish to form a conception of the government of the United States . . . I picture to myself a bloated, swaggering libertine, trampling on the Bible—its own Constitution—its treaties with the Indians—the petitions of its citizens. . . . I have renounced active co-operation with the oppressor on whose territories I live; now I would find a way to put an end to his oppression. But he is manifestly a reprobate: reproof and instruction only aggravate his sins. I cannot attempt to reform him, because I am forbidden to "cast pearls before swine." I must therefore either consent to remain a slave till God removes the tyrant, or I must commence war upon him, by a declaration of independence and other weapons suitable to the character of a son of God.

He then lays down seven reasons for choosing to make war upon the state, amongst which are the following:

1. As a believer in the Bible I know that the territory of the United States belongs to God, and is promised . . . to Jesus Christ and his followers. . . .

6. The Son of God has manifestly, to me, chosen this country for the theatre of such an assault—a country which, by its boasting hypocrisy, has become the laughing-stock of the world, and by its lawlessness has fully proved the incapacity of man for self-government. *My hope of the millennium begins where Dr. Beecher's expires*—viz., AT THE OVERTHROW OF THIS NATION.

I have stated to you only . . . the principal things which God has urged upon me by his Spirit, and by which he has moved me to nominate Jesus Christ for the Presidency, not only of the United States, but of the world. Is it not high time for abolitionists to abandon a government whose President has declared war upon them? I cannot but think that many of them hear the same great voice out of heaven which has waked me, saying, "Come out of her, my people, that ye be not partakers of her sins and of her plagues." . . . Allow me to suggest that you will set Anti-slavery in the sunshine only by making it tributary to Holiness; and you will most assuredly throw it into the shade . . . if you suffer it to occupy the ground, in your mind or in others, which ought to be occupied by UNIVERSAL EMANCIPATION FROM SIN. All the abhorrence which now falls upon slavery, intemperance, lewdness, and every other specific vice, will in due time be gathered into one volume of victorious wrath against *unbelief*. I wait for that time as for the day of battle . . . I counsel you, and the people that are with you, if you love the post of honour—the forefront of the hottest battle of righteousness—to set your face towards *perfect* holiness. (Garrison, *William Lloyd Garrison*, Vol. II, pp. 145–148.)

This curious appeal brought forth its fruit in a Peace Convention, held in 1838, which published a Declaration of Sentiments[5] that was quite as extraordinary a pronouncement—one that serves to explain the utter bewilderment of prosaic souls at the strange progeny of the times. It was only one of many strange conventions, marked by an ebullient faith of which Emerson remarked, "The core of the comet did not seem to be much, but the whole air was full of splendors" (*Journals*, Vol. VII, p. 5), and on which Josiah Quincy

[5] Written by Garrison; see *ibid.*, Vol. II, pp. 230–234.

commented, "Such a mass of free mind as was brought together I have never seen before in any one assembly. . . . There was much talent and a great deal of *soul.*" Men who take their Biblical teachings literally are likely to be curious fellows. Righteousness may prove a potent drink for them that love it, begetting its own particular intemperance; and a conscience that has slipped its leash of the practical will run many a mad chase. If it followed its logic this perfectionism must make short shrift of political parties, of loyalty to government, of the political state itself, and set up instead a social order in which familiar things would be topsy-turvy, with the just sitting in high places and the rich and great of earth brought low; and this is precisely what Noyes did in the Oneida Community— the most successful of the contemporary ventures in communism—of which he was the founder. In spite of his taste for the wine of new vintages Emerson was somewhat taken aback at certain of its ebullitions, and when the sabbatarian Charndon Street Convention in 1840 gathered together the choicest repositories of New England holiness, he shook his head dubiously. His humorous catalogue of the miscellaneous enthusiasts suggests more than a spice of criticism.

Madmen, madwomen, men with beards, Dunkers, Muggletonians, Come-outers, Groaners, Agrarians, Seventh-Day Baptists, Quakers, Abolitionists, Calvinists, Unitarians, and Philosophers,—all came successively to the top, and seized their moment, if not their hour, wherein to chide, or pray, or preach, or protest. ("The Charndon Street Convention," in *Works*, Vol. X, p. 374.)

And even the catholic-minded Edmund Quincy, who was one of the callers of the Convention, confessed that "It was the most singular collection of strange specimens of humanity that was ever assembled." The wine of perfectionism was in high ferment in New England in 1840.

It was a curious anachronism in the midst of the industrial revolution—this revival of the religious Utopianism of 1650, this April renaissance of the faith of a dead *saeculum theologicum.* It was in no sense a by-product of transcendentalism—no lunacy fringe of metaphysical speculation. It owed nothing to French romanticism or German idealism, not in origin at least. It was far more primitive and native, and its affinities run back to Roger Williams and the Fifth Monarchy millennialism, rather than to Rousseau and Kant and Jacobi. It was a breaking through of the

submerged New England spirituality, a volcanic release from
sterile conformity; and it summoned the awakening soul to go
forth and conquer the world for righteousness. Millennialism is the
prophetic hope of a primitive faith. To its disciples it is certain of
fulfillment because God's promises are certain; but to practical
minds, unconvinced that Biblical phrases are authentic divine contracts, any expectation of the speedy coming of the Kingdom of
God seems grotesque. The millennial enthusiast is a fair butt of
ridicule, and the perfectionists came in for a large share. It was
Lowell who leveled at the militant godliness of the new sects the
wittiest attack. Forgetting his English history he found himself
puzzled, and being puzzled he allowed himself to become ill-
natured. His clever sentences explode smartly about his subject,
but there is no light in them.[6]

III

Upon another venture in Utopianism, and one far better known,
the years have laid a pleasant, idyllic haze, softening the prosaic
outlines and clothing them with romance. Brook Farm has been
singularly fortunate in the posthumous fame that has dealt with
it so tenderly as to transmute it into poetry. By virtue of the
light reflected upon it by the transcendental illumination and the
literary skill it commanded, the little communal settlement at
West Roxbury has come to be regarded as a homely Yankee pastoral, a sort of May Day adventure in brown holland tunics, an
inspiring quest of the ideal amongst furrows and manures. It
is a social poem fashioned out of Yankee homespun. No hint of
rude social leveling is associated with its aims; even its communism suggests no stigma. Of the dozens of communistic experiments which marked the first half of the nineteenth century in
America, few were native in origin or ventured upon in New England. They were mostly undertaken by old-world groups, chiefly
German, who sought cheap land and a free environment for primitive religious experiments. But Brook Farm was true Yankee,
using the familiar dialect to clothe its unfamiliar thoughts, and
escaping the prejudice that confronts the uncouth and alien; and
in consequence the vagaries that all New England once laughed at
have become enshrined as a cherished New England possession.
    Perfectionism and Brook Farm embodied diverse phases of the

[6] See the essay on Thoreau.

renaissance and made appeal to different temperaments. Fellow·
ship founded on common ownership and communal labor was
an ideal that left the religious mystic cold, whereas the anarchistic
holiness of perfectionism seemed to the Brook Farmers grotesque.
Present economic maladjustment appeared to the latter the
fundamental problem of the times. They were deeply concerned
for the future that must emerge from the chaotic individualism
of the present. Unless society were brought back to a wiser understanding of values, they foresaw only chaos; and so in a small way
they set about a great experiment. Brook Farm grew out of the
impact of the industrial revolution upon the social conscience of
New England. Industrialism and social speculation were contemporary developments. The first cotton mill in New England
was established at Lawrence in 1822, and the following year the
Merrimac Mills were established in the newly founded city of
Lowell. By absorbing the vast Irish immigration the factory
system brought increasing wealth to Beacon Street homes, but it
brought other consequences in its train which Beacon Street carelessly overlooked. How those consequences affected more sensitive
and intelligent minds—men like William Henry Channing, Theodore Parker and George Ripley—is suggested by their eager talk
of mutualism, association, coöperation, as potential cures for the
growing evils of competition, discussions never before heard in
New England. Describing the state of mind of the Boston group
of social thinkers, John Weiss offers the following explanation:

A mutualism to secure culture and material welfare was consistently
desired by those who believed in a community of the sources of moral and
spiritual welfare. The social evils which result from the struggles of
competitive labour seemed to outweigh all its benefits.   Modern civilization was thought to be the culmination of isolated selfishness, madly
struggling from bread to luxury and refined delights, which the strongest
and least scrupulous only could acquire. Prisons and punishments were
the defences of this artificial system, to repress instincts that were moral
till they become illegal. Hospitals and benevolent institutions were also
mere defences to absorb as much misery as possible ere it became malicious,
to get the social gangrene reduced to limits. The providential impulses
of the human being were forced to act in subversive ways and directions,
when they might all be harmonized by their own inherent laws, and the
blessing of mutualism succeed to the bane of antagonism. Each man
ought to be the guarantee to all men against disorder; the carefully adjusted elements of a selfishness which threatens continually to blow the
social fabric to atoms, would become not only innoxious but salutary in
its proper combination; and a new civilization might arise in fair propor-

tion from the serial development and movement of all possible human tendencies. Then all men and women might labor and be happy; all might earn with a minimum of toil a competence of culture. Property would be the ally of the whole instead of the oppressor of the many; and crime would disappear, because the instincts would no longer have motives to be criminal. (*Life and Correspondence of Theodore Parker*, Vol. I, pp. 106–107.)

The transcendental basis of such social speculation is evident enough. The new social thought was transcendental thought. A common belief in the excellence of human instincts drew these idealists together; but when it came to the vexing problem of reconciling individualism and mutualism, creating an economic fellowship out of electric personalities, the more ardent transcendentalists took fright and prudently kept without the gates of Brook Farm. Organization seemed to them the fatal poison in the bottom of the cup. When a community was planned in Massachusetts in 1841, by liberal Christians of the Universalist sect, a writer in the *Dial* subjected the proposal to sharp criticism:

A true community can be founded on nothing short of faith in the universal man, as he comes from the hands of the Creator, with no law over his liberty but the eternal ideas that lie at the foundation of his being. . . . The final cause of human society is the unfolding of the individual man, into every form of perfection, without let or hindrance, according to the inward nature of each. (Quoted by Frothingham in *Transcendentalism, etc.*, p. 157.)

Such a view is anarchistic rather than collectivistic, and as embodied in Alcott's Fruitlands, it may be regarded as the transcendental type of Utopia. Towards all systems of socialism the transcendentalists were instinctively hostile, as implying an industrial regimentation; and in planning Brook Farm, Ripley rejected industrialism and reduced regimentation to a minimum. With the agrarian background of Brook Farm the transcendentalists were in hearty sympathy, quite oblivious of the fact that agrarianism could offer no solution for industrialism; but they balked at the principle of task allotment as a hindrance to the unfolding of individual differences. Upon the later introduction of the Fourier Phalanx their doubts grew into certainty, and they lost their faith in the experiment. Of all the transcendentalists William Henry Channing was clearly the most confirmed associationist, except perhaps Ripley; to the end of his life he remained a socialist, active in collectivistic movements and clinging fondly to his memory of Brook Farm as a "great college of social students." But few of his fellow transcendentalists shared his faith.

This growing skepticism of organization is clearly shown in the comments of Emerson's *Journals*. In October, 1840, he set down his first reaction to the plan as follows:

Yesterday George and Sophia Ripley, Margaret Fuller and Alcott discussed here the Social Plans. I wish to be convinced, to be thawed, to be made nobly mad by the kindlings before my eye of a new dawn of human piety. But this scheme was arithmetic and comfort; this was a hint borrowed from the Tremont House and United States Hotel; a rage in our poverty and politics to live rich and gentlemanlike, an anchor to leeward against a change of weather; a prudent forecast on the probable issue of the great questions of Pauperism and Poverty. And not once could I be inflamed, but sat aloof and thoughtless; my voice faltered and fell. It was not the cave of persecution which is the palace of spiritual power, but only a room in the Astor House hired for the Transcendentalists. I do not wish to remove from my present prison to a prison a little larger. I wish to break all prisons. I have not yet conquered my own house. It irks and repents me. Shall I raise the siege of this hencoop, and march baffled away to a pretended siege of Babylon? It seems to me that so to do were to dodge the problem I am set to solve, and to hide my impotency in the thick of a crowd. (*Journals*, Vol. V, pp. 473-474.)

In January, 1844, noting the spontaneity of life at Brook Farm, he drew the conclusion "that in the arrangements at Brook Farm, as out of them, it is the person, not the communist, that avails" (*ibid.*, Vol. VI, p. 492). With the introduction of Fourierist organization he became sharply critical. Neither in Fourier nor in Owen did he see any hope.

Fourier learned from him [Owen] all the truth he had, and the rest of his system was imagination, and the imagination of a banker. The Owen and Fourier plans bring no *a priori* convictions. They are come at merely by counting and arithmetic. All the fine *aperçus* are for individualism. The Spartan broth, the hermit's cell, the lonely farmer's life are poetic; but the Phalanstery, the "Self-supporting Village," are culinary and mean. (*Ibid.*, Vol. VIII, pp. 134, 135.)

And a few days later he gave his final judgment, "Dear heart, take it sadly home to thee, that there will and can be no coöperation"— a judgment that explains the clever phrase with which he demolished Brook Farm, "It is the Age of Reason in a patty-pan."

The transcendentalist with his Puritan conscience could understand and sympathize with the perfectionist zeal for universal

righteousness; but collectivistic systems of economy seemed alien
and a community of goods uncongenial to his Yankee individualism. Albert Brisbane, the American apostle of Fourierism,
might bring George Ripley, the least individualistic and most
prosaic of the transcendental group, to his views of organization;
but he got on badly with the others who were quite too fluid to
take a mechanical set. In consequence it was not at Brook Farm
but at the North American Phalanx that the French system found
its fairest experiment and met with its solidest success.

IV

With the awakening interest in social problems the conscience of
New England could not longer remain indifferent to slavery. The
incoming of French humanitarianism, the spread of idealistic
sociology under the teachings of Unitarianism, above all the
stimulus of English Abolitionism that provided argument and
example in the freeing of slaves in the British West Indies, wore
away the indifferentism that had calloused the mind of New England; and with the decay of her provincial particularism the
conscience of New England slowly roused itself. The arrogance
of the slave party nowhere else stirred such deep resentment.
Southern steel, striking the flinty Yankee character, threw off
sparks that would fire whatever combustible stuff lay near; and
such combustible stuff was provided in plenty by the Utopian
enthusiasts who gathered in conventions, each with a plan of
universal reform in his waistcoat pocket. Little conflagrations
were started in many an obscure Yankee soul, and the noise of the
crackling spread over New England, to the anger of the South and
the vast concern of respectable Boston merchants. Sooner or
later Abolition sentiment was bound to make a tremendous stir
amongst the children of Puritanism; and when that time came it
was bound to arouse tremendous antagonism amongst the sons of
Yankees. The dominant commercial group would not tolerate a
movement that was certain to alienate its southern customers.
A mighty collision between the conscience and the self-interest of
New England was inevitable; and in that collision of flinty characters, arguments were likely to be countered with blows.

The New England Abolitionists, men and women, were an
extraordinarily interesting group. They were good fighters, outspoken and tenacious of opinion, unsparing in attack, refusing to

be browbeaten, resilient and tough as seasoned hickory. In them the Yankee Tory met his match; against them coercion and intimidation, all the usual Tory weapons, failed as earlier they had failed with the primitive Quakers. They were daily charged with being social incendiaries. The commercial newspapers thundered against them as atheists, Sabbath-breakers, socialists, anarchists; the absurdest myths were given circulation; the public mind was skillfully poisoned against them. Yet as a matter of sober historical fact, they were the kindliest of men, with generous sympathies and disinterested motives. No blackguard was ever an Abolitionist—no ward-heeler, or mob-inciter, or purse-patriot; all such convenient tools of power were found amongst the baiters and mobsters in the commercial opposition. John Brown was the only direct-action Abolitionist and what befell him is well known among men. There was no money to be made, no place of honor or power to be got by espousing Abolitionism, but only self-sacrifice and social ostracism. Ambitious men, self-seekers, went with the dispensers of social favors. It was the remnant in Israel that gathered to the cause, few in numbers but the best New England had. And what an excellent company they were: Garrison, Samuel J. May, Edmund Quincy, Jonathan Sewall, Theodore Parker, Lydia Maria Child, Mrs. Chapman, Wendell Phillips, Thomas Wentworth Higginson, Whittier, Henry Ward Beecher, Sumner, Maria White and the young Lowell—such a fighting phalanx as the New England conscience had never before mustered, nor has since. To them were gathered heroic souls from other states: Arthur and Lewis Tappan and Gerrit Smith from New York, James Birney from Kentucky, Lucretia Mott from Philadelphia, the Grimké sisters from South Carolina. Harriet Martineau, who knew the group intimately, has left on record her judgment of them: "A just survey of the whole world can leave little doubt," she wrote in 1838, "that the abolitionists of the United States are the greatest people now living and moving in it" (Carpenter, *John Greenleaf Whittier*, p. 107). They gave New England and the country no peace. From their persistent agitation came the Emigrant Aid Society, Sharp's rifles, and the bloody struggle in Kansas; and from it came the temporary overwhelming of the Tory minority in Massachusetts. For a few brief years New England threw off the stifling grip of the commercial mind and was the home of American humanitarianism.

CHAPTER IV

CERTAIN MILITANTS

I

WILLIAM LLOYD GARRISON

THE flintiest character amongst the New England militants, curiously enough, was the son of an immigrant family, brought to Newburyport and abandoned by a shiftless father. William Lloyd Garrison was not an offspring of generations of New England Puritanism, but a waif thrown by chance on the bleak shores of Massachusetts, and left to shift pretty much for himself. Born in Newburyport, half English and half Irish, with a heritage that promised ill, he was disciplined in the sternest of schools. His capable Irish mother had a bitter time providing for her three fatherless children, and the son suffered the privation and found the help that were the mixed portion of the destitute of old New England. Like Horace Greeley he ate the bread of poverty and grew strong on it. There was iron in his nature, and the narrow means that drove his father to drink and desertion, that sent his brother adrift, that broke his mother and killed his sister, only strengthened his will and toughened his fiber. As a lad he was put to the cobbler's bench to learn the trade that Whittier was learning at Haverhill; later he was apprenticed to a carpenter and cabinet-maker. In both trades he was unhappy, and it was not till a freak of fate turned him over to a friendly printer that he found himself. For seven years he stuck to his case, and at the end of the apprenticeship he was not only a first-rate practical printer, but with some little knowledge of books and master of a vigorous and serviceable prose style. With the amazing capacity for self-training so characteristic of the Yankee, he had picked up a sort of education and was ready to do whatever work in the world should come to hand.

Chance threw in his way the job of village editor, and inclination plunged him into politics. His political opinions, which he embraced more ardently than intelligently, were faithful reflections of current Massachusetts partisanship. He was quite ignorant of political principles and the economics that determined political parties, and with unconscious naïveté he espoused the cause of Boston commercialism. He was a dogmatic, unquestioning Whig. Clay was his idol, General Jackson his abomination; and his first political speech was in support of Harrison Gray Otis, the discredited boss of the old Federalist machine. But this was only a vagary of youthful hero worship. Enthusiasm for reform was already setting up a ferment in his ardent soul and preparing him for quite other alliances. The unhappy fate of his father was a lesson that he took home, and he interested himself in the temperance movement then just getting under way, serving for a time as editor of a small temperance paper. Shortly thereafter he stumbled upon his life work. Benjamin Lundy, a homespun hero of the Society of Friends, had long been publishing intermittently his *Genius of Universal Emancipation*, and in the itinerant work of begging support he fell in with Garrison. The two discovered kindred interests and they entered into a compact to go forth together to fight the dragon of slavery. They sought out the den of the beast in Baltimore and delivered their blows lustily; with the result that Garrison was indicted by the grand jury for printing the name of a Newburyport merchant who was picking up some honest dollars in the coastwise slave traffic, and spent seven weeks in jail. On his release he returned to Boston to replenish a lean purse, and January 1, 1831, he issued the first number of *The Liberator*, a little paper that was to make a mighty stir in the world during a long period of hand-to-mouth existence.

Never was there a more foolhardy venture, judged by the wisdom of this world. With no following, no weapon but a borrowed font of type in a mean little print-shop, no money or credit, he flung his defiance at the entrenched enemy with the courage of uncalculating youth. A prospectus issued in the fall of 1830 thus set forth the purpose of the venture:

I shall assume, as self-evident truths, that the liberty of a people is a gift of God and nature:—That liberty consists in an independency upon the will of another:—That by the name of slave we understand a man who can neither dispose of his person or goods, but enjoys all at the will of his master:—That no man can have a right over others, unless it be by them granted to him. . . . That that which is not just is not law; and that which is not law, ought not to be in force:—That he who oppugns the public liberty, overthrows his own. . . . That there is no safety where there is no strength, no strength without union, no union without justice, no justice where faith and truth are wanting:—That the right to be free is a truth planted in the hearts of men, and acknowledged so to be by all that have hearkened to the voice of nature. . . . *Vide Algernon Sidney's Discourses on Government—the Declaration of American Independence—the Constitutions and Bills of Rights of the several States, etc., etc.* (*Life of William Lloyd Garrison, by his Children.* Vol. I, p. 200.)

This pronouncement was amplified in the salutatory address in the first number, as follows:

Assenting to the "self-evident truth" maintained in the American Declaration of Independence, "that all men are created equal, and endowed by their Creator with certain inalienable rights—among which are life, liberty, and the pursuit of happiness," I shall strenuously contend for the immediate enfranchisement of our slave population. . . . I am aware that many object to the severity of my language; but is there not cause for severity? I *will* be as harsh as truth, and as uncompromising as justice. On this subject, I do not wish to think, or speak, or write, with moderation . . . urge me not to use moderation in a cause like the present. I am in earnest—I will not equivocate—I will not excuse—I will not retreat a single inch—AND I WILL BE HEARD. (*Ibid.*, Vol. I, pp. 224-225.)

The young man just turned twenty-six who thus marked out the path he was to follow for thirty-five years was an extraordinarily single-minded and rugged character. His like has too rarely appeared in America. Arrogant, dictatorial, intolerant, he might be, as his warmest friends admitted; but it is a foolish judgment that will dismiss him thus. Unyielding as granite, sheer Yankee will driven by a passionate energy, he was born for hazardous leadership. He was a man utterly unacquainted with fear. Lied about daily, threatened, bullied, charged with every sin in the Decalogue and every crime on the statute-book, he could not be coerced nor intimidated nor turned aside from his purpose. An ascetic who cared nothing for ease or preferment; a pacifist who fought only with the sword of the spirit; a stern moralist prophesying wrath upon a nation of mockers, and pronouncing doom upon a people that had forgotten God, he was an agitator fashioned after the ancient Hebraic pattern. The stature of such a man cannot be measured by conventional standards. Outwardly a somewhat prosaic Baptist, deeply religious and in his younger days bigotedly orthodox, he was in reality a spiritual child of the Old Testament, a modern Puritan on whom had fallen the mantle of the Prophets. New England Calvinism never bred so Puritan a soul. Hebraism was in his marrow—its noble austerity, its consuming passion. He daily walked with righteousness and communed with conscience. He carried God's scales into the market place. He would not accept his law of men. Constitutions and statutes were vain and foolish pronouncements to him if he judged them to be contrary to the divine enactments. He counted property in negroes and cotton as nothing when weighed in the balance of justice. A human soul, whether in black skin or white, was of far greater worth in his eyes than all the warring kingdoms of this world. As fully as John Humphrey Noyes he reëmbodied the root-and-branch righteousness of English Commonwealth times. Others might lash the sins of his generation with whips; he would scourge them with nettles and scorpions. He would raise such a clamor about men's ears that the drowsiest must awake. He would light such a fire in the slave market of America that the evil thing should be consumed as stubble in the white flame of righteousness.

Such primitive Hebraism, quite evidently, is calculated to make troublesome citizens who are certain to get themselves heartily disliked by those who approve of the world as it is. Any invasion of the devil's realms will create an uproar, for the devil is prompt to defend his own. Righteousness may prophesy in the gates, but the buying and selling of the poor goes on as usual. Amongst comfortable folk conscience is rarely at home when justice knocks at the door; it is gone a-visiting, or is busy, or is waiting upon Caesar, or is gone forth to pray. Comfortable folk do not like clamor, even from the prophets, and are content to leave justice to God with the hope that He will not disturb business. If the tithes are duly paid, it is a mean and censorious God that will ask how the money was got. Hence comfortable folk, north as well as south, did not like Garrison; and not liking him they were zealous to damn him. He was made out to be a bogy man, busily engaged in stirring up Nat Turner insurrections, inciting peaceful and contented slaves to discontent, flouting the Constitution and seeking to disrupt the Union. His righteousness was so great a stumbling-block that he was held to be an atheist by eminent formalists who knew of righteousness only by hearsay, and learned of God only from report. It was reckoned to him a major sin that he forgot his manners, for must not the Lord's work be carried on in seemly fashion, and the money-changers be scourged from the temple politely? "The first movement here at the North, was a

rank onset and explosion," said the eminent Dr. Bushnell. "The
first sin of this organization was a sin of ill manners. They did not
go to work like Christian gentlemen. . . . The great convention
which met at Philadelphia drew up a declaration of their sentiments . . . by which they willfully and boorishly cast off the whole
South from them" (Garrison, *William Lloyd Garrison*, Vol. II,
p. 132, Note). What could be done with a fellow who insisted that
the devil is rarely put in a quake by courteous treatment, and who
had never learned that the Hebrew prophets bore themselves
like Christian gentlemen? That he spoke with plebeian directness
was unquestionably true.

These are your men of "caution," and "prudence," and "judiciousness"
[he exclaimed in a speech at Philadelphia, May 14, 1838]. Sir, I have
learned to hate those words. Whenever we attempt to imitate our great
Exemplar, and press the truth of God, in all its plainness, upon the conscience, why, we are very imprudent; because, forsooth, a great excitement will ensue. Sir, slavery will not be overthrown without excitement,
a most tremendous excitement. (*Ibid.*, Vol. II, p. 215. Note.)

If clerical gentlemen disliked Garrison, gentlemen of State
Street disliked him much more heartily, and being the responsible
custodians of law and order, they upheld existing institutions in
their own way. Your Tory is always a Fascist at heart, and the
Boston Tories naturally adopted the principle of direct action.
Unpleasant things happened to Garrison in consequence. He was
denounced at a most respectable meeting in Faneuil Hall, "at
which Washington was cheered for being a slave-holder." He was
mobbed in his print-shop by "gentlemen of property and standing
from all parts of the city," and was thrown into jail by a timid
mayor to save his life. Not since the days of Tom Paine had such
unmeasured vituperation been poured out on the head of an American. It would seem that it was a perilous business to defend the
downtrodden or to remind church-members of the injunction
"to undo the heavy burdens and let the oppressed go free." When
conscience throws down the gauntlet to economics it is certain to
get some hard knocks. It is ill-trained for a rough and tumble
contest; its scruples will not permit it to hit below the belt. But
the Tory suffers no handicap of scruple and plants his blows where
he can. On the occasion of an Abolition convention announced
to be held within the shadows of Wall Street, Bennett's *New York*

Herald exemplified the sweetness and light of the commercial mind in such pronouncements as this:

> What business have all the religious lunatics of the free states to gather in this commercial city for purposes which, if carried into effect, would ruin and destroy its prosperity? . . . Public opinion should be regulated. These abolitionists should not be allowed to misrepresent New York. . . . When free discussion does not promote the public good, it has no more right to exist than a bad government that is dangerous and oppressive to the common weal. It should be overthrown. On the question of the usefulness to the public of the packed, organized meetings of these abolitionists, socialists, Sabbath-breakers, and anarchists, there can be but one result arrived at by prudence and patriotism. They are dangerous assemblies—calculated for mischief, and reasonable in their character and purposes. . . . That half-a-dozen madmen should manufacture opinion for the whole community, is not to be tolerated. (*Ibid.*, Vol. III, pp. 283–284.)

In consequence of which appeals to "prudence and patriotism" the meeting was broken up, public opinion was judiciously regulated, and the Bible and Constitution vindicated by a Bowery mob under the leadership of a ward-heeler. It was from the impact of such ruthless opposition that Garrison's strategy took form; and it was direct and uncompromising and outspoken—as sternly logical as Calhoun's. There were no shades in his thinking but only black and white, righteousness and sin. Expediency was not in his vocabulary. He was as narrow as he was intense. The catholic intellectual interests of the times touched him but little. Transcendentalism lay quite outside his world of thought. He was a religious soul rather than a speculative intellect, and he measured all things by the principles of primitive Christianity. As a young man he preferred the Calvinism of Lyman Beecher to the Unitarianism of Channing, but later he came to perceive the intimate relation between the major premises of Unitarianism and his social ideals. It is idle to seek a political philosopher in a Hebrew moralist. His somewhat naïve political conceptions were an amalgam of French equalitarianism and Yankee perfectionism. The Declaration of Independence was his one political textbook, in the light of which he judged Congressional enactments and interpreted the Constitution. With Channing he assumed an ethical sanction for natural rights, and this assumption conducted straight to the doctrine of the higher law. As early as 1830 his conscience was prepared to appeal from laws and statutes to ethics, on the principle that "that which is not just is not law." By 1837 he had accepted the philosophy of spiritual anarchism as set forth in the new gospel of perfectionism, and from this flowed naturally the doctrines of Nullification and disunion.

With amazing frankness Garrison published his views to friends and enemies, bringing all the hornets of conservatism about his ears. A furious discussion arose within the Abolition ranks on the question of loyalty to the political state, and the scandal of Garrison's Fifth Monarchy doctrine spread far. What that doctrine was he was at great pains to make clear. Writing to Henry C. Wright on the Quaker doctrine of non-resistance, he insisted on the sinfulness of all force whether in a private or public capacity, and then asserted:

Human governments will remain in violent existence as long as men are resolved not to bear the cross of Christ, and to be crucified unto the world. But in the Kingdom of God's dear Son, holiness and love are the only magistracy. It has no swords, for they are beaten into ploughshares— no spears, for they are changed into pruning hooks—no military academy, for the saints cannot learn war any more—no gibbet, for life is regarded as inviolate—no chains, for all are free. And that kingdom is to be established upon the earth, for the time is predicted when the kingdoms of this world will become the kingdoms of our Lord and of his Christ. (Garrison, *William Lloyd Garrison*, Vol. II, p. 149.)

From such premises he deduced the conclusion that government is a cross that God permits men to endure as punishment for their sins. When they shall voluntarily quit their sins political government will cease.

Human governments "are the results of human disobedience to the requirements of heaven; and they are better than anarchy just as a hailstorm is preferable to an earthquake, or the small-pox to the Asiatic cholera." From the silence of the Bible as to the *form* of such governments, he inferred not that each might claim a divine sanction, "but that the kingdom which Christ has established on earth is ultimately to swallow up or radically to subvert all other kingdoms." . . . "Shall we, *as Christians*, applaud and do homage to human government? or shall we not rather lay the axe at the root of the tree, and attempt to destroy both cause and effect together?" Foolish are the speculations about the best form of human government: "What is government but the express image of the moral character of a people?" (*Ibid.*, Vol. II, pp. 150-151.)

This is of course undiluted perfectionism, in which Garrison was the most ardent of believers. Prosaic political theory had lost all significance for him; he had got himself drunk on the new wine and was in no mood to listen to the counsels of expediency. Like John Humphrey Noyes he declared war upon the existing political state. He voluntarily disfranchised himself. He raised the banner of "disloyalty" in the *Liberator*, and summoned the Abolitionists to separate themselves from the unclean government that protected the sin of slavery. That the Constitution recognized the hateful system was sufficient proof to Garrison that the Constitution itself was unclean. Let it be consumed by its own iniquity. In 1843 he began an uncompromising attack upon it by nailing to the masthead of the *Liberator* his famous phrase, "A Covenant with Death and an Agreement with Hell," to which he soon added the words, "No Union with Slaveholders." He broke with many of his oldest friends, with Whittier and Gerrit Smith and James Birney, assailing them bitterly for meddling with third-party movements in the hope of curing the evil by political action. There followed, in consequence, a whirlwind and tempest of debate that brought a disastrous schism upon the Abolition movement. Cries of disloyalty and sedition filled all ears; but Garrison was indifferent to the storms that gathered about his head. He would go forward though he went alone. With every advance of the slave power his hatred of the Constitution, under cover of which its advances were made, grew more bitter. He outran southern fire eaters in advocacy of Nullification and secession. It became his daily work to undo the labors of Webster and bring the fundamental law into common contempt. The doctrine of no compromise with sin made no account of the complexities of social problems—the immediate, root-and-branch eradication of slavery or immediate dissolution of the Union, were his alternatives. "We dissolved the Union by a handsome vote, after a warm debate," wrote Edmund Quincy in 1843; "the question was . . . wrapped up by Garrison in some of his favorite Old Testament Hebraisms by way of vehicle, as the apothecaries say" (*ibid.*, Vol. III, p. 88).

It was at a Fourth of July meeting, following the Anthony Burns affair of 1854, that Garrison made use of the striking appeal that attests his extraordinary boldness and skill as an agitator. After contrasting the principles of the Declaration of Independence and the present state of the Republic, he went on:

He should now proceed to perform an action which would be the testimony of his own soul, to all present, of the estimation in which he held the pro-slavery laws and deeds of the nation. Producing a copy of the *Fugitive Slave Law*, he set fire to it, and burnt it to ashes. Using an old and well-known phrase, he said, "And let all the people say, Amen"; and a unanimous cheer and shout of "Amen" burst from the vast audience. In like manner Mr. Garrison burned the decision of Edward G. Loring in the case of Anthony Burns . . . the multitude ratifying the fiery immolation with shouts of applause. Then, holding up the U. S. Constitution, he branded it as the source and parent of all the other atrocities,—"a covenant with death and agreement with hell"—and consumed it to ashes on the pot, exclaiming, "So perish all compromises with tyranny! and let all the people say, Amen!" A tremendous shout of "Amen" went up to heaven in ratification of the deed, mingled with a few hisses and wrathful exclamations from some who were evidently in a rowdyish state of mind, but who were at once cowed by the popular feeling. (*Ibid.*, Vol. III, p. 412.)

In such fashion did this disciple of the gospel of peace carry the war into Macedonia. The law of conscience had come into collision with the law of the land, and he followed conscience. For Garrison majority votes held no mandate. He had come to regard the political state as the mother of all mischiefs; for behind this thing of shreds and patches he saw unscrupulous politicians whose profession was the deceiving of simple minds, befogging moral issues with their myths and cults—their appeals to patriotism and the Constitution—and bringing the law of God into contempt. It was the spiritual bondage of the North that held the negro in slavery, Garrison had come to believe, and to free the conscience of the North was the great duty devolving upon the Abolitionists. With his intense single-mindedness he saw no other duty, and in doing that duty he would use no other weapon than the sword of the spirit. It is fortunate, perhaps, that the prophet knows so little of the resourcefulness of the market place on which he pronounces judgment, or his zeal might suffer abatement. Slavery was not destroyed by the conscience of Massachusetts, but by the economics of free labor. The free-soilers were more dangerous to it for they fought with material weapons; and old John Brown of Ossawatomie, more Hebraic even than Garrison, was a sterner realist, who took care to load his Sharp's rifle while girding on the sword of the spirit. From the prophet to the soldier is but a step, from the sword of the spirit to musket and ball, from conscience to the Emancipation Proclamation. Single-minded men—the Garrisons and John Browns—marshaling the discontent of their generation, sometimes do succeed in removing mountains; but unfortunately they leave a great scar, and the débris litters the whole country-side. Other mountains may even arise from the waste of the leveling. After the Emancipation Proclamation came the Four-teenth Amendment, and out of that came the triumphant gospel of "due process of law." The devil understands the ways of the world too well to become discouraged at a temporary set-back, for if righteousness succeed in breaking the bonds that bind a genera-tion, he knows that the market place carries an ample stock of new cords to replace those that are broken.

II

JOHN G. WHITTIER
Puritan Quaker

If Garrison was the flintiest character amongst the militant Abolitionists, Whittier was certainly the gentlest. Among many lovable men he was perhaps the most lovable. Bred in a faith that had never been dominant in New England, he escaped the indura-tion that was the price the New England conscience paid for its hard dogma. No thick shell of Calvinism incrusted for him the soul of humanitarian religion. In the Society of Friends righteous-ness was not daily twisted into unloveliness, nor the beauty of holiness forgotten; and in consequence, it was easier for him than for his Calvinist neighbors to fashion his life upon the principles of the New Testament, and set Christ above the Prophets.

Whittier's family escaped many temptations by following quiet paths to their own ends. Prosperity had never wooed the Massa-chusetts Quakers away from the simple life, as it had done with so many Philadelphia Friends, but a narrow domestic economy and social non-conformity had nourished their religion of peace and good will. Long before Channing discovered the religion of love in the teachings of French humanitarianism, the early Quakers had found that primitive gospel in the byways of Carolinian England, and had brought it to the new world. There they had borne testimony in their daily lives to the excellence of Christian fellow-ship, and there they had suffered the reproaches and the blows of bigoted conformists. Their faith had been tried in the fires of persecution, and the Society of Friends had justified its use of that most excellent of sectarian names. In the sincerity of their equali-tarian fellowship the Quakers were the friends of humanity, of the poor and the outcast of this world. Their religion was of the week-day as well as the Sabbath. With its mystical doctrine of the inner light—of the Holy Spirit that speaks directly to the soul without the intermediation of priest or church—it unconsciously spread the doctrine of democracy in an autocratic world. It interpreted literally the principle that members of the Christian fellowship are equals in the sight of God and in each other's eyes— that on earth there is neither high nor low but a common brother- hood in Christ. It quietly set aside the pretentions of priestly hierarchies, and substituted the principle that religion is a matter that lies with the individual and God. Naturally a "hireling ministry" could not look with favor on such doctrine, and the sharp hostility it aroused in theocratic New England, sprang from the realization that the ideals of the Quaker fellowship were dangerous to the ideals of a priestly theocracy. The autocratic rulers of Massachusetts Bay could see little good in the democracy of the Friends.

As became a Quietist, the master passion of Whittier's life was ethical. He was neither a transcendental nor a Utopian visionary, but a primitive Christian, an apostle of good will and a friend of justice. Sprung from a long line of New England yeomen, wholly of the soil, simple in wants, quietly independent, he was the last lineal expression in our literature of the primitive faith, the last authentic echo of the spiritual democracy of the seventeenth century. A thorough Yankee in character, the Yankee never dominated him. As a young man, to be sure, he temporized with his Quakerism and dreamed fond dreams of worldly ambition. The stirrings of youthful romance awakened the desire to be a Byronic poet, and a Yankee knack with politics led him to meddle with the hope of representing his district in Congress. He was hand-in-glove with the time-serving Caleb Cushing, and the temp- tations of political intrigue almost led to his backsliding; but he soon put the devil behind him and gave security for his better behavior by coming out for the cause of Abolitionism. That was the end of his hopes of political preferment, and the more surely to burn his bridges he published in 1833, at his own cost, a little Abolition tract entitled *Justice and Expediency*, which was re- issued by Lewis Tappan in a great edition and scattered broadcast. The same year he attended as delegate the National Anti-Slavery Convention at Philadelphia, and subscribed his name to its pronouncement. Thenceforth for over thirty years he gave his best strength to the cause, writing abundantly in prose and verse, serving as editor of Abolition publications, and suffering the unpleasant experiences common to the group, at one time being hunted by a mob and stoned.

This deliberate alignment with an unpopular cause, this calm response to the summons of conscience, was the fruit of his Quaker training. It was no new experience for the Quaker to dissent. The Whittier family had been Come-outers for generations, sacrificing material well-being for their faith, and he had grown up in dissent. The long struggle for democratic freedom in Massachusetts was a familiar story to him. The record had come down by word of mouth and stories of early persecutions were fireside tales in the Whittier household. His ancestors had lived in the hard old Puritan theocracy, and yet detached from it; and this detachment had rendered them shrewdly critical and sensitive to injustice. With their quiet dissent from what the Quaker conscience regarded as unrighteous, and their practical nullification of unjust authority, Whittier was in full sympathy. His intimate knowledge of early Massachusetts history had taught him certain things which official historians had overlooked, the chief of which was that dissent had been the ally and friend of freedom in New England. From his youth up he had been a loving student of the old annals, of those intimate narratives that preserve the voice and manner of the past; and as he discovered how often persecution had left its stain on the record, he was drawn to consider the superstitious aberrations of a people supposedly devout. In middle life he gathered up in *Leaves from Margaret Smith's Journal of Massachusetts Bay, 1678–79*, materials that he had long been collecting, and which, interpreted by a sympathetic imagination, provides a surprisingly vivid account of life in New England in the second generation.

All in all, it is Whittier's most notable achievement in prose. Pieced together out of old records, it is authentic as the yellow documents from which it was drawn. The soft light of romance lies upon its pages, sobered by historical fact and tempered by creative sympathy. Loving yet critical, quite devastating at times in its implications, it is an amazingly intimate narrative. The mind of Puritan New England is uncovered in these unpretentious pages, and it does not show to advantage. There was

many a knot and seam in the old Puritan life, much that was mean
and ugly woven into the honest web. The Puritan proneness to
Quaker-baiting—aggravated to be sure by the ill manners of the
Ranters; their vulgar credulity that encouraged witch-hunting;
their callous treatment of the Indian and negro; their hardness
of nature that made them grasping and censorious: such knots
and seams in the Puritan character did not escape Whittier's eye,
but they appear in the sketches of avaricious deacons, sour women,
intolerant magistrates—the Deacon Doles and Goody Lakes and
Roger Endicotts, whose bigotry tyrannized over the better natures
of the community. Whittier sifted his materials carefully to
gather up what good wheat there might be, yet the showing it
must be confessed is but paltry. Honest Robert Pine who will
have none unjustly treated, good Mr. Russ who counsels moderation in dealing with the unhappy victims of mob suspicion, Captain
Samuel Sewall who speaks up bravely for the outcast—these are
the remnant in Israel, the generous minority that cannot leaven
the dour and credulous mass. Yet even they are not heroic figures
to Whittier. His heroes are the Come-outers, and in particular
Peggy Brewster—reminiscent evidently of his great-grandmother,
the Quakeress Mary Peaslee, who married Robert Whittier in
1694—who is the good Samaritan of the Puritan neighborhood,
and whose loving-kindness wins a reluctant good will that stops
short of toleration of her non-conformity.

Such intimate studies in the psychology of persecution were a
liberal education, and Whittier would have been no Quaker had
he not learned his lesson. He was justified in not thinking well
of the social conscience of respectable New England. Religious
conformity, he had come to understand, had not kept alive the
torch of freedom in Massachusetts, nor had Puritan righteousness
befriended justice. Not the great of earth but the simple may be
counted on to do God's work. So taking his lesson to heart he
quietly put aside ambition, and like Peggy Brewster numbered
himself among the remnant. Like her he would be a Come-outer
and bear his testimony against the uncleanness of the American
people in this matter of negro slavery. Not with musket and ball
would he fight, like old John Brown; but with the sword of the
spirit. The solution must lie with the conscience of the American
people. As a Friend, a man of peace, he would not deal harshly
with the supporters of slavery; he would not counsel violence.

But as a Yankee with a gift for politics, he would use political means to jog a slothful conscience and marshal its forces. And so Whittier became the politician amongst the Abolitionists. He proved himself a skillful lobbyist. He was active in getting up petitions to Congress. He supported John Quincy Adams and put pressure on the slippery Caleb Cushing. He advocated the policy of boring from within the old parties, but when such methods proved futile he became an active leader in the third party movement. He was an early supporter of the Liberal party—that in 1844 drew enough votes from Clay in New York to defeat him for the Presidency—of the Free-Soil party, and later of the Republican party.

It was this insistence upon the use of political methods that brought about the unhappy break with Garrison. Immediately it was no more than a difference over tactics, but it was embittered by a wide cleavage of political theory. With Garrison's conversion to spiritual anarchism the Abolition movement was sundered by a division between the perfectionists and the political actionists. The principle of non-voting and of refusing allegiance to the Constitution aroused strong opposition, and Whittier went with Birney and Gerrit Smith, with Jonathan Sewall, John Pierpont and the Tappans in rejecting the perfectionist policy. His political common sense turned naturally to political agencies to accomplish his ends. "Moral action apart from political" seemed to him an "absurdity." But when he applied the Quaker principle of Come-outism, and advocated separate party alignment, Garrison attacked him with his habitual intolerance. The latter feared a third party movement as certain to provide a rallying cry for the commercial interest to muster the mob to its support, and overwhelm the minority with the unthinking and selfish mass. "All political minorities," he argued, "are more or less liberal," and by throwing the Abolition strength to such organized minorities, the movement would be "feared and respected by all political parties" (Garrison, *William Lloyd Garrison*, Vol. II, pp. 310–311). The wisest strategy, he believed, was to seek to hold the balance of power between the old parties—rewarding friends and punishing enemies—while laboring to arouse the conscience of America, for ballots without conscience were the enemies of justice.

Whittier was no such root-and-branch spirit as Garrison, and in the political field he was a practical, somewhat prosaic Yankee, little given to abstract speculation, skillful in minor strategical skirmishes, inclined to opportunism. He belonged to no school of political thought. His equalitarianism came as a heritage from his Quaker religion rather than from political theory. To prepare himself for his work he read Milton and Burke. The pamphlets of the great Puritan appealed to him as the voice of the moral fervor of a heroic age, but Milton's aristocratic republicanism he seems to have examined no more critically than Burke's Whiggish legalism. Neither held anything in common with Quaker equalitarianism. Rousseau and Tom Paine and Jefferson, with whom he certainly would have sympathized, he seems not to have been acquainted with. In Whittier's New England they were in ill repute, and the young Whittier was as naïvely provincial in his political partisanship as was Garrison. Economics had no part in his thought, and the economic interests that divided Federalism and Anti-Federalism he seems never to have understood. Though sprung from six generations of farmers who tilled the same acres, he reveals no sympathy with agrarianism. He swallowed Clay and the American System without a qualm, and as a young editor he wrote with pride of the developing industrialism of Massachusetts. Neither in politics nor in economics was he a rebellious soul. He was conscience rather than intellect. He felt rather than thought. Only a moral issue could draw him into strife, and even in such contests he was ill equipped to lead the prosaic debates. His moral indignation found its natural expression in verse, and he early took his place as the poet of the Abolition movement, distilling into ready lyrics the emotion of the moment.

A great, even a noteworthy poet, Whittier certainly was not. Compared with Whitman he is only a minor figure. Among the better known American poets Bryant alone is so narrow in range and barren in suggestion. His austere and meager life bred too little sensuousness of nature and too few intellectual passions. An over-frugal watering of the wine of paganism had left the New England character thin. The sap of humor that ran so boisterously through the veins of the West, exuding a rough wit from Davy Crockett to Mark Twain, was quite gone out of the Yankee blood. His homely imagination was unquickened by a hearty village life as was the case with the English Bunyan and the Scotch Burns. He had become a bundle of Yankee nerves, responding only to moral stimuli. The comment of Whitman sums up the Quaker poet adequately:

Whittier's poetry stands for morality . . . as filtered through the positive Puritanical and Quaker filters; is very valuable as a genuine utterance. . . . Whittier is rather a grand figure—pretty lean and ascetic —no Greek—also not composite and universal enough (doesn't wish to be, doesn't try to be) for ideal Americanism. (Carpenter, *Life of Whitman,* p. 293.)

Never a great artist, rarely a competent craftsman, he wrote for the most part impassioned commonplace, with occasional flashes that are not commonplace.

The high-water mark of lyric indignation was reached in the lines to Webster. Written at white heat, they have the passionate directness of Thoreau's prose. Like other Abolitionists, Whittier had clung to his hopes of Webster in spite of frequent signs of the latter's backsliding. He did not sufficiently appreciate the economic alliances that tied Webster to State Street, and he underrated his presidential ambitions. But when the blow came with the Seventh of March Speech, it staggered him—not alone the defection of Webster, but the demonstrative approval of his wealthy constituents. For having "convinced the understanding and touched the conscience of a nation," Webster was formally thanked by some seven hundred addressers from the most respectable circles of Massachusetts—great men like Rufus Choate, George Ticknor, W. H. Prescott, President Jared Sparks and Professor Felton of Harvard, Moses Stuart and Leonard Woods of Andover Theological Seminary. It was an hour of profound discouragement that laid bare what colossal difficulties stood in the way of Abolitionism. "The scandalous treachery of Webster and the *backing* he has received from Andover and Harvard," wrote Whittier to Garrison, "show that we have nothing to hope for from the great political parties and religious sects" (William Sloane Kennedy, *John G. Whittier,* p. 113).

The scathing lines of *Ichabod* were read throughout the North, and they must have rankled in Webster's heart. Even Whittier was troubled by their severity and thirty years later he wrote a second Webster poem which he set beside *Ichabod* in his collected works. *The Lost Occasion* is a testimony to the kindliness of Whittier's Quaker heart that did not love to offend; but no kindliness of memory could change or soften the just verdict of the lines:

> Of all we loved and honored, naught
>   Save power remains;
> A fallen angel's pride of thought,
>   Still strong in chains.
>
> All else is gone; from those great eyes
>   The soul is fled:
> When faith is lost, when honor dies,
>   The man is dead!
>
> Then, pay the reverence of old days
>   To his dead fame;
> Walk backward, with averted gaze,
>   And hide the shame!

If Whittier was ill acquainted with the Boston of State Street and the Back Bay, and the Cambridge of Harvard culture, he knew intimately the Massachusetts of the village and the farm, and the overwhelming repudiation of Webster and the Whig party, following the Seventh of March Speech, would seem to have justified his lyric confidence expressed in the vigorous heptameters of *Massachusetts to Virginia*. For those who lived in the social world of Commissioner Loring—professor of law at Harvard—and Rufus Choate, it was hard not to think that Massachusetts had come to degenerate days. The fine old-school Federalist, Josiah Quincy, commenting on the Boston that watched Sims returned to slavery, wrote:

> When the [Fugitive Slave] law passed, I did think the moral sense of the community would not enforce it; I said that it never would be. But now I find that my fellow-citizens are not only *submissive* to, but that they are earnestly active for, its enforcement. The Boston of 1851 is not the Boston of 1775. Boston has now become a mere shop—a place for buying and selling goods; and I suppose, also, of *buying and selling men*. (Garrison, *William Lloyd Garrison*, Vol. III, p. 328.)

And Lowell, living in the same mean atmosphere, wrote:

> Massachusetts, God forgive her,
>   She's akneelin' with the rest,
> She, thet ough' to ha' clung ferever
>   In her grand old eagle-nest.
>   (*Biglow Papers*, Part I, 1.)

But Whittier professed to think better of the conscience of New England. A strong pride of the commonwealth runs through the lines that name over the towns of Massachusetts, from "free, broad Middlesex," westward and northward to the hills of Hampshire:

And sandy Barnstable rose up, wet with the salt sea spray;
And Bristol sent her answering shout down Narragansett Bay!
Along the broad Connecticut old Hampden felt the thrill,
And the cheer of Hampshire's woodmen swept down from Holyoke Hill.

The voice of Massachusetts! Of her free sons and daughters,
Deep calling unto deep aloud, the sound of many waters!
Against the burden of that voice what tyrant power shall stand?
No fetters in the Bay State! No slave upon her land!

When at last the long controversy was over and release from the struggle came to Whittier, his poetry grew richer and mellower. He was not made to be a fighter, and it was with a sigh of relief that he turned to the Elysian fields he had dreamed of, while he was turning with his plow the rough stubble of a cause. Looking back upon those arduous days, he sketched half whimsically his own portrait in *The Tent on the Beach.*

And one there was, a dreamer born,
    Who, with a mission to fulfill,
Had left the Muses' haunts to turn
    The crank of an opinion-mill,
Making his rustic reed of song
A weapon in the war with wrong,
Yoking his fancy to the breaking-plough
That beam-deep turned the soil for truth to spring and grow.

Too quiet seemed the man to ride
    The winged Hippogriff Reform;
Was his a voice from side to side
    To pierce the tumult of the storm?
A silent, shy, peace-loving man,
He seemed no fiery partisan
To hold his way against the public frown,
The ban of Church and State, the fierce Mob's hounding down.

For while he wrought with strenuous will
    The work his hands had found to do,
He heard the fitful music still
    Of winds that out of dream-land blew.
The din about him could not drown
What the strange voices whispered down;
Along his task-field weird processions swept,
The visionary pomp of stately phantoms stepped.

> The common air was thick with dreams,—
>   He told them to the toiling crowd;
>   Such music as the woods and streams
>   Sang in his ear he sang aloud;
>   In still, shut bays, on windy capes,
>   He heard the call of beckoning shapes,
>   And, as the gray old shadows prompted him,
>   To homely moulds of rhyme he shaped their legends grim.

Many excellent things he did in those quiet later years; old time pictures like *Snowbound*, with its homely fireside economy long since buried under the snows of forgotten winters; vigorous tales like *Abraham Davenport;* ballads like *Skipper Ireson's Ride*, that have something of the spirit of the primitive. He had given thirty years of his life to the cause of social justice, and surely none would grudge him in old age his rambles in pleasanter fields. It was well that he could turn to the past, for the America of the new exploitative age, the New England of Lowell and Lawrence, he never understood. Black slavery he understood, but wage slavery he comprehended no more than did Garrison. To the end he remained a primitive soul, ill equipped to understand a materialistic philosophy of society. There is something pathetic in his *Songs of Labor*. His economics, like his democracy, was of a bygone time, having no kinship with a scrambling free-soil-ism or a rapacious capitalism. There is scant room in this world for the Friend with his unmilitant dream of the fellowship. With his passion for freedom, established in the gospel of righteousness, the Quaker Whittier was fast becoming an anachronism in indus-trial New England that was concerned about very different things. How old-fashioned he had become is suggested by certain lines that phrase his greetings to later times. Spare, somewhat halting in rhythm, yet transparently sincere, they constitute an apologia that New England need feel no shame for.

> Yet here at least an earnest sense
> Of human right and weal is shown;
>   A hate of tyranny intense,
>   And hearty in its vehemence,
> As if my brother's pain and sorrow were my own.
>
> O Freedom! if to me belong
> Nor mighty Milton's gift divine,
>   Nor Marvell's wit and graceful song,
>   Still with a love as deep and strong
> As theirs, I lay, like them, my best gifts on thy shrine!

III
HARRIET BEECHER STOWE
A Daughter of Puritanism

No more Puritan mind than Mrs. Stowe's ever contributed to the literature of New England. Her remarkable native gifts were unconsciously given specific shape by a rigid environment. For years the artist in her struggled to subdue the moralist, and never quite succeeded. Before she dipped her pen in ink her mind had taken its set. She could not hope to escape being a preacher. Daughter of a minister and wife of a minister, with brothers and sons ministers, she lived all her life in an atmosphere of religion. She was baptized in creeds and prattled the language of sermons as the vernacular of childhood. Born at a critical time for the old New England faith, her youth was passed amid the storm clouds of the Unitarian controversy, in an atmosphere charged with electricity. Connecticut was the very citadel of the Edwardean orthodoxy, and Litchfield was as rugged in its faith as the hills it nestled among; and when the old-school Calvinism of Boston was in danger of utter rout, it naturally turned to a Connecticut Daniel to save the venerable cause. Stout old Lyman Beecher was a host in himself. Son of a Connecticut blacksmith and himself brought up at the forge before he quitted it to seek learning at Yale College under Timothy Dwight, able, kindly, practical, with pronounced literary tastes and a capable pen, he was a stalwart Edwardean, militantly conservative, who damned our perverse human nature with incontrovertible logic. Harriet was eight years old when Channing preached his Baltimore sermon, and fourteen when her father was summoned to Hanover Street Church, Boston. Her childish heart had already been given to Baxter's *Saint's Rest*, and her imagination awakened by Cotton Mather's *Magnalia Christi Americana*. Theocratic New England lay enveloped for her in a haze of romance, more fascinating than any Sir Walter had woven about the Scottish Highlands; she had discovered there noble figures and heroic deeds to kindle an ardent hero worship. At fourteen she was converted—too easily it seems, for she could not demonstrate to the satisfaction of her spiritual counselors that she had been sufficiently under conviction of sin. Thereafter to the end of her life the greatest of all dramas for her was the drama of the soul concerned with the great business of salvation.

The surest clue to Mrs. Stowe's literary secret is to be found in her sympathetic understanding of the spiritual life of Puritan New England. She was a lifelong student of New England psychology, with its "profound, unutterable, and therefore unuttered melancholy" that resulted from open-eyed contemplation of grim fact. The past that lay bleak and stern behind the sober present she understood as few others did. Before her sympathetic eyes it fell into just proportions, and quite naturally she became the historian of her people. The autobiographical material that fills her later work—her husband's recollections in *Old-Town Folks*, and her own in *Poganuc People*—is much more than autobiography; it is intimate history of New England, written by one who in distilling her own experience was writing the chronicle of a race. In a brilliant chapter of the former work she gives a remarkable analysis of the intellectual development of Puritan New England, and provides the setting against which her own intellectual life should be placed. To overlook it is to miss the most suggestive commentary on her work that has ever been written.

This daughter of Puritanism traces her intellectual antecedents back to the long struggle of Puritan rationalism with feudal custom and medieval ideas. The old English Puritans, "by nature the most reverential and most loyal portion of the community," in destroying the divine-right sovereignty of King Charles, were impelled to transfer that sovereignty to a higher King. In pulling down the temporal, they erected a divine sovereignty; and their passionate attachment to the new Sovereign was the natural response to "the pleading and yearning within them of a faculty robbed of its appropriate object, and longing for support and expression." But the theologies to which they yielded intellectual allegiance were a "legacy from past monarchical and medieval ages." To free themselves from this unhappy legacy, and create a democratic theology, was an arduous work that needed two hundred years to accomplish; and not until the Revolution spread a new social philosophy through America, did the work go forward rapidly. Wanting such a democratic philosophy Puritan New England wandered in the old theological fogs. It was Jonathan Edwards who first turned the New England mind to rationalism, and began that long "controversy" that was to unsettle so much. But unhappily the rationalism of Edwards was turned aside to reactionary ends, and his *Treatise on True Virtue* was "one of the strongest attempts to back up by reasoning the old monarchical and aristocratic ideas of the supreme right of the king and upper classes." Nevertheless he set all New England to rationalizing, and it was this severe discipline that carried her people soberly through the Revolutionary War, and preserved them from the excesses which followed the Revolution in France. And it was this same discipline that prepared them for the eventual re-discovery of the humanity of Jesus and the democracy of his religion. New England had been struggling towards democracy through the bog of its feudal theology; it became consciously democratic with the appearance of the new theology (*Old-Town Folks*, Chapter XXIX).

This rationalistic bias of eighteenth-century New England suffices to explain for Mrs. Stowe the stern temper and angular individuality of the old Puritan Yankee. Her particular hero and saint was Jonathan Edwards, and her lesser hero and saint was Samuel Hopkins; and in both it was the courageous rationalism that appealed to her. In them, and more particularly in the former, she discovered the creative force that quickened a religion that was falling into dead formalism, that gave it fresh vitality and made it the central fact of everyday New England life. Across the world of her youth lay the shadow—or the light—of the great Edwards, and the great Hopkins was his intellectual heir. In another chapter of *Old-Town Folks* she sketches the Edwardean influence in bold outline.

The ministers of the early colonial days of New England, though well-read, scholarly men, were more statesmen than theologians. Their minds ran upon the actual arrangements of society, which were in great measure left in their hands, rather than on doctrinal and metaphysical subtleties. They took their confession of faith just as the great body of Protestant reformers left it, and acted upon it as a practical foundation, without much further discussion, until the time of President Edwards. He was the first man who began the disintegrating process of applying rationalistic methods to the accepted doctrines of religion, and he rationalized far more boldly and widely than any publishers of his biography have ever dared to let the world know. He sawed the great dam and let out the whole waters of discussion over all New England, and that free discussion led to all the shades of opinion of our modern days. Little as he thought it, Waldo Emerson and Theodore Parker were the last results of the current set in motion by Jonathan Edwards. (Chapter XIX.)

In this flood let loose by the metaphysical saw of Jonathan Edwards, Mrs. Stowe found the material for her New England tales. In no other pages does one realize so fully the tremendous, vital significance of religion to the children of Puritanism, nor appreciate how narrow a course their lives ran between the farm and the meeting-house. A domestic economy and a parochial theology absorbed their energies, and they took on sharp and angular imprints from a severe routine. It was a school of discipline that created individual character, and Mrs. Stowe possessed a loving eye for the odd and original. She delighted in emphasizing the theological differences that ran through Yankee families, giving little twists to character, and rising to the tongue in scraps of confirmatory Scripture. Large-hearted, motherly Grandmother Badger, in *Old-Town Folks*, was a stern Calvinist who daily threw predestination in the face of her easy-going Arminian husband, and exchanged syllogisms in a Sabbath-day "battle of the Infinities" with her son from Yale. Theology provided the staple of talk in the farmer's kitchen; it was the axis on which turned the simple country life. *Old-Town Folks* and *Poganuc People* are cross sections of old New England, with its lingering prejudices in favor of rank,[1] its Arminian Parson Lothrop in wig and gold cane, and its Calvinist Dr. Cushing hostile to all democratic Jacobinism, its country yokels, its stubborn yeomen who parade their independence by voting the democratic ticket openly in the face of gentlemanly Federalists, its sharp contrasts of a stately old order and a somewhat bumptious new, yet with the hard New England granite snugly laid up and bonded with the mortar of religion —a strange dead world that emerges distinctly through the haze of Victorian sentiment. For Mrs. Stowe was a child of her own romantic generation as well as a daughter of Puritanism, and it was easy for her to discover suggestions of Utopia in a world where minister and people mingled theology with their corn-huskings and apple-bees.

Between these sketches and the Abolition novels stands *The Minister's Wooing*, with its Puritan heroine bleached into pure holiness under the cold sunshine of Hopkinsian theology, and its unworldly minister who demonstrated the sincerity of his creed of disinterested benevolence—of willing to be damned for the glory of God—by voluntarily yielding his betrothed to an earlier lover.

---

[1] " It's a hard struggle for our human nature to give up titles and ranks, though," said Miss Mehitable. "For my part, I have a ridiculous kindness for them yet. I know it's all nonsense; but I can't help looking back to the court we used to have at the Government House in Boston." (*Old-Town Folks*, Chapter VI.)

It is a love story without sex, as befits the wooing of a Puritan nun by her spiritual father, set against a Yankee background of capable housekeeping and dignified tea-drinking, subdued to proper decorum by religion, and touched with tragedy by the shadow of damnation that falls on the unregenerate—a world in which the beauty of holiness is somewhat pale and austere, and where disinterested benevolence finds a thin and obdurate soil to strike root in. Mrs. Stowe was drawn to the theme, very evidently, by the impulse of her two Utopian enthusiasms, her interest in Abolition and her affection for the ways of old New England. Such romance as blossomed under those bleak skies she loved to gather into a Yankee nosegay, and in her sympathetic hands the old slave-running Newport becomes almost lovable and human. She might find the theology hard, but she forgave the sermon out of love for the preacher. As the historian of the human side of Calvinism she tempered dogma with affection. In unsympathetic print those old sermons were almost unbelievably harsh and ungainly; as theologians those bewigged preachers were dry as the chips of last year's woodpile; but as husbands and fathers and neighbors, they were usually kind and unselfish and helpful. Her father Lyman Beecher was an arid dogmatist on the Lord's Day, but on week-days he fished and hunted rabbits and went nutting with his sons, made garden or smoked hams, or helped a neighbor with plowing or haying, and was an unusually capable and cheery member of a busy little world. In the light of such domestic exegesis the bleakness of his theology was softened, and the dogmatic theologian became a very human person.

Thus instructed Mrs. Stowe found no difficulty in discovering the human side of Dr. Samuel Hopkins, or understanding how the hard doctrine might cover the gentlest of souls—that the very intensity of devotion to the logic of a stern creed betokened a depth of religious sincerity that would find issue in generous deeds. A thinker who can dig from the harsh soil of Calvinism the doctrine of disinterested benevolence will discover a tender conscience in his own bosom. One might hazard a guess, indeed, that the story of Samuel Hopkins was an unconscious defense of the New England ministers against the sharp charges of the Abolitionists that the clergy were half-hearted in the cause or openly hostile. With her conviction of the unselfish nobility of their lives, Mrs. Stowe must have taken a secret pleasure in revealing the good Doctor

as a forerunner of the Abolitionists, and in pointing out that the
crabbed logician of the Edwardean school, the theologian immersed
in the abstractions of a grotesque system, was nevertheless a
light set upon a hill, a primitive Christian with heart overflowing
with loving-kindness, who understood the iniquity of slavery and
turned shepherd to the outcast to his own hurt. The figure of the
unworldly minister is drawn with loving hand and his angularities
made less rugged. His noble spirituality shrivels and consumes the
mean excuses of his slave-running parishoner; it spreads quietly
over the countryside, and his daily life is a sermon that quickens
hearts that his theology leaves cold. There is preaching aplenty
in the book—quite too much for later stomachs; but it scarcely
detracts from the significance of the story as a document of Puritan New England, revealing how a tender conscience was stirring
beneath the crabbed exterior of the old Calvinism.

In the light of such antecedents and such training Mrs. Stowe's
passionate concern over slavery becomes easily comprehensible.
Her Puritan conscience was quickened by her warm human sympathies. She had come close to the hateful thing during the years
spent at Cincinnati, where the Abolition sentiment of the Lane
Seminary students aroused such bitter opposition that President
Lyman Beecher was forced to approve the decision of the trustees
to forbid any discussion of slavery, with the result that so great a
hegira of students took place from Lane to Oberlin that the seminary was forced to close. Only the fact that two miles of Ohio mud
provided defensive outworks saved the building and the houses
of the teachers from the hands of the Cincinnati mob. She had
visited in Kentucky; she had been to the slave markets; she had
seen her father and brother aid runaway slaves by means of the
underground railway. A profound sense of the iniquity of the
system oppressed her, and when the Fugitive Slave Bill came to
fill up the measure of her wrath, she poured out her heart in *Uncle
Tom's Cabin*. Despite its obvious blemishes of structure and sentimentalism it is a great human document that stripped away the
protective atmosphere from the sacred institution, and laid bare its
elementary injustice. It brought the system home to the common
feeling and conscience. The strong religious coloring emphasized
the Abolition argument that slavery trafficked in Christian souls,
and rendered it hateful to every humanitarian instinct. It was
noble propaganda, and the humor and pathos, the passion for

social righteousness, still linger in its pages to make a later generation wonder that our fathers should so long have tolerated this evil thing.

Five years later she published *Dred, A Tale of the Great Dismal Swamp*, a thoughtfully elaborated statement of the complex problem, with a suggested solution that only thrust into relief the fact that it had indeed become an irrepressible conflict—the same solution that had been hinted at thirty years before in Kennedy's *Swallow Barn*, namely, a system of paternalistic emancipation, based on the historical analogy of the extinction of English villeinage, the slaves to be treated as wards by the masters and educated for gradual emancipation. It was a feudal solution of a feudal problem, but it took higher humanitarian ground than human nature can, and Mrs. Stowe recognized the complex of passion and interests in which the problem was involved, by removing her southern emancipationist to Canada to try his experiment. More striking, perhaps, is the shift from the Christian pacifism of *Uncle Tom's Cabin* to the economics of *Dred*. The former had made appeal to the humanitarianism of the North; the latter proposed to appeal to the self-interest of the South. The slave states, Mrs. Stowe's heroine argued, were being ruined by slavery, and if they were to expect a sane economic future, they must destroy the wasteful system. The contrast between Yankee thrift under free labor and plantation shiftlessness under slave labor had been pointed out by Whittier in his *Justice and Expediency* as early as 1833 and by Caruthers in his *Kentuckian in New York* in 1834—statements that perhaps drew Mrs. Stowe's attention to the economic phases involved; nevertheless the recognition of the complexity of the problem, and the attempt to deal with it adequately, lessened the popular appeal of *Dred*. The book is more skillfully done than *Uncle Tom*, it is far richer in background material—in vivid sketches of poor whites, of revivalist preachers, of plantation life—it provides in Old Tiff a delightful study of the negro servant and it suggests the perennial fear of a negro uprising; but it lacks the singleness of appeal that makes for telling propaganda. It was not its melodrama that hindered its success. The public had swallowed that in *Uncle Tom* with a hearty appetite. It was rather the dissipation of dramatic interest, the want of a striking figure to capture the imagination and sympathy. It is a better sociological study but a weaker story.

It was hard for the New England conscience to quit the pulpit and turn artist; and it was particularly hard for Mrs. Stowe with her ardent nature and multiplying domestic cares. She could bring her soul under discipline but not her art. She never trained herself in craftsmanship, never learned restraint, but suffered her pen to range freely as her emotions directed. The creative instinct was strong in her but the critical was wholly lacking. Richly endowed though she was her work has suffered the fate that pursues those who forget that beauty alone survives after emotion subsides.

PART THREE: THE TRANSCENDENTAL MIND

CHAPTER I

THE GENESIS OF TRANSCENDENTALISM

From the doctrine of the open mind that was the core of Unitarianism, came the transcendental movement that marked the full flowering of the New England renaissance. It was the native response of the mind of New England to the summons of revolutionary romanticism, and its ardor was the greater for being so long delayed. Creatively influenced though it was by French Utopianism and German mysticism, its manners and mode of thought received a particular impress from an environment long preparing and that was natively congenial. "Practically," says its most penetrating historian, transcendentalism "was an assertion of the inalienable worth of man; theoretically it was an assertion of the immanence of divinity in instinct, the transference of supernatural attributes to the natural constitution of mankind."[1] It was the glowing expression of philosophic Utopianism, the flaring up of old fires of idealism, before the scientific and materialistic reactions destroyed its romantic dreams. It accepted kinship with the social idealism of the Declaration of Independence; it accepted the dynamic principle of equalitarianism; but it sought to go farther and provide a sure defense and justification of an idealism that it professed to find established in human nature, by establishing it in metaphysics.

The explanation of this curious throwback to earlier times in the mind of transcendental New England is clear enough to anyone acquainted with the history of Puritan thought struggling with the mystical element of Christian experience. Since the far-off days of Roger Williams—the seeker and mystic who was so great a puzzle to his realistic brethren—idealism had been starved in New England. Its mystical aspirations had been repressed by dogma, and its elusive dreams brought to nothing. Jonathan Edwards struggled life-long to hold his idealism in subjection to theology, and ended in abortive reaction; a potential Emerson,

[1] See Frothingham, *Transcendentalism in New England*. Chapter VI.

379

another Berkeley, he re-welded the bonds of dogma on the mind of New England, putting off for two generations the day of its release. Even in the freer minds idealism suffered from the repressions of the common rationalism; with Locke and Hume in the ascendancy the mystic found the times uncongenial to his needs. The dawn of a new day seemed to be breaking with the shift of interest from theology to politics, during the stirring days of the Revolution. The submerged idealism of New England came to expression in the dreams of homespun democrats like Sam Adams, and expanded in the sunshine of French Utopianism; but unfortunately Boston Federalism reasserted the old dogmatisms and put a speedy end to the movement. It shut the door upon all democratic aspiration and bade it go about its business. It was from such a narrow environment that the rising movement of Unitarianism received its impress. From a sterile rationalism, a respectable close-fisted conservatism, it could not escape; and in consequence the new movement of liberalism was taken over by Federalism and became a new orthodoxy. "The pale negations of Boston Unitarianism"—to use Emerson's well-known phrase— provided little nourishment for transcendental hopes.

Nevertheless Unitarianism carried within it the seeds of the new faith—in its intellectual attitude, if not in its philosophy. "The Unitarians as a class," remarks Frothingham, "belonged to the school of Locke, which discarded the doctrine of innate ideas, and its kindred beliefs. . . . Unitarianism . . . has rarely, if ever, been taught or held by any man of eminence in the church who was a Platonist" (*Transcendentalism in New England*, Chapter VI). But in spite of its eighteenth-century nurture—because of it, indeed—Unitarianism was a profoundly liberalizing movement. It was a narrow and local phase of a world-wide revolution; the special contribution of Boston to the great work of disintegrating the past to make ready for the future. It loosened the grip of dogma on the Puritan mind and widened the field of reading and thinking. But it did very much more—it recovered the original principle of Protestantism, the principle of individual responsibility, that had been tacitly denied by Calvinistic orthodoxy. It asserted the essential decency of human nature—men may not be the children of God but they are assuredly not children of the devil; and it summoned this decent human nature to live decently in accordance with its nature. It would not coop up the mind in dogma; it would not close all roads to heaven but one. The Unitarians might be instinctively conservative, as was natural to prosperous persons, but they at least acknowledged "themselves to be friends of free thought in religion." Their doctrine was not a creed but an attitude of mind. If they themselves were not Seekers, they professed a willingness for others to become Seekers. Very likely few of them measured up to the full stature of such liberalism; nevertheless they "honestly but incautiously professed a principle broader than they were able to stand by, and avowed the absolute freedom of the human mind as their characteristic faith" (*ibid.*, Chapter VI).

All this was excellent, but it was not enough. It remained to see what the free mind should discover in its venturesome quest into the unknown. Intellectually emancipated, with the bleak dogmas of election and reprobation put away, with the God of wrath dethroned and the God of love lifted up, and with the dynamic principle of freedom of inquiry in their possession, the younger generation of New England intellectuals naturally opened their eyes to discover what winds of new doctrine were blowing in the world. They were pretty much all Unitarians—the young transcendentalists—and largely clergymen; their primary interest was metaphysical and they had already abandoned Locke for Plato. The rationalistic eighteenth century was dead to them and they set forth to discover another age. Hints and suggestions of that better age had come to them from overseas—from Wordsworth and Shelley, from Cousin and Madame de Stael, from Coleridge and Carlyle; and the fresh beauty of that new poetry, the enormous stimulus of that new metaphysic, fired them with a desire to seek this inspiration at its source and drink from the living waters. And so they discovered romantic Germany where the new idealism had quite routed the philosophy of sensationalism, and a great school of transcendental thinkers was in triumphant possession of the field. It was a profoundly stimulating discovery, and from it dated the rise of New England transcendentalism.

The immediate creative influence of the new contact with Germany was to strengthen the incipient Platonism of the rebellious intellectuals, and provide it with an added sanction. Transcendentalism, it must always be remembered, was a faith rather than a philosophy; it was oracular rather than speculative, affirmative rather than questioning; and it went to Germany to find confirma-

tion of its faith, not to reëxamine its foundations. Faith preceded
metaphysics, and if the metaphysics had been lacking intuition
would have supplied its place, poetic inspiration would have
sufficed the needs of transcendental minds. They had found God
for themselves before the philosophers justified them; they took
to Germany what they sought there. Nevertheless it was a
tremendous experience to come upon their own philosophy there,
erected into a system, supported by a complete metaphysic; a
philosophy that had put to rout the fashionable skepticism of
Voltaire and Condillac, established on the sensationalism of Locke,
and offering justification for faith in God and man—faith in a
divinity indwelling in nature and the individual soul—by a
masterly dialectics. That experience determined the development
of New England transcendentalism. The metaphysic of Kant,
the mysticism of Jacobi, the idealistic egoism of Fichte, the transcendentalism of Schleiermacher—the new gospel of the renascent
German spirit—these were the living waters of truth to the thirsty
minds of the New England intellectuals, from which they drank
eagerly, never doubting their sufficiency. They were poets and
prophets; they were young and strong in faith; others might concern themselves with the dialectics of idealism, they would apply
it in their daily lives.

In essence this new transcendental faith was a glorification of
consciousness and will. It rested on the rediscovery of the soul
that had been dethroned by the old rationalism; and it eventuated
in the creation of a mystical egocentric universe wherein the
children of God might luxuriate in their divinity. The Unitarians
had pronounced human nature to be excellent; the transcendentalists pronounced it divine. They endowed it with great potentialities; made of it a dwelling place of the Most High; discovered
the secret voice of God in the buried life that men call instinct;
refused to heed any other command save this inner voice of God.
With ebbing faith men may deny their own divine nature, but the
divinity is not destroyed; the music of the indwelling Godhood
murmurs in the shell till the tide returns to flood it again. The
one great miracle is the daily rebirth of God in the individual
soul; every day is a new day; every act is a fresh wonder; faith,
hope, trust, accompany man in his adventurous journeyings.
Why, therefore, demanded the transcendentalist, should he not
trust himself? Why should he not walk confident in his own high

purpose? Why should he doubt and question the buried compulsions that urge him forward? If he is indeed a child of God, let
him live as unto God; and if it should turn out that there has been
some mistake in the premises and he proves to be a child of the
devil, then let him live as unto the devil. Better so than not to
trust himself.

Quite obviously they were arch-romantics—these young poets
of the new faith; children of an age given over to new hopes and
disintegrating revolutions; inexperienced prophets of a world in
flux, before the scientific spirit had stripped them of their wings.
The fascinating book of nature and of man had been newly opened
to them, and like Miranda they were ready to exclaim,

> O wonder!
> How many goodly creatures are there here!
> How beauteous mankind is! O brave new world,
> That has such people in 't!

They could see only God because in their thinking God had filled
their minds. No evil lurked in the secret places of their hearts to
whisper doubts concerning the goodness of life; no ominous clouds
veiled the divine light that wrapped their universe about. After
two hundred years of discipline in righteousness the old dogmatic pessimism was dissipated, leaving not a rack behind. The
evil was gone and God remained; and in this new world the sons of
God were to be henceforth heirs of the kingdom, free to fulfill that
good which is the final reality. Arch-romantics, they were dreaming a transcendental dream, as other arch-romantics were dreaming
their Jacksonian dream, their imperialistic dream, their Utopian
dream. Romanticism comes to different issues in different men
and different times: Emerson and Jefferson were unlike enough,
as their worlds were unlike; but they were both romantics and
their idealism was only a different expression of a common spirit.

Years after the transcendental ferment had subsided, one of the
lesser prophets of the movement offered a statement of the faith
that deserves to be recalled:

Transcendentalism [he said] relies on those ideas in the mind which are
laws in the life. Pantheism is said to sink man and nature in God; Materialism to sink God and man in nature; and Transcendentalism to sink
God and nature in man. But the Transcendentalist at least is belied and
put in jail by the definition which is so neat at the expense of truth. He
made consciousness, not sense, the ground of truth. . . . Is the soul

reared on the primitive rock? or is no rock primitive, but the deposit of spirit—therefore in its lowest form alive, and ever rising into organism to reach the top of the eternal circle again, as in the well one bucket goes down empty and the other rises full? The mistake is to make the ever-lasting things subjects of argument instead of sight. . . . Our soul is older than our organism. It precedes its clothing. It is the cause, not the consequence, of its material elements; else, as materialists understand, it does not exist. . . . What is it that accepts misery from the Most High, defends the Providence that inflicts its woes, espouses its chastiser's cause, purges itself in the pit of its misery of all contempt of His commands, and makes its agonies the beams and rafters of the triumph it builds? It is the immortal principle. It is an indestructible essence. It is part and parcel of the Divinity it adores. It can no more die than he can. It needs no more insurance of life than its author does. Prove its title? It is proof of all things else. It is substantive, and everything adjective beside. It is the kingdom all things will be added to. (C. A. Bartol, quoted by Frothingham in *Transcendentalism in New England*, Chapter XIV.)

This is sheer mysticism, and mystics in greater or less degree all the transcendentalists were—isolated and lonely in the midst of men, seeking always a larger fellowship, awaiting those fleeting moments of illumination that should light up the meaning of life. "Mine is a certain brief experience," says Emerson, "which sur-prised me in the highway or in the market, in some place, at some time,—whether in the body or out of the body, God knoweth, —and made me aware that I had played the fool with fools all this time, but that law existed for me and for all; that to me be-long trust, a child's trust and obedience, and the worship of ideas, and I should never be fool more" (*The Transcendentalist*). Fleet-ing and incommunicable are such illuminations, yet like the clear sunlight to eyes that are open. "If you do not need to hear my thought, because you can read it in my face and behavior, then I will tell it you from sunrise to sunset. If you cannot divine it, you would not understand what I say" (*ibid.*). And because the realist found himself quite incapable of such understanding, the transcendentalist turned away from him to live by himself. "They feel that they are never so fit for friendship, as when they have quitted mankind, and taken themselves to friend."

Such an attitude of mind may easily become the father of criti-cism. Communing with the ideal rarely begets complacency; the actual seems poor and mean in comparison with the potential. Hence the transcendentalists, willingly or not, were searching critics of their generation. They were impatient of any falling short of the ideal, and their lives in consequence became an open indictment of a Yankee world given over to materialism. "By their unconcealed dissatisfaction," said Emerson, "they expose our poverty, and the insignificance of man to man." "Their quarrel with every man they meet, is not with his kind, but with his degree. There is not enough of him,—that is the only fault. . . . They make us feel the strange disappointment which overcasts every human youth. So many promising youths, and never a finished man!" (*The Transcendentalist.*)

As to the general course of living, and the daily employments of men, they cannot see much virtue in these, since they are parts of this vicious circle; and as no great ends are answered by the men, there is nothing noble in the arts by which they are maintained. Nay, they have made the experiment, and found that, from the liberal professions to the coarsest manual labor, and from the courtesies of the academy and the college to the conventions of the cotillion-room and the morning call, there is a spirit of cowardly compromise and seeming, which indicates a frightful skepticism, a life without love, and an activity without aim. (*Ibid.*)

Idealists though they were, they could not escape meddling with the real which encompassed them on all sides—with institutions, laws, society, with the state itself. They were far more interested in God than in Cæsar, and they found it impossible to divide loyalties that too often clashed. When Cæsar essayed to impose his will upon theirs, when he put their ideals in jeopardy by demanding allegiance to laws they did not approve, they quietly denied him sovereignty and followed their own paths. With such men nothing could be done; their very lives were a criticism and a judgment on New England and America. Transcendentalism may have run into its follies, but foolish in its critical judgment—blind to the gap between profession and reality—it was not. It might be severe, but it was honest and intelligent, and honest intelligent criticism America stood greatly in need of.

CHAPTER II

RALPH WALDO EMERSON
Transcendental Critic

At the age of thirty-six the man who was to become the most searching critic of contemporary America expressed his conception of his mission in the following passage:

> What shall be the substance of my shrift? Adam in the garden, I am to new-name all the beasts of the field and all the gods in the sky. I am to invite men drenched in Time to recover themselves and come out of time, and taste their native immortal air. I am to fire with what skill I can the artillery of sympathy and emotion. I am to indicate constantly, though all unworthy, the Ideal and Holy Life, the life within life, the Forgotten Good, the Unknown Cause in which we sprawl and sin. I am to try the magic of sincerity, that luxury permitted only to kings and poets. I am to celebrate the spiritual powers in their infinite contrast to the mechanical powers and the mechanical philosophy of this time. I am to console the brave sufferers under evils whose end they cannot see, by appeals to the great optimism, self-affirmed in all bosoms. (*Journals*, Vol. V, p. 288.)

Seven days before Emerson set down this transcendental pronouncement, he had written in his journal a different comment:

> A question which well deserves examination now is the Dangers of Commerce. This invasion of Nature by Trade with its Money, its Credit, its Steam, its Railroad, threatens to upset the balance of man, and establish a new, universal Monarchy more tyrannical than Babylon or Rome. Very faint and few are the poets or men of God. Those who remain are so antagonistic to this tyranny that they appear mad or morbid, and are treated as such. Sensible of this extreme unfitness they suspect themselves. And all of us apologize when we ought not, and congratulate ourselves when we ought not. (*Ibid.*, Vol. V, pp. 285–6.)

In such comments and others scattered plentifully through his Journals, Emerson essayed to make clear to himself the function of transcendental criticism as he felt himself called to practice it. It was to be no trivial or easy duty. In the midst of a boastful materialism, shot through with cant and hypocrisy and every insincerity, fat and slothful in all higher things, the critic proposed to try the magic of sincerity, to apply the test of spiritual values

386

to the material forces and mechanical philosophies of the times. His very life must embody criticism; his every act and word must pronounce judgment on the barren and flatulent gods served by his countrymen. He must be a thinker and as such he must summon to the bar of a nobler philosophy the current standards of value and conduct. Men of the greatest reputation must not be spared; he must "issue a *quo warranto* and revoke the characters of fame," overruling the verdict of newspaper editors and the acclaim of the electorate. Here was a revolutionary business indeed, that the critic was proposing to himself; and the calm serenity with which he set about it was disconcerting. A thinker loose in the America of Daniel Webster, a thinker who proposed to test men and measures by the magic of sincerity, was likely to prove an unpleasantly disturbant factor in a world of pretense. Measured by such standards the current philosophies must bate and dwindle, and the common ideals shrink to the mean and paltry. The life of an honest thinker laid on the America of 1840 would reveal how far short it came from the stature of intellectual manhood.

Emerson the critic has been too much obscured to common view by Emerson the brilliant dispenser of transcendental aphorisms. The oracular *Essays* with their confident wisdom—the sententious expression of the middle period of a life that came to late maturity—interpose themselves between the young priest whose intellectual interests quietly detached themselves from Unitarian orthodoxy, and the mature critic whose loyalties quietly detached themselves from the gods of his generation. The very brilliancy of the *Essays* conceals the laborious processes by which their abundant wisdom was distilled. One must go to the *Journals* for that—to those intimate records that reveal how patiently he sought for truth and how honestly he followed it. Wisdom did not come to him of its own accord; it was painfully groped for. As an introspective Puritan youth he began early to keep a diary of his intellectual life, gathering into successive journals the savings from his discursive readings. For years as a quiet student he lived in a world of moral aphorisms, a cold, thin atmosphere where gnomic phrases bloomed and ancient oracles uttered judgment. This was the seedtime of his mind. He was making acquaintance with the noble dead, gathering their utterances to make for himself a new testament. "No man could be better occupied," he said later, "than in making his own bible by harkening to all those sentences which now here, now there, now in nursery rhymes, now in Hebrew, now in English bards, thrill him like the sound of a trumpet." As a young man he made this his chief concern. His early journals are an ample nursery where cuttings from all philosophies are set out, there to grow into such plants as circumstance should permit. The ancestral cult of the book was in his blood, and living as he did under the threat of ill health, none too confident that the years would lengthen out before him, he forced himself to a severe intellectual regimen. To invest his days wisely was his single purpose. He wanted only the best securities for his investments, and what he got he carefully deposited, together with the increments of his own thought, to draw upon at later need. There were no wastrel forays in his intellectual life, no unpruned riot of growth, but the very odds and ends of his meditation were carefully treasured to be used when other materials were lacking. Fortunately the stuff was of good quality that outlasted many makings-over, till finally he got the cut to his liking. From this discipline of years came his superlative mastery of the sententious sentence; his brilliant utterances are rich with the thought he has crammed into them.

The cheerful serenity that never deserted him was a triumph of will over circumstance. It was a singularly cheerless world that bred him, subsisting by sheer will power, eating its heart out with heroic ambitions, too grimly earnest to enjoy what it got so laboriously—the lean aftermath of two centuries of asceticism. The business of plain living and high thinking was a joyless manner of life, and the young Emerson got little pleasure from it. A nature less insulated must have broken under the strain. It was a world stricken with tuberculosis. Of the five brothers one was mentally defective, another burnt up his vitality and went to the West Indies to die, a third of brilliant powers succumbed to consumption, his first wife died of the same scourge, his second wife and Emerson himself were long affected with incipient tuberculosis. To ease such anxious lives there was need of a great solace, and that solace was sought in religion. The ascetic youth ran as naturally to religious meditation as a normal child to play. No call to conversion ever came to him; the natural man postulated in Calvinistic dogma was washed out of him before he was born. The earlier jottings in the journals, before philosophy came to soften the inherited asceticism, and a transcendental revulsion from the common pessimism had turned him into a serene optimist, often are as bleak and austerely introspective as those morbid human documents that fill the old libraries of Puritanism. Such meditations are thin gruel for the nourishment of a vigorous life, and Emerson must have suffered from innutrition if he had not come upon more substantial food.

Fortunately the old Puritan anchors were already dragging, and Emerson was pretty well adrift when the romantic surge caught him and sent him far along new courses. The Puritan moralizer became the transcendental seeker; the curious-minded loiterer in the gates of the temple, who had studied the moral winds by watching the tiny straws of circumstance—erecting unconsidered trifles into ethical signposts—calmly quitted the church and set forth on his intellectual quest. The ties had long been loosening, but it was his year abroad where he discovered ways of thinking unknown to Concord and Boston, that effectively liberalized his mind and released him from the narrow Yankee provincialisms. On that momentous trip Goethe, Landor, Coleridge, Wordsworth, Carlyle, set him speculating on new themes, stimulating afresh the love of Plato, in whom he had long found inspiration. Continental idealism with its transcendental metaphysics refashioned Emerson and put him upon his life-work.

Speaking of the intellectual revival of New England later in life, he remarked that "Goethe was the cow from whom their milk was drawn"; but it would seem that the influence of Wordsworth proved more immediately stimulating, for on his return home Emerson set about the systematic contemplation of nature which left so considerable a deposit in his mind. Before this he had been too intent on his soul to consider the sunshine on the fields, but thereafter he made his pilgrimages into the country with the seriousness of one conducting a novel experiment. In this new concern for nature there was a deliberate self-consciousness. In temperament he was a bookish recluse, in love with the printed page. He was not a Thoreau to love his Walden Pond for its own sake, and it needed an effort of the will to send him as far as Auburn wood, to lie on his back and translate nature into metaphysic. But he had come to the point where his developing philosophy must send him into the fields. He had looked within himself and discovered the divinity of the individual soul; but he had not probed the non-self, the great encompassing universe of matter by which the individual is circumscribed and of which he is a part. To discover there the diffused presence of God, to feel his kinship with man, to understand that the soul is a microcosm, were necessary preliminaries to the unfolding of his transcendental philosophy, and he went about the work with painstaking thoroughness. From this creative contact with nature emerged the Emerson we know, radiant with idealism, glad of life; and this radiant gladness he put into his maiden essay, *Nature*.

This was in 1836 when Emerson was thirty-three years of age. In the next two years he published *The American Scholar*, quintessence of transcendental individualism, and the *Divinity School Address*, the bible of transcendental religion. With the appearance of the second series of *Essays*, six years later, the major ideas of his philosophy were fully elaborated. Stripped of its idealistic phraseology, of its beauty and fervor, the master idea of the Emersonian philosophy is the divine sufficiency of the individual. In accepting himself he accepted his fellows, and he accepted God. The universe he conceived of as a divine whole, whereof each man is his own center from whom flows the life that has flowed in upon him, perennially fresh, perennially a new creation. The law for things is not the law for mind; man is unkinged in acknowledging any lesser sovereignty than the sovereignty of self. Statutes, constitutions, governments, schools, churches, banks, trade—the coercing sum of institutions and customs—these things do not signify; they are only idols with clay feet that blind men worship. The true divinity dwells elsewhere, in the soul of man; and that divinity must rule the world and not be ruled by it. The apotheosis of individualism—such in briefest terms was the gospel of Emerson; new only in its radiant dress and idealistic sanctions, the final transcendental form of a doctrine spread widely by the French romantic school. It was the same revolutionary conception that Channing had come upon, that Jefferson had come upon, that Rousseau had come upon—the idea which in the guise of political romanticism had disintegrated the *ancien régime*, and in the form of philosophical romanticism had disintegrated eighteenth-century rationalism—the idea that was providing Utopian dreams for an ebullient democratic faith.

Thus equipped with a philosophy Emerson was prepared to begin his work as a critic. The ideal he had drunk of was a perennial condemnation of the material. The mean and ignoble ends

pursued by a mean and ignoble society were a challenge to the
serenity of his faith, and he must set himself to analyze the causes
of the low estate to which the potential sons of God had fallen.
Lesser revolutions in thought were implicit in this greater one,
revolutions which Emerson was bound to go through with. Despite
the jaunty optimism of which he was often accused, his eyes were
never blind to reality; to see, and measure, and judge, was to become his life business. He did not shrink from the ugliest fact, and
the unhappy condition he discovered men to be in would have
discouraged a less robust faith. At times even he doubted. At
times he seems half persuaded, with Cotton Mather, that the
potential children of light are "strangely and fiercely possessed
of the devil." "Human nature is as bad as it dares to be," he
commented in his journal; and at another time, "If it were possible to repair the rottenness of human nature . . . it were well"
(*Journals*, Vol. VIII, p. 259).

In seeking an explanation of the tragic gap between the real and
the ideal, he came to attribute a large measure of the cause, like
the eighteenth-century romantics, to pernicious social institutions
which stifle the nobler impulses and encourage the baser; and he
became convinced likewise that the work to which the critic was
called was the work of liberation, setting the mind free from false
and ignoble loyalties that it might serve the true. He prepared
therefore to lay his transcendental yardstick on the little world
of Yankee reality and judge how far short it came of its potential
divinity. New England had never been scrutinized so searchingly,
measured so justly. Serene, imperturbable, he set the ideal in one
pan of the scales, and all the New England realities in the other,
and bade his neighbors see how the balance tipped. For a generation he was the conscience of America, a pricker of inflated balloons,
a gauger of the national brag and cant and humbug. With keen
insight he put his finger on the mean and selfish and the great and
generous. He surveyed his world with the detachment of posterity
and anticipated the slower judgment of time. His penetration
was uncanny and few of his judgments on men and measures have
suffered reversal in the court of final jurisdiction.

So shrewd a critic must concern himself greatly with the Jacksonian revolution that was hurrying America towards the acceptance of political equalitarianism. By every compulsion of
his transcendental philosophy Emerson was driven to accept the

abstract principle of democracy. He understood well what hopes for human betterment were awakened by the principle of majority rule, and as he followed the noise and tumult of the political campaigns he was driven to definition. In 1834 he commented in his journal:

> The root and seed of democracy is the doctrine, Judge for yourself. Reverence thyself. It is the inevitable effect of the doctrine, where it has any effect (which is rare), to insulate the partisan, to make each man a state. At the same time it replaces the dead with a living check in a true, delicate reverence for superior, congenial minds. "How is the King greater than I, if he is not more just?" (*Journals*, Vol. III, p. 369.)

Somewhat later in the same year he suggested:

> Democracy, Freedom, has its root in the sacred truth that every man hath in him the divine Reason, or that, though few men since the creation of the world live according to the dictates of Reason, yet all men are created capable of so doing. That is the equality and the only equality of all men. To this truth we look when we say, Reverence thyself; Be true to thyself. (*Ibid.*, Vol. III, p. 390.)

> When I . . . speak of the democratic element, I do not mean that ill thing, vain and loud, which writes lying newspapers, spouts at caucuses, and sells its lies for gold; but that spirit of love for the general good whose name this assumes. There is nothing of the true democratic element in what is called Democracy; it must fall, being wholly commercial. I beg I may not be understood to praise anything which the soul in you does not honor, however grateful may be names to your ear and your pocket. (*Ibid.*, Vol. IV, p. 95.)

His deepening concern over the state of politics in America— the property-mindedness of the Whigs and the mob-mindedness of the Democrats—drew him into an analysis of political parties and the nature of the political state. He was little read in the political classics, and although he professed a mild approval of Montesquieu and was never tired of praising Burke, he was little influenced by either. The latter's political theory, indeed, was so fundamentally hostile to Emerson's major convictions—so legalistic in its reverence for government from the grave, so explicit in denial of new-born rights—that it is a fair assumption that Emerson never took the trouble to understand him but was content to enjoy his glowing rhetoric. Later commentators are too much given to glossing over Emerson's political theory, not approving its implications; or explaining it away by appeal to certain comments jotted down when his nerves were tried by enthusiasts; [1] but there is no explaining away a theory that was the logical expression of his transcendental philosophy, unless his whole philosophy be explained away. Emerson knew very well where his political theory led, and he had no timid compunction about following it through.

In his speculations on the nature and functions of the ideal republic—a theme that was much in his mind—he elaborated what we may call the transcendental theory of politics, a theory closely akin to philosophical anarchism. All the elaborate machinery devised by political thinkers like Montesquieu and John Adams, with their schemes of checks and balances to preserve the *status quo*, he calmly throws overboard; constitutions he is not interested in, nor the complicated props of coercive sovereignty. The single, vital, principle on which the true republic must found itself, he insists, is the principle of good-will. Since "governments have their origin in the moral identity of men," the recognition of a common human nature with common interests must induce rational men to enter a common political brotherhood; and until men become wise enough voluntarily to coöperate to the common well-being, no good government is possible. The history of governments hitherto is a history of the tragic failure of men to achieve a rational political state. "The idea, after which each community is aiming to make and mend its law," he suggests in the *Essay on Politics*, following Carlyle, "is the will of the wise man. The wise man, it cannot find in nature, and it makes awkward but earnest efforts to secure government by contrivance." But he does not push his "wise man" theory to the patriarchal absolutism of Carlyle; with Channing he postulates an ethical sovereignty above the instrument. "Absolute right is the first governor; or, every government is an impure theocracy."

The doctrine of good-will establishes government in "moral identity"; it "separates the individual from all party, and unites him at the same time to the race"; and in so doing it accepts the sovereignty of the ethical absolute. This major conception of Channing's Emerson took over and made his own. He is explicit in his assertion of the need of a moral interpretation of the doctrine of natural rights. The doctrine of an ethical sovereignty, he asserts,

[1] See, for example, *Journals*, Vol. VII, p. 221.

. . . promises a recognition of higher rights than those of personal freedom, or the security of property. A man has a right to be employed, to
be trusted, to be loved, to be revered. The power of love, as the basis of
a State, has never been tried. . . . There will always be a government of
force where men are selfish; and when they are pure enough to abjure the
code of force they will be wise enough to see how these public ends of the
post-office, of the highway, of commerce and the exchange of property,
of museums and libraries, of institutions of art and science can be answered.

Every man's nature is a sufficient advertisement to him of the character
of his fellows. My right and my wrong is their right and their wrong.
Whilst I do what is fit for men, and abstain from what is unfit, my neighbor
and I shall often agree in our means, and work together for a time to one
end. But whenever I find my dominion over myself not sufficient for me,
and undertake the direction of him also, I overstep the truth, and come
into false relations to him. I may have so much more skill or strength than
he that he cannot express adequately his sense of wrong, but it is a lie, and
hurts like a lie both him and me. Love and nature cannot maintain the
assumption; it must be executed by a practical lie, namely by force. This
undertaking for another is the blunder which stands in colossal ugliness
in the governments of the world. . . . For any laws but those which men
make for themselves are laughable. . . . This is the history of government,—one man does something which is to bind another. . . . Hence
the less government we have the better,—the fewer laws, and the less
confided power. The antidote to this abuse of formal government is the
influence of private character, the growth of the individual . . . the
appearance of the wise man; of whom the existing government, is, it must
be owned, but a shabby imitation. . . . To educate the wise man the
State exists, and with the appearance of the wise man the State expires.
The appearance of character makes the State unnecessary. The wise
man is the State. (*Essay on Politics.*)

Thus in transcendental fashion does Emerson range himself on
the side of Jefferson, in opposition to a coercive sovereignty. A
strong and energetic government he feared as an efficient instrument of tyranny; and of the several contrivancies by which it
enforced its will, he considered the police power the stupidest.
As a sensible man he bore with the state; he would pay his taxes;
he would not strain at gnats; but as a free man he would not suffer
the state to coerce him; he would destroy it first. There is a passage
in his journal, written at the time of the declaration of war against
Mexico—when Alcott and Thoreau refused to pay their taxes—
that states his position with whimsical directness:

The State is a poor, good beast who means the best: it means friendly.
A poor cow who does well by you,—do not grudge it its hay. It cannot

eat bread, as you can; let it have without grudge a little grass for its four stomachs. It will not stint to yield you milk from its teat. You, who are a man walking cleanly on two feet, will not pick a quarrel with a poor cow. Take this handful of clover and welcome. But if you go to hook me when I walk in the fields, then, poor cow, I will cut your throat. (*Journals*, Vol. VII, p. 220.)

With equal emphasis he rejected the economic interpretation of politics. As a child of the romantic revolution he understood quite clearly how the waves of humanitarian aspiration broke on the reefs of property rights, how economic forces were in league against the ideal republic. There could be no true democracy till this matter of economics was put in subordination to higher values. Both the political parties, the respectable Whigs and the voluble Democrats, he was convinced, were debauched by it; the one served property openly, the other secretly. "From neither party, when in power, has the world any benefit to expect in science, art, or humanity, at all commensurate with the resources of the nation." Emerson did not deny the fact of the universal appeal of economics. He could not, of course, accept the theory of economic determinism; but he was convinced that the whole matter must be probed deeply:

The philosophy of property, if explored in its foundations, would open new mines of practical wisdom, which would in the event change the face of the world; would destroy the whole magazine of dissimulation, for so many ages reckoned the Capital art of Government. It would purge that rottenness which has defamed the whole Science until *politic* has come to mean cunning. . . . It would go deep into ethics and touch all the relations of men. (*The Present Age.*)

Pending such exploration it was clear to Emerson that the Federalist-Whig theory of a stake-in-society, or rulership by persons of principle and property, was wholly vicious:

The theory of politics which has possessed the minds of men, and which they have expressed the best they could in their laws and in their revolutions, considers persons and property as the two objects for whose protection government exists. Of persons, all have equal rights, in virtue of being identical in nature. This interest of course with its whole power demands a democracy. Whilst the rights of all as persons are equal, in virtue of their access to reason, their rights in property are very unequal. . . . Personal rights, universally the same, demand a government framed on the ratio of the census; property demands a government framed on the ratio of owners and owning. . . . That principle no longer looks so self-

evident as it appeared in former times, partly because doubts have
arisen whether too much weight had not been allowed in laws to property,
and such a structure given to our usages as allowed the rich to encroach
upon the poor, and keep them poor; but mainly because there is an instinctive sense, however obscure and yet inarticulate, that the whole
constitution of property, on its present tenures, is injurious, and its influence on persons deteriorating and degrading; that property will always
follow persons; that the highest end of government is the culture of men.
(*Essay on Politics.*)

In such suggestions as he offered touching the form of the ideal
republic, where "every child that is born must have a just chance
for his bread," Emerson reveals a pronounced bias in favor of the
Physiocratic theory of society. He was at one with Jefferson in
preferring an agrarian to an industrial order. Manchester economics—the doctrine of the economic man, of the iron law of wages,
and other obscenities of the school—he quite frankly loathed. He
did not, he said, "look with sour aspect at the industrious manufacturing village, or mart of commerce"; but he would not glorify
the machine, nor reduce man to a factory hand. He questioned
the sufficiency or finality of the division of labor. There is more than
a suggestion of William Morris in the doctrine elaborated in *Man
the Reformer;* that the industrial revolution with its factory system,
must be judged in the light of its effect upon the workingman,
that the true function of work must be explored and every man
ply his tool to his own good. The suggestion that "a man should
have a farm or mechanical craft for his culture," was an implicit
denial of industrialism in the days of its first triumphs—a denial
that Morris would have indorsed.

We must have a basis for our higher accomplishments, our delicate
entertainments of poetry and philosophy, in the work of our hands. We
must have an antagonism in the tough world for all the variety of our
spiritual faculties, or they will not be born. Manual labor is the study of
the external world. The advantages of riches remains with him who
produces them, not with the heir.

I should not be pained at a change which threatened a loss of some of
the luxuries or conveniences of society, if it proceeded from a preference
of the agricultural life out of the belief, that our primary duties as men
could be better discharged in that calling. . . . But the doctrine of the
Farm is merely this, that every man ought to stand in primary relations
with the work of the world, ought to do it himself, and not to suffer the
accident of his having a purse in his pocket, or his having been bred to
some dishonorable and injurious craft, to sever him from those duties;
and for this reason, that labor is God's education: that he only is a sincere

learner, he only can become a master, who learns the secret of labor, and who by real cunning extorts from nature its sceptre. (*Man the Reformer.*)

In all this—in the doctrine of the minimized state, of the sacred rights of the individual, of the wholesomeness of an agricultural life; in his concern for social justice and his tenderness for the poor and exploited among men—Emerson proved himself a child of the romantic eighteenth century, who by his own transcendental path had come upon the Utopia that an earlier generation had dreamed of, and which he sketched in the lovely poem prefacing the *Essay on Politics.* Much of Emerson is compressed in these lines:

> Fear, Craft, and Avarice,
> Cannot rear a State.
> Out of dust to build
> What is more than dust. . . .
> When the Muses nine
> With the Virtues meet,
> Find to their design
> An Atlantic seat,
> By green orchard boughs
> Fended from the heat,
> Where the statesman ploughs
> Furrow for the wheat;
> When the Church is social worth,
> When the state-house is the hearth,
> Then the perfect State is come,
> The republican at home.

The contrast between such Utopian conceptions and the realities of America in the forties was calculated to edge the critical judgment with a certain asperity. The older agrarian simplicity of New England was being submerged by the industrial revolution, and in the midst of the change Emerson quietly pronounced judgment upon the new idols of his generation, upon State Street and Beacon Street, upon Webster and Clay and Douglas, upon Everett and Choate, upon black slavery and white, upon the Mexican War and the Fugitive Slave Bill, upon the stolid poor and the callous rich. His judgment was severe but it was never unjust. His later journals are a rich storehouse of critical comment, keen, illuminating, disastrous in its analysis of all cant and humbug. At times—in his comment on Webster, in his hatred of State Street, in his criticism of the common materialism—he is almost savage; at other times he is consumed with a vast sympathy for the long-suffering, exploited mass of the people. "Alas, for the majority," he exclaimed, "that old, inevitable dupe and victim. What a dreary Iliad of woes it goes wailing and mad withal. Some dog of a Cleon or Robespierre or Douglas is always riding it to ruin" (*Journals*, Vol. VIII, p. 449). When the Fugitive Slave Bill passed he wrote: "This filthy enactment was made in the nineteenth century, by people who could read and write. I will not obey it, by God" (*ibid.*, Vol. VIII, p. 236). In smug and prosperous Boston he found no comfort—the Boston that applauded when "Thank-God Choate thanked God five times" in denouncing "the trashy sentimentalism of our lutestring enthusiasts." Emerson would have none of Boston:

> In Boston is no company for a fine wit. There is a certain *poor-smell* in all the streets, in Beacon Street and Mount Vernon, as well as in the lawyers' offices, and the wharves, and the same meanness and sterility, and leave-all-hope-behind, as one finds in a boot manufacturer's premises. (*Ibid.*, Vol. VIII, p. 363.)

With Theodore Parker he judged Boston to be the home of Hunkers, of that "cotton aristocracy" that Webster served. It groveled servilely before State Street; how should the homely moralities get a hearing in such a place? Even Harvard College he charged with being a tool of the Boston counting-houses.[2]

It was the crass materialism of America, of the Democrats equally with the Whigs, of the northern capitalists equally with the southern planters, that drove him to exasperation, and tempered his optimism. There is no jaunty optimism in a passage written during the panic days of '37:

> . . . Society has played out its last stake; it is checkmated. Young men have no hope. Adults stand like day-laborers idle in the streets. None calleth us to labor. The old wear no crown of warm life on their gray hairs. The present generation is bankrupt of principles and hope, as of property. I see man is not what man should be. He is a treadle of a wheel. He is the tassel at the apron-string of society. He is a money-chest. He is the servant of his belly. This is the causal bankruptcy, this the cruel oppression, that the ideal should serve the actual, that the head

---

[2] "Harvard College has no voice in Harvard College, but State Street votes it down on every ballot. Everything will be permitted there which goes to adorn Boston whiggism; . . . but that which it exists for,—to be a fountain of novelties out of heaven, a Delphi uttering warning and ravishing oracles to elevate and lead mankind,—*that* it shall not be permitted to do or to think of. On the contrary, every generosity of thought is *suspected*, and gets a bad name." (*Ibid.*, Vol. IX, p. 215.)

should serve the feet. . . . Pride, and Thrift, and Expediency, who jeered and chirped and were so well pleased with themselves, and made merry with the dream, as they termed it, of Philosophy and Love,— behold they are all flat, and here is the Soul erect and unconquered still. What answer is it now to say, It has always been so? I acknowledge that, as far back as I can see the widening procession of humanity, the marchers are lame and blind and deaf; but to the soul that whole past is but one finite series in its infinite scope. Deteriorating ever and now desperate. Let me begin anew; let me teach the finite to know its master. (*Journals*, Vol. IV, p. 242.)

To be a critic rather than a fighter, and a critic because he was a poet and philosopher—this was the duty laid upon Emerson; and yet he was sorely troubled when men from the skirmish line of social conflict reported to him the need of leaders. Why should he be privileged to remain in his study when slaves were abducted on the streets of Boston and John Brown was fighting at Harper's Ferry? With the extremest reluctance he was drawn into the struggle—it was not his fight.

I waked at night [he recorded in his journal] and bemoaned myself, because I had not thrown myself into this deplorable question of Slavery, which seems to want nothing so much as a few assured voices. But then, in hours of sanity, I recover myself, and say, "God must govern his own world, and knows his own way out of this pit, without my desertion of my post, which has none to guard it but me. I have quite other slaves to free than those negroes, to wit, imprisoned spirits, imprisoned thoughts, far back in the brain of man,—far retired in the heaven of invention, and which, important to the republic of Man, have no other watchman, or lover, or defender, but I." (*Ibid.*, Vol. VIII, p. 316.)

But always in the end he was drawn in, and none spoke wiser or braver words to a careless generation. He never faltered, never compromised; the prophet of the ideal faced the real and told the truth about it, serenely and with clear insight. His heroes were not the heroes of State Street; Horace Greeley, Theodore Parker, Horace Mann, Henry Ward Beecher, he accounted the great Americans of his day, and not Everett and Webster and Clay and Calhoun. A friend of civilization, he was partisan only to the ideal; to justice, truth, righteousness. A Yankee of the Yankees, a Puritan of the Puritans, he had emancipated himself from all that was mean and ungenerous in the one and harsh and illiberal in the other. A free soul, he was the flowering of two centuries of spiritual aspiration—Roger Williams and Jonathan Edwards come to more perfect fruition.

CHAPTER III

HENRY THOREAU
Transcendental Economist

"Wisdom crieth in the streets and no man regardeth her"; yet "she teacheth temperance and forethought, justice and fortitude; than which men can have in their life nothing more profitable."

The single business of Henry Thoreau, during forty-odd years of eager activity, was to discover an economy calculated to provide a satisfying life. His one concern, that gave to his ramblings in Concord fields a value as of high adventure, was to explore the true meaning of wealth. Honest, fearless, curiously inquisitive—a masterless man who would give no hostages to fortune—he proved his right to be called a philosopher by seeking wisdom as a daily counselor and friend, and following such paths only as wisdom suggested. Out of his own experience, tested in the clear light of the Greeks, he wrote a transcendental declaration of independence that may be taken as the final word of the Concord school touching the great issues of practical living. *Walden* is the handbook of an economy that endeavors to refute Adam Smith and transform the round of daily life into something nobler than a mean gospel of plus and minus.

It was the common opinion of his neighbors that Henry Thoreau was a queer fellow who had somehow got all his values topsy-turvy. And yet the more thoughtfully one considers him, the more doubtful it appears whether the queerness lay with him or with his critics. Unfortunately a wholly honest and original man is so rare as to fall under common suspicion. To the inmates of Bedlam a sane man will appear queer. In a society of serfs a masterless man will be accounted an outlaw. To the Concord farmers Thoreau appeared strange only because he applied in his daily life a truth they assented to on the Sabbath. The principle that life is more than the meat and the body than raiment was familiar enough to the Sunday doctrines of Concord; but that a man should seriously apply it on week-days; that he should propose to regulate his mid-week activities by the economy of the Sermon on the

Mount, passed the comprehension of practical Yankees who followed quite another economy. It was Thoreau's conduct that perplexed them, rather than his philosophy.

From first to last that conduct was serenely logical. To this disciple of the ancient wisdom, Sabbath and week-day were one, and in seeking to square his daily life with the ancient precept, Thoreau became the arch-rebel of his group, the most individual amongst the "lunatic fringe" of the transcendental movement, the one who escapes elusively from the grip of an adjective. He slips out of all phrases devised to imprison him. "A bachelor of nature," Emerson, with his gift for cryptic phrase, called him; "poet-naturalist," Ellery Channing who knew him intimately, chose to call him. "I am a poet, a mystic, and a transcendentalist," Thoreau said of himself, disregarding his nature writings. Yet none of these phrases, true as they are, quite adequately sums him up. At the risk of committing a fresh futility, one may perhaps suggest that he was a Greek turned transcendental economist. His life seems to have been a persistent experiment in values. A philosopher of the open air who kept his mind clear and his nerves robust by daily contact with wind and weather; a mystic who pried curiously into the meaning of nature and was familiar with Hellenic and Oriental systems of thought; a Yankee, skilled in various homely crafts, yet rather interested in proving for himself what things were excellent and taking nothing on hearsay—Thoreau's chief business would seem to have been with life itself, and how it might best be lived by Henry Thoreau; how a rational being, in short, might enjoy the faculties God has given him, following the higher economy and not enslaving himself to the lower, so that when he came to die he might honestly say, I have lived.

Amongst the members of the transcendental school Thoreau was the one Concord man, born and bred there, literally of the soil and loving the things of the soil. His tireless rovings were commonly bounded by the familiar Concord horizons. His life had taken deep root in the Concord fields, and he refused to join the restless multitude of the *déracinés*, who seek novel experiences in a succession of transplantings. No English peasant ever clung to the home-acres with more loving tenacity. He was a countryman in instinct, distrusting the great city twenty miles away that disseminated its virus through the outlying villages and farms. The city was wedded to the economy of industrialism and exploitation. But as a child of Jean Jacques, Thoreau chose to believe that the road to heaven ran through the fields and not over the cobble-stones of Boston; he discovered an honest integrity of character oftener in the country than in Lowell mills, yet none too often there. It was easier to be free there, yet even in Concord village the herd mind was always laying springes to catch the unwary; and Thoreau would not be caught. He was poet and philosopher as well as countryman, and he weighed his own life and the life of his neighbors in the scales of Hellenic thought. He was surveyor of broader fields than his neighbor's wood-lot; was acquainted with other mysteries than the mystery of pencil-making. He desired other ends than those his shopkeeping, farm-tending neighbors served; he would not be encumbered as they were. He could not carry such gross impedimenta in his pack and be a free man; the pack was too heavy; and he proceeded to lighten it with a thoroughness that startled Concord. He "signed off" from Dr. Ripley's church; with Alcott, he refused to pay his poll tax: he severed his allegiance to the Commonwealth of Massachusetts and the Federal government; he rid himself of all concern at what Concord thought of his ways; he spoke out his honest convictions in the village Lyceum—convictions about John Brown and slavery and Massachusetts' part in sending negroes back to their masters— quite careless of the disapproval of Judge Hoar and other Concord dignitaries. Such a man had never before walked the village streets, and the spectacle filled his neighbors with amazement.

With so much useless luggage got rid of, Thoreau was ready to set about the high business of living. To outward appearance a somewhat angular Yankee, practical and capable, he was at heart a Greek, with the delight in the simple round of the seasons and a responsiveness to natural beauty that belonged to the older civi-lization. Brought up under the "pale negations" of Dr. Ripley's theology, he emerged a pagan. He was the most widely read in Greek literature of the Concord transcendentalists; had translated *Prometheus Bound*, and much of Pindar; and was completely at home in the clear Greek atmosphere. Who but a Hellenist could utter such words as these which serve as his apology for the Walden experiment?

I went to the woods because I wished to live deliberately, to front only the essential facts of life, and to see if I could learn what it had to teach, and not, when I came to die, discover that I had not lived. I did not wish to live what was not life, living is so dear; nor did I wish to practice resignation, unless it was quite necessary. I wanted to live deep and suck out all the marrow of life, to live so sturdily and Spartan-like as to put to rout all that was not life, to cut a broad swath and shave close, to drive life into a corner, and reduce it to its lowest terms, and, if it proved to be mean, why then to get the whole and genuine meanness of it, and publish its meanness to the world; or if it were sublime, to know it by experience, and be able to give a true account of it in my next excursion. (*Walden,* "What I Lived For.")

To seek Pan in a tired world and recover joys that have long been forgotten is a business that only a romantic will engage in; yet Thoreau set out on the quest with a clear-eyed purpose:

. . . My Good Genius seemed to say,—Go fish and hunt far and wide day by day,—farther and wider,—and rest thee by many brooks and hearth-sides without misgiving. Remember thy Creator in the days of thy youth. Rise free from care before the dawn, and seek adventures. Let the noon find thee by other lakes, and the night over-take thee everywhere at home. There are no larger fields than these, no worthier games than may here be played. Grow wild according to thy nature, like those sedges and brakes, which will never become English hay. Let the thunder rumble; what if it threaten ruin to farmer's crops? that is not its errand to thee. Take shelter under the cloud, while they flee to carts and sheds. Let not to get a living by thy trade, but thy sport. Enjoy the land, but own it not. Through want of enterprise and faith men are where they are, buying and selling, and spending their lives like serfs. (*Ibid.,* "Baker Farm.")

If the day and the night are such that you greet them with joy, and life emits a fragrance like flowers and sweet-scented herbs, is more elastic, more starry, more immortal,—that is your success. All nature is your congratulation, and you have cause momentarily to bless yourself. . . . The true harvest of my daily life is somewhat as intangible and indiscernible as the tints of morning or evening. It is a little star-dust caught, a segment of the rainbow which I have clutched. (*Ibid.,* "Higher Laws.")

To save one's soul has always been accounted in New England a matter worthy of a man's best effort, and Thoreau's days were given over to it with a single-heartedness without parallel even in New England. The Puritan, he believed, had suffered his high spiritual mission to be sacrificed to the economic; he would recover that mission by sacrificing the economic to the spiritual; but he would interpret the spiritual as a Hellenist rather than a Hebraist. The Christian other-worldliness seemed to him unduly regardless of the loveliness of this world. "Christianity," he says in the *Week*, "only hopes. It has hung its harp on the willows, and cannot sing a song in a strange land. It has dreamed a sad dream, and does not yet welcome the morning with joy."

I am not sure but I should betake myself in extremities to the liberal divinities of Greece, rather than to my country's God. . . . In my Pantheon, Pan still reigns in his pristine glory, with his ruddy face, his flowing beard, and his shaggy body, his pipe and his crook, his nymph Echo, and his chosen daughter Iambe; for the great God Pan is not dead, as was rumored. Perhaps of all the gods of New England and of ancient Greece, I am most constant at his shrine. (*The Week*, "Sunday.")

His extraordinarily frank evaluation of the New Testament, and of Calvinistic New England that had too long chewed the cud of conscience—"they did not know when to swallow their cud, and their lives of course yielded no milk"—is the work of a pagan from whom all creeds slip easily. Few more searching sermons have been preached in Massachusetts than the sermon that composed itself as Thoreau's boat floated down the Concord River, past the Billerica meeting-house where the honest villagers were worshiping the God of New England—a sermon that with fine irony summons minister and congregation to consider the deeper teachings of their sacred book.

I know of no book that has so few readers. There is none so truly strange, and heretical, and unpopular. To Christians, no less than Greeks and Jews, it is foolishness and a stumbling-block. There are, indeed, severe things in it which no man should read aloud but once. " Seek first the kingdom of heaven."—" Lay not up for yourself treasures on earth."— "If thou wilt be perfect, go and sell that thou hast, and give to the poor, and thou shalt have treasure in heaven."—"For what is a man profited, if he shall gain the whole world, and lose his own soul? or what shall a man give in exchange for his soul?"—Think of this, Yankees! . . . . Think of repeating these things to a New England audience! thirdly, fourthly, fifteenthly, till there are three barrels of sermons! Who, without cant, can read them aloud? Who, without cant, can hear them, and not go out of the meeting-house? They never *were* read, they never *were* heard. Let but one of these sentences be rightly read from any pulpit in the land, and there would not be left one stone of that meeting-house upon another.
. . . When one enters a village, the church, not only really but from association, is the ugliest-looking building in it, because it is the one in which human nature stoops the lowest and is most disgraced. Certainly, such temples as these shall ere long cease to deform the landscape. . . . Really, there is no infidelity, now-a-days, so great as that which prays, and keeps the Sabbath, and rebuilds the churches. (*The Week*, "Sunday.")

As Thoreau understood the problem of economics there were three possible solutions open to him: to exploit himself, to exploit his fellows, or to reduce the problem to its lowest denominator. The first was quite impossible—to imprison oneself in a treadmill when the morning called to great adventure, to burden oneself with useless fardels when the pack must be kept light, was the folly of a slave mind. He had observed his neighbors closely and found little good in their way of self-exploitation.

> I have travelled a good deal in Concord; and everywhere, in shops, and offices, and field, the inhabitants have appeared to me to be doing penance in a thousand remarkable ways. . . . How many a poor immortal soul have I met well-nigh crushed and smothered under its load, creeping down the road of life, pushing before it a barn seventy-five feet by forty, its Augean stables never cleansed, and one hundred acres of land, tillage, mowing, pasture and wood-lot. . . . The better part of the man is soon ploughed into the soil for compost. (*Walden*, "Economy.")

To exploit one's fellows seemed to Thoreau's sensitive social conscience an even grosser infidelity. The leisure of a slave driver, got by imprisoning his fellows in a treadmill, was an ignoble leisure from which came the empty vulgarity of modern life. "If I devote myself to other pursuits and contemplations," he said, "I must first see, at least, that I do not pursue them sitting upon another man's shoulders. I must get off him first, that he may pursue his contemplations, too." Freedom with abstinence seemed to him better than serfdom with material well-being, for he was only giving up the lesser to enjoy the greater, as was the privilege of the philosopher.

> To be a philosopher is not merely to have subtle thoughts, nor even to found a school, but so to love wisdom as to live according to its dictates, a life of simplicity, independence, magnanimity, and trust. It is to solve some of the problems of life, not only theoretically, but practically. . . . When he has obtained those things which are necessary to life, there is another alternative than to obtain the superfluities; and that is, to adventure on life now, his vacation from humbler toil having commenced. (*Walden*, "Economy.")

It was the reply of the arch-individualist to the tyrannous complexities of society, and it set him apart even in the world of transcendentalism. Other members of the group professed to have found a better way out of the dilemma—the way of Brook Farm and

Fruitland; a richer life was to be achieved not by espousing poverty but by coöperation. But Thoreau could not adopt the coöperative solution; he must either accept society as it was or remove. Convinced that it was not worth accepting—that one made a foolish bargain in selling oneself to it—he was content to remove to Walden Pond. "I came into this world," he said, "not chiefly to make this a good place to live in, but to live in it, be it good or bad." "I desire to speak impartially on this point, and as one not interested in the success or failure of the present economical and social arrangement." He did not advocate that other men should build cabins and live isolated. He had no wish to dogmatize concerning the best mode of living—each must settle that matter for himself. But that a satisfying life should be lived, that the fox should somehow get free even though he left his tail in the trap, he was vitally concerned about. "The youth may build or plant or sail, only let him not be hindered from doing that which he tells me he would like to do." Let him at least rid himself of the false gospel of creature comforts, which men pay too high a price for.

The story of Thoreau's emancipation from the lower economics is the one romance of his life, and *Walden* is his great book. More restrained than the *Week* and lacking the exuberant beauty of the latter—its noble talk and scathing criticism—it is "informed by a more explicit unifying philosophy." It is a book in praise of life rather than of Nature, a record of calculating economies that studied saving in order to spend more largely. But it is a book of social criticism as well, in spite of its explicit denial of such a purpose, and in its speculations much of Carlyle and Ruskin and William Morris crops out. In considering the true nature of economy he concluded, with Ruskin, that "the cost of a thing is the amount of what I will call life which is required to be exchanged for it, immediately or in the long run." Conceive of life as cheap, a poor thing to be exploited, and the factory system becomes the logical economic order; but conceive of it as dear, and the common happiness the great objective of society, and quite another sort of industrialism will emerge. Thoreau did not look with approval on the rising city of Lowell, with its multiplying spindles and increasing proletariat, and he did not understand why Americans should boast of a system that provided vulgar leisure for the masters at the cost of serfdom for the workers.

Where is this division of labor to end? [he asks] and what object does it finally serve? I cannot believe that our factory system is the best mode by which men may get clothing. The condition of the operatives is becoming every day more like that of the English; and it cannot be wondered at, since, as far as I have heard or observed, the principal object is, not that mankind may be well and honestly clad, but, unquestionably, that the corporations may be enriched. (*Walden*, "Economy.")

The whole middle-class philosophy of exploitation was hateful to him, the middleman equally with the manufacturer. "Trade curses everything it touches; and though you trade in messages from heaven, the whole curse of trade attaches to the business." Men have been deceived by a false economy—lured by the bog lights away from the open fields to flounder in the miasmic marshes. While Ruskin was still pottering over Turner, Thoreau was elaborating in *Walden* the text: The only wealth is life.

In other bits *Walden* is curiously like *Hopes and Fears for Art*, and the drift of the whole is one with the revolutionary teachings of Morris, that the abiding satisfactions are those which spring from free creative work. This Yankee Greek had learned that it is a beautiful life back of the tool that creates beauty, and that if the work of our hands is ugly, it is because our lives are mean and sordid, affording no outlet for the free creative spirit. In New England, Puritan and Yankee alike had conspired against beauty, and the gods had taken revenge by clothing life in drab.

Before we can adorn our houses with beautiful objects the walls must be stripped, and beautiful housekeeping and beautiful living be laid for a foundation: now, a taste for the beautiful is most cultivated out of doors, where there is no house and no housekeeping.

What of architectural beauty I now see, I know has gradually grown from within outward, out of the necessities and character of the indweller, who is the only builder,—out of some unconscious truthfulness, and nobleness, without ever a thought for the appearance; and whatever additional beauty of this kind is destined to be produced will be preceded by a like unconscious beauty of life. The most interesting dwellings in this country, as the painter knows, are the most unpretending, humble log huts and cottages of the poor commonly; it is the life of the inhabitants whose shells they are, and not any peculiarity in their surfaces merely, which makes them *picturesque;* and equally interesting will be the citizen's suburban box, when his life shall be as simple and as agreeable to the imagination, and there is no straining after effect in the style of his dwelling. (*Walden*, "Economy.")

Thoreau needed only to have lived in a world that honored craftsmanship to have opened fully the vein of gold that Morris dug his
philosophy from; he had the instinct of the craftsman but not his
training.   His turning from the workshop to the fields, hearing no
call in the humdrum village economy to develop a beautiful
craftsmanship, was an implied criticism of the common sterility
of labor in every-day Concord; yet the honest sincerity of his nature led him to the conclusion that lies at the heart of the philosophy of the great English craftsman:

> None have so pleasant a time as they who in earnest seek to earn their
> bread.   It is true actually as it is true really; it is true materially as it is
> true spiritually, that they who seek honestly and sincerely, with all their
> hearts and lives and strength, to earn their bread, do earn it, and it is
> sure to be very sweet to them.
> In short, I am convinced, both by faith and experience, that to main-
> tain one's self on this earth is not a hardship but a pastime, if we will live
> simply and wisely; as the pursuits of the simpler nations are still the
> sports of the more artificial.   It is not necessary that a man should earn
> his living by the sweat of his brow, unless he sweats easier than I do.
> (*Walden*, "Economy.")

At Walden Pond and on the Merrimac River Thoreau's mind
was serene as the open spaces; but this Greek serenity was rudely
disturbed when he returned to Concord village and found his
neighbors drilling for the Mexican War, and when authority in
the person of the constable came to him with the demand that
he pay a due share to the public funds.   The war to him was a
hateful thing, stupid and unjust, waged for the extension of the
obscene system of negro slavery; and Thoreau was brought sharply
to consider his relations to the political state that presumed to
demand his allegiance, willing or unwilling, to its acts.   Under the
stress of such an emergency the transcendentalist was driven to
examine the whole theory of the relation of the individual to the
state.   He was not political-minded; he had concerned himself
little with political theory; he would gladly let the government
alone if government would let him alone; he was even prepared to
make excuses for government.   But he would not compromise
with his conscience; and when the state applied the principle of
coercion, he applied the counter principle of passive resistance.
It was while he was domiciled in Walden cabin that the hand of
the law seized him and thrust him into Concord jail.   He went
with the constable quietly, but there was a dangerous contempt

in his heart. It seemed absurd that a man could not go to the cobbler's for a pair of mended boots, but he must be interfered with by a neighbor playing the rôle of constable. Constable, jailer, the magistrate on the bench, all the elaborate machinery of the law, Thoreau contemplated quizzically and judged his neighbors fools to have exchanged their freedom for such masquerades. Those who got anything from such instruments—lawyers and propertied men—might think well of them, but they were a mere impertinence to Thoreau who wanted to go huckleberrying. When they let him out he went quietly after his berries, and discovered there was "no state in sight among the berry bushes." "I saw," he remarked casually, "that the state was half-witted, that it was as timid as a lone woman with her silver spoons, and that it did not know its friends from its foes, and I lost all my remaining respect for it and pitied it."

But Thoreau was not done with the comedy. It set him upon thinking, and the result was the essay, *Civil Disobedience*. Taken by itself alone, it is a somewhat astonishing performance. This Yankee transcendentalist quite evidently has turned philosophical anarchist. But read in the light of Emerson's *Journals*, or in the light of Godwin's *Political Justice*, it is easily comprehensible. It is no more than transcendental individualism translated into politics, with all comfortable compromises swept away. Its sources run straight back to eighteenth-century liberalism with its doctrine of the minimized state—a state that must lose its coercive sovereignty in the measure that the laws of society function freely. Very likely Thoreau had never read Godwin, yet his political philosophy was implicit in *Political Justice*. In Godwin's thinking the problem of man in society is the problem of a voluntary adjustment of the individual to the state; and it is only by establishing economics and politics on morality, that political justice is possible. The moral law is the fundamental law, superior to statutes and constitutions; and to it the citizen is bound to render allegiance. "The object of the present state of society is to multiply labor," asserted Godwin; "in another state it will be to simplify it." "The only adequate apology of government is necessity." "Government however reformed" is "little capable of affording solid benefit to mankind." "Give us equality and justice but no constitution. Suffer us to follow without restraint the dictates of our own judgment, and to change our forms of social

order as fast as we improve the dictates of our own judgment."
"The pretense of collective wisdom is the most palpable of all
impostures." "The true reason why the mass of mankind has so
often been the dupe of knaves, has been the mysterious and complicated nature of the social system. Once annihilate the quackery
of government, and the most homespun understanding will be
prepared to scorn the artifices of the state juggler that would
mislead him."

By his own path Thoreau came to identical conclusions. There
is little in *Civil Disobedience* that is not in *Political Justice*. To
neither thinker is there an abstract state, society or nation—only
individuals; and to both, the fundamental law is the law of morality. Political expediency and the law of morality frequently clash,
and in such event it is the duty of the individual citizen to follow
the higher law. Thoreau went even further, and asserted the
doctrine of individual compact, which in turn implied the doctrine
of individual nullification; no government, he said, can have any
"pure right over my person or property but what I concede to it."

I heartily accept the motto,—"That government is best which governs
least"; and I should like to see it acted up to more rapidly and systematically. Carried out, it finally amounts to this, which also I believe,—
"That government is best which governs not at all"; and when men are
prepared for it, that will be the kind of government which they will have.
Government is at best but an expedient; but most governments are usually,
and all governments are sometimes, inexpedient.
A government in which the majority rule in all cases cannot be based
on justice. . . . We should be men first and subjects afterwards. It is
not desirable to cultivate a respect for the law, so much as for the right.
. . . How does it become a man to behave toward this American government today? I answer, that he cannot without disgrace be associated
with it. I cannot for an instant recognize that political organization as
my government which is the *slave's* government also. . . . There is but
little virtue in the action of masses of men. . . . It is not a man's duty,
as a matter of course, to devote himself to the eradication of any, even the
most enormous wrong; he may still properly have other concerns to engage
him; but it is his duty, at least, to wash his hands of it, and, if he gives
it no thought longer, not to give it practically his support. If I devote
myself to other pursuits and contemplations, I must first see, at least,
that I do not pursue them sitting upon another man's shoulders. I must
get off him first, that he may pursue his contemplations too. . . . If
the law is of such a nature that it requires you to be an agent of injustice
to another, then, I say, break the law. Let your life be a counter friction
to stop the machine. . . . As for adopting the ways which the state has
provided for remedying the evil, I know not of such ways. They take

too much time, and a man's life will be gone. . . . Some are petitioning
the State to dissolve the Union. . . . Why do they not dissolve it themselves,—the union between themselves and the state,—and refuse to pay
their quota into its treasury? [1] (*Works*, Vol. X, pp. 131–170.)

"Let your life be a counter friction to stop the machine"—in
this doctrine of individual syndicalism Thoreau's conception of
the relation of the citizen to the state is tersely summed up. In
so far as he was a democrat it was of the transcendental school,
rather than the Jacksonian. He would be governed by the majority
no more than by the minority. The scorn of a fine ethical mind
for practical government by politicians could scarcely be more
tellingly phrased than in the bit of verse he tucks into *Civil Disobedience:*

> A drab of state, a cloth-o'-silver slut,
> To have her train borne up, and her soul trail in the dirt.

Such a man quite evidently would go for Nullification as fiercely
as Garrison. Even though he might wash his hands of society, the
cries of those who suffered injustice followed him, and when the
Fugitive Slave Law passed, it robbed him of his peace, destroying
his pleasure in wonted things. The slave hunters were in Boston
streets, and justice in the person of Commissioner Loring was
sending Anthony Burns back to slavery. As he contemplated the
spectacle his wrath against a coercive government flamed up.
"My thoughts are murder to the state," he complained bitterly,
"and involuntarily go plotting against her."

I would remind my countrymen that they are to be men first, and
Americans only at a late and convenient hour. . . . I hear a good deal
said about trampling this law under foot. Why, one need not go out of
his way to do that. This law rises not to the level of the head or the reason;
its natural habitat is in the dirt. It was born and bred, and has its life,
only in the dust and mire, on a level with the feet; and he who walks with
freedom, and does not with Hindoo mercy avoid treading on every
venomous reptile, will inevitably tread on it, and so trample it under foot,

[1] Compare the following entry in his *Journal* under date of March 26, 1842:
"I must confess I have felt mean enough when asked how I was to act on society,
what errand I had to mankind. Undoubtedly I did not feel mean without a reason,
and yet my loitering is not without defense. I would fain communicate the wealth
of my life to men, would really give them what is most precious in my gift. . . . I
know no riches I would keep back. I have no private good unless it be my peculiar
ability to serve the public. . . . This is the only individual property. . . . It is
hard to be a good citizen of the world in any great sense, but if we do render no
interest or increase to mankind out of that talent God gave us, we can at least
preserve the principal unimpaired."

—and Webster, its maker, like the dirt-bug and its ball. ("Slavery in Massachusetts," in *Works*, Vol. X.)

The law will never make men free; it is men who have got to make the law free. They are the lovers of law and order who observe the law when the government breaks it.

Thoreau was a stern judge, and he held his age in low esteem. His Concord neighbors seemed to him poor fellows with too little spirit to be free men; they were the raw material of standing armies, militia, jailors, constables, and the *posse comitatus*. And then one day into the field of his vision came a plain Yankee, primitive and heroic, John Brown of Ossawatomie. In the contemplation of his life and death Thoreau felt a shock of new faith run like an electric current through his veins. The age was no longer dead to him, for it had bred a man. "I rejoice that I live in this age," he exclaimed, "that I am his contemporary." He had found his hero—not in past times as Carlyle and Emerson had done, but in the present and among his own Yankee kind. He had talked with John Brown in Concord and recognized him as a primitive idealist of rugged mold, a stern moralist who set justice above the law. That this man should be so grossly misunderstood by lesser men, so foully slandered, filled him with sorrow and with wrath also. "When a noble deed is done, who is likely to appreciate it? They who are noble themselves. I was not surprised that certain of my neighbors spoke of John Brown as an ordinary felon, for who are they? They have either much flesh, or much office, or much coarseness of some kind" ("The Last Days of John Brown," in *Works*, Vol. X, p. 241). His trial and conviction Thoreau regarded as a judgment, not on John Brown, but upon America; the lawyers and editors and politicians who judged him were only convicting themselves.

His company was small indeed, because few could be found worthy to pass muster. Each one who there laid down his life for the poor and oppressed was a picked man, culled out of many thousands, if not millions; apparently a man of principle, of rare courage, and devoted humanity; ready to sacrifice his life at any moment for the benefit of his fellow-man. It may be doubted if there were so many more their equals in these respects in all the country,—I speak of his followers only,—for their leader, no doubt, scoured the land far and wide, seeking to swell his troop. These alone were ready to step between the oppressor and the oppressed. Surely they were the very best men you could select to be hung. That was the best compliment this country could pay them. They were ripe for her gallows. She has tried a long time, she has hung a good many, but never found the right one before.

I do not believe in lawyers, in that mode of attacking or defending a man, because you descend to meet the judge on his own ground, and, in cases of the highest importance, it is of no consequence whether a man breaks a human law or not. Let lawyers decide trivial cases. Business men may arrange that among themselves. If they were the interpreters of the everlasting laws which rightfully bind man, that would be another thing. A counterfeiting law-factory, standing half in a slave land and half in a free! What kind of laws for free men can you expect from that? ("A Plea for Captain John Brown," in *Works*, Vol. X, p. 197.)

In Thoreau the eighteenth-century philosophy of individualism, the potent liberalisms let loose on the world by Jean Jacques, came to fullest expression in New England. He was the completest embodiment of the *laissez-faire* reaction against a regimented social order, the severest critic of the lower economics that frustrate the dreams of human freedom. He was fortunate in dying before the age of exploitation had choked his river with its weeds; fortunate in not foreseeing how remote is that future of free men on which his hopes were fixed:

The life in us is like the water in the river. It may rise this year higher than man has ever known it, and flood the parched uplands; even this may be the eventful year, which will drown out all the muskrats . . . such is the character of that morrow which mere lapse of time can never make to dawn. The light which puts out our eyes is darkness to us. There is more day to dawn. The sun is but a morning-star. (*Walden.*)

With the dawning of that day perhaps men will sit once more at the feet of the ancient wisdom and fashion their lives upon the principle that the soul is more than the meat and the body than raiment. Perhaps they may even shape for themselves new heroes—"above and after all, the Man of the Age, come to be called workingman." He and his deeds are looked down upon in our time—"It is obvious that none yet speaks to his condition, for the speaker is not yet in his condition." "Literature speaks how much still to the past, how little to the future; how much to the East, how little to the West" ("Thomas Carlyle and his Works," in *Works*, Vol. X, p. 118). One of the great names in American literature is the name of Henry Thoreau. Yet only after sixty years is he slowly coming into his own.

CHAPTER IV

THEODORE PARKER

Transcendental Minister

THEODORE PARKER was described by one of his biographers as "the best working-plan of an American yet produced," and by a fellow minister as "a conscience since Luther unsurpassed." The two comments suggest still another, that he was completely and adequately New England. Yankee and Puritan contributed equally to his making. His rich and plastic mind was two-sided: one-half was wholly English, practical, logical, concrete, lucid; loving fact and tireless in its acquisition; master of everyday affairs and competent in dealing with this world; the other was emotional, mystical, idealistic, deeply and spontaneously religious, living daily with God as a son with the Father, carrying the sorrows of men in his heart and the wrongs of the world on his conscience. One of the greatest of New England ministers, he was shepherd as well as counselor, pastor as well as teacher. "I wish to stand on the earth," he said with true critical insight, "though I would look beyond the stars. I would live *with men*, but think with philosophers" (Weiss, *Life and Correspondence of Theodore Parker*, Vol. I, p. 115). The generous amplitude of his nature was too large for the narrow walls of a church; he took all Boston for his parish, all New England for his congregation. Amazingly active and vital, he consumed whole libraries in his pursuit of knowledge. "His mind," says Weiss, "was like the republican idea itself; it could afford to be hospitable, but could not afford to be exclusive" (*ibid.*, Vol. I, p. 178). Conversant with many fields of knowledge, with a memory extraordinarily retentive, he was master of many languages—nineteen or twenty, according to Thomas Wentworth Higginson—and at home in the most abstruse subjects. He spent his vast energy with the prodigality of Cotton Mather, and he achieved what Cotton Mather with his inbred parochialism could not achieve, an intellectual cosmopolitanism that judged Boston by broader standards than it could gauge.

A first-class fighting-man was this child of yeoman New England

—none braver, not even Garrison, none more effective; and yet tender-hearted, sympathetic, with the shrewd common sense of his homespun forebears. The son of a Lexington farmer and mechanic, self-trained, endowed with indomitable will, he came of the soundest stock in Massachusetts. His grandfather was captain of the Minute Men who faced the British troops on Lexington Common in April, 1775; and a conscious pride of ancestry broke out frequently in his speech. The words uttered before the Ministerial Conference in May, 1851, in justification of his repudiation of the Fugitive Slave Law, were characteristic: "I am not afraid of men, I can offend them. I care nothing for their hate, or their esteem. I am not very careful of my reputation." He then goes on:

I have had to arm myself. I have written my sermons with a pistol in my desk,—loaded, a cap on the nipple, and ready for action. Yea, with a drawn sword within reach of my right hand. This I have done in Boston; in the midst of the nineteenth century; been obliged to do it to defend the (innocent) members of my church, women as well as men! You know that I do not like fighting. . . . But what could I do? I was born in the little town where the first bloodshed of the Revolution began. The bones of men who first fell in that war are covered by the monument at Lexington, it is "sacred to Liberty and the Rights of Mankind"; those men fell "in the sacred cause of God and their country." This is the first inscription that I ever read. These men were my kindred. My grandfather drew the first sword in the Revolution; my fathers fired the first shot; the blood which flowed there was kindred to this which courses in my veins today. Besides that, when I write in my library at home, on the one side of me is the Bible which my fathers prayed over, their morning and evening prayer, for nearly a hundred years. On the other side there hangs the firelock my grandfather fought with in the old French war, which he carried at the taking of Quebec, which he zealously used at the battle of Lexington, and beside it is another, a trophy of that war, the first gun taken in the Revolution, taken also by my grandfather. With these things before me, these symbols; with these memories in me, when a parishioner, a fugitive from slavery, a woman, pursued by the kidnappers, came to my house, what could I do less than take her in and defend her to the last? (*Additional Speeches*, Vol. I, pp. 13–15.)

With his sensitive conscience visited by such memories—a child of '76 living in the evil days of the Fugitive Slave Law, a devout freethinker borne on the crest of transcendental thought— Theodore Parker became the embodiment and epitome of the New England renaissance. More completely perhaps than any other representative, he gathered up and expressed the major revolu-

tionary impulses of his time and world: the idealistic theism implicit
in the Unitarian reaction from Calvinism; the transcendental
individualism latent in the doctrine of divine immanence; and
the passion for righteousness, to make the will of God prevail in
a world where the devil quite openly kept his ledgers. He was an
eager and thorough iconoclast, impatient to break the false
images—the God of John Calvin with its slanders of human nature,
and the god of State Street with its contempt for justice—which
New England, he believed, had worshiped too long, forgetting
the ideals of the Revolutionary fathers. The mind and conscience
of Boston seemed to him stifled by the strait-jacket of respectability. Righteousness like a fugitive slave, was driven into hiding,
or must walk the open streets with a Derringer in its pocket. As
a free soul loving freedom, and a righteous man loving righteousness, he believed a duty was laid on him to cut away the strait-
jacket, to shame the Boston that sold the poor in the gates for a
pair of shoes. He must labor to set free the mind and conscience
of Boston that they might go forth purified to work a beneficent
work in a world that is God's and not the devil's. His attack was
keen and unsparing; he laid on with gusto; he used homely words;
he was just rather than polite. Impatient of humbug and self-
seeking he dealt in searching criticism rather than conventional
eulogy. At his touch distinguished reputations shrank to the mean
and commonplace, and inflated dignitaries collapsed like a pricked
balloon. Intellectually honest, he spoke the truth he had been at
immense pains to gather, and in consequence those who suffered
the sting of his attack—ministers and lawyers and merchants and
politicians, men in high position, distinguished leaders of Boston
society—were not slack in crying out against him as a demagogue
and agitator. Next to Garrison he became the most hated man in
New England; and something of that contemporary hatred, fierce
and unforgiving, clings to his name still, coloring later estimates
of his worth, hinting that his manners were not on a level with his
morals.[1] An extraordinarily vital and interesting person, in short,
was this Yankee preacher with his Puritan conscience—this transcendental critic with his quiver full of facts; one not to be ignored
in casting up the accounts of the New England renaissance.

　　With his memorable sermon *On the Transient and Permanent
in Christianity*, preached in May, 1841—a sermon that ranks in

---

[1] See Wendell, *Literary History of America*, p. 348.

the history of Unitarianism with Channing's Baltimore sermon—the Unitarian movement entered upon its second broad phase. It abandoned supernaturalism established on the sufficient authority of the Scriptures, and adopted the conception of an evolutionary theism, of God progressively revealing himself to the developing faculties of men and speaking through the conscience. Under Channing's guidance Unitarianism had abandoned the major dogmas of Calvinism—total depravity, predestination, a God of wrath; it had shifted the emphasis from stable will to boundless love; and by such teachings it had captured the greater churches of Boston. By 1830 it had become securely established as the religion of Boston respectability, with implied bounds set to its intellectual liberalism. As the first ardor abated it fell to defining the new orthodoxy, resting content with what already had been won. It was against this new orthodoxy that held fast to the old supernaturalism that Theodore Parker protested. "The defect of the Unitarians was a profound one," he pointed out; "ceasing to fear 'the great and dreadful God' of the Old Testament, they had not quite learned to love the all-beautiful and altogether lovely [God] of the universe." [2] He would have no pausing of the movement of adventurous thought, no settling back into the ruts of dogmatism; and so he threw himself with immense energy into the work of liberating Unitarianism from a premature orthodoxy.

For this work he was admirably equipped. The greatest scholar of his generation of New England ministers, deep in German theology and philosophy, with the latest results of higher criticism on his study table, he was critically trained to separate historical fact from ecclesiastical tradition, and establish his theology on a basis of naturalism. He was at once scientific and transcendental. He had translated De Wette's *Introduction to the Old Testament* and was intimately acquainted with Strauss's *Leben Jesu*. He knew the oriental backgrounds of Hebraic thought, had studied comparative religion with its suggestive record of taboos and fetishism, and was gathering materials for a comprehensive history of religion from primitive times. Intellectually acquisitive and curious, he far outran the less informed and courageous of his Unitarian brethren. But he was far more than a critic, he

[2] See "Letter to the Members of the Twenty-Eighth Congregational Society of Boston," in Weiss, *Life and Correspondence of Theodore Parker*, Vol. II, Appendix II, p. 482. This account of his "Experience as a Minister" constitutes a brief intellectual autobiography, of first importance to the student of Parker.

may well be accounted a religious genius. A convinced intui-
tionist, he tested every authority by appeal to transcendental
experience. He frankly abandoned faith in the supernatural,
with its corollaries of miracles and its "fetishism of the Bible,"
and was far advanced in a theism that compensated for the supernatural by a passionate love of God. Thus established in personal
experience his religion issued in conduct. Love of God was more
to him than historical faith embodied in an historical church;
love to his fellow men was more appealing than dogma. Hence the
profoundly ethical quality of his religion, warm, palpitating,
generous, that set it apart from the colder and austerer ethicism
of the conventional Unitarians. The spirituality of Channing was
enriched in Parker by the ardency of his loving nature.

The three major doctrines of his theism, as elaborated in his
"Letter to the Members of the Twenty-Eighth Congregational
Society," were the infinite perfection of God, the adequacy of
man to all his functions, and the sufficiency of absolute, natural
religion. In his elaboration of these doctrines the controlling
influence of transcendental thought is everywhere apparent.
A metaphysical optimism throws a golden light on all his thinking.
The trinitarian Godhead, equally with the devil, vanishes in "the
infinitely perfect God," "immanent in the world of matter, and in
the world of spirit, the two hemispheres which to us make up the
universe"—a universe created "from a perfect motive, for a perfect purpose, of perfect substance, and as a perfect means." Hence
it follows in Parker's logic, that

there must be a complete solidarity between God and the two-fold universe which He creates. The perfect Creator is thus also a perfect providence; indeed, creation and providence are not objective accidents of
Deity, nor subjective caprices, but the development of the perfect motive
to its perfect purpose, love becoming a universe of perfect welfare. I
have called God Father, but also Mother . . . to express more sensibility,
the quality of tender and unselfish love, which mankind associates with
Mother more than aught else beside. ("Letter," etc., in Weiss, Vol. II,
pp. 470–471.)

The doctrine of the adequacy of man flows logically from the
doctrine of the immanence of God, but Parker was not content to
rest it on such basis alone. The conception of human perfectibility, as it filtered down to him through different strata of thought,
romantic and idealistic, found a high sanction in his transcenden-

talism; but his practical nature demanded that it be established if possible on a scientific foundation. Anthropology must substantiate philosophy. Parker was not convinced that it could be thus adequately established; nevertheless he would travel the objective path as far as it might lead. Darwin's *Origin of Species* was published after Parker was seized with his fatal illness, yet in much of the latter's thinking he was groping his way toward some similar conception of "the unity of life of the human race," with its "progressive development" from "the state of ignorance, poverty, and utter nakedness of soul and sense, the necessary primitive conditions of the race, up to the present civilization." In the deep-buried scattered records of the past, slowly being gathered together and interpreted by science, he found "proof of time immense, wherein man, this spiritual Cosmos, has been assuming his present condition, individual, domestic, social, and national, and accumulating that wealth of things and thoughts which is the mark of civilization." The doctrine of human perfectibility might not be capable of scientific proof, but it was more than a reasonable hope; it was implicit in all the past.

But this progressive development does not end with us; we have seen only the beginning; the future triumphs of the race must be vastly greater than all accomplished yet. In the primal instincts and automatic desires of man, I have found a prophecy that what he wants is possible, and shall one day be actual. . . . What good is not with us is before, to be attained by toil and thought, and religious life. (*Ibid.*, Vol. II, pp. 471-472.)

Of this slowly and painfully evolving man with his expanding ideals, religion Parker believed to be the highest ultimate expression; and religion, as the eyes of men slowly open to larger truths, will be seen to be answerable to the needs of daily life, to embody the highest ideal of social excellence. The noblest religion he believed was not supernatural, but natural. "The absolute religion which belongs to man's nature, and is gradually unfolded thence," "is the idea of humanity, dimly seen but clearly felt, which has flitted before the pious eyes of men in all lands and many an age, and been prayed for as the 'Kingdom of Heaven.'" It is forever refashioning its ideal, re-embodying its vision, in every devout soul, in every creative age. "The religious history of the race is the record of man's continual but unconscious efforts to attain this 'desire of all nations'" (*ibid.*, Vol. II, p. 473). But unhappily every new advance soon crystallizes in dogmas and in-

stitutions; taboos and fetishisms are quick to re-imprison the mind
that struggles to be free. Old forms, therefore, must be daily
broken to make room for evolving experience. Religion must be
free; it must rise spontaneously from the depths of life. Christianity has suffered grievously from a fetishism of the Bible, from
its worship of the supernatural, from an ungenerous sectarianism
beloved of "ecclesiastic skeptics," who believe "there is no place
for the Christian Church or the Bible till they have nullified the
faculties which created both, and rendered Bible-makers and
Church-founders impossible." Every age must write a new Bible
out of its God-given instincts, permeated with the divine love
that is slowly shaping society to the divine purpose.

No more is the atheistic mocker or the ecclesiastic bigot commissioned
to stop the human race with his cry, "Cease there, mankind, thy religious
search! for, thousand-million-headed as thou art, thou canst know nought
directly of thy God, thy duty, or thyself. Pause, and accept my authen-
ticated word; stop, and despair!" (*Ibid.*, Vol. II, p. 475.)

It was this ethical quality of his religion that kept Theodore
Parker so sensitive to wrongs and so generous in response to the
call of social justice. His religion quickened his social conscience
and summoned him to serve the plentiful reform movements of
the day. With Garrison and Wendell Phillips he organized the
militants of Boston radicalism. His political principles were
simple and uncompromising, woven from the strands of English
and French libertarianism of the seventeenth and eighteenth
centuries—from Sidney, Locke, Rousseau, the great leaders of the
natural-rights school. One who accepted as axiomatic the nobility of human nature and the perfectibility of man, might be a political romantic, but he was certain to be a liberal. Parker was a
primitive democrat, whose democracy was bone of his bone and
flesh of his flesh. But the democracy that answered the needs of
his dream of the kingdom was, like Emerson's and Channing's,
ethical rather than political or economic—it was "the enactment
of God's justice into human laws" ("The Nebraska Question," in
Additional Speeches, Vol. I, p. 327). "The democratic idea has
had but a slow and gradual growth even in New England," he
pointed out; nevertheless he was convinced that it was spreading,
and "government becomes more and more of all, by all and for
all" [3] (*ibid.*, p. 33). He hated Federalism with an intensity equal-

[3] This phrase of Parker's was probably the source of Lincoln's phrase.

ing Jefferson's, and ecclesiastical Federalism that twisted the authority of the church to the side of wealthy pewholders, using Scripture as a sanction for exploitation, he denounced as scathingly as Garrison. The power of the political state he feared, because he discovered the political state to be the friend of the rich rather than the poor, of selfish advantage rather than of God's justice. With other Abolitionists he distrusted the machinery of centralization that was being skillfully erected at Washington. "Opposition to centralization of authority is very old in America," he remarked; "I hope it will be always young" (*ibid.*, Vol. II, p. 29). But he was no partisan to the rule of the majority, if it determined contrary to his conscience. A transcendental individualist, he went for the nullification of an immoral statute in the name of the Higher Law.[4]

Parker was never blind to the economic basis of politics. He saw so clearly, indeed, the close alliance between group interests and governmental statutes, that his political activities were almost wholly determined by that recognition. As a political critic he was the shrewdest realist of his generation. He was one constituent whom politicians talking for Buncombe could not befuddle. He was too deeply read in American history, gifted with too keen historical insight, to be impressed by the glittering rhetoric of the Rufus Choates. He had his own views of the American government, and majestic appeals to the Constitution left him cold. The Constitution, he asserted, "is a provisional compromise between the ideal political principles of the Declaration, and the actual selfishness of the people North and South." America was not a democracy. It had thrown off theocracy, aristocracy, and monarchy, only to set in their places the "institution of money—the master of all the rest." The economic basis of society in America he considered to be open and patent. In church and state, money "is this day the strongest power of the nation." He declined to be deceived by party cries and platforms, either Whig or Democratic; both parties served economics rather than justice.

So there is a party organization about the dollar as its central nucleus and idea. The dollar is the germinal dot of the Whig party; its motive

[4] See "The Law of God and the Statutes of Men," in *Additional Speeches*, Vol. II, p. 181.

is pecuniary. . . . It sneers at the poor; at the many; has a contempt for the people. It legislates against the poor, and for the rich . . . the few who are born with the desire, the talent, and the conventional position to become rich. "Take care of the rich, and they will take care of the poor," is its secret maxim. Everything must yield to money. . . . With this party there is no Absolute Right, no Absolute Wrong. . . . There is Expediency and Inexpediency. . . . Accordingly a millionaire is reckoned by this party as the highest production of Society. He is the Whig ideal; he alone has attained "the measure of the stature of a perfect man."

The Democratic party appeals to the brute will of the majority, right or wrong; it knows no Higher Law. . . . There is . . . no vital difference between the Whig party and the Democratic party; no difference in moral principle. The Whig inaugurates the Money got; the Democrat inaugurates the Desire to get money. That is all the odds. . . . There is only a hand rail between the two, which breaks down if you lean on it, and the parties mix . . . a Democrat is but a Whig on time; a Whig is a Democrat arrived at maturity; his time has come. A Democrat is a young Whig who will legislate for money as soon as he has got it; the Whig is an old Democrat who once hurrahed for the majority—"Down with money! there is a despot! and up with the desire for it! Down with the rich, and up with the poor!" The young man, poor, obscure, and covetous, in 1812 was a Democrat, went a-privateering against England; rich, and accordingly "one of our eminent citizens," in 1851 he was a Whig, and went a-kidnapping against Ellen Crafts and Thomas Sims. ("The Nebraska Question," in *Additional Speeches*, Vol. I, pp. 331–335.)

The America of Parker's day was fast becoming middle class and Parker knew it, and like Lincoln he did not disapprove. Honest thrift he found wholly desirable, and wealth if it were honestly got. But speculation dissociated from creative work he regarded with old-fashioned distrust. "If a man fully pay in efficient, productive toil and thought, he is entitled to all he gets, one dollar or many million dollars . . . and if his estate be but what he has thus actually and honestly paid for with service given, equivalent to the service received, what he can virtuously keep or humanely apply and expend, then it will never be too large." [5] But he believed there were other gods, and greater, than the god of getting on; social justice was more desirable than unearned increment; and he set his face like flint against the common materialism of America. "I come to build up piety and morality; to pull down only what cumbers the ground," he said; but he had learned that the temples of State Street were not easily leveled;

[5] Quoted in Weiss, Vol. II, p. 488.

that they would not fall without a mighty crash. A less courageous man would have hesitated, but Parker was utterly fearless. Boston he knew "was a Tory town." "The Mother city of the Puritans is now the metropolis of the Hunkers" (*Additional Speeches*, Vol. I, p. 111). But the spirit of '76 was strong in him and he would "appeal from Boston drunk with gold, and briefly mad with hate, to sober Boston in her hour to come." He would appeal from Whiggish Boston to Revolutionary Boston; from State Street to Lexington common; from the Faneuil Hall of Rufus Choate to the Faneuil Hall of Sam Adams. He would awaken the ancestral idealism of Boston that slept uneasily under the spell of middle-class ambitions—that had sold its Puritan heritage for southern trade profits. Such an appeal Boston had never before listened to, ardent, unsparing, the Hebraic and the Yankee vernacular curiously mingled; and Boston writhed uncomfortably and pronounced the prophet ill-mannered.

When the Fugitive Slave Bill passed, the six New England states lay fast asleep: Massachusetts slept soundly, her head pillowed on her unsold bales of Cotton and of woolen goods, dreaming of "orders from the South." Justice came to waken her . . . and she started in her sleep, and being frightened, swore a prayer or two, then slept again. But Boston woke,— sleeping, in her shop, with ears open, and her eye on the market, her hand on her purse, dreaming of goods for sale,—Boston woke broadly up, and fired a hundred guns for joy. O Boston, Boston! if thou couldst have known, in that thine hour, the things which belong unto thy peace! But no: they were hidden from her eyes. She had prayed to her god, to Money; he granted her the request, but sent leanness into her soul. ("The Boston Kidnapping," in *Additional Speeches*, Vol. I, p. 89.)

But he offended the Boston code of good breeding even more seriously. He became personal. He named names. Before vast congregations, in printed books, he pronounced judgment on Bostonians respected in the Back Bay, mighty in State Street. Boston gentlemen had never before suffered such tongue-lashings. How mercilessly he excoriated Commissioner Loring, judge of probate and Harvard professor, for soiling his hands in the Anthony Burns case! How neatly he pricked the empty culture of Edward Everett for his pro-slavery ardor—"a Cambridge professor of Greek, he studied the original tongue of the Bible to learn that the Scripture says 'slaves,' where the English Bible says only 'servants'!" (*Additional Speeches*, Vol. II, p. 115.) What an

utterly devastating attack he made on the great Webster for the
latter's subserviency to local economic interests! Much honest
realism underlies that criticism, and much honest American history.
The "Nebraska Address" and the "Webster Address" are notable
historical documents, incisive analyses—rare in those romantic
days—done by one who has kept a shrewd eye on current politics,
and understands the hidden springs of party policy. Into the
Webster address he put his vast knowledge, his power of analysis, his
frank idealism. It was "a sad and dreadful day" when duty bade
Theodore Parker speak on the man whose uncommon powers he
had long admired; but he did his work thoroughly, refusing to shut
his eyes to ugly fact, refusing to indulge in commonplace eulogy.
It was the eighteenth-century economic realism of Webster that
stirred the wrath of the transcendentalist—that and the lapses
from integrity. Parker's text was found in Webster's dictum
that "the great object of government is the protection of property
at home, and respect and renown abroad"; and how starkly it
runs counter to his own ideal of government, "the enactment of
God's justice into human laws," is laid bare in page after page of
scathing commentary. To the exacting ethics of Parker, Webster
was wanting in principles; he followed expediency rather than
justice; and how surely expediency digs pitfalls for its own undoing he discovered tragic illustration of in the career of the great
senator. It is a hard fate for a politician, accustomed to the cheap
praise of the gullible public, to fall into the hands of a critic who
is honest and searching; and Webster had too many weak points to
emerge from such an analysis with credit. It is probably the most
critical examination of Webster's career that has ever been made,
and withal just.

Surprisingly modern, far more so than Channing, was this brilliant preacher—impulsive, colloquial, natural, whose every arrow
was pointed with a fact and feathered to fly true; concerned more
with righteousness than with policy; hating the dull commonplace
and empty dignity of Tory ways; careless of convention, somewhat
spectacular, with a keen relish for combat—a vital, vivid man, the
apostle of conscience, the advocate of every unpopular cause. He
possessed an amazing gift of words, yet he was too impatient, too
practical, to become an artist; preferring immediate ends to more
lasting reputation, and spending himself with a free prodigality.
He was always the speaker rather than the writer and his printed

pages bear the unmistakable marks of impetuous oral discourse. Emerson accounted him one of the four great men of the age. Whether or not that judgment holds, whether he was too eager a militant to become a great transcendental philosopher, the historian sees in Theodore Parker one of the greatest, if not the last, of the excellent line of Puritan preachers.

CHAPTER V

MARGARET FULLER

Rebel

THE fame of Margaret Fuller has waned greatly since her vivid personality was blotted out in the prime of her intellectual development. Misunderstood in her own time, caricatured by unfriendly critics, and with significant facts of her life suppressed by her friends out of a chivalrous sense of loyalty, the real woman has been lost in a Margaret Fuller myth and later generations have come to underestimate her powers and undervalue her work. Yet no other woman of her generation in America is so well worth recalling. She was the completest embodiment of the inchoate rebellions and grandiose aspirations of the age of transcendental ferment; for to the many grievances charged against the times by other New England liberals, she added the special grievance of the stupid inhibitions laid upon women. Transcendental radical and critic, like Emerson and Thoreau and Parker, she was feminist also; and to the difficult business of freeing her mind from the Cambridge orthodoxies, she added the greater difficulty of freeing her sex.

The written record that Margaret Fuller left is quite inadequate to explain her contemporary reputation. In no sense an artist, scarcely a competent craftsman, she wrote nothing that bears the mark of high distinction either in thought or style. Impatient of organization and inadequately disciplined, she threw off her work impulsively, not pausing to shape it to enduring form. Yet she was vastly talked about, and common report makes her out to have been an extraordinary woman who creatively influenced those with whom she came in contact. Like Alcott, her power lay in brilliant talk. Her quick mind seems to have been an electric current that stimulated other minds to activity, and created a vortex of speculation wherever she passed. Hungry for ideas, intellectually and emotionally vibrant, she caught her inspirations from obscure impulses of a nature thwarted and inhibited from normal unfolding; and in her sensitive oscillations she was often drawn away from polar principles to which she would later swing back. There was quite evidently a fundamental unrest within her, a conflict of impulses, that issued in dissatisfaction; and this contradiction was aggravated by intense emotions, which both quickened her mind and distorted it.

A product of Cambridge bookishness, Margaret Fuller was both a wonder and a riddle to a generation that made little account of the psychology of sex. She was commonly looked upon as an intellectual monstrosity, the most fearful of Yankee bluestockings, and a later Bostonian has gone so far as to suggest that she was "an unsexed version of Plato's Socrates" (Wendell, *Literary History of America*, p. 300). But to present-day psychology her character is an extraordinarily suggestive document, and a recent critic has read her seeming contradictions like an open book.[1] Before Miss Anthony's penetrating analysis the Margaret Fuller myth vanishes, and a very real, natural, and unfortunate woman takes its place. She came of vigorous stock, independent, outspoken, opinionated. Her grandfather was a clergyman who was unfrocked by his church for being lukewarm in the Revolutionary War. Her father, Timothy Fuller, and her four uncles, worked their way through Harvard. In Timothy Fuller there was a large measure of Puritan grimness and severity that locked the door on the passions of his heart, that none might know of them; yet there seems to have been a volcano in the man who held off the world so brusquely. The rebel was strong in him. The Fullers were not of Brahmin stock and had no wish to please their social superiors. While a Harvard undergraduate, Timothy Fuller turned Jeffersonian republican and lost his place as first honor man by joining in an undergraduate protest against certain hated regulations. As a lawyer and politician he repudiated respectable Federalism, and although he was representative in Congress for four terms and enjoyed certain other offices, his non-conformity in the end cost him dear. No doubt he had counted on that, for he was stubborn oak that might break but would not bend. The tragedy of Margaret Fuller's life seems to have been sketched before in the life of Timothy Fuller.

To an extraordinary degree the daughter was the child of the father, in ideas and sympathies as well as blood. Like him she was a rebel, but for the daughter to turn rebel involved greater

[1] See Katharine Anthony, *Margaret Fuller. A Psychological Biography*.

hazards than for the father. Her sex was a heavy handicap, for the experience of Fanny Wright and Lucretia Mott had revealed that American chivalry had definite bounds; it did not shield the woman who ventured beyond the pale. Yet considering her blood and training, how could she help thus venturing into freer fields without? From her earliest years her father treated her as a comrade and gave her the training of a boy. In her studies he dealt with her as James Mill dealt with his brilliant son. Perhaps it was a mistake to force her into the rigid groove of classical learning when she should have been playing with her dolls. From it she got very unusual acquisitions, but overstimulation broke her health, and isolation turned her mind in upon itself and made her the victim of somnambulism and freaks of imagination. The result was the development, on one side of her nature, of a female counterpart of Cotton Mather—precocious, domineering, moody, visionary, given to long hours of greedy reading, gorging herself on books and well-nigh ruining her intellectual digestion as well as her health. Against this unfortunate overstimulation her vigorous nature struggled for years, and never quite successfully. Her emotions were forever embroiling her intellect. To conceive of her as sexless is curiously to miss the point of her emotionalism. She was rather the victim of sex. Her ardent friendships with other women, her flashes of mystical experience, her fondness for children, her love of luxury and creature comforts, her eager love affair with James Nathan who unchivalrously found safety in flight, her friendship with Mazzini and her more intimate friendship with Count Ossoli, that ended in an unconventional marriage after her situation rendered it necessary—such reactions can be explained on no other hypothesis. Her ardent nature was the victim of disastrous frustrations, rendered the more acute by premature development. If she had married early, as Harriet Beecher did, and her excessive energy had been turned into domestic channels, her life must have been less tragic, whatever the effect might have been on her intellectual development.

The acutest contemporary analysis of her contradictory character is that given by her friend William Henry Channing, who found his clue in the clash between endowment and environment:

Here was one fond as a child of joy, eager as a native of the tropics for swift transition from luxurious rest to passionate excitement, prodigal to pour her mingled force of will, thought, sentiment, into the life of the moment, all radiant with imagination, longing for communion with artists of every age in their inspired hours, fitted by genius and culture to mingle as an equal in the most refined circles of Europe, and yet her youth and early womanhood had passed away amid the very decent, yet drudging, descendants of prim Puritans. Trained among those who could have discerned her peculiar power, and early fed with the fruits of beauty for which her spirits pined, she would have developed into one of the finest lyrists, romancers and critics, that the modern literary world has seen. This she knew; and this tantalization of her fate she keenly felt. (*Memoirs of Margaret Fuller Ossoli*, by R. W. Emerson, W. H. Channing, and J. F. Clarke, Vol. II, pp. 36–37.)

This disastrous clash between endowment and environment is strikingly exemplified in her delight in Europe when at thirty-four she found herself there—in her admiration for Georges Sand, and in particular the extravagance of her love for Rome, where her starved heart found satisfactions she had long dreamed of. "Italy receives me as a long-lost child, and I feel myself at home here," she wrote in 1847; and a few weeks later, "I find how true was the lure that always drew me towards Europe. It was no false instinct that said I might here find an atmosphere to develop me in ways I need. Had I only come ten years earlier! Now my life must be a failure, so much strength has been wasted on abstractions, which only came because I grew not in the right soil" (*ibid.*, Vol. II, p. 225). She was too eagerly pagan to be satisfied with either Puritan or Yankee Cambridge. The pale ethicism of New England was thin gruel for such an appetite for life. Even Emerson she found cold, and her stomach rebelled at the food he throve on. But this was only half the story; the other half was this:

But the tragedy of Margaret's history was deeper yet. Behind the poet was the woman,—fond and relying, the heroic and disinterested woman. The very glow of her poetic enthusiasm was but an outflush of trustful affection; the very restlessness of her intellect was the confession that her heart had found no home. A "book-worm," a "dilettante," a "pedant," I had heard her sneeringly called; but now it was evident that her seeming insensibility was virgin pride, and her absorption in studying the natural vent of emotions, which met no object of life-long attachment. At once, many of her peculiarities became intelligible. Fitfulness, unlooked-for changes of mood, misconceptions of words and actions, substitutions of fancy for fact . . . were now referred to the morbid influence of affections pent up to prey upon themselves. And, what was still more interesting, the clue was given to a singular credulousness, by which, in spite of her unusual penetration, Margaret might be led away blindfold. As this revelation of her ardent nature burst upon me, and . . . I saw how faith-

ful she had kept to her life purposes,—how patient, gentle, and thoughtful of others, how active in self-improvement and usefulness, how wisely
dignified she had been,—I could not but bow to her in reverence. (*Ibid.*,
Vol. II, p. 37.)

The inchoate rebellions in her heart were stimulated and given
form by her reading. From the English, French, and German romantics she drew much of her intellectual food. The long hours
spent with her father over Jefferson's letters were the best of
preparation for Rousseau and Mary Wollstonecraft, and French
romanticism provided an excellent introduction to the German.
Her emotions were in high ferment when she came upon the German
school, and she yielded her heart to it without reserve. Novalis,
Richter, above all Goethe, became a passion and swept her along
the path that Hedge and James Freeman Clarke were following.
For years she gathered materials for a life of Goethe, but a feeling
of self-distrust held back the project. Her love for him was the
great literary enthusiasm of her life. "It seems to me," she wrote
in 1832, "as if the mind of Goethe had embraced the universe. . . .
I am enchanted while I read. He comprehends every feeling I
have ever had so perfectly, expresses it so beautifully; but when I
shut the book, it seems as if I had lost my personal identity; all
my feelings linked with such an immense variety that belongs to
things I had thought so different" (*ibid.*, Vol. I, p. 119). Later,
with more critical analysis of Goethe, she found her enthusiasm
modifying; she was repelled by his calm, aloof intellectuality; [2]
but she never wavered in loyal recognition of his commanding
powers.

Her romantic idealism was in full career when the transcendental
movement caught her up and put its stamp upon her. It came as
an emotional appeal to the vague aspirations of a life inadequately
motivated, and she threw herself eagerly into the new philosophy
and became the most hectic of its expounders. The intellectual
foundations of her transcendentalism were so slight in comparison
with the equipment of Hedge and Parker as scarcely to justify her
pretentions to their fellowship. But what she lacked in knowledge
of Kant and Fichte she made up in enthusiasm, and none questioned her right to speak for the group. The editorship of the
Dial provided a convenient safety valve for her energy, but it
neither absorbed her nor sufficed to satisfy her limitless desires.

[2] See *Life Without and Life Within*, pp. 23-60.

She needed to espouse a cause more concrete and dramatic, personal in its demands, calling for high sacrifice. Abolitionism was at hand, but it repelled her by its narrow dogmatisms. Garrison was never a hero of hers. She regarded him with "high respect" for his "noble and generous" course; but "he has indulged in violent invective and denunciation till he has spoiled the temper of his mind" ("Frederick Douglass," in *Life Without and Life Within*, p. 122). Later, when she was in Europe, she looked back half regretfully at her indifference to the movement.

How it pleases me here to think of the Abolitionists! I could never endure to be with them at home; they were so tedious, often so narrow, always so rabid and exaggerated in their tone. But, after all, they had a high motive, something eternal in their desire and life. (*Memoirs*, Vol. II, p. 229.)

Even Brook Farm repelled her as much as it attracted her. Though she loved many of the members, bore her share in the discussions preliminary to its establishment, and often visited there, she would not join the venture. She had had enough of farm life at Groton. To open a road to Utopia with a common plow was, perhaps, too prosaic a business for her romantic nature, and when the Fourier Phalanx was introduced she grew skeptical. Fourierism seemed to her too mechanical a conception, in spite of her sympathy for the humanitarian spirit that lay behind it. As she looked back upon it from the vantage point of her French experience, she modified her judgment somewhat, although the old transcendental bias that Emerson had voiced still colored her views.

The more I see of the terrible ills which infest the body politic of Europe, the more indignation I feel at the selfishness or stupidity of those in my own country who oppose an examination of these subjects,—such as is animated by the hope of prevention. Educated in an age of gross materialism, Fourier is tainted by its faults; in attempts to reorganise society, he commits the error of making soul the result of health of body, instead of body the clothing of the soul; but his heart was that of a genuine lover of his kind, of a philanthropist in the sense of Jesus; his views are large and noble; his life was one of devout study on these subjects, and I should pity the person who, after the briefest sojourn in Manchester and Lyons, the most superficial acquaintance with the population of London or Paris, could seek to hinder a study of his thoughts, or be wanting in reverence for his purposes. (*Ibid.*, Vol. II, p. 206.)

It was in part from Fourier, certainly from the collectivistic theories discussed so generally by the transcendental group, that she received her equipment for the cause which, more than any other except the dramatic Roman revolution, appealed to the deeper rebellions of her soul. She had dealt much with the woman question in her "Conversations," and in 1844 she published *Woman in the Nineteenth Century*, a work that made a great stir in America. The "little book was the first considered statement of feminism in this country" (Katharine Anthony, *Margaret Fuller*, p. 80), and its novelty was emphasized by its boldness. The question of woman's place had emerged sharply from the Abolition movement, when the appearance of women on the platform had aroused opposition even from radical reformers, and Angelina Grimké had encountered insults when she spoke at Abolition meetings. But Margaret Fuller was the first since Mary Wollstonecraft, fifty years before, to undertake a reasoned defense of the claims of woman to emancipation from man-made custom. It was a somewhat shocking book to fling at respectable Boston bluestockings—male as well as female—for not only did she discuss equality of economic opportunity and equality of political rights for women, but she went further and spoke frankly about sex equality, marriage, prostitution, physical passions—pretty much everything that was taboo in Boston society. It was a bold thing to do, needing more courage even than to engage in a Fourieristic onslaught upon the conventions of private property. Only a first-class rebel would have had the temerity to offer such morsels to wagging tongues.

This was her parting shot at a world that had done its best to stifle her. Thenceforth her field was to broaden out immensely. In 1844 she went to New York to live in the family of Horace Greeley and write critical reviews for *The Tribune*—a shift that marked the beginning of her intellectual maturity, the end of her mystical sentimentalism. She was thirty-four years of age, and she plunged vigorously into the work of criticism, never perhaps very successfully, certainly never with high distinction. Her judgments were penetrating and individual, she awakened some Cambridge animosities by her comment on certain Cambridge poets, but she was not a notable critic. A fine craftsmanship she never attained. A light touch she could never command. Nevertheless the experience was sobering. Honest, practical Horace Greeley, with his pugnacious fondness for social reform, was an excellent antidote to Concord transcendentalism; and an awakening sociological interest discovered ample opportunities in New York for the expression of her mother-instinct. She took to her stormy bosom the inmates of Sing Sing prison, the poor and out-cast of the city. At last she went to Europe, fell in with Mazzini, and found a cause dramatic enough and real enough to satisfy her rebellious instincts. She was profoundly stirred by the Roman revolution, took charge of one of the hospitals, and spent her strength freely. On the tragic failure of the revolt she started home with her husband and child, only to perish on the sandy shores of Fire Island—a fate she did not turn her finger to escape. Perhaps it was well. She had only too good reason to be fearful of her reception and of the future. Tongues that had wagged before would certainly have risen to a virtuous gabble over her misadventure in Italy. On the whole one must be glad that her friends refused to permit her good name to be thrown to the gos-sips. Why shouldn't gentlemen lie stoutly if by so doing they can cheat the salacious?

A sensitive emotional nature offers the best of social barometers, and Margaret Fuller's tragic life, despite its lack of solid accom-plishment, was an epitome of the great revolt of the New England mind against Puritan asceticism and Yankee materialism. She was the emotional expression of a rebellious generation that had done with the past and was questioning the future. Not a scholar like Theodore Parker, not a thinker like Thoreau, not an artist like Emerson, she was a ferment of troubled aspiration, an enthu-siasm for a more generous culture than New England had known—the logical outcome of the romantic revolution which, beginning with Channing's discovery of humanitarian France, and leading thence to idealistic Germany, was to break the indurated shell of life in New England, and release its conscience and its mind. She was the spiritual child of Jean Jacques even more than of Goethe—a fact that she eventually came to realize. Writing from Paris in 1847, she said:

To the . . . Chamber of Deputies, I was indebted for a sight of the manuscripts of Rousseau, treasured in their library. I saw them and touched them,—those manuscripts just as he has celebrated them, written on fine white paper, tied with ribbon. Yellow and faded age has made them, yet at their touch I seemed to feel the fire of youth, immortally glowing, more and more expansive, with which his soul has pervaded this century. He was the precursor of all we most prize. True, his blood was mixed with madness, and the course of his actual life made some *detours* through villainous places; but his spirit was intimate with the fundamental truths of human nature, and fraught with prophecy. There is none who has given birth to more life for this age; his gifts are yet untold; they are too present with us; but he who thinks really must often think with Rousseau, and learn him ever more and more. Such is the method of genius,—to ripen fruit for the crowd by those rays of whose heat they complain. (*Memoirs*, Vol. II, pp. 206–207.)

The rebel pays a heavy price for his rebellions, as Margaret learned to her cost. She suffered much in her daily life, but it was her art that suffered most. She was evidently a far richer nature than her printed works reveal. Intense in her extravagant demands upon life, a radical humanitarian in all her sympathies and instincts, generous in response to whatever was fine and high, living unduly an inner life as became a daughter of Puritanism—Margaret Fuller was too vivid a personality, too complete an embodiment of the rich ferment of the forties, to be carelessly forgotten. The deeper failure of her career—its vague aspirations and inadequate accomplishment—was a failure that may be justly charged against the narrow world that bred her. Perhaps no sharper criticism could be leveled at New England than that it could do no better with such material, lent it by the gods.

PART IV: OTHER ASPECTS OF THE NEW ENGLAND MIND

CHAPTER I

THE REIGN OF THE GENTEEL

I

THE discussion of the New England mind hitherto has kept pretty much to the outskirts of Boston, to Concord and Roxbury and undistinguished precincts; it has not penetrated the Back Bay where dwelt the authentic representatives of Brahminism, nor has it concerned itself greatly with Cambridge that was a lesser Back Bay. Nevertheless there were other ideals than those of transcendentalism and social reform in the New England of the renaissance—ideals of culture, of scholarship, of *belles lettres*, to which the Brahmin mind contributed, and which after the subsidence of the ferment came to dominate genteel New England and for a generation largely influenced American letters. To the revolutionary aspirations of the forties the Back Bay contributed little. Brahmin Boston might turn Unitarian with Channing, but it was at heart neither French romantic nor German idealist; it desired rather culture for its own sake, and scholarship it regarded as the handmaid of culture. It hoped of course that righteousness and the will of God should ultimately prevail in human affairs, but it was not exigent in its demands. Occasion and means it willingly left to God, anticipating that the walls of Jericho must fall of their own weakness. It is surprising how little the greater issues of the time ruffled the serenity of the Brahmin mind, and how uncritical were its judgments on such issues as came under its review. Divided between State Street and the Back Bay, its life ran a smoothly agreeable course with no hint of potential antagonisms between exploitation and culture. It followed so strictly the injunction, let not thy left hand know what thy right hand doeth, that the two were almost total strangers to each other. Like Edith Wharton's contemporary Knickerbockers, the Brahmins conceived the great business of life to be the erection of barriers against the intrusion of the unpleasant. They took it ill when those barriers were assaulted by rude militants, and when indisputable Brahmins—men like Edmund Quincy and Wendell Phillips—took part in the assault, the Back Bay regarded them as more than a little queer.

The immediate consequence of this concern for defensive breast-works was the reign of the genteel in life and letters, a reign that set up a court of critical jurisdiction over the domain of American letters. The essence of the genteel tradition was a refined ethicism, that professed to discover the highest virtue in shutting one's eyes to disagreeable fact, and the highest law in the law of convention. Gone were the franker days of Robert Treat Paine when a wit might find his choicest *bons mots* in the bottom of his cups. Coarse-ness had given way to refinement. It was the romanticism of Brahmin culture, with all Falstaffian vulgarity deleted, and every smutch of the natural man bleached out in the pure sunshine of manners. It was Victorianism of a more maidenly purity than the English strain, so carefully filtered by passing through the close Puritan mesh that the smallest impurities were removed. The first of literary commandments was the commandment of reti-cence. Literature was conceived of as belonging to the library and the drawing-room, and it must observe the drawing-room amen-ities. Only a vulgarian would lug a spade there. Any venture into realism was likely to prove libidinous, and sure to be common. Certainly Margaret Fuller had overstepped the bounds of decency with her remarks about women of the streets. The Adamite school was the vulgar expression of the natural man, and Con-tinental realism—the French and the Russian—was only bringing the gutter into the library. Literature must be fine and pure and noble, and as such it will serve decency and manners; what excuse is there for it otherwise? The case for the true church of lit-erature, as against the Adamite and other heresies, was admirably stated by Lowell:

I have not seen Swinburne's new volume—but a poem or two from it which I have seen shocked me, and I am not squeamish. . . . Why should a man by choice go down to live in his cellar, instead of mount-ing to those fair upper chambers which look towards the sunrise of that Easter which shall greet the resurrection of the soul from the body of this death? *Virginibus puerisque?* To be sure! let no man write a line that he would not have his daughter read. . . . But I have outlived many heresies, and shall outlive this new Adamite one of Swinburne.

The true Church of poetry is founded on a rock, and I have no fear that these smutchy back-doors of hell shall prevail against her. (*Letters*, Vol. I, p. 377.)

II

Though it willingly recognized the superior claims of poetry and the essay, the Brahmin mind found a more congenial field for its literary ambitions in history; and the quiet scholarship that it pursued with exemplary diligence was likely to flower in substantial historical studies. Excellent work much of it is, brilliant in certain instances; yet it too is subtly marked by the psychology of the environment that produced it. The renaissance of Boston scholarship began with Everett and Ticknor, whose German training was imposed on natures instinctively aristocratic, swayed by the older Federalist prejudices. The latter applied himself to Spanish literature, but his colleague and fellow historian, Jared Sparks, proved that in the American field even painstaking scholarship could not subdue the temptation to improve upon reality. Sparks applied Boston ethics to biography and conceived that his mission in writing the life of a great American like Washington was to portray a national hero as a model to the youth of the land. In pursuance of this aim he studiously perfected nature by correcting all the little blemishes of manner and little weaknesses of character in order to produce an immaculate effect. He edited Washington's letters with a free hand, not only correcting the grammar and spelling, but silently deleting such passages as did not become the hero he had in mind. He did not of course go to the absurd lengths of Parson Weems in inventing episodes and effects, but he refused to deal with his materials realistically and the result was a falsifying of the total impression.

The greatest and in certain respects the most characteristic work of the period was George Bancroft's *History of the United States*, to which with single-minded purpose he devoted sixty laborious years. Trained in Göttingen, he gathered his materials with German thoroughness, but the underlying spirit and purpose of his exposition were native to the ardent nationalism of Jacksonian America. Bancroft was the only important member of the New England group of historians who was a militant Democrat, and he set out to justify to the world the ways of democratic America. It was a great undertaking and in the opinion of Ranke, the

German historian, it justified itself. "Your history is the best book ever written from the democratic point of view," [1] he wrote Bancroft. The praise was perhaps not excessive. Conceived in the early days of the Jacksonian triumph, it reflects the grandiose conception of the future of America and the beneficent influence of republican institutions on western civilization, that were common in the golden days of equalitarianism and that even such a scholarly legalist as Hugh Legaré shared. But unfortunately, with his generation Bancroft had lost his economic bearings, and he drove forward somewhat too confidently into the new seas of political idealism trusting to the pole-star of emancipated human nature. As a democrat he was too easily persuaded that democratic America lay in the particular keeping of Providence, and he assumed too readily that the democratic development of American institutions was in response to the divine will. It reflects something of the partisanship of honest patriots who believe God is on their side; but it served to correct the teachings of Federalists like Richard Hildreth who insisted that God was on the side of Federalism. Till Bancroft took up his pen the bias of American chronicles had been anti-democratic. Every Federalist with leisure, a quill, and a smattering of historical knowledge, had added his mite to the Federalist myths that long constituted the body of our history. The democratic interpretation ran so counter to Boston tradition that Bancroft found little congeniality amongst his fellow historians, and he eventually quitted his native state and took up his home in Washington.

More representative of the Brahmin spirit was the work of William H. Prescott, John L. Motley, and Francis Parkman, who constitute what may be called the romantic school of Boston historians. They sought the romantic in theme and aspired to the romantic in treatment quite as consciously as did the contemporary novelists. Of excellent Brahmin strain, with leisure, wealth, opportunity, they were free to pick and choose as they would. Prescott and Motley turned away from the partisanships of America, and while Jacksonianism was in full swing the former wrote his *Ferdinand and Isabella*, and while the country was wrangling over slavery the latter wrote his *Rise of the Dutch Republic*. Broad in conception and dramatic in treatment, they are admirable works, yet they suggest that aloofness from the sordid realities

[1] Quoted in Stanton, *Manual of American Literature*, p. 103.

of America so characteristic of the Brahmin mind. Far more brilliant and significant was the work of Francis Parkman who turned his imagination to the far West over which the struggle for exploration and conquest had long persisted between the French and English. In his twenties he had made a venturesome trip to the great plains, and that experience gave life and vitality to his later historical writings, that were enriched by close research, a brilliant style, and a creative imagination. The theme he set himself was not alone a "history of the American forest," but a clash between civilizations—the "feudal, militant, and Catholic France in conflict with democratic, industrial, and Protestant England"; and with fine tenacity of purpose, in the teeth of ill health, he wrought at his project till the America of the old French War times was gathered into his pages. The Brahmin mind has contributed to American letters no more brilliant work than came from the pen of Francis Parkman.

III

If the highest aspirations of the Brahmin nature sought satisfaction in poetry, Longfellow may be reckoned its most characteristic product. In his work the romantic, the sentimental, and the moralistic, blended in such just proportions, and expressed themselves with such homely simplicity as to hit exactly the current taste and establish a reputation that later generations have difficulty in understanding. A gentle, lovable soul, widely read and in maturer years possessing a ripe literary scholarship, he was a skillful purveyor of gentle, lovable ideals. Although he drew his materials from Spain and Sweden and Italy, from primitive New England and aboriginal America, it was Germany that largely provided the staple of his romance. With Emerson and Margaret Fuller and Theodore Parker, he found Germany a singularly congenial land—not Königsberg with its transcendental metaphysics, nor Weimar with its pagan culture, nor Tübingen with its higher criticism. Such things, transcendental and critical, he was not concerned about; it was the minor romantics, Freiligrath rather than Heine, the gentle melancholy and pervasive *Sehnsucht* of the German folk-nature, that drew him irresistibly and quickened his sympathetic pen. There was little intellect in Longfellow, little creative originality. He was the poet of an uncritical and unsophisticated generation, as yet untroubled by science and

industrialism, and his mind was detached from politics and his
conscience rarely disturbed by social questions. He came of
excellent Federalist stock, his father having been a delegate from
Maine to the Hartford Convention; and with his courteous manners he fitted easily into the little world of Cambridge Brahmins.
However one might question his poetry, none could question that
he was a gentleman amongst gentlemen.

If he was never the omnivorous bookman that Lowell was, he
was distinctly a poet of the library. His placid and singularly
happy life was pretty much bounded by his library walls. One
could scarcely have lived more detached from contemporary
America, more effectively insulated against the electric currents
of the times. Though Thoreau might flee to Walden he carried his
questioning intellect with him; even the constable would not
leave him alone there. But Longfellow's door shut securely
against all intrusion. The winds of doctrine and policy might
rage through the land, but they did not rattle the windows of
his study to disturb his quiet poring over Dante. The translation of the *Divina Commedia* would go forward even while the
country was being torn asunder. In a sense such work was his
refuge against the storm and stress of malignant forces that troubled him. He did not like the tumult and the shouting, and much
of Longfellow is compressed into the sonnets that preface the
translation, much of the gentleness of his evasion, and much of
the finer craftsmanship of his later years.

> Oft have I seen at some cathedral door
>   A laborer, pausing in the dust and heat,
>   Lay down his burden, and with reverent feet
>   Enter, and cross himself, and on the floor
> Kneel to repeat his paternoster o'er;
>   Far off the noises of the world retreat;
>   The loud vociferations of the street
>   Become an undistinguishable roar.
> So, as I enter here from day to day,
>   And leave my burden at this minster gate,
>   Kneeling in prayer, and not ashamed to pray,
> The tumult of the time disconsolate
>   To inarticulate murmurs dies away,
>   While the eternal ages watch and wait.

> How strange the sculptures that adorn these towers!
>   This crowd of statues, in whose folded sleeves
>   Birds build their nests; while canopied with leaves

Parvis and portal bloom like trellised bowers,
And the vast minster seems a cross of flowers!
But fiends and dragons on the gargoyled eaves
Watch the dead Christ between the living thieves,
And underneath, the traitor Judas lowers!
Ah! from what agonies of heart and brain,
What exultations trampling on despair,
What tenderness, what tears, what hate of wrong,
What passionate outcry of a soul in pain,
Uprose this poem of the earth and air,
This mediaeval miracle of song!

A single incursion Longfellow made into the field of Abolition controversy, prompted perhaps by Dickens, whose "grand chapter on slavery" in *American Notes* he had read in London. The seven poems were written to beguile the tedium of a sea voyage. They are unreal enough to seem quite harmless, yet they created a decided stir on their appearance. For a Harvard professsor to express publicly even a mild sympathy with the Abolition movement, may well have been somewhat perilous, considering the fate of Professor Follen; and the sacred institution may have scented a real danger in such romanticisms. Grotesque as these academic poems were, with their burnt-cork figures, they perhaps served to romanticize and sentimentalize the negro for northern minds, as *Uncle Tom's Cabin* did a decade later with tremendous effect. Slavery had no weapon against such an attack, and no doubt Longfellow's contributions proved serviceable to the cause of Abolitionism. But this one venture satisfied him, and having got safely back to his library, he shut the door on the whole vexatious question of slavery. He was not made for battle, and causes commanded an unwilling allegiance. Little remained of his Puritanism save conscience, a sense of struggle against somewhat vague and indolent powers of evil, a pleasant melancholy that transmuted itself into pleasant verse. He lived vicariously the lives of other poets, sharing their emotions, repeating their thoughts, reproducing their pictures; yet adding some individual color from his own sincere nature. Not richly endowed, he was more than an echo. He marked the transition from the nebulous ferment of the creative renaissance to the scholarly culture of Brahmin Cambridge. After Longfellow came Charles Eliot Norton in whose blameless life that culture flowered, and after that came sterility.

CHAPTER II

NATHANIEL HAWTHORNE

Skeptic

AFTER his immersion for some months in the Utopian dreams of Brook Farm, Miles Coverdale in *The Blithedale Romance* discovered that he had drifted far from reality. "No sagacious man," he remarked, "will long retain his sagacity, if he live exclusively among reformers and progressive people, without periodically returning into the settled system of things, to correct himself by a new observation from that old standpoint."

It was now time for me, therefore, to go and hold a little talk with the conservatives, the writers of the North American Review, the merchants, the politicians, the Cambridge men, and all those respectable blockheads who still, in this intangibility and mistiness of affairs, kept a death-grip on one or two ideas which had not come into vogue since yesterday morning.

In this suggestive pronouncement the intellectual position of Hawthorne is revealed. Cool, detached, rationalistic, curiously inquisitive, he looked out upon the ferment of the times, the clash of rival philosophies and rival interests, only to bring them into his study and turn upon them the light of his critical analysis. One after another he weighed the several faiths of New England, conservative and transcendental and radical, and ended skeptic. He was too much of a realist to change fashions in creeds. Time, experience—he is always remembering—have created men as we find them, and very likely only time and experience can make them over into something different. The conservatives would seem to have common sense on their side, for they are seeking to retain what has hitherto been won; but the reformers are not without justification as well, for impelled by an ardent faith they are seeking to win new conquests. But whether that which the conservatives defend so valiantly is worth defending, or whether the goal towards which the reformers drive so furiously is worth the trouble, are questions about which the rationalist may be permitted his doubts. The universe in which he found himself was a moral universe, Hawthorne on the whole believed; and if that were true then man's chief business and urgent problem was the matter of a sufficient morality.

Radical in his intellectual processes, he could never become greatly interested in specific radicalisms. He is often thought of as a transcendentalist, and his association with the Peabodys and his venture into Brook Farm might seem to lend color to such an interpretation. Yet nothing in his intellectual sympathies marks him as of the school. The polar conceptions of transcendentalism repelled rather than attracted him. Political and metaphysical speculation left him cold, and the twin revolutionary forces of the time, French romanticism and German idealism, never deeply affected his thinking. Amid all the flux he retained much of the older Calvinist view of life and human destiny. Though nominally a Unitarian he did not share Channing's faith in the perfectibility of man. The buried voice of God that the transcendentalists professed to have discovered in instinct, he greatly distrusted. Man seemed to him quite as likely to turn out to be a child of the devil as the first-born of God. Perhaps through a long and uncertain process he may grow into something nobler than he now is, but for the present the fact remains that the human heart, if not desperately wicked, is at least on familiar terms with evil; too often it is cold, selfish, malignant, and its secret promptings need watching. Doubting the indwelling presence of the divine Over-soul, he could find no justification for the transcendental faith in the excellence of the universe, out of which came the genial optimism of the Emersonians. Too pronounced a rationalist to comprehend the mysticism that lurked in the heart of the transcendental faith, he remained cold to the revolutionary criticism that was eager to pull down the old temples to make room for nobler. Eager souls, mystics and revolutionaries, may propose to refashion the world in accordance with their dreams; but evil remains, and so long as it lurks in the secret places of the heart, Utopia is only the shadow of a dream. And so while the Concord thinkers were proclaiming man to be the indubitable child of God, Hawthorne was critically examining the question of evil as it appeared in the light of his own experience. It was the central, fascinating problem of his intellectual life, and in pursuit of a solution he probed curiously into the hidden, furtive recesses of the soul.

The isolation in which he chose to brood over the problem,

seeking to take the solution by surprise in unguarded moments, was the natural consequence of his temperament and his habits. He lived singularly remote from common interests, singularly self-sufficient. Both as thinker and artist he suffered from his self-imposed isolation. The twelve years of his apprenticeship, closely immured and given over to spinning cobwebs about the old Puritan rafters, drawing the stuff of his romance out of his own bowels, may have facilitated the development of technic, but it laid narrow limitations on the matter of his art. Intellectually unlocalized in his Yankee world, he was the romancer of a dead but unforgotten past, at home only where the New England conscience brooded over sin—subduing the old nightmares to less terrifying dreams, intruding his doubts into old dogmas yet never emerging from the old shadows. Although he was a child of the liberation and had broken the web that Calvinism had woven about the mind of New England, he did not choose to quit the world from whose bondage he had freed himself. He would examine the old problem in a new light. In rejecting Calvinism as a religion, he retained it as a background for his inquisitive probing. It appealed to his imagination after his reason had rejected its dogmas; it determined his art after it had ceased to command his loyalty. In consequence, all his life Hawthorne dwelt between worlds. Though at times he tried to establish contact with Yankee reality, though he essayed to establish an intellectual *rapport* with his generation, he never quite succeeded, but remained to the last isolated, a frequenter of the twilight.

Only in a narrow and very special sense was Hawthorne a romantic. With the romance of love and adventure he was never concerned; what interested him was the romance of ethics—the distortions of the soul under the tyranny of a diseased imagination. How little he shares in common with other romantics is revealed in his detachment from his native Salem. The place was not lacking in picturesque charm, present and past. During the long years he spent in his Salem study, the city was rising to the zenith of its brisk sea life, with its ships in the China trade, its venturesome fisheries, its echoes of the whaling industry at Nantucket. Materials for romance were lying all about the Salem wharves—such a show of canvas and spars and rigging, such briny smells, such suggestions of far voyages to outlandish places, such strange figures slipping in from the ends of the earth—such romantic promptings in short as would have intoxicated the imagination of Herman Melville, and that Joseph Hergesheimer wove into the rich tapestries of *Java Head*. A romantic could scarcely have found in America a setting better calculated to awaken a sense of brave adventure than in old Salem; yet for three years Hawthorne sat in the Custom House, with such materials all about him, and then turned away to the seventeenth century to write of Hester Prynne. For a man gifted with imagination to fail to lift his eyes to the horizon beyond which the hurrying ships were seeking strange markets, and instead to turn them in upon a shadowy world of half unreal characters; to overlook the motley picturesque in the foreground of the actual, in order to brood over an old adultery and twist it into theological sin, can be explained only on the ground that Hawthorne was concerned with ethical rather than romantic values, that he was interested rather in the problem of evil than in the trappings of romance. Aloofness of time and place served to isolate the problem, stripping away the wrappings of the physical, delocalizing it, transmuting the individual act into the universal. Thus isolated, Hester's sin becomes a symbol of that ancient evil which forever waylays human life and by strange perversions brings havoc to our hopes—the greatest havoc to him whose heart, like Chillingsworth's, is cold, selfish, malignant.

This temperamental aloofness from objective reality was both the strength and the weakness of Hawthorne's art. In choosing to follow the way of the inner life he was true to his Puritan breeding. The perpetual turning-in of the mind upon itself, the long introspective brooding over human motives, came naturally to one who lived in the shadow of a Puritan past. In their anxious concern over sin the Puritans had become in some measure psychologists; how else could the secret impulses of the soul be probed and its dark workings laid bare? Hawthorne was only doing what Jonathan Edwards before him had done in his psychological clinic of the Great Awakening—examining the reactions of sin on conscience and character. From this comes the simplicity of his theme and the compelling unity of his handling. To be sure it is pathological phenomena that he deals with, as the phenomena that Edwards dealt with in his *Narrative of the Surprizing Work of God*, were pathological; and like Edwards, Hawthorne is led into insubstantial and tenuous regions where he breathes with difficulty. The substantial world of Puritan reality that Samuel

Sewall knew, Hawthorne seems scarcely to have been aware of; he created instead his own Puritanism, fantastic and unreal. He was forever dealing with shadows, and he knew that he was dealing with shadows, and this consciousness was a perennial source of doubt and uncertainty that bred self-distrust. In setting himself the task of dramatizing sin rather than sinners, of creating romance out of the problem of evil, he encountered difficulties that oppressed him. The well-springs of his imagination were constantly running dry and he must wait till they filled again slowly. Hence the "development of his art is towards ever greater elaboration of scantier and scantier materials, until the joy of the whole becomes lost at last in the milder pleasures of detail."[1]

From the grave difficulties inherent in his theme came the inveterate habit of sliding into symbolism and allegory—from this and from the narrowness of his emotional life and the restrictions of his sympathies. The cold thin atmosphere of his work, one comes increasingly to feel, was due not alone or chiefly to the severity of his artistic restraint that forbade all rioting of the sensuous imagination; it was due rather to a lack of nourishment, to a poverty of ideas and sensuous imagery. His inveterate skepticism robbed him of much, but his inhibitions robbed him of more. A romantic uninterested in adventure and afraid of sex is likely to become somewhat graveled for matter. Like the Pyncheon fowls, Hawthorne's imagination had suffered from too long inbreeding; it had grown anemic, and every grain of fancy is clucked over and picked at and made much of. Once an idea comes into his head he is loath to let it go, but he must turn it about curiously and examine it from every angle. The striking chapter in *The House of the Seven Gables*, where the death of Judge Pyncheon is played upon so persistently, is only an extreme example of his habitual method. The tongues that wagged over the minister's black veil were no more inquisitive and tireless than Hawthorne's when his imagination is fired by a vivid image. He will not let it go till it is sucked as dry as last year's cider cask. It is the way of one to whom ideas are few and precious. Knowing how little is in the bottle he will linger out the flavor of every drop. Hence his fondness for symbolism, and hence his frequent lapse into allegory when imagination grows dull. Because Hawthorne was an

---

[1] Amy Louise Reed, "Self-Portraiture in the Work of Nathaniel Hawthorne," *Studies in Philology*, Vol. XXIII, No. I.

artist he was saved from the shipwreck that such a method might seem to invite; yet perhaps it is not unreasonable to suggest that he was an artist for the reason that only through the mastery of a refined technic could his scanty stock of ideas make any show at all.

The intellectual poverty that resulted from his long immuring himself in a void is sufficiently revealed in his *American Note-Books*. In the somewhat tedious volume covering the eighteen years between 1835 and 1853—the most vigorous years of the renaissance—there is no suggestion of interest in the creative ideas of the time, in metaphysics or politics or economics or humanitarianism. It is the occasional record of one who lived an unintellectual life, and it makes but a paltry showing when set beside the journals of Emerson for the same years. Few books are referred to; systems of thought lie beyond his ken. Compared with the thinkers and scholars of the time he is only an idler lying in wait for such casual suggestions as he may turn into stories. Almost childish is his delight in marvels. There is something of the spirit of Cotton Mather in his persistent recording of the gruesome and fantastic, in the hope that they will open a quarry for his art. In the year that Emerson wrote *Nature*, Hawthorne set down the following amongst some dozens of similar suggestions: "A snake taken into a man's stomach and nourished there from fifteen to thirty-five years, tormenting him most horribly. A type of envy or some other evil passion." The *Note-Books*, of course, are very inadequate records of his life, and yet that a mind should lie in wait for such grotesqueries, and treasure them, offers food for speculation. After his marriage they are much less frequent and his jottings become more normal—a change which the Freudians, no doubt, would be ready enough to explain.

The one great adventure of Hawthorne's life was the plunge into Brook Farm Utopianism, a plunge that only proved the waters colder and less hospitable than he had hoped. It was a curious adventure for one of his temperament to engage in, and his eventual disillusion might have been foretold. Perhaps it may be explained as reaction from his long isolation. The glowing enthusiasms of the times must often have tempted him to leave his narrow walls, and share the intellectual and emotional stimulus that others professed to discover in the work of making society over. Whatever the explanation the venture turned out to be a failure. His skepticism followed him there and came to later expression in *The Blithedale Romance*, a work as thin and unreal as anything he ever did. It is worse. There is in its pages more than a hint of ill humor that colors his interpretation of the Fourieristic stage of the experiment, and slips out in his portraiture of the major characters. Hollingsworth both fascinates and repels him. A dramatization of the intransigent spirit of reform, his single-minded zeal for righteousness, is subtly fused with an intolerant egotism that destroys Zenobia, cows Priscilla, and wrecks the venture. Perhaps Albert Brisbane may have been in the background of Hawthorne's mind when he drew Hollingsworth, for it was Brisbane who influenced the change he seems to have resented; perhaps Garrison may have served to fill out the picture. Whoever it was, the figure of Hollingsworth is Hawthorne's reply to the summons of the social conscience of the times, done by a critic whose insistent skepticism will not shut its eyes, but discovers under a new masquerade the ancient evil of a cold imperious heart. Seventeen years before he wrote *The Blithedale Romance*, he had jotted down in his *Note-Book* the conception out of which came the later portrait:

A sketch to be given of a modern reformer,—a type of the extreme doctrines on the subject of slaves, cold water, and other such topics. He goes about the streets haranguing most eloquently, and is on the point of making many converts, when his labors are suddenly interrupted by the appearance of the keeper of a mad-house, whence he has escaped. Much may be made of the idea. (*American Note-Books*, pp. 20–21.)

Hawthorne's interpretation of Margaret Fuller is not so easily explained. Perhaps it came out of a subconscious personal spleen. Her rich paganism may well have disturbed a nature so reticent as his, so restrained by certain Puritan inhibitions. In an early sketch he commented on the unfitness of authorship for women, on the ground that "there is a delicacy . . . that perceives, or fancies, a sort of impropriety in the display of woman's natal mind to the gaze of the world, with indications by which its inmost secrets may be searched out" (quoted by Amy Louise Reed, "Self-Portraiture in the Work of Nathaniel Hawthorne"). Margaret's frankness in displaying her natal mind to the gaze of the world, her bold discussion of prohibited subjects like prostitution, could not fail to rub across Hawthorne's deepest prejudices.

She was too vigorous and outspoken, too consciously endowed with sex, too frankly feminist, not to have ruffled his instinctive squeamishness. It was not her radical feminism in the abstract that offended him, if he may be trusted; but certainly in the concrete. A sexless feminism would not greatly disturb a mind tolerantly familiar with the current radicalisms; but the frank avowal of sex touched a sensitive nerve. It offended certain latent Puritanisms in him. He was fascinated by Zenobia and yet afraid of her—or of himself; so his hero falls in love with the anemic and witless Priscilla. How characteristic of a mind long fed on symbols, to turn away from the wealth of reality and prefer a shadow!

After Brook Farm came no further experiments in the unsatisfactory business of a *rapprochement* with his generation. His marriage with Sophia Peabody brought with it the prosaic duties of providing for a family, and he had no leisure to play with social reform. Abolitionism he would have none of, nor perfectionism, nor Jacksonianism—the futility of such things became for him a fixed idea. That he once had the courage to make his plunge he seems to have rejoiced over: "Whatever else I may repent of," Miles Coverdale wrote, "let it be reckoned neither among my sins nor follies that I once had faith and force enough to form generous hopes of the world's destiny,—yes!—and to do what in me lay for their accomplishment." Yet the truer Hawthorne is to be found in the judgments set down in the *Note-Book:* "It is my opinion that a man's soul may be buried and perish under a dung-heap, or in a furrow of the field, just as well as under a pile of money." "Oh, labor is the curse of the world, and nobody can meddle with it without becoming proportionably brutified." The man who wrote that had much to learn about life and society, much that he might have learned from Thoreau. But Hawthorne never grappled with economics as Thoreau did, and he learned no more from him than from Melville, or from Emerson, or from any of the books he read by the wise of other days. Self-sufficient he remained to the last, hard-headed and practical, yet missing many a deeper truth that more receptive minds discover. He was traveling the path that leads to sterility, and the lifelong business of playing Paul Pry to the secrets of the conscience brought him at last to the comment, "Taking no root I soon weary of any soil in which I may be temporarily deposited. The same impatience I sometimes feel, or conceive of, as regards this earthly life." He was the extreme and finest expression of the refined alienation from reality that in the end palsied the creative mind of New England. Having consumed his fancies, what remained to feed on?

CHAPTER III

THE AUTHENTIC BRAHMIN

I

OLIVER WENDELL HOLMES
Beacon Street Wit

SINCE the death of Holmes in 1894, his reputation has shrunk and dwindled with that of his group. With the rise of other literary schools, New England standards have been submitted to a somewhat rude overhauling, and Brahmin ideals are no longer reckoned so authoritative as they were once believed to be, nor the supremacy of Boston genius so indisputable. Concord has risen as Cambridge and Beacon Street have declined, and in the shadow of Emerson and Thoreau, the wit of Back Bay is in danger of being obscured. Unsupported by his physical presence, his writings seem far less vital than they did when the echoes of his clever talk were still sounding through them. Certain intellectual shortcomings are more obvious when his works are brought together in a library edition: in the mass his prose seems far more discursive and his verse thinner and more jingly than when the several bits appeared singly, personally sponsored by the author in whose cleverness everybody delighted. Read with sprightly vivacity to a group of sympathetic listeners at the mellowest hour of the dinner, his occasional verse must have sparkled brightly and have gone off with such a crackle of laughter as to convince the Back Bay that the asthmatic little gentleman with bubbling spirits was a veritable poet, on the same friendly footing with the muse that he was with Beacon Street. So frequently on pleasant occasions did Holmes appear before his classmates and friends copy in hand, so often and so happily did he respond to the invitation to write something, that it would have been ungenerous of Boston—and Boston meant the Back Bay, the Saturday Club and Harvard College—not to have crowned him with a wreath of her own ivy.

For upwards of half a century, throughout the prime and on past the Indian Summer of the New England renaissance, Holmes was Boston's own wit, inexhaustible in clever sayings, bubbling

over with satire and sentiment, the autocrat of her social gatherings, the acknowledged head of her mutual admiration society.
Not since Robert Treat Paine had there been such a master of
Yankee small talk.   If he monopolized the conversation he dealt
generously with his listeners.   The stream was copious and the
waters were never bitter or astringent, but with just enough effervescence to suit the Boston palate.   As a young man the wit
sparkled more brightly; as an old man the humor exuded more
gently.   At twenty-five he described William IV of England with
republican irreverence: "The King blew his nose twice, and wiped
the royal perspiration repeatedly from a face which is probably
the largest uncivilized spot in England"; late in life he commented
on his obvious fondness of praise: "I was always patient with those
who thought well of me, and accepted all their tributes with something more than resignation."   Taste had changed with the times
in Boston.   Wit was yielding place to humor; eighteenth-century
frankness had given way to nineteenth-century refinement; Victorianism was in full and vigorous bloom in the Beacon Street of
1850, and so Holmes became a Yankee Victorian.   The morals
of an impeccable society required no castigation, and he was under
no obligation to satirize vice.   Audacious sallies would have been
reckoned in bad taste.   If the old-fashioned masculine wit of Robert Treat Paine, with its echoes of Charles Churchill, had presumed to intrude itself into the teacup society of Back Bay drawing-rooms, the indignant Doctor would have shown it the door,
and the small talk would have flowed again, decorous and clean
and amiable, far more refined than the wit that had delighted their
fathers.

And yet, though a full-blown Victorian in manners and tastes,
Holmes was something of a child of the eighteenth century at
heart.   The situation in which he found himself might have proved
disconcerting if he had chosen to speculate upon it.   By nature
a thoroughgoing rationalist, he lived in a romantic age.   A gentleman of "parts and learning," with a quick and lively fancy that
blossomed in the pat phrase and neat couplet, he loved wit and
hated dullness with true Augustan zeal.   The great days of Queen
Anne were a perennial inspiration to him.   He clung to the heroic
couplet through all the changes of romantic styles.   He moralized
in rime with the fluency if not the finish of Pope.[1]   He satirized

---

[1] See *A Rhymed Lesson.*

Calvinism with an honest wrath that he might have learned of
Swift. He commented in his table-talk on the manners of the
times with the chatty discursiveness of Addison. Like the earlier
wits, he discovered a deep sympathy for the maturity and ripe
wisdom of the classics. Writing to his friend John O. Sargent, he
remarked:

> I wish I had become as familiar with some classic author as you are
> with Horace. There is nothing like one of those perennial old fellows for
> good old gentlemenly reading; and for wit and wisdom, what is there to
> compare with the writings of Horace? You make me envious,—I vow I
> shall have to get up Juvenal or Catullus, naughty but nice, or somebody
> that nobody else knows. . . . I get so tired of the damp sheets of all
> sorts of *literati* (worse than the "screeching women of Marblehead") and
> clamorous essayists, that I want something always by me, calm, settled
> beyond cavilling criticism,—a cool, clear draught of Falernian that has
> been somewhere near two thousand years in the cellar. (Morse, *Life and
> Letters*, Vol. II, p. 311.)

But unhappily what could he do? He was the most sociable of
persons, and he lived and moved in an atmosphere surcharged with
various and sundry romanticisms. How could he preserve the
spirit of quiet rationalism, or assure himself gentlemanly leisure,
with a host of "isms" clamoring in his ears? He was amongst
them even if he was not of them. He strove to keep himself aloof,
unfuddled by heady idealisms and untroubled by strident reforms,
but he could not shut his study door against the infection. He
could not deny his generation, and inevitably he suffered his
thought to be streaked and pied with the current romanticism.
He gave Lyceum lectures on Wordsworth and Keats and Shelley,
and their influence seeped into his verse. The Longfellow fame
was all about him, and he fell to composing ballads and idyls and
tales, quite as if he did not know better. Romantic garments
fitted him ill, yet he persisted in trying them on. He even got to
like them, and came finally to prefer *The Chambered Nautilus*
above his other poems—a strange perversion of taste for a rationalist. *The One-Hoss Shay* is worth a volume of such pretty moralizing. *Parson Turell's Legacy* and *The Moral Bully* are in better
vein—witty, lucid, critical—than any half-hearted ventures in
romanticism. The eighteenth-century wit does not appear to
advantage patched with Victorian sentiment, and he should have
been rationalist enough to know it.

As a Beacon Street Victorian Holmes was as full of virtuous prejudices as an egg is full of meat; but as a rationalist, with a modest scientific equipment that came from his professional training, he kept the windows of his mind open to the winds of scientific inquiry that were blowing briskly to the concern of orthodox souls. Many a barnacled craft was foundering in those gales, and Holmes watched their going-down with visible satisfaction. He was perhaps the most militant Unitarian amongst Boston laymen. Hatred of Calvinistic dogma was an obsession with him; it dominated his thought and colored much of his work, *Elsie Venner* and his table-talk as frankly as *The One-Hoss Shay*. The criticism to which he subjected the old-school dogmas was always vehement, often vindictive. Long after the battle had been won he kept annoying the retreating enemy. His father, Abiel Holmes, was a rigorous follower of the Edwardean school, who after nearly forty years' service lost his pulpit for refusing to compromise with Unitarian liberalism that had gained the fortress of the near-by College Yard; and the stalwart among his congregation, having to yield the building, the endowment and the communion plate, were forced to establish themselves anew. In this unhappy schism that came about the time Oliver Wendell Holmes was graduating from Harvard in 1829, the latter went with the liberals. He had broken with the Calvinism of his father, and in the reaction he went further than most along the path of Unitarian rationalism—not the path of Channing that led to French romanticism and transcendentalism, but the path of Andrews Norton that led to a harder-headed rationalism. The reasons for this shift are sufficiently evident in his writings. At his father's table he had watched too many "whey-faced" brethren to like the breed—men with "a weedy flux of ill-conditioned hair," whose

> acrid words
> Turn the sweet milk of kindness into curds,
> Or with grim logic prove, beyond debate,
> That all we love is worthiest of hate,
> As the scarred ruffian of the pirate's deck,
> When his long swivel rakes the staggering wreck!
>
> (*The Moral Bully*.)

The words are bitter, but they reveal the length of his reaction from the Calvinism on which he had been over-fed at home and at Phillips Andover Academy; and they suggest also why, next to Theodore Parker, Holmes came to be the best hated of Boston Unitarians amongst the orthodox. On this one subject he was militantly radical, never shirking debate, but whetting the edge of his satire and impaling his victim neatly with his logic. He took sardonic delight in turning Calvinism against itself, in the clever *reductio ad absurdum* of the Edwardean argument. Perhaps this major intellectual interest appears most adequately in his picture of the Master, the autobiographical rationalist whom he introduces into *The Poet of the Breakfast Table*. A dabbler in the law, theology and medicine, a philosophic contemplator of the Order of Things, who refused to permit "the territory of a man's mind" to be "fenced in," who agreed with the Poet in thinking somewhat ill of the specialist who dedicated his life to the study of beetles, preferring to range widely through time and eternity, who followed Darwin and was deep in bacteriology, trying "curious experiments in spontaneous generation"—this was Holmes on the intellectual side, a genial disseminator of the latest scientific speculations, a tolerant amateur of the things of the mind, a friendly dabbler in absolute moralities, who hoped "to do some sound thinking in heaven" if he ever got there, but who was too pleasantly engaged with Beacon Street to settle things now.

In his own special way, then, as a Brahmin of the Brahmins, Holmes was a rebel, a puller-down of worm-eaten structures, a freethinker rejoicing when free thought tossed a cargo of obsolete dogma into Boston Bay, or drew out a linchpin of some respectable social coach. He loved Boston the more because he believed that Boston was the home of free thought and free speech, the capital of American brains, the intellectual rebel of the continent. He did not agree with Emerson's strictures, or Parker's. He would not concede that Boston was the "home of the Hunkers." It was provincial; it had crooked little streets; but

I tell you Boston has opened, and kept open, more turnpikes that lead straight to free thought and free speech and free deeds than any other city of live men or dead men—I don't care how broad their streets are, nor how high their steeples. (*The Professor at the Breakfast Table*, p. 4.)

When he contemplated the future of America, with Boston as its intellectual leader, he was carried on the crest of an exuberant optimism:

A new nursery, Sir, with Lake Superior and Huron and all the rest of 'em for washbasins! A new race, and a whole new world for the new-born human soul to work in! And Boston is the brain of it, and has been any time these hundred years! That's all I claim for Boston—that it is the thinking centre of the continent, and therefore of the planet. (*Ibid.*, p. 104.)

If the mind is free other things will take care of themselves—this pretty much sums up Holmes's social philosophy. Only, he would add, when the mind is used to its freedom, it will create a culture that is well-mannered, that does not run to extravagant agitation, that considers time, place, and outward circumstance in effecting needful changes—the quiet decency of Channing rather than the noisier way of Parker. The Brahmin way, after all, was the better way, Holmes believed; and Channing was a Brahmin:

Parson Channing put a little oil on one linchpin, and slipped it out so softly, the first thing they knew about it was the wheel of that side was down. T'other fellow's at work now; but he makes more noise about it. When the linchpin comes out on his side, there'll be a jerk, I tell you! Some think it will spoil the old cart, and they pretend to say that there are valuable things in it which may get hurt. Hope not—hope not. But this is the great macadamizing place—always cracking up something. (*Ibid.*, p. 19.)

Certainly not on the intellectual side could Holmes be set down as a conservative. He did not relish any such imputation and defended himself with vigor:

If to be a conservative is to let all the drains of thought choke up and keep the soul's windows down—to shut out the sun from the east and the wind from the west—to let the rats run free in the cellar, and the moths feed their fill in the chambers, and the spiders weave their lace before the mirrors, till the soul's typhus is bred out of our neglect, and we begin to snore in its coma or rave in its delirium—I, Sir, am a *bonnet-rouge*, a red-cap of the barricades, my friends, rather than a conservative. (*Ibid.*, p. 18.)

It was this spirit of rationalism that made him—at some risk of unpopularity—an unsparing critic of romantic equalitarianism. Here again is an echo of the older century. Neither the Jacksonian nor the transcendental version of the new gospel found favor in his eyes; both seemed to run counter to the open facts of history. As a realist he discovered justification for John Adams's doctrine of economic determinism: all society, he was convinced, tends to stratify in lines of wealth distribution, in America as well as in Europe, and no dogmas can prevent it. He went further and insisted that the possession of wealth makes possible comfort, ease, leisure, culture; that those lacking wealth are necessarily unfree and their lives in consequence are meaner and narrower. Much of his criticism of Yankee villagers and countrymen—and except Cooper, he was perhaps the most critical commentator on Yankee provincialisms of speech and manners—springs from the conviction that a niggardly economics had created a niggardly society. He desired more wealth to the end of more culture. He was too completely Brahmin to set material well-being as the ultimate goal of the competitive struggle; that seemed to him the object of State Street and of the plutocracy he frankly detested. In *The Poet at the Breakfast Table* he apologizes for calling one of his characters a capitalist, on the ground that "the word seems to be equivalent to highway robbery in the new gospel of Saint Petroleum." Wealth as a means to power he would have none of; but wealth as a means to leisure, and leisure as a means to cultivated living, he was fond of extolling. The machinery of Brahmin life must be well oiled, but the life is more than the machinery. Always he returned to the intellectual as the hallmark of every society that may be accounted excellent, and his instinctive dislike of the middle class was founded on its intellectual sterility. It lived opulently but meanly; its rich dinners wanted the spice of wit, its ostentatious display lacked the salt of manners. It was vulgar at heart, and Holmes hated vulgarity even more than he hated John Calvin's dogmas.

Unfortunately his Brahminism sealed pretty tightly certain windows of his mind that might better have been kept open. A radical in the field of theology where personal concern brought him to serious grappling with the problem, a tolerant rationalist in the realm of the intellect, he remained a cheerfully contented conservative in other fields. He was unconsciously insulated against the currents of social and political thought flowing all about him. Economic inequality he accepted rather too complacently. His daily life ran so easy and comfortable a course as never to prod him into questioning how other lives might be running. By instinct and training he was an aristocrat, and he was never at pains to conceal his preference for the well born and well mannered. He professed a philanthropic sympathy for the cause of the slave, but he shared the Beacon Street dislike of agitation—it was not well bred and it might bring down more things than he cared to have brought down. The most completely class-conscious of the

Boston writers, he deprecated all proletarian appeals. They were not, in his opinion, "wholesome moral entertainment for the dangerous classes. Boys must not touch off their squibs and crackers too near the powder-magazine." The less said about the wrongs of labor, the better—at least publicly. Social strata being determined by economics, the agitator is little better than a firebrand.

You can't keep a dead level long, if you burn everything down flat to make it. Why, bless your soul, if all the cities of the world were reduced to ashes, you'd have a new set of millionaires in a couple of years or so, out of the trade in potash. In the meantime, what is the use of setting the man with the silver watch against the man with the gold watch, and the man without any against them both? . . . Here we are travelling through the desert together like the children of Israel. Some pick up more manna and catch more quails than others, and ought to help their hungry neighbors more than they do; . . . but we don't want the incendiary's pillar of a cloud by day and a pillar of fire by night to lead us in the march to civilization, and we don't want a Moses who will smite the rock, not to bring out water for our thirst, but petroleum to burn us all up with. (*The Poet at the Breakfast Table*, pp. 5–6.)

In his attitude toward the present comfortable arrangement of society, Holmes was no rebel. He was not callous to the evils of society, but he was willing to take a longer time in the march towards civilization than more exigent souls wished; it was a pleasant march on the whole, and why quarrel over the difference in packs? If his attitude was not the indifferentism of the well-to-do, it was near kin to it. He reflected the negative qualities of Unitarianism, rather than the positive, the free mind rather than the tender conscience. His social bias is sufficiently revealed in the tributes of praise he bestowed so generously. Among those whom he delighted to honor, the names of Garrison, Phillips, Parker, Thoreau, Greeley, John Brown, do not appear; instead he offered his praises to Everett, Webster, Bryant, Whittier, Agassiz, Parkman, Wilkie Collins, the Grand Duke Alexis, and a host of lesser celebrities known to the Back Bay. His heroes were respectable souls rather than militant. As a critic his vision seems to have been blurred by certain astigmatisms, and he discovered heroic qualities more readily in the militant dead than in the militant living. He delighted in the Boston of '76, but it is reasonably certain that if he had lived then he would have walked the streets of that older Boston as a genial Tory, and would have suffered the fate of other gentlemen who found it desirable to withdraw with Gage's Redcoats—unless, indeed, his love of the place had held him despite his politics.

In his literary work Holmes was always the talker rather than the writer. The charm of the vivid and racy colloquial marks every page. A clever aphorism or telling pun is the objective of every paragraph, and it explodes with a brilliant shower of sparks. But like every talker his discursiveness is inveterate; he wanders far in pursuit of his point and sometimes returns empty-handed. He was always an amateur; life was too agreeable for him to take the trouble to become an artist. The essay was his most congenial form—his novels are to be taken no more seriously than his occasional verse. *Elsie Venner* wraps up the familiar problem of moral determinism in pleasantly discursive chat of Yankee bumpkinism in contrast with Yankee Brahminism, and he returns his impeccable hero to Beacon Street, after his sojourn in the provinces, to reward him with the Brahmin rewards—a munificent practice, a charming wife, and an exalted social position. What richer reward could be desired by one who had tasted to the full the mellow flavor of that society? Staid, delightful, self-satisfied, righteous little Beacon Street! Last refuge and citadel of the old Brahmin respectability; basking in the afternoon sunshine of its culture, not realizing that its sun is already well past the meridian; in love with its own virtues and unaware that the morrow will see the invasion of the Huns and Vandals of plutocracy, to whose plethoric bank books Brahmin culture must eventually bow— who would not have liked it? It was something after all to have been its favorite wit, its ready oracle, its clever poet, who in praising his fellow Brahmins was well aware that he discreetly praised his own admirable qualities. Kindly, delightful, fortunate Dr. Holmes! chief citizen of the Hub of the Universe! He was born and lived with a silver spoon in his mouth, and if a grudging posterity inclines to rate him and his little world somewhat lower than he rated them, what difference can that make to him? Tolerant himself, we should perhaps emulate his example, and not insist too rudely that he is only a minor figure in American literature.

II

JAMES RUSSELL LOWELL
Cambridge Brahmin

Whatever the critics may eventually come to say about Lowell, he was certainly the ablest and most distinguished of the old Cambridge breed, in the days when the Brahmin caste was disintegrating and Brahmin ideals losing their hold on New England —a man of fine native abilities in whom Harvard culture did its best to strike fire and light and understanding to serve as a beacon to the rest of America. He was not of the Concord line of transcendental individualists, nor of the militant strain of reforming enthusiasts; but of the true Brahmin line of Josiah Quincy and Edward Everett and Oliver Wendell Holmes—men of sound culture who could serve God valiantly in the social station in which He had placed them, without wanting to pull down the old church to build a new. Like Charles Eliot Norton—*clarum et venerabile nomen*—he had no plans of a new building in his pocket, but was content to enlarge and embellish the old. He would serve culture rather than causes. His gifts were Brahmin gifts, his prejudices were Brahmin prejudices; and so in spite of a "certain sprightliness of brain" that tempted him to rebel at the aridity of the scholastic commons on which he fed, and in spite of certain youthful vagaries and incursions into indiscreet places, he remained at bottom a Harvard conservative, content with his birthright, hopeful that his ways were God's ways. This suffices to explain the extraordinary reputation of Lowell in Cambridge circles, and the difficulty with which it made headway elsewhere. Though he traveled much in his library—as Thoreau would say—his prejudices remained narrowly local. To the last he remained extraordinarily parochial.

Yet the culture he served so faithfully never fruited in wisdom. He was never quite certain of himself, of what he really believed. He was fond of standing off and studying himself quizzically, to learn what sort of person he was; yet he was swayed by so many impulses he was never quite sure what sort of legs were under him. He was hopelessly bewildered by his own vast disorder. His mind was as cluttered as a garret, filled with an endless miscellany of odds and ends. Life puzzled him, as it puzzles every serious mind; but he allowed himself to be too easily discouraged by his inveterate unwillingness to think. He never speculated widely or analyzed critically. Ideas, systems of thought, intellectual and social movements, he had no interest in; he was content to remain a bookish amateur in letters, loitering over old volumes for the pleasure of finding apt phrases and verbal curiosities. With all his reading, history remained a blank to him; and science he would have none of. "I hate it," he confessed late in life; "I hate it as a savage hates writing, because I fear it will hurt me somehow." A good many things hurt him in those later years, and it was characteristic of him to say, "I continue to shut my eyes resolutely in certain speculative directions." He defined culture as "intelligent purpose"; yet of such intelligent purpose his intellectual life revealed little. Naturally he did not relish the theological unsettlement that came with the advance of scientific inquiry. Leslie Stephen's rationalism troubled him, and after reading the former's *English Thought in the Eighteenth Century*, he wrote, "I am very much in the state of mind of the Bretons who revolted against the Revolutionary Government and wrote upon their banners, 'Give us back our God!'" (*Letters*, Vol. II, p. 168.) Neither did he relish the economic unsettlement the industrial revolution was bringing to Cambridge and America, but he looked back longingly to the quiet days "before our individuality had been trampled out of us by the Irish mob." Standing between the older America and the new, with the foundations disintegrating under his feet, he confused the disorder in his own mind with the disorder in the external world of society, and desperately sought to cling to his ancient hopes. A pathetic yearning for orderliness in an age that has grown heedless of it was natural enough in a mind that had come to expect little of life; but surely orderliness, like charity, should begin at home.

It was, perhaps, not altogether his fault. His impulses were liberal and his mind generous, but he was never strong enough to overcome the handicap of the Lowell ancestry and training. When he spoke of himself half whimsically as a natural Tory, he was putting his finger on the Brahmin strain. The sanctity of the Lowell blood is a commonplace in New England; but that it was Tory blood is less frequently remarked. His grandfather, John Lowell, to be sure, was visited by certain humanitarian compunctions, and in 1772 convinced himself that at Common Law slavery could not stand, and was eager to put it to the test in Massachusetts. But John Lowell was high in the councils of the Federalist party, and a judge, and it is a safe guess that his radicalism did not go deep. Certainly, the next generation was stalwartly conservative. The three brothers represented the three major professions of law, theology, and business, that constituted the New England hierarchy. His father, Charles Lowell, after traveling abroad, was settled as pastor of the West Church, Boston— Jonathan Mayhew's church—a post he held for fifty-six years. He was a stout Federalist, a good hater of Jefferson,[2] a pleasant, cautious gentleman who refused to be drawn into the bitter Unitarian-Trinitarian controversy of the day—as unlike the militant Mayhew as a conventional soul could well be.[3] His uncle, John Lowell, was a capable lawyer-politician, one of the directing minds of the Federalist machine, earnestly engaged in defending Massachusetts against the wicked Republicans. Another uncle, Francis Cabot Lowell, was an enterprising capitalist, founder of the city of Lowell, whose multiplying spindles, it was hoped, would turn the wives and daughters of Yankee farmers, and the poverty-stricken Irish immigrants, into efficient revenue-producers for State Street securities.

From this pleasant background of Brahmin conservatisms, Lowell went forth into a world given over to momentous changes, contemptuous of all Brahmin standards, to find his way as he might. An original mind would have marked out its own path, as Emerson did; a conventional mind would have gone with the better sort, as Josiah Quincy did; but Lowell was neither Emerson nor Quincy. Sensitive to change, he was rarely self-reliant; generous in sympathies, he was timid in convictions. He was no Come-outer to stand alone against the world, but unconsciously he took color from his environment and was always glad to find a staff to lean on. It was fortunate for his peace of mind that he never realized how frequently he was no more than an echo of other minds; yet the confusions and contradictions that mark off the several periods of his life can be explained in no other way. From Brahminism he drifted to radicalism, and from radicalism back to a modified Brahminism; and these changes resulted from no native intellectual unfolding, but from certain dominant personalities who drew him aside from his natural or-

---

[2] See *Letters*, Vol. I, p. 82.
[3] See Hale, *James Russell Lowell and His Friends*, p. 10.

bit. He quitted college as a pleasant young Tory, who paused in his Commencement Poem to address some pointed remarks at Abner Kneeland—the last man imprisoned in Massachusetts for religious opinion—upon the wickedness of an atheism that denied the faith of Charles Lowell. But the ferment of the times was already working in him, and when he was nineteen he wrote with youthful fervor, "I am fast becoming ultra-democratic. . . . Liberty is now no longer a cant word in the mouths of knaves and fools" (*Letters*, Vol. I, p. 33). Within a year he had met Maria White, whose influence till her death in 1853 was the determining factor in his intellectual life. She was an ardent Abolitionist and reformer, and under her pleasant tutelage Lowell was indoctrinated in the current philosophy of radicalism. He spoke at Abolition meetings, and contributed to the Abolition press. More important, he conceived that he had come upon his true mission in letters. In an ode beginning "In the old days of awe and keen-eyed wonder," he put into verse his new creed, a prose statement of which he elaborated in a letter explaining his *Prometheus* in 1843, a year before his marriage to Miss White:

Although such great names as Goethe, Byron, and Shelley have all handled the subject in modern times, you will find that I have looked at it from a somewhat new point of view. I have made it *radical*, and I believe that no poet in this age can write much that is good unless he give himself up to this tendency. For radicalism has now for the first time taken a distinctive and acknowledged shape of its own. So much of its spirit as poets in former ages have attained (and from their purer organization they could not fail of some) was by instinct rather than by reason. It has never till now been seen to be one of the two great wings that upbear the universe. . . . The proof of poetry is, in my mind, that it reduces to the essence of a single line the vague philosophy which is floating in all men's minds, and so renders it portable and useful and ready to the hand. (*Letters*, Vol. I, p. 73.)

Six years later he asserted confidently, "I am the first poet who has endeavored to express the American Idea, and I shall be popular by and by." Yet within a few months he found the vein nearing exhaustion. In a survey of his course up to 1850, he remarked that he had served love and freedom hitherto, and he now proposed to serve beauty, adding the significant comment, "I find that Reform cannot take up the whole of me, and I am quite sure that eyes were given us to look about us sometimes, and not to be always looking forward. . . . I am tired of controversy" (*ibid.*,

Vol. I, p. 173). Between these several confessions lies the bulk
of Lowell's contribution to the "causes" of the times, and how
adequately he served them is revealed in the successive poems that
came from his pen.[4] Their equal as a whole is not to be found in
the work of other contemporary radicals. The better work is
solidly vigorous, with competent iambs that often rise to the dignity of such lines as "Slowly the Bible of the race is writ." The
eager rhetoric of *The Present Crisis* was the highwater mark of
Abolition argument in verse; but its serviceableness for quotation
cannot make it so good a poem as *Prometheus* with its muscular
blank verse, or as *A Glance behind the Curtain* with its portrait
of Cromwell, strong in his faith, ready for all needful iconoclasms:

> I have no dread of what
> Is called for by the instinct of mankind;
> Nor think I that God's world will fall apart
> Because we tear a parchment more or less."

This is frank transcendental radicalism, yet the truer Lowell of
those days of youthful enthusiasm is found in the *Biglow Papers*,
first written with spontaneous gusto out of his hatred of the imperialism of the Mexican war, and later carefully embedded in
the heavy machinery of the prose setting. The native clutter of
Lowell's mind is there laid bare—the grotesque mixture of homely
satire, moral aphorisms, Yankee linguistics, literary criticism—
an unwieldy mass that he could neither simplify nor reduce to
order. The machinery spoils the propaganda and weighs down
the satire; yet the verse has survived because for once Lowell let
himself go and hit such heads as he had a mind to.

Lowell saw fit to retain most of his radical verse in the definitive
edition of his works, but his radical prose he disowned, and it was
left for pious hands to gather together long after his death. It
was perhaps as well for his reputation that the ambassador at
the Court of St. James's should not be plagued by his youthful
indiscretions. In those prose writings were combustible materials.
He went with the Abolitionists in their brisk assaults on law,
order, and the Constitution. Whatever revolution was stirring
anywhere found him sympathetic. He was strong for the work-

---

[4] The more significant titles are: *Prometheus* and *A Glance behind the Curtain*,
1843; *Columbus* and *The Present Crisis*, 1844; *On the Capture of Fugitive Slaves near
Washington*, 1845; *Biglow Papers*, begun in 1846; *The Pioneer*, 1847; *Bibliolâtres*,
1849; *Anti-Apis*, 1851.

ingman's revolution of 1848 in France; it was social injustice that was to blame for mob violence, and the fetish of *laissez faire* was a sorry enough god to worship.

> The great problem of the over-supply of labor is not to be settled by a decimation of the laboring class, whether by gunpower or starvation. . . . The giant Labor did not merely turn from one side to the other for an easier position. Rather he rose up, "Like blind Orion hungry for the morn." . . . They had learned by bitter experience that it was on the body of old King Log *Laissez-faire* that King Stork perched to devour them. *Let-alone* is good policy after you have once got your perfect system established to let alone. (Quoted in Scudder, *James Russell Lowell*, Vol. I, pp. 205–206.)

In common with the Abolitionists, Lowell appealed to the Declaration of Independence against the Constitution. He took delight in satirizing his Federalist forebears, who, he asserts, beginning to fear the light of freedom, ingeniously constructed a "Sacred Parasol" for the new Goddess of Liberty, "to prevent her from being tanned":

> A stout machine of parchment was accordingly constructed, and, under the respectable name of a Constitution, was interposed wherever there seemed to be danger from the hostile incursions of light. Whenever this is spread, a dim twilight, more perplexing than absolute darkness, reigns everywhere beneath its shadow. . . . This contrivance of ours, though the work of our own hands, has acquired a superstitious potency in our eyes. (*Ibid.*, Vol. I, p. 210.)

No wonder Lowell later disowned such apostasies, for after Maria White's death in 1853 came the dun professorial period of his life, when Harvard laid hands on him and came near to reducing him to its own ways. It revived the old Brahmin instincts that had lain dormant during the years of his Abolitionism, without reviving the old sanctions. Left without a cause, half ashamed of his youthful indiscretions yet ill content to drift, he turned bookman and for twenty-one years wandered with Norton and Longfellow and Child in the Sahara of medieval scholarship. It was not a happy time with him. There is plenty of evidence of his restlessness and dissatisfaction that occasionally prompted the wish to turn wholly scholar and keep his note-books in order; that prodded him to salvage the mass of his accumulation by turning his lecture-notes into literary essays; and that in other moods induced him to turn half savagely upon his dead enthusiasms and find solace in clever satire. His vigorous salvagings were scarcely worth the trouble. He had nothing important to say about Dante or Pope or Wordsworth, and he said it with a good deal of needless verbal exertion. The essay on Thoreau, written in 1865, was a different matter. Here he was brought face to face with a past which it still hurt him to remember; and the ill nature that colors his comment is sufficient testimony to the painfulness of his memories. Certainly he did not understand Thoreau, was incapable of understanding him; yet might not his dislike have been prodded by the consciousness that Thoreau had refused to make terms with Harvard culture as he had done? An intelligent reading of Thoreau must have been an unpleasant experience in Lowell's mood, keenly aware of certain backslidings of his own; and the essay is suggestive for the light it throws on Lowell, not on Thoreau.

To this period belong most of the essays on which rests Lowell's reputation as a critic of letters and politics. Bright as that reputation long was, it is beginning to show tarnish. Subjected to the scrutiny of eyes unblinded by the congenialities of the Cambridge coterie, it appears that Lowell's brilliancy covered over certain grave shortcomings that unfitted him for serious critical judgment.[5] He had no standards other than ethical, only likes and dislikes; no interest in ideas, only a pottering concern for the text; no historical backgrounds, only isolated figures dwelling in a vacuum. He was puzzled over new schools and unfamiliar technic, and was at ease only in praising established reputations and confirming approved judgments. He scoffed at Taine instead of going to school to him, and made merry over Masson's *Life of Milton;* yet he was wholly incapable of dealing with men from whose fruitful minds came ideas that summoned throngs of followers. In almost the last year of his life he spent weeks rereading Rousseau, and was satisfied to dismiss him with the comment, "a monstrous liar, but always the first dupe of his own lie" (*Letters*, Vol. II, p. 424). *Leaves of Grass* he dismissed as affected, not original. He was shocked at Swinburne's "Adamite" heresy —"When a man begins to lust after the Muse instead of loving her, he may be sure that it is never the Muse that he embraces" (*ibid.*, Vol. I, p. 377). He admired Howell's prose style and loved

[5] See C. Hartley Grattan, "Lowell," in *The American Mercury*, Vol. II, pp. 63–69.

:he man, but he could not bring himself to approve his literary and social theories.

During those sterile professorial years he was closing one door after another. Scarcely an important movement of contemporary thought awakened his interest. The hypothesis of evolution he rejected somewhat flabbily. "I think the evolutionists will have to make a fetish of their protoplasm before long," he said in 1879. "Such a mush seems to me a poor substitute for the Rock of Ages —by which I understand a certain set of higher instincts which mankind have found solid under their feet in all weathers" (*ibid.*, Vol. II, p. 245). And as late as 1886 he wrote, "I am a conservative (warranted to wash) and keep on the safe side—with God as against evolution." Naturally so provocative a doctrine as economic determinism never showed its face in his study; Karl Marx was not one of his intellectual companions. Even the home-bred knight-errant, Henry George, did not greatly interest him. "Why, who in the world buys such a book as that," he exclaimed of *Progress and Poverty;* and learning that a friend had subscribed for a thousand copies, he remarked, "He *must* be getting eccentric." [6]

The political principles that he discovered in the smoke of his professor's pipe were equally naïve. He took himself seriously as a guide and mentor in matters political. He was fond of talking about the "noble science of politics"; yet he never took the trouble to ground himself in the elements of the subject. He had scarcely read the primer of political theory. Burke was probably the only political writer who ever made any impression on his mind. Of American constitutional history he was as ignorant as a politician, and when in Civil War days he began to scratch the field of politics, he only uncovered certain old Federalist prejudices that lay hidden under his later accumulations. The extreme parochialism of the Brahmin mind is revealed in Lowell's incapacity to understand the South. The comment on Sibley's *Harvard Graduates*—"I do not know when the provincialism of New England has been thrust upon me with so ineradicable a barb"—should be turned upon Lowell's dogmatic essays in American politics. He had not the slightest comprehension of Calhoun's doctrine of majorities; yet he dismissed it contemptuously, after attribut-

[6] Five years later he was more sympathetic, but hopelessly confused. See *Democracy*, Vol. VI, p. 35.

ing it to one of Calhoun's followers.[7] He speaks of the "weak and wicked element" of states rights—which he supposes the South owed to "the unhappy ingenuity of Mr. Jefferson"—as an unhistorical repudiation of the principle of coercive sovereignty established by the fathers, quite overlooking the Hartford Convention. His treatment of Jefferson Davis and Andrew Johnson is marked by the dogmatisms of one who is defending God's will against the devil's sophistries. He will have no other interpretation of history than an ethical interpretation, in which good and evil are eternally at combat; and he closes his volume of political essays with a comment that embodies for him the sum of all political wisdom:

> We have only to be unswervingly faithful to what is the true America of our hope and belief, and whatever is American will rise from one end of the country to the other instinctively to our side, with more than ample means of present succour and of final triumph. It is only by being loyal and helpful to Truth that men learn at last how loyal and helpful she can be to them. (*Ibid.*, Vol. V, p. 326.)

Into the stagnant atmosphere of the Elmwood study came on a happy day in the middle sixties the vibrant personality of Edwin Lawrence Godkin, and under the stimulus of his crisp thinking there began for Lowell what may perhaps be reckoned an intellectual renaissance. Godkin was a moderate English liberal, a man of complete self-assurance, whose tart comment on politics and economics was pointed by a conviction of the finality of his own conclusions. Under such teaching Lowell made rapid progress in the new school of criticism fathered by *The Nation*. The delight with which he read Godkin's comment and the eager faith with which he greeted his ideas suggest that his own ethical interpretation of politics was giving way under the strain of post-war experience. From Godkin he got some casual instruction in *laissez faire*, and certain of its teachings snuggled down comfortably in his mind beside the principles of coercive sovereignty and a centralizing state, without awakening any suspicion of their incompatibility of temperament. He never went over wholly to *laissez faire*; he was too strongly Brahmin Federalist for that; but his leanings often carried him into the English camp. It was a tonic to his native conservatism that was troubled about the new theories of collectivism, and

[7] See "The Rebellion," in *Prose Works*, Vol. V, p. 134.

it awakened strong doubts about the experiment in democracy. The reaction against the radicalism of his Abolition days became sharp and final. "We have got to work back from a democracy to our original institution as a republic again," he wrote Leslie Stephen in 1879 (*Letters*, Vol. II, p. 161); and in 1888 he asserted that the republic would endure only "so long as the ideas of the men who founded it continue dominant" (*The Independent in Politics*, Vol. VI, p. 207). He warned Thomas Hughes against the extension of suffrage in England,[8] and he was more and more inclined to think that democracy meant a slough of mediocrity underlain with the mud of corruption—that it might prove to be "a Kakistocracy rather, for the benefit of knaves at the cost of fools" (*Letters*, Vol. II, p. 159).

From the vigorous movements of protest of the seventies and eighties, the agrarian uprising of the Middle Border and the proletarian organization in the industrial centers, he drew added confirmation of his fears. In his attitude towards both he was little more than an echo of Godkin, who was laying about him briskly, hitting both farmer and workingman with fine impartiality. He shared the latter's contempt for all agrarian programs, without quite understanding them. He knew little of America. The continent was scarcely more than a hinterland to Cambridge, a hinterland that he explored with some bewilderment on a trip that carried him as far as Cincinnati. Equally ignorant of economics and of the Middle Border, he had no basis for any opinion; a juster man would have put the agrarian question aside as beyond his competency; at least he would have been careful to clear his mind of prejudice. But Lowell was as much a victim of capitalistic prejudice as Thomas Bailey Aldrich and other Boston pseudo-intellectuals. The old Brahminism was close to the surface in those later years, and a scratch would reveal it. In the matter of the "Haymarket Riot" he wrote Howells that "he thought those Chicago ruffians well hanged"—a comment that recalls the Abner Kneeland episode of fifty years before. Physically Lowell was in close proximity to the labor problem, but intellectually he was worlds removed. He looked upon the labor unions with heavy misgivings. He frankly feared the power of the proletariat and was bitter in denunciation of social legislation. In 1869 he wrote Godkin, "Pray give Henry Wilson a broadside for dipping his

[8] See *Letters*, Vol. II, p. 175.

flag to that piratical craft of the eight-hour men. . . . I have a thorough contempt for a man who pretends to believe that eight is equal to ten" (*Letters*, Vol. II, p. 31). And somewhat later he wrote Norton:

> I sometimes feel a little blue over the outlook here, with our penny-paper universal education and our workingmen's parties, with their tremendous lever of suffrage, decrying brains. . . . But the more I learn, the more am I impressed with the wonderful system of checks and balances which history reveals (our Constitution is a baby-house to it!) and the more my confidence in the general commonsense and honest intention of mankind increases. . . . I take great comfort in God. I think He is considerably amused with us sometimes, but that He likes us, on the whole, and would not let us get at the match-box so carelessly, as He does, unless He knew that the frame of His Universe was fire-proof. How many times have I not seen the fire-engines of Church and State clanging and lumbering along to put out—a false alarm! And when the heavens are cloudy what a glare can be cast by a burning shanty! (*Ibid.*, Vol. II, p. 51.)

The ways of the Gilded Age were a rude shock to Lowell's ill-grounded idealism. The crude post-war exploitation and the political corruption that marked the buccaneer stage of the rising plutocracy filled him with anxiety. As an honest man he was angered by the common scoundrelism of the politicians and the press and troubled at the apathy of the public, but his dislike for economics did him a grave disservice. In seeking out the guilty he went wide of the mark. To trace the source of the virus that was poisoning the public life to an exploiting economics, would have brought him close home. He chose to think it was spread rather by western agrarians and city ringsters, than by respectable New Englanders; yet after passing through the *Crédit Mobilier* scandal he was visited by unpleasant suspicions. "I suspect," he wrote after his return from the Cincinnati Convention in 1876, "that few of our Boston men who have had to do with Western railways have been more scrupulous [than the western Grangers.] I rather think they set the example of tempting legislators with the hope of questionable gains" (*Letters*, Vol. II, p. 170). With the open facts of a Congressional investigation before him, Lowell got no deeper than that. Yet his indignation must find outlet and he contributed two poems to *The Nation*—"The World's Fair, 1876," and "Tempora Mutantur"—in one of which he wrote:

Show 'em your Civil Service, and explain
How all men's loss is everybody's gain; . . .
Show your short cut to cure financial ills
By making paper-collars current bills;
Show your new bleaching-process, cheap and brief,
To wit: a jury chosen by the thief;
Show your State legislatures; show your Rings;
And challenge Europe to produce such things
As high officials sitting half in sight
To share the plunder and to fix things right;
If that don't fetch her, why, you only need
Your latest style in Martyrs—Tweed:
She'll find it hard to hide her spiteful tears
At such advance in one poor hundred years.

(*Letters*, Vol. II, p. 155.)

This is Godkin translated into the Lowell vernacular, and what issued from his indignation was Godkin also—an apostolic ardor for civil service reform. He had learned at least, that democracy had not yet been achieved in America; that, indeed, such spontaneous liberalism as had been bred by free land was in danger of being destroyed by evils that issued from the loins of this same heedless frontier order.[9] In 1876 he wrote, "Let us all work together (and the task will need us all) to make Democracy possible. It certainly is no invention to go of itself any more than the perpetual motion" (*Letters*, Vol. II, p. 159). Yet in spite of his zeal, one may be permitted to doubt that Lowell really desired any other than a Brahmin democracy. In those later years his conception of an ideal society was unconsciously colored by memories of Cambridge fifty years before—a simple, patriarchal world, amenable to the rule of the better sort. In such a world democracy seemed possible; but in the rising proletarian-plutocratic order, what reasonable hope was there?

From his growing perplexities Lowell found a happy relief in his mission abroad. The experience was a godsend to a mind that was growing torpid. In 1869 he had written, "I fancy if I were suddenly snatched away to London, my brain would prickle all over, as a foot that has been asleep when the blood starts in it again. Books are good dry forage; we can keep alive on them; but, after all, men are the only fresh pasture" (*ibid.*, Vol. II, p. 24). London, in this mellow autumn of his life, ripened Lowell. He slipped into the congenial environment as easily as Irving had

[9] See *The Independent in Politics*, Vol. VI, pp. 204–209.

done a generation before, and found English society as delightful. He loved England with unaffected heartiness, and under the stimulating experience he expanded into a kindly English Liberal. The extreme Liberals—men like Mill and Arnold and John Morley—he found less sympathetic; and radical thinkers like William Morris he seems not to have known of. But English Liberalism of the Gladstone type was own cousin to Cambridge Brahminism; it united dignity and conscience; it seemed to him the ideal type of government—the rule of God-fearing gentlemen who strove to be faithful to their trusteeship, and who ruled because they were best fitted to rule. Into such a world no other American of the times could have entered more appreciatively than Lowell. If congeniality to the host be a prime requisite in an ambassador, President Hayes made no mistake in sending him to the Court of St. James's. He was a distinguished representative of Brahmin culture; but whether he was a representative of the solid realities of America is not so certain.

CONCLUSION

To the ebullient romanticisms with which the foregoing pages have dealt, the Civil War brought diverse fortunes; and from the titanic conflict emerged an America rid of one of the feculent sources of domestic schism. The romantic imperialisms of the slave economy were gone forever. So much at least was cleared from the path of its destiny, and the field of potential conflict was narrowed to the rival imperialisms of eastern capitalism and western agrarianism. Both had been vastly strengthened by the war. In the eastern centers was a greatly stimulated industrialism, fed from the reservoirs of liquid capital gathered in the process of financing the northern armies, ready to turn to transcontinental railway-building, large-scale manufacture, and a gigantic exploitation of the raw materials of mine and forest and field. Along the Middle Border the old romance of the settlement came to new life as the flood of homesteaders, augmented by disbanded soldiers, poured over the prairie spaces beyond the Mississippi, to repeat there the story of commonwealth building. East and West would eventually clash, for their diverse economic needs were driving towards a collision; but that would not come for a generation till the conflict of interests was thrust into sharper relief.

In the meantime many familiar things were becoming anachronisms over night, though they might linger on for years. As the romantic revolution began with the laying aside of the small-clothes and tie-wig of eighteenth-century aristocratic conservatism, so the new age began with the putting away of the outworn dress of eighteenth-century romantic liberalism. In the hurrying new days there was no time or place for abstract theories of natural rights, for equalitarian democracy, for local home rule—these relics of the past were thrust aside in the scramble for wealth and power. The old philosophies were swept out on the rubbish heap—Jefferson and Lincoln with Calhoun and Stephens—and Hamilton and Marshall came to their own again. The lost cause carried down to defeat much more than slavery, it carried down the old ideal of decentralized democracies, of individual liberty; and with the overthrow of the traditional principles in their last refuge, the nation hurried forward along the path of an unquestioning and uncritical consolidation, that was to throw the coercive powers of a centralizing state into the hands of the new industrialism. Here was a revolution that was to engulf the older romantic America, its dignified literary ideals as well as its democratic political theory. In the world of Jay Cooke and Commodore Vanderbilt, the transcendental dream was as hopelessly a lost cause as the plantation dream; it was in even worse plight, for it left no tragic memories to weave a new romance about the fallen hopes. Emerson in Concord was as much out of date as Lowell in Cambridge, or Gilmore Simms in Charleston. A new age had come and other dreams—the age and the dreams of a middle-class sovereignty, that was busily surveying the fields of its future conquests. From the crude and vast romanticisms of that vigorous sovereignty emerged eventually a spirit of realistic criticism, seeking to evaluate the worth of this new America, and discover if possible other philosophies to take the place of those which had gone down in the fierce battles of the Civil War. What form this critical spirit assumed, and what replies it returned to the strident challenge of the time, are questions not to be answered here.

BIBLIOGRAPHY

Only the more important titles dealt with in the present study are listed hereunder, together with selected biographical and critical material. The invaluable bibliographies in the *Cambridge History of American Literature*, 4 vols., New York, 1917–22, cover most of the writers considered, and the reader is referred to them.

BOOK I: PART I

Information will be found in the *Library of Southern Literature* by E. A. Alderman and others (16 vols., New Orleans, 1908–13) and in Montrose J. Moses, *Literature of the South* (New York, 1910). See also Carl Van Doren, *The American Novel* (New York, 1921).

I. THE OLD DOMINION. See Thomas J. Wertenbaker, *Patrician and Plebeian in Virginia* (Charlottesville, Va., 1910).

II. For the economics of Jeffersonianism, see Charles A. Beard, *The Economic Origins of Jeffersonian Democracy* (New York, 1915; Chapter XII). Also Charles Gide and Charles Rist, *A History of Economic Doctrines* (translated by W. Smart and R. Richards, Boston).

JOHN TAYLOR: His works are out of print. Important titles are: *An Inquiry into the Principles and Policy of the United States* (Fredericksburg, Va., 1814). *New Views of the Constitution of the United States* (Washington, 1823). *Correspondence* (edited by W. E. Dodd, Richmond, 1908).

See "John Taylor, Prophet of Secession" (by William E. Dodd, in *Branch Historical Papers*, II, Richmond, 1908). See also Beard, *Economic Origins of Jeffersonian Democracy*.

III. JOHN MARSHALL: Sufficient materials will be found in Albert J. Beveridge, *Life of John Marshall* (4 vols., New York, 1916–19).

IV. For the plantation tradition, see Francis Pendleton Gaines, *The Southern Plantation* (New York, 1924).

WILLIAM WIRT: His works are out of print. *Letters of a British Spy* (Richmond, 1803). *The Old Bachelor* (2 vols., Richmond, 1810). *Life and Character of Patrick Henry* (Philadelphia, 1817; also several later editions).

See John P. Kennedy, *Memoirs . . . of William Wirt* (Philadelphia, 1849).

NATHANIEL BEVERLEY TUCKER: His works are out of print. *George Balcombe; a Novel* (2 vols., New York, 1836).—*The Partisan Leader; a Tale of the Future*, by Edward William Sidney (printed for the publishers, by J. Caxton, 1856 [*i. e.*, Washington, printed by Duff Green, 1836], 2 vols.); reissued as *A Key to the Disunion Conspiracy: The Partisan Leader* (2 vols. in one, New York, 1861); edition issued at Richmond, 1862.

Some information about Tucker will be found in W. P. Trent, *William Gilmore Simms* (Boston and New York, 1892).

V. WILLIAM ALEXANDER CARUTHERS: *The Kentuckian in New York. Or, the Adventures of Three Southerns. By a Virginian* (2 vols., New York,

1834).—*The Cavaliers of Virginia, or the Recluse of Jamestown. An Historical Romance of the Old Dominion* (2 vols., New York, 1834–1835).—*The Knights of the Horse-Shoe; a Traditionary Tale of the Cocked Hat Gentry in the Old Dominion* (Wetumpka, Ala., 1845; New York, 1882, 1909).

JOHN P. KENNEDY: *Works* (3 vols., New York, 1854; 9 vols., New York, 1871, with life by H. T. Tuckerman, Vol. X). *Swallow Barn, or a Sojourn in the Old Dominion* (2 vols., Philadelphia, 1832; several later editions). *Horse-Shoe Robinson; a Tale of the Tory Ascendency* (2 vols., Philadelphia, 1835; numerous later editions, the latest in 1906). *Rob of the Bowl; a Legend of St. Inigoe's* (2 vols., Philadelphia, 1838; later editions). *Quodlibet: Containing Some Annals Thereof* ... (Philadelphia, 1840; 1860).

EDGAR ALLAN POE: The bibliography is extensive. See the *Cambridge History of American Literature.*

BOOK I: PART II

II. JOHN C. CALHOUN: *Works* (6 vols., Columbia, S. C., 1851; New York, 1853–55). *Correspondence,* edited by J. F. Jameson (American Historical Association, *Annual Report,* 1899, Vol. II).

Biographies: W. E. Dodd, in *Statesmen of the Old South* (New York, 1911). H. von Holst, *John C. Calhoun* (*American Statesmen Series,* Boston, 1882, 1899). W. M. Meigs, *Life of John Caldwell Calhoun* (2 vols., New York, 1917). G. M. Pinckney, *Life of John C. Calhoun* (Charleston, 1903). W. P. Trent, *Southern Statesmen of the Old Régime* (New York, 1897).

ALEXANDER H. STEPHENS: *Constitutional View of the War between the States* (2 vols., Philadelphia, 1868).

See L. B. Pendleton, *Alexander H. Stephens* (Philadelphia, 1908).

FRANCIS LIEBER: *The Stranger in America* (2 vols. in one, London, 1834). *Political Ethics* (Philadelphia, 1838; edited by Theodore D. Woolsey, Philadelphia, 1890; with introduction by Nicholas Murray Butler, Philadelphia, 1911). *Essays on Property and Labor* (New York, 1841). *Civil Liberty and Self-Government* (2 vols., Philadelphia, 1853; London, 1859; edited by Theodore D. Woolsey, Philadelphia, 1891). *Miscellaneous Writings* (2 vols., Philadelphia, 1881; edited by Daniel C. Gilman, Philadelphia, 1916).

See L. R. Harley, *Francis Lieber: His Life and Political Philosophy* (New York, 1899).

III. For the southern position, see Jeannette Reid Tandy, "Pro-Slavery Propaganda in American Fiction in the Fifties" (in *South Atlantic Quarterly,* January March, 1922). Francis Pendleton Gaines, *The Southern Plantation* (New York, 1924; Chapter III).

WILLIAM J. GRAYSON: *The Hireling and the Slave* (Charleston, 1856).

IV. WILLIAM CRAFTS: *A Selection in Prose and Poetry, from the Miscellaneous Writings of the Late William Crafts. With Memoir by Samuel Gilman* (Charleston, 1828).

HUGH SWINTON LEGARÉ: *Writings* (2 vols., Charleston, 1846; with memoir).

WILLIAM GILMORE SIMMS: His works have never been collected and most of them are out of print. *Border Romances* (17 vols., New York, 1859, 1866, 1879; 10 vols., New York, 1882; 15 vols., Chicago, 1885; 17 vols., Chicago, 1888; 17 vols., Atlanta, 1901 [?]).

See W. P. Trent, *William Gilmore Simms* (New York, 1892)—an excellent study. Also see J. Erskine, *Leading American Novelists* (New York, 1910).

BOOK I: PART III

Excellent bibliographical material for western literature will be found in Ralph Leslie Rusk, *The Literature of the Middle Western Frontier* (2 vols., New York, 1925). See also W. H. Venable, *The Beginnings of Literary Culture in the Ohio Valley* (Cincinnati, 1891).

II. Interesting material will be found in Claude G. Bowers, *Party Battles of the Jackson Period* (Boston, 1922).

III. TIMOTHY FLINT: His works are out of print and rare. *Recollections of the Last Ten Years* (Boston, 1826). *Francis Berrian, or the Mexican Patriot* (Boston, 1826; Philadelphia and London, 1834). *The Life and Adventures of Arthur Clenning* (Philadelphia, 1828). *George Mason, the Young Backwoodsman; or, "Don't Give up the Ship"* (Boston, 1829; with changed title, London, 1833). *The Shoshonee Valley; a Romance* (Cincinnati, 1830).
See John Ervin Kirkpatrick, *Timothy Flint, Pioneer, Missionary, Author, Editor* (Cleveland, 1911)—an excellent study with bibliography.

JAMES HALL: *Works* (4 vols., New York, 1853–56). *Legends of the West* (Philadelphia, 1832, 1833; five later editions).—*The Soldier's Bride; and Other Tales* (Philadelphia, 1833).—*The Harpe's Head; a Legend of Kentucky* (Philadelphia, 1833); as *Kentucky. A Tale* (London, 1834, 2 vols.).—*Tales of the Border* (Philadelphia, 1835). *The Wilderness and the War Path* (New York, 1846; New York and London, 1849).
See J. L. Davis, "Judge James Hall, a Literary Pioneer of the Middle West" (in *Ohio Archæological and Historical Society Publications*, October, 1909).

AUGUSTUS LONGSTREET: *Georgia Scenes* (Atlanta, Ga., 1835; New York, 1840; several later editions).
See John Donald Wade, *Augustus Longstreet, a Study of the Development of Culture in the South* (New York, 1924), an excellent study with bibliographical material.

DAVY CROCKETT: Five titles are grouped under the name of Crockett: *Sketches and Eccentricities of Col. David Crockett, of West Tennessee* (1833). *A Narrative of the Life of David Crockett, of the State of Tennessee* (Philadelphia, 1834; seven editions in one year). *Life of Martin Van Buren* (1835). *An Account of Col. Crockett's Tour to the North and Down East* (1835). *Col. Crockett's Exploits and Adventures in Texas* (1836). The *Narrative* is reprinted with an introduction by Hamlin Garland, in *The Modern Student's Library*, under the title, *The Autobiography of David Crockett* (New York, 1923).
There is no life of Crockett; such so-called works are uncritical jumbles of fact and fiction. Some information will be found in John Donald Wade, "The Authorship of David Crockett's Autobiography" (*Georgia Historical Quarterly*, September, 1922); S. H. Stout, "David Crockett" (*American Historical Magazine*, Vol. VII, No. I, Jan., 1902)—uncritical; Chester T. Crowell, "Davy Crockett" (*American Mercury*, Vol. IV, No. 13).

BOOK II

For Philadelphia, see Ellis Paxson Oberholtzer, *The Literary History of Phila-delphia* (Philadelphia, 1906). Also H. M. Ellis, "Joseph Dennie and His Cir-cle" (*University of Texas Bulletin*). For the politics of New York, see Dixon Ryan Fox, *The Decline of Aristocracy in the Politics of New York* (New York, 1918).

I.   CHARLES BROCKDEN BROWN: *The Novels of Charles Brockden Brown. . . with a Memoir* (Boston, 1827; Philadelphia, 1857, 1887). *Wieland; or the Transformation* (New York, 1798; best recent edition in *Ameri-can Authors Series*, New York, 1926). *Arthur Mervyn; or, Memoirs of the Year 1793* (Philadelphia, 1799; Second Part, New York, 1800; numerous later editions).

No adequate life has been written. The best is by William Dunlap, *The Life of Charles Brockden Brown* (2 vols., Philadelphia, 1815). See John Erskine, *Leading American Novelists* (New York, 1910), and Annie R. Marble, in *Heralds of American Literature* (Chicago and London, 1907).

ROBERT MONTGOMERY BIRD: For a list of his plays, see A. H. Quinn, *A History of the American Theatre* (New York, 1923). *Calavar; or, the Knight of the Conquest: a Romance of Mexico* (2 vols., Philadelphia, 1834; about ten later editions).—*The Hawks of Hawks-Hollow. A Tradition of Pennsylvania* (2 vols., Philadelphia, 1835; two London editions).—*The Infidel; or, The Fall of Mexico* (2 vols., Philadelphia, 1835; London, 1835).—*Nick of the Woods, or, the Jib-benainosay. A Tale of Kentucky* (2 vols., Philadelphia, 1837; upward of twenty later editions).

For his life, see Clement Foust, *Life and Dramatic Works of Robert Montgomery Bird* (1919).

II. JAMES KENT: *Commentaries on American Law* (4 vols., New York, 1826-1830; many later editions).

For his life, see William Kent, *Memoirs and Letters of James Kent* (Bos-ton, 1898).

FITZ-GREENE HALLECK: *Poetical Works* (New York and Philadelphia; eight editions between 1847 and 1859). *Poetical Writings with Ex-tracts from those of Joseph Rodman Drake* (edited by J. G. Wilson, New York, 1869, 1885).

For a life, see J. G. Wilson, *The Life and Letters of Fitz-Greene Halleck* (New York, 1869). Also see W. C. Bryant, *Some Notices on the Life and Writings of Fitz-Greene Halleck* (New York, 1869).

III. WASHINGTON IRVING: The standard edition of his works is in forty volumes, New York, 1887.

The standard life is by Pierre M. Irving, *The Life and Letters of Washing-ton Irving* (4 vols., London, 1864; New York, 1879, 1883).

See also *The Letters of Washington Irving to Henry Brevoort* (edited by George S. Hellman, 2 vols., New York, 1915). A recent study is George S. Hellman, *Washington Irving, Esq.* (New York, 1925).

JAMES KIRKE PAULDING: *Works* (15 vols., New York, 1834-1839; 4 vols., 1867-1868).—*The Diverting History of John Bull and Brother Jonathan* (New York, 1812).—*Letters from the South* (2 vols., New York, 1817).—*The Backwoodsman. A Poem* (Philadelphia, 1818).—*Salmagundi, Second Series* (2 vols., New York, 1820).—*Koningsmarke, the Long Finne, A Story of the New World* (New York, 1823; 2 vols.,

New York, 1834; three London editions, and a German).—*Westward Ho! A Tale* (2 vols., New York, 1832, 1845; three London editions, a French and a German).—*The Dutchman's Fireside. A Tale* (2 vols., New York, 1831; latest edition, 1900).—*The Puritan and his Daughter* (New York, 1849, 1850; also London, 1849, two editions, and one German).

No adequate life has been written, but see W. I. Paulding, *Literary Life of James K. Paulding* (New York, 1867).

IV. JAMES FENIMORE COOPER: The editions of Cooper's novels are numerous; as good as any is the one in thirty-two volumes (New York, 1895, 1896–97). Much of his controversial work and critical articles have not been reprinted. See *Notions of the Americans; Picked up by a Travelling Bachelor* (2 vols., Philadelphia, 1829). *A Letter to His Countrymen* (New York, 1834). *The American Democrat; or Hints on the Social and Civic Relations of the United States* (Cooperstown, 1838). *The History of the Navy* (2 vols., Philadelphia, 1839). Also his eight volumes of European travels.

No satisfactory life has been written. The best is by T. R. Lounsbury, *James Fenimore Cooper* (New York, 1883). See also *Correspondence of James Fenimore-Cooper* (edited by his grandson, James Fenimore Cooper, 2 vols., New Haven, 1922). W. C. Brownell, in *American Prose Masters* (New York, 1909). Carl Van Doren, in *The American Novel* (New York, 1921).

V. WILLIAM CULLEN BRYANT: The standard edition is edited by Parke Godwin (6 vols., New York, 1883–1889: 1–2, *Biography*, 1883; 3–4, *Poetical Works*, 1883, 1901; 5–6, *Prose Writings*, 1884–1889). Much information on his work in journalism will be found in Allan Nevins, *A Century of Journalism* (New York, 1921).

HORACE GREELEY: His works have not been collected. See *Hints towards Reform* (New York, 1850). *Recollections of a Busy Life* (New York, 1868). *Essays Designed to Elucidate the Science of Political Economy* (Boston, 1870). *The American Conflict* (Hartford and Chicago, 1864–1866).

For his life, see James Parton, *The Life of Horace Greeley* (Boston, 1868). Charles Sotheran, *Horace Greeley* (New York, 1915). See also John R. Commons, "Horace Greeley and the Working-Class Origins of the Republican Party" (*Political Science Quarterly*, Vol. XXIV, pp. 468–488).

HERMAN MELVILLE: The best edition is The Standard (16 vols., London, 1922–23). Also see *Works* (4 vols., edited by A. Stedman, New York, 1892, 1896; Boston, 1900, 1910). Convenient editions of *Typee, Omoo,* and *Moby-Dick* are plentiful.

The indispensable life is Raymond Weaver's *Herman Melville: Mariner and Mystic* (New York, 1921), with bibliography. Also see John Freeman, *Herman Melville (in English Men of Letters Series,* New York, 1926).

BOOK III: PART I

I. For the political backgrounds, see A. E. Morse, *The Federalist Party in Massachusetts to the Year 1800* (Princeton, 1909). W. A. Robinson, *Jeffersonian Democracy in New England* (New Haven, 1916). Samuel Eliot Morison, *Life and Letters of Harrison Gray Otis* (2 vols., Boston, 1913).

FISHER AMES: *Works* (with memoir by J. T. Kirkland, Boston, 1809). *Works, with a Selection from his Speeches and Correspondence* (edited by his son, Seth Ames, 2 vols., Boston, 1854).

ROBERT TREAT PAINE: *Works in Prose and Verse* (with memoir, Boston, 1812).

II. JOSEPH STORY: *Commentaries on the Constitution of the United States* (3 vols., Boston, 1833; numerous later editions).
See W. W. Story, *Life and Letters of Joseph Story* (2 vols., Boston, 1851).

DANIEL WEBSTER: The best edition of his works is The National— *The Writings and Speeches of Daniel Webster* (18 vols., Boston, 1903). *Private Correspondence of Daniel Webster* (2 vols., Boston, 1857). *Letters* (edited by C. H. Van Tyne, New York, 1902).
See George Ticknor Curtis, *Life of Daniel Webster* (2 vols., New York and London, 1870). For a critical contemporary estimate see Theodore Parker, *Discourse Occasioned by the Death of Daniel Webster* (Boston, 1853). See also Charles A. Beard, *The Economic Basis of Politics* (New York, 1922).

BOOK III: PART II

I. UNITARIANISM: See George Willis Cooke, *Unitarianism in America: A History of its Origin and Development* (Boston, 1902). Williston Walker, *A History of the Congregational Churches in the United States* (New York, 1894).

WILLIAM ELLERY CHANNING: *Works* (5 vols., Boston, 1841; sixth volume added in 1843; numerous later editions).
An excellent life is J. W. Chadwick, *William Ellery Channing, Minister of Religion* (Boston, 1903). See also William H. Channing, *Memoir of William Ellery Channing* (3 vols., Boston, 1848).

II. PERFECTIONISM: For materials see Garrison, *Life of William Lloyd Garrison* (4 vols., New York, 1885–1889).

BROOK FARM: See Lindsay Swift, *Brook Farm; Its Members, Scholars and Visitors* (New York, 1906; contains bibliography). J. T. Codman, *Brook Farm: Historic and Personal Memoirs* (Boston, 1894). Nathaniel Hawthorne, *Blithedale Romance.*

ABOLITIONISM: Sufficient materials will be found in Garrison, *Life of William Lloyd Garrison* (4 vols., New York, 1885–1889). See also Catherine N. Birney, *Sarah and Angelina Grimké* (Boston, 1885); and *James G. Birney and His Times, by His Son, William Birney* (New York, 1890).

III. WILLIAM LLOYD GARRISON: See Garrison, *Life of William Lloyd Garrison* (4 vols., New York, 1885–1889).

JOHN G. WHITTIER: *The Writings of John Greenleaf Whittier* (Riverside Edition, 7 vols., Boston, 1885–1889).
See G. R. Carpenter, *John Greenleaf Whittier* (in *American Men of Letters Series*).—T. S. Pickard, *Life and Letters of John Greenleaf Whittier* (2 vols., Boston, 1894).—F. H. Underwood, *John Greenleaf Whittier. A Biography* (Boston, 1884).

HARRIET BEECHER STOWE: *Works* (Riverside Edition, 16 vols., Boston, 1896; with life by Mrs. Field, 17 vols., 1898).
See Mrs. J. T. Fields, *The Life of Harriet Beecher Stowe* (Boston, 1897).

BOOK III: PART III

I. TRANSCENDENTALISM: The literature is abundant. See *The Dial* (4 vols., Boston, 1840–1844).—*The Harbinger* (4 vols., New York, 1844–1848).—Harold Clarke Goddard, *Studies in New England Transcendentalism* (New York, 1908).—O. B. Frothingham, *Transcendentalism in New England. A History* (New York, 1876).—See also Sylvester Judd, *Margaret. A Tale of the Real and Ideal* (2 vols., Boston, 1845; revised edition, 1851).

II. RALPH WALDO EMERSON: *Works* (Riverside Edition, edited by James Eliot Cabot, 12 vols., Boston, 1884–1893; London, 1884–1893; Centenary Edition, with biographical introduction and notes by E. W. Emerson, 12 vols., Boston, 1903–04; London, 1904).—*Journals of Ralph Waldo Emerson, with Annotations* (edited by Edward Waldo Emerson and Waldo Emerson Forbes, 10 vols., Boston, 1909–1914).—*Uncollected Writings. Essays, Addresses, Poems, Reviews and Letters by Ralph Waldo Emerson* (New York [1912]).

See George Willis Cooke, *Bibliography of Ralph Waldo Emerson* (Boston, 1908). James Eliot Cabot, *A Memoir of Ralph Waldo Emerson* (2 vols., Boston, 1887). George Willis Cooke, *Ralph Waldo Emerson; His Life, Writings, and Philosophy* (Boston, 1881). Oscar W. Firkins, *Ralph Waldo Emerson* (Boston, 1915). W. C. Brownell, *American Prose Masters* (New York, 1909).

III. HENRY DAVID THOREAU: *Works* (Riverside Edition, 11 vols., Boston, 1894; Manuscript Edition, 20 vols. [Vols. VII–XX contain the Journals], Boston, 1906).

See Francis H. Allen, *A Bibliography of Henry David Thoreau* (Boston and New York, 1908). William E. Channing, *Thoreau, the Poet-Naturalist* (Boston, 1873, 1902). F. B. Sanborn, *Henry D. Thoreau* (in *American Men of Letters Series*, Boston, 1882, 1910); *The Personality of Thoreau* (Boston, 1901); *The Life of Henry David Thoreau* (Boston and New York, 1917). Léon Bazalgette, *Henry Thoreau—Bachelor of Nature* (translated by Van Wyck Brooks, New York, 1924).

IV. THEODORE PARKER: *Collected Works* (edited by F. P. Cobbe, 14 vols., London, 1863–71). *The Critical and Miscellaneous Writings of Theodore Parker* (Boston, 1843). *Speeches, Addresses and Occasional Sermons* (2 vols., Boston, 1876). *The American Scholar* (with notes by George Willis Cooke, Boston, 1907).

An excellent study is J. W. Chadwick, *Theodore Parker, a Biography* (Boston, 1900), containing a bibliography. John Weiss, *Life and Correspondence of Theodore Parker* (2 vols., New York, 1864)—indispensable.

V. MARGARET FULLER: Her works have not been collected. Important titles are: *Woman in the Nineteenth Century* (New York and London, 1845; with additional papers and introduction by Horace Greeley, New York, 1855). *Life Without and Life Within* (Boston, 1860; New York, 1869). *Papers on Literature and Art* (2 vols., New York and London, 1846).

An excellent study is Katharine Anthony, *Margaret Fuller: A Psychological Biography* (New York, 1920). See also R. W. Emerson, W. H. Channing, and J. F. Clarke, *Memoirs of Margaret Fuller Ossoli* (2 vols., Boston, 1852). Thomas Wentworth Higginson, *Margaret Fuller Ossoli* (in *American Men of Letters Series*, Boston, 1884), containing bibliography.

BOOK III: PART IV

I. HENRY W. LONGFELLOW: *The Writings of . . . with Bibliographical
and Critical Notes* (11 vols., Boston, 1886 [Vols. I–VI, *Poetical Works;*
VII–VIII, *Prose Works;* IX–XI, *Dante*]).

See Samuel Longfellow, *Life of Henry Wadsworth Longfellow* (3 vols.,
Boston and New York, 1891). T. W. Higginson, *Henry Wadsworth
Longfellow* (in *American Men of Letters Series*, Boston and New York,
1902).

II. NATHANIEL HAWTHORNE: *Works* (12 vols., Boston, 1871–76; Fireside
Edition, 12 vols., Boston, 1879; Riverside Edition, 12 vols., Boston,
1883; Standard Library Edition, 15 vols., Boston, 1891 [contains
Nathaniel Hawthorne and his Wife, by Julian Hawthorne]; New
Wayside Edition, 13 vols., Boston, 1902).

The best-known life is Julian Hawthorne, *Nathaniel Hawthorne and His
Wife* (2 vols., Boston, 1885). Henry James, *Nathaniel Hawthorne*
(in *English Men of Letters Series*, London, 1879; New York, 1885, 1887).
See also W. B. Brownell, *American Prose Masters* (New York, 1909).
John Erskine, *Great American Novelists* (New York, 1910). Carl Van
Doren, *The American Novel* (New York, 1921); Stuart P. Sherman,
Americans (New York, 1923).

III. OLIVER WENDELL HOLMES: *Works* (Riverside Edition, 13 vols.,
Boston, 1891, additional volume, 1892; Autocrat Edition, 13 vols.,
Boston and New York, 1904).

See George B. Ives, *A Bibliography of Oliver Wendell Holmes* (Boston
and New York, 1907).—John T. Morse, *Life and Letters of Oliver
Wendell Holmes* (2 vols., Boston and New York, 1896).—Lewis W.
Townsend, *Oliver Wendell Holmes. Centenary Biography* (London,
1909).

JAMES RUSSELL LOWELL: *Works* (Riverside Edition, 13 vols., Boston
and New York, 1902 [contains Scudder's *Life*]; Elmwood Edition,
16 vols., Boston, 1904 [four volumes of letters]). *Anti-Slavery Papers*
(2 vols., Boston and New York, 1902). *Letters of James Russell Lowell*
(edited by Charles Eliot Norton, 2 vols., New York, 1893; 3 vols.,
Boston, 1904). *Early Prose Writings of . . .* (2 vols., New York, 1903).

G. W. Cooke, *A Bibliography of James Russell Lowell* (Boston and
New York, 1906). H. E. Scudder, *James Russell Lowell: A Biog-
raphy* (2 vols., Boston, 1901). Ferris Greenslet, *James Russell Lowell:
A Biography* (2 vols., Boston, 1901). Ferris Greenslet, *James Russell
Lowell: His Life and Work* (Boston, 1905). See also C. Hartley
Grattan, "Lowell" (*The American Mercury*, Vol. II, p. 69); Harry
Hayden Clark, *Lowell's Criticism of Romantic Literature* ("Publications
of the Modern Language Association," March, 1926); W. D. Howells,
Literary Friends and Acquaintances (New York, 1902); Henry James,
Essays in London and Elsewhere (New York, 1893); J. J. Reilly,
James Russell Lowell as a Critic (New York, 1915); and John M.
Robertson, *Lowell as a Critic* (*North American Review*, February, 1919).

INDEX

483

THE
BEGINNINGS OF CRITICAL
REALISM IN AMERICA

VERNON LOUIS PARRINGTON

THE sudden death of Professor Vernon Louis Parrington in England, June 16, 1929, cut tragically short his labors on the last volume of *Main Currents in American Thought*. Of this third volume approximately the first half had been completed, which, together with the outline of the work and some scattered essays in sections otherwise undeveloped, constitutes all that the author left. Unfinished it is, yet no completion by another can be justified. That anyone could duplicate his felicity of style, so unobtrusively individual, so sensitively adjusted to the freighted thought, is hardly to be hoped for; and more important, that another scholar could accurately reproduce his interpretation is an assumption not to be warranted. The decision to publish the author's incomplete work is a tribute to his brilliance.

Nevertheless it is possible to know Professor Parrington's chief intentions, particularly when one understands, as his associates did, his principles for organizing materials and his standards of value. Students as well as associates first of all noticed beneath the richness and complexity of his thought a constancy of purpose as clear as the treatment of mass in a Gothic cathedral. Indeed it was through a delight in architecture pursued as a hobby for many years that Parrington expressed this desire for a unity, balanced, harmonious, and properly proportioned.

This architectonic feeling, abundantly illustrated in his writing habits, was carried over not only into his classroom procedure and conversation, but also into his varied interests. Painting as well as architecture had long intrigued him. Though few people knew it, he wrote poetry distinguished for restraint in expression and clarity of form; while in conversation he persistently sought the appropriate phrase, spiced it with wit, salted it with homely realism; for no gentleman of the eighteenth century was more conscious of the charms of good discourse.

Professor Parrington's classroom procedure had a reputation that attracted students not much interested in literature and which appealed to all ranges of intellect. The source of that popularity

was the personality of the teacher, together with his gift for presenting ideas and evoking a response. By means of a Socratic cross-
examination Parrington made the student discover his intellectual
deficiencies; while the class, to its astonishment and delight, found
the quest for truth both elusive and exciting. Surprise and satisfied
expectation kept the easily bored from sinking into apathy, for
there was no telling from day to day just what Professor Parrington
was going to do. He paired every occasion with a fitting response;
yet this flexibility did not degenerate into an aimless drifting, since
he persistently simplified his main objectives and concentrated the
material to be studied, while expressing its meaning through a
significant symbol or a telling phrase. His classes in the eighteenth
century, for example, were given the concept of harmony, balance,
and proportion. They found it in architecture, they saw it in dress,
they heard it in conversation, they watched it work out in the
heroic couplet, they pursued it in Addison, Pope, and Swift; in
short, they analyzed the whole social structure of the age and discovered it everywhere. A germinal idea, Parrington liked to call
it, while he held it before the class like a many-faceted crystal,
slowly turning it around and around so the student could see every
face. As a result no student who had taken the course ever forgot
the significance of this architectonic trilogy.

In writing habits there was a similar all-encompassing purpose.
He habitually began with his thesis—a phrase, a sentence, or a
revealing figure. This was examined and stripped of its implications
as one would peel an onion layer by layer. So imperious was the
habit of this procedure that his ability to write would be blocked
until he had in mind a perfectly crystallized concept expressible at
the maximum in one sentence. An example of this occurred shortly
before he left on his trip to England. He had been working on the
period that Mark Twain had labeled the "Gilded Age," but found
the title inadequate to his idea, and, as a result, his writing did not
get on. Another day some weeks later there was an obvious satisfaction expressed in his bearing and an exceptionally pronounced
twinkle in his eye. "I have found the phrase," he said; "I will
call it The Great Barbecue." Similarly, the three volumes of this
work began in a single paragraph which by progressive unfoldings
he expanded to its present scope.

After having made a provisional outline, with each section con-
densed into a single sentence, he began writing, completing a unit

here or there as circumstance and mood directed. When it was completed the process of readjustment began. Each portion was inspected for its length, which had to be fitted to its relative importance; an emphasis here was shifted to balance an emphasis there; the mood of one part was altered to make it harmonize with the mood of its neighbor. As many as twelve times he rewrote a single section in this complex and delicate effort for harmonious adjustment. Finally, he made from this his finished outline.

Knowing Professor Parrington's methods one can now understand the problem he faced and the solution he found when bent on the task of writing a history of American literature. Although he was by nature partial to the claims of aesthetics, yet it was obvious to him that such an approach was foredoomed to failure. All too few of the American writers would deserve treatment on any aesthetic test, while many who were undeniably significant could not possibly be left out even though inferior artistically. Moreover, one only had to look at the numerous attempts already made to see the failure of the belletristic interpretation. What were these histories of American literature? Sprawling lists of names arranged in a fashion that gave little save conventionalized data and some dubious evaluations. Already there was a widespread demand for a new interpretation growing out of these past failures.

Professor Parrington found the first step to a solution when he remembered the day he opened Taine's *Histoire de la littérature anglaise*. It had come as a new and inspiring discovery to find a method that envisaged the literature of a people as the inevitable outgrowth of their racial peculiarities, environment, and epoch. It is true that the claim set up by Taine, that his method was scientific and could account for every phenomenon, proved to be unfounded; but nevertheless his work was epoch-making; it gave a unity and a significance never before attained, and this was what attracted Parrington. Nothing less unifying than Taine's method was thinkable.

A second source of inspiration came from a close friend and colleague, J. Allen Smith, another pioneer figure, who applied to the abstract theorizings of political science the economic realities that underlie and determine them. The method was so fruitful of results that it quickly spread to a group of American political scientists, from whose findings much of Parrington's significant work received its first flattering confirmation. Under such a stimu-

Ius Parrington was quick to realize the fruitfulness of economic determinism when applied even to literature.

A third idea completed the synthesis. When he envisaged American literature as American thought, the trammel of the belletristic was broken and he was free to reëvaluate American writers, to follow the trail of their work wherever it led; for at last he had found a method true to facts, yet one which would satisfy his insatiable demand for a significant unity, balanced, harmonious, and properly proportioned. The economic forces imprint their mark upon political, social, and religious institutions; literature expresses the result in its thought content.

But a technique, though vitally necessary, is not the end of the story. There still remains, even for the most impartial scholar, the final and, be it admitted, inescapable evaluation. Parrington was too honest with himself to dodge the issue; he made his choice and abided the result. In the foreword to the first volume he made his confession: "The point of view from which I have endeavored to evaluate the materials is liberal rather than conservative, Jeffersonian rather than Federalistic; and very likely in my search I have found what I went forth to find, as others have discovered what they were seeking. Unfortunately the *mens aequa et clara* is the rarest of attributes, and dead partisanships have a disconcerting way of coming to life again in the pages of their historians. That the vigorous passions and prejudices of the time I have dealt with may have found an echo in my judgments is, perhaps, to be expected; whether they have distorted my interpretation and vitiated my analysis is not for me to determine."

Professor Parrington's *Main Currents in American Thought* has, then, for its subject the adventures of American liberalism. To anyone alive to the issue an adventurous story it is, as becomes more apparent when the author's own liberalism is completely understood. Those sections where his sympathies are kindled, where he stamps his seal of enthusiastic admiration, provide the clue which his treatment of Roger Williams, Benjamin Franklin, Tom Paine, Jefferson, Emerson, Thoreau, Channing, and Theodore Parker assuredly verifies. All of his latent enthusiasms burst into bloom until, as in his essay on Roger Williams, nothing less than the cadence and passion of the Song of Solomon would express it. "Running through his writings is a recurrent echo of the Hebrew love-song that Puritan thought suffused with glowing mysticism:

'I am my beloved's and my beloved is mine: he feedeth among the lilies. . . . I will arise now, and go about the city in the streets, and in the broad ways I will seek him whom my soul loveth.' But when he went into the broad ways of Carolinian England, seeking the rose of Sharon and the lily of the valley, he discovered only abominations. The lover was tempted by false kisses; the Golden Image was set up in the high places, and the voice of authority commanded to bow down to it. And so as a Christian mystic Roger Williams became a Separatist, and set his mind upon the new world where the lover might dwell with his bride."[1]

The liberalism of Parrington had this great virtue, which all too many creeds lack: it was built on an obligation first to examine and understand all points of view before exercising the right to condemn them. Although he disliked the personalities and groaned at the dreary pages of men like Cotton Mather, yet he was not satisfied until he got at their marrow. And again there was an abiding sense of the humane in Parrington before which all abstractions, generalizations, and logical systems had to pass in review. He feared above all, as did the sensitive Jefferson, the cancer of power. "Man," he used to say, "has never proved himself worthy of an unrestrained control of his fellows, nor has any special group of men ever been dominant without injustice to others." Combined with this love of freedom was an urbanity and a sense of personal integrity not subject to the interference of outside forces in convention or mob—an integrity which so impressed everyone having contact with the man, that he has been often called an aristocrat. Parrington would not have objected to the label, nor have seen it as contradictory to the principles of liberalism, since in his opinion only liberalism expressing itself in a democratic society provides for the free exercise of personal rights. Elevating oneself by riding on the shoulders of others, a common device of the pseudo-aristocrat, was to him but a vulgar gymnastic performance.

When he described Jefferson "with his aristocratic head set on a plebeian frame"[2] he was unconsciously describing himself, for there was a deep love of the soil in Parrington. One saw it, surprisingly, in his hands. They were thick and sturdy, blunted at the ends as if from too much delving into the black loam of his flower garden, where roses, peonies, and crocuses were cherished companions, and the delight of his leisure hours. He secretly suspected

---

[1] Vol. I, p. 65. [2] *Ibid.*, p. 343.

the apartment dweller as any true farmer would; and though there was a twinkle in his eye when he called New York a Babylon or spoke of its corrupting influence on scholar and artist, yet there was a meaning implied more serious than the jest.

It was Parrington's hope to vindicate this liberalism "stemming," as he said, "from the fruitful loins of the eighteenth century." As he diagnosed it, that era had two creative currents of thought: a hopeful, vigorous liberalism, together with a sturdy realism which did not balk at men's selfishness or deny the economic basis of social forces. Unfortunately the nineteenth-century liberal attended only to hopes and neglected the realism, while the swelling forces of industrialism accepted the economic realities but cynically brutalized them. Failure was the inevitable result; the liberals despair while Babbitt, regnant, infests the country with his blustering agents. In the unfinished section of this last volume it was Parrington's purpose to show this parlous state of twentieth-century America, to discern the hopeful gleam in the darkness, and to uncover the hidden forces working for a more stable and just society. Parrington's point of view then, was that of a staunch and kindly liberalism, the motif in the three volumes, the theme never absent from a page of the whole composition. It is a liberalism not to be found in any program yet formulated by political party or economic sect; it is rather a generous idealism that can envisage a future richer in values, more humane in distribution of favors than any known past. Wise to the ways of man, such a liberalism refuses confinement in the strait-jacket of any set formula, yet escapes the emasculation awaiting mere enthusiasm; for it can separate foes from friends and recognize the point where compromise means surrender.

If my analysis thus far is to any purpose it will suggest what these main objectives that Parrington never completed were to have been. The unfinished Book Two was to chronicle three parties of revolt against the plutocracy born of the Gilded Age. Of these rebellions the first was engendered on the Middle Border, where the farmers, beset by hard times, struck out against the source of their ills. As the agrarians diagnosed the situation, these economic maladjustments were brought on by a currency manipulated for the benefit of creditors, and further enhanced by capitalistic control of the political machine. One of the last of Parrington's completed units deals with the economic phase of the revolt; the next section was to record the farmer's effort to democratize the government. Through pressure of third-party movements the farmers tried to inject such reforms as the initiative and referendum, the recall, the direct primary, and the income tax; until, seduced by Bryan's oratory, they joined with the Democrats in an attack upon the intrenchments of capitalism. As Parrington saw it, these agrarian descendants of Jefferson, lacking the intellectual leadership which the South had contributed in earlier days, at a tactical disadvantage, and already a minority economic group, were fated to lose their last great uprising.

Also out of the valley of the Mississippi came a literature of the Middle Border. Such writers as Edward Eggleston and E. W. Howe had already initiated a realism that revealed the drabness of frontier life and suggested its smoldering discontent, although the pastoral note fathered by the genial and romantic James Whitcomb Riley did not lack its prose children. Notably did Meredith Nicholson, William Allen White, and Booth Tarkington[3] portray the village neighborliness, its wholesomeness, its spirit of democracy, until they cast such a fog of sentiment over the scene as to blur all the realities. But the true spirit of Populism is represented in the impassioned work of Hamlin Garland, whose "admirable realism and passionate democracy" Parrington depicts in a chapter that he completed.

The second chorus of dissent came from the very citadels of plutocracy, for the wage-earners, unable to escape slavery by flight to an unshackled frontier that no longer existed, were brought to bay. The doctrine of class war, which had been ignored since the eighteenth century, was revived by the German socialists and given an added plausibility by the employers' unscrupulous use of injunction, black list, and lockout. T. V. Powderly, who found a solution to the labor problem in syndicalism, organized the Knights of Labor. Although this union had a promising inception, it was soon wrecked, while the craft unionism recommended by Samuel Gompers forged to the front because of its middle-class ideology and spirit of compromise. On the other hand the left wing of the labor cause embraced various brands of socialism. The tragic flare-up of the Haymarket riot, which resulted in a "red" scare and persecution of the humane Governor Altgeld, served Parrington as a dramatic illustration of the obloquy that descended upon the

[3] See Addenda for notes on these men.

leaders of socialism, Daniel De Leon, Eugene V. Debs, and Victor Berger. Needless to say, Parrington had planned a vindication of them born of his desire to see more justice in the world.

There were echoes of this proletarian strife manifested in the world of letters. Certain writers following Edward Bellamy joined the quest for a socialistic Utopia. Parrington had completed his passage on Bellamy, but of the party formed to agitate for principles advanced in *Looking Backward* and of the other writers of Utopian novels, such as Tourgee, he left no treatment. A second set of writers were grouped together by reason of their common concern over the darkening future of American civilization. Edwin Markham, his humanitarian sympathies aroused, penned an indictment of wage exploitation in his "The Man with the Hoe" that caused no little concern in its day and spurred defenders of the existing economic system to offer liberal prizes for an equally convincing reply. The emergence of naturalism, seen in Stephen Crane[4] and Frank Norris,[4] was also a response to the darkening social outlook. Parrington defined naturalism as "a pessimistic realism that sets man in a mechanical world." He traced this pessimistic determinism to the machine industrialism so overwhelming in its power as to impress man with his own impotence, to the centralization of wealth, which causes a caste regimentation of society, and finally to the great city, which reduces the inhabitant to an infinitesimal unit of a vast beehive. Other writers, equally oppressed by this state of affairs, concentrated on the phenomena of the city. It was here that Parrington intended to discuss Henry B. Fuller, Harold Frederic, Robert Grant, and Edith Wharton.[5]

The third party of revolt was a hesitant one—the South, still convalescing from the Civil War and further weakened by divisions in its counsels. Though burdened by parochial creeds, weakened by lack of intellectual leadership, the agrarian South, largely plebeian, joined the Middle Border in its uprising. The middle-class South, represented by Henry W. Grady, proposed a surrender to the Yankee principle of industrial exploitation, while the remnant of the old aristocracy resisted the new and clung to the traditions of the past. Thomas Nelson Page, Joel Chandler Harris, Mary Murfree, and George Washington Cable attended to these romantic traditions of the plantation, the negro, the mountaineer, and

---

[4] See Addenda for lecture notes on these writers.
[5] See Addenda for brief notes on these writers.

the creole; while Sidney Lanier [5] became the poet of southern landscape and sunrise. Far more significant in Parrington's eye was the rebirth of a southern intelligentsia represented in letters by Ellen Glasgow, W. W. Woodward, the debunker, and James Branch Cabell,[6] the ironic romanticist. Professor Parrington, who had been among the first to appreciate Cabell, admired the competence of his style and the effectiveness of his ironic commentary on American civilization.

Book Three was to present the movement of liberalism from 1903 to 1917, and the reaction to it following the war. Parrington called this period of liberalism the "great stock-taking venture." These liberals announced that the democratic hopes of earlier days had not been fulfilled, that the Constitution is not a democratic instrument nor was it intended to be, and that while Americans were professing to create a democracy, they had been creating in fact a plutocracy. They then determined upon a new program based on their discovery of the relations between economics and politics. Such relations made necessary the control of property by the collective will, and to that end they endeavored to squeeze the Hamiltonian state into a Jeffersonian mold.[7]

The muckrakers of 1903 to 1910 attacked the plutocracy where its joints creaked. In effect this group of writers from Henry D. Lloyd to Charles Edward Russell, Gustavus Meyers, and A. M. Simons popularized economics and made the liberals conscious of what was going on behind the closed doors of the directors' meetings. On the other hand, the movement of Progressivism, engaged in the hopeless task of directing the political machinery to democratic ends, was typified by Robert LaFollette, Theodore Roosevelt, and Woodrow Wilson. Only one, LaFollette, remained true to the colors; the other two compromised, then surrendered, and the hopes of liberalism went down in a tragic débâcle.

In the realm of letters this liberalism found expression in three major groups of writers. A set of intellectuals turned critical began to scrutinize the economic, political, and social institutions of America. Of these critics Parrington considered Randolph Bourne and Charles A. Beard [8] the most important. Another set turned

[5] See Addenda for brief notes on these writers.
[6] See Addenda for magazine article on Cabell.
[7] "A Chapter in American Liberalism," which is included in the Addenda, deals with this subject, with the muckraking movement, and with post-war realism.
[8] See Addenda, "A Chapter in American Liberalism."

to fiction, shifting their point of view from liberalism to radicalism, from politics to economics. Winston Churchill [9] had discovered the emptiness of the profit motive with its resultant destruction of beauty, freedom, and creative craftsmanship. Similarly Robert Herrick [9] became a pathologist of the city, investigated its ethics, and then rebelled at the predatory egoism which ruled its life to the destruction of all ethical integrity. At his best Jack London [10] wrote of the revolution, though later selling out to bigger and better royalties; while Upton Sinclair became the revolutionary sleuth spying upon the indecencies of the capitalist system. Perhaps these novelists were too seriously engaged in social criticism and reform propaganda to become great craftsmen, yet they were to Parrington important writers, because they were in touch with deep currents of American thought.

Still a third set of writers turned to a realistic technique appropriate to the times, yet avoided the weakness inherent in direct propaganda. The poets Masters, [11] Sandburg, Frost, and Robinson, Parrington chose for consideration as realists with an art, an underlying criticism of conditions, and a philosophy that set them above the other poets of the time. For the same reasons he had planned a section on Huneker. Theodore Dreiser, [12] because of his massive documentation, his deterministic philosophy, and his sense of the inevitable tragedy inherent in life, Parrington labeled a modern, meaning by this that Dreiser most adequately and most thoroughly represented modern America.

The last section of the book was to be a consideration of the post-war reaction to the liberalism of the preceding period. The economic democracy which liberals had marked for their goal was now attacked by the younger intellectuals. H. L. Mencken turned to farce and burlesque for methods adequate to express his contempt of American democracy. Biologists pointed to the inescapable laws of heredity as a refutation of the liberals' hopes for social improvement; while some psychologists, discovering morons, ruled out all equalitarian Utopias. Parrington could find little sympathy in his heart for a return to the spirit of aristocracy. This narrow, doctrinaire biology, denied by the more careful biologists and

[9] See "The Problem Novel and the Diversion from Naturalism," in the Addenda.
[10] See Addenda for notes on London.
[11] See Addenda, "Ole Rölvaag's *Giants in the Earth* "
[12] See Addenda for lecture notes on Dreiser.

the behaviorists who assert that environment is determining, cannot rule out all environmental changes. As long as the *milieu* is an effective force in molding the organism, room is left for social betterment by social readjustments. A disputed psychology dealing in primitive sex drives, gland secretions, and intelligence scores is no more conclusive on the subject.

The attack on industrialism is nearer to the heart of Parrington's ideals, because it proved to him that liberalism is not by any means dead. Such a comprehensive movement enlisting first-class minds —intellectuals, poets, novelists, dramatists—revealed clearly to him the increasing criticism of a dehumanized economics, and such criticism proceeds from an implicit liberalism.

The attack on the middle class is seen best in Zona Gale,[12] Evelyn Scott, and particularly in Sinclair Lewis,[14] whom Parrington rated the chief of our younger satirists. This satire is a searching criticism of the *bourgeois* ideals and habitat, its tyrannical herd-mind, its povery-stricken materialism. By its nature this satire clearly suggests a set of new ideals which grow out of a free individualism rather than a political or economic socialism. The emphasis is shifted by implication from externalities to things of the spirit. This is more clearly seen in the new philosophies just now arising, which deny the finality of economic law, turn in politics to the ideal of a decentralized state, and in science to new syntheses emphasizing the pragmatic and relative aspects of scientific law.

The latest literary fashions that Parrington intended to consider embody a psychological emphasis seen in the impressionism of biography, in the brutal but frank pacifism of war novels,[13] and most significantly of all in the impressionism and expressionism of Sherwood Anderson.[14] Parrington felt that there were rich potentialities latent in these new methods although the writers of the new school were themselves painfully at sea. In technique as well as in direct statement there was to be seen, though obscurely, a renewed emphasis upon individual integrity, the necessity for creative expression, and the reaffirmation of what some may choose to call spiritual values.

In effect he believed that all is not lost. Through the influence of science we are recovering the neglected realism of the past; we

[13] See Addenda for brief notes.
[14] See Addenda, " Sherwood Anderson: a Psychological Naturalist."

are not only reaffirming it but making its acquaintance more intimately than ever before. Weld that science to enlightened and humane aspirations (Parrington believed that there was nothing in the findings of science that prevented the union) and a revivified liberalism will make the world a fit place to live in. It is by no means an easy program, for it requires knowledge of fact, and ability to carry knowledge into the sphere of effective action. It is made doubly difficult by the untimely death of one of its chief proponents, yet in the young men and women whom he liked to have around him there must be, however obscurely, a feeling and a groping for the way out. They will be guided and inspired by such utterance as Parrington's diagnosis of Sinclair Lewis, where he quarries out a vein of his own enduring liberalism.

"Some lingering faith in our poor human nature he still clings to. In the great American mass that human nature is certainly foolish and unlovely enough. It is too often blown up with flatulence, corroded with lust, on familiar terms with chicanery and lying; it openly delights in hocus pocus and discovers its miracle-workers in Comstocks and Aimee Semple McPhersons. But for all its pitiful flabbiness human nature is not wholly bad, nor is man so helpless a creature of circumstance as the cynics would have us believe. There are other and greater gods than Mumbo Jumbo worshiped in America, worthier things than hocus pocus; and in rare moments even Babbitt dimly perceives that the feet of his idol are clay. There are Martin Arrowsmiths as well as Elmer Gantrys, and human nature, if it will, can pull itself out of the trap. Bad social machinery makes bad men. Put the banker in the scullery instead of the drawing-room; exalt the test-tube and deflate the cash register; rid society of the dictatorship of the middle class; and the artist and the scientist will erect in America a civilization that may become, what civilization was in earlier days, a thing to be respected. For all his modernity and disillusion learned from Pullman-car philosophers, Sinclair Lewis is still an echo of Jean Jacques and the golden hopes of the Enlightenment—thin and far-off, no doubt, but still an authentic echo."

"Thin and far-off, no doubt," is this contemporary liberalism, yet Parrington found hints of it in the midst of the war fiasco that culminated in reaction and despair. Death did not grant him the opportunity to show what he found, but the young men who learned from him the love of sound craftsmanship, who were inspired by his enlightened dreams, will some day complete the monument. In the meantime Vernon Louis Parrington would like to be held in memory as he held his friend, J. Allen Smith—as a "scholar, teacher, democrat, gentleman."

E. H. EBY

University of Washington
Seattle, Washington
March, 1930

FOREWORD

WITH the present volume I bring to a close my studies in the main currents in American thought. The broad drifts of American opinion, as I interpret that opinion, should now be sufficiently clear. The volume immediately preceding the present one dealt with the romantic revolution in America—one of the most stimulating experiences the American mind has undergone—which was traced to twin forces: the influence upon an expansive generation of French romantic thought, and the spirit of robust individualism resulting from a fluid economics; and the creative result was the spontaneous emergence in America of a buoyant spirit of hopefulness that expressed itself in democratic programs and faith in a benevolent progress. The present volume deals with the slow decay of this romantic optimism in more thoughtful minds, and the cause of that decay is traced to three sources: the stratifying of economics under the pressure of centralization; the rise of a mechanistic science; and the emergence of a spirit of skepticism which, under the pressure of industrialism, the teachings of the physical sciences, and the lessons of European intellectuals, is resulting in the questioning of the ideal of democracy as it has been commonly held hitherto, and the spread of a spirit of pessimism. The custodianship of America by the middle class has brought unsuspected consequences in its train.

Thus after three hundred years' experience we have returned, intellectually, to the point from which we set out, and the old philosophy brought to the new world from the compact societies of Europe, with its doctrine of determinism and its mood of pessimism, has come back in changed form to color the thinking of our generation. Emersonian optimism, that was the fullest expression of the romantic faith, is giving way to Dreiserian pessimism, and the traditional doctrine of progress is being subjected to analysis by a growing skepticism. Our intellectual history thus conceived falls into three broad phases: Calvinistic pessimism, romantic optimism, and mechanistic pessimism. Between the first and the last lies the America of yesterday that shaped the American mind and American institutions; and with the submergence of that native world we are in the way of repeating here the familiar history of Europe, with its coercive regimentations reproduced on a larger scale and in more mechanical fashion. Once more a gloomy philosophy stands on the threshold of the American mind. Whether it will enter and take possession of the household, no one can predict as yet. This much nevertheless is clear: an industrialized society is reshaping the psychology fashioned by an agrarian world; the passion for liberty is lessening and the individual, in the presence of creature comforts, is being dwarfed; the drift of centralization is shaping its inevitable tyrannies to bind us with. Whether the quick concern for human rights, that was the noble bequest of our fathers who had drunk of the waters of French romantic faith, will be carried over into the future, to unhorse the machine that now rides men and to leaven the sodden mass that is industrial America, is a question to which the gods as yet have given no answer. Yet it is not without hope that intelligent America is in revolt. The artist is in revolt, the intellectual is in revolt, the conscience of America is in revolt.

·   ·   ·   ·   ·   ·

It ought not to be necessary to add that in these volumes I have not essayed to write a history of American literature—that rather difficult task for which no scholar is as yet equipped. But I have suffered so many gentle reproofs for failing to do what I did not set out to do, that it may be well to repeat what I said in the Foreword to Volume I, that I have been concerned in the present study with the total pattern of American thought—the broad drift of major ideas—and not with vagrant currents or casual variations. In particular I have been repeatedly taken to task for a seeming slight put upon certain of our artists, and it has been inferred that I slighted them because I chose to ignore whatever did not fit into a rigid scheme of economic determinism. Let me say in rebuttal that I hold no brief for a rigid scheme of economic determinism. I recognize the rich culture potentialities that inhere in individual variation from type, and I realize that the arts are likely to receive their noblest gifts from men who should be classed biologically as cultural sports or variations from the cultural type. But in such a study as I have undertaken, individual variation is significant not for its own sake, but rather for the help it may offer in determining the type. After due consideration I see no cause to apologize for my treatment of Poe, for example, if indeed I have done so. I am content to have placed him historically and culturally in relation to the whole, leaving the fascinating problem of his variation from type to those who deal with such problems.

V. L. P.

INTRODUCTION *

In the second volume of my studies I laid down the thesis that
at the beginning of our national existence two rival philosophies
contended for supremacy in America: the humanitarian philosophy
of the French Enlightenment, based on the conception of human
perfectibility and postulating as its objective an equalitarian democracy in which the political state should function as the servant
to the common well-being; and the English philosophy of *laissez
faire*, based on the assumed universality of the acquisitive instinct
and postulating a social order answering the needs of an abstract
"economic man," in which the state should function in the interests of trade. And I pointed out further, with adequate backing
up, I hope, that the first of these antagonistic philosophies was
accepted by the agrarian leaders of America and found issue in
the Jeffersonian program; that the second came to dominate the
thinking of the mercantile, capitalistic America and took form in
Hamiltonian Federalism. Unfortunately this logical alignment of
diverse economic groups was obscured by the needs of practical
politics, and in passing through the explosive Jacksonian revolution both philosophies underwent subtle changes. Jacksonianism
imposed upon America the ideal of democracy to which all must
thereafter do lip service, but it lost its realistic basis in a Physiocratic economics and wandered in a fog of political equalitarianism;
and the Whiggery that issued from Federalism turned to the work
of converting the democratic state into the servant of property
interests. Both political parties contented themselves with an
egoistic individualism that took no account of social ends, forgetful
of the humanitarian spirit that underlay the earlier democratic
program. The finer spirit of the Enlightenment was lost, and in
consequence the major parties chose to follow the economic interests of master groups, heedless of all humanitarian issues.

* The Introduction, as will be readily seen by the reader, is not complete, yet it
undoubtedly contains the gist of what Professor Parrington intended to include in
it. He wrote several forms of some parts, from which the Introduction as it stands
has been pieced together in logical order. It is probable that the last words he wrote
were the significant closing words here—" to summon forth the potential intelligence
of the younger generation."—*Publisher.*

But the spirit awakened by the earlier democratic enthusiasm could not be kept in political strait-jackets. The Jacksonian revolution overflowed all narrow party dikes, expressing itself in diverse humanitarian and reform movements and quickening the minds of ardent Americans with larger democratic aspirations. The noble idealism of successive third parties that have sprung up reasserted the democratic principles flouted by the major parties. The Locofoco movement, the Free-soil Party, the early Republican Party, the Greenback Party, the Populist Party, the Progressive Party, have had a common objective, namely to carry further the movement inaugurated by the Jeffersonians to make of America a land of democratic equality and opportunity—to make government in America serve man rather than property. The third-party movements have always been democratic movements, and though they have failed in their immediate objectives they have served the purpose of reminding the major parties—oftentimes rudely— that America presumes to be a democratic country. Thus interpreted the history of the political struggle in America since 1790 falls into three broad phases: the Jeffersonian movement that asserted the ideal of political democracy; the Jacksonian movement that established it crudely in practice; and the successive third-party movements that attempted to regain such ground as had been lost, to extend the field, and to perfect the machinery of democratic government.

As a result of the long struggle the abstract principle of democracy—during the period under consideration—was firmly established in the popular mind; but as it fell under the successive custodianship of different economic groups it came to receive strangely diverse interpretations. Interpreted by the coonskin Jacksonians it meant political equalitarianism; by the slave economy it meant a Greek democracy; by the industrial economy it meant the right of exploitation. It has changed service with each new master. Always the principles of Jeffersonianism—of democracy as a humane social order, serving the common well-being— have been lost out of the reckoning, and except in so far as the tendency has been checked by the third-party threat, democratic professions have been only a thin cover under which the old class warfare has gone forward vigorously. In the decades immediately following the Civil War democracy passed under the custodianship of the middle class, who were busily engaged in creating a plutocracy, and the major ideas of the earlier movement took on a characteristic middle-class coloring. The idea of a beneficent progress, which was the flower of the doctrine of human perfectibility, came to be interpreted as material expansion with constantly augmenting profits; and the idea of democracy came to be interpreted as the right to use the government of the whole for the benefit of the few.

.   .   .   .

Considered historically perhaps the chief contribution of the Progressive movement to the democratic cause is to be found in its discovery of the fundamentally undemocratic nature of the federal Constitution. That so obvious a fact so long escaped recognition was due to political causes easily understood. For a century the Constitution had been a symbol of national unity, a cohesive force amidst the drift of expansion, a counter influence to the disintegrations of states-rights particularisms; and as such it had appealed to the national loyalties of men in every commonwealth. To criticize it was reckoned disloyal. The long process of interpretation had remained in the hands of the lawyers and had been wholly legalistic and antiquarian. In all this earlier commentary—except for a small group of left-wing Abolitionists who repudiated the entire instrument—no question as to the democratic spirit of the Constitution was raised, no doubts as to its sufficiency as a fundamental democratic law were suggested. The class divisions that presided at its making were ignored, and the aristocratic spirit of its creators was forgotten. But with the rising revolt against the custodianship of government by financial and industrial interests came a new critical interest in the fundamental law. Discovering that its hands were tied the democracy began to question the reason for the bonds that constrained its movements. The latent distrust was quickened by what was regarded by many as judicial usurpations of power, such as the act of the Supreme Court in declaring unconstitutional the federal income-tax law, and the question of the desirability of an eighteenth-century document that by its complexity unduly impeded the functioning of the democratic will, was thrust into the foreground of political debate. It was the struggle of 1789 over again.

The new school of criticism was historical rather than legalistic. It was concerned primarily with origins—and it must take into account the political theories and class interests of the eighteenth-

century gentlemen who framed the document. It refused to look
upon the Fathers as supermen, devoted unselfishly to high patriotic
duty, but chose to regard them as capable statesmen, saturated
with aristocratic prejudices, who fearful of losing control of the
new venture in republicanism, took care to shape an instrument
that threw sharp restrictions about the majority will.

. . . .

The theme of the present volume is the industrialization of
America under the leadership of the middle class, and the consequent rise of a critical attitude towards the ideals and handiwork
of that class. It concerns itself primarily with the spirit of realism
that under the constrictions of industrialism and with the spread of
scientific modes of thought emerged to question the ardent romanticisms of an earlier age, and bring under doubt the excellence
of a social order created by the Industrial Revolution.

The field to be traversed is thus predetermined. The interpretation of our literature since 1860 must be fitted into the broad lines
of our national experience and will follow the main divisions of
development.

I. The conquest of America by the middle class and its custodianship of democracy. The philosophy of the middle class.
II. The challenge of that overlordship by:
1. The older democratic agrarianism as expressed chiefly in
the third-party movements.
2. The new proletarian philosophy that came likewise out of
the ferment of the French Revolution, but that traveled a different course—through Europe and the earlier continental Industrial Revolution, and thence to
America.
III. The intellectual revolution brought about by science with
the results:
1. The recovery of a spirit of realism.
2. The appropriation of science by the middle class.
IV. The rise of a detached criticism by the younger intellectuals.

In dealing with this material it will be necessary to follow sectional lines in the earlier decades until the encompassing movement
of centralization finally obliterated them and produced a common
national spirit and purpose.

In the welter that is present-day America militant philosophies with their clear-cut programs and assured faiths are wanting, and many feel, as Matthew Arnold felt fourscore years ago, that they are dwelling between worlds, one dead, the other powerless to be born. The old buoyant psychology is gone and in the breakdown and disintegration of the traditional individualism no new philosophies are rising. Builders of Utopias are out of a job. Political and economic theory is in charge of paymasters and is content with the drab rim of the familiar landscape. Retainer-fees have blotted out for it the lovelier horizons that earlier thinkers contemplated. Academic political scientists and economists have largely joined the Swiss guards, and abdicated the high prerogative of speculative thought. It is the men of letters—poets and essayists and novelists and dramatists, the eager young intellectuals of a drab generation—who embody the mind of present-day America; not the professional custodians of official views. They at least decline to block the path to the Promised Land with retainer-fees; they at least are free souls, and in the measure of their abilities, free thinkers. It is to them therefore that one must turn to discover the intellectual currents of later America—to their aspirations as well as to their criticisms. Literature at last has become the authentic voice of this great shapeless America that means so much to western civilization. Not theologians any longer, nor political philosophers, nor industrial masters, nor bankers, are the spokesmen of this vibrant life of a continent, but the intellectuals, the dreamers, the critics, the historians, the men of letters, in short; and to them one may turn hopefully for a revelation of American life.

The period dealt with in the present study marks the complete triumph of the middle class and the final defeat of the traditional agrarianism. The disintegration of the earlier romanticisms, both native and imported, has run its course. The philosophy of Jefferson and John Taylor, with its physiocratic bias, its antipathy to a money economy, its love of local autonomy, has been buried in the potter's field.

.   .   .   .

Amidst all the turmoil and vague subconscious tendencies, certain ideas slowly clarified: first, that the earlier democratic aspirations had somehow failed, that an equalitarian philosophy adapted to frontier conditions could not easily be carried over into a centralizing and stratifying America and was doomed to eventual defeat; second, that even in the supposed heyday of our democracy, we had never achieved a democracy, but rather a careless individualism that left society at the mercy of a rapacious middle class; third, that we must take our bearings afresh and set forth on a different path to the goal. As these convictions slowly rose into consciousness, a quick suspicion of our earlier philosophies arose to trouble us. With the growing realism of the times came a belief that our French romantic theories were mainly at fault and we must somehow go back to the rationalistic eighteenth century and start once more to recreate a democratic philosophy. The crux of the matter seemed to lie in the romantic conception of human nature. Rousseau and Godwin were the false prophets who led us astray, and we must return to the solid realism of John Locke. In the light of a realistic psychology, with its discovery of morons, and its study of mob tendencies, it was no longer possible to take seriously that attractive figment of the romantic imagination—man in the state of nature, perfectible by following the light of reason, seeking justice. Morons do not fit nicely into the older theory— they jar one's faith in human perfectibility. In the light of intelligence tests perhaps the whole romantic theory of democracy was only a will-o'-the-wisp. With the very foundations of our traditional philosophy turning to quicksand under our feet, no wonder we are bedeviled by doubts and uncertainties. Utopias no longer seem so near at hand as they did; plans and specifications of the ideal commonwealth no longer seem simple matters to be drawn by any competent social carpenter. Our jauntiness is gone, speculation is less important than investigation, and in the spirit of sober realism we are setting about the serious business of thinking.

In this thinking two major forces are at hand: economics and psychology. In our economic realism we are returning to the spirit of the eighteenth century, and adapting the determinism that marked political thought from Harrington and John Adams to Webster and Calhoun; but we are equipped with a psychological knowledge that those earlier thinkers lacked. Wedding the new psychology to the older economic determinism, we may hope in a spirit of sober realism to make some progress in our thinking.

Yet not too hastily should we abandon our earlier faith: the eighteenth-century conception of environment as a creative influence in determining character is a vital idea not yet adequately explored. Even morons may be traced back to adenoids or diets of salt pork and whisky or to later machine labor, and aristocracies are still seen to be economic. And aristocratic albinos may well breed mobs and morons. Jefferson was not as foolish as many of his disciples have been, and Jeffersonian democracy still offers hope. Education begins to fail—except education to individualize and to summon forth the potential intelligence of the younger generation.

CONTENTS *

* This is given in full, as Professor Parrington left it, with those parts not completed by him in brackets. Some revision has been made for the parts he completed,
but notes have been added to the text to show his original intention. For some of the
bracketed headings after Part II of Book II some material is given in the Addenda
from other work of Parrington's.—*Publisher.*

BOOK TWO: THE OLD AND THE NEW: STORM CLOUDS

PART I

The Middle Border Rises

[1] See "Naturalism in American Fiction," in the Addenda—lecture notes including Crane and Norris.

BOOK THREE: THE NEW AMERICA

PART I

The Rise of Liberalism [4]

[2] See Addenda for lecture notes on Lanier.
[3] See Addenda for magazine article on Cabell.
[4] See "A Chapter in American Liberalism," the last of the Addenda.

[5] See *Ibid.*
[6] See Addenda, "The Problem Novel and the Diversion from Naturalism."
[7] See Addenda for brief notes.
[8] See Addenda for notes of lecture on Dreiser.

PART III

Reaction   PAGE

[9] See Addenda for reprint of pamphlet on Lewis.
[10] See Addenda for brief notes.

CONTENTS

CONTENTS

BOOK ONE: CHANGING AMERICA

BOOK ONE

CHANGING AMERICA

When America laid aside its arms after Appomattox and turned back to the pursuits of peace it was well advanced toward the goal set by Alexander Hamilton three-quarters of a century before. The great obstacle that had withheld its feet hitherto had been swept from its path. A slave economy could never again thwart the ambitions of the capitalistic economy. The jealous particularism that for a generation had obstructed the inevitable drift toward a coalescing national unity had gone down in defeat. The agrarian South was no longer master in the councils of government; the shaping of the future had fallen to other hands and the unfolding of the new order could go forward without southern let or hindrance.

Other obstacles were falling away of themselves. North as well as South, the traditional domestic economy was already a thing of the past. An easier way to wealth, and one enormously more profitable, had been discovered. The future lay in the hands of the machine that was already dispossessing the tool. In the hurry of the war years the potentialities of the factory system had been explored and the ready resources of liquid capital had been greatly augmented. From the smoke of the great conflict an America had emerged unlike any the earlier generations had known. An ambitious industrialism stood on the threshold of a continental expansion that was to transfer sovereignty in America from a landed and mercantile aristocracy to the capable hands of a new race of captains of industry. Only the western farmers, newly settled in the Middle Border and spreading the psychology of the frontier through the vast prairie spaces of a greater Inland Empire, remained as a last stumbling-block. Other battles with agrarianism must be fought before capitalism assumed undisputed mastery of America; but with the eventual overthrow of the agrarian hosts in their last stronghold the path would lie broad and straight to the goal of an encompassing industrialism, with politicians and political parties its willing servants. There would be no more dissensions in the household. With southern Jeffersonians and western agra-

3

rians no longer sitting as watch dogs to the Constitution, the political state would be refashioned to serve a new age, and the old dream of a coalescing national economy become a reality. The American System was in the way of complete establishment.

Other changes impended, and greater. The enthronement of the machine was only the outward and visible sign of the revolution in thought that came with the rise of science. As a new cosmos unfolded before the inquisitive eyes of scientists the old metaphysical speculations became as obsolete as the old household economy. A new spirit of realism was abroad, probing and questioning the material world, pushing the realm of exact knowledge into the earlier regions of faith. The conquest of nature was the great business of the day, and as that conquest went forward triumphantly the solid fruits of the new mastery were gathered by industrialism. Science and the machine were the twin instruments for creating a new civilization, of which the technologist and the industrialist were the high priests. The transcendental theologian was soon to be as extinct as the passenger pigeon.

With the substitution of the captain of industry for the plantation master as the custodian of society, the age of aristocracy was at an end and the age of the middle class was established. A new culture, created by the machine and answering the needs of capitalism, was to dispossess the old culture with its lingering concern for distinction and its love of standards—a culture that should eventually suffice the needs of a brisk city world of machine activities. But that would take time. In the meanwhile—in the confused interregnum between reigns—America would be little more than a welter of crude energy, a raw unlovely society where the strife of competition with its prodigal waste testified to the shortcomings of an age in process of transition. The spirit of the frontier was to flare up in a huge buccaneering orgy. Having swept across the continent to the Pacific coast like a visitation of locusts, the frontier spirit turned back upon its course to conquer the East, infecting the new industrialism with a crude individualism, fouling the halls of Congress, despoiling the public domain, and indulging in a huge national barbecue. It submerged the arts and created a new literature. For a time it carried all things before it, until running full tilt into science and the machine, its triumphant progress was stopped and America, rejecting individualism, began the work of standardization and mechanization. It is this world in transition from an aristocratic to a middle-class order, turmoiled by the last flare-up of the frontier spirit, shifting from a robust individualism to a colorless standardization, which the chapters that follow must deal with. A confused and turbulent scene, but not without its fascination to the American who would understand his special heritage—perhaps the most characteristically native, the most American, in our total history.

transition from an aristocratic to a middle-class order, transpired by the breakup of the frontier spirit; shimmer from a coarse individualism in a colorless standardization, which the chapters that follow must deal with. A confused and unhelpful scene that not venomous historian to the American who would understand his age at least, perhaps the most characteristically native, the most American, in our total history.

PART ONE: THE GILDED AGE

CHAPTER I

THE AMERICAN SCENE

I

FREE AMERICA

The pot was boiling briskly in America in the tumultuous post-war years. The country had definitely entered upon its freedom and was settling its disordered household to suit its democratic taste. Everywhere new ways were feverishly at work transforming the countryside. In the South another order was rising uncertainly on the ruins of the plantation system; in the East an expanding factory economy was weaving a different pattern of industrial life; in the Middle Border a recrudescent agriculture was arising from the application of the machine to the rich prairie soil. All over the land a spider web of iron rails was being spun that was to draw the remotest outposts into the common whole and bind the nation together with steel bands. Nevertheless two diverse worlds lay on the map of continental America. Facing in opposite directions and holding different faiths, they would not travel together easily or take comfort from the yoke that joined them. Agricultural America, behind which lay two and a half centuries of experience, was a decentralized world, democratic, individualistic, suspicious; industrial America, behind which lay only half a dozen decades of bustling experiment, was a centralizing world, capitalistic, feudal, ambitious. The one was a decaying order, the other a rising, and between them would be friction till one or the other had become master.

Continental America was still half frontier and half settled country. A thin line of homesteads had been thrust westward till the outposts reached well into the Middle Border—an uncertain thread running through eastern Minnesota, Nebraska, Kansas, overleaping the Indian Territory and then running west into Texas —approximately halfway between the Atlantic and the Pacific. Behind these outposts was still much unoccupied land, and beyond stretched the unfenced prairies till they merged in the sagebrush

7

plains, gray and waste, that stretched to the foothills of the Rocky Mountains. Beyond the mountains were other stretches of plains and deserts, vast and forbidding in their alkali blight, to the wooded coast ranges and the Pacific Ocean. In all this immense territory were only scattered settlements—at Denver, Salt Lake City, Sacramento, San Francisco, Portland, Seattle, and elsewhere—tiny outposts in the wilderness, with scattered hamlets, mining camps, and isolated homesteads lost in the great expanse. On the prairies from Mexico to Canada—across which rumbled great herds of buffalo—roved powerful tribes of hostile Indians who fretted against the forward thrust of settlement and disputed the right of possession. The urgent business of the times was the subduing of this wild region, wresting it from Indians and buffalo and wilderness; and the forty years that lay between the California Gold Rush of '49 and the Oklahoma Land Rush of '89 saw the greatest wave of pioneer expansion—the swiftest and most reckless—in all our pioneer experience. Expansion on so vast a scale necessitated building, and the seventies became the railway age, bonding the future to break down present barriers of isolation, and opening new territories for later exploitation. The reflux of the great movement swept back upon the Atlantic coast and gave to life there a fresh note of spontaneous vigor, of which the Gilded Age was the inevitable expression.

It was this energetic East, with its accumulations of liquid capital awaiting investment and its factories turning out the materials needed to push the settlements westward, that profited most from the conquest of the far West. The impulsion from the frontier did much to drive forward the industrial revolution. The war that brought devastation to the South had been more friendly to northern interests. In gathering the scattered rills of capital into central reservoirs at Philadelphia and New York, and in expanding the factory system to supply the needs of the armies, it had opened to capitalism its first clear view of the Promised Land. The bankers had come into control of the liquid wealth of the nation, and the industrialists had learned to use the machine for production; the time was ripe for exploitation on a scale undreamed-of a generation before. Up till then the potential resources of the continent had not even been surveyed. Earlier pioneers had only scratched the surface—felling trees, making crops, building pygmy watermills, smelting a little iron. Mineral wealth had been scarcely touched. Tools had been lacking to develop it, capital had been lacking, transportation lacking, technical methods lacking, markets lacking.

In the years following the war, exploitation for the first time was provided with adequate resources and a competent technique, and busy prospectors were daily uncovering new sources of wealth. The coal and oil of Pennsylvania and Ohio, the copper and iron ore of upper Michigan, the gold and silver, lumber and fisheries, of the Pacific Coast, provided limitless raw materials for the rising industrialism. The Bessemer process quickly turned an age of iron into an age of steel and created the great rolling mills of Pittsburgh from which issued the rails for expanding railways. The reaper and binder, the sulky plow and the threshing machine, created a large-scale agriculture on the fertile prairies. Wild grass-lands provided grazing for immense herds of cattle and sheep; the development of the corn-belt enormously increased the supply of hogs; and with railways at hand the Middle Border poured into Omaha and Kansas City and Chicago an endless stream of produce. As the line of the frontier pushed westward new towns were built, thousands of homesteads were filed on, and the speculator and promoter hovered over the prairies like buzzards seeking their carrion. With rising land-values money was to be made out of unearned increment, and the creation of booms was a profitable industry. The times were stirring and it was a shiftless fellow who did not make his pile. If he had been too late to file on desirable acres he had only to find a careless homesteader who had failed in some legal technicality and "jump his claim." Good bottom land could be had even by late-comers if they were sharp at the game.

This bustling America of 1870 accounted itself a democratic world. A free people had put away all aristocratic privileges and conscious of its power went forth to possess the last frontier. Its social philosophy, which it found adequate to its needs, was summed up in three words—preëmption, exploitation, progress. Its immediate and pressing business was to dispossess the government of its rich holdings. Lands in the possession of the government were so much idle waste, untaxed and profitless; in private hands they would be developed. They would provide work, pay taxes, support schools, enrich the community. Preëmption meant exploitation and exploitation meant progress. It was a simple philosophy and it suited the simple individualism of the times. The Gilded Age knew nothing of the Enlightenment; it recognized only the acquisitive instinct. That much at least the frontier had taught the great American democracy; and in applying to the resources of a continent the lesson it had been so well taught the Gilded Age wrote a profoundly characteristic chapter of American history.

II

FIGURES OF EARTH

In a moment of special irritation Edwin Lawrence Godkin called the civilization of the seventies a chromo civilization. Mark Twain, with his slack western standards, was equally severe. As he contemplated the slovenly reality beneath the gaudy exterior he dubbed it the Gilded Age. Other critics with a gift for pungent phrase have flung their gibes at the ways of a picturesque and uncouth generation. There is reason in plenty for such caustic comment. Heedless, irreverent, unlovely, cultivating huge beards, shod in polished top-boots—the last refinement of the farmer's cowhides—wearing linen dickeys over hickory shirts, moving through pools of tobacco juice, erupting in shoddy and grotesque architecture, cluttering its homes with ungainly walnut chairs and marble-topped tables and heavy lambrequins, the decade of the seventies was only too plainly mired and floundering in a bog of bad taste. A world of triumphant and unabashed vulgarity without its like in our history, it was not aware of its plight, but accounted its manners genteel and boasted of ways that were a parody on sober good sense.

Yet just as such comments are, they do not reach quite to the heart of the age. They emphasize rather the excrescences, the casual lapses, of a generation that underneath its crudities and vulgarities was boldly adventurous and creative—a generation in which the democratic freedoms of America, as those freedoms had taken shape during a drab frontier experience, came at last to spontaneous and vivid expression. If its cultural wealth was less than it thought, if in its exuberance it was engaged somewhat too boisterously in stamping its own plebeian image on the work of its hands, it was only natural to a society that for the first time found its opportunities equal to its desires, a youthful society that accounted the world its oyster and wanted no restrictions laid on its will. It was the ripe fruit of Jacksonian leveling, and if it ran to a grotesque individualism—if in its self-confidence it was heedless of the smiles of older societies—it was nevertheless by reason of its uncouthness the most picturesque generation in our history; and for those who love to watch human nature disporting itself with naïve abandon, running amuck through all the conventions, no other age provides so fascinating a spectacle.

When the cannon at last had ceased their destruction it was a strange new America that looked out confidently on the scene. Something had been released by the upheavals of half a century, something strong and assertive that was prepared to take possession of the continent. It did not issue from the loins of war. Its origins must be sought elsewhere, further back in time. It had been cradled in the vast changes that since 1815 had been reshaping America: in the break-up of the old domestic economy that kept life mean and drab, in the noisy enthusiasms of the new coonskin democracy, in the romanticisms of the California gold rush, in the boisterous freedoms discovered by the forties and fifties. It had come to manhood in the battles of a tremendous war, and as it now surveyed the continent, discovering potential wealth before unknown, it demanded only freedom and opportunity—a fair race and no favors. Everywhere was a welling-up of primitive pagan desires after long repressions—to grow rich, to grasp power, to be strong and masterful and lay the world at its feet. It was a violent reaction from the narrow poverty of frontier life and the narrow inhibitions of backwoods religion. It had had enough of skimpy, meager ways, of scrubbing along hoping for something to turn up. It would go out and turn it up. It was consumed with a great hunger for abundance, for the good things of life, for wealth. It was frankly materialistic and if material goods could be wrested from society it would lay its hands heartily to the work. Freedom and opportunity, to acquire, to possess, to enjoy—for that it would sell its soul.

Society of a sudden was become fluid. With the sweeping-away of the last aristocratic restraints the potentialities of the common man found release for self-assertion. Strange figures, sprung from obscure origins, thrust themselves everywhere upon the scene. In the reaction from the mean and skimpy, a passionate will to power was issuing from unexpected sources, undisciplined, confused in ethical values, but endowed with immense vitality. Individualism was being simplified to the acquisitive instinct. These new Americans were primitive souls, ruthless, predatory, capable; single-minded men; rogues and rascals often, but never feeble, never hindered by petty scruple, never given to puling or whining—the raw materials of a race of capitalistic buccaneers. Out of the drab mass of common plebeian life had come this vital energy that erupted in amazing abundance and in strange forms. The new freedoms meant diverse things to different men and each like Jurgen followed after his own wishes and his own desires. Pirate and priest issued from the common source and played their parts with the same picturesqueness. The romantic age of Captain Kidd was come again, and the black flag and the gospel banner were both in lockers to be flown as the needs of the cruise determined. With all coercive restrictions put away the democratic genius of America was setting out on the road of manifest destiny.

Analyze the most talked-of men of the age and one is likely to find a splendid audacity coupled with an immense wastefulness. A note of tough-mindedness marks them. They had stout nippers. They fought their way encased in rhinoceros hides. There was the Wall Street crowd—Daniel Drew, Commodore Vanderbilt, Jim Fisk, Jay Gould, Russell Sage—blackguards for the most part, railway wreckers, cheaters and swindlers, but picturesque in their rascality. There was the numerous tribe of politicians—Boss Tweed, Fernando Wood, G. Oakey Hall, Senator Pomeroy, Senator Cameron, Roscoe Conkling, James G. Blaine—blackguards also for the most part, looting city treasuries, buying and selling legislative votes like railway stock, but picturesque in their audacity. There were the professional keepers of the public morals—Anthony Comstock, John B. Gough, Dwight L. Moody, Henry Ward Beecher, T. De Witt Talmage—ardent proselytizers, unintellectual, men of one idea, but fiery in zeal and eloquent in description of the particular heaven each wanted to people with his fellow Americans. And springing up like mushrooms after a rain was the goodly company of cranks—Virginia Woodhull and Tennessee Claflin, "Citizen" George Francis Train, Henry Bergh, Ben Butler, Ignatius Donnelly, Bob Ingersoll, Henry George—picturesque figures with a flair for publicity who tilled their special fields with splendid gestures. And finally there was Barnum the Showman, growing rich on the profession of humbuggery, a vulgar greasy genius, pure brass without any gilding, yet in picturesque and capable effrontery the very embodiment of the age. A marvelous company, vital with the untamed energy of a new land. In the presence of such men one begins to understand what Walt Whitman meant by his talk of the elemental.

Created by a primitive world that knew not the machine, they were marked by the rough homeliness of their origins. Whether wizened or fat they were never insignificant or commonplace. On the whole one prefers them fat, and for solid bulk what generation has outdone them? There was Revivalist Moody, bearded and neckless, with his two hundred and eighty pounds of Adam's flesh, every ounce of which "belonged to God." There was the lyric Sankey, afflicted with two hundred and twenty-five pounds of human frailty, yet looking as smug as a banker and singing "There were ninety and nine" divinely through mutton-chop whiskers. There was Boss Tweed, phlegmatic and mighty, overawing rebellious gangsters at the City Hall with his two hundred and forty pounds of pugnacious rascality. There was John Fiske, a philosophic hippopotamus, warming the chill waters of Spencerian science with his prodigious bulk. There was Ben Butler, oily and puffy and wheezy, like Falstaff larding the lean earth as he walked along, who yearly added more flesh to the scant ninety-seven pounds he carried away from Waterville College. And there was Jim Fisk, dressed like a bartender, huge in nerve as in bulk, driving with the dashing Josie Mansfield down Broadway—prince of vulgarians, who jovially proclaimed, "I worship in the Synagogue of the Libertines," and who on the failure of the Erie coup announced cheerfully, "Nothing is lost save honor!"

Impressive as are the fat kine of Egypt, the lean kine scarcely suffer by contrast. There were giants of puny physique in those days. There was Uncle Dan'l Drew, thin as a dried herring, yet a builder of churches and founder of Drew Theological Seminary, who pilfered and cheated his way to wealth with tobacco juice drooling from his mouth. There was Jay Gould, a lone-hand gambler, a dynamo in a tubercular body, who openly invested in the devil's tenements as likely to pay better dividends, and went home to potter lovingly amongst his exotic flowers. And there was Oakey Hall, clubman and playwright, small, elegant, and unscrupulous; and Victoria Woodhull who stirred up the Beecher case, a wisp of a woman who enraged all the frumpy blue-stockings by the smartness of her toilet and the perfection of her manners; and little Libby Tilton with her tiny wistful face and great eyes that looked out wonderingly at the world—eyes that were to go blind with weeping before the candle of her life went out. It was such men and women, individual and colorful, that Whitman and Mark Twain mingled with, and that Herman Melville—colossal and dynamic beyond them all—looked out upon sardonically from his tomb in the Custom House where he was consuming his own heart.

They were thrown up as it were casually out of the huge caldron of energy that was America. All over the land were thousands like them, self-made men quick to lay hands on opportunity if it knocked at the door, ready to seek it out if it were slow in knocking, recognizing no limitations to their powers, discouraged by no shortcomings in their training. When Moody set out to bring the world to his Protestant God he was an illiterate shoe salesman who stumbled over the hard words of his King James Bible. Anthony Comstock, the roundsman of the Lord, was a salesman in a dry-goods shop, and as careless of his spelling as he was careful of his neighbors' morals. Commodore Vanderbilt, who built up the greatest fortune of the time, was a Brooklyn ferryman, hard-fisted and tough as a burr-oak, who in a lifetime of over eighty years read only one book, *Pilgrim's Progress*, and that after he was seventy. Daniel Drew was a shyster cattle-drover, whose arid emotions found outlet in periodic conversions and backslidings, and who got on in this vale of tears by salting his cattle and increasing his—and the Lord's—wealth with every pound of water in their bellies—from which cleverness is said to have come the Wall Street phrase, "stock-watering." Jim Fisk was the son of a Yankee peddler, who, disdaining the unambitious ways of his father, set up for himself in a cart gilded like a circus-wagon and drove about the country-side with jingling bells. After he had made his pile in Wall Street he set up his own opera house and proposed to rival the Medici as a patron of the arts—and especially of the artists if they were of the right sex. A surprising number of them—Moody, Beecher, Barnum, Fisk, Comstock, Ben Butler—came from New England; Jay Gould was of Connecticut ancestry; but Oakey Hall was a southern gentleman; Fernando Wood, with the face of an Apollo and the wit of an Irishman, was the son of a Philadelphia cigar-maker and much of his early income was drawn from sailors' groggeries along the waterfront; Tweed was a stolid New Yorker, and Drew was a York State country boy.

What was happening in New York was symptomatic of the

nation. If the temple of Plutus was building in Wall Street, his devotees were everywhere. In Chicago, rising higgledy-piggledy from the ashes of the great fire, Phil Armour and Nelson Morris were laying out stockyards and drawing the cattle and sheep and hogs from remote prairie farms to their slaughter-houses. In Cleveland, Mark Hanna was erecting his smelters and turning the iron ore of Michigan into dollars, while John D. Rockefeller was squeezing the small fry out of the petroleum business and creating the Standard Oil monopoly. In Pittsburgh, Andrew Carnegie was applying the Bessemer process to steel-making and laying the foundations of the later steel trust. In Minneapolis, C. C. Washburn and Charles A. Pillsbury were applying new methods to milling and turning the northern wheat into flour to ship to the ends of the earth. In San Francisco, Leland Stanford and Collis P. Huntington were amassing huge fortunes out of the Southern Pacific Railway and bringing the commonwealth of California to their feet. Everywhere were boom-town and real-estate promoters, the lust of speculation, the hankering after quick and easy wealth.

In the great spaces from Kansas City to Sacramento the frontier spirit was in the gaudiest bloom. The experiences of three centuries of expansion were being crowded into as many decades. In the fifties the highway of the frontier had run up and down the Mississippi River and the golden age of steamboating had brought a motley life to Saint Louis; in the seventies the frontier had passed far beyond and was pushing through the Rocky Mountains, repeating as it went the old frontier story of swagger and slovenliness, of boundless hope and heroic endurance—a story deeply marked with violence and crime and heart-breaking failure. Thousands of veterans from the disbanded armies, northern and southern alike, flocked to the West to seek their fortunes, and daily life there soon took on a drab note from the alkali of the plains; yet through the drabness ran a boisterous humor that exalted lying to a fine art— a humor that goes back to Davy Crockett and the Ohio flatboatmen. Mark Twain's *Roughing It* is the epic of this frontier of the Pony Express, as *Life on the Mississippi* is the epic of the preceding generation.

The huge wastefulness of the frontier was everywhere, East and West. The Gilded Age heeded somewhat too literally the Biblical injunction to take no thought for the morrow, but was busily intent on squandering the resources of the continent. All things

were held cheap, and human life cheapest of all. Wild Bill Hickok
with forty notches on his gun and a row of graves to his credit in
Boot Hill Cemetery, and Jesse James, most picturesque of des-
peradoes, levying toll with his six-shooter on the bankers who were
desecrating the free spirit of the plains with their two per cent. a
month, are familiar heroes in Wild West tales; but the real plains-
man of the Gilded Age, the picturesque embodiment of the last
frontier, was Captain Carver, the faultless horseman and faultless
shot, engaged in his celebrated buffalo hunt for the championship
of the prairies. Wagering that he could kill more buffalo in a day
than any rival hero of the chase, he rode forth with his Indian
marker and dropping the miles behind him he left an endless trail
of dead beasts properly tagged, winning handsomely when his
rival's horse fell dead from exhaustion. It was magnificent. Davy
Crockett's hundred and five bears in a season was but 'prentice
work compared with Captain Carver's professional skill. It is
small wonder that he became a hero of the day and his rifle, turned
now to the circus business of breaking glass balls thrown from his
running horse, achieved a fame far greater than Davy's Betsy.
With his bold mustaches, his long black hair flying in the wind, his
sombrero and chaps and top-boots, he was a figure matched only by
Buffalo Bill, the last of the great plainsmen.

Captain Carver was picturesque, but what shall be said of the
thousands of lesser Carvers engaged in the same slaughter, market-
hunters who discovered a new industry in buffalo-killing? At the
close of the Civil War the number on the western plains was estimated at fifteen millions. With the building of the Union Pacific
Railroad they were cut asunder into two vast herds, and upon these
herds fell the hunters with the new breech-loading rifles, shooting
for the hide market that paid sixty-five cents for a bull's hide and a
dollar and fifteen cents for a cow's. During the four years from 1871
to 1874 nearly a million head a year were slain from the southern
herd alone, their skins ripped off and the carcasses left for the
coyotes and buzzards. By the end of the hunting-season of 1875
the vast southern herd had been wiped out, and with the building
of the Northern Pacific in 1880 the smaller northern herd soon suffered the same fate. The buffalo were gone with the hostile Indians
—Sioux and Blackfeet and Cheyennes and a dozen other tribes.[1]

[1] See Allan Nevins, "The Taming of the West," in *The Emergence of Modern
America.*

It was the last dramatic episode of the American frontier, and it wrote a fitting climax to three centuries of wasteful conquest. But the prairies were tamed, and Wild Bill Hickok and Captain Carver and Buffalo Bill Cody had become romantic figures to enthrall the imagination of later generations.[2]

It was an abundant harvest of those freedoms that America had long been struggling to achieve, and it was making ready the ground for later harvests that would be less to its liking. Freedom had become individualism, and individualism had become the inalienable right to preëmpt, to exploit, to squander. Gone were the old ideals along with the old restraints. The idealism of the forties, the romanticism of the fifties—all the heritage of Jeffersonianism and the French Enlightenment—were put thoughtlessly away, and with no social conscience, no concern for civilization, no heed for the future of the democracy it talked so much about, the Gilded Age threw itself into the business of money-getting. From the sober restraints of aristocracy, the old inhibitions of Puritanism, the niggardliness of an exacting domestic economy, it swung far back in reaction, and with the discovery of limitless opportunities for exploitation it allowed itself to get drunk. Figures of earth, they followed after their own dreams. Some were builders with grandiose plans in their pockets; others were wreckers with no plans at all. It was an anarchistic world of strong, capable men, selfish, unenlightened, amoral—an excellent example of what human nature will do with undisciplined freedom. In the Gilded Age freedom was the freedom of buccaneers preying on the argosies of Spain.

III

POLITICS AND THE FAIRY GODMOTHER

Certainly the Gilded Age would have resented such an interpretation of its brisk activities. In the welter of change that resulted from the application of the machine to the raw materials of a continent, it chose rather to see the spirit of progress to which the temper of the American people was so responsive. Freedom, it was

[2] It is the same story in the matter of the passenger pigeon. In early days the flights of these birds ran to untold millions. The last great nesting was at Petoskey, Michigan, in 1878, covering a strip forty miles long and from three to ten miles wide. Upon the nests fell the market-hunters and a million and a half squabs were shipped to New York by rail, besides the thousands wasted. Within a generation the passenger pigeon had become extinct. See W. B. Mershon, *Outdoor Life and Recreation,* February, 1929, p. 26 ff.

convinced, was justifying itself by its works. The eighteenth
century had been static, the nineteenth century was progressive.
It was adaptable, quick to change its ways and its tools, ready to
accept whatever proved advantageous—pragmatic, opportunist.
It was not stifled by the dead hand of custom but was free to adapt
means to ends. It accepted progress as it accepted democracy,
without questioning the sufficiency of either. The conception
accorded naturally with a frontier psychology. Complete opportunism is possible only amongst a people that is shallow-rooted, that
lives in a fluid society, scantily institutionalized, with few vested
interests. In a young society it is easy, in a maturing society it
becomes increasingly difficult.

Dazzled by the results of the new technique of exploitation
applied on a grand scale to unpreëmpted opportunities, it is no
wonder the Gilded Age thought well of its labors and confused the
pattern of life it was weaving with the pattern of a rational civilization. It had drunk in the idea of progress with its mother's milk.
It was an inevitable frontier interpretation of the swift changes
resulting from a fluid economics and a fluid society in process of
settling into static ways. It served conveniently to describe the
changes from the simplicities of social beginnings to the complexities of a later order. It was made use of following the War of 1812
to explain the stir resulting from the westward expansion and the
great increase in immigration; but it was given vastly greater
significance by the social unsettlements that came with the industrial revolution. With the realization of the dramatic changes
in manner of living—the added conveniences of life, release from
the laborious round of the domestic economy, ease of transportation—that resulted from the machine order, it was inevitable that
the idea of progress should have been on every man's tongue. The
increase of wealth visible to all was in itself a sufficient sign of
progress, and as the novelty of the industrial change wore off and
the economy of America was more completely industrialized, it
was this augmenting wealth that symbolized it.

In such fashion the excellent ideal of progress that issued from
the social enthusiasms of the Enlightenment was taken in charge
by the Gilded Age and transformed into a handmaid of capitalism.
Its duties were narrowed to the single end of serving profits and its
accomplishments came to be exactly measured by bank clearings.
It was unfortunate but inevitable. The idea was too seductive to

the American mentality not to be seized upon and made to serve a rising order. Exploitation was the business of the times and how better could exploitation throw about its activities the sanction of idealism than by wedding them to progress? It is a misfortune that America has never subjected the abstract idea of progress to critical examination. Content with the frontier and capitalistic interpretations it has confused change with betterment, and when a great idealist of the Gilded Age demonstrated to America that it was misled and pointed out that the path of progress it was following was the highway to poverty, he was hooted from the market-place.

Having thus thrown the mantle of progress about the Gold Dust twins, the Gilded Age was ready to bring the political forces of America into harmony with the program of preëmption and exploitation. The situation could hardly have been more to its liking. Post-war America was wholly lacking in political philosophies, wholly opportunist. The old party cleavage between agriculture and industry had been obscured and the logic of party alignment destroyed by the struggle over slavery. Democrat and Whig no longer faced each other conscious of the different ends they sought. The great party of Jefferson and Jackson was prostrate, borne down by the odium of slavery and secession. In the North elements of both had been drawn into a motley war party, momentarily fused by the bitterness of conflict, but lacking any common program, certain indeed to split on fundamental economic issues. The Whig Republican was still Hamiltonian paternalistic, and the Democrat Republican was still Jeffersonian *laissez faire*, and until it was determined which wing should control the party councils there would be only confusion. The politicians were fertile in compromises, but in nominating Lincoln and Johnson the party ventured to get astride two horses that would not run together. To attempt to make yoke-fellows of democratic leveling and capitalistic paternalism was prophetic of rifts and schisms that only the passions of Reconstruction days could hold in check.

In 1865 the Republican party was no other than a war machine that had accomplished its purpose. It was a political mongrel, without logical cohesion, and it seemed doomed to break up as the Whig party had broken up and the Federalist party had broken up. But fate was now on the side of the Whigs as it had not been earlier. The democratic forces had lost strength from the war, and democratic principles were in ill repute. The drift to centralization, the enormous development of capitalism, the spirit of exploitation, were prophetic of a changing temper that was preparing to exalt the doctrine of manifest destiny which the Whig party stood sponsor for. The middle class was in the saddle and it was time to bring the political state under its control. The practical problem of the moment was to transform the mongrel Republican party into a strong cohesive instrument, and to accomplish that it was necessary to hold the loyalty of its Democratic voters amongst the farmers and working-classes whilst putting into effect its Whig program.

Under normal conditions the thing would have been impossible, but the times were wrought up and blindly passionate and the politicians skillful. The revolt of Andrew Johnson came near to bringing the party on the rocks; but the undisciplined Jacksonians were overthrown by the appeal to the Bloody Flag and put to flight by the nomination of General Grant for the presidency. The rebellion of the Independent Republicans under Horace Greeley in 1872 was brought to nothing by the skillful use of Grant's military prestige, and the party passed definitely under the control of capitalism, and became such an instrument for exploitation as Henry Clay dreamed of but could not perfect. Under the nominal leadership of the easy-going Grant a loose rein was given to Whiggish ambitions and the Republican party became a political instrument worthy of the Gilded Age.

The triumph of Whiggery was possible because the spirit of the Gilded Age was Whiggish. The picturesque embodiment of the multitude of voters who hurrahed for Grant and the Grand Old Party was a figure who had grown his first beard in the ebullient days before Secession. Colonel Beriah Sellers, with his genial optimism and easy political ethics, was an epitome of the political hopes of the Gilded Age. With a Micawber-like faith in his country and his government, eager to realize on his expansive dreams and looking to the national treasury to scatter its fructifying millions in the neighborhood of his speculative holdings, he was no other than Uncle Sam in the boisterous days following Appomattox. The hopes that floated up out of his dreams were the hopes of millions who cast their votes for Republican Congressmen who in return were expected to cast their votes for huge governmental appropriations that would insure prosperity's reaching certain post-office addresses. Citizens had saved the government in the trying days that were past; it was only fair in return that government should aid the patriotic citizen in the necessary work of developing national resources. It was paternalism as understood by speculators and subsidy-hunters, but was it not a part of the great American System that was to make the country rich and self-sufficient? The American System had been talked of for forty years; it had slowly got on its feet in pre-war days despite the stubborn planter opposition; now at last it had fairly come into its own. The time was ripe for the Republican party to become a fairy godmother to the millions of Beriah Sellerses throughout the North and West.

It is plain as a pikestaff why the spirit of Whiggery should have taken riotous possession of the Gilded Age. With its booming industrial cities America in 1870 was fast becoming capitalistic, and in every capitalistic society Whiggery springs up as naturally as pigweed in a garden. However attractive the disguises it may assume, it is in essence the logical creed of the profit philosophy. It is the expression in politics of the acquisitive instinct and it assumes as the greatest good the shaping of public policy to promote private interests. It asserts that it is a duty of the state to help its citizens to make money, and it conceives of the political state as a useful instrument for effective exploitation. How otherwise? The public good cannot be served apart from business interests, for business interests are the public good and in serving business the state is serving society. Everybody's eggs are in the basket and they must not be broken. For a capitalistic society Whiggery is the only rational politics, for it exalts the profit-motive as the sole object of parliamentary concern. Government has only to wave its wand and fairy gifts descend upon business like the golden sands of Pactolus. It graciously bestows its tariffs and subsidies, and streams of wealth flow into private wells.

But unhappily there is a fly in the Whiggish honey. In a competitive order, government is forced to make its choices. It cannot serve both Peter and Paul. If it gives with one hand it must take away with the other. And so the persuasive ideal of paternalism in the common interest degenerates in practice into legalized favoritism. Governmental gifts go to the largest investments. Lesser interests are sacrificed to greater interests and Whiggery comes finally to serve the lords of the earth without whose good will the

wheels of business will not turn. To him that hath shall be given.
If the few do not prosper the many will starve, and if the many
have bread who would begrudge the few their abundance?   In
Whiggery is the fulfillment of the Scriptures.

Henry Clay had been a prophetic figure pointing the way America was to travel; but he came a generation too soon. A son of
the Gilded Age, he was doomed to live in a world of Jacksonian
democracy. But the spirit of Henry Clay survived his death and
his followers were everywhere in the land. The plain citizen who
wanted a slice of the rich prairie land of Iowa or Kansas, with a
railway convenient to his homestead, had learned to look to the
government for a gift, and if he got his quarter-section and his
transportation he was careless about what the other fellow got.
A little more or less could make no difference to a country inexhaustible in resources. America belonged to the American people
and not to the government, and resources in private hands paid
taxes and increased the national wealth. In his favorite newspaper,
the *New York Tribune*, he read daily appeals for the adoption of
a patriotic national economy, by means of which an infant industrialism, made prosperous by a protective tariff, would provide
a home market for the produce of the farmer and render the
country self-sufficient. Money would thus be put in everybody's pocket. Protection was not robbing Peter to pay Paul,
but paying both Peter and Paul out of the augmented wealth of
the whole.

The seductive arguments that Horace Greeley disseminated
amongst the plain people, Henry Carey purveyed to more intelligent ears. The most distinguished American economist of the
time, Carey had abandoned his earlier *laissez-faire* position, and
having convinced himself that only through a close-knit national
economy could the country develop a well-rounded economic program, he had become the most ardent of protectionists. During the
fifties and later he was tireless in popularizing the doctrine of a
natural harmony of interests between agriculture and manufacturing, and to a generation expanding rapidly in both fields his
able presentation made great appeal. It was but a step from protectionism to governmental subsidies. Beriah Sellers and Henry
Clay had come to be justified by the political economists. (Note
that amongst Carey's converts were such different idealists as
Wendell Phillips and Peter Cooper.)

THE GREAT BARBECUE

Horace Greeley and Henry Carey were only straws in the wind that during the Gilded Age was blowing the doctrine of paternalism about the land. A Colonel Sellers was to be found at every fireside talking the same blowsy doctrine. Infectious in their optimism, naïve in their faith that something would be turned up for them by the government if they made known their wants, they were hoping for dollars to be put in their pockets by a generous administration at Washington. Congress had rich gifts to bestow—in lands, tariffs, subsidies, favors of all sorts; and when influential citizens made their wishes known to the reigning statesmen, the sympathetic politicians were quick to turn the government into the fairy godmother the voters wanted it to be. A huge barbecue was spread to which all presumably were invited. Not quite all, to be sure; inconspicuous persons, those who were at home on the farm or at work in the mills and offices, were overlooked; a good many indeed out of the total number of the American people. But all the important persons, leading bankers and promoters and business men, received invitations. There wasn't room for everybody and these were presumed to represent the whole. It was a splendid feast. If the waiters saw to it that the choicest portions were served to favored guests, they were not unmindful of their numerous homespun constituency and they loudly proclaimed the fine democratic principle that what belongs to the people should be enjoyed by the people—not with petty bureaucratic restrictions, not as a social body, but as individuals, each free citizen using what came to hand for his own private ends, with no questions asked.

It was sound Gilded Age doctrine. To a frontier people what was more democratic than a barbecue, and to a paternalistic age what was more fitting than that the state should provide the beeves for roasting. Let all come and help themselves. As a result the feast was Gargantuan in its rough plenty. The abundance was what was to be expected of a generous people. More food, to be sure, was spoiled than was eaten, and the revelry was a bit unseemly; but it was a fine spree in the name of the people, and the invitations had been written years before by Henry Clay. But unfortunately what was intended to be jovially democratic was marred by displays of plebeian temper. Suspicious commoners with better eyes than

manners discovered the favoritism of the waiters and drew attention to the difference between their own meager helpings and the
heaped-up plates of more favored guests. It appeared indeed that
there was gross discrimination in the service; that the farmers'
pickings from the Homestead Act were scanty in comparison with
the speculators' pickings from the railway land-grants. The *Crédit
Mobilier* scandal and the Whisky Ring scandal and divers other
scandals came near to breaking up the feast, and the genial host—
who was no other than the hero of Appomattox—came in for some
sharp criticism. But after the more careless ones who were caught
with their fingers where they didn't belong, had been thrust from
the table, the eating and drinking went on again till only the great
carcasses were left. Then at last came the reckoning. When the
bill was sent in to the American people the farmers discovered that
they had been put off with the giblets while the capitalists were
consuming the turkey. They learned that they were no match at a
barbecue for more voracious guests, and as they went home unsatisfied, a sullen anger burned in their hearts that was to express
itself later in fierce agrarian revolts.

What reason there was for such anger, how differently rich and
poor fared at the democratic feast, is suggested by the contrast
between the Homestead Act and the Union Pacific land-grant.
Both were war-time measures and both had emerged from the
agitations of earlier decades. By the terms of the former the homesteader got his hundred and sixty acres at the price of $1.25 an
acre; by the terms of the latter the promoters got a vast empire for
nothing. It was absurd, of course, but what would you have? The
people wanted the railway built and Collis P. Huntington was
willing to build it on his own terms. The government was too
generous to haggle with public-spirited citizens, and too Whiggish
to want to discourage individual enterprise. Ever since the cession
of California there had been much talk of a continental railway
to tie the country together. In the first years the talk in Congress
had all been of a great national venture; the road must be built by
the nation to serve the common interests of the American people.
But unfortunately sectional jealousies prevented any agreement as
to the route the survey lines were to run, and the rising capitalism
was becoming powerful enough to bring into disfavor any engagement of the government in a work that promised great rewards.
Under its guidance political opinion was skillfully turned into the

channel of private enterprise. The public domain backed by the public credit, it was agreed, must pay for the road, but the government must not seek to control the enterprise or look to profit from it directly; the national reward would come indirectly from the opening-up of vast new territories.

The definite shift in policy came about the year 1855. In 1837 Stephen A. Douglas had been the driving force behind the state enterprise of building the Illinois Central Railway. In 1853 he proposed that the Pacific Railroad should be built by private enterprise. With the change promptly came a request for a patriotic land-grant. The government was expected to provide the road, it appeared, but private enterprise was to own it and manage it in the interest of speculators rather than the public. For old-fashioned souls like Thomas A. Benton, who still remembered the Jeffersonian concern for the common well-being, it was a bitter mess to swallow.

I would have preferred [he said] that Congress should have made the road, as a national work, on a scale commensurate with its grandeur and let out the use of it to companies, who would fetch and carry on the best terms for the people and the government. But that hope has vanished . . . a private company has become the resource and the preference. I embrace it as such, utterly scouting all plans for making private roads at national expense, of paying for the use of roads built with our land and money, of bargaining with corporations or individuals for the use of what we give them.[3]

With this speech the old Jeffersonianism pulled down its flag and the new Whiggery ran up its black banner. The Gilded Age had begun and Old Bullion Benton had outlived his time. In the tumultuous decades that followed there was to be no bargaining with corporations for the use of what the public gave; they took what they wanted and no impertinent questions were asked. The hungriest will get the most at the barbecue. A careless wastefulness when the supply is unlimited is perhaps natural enough. There were hard-headed men in the world of Beriah Sellers who knew how easy it was to overreach the simple, and it was they who got most from the common pot. We may call them buccaneers if we choose, and speak of the great barbecue as a democratic debauch. But why single out a few, when all were drunk? Whisky was plentiful at barbecues, and if too liberal potations brought the

[3] Quoted in J. P. Davis, *The Union Pacific Railway*, pp. 67–68.

Gilded Age to the grossest extravagancies, if when it cast up accounts it found its patrimony gone, it was only repeating the experience of a certain man who went down to Jericho. To create a social civilization requires sober heads, and in this carousal of economic romanticism sober heads were few—the good Samaritan was busy elsewhere.

The doctrine of preëmption and exploitation was reaping its harvest. The frontier spirit was having its splurge, and progress was already turning its face in another direction. Within the next half-century this picturesque America with its heritage of crude energy —greedy, lawless, capable—was to be transformed into a vast uniform middle-class land, dedicated to capitalism and creating the greatest machine-order known to history. A scattered agricultural people, steeped in particularistic jealousies and suspicious of centralization, was to be transformed into an urbanized factory people, rootless, migratory, drawn to the job as by a magnet. It was to come about the more easily because the American farmer had never been a land-loving peasant, rooted to the soil and thriving only in daily contact with familiar acres. He had long been half middle-class, accounting unearned increment the most profitable crop, and buying and selling land as if it were calico. And in consequence the vigorous individualism that had sprung from frontier conditions decayed with the passing of the frontier, and those who had lost in the gamble of preëmption and exploitation were added to the growing multitude of the proletariat. It was from such materials, supplemented by a vast influx of immigrants, that was fashioned the America we know today with its standardized life, its machine culture, its mass psychology—an America to which Jefferson and Jackson and Lincoln would be strangers.

v

FOLK HEROES

Perhaps one cannot penetrate more directly to the heart of the Gilded Age than in taking account of certain of its heroes, figures of earth whom it accounted great in its generation, and to whom its admiration flowed out in unstinted measure. It is our own secret desires we attribute to our gods, and if from the muck of the times a queer lot of heroes was singled out, if an undisciplined generation rioting in its new freedoms chose to honor men who had scrambled upward in uncouth ways, it only suggests that such figures were a composite picture of the secret desires of an age vastly concerned with getting on. From a host of striking personalities two must suffice to suggest the spirit of the times, authentic folk-heroes of the Gilded Age, fashioned out of the commonest stuff and realizing such greatness as multitudes of Americans were then dreaming of; and over against them a third figure, a mordant intellectual, who sardonically swam with the stream of tendency and in serving all the gods of the Gilded Age gained for himself a brilliant career.

I

GENERAL GRANT

Greatest of all the heroes of the age was the victor of Appomattox. His fame was in all men's mouths, and his reputation was substantial enough to withstand the attacks of enemies and the gross shortcomings of his own character. It was not for any singular or remarkable qualities of mind or personality that General Grant was taken to the heart of his generation, but rather because he was so completely a product of the times, so strikingly an embodiment of its virtues and weaknesses. In his spectacular career were the sharp contrasts that appealed to a plebeian people wanting in fine and discriminating standards of appraisal. He had come up from the people and the marks of his origins—the slovenly manners and uncritical force of frontier folk-ways—were stamped on him as indelibly as they were stamped on his fellow soldiers who proclaimed his greatness. To a later generation he seems an odd and unaccountable figure for the high rôle of national hero, yet he was as native and homespun as Lincoln, like him sprung from the common stock and learning his lessons from harsh experience, a figure blown to huge dimensions by the passions of civil war. A generation that discovered something praiseworthy in the "smartness" of Jim Fisk, in the burly acquisitiveness of Commodore Vanderbilt, or in the clever humbuggery of Barnum the Showman, certainly would judge with no very critical eyes the claims to greatness of a grim leader of armies who succeeded where so many before had failed.

General Grant was no conventional military hero. It was not the gold stars on his epaulets that dazzled his generation. The people of the North had seen too many gold stars rise and set on the military horizon, they had been stricken too sorely by the bitter struggle, to be caught by military popinjays. They had gone through the fire and any hero of theirs must himself have passed through the fire. It was something veracious in the man, something solid and unyielding in the soldier, something plain as an old shoe in the field marshal of bloody battles, that caught the imagination of the North and made Grant a hero—this together with a certain gift of pungent phrase, befitting the leader of democratic hosts, that served to spread his fame amongst the common people. Vicksburg did much for his reputation, but the demand for "unconditional surrender," sent to a Confederate leader, did far more. The words fixed his character in the popular mind. Here at last was a fighting man who instead of planning how to fall back, as other generals did, thought only of going ahead; so the popular judgment shut its eyes to his dull plebeian character and set a wreath on his brows. It rested there somewhat grotesquely. In spite of a deep unconscious integrity and a stubborn will that drove him forward along whatever path his feet were set on, he was the least imposing of military heroes. Short, stooped, lumpish in mind and body, unintellectual and unimaginative, devoid of ideas and with no tongue to express the incoherent emotions that surged dully in his heart, he was a commonplace fellow that no gold braid could set off. He hated war and disliked soldiering, yet accepting life with a stolid fatalism he fought his bloody way to ultimate victory.

Graduated from West Point after four sterile years of drill, quite uneducated and unread even in his profession, he served for a time at different army posts, went through the Mexican War—which he looked upon as a stupid imperialistic debauch—as quartermaster without gaining distinction, and eventually, oppressed by the eventless routine of garrison life, he fell into the habit of solitary drinking and was dismissed from the service. Misfortune that it seemed, it was his making. Only as a volunteer could he have risen so quickly to high command; as a captain or major in the regular army he would have been detailed as drill-master to the raw troops and have had no chance. Nevertheless hard times came with his dismissal. Indolent by nature and inclined to drift, he was as incompetent a man in practical affairs as one could find in a frontier township. But with a wife and children to support he must turn his hand to something, so he tried his luck at farming, selling real estate, and various odd jobs, yet all the time growing poorer and seedier, till the war came and picking him up flung him to mountain heights of popularity and reputation. Thereafter till his death he was accounted the greatest American of his generation. No accumulating evidence of his well-meaning but witless incapacity in civic and political affairs could pluck from his brows the wreath that had been thrust upon him.

In his spectacular career Grant was an embodiment of the dreams of all the Beriah Sellerses of the Gilded Age. He was a materialistic hero of a materialistic generation. He was dazzled by wealth and power, and after years of bitter poverty he sat down in the lap of luxury with huge content. He took what the gods sent, and if houses and fast horses and wines and cigars were showered upon him he accepted them as a child would accept gifts from a fairy godmother. He had had enough of skimping meanness; with his generation he wanted to slough off the drabness of the frontier; he wanted the good things of life that had so long been denied him, and he was not scrupulous about looking a gift horse in the mouth. He sought out the company of rich men. He was never happier than when enjoying the luxury of Jay Cooke's mansion in Philadelphia or riding with A. T. Stewart in Central Park. As he grew fat and stodgy the vulgar side of his plebeian nature was thrown into sharper relief. He accepted gifts with both hands, and he seems never to have suspected the price that would be exacted of the President for the presents to the General. He never realized how great a bill was sent to the American people for the wine he drank or the cigars he smoked with his wealthy hosts; yet if the wine had been molten gold and the cigars platinum they would have been far cheaper. In return for a few boxes of choice Havanas, Jay Cooke laid his hands on millions of western lands for the Northern Pacific Railway. It was the way of the Gilded Age, and Grant was only doing what all his friends and associates were doing. If he accepted a fifty-thousand-dollar house in Philadelphia, his comrade General Sherman accepted a hundred-thousand-dollar house at Washington. Such gifts were not bribes; they were open and aboveboard; it was the free and easy way of the times. What the age was careless about is the fact that it is hard to refuse a reasonable request from one's fairy godmother, and what the General never understood is that if one is President such a godmother is certain to be a very dangerous member of the family.

There was far too much of that sort of thing all about him for Grant to serve as President with credit to himself or profit to the country. Honest himself, he was the source of more dishonesty in others than any other American President. His eight years in the White House marked the lowest depths—in domestic affairs at least—to which any American administration has fallen. They were little better than a national disgrace. All the festering evils of post-war times came to a head and pock-marked the body politic from head to foot. Scandal and corruption whispered all about him, the hands of his closest advisers were dirty; yet he stubbornly refused to hear the whispers or see the dirt. In judging men and policies he was no more than a child. He could never distinguish between an honest man and a rascal. He was loyal to his friends and open-handedness he regarded as a mark of friendship. In the end it turned out that like the thieves of Jericho his blatant followers despoiled him of pretty nearly everything.

In what must pass for his political views Grant was as naïvely uninformed as a Wyoming cowboy. Utterly wanting in knowledge of political principles, he was a fit leader for the organized mob that called itself the Republican party, whose chief objective was the raiding of the treasure-box of which it was the responsible guardian. He had been nominally a Democrat and the first vote he cast for President he cast for Buchanan. After Lincoln's death he turned naturally to President Johnson and was one of his supporters till the wily Radical group got his ear and carried him over to the rival camp. They wanted his reputation to hide under, and they took possession of it with no great credit to the General's reputation. Thereafter he was a Republican of the Whig wing. It was where he belonged. He was swayed politically by his emotional reactions and it was natural for him to drift into the opulent camp of money and power. His frontier democracy sloughed away and with his generation he went over easily to a buccaneer capitalism. No social conscience obtruded itself to give him trouble. His millionaire friends were Whig Republicans and with his respect for rich men, his admiration for material success, he found himself in congenial company amongst the Whig group. About the only political policy he ever interested himself in was the policy of a protective tariff, and his Whig associates took care that his interest did not wane. Yet so completely did the naïve General reflect the spirit of the Gilded Age that his noisy followers, conspiring to confuse in the public mind southern reconstruction and capitalistic expansion, and hiding a precious set of rascals in the folds of the bloody flag, came near to making him President for a third term. The General was bitterly disappointed at their failure, and the General's wife, who liked to live in the White House, was even more disappointed. To millions of Americans Grant was an authentic hero, to Mark Twain he was a very great man, and to Jay Cooke he was a pawn to be used in the noble strategy of fortune-seeking. What a comedy it all seems now—yet one that leaves an unpleasant taste in the mouth.

Yet to dismiss the stolid General thus is scarcely to do justice to the substantial core of the man. There remains the work written in pain during his last days, the two volumes of *Memoirs* that in their plain directness—as uninspired, says a late biographer, as "a bale of hay"— laid bare his honest simplicity and rugged meagerness. No blackguard and no charlatan could have written such pages. If General Grant was not the great man so many thought, he was a native growth from American soil, endowed like his age with a dogged will and a plodding energy, and he gave his country what he had. Though the branches of the tree were ungainly and offered too hospitable shelter to unseemly birds of the night, the gnarly trunk was sound at the heart.

2

JAY COOKE

Another hero of the times likewise was flung up as it were casually out of obscurity and reaped an amazing harvest from the gigantic struggle. In those difficult years the name of Jay Cooke— "the financier of the Civil War," as his biographer calls him— became as familiar to the people of the North as the names of Grant and Lincoln, and was often joined with theirs as that of one of the saviors of the Union. He was the first great American banker, and good fortune sent him into the world at a moment when his skill in brokerage found opportunity for free play. The war was as great a godsend to Jay Cooke as it was to Grant, for alone amongst our money-lenders he realized the problems and foresaw the profits in a popular system of war financing. He was a pioneer in exploring all the potentialities of the banker's trade, and in his dramatic exploitation of salesmanship and his skillful manipulation of money and credit he marked out the highway our later financiers have traveled. Jay Cooke occupies too significant a place in the history of American capitalism to be overlooked in casting up the accounts of the Gilded Age.

Of Yankee-Puritan stock, he was born in the frontier hamlet of Sandusky, Ohio, when the Western Reserve was at the beginning of its development. His father was a country lawyer of Federalist-Whig affinities, proficient in high-flown western oratory, who liked to be much in the neighborhood eye. He was a pushing, self-confident fellow, highly patriotic, soberly moral, fearing God and loving his country, who felt that the government he supported so heartily should serve him and his town with equal heartiness. His readiness in florid speech won him a single term in Congress, and he used his position as a heaven-sent opportunity to promote a government road from Sandusky—which it seems was not prospering as its inhabitants had expected it would—deep into the Indian country. It was a good Clay-Whig scheme of internal improvement; it would open up a rich timber country, and be highly profitable to the real-estate promoters of Sandusky. Cradled thus in speculation and faith in a benevolent government, his three sons grew up native Whigs, with vigorous Puritan-Yankee minds, who found no difficulty in reconciling the interests of God and Mammon. Eager to get on "the right side of fortune," they went into the three professions of banking, journalism, and the law. The eldest, Pitt, found the law little to his liking; the youngest, Henry, labored diligently at journalism, at Sandusky and later at Columbus, where he was part owner of the *Ohio State Journal* and "boss" of young William Dean Howells, who was likewise seeking to rise through the medium of journalism. It was the family itch for politics that took him to Columbus, and although the venture was financially unsuccessful it brought him influential connections. He was useful to Governor Salmon P. Chase, afterwards to be Lincoln's Secretary of the Treasury, and to John Sherman, who was later to become a great influence on financial policies at Washington. His reward came in the shape of an appointment to do the government binding, reputed to be worth $25,000—a commission that allowed him to unload his paper on some investors who speedily lost the $20,000 they put into it.

Henry Cooke's Whiggery was justifying itself, yet to both Pitt and Henry it soon became clear that Jay had hit upon the true road to wealth. At twelve years of age he had begun his career in his father's store at Sandusky, and with characteristic enterprise

he put in some side lines and became "quite a capitalist." At
fourteen he ventured so far as St. Louis to help in a general store,
and at the age of seventeen he went to Philadelphia and took a
place in a broker-banker's office. That was in 1839, a golden time
for brokers, when every business man must keep a sharp eye on
the table of banknote discounts and see to it that bad paper was
worked off. Into this world of discounts and premiums the young
clerk plunged with immense zest. "The business I am engaged in
is of the most respectable kind and the house is the first in the
city," [4] he wrote to Pitt Cooke. "He was ambitious, industrious,
and faithful to each day's duties," his biographer reports of him.
His quick mind ran to calculations and his slender sensitive fingers
seemed made for telling money. He was soon the admiration of
the office, an expert in detecting counterfeits, a walking table of
"wild-cat" currency, with a genius for smelling out possible commissions. Every art of extracting profits from note-shaving, gold-
juggling, delayed payments, and other devices known to the world
of brokerage, he speedily made himself master of. When he reached
his majority he was entered a member of the firm, and before he
was thirty he aided his partners—"noble" fellows he called them,
of honest Puritan extraction—in squeezing huge commissions out
of the financing of the Mexican War. "It was a grand time for
brokers and private banking," he remarked; and late in life he
wrote glowingly of his cleverness in twice overreaching the Secretary of the Treasury. It was quite legal and the patriotic banker
was vastly pleased to report, "So we victimized him again." [5]
He was the brains of the company and under his guidance the business piled up profits at an astonishing rate. During the panic of
1854 he wrote: "We use our money at 1 1/2 to 3 per cent. per
month from day to day and frequently it pays 1/8 to 1/4 a day.
We have done a noble business since 1st of January; profits up to
1st July $135,000." [6] On the reorganization of the firm in 1858
he withdrew, and three years later, on January 1, 1861, he opened
the doors of what was soon to become the greatest banking-house
in America, Jay Cooke and Company of Philadelphia.

He was then in his fortieth year and his private fortune he reckoned at $150,000. But with the breaking-out of the war, oppor-

[4] E. P. Oberholtzer, *Jay Cooke, Financier of the Civil War*, Vol. I, p. 52.
[5] *Ibid.*, Vol. I, pp. 81 and 83.
[6] *Ibid.*, Vol. I, p. 85.

tunity knocked at the door of the new bank. Ardently patriotic, Jay Cooke was anxious to do his bit for the cause, but he seems never to have thought of going to the front. He came of fighting Revolutionary stock, but love of the battlefield had died out of the family. His father had been drafted for the War of 1812, but hired a substitute who was unfortunate enough to be killed, and none of the three sons got nearer the front than the Treasury Department at Washington. It was there that the battles of the Cooke brothers were fought. Henry Cooke went to Washington to attend the inauguration of the new administration, and twenty-one days later Jay Cooke modestly proposed a plan for mobilizing the resources of the firm in defense of the country. On March 25, he wrote to his brother:

What we wish to do with the Treasury is to have the Department allow us to make the frequent transfers that are made from point to point instead of giving the business to Adams and Company [Express]. We can make those transfers and the Department when flush can give us 30, 60, 90 or 120 days time, as it is no loss to them, and the interest in the meantime would be clear profit and to be divided.[7]

When the magnitude of the task in which the country was engaged became clear to him he was no longer content with a single banking-house at Philadelphia. A branch at Washington under the shadow of the Treasury was highly desirable, and Henry Cooke was the man for the business. A born lobbyist, a close friend of John Sherman—who was looking out for a profitable opening in some war business for a brother—and of Secretary of the Treasury Chase, he let no grass grow under his feet. The war loans had not been taken freely and in July, Jay Cooke wrote to Chase suggesting a close alliance between the Treasury and two Philadelphia firms, Jay Cooke and Company and Drexel and Company.

We would wish to make our business mostly out of the Treasury operations and we feel sure that we could by having a proper understanding with yourself greatly help you in the management of your vast negotiations. . . . We could not be expected to leave our comfortable homes and positions here without some great inducement and we state frankly that we would, if we succeeded, expect a fair commission from the Treasury in some shape for our labor and talent. If you feel disposed to say to us . . . that you will give us the management of the loans to be issued by the government during the war, allowing us a fair commission on them, . . . we are ready to throw ourselves into the matter heartily. . . .[8]

[7] *Ibid.*, Vol. I, pp. 132–133.   [8] See *Ibid.*, Vol. I, pp. 143–144.

It was quite an amazing proposal and one that Secretary Chase dared not accept. Bankers and brokers in New York and Boston would scarcely approve a monopoly of loan-commissions granted to two Philadelphia houses. But Jay Cooke would not acknowledge defeat. He cultivated the acquaintance of the Secretary, lent him money, entertained his family, presented him with gifts, and gave him sound advice. He took the harassed servant of the people to his warm and generous heart and was vigilant in keeping him out of the clutches of Copperhead profiteers. His opportunity came in October, 1861, when in competition with other brokers he undertook the sale of a new bond-series. His success was so great that he won the complete confidence of Secretary Chase, and it was only a matter of time when he should secure his coveted monopoly. In February, 1862, he opened the branch house at Washington, immediately opposite the Treasury building, and Henry Cooke soon made its offices an indispensable club for Congressmen and government employees. He was charmingly cordial and during the next ten years he knew everybody and every political move at the Capital. With the same bland and deacon-like appearance as his brother, he was master of the art of ingratiating himself into the confidence of influential men, and successive Secretaries of the Treasury—Chase and Fessenden and McCulloch—were easily induced to look with partial eye upon the firm of Jay Cooke and Company. When Grant returned to Washington after the war he was soon like a brother to Henry Cooke, and when the General had tasted the quality of cigars kept for his use at Jay Cooke's Philadelphia home, his heart warmed to the kindly banker.

Meanwhile the firm was discovering innumerable ways to help win the war; amongst others Henry Cooke put through a congressional franchise for a street railway at Washington, and the new cars were soon carrying citizens and soldiers to and fro, to their great content and the company's great profit. He was hourly in and out of the Treasury and he knew as much about the government business as the Secretary. The interests of the firm extended with amazing rapidity; other banks came under their control and their agents were everywhere. Their later successes in selling bonds were a revelation to older-fashioned brokers. On the day that Richmond fell the "financier of the Civil War" marked out the lines of a pretentious country house that was to cost a million dollars and to become a show place of America, where Secretaries of the Treasury,

Presidents, and great men from every walk of life were to find a welcome release from their cares. "As rich as Jay Cooke" had become a common saying from the Atlantic to the Pacific. The gigantic war had been no ill wind to the money-teller of 1861.

In certain aspects Jay Cooke may be reckoned the first modern American. He was the first to understand the psychology of mass salesmanship. It was his fertile brain that created the syndicate and conceived and executed the modern American "drive." Under his bland deacon-like exterior was the mind of a realist. He assumed that every man has his price, but he knew that few men like to acknowledge the fact even to themselves; so he was at immense pains to cover our poor human nakedness with generous professions. If he were to lure dollars from old stockings in remote chimney-corners he must "sell" patriotism to his fellow Americans; and to do that successfully he must manufacture a militant public opinion. The soldier at the front, he announced in a flood of advertisements, must be supported at the rear. It was every loyal American's war, and patriotism demanded that idle dollars—in greenbacks—should be lent to the boys in blue, and a grateful government would return them, both principal and interest, in gold. To induce slacker dollars to become fighting dollars he placed his agents in every neighborhood, in newspaper offices, in banks, in pulpits—patriotic forerunners of the "one-minute men" of later drives. They also served their country, he pointed out, who sold government bonds on commission. He subsidized the press with a lavish hand, not only the metropolitan dailies but the obscurest country weeklies. He employed an army of hack-writers to prepare syndicated matter and he scattered paying copy broadcast. His "hired friends" were everywhere. In a hundred delicate ways he showed his appreciation of patriotic coöperation in the bond-sales—gifts of trout caught with his own hand, baskets of fruit from his own garden. He bought the pressings of whole vineyards and cases of wine flowed in an endless stream to strategic publicity-points. Rival brokers hinted that he was debauching the press, but the army of greenbacks marching to the front was his reply. It all cost a pretty penny, but the government was liberal with commissions and when all expenses were deducted perhaps two millions of profits remained in the vaults of the firm, to be added to the many other millions which the prestige of the government agency with its free advertising brought in its train.

With such prestige and with the greatest fluid resources as yet accumulated by any American, it was inevitable that the Rothschild of the North should play a bold part in the speculations of the Gilded Age. Jay Cooke vastly enjoyed the game and it was idle to expect him to sit back quietly when others were playing for high stakes. In those halcyon days promoters were as thick as flies about a dead carcass; wild-cat railroads had succeeded wild-cat banks as short-cuts to wealth; and in an unlucky moment Jay Cooke was tempted. He had expected to be made Secretary of the Treasury by President Grant, but failing of appointment in spite of countless boxes of twenty-five-cent cigars provided for the General's pleasure, he determined to back the Northern Pacific Railway enterprise. The company had been chartered in July, 1864, receiving a congressional grant of 12,800 acres of public land for every mile of track laid in the states, and double that amount in the territories. As the proposed line would run almost entirely through territories the grand total was reckoned at 47,360,000 acres.[9] Early land-sales were at the rate of $6 an acre. At such valuation the prospective value of the grant through the territories was $153,600 for every mile of track, yet in portions of an earlier line absorbed by the company the road had been built for $8,225 a mile, and a stretch of 112 miles at the rate of $9,500.[10] To be sure there were great stretches of unsalable land, but in compensation the company was free to run its surveys so as to embrace choice mineral deposits, virgin timber, water-power, and town sites.

As Jay Cooke contemplated the possibilities his buoyant temperament took fire, and he dreamed of empire-building. He quickly rationalized the project into a great patriotic undertaking that would carry the blessings of civilization to the farthest Northwest. He would lay open to the poor man the rich wheat lands of the Dakotas, the mineral wealth of the Rockies, the vast timber resources of the Puget Sound territory. He would annex western Canada by benevolent absorption. It was a dream worthy of the Gilded Age and Jay Cooke was chief amongst the Beriah Sellerses of the day. He threw himself into the project with boundless optimism, and proved again his right to be called a great financier. He proposed to sell the Northern Pacific as he had sold govern-

[9] See *Ibid.*, Vol. II, pp. 97–98.
[10] C. E. Russell, *Stories of Great Railroads*, p. 19.

ment bonds. He had learned that to catch the little fish he must first catch the big fish, for the shilling is timid till the pound shows the way. He must create confidence, cost what it would, and to that end he opened a huge pool and created a special syndicate. Stocks, jobs, cash, influence, were distributed judiciously where they would do good. In the language of stock-jobbing much "sweetening" was used.[11] And there was need of much "sweetening," for the times were inauspicious. Jay Cooke drove the publicity work with his old vigor, but sales were slow, and as the great patriotic venture showed signs of lagging he turned for help to a sympathetic government.

His engineer had made a careful estimate of the prospective cost of the road, which including rolling-stock, terminals, a branch line to Portland, and interest on bonds during the construction, came to $42,638 a mile for the entire line.[12] But the financier was not satisfied "with the magnificent property the government has given us," and made ready to buy from Congress a revision of the terms of the charter, which amongst other things would widen the land-grant belt through the territories to 120 miles, convey a second right-of-way zone from the Rocky Mountains to the Pacific, and permit the company to hypothecate the whole before the terms of the contract were fulfilled. It was an audacious proposal even to a generation used to audacious proposals. There was bitter opposition, for the rumblings of the *Crédit Mobilier* scandal were already disturbing the halls of Congress; but his lobbyists used "the company's money freely" to bring in the common breed of Congressmen, and the Cooke brothers employed their well-practiced skill to take care of such important persons as Speaker Blaine of the House, Vice-President Colfax of the Senate, and President Grant. The matter was handled with great delicacy in the case of the latter—"the glorious honest man," the banker called him. "He sent a fishing-rod and creel to the President's little son Jesse, for which he was duly thanked in a childish hand." He invited

---

[11] The list of his "beneficiaries," some of whom were drawn in delicately and some realistically, included, according to his biographer, Vice-President Colfax, Speaker Blaine and James A. Garfield of the House, Governor Rutherford B. Hayes of Ohio and Governor Geary of Pennsylvania, General Horace Porter, President Grant's private secretary, Senators John Sherman, William Windom, and Ben Wade, Delegate Garfielde of Washington Territory, Bayard Taylor. Amongst the papers were Henry Ward Beecher's *Christian Union*, Greeley's *Tribune*, the *Philadelphia Press*, the *Washington Chronicle*, the *London Times*.

[12] See Oberholtzer, Vol. II, p. 154.

the General to a day's fishing-trip, and together the heroes whipped the trout stream in the most charming comradeship. "It may be thought," remarks his biographer, "that such machinations were unbecoming in a man of Mr. Cooke's moral dimensions." [13] But surely delicate "machinations" were not unbecoming to such "moral dimensions." "We let the other side do most of the talking," wrote the deacon-like Henry Cooke, who kept the Sabbath as strictly as his brother, "and we do the voting." The President's cabinet was bitterly divided on the issue, but wheels turn on well-greased axles and delicate attentions have their reward. The bill was signed and the building of the Northwest empire could go forward.

Unfortunately, however, black days were pressing hard on the great success. The money of the company ran in fructifying streams through Europe and America but the expected crop was short. Thirty papers were subsidized in Germany; agents lived in ducal palaces; commissions, stocks, bonuses, were plowed in for manure; but the crop of bond-sales was still scanty. Ugly rumors were abroad. There was talk of a congressional investigation, and when General Banks offered a resolution of inquiry Jay Cooke was hurt to the quick. An investigation he regarded as no other than persecution of legitimate business, and he wrote to his brother: "He ought to be expelled from Congress for such outrageous attacks upon the great interests of the country. . . . If I get at him I will give him a piece of my mind, and no mistake, for his impertinence and foolishness." [14] Then the *Crédit Mobilier* scandal broke and in a panic he wrote to Henry Cooke denouncing the proposal to stop payment on the interest-coupons of the Union Pacific.

Now I want you to go to the Attorney General at once and tell him how wrong this whole procedure is. This whole persecution of the Union Pacific is nonsense, and is damaging our credit abroad. If the government sets the example of enjoining the payment of interest coupons, who will buy a bond abroad? The whole thing is wrong, ill advised and scandalous. . . . Williams ought to make a public apology for such an attack and instruct the lawyers to desist from anything of the kind. The bonds are long since in the hands of innocent holders, and, if they were not, they could never reach them in this way. Some wily speculators have put the idea into the heads of the government lawyers and they, without knowing anything of its effect upon business, have made this attack. It will damage us hundreds of millions unless withdrawn at once. No man of sense

[13] *Ibid.*, Vol. II, p. 176.   [14] *Ibid.*, Vol. II, p. 322.

would buy a railroad bond or anything else in this country if such legal proceedings are to be permitted under the sanction of the highest officer of the government.[15]

Jay Cooke's ethics were simple. Whatever helped bond-sales was patriotic and right; whatever hurt them was wicked and immoral. Let government take care of business and business will take care of the country. That the newspapers could not see this great truth, but often indulged in wild demagoguery, was painful to one who had been generous to them. "It is too bad," he wrote of a certain attack, "that these newspapers are permitted by the law thus to interfere with great public works."[16] But the black days were at hand. The *Crédit Mobilier* scandal was a whirlwind reaped from the sowings of the Gilded Age. With the outbreak of the Franco-Prussian war bond-sales stopped short in Europe and the firm of Jay Cooke and Company was broken. September 18, 1873, the New York house suspended payment; the house of cards tumbled to pieces; and a panic swept the country. The crash was as spectacular as the rise; it had been built on credit and when credit was shaken it fell.

Because he had amassed a great fortune Jay Cooke was regarded by his fellow Americans as an intelligent man whose opinions were entitled to heedful consideration. A national figure in finance must become a national figure in the public councils; and this added function he assumed with the utmost seriousness. As the power behind the United States Treasury he regarded himself as responsible for the program of the Treasury; and he made use of his immense publicity-machine to shape public opinion in regard to taxation, funding, and the currency. His "views" of those questions were as simple as a child's primer. In brief they were: no taxes for the extinction of the debt; consolidate the debt and fund it in a form attractive to capital; retire the greenbacks and return at once to specie payments. Like others who had made money out of the war he did not take kindly to the idea of returning a part of it in taxes to pay off a debt that was highly profitable to him as a broker and banker. The men of '65 had fought and suffered to secure the blessings of liberty to their posterity, and it was only fair that posterity should help pay the bills. To popularize this pregnant thought he subsidized a pamphlet contributed by one of his hack-writers, entitled *Our National Debt a National Blessing;*

but the Hamiltonian argument overshot the mark and aroused bitter opposition. In this as in his attitude towards currency-contraction and funding he was thinking exclusively in terms of the money-lender. Very likely he was probably not so much self-seeking as ignorant. Intellectually he was poverty-stricken and outside the narrow realm of brokerage and banking he was only a child. He read nothing, thought little and was unconcerned with social or economic principles. His business life was regulated by a set of ready-made formulas, in which ideas played no part. William Cullen Bryant rightly judged him in the following comment:

> We counsel Mr. Jay Cooke in all good will, not to abandon his proper vocation of dealing in stocks and government securities, for the sake of giving lectures on political economy—a subject which he does not understand. We do not say that he might not understand it if he had given it his attention, but that he has evidently never done, and knows no more of the matter than Red Jacket knew of Greek. We advise all who have any money to invest to take Mr. Jay Cooke's seven-thirty bonds, and eschew his political economy. His seven-thirties are first rate, his political economy is a tissue of mistakes.[17]

Any program that lay outside the bounds of his formulas he regarded as dangerous radicalism, and any policy that threatened to reduce his commissions he regarded as unchristian. He bitterly disliked Secretary Boutwell of the Treasury, who rejected his guidance, and he wrote to his brother:

> I observe . . . that Boutwell is to leave the Treasury. I think that if he does not propose to do any better than he has in the past it will be a grand move for Grant to put some more practical person in his place. A man who has no more breadth of thought . . . and no more spunk than to let the country drift along without even an attempt at funding the debt, and who insists upon keeping up an enormous taxation for the foolish object of paying off rapidly a debt that no one wants paid off, excepting gradually, it will be a great benefit to have replaced by some one who will take an opposite course.[18]

A month later one of the causes of the hostility was suggested by a member of the firm:

> All of our transactions with Boutwell have shown conclusively that he will never permit one dollar to be made out of the business of the Treasury, if he can possibly prevent it. With all his friendly feelings I cannot remember a single dollar that we have made directly or indirectly out of his administration of the Treasury, . . .[19]

[17] *Ibid.*, Vol. I, pp. 643–644.   [18] *Ibid.*, Vol. II, pp. 267–268.
[19] *Ibid.*, Vol. II, p. 269.

Against the Greenback movement his hostility was bitter. He regarded it as an attempt to repudiate the "plighted faith" of the nation, and in 1867 he issued a pamphlet, written to order, aimed at combating the movement. In the opinion of a subsidized admirer it was "able, unanswerable and timely," calculated to do immense good in a country where universal suffrage encourages the "attempts of demagogues to excite the poor against the rich, labor against capital, and all who haven't money against the banks who have it." [20] How deeply the members of the firm felt in presence of any threat to the money interests is suggested in a letter from Henry Cooke of October 12, 1867.

You know how I have felt for a long time past in regard to the course of the ultra infidelic radicals like Wade, Sumner, Stevens, *et id omne genus.* They were dragging the Republican party into all sorts of isms and extremes. Their policy was one of bitterness, hate, and wild agrarianism without a single Christian principle to give it consistency, except the sole idea of universal suffrage. . . . These reckless demagogues have had their day and the time has come for wiser counsels. With Wade uttering agrarian doctrines in Kansas and fanning the flame of vulgar prejudices, trying to array labor against capital and pandering to the basest passions; with Butler urging wholesale conscription throughout the South and wholesale repudiation throughout the North so far as the national debt is concerned; with Stevens joining hands with the traitor Vallandigham and advocating the idea of a flood of irredeemable paper money sufficient in volume to drown the whole country; with Pomeroy and Wade and Sprague and a host of others clamoring for the unsexing of woman and putting the ballot in her hand . . . what wonder it is that the accumulated load was too heavy for any party to carry and that it broke down under it? [21]

There can be little doubt that the spectacular career of Jay Cooke quite dazzled his contemporary fellow citizens. Nothing like it had before appeared in America. The greatest salesman that the rising middle class had yet produced, a financier who understood the psychology of mass appeal, a propagandist of truly heroic proportions, he was reckoned no other than a magician by all the lesser money-grabbers of the Gilded Age. From nothing he built up a vast fortune. Scrupulous in all religious duties, a kind husband, a generous friend, benevolent in all worthy charities, simple and democratic in his tastes, ardently patriotic, uncreative and unintellectual, he exemplified all the substantial middle-class virtues of a people newly given to the worship of a sterile money economy.

[20] *Ibid.*, Vol. II, p. 56 note.   [21] *Ibid.*, Vol. II, p. 28.

To call him a vulgarian and the chronicle of his life nauseous would scarcely be charitable. The record of his days has been laid before us, naked and mean, by his biographer, who has done his best to construct a hero from the poor materials. No doubt he was a hero of his generation—and perhaps of ours also.

3

CHARLES A. DANA

If General Grant and Jay Cooke were naïve heroes, ignorant as the generation that delighted to honor them, Charles A. Dana, the journalist of the Gilded Age, was a disillusioned intellectual who after immersing himself in the golden dreams of the forties, put away all Utopian hopes and made use of his brains to serve himself. Disappointed with idealism, he turned materialist and dedicated to capitalistic exploitation the abilities that before had been given to a venture in coöperative living. A brilliant fellow, playing the new game in Gilded Age fashion and winning a brilliant success, he was a conspicuous victim of the bankruptcy of idealism that is the price of all wars, and his later triumph as editor of the *New York Sun* only served to measure the greatness of his fall. The career of Dana is a cynical commentary on the changing spirit of America from the days of Brook Farm to the days of Mark Hanna.

A child of the Puritan frontier, Dana early crossed over into New York State and became a shop-boy in the backwoods village of Buffalo at a time when the Indian trade was important enough to justify him in learning Algonquin. In these early manhood days he was living in the midst of the coonskin democracy, and falling in with the frontier spirit he became an ardent Jacksonian. He was eager for an education and quitting Buffalo he went to Harvard, but his eyes failing him after two years, he joined the Brook Farm community where he speedily became one of the chief counselors, and was deeply concerned for the success of the experiment. In those generous years he was a militant idealist, widely read in socialist literature and warmly espousing associationism as a cure for the evils of competition. Upon quitting Brook Farm after the burning of the Phalanstery he joined Greeley and for fifteen years was one of the directing minds on the *Tribune*. In 1848 he went abroad as foreign correspondent, saw much of the revolutions of

that great year, studied the temper of the French and German
people, analyzed the popular leaders and programs with singular
acuteness, and found his sympathies warmly enlisted in the cause
of the lower classes. He was then thirty-nine, and his active mind
had gathered up all the diverse radicalisms—Jacksonian, Utopian,
European proletarian—of his revolutionary generation. Shrewdly
observant and with a sensitive social conscience, he was amply
equipped to become such another critic of the Industrial Revolution as England had bred from its bitter experience.

But the war intervened, and after the war a dun twilight gathered about the hopes of the forties. Few generous enthusiasms
survived those years of struggle and Dana in his editorial rooms
underwent successive changes of heart. The realist slowly dispossessed the idealist and then the cynic swallowed up the realist.
The last forty years of his life were spent undoing the work of his
earlier years. His political philosophy went to pieces and the policy
of the *Sun* became a mere hodge-podge of jingo programs, an irrational bundle of personal prejudices and private interests. His
reaction from associationism carried him over to a stark and
ruthless individualism. He saw all about him the strong and capable as the masters of the earth, with social justice an outcast and
mendicant begging from house to house. The millennium to which
belongs the ideal of social democracy which he had earlier served,
he could no longer make out from any present bend in the road,
and putting away his faith he went with the masters. The reaction
began during the *Tribune* days with his espousal of the American
System—the first outcropping of the middle-class qualities of his
mind—and thereafter he drifted steadily to the right and the
Dismal Swamp of exploitation. With augmenting wealth and the
sense of power that came from the great success of the *Sun* he
became the apologist and defender of capitalism, phrasing with
clever vivacity all the sophistries of Gilded Age argument. Professing to be a Democrat, he made much of states rights and governmental *laissez faire*. He would countenance no interference
with the principle of free competition, but would reduce the government to the rôle of policeman to keep the peace. He professed
to believe that the dry bones of Manchesterism were a living
democratic faith. He ridiculed the proposal for pure-food legislation, civil service reform, the control of monopolies, professing
to see in every such move the insidious beginnings of an un-Ameri-

can bureaucracy. No social pretext justified in his eyes the regulation of business enterprise. Centralization of economic power he
accepted as in the nature of things, and the popular denunciation
of trusts he called "the greatest humbug of the hour." His argument was simple and to the Gilded Age wholly satisfactory.

The objects of trade being to buy as cheap as possible, to sell as dear as
possible, and to get control of the market as far as possible, the formation
for these purposes of these gigantic and widely extended partnerships is
just as natural and regular as the partnership of two shoemakers or of
two blacksmiths.[22]

Thus far Dana must be reckoned a belated disciple of the
Manchester school. The days of transcendental and Utopian
idealism were past and he knew it. The Gilded Age had traveled
far from such naïve enthusiasms and it was time to face reality.
But his realism was only a gesture to cover his surrender to capitalism. It was not honest. When his principle of individualism trod
on his own toes he threw it aside with no compunctions. He was
a *laissez-faire* Democrat only when a free field favored business,
but when business desired government assistance he made no
scruple to turn Whig. Accepting the principle of private exploitation under the drive of the acquisitive instinct, and content with
the social ethics of Captain Kidd, he would weaken government
or strengthen government as business profits dictated. In these
later years he became cynically class-conscious, while professing
to deny the existence of classes. He would disarm the government
as against the capitalist, but he would triple-arm it against the
farmer and workingman. He was shrill in his demands for a high
protective tariff for the manufacturers, huge grants of public lands
for speculative railway companies, and a monetary system in the
control of the bankers. But for the economic demands of the western farmers he had only contempt—the agrarians were flying in the
face of economic law as economic law was understood by the high
priests of capitalism. When he talked about "honest money" he
laid his brains on the shelf. He would have no other money than
the gold standard, and to achieve that object he never suffered
candor to weaken his plea. He bitterly opposed the income tax
and when the Democratic platform of 1896 suggested the reorganization of the Supreme Court to reverse the decision on its con-

[22] See James Harrison Wilson, *The Life of Charles A. Dana*, p. 479.

stitutionality, he turned demagogue and indulged in talk about "the destruction of the independence of the judiciary." When it was proposed that the railways be nationalized he protested that he could not "imagine anything more absurd, unpatriotic, and dangerous"—on the assumption no doubt that railways existed to pay dividends on their stock. "Still more alarming" to him was the "clearly implied approval of lawless violence contained in the denunciation of what is denominated in the [Democratic] platform 'government by injunction.' Veiled in the language of moderation, the wild light of anarchy shines through." [23] He urged upon government the necessity of holding the labor unions in strict control, he was eloquent in defense of the individual laborer's sacred right of "free contract," and he was loud in applause of President Cleveland's lawless suppression of the Pullman strike. When it came to Bryan and Populism he lost his head and became quite maudlin.

Dana was no fool to be deceived by his own insincerity. On the contrary he was highly intelligent and knew perfectly well what he was about. Having gone over to capitalism, he would fight its battles with whatever weapons came to hand, and like a son of New England he would cover his breast with a shield of morality. He became the chief journalistic exponent of the "lawless violence" he was fond of attributing to other social classes. He turned into a flaming jingo imperialist, talked patriotically about "adequate" coast defenses, demanded a great navy, and was the loudest spokesman of the blowsy doctrine of "Manifest Destiny." He was always peering through his glasses to discover some fresh territory to annex—Haiti, Cuba, Mexico—and so late as 1887 he was still calling for the annexation of Canada. Naturally he approved President Cleveland's Venezuelan proclamation and he probably would have enjoyed a tussle with the British lion. In his morality he was quite as truculent as in his patriotism and in his advocacy of capitalism. Perhaps it was a salve to a conscience that could not have been easy. He hated political corruption and he attacked the sordid looting that marked President Grant's administration with gusto. He took sardonic delight in giving the widest publicity to the classic corruptionist phrase of the day— "He understands addition, division, and silence." He erected into a fetish the cry "Turn the rascals out!" yet while helping to pry

[23] See *Ibid.*, p. 491.

loose one set of rascals from their spoils he was busily providing another set with his demand for subsidies and tariffs. It was a situation that must have amused the cynical Dana. He had long since left off worrying about the damned human race. It was more sensible to pile up one's plate at the barbecue and send the bill to the American people. He had made a huge success and what mattered it if his old Brook Farm associates, Ripley and Curtis, no longer spoke to him when they met?

CHAPTER II

THE CULTURE OF THE SEVENTIES

IT was in the seventies that good taste reached its lowest ebb. Not only in America, but in England as well, where rebels like William Morris were contemptuously rejecting a machine civilization. A veritable *débâcle* of the arts was in process, the lesser as well as the greater, in New York and Boston as well as in Chicago and San Francisco, from which literature could not wholly escape; and that *débâcle* was an expression of profound changes taking place at the bases of society. The dignified culture of the eighteenth century, that hitherto had been a conserving and creative influence throughout the Jeffersonian revolution, was at last breaking up. The disruptive forces that swept out of the great West, bringing the frontier spirit to every threshold, and the factory economy that displaced the wares of the craftsman with the products of the machine, were destroying that earlier culture and providing no adequate substitute. Distinction of manners and dress was gone, dignity and repose were gone, traditional standards were gone; and in their stead a bumptious restlessness, a straining for originality and individuality that exuded in a shoddy and meaningless grotesque. It was not without justification that Godkin contemptuously applied the phrase, "a chromo civilization," to the works of that singular generation dwelling between worlds, the one dead, the other seeming powerless to be born.

How much was lost in the break-up of the excellent culture of the eighteenth century the children of the seventies neither knew nor cared. Generations of growth had gone to its shaping. It had been formed by the needs of men and women conscious of the ties that linked them with the past. It was bound back upon the rich cultural life of medieval times, and in the aristocratic eighteenth century it had come to flower in forms of fine distinction and dignity. Touch that century on any side—dress, architecture, furniture, manners, letters—and the same note of refinement, of grace, of balanced harmonious form, is everywhere evident. The culture of the times of the Coffee House Wits was all of a piece, held to-

gether by an inner pervasive unity. The formality of the wig and
the heroic couplet was symbolic of a generation that loved dignity,
and the refinement of the Chippendale sideboard, wrought in
slender Honduras mahogany, was the expression of a society that
cultivated the graces of life. But when the tie-wig and smallclothes
disappeared before the social revolutions of the end of the century,
when the gentleman was pushed from his place by the banker and
manufacturer, and broadcloth gave way to tweeds, the culture of
the eighteenth century was doomed; and until another culture
should impose its standards upon society and reëstablish an inner
spiritual unity, there would be only the welter of an unlovely transition.

In no other field is the sprawling formlessness of the seventies
more grotesquely suggested than in its architecture and in interior
decoration, which is a lesser form of architecture. Upon the buildings of the times the hallmark of the Gilded Age is stamped in
gaudy colors. By the end of the thirties the fine traditions of
colonial craftsmanship were gone and the builders set forth on a
foolish quest for historical styles. Revivals followed on each other's
heels. The Greek revival and the Gothic revival marked the successive decline of the noble art of building, until at last, turning
away from the past, architecture erupted in what it conceived to be
a new American style, the expression of a free democratic people,
but which later generations reckon a sign and proof of cultural
bankruptcy. It was the golden age of the jig saw, of the brownstone
front, of the veranda that ran about the house like a spider web, of
the mansard roof, the cupola, the house of stilts. Flamboyant lines
and meaningless detail destroyed the structural unity of the whole;
tawdry decoration supplanted beauty of materials and a fine balance
of masses. A stuffy and fussy riot of fancy, restrained by no feeling
for structural lines, supplied the lack of creative imagination, and
architecture sank to the level of the jerry-builder. Bad taste could
go no further.

With this decay of aristocratic culture and the attendant disintegration of the earlier cultural unity, three diverse strands of
cultural impulse remained, each of an individual fabric that could
not easily be woven into a harmonious pattern: a decadent Federalistic culture that occupied the seats of authority in New England and wherever New England opinion was respected; the body
of social aspiration that had come from the French Enlighten-

ment, from which individual dreamers still drew nourishment; and
the vigorous individualism of the frontier that bit so deeply into
the psychology of the age. Behind these diverse impulses lay still
another that would eventually shoulder them aside and provide the
pattern for the America that was rising—the culture of an urbanized and mechanized society that in its vast warrens of business
was creating the psychology and manners of a standardized,
middle-class world of salesmanship.

I

NEW ENGLAND IN DECAY

In one spot in America, at least, the disruption of the fine old
aristocratic culture would not be suffered without a protest. Brahmin New England would cling to its traditional standards though
all the rest of America should go whoring after strange gods. The
welter of the seventies it looked upon with undisguised contempt.
It would not follow the way that other portions of the country were
hastening. It would have nothing to do with a bumptious frontier
spirit that recognized no obligations to the past—for the excellent
reason that it had no past. It had had its fill of the visionary Enlightenment that had come to logical fruit in the vagaries of Thoreau and the grotesque vaporings of Alcott. It had had more than
its fill of the strident causes that spawned like mushrooms in the
rank soil of French romanticism. Emerson it could forgive, for
Emerson was a Brahmin, but it quietly ignored his philosophic
anarchism and chose to dwell on pleasanter aspects of his teaching.
Wendell Phillips it regarded as a common nuisance, but Edmund
Quincy it forgave, for after a season of vagrant wanderings he
returned to the placid ways of his ancestral Brahminism. Of all
these things, whether frontier or Utopian or what not, it had had
enough, and so it turned back lovingly to the culture of earlier
times and drew comfort from a dignified Federalism—enriched now
by a mellow Harvard scholarship that was on intimate terms with
Dante and Chaucer and Cervantes and Shakespeare—a Federalism
that fitted the dignified Brahmin genius as comfortably as an old
shoe.

It was an excellent heritage—that old culture. Never richly
creative, never endowed with a fleshly paganism, it possessed
nevertheless a solidity got from long wrestling with the eternities,
a pleasantly acrid flavor got from crotchety old books, and a sober

morality got from much contemplation of the sinfulness of the children of Adam. It was as native to New England as Boston brown bread, and it issued in self-respecting and dignified character. Underneath all transcendental and other eruptions it had lain unmoved like the granite foundations of the New England fields; and now after those eruptions had subsided it provided the solid footing on which the later culture might rear its chaste temples. But unhappily the building days of New England were over. Matters were going ill there. Emigration to the West was draining the vitality from farm and village, and in Boston disastrous changes were under way. The familiar places where Sam Adams and Josiah Quincy had dwelt with their fellows were being invaded by immigrants who brought with them another faith and discordant manners. The Roman Catholic church grew strong as the Old North declined; the Irish brogue displaced the Yankee on Boston Common; Faneuil Hall was given over to alien fishmongers. The Brahmin remnant was absorbed in banking and brokerage and railway investments. It still held the Boston purse but it was fast losing the Boston vote. The capital of the Puritan fathers was being destroyed by the Industrial Revolution that their descendants had set on foot. New England was visibly falling into decay and the years of its intellectual leadership in America were numbered.

The days of high thinking were over and the familiar home of humanitarian causes was inhabited by other tenants. All that remained of the golden forties was the quiet atmosphere of good breeding. Unitarianism, that Theodore Parker had kept open-minded and militant, settled into a staid and respectable orthodoxy, its pale negations sufficing to soothe its placid congregations. Transcendentalism, that had thrown a lovely mist about the lean New England character, was evaporating in the rising sun of science; and the ardor of reform, that had burned fiercely in the Puritan heart, subsided into a well-bred interest in negro schools and foreign missions. The Abolition leaders laid aside their pens, convinced that the last injustice had been removed from American society. Their work was done and they turned unwilling ears to calls for new crusades. The New England conscience was tired. It had borne the burden and heat of a long day and was glad to be released from its cares to set up monuments to its sacred dead and to write the chronicles of its past. New England lost interest in

ideas and turned away from creative intellectual life to catalogue
its libraries and revere the men who had written those libraries.
The Enlightenment was over in Boston and the stir of reform
passed to New York and the West, where Amelia Bloomer and Elizabeth Cady Stanton carried forward the great crusades for temperance and women's rights, and Henry George was preaching the
gospel of a new social economics. Whatever militants existed in
New England were not likely to be Brahmins and their labors did
not roil the quiet waters. Clamorous distractions no longer disturbed the calm of Federalistic culture, and Cambridge and the
Back Bay quietly appropriated the literary earnings of Concord
and lived pleasantly on its revenues.

The inevitable fruit of such thin soil was the genteel tradition,
the excellence of which in the seventies New England maintained
in the face of all frontier leveling and romantic liberalisms—a
timid and uncreative culture that lays its inhibitions on every generation that is content to live upon the past. It was a penalty for
backsliding. The men of the preceding generation had got their
cheeses made—and excellent cheeses they were, with a fine native
flavor. But the transcendental cow had gone dry and with no
fresh cows coming in the Brahmins of the seventies were hard put
to it to live an adequate intellectual life. Translations and medieval
scholarship were no better than remainder biscuit after voyage.
Ever since Lowell put away his youthful radicalisms and turned
bookman, Brahmin culture had been undernourished. The story
of intellectual New England after 1870 is little more than a repetition of the story of New England after 1790—a resurgence of the
traditional Toryism that assumed an unquestioned custodianship
of all matters intellectual.

That was her own business, of course, and it would have been of
no great concern to the rest of the country if New England had
not set up a cultural dictatorship over American letters. It was
not content to follow its own path to sterility, but was bent on
dragging the country with it. Boston taste determined American
literary standards, and Boston taste rejected most of the new
movements then getting under way. Stoddard and Stedman in
New York, Boker in Philadelphia, and Aldrich in Boston, stoutly
upheld the genteel tradition, of which the *Atlantic Monthly* was
the authoritative spokesman. Great figures from the past—Emerson, Longfellow, Lowell. Whittier, Holmes, Motley, Parkman—

still walked the streets of Boston, and their extraordinary reputations were little less than tyrannous in the inhibitions they laid on younger men. It is incomprehensible today, the authority of these great reputations. Young William Winter walking twenty miles to stand in the moonlight at Craigie House gate and view reverently the silent walls within which the great Longfellow was sleeping; Mark Twain in the fullness of his powers abashed and put out of countenance at his temerity in speaking humorously of Emerson and Longfellow and Holmes at the *Atlantic* dinner—one understands such things with difficulty now that those reputations have so much bated and dwindled. Yet to the generation of the seventies the inhibitions of the genteel tradition were all-powerful, and the little Boston group set themselves up as a court of final jurisdiction over American letters. New England parochialism had become a nation-wide nuisance.

The genteel tradition, as Professor Santayana has pointed out, had long been a disease in New England. Some of the finest minds of the Renaissance—Emerson and Hawthorne in particular—had suffered from it; their mental processes "had all a certain starved and abstract quality," a lack of the rich paganism that endows life and art with sensuous beauty.

They could not retail the genteel tradition [he goes on]; they were too keen, too perceptive, and too independent for that. But life offered them little digestible material, nor were they naturally voracious. They were fastidious, and under the circumstances they were starved. . . . Therefore the genius of . . . Hawthorne, and even of Emerson, was employed in a sort of inner play, or digestion of vacancy. It was a refined labor, but was in danger of being morbid, or tinkling, or self-indulgent. It was a play of intra-mental rhymes. Their mind was like an old music-box, full of tender echoes and quaint fancies. These fancies expressed their personal genius sincerely, as dreams may; but they were arbitrary fancies in comparison with what a real observer would have said in the premises. Their manner, in a word, was subjective. In their own persons they escaped the mediocrity of the genteel tradition, but they supplied nothing to supplant it in other minds.[1]

If the thin pale atmosphere in which the genteel tradition throve starved the minds of greater men in a more vigorous age, it would play havoc with smaller men in an imitative age. After Emerson and Hawthorne came Stedman and Stoddard and Aldrich, upon

[1] *The Genteel Tradition in American Philosophy, University of California Chronicle,* Vol. XIII, Number 4.

whose studiously correct pages the genteel tradition laid a hand of death. In the seventies it had become the refuge of a stale mentality, emptied of all ideals save beauty, and that beauty become cold and anemic. Its taboos were no more than cushions for tired or lazy minds. The idea of morality—with its corollary of reticence—and the idea of excellence were well enough in the abstract, but become empty conventions, cut off from reality, they were little more than a refuge for respectability, a barricade against the intrusion of the unpleasant. In compressing literature within the rigid bounds of a genteel morality and a genteel excellence, New England was in a way of falsifying it. Highways are easy traveling, but the artist who will not venture from them misses much. In the seventies and eighties the incurious Boston mentality missed pretty much everything vital and significant in American life, and the more daring children of Boston—men like Henry Adams and, shall we add, Henry James—sought congenial atmosphere elsewhere.

I

THOMAS BAILEY ALDRICH AND THE GENTEEL

In the expansive days of Walt Whitman and Mark Twain the official custodian of the genteel in letters was Thomas Bailey Aldrich, who as editor of the *Atlantic* from 1881 to 1890 sturdily combated all literary leveling. Sitting in the high seat of Boston authority he would countenance none of the "Josh Billingsgate" corruptions of the English language that he professed to believe were sullying the purity of American literary taste. A Portsmouth, New Hampshire, boy, early transplanted to New York City, he lisped in numbers before he learned to think. At the age of nineteen he published a volume of poems entitled *The Bells*, *A Collection of Chimes*, the tintillations of which were little more than faint echoes of Keats, Chatterton, Tennyson, Poe, Bryant, Willis, and Longfellow; and to the end of his life his state of ideal felicity was to be "loaded to the muzzle with lyrics and sonnets" wherewith to do execution on all purveyors of realism with its "miasmatic breath blown from the slums." Transplanted to Boston from the Bohemian world of Pfaff's restaurant where Willis held court, he settled down into the staid atmosphere of the Back Bay with immense content. Though he was fond of calling himself only Boston-plated he was soon as completely Bostonian as the Autocrat himself. Intellectually and esthetically he had been Cambridge

bred, and the influence of Longfellow, Lowell, and Holmes determined his every literary endeavor. Like the returned prodigal he
wandered no more but was satisfied to feast on the dainties of
Back Bay culture. He immersed himself in the genteel. His one
ambition as editor of the *Atlantic* was to keep it as Lowell wished
it kept. To the end of his life he remained completely insulated
against the creative forces of the times, and in the year that
Stephen Crane was writing *Maggie* he published *The Sisters'*
Tragedy. He would have been shocked by *Maggie*, if he had read
it, as a later generation wonders at *The Sisters' Tragedy.*

It is easy to see why Aldrich should have been taken to Boston's
heart. His refined and delicate technique more than compensated
for an intellectual sterility that seems never to have been apparent
to his ardent admirers. Witty, charming in manners, in love with
art and devoted to a painstaking craftsmanship, he was a hollow
reed through which blew into flawless form the refinements of his
world and group. Good taste found nothing to offend in his scanty
pages. If he worshiped at the altar of beauty, beauty to him was
always a chaste goddess, severe and pale and slight. A blowsy goddess like Whitman's, or a slattern like Mark Twain's, he would have
none of. As a youthful poet, to be sure, he sometimes hinted that
she had red cheeks and plump breasts and rounded limbs, but on his
removal to Boston he discovered that she was quite Beacon Street
with her slender form and modest reserve—no Greek but a lovely
Puritan maiden; and the mature Aldrich came to prefer her chaste
reticence to the freer ways the younger generation liked. They were
destroying beauty—this younger generation—with their vulgar realism, besmirching the goddess with their vulgarities. In an interlude
entitled "Realism" he gave voice to the following pastoral lament:

> Romance beside his unstrung lute
>   Lies stricken mute.
> The old-time fire, the antique grace,
> You will not find them anywhere.
> To-day we breathe a commonplace,
> Polemic, scientific air:
> We strip Illusion of her veil;
> We vivisect the nightingale
> To probe the secret of his note.
> The Muse in alien ways remote
>   Goes wandering.[2]

[2] *Poetical Works*, Vol. I, p. 45.

And in a dramatic monologue, quite evidently suggested by *The Grammarian's Funeral*, he voiced the following protest against an age enslaved to realism:

> A twilight poet, groping quite alone,
> Belated, in a sphere where every nest
> Is emptied of its music and its wings.
> Not great his gift; yet we can poorly spare
> Even his slight perfection in an age
> Of limping triolets and tame rondeaux.
> He had at least ideals, though unreached,
> And heard, far off, immortal harmonies,
> Such as fall coldly on our ear to-day.
> The mighty Zolaistic Movement now
> Engrosses us—a miasmatic breath
> Blown from the slums. We paint life as it is,
> The hideous side of it, with careful pains,
> Making a god of the dull Commonplace.
> For have we not the old gods overthrown
> And set up strangest idols? We would clip
> Imagination's wing and kill delight,
> Our sole art being to leave nothing out
> That renders art offensive. Not for us
> Madonnas leaning from their starry thrones
> Ineffable, nor any heaven-wrought dream
> Of sculptor or of poet; we prefer
> Such nightmare visions as in morbid brains
> Take form and substance, thoughts that taint the air
> And make all life unlovely. Will it last?
> Beauty alone endures from age to age,
> From age to age endures, handmaid of God.[3]

It was not the realists alone, he thought, who were fouling their own nests, but all who turned aside from the narrow path of Victorianism to explore new ways. Whitman he regarded as a charlatan whose mannerisms were a "hollow affectation" representing "neither the man nor the time." Riley's formal verse he preferred to his dialect poems—"The English language is too rich and sacred a thing to be mutilated and vulgarized," he wrote, overlooking the *Biglow Papers*. He held Kipling's cockneyisms in contempt and said he would not have opened the pages of the *Atlantic* even to the "Recessional." Lanier he thought a less significant figure than Fitz-Greene Halleck, and of Poe he remarked that if he "had been an exemplary, conventional, tax-

---

[3] "At the Funeral of a Minor Poet," *Ibid.*, Vol. II, p. 94.

oppressed citizen, like Longfellow, his few poems, as striking as they are, would not have made so great a stir."[4]   In such literary judgments the arch-conservative is engaged in defending the genteel tradition against every assault, convinced that the portals of creative literature open into the past and that in following in the footsteps of the dead we shall come upon a living world. The sterility of his own refined craftsmanship is perhaps sufficient commentary upon his faith.

When in later years he turned to prose his work revealed the same negative qualities. His prose style is finished, clean, and thin, wanting in homely idiom and a rich suggestiveness. The water trickled gently from the spring of his invention, cool and unroiled, but never abundant. The dignity that results from a strong nature held in restraint, he never achieved. There were no depths in him. He waited patiently for his vessel to fill and measured it out carefully. As a short-story writer he gained a surprising repute, and admirers like Sarah Orne Jewett were never tired of praising the sprightliness of his humor. Nevertheless his most celebrated story scarcely explains today the immense stir it made. *Marjorie Daw* is a clever *jeu d'esprit* but a bit thin and artificial, too consciously written backwards from its surprise ending. Other distillings of his wit and wisdom, done in the sententious manner and gathered up in *Ponkapog Papers*, are slight in content, and the effervescence is long since gone out of them. *The Story of a Bad Boy*, with its pleasant recollections of his Portsmouth youth, remains his most important work in prose and deserves much of the praise that has been lavished upon it; but set over against *Huckleberry Finn* its shortcomings are evident.

It is absurd, of course, to expect an aesthete to concern himself with ideas, or to care greatly about what goes on outside his ivory tower. The rumblings of the vulgar world beat ineffectually against the gate behind which he sits and dreams. For years the editor of the *Atlantic* was scarcely conscious of his complete aloofness from the world of reality, and he wrote in some surprise to Hamilton Wright Mabie, in 1897:

I like to have you say that I have always cared more for the integrity of my work than for any chance popularity. And what you say of my "aloofness" as being "due in part to a lack of quick sympathies with contemporary experience" (though I had never before thought of it) shows

[4] Ferris Greenslet, *Life of Thomas Bailey Aldrich*, p. 215.

true insight. To be sure, such verse as "Elmwood," "Wendell Phillips,"
"Unguarded Gates" and the "Shaw Memorial Ode" would seem somewhat to condition the statement; but the mood of these poems is not
habitual with me, not characteristic. They did, however, grow out of
strong conviction.[5]

Yet though he spoke rarely on social themes, during the long
years in Boston most of the Back Bay prejudices seemed to have
seeped into his mind and when the "strong convictions," to which
he refers, found utterance they proved to be Brahmin convictions.
In the vigorous poem "Unguarded Gates"—a poem tense, outspoken, almost unique in its deliberate declamation—he sallied
forth from his ivory tower to speak to the American people on the
dangers of uncontrolled immigration, a subject that Boston Brahmins had been talking about since the days of Harrison Gray Otis.

> Wide open and unguarded stand our gates,
> And through them presses a wild motley throng—
> Men from the Volga and the Tartar steppes,
> Featureless figures from the Hoang-Ho,
> Malayan, Scythian, Teuton, Kelt, and Slav,
> Flying the Old World's poverty and scorn;
> These bringing with them unknown gods and rites,
> Those, tiger passions, here to stretch their claws.
> In street and alley what strange tongues are loud,
> Accents of menace alien to our air,
> Voices that once the Tower of Babel knew!
>
> O Liberty, white Goddess! is it well
> To leave the gates unguarded? On thy breast
> Fold Sorrow's children, soothe the hurts of fate,
> Lift the down-trodden, but with hand of steel
> Stay those who to thy sacred portals come
> To waste the gifts of freedom. Have a care
> Lest from thy brow the clustered stars be torn
> And trampled in the dust. For so of old
> The thronging Goth and Vandal trampled Rome,
> And where the temples of the Caesars stood
> The lean wolf unmolested made her lair.[6]

What emotions lay back of the measured words of the poem, and
how deeply they were colored by the social passions of the times, he
tells in a letter to George E. Woodberry, written May 14, 1892:

> I went home and wrote a misanthropic poem called "Unguarded Gates"
> , . . in which I mildly protest against America becoming the cesspool of

Europe. I'm much too late, however. I looked in on an anarchist meeting the other night . . . and heard such things spoken by our "feller citizens" as made my cheek burn. These brutes are the spawn and natural result of the French Revolution; they don't want any government at all, they "want the earth" . . . and chaos. My Americanism goes clean beyond yours. I believe in America for the Americans; I believe in the widest freedom and the narrowest license, and I hold that jail-birds, professional murderers, amateur lepers . . . and human gorillas generally should be closely questioned at our Gates. Or the "sifting" that was done of old will have to be done over again. . . . A certain Arabian writer, called Rudyard Kipling, described exactly the government of every city and town in the . . . United States when he described that of New York as being "a despotism of the alien, by the alien, for the alien, tempered with occasional insurrections of decent folk!" [7]

Two years later he again gave private expression to one of his rare judgments on matters political and social:

When not otherwise engaged I sit and smoke, and smile at the present administration [President Cleveland's]. . . . The best kind of Democracy (as per sample) is no better than the worst kind of Republicanism. The Income Tax is the deformed child of Coxey and his brother scalawags. I vote for McKinley. We shall have bloody work in this country some of these days, when the lazy *canaille* get organized. They are the spawn of Santerre and Fouquier-Tinville. In about twenty years we shall bring out an American edition (illustrated with cuts) of the beautiful French Revolution.[8]

And again in 1899:

Personally I must confess that I have never been very deeply impressed by the administrative abilities of what we call the lower classes. The Reign of Terror in France is a fair illustration of the kind of government which the masses give us when they get the happy opportunity.[9]

The literary conservative, it appears, was no better than a social and political Tory. He has traveled back a hundred years and speaks again the very language of Robert Treat Paine. *Canaille* is not a nice word to apply to American workingmen, and the French Revolution has never been well thought of by the children of the *ancien régime*. Thomas Bailey Aldrich was a cultivated gentleman, on the pleasantest terms with the Muse of Beacon Street. Twice he traveled around the world; innumerable summers he spent in Europe; yet of many things that concern men greatly he was very, very ignorant. Of the American people beyond the

[7] Ferris Greenslet, *Life of Thomas Bailey Aldrich*, pp. 168–169.
[8] *Ibid.*, p. 176.   [9] *Ibid.*, p. 205.

Hudson River, he knew nothing. Of social economics he knew nothing. Fearful lest his art should get a smutch from the streets, he withdrew within his tower, where perhaps it is well to leave him. Yet it is odd to recall that he was once regarded as a significant literary figure and that intelligent people listened to him seriously.

2

THE NEW ENGLAND SCENE

In fields less distinguished than poetry and the essay the sway of the genteel was neither so magisterial nor so repressive. As fiction somewhat tardily encroached upon the older literary preserves of New England it brought with it a fresher and more realistic spirit that was eventually to deny the validity of the traditional standards. The group of fiction writers that arose in the seventies and eighties to chronicle the life of New England, was greatly concerned with the decay of the old New England world, and with the causes of that decay. As it set down with loving fidelity the characteristics of an earlier order it could not fail to consider the unloveliness of the new world that was rising on the decay of the old—the alien industrial towns with their polyglot workers that were flourishing as the native villages and quiet countryside declined. New England fiction, therefore, came to embody two main features, chronicle and criticism. It gathered up such picturesque bits of the past as time and change had left, and it questioned with some anxiety the ways of an industrialism that was destroying what it loved. It was not Boston fiction, but up-country fiction, given to exploring quiet villages and decaying towns; and in both its chronicles and its criticisms the spirit of realism became more searching as the years passed.

In its own fashion such fiction would finally be brought into service to the social conscience and issue as sociological studies. As the evils of sweated labor under the factory system were brought home to the common knowledge, one would suppose that New England would have been the first to conscript the novel to arouse the public conscience. There had been anxious discussion amongst the Concord intellectuals on the evils of industrialism, and in the early forties the talk had turned upon associationism as the likeliest cure; but though from such discussions came Brook Farm and other Utopian ventures, no fiction resulted. It was elsewhere, in the Pennsylvania iron district where exploitation was harsher and more brutal than in the textile mills, that fiction first turned to consider the ways of industrialism. In 1861 Rebecca Harding contributed to the *Atlantic* a story entitled "Life in the Iron Mills," that was stark and fierce in its drab realism.[10] Nevertheless ten years were to pass before Elizabeth Stuart Phelps published *The Silent Partner* (1871), a dithyrambic plea for justice for the mill-hands.

If this was not the first New England novel of industrialism it was certainly one of the earliest. In conception, temper, and technique it belongs to the emotional fifties, and is almost primitive in comparison with Rebecca Harding's work. Underlain with religion, it is sticky with sentiment. Although Miss Phelps professed to base her work on the Reports of the Massachusetts Bureau of Statistics of Labor, to which she says she was "deeply in debt for the ribs" of her story, the result is more a tract than a study. There is no realistic grasp of the materials. She was grieved that the mill-masters should reveal so little Christian understanding of the hard lot of the hands and so little sympathy with their poverty. "I believe," she said, "that a wide-spread ignorance exists among us regarding the abuses of our factory system, more especially, but not exclusively, as exhibited in many of the country mills." "Had Christian ingenuity been generally synonymous with the conduct of manufacturing corporations, I should have found no occasion for the writing of this book."[11] It was to lessen such ignorance and encourage Christian sympathy between the classes that she offered her study.

The book is a closet study done with more unction than skill. It is the work of an emotional woman who lived in a world of sentiment rather than reality. Miss Phelps was an Andover Brahmin, highly sensitive, whose deeply religious nature was ruffled by every vagrant wind. She was tremulous in her eager desire to lessen the injustice of men. *The Silent Partner* is a story of a young woman brought up in luxury, daughter of a manufacturer, who on her father's death wishes to join in the management of the factory, but on being politely rejected by her partners she engages in personnel work amongst her employees. There she comes upon

---

[10] Fred Lewis Pattee, *The Development of the American Short Story*, pp. 171–172. See the entire chapter for a discussion of early realism in the *Atlantic*.
[11] Preface, p. 5.

poverty as a sordid fact, and that discovery works a moral change in her life. She is overwhelmed by it and cannot understand why the conscience of the world is not overwhelmed. "Sometimes I do not see," she exclaimed, "what else there can *be* to talk about in such a world as this! I've stepped into it, as we have stepped out into this storm. It has wrapped me in. . . ." [12] Of the complexity of the problem she is wholly ignorant. Surely there must be some road that leads to justice—justice based on understanding and Christian kindliness; and the working girl whom she singles out for heroine becomes in the end a street preacher to the textile workers, after refusing to marry and bring children into a world of factory toil. *The Silent Partner* is an emotional Puritan document that was out of date when it came from the press.

While Miss Phelps was thus summoning the New England conscience to cleanse the textile mills, her Brahmin sisters were little inclined to engage in such thankless labors, but preferred to gather up and preserve such fragments of the homely traditional New England as had not been swept away in the engulfing stream of industrialism. Female writers, from the days of Mrs. Sarah Wentworth Morton, had long been busy in New England but never had they written so well or so understandingly as in the days of the New England decline. Harriet Beecher Stowe, Elizabeth Stuart Phelps, Harriet Prescott Spofford, Rose Terry Cooke, Mary Wilkins Freeman, and Alice Brown were not great writers, but they essayed to be faithful recorders of what came under their eyes. It was the earlier New England that quickened their imaginations, the rugged Yankee character that had taken form under a homely domestic economy. They had no liking for the New England that was rising in the shadow of the mills; the cleavages of race and religion that were sundering the old homogeneous society were bitterly distasteful to them. The Irish, the French-Canadians, the masses of raw immigrants that were swept into the hoppers of the mills, were unwelcome gobbets to the Brahmin stomach. And so these recorders of the New England decline turned away from the sordid industrial scene, and it was not till thirty years later that Mary Wilkins Freeman, in *The Portion of Labor* (1901), essayed to do more adequately what Elizabeth Stuart Phelps had first sketched.

From Catherine Sedgwick to Mrs. Freeman the note shifted

[12] Chapter VIII. p. 183.

from the moralistic to the sentimental, then to the idyllic, then to the realistic; and the successive changes are sufficiently marked by three writers, Harriet Beecher Stowe, Sarah Orne Jewett, and Mary Wilkins Freeman. Seeking their materials remote from Boston, amidst the old native stock pottering through the traditional round of life, they discovered a world of angular figures that had grown knotty and gnarly from a harsh climate and a meager soil. The stoic repressions that were a heritage from Puritan ancestors had bred a hard race that any twist of circumstance was likely to turn into grotesques. Calvinists have always at hand a providential justification of any freakish outcome to men's struggles, and in piously denying freedom of the will they often put the seal of God's approval on their own willfulness. Mrs. Freeman's *Pembroke* is not unlike *Winesburg, Ohio*, as a record of abortive lives; and Sarah Orne Jewett, in spite of a Brahmin temperament that chose to see the idyllic rather than the grotesque, could not overlook what New England provided so abundantly. In *A Country Doctor* a visitor in the village of Oldsfield thus analyzed the New England character:

. . . for intense, self-centred, smouldering volcanoes of humanity, New England cannot be matched the world over. It's like the regions in Iceland that are full of geysers. I don't know whether it is the inheritance from those people who broke away from the old countries, and who ought to be matched to tremendous circumstances of life, but now and then there comes an amazingly explosive and uncontrollable temperament that goes all to pieces from its own conservation and accumulation of force. By and by you will all be blown up,—you quiet descendants of the Pilgrims and Puritans, and have let off your superfluous wickedness like blizzards; and when the blizzards of each family have spent themselves you will grow dull and sober, and all on a level, and be free from the troubles of a transition state. Now, you're neither a new country nor an old one. You ought to see something of the older civilizations to understand what peace of mind is. Unless some importation of explosive material from the westward stirs them up, one century is made the pattern for the next.[13]

They deal wholly with the past—these chronicles of a decaying New England—concerning themselves with a "primitive and Biblical people" who dwelt in quiet inland towns or about the lonely shores of the Maine coast; yet always under the shadow of the meeting-house, with few defenses betwixt them and the eter-

[13] Chapter IX, p. 100.

nities. The age had traveled far beyond them and they were left pottering about in their narrow Hebraic world, unaware that science and industrialism were undermining the foundations on which village and meeting-house rested. "In that handful of houses," said old Captain Littlepage in *The Country of the Pointed Firs*, "they fancy that they comprehend the universe." But if they understood God's plan of redemption they knew nothing of the ways of capitalism. A certain romantic quaintness colors the realism of these country tales and imparts a note of the idyllic. Harriet Beecher Stowe first discovered the literary possibilities of decaying New England, and in *Old-Town Folks*, *Poganuc People*, and *The Minister's Wooing*, she turned back to the days of its prime and sketched the scene with a loving hand. But it was rather in *The Pearl of Orr's Island*, especially the first part before the heavy moralism that was always entrapping her art had closed upon the tale, that she revealed its possibilities to later writers. In a letter of July 5, 1889, Sarah Orne Jewett suggests the source of her own more finished work:

I have been reading the beginning of *The Pearl of Orr's Island* and finding it just as clear and perfectly original and strong as it seemed to me in my thirteenth or fourteenth year, when I read it first. I never shall forget the exquisite flavor and reality that it gave me. . . . It is classical—historical—anything you like to say, if you can give it high praise enough.[14]

But Miss Jewett desired a more adequate realism and so she turned curiously to consider the technique of the great continental realists of the eighties. She read Zola and Flaubert, Tolstoi and Turgenev, and oddly enough was persuaded that she had long been trying to do what Tolstoi was doing. In a letter of 1888 she wrote:

That story of Tolstoi's was such an excitement that I did not sleep until almost morning. What a wonderful thing it is! . . . It startled me because I was dimly feeling the same kind of motive (not the same plan) in writing the "Gray Man.". . . I have felt something of what Tolstoi has been doing all the way along. I can tell you half a dozen stories where I tried to say it, "Lady Terry," "Beyond the Toll-Gate," and this "Gray Man." Now and then it came clearer to me. I never felt the soul of Tolstoi's work until last night . . . but now I know what he means, and I know that I can dare to keep at the work I sometimes have despaired about. . . .[15]

---

[14] *Letters of Sarah Orne Jewett*, pp. 46–47.   [15] *Ibid.*, pp. 38–39.

Yet to later readers the tie that drew her to Tolstoi seems the thinnest of gossamers. The roots of her character—and of her art—went down too deep into Brahmin soil, she was too completely under the critical sway of Lowell and Fields and Aldrich, for her to turn naturalist. Her realism—if one may use the word—was as dainty and refined as her own manners—bleached out to a fine maidenly purity. In *The Country of the Pointed Firs*—a story that Willa Cather would destine for immortality in the select company of *Huckleberry Finn* and *The Scarlet Letter*—she discovers an innate gentility, or at least gentleness, in the simple fisherfolk of the Maine village, and she suggests as its source a primitive environment supplemented by an encompassing religion. Nowhere does she paint in the smutch of vulgarity, for in these eddies of New England life she discovers no vulgarity either of mind or manners. But in the cities it is different. There she found evidence in plenty of what she called the "cheap side of life," and she attributed it to the increasing material well-being of the country. Of the new middle class she held a low opinion—

Their grandparents or even their own parents went hungry and ill clothed, and it will take some time for these people to have their fling, to eat all they want and to wear fine raiment, and flaunt authority. They must get to a state, and by slow stages too, where there is going to be something fit for education. . . . The trouble is to us old-fashioned New Englanders that "the cheap streak" so often spoils what there is of good inheritance, and the wrong side of our great material prosperity is seen almost everywhere.[16]

There spoke the Brahmin. That this "cheap streak" should have spread so far through American life, that the vulgar middle class should have taken over the rule of the country, gave her concern. To one brought up on Carlyle and Lowell and Arnold the ways of the plutocracy were abhorrent, and she clung the more tenaciously to the land of her memories, where the gentry ruled, where the plain people respected themselves and their betters, and where vulgar display was unknown. "I think as Mr. Arnold does," she wrote in 1884, "and as Mr. Lowell did, that the mistake of our time is in being governed by the ignorant mass of opinion, instead of by thinkers and men who know something." [17] Though she disliked and distrusted the America that was submerging the old landmarks, she was as ignorant as her Maine fisherfolk of the

[16] *Ibid.*, pp. 186–187.   [17] *Ibid.*, p. 23.

social forces that were blotting out the world of her fathers, and she clung with pathetic futility to such fragments of the old order as remained. Like Lowell in his later years her heart was given to a Brahmin democracy where gentlemen ruled and where "the best traditions of culture and manners, from some divine inborn instinct toward what is simplest and purest," were held in universal respect.

What Miss Jewett with her love of the idyllic did not see—the grim and stark ugliness that resulted from the long Puritan repression—Mary Wilkins Freeman was to make the very warp of her work. She did not come of Brahmin stock. Bred up in the narrow village world of New England, she was a part of that world and she knew it as Miss Jewett could not. The decay of a social order was all about her in her youth. The more ambitious were drifting to the cities or to the new West, and those who remained were deeply marked by the constricting round of duties. Catastrophe seems always to be lying in wait for the characters that fill her meager pages. They are either timid and querulous, or fiercely "sot," yet in either case happiness has a way of slipping through their fingers. There was too little of the wine of paganism in their veins for them to enjoy what life offers. They held themselves in with too tight a rein. The New England conventions were always building higher the dams of their emotions until they broke and the roily waters rushed out in a wasting flood. Potential disaster peeps out of every page of her stories. *Pembroke* is an extraordinary collection of mean and petty and tragic lives, besotted with stubborn willfulness, without grace or comeliness, extracting no pleasant flavors from the crushed grapes of life. In that narrow world daily existence demands an unending struggle and the pinching meanness breeds miserly instincts and dour ways. *A Humble Romance* is a stark bit of sordid futility, and in many another of her short stories Mrs. Freeman etched in the familiar scene with a mordant pen. Drawn with realistic strokes the picture of New England in decay is not so lovely as Miss Jewett found it to be.

Realizing poignantly what was happening in the home of Puritanism, Mrs. Freeman turned eventually to deal with the problem of industrialism that was subduing New England to its will. *The Portion of Labor* picks up the theme where it had been dropped a generation before by Miss Phelps, and attempts in realistic manner to portray the life of the New England villager in the shoe factory. It is a tract rather than a story, and it finds no difficulty in reconciling industrialism with morality. It revives the old Puritan ethics of work—preached by Richard Baxter to his Kidderminster weavers two hundred and fifty years before; it discovers in discipline of character the great end of life; and it accepts the factory as a necessary instrument of civilization. It is the Cinderella story of a village girl who, refusing a chance to be sent to Vassar, enters a shoe factory, becomes a proletarian leader, engineers a strike, gains a wider vision of the function of labor, accepts the principle of exploitation, and is rewarded by marriage into the exploiting class. In her girlhood she was a radical in an untaught way, and from her valedictory essay at the High School Commencement to her organization of the factory workers she boldly attacked the factory owners. With the machine itself she had no quarrel. This is how she felt when she took her place for the first time in the mill:

> Scared she was not; she was fairly exultant. All at once she entered a vast room in which eager men were already at the machines with frantic zeal, as if they were driving labor herself. When she felt the vibration of the floor under her feet, when she saw people spring to their stations of toil, as if springing to guns in a battle, she realized the might and grandeur of it all. Suddenly it seemed to her that the greatest thing in the whole world was work and that this was one of the greatest forms of work—to cover the feet of progress of the travellers of the earth from the cradle to the grave. She saw that these great factories, and the strength of this army of the sons and daughters of toil, made possible the advance of civilization itself, which cannot go barefoot. She realized all at once and forever the dignity of labor, this girl of the people, with a brain which enabled her to overlook the heads of the rank and file of which she herself formed a part. She never again, whatever her regret might have been for another life for which she was better fitted, which her taste preferred, had any sense of ignominy in this. She never again felt that she was too good for her labor, for labor had revealed itself to her like a goddess behind a sordid veil.[18]

Nevertheless she is ready to fight for control of the machine— for a return to the workers of a larger share of their earnings; but when the strike fails and she contemplates the misery that it has spread amongst the workers, she recants:

> Her youthful enthusiasm carried her like a leaping-pole to conclusions beyond her years. "I wonder," she said to herself, "if, after all, this

[18] Chapter XXXV, p. 350.

inequality of possessions is not a part of the system of creation, if the righting of them is not beyond the flaming sword of the Garden of Eden? I wonder if the one who tries to right them forcibly is not meddling, and usurping the part of the Creator, and bringing down wrath and confusion not only upon his own head, but upon the heads of others? I wonder if it is wise, in order to establish a principle, to make those who have no voice in the matter suffer for it—the helpless women and children?" . . . She reflected, as she had so many times before, that the world was very old—thousands of years old—and inequality was as old as the world. Might it not even be a condition of its existence, the shifting of weights which kept it to its path in the scheme of the universe? [19]

Mrs. Freeman wisely chose a girl in her teens as the leader in a fierce labor battle, for Mrs. Freeman's own thinking on social questions was still in its teens. She had the warmest sympathy for the exploited poor; her conscience was as tender as Miss Phelps's; but her inadequate knowledge of economics served her ill. If economic inequality is necessary to keep the world from flying from its orbit, it serves the purpose likewise of character development. When an old factory-hand looks back upon a long life of futile labor he thus philosophizes:

Andrew quoted again from the old King of Wisdom—"I withheld not my heart from any joy, for my heart rejoices in all my labor, and that was my portion of labor." Then Andrew thought . . . of all the toilsome lives of those beside him, of all the work which they had done with their poor, knotted hands, of the tracks which they had worn on the earth towards their graves, with their weary feet, and suddenly he seemed to grasp a new and further meaning for that verse of Ecclesiastes.

He seemed to see that labor is not alone for itself, nor for what it accomplishes of the tasks of the world, not for its equivalent in silver and gold, not even for the end of human happiness and love, but for the growth in character of the laborer.

"That is the portion of labor," he said. [20]

So the book ends on a Hebraic note. In 1901 when Mrs. Freeman wrote *The Portion of Labor* the psychology of work had been pretty well explored. For years William Morris had been preaching a very different doctrine, pagan rather than Hebraic, yet Mrs. Freeman seems to have been acquainted with Morris no more than was Ellen Brewster, her girlish heroine. Even the starkest New England realism was not very critical of the industrialism that was destroying the traditional New England. A cynical reader

---

[19] Chapter LVII, pp. 519–520.   [20] *Ibid.*, p. 563.

might perhaps suggest that the explanation is to be found in the fact that the Yankee was profiting enormously from this fouling of the Puritan nest.

II

THE AFTERGLOW OF THE ENLIGHTENMENT— WALT WHITMAN

If the philosophy of the Enlightenment was fast disintegrating in the America of 1870, it still numbered its picturesque followers who sought to leaven the age with the social spirit of an earlier generation. It was a noble bequest—this gift of the French thinkers—with its passion for liberty, its faith in man, its democratic program. From that great reservoir had come pretty much all that was generously idealistic and humanitarian in the life of the two preceding generations. Its persuasive idealism had woven itself so closely into the fabric of national thought that our fathers had come to believe that America was dedicated in a very special sense to the principles of a free society. The democratic movement returned to it constantly to refresh its strength and take new bearings. At every great crisis the familiar pronouncement of the Declaration of Independence had been confidently appealed to in furtherance of social justice. And now in the days of an acquisitive individualism, when idealism was begging alms in the market-place, it still threw flashes of romantic splendor on the crude American scene. Old Peter Cooper still dreamed his dreams of social justice after eighty years had passed over his head; and Thaddeus Stevens, grown crabbed and surly from bitter struggles, mutely testified to his passionate equalitarianism on the day of his burial. But it was Walt Whitman in his den at Camden— culturally and in the things of the spirit countless leagues removed from Boston—who was the completest embodiment of the Enlightenment—the poet and prophet of a democracy that the America of the Gilded Age was daily betraying.

In his somewhat truculent pose of democratic undress Whitman was a singular figure for a poet, and especially an American poet. The amplitude and frankness and sincerity of his rich nature were an affront to every polite convention of the day. Endowed with abundant sensuousness and catholic sympathies, he took impressions as sharply as wax from the etcher's hand; and those impressions he transcribed with the careful impartiality of the modern expressionist. His sensitive reactions to experience were emotional rather than intellectual. A pagan, a romantic, a transcendentalist, a mystic—a child of the Enlightenment yet heeding the lessons of science and regarding himself as a realist who honored the physical as the repository of the spiritual—to an amazing degree he was an unconscious embodiment of American aspiration in the days when the romantic revolution was at flood tide. His buoyant nature floated easily on the turbulent stream of national being, and his songs were defiant chants in praise of life—strong, abundant, procreative—flowing through the veins of America.

Oracular and discursive, Whitman lived and moved in a world of sensuous imagery. His imagination was Gothic in its vast reaches. Thronging troops of pictures passed before him, vivid, vital, transcripts of reality, the sharp impress of some experience or fleeting observation—his own and no one's else, and therefore authentic. Delighting in the cosmos he saw reflecting its myriad phases in the mirror of his own ego, he sank into experience joyously like a strong swimmer idling in the salt waves. Borne up by the caressing waters, repressing nothing, rejecting nothing, he found life good in all its manifestations. As an Emersonian he was content to receive his sanctions from within, and as he yielded to the stimulus of the environing present his imagination expanded, his spirits rose to earth's jubilee, his speech fell into lyric cadences, and from the exalted abandon of egoistic experience there issued a strong rich note of the universal. His like had not before appeared in our literature for the reason that the childlike pagan had not before appeared. Emerson with his serene intelligence almost disencumbered of the flesh, and Hawthorne with his dessicating skepticisms that left him afraid of sex, were the fruits of a Hebraized culture that Puritan America understood; but Walt Whitman the caresser of life, the lover who found no sweeter fat than stuck to his own bones, was incomprehensible, and not being understood, it was inevitable that he should be inexorably damned. The most deeply religious soul that American literature knows, the friend and lover of all the world, the poet of the democratic ideal to which, presumably, America was dedicated, Whitman was flung into outer darkness by the moral custodians of an age that knew morality only from the precepts of the fathers.

The early stages of Whitman's intellectual development are obscure, but that in his twenties he caught most of the infections of the times, literary, political, and social, is clear enough. The young printer-editor in frock coat and tall hat, with cane and boutonnière, who often joined the Bohemian society at Pfaff's restaurant, was a callow romantic, practicing the conventional literary arts of the time, writing formal verse, spinning romantic tales,[21] and seeking to approve himself a reputable littérateur. But the passion of reform was already stirring within him and a succession of causes—temperance, anti-capital-punishment, abolitionism—recruited his pen. As a child of Manhattan and of the Jacksonian revolution it was inevitable that his first great passion should have been political, and when in the late forties he found a suitable vehicle of expression in the *Brooklyn Eagle*, his native Jeffersonianism took stock of current political programs. His political master was the radical equalitarian William Leggett—whose praises in after life he never stinted—and from Leggett and the *Evening Post*, supplemented by Fanny Wright and Tom Paine and other disreputable influences, he seems to have got the first clear expression of the sweeping democratic postulates on which later he was to erect his philosophy. The times were stirring everywhere with revolution and on Manhattan Island Locofocoism, with the newfangled matches, ten years before had started its little local bonfire by way of preparation for a general conflagration that should consume the accumulated mass of wrong and injustice. The ardent young Whitman was deeply infected with Locofoco enthusiasm and his editorials for the *Eagle* were the pronouncements of an extreme left-wing Democrat, as became a disciple of Leggett.

In this early phase of his democracy he fixed his hopes on the great West where, he believed, a freer and more democratic America was taking shape. He was an expansionist, full of ardent hopes, an apostle of "manifest destiny." In such lesser matters as finance and governmental subsidies he was a good Jacksonian, following Old Bullion Benton in his preference for hard money and dislike of shin-plasters. He was opposed to the bankers and monopolists. He called himself a "free-trader by instinct," and so late as 1888 he said, "I object to the tariff primarily because it is not humanitarian—because it is a damnable imposition upon the masses."[22] But these lesser things were inconsequential in comparison with the

[21] See Mabbott, *Short Stories by Walt Whitman*, Columbia University Press, 1927.
[22] For his late views see Horace Traubel, *With Walt Whitman in Camden*, Vol. I, p. 99, and elsewhere.

great objective towards which America was moving—the ever-widening freedom of men in society. "There must be," he wrote in those early years, "continual additions to our great experiment of how much liberty society will bear."[23] On that grand theme he was never tired of speaking. With Tom Paine he believed that just government was a simple thing, fitted to the capacity of many heads; it is made complex to hide its dishonesty. After commenting on the "once derided, but now widely worshipped doctrines which Jefferson and the glorious Leggett promulgated," he went on:

... this one single rule, rationally construed and applied, is enough to form the starting point of all that is necessary in government: *to make no more laws than those useful for preventing a man or body of men from infringing on the rights of other men.*

And again:

There is not a greater fallacy on earth than the doctrine of *force*, as applied in government. . . . Sensible men have long seen that the best government is that which governs least.[24]

Such comments, of course, are only familiar echoes of the Enlightenment—echoes that run through all the thinking of the naturistic school, from Godwin and Paine to Channing and Emerson and Thoreau. In the minds of the children of the Enlightenment the creative ideal of individualism was always pointing toward the ultimate end of philosophic anarchism, and Whitman with his assured faith in the average man accepted the Godwinian political theory as naturally as did Thoreau. What other politics, indeed, was possible for those who built upon the postulates of the innate excellence of human nature and the measureless potentialities of men when vicious social codes have been swept away and the plastic clay is molded by a kindly environment? The perfectibility of man was no romantic dream to the disciples of the French school, but a sober statement of sociological fact, based on a rationalistic psychology; and Whitman was convinced that he was a competent realist in thus envisaging the social problem. If man's instincts are trustworthy, what justification is there for narrow repressions laid on his freedom? Hitherto those repressions have only maimed and distorted him, encouraging his baser rather than his better impulses; and before he can realize his potentialities he

[23] Cleveland Rogers and John Black, *The Gathering of the Forces*, Vol. I, p. 12.
[24] *Ibid.*, Vol. I, pp. 53, 54, 57.

must put away all external compulsions and learn to rely solely upon himself. Hence the immediate objective of the democratic revolution was individual freedom, the breaking of all chains, to the end that free men may create a society worthy of them.

So it was as a revolutionary that Whitman began his work; and a revolutionary he remained to the end, although in his last years he chose to call himself an evolutionist. A born rebel, he was always preaching the gospel of rebellion. "I am a radical of radicals," he said late in life, "but I don't belong to any school." [25] It was this revolutionary spirit that made him the friend of all rebellious souls past and present. "My heart is with all you rebels—all of you, today, always, wherever: your flag is my flag," [26] he said to a Russian anarchist; and it was this sympathy that enabled him to understand Fanny Wright and Tom Paine and Priestley, who "have never had justice done them." [27] "The future belongs to the radical," and so *Leaves of Grass*—he says in "Starting from Paumanok"—"beat the gong of revolt." Conventional law and order he frankly despised and those individuals who sought their own law and followed it awoke his admiration. Thoreau's "lawlessness" delighted him—"his going his own absolute road let hell blaze all it chooses." It is a coward and a poltroon who accepts his law from others—as true of communities as it is true of individuals. He was a good Jeffersonian in his fear of Federalistic consolidation that must put an end to local rights and freedoms.

> To the States or any one of them, **or** any city of the States,
>   *Resist much, obey little,*
> Once unquestioning obedience, once fully enslaved,
>   . . . no nation, state, city of this earth, ever afterward resumes
>   its liberty.[28]
> I am for those that have never been master'd,
> For men and women whose tempers have never been master'd,
> For those whom laws, theories, conventions can never master.[29]

This is the spirit of the radical forties when men were prone to repudiate their allegiance to the political state; when left-wing Abolitionists were dissolving the Union by resolutions; and tran-

[25] Traubel, *op. cit.*, Vol. I, p. 215.
[26] *Ibid.*, Vol. I, p. 65.
[27] *Ibid.*, Vol. I, pp. 79–80.
[28] *Leaves of Grass*, inclusive edition ed. by Emory Halloway, Garden City, N. Y., 1927. Hereafter called *Leaves*. "To the States," p. 8.
[29] *Ibid.*, "By Blue Ontario's Shore," p. 297, ll. 21–23.

scendentalists were proclaiming the doctrine of nullification of unrighteous law. It had come out of the Jacksonian upheaval, but it was daily discovering fresh sanctions as the anarchistic premises of the Enlightenment were more adequately explored and the revolutionary spirit of Europe broke in upon America. During these turbulent years Whitman's great plan was in gestation, but before *Leaves of Grass* came to print in the first slender edition of 1855 other influences had been at work, confirming his earlier views, endowing them with lyric passion and expanding them into a grandiose whole. Those influences would seem to have been the fervid emotionalism of the fifties, the monistic idealism of the transcendental school, and the emerging scientific movement. On the whole perhaps it was the first, with its vague and expansive Utopianism, that bit most deeply, stimulating his rich pagan nature to unconventional frankness and encouraging him to throw off the inhibitions of a Puritan ethicism that held American thought in narrow bondage. The rude and ample liberalisms that so shocked his early readers were in no sense peculiar to Whitman, despite common opinion, but the expression of the surging emotionalism of the times, and *Leaves of Grass*, can best be understood by setting its frank paganism against the background of the lush fifties.

With its Calvinistic antecedents—Scotch-Irish and Huguenot as well as New England Puritan—America had always been unfriendly to a pagan evaluation of man's duties and destiny, and the revolutionary movement of the forties had been kept within sober ethical bounds. John Humphrey Noyes was probably the most radical American of the times, yet the Perfectionism of his earlier years, with its ascetic religiosity, bore little resemblance to the later communism of the Oneida Community. But the liberalism of the fifties was casting off all Hebraic restraints and running wild, proclaiming a new heaven about to appear on the free continent of America, and bidding the youth of the land live joyously as children of the earth. Paganism for the first time lifted up its head and surveyed the American scene—a youthful paganism, lusty and vigorous, that suggested amazing applications of the respectable doctrines of freedom and individuality, to the scandal of older-fashioned folk. From the free spaces of the West, carried on the tide of the Gold Rush, had come a spontaneous reaction from the earlier repressions. Liberalism was passing from the political to the social—a free welling-up of repressed desires, a vast expansiveness. Too long had the natural human emotions been under the ban of asceticism; too long had a God of wrath dispossessed a God of love. Life is good in the measure that it is lived fully, and to live fully is to live in the flesh as well as the spirit. Emerson the prophet of the earlier decade had suffered from an extreme unfleshliness; Whitman the prophet of the fifties would recover the balance. As the current of emotionalism gathered force a frank *joie de vivre* submerged the old reticences; candor, frankness, a very lust of self-expression, was the new law for free men and women—a glorification of the physical that put to rout the traditional Hebraisms. A riotous sentimentalism ran about the land until it seemed to timid souls as if liberty were quite running away with decency. Freedom for black slaves was one thing, but freedom for women—the loosening of social convention—suggested terrifying eventualities like free love and the disruption of the family. They would countenance no such immoral freedom and under the leadership of young Anthony Comstock the forces of reticence and respectability made ready to do battle with the new liberalisms.

It was not alone Walt Whitman who threw down the gage to the Comstockian watchmen in the gates. The apostle of the new freedom, the high priest of emotional liberalism, was Henry Ward Beecher, lately come out of the West, who from the pulpit of Plymouth Church swept his thousands of idolizing followers along the path of Utopian emotionalism. With a rich amplitude and golden vagueness of metaphor he preached the new gospel. From his lips flowed a lyric chant, a vast paean, a very shout in praise of liberty and love, of godlike man and a manlike God. "Life— affirmative, immediate, in a highly ornamented Mayday world— he acknowledged and commemorated life!" [30] He bathed in a "perpetual tropical luxuriance of blessed love." "I never knew how to worship until I knew how to love," he cried; "and to love I must have something . . . that touching my heart, shall not leave the chill of ice but the warmth of summer." Like a good Emersonian he discarded reason—the discipline of the ancestral Calvinism—to follow the "secret chords of feeling," the "heart's instincts, whose channels you may appoint but whose flowing is

[30] Constance Mayfield Rourke, *Trumpets of Jubliee*, p. 171.

beyond control." A "magnificent pagan"—so Thoreau called him—he reveled in sensuous beauty. His emotions mounted as he contemplated this new land, this new people, the golden future that beckoned—with all shackles broken, dedicated to freedom, warm and palpitating from abundant life—a radiant world of lovely women and manly men. He dwelt on Pisgah and from the heights looked out on a divine democracy. "The life of the common people is the best part of the world's life," he exclaimed; "the life of the common people is the life of God." And to his congregation intoxicated with his rhetoric he shouted, "Ye are gods! You are crystalline, your faces are radiant!" [31] And the end and outcome envisaged by this prophet of the American Idea was a vaguely grandiose fellowship, not of the Saints alone, but of all the thronging children of men, for of such is God's kingdom of this world.

As such lyric chants fell on Whitman's ears, they must have quickened the ferment of thought that was eventually to clarify for him the ideal of democracy, exalting it by making it warm and human and social. The old Jacksonian leveling had been negative; its freedoms had been individual, its anarchism selfish and unsocial. The great ideal of the fellowship had been lost in the scramble for rights. Even transcendental democracy had narrowed its contacts. The hermit Thoreau in his cabin at Walden Pond was no symbol of a generous democratic future. In the struggle for liberty and equality the conception of fraternity had been denied and the golden trinity of the Enlightenment dismembered. It was this idea of fraternity, made human and hearty by his warm love of men and women, that Whitman got from the expansive fifties and built into his thinking. The conception of solidarity, then entering the realm of proletarian thought through the labors of Friedrich Engels and Karl Marx, was his response to the new times—a response that infused his democratic faith with a glowing humanism. Democracy spiritualized by Channing and Emerson and Parker had suffered limitations from their lingering Hebraisms—the Puritan passion for righteousness had imposed strict ethical bounds on the democratic will. In Thoreau it had been subjected to caustic skepticisms—the transcendental individualist quizzically asked, "What *is* your people?" and refused to subject himself to the mass. But in Whitman all limitations and skepticisms were swept away by the feeling of comrade-

[31] *Ibid.*, p. 172.

ship. Flesh is kin to flesh, and out of the great reserves of life is born the average man "with his excellent good manliness." Not in distinction but in oneness with the whole is found the good life, for in fellowship is love and in the whole is freedom; and love and freedom are the law and the prophets. The disintegrations of the earlier individualism must be succeeded by a new integration; fear and hate and jealousy and pride have held men apart hitherto, but love will draw them together. After all solidarity—the children of America merging in the fellowship, sympathetic, responsive, manlike yet divine, of which the poet should be the prophet and literature provide the sermons.

It was a noble conception—washing away all the meanness that befouled Jacksonian individualism—and it somewhat slowly found its way to parity with his first master conception, the universal ego, and settled into place in those later opening lines of *Leaves of Grass:*

> One's-self I sing, a simple separate person,
> Yet utter the word Democratic, the word En-Masse.[32]

Then came the war to strengthen his faith in the common man. As he watched the soldiers marching, fighting, suffering, he was deeply impressed with their courage, patience, kindness, manliness, and came to reverence the deep wellspring of national being from which issued such inexhaustible waters. It was not the few but the many that gave him hope. "I never before so realized the majesty and reality of the American people *en masse*," he wrote of some regiments returning from the front. "It fell upon me like a great awe." [33] And as he contemplated this fecund people, with its sons and daughters issuing strong and wholesome from every part of the land, there came to him a new conception of unity—the Union that Lincoln loved—the drawing together into an indissoluble whole of the far-flung commonwealths—a realization of the perfect State where reign liberty, equality, fraternity. Solidarity had taken on a political complexion but its life-blood was in the veins of a free people.

But pagan though he was in his deeper nature, a child of the emotional fifties, he was a transcendentalist also and his democratic philosophy, as it took shape, bears unmistakable marks of the New England school, supplemented perhaps by Quakerism. His well-

[32] *Leaves,* "One's-Self I Sing," p. 1, ll. 1–2.
[33] *Autobiographia,* p. 73. See also *Democratic Vistas,* p. 74.

known comment, "I was simmering and simmering; it was Emerson brought me to boil," suggests much, and in particular that the Enlightenment as it had come to him through the Jeffersonian heritage was supplemented and spiritualized by the Enlightenment as it had taken special form in passing through the transcendental mind. To this latter source must be traced the philosophic monism that served to draw his speculations together—a mystic sense of the divine oneness of life that took his major postulates in golden hands and fused them into a single spiritual whole. Thus instructed the "great Idea, the idea of perfect and free individuals," became curiously Emersonian in all its amplifications. There is the same glorification of consciousness and will, the same exaltation of the soul, the same trust in the buried life that men call instinct, the same imperious call to heed the voice of innate Godhood; and round and about this "perfect and free individual" is a mystical egocentric universe wherein the children of men may luxuriate in their divinity. The body is excellent as the soul is excellent; away, therefore, with all shamefacedness—the mean secretiveness, the putting of fingers to the lips in presence of the naked, the lies in presence of open palpable fact! For if this be indeed God's universe, and He is in and through it all, the children of Adam may stand in His presence unafraid—nay, rather with pride in their own excellence. "I exist as I am, that is enough," for "Divine am I inside and out, and I make holy whatever I touch or am touch'd from."

Whitman not only accepted Emerson with ungrudging loyalty but he dwelt much with Hegel and the German idealists, and with their help he penetrated curiously to the core of things, discovering there an inner spiritual reality that is the abiding substance behind the external manifestation. He had come upon food to sustain his faith in presence of the mean and base that compassed him about, and the puzzling contradictions of life no longer troubled him. If man be perfectible, if he be indeed a child of God though still in his infancy, how glorious must be the future toward which he is pressing! The evil will pass and the good remain.

Roaming in thought over the Universe, I saw the little that is Good
    steadily hastening towards immortality,
And the vast all that is call'd Evil I saw hastening to merge itself and
    become lost and dead.[34]

[34] *Leaves*, "Roaming in Thought," p. 233.

When he turned from the oracular utterance of *Leaves of Grass* to sober exposition, he phrased it thus:

There is, apart from mere intellect . . . a wondrous something that realises without argument . . . an intuition of the absolute balance, in time and space, of the whole of this multifarious, mad chaos of fraud, frivolity, hoggishness—this revel of fools, and incredible make-believe and general unsettledness, we call the *world;* a soul-sight of that divine clue and unseen thread which holds the whole congeries of things, all history and time, and all events however trivial, however momentous, like a leash'd dog in the hands of the hunter.[35]

To discover this divine clue and be drawn by the unseen thread into the orbit of things, to suffer the Me—the "human identity of understanding, emotions, spirit"—to fuse with the Not Me—"the whole of the material, objective universe and laws, with what is behind them in time and space"—became therefore for Whitman the grand objective of man's life and effort. This for him was the sum and substance of religion, which was no other than the binding of the individual back upon the whole. "A vast similitude interlocks all." And so from his conception of social solidarity he went forward to the conception of spiritual solidarity, and discovered religion to be the crown and glory of the "American Idea." Walt Whitman and America were to be the prophets of religion. "Easily at home in a natural world of prodigious brightness and scale, he . . . saw 'the most splendid race the sun ever shone upon,' and was urging the life of instinct and impulse. Love was the key—taking form and in 'Starting from Paumanok' he asserted his Love, Democracy, Religion—a new religion." [36] His message was purpose.

The soul,
Forever and forever—longer than soil is brown and solid—longer than
    water ebbs and flows.

I will make the poems of materials, for I think they are to be the most
    spiritual poems,
And I will make the poems of my body and of mortality,
For I think I shall then supply myself with the poems of my soul and of
    immortality.

I will make a song for these States that no one State may under any
    circumstances be subjected to another State,

.   .   .   .

[35] "Carlyle from the American Point of View," in *Specimen Days, Prose Works,* pp. 174–175.   [36] Rourke, *op. cit.,* p. 173.

I will sing the song of companionship,

     .   .   .   .   .   .

I will write the evangel-poem of comrades and of love,

     .   .   .   .   .

I am the credulous man of qualities, ages, races,
I advance from the people in their own spirit,

     .   .   .   .   .

I, too, following many and follow'd by many, inaugurate a religion, . . .

     .   .   .   .   .

Each is not for its own sake,
I say the whole earth and all the stars in the sky are for religion's sake.

I say no man has ever yet been half devout enough,
None has ever yet adored or worship'd half enough,
None has begun to think how divine he himself is, and how certain the future is.

I say that the real and permanent grandeur of these States must be their religion,
Otherwise there is no real and permanent grandeur;

     .   .   .   .   .   .

My comrade!
For you to share with me two greatnesses, and a third one rising inclusive and more resplendent,
The greatness of Love and Democracy, and the greatness of Religion.[37]

But this new religion of the mystical Whitman, in harmony with post-transcendental thought, was deeply impregnated with the spirit of science. He was in the very fullness of his powers when the conception of evolution came to him and he greeted it gladly, weaving it into all his thinking and discovering in it a confirmation of his idealistic philosophy. It was the evolution of Herbert Spencer, it must be remembered, that Whitman accepted—teleological, buoyantly optimistic, dominated by the conception of progress, shot through with the spirit of the Enlightenment; and such an evolution was a confirmation and not a denial of his transcendental premises. It supplemented rather than contradicted the tenets of his faith. Like Emerson as he saw the bounds of the material universe slowly pushed back by science he discovered amidst the constant change the presence of growth, development, the natural passage from the simple to the complex;

[37] *Leaves*, "Starting from Paumanok," p. 14, ll. 22–26; p. 15, ll. 1, 13, 19, 22–23; p. 16, ll. 2, 5–11; p. 17, ll. 7–10.

and like Theodore Parker he felt that this slow unfolding was no other than the unfolding of God, making Himself evident and unmistakable to man. Evolution was God's great plan. "The law over all, the law of laws, is the law of successions," he was persuaded; "for what is the present after all but a growth out of the past?" But noble as is the evidence of God's work discoverable by science, the soul is not content to rest with such evidence; it must seek out the reality behind the manifestation; and for this work the poet alone is fitted. The poet must complete the work of the scientist. The noble "Passage to India" is a lovely chant of human progress, the adventurous soul conquering the earth; but it must not pause there; it must seek God through the universe until it finds Him, and "Nature and Man shall be disjoin'd and diffused no more," and "All these hearts as of fretted children shall be sooth'd."

> Bathe me O God in thee, mounting to thee,
> I and my soul to range in range of thee.[38]

It was in this profoundly religious spirit that Whitman accepted science, built it into his poetry, rested confidently upon it; and it is this spirit that explains his formal statement in the "Song of Myself."

I accept Reality and dare not question it,
Materialism first and last imbuing.

Hurrah for positive science! long live exact demonstration!
Fetch stonecrop mixt with cedar and branches of lilac,
This is the lexicographer, this the chemist, this made a grammar of the
   old cartouches,
These mariners put the ship through dangerous unknown seas,
This the geologist, this works with the scalpel, and this is the mathema-
   tician.

Gentlemen, to you the first honors always!
Your facts are useful, and yet they are not my dwelling,
I but enter by them to an area of my dwelling.[39]

Equipped with such a philosophy and supported by such a faith Whitman accepted the twin duties laid upon him: to make clear to America her present failure in the great adventure—how far she had fallen short hitherto of any adequate democratic

[38] *Leaves*, p. 349, ll. 18–19.   [39] *Leaves*, p. 43, ll. 9–17.

reality; and to mark out afresh the path to the Canaan of democratic hopes—reviving the early hopes of the Enlightenment and
drawing in lovelier colors the democratic Utopia dreamed of for a
hundred years. To be both critic and prophet—that he conceived
to be his mission, a mission that he was faithful to for upwards of
forty years. For the first duty he was admirably equipped. No
other knew this America so intimately or so broadly—had penetrated so lovingly to the common heart and read so clearly its
secret hopes and fears. That America was not yet a democracy—
was very far indeed from a democracy—that it was a somewhat
shoddy *bourgeois* capitalistic society shot through with cant and
hypocrisy and every meanness, he saw with calm, searching eyes.
No contemporary critic, not Godkin, not Emerson, saw more
clearly the unlovely reality or dealt with it more scathingly, not
only in *Leaves of Grass* but especially in his prose writings and in
casual talk. Amongst scores of such passages a single one must
serve for illustration.

I say that our New World democracy, however great a success in uplifting the masses out of their sloughs, in materialistic development,
products, and in a certain highly-deceptive superficial popular intellectuality, is, so far, an almost complete failure in its social aspects, and in really
grand religious, moral, literary, and esthetic results. . . . Shift and turn
the combinations of the statement as we may, the problem of the future
of America is in certain respects as dark as it is vast. Pride, competition,
segregation, vicious wilfulness, and license beyond example, brood already
upon us. Unwieldy and immense, who shall hold in behemoth? who bridle
leviathan? Flaunt it as we choose, athwart and over the roads of our
progress loom huge uncertainty, and dreadful threatening gloom. It is
useless to deny it: Democracy grows rankly up the thickest, noxious, dead-
liest plants and fruits of all—brings worse and worse invaders—needs
newer, larger, stronger, keener compensations and compellers. Our lands
embracing so much . . . hold in the breast that flame also, capable of consuming themselves, consuming us all. . . . Even today, amid these whirls,
incredible flippancy, and blind fury of parties, infidelity, entire lack of
first-rate captains and leaders, added to the plentiful meanness and vulgarity of the ostensible masses—that problem, the labor question, beginning to open like a yawning gulf, rapidly widening every year—what
prospect have we? We sail a dangerous sea of seething currents, cross and
under-currents, vortices,—all so dark and untried.[40]

As a realist Whitman granted the worst charges of the critics of
democracy, but he probed deeper and brought other facts to light
that modified the equation. It was the difficult question the old

[40] *Democratic Vistas, Prose Works*, pp. 254–255.

Federalists had posed and that Carlyle had lately revived—the question, is not this meanness inseparable from democracy? is not your people in fact a great beast, requiring the lash and the curb? It was the crux of the long debate over democracy and to it Whitman gave anxious and frequent consideration. In fighting the battle of 1790 over again, like Jefferson he rested his case on the native integrity and measureless potentiality of the "bulk-people"—they are the deep soil from which spring the abundant fruits and flowers of civilization. Gentle-nurtured folk do not understand this—they do not like the rank qualities of vital being. Matthew Arnold "always gives you the notion that he hates to touch the dirt—the dirt is so dirty! But everything comes out of the dirt—everything: everything comes out of the people . . . not university people, not F.F.V. people: people, people, just people!" In the rude, vital, natural man is the inexhaustible wellspring of good and evil; "He's got it all . . . not only the cruel, beastly, hoggish, cheating, bedbug qualities, but also the spiritual—the noble—the high-born"; [41] in "some ways" he is a "devil of a fellow," but he is not "all devil or even chiefly devil." [42] And because he is not chiefly devil such love and beauty and justice and comradeship as there is in the world, such progress in civilization as has been made hitherto, have been possible—how otherwise? If he has journeyed thus far out of the primeval slime, what bounds shall be set to his eventual journeyings? Why put out one's eyes with a mere handful of years?

So Whitman projected his democratic commonwealth far into the future; he would not have us believe that it had been realized here in America. Political democracy, the struggle for political rights that had engaged America hitherto, was only negative, a necessary preliminary to the ultimate reality. "I submit," he said, "that the fruition of democracy, on aught like a grand scale, resides altogether in the future," and its realization depends upon the use to which the people put their freedom. If from it emerges a proud and self-conscious individualism—"the quality of Being, in the object's self, according to its own central idea and purpose, and of growing therefrom and thereto—not criticism by other standards, and adjustments thereto"—then democracy on a grand scale will be possible and the self-reliant citizen will take his place in a free creative society. The ideal of the growing man, and the

[41] Traubel, *op. cit.*, Vol. I, p. 174.   [42] *Ibid.*, Vol. I, p. 285.

ideal of the perfect State—broadly social rather than narrowly political—these were his twin ideals; and the tie that is to bind men together in spontaneous solidarity is love. How characteristic is his sketch of the perfect city, and how deeply saturated with the Enlightenment! There is wanting only a physiocratic economics to make it perfect.

A great city is that which has the greatest men and women,

. . . . . .

Where the city stands with the brawniest breed of orators and bards,
Where the city stands that is belov'd by these, and loves them in return and understands them,
Where no monuments exist to heroes but in the common words and deeds,
Where thrift is in its place, and prudence is in its place,
Where the men and women think lightly of the laws,
Where the slave ceases and the master of slaves ceases,
Where the populace rise at once against the never-ending audacity of elected persons,

. . . . . .

Where outside authority enters always after the precedence of inside authority,
Where the citizen is always the head and ideal, and President, Mayor, Governor and what not, are agents for pay,
Where children are taught to be laws to themselves, and to depend on themselves,
Where equanimity is illustrated in affairs,

. . . . . .

Where the city of faithfulest friends stands,
Where the city of the cleanliness of the sexes stands,

. . . . . .

There the great city stands.[43]

Individualism, solidarity—on such strong bases he erected his ideal democracy, and the heaven-reaching temple will be overlaid with the rich arts and graces of a civilization worthy at last of the name. Such was the Enlightenment as it came to flower in the passionate idealism of Walt Whitman—a dream that was mocked and flouted and nullified by the Drews and Fisks and Goulds—the "hoggish, cheating, bedbug qualities" of a generation that scorned him for a beast. Even his stout faith was shaken at times

[43] *Leaves*, "Song of the Broad Axe," p. 160, ll. 7, 14–20, 21–22; p. 161, ll. 1–2, 6–7, 10.

by the infidelities of the Gilded Age. He was troubled by the gap that opened between the free individual and the perfect State. "I seem to be reaching for a new politics—for a new economy," he confessed in 1888; "I don't quite know what, but for something." [44] Although he protested, "The older I grow . . . the more I am confirmed in my optimism, my democracy," he projected his hopes farther into the future. He sympathized with the socialists but he was not one of them. His revolutionary ardor abated and he preferred in later years to call himself an evolutionist.[45] "Be radical—be radical," he said to Traubel, "be not too damned radical." [46] With his catholic sympathies that refused all bitterness he could not be a partisan—"after the best the partisan will say something better will be said by the man." [47]

So in the twilight of the romantic revolution Whitman quietly slipped away. The great hopes on which he fed have been belied by after events—so his critics say;[48] as the great hopes of the Enlightenment have been belied. Certainly in this welter of today, with science become the drab and slut of war and industrialism, with sterile money-slaves instead of men, Whitman's expansive hopes seem grotesque enough. Democracy may indeed be only a euphemism for the rulership of fools. Yet in a time of huge infidelities, in the dun breakdown and disintegration of all faiths, it is not wholly useless to recall the large proportions of Walt Whitman, his tenderness, his heartiness, his faith, his hope. There was in him no weak evasion, no sniveling over the shards of the goodly vessel broken at the well, but even when "old, alone, sick, weak-down, melted-worn with sweat," a free and joyous acceptance of life.

Thanks in old age—thanks ere I go,
For health, the midday sun, the impalpable air—for life, mere life,

      .   .   .   .   .   .

For all my days—not those of peace alone—the days of war the same,
For gentle words, caresses, gifts from foreign lands,
For shelter, wine and meat—for sweet appreciation,

      .   .   .   .   .   .

[44] Traubel, *op. cit.*, Vol. I, p. 101.
[45] *Ibid.*, Vol. I, pp. 193, 215.
[46] *Ibid.*, Vol. I, p. 223.
[47] *Ibid.*, Vol. I, p. 363.
[48] See Norman Foerster, *American Criticism*, pp. 211–222; Lucy Lockwood Hazard, *The Frontier in American Literature*, pp. 170–177.

For beings, groups, love, deeds, words, books—for colors, forms,
For all the brave strong men—devoted, hardy, men—who've forward
    sprung in freedom's help, all years, all lands,
For braver, stronger, more devoted men—(a special laurel ere I go, to
    life's war's chosen ones,
The cannoneers of song and thought—the great artillerists—the foremost
    leaders, captains of the soul:)
As soldier from an ended war return'd—As traveler out of myriads, to the
    long procession retrospective,
Thanks—joyful thanks!—a soldier's, traveler's thanks.[49]

   A great figure, the greatest assuredly in our literature—yet perhaps only a great child—summing up and transmitting into poetry
all the passionate aspirations of an America that had passed through
the romantic revolution, the poet of selfhood and the prophet of
brotherhood, the virile man and the catholic lover—how shall
Walt Whitman become dumb or cease to speak to men unless the
children of those who are now half-devil and half-God shall prove to
be wholly devil—or wholly moron?

III

THE BACKWASH OF THE FRONTIER—MARK TWAIN

   As Whitman contemplated the feeble literature purveyed by the
worshipers of the genteel he asked with some irritation: "What is
the reason in our time, our lands, that we see no fresh local courage,
sanity, of our own—the Mississippi, stalwart Western men, real
mental and physical facts, Southerners, etc., in the body of our
literature?" That was in 1870 and the answer was at hand in the
person of Mark Twain. Here at last was an authentic American—
a native writer thinking his own thoughts, using his own eyes,
speaking his own dialect—everything European fallen away, the
last shred of feudal culture gone, local and western yet continental.
A strange and uncouth figure in the eyes of Thomas Bailey Aldrich,
yet the very embodiment of the turbulent frontier that had long
been shaping a native psychology, and that now at last was turning
eastward to Americanize the Atlantic seaboard. Yet in spite of a
rare vein of humor, the outcropping of a rich and whimsical imagination, he made his way slowly to polite recognition. For years he
was regarded by authoritative critics as little more than a buffoon,
an extravagant fun-maker with a broad streak of western coarseness; and it was not till near the end, when he had long been an in-

[49] Leaves, "Thanks in Old Age," p. 435.

ternational figure, that the culture of the East accepted him. It was Howells then who pronounced him "the sole, the incomparable, the Lincoln of our literature . . . the very marrow of Americanism."

Just as that judgment was at the time, it needs qualification now. The marrow of Americanism is not the same substance from generation to generation. The outer environing life of a people works itself slowly into the bones and brings about subtle changes. Mark Twain was indubitably an embodiment of three centuries of American experience—frontier centuries, decentralized, leveling, individualistic; but the Americanism that issued from them came to its flower and was quickly succeeded by another kind as the fields of experience were re-plowed by industrialism and sowed to a different grain. Mark Twain was the child of a frontier past—as Lincoln was, as the Gilded Age was—and the America of today could no more breed him than it could breed Lincoln, or Greeley, or Whitman; his Americanism was the reflection of an environment that is no longer ours, in the slack folk-ways of the frontier that we have outgrown. Child of the Southwest in its early boom days, he was cradled in profitless schemes and nourished on dreams of vast potential wealth. The frontier spirit was an effervescence in his blood and golden expectations flung their mirage over the drab reality. As a boy he took impress from a kindly, ignorant, slave-holding, Calvinistic village world, and he quitted the slattern village life to plunge into the picturesque traffic of the Mississippi in the boom days when every river pilot drove his boat full steam ahead. Then the Far West of silver mines and the Golden Gate took him in hand—a gambling, romantic, optimistic frontier, feverish with flush times, "a beggar's revel of potential millionaires without the price of a square meal." [50] And finally this buoyant, irreverent adolescent was taken in hand by the Far East: by New England respectability in the persons of Olivia Langdon of Elmira, William Dean Howells of Cambridge, Twitchell and Warner of Hartford; and by New York in the persons of Carnegie and Gilder and Whitelaw Reid and Henry H. Rogers, to be made over into a man of the world.

Such were his origins and his schooling. All his life he remained a boy, with the imitativeness of youth, and yet with something deep within him that cherished its own integrity. Quick to take color from his environment and at home in crowds, he lived nevertheless in the solitude of his own heart. Acutely conscious of his

[50] Lucy Lockwood Hazard, *The Frontier in American Literature*, p. 223.

rough western ways, he admired the culture of the Langdons and the refined art of Howells, and he wanted to be approved by them. A kinsman of Beriah Sellers, he delighted in the great barbecue and wanted to carve great portions for himself, to heap up his plate as others were doing. His reactions to experience were always emotional. He was not a Walt Whitman to penetrate curiously to the core of his own being and grow thence outwardly, content to wait till the world came round to him. He loved to make a splurge, to be talked of, to be in the public eye, to live on an ample scale; he accepted the world's standards and wished to be measured by them. It was characteristic of the frontier. Wanting other standards, the frontier measured success by obvious material standards. Its aggressive individualism was never spiritual or intellectual or cultural. So with all his heritage of generations of frontier individualism he never achieved an intellectual or spiritual unity, an untroubled conscious integrity, as Emerson did and Whitman did. He never was at home in the world of catholic thought, but all his life he suffered from the petty inhibitions of his origins. He could not throw off the frontier—its psychology and its morality were too deeply intertwined with his primitive self; and the result was a harassing inner conflict that left him maimed.

Yet with all his shortcomings—because of them indeed—Mark Twain is an immensely significant American document. He is a mirror reflecting the muddy cross-currents of American life as the frontier spirit washed in, submerging the old aristocratic landmarks. To know Mark Twain is to know the strange and puzzling contradictions of the Gilded Age. With unconscious fidelity he reveals its crudity, its want of knowledge, discipline, historical perspective; its intellectual incapacity to deal with the complexities of a world passing through the twin revolutions of industrialism and science. And he reflects with equal fidelity certain other qualities that go far to redeem the meanness: a great creative power; an eager idealism, somewhat vague but still fine; a generous sympathy; a manly independence that strove to think honestly; a passionate hatred of wrong and injustice and an honest democratic respect for men as men. A significant if not an unsoiled or heroic document!

That in his later years an impassable gulf opened between Mark Twain and his generation, that the buoyant humorist of the sev-

enties ripened into the bitter satirist of the nineties, is a matter
that has been much remarked upon. The fact is clear enough but
the explanation is not so clear. In part no doubt—as Van Wyck
Brooks has pointed out—the change resulted from a thwarting
of the creative artist by a disastrous surrender to the ideals of the
Gilded Age; in part, also, it was the inevitable toll exacted by the
passing years. A humane and generous spirit cannot long watch
with indifference the motley human caravan hastening to eternity—cannot find food for laughter alone in the incredible meanness
and folly of men cheating and quarreling in a wilderness of graves.
Tenderness, chivalry, love of justice, are poor bucklers to withstand the blows of fate, and Mark Twain had little skill in defense.
The humorist like the poet is sensitively responsive to life and the
scars multiply fast. Endowed with a nature not unlike Swift's
in its fierce rage at inhumanity, not unlike Sir Philip Sidney's in
its romantic chivalry, he was not a stoic to endure with equanimity. He was foredoomed to suffer vicariously. The comment he
wrote Howells in 1899 throws a white light on the man. "I have
been reading the morning paper," he said. "I do it every morning—well knowing that I shall find in it the usual depravities and
basenesses and hypocrisies and cruelties that make up civilization,
and cause me to put in the rest of the day pleading for the damnation of the human race."

Yet granting so much, and granting also a morbid conscience
that harassed him with self-condemnation—"What a man sees in
the human race is merely himself in the deep and honest privacy of
his own heart"—it still remains true that the bleakness of his later
years was due in part, at least, to the insubstantial dwelling he chose
to live in. The architects of the Gilded Age were jerry-builders,
and Mark Twain found his jerry-built house a poor protection
against the winter winds. It was perhaps not greatly his fault that
he built so flimsily. He was too willing to be caught in the web of
material things. He could not reach out for companionship with
the great earth. Hamlin Garland in a bleak Dakota shack found
help and comfort in the philosophy of Taine, but Mark Twain
could not get outside his own skin. He could not break a path
through the provincialism of his environment. He was held
prisoner to his own thoughts and his only release was through the
window of imagination. When harassed beyond endurance he
sought release in writing that hid the evidence of his rebellion.

What would Livy say, what would the American public say, if they knew he had come to deny all the tribal gods!

There is no more pathetic figure in American literature than Mark Twain, alone and solitary amid the blatant American crowd, living in a dreary wash of speeches and banquets, spinning the threads of a rebellious philosophy out of his own bowels, unaware of what others were spinning, regarding himself as a dangerous fellow and stowing away in his strong-box intellectual bombs that he thought too explosive for the Gilded Age to play with. In his intellectual isolation he could not take the measure of his speculations and he did not realize how common were such conclusions— that his own generation indeed, under the tutelage of the physical sciences, was fast drifting in the same direction, and that the clouds of pessimism were obscuring for many the brighter horizons of an earlier day. If he had known Henry Adams as intimately as he knew Henry H. Rogers, very likely his eyes would have been opened to many things that would have done him good. As it was he knew only that his speculations ran counter to the formal creed of his middle-class neighbors and friends. To deny the dogmas of the conventional orthodoxy and in the face of a smug optimism to assert a mechanistic pessimism, was an unpleasant business that he would have avoided if he could.

But he couldn't avoid it wholly, and in that fact is to be found the thread that runs through his later life, giving to it such unity and coherence as it possessed. It is this: here was a thoroughly honest mind, that hated all sham and quackery and humbug, and a singularly warm heart, that hated all wrong and cruelty and injustice; and this honest mind and chivalrous heart, deceived and led astray by the mass *mores*, espoused and defended such fragments of ideals, such bits of truth, as he came upon in his solitary brooding, until driven from one stronghold after another he came to doubt the adequacy of all strongholds and took refuge in a black pessimism—God is a malignant being, the universe is a machine, and man is a creature of determinism. It was a fierce and stark reaction from the emotionalism of the fifties—from Beecher's God of love and Whitman's religion of democracy. His earlier loyalty to half-gods had brought him at last to deny all the gods. And so a maimed giant, stumbling and uncertain, he made such way as he could; and his journeyings wrung from him many a fierce comment that his generation did not understand.

When the milk of western humor curdled in his veins, a Mark Twain emerged who was a puzzle to the Gilded Age. A humorist who was a good Republican and business man, the Gilded Age could understand; but a satirist who launched his shafts at sacred things —at evangelical religion, the Republican party, the government at Washington, the damned human race itself—it could not understand. The professional fun-maker had outgrown his audience. Expecting the familiar exaggeration, they accounted his bitterest sally a characteristic whimsy, and laughed when he commented bitterly on "this plodding sad pilgrimage, this pathetic drift between the eternities," or when he exclaimed, "Everything human is pathetic. The secret source of Humor is not joy but sorrow. There is no humor in heaven." But the significant thing is that in the end the tyrannizing *mores* did not conquer, they did not destroy him wholly; but such convictions as he had hewn from puzzling experience, however bleak or repellent they might be, he clung to firmly, desperately, and at last flung them in the face of the Gilded Age that had kept him prisoner.

The slow drift of Mark Twain's thought from humor to satire— it smacks of Philistinism to call it progress with its many false alarums and excursions and its huge frontier wastefulness—is plain enough to anyone who will take the trouble to chart his course. Roughly it falls into definite stages: the swaggering gayety of western youth in *Innocents Abroad* and *Roughing It*—the mood of flush times, down-grade with the brakes off; then a gay plunge into satire in *The Gilded Age;* then the West recalled in middle life—*Tom Sawyer, Life on the Mississippi, Huckleberry Finn*— living over again a youth that is gone; then an excursion into the Middle Ages—*The Prince and the Pauper* and *A Connecticut Yankee in King Arthur's Court*—a romantic flare-up of the democratic passions of the Enlightenment; then the search for the ideal in *Joan of Arc*—the dream of the perfect woman, the Domnei of James Branch Cabell; and finally *The Mysterious Stranger* and *What is Man?*—a fierce satire of disillusion, the cry of an idealist who realizes at last how greatly he has been cheated by his dreams.

That he should have begun by burlesquing life was itself a broad sign of his frontier origins. Since the first crossing of the Allegheny Mountains a swaggering extravagance of speech had been a hallmark of the Westerner. In part this swagger was an unconscious defense-mechanism against the drabness of frontier

life; and in part it was the spontaneous expression of new experiences in an untrammeled world, the spirit of wilderness-leveling.
Its procreative source would seem to have been the Ohio River
where the rough flatboatmen bequeathed the Mike Fink legend
to literature; and it expanded in the huge Davy Crockett hoax—
a hoax that would have tickled the ribs of Mark Twain had he
traced its genesis and progress, as a colossal example of how the
damned human race loves to be humbugged. It developed further
in Gus Longstreet's *Georgia Scenes* with its grotesque Ransy Sniffle
—sorriest of backwoods heroes, too mean-spirited to ruffle like
Canebrake Davy; and in Joseph Baldwin's *Flush Times of Alabama and Mississippi*, with its greasy frontier blackguard, Colonel
Simon Suggs.

This earliest backwoods humor had been done in realistic colors
and bears the impress of authenticity. But the school that succeeded—John Phoenix, Artemus Ward, Petroleum V. Nasby—
quickly conventionalized its technique, relying on burlesque, tall
lying, distorted spelling, genial philosophy. The picaresque strain
was softened and perverted by deliberate human-interest touches—
a better case must be made out for the untutored children of nature. It was this humor that Mark Twain inherited, and he enriched it with a wealth dug from his own large and generous
nature. An incorrigible idealist, as all great humorists must be,
he recreated some of the earlier types, translating Colonel Simon
Suggs into Colonel Sellers, and Ransy Sniffle into Huck Finn. It
was a glorious transformation, but the result lacked something
of the soiled reality of the earlier blackguards. Yet underneath
his idealism was a generous deposit of the common mud of life.
The spirit of Mike Fink was never far from Mark Twain. It
haunted him like an evil genius, refusing to be exorcised by Olivia
Clemens, and it found vent in sly literary sprees that begot offspring to be handed about furtively and chuckled over by the sons
of Adam; but for the most part it was kept in strict subjection to
the proprieties of Elmira and Hartford.

Roughing It and *The Gilded Age* are brilliant complementary
pictures of the gaudy frontier spirit that was washing in upon the
staid realm of the genteel, to the vast concern of such genteelists
as Thomas Bailey Aldrich. The former is a buoyant chronicle of
the West of Captain Carver and Wild Bill Hickok, the West of
the Pony Express, the Comstock lode, the bad man and the lynch

law, a land of young men in red flannel shirts, heavy boots, and six-shooters, who feared neither God nor the devil. Bret Harte in San Francisco first realized the literary possibilities of this picturesque world, and his tales of life in the mining-camps were received with a shout of approval. But Bret Harte had never been a miner. He was not realist enough, nor honest enough, to portray the West in its stark, grotesque reality. He was only a literary middleman who skillfully purveyed such wares as his eastern readers wanted. In consequence he coated his tales with a sentimental picaresque—pandered to the common taste by discovering nuggets of pure gold in the dregs and outcasts of the mining-camps. But Mark Twain was too honest for that. He had been a part of the flush times and had seen the economic process work itself out. He had seen the grub-stake prospector succeeded by the wild-cat speculator, and him in turn followed by the eastern capitalist. He had seen the mining frontier become a thing of the past in a single decade, with the Comstock lode in the hands of competent exploiters and the pick-and-shovel miners plunging deeper into the mountains to pursue their feverish hopes. From that experience he had learned a lesson he was to carry East with him. "Because we judged that we had learned," he said, "the real secret of success in silver mining, which was, not to mine the silver ourselves by the sweat of our brows and the labor of our hands, but to *sell* the ledges to the dull slaves of toil and let them do the mining." [51]

It was the great lesson of his generation, and thus instructed he proposed to sell his brains in the best market. Exploitation was the royal road to wealth and he was eager to exploit both himself and his fellows. Yet not all of Mark Twain was thus eager. Deep in his heart was another Mark Twain, the artist, the chivalrous lover of justice, the simple child puzzled at life—and this Mark Twain was already plotting treason against the exploiting Mark Twain. For the first time this deeper self got out of hand in *The Gilded Age*. As he contemplated the common scoundrelism at Washington and elsewhere, his anger exuded in scathing satire. He hated the dirty thing, yet he seems never to have realized that such scoundrelism was only the backwash of the spirit of exploitation and that he himself was riding on its waves. With the soap-bubble dreams of Colonel Sellers he dealt lovingly, for he was sketching his own

[51] Vol. I, Chapter XXXIII, p. 237.

origins; the Colonel and the Hawkinses were his own flesh and blood and the Tennessee lands were an old investment about which the family dreams of wealth had been woven for years. He delighted in the Colonel's childlike faith that prosperity only awaited a vote of Congress—with adequate appropriations, of course. He asked no questions about unearned increment; to question that would have been treason to the frontier philosophy. So into Colonel Sellers he put all that was naïve and lovable in the Gilded Age. But Senator Dillworthy was another matter. Hypocrite and corruptionist, he was laying obscene hands on sacred things, betraying his high trust for sordid ends. Mark Twain hated graft—the word had not been coined but the ugly thing was there—and with the innocence of his generation he damned the agent and overlooked the principal. It was not his fault. The economics of history was a closed book to Americans of the seventies, and even Henry Adams in his analysis of the current corruption in his novel *Democracy* was no better than a mole nosing blindly underground.

He had opened another door to his genius and discovered the satirist. There lay the real Mark Twain. But the wares of the satirist were not in demand at the barbecue, so he closed the door and fell to purveying what the public wanted. *Tom Sawyer* was in part a malicious thrust at the Sunday School tale, and in part a whimsical pronouncement of the natural rights of the small boy. But it is in *Huckleberry Finn*—the one great picaresque tale of the frontier—that the western philosophy of Mark Twain, a philosophy that derives straight from the old naturistic school, crops out most sharply. It is a drama of the struggle between the individual and the village *mores*, set in a loose picturesque framework, and exemplifying the familiar thesis that the stuff of life springs strong and wholesome from the great common stock. Huck Finn is a child of nature who has lived close to the simple facts of life, unperverted by the tyrannies of the village that would make a good boy of him. He had got his schooling from the unfenced woods, from the great river that swept past him as he idly fished, from the folk-tales of negroes and poor whites, from queer adventures with Tom Sawyer; and from such experiences he had got a code of natural ethics. Then he found himself on the raft with Jim the runaway nigger, and his little pagan soul felt the stirrings of the problem of right and wrong. The village code and the natural code clashed and the conflict was terrifying. The village code warned him that hell yawned for one who helped a slave escape, and the human code warned him that betrayal was a blackguardly thing. With the fear of hell upon him he wrote to Miss Watson, and then his sense of the kindliness of Jim, the honest humanity under the black skin, rose up in fierce protest.

It was a close place. I took [the letter] up, and held it in my hands. I was a-trembling, because I'd got to decide, forever, betwixt two things, and I knowed it. I studied for a minute, sort of holding my breath, and then says to myself:

"All right, then, I'll *go* to hell"—and tore it up.

It was awful thoughts and awful words, but they was said. And I let them stay said; and never thought no more about reforming.[52]

It was a triumph over the sacred tribal law of conformity—the assertion of the individual will in opposition to society—and it reveals the heart of Mark Twain's philosophy. The rebel Huck is no other than the rebel Mark Twain whose wrath was quick to flame up against the unrighteous customs and laws of caste. If men were only honest realists—that is, if they were men and not credulous fools—how quickly the stables might be cleansed and life become decent and humane. If only the good brains could be segregated and trained in a real "man-factory," the history of civilization might become something the angels need not weep over as they read it. It all comes back to an honest realism that in accepting fact will clear away the superstitious fogs in which men have floundered and suffered hitherto. The one sacred duty laid on every rational being is the duty of rebellion against sham—to deny the divinity of clothes, to thrust out quack kings and priests and lords, to refuse a witless loyalty to things. This creed of the rebel is written all through Mark Twain's later work, edging his satire and lending an Emersonian note to his individualism. In such a passage as this it emerges sharply:

You see my kind of loyalty was loyalty to one's country, not to its institutions or its office-holders. The country is the real thing, the substantial thing, the eternal thing; it is the thing to watch over, and care for, and be loyal to; institutions are extraneous, they are its mere clothing, and clothing can wear out, become ragged, cease to be comfortable, cease to protect the body from winter, disease, death. To be loyal to rags, to shout for rags, to worship rags—that is a loyalty to unreason, it is pure animal; it belongs to monarchy, was invented by monarchy; let monarchy keep it. I was from Connecticut, whose Constitution declares "that all

[52] Chapter 31.

political power is inherent in the people, and all free governments are founded on their authority and instituted for their benefit; and that they have *at all times* an undeniable and indefeasible right to *alter their form of government* in such manner as they may think expedient."

Under that gospel, the citizen who thinks he sees that the commonwealth's political clothes are worn out, and yet holds his peace and does not agitate for a new suit, is disloyal; he is a traitor. That he may be the only one who thinks he sees this decay, does not excuse him; it is his duty to agitate anyway, and it is the duty of others to vote him down if they do not see the matter as he does.[53]

In the Middle Ages clothes-worship had been exalted to a religion, he believed, and he turned with gusto to reply to the aristocratic romanticism of Sir Walter, who, delighting in the picturesque company gathered in the great hall, forgot to penetrate to the *oubliettes*—is not the word commentary enough on the ways of the seigneur?—where nameless wretches were rotting under the walls of the castle. He had small patience with the cult of medievalism that was turning such men as Henry Adams and William Morris back to the Middle Ages as to their lost home. He had the frontier contempt for medieval ways, and for the *ancien régime* that was the last rags of the Middle Ages. The French Revolution had thrust the abomination away forever, and he thanked God for that "ever memorable and blessed Revolution, which swept a thousand years of . . . villainy away in one swift tidal wave of blood." He had no tears for Marie Antoinette. What was the Terror but "a settlement of that hoary debt in the proportion of half a drop of blood for each hogshead of it that had been pressed by slow tortures out of that people in the weary stretch of ten centuries of wrong and shame and misery the like of which was not to be mated but in hell . . . that unspeakably bitter and awful Terror which none of us has been taught to see in its vastness or pity as it deserves."[54] The past that had been consumed in that fierce conflagration had been a brutal, tyrannical, superstitious past, and not till king and priest had been flung out on the dungheap did the people walk their native soil as free men. The whole king business was preposterous to him; with Freneau he cried, "Kings are the choicest curse that man e'er knew." The battle against medievalism had been fought and won and why go maundering back over past battlefields, when other battles await?[55]

[53] *The Connecticut Yankee*, N. Y., 1917, p. 107.
[54] *Ibid.*, Chapter XIII, pp. 105–106.
[55] Cf. Whitman's view, *The Gathering of the Forces*, Vol. II, pp. 284–286.

Mark Twain's passionate republicanism was a product of the Enlightenment as it had passed into the psychology of western Americans, and it retained the militant idealism of Jeffersonian times. It is shot through with the nature philosophy. In *The Prince and the Pauper*, the heir of Offal Court and the heir of the Tudors are both children of nature, endowed with warm hearts, generous sympathies, and clever wits. Put rags on the prince and robes on the pauper and their own kin cannot tell them apart. The latter, indeed, promises to make the better king, for he has suffered the lot of the subject, and not till the prince has put on rags does he come to know his people. It is caste that breeds cruelty and wrong; the brutalities of the English criminal code were deviltries devised by king and nobles to safeguard their stealings. Only when the laws spring from the people are they just. "The world is made wrong," cried the young king when he was brought out of prison to watch the burning at the stake of two women who had befriended him—women whose only crime was that of being Baptists—"the world is made wrong, kings should go to school to their own laws, at times, and so learn mercy." And this great lesson of mercy is exemplified in the acts of the pauper king, who during his brief reign tempers the harshness of the law with a sense of justice learned, like Huck Finn's, from sharp contact with reality.

It is in *A Connecticut Yankee in King Arthur's Court*—a curious medley, half philippic and half farce—that Mark Twain's passion for justice rises to white heat. The book has been grossly misunderstood. It is not an attack on chivalry—at least not primarily; it is rather an attack on thirteen centuries of reputed Christian civilization that under pretense of serving God has enslaved and despoiled the children of God. The keen satire is given point and edge by the long tragic perspective. Thirteen centuries heavy with sorrow and misery and frustrated hopes—a meaningless succession of foolish and futile generations, wandering in fogs of their own brewing, hagridden by superstitions, deceived and exploited by priest and noble, with no will to be free—here is a perspective to correct our callow enthusiasms, our revolutionary hopes! Why indeed should we expect men to possess the will to freedom, seeing that each generation is molded after the likeness of the past and none has been free? There is change, advance and recession, but the story of the generations is no more than a "sad drift between

the eternities," without purpose or meaning. In the brain of the
Connecticut Yankee are secrets hidden from the children of King
Arthur's time—a curious ability to use the forces of nature, some
glimmerings of social justice. But to what purpose have Hartford
and the nineteenth century used their knowledge? It is a world of
slaves still as it was in King Arthur's day. The human animal
cannot lift himself to heaven by his own bootstraps, and heaven
will not stoop to lift him. For a "clammy atmosphere of reverence,
respect, deference," it has substituted smartness, vulgarity, irreverence.

As one slips back and forth between the two worlds the satire
takes on vaster perspectives; it cuts deep into all civilizations, for
all alike are sham, all have issued from the conquest of man's native
intelligence by his superstitions that are too useful to his masters
to be dissipated. Clearly in Mark Twain's philosophy of history
the hopes of the Enlightenment are fading. Passionately dedicated
to the program of the Enlightenment—freedom, individuality,
humanitarianism, democracy—his faith in reason, free will,
progress, was burning low, in presence of the historical record.
The determinism that lurked at the bottom of John Locke's
psychology, unperceived by the French idealists, was revealing
itself to Mark Twain and he was already trimming his sails to the
chill winds blowing from the outer spaces of a mechanistic cosmos.

More immediately of course *A Connecticut Yankee* is an attack on the aristocratic romanticism of Sir Walter. There is little
loitering in the great hall—except to comment on the coarseness
of the knights and ladies—and much poking about in unlovely
secret places where one comes upon a rare collection of human
animals thrust away in the *oubliettes* or pigging together in mean
huts. Few chapters in American literature are so noble in their
saeva indignatio, so beautiful in their stern simplicity, as certain
sketches of the king's progress through his realm—not a royal
progress but a peasant's. There are no tears in them, they go far
beyond that. The scene in the smallpox hut where the wife is glad
her husband and daughters are dead—they are either in heaven or
hell, it makes little difference, for they are no longer in Britain
and so are happy; and the scene of the young mother hanged for
stealing a piece of cloth of an ell's length or so, hanged that property in Britain might be safe—such pictures reveal how far he had
traveled from the days of *Roughing It*. He was no longer a good

Federalist-Whig concerned about exploitation and the safeguards of property. Although he voted the Republican ticket he made merry over the tariff [56] and he frankly hated the dominant Republican property-consciousness. Like Lincoln he was for the man rather than the dollar when the rights of the two clashed. In these later years he was steadily drifting to the left, on the side of the social underling, sympathetic with those who do the work of the world. "He never went so far in socialism, as I have gone," said Howells, "if he went that way at all . . . but from the first he had a luminous vision of organized labor as the only present help for workingmen. . . . There was a time when I was afraid that his eyes were a little holden from the truth; but in the very last talk I heard from him I found that I was wrong, and that this great humorist was as great a humanist as ever." [57]

It is good for an American to read *A Connecticut Yankee*—and *Joan of Arc* as well; for in them is a flame that sears and shrivels the mean property-consciousness which lays a blight on every civilization. In the peasant girl of Domrémy, the rapt mystic led by her Voices, Mark Twain found his ideal, the lily that bloomed out of the muck of medieval times; and as he contemplated her life and work he was lifted to the plane of worship. She had waged heroic warfare against the embattled lies and shams and treacheries of a sordid age, and that she should have died at the stake was inevitable. What other reward was to be expected from bishops and kings and suchlike spawn of the devil? Not till the people grow to manhood can any savior help them, and in that day they will need no savior but themselves. The Sieur Louis de Conte struggles with the idea confusedly.

I believe that some day it will be found out that peasants are people. Yes, beings in a great many respects like ourselves. And I believe that some day *they* will find this out, too—and then! Well, then I think they will rise up and demand to be regarded as a part of the race, and that by consequence there will be trouble. Whenever one sees in a book or in a king's proclamation those words 'the nation,' they bring before us the upper classes; only those; we know no other 'nation;' for us and the kings no other 'nation' exists. But from the day I saw old D'Arc the peasant acting and feeling just as I should have acted and felt myself, I have carried the conviction in my heart that our peasants are not merely animals, beasts of burden put here by the good God to produce food and comfort for the 'nation,' but something more and better. You look incredulous.

[56] See Chapter 33.   [57] W. D. Howells, *My Mark Twain*, p. 43.

Well, that is your training; it is the training of everybody; but as for me, I thank that incident for giving me a better light, and I have never forgotten it.[58]

No Bayard ever did his devoir more knightly to his lady than Mark Twain to Joan, finding in the noble drama of her life the romance he had not found at Arthur's court. The knights of the Round Table were "but ghosts fighting in the fog," but Jeanne D'Arc was human and lovable and divine. And then the outlet through which his idealism had found release slowly closed in, and he was left alone with his comfortless speculations. What profits it to rail at the damned human race when man has about as much chance for happiness as a blind puppy in a sack? The bitter lot of humanity is due not to institutions alone or chiefly, it is a part of the mad plan of a bleak mechanical universe. For Mark Twain the solid earth was dissolving, leaving only a rack behind. It is futile to lament. A sympathetic heart, indeed, is the last and bitterest irony—for why weep over an evil exhalation! *"Life itself is only a vision, a dream . . . Nothing exists save empty space— and you."*

In a little while you will be alone in shoreless space, to wander its limitless solitudes without friend or comrade forever—for you will remain a *thought*, the only existent thought, and by your nature inextinguishable, indestructible. But I, your poor servant, have revealed you to yourself and set you free. Dream other dreams, and better. Strange, indeed, that you should not have suspected that your universe and its contents were only dreams, visions, fiction! Strange, because they are so frankly and hysterically insane—like all dreams . . . the silly creations of an imagination that is not conscious of its freaks—in a word that they are a dream, and you the maker of it. . . .[59]

So, like Cabell, Mark Twain asserts that man must build within and by letting his dreams flow out create for himself such shelter as he can against the chill of the eternal void. A flea on the epidermis of earth, nevertheless he is thought and thought is deathless. To such a conclusion did the buoyant youth of *Roughing It* arrive in the dun twilight years. *The Mysterious Stranger* is only *Tom Sawyer* retold in the midnight of his disillusion.

What an ending for a child of the Gilded Age! In his youth a complete frontiersman, with vast potential wealth within him, he hewed and hacked at his genius, working the easiest veins,

[58] *Joan of Arc*, Chapter 37, p. 290.
[59] *The Mysterious Stranger*, p. 151.

exploiting the most accessible resources, wasting much to cash in on a little. And when in the end the fool's gold turned to ashes in his mouth, as a frontiersman still he pursued his way alone, a solitary pioneer exploring the universe, seeking a homestead in an ironical cosmos, until overwhelmed by the intolerable solitude he made mock at all the gods. What a commentary on the Gilded Age!

CHAPTER III

CHANGING THEORY

UNLIKE as were Thomas Bailey Aldrich, Walt Whitman, and Mark Twain, they belonged equally to an America that was passing. In consequence of the silent drift towards consolidation new philosophies were preparing that were to rephrase the familiar American ideals and adapt current political and economic theory to the needs of the new order. For a decade or more the significance of that drift was obscured by the last great wave of decentralization that swept across the prairie commonwealths; but when the frontier had been pushed to the Pacific Northwest and the free lands had passed into private ownership, the movement of consolidation gathered momentum swiftly. Primarily economic in its origins, it went forward on even foot with the industrial revolution. The vast increase in population, the unprofitable expansion of agriculture, the augmenting resources of liquid capital, the new potentialities revealed by industrialism, were all engaged in the work of transforming a scattered agricultural people into an urbanized industrial people.

And then came the railways to hasten a movement that was implicit in the nature of things. Effective nationality in America issued more immediately from fluid communication than perhaps any other cause. A depressing spirit of isolation—of provincial aloofness—had lain like a heavy weight on the colonial mind. The barriers of distance were made formidable by a rugged untamed country, and to open up free communication was an arduous undertaking. Yet easy communication must be provided if economic development were to go forward. In the early years of the nineteenth century vast plans and great outlays of money went into the work of linking the sundered portions of the country by a system of waterways. The Erie canal, the great lakes, the Ohio and the Mississippi, were creating their own America, picturesque and individual, when the process of differentiation was rudely broken across by the iron rails that ran East and West, disregarding natural barriers and breaking down traditional frontiers. It was the railways that tied the continent effectively together, providing the needed transportation to make possible a national economic system. With the laying of the Union Pacific rails in the late sixties the destiny of America as a self-sufficient economic unity was fixed. Henceforth for an indeterminate period the drift of tendency would be from the outlying frontiers to industrial centers, and with that drift would come far-reaching changes in the daily routine of life. The machine would reach into the remotest villages to disrupt the traditional domestic economy, and the division of labor would substitute for the versatile frontiersman the specialized factory-hand. A new urban psychology would displace the older agrarian, and with the new psychology would come other philosophies in response to the changing realities.

I

WINDS OF ECONOMIC THEORY

So profound a revolution could not fail to dislocate the foundations of all traditional schools of thought. Economic and political theory were both thrown out of their earlier beds to flow in new channels. By force of gravitation the main stream of economic theory—like the main stream of political theory—poured into the broadening channels of capitalism, and only the lesser vagrant currents followed the old channels of agrarianism or the new channels of proletarianism. There was much speculation on the disturbing phenomena of the great change, and current economic theory was slow to settle into the conformities of a school. It divided sharply, not only between the advocates of capitalism and agrarianism, but between those who accepted the classical English theory and those who believed that economic conditions in America warranted an independent American school. The first group of professional economists—Henry C. Carey, Francis A. Walker, David A. Wells—made its appearance, and a very considerable group of amateurs—free-lance economists and fireside theorists—contributed to the speculation of the times in the measure of their intelligence. These latter have received scant attention, since the battle went against them; nevertheless they do not deserve to be forgotten, for most often they were an expression of the social conscience of the times—a homely protest against the exploitation of farmer and workingman by the rising capitalism.

But because they essayed to turn the course of "manifest destiny" they were ignored or roughly ridden down, and only one of them— Henry George—is still widely influential.

In the primitive early days of America economic theory had been a simple homespun product, woven on fireside looms, and following simple domestic patterns. With the rise of industrialism it passed into the keeping of stockbrokers and textile manufacturers and retail merchants who were looked upon as authoritative expounders of the new science of wealth. In his *Elements of Political Economy*, first published in 1837 and for forty years a standard textbook in American colleges, Francis Wayland accepted this view and offered an apology for treating of the subject at all. "It may possibly be urged," he said, "that the Author, having had no experience in mercantile business, should have left this subject to be treated of by practical men." In the days of Henry Clay this view established itself in the halls of Congress, where politicians who had never heard of Ricardo were on profitably intimate terms with Nick Biddle, and respected the interests of influential constituents far more than the principles of Manchesterism. With the appearance of professional economists the breach between economic theory and legislative votes widened to a chasm. Ignored by the politicians except in so far as their views fell in with the current paternalism, the economists retreated to the quiet of the schools and there spun their webs quite harmlessly. Youthful undergraduates were fed on a modified English classical theory in which the pessimism of Ricardo and Malthus, bred of the bitter dislocations of English industrial life, was diluted with an optimism more suited to the temper of the new world.

The academic economists, it must be confessed, were in an unhappy position, not unlike that of the earlier Calvinists. They lived as remote from the realities of life as did those old ministers. Trained in the orthodox English school they felt bound to defend *laissez faire;* yet as members of universities dependent on wealthy patrons they could not well offend powerful interests that wanted none of their free-trade theory. On the whole they stuck pretty manfully to their guns, and from Wayland to Sumner they upheld the abstract principle of free competition; but what they could do in other ways to appease the wrath of the protectionists they did heartily, and the steady rapprochement of academic economic theory and capitalism was foreordained in the nature of things academic. Agrarian and proletarian economics were granted no hearing in the colleges. Other schools than the English classical were not countenanced, Henry George was ridiculed and the left-wing European economists—great thinkers like Sismondi, Saint-Simon, Louis Blanc, Bastiat, Proudhon, Engels, and Karl Marx—were pretty much ignored by professors of economics in the America of the Gilded Age. Something of the intellectual sterility of the genteel tradition descended upon our academic economists; yet amongst them were vigorous and capable minds that must not be overlooked.

I

HENRY C. CAREY

Henry C. Carey, son of the vigorous Irish Republican, Matthew Carey, who made *The American Museum* one of the ablest of the eighteenth-century American magazines, may perhaps be justly called our first professional economist. The eighty-six years of his life were filled with enormous labors in the twin fields of economics and sociology. He did his own thinking from a basis of facts that he was at great pains to gather and tabulate, and his intellectual unfolding followed naturally the current material development of the mid-century. His statistics, of which he was excessively fond, no doubt were as unreliable as most statistics that economists love to dabble in, and like other purveyors of columned figures and impressive charts he certainly leaned too heavily on his knotty staff; but unlike academic economists such as Francis Wayland he tried to keep his thinking in contact with reality and in consequence his studies possess a solidity that is still impressive.

Although his father had early been interested in Hamilton's national system and for a time was president of a Philadelphia society concerned in furthering a protective tariff—for which the great German protectionist List published a number of letters in 1827—Carey began as a follower of the classical school, and in the thirties he published a treatise on political economy that expounded the Manchester doctrine of free-trade. But under the stirring leadership of Henry Clay the American System was making headway fast, and the facts of American expansion impressed him as earlier they had impressed the young List on his visit here. Turning statistician, he soon discovered, as he believed, certain fallacies in the English classical school, and he proceeded to examine afresh the Ricardian theory of rent. (The change came in 1848.) According to this most celebrated of all economic doctrines rent is measured by the difference in productivity between the best land, which is settled first, and the poorest, which social need later brings under cultivation; and hence in every growing community the increment of rent constantly increases at the expense of both labor and capital. But in the America which Carey was acquainted with, and where the story of social development was being swiftly recapitulated, the facts seemed to him to prove quite otherwise. Here the poorer lands were settled first, because their physical condition made them more easily available, and only later, when social pressure increased and larger means were available, were the rich bottom-lands cleared and the marshes drained.

As a result of his narrow interpretation of Ricardo's doctrine of social fertility, Carey lost faith in the Ricardian theory and turned frankly to the American scene to discover, if possible, a more adequate explanation. Soon the seeds of his intense nationalism were bearing their fruit. An inherited dislike of England led him to fear its industrial preëminence, and he abandoned the ideal of an international division of labor for the ideal of independent nationality, with America developing its individuality through the exploitation of its own resources. Free-trade, he came to believe, is international, it results in establishing a "single factory for the whole world, whither all the raw produce has to be sent whatever be the cost of transport"; whereas any society waxes individual and strong in the measure that it develops variety of employment with its demand for mutual help and service. Only through such associations can man develop his capacities and further his mastery of nature. His patriotism thus became involved in his economics and for years he waged a relentless warfare against Manchesterism. Not only were the English doctrines false to American fact, he pointed out, but they were vicious Tory doctrines which if followed here would keep America poor for the benefit of England. The great idea which came finally to dominate his thinking is suggested by the title of a pamphlet, written in 1852, *The Harmony of Interests: Agricultural, Manufacturing, and Commercial*—a work that suggests Frédéric Bastiat's *Les harmonies économiques*, published in 1850, and influenced by Carey's earlier speculations.[1] It was an age much given to discovering harmonies and Carey was

[1] See Gide and Rist, *A History of Economic Doctrines*, pp. 282–284, 327–331.

not behindhand in the business. In the introduction he traced the
ills of contemporary economic life to the Manchester theories of
rent and population—theories which had thrown their black
shadows over English Parliamentary programs of relief and perverted the normal unfolding of western civilization. In consequence the "tendency of the whole British system of political economy is the production of discord among nations." [2]

In the background of Carey's mind was a Physiocratic dislike
of the sterile middleman which sharpened his antagonism to an
international division of labor, and a sensitive social conscience
that was concerned at the ruthless exploitation of English mill-
hands. An ardent believer in natural liberty and convinced of its
beneficence, he restricted economic freedom within national
boundaries. The harmony of interests is local and not international—the tying together of the several parts of the whole. Beyond the national boundaries it ceases. The pessimism of the
English school with its iron law of wages and its Malthusian law
of population was harshly repugnant to his buoyant optimism.
From these vicious roots, he was convinced, sprang the principle
of isolation and differentiation—that producer and consumer must
live apart, with the corollary that the poor must seek new lands in
far countries to supply the places of those from which they have
been thrust, there to produce agricultural staples to exchange for
the manufactured goods produced in thickly settled countries—a
principle that taxes both producer and consumer in the exact
measure of transportation tolls, and benefits exclusively the sterile
middleman. Applied to America the policy of free-trade must keep
this country dependent upon England—keep it agricultural for the
benefit of British merchants; and the program that Carey outlined, the complete sufficiency of which he never doubted, was a
return to the policy of Adam Smith, to that "general harmony of
interests" that must result from bringing the farmer and artisan
into neighborhood communities, fashioning the raw materials
where they are produced and consuming the farmer's produce
where it is grown. Adam Smith "saw well," says Carey, "that
when men came thus together, there arose a general harmony of
interests, each profiting his neighbor, and profiting by that neighbor's success, whereas the tendency of commercial centralization
was toward poverty and discord, abroad and at home." [3]

[2] *Miscellaneous Works*, Preface to *Harmony of Interests*.   [3] *Ibid.*

To his death in 1879 Carey was the most distinguished as he had been the most tireless advocate of a system of protection for American manufactures.   He was one of the most pugnacious pamphleteers of a pugnacious generation.[4] He was a co-worker with Horace Greeley in the labor of convincing a suspicious people of the common benefits to be got from a subsidy to a class; and their joint influence gave respectability and popularity to the appeals of business men and politicians.   Between 1849 and 1857 he "was the virtual editor of the *New York Tribune*" in all matters regarding protection.   His chief antagonist in the long struggle was William Cullen Bryant and the *Evening Post;* and he made frequent appeal to Bryant to meet him in a pamphlet debate that should bring before the public both sides of the great question of protectionism.   Bryant's refusal did not lessen his ardor, and in successive pamphlets he laid before the American people a well-rounded argument for tariff subsidies that ranks him in the history of economic thought with Friedrich List, the great German apostle of a nationalist economic system.   American manufacturers owe a heavy debt to Henry Carey.

In these early years of industrialism the manufacturer was still dependent on the banker, and industrial development was held back, Carey came to believe, by a false financial policy imposed on the county by the bankers.   From his boundless enthusiasm for the ideal of a national economy sprang likewise his unorthodox views on money that so greatly annoyed his fellow economists. Individual in his thinking on this as on other subjects, he espoused theories that to dogmatic bullionists like David A. Wells seemed incendiary at a time (during the post-war years) when so many Americans were bitten with "money heresies." On this theme his patriotism and his democratic sympathies ran together.   He was opposed to the bullion system because it struck at nationalism. An English system, devised by Lombard Street, did not answer the needs of America.   The price of gold is established in a world market and the flow of bullion is always toward the great centers already glutted with money.   To throw the money of the world into a common pool was to subject the money of poorer and remoter countries to the control of the great financial capitals.   Free-trade and the gold standard were the twin weapons forged by England for world-

---

[4] All told he published at his own print-shop some 3000 pages of pamphlet mate-rial of his own writing.

wide economic conquest, and for America to adopt a financial policy that held her subject to Lombard Street, seemed to Carey the height of folly. Gold follows the balance of trade, and until America had built up an adequate domestic economy her specie would continue to drain off, leaving too scanty a supply to do the necessary work of society.

The solution, he believed, lay in the creation of an independent national currency; and an efficient national currency, he held with Bishop Berkeley, was one that was non-exportable, that remained at home to do the day's work instead of gadding about. To provide such a medium of exchange he proposed a currency founded on the national credit—a "national system," he argued, "based entirely on the credit of the government with the people, and not liable to interference from abroad." [5] It was on such grounds that Carey supported the greenback issues and favored the remonetization of silver. The ideal of "societary circulation," he pointed out, was credit—"that great step towards civilization which consists in substituting *letters of credit* for material money"; and because "the steady and regular use of the *letter of credit* known to the world as the 'greenback,' or that other known as the 'national bank note,'" [6] tended to wean the minds of men from dependence on specie, he was warm in their favor.

With a sound national system, let foreigners take our gold for whatever balance of trade they can impose upon us, having no use among ourselves for any coin money except what we can retain under a wholesome foreign commerce.

What we most need today is the establishment of that monetary independence which results from maintaining absolute command over the machinery of exchange used within our borders, leaving to the gold dollar the performance of its duty of arranging for the settlement of balances throughout the world.[7]

Carey's insistence on a plentiful supply of money laid him under the charge of being an advocate of "cheap money," and therefore one of those wicked persons known as "inflationists." The charge in the main was true. He was pungent in his contrast between the prosperity of war times when an abundant currency released all the energies of the American people, and the stagnation that

[5] *Contraction or Expansion? Repudiation or Resumption? Letters to the Hon. Hugh M'Culloch, Secretary of the Treasury*, Philadelphia, 1866, p. 20.
[6] *Ibid.*, p. 22.
[7] Quoted in W. Elder, *Memoir of Henry C. Carey*, p. 13 (Philadelphia, 1880. With bibliography).

followed upon contraction. "Cheap money—low interest—enabled our working men to prosper," whereas dear money—high
interest—was bringing distress and hardship. Every reduction
in the amount of currency decreases the purchasing power of the
people, and slows down the circulatory system. The attempt to
retire the greenbacks he regarded as a class attack on the common
welfare of the country. "To that end the greenback, everywhere
claimed as the people's money, has by those in high places been
denounced, small as is the quantity, when compared with the real
need for it." [8] Paper money is "democratic in its tendencies,"
passing from hand to hand and never seeking a bank vault to
hide in.

A war upon what is called "paper money" is . . . a war upon the poor
in favor of the rich; and that the war being made upon it has precisely that
effect is proved by the fact, that the western farmer is now being so impoverished by reason of such a reduction in the price of corn and oats
that the former is being used as fuel, while the latter sold at 8 cents a
bushel, [while] houses and lots in the neighborhood of Wall Street [are]
commanding . . . prices such as had never before been heard of.[9]

Considering Carey's reputation as an economist and his wide
influence, such doctrine, in the eyes of all "sound-money men,"
was distinctly pernicious. He was giving aid and comfort to the
apostles of inflation and repudiation, and he suffered many a sharp
attack. But that would not deter a warrior grown gray in battle,
and in the very last year of his life he fell upon the bullion theory
with the ardor of a young man. He would not suffer the bankers
to go unrebuked in their mad attack on the prosperity of the
country; he would not be silent while a policy of contraction, that
so early as 1866 had reduced the per capita circulation to $12.50—
according to his statistics—was still in full swing after the disastrous lesson of 1873. He had much in common with Peter Cooper,
who in 1876 took up the battle against Wall Street for a "democratic" monetary system. The blood of the two old men, both born
in the last decade of the eighteenth century, had not grown cold
or sluggish with long years, but responded ardently to the great
cause of democracy that had inspired their youth. That Carey's
national system was a house divided against itself—that industry
and finance were engaged in a mortal combat for supremacy—he

[8] *Shall We have Peace? Letters to President-elect Grant*, p. 39.
[9] *Contraction or Expansion? etc.*, p. 20.

probably never quite realized. He was concerned that America should be free to create and enjoy the wealth that lay in the potentialities of the continent, and to that end he would have money serve industry, and not industry money.

2

FRANCIS A. WALKER

The social conscience of Carey was colored with an optimism that was the spontaneous expression of a generation that set no limits to the beneficent development of American industrialism. No storm-clouds had yet gathered on the horizon; no hostile systems challenged the sufficiency of capitalism. But a change was at hand. By the end of the seventies the complacency of the Gilded Age was disturbed by the rise of pestilent heresies in the shape of new economic dogmas. The surplus-value theory of Marx and the unearned-increment theory of Henry George were spreading widely through America, to the unsettlement of susceptible minds; and the Knights of Labor were preparing to launch a general attack against the whole system of capitalistic exploitation. Carey had sufficed the wants of his simpler day, but there was need of a new champion to wield the sword of pure Ricardian doctrine against these later heresies.

Francis A. Walker, son of the economist Amasa Walker, Brigadier General in the Civil War, Professor at Sheffield Scientific School and later President of the Massachusetts Institute of Technology, was to be the self-appointed champion of industrialism, the official economist of the Gilded Age, and forerunner of a long line of academic purveyors of economic dogma. As the author of a college textbook that superseded Francis Wayland's naïve *Elements of Political Economy*—a work that had served innumerable college generations as a quarry of economic doctrine— he elaborated a complete system of economics with a geniality that went far to popularize the "dismal science" with vast numbers of undergraduates; and as an authoritative apologist for entrepreneur profits he rendered a service to capitalism that quite erased his little Ricardian peccadillo of free-trade prejudice. There runs through his solid pages the confident optimism of his generation— an optimism that discovers in the heresies of socialism and single-tax the only storm-clouds on the fair American horizons. He saw no reason to question the ultimate good of industrialism, or to fear any deep-seated clash between labor and capital. He carried water easily on both shoulders, for he was so fortunate as to have worked out to his complete satisfaction, a magic economic formula that should return both to master and workman their just shares of the total production. In the light of his exegesis there could be no Marxian struggle of the classes. The captain of industry must no longer be regarded with sour aspect as a parasite upon labor, but as a fellow worker, the creator of those profits which are not subtracted for his benefit from the portion of labor. From Ricardo to Marx the economists had been barking up the wrong tree in their analysis of the rewards of the entrepreneur.

The classical school of the Gilded Age was in like position with the eighteenth-century Calvinists; they must either abandon their dogmas or reinterpret them to meet current needs. Walker was too good a Ricardian to abandon them, so he proposed to reinterpret them. The urgent problems to which he addressed himself were the sources of profits and of wages; and the examination of those problems led him to his theory of the function of the entrepreneur and to a rejection of the classical wage-fund theory. He refused to discard his suit of Ricardian clothes as Carey had done. They could never go out of style, he believed, so long as honest thinking was respected. He accepted most of the Ricardian dogmas without question. "Capital," he asserted soberly, "arises solely from saving. It stands always for self-denial and abstinence," and interest is the "reward of abstinence." But one important dogma, the classical wage-fund theory, he insisted on stripping away. He was too genial an optimist to rest content with the bleak conception that the margin of subsistence circumscribes the rewards of labor, and too enlightened an apologist of industrialism to assert that "profits are the leavings of wages." He could not hope to erect a theory suitable to the Gilded Age on such skimpy hypotheses, and he scourged them from the temple of economic law. Wages, to be sure, are the leavings after rent, interest, and profits have been deducted from the total production; but vast and dangerous misconceptions have arisen in regard to the portions that accrue to these several partners, and in particular mischievous perversions touching the share of profits. This was the crux of the problem of distribution and until the nature of profits should be determined the question of wages would remain to befuddle weak heads.

The heart of Walker's doctrine, therefore, is his theory of profits. He proposed to show that according to the true law of profits this flexible increment is never a moiety wrested from labor, but an additional earning of management that justly accrues to him who creates it. The doctrine from which he deduced his theory of the entrepreneur was the Ricardian theory of rent. On this point Walker was the most loyal of Ricardians, and he violently attacked Carey for repudiating the classical dogma. In a word "Ricardo's doctrine can no more be impugned than the sun in the heaven," he asserted, "and those who mouth at it simply show that they do not know what it was Ricardo taught." [10] What was needed was to understand its wide implications rather than to seek to destroy it—to trace in all its reaches the doctrine of fertility and discover how in other spheres than land the difference between fertile and unfertile measures the return upon economic endeavor. For the great doctrine of fertility, Walker pointed out, following Mill, is capable of expansion to cover wider fields than rent; it applies equally to management and labor; it broadens out into a comprehensive principle that exactly measures the most bitterly disputed of the several increments, the increment of profits.

This theory of fertility, introduced into the law of distribution, is Walker's most interesting contribution to economic speculation. By it he supplemented the trinity of land, capital, and labor—or in terms of distribution, of rent, interest, and wages—with a new entity—management and the earnings of management. The argument is highly ingenious. Assuming a no-profits employer at the lowest scale of the entrepreneur system, by analogy from the Ricardian no-rent grade of land, he asserted that similarly "profits are measured upwards from the level of the no-profits class of employers," and hence "it appears that the gains of the employer are not taken from the earnings of the laboring class, but measure the difference in production between the commonplace or bad, and the able, and shrewd, and strong management of business." [11] Profits, then, are an added increment of management, secured by foresight and business skill, the fruit of managerial fertility; and since they flow solely from the entrepreneur they belong to him alone and no portion may be justly claimed for rent, interest, or wages. The complete theory he states thus:

[10] *Land and its Rent*, p. 108.
[11] *Political Economy*, pp. 242, 348.

Under free and full competition, the successful employers of labour would earn a remuneration which would be exactly measured, in the case of each man, by the amount of wealth which he could produce, with a given application of labour and capital, over and above what would be produced by employers of the lowest industrial, or no-profits, grade, making use of the same amounts of labour and capital, just as rent measures the surplus of the produce of the better lands over and above what would be produced by the same application of labour and capital to the least productive lands which contribute to the supply of the market, lands which themselves bear no rent.[12]

It is a persuasive argument of which Walker was vastly proud. The germ of it later historians of economic thought have traced to Senior and John Stuart Mill, who had suggested the idea of "differential rent," or "rent of ability," which is the reward of "all peculiar advantages of extraordinary qualities of body and mind." [13] From whatever source it issued, the usefulness of such doctrine in the days of an expanding industrialism, and the ends it might serve in counteracting proletarian philosophies, are too evident to need comment. The Marxian dogma of surplus value—that profits are stealings from wages—was certainly calculated to breed dissatisfaction in weak proletarian heads. Marx was a good Ricardian in his major postulates and the Ricardians had failed to analyze adequately the true sources of profits; because of such failure the classical school had underestimated the social beneficence of the capitalistic system. Chained to the iron law of wages the school had been forced to envisage a bleak future with labor kept always at the margin of subsistence. From this pessimism Walker proposed to rid economic theory, by showing that entrepreneur profits augment the wage fund and hence that the entrepreneur is the benefactor rather than the exploiter of labor. With his business skill the captain of industry, like the inventor of a new machine, lays open new sources of wealth for all, and if he gains much for himself he gives more to society; for every improvement in business methods accrues in the end to society as a whole, for the new technique soon becomes a common possession.

The validity of Walker's theory of profits does not concern us here; it is a matter for economists to determine. To one who is under the spell of no doctrinaire system the theory seems some-

---

[12] *Quarterly Journal of Economics*, April, 1887. Quoted in Gide and Rist, *A History of Economic Doctrine*, p. 551.
[13] *Ibid.*, p. 549.

what too neat with its assumption of "free and full competition";[14] and in its conscious purpose to glorify the captain of industry it is freighted rather too heavily with the spirit of the Gilded Age. It not only throws the door wide to exploitation but it invites everybody to the feast. Yet the work of the apologist was only half done. Having established to his satisfaction the law of profits, Walker was prepared to take equally high ground in determining the increment that falls to labor. To glorify profits and at the same time defend the pessimism of the wage-fund theory, would have been foolish tactics in presence of the Marxian surplus-value theory; proletarian discontent must be dealt with and Walker was prepared to deal with it. Having ascertained exactly the several increments due to rent, interest, and profits—which in his system are rigidly determined by economic law—he confidently assigned all the residual increment to wages. Labor not only gets all it earns, he argued, but far more, since what does not fall to the just shares of the other partners falls to it—that is the "whole remaining body of wealth." If it be recalled that the total social fund of inventions, machinery, trade processes, systems of transportation, business methods, are alike in the service of all employers—the no-profit entrepreneur equally with the high-profit—it follows that the individual employer can derive from such social wealth no modicum of profit above and beyond what his individual fertility has produced. Where then can the income from such social fund flow except to wages? "Every invention in mechanics, every discovery in the chemical art, no matter by whom made, inures directly and immediately" to the benefit of labor.[15] This, to be sure, on the hypothesis of "full and free competition," which may be interfered with by various means but which in the long run prevails. How else shall one explain the constant rise in the wage-scale that has marked the Industrial Revolution and that has gone hand in hand with vast profits to the entrepreneur class?

It was a robust optimism that could lay down the theory that labor is "the residual claimant to the product of industry." Although Walker prided himself on his discovery, it seems to have made slight impression on later economic thought. Like too many members of the classical school the apologist of the Gilded Age

[14] For a critical examination see Gide and Rist, *A History of Economic Doctrine*, pp. 551-558.
[15] *Political Economy*, pp. 251-258.

failed to keep his feet on the plebeian earth; and his conclusions
suggest how great mischief *a priori* reasoning may work in the
speculations of academic gentlemen. A moderate dash of realism
might have lessened his buoyant optimism; but Walker was too
warm an admirer of capitalism, too eager to assert the beneficence
of industrialism, to inquire curiously into the everyday facts of
current exploitation. As a realistic statistician he was far inferior
to Carey. But why demand a plodding realism of the economist
when all America was romantic? If the economic theory of General
Walker was a pleasant blend of Ricardo and Colonel Sellers, would
it not hit the taste of the age to a nicety? Its sturdy optimism was
a soothing antidote to the Jeremiads of the Marxians and the
shrill demands of the single-taxers. The Gold Coast of America
looked to its official economists for a confutation of all economic
heresies, and who was so well equipped for that business as a
doughty Colonel Sellers armed with a sharp Ricardian sword?

In this brisk work Walker engaged with gusto. In his onslaught
upon Marx and Henry George he was untroubled by doubt. He
first demolished the structure of their theory and then impugned
their honesty. His condemnation of single-tax is bold and sweeping.
There is a bitter asperity in his denunciation of the economic heresies of *Progress and Poverty*, and he dismisses the proposal to tax
unearned increment with the comment, "Every honest man will
resent such a proposition as an insult."[16] His discussion of the
economics of the question is only casual and he hastens back to the
safe haven of Ricardian doctrine.[17] In his commentary on the
Knights of Labor he is somewhat vindictive for a well-bred gentleman. He charges the syndicalistic attack on the profits system to
immigrant foreigners, asserts that the law of profit fertility is an
insuperable obstacle to any proletarian control of industry, and
finally damns it as un-American. The honest, native American
"knows that for himself and his children the way is open clear to
the top"; his "spirit is that of civility, reciprocity and fair play";
and he concludes:

Had it been left to our native population alone, not one of those violent
and reckless attacks upon production and transportation, which have,
within the past two or three years, shocked the whole industrial system
and have come near to produce a general crisis of trade, would ever have
taken place.[18]

[16] *Land and its Rent*, Preface, p. vi.   [17] *Ibid.*, pp. 181-182.
[18] *Political Economy*, p. 394.

Yet in spite of his genial optimism he discovered specks on the fair picture of society. To the Ricardian logic the stupidity of men is a constant irritant; if only men were rational the path of progress would be so much easier! After economic law has been demonstrated with the finality of a Euclidian theorem, it is disconcerting to see how the multitude will not be reasoned with, but persist in following after the last false prophet who cries in the marketplace. The clamor raised by single-tax was especially annoying. "That such an argument," he remarked a bit testily, "should for a moment have imposed upon anybody, is enough to give one a new conception of the intellectual capabilities of mankind." [19] Fortunate it is for society, he concludes, that while man proposes, economic law disposes. False prophets will have their little day, but from their secure watch-tower the Ricardians calmly look out upon a world of which they alone hold the key.*

II

THE CONSCRIPTION OF POLITICAL THEORY

When the social fabric is being torn rudely across by a changing economics, political theory and practice will suffer from the attendant confusions. The America of the Gilded Age accounted itself a democracy and was outwardly content to make use of the familiar democratic machinery; but until it was determined whether majority or minority rule should prevail, whether the well-being of the many or the property of the few should be the chief object of government, there would be no serious effort to create a political state for adequate social control. In the meantime the old individualisms would range the land seeking what they might devour, and the common attitude toward the political state would remain one of good-natured contempt. A shambling government, corrupt and incompetent, awakened no man's hope or pride, and amidst the slovenly anarchisms of the times, with a crude exploitation in the saddle, the state would be pretty much ignored except when its services might prove useful to such exploitation. The plutocracy would oppose the erection of a vigorous state until such time as it felt strong enough to control its activities. The principle of the majority-will held grave potentialities that

[19] *Ibid.*, p. 433.
* In his original plan Professor Parrington included a third subsection on W. G. Sumner, but evidently decided against its inclusion.—*Publisher.*

might threaten the eventual mastership of wealth, and until the
plutocracy had created its strongholds within the framework of
the democracy it would bitterly oppose any extension of democratic
control.

Broadly two great movements were going forward side by side
in the unconscious drift of political tendency—the democratic and
the plutocratic. The former, drawn chiefly from agrarian and
labor elements with a considerable following of the middle and
professional classes, was determined to carry forward and supplement the Jacksonian movement. It was honestly concerned for
the development of the democratic principle. It would purify
government by the application of civil service reform, it would
steadily enlarge the bounds of social control of economic forces,
and it would strengthen the political state to enable it to cope with
corporate wealth and constrain the ambitions of the plutocracy
into conformity with democratic ends. To such a democratic
program the plutocracy was necessarily opposed. It professed the
warmest loyalty to the abstract principle of democracy while
bending every energy to emasculate effective democratic control.
The problem confronting it was the familiar Federalistic problem—
how to protect the minority from the majority and set property
interests above human interests; but the problem had been immensely complicated by the strategic advances made by democracy. The democratic principle could not be easily thrust aside,
it must be undermined. And so while awaiting the time when it
should be strong enough to set up boldly its mastery of society,
plutocracy took refuge in two principles, the superman theory
and the *laissez-faire* theory, both of which it asserted to be democratic, the very essence of democracy. The former was "The public
be damned" theory, which held that the economic leaders of society must be left free to manage their properties as they saw fit;
and the latter was the familiar doctrine of individual initiative,
that looked with suspicion on any interference by the political
state with economic activity. If a bureaucracy may stick its nose
into the citizen's private affairs what becomes of individual liberty?

But the plutocracy was building its real defenses elsewhere.
Shrewdly aware of the potentialities of a Constitution that had
been designed for the protection of property interests, it followed
two main lines of development: it furthered the popular develop-

ment of a cult of the Constitution by praising the excellence of a system of checks and balances, and spreading the view that to tamper with any provisions of the instrument was little short of sacrilege; and at the same time it bent every energy to extend the range of judicial prerogative and bring the legislative branch under control of the judiciary. It sought extra-constitutional indulgences that were dispensed by the courts in the name of the police power. The way had been prepared by Marbury vs. Madison and Dred Scott vs. Sanford, and during the Gilded Age a broad path to judicial control was opened by the elaboration of the "due process of law" principle discovered in the fourteenth amendment. With the development of the plutocracy the extension of the doctrine of judicial review went forward rapidly, providing an impregnable defense for property interests that promised ill for the principle of democratic control in the interests of the common well-being. The democracy was being driven from the inner keep of the castle.

While the real struggle was thus going on in the court-room, with the outcome in the hands of the judges, political speculation was playing havoc with certain of our oldest and most cherished doctrines. Pursuing the path suggested by Webster and Francis Lieber, it turned away from the particularism of Calhoun to explore the reaches of a consolidating nationalism. The inevitable drift towards unity—whether democratic or plutocratic—was daily gathering momentum. The destruction of the states-rights program and party had cleared the ground for a new conception of the dignity and powers of the political state. With the social shift from dispersion to centralization the federal government was destined to grow in authority; and political theory was destined to follow the same course, seeking to justify in principle what was being accomplished in fact. The end of the philosophy of dispersion was in sight. The tide was running toward an exaltation of the doctrine of sovereignty, with the consequent exaltation of the abstract political state. As the individual coalesced in the mass, the rights and dignity of the individual would lessen in the presence of an engulfing sovereignty. The traditional doctrine of natural rights was in for a slashing attack. Centralization must destroy the shambling Jacksonian structure and erect in its place a grandiose organic theory.

During the Gilded Age a number of systematic studies of political theory appeared, amongst which the most significant were, Woolsey's *Political Science, or the State* (1877), Bryce's *The American Commonwealth* (1888), Woodrow Wilson's *The State* (1889), and Burgess's *Political Science and Constitutional Law* (1891). Of these the formal studies of Woolsey and Burgess may serve to illustrate the changing thought of the times. Both are academic reflections of the current drift of tendency, and both reveal the academic sympathy with the master movement of centralization. The work of Woolsey was a revision of classroom notes used between 1846 and 1871 and strongly colored by pre-war views; the work of Burgess was the first-fruits of the influence of German speculation on the nature of the leviathan state.

I

THEODORE WOOLSEY

Theodore Dwight Woolsey, professor of Greek and president of Yale, was an heir in direct succession of Connecticut Federalism. Nephew of Timothy Dwight, a minister, and distinguished member of the social oligarchy that in its decadence still held Connecticut opinion in a strong grip, he could scarcely escape a predilection for the moralistic authoritative dogmatisms that marked the old Connecticut *régime*. The principle of coercive authority had lain at the heart of the political theory of Timothy Dwight, and Theodore Woolsey was true to his Puritan antecedents in asserting the supremacy of authority over liberty. The only important element in his thinking that sets him apart from his uncle was the influence of Francis Lieber, whose conception of organic growth in social custom he made his own, and whose disciple he professed to be. Naturally he retained the old Puritan dislike of leveling—the traditional Connecticut distrust of democracy. He would have no weakening of authority, no Jacobean license; and for anarchism, socialism, communism, which he reckoned the nastiest spawn of Jacobinism, his abhorrence was what one would expect of a Connecticut Federalist. The two ponderous volumes that he issued in 1877 are learned studies that bear on their dun pages many a tell-tale mark of earlier times. In them Theodore Woolsey was renewing the fight against an infidel philosophy that with its doctrine of natural rights denied the authority of the godly to police society.

In harmony with Lieber and Calhoun he rejected the romantic

doctrine of natural rights, and substituted a composite social-moralistic conception, that from John Winthrop and Roger Williams to Channing and Emerson had colored the Puritan thought of New England. Natural rights, he asserted, are those which belong to man by reason of the nature God has endowed him with; and the state is a moral agent, arising out of custom, to secure and guarantee such rights. It is "as truly natural as rights are, and as society is"; for established in the social nature of man it is the natural repository and guardian of his rights in a social order. It is an expression of the teleological purpose that underlies all things. The manner in which Woolsey elaborated his moralistic theory will be evident from the following passages:

> The considerations that men exist together in society, that they have an irresistible impulse towards society, that their perfection of soul and of outward condition can be secured only in a social life, and, on the other hand, that recognition of rights and obligation alone make a social life a tolerable or even a possible thing, and that wherever men reflect on their own nature they admit the existence of certain classes of rights and shield them by public power, show a divine purpose which none who believe in a Creator of the world can deny. The Creator of man, having made him such that his temporal, moral, and spiritual perfection can be found only in society, prepared his moral feelings for the life for which he was destined. The destination for society; the means within human nature by which it is fulfilled; the means by which the individual and the community, when brought into society, are able to secure the good and avoid the evils possible in a state of coexistence—these form a complete, harmonious whole, which manifest comprehension of view and forethought. It is provided in our nature, when it is not perverted—that is, when it does not swerve from the true idea of human nature—that we shall form societies under law. A state of society is a state of nature, and the only true one.
>
> When therefore *natural* rights are spoken of, we can accept the term, if it be used to denote such rights as grow out of our nature, and may be inferred from the destination to which it points us. Another and a heathenish kind of sense was attached to the words, when they were taken to mean the rights, or rather uncontrolled liberties, which men possessed in a state of human nature in which there was no organized society or government. . . . [Such a theory] contemplates men as enjoying certain powers of free action in this state of nature, and these powers must serve for a foundation of their state as members of society, or so many of them as it cannot be shown that they gave up, in order to make a state of law and order possible. In other words, the theory of the derivation of these rights from a state of nature may take a hypothetical shape, and deduce rights from what a man could do in a state of things which exists only in a jural fiction. . . .

We find no fault with the objects which the theories had in view, but with the want of conformity to truth. It must be pronounced, in *the first place*, contrary to fact, that such a state of nature ever existed. Man has always been under law; he is a ζῷον πολιτκον. . . .

Secondly, if it could be shown that he had such an origin, it would prove nothing.[20]

Having thus established both society and the state in the nature of man, and dismissed the romantic interpretation of natural rights as heathenish, Woolsey turned to examine the true sphere and function of the political state. He rejected in the main the *laissez-faire* view of Mill and Spencer, but he refused to go so far as Burgess. He will have no omnicompetent state. A just mean must be laid down between authority and liberty, and that mean he discovered in the dictum, "The sphere of the state . . . may reach as far as the nature of man and needs of man and of men reach";[21] that is to say, its control runs far beyond mere police powers, and concerns itself not only with material ends but with the "intellectual and aesthetic wants of the individual, and the religious and moral nature of its citizens." A state swollen to great powers he regarded as likely to swallow up liberty in paternalism, and a state immediately responsive to the popular will is certain to run into "extreme democracy." His ideal government he discovered in the rule of the Connecticut oligarchy, under which a homogeneous people, with simple agrarian habits, disciplined by religion and responsive to moral leadership, enjoyed a stable government administered by proved executives. Unfortunately with the nineteenth century began a decline in American government, resulting from economic changes, the growth of cities, lower-class immigration, and the "gradual reception of doctrines of political rights, which belong to extreme democracy." Such pernicious doctrines, in his judgment, were: the short term of office, popular election of judges to hold for a fixed period instead of for life, the debasement of the representative system by subjecting the representative to his constituents, and the spoils system.[22] In a later study he added two other evils: direct legislation through the initiative, and a popular referendum on war and peace.[23]

In spite of an imposing display of classical learning these two stout volumes reveal a childlike ignorance of *Realpolitik*, a naïve

[20] *Political Science*, Vol. I, pp. 23–25.   [22] *Ibid.*, Vol. II, p. 141.
[21] *Ibid.*, p. 216.   [23] *Communism and Socialism*, p. 232.

inability to grasp the significance of economic groupings that under-lie all political alignments. Neither as minister nor as college pres-ident did Theodore Woolsey learn anything about the robust materialisms which any realistic political theory must take into great account. His knowledge of ancient Greek institutions no doubt was adequate, but his knowledge of American constitutional development was singularly inadequate. He accepted without question the argument of Story and Webster that the phrase, "We the people," proves the original, consolidating intention of the document; he discussed the history of party government in the United States without touching on the economic alignment of agrarianism and capitalism; and he could discover only one thor-oughly admirable political party—"the upright federal party." He extols the Supreme Court as the triumph of the American Constitution, without considering the desirability of a judicial veto on legislative enactments, or suggesting a potential alignment of the judiciary with the master forces of a generation. The moralistic bias of his thought is perhaps sufficiently revealed in a comment on the functions of the judges. "In a higher sense, they are not representatives of the community nor of its chief magistrates, but of justice and of God. . . . They are in fact more immediately servants of God than any other men who manage the affairs of a country, because expediency, departure from law or from the con-stitution, is for them in no circumstance a thing to be conceived of."[24] Mark Twain, it would seem, was not the only humorist of the Gilded Age.

In his later years Woolsey was much disturbed by the spread of collectivist doctrine, and in the thick of the economic unrest of the times he felt it to be his duty to assist in stemming the advance of such doctrine. In his great work on political theory, he demolished the communist-anarchist-socialist arguments in a few pages, and then remarked with excellent candor, "There is an extensive literature, relating to the subject . . . with much of which I am not familiar." Fearful that he might not have delivered a death-blow, after further reading he returned to the attack three years later, and in 1880 published a volume entitled *Com-munism and Socialism*. For so difficult a business he was even then inadequately equipped. He did not realize the magnitude of his task. Marx's *Capital* could not be undermined in ten pages,

[24] *Political Science*, Vol. II, pp. 330–331.

even with the help of Cairnes, Mill, and Ricardo, and a political
scientist with a theological background was scarcely competent
to untie the close-knit threads of the Marxian economics. His
exposition in consequence is incomplete and faulty; it largely overlooks the Marxian philosophy of history and ignores the doctrine
of economic determinism. What troubles him most is the lack
of religious faith amongst socialists. The validity of a theory he
is satisfied to test by the morality of the theorist. One can easily
guess that President Woolsey's opinions had turned into dogmatic
conviction before a page of the literature to be examined had come
under his eyes. Yet that so shallow a book should have issued from
an academic pen will surprise no one who is aware of the incredible
number of shallow books that actually have issued from academic
pens. Provocative social thinking and the American university
seem never to have got on well together.

In the fact that Woolsey's speculations on the nature of the
state were accounted significant contributions to political science
by his generation of Americans, the historian may find added
confirmation of the shallowness of the Gilded Age. A stale Connecticut Calvinism, molding in the corner of the cupboard, is
poor food to nourish thinking, and a man who knows nothing
about the deeper springs of political struggle is singularly un-
qualified to elaborate a science of the state. Theodore Woolsey's
weighty volumes were a dignified attempt to rehabilitate the old
Connecticut Federalism and suit it to the taste of a new age. But
what measure of political intelligence can one expect of a people
fed on pious fictions by their most authoritative expounder of the
noble art of government?

2

JOHN W. BURGESS

Woolsey has little to say about sovereignty. The speculations
of Austin had not reached his quiet study, and the need for a
coercive state in harmony with a centralizing industrialism was
not likely to be realized by a man whose eyes were turned back
fondly to a simple village life. It was left for a younger generation
to examine the problem of sovereignty, and to that business John
W. Burgess turned with zest. A thoroughgoing Austinian, a disciple
of the German state-cult, a Hegelian, he would seem to have been

ill fitted to interpret the functions of the state to America. And
yet by virtue of his European detachment he saw clearly the direction in which America *

IV

BUTTRESSING THE DEMOCRATIC THEORY

I

A DEMOCRATIC ECONOMICS—HENRY GEORGE

While the academic economists were thus providing a new body
of capitalistic theory, from the ranks of the people came a group
that was bent on bringing economic principles into greater conformity to what they considered democratic needs. The economics
of bankers and manufacturers they regarded as a selfish class
economics and they proposed to democratize the body of economic
thought as Tom Paine and Jefferson had democratized the body
of political thought. Since the days of John Taylor such amateur
economists had been plentiful in America, and in the post-war days
when the country was in the throes of the Industrial Revolution,
they sprang up at every cross-roads.   George Henry Evans,
Horace Greeley, Peter Cooper, Parke Godwin, Wendell Phillips,
Albert Brisbane, Hinton R. Helper, "Coin" Harvey, were only
a few out of the many who in their own way were seeking in economics a road to freedom. They were not formal economists; they
were little read in the history of economic thought; in so far as
they may be accounted a school they were mostly the unclaimed
progeny of French Physiocratic theory who did not recognize their
own father. Yet they were vastly concerned to bring economic
theory into some sort of realistic contact with the facts of American
experience and the ideals of democracy; and their immediate objective was the overthrow of current Manchester principles and
the erection in their stead of a body of theory based on the needs
of the producer and the consumer rather than the middleman.

Of this characteristic native group, largely ignored by our formal
historians, by far the ablest and most influential was Henry George,
a thinker created by the impact of frontier economics upon a mind
singularly sensitive to the appeal of social justice, singularly self-

* The discussion of Burgess was not completed by Professor Parrington. At this
point he planned a third section, "The New Ally: the courts: the police power
and the fourteenth amendment; the injunction." None of this section was written,
but he has dealt with these subjects *passim.—Publisher.*

sufficient in its logic. He remains still our most original economist. Beyond the Ricardian theory of rent, with its corollary of unearned increment, he owed little to Europe and nothing to academic American economists. From the first he was a free-lance, returning to the origins of things—as Tom Paine had advised long before— and thinking "as if he were the first man who ever thought." His major doctrines he arrived at largely independently, ignorant of the fact that his *impôt unique* had been earlier elaborated by the Physiocratic school, till long after he had come to identical conclusions. His matured philosophy was the outcome of the meditations of a Jeffersonian idealist contemplating the divergence between the crude facts of exploitation all about him and the eighteenth-century ideal of natural justice; and he became, in consequence, the voice of idealistic America seeking to adjust the economics of a rapidly changing society to the ends of democratic well-being. The passion of the reformer was in him, but wedded to the critical mind of the analyst; and this accounts for the wide appeal of *Progress and Poverty* that for thousands of Americans removed economic theory from the academic closet and set it in the thick of political conflict. Henry George humanized the dismal science and brought it home to the common interest. With his extreme simplification no doubt he fell into the same error the classical school had fallen into before him; he left too many elements out of his equation; but he succeeded in the same way they had succeeded—he made of economic theory a weapon to use in the struggle between the exploiters and the exploited. After *Progress and Poverty* the social economist could cross swords with the Ricardians.

Henry George is readily enough explained in the light of his environment. He was intellectually native to the West, but it was the West of the Gilded Age with its recollections of an earlier agrarian order. Upon the gigantic exploitation of post-war times, carried forward in the name of progress, he threw the experience of two hundred and fifty years of continental expansion. That experience had undergone a subtle change as the settlements moved through the Inland Empire, a change marked by the spirit of capitalistic expansion with its crop of unearned increment. On the frontier, land speculation was often the readiest means to wealth. To the west of the Allegheny Mountains land had long been the staple commodity, with the buying and selling of which every community was deeply concerned; and from the dramatic repetition of that experience in California, Henry George clarified the principle upon which he erected his social philosophy, namely, that a fluid economics begets an equalitarian democracy and homespun plenty, and that with the monopolization of natural resources a static economy succeeds, with its attendant caste regimentation and augmenting exploitation. In the days when he was meditating his social philosophy, California was still in the frontier stage of development, but amidst the hurrying changes a fluid economics was visibly hardening to the static, with a swiftness dramatic enough to impress upon him the significance of a story that had been obscured in earlier telling by the slowness of the dénouement. The vast cupidity of business in preëmpting the virgin resources of California, and in particular the technique of Leland Stanford and the Central Pacific Railway group, provided an eloquent object-lesson that set him to examining the long history of land-jobbing in America in its remoter social bearings. From such inquiry emerged the cardinal principles of an economic theory that must be reckoned the ultimate expression of a school of thought that beginning with Quesnay a hundred years before, and first interpreted for America by John Taylor and the Jeffersonians, was finally buried in a common grave with the kindred doctrine of natural rights.

It was no accident that his mind fastened upon land monopoly as the deeper source of social injustice. As a child of the frontier he thought in terms of land as naturally as the money-broker thinks in terms of discounts. His psychology was that of the producer rather than the middleman. Land, with all its potential wealth of field and orchard and forest and stream, with its unmeasured resources of coal and iron and oil and timber, was the fruitful gift of nature to man; and the true measure of social well-being, he believed, is the measure in which labor is free to use such natural resources for productive purposes. Land monopoly was an ancient evil that had laid its blight on every civilization. The expropriation of natural resources was the origin of rent, and rent was a social tax parasitic in nature. Unearned increment was a moiety wrested from the producer, that waxed ever greater with the increase of production. Henry George was well aware how deeply rooted in American psychology was the love of unearned increment. Since the far-off days when the agent of the Transylvania Land Company wrote in 1775 that the Ohio Valley abounded in land-mongers, the rage for expropriative speculation had mounted steadily; and the railway land-grants of his day were a fitting climax to a policy that in every generation had brought forth such fruits as the Yazoo frauds. The land question was a perennial western problem. For years Horace Greeley in the *Tribune*, had spread amongst the farmers the "Vote Yourself a Farm" propaganda. The protest of the small western settler against the middleman policy of the government in alienating great blocks of the public domain to speculative companies, had added thousands of votes to the Republican party, and the result was the Homestead Act of 1862. But the fruits of the Act were partly destroyed by huge grants to railway promoters, and the time had come, George believed, when the problem must be envisaged in all its complexities and the American people brought to understand how great were the stakes being gambled for.

The disease had so long been endemic in America that the remedy must be drastic. No patent nostrums would serve. The vividness of his experience in the West had thrown into sharp relief his earlier experiences in the East, and made him distrustful of all social panaceas that hopeful idealists were seeking in Europe. With any form of collectivistic theory he would have nothing to do. Marxian socialism he looked upon as an alien philosophy, inadequate in its diagnosis and at fault in its prescription. The ills of America—perhaps of Europe as well—must be cured by another regimen. *Progress and Poverty* grew out of his experience as he watched the heedless alienation of the public domain. It was his reply to the policy of preëmption, exploitation, and progress of the Gilded Age. Philadelphia-born, he early suffered in his personal fortune from the periodic hard times that ran so disastrous a cycle in the days when America was in thoughtless transition from an agrarian order to an industrial. His scanty schooling came to an end before he had reached his fourteenth year, and at sixteen he saw no better opening in life than to ship before the mast to Australia. On his return he learned to set type, but times were bad and opportunity declining to knock at his door, he worked his way through the Straits of Magellan, landing in San Francisco in 1858, on his way to Salem, Oregon, where he worked for a time in a shop. With the exhaustion of the diggings he made his way back to San Francisco, and began a long series of restless ventures in the newspaper field, with only his hands for capital—none very successful, none quite a failure, but returning him useful dividends in the form of a serviceable prose style. At twenty-two he plunged into an improvident marriage with a girl of eighteen, and the next dozen years brought many privations to the little family.

Fate had not yet taken Henry George in hand to lead him into his life work. All the economics he then knew had been learned in the rough and tumble ways of a western print-shop. In 1869, at the age of thirty, while on a business trip to New York City, he was confronted by the contrast between wealth and poverty there nakedly exposed—so unlike what he had known at San Francisco. It was a prod to his social conscience, and as he contemplated the wretchedness of the East Side he registered a vow to explore the hidden causes of social disease. He had given no serious thought to economic questions, and now almost casually he went to the Philadelphia public library to look into John Stuart Mill's *Political Economy*. He accepted Mill's views on wages without critical examination, and wrote his first important article—on the Chinese question in California. In the meantime a group of California railway promoters had been buying and selling legislators in their work of building up private fortunes out of a public monopoly; and it was the contemplation of wealth acquired by such methods, together with the gamble of land speculation in Oakland in consequence of the proposal to establish there the western terminal of the continental railway, that clarified for Henry George the great principle he was to expound in *Progress and Poverty* ten years later.

The first drift in his intellectual development had been a drift back to the old Jeffersonianism from which the country was swiftly moving. As an editor he was an outspoken Democrat of the primitive school, opposed to protectionism, subsidies, a centralizing political state, and the corruption that follows in the train of paternalism as sickness follows infection. In a pamphlet written in 1870, he expounded his political faith thus:

Railroad subsidies, like protective duties, are condemned by the economic principle that the development of industry should be left free to take its natural direction. They are condemned by the political principle that government should be reduced to its minimum—that it becomes more corrupt and more tyrannical, and less under the control of the people, with every extension of its powers and duties. . . . They are condemned by the experience of the whole country, which shows that they have invariably led to waste, extravagance and rascality; that they inevitably become a source of corruption and a means of plundering the people.[25]

[25] George, *Life of Henry George*, pp. 216–217.

Having thus indoctrinated himself in the Jeffersonian liberalism with its foundations laid in natural rights and its conception of a decentralized society, the following year, at the age of thirty-two, he sat down to the serious elaboration of his views. *Our Land and Land Policy, National and State*, was an explorative pamphlet that went to the heart of the problem as he had come to understand it. The kernel of the work is the question of the relation of land to labor, of rent to wages; and the conclusion to which it led was the doctrine of the social ownership of socially created values, which justice requires shall return to society in the form of an equalized tax that shall absorb the unearned increment. Around this fundamental doctrine was grouped a considerable body of ideas that had been expounded by earlier liberals. How much he borrowed and how much he arrived at independently, cannot easily be determined; such diverse thinkers as James Harrington, Locke, the Physiocrats, Tom Paine, Karl Marx, John Stuart Mill, William Ellery Channing, might well have contributed to this provocative document, if George had been acquainted with them. Like Harrington was the assumption of economic determinism—that ownership of the land implies the rulership of society. From the school of Locke came the conception of natural rights, but interpreted rather in terms of Tom Paine and of William Ellery Channing. From Mill came the conception of unearned increment; from Marx the law of concentration; and from the Physiocrats the conception of a natural order and the doctrine of an *impôt unique*. And all this set in a framework of American economic history, which reveals with shrewd insight the disastrous tendency of the traditional policy of land alienation in great blocks to middle-men, with the attendant rise of rent.

How intimately he was related in his thinking to the French liberals of the eighteenth century, may perhaps be sufficiently suggested in his interpretation of the doctrine of natural rights—a doctrine the new realistic school from Calhoun to Woolsey and Burgess was subjecting to critical analysis. By uniting the individualism of Locke's doctrine of property with the Physiocratic doctrine of social well-being, he gave a sharp turn to the conception that, like Jefferson's, set it widely apart from the exploitative interpretation preferred by the Hamiltonian followers of Locke. The gist of his conception is thus set down:

Now the right of every human being to himself is the foundation of the right of property. That which a man produces is rightfully his own, to keep, to sell, to give or to bequeath, and upon this sure title alone can ownership of anything rightfully rest. But man has also another right, declared by the fact of his existence—the right to the use of so much of the free gifts of nature as may be necessary to supply all the wants of that existence, and which he may use without interfering with the equal rights of anyone else; and to this he has a title as against all the world.[26]

Much of Henry George is compressed within these few lines, that suggest as well the diverse liaisons of his thought. In his conception of the right of every man to himself he is in agreement with William Ellery Channing, who used the argument in his attack on slavery, and with Emerson, Parker, and the Transcendental radicals generally. It is an interpretation of natural rights that sprang easily from the Unitarian-Transcendental conception of the sacredness of the individual, and that was given wide currency by the anti-slavery propaganda. From his deduction that the right to property flows from the right to self, came his theory of tax-equity that was to play a major rôle in the formulation of his principle of taxation. If society may not justly take from the individual what the individual has created, it must seek its revenues elsewhere than in a personal-property tax; and where should it look if not to those values which society has created? The inalienable right of the individual to what he has produced does not extend to the appropriation of wealth he has not produced, and a sharp line is drawn between the rights of the individual and the rights of society, between production and exploitation. Herein lies the justification of the single-tax—a principle derived by crossing Locke with the New England school.

From the classical economists Henry George got little. He had a quiet contempt for them he was never at pains to conceal. He was convinced that they had distorted the whole science of economics. As the earlier Tories with their sacred *arcana imperii* had done with political government, they had involved economics in abstract theory, removing it from the comprehension of the common man. At the best they had dehumanized it to the status of a dismal science, with their postulate of an economic man and their pessimistic outlook. At the worst they had shaped it into a potent weapon for the exploiting class, who gravely invoked economic law—which none understood—to justify class policies of

[26] *Ibid.*, p. 223.

state. In an address delivered at the University of California, Henry George paid his respects to the classical school in these words:

> The name of political economy has been constantly invoked against every effort of the working classes to increase their wages or decrease their hours of labour. . . . Take the best and most extensively circulated textbooks. While they insist upon freedom for capital, while they justify on the ground of utility the selfish greed that seeks to pile fortune on fortune, and the niggard spirit that steels the heart to the wail of distress, what sign of substantial promise do they hold out to the working man save that he should refrain from rearing children? . . .[27]

For political economy thus degraded from its high place and become the slut of private interest, Henry George proposed to do what Tom Paine had done for political theory a hundred years before—he would transfer it from the closet to the market-place by exposing the shabby *arcana imperii* and bringing it within the comprehension of common men. He would bring home to the popular intelligence a realization of the dynamics of economic law and its bearing upon social well-being, that men might plot a fairer course for society. This was the deeper purpose of *Progress and Poverty*—to humanize and democratize political economy, that it might serve social ends rather than class exploitation. *The Rights of Man* and *Progress and Poverty* may be reckoned complementary works, applying to related fields the spirit released to the modern world by the great thinkers of Revolutionary France. The foundations on which they both rest is the eighteenth-century conception of natural law, all-comprehensive, beneficent, free, enshrined in the common heart of humanity, and conducting to the ultimate of social justice.

As a necessary preliminary to his purpose, Henry George was forced to clear the ground of old growths. Before he could declare the truth he must uproot certain of the Malthusian and Ricardian heresies. He must substitute a sociological interpretation, based on historical reality in western civilization, for a set of economic abstractions, based on the political and economic accidents of England in post-Napoleonic days. The Manchester school, it must be remembered, was an embodiment of the aspirations of the rising middle class; it was a philosophical attack upon the vexatious restrictions laid upon capitalism by government in the hands of the landed aristocracy. It conceived of economic principles as of con-

[27] *Ibid.*, p. 277.

cern only to the owning classes, and its theory took a special and narrow form from the current struggle between the landed and capitalistic interests. In a Parliamentary debate over the corn laws in 1814, Alexander Baring, the banker, assumed that the working classes had no interest at stake. To argue that they were affected, he said, was "altogether ridiculous; whether wheat was 130s. or 80s., the laborer could only expect dry bread in the one case and dry bread in the other."[28] In Francis Wayland's *Elements of Political Economy*, published in 1837, a similar narrow view of the field of economics was expressed. That an adequate political economy must be social, that it must be something very much more than a merchant's *vade mecum*, or handbook of profit rules, Henry George grasped as clearly as Ruskin; and he attacked certain of the Manchester principles with the ardor of a social prophet. Of these the classical wage-fund theory seemed to him the most vicious, and he was at vast pains to prove that wages are drawn from the produce of labor and not from a preëxistent capital-fund. Having established this to his satisfaction, he turned to consider the economic effects of monopolistic expropriation of natural resources, and discovered the explanation of the augmenting poverty of civilization in the shutting out of labor from the sources of subsistence, that is in land monopoly.

The argument is based on the Ricardian theory of rent. Though George rejected the classical wage-fund theory, he accepted without qualification the classical rent-theory, and discovered the kernel of his philosophy in the doctrine of social fertility. If rent is the difference between the income-value of a given piece of land and that of the least valuable in the neighborhood, it measures the difference between the yields per acre on the richest and the leanest soil with a like outlay of labor and capital. So in an urban community rent arises from what may be called social fertility— that is, from a monopoly-value in a given neighborhood. Such monopoly-value arises from strategic location; the desirability of a given tract for dwelling, factory, or shop. The number of persons daily passing will determine the rental value for shop purposes; the the accessibility to docks, railways, raw material, power, markets, labor-surplus, will determine its rental value for factory purposes. In every such case, however, it is society and not the individual

---

[28] Quoted by Wesley Clair Mitchell in *The Trend of Economics*, edited by R. G. Tugwell, p. 5.

that augments rent, and this unearned increment increases with the growth of the community. From every advance of civilization it is the landlord who profits. He is a social parasite, the nether millstone between which and material progress the landless laborer is ground.

In every direction, the direct tendency of advancing civilization is to increase the power of human labour to satisfy human desires—to extirpate poverty and to banish want and the fear of want. . . . But Labour cannot reap the benefits which advancing civilization thus brings, because they are intercepted. Land being necessary to labour, and being reduced to private ownership, every increase in the productive power of labour but increases rent—the price that labour must pay for the opportunity to utilise its power; and thus all the advantages gained by the march of progress go to the owners of land, and wages do not increase. . . [29]

Labour and capital are but different forms of the same thing—human exertion. Capital is produced by labour; it is, in fact, but labour impressed upon matter. . . . The use of capital in production is, therefore, but a mode of labour. . . . Hence the principle that, under circumstances which permit free competition, operates to bring wages to a common standard and profits to a substantial equality—the principle that men will seek to gratify their desires with the least exertion—operates to establish and maintain this equilibrium between wages and interest. . . . And this relation fixed, it is evident that interest and wages must rise and fall together, and that interest cannot be increased without increasing wages, nor wages be lowered without depressing interest.[30]

There is no inherent antagonism between labor and capital, Henry George was early convinced. The Marxians with their theory of a class war were mistaken in their analysis. It is rent that is the true source of social injustice, and the clash of interests in society lies between the producer and the parasitic rent-collector. In every society the appropriation of measured increment has enslaved the ownerless. In all civilizations, from ancient Peru to modern Russia, it has subjected the worker to exploitation. Helot, villein, serf, are only different names for a common slavery, the profits of which go to the landlord. In modern times the Industrial Revolution has changed the form of serfdom, only to intensify and embitter it. The Manchester factory-hand was in worse plight than the medieval villein after the Black Plague. Dispossessed of his acres by the enclosure movement, he had been thrown into the hoppers of industrialism and ground to pieces. He was helpless in

[29] *Progress and Poverty*, Book IV, Chapter 4.
[30] *Ibid.*, Book III, Chapter 5.

the hands of the masters, who with their monopoly of land and the machine, in control of the common heritage of trade processes, raw materials, transportation, credit, and the law-making and law-enforcing machinery, were taking from labor an augmenting toll of its production. Hence the close correlation between material progress and proletarian poverty. Hence the logical outcome of the Industrial Revolution, when it should have run its course, was the reduction of the worker to the level of a slave, compared with whose material condition the status of the southern bond-slave was enviable. The southern apologists of slavery had been right; the negro on the plantation enjoyed advantages denied to wage-labor under industrialism.[31]

Having thus analyzed the forces at work in modern society, and wedded a flamboyant material progress to a slattern poverty, Henry George proposed his sovereign remedy—the return to society of social values, hitherto expropriated by means of the private ownership of land, and the removal of the burden of indirect taxation from the back of productive labor. The Ricardian theory of rent, interpreted in the light of eighteenth-century *laissez faire*—of free competition, of a beneficent natural law, of social justice—conducted to unforeseen social issues. If labor and capital are individual, the fruits of both should return to their producers. Society has no just claim on what society has not produced, and the individual has no just claim to that which his labor or capital has not produced. Render unto Cæsar the things that are Cæsar's, and to the individual citizen the things that are his—such to Henry George was the sum of the law of distribution. Land monopoly was a refined denial of natural rights. "The equal right of all men to the use of the land is as clear as their equal right to breathe the air—it is a right proclaimed by the fact of their existence."[32] Unearned increment was the shackles wherewith labor was bound. In the name of social justice strike those shackles from the limbs of men and progress would never again have its ears filled with the wailings of poverty. The workman would once again sing at his work, and the sunshine of well-being fall pleasantly on the land.

A brilliant thinker, with a passionate sympathy for the exploited of earth, this knight-errant from out the newest West ardently believed in the sufficiency of his social philosophy to all

[31] See *Ibid.*, Book VII, Chapter 2. [32] *Ibid.*, Book VII, Chapter I.

needs. In him the French Revolutionary doctrine came to its most original expression in America. No doubt, like his progenitors, he oversimplified the problem. Society is more complex than he esteemed it; individual motives are more complex. It is perilous to subordinate psychology to abstract theory; the ideal of justice is always running afoul of immediate and narrow interest. Later academic economists have dealt sharply with Henry George, but what have they done to justify their magisterial tone? The science of economics is still cousin-german to philosophy in its fondness for spinning tenuous subtleties; it is still system-ridden, still too much the apologist for things as they are. From its servitude to a class Henry George essayed to deliver it. In fastening upon monopoly as the prime source of social injustice, he directed attention to the origins of exploitative capitalism. He did more than any other man to spread through America a knowledge of the law of economic determinism. He opened a rich vein and one that needs further exploring. The suggestive principle of unearned increment calls for further expansion to embrace other forms than rent, to fit it to the needs of a complex society. What he seems not to have seen was the wider range of economic determinism—that changes come only when the existing order has become intolerable to great classes, and the grip of use and wont is loosened by the rebellions born of exigent need. "For ever the fat of the whole foundation hangeth to the priest's beard," asserted a quaint Beggars' Petition in appeal to Henry VIII against the monasteries, and in that comment were the seeds of the Reformation. When the beards are few to which the fat hangs, the time is ripe for an upheaval. An arch-idealist, Henry George would hasten the change by appeal to reason. Like Godwin and Tom Paine he believed that reason will make its own way, forgetting that reason waits upon interest, and the day of its freedom is long delayed. Yet if he was oversanguine, why account that to his discredit? *

* The discussion of Henry D. Lloyd, planned as the second subsection, was not written.—*Publisher.*

CHAPTER IV

THE BEGINNINGS OF CRITICISM

For many thoughtful Americans the welter of frontier individualism was a severe trial to their faith in American institutions. An ambitious industrialism colliding with a shambling Jacksonian democracy was forecasting consequences to government and to society that intelligent men could not shut their eyes to. The America of Fisk and Gould, of Boss Tweed and the *Crédit Mobilier* scandal, was far from satisfying the requirements of any rational civilization. After a hundred years to have come to such heroes, to have bogged down in such filth, was an outcome to the great experiment that one could not contemplate with pride. It was no time to be silent. No people was ever saved by dumb preachers. The present generation was answerable for the new evils that were springing from the graves of the old, and intelligent Americans must not lose their heads in the thick of the common hurly-burly. So amidst the ruck and clamor of the times a tiny note of criticism was lifted up, timid and uncertain at first, but growing more confident and more strident as the decade grew older. It was not searching criticism. Sooner or later it was pretty certain to run into a blind alley of moral indignation, overlooking the major issues and leaving the vital factors of the problem unconsidered. Yet such as it was—shallow and feeble enough often to excite wonder in a later generation—it marks the rise of a spirit of skepticism towards the blowsy doctrine of manifest destiny that since the fifties had been blowing about the land.

The determining factors in the situation confronting criticism were political and economic, and the immediate problem that pressed for solution was the problem whether an undisciplined people, wedded to an old-fashioned agrarian democracy, could cope with an ambitious industrialism that was quite cynically buying and selling the political state. To deal with that problem most of the critics were singularly ill equipped. Two generations of constitutional debate, seasoned with a dash of equalitarian dogma, had left them intellectually lean and impoverished. They had forgotten the sober realism of the eighteenth century that never overlooked the intimate ties between economics and politics, and with no anchors down in the plebeian mud they were likely to drift helplessly in the moral squalls they were always blowing up. The more distinguished critics—those who commanded the most serious attention—were in a particularly unfortunate situation, for not only were they uninstructed idealists with no understanding of *Realpolitik*, but they had been reared in the classical tradition and their minds were saturated with a decadent aristocratic culture. To many of them the present evils of America served only to quicken an inherited skepticism of democracy. How can society expect to function adequately, they asked, without capable and honest leadership; and how can such leadership be hoped for in a rough and tumble democracy that loves the noisiest demagogue? Of this very considerable group of belated Federalists James Russell Lowell was the most distinguished representative. In the middle seventies he had come to believe that America was suffering from too much democracy, and that competent government could be had only by working back to the responsible Federalism of earlier times, with leadership reclaimed by the better elements of society. To the economics of the problem—the antagonistic interests of capitalist, proletarian, and farmer, with their struggles to control the political state—he gave no serious thought, but he viewed with instinctive suspicion the mounting ambitions of labor and he foresaw only evil from the bitter unrest of the farmers.

A second very considerable group, of which George William Curtis may be taken as spokesman, rejected all such antiquated Federalistic hopes as the foolish dreams of defeatists. They held fast to their faith in democracy, but they were convinced that more adequate democratic machinery must be provided. The root of the evil, they had come to believe, was political and must be sought in the vicious Jacksonian spoils system. With every change of administration to turn over the country to hungry partisans to devour, was not democracy but the negation of democracy? Government would not function satisfactorily until a trained civil service was provided, and the need of the hour, they pointed out, was an honest civil service reform. A third group, very much smaller than the others, of which Edwin Lawrence Godkin was the spokesman, was inclined to trace the plentiful evils of the times to an unwise paternalism, asserting that the real source of the common political scoundrelism was the lauded Amer ican System devised by Henry Clay, as a result of which govern ment was seduced from its proper business of keeping the peace and was turned into a fairy godmother to shower gifts on favored interests. The only cure for the evil was to divorce business and politics and reëstablish in practice the police theory of government.

In the thinking of all three groups little consideration was given to the social consequences of the venture on which America had entered with the vigor of thoughtless youth. Concerning the ultimate consequences of the collision between a shambling democracy and an ambitious industrialism, few troubled themselves greatly. To find those who confronted the problem frankly and realistically, one must search out obscure men, labor leaders for the most part, or *déclassé* radicals like Wendell Phillips. The middle-class mind refused to see what its feet were stumbling over. In consequence the Gilded Age produced no critics of industrialism comparable to the great English critics—Carlyle, Kingsley, Ruskin, Morris, Tawney; no social philosophers like the great continental expounders of proletarian ideals—Marx, Engels, Bakunin, Sorel; no left-wing economists like the great French school—Louis Blanc, Bastiat, Proudhon. The genteel culture of America was no better than bankrupt in presence of brutal reality, quite unequipped to interpret the sprawling America that was transforming itself before its eyes into something it hated but did not understand. The time for searching criticism had not come, and would not come until the Industrial Revolution had created in America a proletariat such as swarmed in the English black country and amongst the hovels of continental cities. Nevertheless such criticism as there was must be taken into consideration, and for our present purpose it will suffice to single out three spokesmen—a grizzled warrior of the earlier renaissance who had the courage to face unpleasant fact, and two critics who brought to bear on political themes the best culture of the time. With these may be conveniently grouped certain novelists who more or less casually suffered their pens to deal with social problems.

I

THE NEW ENGLAND CONSCIENCE AND CAPITALISM—
WENDELL PHILLIPS

Social criticism was by no means a new thing in America. For half a century it had filled all ears with its strident clamors, and from it had issued the motley group of reform movements that had been cheered or mocked at by thousands. From Channing and Cooper down to Parke Godwin and Horace Greeley it had been mustering its forces, vivid and picturesque figures for the most part—men and women like Fanny Wright, George Henry Evans, and Hinton R. Helper; ardent souls who beyond the dun horizon discovered a golden morrow that only awaited the rising of a new sun, and who lectured and wrote and argued till pretty much all America had caught something of their contagious enthusiasm. In this work New England came eventually to take the lead, and the golden forties were a time when in many an obscure Yankee head programs of reform were fermenting like a vat of malt. But unfortunately an excess of eagerness wore out the first enthusiasm, and when the shackles had been loosened from the negro bondmen the militancy of the New England leadership subsided and the tired New England conscience went on vacation.

But in these slothful times the conscience of one great New Englander was not tired, though he gave it no rest while life lasted. Wendell Phillips was a soldier of Puritan soul who did not lay down his arms in '65, but for nearly a score of years warred upon the injustices of the Gilded Age as he had warred before upon the obscenities of negro slavery. No sooner was the cause of abolitionism won—a cause to which he had sacrificed much in ease and the good opinion of Beacon Street, but from which he had gained more in self-respect and the decent opinion of mankind—than he turned to whatever new work offered. The lovers of justice, he knew very well, can indulge themselves in no vacations, for the devil is on the job day and night, and while the assailants sleep he is at work repairing any breaches in the walls of his citadel. When conscience is tired he counts on gaining his greatest victories.

The love of freedom has always been a dangerous possession in Massachusetts, given to exploding in unforeseen moments and unexpected places. No one could have foretold—certainly not he himself—that Wendell Phillips would put away all his Brahmin

loyalties and devote forty-seven years to an unresting attack on the
diverse Toryisms from which he and his class had hitherto prospered. Son of the first mayor of the city and a distinguished member of the Boston gentry, he was a patrician in the fullest Boston
sense. All the loyalties of his caste summoned him to uphold the
Brahmin authorities, but something deep within him, a loyalty to
other and higher ideals, held him back. When a frock-coated mob
laid its hands on Garrison to lynch him for abolition propaganda,
he drew back; he refused to follow the Mayor and the Colonel of
his regiment and other gentlemen if they betrayed the Boston for
which their grandfathers had fought. An instinctive love of justice
held him back. A fierce indignation flamed up within him at the
wrong done a citizen of Massachusetts for exercising his natural
right of free speech, and in that wild hour he discovered that he was
a child of '76 with the mentality of a revolutionist. His conscience
was aroused and he proceeded to put it in the safe keeping of Ann
Terry Greene, a brilliant young woman of radical mind, who quickened his sense of social justice as Maria White was to quicken
Lowell's. There was to be no backsliding in his case. From the
December day in 1837 when he replied to Attorney-General
Austin's slanders of the Revolutionary fathers in Faneuil Hall, to
the end of a life filled with enormous labors—a life daily stabbed by
Tory hornets, and that at the last is said to have inspired the re-
mark of Judge Hoar that he did not attend the funeral of Wendell
Phillips but he approved of it [1]—he followed his conscience into
many an unpopular cause and spoke for those for whom few were
willing to speak.

The story of his anti-slavery labors belongs to an earlier time and
need not be recounted here. His devotion to abolitionism equaled
Garrison's and his services were as great. It is rather the nineteen
years that remained to him after Appomattox that are of present
concern—what later battles he fought and how he bore himself in
those battles. It was a difficult time for Puritan liberalism, face to
face with a new age that had forgotten the old liberalisms. The
Grand Army of Abolitionism had disbanded and new armies of
other causes had not yet been recruited. Garrison and Edmund
Quincy and Whittier had laid aside their arms, and Lowell had long
since settled back into a comfortable Brahminism; the long struggle
had left them drained of their energy. But for Wendell Phillips the

[1] See Charles Edward Russell, *The Story of Wendell Phillips*, p. 53.

battle was not over; it was unending and he was enlisted for life. At a vast meeting that marked the formal close of the abolition movement he took leave of his old associates with these words: "We will not say 'Farewell,' but 'all hail.' Welcome, new duties! We sheathe no sword. We only turn the front of the army upon a new foe." [2] He had long spoken for prohibition, woman's rights, the abolition of capital punishment, and he now joined heartily with the courageous women engaged in such reform work. But more provocative business was at hand, and more dangerous—causes that touched the northern pocketbook as abolitionism had touched the southern. The banker's exploitation of the national currency, and the manufacturer's exploitation of factory labor—these were issues that a cautious man who was careful of his good name would not meddle with. But Wendell Phillips was never cautious and his good name had long since been flung to the wolves. And so in the evening of his days, with a courage that took little counsel of expediency, he embarked on a campaign that had for its ultimate objective the impregnable citadel of State Street. He would destroy capitalistic exploitation in all its works. It was as hopeless a battle as King Arthur's "last, dim, weird battle of the west," and entered upon as courageously.

How he came to hold the heretical views on money and labor that he expounded from the lecture platform cannot easily be traced. Perhaps they came from the radical fringe that envelops every great social movement; perhaps they were the inevitable expression of his left-wing temper. A man who had fought all Tory programs for thirty years must eventually come to hate the ways of capitalism, and so confirmed a democrat as Wendell Phillips would be certain to espouse the doctrine of thorough. One who had passed through the fires of abolition nullification, who had spoken of the Union as "built i' the eclipse and rigged with curses dark," who had repudiated his citizenship and equaled Garrison in contempt for a slave-protecting Constitution, would have pretty well cleared his mind of conventional respect for capitalistic law and order. He was not impressed by political cant. He had taken the measure of existing law and order and was casting about for a juster law and a more generous order.

In these later years, as a program of social reconstruction took shape in his mind, he was coming to essential agreement with the

[2] Quoted in Martyn, *Wendell Phillips: The Agitator*, p. 372.

program of socialism. With the Marxians he based his thinking
upon economics, and his final objective came to be the substitution
of coöperation for the profit-motive. As ardently as Horace Greeley
he asserted the rights of labor. As early as 1860–1861 he had come
to recognize a similarity in the economic status of the wage-slave
and the bond-slave, and in 1865, in a speech on the eight-hour
movement, he accepted as true the southern thesis that in western
civilization all labor, whether bond or wage, was unfree, held in
the grip of a master, bought and sold in the market; [3] and now that
the shackles had been struck from the negro, it remained to strike
them from the wage-earner. To turn the negro from a bond-slave
to a wage-slave would be a sorry ending of abolitionism; but such
must be the inevitable outcome, he believed, unless all labor should
win freedom. The question of the hour for Wendell Phillips had
become the question of the relation of labor and capital.

In his thinking on the currency question—a question that became acute in the seventies—he was soon caught up by the Greenback movement. It may have been that his contact with Thaddeus
Stevens helped to mold his views on the money question; yet that
he should have become a Greenbacker was foreordained. He had
no amiable illusions in regard to State Street. As a tribune of
the people he had long been intimately acquainted with its ambitions, and he would not turn over the country to its custodianship.
He would have no bankers' control of the national currency, to
augment or deflate as banking profits dictated. His democratic
sympathies recoiled from a class control of the common medium
of exchange, and in 1875 he offered a drastic solution of the vexing
question that brought down on his head all the wrath of State
Street. His plan provided for three things: the rejection of the
national banknote system; the issue of honest greenbacks, secured
by the wealth of the country, and receivable in payment for all
debts public and private—not dishonest greenbacks like the old,
which the government had repudiated at issue by refusing to accept them in payment of custom dues; and finally the retirement
of interest-bearing bonds and the return to a cash basis for government business. How deeply he felt in the notorious matter of
credit manipulation is suggested in the following passage with
its echoes of an older America that looked with suspicion on a
consolidating capitalism.

[3] See *Speeches*, Second Series, p. 139.

Three times within a dozen years, [he said] capitalists with their knives on the throat of the Government, have compelled it to cheat its largest creditor, the people; whose claim, Burke said, was the most sacred. First, the pledge that greenbacks should be exchangeable with bonds was broken. Secondly, debts originally payable in paper . . . were made payable in gold. Thirdly, silver was demonetized, and gold made the only tender. A thousand millions were thus stolen from the people.[4]

At other times he went further. Speaking on the labor question in 1872, he said:

I say, let the debts of the country be paid, abolish the banks, and let the government lend every Illinois farmer (if he wants it), who is now borrowing money at ten per cent., money on the half-value of his land at three per cent. The same policy that gave a million acres to the Pacific Railroad, because it was a great national effort, will allow of our lending Chicago twenty millions of money, at three per cent., to rebuild it.[5]

When we get into power, there is one thing we mean to do. If a man owns a single house, we will tax him one hundred dollars. If he owns ten houses of like value, we won't tax him one thousand dollars, but two thousand dollars. . . . We'll double and treble and quintuple and sextuple and increase tenfold the taxes. . . . We'll crumple up wealth by making it unprofitable to be rich. . . . You will say, "Is that just?" My friends, it is safe. Man is more valuable than money. You say, "Then capital will go to Europe." Good heavens, let it go! If other States wish to make themselves vassals of wealth, so will not we. We will save a country equal from end to end. Land, private property, all sorts of property, shall be so dearly taxed that it shall be impossible to be rich; for it is in wealth, in incorporated, combining, perpetuated wealth, that the danger of labor lies.[6]

The mad wicked ravings of a demagogue, such talk was accounted by sober financiers of Boston. But it was rather the talk of an honest equalitarian who understood how incompatible was property rule and the ideal of equality. The arch-enemy of a worthy civilization, Wendell Phillips had become convinced, was private capitalism with its dehumanizing profit-motive. There could be no adequate civilization, no Christianity, until coöperation had displaced competition, and men were become equal in economic rights as they were in franchise rights. At a Labor-Reform Convention held at Worcester on September 4, 1871, resolutions drafted by him were adopted—resolutions that reveal "just where Mr. Phillips stood for the last thirteen years of his life."

[4] Quoted in Martyn, *op. cit.*, pp. 412–413.
[5] *Speeches*, Second Series, p. 176.
[6] *Ibid.*, p. 167.

In this "full body of faith," and in two later speeches—*The Foundation of the Labor Movement,* and *The Labor Question*—the man who called himself "a Jeffersonian democrat in the darkest hour," wrote down as the great objective of the labor party the principle that has long been accepted as the cardinal plank of the Socialist platform.

We affirm, as a fundamental principle, that labor, the creator of wealth, is entitled to all it creates.

Affirming this, we avow ourselves willing to accept the final results of the operation of a principle so radical,—such as the overthrow of the whole profit-making system, the extinction of all monopolies, the abolition of privileged classes, universal education and fraternity, perfect freedom of exchange, and . . . the final obliteration of that foul stigma upon our so-called Christian civilization—the poverty of the masses. . . . *Resolved,* —That we declare war with the wages system, which demoralizes alike the hirer and the hired, cheats both, and enslaves the workingman; war with the present system of finance, which robs labor, and gorges capital, . . . war with these lavish grants of the public lands to speculating companies, and whenever in power, we pledge ourselves to use every just and legal means to resume all such grants heretofore made; war with the system of enriching capitalists by the creation and increase of public interest-bearing debts. We demand that every facility, and all encouragement, shall be given by law to co-operation in all branches of industry and trade, and that the same aid be given to co-operative efforts that has heretofore been given to railroads and other enterprises. . . .[7]

When he was about to take the platform on another occasion his wife is reported to have said to him, "Wendell, don't shilly-shally!" Certainly in this pronouncement, and in the speeches supporting it, there is no shilly-shallying. He will have no halfway measures, but goes straight to the economic core of the problem. Pretty much all of Marxianism is there, even to the class war. The capitalists had whetted their swords and he would have labor put its sword likewise to the grindstone. If the war were cruel, where did labor learn it—"learned it of capital, learned it of our enemies." In a world of economic concentration where caste follows property accumulation he had come to rest his hopes on the international solidarity of labor. The cause of democratic justice was committed to the keeping of the workingman, and if he were defeated in his hopes the future was black indeed. The American Revolution and the French Revolution had prepared the way gloriously for a greater event, the revolution of labor.

[7] *Ibid.,* pp. 152–153.

He was not afraid of revolution. In America he hoped the battle would be fought with ballots, but if it must come to bullets, so be it. The Paris Commune met with his heartiest approval: "I have not a word to utter—far be it from me!—against the grandest declaration of popular indignation which Paris wrote on the pages of history in fire and blood. I honor Paris as the vanguard of the Internationals of the world." [8] And in the Phi Beta Kappa address, delivered in 1881 before all the assembled conservatisms of Boston, the old warrior with seventy years upon his head, went so far as to defend Russian Nihilism.

Nihilism is the righteous and honorable resistance of a people crushed under an iron rule. Nihilism is evidence of life . . . the last weapon of victims choked and manacled beyond all other resistance. . . . I honor Nihilism, since it redeems human nature from the suspicion of being utterly vile, made up only of heartless oppressors and contented slaves. . . . This is the only view an American, the child of 1620 and 1776, can take of Nihilism. Any other unsettles and perplexes the ethics of our civilization. Born within sight of Bunker Hill, in a commonwealth which adopts the motto of Algernon Sydney, *sub libertate quietem* ("accept no peace without liberty"); son of Harvard, whose first pledge was "Truth"; citizen of a republic based on the claim that no government is rightful unless resting on the consent of the people, and which assumes to lead in asserting the rights of humanity,—I at least can say nothing else and nothing less; no, not if every tile on Cambridge roofs were a devil hooting my words! [9]

"It was a delightful discourse," said one gentleman, "but preposterous from beginning to end." The doctrine was strange to Harvard ears—wicked and perverse. And strange and disconcerting also was his roll-call of great and noble deeds done in America in which Harvard scholarship had had no part. To an audience of Brahmin scholars it was not kind to say, "The greatest things have not been done for the world by its bookmen"; nor this, "It is not the masses who have most disgraced our political annals. I have seen many mobs . . . I never saw or heard of any but well-dressed mobs, assembled and countenanced, if not always led in person, by respectability and what called itself education." [10]   It was a curious scene—that gathering in a Harvard hall listening to a son of Harvard who had gone to school to other teachers than those brought up on Brahmin culture. The liberalism of the forties was speaking to a generation that was concerned about other

[8] *Ibid.*, p. 154.   [9] See *Ibid.*, pp. 356–359.   [10] See *Ibid.*, p. 347.

things than a just and humane civilization. Wendell Phillips was hopelessly old-fashioned in America of the Gilded Age—a lone Puritan in a land of Yankees. He used to speak of himself grimly as "that Ishmael"; his home, he said, was the sleeping-car and his only friends the brakeman and the porter. He spent his strength and his earnings with generous prodigality, and when he died the only treasures he had laid up were in heaven. He was the last survivor of the great age of Puritan conscience, and the words he spoke of Theodore Parker may well stand for his epitaph: "The child of Puritanism is not mere Calvinism—it is the loyalty to justice which tramples under foot the wicked laws of its own epoch."

II

MORALITY AND POLITICS—GEORGE WILLIAM CURTIS

A child of Puritan conscience also was George William Curtis, like Wendell Phillips sprung from the Puritan gentry, but unlike him wanting in a passionate Hebraism that sought justice in all the byways and would not turn aside from pursuing it. A reformer but never a radical, he was a gentleman who was a lifelong friend of civilization. An idealist, he refused to serve the gross materialisms that swept so many of his fellows from the old moorings, but throughout a long and honorable career he preserved unshaken his early faith in republican ideals and the way of liberty. As an abolitionist he faced hostile audiences with admirable poise, and as a civil service reformer he fought off the attacks of greasy politicians with quiet contempt. A cultivated gentleman, high-bred if not heroic, was George William Curtis.

Born in Providence, Rhode Island, of excellent stock, living most of his life in New York City whither his father had removed to engage in the banking business, he was brought up in affluence and spent his days amidst dignified surroundings. Broad-minded and generous, with wide sympathies and urbane manners, he followed his conscience and weighed life in the scales of Puritan morality. He was no friend to compromise or expediency, yet he was content to serve God in the station whereunto he had been called, declining to turn rebel and become an outcast and pariah. Endowed with excellent parts, his training was unusually fortunate. At eighteen with his brother Burrill he went to Brook Farm, where he spent two profitable years in an atmosphere he found stimulating. After

quitting Brook Farm he passed the better part of two years at
Concord with his brother, living at farmhouses, helping with the
crops, and for a time indulging in an experiment not unlike Thoreau's at Walden Pond. Then followed four years overseas—from
1846 to 1850—rambling about the continent, sloughing off the
provincial asceticism of New England, and practicing his pen by
means of letters and diaries. On his return he drifted into journalism, wrote several volumes of travel essays and social satire,
caught the Lyceum infection, then at its malignant stage, lectured
voluminously to pay off an unfortunate debt, wrote for *Putnam's
Magazine*, became connected with *Harper's Weekly*, finally settling
into the Easy Chair of *Harper's Magazine*, from which comfortable
seat for years he sent forth gracefully pointed comments on manners, society, politics, life, yet more and more turning to politics as
his particular field and serving as volunteer political mentor and
critic to the Gilded Age.

Of his several early ventures into the field of polite letters little
need be said. The work of a high-spirited young man, they were
a cross between Nathaniel Parker Willis and Thackeray with a
suggestion of Disraeli. He took his place naturally as a member of
the New York group of littérateurs who were gaily exploiting the
conventional sentimentalism of the fifties. With its pose of clever
sophistication the New York school could do no good to a serious
young writer, and the pretensions of the new-rich society of the
town were a cordial invitation to go wrong. *Nile Notes of a Howadji*
(1851), written before the young traveler had caught the current
note of social satire, was a conscious correction of the ascetic
Puritanism imbibed at Concord, and with its frank delight in the
sensuousness of the East it gave offense to the professional blue-
stockings of the time. But in *The Potiphar Papers* (1853) he turned
to satirize New York society, then hastening to transform itself
from a staid Knickerbocker world into a Gold Coast of social
climbers. That his treatment of the theme should have been a
slighter edition of Thackeray's *Vanity Fair*—less searching and
more sentimental—might be guessed even if we did not know how
greatly Curtis loved and admired the English satirist. "He seems
to be the one of all authors who takes life precisely as he finds it,"
he wrote of him. "If he finds it sad, he makes it sad: if gay,
gay. You discover in him the flexible adaptability of Horace,
but with a deep and consuming sadness which the Roman never

knew, and which in the Englishman seems to be almost senti-mentality.[11]

But in spite of their excellent model these sketches do not now seem so sprightly as they seemed to his fellows on the staff of *Putnam's Magazine*. Moralism scented with patchouli is no longer the vogue, and they have long since been laid away with the hoops and crinoline of the fifties. His most important venture in polite literature—if indeed even that deserves the name important—was *Prue and I* (1856), written in a golden summer when his pen was dipped into the inkwell of love and he foresaw the years of his life lengthening out in the most intimate of companionships. They are charming essays in contentment that teach the familiar lesson that the only abiding riches are the riches of mind and character. The old bookkeeper in black coat and white tie who voyages to the realms of romance while watching from the Battery outgoing ships, has discovered the vicarious pleasure of the imagination, and the Aurelia of his dreams is Prue as she was in her youth, and both are Anna Shaw to whom soon after he was married. The first three sketches—"Dinner Time," "My Chateaux," and "Sea from the Shore"—are humorous and tender fancies in the graceful Victorian manner; but "Titbottom's Spectacles" is Hawthorne-like in the tenuous play of a grotesquely moralistic fancy, and the succeeding sketches reveal the exhaustion of the vein. Later he tried his hand at a novel—*Trumps*—but it refused to turn into anything but a tract and in the early sixties he settled down in the Easy Chair which he had first occupied as early as 1853.

Thereafter to his death in 1892 his work followed three diverse lines. For thirty years he was essayist, orator, and political critic, to a generation sorely in need of wise and urbane counsel. His audience was wide and his influence great, and to his work he brought the weight of his sane and just character. Not a great scholar and not an acute critic, he was an enlightened and sensitive conscience, and to the bar of his conscience he summoned the parties and policies of a heedless and selfish generation. From the Easy Chair he sent forth his genial comment on matters of current interest, satisfying his love of creative writing by the grace of his talk, and recognizing his kinship with the age of Queen Ann by adopting the words of *The Tatler*, "I shall from time to time Report and Consider all Matters of what Kind soever that shall occur to

[11] Edward Cary, *George William Curtis*, p. 78.

me." But such work at the best is ephemeral, and ephemeral likewise were the polished pronouncements of the occasional orator on
which far too much time and labor were expended. But New York
City must have its spokesman for formal occasions, and after
Bryant's death George William Curtis was summoned with increasing frequency. The rich context of his speeches, elaborated
with formal dignity and embellished with literary allusions, hit to
a nicety the taste of a generation that still delighted in oratory and
preferred dignity to informality. His addresses on Charles Sumner,
Wendell Phillips, Bryant, and Lowell, are excellent examples of a
style that is no longer the fashion. In their polished sentences
eulogy is tempered with criticism, but the criticism is sympathetic
and refuses to render judgments that may strike his hearers as
severe. It would be ungracious to intrude unpleasant facts on dignified occasions.

But his most significant work during these busy years lay in the
field of political criticism, and it was as editor of *Harper's Weekly*,
from 1863 to his death, and as a leader in the movement of civil
service reform, that he made the deepest impress on the age. The
Weekly, with Nast as cartoonist, was then at the height of its
popularity and influence, and by means of its editorial page Curtis
was able to marshal a very considerable following for whatever
cause or party he espoused. He had long taken part in practical
politics, was active in caucuses and conventions, was much on the
stump and kept his fingers on party wires. Yet influential as he
was—the scholar in politics, as his own generation loved to say—he
was never a serious student of politics in the broader meaning. He
was essentially an English gentleman politician, with a fine scorn
of mean and sordid policies, a warm love of country but an equally
warm love of civilization, devoted to the cause of liberty, a friend of
justice, yet with all his excellent traits an inadequate political philosopher. Like Lowell's his horizon was curiously limited. Abstract
political theory did not interest him and he never critically examined
diverse systems of government. Of economics he was as ignorant
as his generation. Again like Lowell the single standard by which he
judged politics was the moral standard, and in his anxious concern for
"good government" he failed to probe deeply the sources of "bad
government." In presence of the vast corruptions of the Gilded
Age he was as helpless in diagnosing the evil as Lowell or Norton.
Such helplessness is the more surprising considering what rare

opportunities he had enjoyed for intelligent understanding. During the impressionable years of youth he daily associated with the most militant group of intellectual radicals in America and heard the ideas of Saint-Simon and Fourier and Owen eagerly canvassed. Associationism as a cure for the evils of competition was the cardinal doctrine of the Brook Farmists; yet his individualism passed unaffected through all such discussions. He seems to have sympathized with the skepticism of Hawthorne rather than the faith of Ripley and Dana. Writing to his father from Brook Farm he fell into the genial transcendental vein and gaily poked fun at those who would make the world over.

> No wise man is long a reformer, [he wrote] for Wisdom sees plainly that growth is steady, sure, and neither condemns nor rejects what is, or has been. Reform is organized distrust. It says to the universe fresh from God's hand, "You are a miserable business; lo! I will make you fairer!" and so deputes some Fourier or Robert Owen to improve the bungling work of the Creator.[12]

It was as a transcendental optimist that he set out on his travels in 1846. The Europe he visited at the age of twenty was seething with discontent that was to flame up in the revolutionary year of '48, yet though he wandered leisurely through Italy, Hungary, Germany, France, and was at Paris during the great overturn, the evidence that his biographer has gathered indicates that he was not deeply affected by the experience. Unlike his friend Margaret Fuller, who was a passionate volunteer in the struggle of Mazzini at Rome, or like Dana, who followed the movement closely as foreign correspondent, he felt none of the promptings of a revolutionist. A romantic sympathy for Kossuth is clearly indicated, but his feelings carried him little further than that. Even in England, seething as it was with the proletarian unrest that culminated in the great Chartist movement, he came upon little to quicken his transcendental pulse. It was not till he got back home and found himself in presence of negro slavery that his reforming ardor took fire and he proposed to engage in the business of "organized distrust." He threw himself into the cause with enthusiasm and spoke from many an abolition platform. Then came the war and during those passionate years he was swept unconsciously along the path of consolidation, emerging from the fire a confirmed Hamiltonian with transcendental democratic leanings.

[12] See *Ibid.*, pp. 25–26.

Have you thought [he wrote Charles Eliot Norton in 1864] what a vindication this war is of Alexander Hamilton? I wish somebody would write his life as it ought to be written, for surely he was one of the greatest of our great men, as Jefferson was the least of the truly great; or am I wrong? Hamilton was generous and sincere. Was Jefferson either? [13]

Such Hamiltonian sympathies suffice to explain some of his votes in the New York Constitutional Convention of 1867, of which he was a member. He advocated the appointment of the attorney-general and certain other state officers, opposed the principle of municipal home rule, and approved the extension of the authority of the state over local police systems. With Tammany Hall and Boss Tweed before his eyes it was perhaps natural that he should have sought in the power of the up-state voter some external control over the city machine. But in spite of such obvious leanings towards the Whig branch of the Republican party Curtis was never a Whig. The transcendentalism he had imbibed at Brook Farm remained with him to color much of his thinking and restrain him from an uncritical advocacy of capitalism. He never went over body and soul to the new gospel of exploitation. He never lent a willing ear to the seductive appeals of the American System. He early became a free-trader and throughout his life was opposed to all tariffs and grants and subsidies. Discovering in the principle of liberty the cardinal principles of American democracy, he was disposed to accept a wide application of *laissez faire;* yet when it opened the door to extortion he was willing to curb an anti-social individualism. When in the seventies it was proposed by the western farmers that a national railroad should be built from Chicago to the Atlantic seaboard, Curtis looked upon the proposal with sympathy as likely to rescue the farmer from extortionate tolls. [14] Unlike Dana and Godkin, he declined to grow bitter and lose his head over the economic proposals of the western agrarians. In the sharp alignment between agrarianism and capitalism he stood in the main outside both parties, and although opposed to greenbackism he discussed the question with moderation and good sense—a rare thing in those blatant times.

But it was political decency rather than capitalistic or agrarian programs that he was chiefly concerned about. He looked to his conscience as guide and as editor of *Harper's Weekly* he used his influence to cleanse America of the corruption he abhorred. Week after week he appealed to the American voter to turn rascals out of office and put honest men in. The corrupt political machine was the source of the evil, and the machine had grown powerful through its control of patronage. There would be vicious government so long as politicians could create a machine by means of the spoils system. Two remedies, he believed, were necessary to cure the evil—independent voting and civil service reform; and to the spread of these two ideas he devoted the last twenty years of his life, thereby bringing on his head much abuse and incurring eventually a break with the Republican party.

His troubles began with his proposal of independent voting. To that party-ridden generation on whom the passions of war had fastened a tyrannical machine, the scratching of the party ticket seemed no better than treason. It was a Copperhead device to undo the results of the war and reëstablish the rebel leaders at Washington, and it needed courage to advocate it publicly. Curtis put the matter fairly in a speech to Independent Republicans at New York in 1880:

The first powerful and conclusive remedy for the tyranny of the machine . . . is scratching. The word has become a sneer, a taunt, a bitter reproach, but the test of the power and effectiveness of the remedy is the fury with which it is assailed. . . . The machine denounces scratchers as lustily as Laud denounced the Puritans, or George III the rebellious Yankees, or slave-driving Democrats Republican woolly heads. . . . The scratcher is the minute-man of politics. He is always in light marching order. He has only to consult his own knowledge and conscience, and with one stroke his work is done. Fortunately, also, his stroke may be as secret as his ballot. Those who do not choose to publish the fact need not be known, and may smile serenely at the blind fury of those whose plots are quietly foiled. This is the reason of the impotent anger with which scratching is assailed. It cannot be reached. . . . Scratching is denounced as dishonorable. Oh, no! the secret ballot is not dishonorable. The shot of the Middlesex farmer from behind a tree was no more dishonorable than the immortal volley from behind the breastworks of Bunker Hill.[15]

He then proceeded to lay open what seemed to him the core of the problem:

But useful as scratching is as a corrective, it does not strike at the heart of the machine, and it is therefore *only* a corrective and not a radical remedy. That remedy can be found only by finding the source of the power of the machine, and that source is official patronage. It is the command of millions of the public money spent in public administration; the control

[15] *Orations and Addresses*, "Machine Politics and the Remedy," Vol. II, pp. 157–159.

of the vast labyrinth of place, with its enormous emoluments; the system which makes the whole Civil Service, to the least detail and most significant position, the spoils of party victory; which perverts necessary party organization into intolerable party despotism. It is upon this that the hierarchy of the machine is erected. Strike at this system strongly, steadily, persistently, and you shiver the machine to pieces.[16]

Seeing his duty clearly, Curtis did not spare himself, but while most of his fellows were seeking fame or wealth for themselves he gave his time and strength without stint to the cause, and it was due to his efforts more than to those of any other man that a reform in the civil service was eventually brought about. He had to fight his way against bitter opposition. It was charged that he was seeking to create in America an undemocratic bureaucracy. His old friend Charles A. Dana—from whom he had become estranged—was quite frank. "Above all I do not believe," he said, "in the establishment in this country of the German bureaucratic system, with its permanent staff of office-holders who are not responsible to the people, and whose tenure of place knows no variation and no end except the end of life." [17] But it was the politicians who fought most bitterly, and when to civil service reform he added the sin of bolting the party, throwing over Blaine and supporting Cleveland, he was subjected to plentiful insults. Nevertheless as the leader of the Mugwumps, preaching to a party-ridden generation the gospel of independency, he did his country a real service. He could not foresee, of course, how easily the menace of the independent voter was to be met; how through the control of both party machines and both nominees by the political bosses the independent would have only the choice betwixt tweedledum and tweedledee, and in disgust would largely refrain from voting. But the open and crying political evils of the Gilded Age he saw clearly, and in seeking to lessen them he proved himself a useful citizen as well as a cultivated American.

III

ENGLISH LIBERALISM AND POLITICS—GODKIN AND "THE NATION"

The severest critic of the Gilded Age was Edwin Lawrence Godkin, founder of the *Nation*. More caustic than George William Curtis, equipped with a complete social philosophy, and armed with

[16] See *Ibid.*, p. 160.   [17] J. H. Wilson, *The Life of Charles A. Dana*, p. 466.

perfect self-assurance, he devoted thirty-five years to the task of instructing America in the principles of government as those principles were understood by John Stuart Mill. He was at once an idealist and a realist, and the intellectual history of the critic is revealed in the shift from the one to the other. To Godkin the English liberal—who had studied the American experiment from overseas—as to Karl Schurz the German liberal, America was the torchbearer of the democratic faith; and any defection from the cause, any betrayal of that faith, was a desecration of the temple of liberalism by its own priesthood. Liberalism, he was persuaded, was the handmaid of civilization; the hope of any rational progress, rested on the principle of free inquiry and free endeavor. To Godkin, therefore, and to Schurz and the hundreds of European liberals who sought refuge here following the *débâcle* of the revolutionary hopes of 1848, it was a matter of deep import that America should remain true to its liberal tradition, trusting freedom, refusing to repeat the unhappy experience of a Tory Europe. He would say to America what John Wise had said nearly two centuries before: "Ye have been called unto liberty, therefore hold your hold, brethren! Pull up well upon the oars, you have a rich cargo, and I hope . . . day-light and good piloting will secure all." But he would do more than that; he would pull an oar himself; and with high hopes, at the age of twenty-five, he cast in his lot with America to serve the cause in whatever ways might offer.

Godkin came of an English Protestant strain that for seven centuries had lived in County Wexford, at the extreme southeastern point of Ireland. He was neither Scotch like the men of Ulster, nor Irish like his neighbors of Kilkenny and Wicklow, but as English in blood and temperament as Jonathan Swift. Educated at Queen's College, Belfast, he studied law for a time at Lincoln's Inn, went through the revolutionary years of 1848–1851 with their great hopes, and entered the field of journalism as correspondent for the London *Daily News* during the Crimean War. In 1856 he came to America with the intention of entering the law, but returned to journalism. During the Civil War he was correspondent for the *Daily News* of London, laboring to counteract British Tory opinion that ran strongly pro-South, and marshal the forces of English liberalism on the side of the North. Three months after Appomattox he founded the *Nation* as an organ of criticism, through the columns of which he proposed to appeal to the intelligence and the conscience of America in support of the principles of Victorian liberalism.

For this excellent work of criticism Godkin was provided with a sound equipment. Endowed with a vigorous intellect, he kept his mind free from shifting fogs and rarely mistook immediate for ultimate ends. His training had been in a distinguished tradition. His father was a Presbyterian minister and journalist, and the strain of robust dissent that contributed so richly to Victorian liberalism came to him as a birthright. He was "brought up," he said, "in the Mill-Grote school of radicals." "When I was in college," he wrote in later years, "I and the young men of my acquaintance were Liberals, in the English sense. John Stuart Mill was our prophet, and Grote and Bentham were our daily food." [18] Already his heart was overseas; America as it had been described by de Tocqueville was his "promised land," the home of a free democracy on which his hopes for civilization were fixed. His first book, written at the early age of twenty-two, was a history of the land Kossuth was striving to set free, and he there defined the word democrat as he had come to interpret it—the democrats, he said, are "all those whose hopes and sympathies are not bound up in a party or class, but look for the welfare and progress of humanity as the goal of their striving." [19]

Thus he wrote in the aftermath of the revolutionary years of 1848–1851. But the glowing idealism of the young radical was to suffer discouragements and setbacks from the experience of later years. One suspects that his liberalism never possessed the whole of him, never grew from within out, but was overlaid on a nature fundamentally aristocratic that at heart preferred Tory to liberal ends. Though as a young man he spred his canvas to the winds of liberalism, he was always a little distrustful of the bellying sails and he never quite liked the crew. There is a curious suggestiveness in his changing attitude towards England and English society. He had quitted the old world out of dislike for it, and a dozen years later he declined to go back except as a "last extremity." "It would be going back," he said, "into an atmosphere that I detest and a social system that I have hated since I was fourteen years old."[20] At the bottom of this repugnance was an obstinate pride. He was ambitious, capable, and sensitive, and a caste society that refused

[18] Ogden, *Life and Letters of Edwin Lawrence Godkin*, Vol. I, p. 11.
[19] *Ibid.*, Vol. I, p. 17.   [20] *Ibid.*, Vol. II, p. 140.

to open its doors to him he looked upon as pernicious. To assert that his espousal of democracy was due to his brusque rejection by a more distinguished mistress, is a severe judgment, yet it is a judgment that his friend Henry Holt quite frankly implied.[21]

He had come to America in the hope of getting on in the world. He had a strong regard for social position. His standards were severe and his sympathies so narrow as to lay him open to the frequent charge of snobbery. He would mingle in none but good society, and it was easier in America than in England to gain entrance to good society. Until he had made his mark he would not go back; but when as a distinguished editor he ventured to return, and found himself accepted by the best people, his hatred for the English social system oozed away, and the eager delight he experienced in upper-class society was an unconscious testimony to the value he had set upon a system from which as a young man he had been excluded. Godkin was too English to make himself over into an American, too natively aristocratic to be a democrat. A disciple of John Stuart Mill, he lacked the complete intellectual integrity of Mill that brushed aside all caste prejudices and personal ambitions, as he lacked his vast intellectual accumulation. Godkin's liberalism was founded on Mill, but it was never quite Mill.

The philosophy to which, as a disciple of the Bentham-Mill-Grote school, the young Godkin gave his allegiance, was a Utilitarian adaptation of *laissez faire*—the doctrine that the greatest happiness of the greatest number is the ultimate social objective, and that such objective can be attained only through the completest liberty under the sway of reason and justice. As presented by John Stuart Mill it was a singularly persuasive philosophy that awakened a response in every generous mind. Liberty, he insisted, is the thing chiefly to be desired, for where men are free they will shape social organisms to their needs. Man is both an economic and a political animal, and the difficult problem of the political philosopher is to keep the one from trespassing upon the rights of the other. The economic man, under the drive of the acquisitive instinct, regards the political state as an ally in the present business of acquisition; and the political man looks upon business as subject to strict regulation and control in the interests of the state. To prevent this meddlesome interference of each with the other, Mill laid down the principle of liberty in terms as uncompromising as

[21] *Nation*, July 8, 1915, p. 47.

those of the Physiocrats. The "sole end," he asserted, "for which mankind are warranted, individually or collectively, in interfering with the liberty of action of any of their number, is self-protection," and "the only purpose for which power can be rightfully exercised over any member of a civilized community, against his will, is to prevent harm to others. His own good, either physical or moral, is not a sufficient warrant." [22]

From this excellent school the young Godkin emerged a political theorist of no mean ability; somewhat too dogmatic, perhaps, a bit overconfident of the finality of his logic, but with a shrewd dialectic, quick to separate reality from pretense, severe upon all flummery and buncombe. That his philosophy was sharply opposed to the current tendencies of American political life he saw clearly: to Whiggery with its ambitious paternalisms; to centralization with its glorification of a Bismarckian state. His thought was erected on a foundation of *laissez faire*, and he sharply differentiated economics and politics. As a realist he recognized differences in individual capacity, but he was keenly suspicious of any attempt on the part of government to compensate for such differences. Any interference with natural law, he was convinced, entailed greater evils than benefits. Economic competition is a struggle between individuals, and government must content itself with its proper rôle of policeman to keep the peace. With Mill he refused to recognize the state as a separate entity. He never confused the personnel of government with "what is called 'the state'"; and as he contemplated the honesty and capacity of the several members who administered government in a given commonwealth, he was disinclined to entrust them with regulative powers. Disinterested honesty and capacity, it seemed, too rarely got into office, governments were too little acquainted with common morality, to justify hopes of equalizing the inequality of nature by political means.

To the sound philosophical equipment brought from England Godkin added a very considerable understanding of American political history. The ten years spent here before the founding of the *Nation*, had been employed in getting at home upon the new scene. He had carefully checked the findings of de Tocqueville and was convinced that the French critic had gone far astray in his interpretation of the great American experiment. In his analysis of democratic tendencies he had fallen into the fallacy of *post hoc*

[22] *On Liberty*, Chapter I.

ergo propter hoc, with the result that he had got the cart before the horse; and in an article published in the *North American Review* of January, 1865, Godkin entered the lists in defense of America against the criticisms of English Tories founded on such fallacies. In its emphasis on historical realism "Aristocratic Opinions of Democracy" is a surprisingly modern study that might almost have been written by one of our younger historians. It is an interpretation of our political development in terms of environment, and it traces the rise of democracy to the leveling influence of decentralization. For a hundred and fifty years, he pointed out, old-world habits and customs, the spirit of aristocracy, prevailed in the closely grouped settlements along the Atlantic seaboard, where physical conditions restrained the tendency to social disruption; but with the breaking through of the Appalachian barrier, and the influx of new waves of immigration, the conditions were prepared for a vast movement of decentralization. It was the Inland Empire that made possible the democratic revolution in America. "How was it," he asks, "that that democratic tide, which within the last fifty years, has overwhelmed everything, during the previous hundred and fifty years gave so few signs of rising?" And his reply to the question antedates Professor Turner's theory of the frontier by thirty years:

If we inquire what are those phenomena of American society which it is generally agreed distinguish it from that of older countries, we shall find . . . that by far the larger number of them may be attributed in a great measure to what, for want of a better name, we shall call "the frontier life" led by a large proportion of the inhabitants, and to the influence of this portion on manners and legislation, rather than to political institutions, or even to the equality of conditions. In fact, we think that these phenomena, and particularly those of them which excite most odium in Europe, instead of being the effect of democracy, are partly its cause, and that it has been to their agency more than aught else, that the democratic tide in America has owed most of its force and violence.

The agency which, in our opinion, gave democracy its first great impulse in the United States, which has promoted its spread ever since, and has contributed most powerfully to the production of those phenomena in American society which hostile critics set down as peculiarly democratic, was neither the origin of the Colonists, nor the circumstances under which they came to the country, nor their religious belief; but the great change in the distribution of the population, which began soon after the Revolution, and which continues its operation up to the present time.[23]

[23] "Aristocratic Opinions of Democracy," in *Problems of Modern Democracy,* pp. 25–26, 30–31.

Godkin was thirty-four when he entered upon his life work of pouring a stream of fresh and free thought upon the ways of the Gilded Age. It was somewhat in the spirit of Matthew Arnold that he interpreted the function of criticism. "The highest allegiance of every man," he wrote Norton in 1865, "is due to liberty and civilization, or rather civilization and liberty"; [24] and the creed of the *Nation*, which Godkin unconsciously modified as culture dispossessed liberty in his affections, may be summed up in the words democracy, individualism, morality, culture, to the end of a free life in a humane and well-ordered society. Throughout the Gilded Age this transplanted English liberal was the high priest of criticism in America. His caustic intelligence played ironically about the current shibboleths and fetishes, reducing them to shreds and patches. He could discover little that was good in the Gilded Age, in its tariffs and land grants, its *Crédit Mobilier* and other scandals, its buccaneer plutocracy, its undisciplined proletarianism, its bitter agrarianism; and he was prompted to a severity of judgment that easier-going natures thought harsh. Enemies sprang up in his every footprint; but too much was at stake, he believed, to temper his criticism to flabby minds, and he laid about him with what he considered a fine impartiality.

It was a cold plunge into a dirty pool, and a nature less robust would have scrambled out quickly. His realism was a profound discouragement to his idealism, and his native aristocracy of temperament closed his mind to the virtues of certain homely American liberalisms. As an intellectual he distrusted all Jacksonian frontier freedoms. The doctrine of liberty did not appear to advantage in the garb of agrarians and proletarians; Thaddeus Stevens and Terence V. Powderly were an ungainlier breed of libertarians than Gladstone and Mill; with such leadership it seemed to Godkin that liberty was running away with civilization and a smash-up was likely. It was the duty of the *Nation*, therefore, to arouse the culture of America to its political obligations, to the end that the custodianship of liberty should be taken over by the intelligence of America. It proved a discouraging job, and slowly on the horizon of his mind rose the shadow of the doubt that had troubled de Tocqueville and Cooper and Fisher Ames— must a democracy prove a leveling influence that destroys a fine individuality and a generous social culture? Careless of his trus-

[24] Ogden, *op. cit.*, Vol. II, p. 48.

teeship, was not the American democrat throwing his heritage to the demagogue and the spoilsman?

As he watched the scrambling heedlessness of the times his liberalism oozed away, his democratic faith lost its sanctions, and he slowly drifted to the right and the dead-sea of pessimism. The mass was too powerful in America, and the mass was shot through with the spirit of selfish leveling. The democracy had been distorted by the frontier, and the sense of responsibility, of individual duty, was well-nigh atrophied. The vulgar West threw its crudity upon all America. "I do not like the western type of man," Godkin confessed to Norton; and to another friend who praised California, he wrote, "No scenery or climate I had to share with western people would charm me." He never spared his mordant adjectives in commenting privately on all America west of the Hudson River. In his gloomy later years he found consolation in Brahmin culture. For years he lived in Cambridge, and in the company of Lowell and Norton he felt at home. Here were democratic gentlemen worthy of his ideal. If all America were only like Cambridge his faith in a cultivated liberalism would be justified. In those years he called himself "an American of the *vieille roche*," which being interpreted, meant a liberal of the Brahmin school.

The immediate problems on which Godkin was called to pass judgment brought him into the thick of the struggles of the Gilded Age. As an editor he confronted the bitter antagonisms that sprang from the rivalries of the farmer, the wage-earner, and the industrial capitalist. Each group was seeking to enlist government on its side and use the political state for special and narrow ends. To a disciple of Mill all such attempts were no better than treason to democracy, and when such treason was justified by what he considered specious economic theory Godkin's hostility was edged with acerbity. All the trenchant dogmas of his philosophy—his police theory of the state, his Ricardian *laissez faire*, his individualism—rushed to the attack of such impudent impostors. With no organized forces at his back he made war on every major group in America. He essayed to rally the scattered minority of the intellectuals and overthrow the citadel of economic power by appeal to reason. It was magnificent but it was scarcely war. The culture of the Gilded Age was undisciplined, lacking faith and unnurtured in philosophy, fastidious rather than vigorous—the poorest of material for shock troops. It applauded every clever thrust of its captain, but preferred to keep its own hands unsoiled. In consequence, to the end of his life Godkin was a leader without a following, little more than a voice crying in the wilderness.

For the rising plutocracy Godkin felt the scorn of a gentleman for the vulgar new-rich. Its hands were dirty, and it was soiling all American life. Its gospel of Whiggery, that under pretense of furthering prosperty had turned Congress into an auction room, was an insult to his Manchester liberalism. Just as surely as government meddles with subsidies and tariffs and grants, he pointed out, will it be defiled. Men are but indifferent honest, and if statesmen are not to become mere political hucksters they must stand apart from the temptations of business. The plea for a national economy had brought Congress to the *Crédit Mobilier* scandals, and it would breed other scandals so long as it was heeded. The only cure for Whiggery was to destroy it. In a scathing leader he early paid his respects to the Whiggish system of governmental subsidies:

The remedy is simple. The Government must get out of the "protective" business and the "subsidy" business and the "improvement" and the "development" business. It must let trade, and commerce, and manufactures, and steamboats, and railroads, and telegraphs alone. It cannot touch them without breeding corruption. We care nothing about the wonderful stories we hear about what can be achieved in the way of "promoting industry" by all these canal and steamboat and railroad schemes. Were the material prospect twice as tempting, the state could not profitably meddle with them, because neither it nor any other government in the world *can command the virtue necessary to carry them on.* This is not a matter of speculation; we know it as a matter of experience. It is almost as much as this Government can do to maintain order and administer justice. It may one day be able to do a great deal more, but not until a great change has occurred in the social condition of the country. We have gone far enough, heaven knows, on the road of "protection" and "promotion," and have found at every step that it leads straight to the bottomless pit; that for every hundred dollars voted by these poor men to whom we pay scanty wages for passing bills at Washington, we lessen, and perceptibly lessen, the stock of individual honor, of self-respect, and of public spirit, of a loyalty to ideals, to which far more than to any triumphs of material industry, we must look for continued national greatness. We are making money fast enough in all conscience; what needs fostering just now is honesty.[25]

Godkin found it exceedingly difficult to foster the austere honesty that he desired in the body politic, and in his fury at the

[25] *Nation,* January 30, 1873, p. 68.

common political scoundrelism he came to ascribe much of the
virus that was poisoning America to the party of western agrarians.
He was rapidly drifting to the right and the defense of capitalism,
and as the agrarian platform was slowly built up of successive
planks—greenbacks, free silver, subtreasuries, railway regulation,
the income tax—he turned upon it all the batteries of his wrath.
Godkin never understood the American farmer, but he professed
to understand economics and political science, and the agrarian
platform aroused his implacable hostility. In his frequent discussions of the currency question, a question that for thirty years
was a subject of passionate debate, he was at some disadvantage.
Intellectually he was ill equipped to deal with it. Although a
Ricardian he failed to grasp Ricardo's quantitative principle of
money or the function of paper currency. As a gold-standard
advocate he accepted the English monetary system as it was
given form by the Parliamentary Bank Act of 1844, and he would
have no tampering with it. To Godkin money was a measure of
value, and a fluctuating standard, implied in the quantitative
theory, was as immoral as a fluctuating yardstick. The use of
greenbacks—"rag money"—he reckoned a scheme by which dishonest debtors might cheat their creditors.[26] He was forced to regard gold and silver as commodities, fluctuating in price with
supply and demand; but he looked upon them as possessing a stable
natural value that placed them beyond political manipulation.
Any attempt to disturb this natural value by artificial means he
called dishonest.[27] He was almost indecent in the vehemence of
his adjectives applied to the "dishonest money men." He called
the Greenbackers "communists,"[28] and speaking of the Grangers,
he said, "There is nothing unnatural or deplorable in a Granger
turning from one form of swindle to another."[29]

By the middle nineties it was hard to distinguish Godkin's views
on the agrarian program from those of a Wall Street banker. In
discussing free silver he abandoned economic principles and fell
to mouthing like any newspaper writer. The currency question
he regarded as a simple question of public morality. There was
only one issue, the issue between honest and dishonest money.

[26] See "Public Opinion and the Currency," *Ibid.*, February 27, 1873; "The Political Situation in 1896," in *Problems of Modern Democracy*.
[27] See "On Gold and Silver," *Ibid.*, July 6, 1876.
[28] *Ibid.*, May 25, 1876.
[29] *Ibid.*, June 1, 1876.

"The demand for free-silver coinage is a demand for a division of property," [30] he said in the early days of the campaign of 1896, and a fortnight later he took extreme ground:

. . . the bold and wicked scheme of repudiation . . . is presented without a blush in the platform. Upon this question the campaign must be fought. If the party of repudiators cannot be put down, the republic cannot be preserved and is not worth preserving. [31]

Such pronouncements bear none of the earmarks of dispassionate criticism. It may seem severe to suggest that they are the comments of a very ignorant or shallow critic, blinded by his prejudices; yet it is true. The equipment of Manchester economics with which he had outfitted himself in the late forties, was no longer adequate in the nineties; yet he seems not to have been aware of the fact. The mid-Victorian still regarded himself as an authority on all economic questions, although he seems to have done no serious reading in economic theory for half a century, and was scarcely conscious how far he had drifted towards the right. The old liberal was fighting the battles of capitalism with weapons as antiquated as the old cap-and-ball musket. "The great trouble with all silverites and currency lunatics, North and South," he said, "is that, when monetary crises arise, they cannot be got to go to the right quarter for information"—a comment that one might retort upon Godkin himself. The intellectual knew far less about money than "Coin" Harvey, whom he would have laughed at.

The same drift to the right is evident in the pronouncements on the Populist movement of the times. Writing on "The Kansas Situation," when the farmers' unrest was becoming militant, he remarked:

Such an unexpected outbreak as this of the last two or three years shows at least that it is not only in the cities, where the foreign-born swarm, that demagogues may thrive and the doctrine of revolution be preached. [32]

The "ravings of the Farmers' movement" he regarded as no more than a "vague and visionary discontent," that was seeking political cures for its economic ills. The hard times from which the West was suffering were the result of economic law. It was not the currency or excessive railway rates that were the cause. The vast

[30] "The Issue of the Campaign," *Ibid.*, July 2, 1896.
[31] "The Platform of Revolution," *Ibid.*, July 16, 1896.
[32] *Ibid.*, January 19, 1893.

extension of railway systems had brought under cultivation too many acres, and the reduction of transportation costs would serve only to bring additional acres under cultivation, thereby increasing competition and forcing prices still lower. High railway rates were the surest safeguard against further extension of an industry much overdeveloped; and for state legislatures to attempt to fix railway tariffs by law—to attempt to control economic forces by statutes—was sheer folly. In discussing the celebrated Illinois railway legislation Godkin spoke in defense of the roads:

> The locomotive is coming in contact with the framework of our institutions. In this country of simple government, the most powerful centralizing force which civilization has yet produced has within the next score years, yet to assume its relation to that political machinery which is to control and regulate it. . . . The corporations of course contested the validity of the law. If the legislature could establish one rate at which they should do the work of transportation, it could establish another. They were fighting for their lives and property; it was against taxation without representation. . . . An arbitrary power is claimed in the supreme legislative body to decide on the reasonable rates of the cost of private services. Just as three hundred years ago the price of bread and labor was regulated by act of Parliament, so now the cost of transportation is to be fixed by a jury of twelve men. . . . Thus far, therefore, the results of the Illinois railroad war must be regarded as rather portentous than satisfactory.[33]

The "watered-stock hallucination," that had taken possession of the agrarian mind and aroused such bitterness, he dismissed with a curious comment that did no great credit to his intelligence.

> There is . . . one difficulty in the way, which is the difficulty common to many of the proposed reforms in railroad management—the practice alleged has absolutely no existence except in the heated brain of the agitators who have imagined it. There are no roads in the United States on which any attempt has been made to increase the freight earnings in proportion to the watered stock or debt.[34]

The passions aroused by the campaign of '96 swept Godkin from his moorings and left him adrift. He quickly convinced himself that the real issue at stake was the moral integrity of the nation. As he studied the platforms and leaders he found little comfort in either. For McKinley he had the contempt of the intellectual for a purveyor of heavy platitudes, and he flayed him in a two-

[33] *Ibid.*, April 10, 1873.
[34] "The Watered Stock Hallucination," *Ibid.*, October 9, 1873.

column leader with his old skill.[35] But for Bryan, the "boy orator of the Platte," his dislike passed the bounds of decency; and for the Chicago convention that put him in nomination—"the roaring mob" with its "Populistic, anarchistic platform"—his contempt outran his command of invective.

> No such collection of inflammatory and reckless men ever put themselves on exhibition in a national convention. Beside them the Populists are lamb-like, and the socialists sucking doves. The country has watched their mad proceedings with disgust and shuddering, only impatient for the coming of November to stamp out them and their incendiary doctrines.[37]

To what lengths his overheated brain carried him in those political dogdays, how starkly reactionary he had become, is suggested by his comment on the plank in the Democratic platform attacking the scandal of injunctions:

> This blow at the courts shows how true are the instincts of the revolutionaries. They know their most formidable enemies. Judicial decisions have again and again drawn the fangs of confiscatory and revolutionary legislation, and the courts have come more and more to stand as the great bulwarks of property and personal rights.[37]

Godkin's last years were not happy. The wave of imperialism that swept over England and America, with its Boer War and Spanish War, brought him acute concern. The world that he knew was slipping from its moorings, and he was fearful of the seas into which it was plunging. The conquest of the Philippines seemed to him a badge of national degradation. Writing in November, 1899, he said:

> We are dragging wearily in the old way, killing half a dozen Filipinos every week, and continually "near the end." The folly of ignorance and rascality we are displaying in the attempt to conquer and have "subjects" would disgrace a trades union.[38]

As he watched the tedious process of subjugation he inclined to attribute to Kipling a large share of the current imperialism. "I think most of the current jingoism on both sides of the water is due to him," he wrote a few weeks later. "He is the poet of the barrack-room cads," a "most pernicious, vulgar person"; and his

[35] "Prosperity's Advance Orator," *Ibid.*, June 18, 1896.
[36] "The Chicago Platform," *Ibid.*, July 16, 1896.
[37] "The Platform of Revolution," *Ibid.*, July 23, 1896.
[38] Ogden, *op. cit.*, Vol. II, pp. 238–239.

"White Man's Burden," cabled to America and printed on the
front pages of the newspapers as a message to imperialist America,
must have rubbed across Godkin's raw nerves. The pious cant
of Kipling's imperialism was a bitter cup for a disillusioned liberal.
The Jubilee with its fulsome laudation of "fat, useless royalty,"
was fittingly commemorated by this noisy poet of imperialism,
and Godkin turned away from it all in disgust.

But turn where he might he found no comfort. His old dreams
of a free and enlightened democracy rising in America, were dead.
Victorian liberalism had been laid away in the grave of John Stuart
Mill, and only its ghost was walking in these latter times. Godkin's
last days were bitter, and the gloom that was settling upon him
crept into his letters. It is a malady common amongst liberals, and
how deeply it had struck in is revealed in such passages as these:

> I am not sanguine about the future of democracy. I think we shall have
> a long period of decline . . . and then a recrudescence under some other
> form of society.[39]
> I do not know what the future of our modern civilization is to be. But
> I stumble where I firmly trod.[40]
> Things look very black. I think that while money-making will long
> continue on a great scale, the government will shortly undergo great
> changes which will be presided over not by men of light and learning, but
> by capitalists and adroit politicians.[41]
> I came here fifty years ago with high and fond ideals about America.
> . . . They are now all shattered, and I have apparently to look elsewhere
> to keep even moderate hopes about the human race alive.[42]

The idealist is prone to be exigent in his demands upon civilization. He marks out a straight path to the goal of his hopes, and
takes it greatly to heart when society chooses to follow other ways
to other ends. Godkin's mind was keenly critical, but his sympathies were narrow and his prejudices great. It is well to be a friend
to civilization, but it is foolish to set up as a custodian; for civilization, like Topsy, will shift for itself. A just and liberal government
is an excellent ideal, but it is one for which few amongst the mass
of men greatly care; and because America chose to follow its own
nose, because it would not become like the America of his dreams,
Godkin allowed his heart to fill with bitterness. It is true that his
recompense for long years of labor was scanty; the Gilded Age

[39] *Ibid.*, Vol. II, p. 199.
[40] *Ibid.*, Vol. II, p. 217.
[41] *Ibid.*, Vol. II, p. 243.
[42] *Ibid.*, Vol. II, p. 237.

was not to be frightened from its fleshpots by his warnings. But
long ago it was said, "Wisdom crieth in the streets and no man
regardeth her," and why should Godkin have become discouraged
with civilization because certain blackguard years clove to their
blackguardry, instead of mounting to the somewhat arid heights
he pointed out? One must choose at the last between tolerance
and pessimism, and Godkin chose pessimism.

It is difficult today to understand his great influence with cultivated readers of his generation. In part perhaps it was due to
his crisp assurance. He put things so plumply, he wrote so brilliantly, that his readers were persuaded he must think as neatly.
Yet his trenchant prose style cannot hide a certain slightness of
matter. His later comments tended to become ever thinner and
shriller—not criticism at all, but the sharp expression of aging
prejudice. When he talked about the tariff he had Mill at his
elbow; but when he talked about the agrarian or the proletarian
movements he was little more than a blue-jay scolding at a world
he disliked. Unlike his great master he did not go forward to meet
new times; he did not reinterpret Victorian liberalism in the light
of the lessons taught by the Industrial Revolution; but by standing
still he did liberalism a real disservice.

IV

FICTION CONSIDERS THE STATE OF THE COUNTRY

It was only a question of time before the novel would throw off
the inhibitions of the genteel and turn to consider the state of the
country. A changing social order would not fail of reflection in the
pages of fiction, and as the novelists fell to scrutinizing the familiar
scene, comparing the reality with the patriotic professions, it was
certain that the workings of democracy would come in for sharp
criticism. In the last decades of the century the problem novel
spread swiftly, expanding the field of its inquiry, and seeking to
understand the new ways. Making its first essays in the familiar
field of the political, it soon turned to consider the economic problems arising out of the new industrialism, espousing either capitalism or labor as the social sympathies of the author might determine. The class passions of the times found a reflection in its
pages, and in consequence the sociological novel became increasingly a repository of the social ideas of a perplexed and troubled
generation.

I

THE POLITICAL NOVEL

Of the early political novels three are of sufficient interest to reward attention: *The Gilded Age* (1873), *Democracy* (1881), and *An American Politician* (1884). The first, written by Mark Twain in collaboration with Charles Dudley Warner, is a satire of Gilded Age ways with particular attention to the political corruption of General Grant's administration. The fictional disguise is slight. The actual Washington is presented vividly and familiar figures —Ben Butler, Oakes Ames, President Grant, Secretary Boutwell —move through the scene. The central figure, Senator Dillworthy, was modeled upon Senator Pomeroy of Kansas, who had recently lost a reëlection through an unlucky exposure of an attempt to bribe the Kansas legislature. The heroine, Laura Hawkins, is a western lobbyist who in order to put through a congressional steal under pretense of providing an industrial school for the freedmen, twists Congressmen about her fingers, turns adventuress and ends in tragedy. Out of the West comes the spirit of corruption that the respectable East is unable to withstand, until the itch of speculation infects the whole country. It is Colonel Sellers who embodies the slackness of frontier political morals, that in turn vitiates his political principles. The genial Colonel is quite frankly a Greenbacker.

The country is getting along very well, [he said] but our public men are too timid. What we want is more money. I've told Boutwell so. Talk of basing the currency on gold; you might as well base it on pork. Gold is only one product. Base it on everything! You've got to do something for the West. How am I to move my crops? We must have improvements. Grant's got the idea. We want a canal from the James River to the Mississippi. Government ought to build it.[43]

The analysis is not penetrating. The real sources of political corruption—the rapacious railway lobbyists that camped in brigades about the capitol building—are passed over, and attention is fastened on small steals—the Knobs University bill and the Columbus River Navigation scheme—that do not touch the real rascals of the day. The implication is unmistakable that the source of corruption is the Jacksonian West with its heritage of the spoils spirit. The Federalistic East is victimized by the rapacities

[43] Vol. II, Chapter 13, p. 128.

of mid-western politicians with their religious cant, their talk of
the rights of the people and the greatness of the plain democracy.
Senator Dillworthy is fairly unctuous in his oily Christian spirit,
and Brother Balaam is his fellow. The portraits, one suspects,
need not be taken seriously as pictures of the chief apostles of
preëmption and exploitation. To have sketched the real leaders of
the great barbecue might have involved too many unpleasantries.

Democracy, written seven years later, is an inferior book in every
way, less penetrating, less amusing, less creative. To essay to penetrate the dark places of political jobbery through the eyes of a
society woman, too high-bred to turn lobbyist and inveigle secrets
out of ambitious politicians, is sufficiently absurd, yet not un-
characteristic of the Henry Adams whose home was a distinguished
salon and who in pottering about the political world of Washington
deceived himself in thinking he had his finger on the web of intrigue. It is an amazing book for such a man to write. The attitude
is that of the kid-gloved reformer who goes in for civil service reform, and who views the uncultivated West as the source of all
political corruption. The hero, Senator Silas Ratcliffe of Peoria,
Illinois, like Senator Dillworthy, is a past master in political
organization who covers his dishonesty with religious cant. The
economic sources of political corruption are ignored, and the
evil is traced to the principle of democracy. Whatever political
convictions are in the book are expressed by Representative Gore,
a civil service reformer from Massachusetts, and quite evidently
Henry Adams himself; and the conclusion is thus set forth:

"Do you yourself think democracy the best government, and universal
suffrage a success?"

Mr. Gore saw himself pinned to the wall, and he turned at bay with almost the energy of despair:

"These are matters about which I rarely talk in society. . . . But
since you ask for my political creed, you shall have it. I only condition
that it shall be for you alone, never to be repeated or quoted as mine. I
believe in democracy. I accept it. I will faithfully serve and defend it.
I believe in it because it appears to me the inevitable consequence of what
has gone before it. Democracy asserts the fact that the masses are now
raised to a higher intelligence than formerly. All our civilization aims at
this mark. We want to do what we can to help it. I myself want to see
the result. I grant it is an experiment, but it is the only direction society
can take that is worth its taking; the only conception of its duty large
enough to satisfy its instincts; the only result that is worth an effort or a
risk. Every other step is backward, and I do not want to repeat the past.

I am glad to see society grapple with issues in which no one can afford to be neutral."

"And supposing your experiment fails," said Mrs. Lee; "suppose society destroys itself with universal suffrage, corruption, and communism."

". . . I have faith; not perhaps in the old dogmas, but in the new ones. . . . faith in science; faith in the survival of the fittest. Let us be true to our time, Mrs. Lee! If our age is to be beaten, let us die in the ranks. If it is to be victorious, let us be first to lead the column. Anyway, let us not be skulkers or grumblers. There! have I repeated my catechism correctly? You would have it! Now oblige me by forgetting it. I should lose my character at home if it got out."[44]

And the conclusion of the matter is thus summed up:

"I want to go to Egypt," said Madelaine, still smiling faintly; "democracy has shaken my nerves to pieces. Oh, what rest it would be to live in the Great Pyramid and look out forever at the polar star!"

Not a hint of the Industrial Revolution; not a hint of the sordid Whiggery that was fouling American politics; not a suggestion of any creative social philosophy on which to establish an adequate theory of democracy. A dreary place at best, with no faith in human nature and no trust in democratic machinery, but only a gentlemanly belief that an antiquated Federalism may somehow pull this venture in republicanism out of the bog in which Jacksonianism had mired it. No wonder Henry Adams would not set his name on the title-page, but left it an orphan to make its own way in the world. In his life of John Hay, William Roscoe Thayer has explained the situation thus:

The Adamses, the Hays, and Clarence King formed an inner circle, which somebody named "The Five of Hearts," and out of this came, in 1882, a novel entitled *Democracy*, a strikingly clever satire on Washington society. Its authorship was at once attributed to them, but one after another denied it. If it was a joint product no individual could monopolize the credit; and as it seems to have been read chapter by chapter to the group, and discussed by them all, it might be said, technically, to be a composite. Clarence King is still commonly regarded as its author; and there are many supporters of Hay; but I believe that only Mr. Adams possessed the substance, and style, and the gift of Voltairean raillery which distinguish it.[45]

Mr. Thayer is generous in his praise.

An American Politician is even less consequential as a political study than *Democracy*. Marion Crawford was a professional ro-

[44] Chapter 4, p. 78.   [45] Vol. II, pp. 58–59.

mancer and in this naïve venture into a field little known to him he
carried his complete romantic kit. The political theme is tied about
with so many love strands as almost to strangle it. The hero, John
Harrington, we are assured is a very remarkable man, a Bostonian
with a Mayflower teapot in his family treasures, an idealist of
primitive Puritan intensity. But we must take him upon hearsay.
Nothing that he does or says suggests his greatness. Politically the
book is reduced to a little glimpse of the methods of selecting a
United States senator—an Irish ward boss with twenty votes in his
belt, a gentlemanly railway attorney who handles offal skillfully
with a handkerchief at his nose—set in between two set speeches by
the hero. The rest is Newport and the Back Bay, not quite stupid
yet with no distinction. The romancer does not move easily in an
unfamiliar field, and he sends his hero forth to battle for righteousness with small intellectual equipment. His speeches are heavily
oratorical and his political philosophy is naïve; it is pretty much
George William Curtis, the sufficiency of civil service reform and
the virtues of non-partisanship.

The unreality of the book is furthered by a conception worthy of
Poe—a mysterious council of three that meets in London and
directs political movements in America. We are dimly aware that
the council is both ancient and honorable; that it goes back historically to post-Revolutionary days and is self-perpetuating; and
its uncanny power has resulted from supreme intelligence supplemented by exact information gathered during many years. In its
secret archives every public man in America is tagged and docketed;
his political and financial affiliations are set down in detail; and on
the basis of this knowledge the cryptic three send forth instructions
that are faithfully carried out. The danger to America lies in sectionalism—North, South, and West struggling for supremacy in
the national councils; and upon the three rests the self-imposed
responsibility of saving America from itself. The idea is sufficiently
absurd, as the book is absurd. Crawford was a cosmopolitan who
knew little about American political conditions, and the crisis of the
novel is the Hayes-Tilden *impasse* of 1876. The influence of the
novel, one may safely assume, was negligible.*

* In his original scheme Professor Parrington included Tourgée's *A Fool's Errand,*
but the text shows that he decided against its inclusion.—*Publisher.*

2

THE ECONOMIC NOVEL

The theme of these earlier novels was politics as revealed by the Gilded Age; on the other hand *The Bread-winners* was one of the early economic novels. Like *Democracy* it was an outcome of the discussions of the vivacious trio, John Hay, Clarence King, and Henry Adams. Written in 1882 by Hay, it was published anonymously in the *Century Magazine* from August, 1883, to January, 1884. Hay never publicly acknowledged the authorship, and it was not until the edition of 1915 appeared with an introductory note by his son, that his name appeared on the title-page. It achieved a notable success—far beyond that of *Democracy;* was warmly praised and sharply criticized; was replied to in other novels; all of which goes to show that it fanned the coals that were smoldering in the industrial life of the day, threatening a general conflagration. It was the first recognition on the part of literature that a class struggle impended in America—a first girding of the loins of polite letters to put down the menace that looked out from the underworld of the proletariat; and as such it assumes importance as an historical document quite beyond its significance as a work of art.

The motive of *The Bread-winners* is the defense of property against the "dangerous classes"; its immediate theme is a satire of labor unions. In an introductory note to the later edition, Clarence Leonard Hay explicitly denies this. "*The Bread-winners*," he says, "is not directed against organized labor. It is rather a protest against the disorganization and demoralization of labor by unscrupulous leaders and politicians who, in the guise of helping the workingman, use his earnings to enrich themselves." He then states the theme thus:

> It is a defense of the right of an individual to hold property, and a plea for the better protection of that property by law and order. Civilization rests upon law, order, and obedience. The agitator who preaches that obedience to lawful authority is a sin, and patriotism an illusion, is more dangerous to society than the thief who breaks in at night and robs the householder.

The editor thinks well of the American workingmen. At heart they are sound; their motives are honest; but their ignorance of fundamental economic principles too easily suffers them to fall victim to unscrupulous demagogues whose only object is their exploitation. To prevent such "disorganization and demoralization of labor," which can bring only suffering and failure upon men ill prepared to endure them, is therefore the patriotic duty of the educated classes. The proletariat is groping blindly for leadership; it is stirring uneasily; if the educated classes do not offer an enlightened leadership, the laborer will follow low cunning to immoral ends and blind leaders of the blind will bring irretrievable disaster upon civilization. Selfish appeal will kindle envy and hate; the rich and prosperous will go down before brute force; the rights of property will be destroyed; law, order, and obedience will give place to anarchy.

Such, briefly developed, is Clarence Hay's exposition of *The Bread-winners;* and the exposition seems to suggest the social views of John Hay. He probably had no antipathy to labor unions which are guided in their policy by "sound economic principles" and right "morality"—as the capitalist understands such things. But labor unions which follow their own leaders, which persist in thinking out a proletarian economy, which are bent on substituting a social morality for a property morality, which refuse to be led by the "educated classes," he was bitterly hostile to. It is the unrest furthered by rebellious labor unions that he fears, and it is this that gives point and animus to his satire. That *The Bread-winners* was conceived in a spirit of beneficent paternalism towards the proletariat, the present-day reader will have difficulty in discovering. It is too frank in defense of vested interests, it looks with too stern a disfavor upon all labor leaders who refuse to accept the finality of the present industrial order, it exudes too strong an odor of property-morality, to deceive an intelligent reader. Read today it is clearly a partisan defense of economic individualism, an attack upon the rising labor movement, a grotesque satire smeared with an unctuous morality—and because of this, a perfect expression of the spirit of upper-class America in those uneasy eighties with their strikes and lockouts and Haymarket riots.

The plot of the book is slight—it is the story of the oily machinations of Ananias Offitt, a professional agitator who lives off simple honest workmen whom he seduces, organizes a secret Brotherhood of the Breadwinners, urges on riot and robbery at the time of a great strike, is checkmated by the hero—a cultivated and elegant clubman by the name of Captain Arthur Farnham—betrays his tool, and in the end is murdered by him. Fortunately for the welfare of property interests there are "honest" workmen, men like Leopold Grosshammer, who rally to the support of law and order and eventually break the strike. The love-story is provided with two heroines, and the contrast between them emphasizes the class line which property draws. The upper-class heroine is as correct and colorless as Cooper's Eve Effingham: the lower-class heroine is as vulgarly handsome and as brazen as "such people" are supposed to be. A high-school education has spoilt her for the factory or domestic service, filling her empty head with foolish ambitions, but it could not make a lady of her.

Hay was in Cleveland at the time of the great strike in 1877, and he was profoundly disturbed by the experience. Writing to his father-in-law, he said:

> The prospects of labor and capital both seem gloomy enough. The very devil seems to have entered into the lower classes of workingmen, and there are plenty of scoundrels to encourage them to all lengths. . . . I am thankful you did not *see* and *hear* what took place during the strikes. You were saved a very painful experience of human folly and weakness, as well as crime.[46]

The crying evils of a buccaneer industrialism which lay behind the strikes, Hay ignored completely. To provide his idyllic background of contented labor before it is seduced by demagogues, he goes back to a decadent domestic economy. His "honest and contented workman" is a carpenter who works for another carpenter—not a factory-hand tending a machine; and when the demagogue comes with his specious appeal he is triumphantly refuted.

> "What are we, anyhow?" continued the greasy apostle of labor. "We are slaves; we are Roossian scurfs. We work as many hours as our owners like; we take what pay they choose to give us; we ask their permission to live and breathe."
> "Oh, that's a lie," Sleeny interrupted, with unbroken calmness. "Old Saul Matchin and me come to an agreement about time and pay, and both of us was suited. Ef he's got his heel onto me, I don't feel it."[47]

John Hay was convinced that an "educated leadership" alone could save American democracy. But unfortunately—despite his great reputation in diplomacy and statesmanship—his own education seems to have been faulty. He had lately risen into the exploiting class, and he accepted the ready-made opinions of that

[46] William Roscoe Thayer, *Life and Letters of John Hay*, Vol. II, pp. 5–6.
[47] Chapter V

class. His biographer has admirably stated his position during the days of the strike riots when he was clarifying his views:

> Those riots of 1877 burnt deep into Colonel Hay's heart. Like the rest of the world, he had theorized on the likelihood of war between Capital and Labor; but he had reassured himself by the comfortable assumption that under American conditions—equal opportunity for all, high wages, equal laws, and the ballot-box—no angry laboring class could grow up. The riots blew such vaporing away: for they proved that the angry class already existed, that the ballot-box instead of weakening strengthened it, and that not only the politicians of both parties but also the constituted authorities would avoid, as long as possible, grappling with it.
>
> The event was too large to be dismissed as an outburst of temper: it must be accepted as a symptom, a portent. Did it mean that a cancer had attacked the body politic and would spread to the vital organs? Was Democracy a failure,—Democracy—for more than a century the dream of the down-trodden, the ideal of those who loved mankind and believed in its perfectibility, the Utopia which good men predicted should somehow turn out to be a reality? Hay had sung his paean to liberty; Hay had throbbed at the efforts of patriots in Spain and in France to overthrow their despots; he had even exulted over the signs of democratization in England. Had he been the victim of mirage? Was Democracy not the final goal of human society, but only a half-way stage between the despotism of Autocracy and the despotism of Socialism?
>
> These questions he could not evade. . . . But he held, as did many of his contemporaries, that the assaults on Property were inspired by demagogues who used as their tools the loafers, the criminals, the vicious,—Society's dregs who have been ready at all times to rise against laws and government. That you have property is proof of industry and foresight on your part or your father's; that you have nothing, is a judgment on your laziness and vices, or on your improvidence. The world is a moral world; which it would not be if virtue and vice received the same rewards.[48]

John Hay, it must be recalled, had enjoyed a college education through the aid of relatives, he had been taken under the wing of Lincoln and become his private secretary, he had been thrust forward by influential politicians, and finally he had married wealth—were these things proofs of virtue in a moral world that rewards foresight and punishes improvidence? Or were they rather the marks of a skillful climber? John Hay was a charming and cultivated gentleman, but he was also a child of the Gilded Age, with the materialisms of his generation in his blood. The young man had been an Abolitionist and a political radical; the old man was a McKinley conservative whose chief claim to reputation lay in

[48] Thayer, *op. cit.*, Vol. I. pp. 6–7.

the "open-door" policy in China. The beginnings of this shift to conservatism seem to have coincided with his marriage to Miss Stone, daughter of a Cleveland capitalist whose interests were threatened by the great strike. He was temperamentally one of John Adams's "natural aristocrats," and having gained entrée into aristocratic circles he took the coloring of his new environment. A son of the frontier, he became a man of the world. Prosperity was necessary to him.

Professing a deep attachment to democratic institutions and hatred of all monarchical principles—in Spain and France—John Hay ceased to be a Lincoln democrat, and took his place amongst the ruling class, accepting the principles of the rising plutocracy. *The Bread-winners* is a dramatization of the Federalistic principle that government exists for the protection of property. "Remembering the date when *The Bread-winners* was written," says his biographer, "we must regard it as the first important polemic in American fiction in defense of Property." [49] John Hay had become a thoroughgoing Hamiltonian. In his younger days his sympathies had gone out to radical republicans everywhere, and he watched the rising tide of liberalism with great satisfaction. In his first visits to Europe he followed closely the liberal movements. He was a warm admirer of Castelar, eulogizing him as one of the heroic figures of modern times. In a lecture in 1869 on "The Progress of Democracy in Europe" he spoke with the zeal of an advanced liberal. But soon thereafter the ardor of his zeal lessened. On later trips to Europe he did not display a like sympathy with the program of the Social Democrats. As economic unrest crept into politics, as strikes and boycotts began to disturb his father-in-law's business, he discovered less sympathy for revolutionary movements. Political revolutions sponsored by respectable middle-class leaders, were one thing; economic revolutions sponsored by the proletariat were quite another thing. A democracy that breeds more democracy is clearly dangerous. So much as has already been accomplished is excellent, of course; but nothing further must be attempted.

There is sound strategy in offensive epithets. And so, taking counsel of fear, he applied to the current economic unrest the words most offensive to polite American ears, and called it socialism, anarchism. Without pausing to weigh the demands of the farmer

[49] *Ibid.*, Vol. II, p. 15.

and the workingman, with no understanding of the meaning of the great proletarian movement then going forward in Europe, he appealed in defense of property to the specter of economic leveling before which every good American of the eighties recoiled in horror. As early as 1869, speaking of Castelar, he said: "He has too much sense and integrity to follow the lead of the Socialist fanatics."[50] Commenting on the unsettled state of things in Paris in 1883, he wrote: "The laborers have had the mischief put into their heads by trade-unions."[51] As he contemplated the agrarian unrest of the seventies and later, he discovered in Greenbackism and Populism only another form of this hateful socialism. It was the work of agitators who were plain rascals.

He was greatly disturbed in 1875 at the state of politics, "with half the Republicans and all the Democrats inflationists at heart, and carrying on a campaign on the bald issue whether the nation shall be a liar and a thief or not."[52] And so late as 1900 he exclaimed petulantly: "This last month of Bryan, roaring out his desperate appeals to hate and envy, is having its effect on the dangerous classes. Nothing so monstrous has as yet been seen in our history."[53] Unhappily even in free America with its equal opportunity, and equal laws, there had come to be "dangerous classes"—rather a good many of them, taking the populistic farmers and discontented wage-earners into the account—so many, indeed, that John Hay grew gloomy over the outlook. And the outlook was all the gloomier because of our form of government; for is not the ultimate test of our democratic institutions the test of whether they are adequate to protect the property and "civilization" of the few against the "hate and envy" of the discontented many?

That *The Bread-winners* was a dishonest book Hay certainly could not have been brought to believe; nevertheless a Tory who covers his Tory purpose with a mantle of democracy can scarcely be reckoned intellectually sincere. The men of the seventies and eighties—cultivated and intelligent gentlemen like Godkin and Aldrich and Hay—were little more than demagogues in their fustian attacks on agrarian Greenbackers and militant labor unions; they feared and hated them too much to understand them, and they took advantage of their social position to cry them down. The "educated leadership" of the Gilded Age was a somewhat

[50] *Ibid.*, Vol. I, p. 321.
[51] *Ibid.*, p. 414.
[52] *Ibid.*, p. 426.
[53] *Ibid.*, Vol. II, p. 256.

sorry thing; it was ethically bankrupt while appealing to high moral standards. The best of such leaders were second-rate men—mediocre minds cramped by a selfish environment, imbued with no more than a property-consciousness. Of such a world John Hay in his *Bread-winners* was a distinguished spokesman and representative.*

3

THE BEGINNINGS OF THE SOCIOLOGICAL NOVEL

It was in the nineties that the sociological novel expanded into a great movement that in the next decade and a half was to engulf pretty much all American fiction and bring it into service to the social conscience. Such a development was in the nature of things. The artist would not sit forever in his ivory tower, content to carve his statuettes while the country without was turmoiled with revolution. Sooner or later he would venture forth and once he had been caught up in the swirl his art would take new forms and serve other purposes than the traditional genteel. Realism was in the air, the realism of Zola and the Russians, and from such a realism would come in America a more critical attitude towards the social revolution at work in the land.

It was the city that played havoc with our older fictional methods, as it played havoc with our traditional social philosophy. America was late in discovering the import of the huge Babbitt warrens it had been building with such fierce energy; but slowly the realities of the economic city rose to challenge the respectability of the romantic city. It was the discovery of this new lair of business that created the school of sociological fiction. The older city of literature had been a polite world wherein ladies and gentlemen drank tea and made love and talked proper scandal—a pleasant background of clubs and drawing-rooms, against which moved well-dressed figures. It was an echo of Thackeray—the world of the West End and Beacon Street and Fifth Avenue, too well-bred and prosperous to recognize slums or stockyards or stock-gambling. But with the nineties the old complacency was disturbed. A note of unrest crept into the current fiction. As the *protégés* of Mr. Howells looked out upon their world in search of reality, they discovered that polite society was being undermined. Too many

* In his plan Professor Parrington included here H. F. Keenan's *The Money-Makers,* but apparently he decided against its inclusion.—*Publisher.*

social climbers were thrusting themselves forward; too much vulgarity was displayed by the new-rich. The social primacy of the
old families was being challenged by western pork-packers. Here
was a rich field to harvest. *Le document humain* was the latest cry
of realism, and so under the inspiration of M. Paul Bourget a new
crop of realism came to fruit—clever studies in feminine psychology—the last word in contemporary reality. The social climber
was analyzed mercilessly, her shallow and silly ambitions revealed
to the least petty maneuver; her blighting influence upon an
idealistic husband or her stimulus to a money-grabbing mate, is
traced shrewdly. Such are Boyesen's *Mammon of Unrighteousness*,
Robert Grant's *Unleavened Bread*, and Edith Wharton's *House of
Mirth*—studies that were symptomatic of a generation disturbed by
the consciousness of a vulgar plutocracy rising in its midst, and yet
ignorant of the nature of the disease.

Nevertheless their vogue was brief. As economic unrest rose
more menacingly upon the horizon of the new century, realism
quickly tired of its Kate Van Schaaks and Selma Whites and Lily
Barts, and turned away to prospect for a richer vein. Psychology
was losing its fascination and social analysis was supplying a new
inspiration; M. Bourget was yielding authority to Emile Zola. Even
so whole-hearted a romantic as Mary Johnston was to turn from
tales like *To Have and to Hold* to write *Hagar*, a novel of suffrage
propaganda. There was to be not less realism but more. The
change may be summarized in the word *background*. The old
individualism had unconsciously insulated its hero from economic
contacts; he moved in a polite environment detached from the
larger play of social forces. An individualism so wanting in sociological verity could make scant appeal to the new spirit of sociology.
That old world is dead. With the rise of the philosophy of determinism came another mood. To the realism of environment that
conceived of the individual as a pawn on the chessboard of society,
M. Zola had given the name *naturalism*. It was realism wedded to
a deterministic sociology—the first reaction of a generation awakening to the subjugating power of the mass, and bent on studying the
resultant phenomena in the clear light of science. The change was
no less than revolutionary. The new school thought in terms of
group and class and movement, rather than in terms of individuals
each nursing his petty hopes and fears. The individual counts for so
little in the enveloping stream of social tendency. Let us have no

more shoddy heroes, foolish little egoisms in an unreal world; but figures of men and women, encompassed by the great stream, carried along on a resistless current. If they prove to be little better than puppets the novelist is not to blame, but society that reduces them to impotency. So the emerging school abandoned Howells and James and followed Frank Norris into the camp of the naturalists. Their work might be bad art—as the critics love to reiterate —but it was the honest voice of a generation bewildered and adrift.

The discovery of environment led imperceptibly to another discovery—the economic basis of society; and this in turn led to the rejection of the polite city of older literature. Once the eyes of the novelist opened to the significance of the economic, the world of the spenders became less significant than the world of the makers, the drones became less interesting than the workers. If a novel were to be true to American life, it must adjust its perspectives to the facts of the great American game of money-chasing; it must shift its habitat from Fifth Avenue to Wall Street, from the club to the factory. So the business man entered the portals of fiction, no longer the stock figure in broadcloth and top-hat who discarded business with his dirty collar in order to shift into respectability; but bringing with him his talk of deals and squeeze-outs, playing the great game of exploitation at his mahogany desk—the central, dominating figure in a capitalistic world. He was subjected to acute analysis—his philosophy, his ethics, the machine of industrialism he was creating, the intricate system of exploitation that he had elaborated, the jungle city that was his lair where he fought his battles. The more acutely he was analyzed the clearer it became that here was a figure greater than kings or presidents—a figure that had taken our traditional American life in his hands and was reshaping it to his ends; and that if realism were to be true to its ideal it must paint him as he was without detraction and without glorification. So of necessity the younger novelists turned from polite society to economics, and fell to dramatizing the life of the city jungle where business men fought their fierce battles.

The forerunner of the new school was a Norwegian-American, Hjalmar Hjorth Boyesen. An essayist and philologist, for a number of years professor of German at Columbia University, Boyesen began publishing as early as 1874, and thereafter contributed freely to the several fields of the essay, poetry, and fiction; but it was not until 1891 that he opened the new vein of realism which he worked

industriously the remaining four years of his life, the life brought to
a premature close in 1895. Three novels belong to this last phase of
his work: *The Mammon of Unrighteousness* (1891), *The Golden Calf*
(1892), and *The Social Strugglers* (1893). The books made considerable stir upon their publication, for they were the nearest approach
to the Tolstoian type of realism which till then had appeared in
America. They contain in germ many of the ideas which the later
city realists were to amplify and develop; but these ideas were still
entangled in the mesh of the current psychological realism and their
sociological bearings obscured. In consequence they largely failed
of their purpose, and within a decade they had fallen into oblivion.
They are of interest today chiefly as historical documents of the
early nineties.

In the preface to *The Mammon of Unrighteousness* Boyesen sets
forth his purpose thus:

> My one endeavor in this book has been to depict persons and conditions
> which are profoundly and typically American. I have disregarded all ro-
> mantic traditions, and simply asked myself in every instance, not whether
> it was amusing but whether it was true to the logic of reality—true in
> color and tone to the American sky, the American soil, the American char-
> acter.

This, very evidently, is the realism of *milieu*—an endeavor to
catch the reality of atmosphere; and as such it is of no great significance. In his choice of "types," moreover, he reflected the current taste. The crude self-made millionaire who dimly conscious
of failure founds a university; the young idealist who fails because
he is conscientious and the young realist who succeeds because he
has no scruples against playing the game; and the aristocratic
climber who marries to further her social ambitions—these are the
stock figures of the realism that was to culminate in Robert Grant's
Unleavened Bread, nine years later. But in the delineation of the
character of Horace Larkin—the hero of a book that does not
realize its promise—the note of the new realism is heard distinctly
for the first time. The business man frankly breaks with the old
ethics and erects a new ethics in conformity with his ambition; and
it is the elaboration of the ethics of the Will to Power that justifies
one in regarding *The Mammon of Unrighteousness* as a first study
in the new city realism.

Horace Larkin, like Herrick's Van Harrington, is a Nietzschean
who learned his ethics not from the German philosopher, but from

the world of cut-throat business. It is the flower of the competitive system. The old pretense that business is an uplifting and civilizing agency—that trade breaks down barriers and carries in its shipments the gospel of fraternity and good will—is flung out on the scrap heap. Horace Larkin is no smug hypocrite. He faces the facts frankly; he will not deceive others any more than himself.

He was a beast of prey, asserting his right of survival; nothing more. If he succumbed to sentiment (and it is far easier to succumb to it than to resist it) he would merely be eliminating himself from the battle of existence as a potent and considerable force, and consigning himself to the rear ranks. And he felt in every fibre of his being that he was born for leadership.[54]

. . . nobody has a right to sacrifice himself to anybody else. If he does he simply eliminates himself from the struggle for existence, proves his unfitness to survive. It is natural for every strong man to try to make every other life tributary to his own; but the man who consents to make his life tributary to somebody else's is from Nature's point of view a weak man. . . . She may allow him to exist in a small way; but what is existence without predominance? . . . The man who is in advance of the morality of his age is, for practical purposes, a fool. It is no use quarreling with Fate; and in the United States the average man is the Fate that rules us and determines our place in the world.[55]

"The majority of our politicians are a low-lived lot, and many of them corrupt. But they have the courage to be American—crudely and uncompromisingly American—and that is, in my eyes, a virtue which is not to be lightly rated."

"And may I ask, Mr. Larkin, what do you mean by being American?"

"Being frankly, ably, enterprisingly plebeian. It is the plebeian after all, who shall inherit the earth—"

"I beg your pardon. According to the Bible it is the meek."

"I must differ with the Bible, then; for the meek, in my experience, if they inherit anything, never manage to keep it. It passes, sooner or later, into the hands of the strong, the self-assertive, the grasping. But these, as you will admit, are plebeian characteristics. A universally prosperous, comfortable, impudent, and enterprising mob—that is the goal toward which we are steering; and in my opinion it is a good and desirable one." [56]

This is a note that is to be heard more insistently as the new realism went further in its probing. Armed with this conviction Horace Larkin set forth as a conqueror, and it only adds to the dramatic fitness of things that in his rise he came across a will to power stronger, cleverer, than his own. Kate Van Schaak climbs upon his back to rise with him; she buys him with her money and social position, and having made the deal she realizes on the invest-

[54] Chapter XXXI.   [55] Chapter XXXVI.   [56] Chapter XXXIII.

ment. She is mistress henceforth, and the Nietzschean smiles at the irony of the situation.

In the third work Boyesen fails to maintain the level of *The Mammon of Unrighteousness*. *Social Strugglers* is simpler, more dramatic, better told. It carries the reader forward more easily. But it belongs with such novels of social analysis as Charles Dud-- ley Warner's *The Golden House*—mildly critical of the vulgarizing influence of the new-rich, mildly sympathetic with the slum workers —rather than to the new realism. The heroine—daughter of a new- rich family that has come to New York to climb socially—awakens to the realization of parting ways: one the path of luxury which the four hundred travel, the other the path of service which leads to the slums and settlement work. It is a sentimental awakening, not an intellectual, induced by the hero, who on the fringe of the four hundred is mildly discontented with the ways of luxury. The vague idealism of the latter has been stirred by the Toynbee Hall experiment in London, and the persuasiveness of the lover rather than the conclusions of the thinker carries Maud Bulkley away from her conventional moorings.

The movement of the book is little clogged with sociological discussions; there is too little, indeed, to justify the conclusion. Only once does Philip Warburton lift the curtain upon the idealism which ostensibly is the determining factor in his life.

"I frankly confess that I am something of a red. I think the world is out of gear, and I can perfectly well conceive of a civilization far better than ours, without yet proposing any radical amendment to human na- ture. . . ."

There was to Maud something so wholly unexpected in this ebullition that she scarcely knew what to say. She had never philosophized concern- ing life and its problems; nay, she had never suspected that to a person who had money enough, and the access to good society, it could present any problems whatever. She knew that some terribly disreputable, shaggy, and wild-faced foreigners came here from Europe and proposed to turn our admirable civilization upside down; but that a gentleman of Warbur- ton's culture and social standing could sympathize with such criminals had never occurred to her as a remote possibility. . . .

After this disturbing introduction Warburton proceeds to dis- close what being "a red" means to him in the way of social revolu- tions:

"Have you ever heard of a London experiment known as Toynbee Hall?" he asked. . . .

"Yes: it's a place in the slums, where young men of good family go to live; isn't that it?"

"Yes; and, do you know, that is to me the most beautiful modern instance of a real desire to help the poor and helpless—to lift the world to a higher level. It is what I should like to do myself—and what I shall hope some day to do. . . ."

"Then you really think it a misfortune to be rich?" she ejaculated. . . .

"Yes, if wealth entails the loss of human sympathies, as in nine cases out of ten it seems to do, I regard it as a misfortune. If it means, as in this country it seems to mean, the loss of vital contact with humanity, the contraction of one's mental and spiritual horizon, a callous insensibility to social wrongs and individual sorrows, a brutal induration in creature comforts and mere animal well-being, the loss of that divine discontent and noble aspiration which alone makes us human—if it means this or any part of it, it is the greatest calamity which can befall a man. And it is because Christ foresaw that these were the natural effects of great wealth, and the security and ease which it engenders, that he declared that it was easier for a camel to pass through the eye of a needle than for a rich man to enter the kingdom of heaven." [57]

That is all. There is no dramatic justification of Warburton's views; they are without motive and foundation. *Social Strugglers* does not advance far along the path of the new realism.

As the years drew nearer the new century, the business man usurped an ever larger place in American fiction; the romance which had been sought in the deeds of 1776 was now discovered in the achievements of enterprise. It was the unconscious testimony of literature to the hold which business had got on the imagination of Americans. In the golden days of the "full dinner-pail," following the great victory of '96, the Captain of Industry reached the apogee of his fame. The voice of detraction had not yet been lifted against him; the muckraker had not yet set forth on his devastating career. To young reporters on city papers looking ambitiously towards fiction as the goal of success, what could offer greater appeal than the unwritten romance of Wall Street and the Stock Exchange? They had described it for the daily news columns, they had seen it extolled on the editorial page, why not dramatize it in fiction? Here was the real interest of America—the only reality that signified; yet the novelists had stupidly overlooked it, because they lacked the journalist's sense of news values, his *flair*.

Of the abundant crop of fiction which resulted from this discovery, no more characteristic examples need be sought than *The*

[57] Chapter VII.

Short Line War (1899) and *Calumet "K"* (1901), written in collaboration by Samuel Merwin and H. K. Webster. Their popular
success was immediate and maintained surprisingly. The former
ran to six editions, the last in 1909; the latter, to twelve editions,
the last so late as 1915. They are brisk stories, all action stripped
of descriptive superfluities, with plenty of newspaper punch:
dramatizations of hustle and bluff and the tricks of a cut-throat
game. Charlie Bannon, hero of *Calumet "K,"* is the boss who does
things, who is on the job, who takes long shots and "makes good"
—a "movie" hero of efficiency. He has no time nor inclination to
think, possesses no philosophy, asks no questions and is troubled by
no doubts or scruples; his fertile brain and cool nerve make him a
first-class fighting man, and he fights as the good soldier should on
orders from above. The hero of *The Short Line War*, Jim Weeks, is
another Bannon with the same fertile brain, cool nerve, calm
tenacity of purpose, quick decisiveness, and the same lack of
intellectual interests. In war it is sound strategy to strike quick
and hard; and the Captain of Industry, let it be clearly known, is a
war captain. To play the game hard, to beat the other fellow by
whatever means serve, that is the ideal of a competitive *bourgeoisie:*
not to be too nice about the law, for everybody knows that the law
is the chief weapon of the strong; not to cherish foolish idealisms,
for everybody knows that success alone pays. No more heartless,
brutal, anarchistic books could be conceived—a mad philosophy for
a mad world.

The broad movement towards a realistic portrayal of the economic city produced its eddies and minor currents, which at times
brought such a commotion of the waters as to appear like the main
current. Such was the flood of political novels which came with the
new century and lasted well upwards of a decade. These were a by-
product of the muckraking movement—a part of the propaganda
of the group of young insurgents within the Republican party who
were bent on rescuing the party from control of the old bosses, and
who prepared the way for the more significant movement of Progressivism which followed. Such studies as Francis Churchill
Williams's *J. Devlin—Boss* (1901), and Elliott Flower's *The Spoils-
men* (1903), were early examples; and Winston Churchill's *Coniston*
and *Mr. Crewe's Career* were probably the most notable. They were
journalistic for the most part, *exposés* of the "Boss" and the evils
of the political machine. The "Boss" is painted in various guises, as

brutal, cunning, thoroughly vicious, or as a man who plays the game with the same unsocial conscience that marks the capitalist. Most frequently Lincoln Steffens is followed and the human side of the "Boss" is "played up" equally with his political cunning. It is the characteristic journalistic touch—a bit cheap but immensely effective. As the movement of naturalism gained headway it became increasingly apparent that the "Boss" was only a part of the "System," and the political novel merged in the economic. These brisk studies constitute, however, a suggestive episode in our history—the literary echo of our political history between the years 1900 and 1910.

Little in the way of social analysis was to be expected from a group of clever journalists. They were reporters of fact, transcribers of externals. They n ote the social unrest, but it is little more than an undertone of the chorus of prosperity—a snarl of inconsequential criticism. It is the sting of a troublesome mosquito that is brushed off by the Captain of Industry who is too busy with big projects to bother about insects. Such is Will Payne's *Mr. Salt* (1903)—a sympathetic study of a coal-baron who is caught in the panic of '93 but pulls out and rises higher. To provide dramatic contrast there is the ineffective idealist who is growly and surly— "The whole thing is rotten—the whole business scheme. It's just a gold brick game operated by Salt and his kind. I'd like to stick a fuse to it and touch it off." [58] It is feeble enough—this protest. The rebel joins wildly in the great strike, is struck down by the hand of the law, rebels and strikes again and gets nowhere. Only a bitter, ineffective hate rankles in his heart, while Salt goes on triumphantly to greater power and a sort of moral regeneration through love—a regeneration that does not interfere with his keeping the title-deeds to his loot. An earlier study—*The Money Captain* (1898)—seemed to give promise of honester work than this. It is the story of a struggle between a corrupt gas-magnate and an enterprising editor whose *exposé* puts the magnate afoul of the law as interpreted by the magnate's judges, and who is saved from disaster by the timely death of the "duke." At the end is a touch of prophecy, quite startling in its forecast. These money-kings with their strong prehensile fingers are the spawn of a common plebeian America; the world of the makers is vulgarly democratic; but there follows the age of the spenders, and that shall be finely, altruistically

[58] Chapter IX.

aristocratic. The death of the hero "expunged from his fortune that color of greedy vulgarity and left its gold untarnished."

Dexter, for all his success, was a figure in the common democratic foreground of business; he was intimately and solely of the great everyday warp and woof of toil. He bore all his fruit at once—when he died. An heirship was required to give the fortune value. . . .

In a way it was fine and beautiful—all that huge accumulation of pillage coming to the white, firm hands of this pretty, amiable capable, good-hearted woman. The sudden substitution of her graceful and gracious figure for the swart and iron figure of the duke was like an apt transformation scene, prophetic of the future.[59]

These earlier books are mere preliminary sketches—first studies in economic backgrounds, hesitating between admiration and censure—satisfied to exploit the "human interest" in the dour figure of the money-grabber. The clever newspaper men did not know enough to do better, more realistic work; they saw the daily activities of business but they understood little of economics, less of sociology. And the new realism was soon to yield itself captive to sociology—to inscribe the name of Zola boldly on its pennant and go forth to conquer. It was Frank Norris who wrote the pronunciamiento of the new school, boldly, magnificently, with immense faith in the finality of his own conclusions. *The Responsibilities of the Novelist* was to become the textbook of the young naturalists.

[59] *The Money Captain*, Chapter 22.

CHAPTER I

DISINTEGRATION AND REINTEGRATION

THE figures of the Gilded Age, colossal yet grotesque, belonged to an America that was passing. Another world of thought and experience was rising above the horizon—a world in which the divinities were science and the machine—that was to disintegrate the traditional society of the dispersion and reshape the plastic materials in new forms. The long tide that for two centuries and a half had been running out had come at last to the turn. For six generations the pattern of life had been woven by the impulse of dispersion that in scattering men along a wide frontier had disintegrated the philosophies and rejected the social order brought from the old world, transforming America into such a society of free men as the Enlightenment had dreamed of—decentralized, individualistic, democratic. Dispersion, disintegration, individualism, anarchism—such was the inevitable drift under the compulsions of a fluid economics and frontier ways, of which the ultimate philosophical expression had been Thoreau at Walden Pond, discovering in his bean patch the same anarchistic principles that Godwin had learned of the French naturists—of which the prophet had been Walt Whitman, dreaming amidst the formless crowds of Manhattan his generous dreams of the democratic brotherhood— and of which Jay Gould the sordid wrecker in Wall Street was the prosaic reality.

Then had come the Industrial Revolution that in creating great cities and in drawing men from the plow to the machine was to undo in a few brief years the long work of the dispersion, repudiate the ideals of the Enlightenment, and provide a new pattern for a consolidating urban society. Thenceforward the drift was increasingly toward concentration, with its compulsions to reintegration and conformity—the imperious subjection of the individual to a standardizing order, the stripping away of the slack frontier freedoms in the routine of the factory, the substitution of the ideal of plutocracy for the ideal of Jacksonian democracy. And this revolutionary work of the machine was hastened by the new spirit of science that spread silently through the land, effecting a revolution in men's thinking as great as the machine was effecting in men's lives. Provincial America had been theological- and political-minded; but with the staying of the dispersion and the creation of an urban psychology, the ground was prepared for the reception of new philosophies that came from the contemplation of the laws of the material universe. The incoming of science had two immediate results: the application of technology to industry that was to further the Industrial Revolution; and the impact on speculative thought of the newly discovered laws of science that was to create a new philosophy. In the second of these twin influences lay an intellectual revolution that was to disintegrate the old theological cosmos, push far back the boundaries of space and time, reorient the mind towards all ultimate problems, and bring into question all the traditional faiths—political and social as well as theological and philosophical. Out of science was to come a new spirit of criticism and realism that was to set the pattern for later thought.

The story of disintegration and reintegration is a striking chapter in American life, a story that runs through two generations—the generation that came to maturity in the seventies, and the generation that came to maturity in the nineties. Between 1870 and 1900 the broad movement of thought passed through two sharply differentiating and contradictory phases: the extension of the philosophy of the Enlightenment, and the final rejection of the Enlightenment in consequence of a more rigid application of the law of causality in the light of a mechanistic universe. During the seventies biological evolution was interpreted in the light of earlier philosophies that had come out of the eighteenth century. It was reckoned a fulfillment and justification of the ideals of the Enlightenment, sanctioning the doctrine of progress that had risen from the conception of human perfectibility by a teleological conception of cosmic progress, glorifying the ideal of democratic individualism, and putting the seal of scientific approval on the philosophy of anarchism that had been the flower of two and a half centuries of the dispersion. And then in the nineties the clouds drew over the brilliant Victorian skies. With the substitution of physics for biology came a more somber mood that was to put away the genial romanticism of Victorian evolution, substitute a mechanistic conception for the earlier teleological progress, and reshape its philosophy in harmony with a deterministic pessimism that denied purpose or plan in the changing universe of matter. It was an unconscious return to the dark spirit long before brought hither by Puritanism from the complexities of English society—the spirit that dominated Calvinistic dogma before it disintegrated in the freedoms made possible by the great dispersion.

The great changes came swiftly because the machine had made ready the soil. Farmers and bankers do not think alike; country and town create different psychologies. A simple, decentralized America had been content with theology and metaphysics, and the intellectual history of New England for two hundred and forty years is not greatly skimped by being compressed into three words, Calvinism, Unitarianism, Transcendentalism. What was true of New England was true of America generally, except for the lesser influence of metaphysics. So long as society was mainly agricultural—and in those portions where the frontier spirit lingered on into later days—the church would retain its dominant influence and theology would still bound men's thought. But with the revolutions in economics and industry, with the rise of an urban society, the mind of America was making ready for the reception of science and the realism that was eventually to spring from science.

Venturesome pioneers had been at work long before, digging about under the thick crust of theology. Even in theocratic Massachusetts Increase and Cotton Mather had professed a zeal for scientific investigation, and the latter was vastly proud of his membership in the Royal Society. In the eighteenth century Franklin and Rittenhouse and William Bartram were evidences of a new spirit, and at Yale College President Ezra Stiles made a small beginning of scientific study that was swept away by his successor Timothy Dwight. In the early decades of the nineteenth century an interest in science was spreading widely, as *Silliman's Journal* witnesses. Asa Gray, Le Conte, and Agassiz encouraged the general interest in geology, and in the sixties and seventies Lewis H. Morgan turned to anthropology and R. L. Dugdale stimulated sociology by his significant study of the Jukes family.

Our present concern, however, is not with the contributions of America to abstract science, but rather with the changing mental attitude that resulted from familiarity with scientific methods—the shift from deductive reasoning to inductive investigation, with the consequent breakdown of theology and the slow drift from metaphysical idealism to scientific materialism; and such a changing attitude concerns us because of its enormous influence on the fabric of our later thinking, the total body of our intellectual and cultural life. Considered in this light the intellectual revolution that resulted when the mind of America, long shaped by theological dogmas, turned away from those dogmas to consider the new universe presented by science, cannot be made too much of. With the pushing out of the frontiers of space and time, the discovery of a vast impersonal cosmos that annihilated the petty egocentric world of good and evil postulated by the theologians, the substitution of universal energy for a beneficent providence, the conception of a ceaseless flux and flow that took no account of teleological ends, the assumption of universal law and universal causality, the mind of America quitted its quiet theological retreats and set forth on a great adventure that was to carry far and the results of which were to unsettle what before had been sure.

In this great work we have been engaged since European science first rose on our horizon a half-century and more ago. To speak exactly, it is not so much science that has taken possession of the mind, as certain postulates of science, certain philosophies presumably derived from science and justified by science, which we have felt bound to incorporate in our thinking as a hundred years before the conclusions of the Enlightenment had been incorporated. In that earlier philosophy of the Enlightenment the whole drift had been towards a dissolvent individualism, a disintegration of the earlier integration. In the new interpretation after 1870 the emphasis came to rest on the whole rather than the parts: in sociology, upon the historical growth of human societies; in biology, upon the evolution of the higher from lower forms. The individual, thus conceived of socially and politically, is no longer an isolated, self-determining entity, but a vehicle through which is carried the stream of life, with a past behind and a future before. He is a portion of the total scheme of things, tied by a thousand invisible threads to the encompassing whole. From the parts to the totality, from freedom to determinism—such has been the drift of thought that science has laid upon us and from which there is no easy escape.

With the advent of such a conception the long movement towards philosophical anarchism was brought to a stop. The integrating principle of unity must eventually shoulder aside the disintegrating principle of individualism; order must supersede willfulness. In the outcome a conception so coercive was to deny all the aspirations of our traditional social philosophy, surrendering society to a new regimentation and reducing the individual to an impotent victim of things as they are. Out of it was to spring the passionate protests of later rebels like Theodore Dreiser and Thorstein Veblen. Yet for the moment the rigid determinism of the premise was overlooked and man was accepted as the first-born and heir of God's benevolent universe. In the seventies the new postulates of science were looked upon as no other than fresh sanctions for the Comtean principle of continuity—of evolution from lower to higher in biology, of growth and progress in sociology. It was this middle ground that Herbert Spencer came to occupy in the minds of his American disciples—holding to the older individualism with its implications of anarchism, yet creating a cosmic philosophy that foreshadowed the eventual dwarfing of the individual.

I

THE VICTORIAN MOOD

The sturdy optimism that was a genial hallmark of the Victorian, was erected on more substantial foundations than a middle-class prosperity arising out of the Industrial Revolution; it was founded on a systematic philosophy, built of excellent materials and laid up with nice mortar-work, to which many hands contributed and in the finality of which many minds believed. Its master idea was the conception of growth, a conception that by contrast with the ideal of the static of earlier times, was profoundly revolutionary. Perhaps the most stimulating suggestion that came out of the Enlightenment, it was evolved by Turgot in France and by Price and Priestley in England, from the psychology of John Locke. If the human mind at birth is an empty vessel, wanting in innate ideas and waiting to be filled by sense perceptions, or if—to accept the familiar figure—it is a clean slate on which the finger of experience writes what it will, then it follows from the philosophy of Locke that the shaping of the individual is determined by the environment that cradles him. It is not an unfolding from within but a molding from without. Hence the idea of growth, and hence the vast preoccupation of the Enlightenment with sociology—or the science of environment—the hand of the sculptor that models the plastic clay. From such a conception the principle of progress was an inevitable deduction.

I

SOCIOLOGY AND THE ENLIGHTENMENT

It is convenient, if not quite exact, to trace the rise of the new gospel to Condorcet, who in the midst of the Terror and whilst in hiding from the Jacobins, wrote his stimulating *History of the Progress of the Human Mind* [1]—a work that was early reprinted in America and profoundly influenced Jefferson, who professed to find its principles exemplified in the history of his native Virginia. Condorcet was a humane and liberal spirit, a mathematician, a physicist, a sociologist, one of those eager Revolutionary minds passionately devoted to the creation of a more generous social order; and his celebrated work deserves a distinguished place in the history of social thought. He begins as a good Lockean with the psychology of sense perception, on which he erects his entire superstructure. Here is his opening paragraph:

Man is born with the faculty of receiving sensations; of perceiving and distinguishing the simple sensations of which they are composed; of retaining them, reproducing them, combining them; of comparing these combinations; of grasping what they have in common and what sets them apart; of fixing signs on all such objects in order to reproduce them more clearly and to facilitate new combinations. [2]

He then proceeds to trace the growth of the scientific attitude from the time of Bacon, till it culminated in the rise of social science, with the new politics of natural rights and the new conception of man as perfectible. It is commonly believed that the philosophers of the Enlightenment were speculative dreamers who created a fantastic natural man that flouted the sober realism of experience. Such a notion is grossly absurd. Condorcet was immersed in the scientific spirit of his age; it was to science that he looked for guidance and he had acquired a remarkable understanding of the data already gathered in western Europe. When he set down the following passages, therefore, he was writing not as a speculative dreamer, but as a sociologist who relied solely on

[1] The French title is, *Esquisse d'un tableau historique des progrès de l'esprit humain.* See *Œuvres*, Vol. VI, Paris, 1847.
[2] *Œuvres*, Vol. VI, p. 11, Paris, 1847.

scientific inquiry to find a way out of the social mess into which western civilization was plunged by the selfish stupidity of rulers who were hostile to scientific truth.

After long errors, after having lost their way in incomplete or vague theories, the publicists have finally come to recognize the true rights of man, to deduce them from this single truth, that he is a being endowed with sense perceptions (*un être sensible*), capable of shaping a train of reasoning (*capable de former des raisonnements*), and of acquiring moral ideas.[3]

Finally, we have seen a new doctrine appear. . . . It is that of the indefinite perfectibility of the human species, a doctrine of which Turgot, Price and Priestly, were the first and most distinguished apostles; it belongs to the tenth epoch, in which we shall develop it broadly.[4]

In such passages is contained the kernel of Condorcet's philosophy, the grounds of that hope for human betterment which awakened his generous sympathies. The *Esquisse* is a noble contribution to the work which the heirs of the Enlightenment, from Turgot to Comte, so eagerly and hopefully engaged in—the work of tracing scientifically the changes of the past in order to forecast the path of the future. After dividing the history of social evolution into nine periods, Condorcet projects the outlines of the tenth which is still to come.

If man can predict, with almost complete assurance, the phenomena of which he knows the laws; if, while they are still unknown in him, from the experience of the past he can forecast, with much probability, the events of the future; why should one regard as a chimerical undertaking the attempt to trace with some likeness the picture of the future destiny of the human species, in accordance with the facts of its history (*d'après les résultats de son histoire*)? The sole ground of faith in the natural sciences is this idea, that the general laws, known or unknown, that rule the phenomena of the universe, are necessary and constant; and on what grounds would this principle be less true for the development of the intellectual and moral faculties of man, than for the other operations of nature? Finally, since opinions formed from the experience of the past, in matters of the same kind, are the sole rule of conduct for the wisest men, why should one deny the philosopher the right to rest his conjectures on the same base, provided he does not attribute to them a certainty beyond that which springs from the number, the constancy and the exactness of his observations?

Our hopes for the future state of the human species may be reduced to these three important points: the destruction of inequality between nations; the progress of equality amongst a common people; finally, the

[3] *Ibid.*, p. 176.   [4] *Ibid.*, Vol. VI, pp. 194–195.

growth of man towards perfection (*le perfectionnement réel de l'homme*). May not all nations one day approach the state of civilization to which have arrived the most enlightened peoples, the freest, the most emancipated from prejudice, such as the French and the Anglo-Americans? The vast distance that divides these peoples from the servitude of nations subject to kings, from the barbarism of African tribes, from the ignorance of savages, must it not gradually disappear? [5]

Condorcet was an idealist, and the grand object towards which he was working was an adequate social philosophy that should interpret justly the evolution of civilization. True to the genius of the Enlightenment he believed that in reason and in the moral sense man possessed the keys to his own progress—that the general reason under the guidance of humane feeling must assure a progressive amelioration of life that will eventuate in the common well-being of men in a rational society. The age of the Enlightenment, he believed, had "opened new paths to the political and moral sciences," and laid bare what to him were "the true principles of social happiness." The American Federalists, who were prodigal of vituperative rhetoric in assailing all French theorists, might have read the pages of Condorcet with profit.

The idea of progress with its corollary of a philosophy of history, thus elaborated by Condorcet, was taken over by Saint-Simon, but came to its most elaborate expression in the work of Auguste Comte. The grandiose philosophy of history to which Comte gave the name of Positivism, was an attempt to formulate the law of progress in civilization; and his dynamic sociology, which emerged naturally from his conception of history, was an attempt to apply that law to society. That the principle of progress is the law of nature Comte professed to discover in the unity of all natural processes and the historical unfolding of all systems; there are no breaks and no fresh beginnings, but everywhere and always, continuity. From this principle emerged the Comtean law of historical evolution with its three phases: the theological, the metaphysical, and the scientific-industrial. If continuity is the law of nature, such continuity presupposes an objective—presumably benevolent; and in view of such continuity towards a benevolent objective, it is only logical to endeavor to dispose the forces of society in harmony with the teleological purpose, and through the application of positive knowledge hasten the advent

[5] *Ibid., Dixième Époque,* pp. 236–237.

of the Golden Age. Hence the grand science, hitherto neglected, is sociology. Earlier generations had placed the Golden Age in a dim past; Comtean philosophy, in harmony with the Enlightenment, placed it in the future as the ultimate goal of an evolving society. To forecast the lines along which such progress will move, to read the future as a child of the past, became therefore a prime objective of the new school of history. The tracing of social laws was the great business at hand, and as the founder of a new social science Comte carried further and systematized the work begun by the Physiocrats. Before Comte history had been little more than chronicles, without pattern or meaning, unconcerned with the sources of change and providing no basis for forecast; after Comte history became an interpretation and a philosophy.

One would have supposed that Positivism would have appealed to American intellectuals, as it appealed to liberal English thinkers like Mill and Spencer. Not only has the American mind taken kindly to sociology, but the history of America, as Woodbridge Riley has pointed out, offers too pat an illustration of the Comtean law of progress to be overlooked.[6] The three centuries of American existence—the seventeenth with its theocracy, the eighteenth with its abstract theories of political rights and its faith in constitutions, and the nineteenth with its industrialism based on science—would seem to be pages out of the Positivist philosophy of history. That Comte made so slight an impression on the mind of New England was due, no doubt, to the current influence of transcendentalism with its metaphysical backgrounds. Although eager young intellectuals like John Fiske might accept it while awaiting a more adequate evolutionary philosophy, the country was not yet ripe for Positivism. When that time came it was Spencer rather than Comte who became the master of American intellectuals—Spencer and in a lesser degree John Stuart Mill. Both Spencer and Mill had come under the influence of the French sociological school, and it was through their writings that the new social philosophy penetrated America.[7]

2

BIOLOGY AND THE ENLIGHTENMENT

The appeal of Spencer to the generation born after the Civil War was extraordinary. Ardent young minds, for whom the candles

---

[6] *American Thought*, p. 172, New York, 1915.
[7] Woodbridge Riley, *American Thought*, Chapter XI.

of theology were burnt out and who were seeking new light to their
feet, were drawn to him irresistibly. Young rebels who had thrown
off the guidance of their elders and were bent on discovering fresh
paths through the tangle of dead faiths—independent souls like
Hamlin Garland and Jack London and Theodore Dreiser who were
to become leaders of the realistic revolt against the genteel tradition
in life and letters and faith—went to school to him to prepare
themselves for the great work of freeing the American mind from
the old theological inhibitions. Young men in colleges no longer
read *Butler's Analogy*, as their fathers had done before the war,
but turned with zest to Spencer's *Data of Ethics* to discover a more
scientific theory of conduct. Everywhere the influence of the great
Victorian penetrated, and wherever that influence spread the old
theological prepossessions disintegrated. It is probably no exaggeration to say that Spencer laid out the broad highway over which
American thought traveled in the later years of the century.

If the supreme excellence of Comte, as has been suggested by
Lester F. Ward, was his insistence on the ultimate unity of all
processes of nature,[8] if before him the continuity of forces had been
inadequately understood, his intellectual kinship with Spencer cannot fail to be remarked. The latter's master conception, which he
arrived at independently of Darwin and which life-long he applied
systematically to the several fields of thought, was the master
creative conception of the nineteenth century—the conception of
pervasive unity and organic growth. In his well-known phrase it
was the law of continuous development from the homogeneous to
the heterogeneous, from the simple to the complex; and this
principle he found exemplified in the total history of nature and
man. Here then is the Comtean law of continuity, but vastly
strengthened and given a cosmic significance by deductions from
the new science. Lamarck and Darwin laid the foundations for
Spencer's philosophy, as Condorcet and Saint-Simon had provided
the backgrounds for Comte. Trained thus in the new school of
biology, Spencer erected his synthetic philosophy upon the broad-
est foundations; the principle of organic evolution sufficed to explain for him not only the history of civilization, but the total
history of life in a physical universe; and biology, psychology,
sociology, politics, ethics—all the congeries of ideals and institutions and bodies of knowledge that shape civilization—were but

[8] *Ibid.*, p. 401.

variant expressions of the development from the homogeneous to the heterogeneous.

The final effect of the synthetic philosophy was not to overset but to confirm the major postulates of the Enlightenment. In his social theory are unforeseen confirmations of the glowing hopes of Turgot and Condorcet. From his studies in biology Spencer had come to think primarily in terms of the individual, and only secondarily in terms of the species and the genus. Now variation is the mark of the individual, for strictly considered, nature knows no duplication of life forms, but always and everywhere individual differentiation; yet since likenesses are far greater and more cohesive than unlikenesses, the instinct of gregariousness impels individuals to associate in ever larger groups, interacting through association and coöperation, whence arises a human society that tends continuously to pass from the simple to the complex. On these two major premises then—individual variation and the instinct of association—Spencer established his social and political theory; and when the elaborate data drawn from biology and ethnology and psychology are stripped away, the underlying conceptions reveal a curious likeness to the master principles of French romantic philosophy. This likeness becomes more striking as he explores the fields of sociology and politics; and his final deductions tally so closely with earlier theory as to warrant a disciple of Jefferson in becoming a disciple of Spencer.

There is no break between Condorcet and the synthetic philosophy. The great Victorian completed the work of the Enlightenment. In establishing his individualism on the principle of biological variation, Spencer was only restating in scientific terms the earlier metaphysical individualism; in establishing his psychology upon an unbroken sequence "from the simple reflex action by which an infant sucks, up to the elaborate reasoning of the adult man," with its corollary of continuously expanding powers, he was rebuilding on the foundation of Locke a fresh argument for the doctrine of indefinite development, or perfectibility; in establishing his sociology on the organic principle of "natural development," which shapes the individual to social ends, with an accruing wealth of individuation that is the final objective of true social life, he justified the French enthusiasm for liberty as the great desideratum, but liberty enriched and augmented by association in a free society; and finally, in establishing his ethics on the principle that "increas-

ing fullness of life is the 'end' of evolution," and the "highest conduct is that which conduces to the greatest length, breadth, and
completeness of life"—that the ultimate criterion of social ethics is
justice and that "every man is free to do that which he wills, provided he infringes not the equal freedom of any other man"—he
rephrased the earlier Godwinian principle that rational liberty
under the reign of justice is the ultimate end of society.[9]

That Spencer's social theory should have been shot through with
older ideals is not surprising when one considers his origins and
training. Sprung from radical nonconformist stock, a congenital
rebel, extraordinarily self-sufficient and coming to intellectual maturity in the tempestuous forties with their Benthamism, their
Chartism, their exigent democracy, he was molded by forces that in
large part were a reëmbodiment of the aspirations nullified by the
Napoleonic wars and the Tory reaction, and now come again to
birth. As a consequence his political theory, like Mill's, was deeply
affected by the revolutionary heritage. He accepted the social
contract as a "theoretical, though not a historical, basis of political
authority and institutions";[10] the doctrine of natural rights, which,
with Jefferson, he interpreted in terms of the rights to life, liberty,
and the pursuit of happiness; and the theory of a constantly
diminishing political state, on the hypothesis that the ultimate
form of society—as in Godwin's *Political Justice*—will, be anarchistic.

At least, such he conceives to be the forecast suggested by the
law of social evolution. As the coercive authority of the political
state diminishes, its place will be supplied by the cohesive force of
association, until voluntary coöperation extends to all the necessary
functions of society; and since the state tends to disappear with the
growth of a rational society, the great desideratum is an adequate
sociology rather than a political theory. The net result, therefore,
of Spencer's wide studies was a fresh justification, based on the
findings of Victorian science, of the master principles of eighteenth-
century speculation; its individualism, its liberalism, its passion for
justice, its love of liberty and distrust of every form of coercion.
The power of the majority must be curbed equally with that of the
minority and he concluded his *The Man versus the State* with the

---

[9] For a brief exposition of Spencer's major ideas see, William Henry Hudson,
"Herbert Spencer," in *Philosophies Ancient and Modern*, London, 1908.
[10] William Archibald Dunning, *A History of Political Theories from Rousseau to
Spencer*, New York, 1920, p. 400.

well-known words, "The function of Liberalism in the past was that of putting a limit to the powers of kings. The function of true Liberalism in the future will be that of putting a limit to the powers of Parliament." In the scientific speculations of the great Victorian the aspirations of romantic thought came to fresh vitality; embodied in a comprehensive evolutionary system they were given a fresh currency. Herbert Spencer completed the work begun by Locke a hundred and fifty years before, and his *Synthetic Philosophy* brought to conclusion the greatest intellectual movement of modern times.

As the young intellectuals, trained in the school of Spencer, looked out on the universe in the last quarter of the nineteenth century, they discovered, amid all its complexities an encompassing unity, a continuous growth, a creative purpose; and from such assumptions they justified the theory of progress, cosmic in scope and plan, that opened wide the doors to a vaster future. If in the backgrounds of their minds lurked the conception of determinism, it gave them no concern, for a benevolent determinism that shapes all things to a divine end, is no monster to be feared. In the evolutionary science were the grounds of a genial optimism that nothing could shake. If they had lost something of the jauntiness of the transcendental faith that beheld God plowing furrows at Brook Farm, they were armed with a scientific faith that by tapping stones and comparing fishes they should find His plan in an evolving series of life forms. Browning's Fra Lippo was a good Spencerian in his vigorous pronouncement:

> This world's no blot for us,
> Nor blank; it means intensely, and means good:
> To find its meaning is my meat and drink.

That progress was the law of the universe was held to be axiomatic by the new evolutionary school, and the American read in the new philosophy an added confirmation of a prepossession common to all Americans since Franklin and Jefferson, and become the common faith after the War of 1812. In sober minds it led to a complete reshaping of the outlook upon life, and in unbalanced minds it ran riot in all sorts of blowsy enthusiasms. Freedom, love, benevolence, progress towards a millennial perfection—these were the clarion notes in a huge symphony in praise of human perfectibility that assaulted American ears in the Gilded Age. Not Henry

Ward Beecher alone was the prophet of the new day. In the early seventies Mrs. Victoria Woodhull, one of the minor prophetesses, established a paper dedicated to the high end of "the Universal Religion of the Future . . . the Universal Home . . . the Universal Science, called Universology, based on the discovery and demonstration of Universal Laws . . . and an accompanying Philosophy of Integralism"—the "organ of the most advanced thought and Purpose in the World . . . the Organ of Cardinary News . . . News of the Aspiration and Progression of Mankind toward Millennial Perfection." [11] By contrast with such rhythmic enthusiasms the familiar lines of Tennyson are sober prose.

> Yet I doubt not thro' the ages one increasing purpose runs,
> And the thoughts of men are widen'd with the process of the suns.

How logically to young intellectuals of the seventies it all followed from the premises! If man is a rational being, potentially excellent and capable of indefinite development, the idea of a humane and rational progress in civilization is an inevitable deduction; and the evolutionist above all men was certain to build into his philosophy the cardinal idea of a unified progress, but given a cosmic sweep, accepted as the master principle in all fields of the material and the spiritual. It was the law of life, as the static was the law of death. No thinker who had grasped the idea of organic growth, could escape its larger implications; and no student in the seventies could think seriously without coming upon it.

3

THE END OF THE HOPES OF THE ENLIGHTENMENT

Then a film of haze slowly gathered upon the face of the brilliant sun and the light of men's hopes grew dimmer. As physics encroached upon the interest in biology, and leadership in speculation based on scientific findings passed from Spencer to Ernst Haeckel, young Americans of the next generation found the membership of the current philosophical trinity changed for them, and instead of unity, growth, purpose, they discovered unity, flux, chance. Purpose had disappeared from the grim face of the material universe, and they found themselves in the coils of a determinism that was more likely to prove malignant than benevolent. The idea of

[11] Quoted in Constance Mayfield Rourke, *Trumpets of Jubilee*, p. 201.

progress slipped quietly from their minds, and in its stead was only a meaningless and purposeless flux of things. But unity remained to bind the individual upon the whole and dwarf him to a pin-point in a vast macrocosm. The intellectual history of the last quarter of the nineteenth century—in America as well as elsewhere —in its teleological aspects is the history of the shift from the benevolent evolutionism of Spencer to the mechanistic materialism of Haeckel, with all the dislocations and readjustments involved in the cataclysmic change; and *The Education of Henry Adams*, that curiously suggestive study in disillusion, is saturated with the pessimism that followed upon the transition—a pessimism exuding from the contemplation of the bleak unity of a mechanistic universe. Of the earlier period before hope was gone, he wrote thus:

> For the young men whose lives were cast in the generation between 1867 and 1900, Law should be Evolution from lower to higher, aggregation of the atom in the mass, concentration of multiplicity in unity, compulsion of anarchy in order; and he would force himself to follow wherever it led, though he should sacrifice five thousand millions more in money, and a million more lives.[12]

Was there purpose in it all? To this Adams and the younger men more and more declined to make answer. Yet this much is clear, for them the end of the theological age had come, and the end also of the great hopes of the Enlightenment. The idea of progress was given over henceforth to the middle class to become the plaything of material expansion.

II

THE SCHOOL OF SPENCER—JOHN FISKE

Of the distinguished group that labored to naturalize in America the philosophy of evolution John Fiske was the most authoritative spokesman. As a brilliant popularizer of the Synthetic Philosophy, and an historian who applied the Comtean law of continuity to the American past, he brought to the Gilded Age the revolutionary influence of English and French thought. Deeply immersed in Victorian speculation, he threw over his acquisitions the genial mood of his generation and infused the doctrines of evolutionary science with the spirit of religion. He reveled in the cosmic philosophy of Herbert Spencer, but within the material cosmos the scientists were revealing, controlling its eternal flux, he perceived a

[12] *The Education of Henry Adams*, p. 232.

directing will that was shaping man's destiny to noble ends. New England scholarship had served God for too many generations to put aside its teleological prepossessions, and John Fiske was too completely New England to deny his spiritual obligations. The duty laid upon his conscience was plain. It was not enough to lay open to the New England mind the wealth of evolutionary science; he must justify its conclusions by binding them back upon the old faith and discover God revealed in biology as before he had been revealed in the Bible. And so in the heyday of Spencerian influence, before the bleak conception of a mechanistic universe had risen upon the horizon of men's thought to disperse the genial glow of optimism, this learned son of Connecticut was the prophet in America of the new order of thought.

John Fiske was a brilliant Yankee with a voracious appetite for ideas and a passion for cosmic syntheses. In certain respects he was the most richly endowed of the young students of his generation of Americans. Intellectually curious and acquisitive, he refused to be confined by orthodox fences but ranged far in pursuit of knowledge. The pale negations of the current New England theology, on which he had fed in his youth, soon lost their savor, and following his natural impulses he sought out the strongest food available. While still in his teens he had absorbed Emerson, Theodore Parker, and other New England radicals, and was reaching out for an ampler diet. That was in the late fifties, when a new cosmos was taking shape in men's minds and old faiths were disintegrating. The several rivulets of science—geology, zoölogy, chemistry, physics— that hitherto had followed diverse and vagrant courses, were slowly converging and making ready to mingle their waters in a vast common stream. Some further dredging needed to be done first, and on that great job Darwin had long been patiently engaged. It was a time of high hopes and young John Fiske, about to enter Harvard College, was not one to miss the significance of so great an awakening.

Amidst his quiet Connecticut lanes he had already been making his own discoveries. Although he had early gone through a form of conversion to dogmatic Calvinism he had not long been content with its arid provender, but turned to the English disciples of Positivism—George Henry Lewes, Buckle, Mill—and was absorbing Comte with the help of Voltaire and Goethe. In June, 1860, two months before taking his examinations for advanced standing at Harvard, he came upon a prospectus of Herbert Spencer's proposed system of philosophy, and this boy of eighteen was one of the first dozen Americans to subscribe to the undertaking. It was a golden day in his life, that was to determine his whole intellectual development. He became a devoted disciple of Spencer, dedicating his labors to the great cause of evolution. To that end he felt called to study prodigiously. As a Harvard undergraduate he found it difficult to treat his conventional instructors with due respect, for while his classmates were struggling with Greek roots he was exploring the whole field of philology and rioting in Comtean sociology. Instead of exhausting his energies with the usual undergraduate themes, he wrote in his junior year, at the age of nineteen, a critical examination of *Buckle's History of Civilization* for the *National Quarterly Review;* and while preparing for his final examinations he wrote a learned article on "The Evolution of Language" that was accepted by *The North American Review*.

Such intellectual precocity, suggesting to timid souls a lack of respect for orthodox opinions, was not without its dangers. From his first entrance to Harvard he was marked by certain tutors as a dangerous influence. Positivism and evolution were in ill repute in the college circles, and he was eventually summoned before the faculty and admonished for undermining the faith of Harvard undergradugtes. Outside the college he was becoming known as the "young atheist of Cambridge." The reasons for such a reputation were quite sufficient to Unitarian dogmatists who had forgotten the cardinal principle of Unitarianism—the principle of devout free thought—for young John Fiske had already gathered a huge pile of combustible materials that threatened the established orthodoxy. Before entering Harvard he had planned to write a history of early Christianity, but his interest in science drew him into other fields— the new sociological interpretation of history that he discovered in Grote's *History of Greece*, and the broad field of scientific speculation that opened to him in Humboldt's *Cosmos*. To this latter field he turned greedily, reading amongst other works Cuvier's *Règne Animal distribué d'après son Organisation,* Herschel's *Outlines of Astronomy*, Laplace's *Système du Monde*, Agassiz's *Zoölogy* and his *Essay on the Classification of the Animal Kingdom* (1857), and with the joy of a great discovery Darwin's *Origin of Species* (1859). From Agassiz's defense of special creation he dissented vigorously, and this dissent prepared him for an enthusiastic re-

ception of Darwin's careful exposition. Certainly no other young
student in America followed so closely or so intelligently the unfolding of the English school of evolutionary thought. In solid
acquisition and in intellectual curiosity he was far in advance of
Henry Adams, then a young diplomat in London.

Upon his graduation in 1863 he determined upon the law, read
through the two-year course of the Harvard Law School in nine
months, was admitted to the bar, waited two years for clients who
never came, threw it over, and turned to his first love, the life of the
scholar. He had his eye on a chair at Harvard, but so long as the
old orthodox *régime* lasted no opening offered there. In the first
year of President Eliot's administration (1869) an opportunity was
provided and he was invited to give a course of lectures in Holden
Chapel on the Positive Philosophy. The opposition was still too
strong to permit the offer he sought—a chair in history—but he was
eventually given a place as Assistant Librarian, where he spent
five years amongst the books of Gore Hall. Driven to other means
of support he turned to lecturing, was received with immense applause in London, and thereafter to the end of his life he suffered
much of his vast energy to drain off into that most fruitless of jobs
for a creative mind. A certain genial egoism was to blame for his
playing willingly the rôle of lackey to women's clubs. He liked to
talk to sympathetic audiences, and he was greatly effective on the
platform. The inevitable result was that he fell short in accomplishment of the fine promise of his early years. His style became
diffuse, his materials picturesque rather than solid, his thinking
flabby. Pretty much all his significant work was done before he was
forty.

The greater part of Fiske's intellectual life, despite his later incursions into certain waste places of history, was dedicated to the
indoctrination of the American people in the principle of evolution
as that principle was outlined in Spencer's *Synthetic Philosophy*.
He was a man of one idea, but that idea was so vast and germinal,
so comprehensive in its implications and so constructive in its suggestions, as to set afoot the greatest intellectual revolution in
western civilization. He called himself a philosopher, but he meant
by the term not a metaphysician, but a cosmic historian whose
business was to interpret the universe in the light of the great laws
that science was revealing. By 1860 science had revealed three such
general laws: the law of gravitation, the law of biological variation

and the survival of the fittest, and the law of the conservation of energy; and from them Spencer had deduced the principle of a unitary cosmos, with a common force sustaining both the organic and the inorganic, working to a single "far-off divine event, to which the whole creation moves." An intimate friend of Fiske's, and an ardent Spencerian, puts the intellectual situation in these terms:

The conceptions of the Universe generally held at the time when Fiske was in college were fragmentary and chaotic, each phenomenon or each group of phenomena being, like language, a special creation of an anthropomorphic God, turning out different jobs piecemeal like a man. The conception of one power behind all had been a dream of not a few philosophers and poets, but as a fact comprehensible by the average mind, it was not known until the discovery about 1860 of the Conservation of Force. About the same time was discovered the unity of all organic life, in its descent from protoplasm, and the identity of its forces with those of the inorganic universe. The nebular cosmogony, the persistence of force and the biologic genesis, united together, showed the power evolving, sustaining and carrying on the entire universe known to us, to be *one*, and constantly acting in one unified process; and that every detail—from the most minute known to the chemist, physicist and biologist, up to the greatest known to the geologist and astronomer, and including all known to the psychologist, economist, and historian—was caused by a previous detail. It having been established that the same causes always produced the same results, these uniformities were recognized as Laws, and it was also recognized that conduct in conformity with these laws produced good, and conduct counter to them produced evil. . . .
These great discoveries were at once grasped by Fiske's great intelligence, and welcomed with enthusiasm. To their dissemination he mainly devoted his next twenty years, and to their illustration in the origins and foundation of our national commonwealth, the rest of his career.[13]

While still at Harvard, as a result of the publication of his two undergraduate essays already referred to, he was sought out by Edward L. Youmans and urged to join with him in spreading the new evolutionary philosophy.[14] Youmans was an ardent proselytizer who had volunteered for the job of instructing the American people in the meaning of science. He attached himself to Spencer as spokesman and publicity agent, and was on the lookout for helpers. Encouraged thus by Youmans, Fiske threw himself impetuously into the work of furthering the new philosophy of

[13] Henry Holt, *Garrulities of an Octogenarian Editor, with Other Essays somewhat Biographical and Autobiographical*, Boston, 1923, pp. 327–328.
[14] See John Spencer Clark, *Life and Letters of John Fiske*, Vol. I, pp. 273–278.

evolution. As the task unfolded before his maturing mind it came
to involve three major problems: to dissociate in the popular mind
the potential theism of Spencer's *First Principles* from the materialism of Comte's Positivism, with which it was widely confused; to
elaborate the teleological implications of evolution and demonstrate that the grand objective of all natural processes was "the
production of happiness, and that, despite occasional lapses, all
records of them prove that, on the whole, they tend not only to
produce happiness, but to increase it";[15] and finally to apply the
principles of the cosmic philosophy to historical writing and reveal
how the law of evolution determines the forms of social institutions
—to do more adequately in the field of American history what
Buckle had tried to do in a larger field without the aid of evolution.

In all his intellectual interests and attitudes Fiske was a complete
New England Victorian, but scarcely a British Victorian. In his
erection of the doctrine of progress into a cosmic law, and in his
resultant optimism, he was at one with Spencer and the English
group. But he was a son of New England before he was an evolutionist, and although he had broken with the grotesque, anthropomorphic dogmas of Calvinism, he remained profoundly religious,
and like Henry Drummond he sought to transfuse science with
spiritual qualities. He was effectively a Unitarian, the leader of the
Cambridge intellectuals who were carrying on the work that
Theodore Parker would have done had he lived twenty years
longer—the work of bridging the chasm between science and religion. To that end his vast concern with teleology—that God is
the great wellspring out of which flows the unfolding cosmos, and
that the unfolding is guided and controlled to beneficent ends.
Natural law, working in a realm of causation, and shaping matter
to forms more and more complex, to John Fiske was no other than
the beneficent purpose known to theology as Divine Providence.

Pretty much all that he had to say on the question is contained in
the four volumes of *Outlines of Cosmic Philosophy*, published when
he was only thirty-two. Written with great enthusiasm and
complete confidence, it was an attempt to summarize and restate
the conception of cosmic evolution as Spencer had defined it in
First Principles, and partly elaborated it in his *Biology* and *Psychology*. It was a timely presentation, and with its lucid exposition of
the evidence drawn from the several fields of science it furthered

[15] Henry Holt, *op. cit.*, p. 328.

the spread of the evolutionary philosophy. But it sought to do more. Not content with arraying in due order the scientific proofs of a vast unitary cosmos—as Spencer had done—Fiske essayed the rôle of apologist and supplemented the facts of science with ontological and teleological speculations. Whereas Spencer had remained agnostic, refusing to speculate on the unknowable, and clearly implying a deterministic cosmos, Fiske took high theistic ground, asserting that evolution implies the existence of a creative mind, vaster than the anthropomorphic conceptions of theology and far nobler, whose cosmic plan unfolding in the material universe compels a belief in a benevolent God, and a belief also in the "eternal source of a moral law which is implicated with each action of our lives, and in obedience to which lies our only guarantee of the happiness which is incorruptible." And this "eternal Power, not ourselves, that makes for righteousness"—to use Arnold's phrase which Fiske was fond of quoting—is making also for altruism and the spirit of love that lies at the heart of Christianity; for is not the prolongation of infancy with its demands on altruism—a principle that was Fiske's contribution to evolution, of which he was justly proud—a master biological device for individual variation? In consequence the evolutionist becomes not only a theist, but a Christian in the truest meaning of the term. The fatherhood of God and the brotherhood of man—to which New England Unitarianism had come to restrict its dogmas—are in reality "two great interrelated cosmic truths—the existence of righteousness as an active principle in the Infinite Power or Reality back of the cosmos, and its correlative manifestation in the altruistic consciousness of man."[16]

Such speculation concerning the unknowable exercised an increasing fascination for Fiske as his deeply religious nature slowly colored the acquisitions of the scientist, and in a succession of tracts—*The Destiny of Man* (1884), *The Idea of God* (1885), *Through Nature to God* (1899), and *Life Everlasting* (1900)—he definitely rejected the negative attitude of agnosticism that was a common mark of the English evolutionary school, and turned to outline the religious faith of an evolutionist. George Eliot's dictum that God is unknowable and immortality is unthinkable, was too thin a diet for his robust nature; instead he elaborated the argument that faith in God and immortality is reasonable in the light of

[16] John Spencer Clark, *op. cit.*, Vol. II, p. 50.

the evolving cosmos that science was revealing. To John Fiske
that cosmos was not bleak and impersonal, a vast congeries of
physical forces that reduced man to the status of a flea on the
epidermis of earth, but the expression rather of a benevolent will
unfolding in accordance with a divine purpose. "The process of
evolution is itself the working out of a mighty Teleology, of which
our finite understandings can fathom but the scantiest rudiments."
To Henry Holt this recovery of teleology was Fiske's great contribution to evolutionary thought.

> He did more just there than any modern philosopher, perhaps than any
> philosopher, to show that this teleology is beneficent, and to restore in this
> way the attitude of mind which it may not yet be too late to call Faith
> in God and Immortality.[17]

No doubt it was due to such emphasis on the theistic implications
of evolution that the doctrine was so quickly accepted in New England amongst the Unitarians and liberals; but for Fiske it marked
the end of his intellectual leadership. After the battle had been
won he turned away to engage in less fruitful activities, no longer
followed keenly the new discoveries of science, and finally set himself to write the history of America. The venture on the whole was
not fortunate. In his attempt to reinterpret the American past he
suffered from grave handicaps, an inadequate knowledge and an
inadequate philosophy. He was led into the field of history by his
interest in the English school of Grote and Maine and Stubbs and
Freeman, and his ultimate purpose was to present "the drama of
American civilization, of which the political organization of the
United States was the crowning feature, as an evolutionary development from antecedent causes and of great significance to
the future civilization of the world." [18] But for this undertaking
he was inadequately equipped and his conscious search for a Comtean continuity in social growth did him a real disservice. The
economics of historical change he seems never to have considered,
and his analyses of social forces are never acute or penetrating.
Although he attempted to apply sociological evolution to history
he was really little more than a political and military historian
with a special fondness for wars and the details of battle strategy.
In his first venture, *American Political Ideas*—written for his
London lectures of 1880—he simplified American political develop-

[17] Henry Holt, *op. cit.*, p. 339.
[18] John Spencer Clark, *op. cit.*, Vol. II, p. 456.

ment to two germinal ideas—the town meeting and the principle of federation, and these two conceptions he traces back to the Teutonic folkmote and the Teutonic principle of shire representation. The theme with which he deals is thus stated in the preface:

> The government of the United States is not the result of special creation, but of evolution. As the town-meetings of New England are lineally descended from the village assemblies of the early Aryans; as our huge federal union was long ago foreshadowed in the little leagues of Greek cities and Swiss cantons; so the great political problem which we are (thus far successfully) solving is the very same problem upon which all civilized peoples have been working ever since civilization began. How to insure peaceful concerted action throughout the Whole, without infringing upon local and individual freedom in the Parts,—this has ever been the chief aim of civilization, viewed on its political side; and we rate the failure or success of nations politically according to their failure or success in attaining this supreme end. When thus considered in the light of the comparative method our American history acquires added dignity and interest, and a broad and rational basis is secured for the detailed treatment of political questions.[19]

Only a New England historian could write so naïvely as that, for only to a New Englander does the town meeting become a germinal source of American democracy. Not a great historian, Fiske ceased to be in his wandering later years a great intellectual influence. The rare promise of his young manhood he never fulfilled, but like his generation he suffered his energies to be dissipated and he ended in a somewhat blowsy optimism. To Henry Holt he was a very great and learned man, but to a later generation it is difficult to make out his vast stature. Nevertheless as a purveyor of Victorian science to the American people he did a useful and important work.

[19] John Fiske, *American Political Ideas*, Preface, pp. 4–5.

CHAPTER II

THE SKEPTICISM OF THE HOUSE OF ADAMS

In the welter of change that resulted from the revolutionary transi-
tions of the Gilded Age, one man at least stood apart, skeptical
about the worth of the current revolutions, unconvinced that all
the hurly-burly meant a rational progress. To Henry Adams
skepticism early became a habit. Doubt persistently dogged his
footsteps and the more critically he examined the ways of his
generation of Americans, the more certain it seemed to him that any
were unworthy the name of civilization. He was not at home in the
new world of the Gilded Age; and as he watched the disintegrations
of the older New England in which he had been brought up, an incurable nostalgia seized upon him and he set about seeking another
home where he might live the good life he had not lived heretofore.
The America of the Gilded Age was alien to him; its gods were not
his gods, nor its ends his ends. And so began for him a long pilgrimage of the spirit that was to carry him far and return him at
last with no solider gains than a handful of curious relics in his
pilgrim's scrip.

The sturdy New England character, with its self-sufficing individualism and granite integrity, never came to finer flower than
in the Braintree-Quincy house of Adams. Intellectually curious,
given to rationalism, retaining much of the eighteenth-century
solidity of intellect and honest realism, refusing to barter principle
for the good will of men, the Adams line produced no more characteristic offshoots than came in the fourth generation. In Charles
Francis Adams, Jr., Henry Adams, and Brooks Adams, the family
virtues of independence, intellectual integrity, and disinterested
criticism, found abundant expression. All three were children of an
earlier century, endowed with the solidest Yankee-Puritan qualities
of mind and heart, unyielding as the rock ledges of their native
fields; and they found the experience of living in the late nineteenth
century, of adjusting their eighteenth-century minds to the demands of a sordid capitalistic order, a difficult business. Though
they tried to bridge the chasm between the two worlds, though they

honestly sought some working compromise that would suffer them to share in the work of their generation, they met with failure. It was not possible for the House of Adams, with its old-fashioned rectitude, to accept the ways of the Gilded Age, and in the end they turned aside from the main-traveled road to follow their own paths.

I

CHARLES FRANCIS ADAMS—THE BUSINESS FAILURE

Of the three Charles Francis Adams most nearly succeeded in his experiment of a *rapprochement* with capitalism, with the result that his life came nearest to shipwreck. Perhaps there was less of the Adams granite in his character. He refused to turn rebel but consciously sought to win the prizes offered by his generation, training himself to serve financial interests, making overtures to business, and achieving a very considerable financial success. Yet nothing was more incongruous than an Adams serving as lackey to State Street, and when after abundant experience he came finally to realize it he turned away to pick up the scattered threads of a life largely wasted. For years he had suffered from a long maladjustment. When he quitted the army at the close of the war with the brevet rank of brigadier-general, he found himself adrift. The world of his youth was gone and the future seemed drab and unpromising. Intellectually he was caught between tides. The traditional idealisms had burnt out in the bitter struggle, and in the sterile post-war years his Puritan nature found no adequate nourishment. The crusading ardor was gone, and the new world of science had not yet risen on the horizon of young men who had given their youth to the army. In 1865 he came upon John Stuart Mill's essay on Auguste Comte, which he said revolutionized his whole mental attitude—"I emerged from the theological stage, in which I had been nurtured, and passed into the scientific. . . . From reading that compact little volume of Mill's . . . I date a changed intellectual and moral life." Yet from this accidental foray into Victorian rationalism he got little more than a sense of release from a dead Puritanism. Creative intellectual enthusiasms were not to be his portion.

Disillusioned with the law, over which he had been pottering, and wanting to ally himself with the dominant forces of his generation, he "fixed on the railroad system as the most developing force and largest field of the day." He delved into the history of certain railways and established a reputation as a student of transportation. For upwards of a quarter century—from 1866 to 1890—as a member of different public commissions and finally as president of the Union Pacific system—Jay Gould's road—he devoted his best energy to the work, only to be disillusioned in the end. In 1912 he wrote this confession:

> Indeed, as I approach the end, I am more than a little puzzled to account for the instances I have seen of business success—money-getting. It comes from a rather low instinct. Certainly, as far as my observation goes, it is rarely met with in combination with the finer or more interesting traits of character. I have known, and known tolerably well, a good many "successful" men—"big" financially—men famous during the last half-century; and a less interesting crowd I do not care to encounter. Not one that I have ever known would I care to meet again, either in this world or the next; nor is one of them associated in my mind with the idea of humor, thought, or refinement. A set of mere money-getters and traders, they were essentially unattractive and uninteresting. . . . In the course of my railroad experiences I made no friends, apart from those in the Boston direction; nor among those I met was there any man whose acquaintance I valued. They were a coarse, realistic, bargaining crowd.[1]

Yet not till he had reached his late fifties did he finally cut the ties that held him to the "bargaining crowd," and turn to the business of salvaging the remnant of his days. He gave himself over with zest to the writing of Massachusetts history, but it was then too late to do notable work. He had laid too many offerings on an altar he had come to loathe. Not a lifelong student like Henry, he had been unable to gather great stores of knowledge. Not a militant rebel like Brooks, he had never been given to searching inquiries into the laws of civilization. And so when he found himself free at last, he set himself to the business of local chronicles. That was better than nothing; it was the one thing in his life he took solid pride in; the work was honestly and capably done; but it was small savings from a lifetime of conscientious work. His venture into the realm of business had been a disaster.

II

HENRY ADAMS—INTELLECTUAL

From a similar disaster Henry Adams was saved by an early disillusionment. His efforts at *rapprochement* were little more than a gesture. While casting about after the war for a promising opening

[1] *Autobiography*, pp., 190–195.

for a career he hit upon finance as a likely field and published a number of essays that drew attention to him. But it was quite impossible for him to go forward along such lines. He was too completely the intellectual, too aloof from his generation in spirit and will, to ally himself with the economic masters of the Gilded Age. Sooner or later he would go his own way, and luckily good fortune took the matter in hand promptly. No suitable opportunity offering, he was dragooned by family and friends into an assistant-professorship at Harvard, where he spent seven years trying to explain to himself and his students the meaning of the Middle Ages. Those years were his introduction to history. The passion of the student was in his blood, and he turned with zest to brood over the scanty records of past generations, seeking a clue to the meaning of man's pilgrimage on earth, trying to arrange the meaningless fragments in some sort of rational pattern, in the hope of discovering an underlying unity in what seemed on the face only a meaningless welter of complexity and irrationality. A rationalist, he followed his intellect in an eager quest for the law of historical evolution, and he ended fifty years later in mysticism. It was a natural outcome for a lifetime of rationalizing—a compensation for the mordant dissatisfactions that issued from the restless play of mind.

Dissatisfied with his labors he quitted the Harvard post in 1879 and thereafter made his home at Washington in the atmosphere of politics. From the Middle Ages he turned to the American past and set out to explore the period during which the first Adams had played his part. He could not deal with narrow parochial themes; he would not fall into the "sink of history—antiquarianism," that satisfied Charles Francis Adams. From the beginnings of his intellectual life he had been concerned with the ideas and ideals that presumably lie behind periods and civilizations; so he went back to what he regarded as the great age of American political history, to inquire into the meaning of the struggle between Federalism and Jeffersonianism for control of the venture in republicanism. But finding little satisfaction there, as he had earlier found none in Victorian England, where he had studied closely contemporary English statesmen—Palmerston and Lord Russell and Gladstone— only to convince himself that they were bankrupt of ideas and morality, and had nothing to teach concerning the good life, he abandoned the field, threw over his familiar studies, and set about the great business of reëducating himself.

From his long studies in the American past one significant thing had emerged—he had come to understand the source of certain of his dissatisfactions with current American ideals that set him apart from his fellows. He had gone back to his own origins and had traced the rise of the defiant Adams prejudices that were as strong in the fourth generation as they had been in the first. The Adams family was eighteenth-century—Henry Adams had come to understand—and he himself in mind and education and prejudices, was of that earlier time. He was a child of Quincy rather than Boston—a simple world with simple virtues that capitalism and industrialism were destroying in the name of progress. From such village loyalties he could not rid himself. Perhaps in reason he should not have preferred that earlier homespun world; but affection does not heed logic, and as Henry Adams traced the decline of Quincy to Hamilton's financial policy that started the new capitalism on its triumphant career, he was filled with bitterness. It was a vulgar order that was rising and an evil day. Since 1865 the bankers had ruled America, and they were coming finally to cajole the American people into accepting their vulgar ideals and putting their trust in a bankers' paradise. As he watched the temples of the new society rising everywhere in the land, his gorge rose at the prospect. He had no wish to dwell in a bankers' paradise. Dislike of a capitalistic society was in his blood. From father to son all the Adamses had distrusted capitalism and hated State Street. The "only distinctive mark of all the Adamses," he said late in life, "since old Sam Adams's father a hundred and fifty years before, had been their inherited quarrel with State Street, which had again and again broken out into riot, bloodshed, personal feuds, foreign and civil war, wholesale banishments and confiscations, until the history of Florence was hardly more turbulent than that of Boston."[2]

And so when at the climax of the capitalistic revolution he watched the change going on noisily all about him, when the transition to the bankers' paradise was called progress and capitalistic feudalism was hailed as the advent of Utopia, he seemed to himself a somewhat pathetic anachronism. Shades of the prison house were falling about him. "He had hugged his antiquated dislike of bankers and capitalistic society," he said bitterly, "until he had become little better than a crank."

[2] *The Education of Henry Adams*, p. 21.

He had known for years that he must accept the régime, but he had known a great many other disagreeable certainties—like age, senility, and death—against which one made what little resistance one could. . . . For a hundred years, between 1793 and 1893, the American people had hesitated, vacillated, swayed forward and back, between two forces, one simply industrial, the other capitalistic, centralizing, and mechanical. In 1893, the issue came on the single gold standard, and the majority at last declared itself, once for all, in favor of the capitalistic system with all its necessary machinery. All one's friends, all one's best citizens, reformers, churches, colleges, educated classes, had joined the banks to force submission to capitalism; a submission long foreseen by the mere law of mass. Of all forms of society or government, this was the one he liked least, but his likes and dislikes were as antiquated as the rebel doctrine of State rights. A capitalistic system had been adopted, and if it were to be run at all, it must be run by capital and by capitalistic methods.[3]

But while he clung tenaciously to his obsolete prejudices in favor of an earlier century, the pugnacious realism of that century was oozing out of him. The middle years of his life, between the acceptance of the Harvard post in 1870 and the final break with Victorianism in 1892, were intellectually an unhappy period. He was losing his grasp on realities and becoming narrowly and exclusively political-minded. It was not good for him to live daily in the presence of politics. In so "far as he had a function in life," he said of the Henry Adams of 1877, "it was as stable-companion to statesmen, whether they liked it or not."[4] The term "statesmen" was of course only a polite euphemism for the breed of politicians who played their sordid game under his critical eyes. He was rarely under any illusions in regard to them except when blinded by friendship. Certainly his etchings of Grant and Blaine and Sherman and Conkling and other servants of democracy were done with acid.

Yet in all his penetrating comment on men and measures there is a curious failure to take into account the economic springs of action. He had let slip the clue old John Adams had followed so tenaciously. An acute historian, not thus wanting, would never have traced the triumph of the gold standard to the "mere law of mass," would never have substituted a physical determinism for an economic, would never have confused the principle of mass with a minority. How far an intelligent man and a competent historian could go astray in his criticism of current ways is suggested by the curious novel *Democracy*, that he wrote in 1880 while living in the

[3] *Ibid.*, pp. 343–344.   [4] *Ibid.*, p. 317.

daily companionship of John Hay and Clarence King. In dealing with the phenomena of political corruption he had none of the acuteness of old John Taylor of Carolina, who would have put his finger unerringly on the cause, or of the first Adams. If he had written *Democracy* after he had studied the funding operations of the Federalists under Hamilton's leadership, very likely he would have dealt with the problem more searchingly; but in 1880 Henry Adams revealed no more critical intelligence than did Godkin or Lowell or other critics of the Gilded Age.

The historical work done during those middle years at Washington was abundant and excellent, marked by rigorous use of sources, a dispassionate attitude towards partisan issues, and excellent form. It was easy for an Adams to take middle ground between Jefferson and Hamilton, however much his sympathies inclined to the former. In all this work, however, in the *Life of Albert Gallatin* (1879), in *John Randolph* (1882), as well as in the nine-volume *History of the United States during the Administrations of Jefferson and Madison* (1889–1891), the point of view remains too narrowly political, with the result that it fails to thrust into adequate relief the economics of the great struggle between agrarianism and capitalism; and without that clue the interpretation is wanting in substantial realism.

By 1891 he was convinced that he had got all he could from the curdled milk of politics, and he became dissatisfied with his work. There can be little doubt that it was a growing realization of the inadequacy of his analysis of social forces that determined him to abandon the field he had tilled so long and set about the business of reëducating himself. If *Mont-Saint-Michel and Chartres* and *The Education* tell anything about Henry Adams they reveal that his dissatisfactions welled up from deep springs within himself— from the consciousness of his failure to penetrate beneath the surface, to probe the hidden forces that move the puppets on the historical stage. He had long been seeking an adequate philosophy of history—for a unity behind the multiplicity—and in these early years of the nineties he was stimulated by Brooks Adams, who was then deep in his theory of the law of civilization and decay and had come to lean heavily on the principle of economic determinism.[5] "Brooks Adams had taught him," he said later, "that the relation between civilizations was that of trade," and stimulated by this

[5] *Ibid.*, pp. 338–339.

rediscovery of the philosophy of the first Adams he set about the business of orienting himself to the realm of science, of substituting for a meaningless political interpretation a broader philosophical interpretation.

Very likely it was his reading in the sociology of the Enlightenment that first turned his thought to the philosophy of history—chiefly Turgot and Comte. Speaking of the years 1867–1868 he said he "became a Comteist, within the limits of evolution."[6] He had long been interested in such clues as science offered—in the geological theories of Sir Charles Lyell and the biological deductions of Darwin. But the theory of biological evolution with its implications of a benevolent progress from the simple to the complex, failed to satisfy him; and he turned to the physical sciences for a guide, discovering as the ultimate reality behind all appearances—force. This physical principle he transferred to the field of sociology. Coal-power, electrical power, he concluded, were to civilization what the gaseous theory was to physics. It was a creative suggestion and it revolutionized his conception of history. It runs through all his later speculations and provided the basis of his thinking. "Adams never knew why," he said, "knowing nothing of Faraday, he began to mimic Faraday's trick of seeing lines of force all about him, where he had always seen lines of will."[7] "To evolutionists may be left the processes of evolution; to historians the single interest is the law of reaction between force and force—between mind and nature—the law of progress."[8] "The great division of history into phases by Turgot and Comte first affirmed this law in its outlines by asserting the unity of progress."[9]

Thus by the aid of the physical sciences Henry Adams came back to the philosophy of determinism—a conception that may lead either to pantheism or to mechanism as one's temperament determines. In such a choice there would be no doubt which way Henry Adams would go; he must somehow reconcile determinism and progress, he must discover unity in multiplicity—and that unity and progress he found in a mystical pantheism. "Continuous movement, universal cause, and interchangeable force. This was pantheism, but the Schools were pantheist . . . and their deity was the ultimate energy, whose thought and action were one."[10]

[6] *Ibid.*, p. 225.
[7] *Ibid.*, p. 426.
[8] *Ibid.*, p. 493.

[9] *Ibid.*, p. 493.
[10] *Ibid.*, pp. 428–429.

How creatively this pantheistic mysticism was to determine his later thinking is sufficiently revealed in the pages of *Mont-Saint-Michel and Chartres*. With incredible labor Henry Adams had at last made his way out of the Sahara of politics in which he had long wandered.

Phrased in less transcendental terms his philosophy of history, as he came finally to understand it, was expressed thus:

> The work of domestic progress is done by masses of mechanical power—steam, electric, furnace, or other—which have to be controlled by a score or two of individuals who have shown capacity to manage it. The work of internal government has become the task of controlling these men, who are socially as remote as heathen gods, alone worth knowing, but never known, and who could tell nothing of political value if one skinned them alive. Most of them have nothing to tell, but are forces as dumb as their dynamos, absorbed in the development or economy of power. They are trustees for the public, and whenever society assumes the property, it must confer on them that title; but the power will remain as before, whoever manages it, and will then control society without appeal, as it controls its stokers and pit-men. Modern politics is, at bottom, a struggle not of men but of forces. The men become every year more and more creatures of force, massed about central power-houses. The conflict is no longer between the men, but between the motors that drive the men, and the men tend to succumb to their own motive forces. This is a moral that man strongly objects to admit, especially in mediaeval pursuits like politics and poetry, nor is it worth while for a teacher to insist upon it.[11]

From a civilization thus tyrannized over by coal-power and electrical power, he turned away to discover if possible a civilization in which men had lived the good life that he longed for; and in his second incursion into medieval times he found what he had long been seeking. Two centuries, from 1050 to 1250, came to represent for him in the evening of his days the crown and glory of all human endeavor; the first century with its Norman Mont-Saint-Michel and its *Chanson de Roland*, with its forthright strength and simplicity, its uncritical acceptance of life and God, its hope encompassed by a sufficing unity—a strong, naïve, credulous world, yet with men's minds buttressed like their cathedrals by a faith that held in equilibrium the soaring arches of their aspirations, with every cranny and nook flooded with radiant color: and the second century, that expressed itself in the cathedral of Chartres, with its adoration of the Virgin, its courtly love of Guillaume de Lorris and Marie de Champagne, its passionate mysticism of Saint Louis and

[11] *Ibid.*, pp. 421–422.

Saint Bernard and Saint Francis, and its soaring scholasticism of Thomas Aquinas—a tender, feminine age, that worshiped woman and erected its altars to Our Lady of Love rather than to Our Lady of Sorrows, that found in Isolde the ideal woman and expressed itself in Eleanor of Guienne and Blanche of Castile, in Héloïse and Marie de Champagne, more adequately than in Richard Cœur-de-Lion, till it finally went the way of mortality "with the death of Queen Blanche and of all good things about the year 1250":—to such idealization of medievalism did this child of Puritanism come in the wistful twilight of his days. He had never evaded life, nor professed himself satisfied with mean or cheap substitutes, but had sought persistently till he had come to believe that the good life had been lived once, though it might not ever be lived again. So much at least was clear gain, even though it should end in wistfulness.

Mont-Saint-Michel and Chartres is a beautiful book, the more beautiful because of its wistfulness; and the theme that runs through its pages is a denial of the values that embodied for his countrymen the sum of all excellence. It is an account of certain happy generations—so few amongst the countless many—who worshiped in love, before fear had come to the western world and crept into the message of the church; a love that elevated Mother Mary above the Christ of the Cross, and that in her shrine at Chartres would allow no hint of sorrow or suffering to appear, but represented her as looking out upon the world with a gracious and regal kindliness and mercy, quick to succor and to forgive—the spirit of love that suffices life in all its needs. *Mont-Saint-Michel and Chartres* is rich and tender and wise, perhaps beyond anything else that his generation of Americans wrote, with a mellow scholarship that walks modestly because it has learned how little it knows. Yet in its every implication it is a sharp and searching criticism of Boston and America of the nineteenth century. It repudiates every ideal of a generation that had gambled away the savor of life—that does not comprehend "and never shall," the greatness of that earlier time, "the appetite" for living, the "greed for novelty," "the fun of life." [12] It was precisely these things, unimportant though they might seem to the acquisitive mind, that Henry Adams had missed in his own life and passionately resented having missed. To come to know great men and great deeds and great ages is perhaps of doubtful expediency for one who must live amongst small men; and Henry

Adams was forced to pay a heavy penalty for his catholic understanding and sympathy.

The profound suggestiveness of *Mont-Saint-Michel and Chartres*
lies in the skill with which the brilliant threads of medieval art and
thought and aspiration are woven into a single pattern, and the
splendor of its unity traced to a mystical *élan* that found its highest
expression in faith. It was the ideal of love that he discovered in the
golden twelfth century—love above law, above logic, above the
church and the schools: a love that explains for him the passionate
worship of Mother Mary, together with the new *"courtoisie"* that
sought to shape manners and morals to humane ends. The humanity of the Virgin set her above the Trinity, as the humanity of Saint
Francis set him above Thomas Aquinas, for all the latter's soaring
scholasticism. To one who entered those bygone times through the
portals of Chartres cathedral, it was natural to interpret the total
age in the light of the gentle smile of the Mother of God, and to feel
her presence as a transforming spirit amongst men. Has any other
Yankee interpreted so lovingly the mission of the Virgin, as Henry
Adams analyzed it in such a passage as this?

True it was, although one should not say it jestingly, that the Virgin
embarrassed the Trinity; and perhaps this was the reason, behind all the
other excellent reasons, why men loved and adored her with a passion
such as no other deity has ever inspired: and why we, although utter
strangers to her, are not far from getting down on our knees and praying
to her still. Mary concentrated in herself the whole rebellion of man against
fate; the whole protest against divine law; the whole contempt for human
law as its outcome; the whole unutterable fury of human nature beating
itself against the walls of its prison-house, and suddenly seized by a hope
that in the Virgin man had found a door of escape. She was above law;
she took feminine pleasure in turning hell into an ornament; she delighted
in trampling on every social distinction in this world and the next. She
knew that the universe was as unintelligible to her, on any theory of
morals, as it was to her worshippers, and she felt, like them, no sure conviction that it was any more intelligible to the Creator of it. To her, every
suppliant was a universe in himself, to be judged apart, on his own merits,
by his love for her,—by no means on his orthodoxy, or his conventional
standing in the Church, or according to his correctness in defining the
nature of the Trinity. The convulsive hold which Mary to this day maintains over human imagination—as you can see at Lourdes—was due much
less to her power of saving soul or body than to her sympathy with people
who suffered under law,—divine or human,—justly or unjustly, by accident or design, by decree of God or by guile of Devil. She cared not a
straw for conventional morality, and she had no notion of letting her

friends be punished, to the tenth or any other generation, for the sins of their ancestors or the peccadilloes of Eve.

So Mary filled heaven with a sort of persons little to the taste of any respectable middle-class society, which has trouble enough in making this world decent and pay its bills, without having to continue the effort in another. Mary stood in a Church of her own, so independent that the Trinity might have perished without much affecting her position; but, on the other hand, the Trinity could look on and see her dethroned with almost a breath of relief. . . . Mary's treatment of respectable and law-abiding people who had no favours to ask, and were reasonably confident of getting to heaven by the regular judgment, without expense, rankled so deeply that three hundred years later the Puritan reformers were not satisfied with abolishing her, but sought to abolish the woman altogether as the cause of all evil in heaven and on earth. The Puritans abandoned the New Testament and the Virgin in order to go back to the beginning, and renew the quarrel with Eve.[13]

Thus at last, in another land and a remote age, Henry Adams found the clue that explained for him his own failure and the source of the dissatisfactions that had tracked him doggedly through his far wanderings. He had come to understand the reasons for the sterility of his Massachusetts past, and the last shreds of his Puritan-Federalist heritage were cast off. In comparison with the vision that came to him in the choir of Chartres, how unspeakably poor and mean were the activities he had portrayed in *Democracy*, or even those he had dealt with in his history of the early days of the republic. He had discovered the highest existence in emotional response to noble appeal; the good life was the unified life, possible only on a grand scale in those rare and great periods of social *élan* when the individual is fused in an encompassing unity. Of that golden age of the Transition—so he finally cast up the account— "the sum is an emotion—clear and strong as love and much clearer than logic whose charm lies in its unstable balance."

The Transition is the equilibrium between the love of God—which is faith—and the logic of God—which is reason; between the round arch and the pointed. One may not be sure which pleases most, but one need not be harsh toward people who think that the moment of balance is exquisite. The last and highest moment is seen at Chartres, where, in 1200, the charm depends on the constant doubt whether emotion or science is uppermost. At Amiens, doubt ceases; emotion is trained in school, Thomas Aquinas reigns.[14]

Of all the elaborate symbolism which has been suggested for the Gothic cathedral, the most vital and most perfect may be that the slender

---

[13] *Mont-Saint-Michel*, pp. 276–277.   [14] *Ibid.*, pp. 321–322.

nervure, the springing motion of the broken arch, the leap downwards of the flying buttress,—the visible effort to throw off a visible strain,—never let us forget that Faith alone supports it, and that, if Faith fails, Heaven is lost. The equilibrium is visibly delicate beyond the line of safety; danger lurks in every stone. The peril of the heavy tower, of the restless vault, of the vagrant buttress; the uncertainty of logic, the inequalities of the syllogism, the irregularities of the mental mirror,—all these haunting nightmares of the Church are expressed as strongly by the Gothic cathedral as though it had been the cry of human suffering, and as no emotion had ever been expressed before or is likely to find expression again. The delight of its aspiration is flung up to the sky. The pathos of its self-distrust and anguish of doubt is buried in the earth as its last secret. You can read out of it whatever else pleases your youth and confidence; to me, this is all.[15]

One may enter the past, of course, through such portals as one chooses; but one is likely to choose the portals that promise to open upon the world of one's desires. It was a fortunate accident, no doubt, that led Henry Adams to Chartres to study the cathedral glass under the guidance of John La Farge; nevertheless it finally determined for him his total interpretation of the Middle Ages and of all history, and that interpretation followed naturally a subtle ancestral bias. Even in his rebellion against his past he could not get away from it, but like Ruskin and John Henry Newman he came to affirm—whether rightly or wrongly, who shall say?—that the singular glory of the Middle Ages was the mystical *élan* that came to expression in the adoration of the Virgin. As a child of generations of Puritans he came back finally, in the twilight of his studies, to the great ideal of faith. And yet it is not without suggestion that William Morris, who more nearly than any other modern expressed in his daily life the spirit of the Middle Ages, never concerned himself much with the medieval church—neither its cathedrals nor its scholasticism nor its miracles—never talked about an age of faith, would scarcely have understood, indeed, what was meant by the drive of a mystical *élan;* but discovered the secret of that earlier civilization in the gild rather than the church, and traced the source of the haunting beauty that clings to all its works to the psychology of craftsmanship that found delight in shaping the raw material to the craftsman's dreams.

The difference between Morris and Adams is great enough, and at bottom it is the difference between the artist and the intellectual; yet it is a pity that Henry Adams, with his wide acquaintance in

[15] *Ibid.*, p. 383.

England, should never have known the one Victorian he should most have delighted in—the nineteenth-century craftsman who found in his workshop the good life the historian dreamed of, and was unhappy because it had been lost. Perhaps it would not have greatly changed the latter's interpretation. He was not a pagan in temperament to enter sympathetically into the medieval world that Morris had discovered and of which the Church was only a drapery—a drapery that never quite covered a frank *joie de vivre* that was an emotion far more realistic and human than any mystical *élan*, and that persisted long after the apogee of faith in the early twelfth century, filling all the later Middle Ages with its abundant beauty till it was finally destroyed by the economic revolution that came out of the Reformation. But at any rate he might have been led by such knowledge to set the craftsman beside the poet and the schoolman and the mystic—the nameless artist who wrought such marvels beside the patron who took care to have his name and his arms emblazoned on window and wall to remind posterity of his generosity; and certainly, his interpretation of the Middle Ages would not have suffered by such addition. Instead, an excessive intellectualism drove him back upon the naïve.

The disillusion of Henry Adams is abundantly instructive to the student of our flamboyant transition, so different from the golden Transition. Here was an honest man and an able—none honester and none abler in his generation—who devoted his life to finding a path out of the maze of middle-class America, that should lead to a rational and humane existence. He was never overconfident of his conclusions. All arrogant dogmatisms he had long since left behind; they had become for him pathetically futile and foolish. Creeds and faiths, whether in religion or politics or economics, he no longer subscribed to; but a certain residuum remained, from his long meditations—a sense of interfusing unity, mystical, pantheistic, that his lurking skepticism dealt tenderly with. "*Inter vania nihil vanius est homine*," he asserted as a skeptic, and as a mystic he replied, "Man is an imperceptible atom always trying to become one with God. If ever modern science achieves a definition of energy, possibly it may borrow the figure: Energy is the inherent effort of every multiplicity to become unity." [16] In these later years he called himself half whimsically a "conservative Christian Anarchist" [17] and the explanation probably is to be found in his

---

[16] *Mont-Saint-Michel*, p. 332.　　　　[17] *The Education*, p. 405.

shift from intellectualism to emotion as the crown of a satisfying life. "The two poles of social and political philosophy seem necessarily to be organization or anarchy; man's intellect or the forces of nature." [18] In rare and happy periods—as in the glorious Transition—freedom finds its fullest life in a spontaneous drawing together of the whole; but as the social *élan* dies away, institutions, organization, remain. Thomas Aquinas follows Saint Francis, form remains after emotion has subsided. Nevertheless the free man must cling to his freedom, in spite of society, in spite of the political state.

Absolute liberty is absence of restraint; responsibility is restraint; therefore, the ideally free individual is responsible only to himself. This principle is the philosophical foundation of anarchism, and, for anything that science has yet proved, may be the philosophical foundation of the universe; but it is fatal to all society and is especially hostile to the State. [19]

Though he lived in the midst of a centralizing politics and found his friends in such servants of centralization as John Hay and Henry Cabot Lodge, Henry Adams had no faith in the dominant ideals. He was never a friend to an acquisitive society with its engrossing political state. In the light of his favorite dictum that "Power is poison," he may perhaps be regarded as an old-fashioned Jeffersonian; it is another evidence of the persistence of his eighteenth-century mind. He was an arch-individualist who would go his own way and reach his own conclusions, quite unconcerned that his views were wholly at variance with those of his generation. How could it be otherwise? How should men who lived in the counting-house understand even the language of this pilgrim returned from other and greater worlds? It was foolish to talk of what he had seen. And so when he wrote *Mont-Saint-Michel and Chartres* he published it privately, and was incredulous when it was proposed to republish it and give it to the world. What had he, or the twelfth century, to say to the land of Theodore Roosevelt and Pierpont Morgan? Was not this America of theirs peopled by the descendants of the *bourgeoisie* who, six hundred years before, resentful at having been cheated—as they supposed—in their heavy investments in shrines and churches of Our Lady, had turned away from all such unprofitable business, and put their savings in lands and houses and ships and railways and banks—of which

[18] *Mont-Saint-Michel*, p. 344.   [19] *Ibid.*, p. 372.

things politics was the sluttish servant? How should one who had known Saint Francis and Eleanor of Guienne take such men or such a world seriously?

III

BROOKS ADAMS—REBEL

The difference between Henry Adams and Brooks Adams is, perhaps, sufficiently revealed in the distinction between the intellectual and the rebel. The youngest of the brothers was a militant nonconformist, a searching and outspoken critic of all the faiths of his generation. In Brooks Adams the family skepticisms were pointed and barbed, and the family distrust of capitalism issued in a broadside attack upon the hateful system. Few Americans of his day were so little pleased with the bankers' Utopia dreamed of by the middle class, or subjected the capitalistic mind to such critical analysis. Not content with rejecting that Utopia, he pursued his studies in the history of western civilization with a view to determining whether the economic mind, instead of being the friend and ally of a human society—as it professed to be—were not rather the foul wellspring of a disintegrating egoism that must destroy every civilization that yields to its siren appeal. In the theory he eventually elaborated, the capitalistic mind proves to be a greedy spider spinning his web to catch the simple imaginative minds—warrior and priest and artist and craftsman—and suck them dry. The sterile middleman becomes master of society and with the inevitable enslavement of the producer, and the drying-up of production at its source, civilization withers and decays, to be followed by another cycle in the long struggle between the creative and acquisitive instincts.

None but a congenital rebel could have arrived at such conclusions from the studies in which his youth was passed. As a son of the house of Adams the profession of the law was the predestined path to politics and diplomacy, and like Charles and Henry he devoted his younger years to the ancestral study, receiving such training as the Harvard Law School could give. He made greater progress than his brothers, eventually getting so far as to write legal treatises; but finding such work a bit arid he supplemented his legal studies with the writing of Massachusetts chronicles. His dissatisfactions seem to have culminated in the late eighties, during the lean years that preceded the crash of 1893; and he turned away from local chronicles to speculate on the deeper causes of social vigor and decline. The result was the publication in 1895 of *The Law of Civilization and Decay*, a study in social dynamics that took its point of departure from psychology, and based its conclusions on physics and economics. Before Henry Adams he elaborated the theory that civilization is the product of social energy, and social energy obeys the physical law of mass, accelerating or retarding in ratio to the density of population reduced to order. As society draws together in great centers its activity increases until exhaustion finally slows it down; whereupon follows a period of disintegration that breaks up the integrated mass and disperses its energy. The social ebb and flow, therefore, is always from decentralization to centralization and back again to decentralization, and as it flows it thrusts into the foreground different types of mind that express themselves in diverse ideals.

The master types that appear and disappear in this ceaseless flux are determined by two psychological drives that always and everywhere shape human activity—fear and greed: the one culminating in the social rule of the priest, the other in the social rule of the usurer. Decentralization with its isolation breeds the imaginative mind which, seeing more devils than vast hell can hold, turns to the priest for succor—to one who deals in miracles and professes to be able to fend off malignant powers, and who in consequence grows rich by his traffic in relics and rises to economic power. But imagination produces as well the creative mind that finds in isolation the promptings to revery, expresses its dreams in terms of beauty, and fashions a realm of art in which to dwell. Priest, artist, and warrior,—shrine, cathedral, and castle—were the creation of medieval times, the naïve products of the golden age of decentralization. Whereas centralization, with the rubbing away of singularity by daily contact and the greater rewards that lie open to activity, breeds automatically the economic mind—a mind that is necessarily unimaginative, practical, competitive, acquisitive, skeptical, preferring administration to creation, and setting exploitation as the single object of activity. And since centralization offers increasing rewards to greed, the economic mind subdues the imaginative, and the money-lender with his control of wealth rises to mastery. As he expropriates the resources of society he inevitably dominates the political state. His wealth enables him to maintain a hired police to safeguard his gains, until expropriation having run its course, the police fail to hold in check the mass of the exploited, and an unmartial class discovers that money can no longer buy security against the strength of numbers. The usurer is overthrown, his wealth is expropriated, and the social cycle must be run again.

This suggestive theory, which he works out with conspicuous skill in his interpretation of the Middle Ages and the rise of capitalism, implies a perennial conflict between fear and greed, that turns finally upon the relative development of the arts of attack and of defense. Centralization, it is clear, results from the superiority of the former; when attack is superior to defense the lesser strongholds of exploitation must fall and the defeated must become subject to the coalescing masters. After the disruption of the Roman Empire western Europe created its feudal system, by means of which the baron in his stout castle flouted the centralizing ambitions of the impotent monarchy; and it was not till the wealth of the church and of the *bourgeoisie* was thrown on the side of the king, and the development of the art of attack through the use of gunpowder, that the rise of the monarchical state was possible. But having aided the king to reduce the power of the barons, thereby rendering trade secure on a large scale, the *bourgeoisie* turned against the medieval church with its vast wealth that invited expropriation. In the primitive age of faith, under the dominion of fear, the burgesses had spent their money prodigally to build shrines and churches and cathedrals—in France alone between the years 1170 and 1270, eighty cathedrals and nearly five hundred large churches had been built, that by a calculation made in 1840, would cost a billion dollars to replace [20]—but with the development of the economic mind such amazing expenditures seemed wasteful, and the *bourgeoisie* looked about for a cheaper way of salvation. The money cost to the worshipers of saints and relics was a sharp prod to their skepticism as to the efficacy of such worship. This explains for Brooks Adams the origins of the Reformation; it was due to the economic dissatisfaction of the burgess class; the church had grown rich and grasping from its monopoly power. Speaking of the rise of English Lollardry, he argued:

The Lollards were of the modern economic type, and discarded the miracle because the miracle was costly and yielded an uncertain return . . . gifts as an atonement for sin were a drain on savings, and the econo-

[20] See Henry Adams, *Mont-Saint-Michel*, pp. 94–95.

mist instinctively sought cheaper methods of propitiation. The monied
class, therefore, proceeded step by step, and its first experiment was to
suppress all fees to middle-men, whether priests or saints, by becoming
their own intercessors with the deity . . . [and] as the tradesman replaced
the enthusiast, a dogma was evolved by which mental anguish, which cost
nothing, was substituted for the offering which was effective in proportion
to its money value. This dogma was "Justification by Faith," the corner-
stone of Protestantism. . . .

But the substitution of a mental condition for a money payment led
to consequences more far-reaching than the suppression of certain clerical
revenues, for it involved the rejection of the sacred tradition which had
not only sustained relic worship, but which had made the Church the
channel of communication between Christians and the invisible world.
That ancient channel once closed, Protestants had to open another, and
this led to the deification of the Bible. . . . Thus for the innumerable
costly fetishes of the imaginative age were substituted certain writings
which could be consulted without a fee. The expedient was evidently the
device of a mercantile community, . . . and made an organized priesthood impossible. When each individual might pry into the sacred mysteries at his pleasure, the authority of the clergy was annihilated.[21]

With warrior and priest superseded by the tradesman as the
dominant type—the imaginative mind by the economic—came the
inevitable triumph of greed over fear. The ancient defenses of the
church were razed and it stood naked to its enemies. In presence
of the skepticism of the burgesses it could no longer sell its miracles
in the open market, could no longer persuade men that it was God's
vicegerent with powers of binding and loosing; and with its divine
sanctions gone, its wealth-hoards lay unprotected before the cupidity of king, noble, and commoner. The spoliation of the monasteries was the prelude to the long movement of the Reformation in
England, and made possible its success. So long as the church retained its lands and treasure it could not easily be overturned; so a
greedy King and greedy nobles took effective measures to disarm
it, and having got their hands on the substantial plunder they left
to Genevan ministers the lesser business of disputing over the form
and doctrine of the new church. The revolution had already been
accomplished; and this revolution—the transfer from priest to layman of a third of the wealth of England—was but prelude to still
greater revolutions that were preparing, and which began with the
pouring into England of the gold and silver from the Spanish treas-
ure-ships. The spoiling of Rome and the spoiling of the Spaniard
were both buccaneering adventures undertaken by zealous Protes-

[21] *The Law of Civilization and Decay*, pp. 150–151.

tants. Drake and Hawkins—pirate and slaver—were "hot gospel-
lers," ready to fight, plunder, or rape for the glory of God and the
profit of England; and it was such men who diverted to London the
flood of Spanish-American silver that issued from the rich mines of
Potosi.

Potosi was discovered in 1545, and from that event Adams dates
the rise of the commercial activity that was to prepare the way for
the Industrial Revolution, which came to flower two centuries later.
This vast upheaval that destroyed the older feudal England, was
the immediate outcome of the plundering of India that brought to
London the vast treasure-hoards of the East. The eviction of the
peasants from their lands had already provided a plentiful supply
of cheap labor, the machinery of credit and exchange had been
created, and with this immense influx of capital the Industrial
Revolution was a matter of course. The manufacturers seized
control of England and ruled till approximately 1810, when their
authority was disputed by the financiers who gradually displaced
them. The Bank Act of 1844, which yielded the control of the
currency to the bankers, marked the definite transfer of sovereignty
to Lombard Street; Samuel Lloyd, the banker, completed the
work begun in 1523 by Thomas Cromwell, burgess-adventurer—the
work of bringing England under the authoritative sway of the
principle of greed. Since 1844 western civilization has lain helpless
under the heel of the usurer, who levies his tax upon production by
expanding and contracting the currency at will, and rules society
through his control of the political state. The triumph of the
economic mind is complete.

The aristocracy which wields this autocratic power is beyond attack,
for it is defended by a wage-earning police, by the side of which the legions
were a toy—a police so formidable that, for the first time in history, revolt is hopeless and is not attempted. The only question which preoccu-
pies the ruling class is whether it is cheaper to coerce or bribe.[22]

The Law of Civilization and Decay is an extraordinarily provocative study, the main principles of which he elaborated and applied
in later historical studies, the result of which was to emphasize for
him the determining influence of economics and geography in the
rise and fall of empires.[23] Equipped thus with a comprehensive

[22] *Ibid.*, p. 292.
[23] See *America's Economic Supremacy*, New York, 1900; *The New Empire*, New
York, 1902.

philosophy of history, he turned in a later work to examine certain aspects of the play of social forces in America, in the light of universal social experience. The particular object of his inquiry in *The Theory of Social Revolutions* is the machinery of social control developed in America during the movement of capitalistic centralization, and its probable adequacy to meet the future stresses of acceleration. The problem of security for the capitalistic order resolves itself, he decides, into the problem of a sufficient protective police; and since every non-military master class must depend upon some form of mercenary Swiss guard, the solution in America has assumed a form not uncommon in earlier European experience, but which every European country has learned at bitter cost to reject. In the face of a strong anti-militaristic public sentiment that forbids a coercive army and navy, the financial masters have had recourse to the courts; and it is the eventual effect of such perversion of the courts to non-judicial ends that he considers in this frank inquiry.

Historically, he points out, the courts have at times exercised two diverse functions, the judicial and the political; and the problem of justice and equity before the law, it has been found by long and bitter experience, resolves itself into the total separation of the one from the other. The judicial function is that of impartial arbitrament in accordance with an established *corpus juris;* it is judgment and not will. The enactment of the law, on the other hand, is a political function, residing in the legislature. When therefore, the courts exercise the political function, they not only assert that the judicial will is sovereign, but they engage in a perilous struggle for mastership and involve themselves in all the passions of partisan objectives. Every "dominant class, as it has arisen, has done its best to use the machinery of justice for its own benefit." The temptation to such perversion is perennial; it is the particular and besetting temptation of an unmartial monied class; and in times of social stress it becomes acute. In revolutionary crises—as in England under Lord Chief-Justice Jeffreys and in France under the Revolutionary Tribunal—the political function overrides the judicial, the last protection of the individual is swept away, and society lies helpless before the ruling power. Thus to pervert the legitimate functions of the courts is a dangerous game to play—most dangerous for a non-military group for whom the courts are protectors; and yet it is precisely this game that capitalism in America, heedless of the teachings of experience, has long been playing. Using the courts as a police power it has brought contempt upon them and thereby weakened the arm upon which alone it can hope to rely in periods of acute stress. In short, capitalism has assumed the functions of sovereignty in America, but it has refused to assume the responsibilities of sovereignty. To gain immediate ends it has shut its eyes to future consequences; and what those future consequences are likely to be Brooks Adams is at pains to point out.

The kernel of his argument, obviously, lies in the thesis that the federal courts have assumed political functions; and into this question he delves with the equipment of the lawyer added to that of the philosophical historian. "Politics," he asserts realistically, "is the struggle for ascendancy of a class or a majority." Under the "American system, the Constitution . . . is expounded by judges, and this function, which, in essence, is political, has brought precisely that quality of pressure on the bench which it has been the labor of a hundred generations of our ancestors to remove."[24] Hence, "from the outset, the American bench, because it deals with the most fiercely contested of political issues, has been an instrument necessary to political success. Consequently, political parties have striven to control it, and, therefore, the bench has always had an avowed partisan bias."[25] From so anomalous a situation two curious developments have resulted: in the rôle of guardians of the Constitution the courts have assumed sovereign powers over the legislature, and at the same time, by a clever non-judicial hocus-pocus they have declared themselves superior to the Constitution, possessed of the prerogative of dispensation. How the first came into being Adams traces in detail from the time of Marbury vs. Madison in 1803, when Marshall asserted a supervisory jurisdiction over Congress, to Standard Oil Company vs. United States in 1911, when the Court amended an act of Congress that Congress had declined to amend. How the second came into being is a curious story. It arose, according to Adams, from the rigidity of a written constitution, that having been interpreted narrowly must somehow be stretched to meet public needs. In such an emergency the "Supreme Court of New York imagined the theory of the Police Power," saying in effect, "in our discretion, we suspend the operation of the Constitution, in this instance, by calling your act an exercise of a power unknown to the framers of the Constitution."[26]

[24] *The Theory of Social Revolution*, p. 45.   [25] *Ibid.*, pp. 47–48.   [26] *Ibid.*, p. 128.

In other words, having, by the assumption of sovereignty, nullified the legislative power from which relief would naturally come,
and having awakened a hostile public opinion by its narrow interpretation of contractual rights, the court was embarrassed and
looked about for a loophole of escape; and the most convenient
loophole was the novel doctrine of judicial prerogative:

> No legislature could intervene, and a pressure was brought to bear which
> the judges could not withstand; therefore, the Court yielded, declaring
> that if impairing a contract were, on the whole, for the public welfare,
> the Constitution, as Marshall interpreted it, should be suspended in favor
> of the legislation which impaired it. They called this suspension the opera-
> tion of the "Police Power." It followed, as the "Police Power" could
> only come into operation at the discretion of the Court, that, therefore,
> within the limits of judicial discretion, confiscation, however arbitrary
> and to whatever extent, might go on.[27]
> The effect of the adoption by the Supreme Court of the United States
> of the New York theory of the Police Power was to vest in the judiciary,
> by the use of this catch-word, an almost unparalleled prerogative. They
> assumed a supreme function which can only be compared to the Dispensing
> Power claimed by the Stuarts, or to the authority which, according to the
> Council of Constance, inheres in the Church, to "grant indulgences for
> reasonable causes." I suppose nothing in modern judicial history has ever
> resembled this assumption. . . .[28]

It is this amazing principle of the judicial prerogative which
sets the Courts above the Constitution and grants them the privilege of dispensing Indulgences, that has perverted their functions
from the judicial to the political. If Indulgences are for sale, naturally the wealthy will buy them. And since corporate wealth is regarded by the judiciary with a more than friendly eye, it rarely
finds difficulty in securing such Indulgences as it seeks. The
Courts have become, in consequence, not so much the Swiss Guards
of capitalism, as a pliant sovereign lord who dispenses rewards to
his favorites. The capitalist is "the most lawless" of citizens. In
his attitude towards the state he is essentially anarchistic; he
evades or nullifies a law that he does not like, while clamorous for
the enforcement of a law that works in his favor.

> If the capitalist has bought some sovereign function, and wishes to
> abuse it for his own behoof, he regards the law which restrains him as a
> despotic invasion of his constitutional rights, because, with his specialized
> mind, he cannot grasp the relation of a sovereign function to the nation

[27] *Ibid.*, p. 93.   [28] *Ibid.*, pp. 91–92.

as a whole. He, therefore, looks upon the evasion of a law devised for public protection, but inimical to him, as innocent or even meritorious.

This attitude of capital has had a profound effect upon shaping the American legal mind. The capitalist, as I infer, regards the constitutional form of government which exists in the United States, as a convenient method of obtaining his own way against a majority, but the lawyer has learned to worship it as a fetish. Nor is this astonishing, for, were written constitutions suppressed, he would lose most of his importance and much of his income. Quite honestly, therefore, the American lawyer has come to believe that a sheet of paper soiled with printers' ink and interpreted by half-a-dozen elderly gentlemen snugly dozing in armchairs, has some inherent and marvellous virtue by which it can arrest the march of omnipotent Nature. And capital gladly accepts this view of American civilization, since hitherto capitalists have usually been able to select the magistrates who decide their causes.[29]

The skepticisms of the House of Adams came to their frankest expression in the writings of Brooks Adams. The passion for social justice had brought him at last to a philosophy of history that made him a trenchant critic of the American of his generation. He rejected alike the humanitarian optimism that, from Condorcet to Herbert Spencer, had inspired generous souls with hope for future progress—and that even Henry Adams clung to—and the economic optimism that from the beginnings of the westward movement had inspired acquisitive souls with the hope of continuous gain. Nothing perhaps marked him more clearly as a rebel than his denial of the god worshiped by his fellows. The gospel of progress was for him no more than a fetish of the economic mind. In the ebb and flow of civilizations under the attraction of fear and greed, what justification was there for faith in a benevolent progress? His lot had been cast, unfortunately, in an age of capitalism, when the acquisitive mind was triumphing over the imaginative, the banker over the priest and craftsman and mystic; but he could see no reason in heaven or earth to brag of that fact, and he would have held himself a fool to apply the term progress to the spread of greed that was crowning the usurer as master of men. A thorough skeptic, with the comfortable illusions of his generation dissipated, he was in worse plight than Henry Adams, for he had created no golden twelfth century as a refuge against the present.

But if he was under no illusions, he was under no intellectual tyrannies; he had cleared his mind of all middle-class fetishes and could look out calmly upon a mad world. After a century and a

[29] Ibid., pp. 213–215.

quarter this youngest of the House of Adams was still true to the
sturdy intellectual honesty of his race. He refused to cry up a
fool's paradise where his fellows were crowning the banker as
king—professing to serve high ends while seeking vulgar profits:
he would not shut his eyes to disagreeable truth or hold his tongue.
In Brooks Adams one can almost hear the voice of the first Adams
elaborating his doctrine of determinism, pointing out to a romantic
generation the unpleasant realities that confuted its optimism, ex-
patiating on the abundant follies of men that lay snares in their own
path, yet clinging to a faith in justice that has become old-fashioned. Possibly Brooks Adams is not to be reckoned a great figure,
but he was an honest man and worthy of his name—no mean accomplishment, for all in all the Adams family is the most distinguished in our history.

CHAPTER III

VICTORIAN REALISM

IT was not till the eighties that the movement of realism in fiction began to excite wide interest, and then began a brisk and often acrimonious discussion of the merits and shortcomings of the new technique that filled the pages of the literary magazines. The prejudices against it were many and robust. To most Victorians realism meant Zola, sex, and the exploitation of the animal, and all the pruderies of the Age of Innocence rose up in protest against defiling letters with such themes. The judgment of Aldrich's on realism—"A miasmatic breath blown from the slums"—was a characteristic Yankee echo of Tennyson's condemnation, "wallowing in the slough of Zolaism." All the high priests of the genteel rallied to combat such a desecration of literature, and when it knocked at the door of a respectable magazine in the person of Stephen Crane's *Maggie* the editor could do nothing else than turn it into the street. In the late nineties, when *Jude the Obscure* appeared in one of the family magazines, even the great reputation of Hardy was reckoned a poor excuse for such an offense to morality.

American taste was still romantic, and from his villa at Florence, F. Marion Crawford regularly sent forth heavy romances that were regarded as contributions to our literature. In defense of his wares he threw into the discussion of realism a compact little volume, *The Novel; What It Is*, in which he defined the novel as a pocket drama, the chief interest of which lies in the plot—a retort courteous to Howells's contention that plot is childish and a story ends well that ends faithfully; wedding bells at the end are of no interest to grown men and women, but rather what life brings after the wedding bells. To the aid of Crawford came the brilliant Scot, Robert Louis Stevenson, the literary idol of America in the nineties, whose brave tales were on every center-table. A confirmed romantic, Stevenson could not resist breaking a lance in the cause, and his *Humble Remonstrance* was a persuasive defense of the perennial appeal of romance.

But in spite of protests the spirit of realism spread quietly through the lesser works of fiction and the high-flown romantic was laid away in the grave of John Esten Cooke. The new realism was a native growth, sprung from the soil, unconcerned with European technique. In its earlier expression it inclined to a romantic or idyllic coloring, but as it developed it came to rely more and more on the beauty of truth. This primitive realism issued chiefly from the local color school of the short story, but it was supplemented by the sociological school. The influence of Lowell and the *Atlantic Monthly* on the development of the realistic short story had been encouraging, and in the next decade that development was to go forward swiftly. With the exploitation of local materials came a sharp division on sectional lines, and as Howells pointed out, America was soon parceled out geographically into local groups. Edward Eggleston in southern Indiana, George Washington Cable in New Orleans, Charles Egbert Craddock in eastern Tennessee, James Lane Allen in Kentucky, Octave Thanet in Arkansas, Sarah Orne Jewett and Mary Wilkins Freeman in New England, were representative of the new concern for local truth in fiction that was to tell against the romantic. In fixing attention on narrow and homely fields they were turning towards realism, for the charm of their work lay in fidelity to the *milieu*, the exact portrayal of character and setting. With the spread of an interest in the local the vogue of the strange and the remote declined and a quiet sobriety of tone displaced the romantic. The way was being prepared for a more adequate realism. "Nothing could testify with more force," said H. H. Boyesen in 1894, "to the fact that we have outgrown romanticism than this almost unanimous desire, on the part of our authors, to chronicle the widely divergent phases of our American civilization." [1]

But that waited upon profound changes in the American outlook on life. In the seventies and eighties conditions were not ripe for it and the naturalism that in France, Russia, Germany, and Scandinavia, was carrying everything before it, was still alien to the American temper. It was not so much that it offended our innate Puritanism as that it seemed to us belied by the open facts of American life. The psychology of the dispersion still marked us. Although we were feverishly building great cities we were still emotionally a country people, far from urban-minded. We still thought in terms of the slack earlier freedoms, uncritical of our

[1] *Literary and Social Silhouettes*, p. 73.

ways, untroubled about the future. For the American born before the Civil War, naturalism was impossible; his mind had not been shaped by the industrial city or come under the dominion of science. The traditional outlook on life was unchanged; he still clung to the old moralities, the old verities, the old faith in the goodness of life in America. The intellectual revolution must be gone through with before naturalism should be at home in America, a native expression of native conditions; and it would then be a vehicle only for writers born and bred in the new city environment. In the meanwhile—in the genial years when the earlier optimisms still veiled the harsher realities of science and industrialism—the movement of realism got under way in the work of two distinguished craftsmen who, bred up in Victorian culture, interpreted life in terms of the middle and upper classes.*

II

HENRY JAMES AND THE NOSTALGIA OF CULTURE

There is a suggestion of irony in the fact that one of our earliest realists, who was independent enough to break with the romantic tradition, should have fled from the reality that his art presumably would gird itself up to deal with. Like his fellow spirit Whistler, Henry James was a lifelong pilgrim to other shrines than those of his native land, who dedicated his gifts to ends that his fellow Americans were indifferent to. Life, with him, was largely a matter of nerves. In this world of sprawling energy it was impossible to barricade himself securely against the intrusion of the unpleasant. His organism was too sensitive, his discriminations too fine, to subject them to the vulgarities of the Gilded Age, and he fled from it all. He early convinced himself that the American atmosphere was uncongenial to the artist.[2] The grotesqueries of the frontier irruption, the crude turmoil released by the new freedoms, were no materials to appeal to one in search of subtleties, to one who was a lover of nocturnes in gray. And so, like Whistler, he sought other

---

* The first subsection of this chapter in the Contents is entitled "William James and Pragmatism." None of this appears in the manuscript, and it seems likely that Professor Parrington planned to transfer the subject to a later part of the book. The numbering is, however, left as it is given in the Contents.—*Publisher.*

[2] "Civilization at its highest pitch was the master passion of his mind, and his preoccupation with the international aspects of character and custom issued from the conviction that the rawness and rudeness of a young country were not incapable of cure by contact with more developed forms." Pelham Edgar, *Henry James, Man, Author,* pp. 40–41.

lands, there to refine a meticulous technique, and draw out ever thinner the substance of his art.

The explanation of the curious career of Henry James, seeking a habitation between worlds and finding a spiritual home nowhere, is that he was never a realist. Rather he was a self-deceived romantic, the last subtle expression of the genteel, who fell in love with culture and never realized how poor a thing he worshiped. It was the first mistake of Henry James that he romanticized Europe, not for its fragments of the medieval picturesque, but for a fine and gracious culture that he professed to discover there. With the naïveté of the Age of Innocence he assumed that an aristocratic society—shall we say that of Mayfair or the Quartier Saint Germain?—is a complex of subtle imponderables that one comes to understand and embody only through heritage; and it was an assumption even more romantic that these imponderables were so subtly elusive as to escape any but the subtlest art. Like Edith Wharton he erected this supposititious culture into an abstract *tertium quid*, something apart from social convention or physical environment, something embodied in the choicer spirits of a class that for generations presumably had cherished them. Born of an unconscious inferiority complex in presence of a long-established social order to which he was alien, this romanticization of European culture worked to his undoing, for it constrained the artist to a lifelong pursuit of intangible realities that existed only in his imagination. The gracious culture that James persistently attributed to certain choice circles in Europe was only a figment of his romantic fancy—a fact that after long rambling on the Continent and nearly forty years' unbroken residence in England, he came finally to recognize. It was this failure to find the substance of his dream that imparted to his work a note of wistfulness. He had quitted the land of his birth to seek his spiritual home elsewhere, yet increasingly he came to question the wisdom of his act. He suffered the common fate of the *déraciné;* wandering between worlds, he found a home nowhere. It is not well for the artist to turn cosmopolitan, for the flavor of the fruit comes from the soil and sunshine of its native fields.

The spirit of Henry James marks the last refinement of the genteel tradition, the completest embodiment of its vague cultural aspirations. All his life he dwelt wistfully on the outside of the realm he wished to be a free citizen of. Did any other professed

realist ever remain so persistently aloof from the homely realities
of life? From the external world of action he withdrew to the inner
world of questioning and probing; yet even in his subtle psychological inquiries he remained shut up within his own skull-pan. His
characters are only projections of his brooding fancy, externaliza-
tions of hypothetical subtleties. He was concerned only with
nuances. He lived in a world of fine gradations and imperceptible
shades. Like modern scholarship he came to deal more and more
with less and less. It is this absorption in the stream of psychical
experience that justifies one in calling Henry James a forerunner of
modern expressionism. Yet how unlike he is to Sherwood Anderson, an authentic product of the American consciousness!

III

WILLIAM DEAN HOWELLS AND THE REALISM OF THE COMMONPLACE

From such nostalgia, that left a note of wistfulness in his pages,
William Dean Howells was saved by his frank and undivided
loyalties. Intellectually and emotionally he was native to the
American soil, and however widely he might range he remained
always a conscious American. He had no wish to Europeanize his
mind; he felt no secret hankerings for the ways of Mayfair or the
culture of the Quartier Saint Germain. The homely American
reality satisfied the needs of his art, and he accepted it with the
finality of Walt Whitman. If he failed to depict it in all its sprawling veracity, if much of its crude robustness never got into his
pages, the lack was due to no self-imposed alienation, but to the
temperament of the artist and the refined discretions of his environment.

The current school of realism is inclined to deal harshly with
Howells. His quiet reticences, his obtrusive morality, his genial
optimism, his dislike of looking ugly facts in the face, are too old-
fashioned today to please the professional purveyors of our current
disgusts. They find his writings as tedious as the gossip of old
ladies. To their coarser palates his respectable commonplace is
as flavorless as biscuit and tea. Yet it must not be forgotten that
for years he was reckoned new-fashioned. Whatever may be one's
final judgment on his work it is certain that for twenty years he was
a prophet of realism to his generation, the leader of a movement to

turn American literature from the path of romanticism and bring it
face to face with the real and actual. It was not his fault that the
ways of one generation are not those of another, and it is well to
remember that if his realism seems wanting to a generation bred up
on Theodore Dreiser, it seemed a debasement of the fine art of
literature to a generation bred up on Thomas Bailey Aldrich. Realism like dress changes its modes.

The Howells we know best was not a simple child of the frontier,
like Mark Twain, whom all could laugh with and love because the
sallies of his wit awakened a native response. He did not remain
completely native to the older folk-ways. He was rather a composite of the ideals reckoned excellent by the post-war generation—
an American Victorian, kindly, urbane, tolerant, democratic,
accepting America as a land that God's smile rests on, and convinced that here, wedded to a generous democracy, culture must
eventually produce offspring finer than the world has hitherto
known. Bred up in the mystical Swedenborgian faith, he shrank
from all fleshliness and loved purity with the devotion of a Galahad.
A child of the Ohio frontier, he retained to the last the western
feeling of democratic equality. An adopted son of Brahmin Cambridge, he immersed himself in culture—Italian, English, Yankee—
and served the ideal of excellence with a lifelong devotion; a
reverent pilgrim to the shrine of truth, he followed such paths as
his generation knew to lay his art at the high altar. In all these
things—in his ample culture, his kindly democracy, his high standards of workmanship—as well as in the instinctive reverences of a
clean and sweet nature, he was an embodiment of the best in
American life, a child of Jacksonian democracy who made use of
his freedoms to serve the excellent cause of culture.

But he was much more than that, and if the critics who are wont
to damn his Victorian squeamishness would penetrate to the inner
core of Howells they would discover an intellectual, alert and sensitive to changing currents of thought, seeing with his own eyes,
pursuing his own ends, who wrought out for himself a culture that
was individual and native. If he was not, like Henry Adams,
plagued with an itch of curiosity, he traveled widely in the realm
of the mind. Culture meant to him open-mindedness, familiarity
with diverse schools of thought, a willingness to venture upon the
unorthodox and to defend the unpopular. He was never a child of
the Gilded Age. He was unsoiled by its vulgarity, unconcerned

with its sordid ambitions. Neither at heart was he a child of Brahmin culture. He loved Lowell and Norton and Godkin and Aldrich, and he wanted to be approved by them; but he ranged far more widely than they, into places they thought indiscreet. The mature Howells came to stand apart from Brahminism, dissatisfied with a literary Toryism, convinced that a sterile genteel tradition could not suffice the needs of American literature. His very drift toward realism was a negation of the Brahmin influence. On the whole it was unfortunate that he lived so long in the Cambridge atmosphere. The New England influence may not have been a factor in shaping his too leisurely technique, but certainly it postponed the day of his intellectual release. If he had removed to New York a decade earlier, before his literary method hardened into rigidity, his technique might have changed with his more radical intellectual outlook and become the vehicle of a more adequate realism than he ever achieved.

But the significant thing is that the mind of Howells refused to imprison itself in Brahmin orthodoxies, but set forth on perilous expeditions while Lowell and Norton were discreetly evading the intellectual heresies raging outside their libraries. While Henry James was moving towards aristocratic Mayfair, Howells was journeying towards the proletarian East Side. The scientific revolution seems early to have washed in upon him, undermining the theological cosmos of his youth and turning him into a liberal freethinker. His scientific views very likely came to him secondhand, through the medium of literature; but with his wide reading in Continental fields—Spanish, French, German, Scandinavian— he could not fail to become saturated with the evolutionary view then permeating all current letters. In this he was only following with John Fiske and Henry Holt and Henry Adams the path of a new orthodoxy; nevertheless in applying the scientific spirit to fiction and espousing an objective realism, he quite definitely broke with Brahmin tradition. And when, under the guise of fiction, he turned to social questions, and wove into the placid texture of his work the vexing problem of social justice, he ventured on perilous ground where his Brahmin friends would not follow. To espouse the teachings of Herbert Spencer was one thing, to espouse the teachings of Karl Marx was quite another.

Howells came late to an interest in sociology, held back by the strong literary and aesthetic cast of his mind. But in the eighties, when he had reached middle life, he was no longer able to ignore or evade the economic maladjustments of the Gilded Age. The social unrest that was coming to bloody issue in strikes and lockouts gave him acute concern, and slowly under pressure of a sensitive social conscience there began a quiet intellectual revolution that was to transform the detached observer of the American scene into a Marxian socialist. A democrat, a lover of his kind, a just soul endowed with a tender conscience, an idealist who dreamed of a brotherhood of free men who should create in America a civilization adequate to human needs, what else could he do? He loved peace but war was all about him. And so in the mid-afternoon of life he turned to the work of spreading the gospel of social democracy in the America of the Gilded Age. He had no private or personal causes to serve. He had not, like Godkin and Dana, given hostages to fortune in the shape of a newspaper or magazine; he had no call to be partisan to his own interests. He was free to plead the cause of justice in his own way and at his own time. It is easy for the later radical to sneer at him as a parlor socialist who talked well but carefully refrained from disturbing the capitalistic machine from which he drew his income; but that is to ignore the courage of the artist in confronting a hostile world. He stood stoutly for the rights of workingmen that the passions of the times swept rudely away. When the Haymarket Riot in Chicago brought its shameful hysteria, and all respectable America was crying for blood, Howells was one of the few intellectuals who spoke for justice, one of the few who held aloof from the mob spirit, thereby bringing on his head a wave of criticism. It was a brave thing in 1886 to speak for the "Chicago anarchists."

But it was not till his removal to New York, where he found himself at the center of the great revolution, that he set about seriously studying the ways of plutocracy. For the student of Cambridge society it involved a mental upheaval. The urbanity of his literary-manner conceals for most readers the intensity of emotion that underlies his quiet style; yet it is clear enough that having examined the ways of private capitalism and considered its works, he rejected it. Thenceforth to the end of his life he hated the thing and quietly preached against it. His affections went back fondly to the earlier agricultural order that had shaped his youth, and in the character of Dryfoos, in *A Hazard of New Fortunes*, he suggests the moral degeneration that he believed followed in the train of the substitution of a speculative capitalist economy for the wholesomer agrarian economy. But though, remembering his frontier youth, he might prefer the older ways, he was realist enough to understand that capitalism was the order of his generation, and he turned eagerly to explore the new proletarian philosophies that came out of Germany. Howells was the first distinguished American man of letters to espouse Marxian socialism. For a cultivated American in the Gilded Age to sympathize with proletarian theory and to proclaim himself a socialist, was enough to excite amazement in his fellows. In the eighties American social thought was still naïve and provincial. Old-world theories were as alien as old-world institutions, and in spite of the wide interest aroused by *Looking Backward* the intelligent American in 1890 knew as little about Marxianism as he knows today about Bolshevism.

The doubts and hesitations that troubled Howells during these years of changing outlook, are skillfully dramatized in *A Hazard of New Fortunes*. The story of the removal of the Marshes from New England to New York, told with more than usual leisureliness, is the story of the transition from the peacefulness of his earlier literary life to the anxieties of his later thought. Slowly into a story of the familiar Howells commonplace comes the note of social dissension. Antagonistic social philosophies meet and clash, and the movement draws inevitably to the great climax of the strike that brings tragedy into the scene. Of the mood that grew upon him as he wrote he afterwards said:

It became, to my thinking, the most vital of my fictions; through my quickened interest in the life about me, at a moment of great psychological import. We had passed through a period of strong emotioning in the direction of humaner economics, . . . the rich seemed not so much to despise the poor, and the poor did not so hopelessly repine. That shedding of blood which is for the remission of sins had been symbolized by the bombs and scaffolds of Chicago, and the hearts of those who felt this bound up with our rights, the slavery implicated in our liberty, were thrilling with griefs and hopes hitherto strange to the average American breast. Opportunely for me there was a great street-car strike in New York, and the story began to find its way to issues nobler and larger than those of the love-affairs common to fiction.[3]

The years of unrest marked by the great agrarian revolt were years of great intellectual activity for Howells, during which his

[3] Quoted in " The Social Consciousness of William Dean Howells," *New Republic,* Vol. 26, p. 193.

thought ripened and mellowed. His own liberal spirit drew to him the liberal spirits of the younger generation, and he became the counselor and friend of many of the young rebels of the day. His sympathy went out to all who were concerned at the injustice of the world. He questioned the right of none to uphold his creed, nor sought to impose his own beliefs upon others. As he watched the great struggle of the times his heart was always on the side of the weak and exploited. Very likely he knew little about the economics of money and finance, over which rival partisans were quarreling savagely, but he understood the human side of the farmers' problem and it was always the balance in the human ledger that weighed with him.

He was a friend of Hamlin Garland and rejoiced when *Main-Travelled Roads* was given to the world, writing for it an introduction warmly and tenderly sympathetic. As an artist he grew concerned lest under the stimulus of B. O. Flower the zeal of the propagandist should submerge the art of the story-teller; but he had no quarrel with the "causes" that were fermenting in the mind of the young Populist, and would not lessen one whit the ardor of his social faith. Throughout the passionate campaign of 1896, that brought most of his friends to a blind and scurrilous partisanship of the gold standard, his heart kept his mind just and his sympathy for the unrequited producers served as counterbalance to the shrill vituperation of his friend Godkin. He had thought too long and too honestly to be moved by the *claque* of the press.

It was in the black days of the panic of '93 that he seems to have brooded most thoughtfully over the ways of capitalistic America, and in the following year he published *The Traveller from Altruria*, the first of his two Utopian romances in which he subjected the system of capitalism to critical analysis. It is a clever book that quite disarms the reader. Howells delivers no broadside attack on the capitalistic system, and he suggests its mean and selfish exploitation with such genial urbanity, such sly satire, as to arouse no sleeping lions. The concern in his heart is belied by the twinkle in his eye. He hints that the Altrurian critic is only the figment of a dream, and he smilingly suggests the sources of the Altrurian commonwealth in the long line of Utopian dreamers from Plato and Sir Thomas More to Bellamy and William Morris. But the urbanity is only a mask. Protected by it Howells delivers many a shrewd thrust at the ways of capitalism. American democracy does not show to advantage under his analysis. The Altrurian comes upon the canker of social injustice in every chink and cranny of life—a canker that is slowly destroying democratic America; and Howells takes a sly pleasure in contrasting our democratic professions with our plutocratic practice. There is a delightful irony in his attack on the professional classes—the professor, the minister, the writer—for their quick defense of the exploiting classes. What may we expect of the science of economics, he suggests, when our academic economists are only apologists for the existing order?

The Traveller from Altruria is a shrewd analysis of American life set against a Marxian background, and in forecasting the future Howells follows the Marxian law of concentration. The Age of Accumulation, with its gigantic monopolies gathered in ever fewer hands, prepared the way for a new order when industrialism, grown overbig, falls into the control of the state as naturally as the harvest is gathered into the granary. There was no need of a class war. When the times were ripe political means sufficed, for the democracy retained the effective weapon of the vote. Thirteen years later Howells completed his Utopian venture with *Through the Eye of the Needle*, in which he sketches in fuller detail the order of life in Altruria. It was not till men learned that coöperation is a better social cement than competition, altruism than egoism, that the new order was possible; and in this later work he depicts the kindly, rational society that emerged when men left off fighting each other and turned to working together instead. On every page the influence of William Morris is revealed—not only in the rejection of an urban society founded on the machine and a return to a decentralized anarchistic order, but in the emphasis on the psychology of work and the satisfactions that spring from free creative labor. *Through the Eye of the Needle* is curiously reminiscent of *News from Nowhere* and suggests how sympathetically Howells followed English social thought in its reaction against industrialism.

It was while he was thus engaged that he put into compact form his speculations on the theory of realism. For more than a decade he had been the most distinguished advocate of realism in America, and for longer still his successive novels had revealed to a critical world what substance and form he believed the realistic novel should possess. The immediate sources of his theory are obscure, though it is clear enough that the work of Jane Austen was a creative influence. From the school of French and Russian naturalism, then at the height of its vigor, he drew back in repulsion, and it was not till after his technique was matured that Tolstoi became an influence in his intellectual life. It is reasonable to assume that his realism was a native growth, the result of temperament unfolding through quiet years of reading in the English classics. A quizzical observer with the gift of humor is not likely to run into romanticism, and a youthful passion for Pope and Heine is not the best preparation for it. His intense dislike of the romantic, that led him to an inadequate and partial conception of it, seems to have sprung from certain instinctive feelings and convictions that strengthened with the years: a deep and sincere love of truth, a native sympathy with the simple homely phases of life, a quiet loyalty to American fact, and a sharp distrust of the aristocratic spirit. Endowed with such feelings he came to ascribe his own partisanships to literary methods; the romantic became for him the aristocratic, and the realistic became the democratic. As an American he was content to take the common stuff of life, as he found it in America, and depict it in unpretentious sincerity. Plain American life was not only worthy of literature, he was convinced, but the only material worthy of American literature. The path to the universal runs as directly through the commonplace American parlor as through the hall of the medieval baron or the drawing-room of Mayfair.

In *Criticism and Fiction* (1894), Howells ascribes the rise of modern realism to the twin sources of science and democracy. From science it derives its passion for truth, for "realism," he asserts, "is nothing more and nothing less than the truthful treatment of material." "We must ask ourselves before we ask anything else, Is it true?—true to the motives, the impulses, the principles, that shape the life of actual men and women." The question, what is essential truth, that has been the apple of discord amongst the realists, Howells answers in democratic fashion by appealing to the average. The "foolish man," he says, "wonders at the unusual, but the wise man at the usual." The realist, therefore, will deal objectively with the usual and common rather than with the unusual or strange, and in so doing he draws closer to the common heart of humanity, and learns the respect for simple human nature that is the source and wellspring of democracy. In delineating truthfully the prosaic lives of common people realism reveals the essential dignity and worth of all life. The romantic, on the other hand, is aristocratic. "It seeks to withdraw itself, to stand aloof; to be distinguished and not to be identified." "The pride of caste has become the pride of taste," and romance is the last refuge of the aristocratic spirit that, defeated elsewhere, has taken refuge in culture. Not aloofness, but comradeship, is the need of the world; not distinction, but identity. Realism is the child of democracy because the realist is one who "feels in every nerve the equality of things and the unity of men," and the great artist is one with a talent "robust enough to front the everyday world and catch the charm of its work-worn, care-worn, brave, kindly face."

To this characteristic conception that realism is democratic Howells adds certain other dicta that to his own generation seemed as true as to ours they seem doubtful: that art must serve morality, that it must teach rather than amuse, and that truthfulness to American life requires a note of cheerfulness. Art cannot flout the "eternal amenities," Howells asserted, for "morality penetrates all things, it is the soul of all things." Nor can it stand aloof, disdaining the office of teacher, for unless it "tends to make the world better and kinder" it is empty and futile; and it can do this only "from and through the truth." But the truth that will uplift society does not dwell in the kennel and pigsty; it will not be come upon by exploring the animal in man, or in wrapping the shroud of pessimism about life. In America at least, realism must concern itself with the "large cheerful average of health and success and happy life," for after all "the more smiling aspects of life" are "the more American." From such postulates Howells developed his familiar technique, which in minimizing plot, rejecting the unusual and strange and heroic, reduced his stories to the drab level that bores so many of his readers, and evokes the criticism that in elaboration of the commonplace he evades the deeper and more tragic realities that reach to the heart of life.

The criticism is just. More than any other thing this concern for the usual weakens Howells's work and renders it trivial. He does not probe the depths of emotional experience. Neither the life of the spirit nor the passions of the flesh is the stuff from which he weaves his stories. The lack—and allowing for all his solid excellence it remains grave—sprang in part from his own timid nature that recoiled from the gross and the unpleasant, and in part from the environment in which he perfected his technique. For years he

lived in an atmosphere of complacent convention, a society dominated by women, culture, and conscience. Cambridge and Boston
in the seventies and eighties were still in the Age of Innocence
greatly concerned with erecting defenses against the intrusion of
the unpleasant, reverencing the genteel in life and letters, soberly
moral and making much of the eternal verities. In such a world of
refined manners and narrow outlook what should the realist do but
report faithfully of what he saw and heard? And so Howells,
perforce, became a specialist in women's nerves, an analyst of the
tenuous New England conscience, a master of Boston small-talk.
It was such materials that shaped his leisurely technique until it
falls about his theme with the amplitude of crinoline.

Through these chronicles of the Age of Innocence runs a persistent note of the neurotic. There are more scruples to a page of
Howells than in any other writer except Henry James—for the
most part filmy cobwebs invisible to the coarser vision of a later
generation. The action percolates through the sand of small-talk,
welling up from the tiniest springs and stopped by the smallest
obstruction. Like Franklin's two-headed snake his characters are
in danger of dying from thirst because of much argument over the
right path to water. It is hard to weave a substantial fabric from
such gossamer threads, and when in *The Rise of Silas Lapham* endless pages are devoted to the ethical subtleties of a woman's accepting the hand of a man who the family had believed was in love with
her sister, or when in *April Hopes* the fantastic scruples of a neurotic girl are elaborated with a refinement of art worthy of a Fra An-
gelico Madonna, the stuff is too filmy to wear well. Commonplace
men and neurotic women are poor materials from which to fashion
an adequate realism, and with the passing of the Age of Innocence the scruples of Howells went out of fashion.

The fault, in part at least, must be traced to the artist's deep
reverence for New England. From his youth he had cherished an
exalted notion of the sufficiency of New England culture, and had
accepted its parochialisms as ultimate standards. To a bookish lad,
inclined to be too consciously literary, such loyalty to a declining
school could only accentuate his native aloofness from life. His
four years at Venice had been given over to an ardent pursuit of
culture, as culture was understood by Lowell and Norton. It was
the natural impulse of a sensitive mind, conscious of its limitations,
reveling for the first time in the wealth that had been denied his

frontier boyhood. His poetic *Venetian Days* was an infallible passport to Boston favor, and when after his return he was taken up
by the *Atlantic* group he carried with him to Boston an unconscious
inferiority complex that did his genius an evil turn. It was natural
for the self-taught western youth to be reverent in presence of the
great of earth; but it is not well for the artist to be humble in the
presence of his masters. Unless he is something of a rebel, given to
questioning the dogmas of the schools, he will never ripen into
creative originality.

An inferiority complex is a common mark of the frontier mind
that finds itself diffident in presence of the old and established, and
Howells suffered from it greatly. For years his keen eyes lacked
their usual shrewdness in judging Boston ways, and to the end of
his life he overestimated the greatness of the men to whom his
youthful loyalty had gone out. Not only did he accept Lowell and
Holmes and Longfellow at the Boston rating, but he regarded the
lesser group of cultivated Boston gentlemen with partial eyes. It
would have been far better for his art if like Hamlin Garland he
had never been received within the charmed circle; if he had had
to make his way alone. To justify his acceptance Howells felt that
he must prove himself as completely Bostonian as the best, and in
consequence he sloughed off his western heritage, perverted his
genius, and shaped his realism to the slender materials discovered in
Back Bay drawing-rooms. The genteel tradition was in the way of
strangling his realism.

Subjected to such refinements his realism in the end became little
more than technique—a meticulous transcription of New England
conventions, the casual action submerging itself in an endless
stream of talk. No doubt Howells was true to what he saw; certainly no one has ever fixed more exactly the thin substance of the
Age of Innocence. Nevertheless the fidelity of his observation, the
refinement of his prose style, and the subtlety of his humor that
plays lambently about the edges of his words, do not compensate
for the slightness of his materials. The record he has left is not
that of a great soul brooding over the meaning of life, puzzled,
uncertain, yet tender toward the victims that fate has seized and
crushed. He was restrained by too many inhibitions to deal frankly
with natural human passions. He felt deeply and tenderly, but he
was too diffident to let himself go. It is likely that Howells never
realized the inadequacy of his temperament and the futility of his

method to any serious realism. Even in his acutest study *A Hazard of New Fortunes*, which comes upon brutal economic reality, the story is entangled in a mass of minute detail and never quite breaks through. The indecisions, the repetitions, the whimsical descriptions, the drifting talk, are all true to life, but they are not essential or vital truth. The real issue toward which the story moves—the problem of social justice and the contrasting systems of wage-slavery, bond-slavery, and social democracy—is obscured in a welter of asides and never quite reaches the front of the stage. He is more effective in such works as *Indian Summer*, when he deals with characters on vacation who play whimsically with love, and in *April Hopes*, when he dwells fondly on the infinitely eloquent trivialities of young love-making. In such studies the minute fidelity to word and gesture, the humorous playing with invisible scruple, is a pleasant substitute for solider material.

Howells had real gifts, of which he made the most. Refinement, humor, sympathy—fidelity to external manner and rare skill in catching the changing expression of life—a passion for truth and a jealous regard for his art: he had all these qualities, yet they were not enough to make him a great realist. He belonged to the Age of Innocence and with its passing his works have been laid away. He has had no followers to keep his method alive. If one may hazard an explanation of the lot that has befallen him, it would be this. Howells the artist mistook his calling. He was not by temperament a novelist. He lacked the sense of drama, a grasp of the rough fabric of life, the power to deal imaginatively with the great and tragic realities. His genius was rather that of a whimsical essayist, a humorous observer of the illogical ways of men. He was an eighteenth-century spirit—a subtler Goldsmith—set down in another age and an uncongenial world. In his later years he must have come to realize this, for more and more he turned to the essay form. There his quiet humor and shrewd observation fitted his sinuous prose style to a nicety. In such sketchy autobiography as *My Literary Passions*, and more whimsically in such genial travel essays as *Certain Delightful English Towns*, his refined art arrived at its most perfect expression. Not an original genius like Mark Twain, far from a turbulent soul like Herman Melville, Howells was the reporter of his generation—the greatest literary figure of a drab negative age when the older literary impulse was slackening, and the new was slowly displacing it. He marks the transition between the earlier idealism and the later naturalism. A humane and lovable soul, he was the embodiment of all that was kindly and generous in an America that was not wholly given over to the ways of the Gilded Age—an America that loved beauty and served culture even amidst the turmoil of revolution.

BOOK TWO: THE OLD AND THE NEW: STORM CLOUDS

THE OLD AND THE NEW: STORM CLOUDS

THE quarter-century between the panic of 1873 that rudely disturbed the revelry of the Great Barbecue, and the campaign of 1896 that broke the agrarian opposition to capitalism, was marked by a fierce agrarian attempt to nullify in America the law of concentration. The silent drift toward plutocracy was too evident to escape comment even in the Gilded Age, and the ideal of plutocracy was too repugnant to a people drenched in Jeffersonian and Jacksonian prejudices to escape bitter hostility. The pursuit of wealth was an accepted democratic right, but it was assumed to be a fair race and no favors. The use of the political state by greater wealth to lay handicaps on lesser wealth had not been in the reckoning, and the law of progress that diminished the number of beneficiaries from the national policy of preëmption and exploitation had not been so interpreted. Something was wrong with a progress that augmented poverty as it increased wealth, and with the alarmist cry in their ears—the rich are growing richer and the poor poorer—the untutored democracy of the seventies and the eighties turned to question the drift of tendency that quite evidently was transforming a democratic people into a vast engulfing plutocracy. An older agrarian America was confronted by a younger capitalistic one, and the conflict of ideals and purposes was certain to bring on a bitter debate.

In the fierce struggle that turmoiled the politics of three decades the democracy went into battle as ill-equipped intellectually as it had been a hundred years before in the struggle over the Constitution. It was reaping the harvest of the long Jacksonian slackness that, content with the vote, had given no thought to the ultimate program of democracy but had suffered the lawyers to have their way. The Enlightenment had long since been submerged by Whiggish ambitions, and since the days of the Abolition Movement there had been no serious consideration of political theory. The success of the Jacksonian revolution had brought about its undoing. The abstract principle of democracy having won common acceptance, it was assumed to be competent to shift for itself. But unfortunately a supposedly democratic state was functioning under a Constitution designed to thwart democracy, and, interpreted by lawyers, it buttressed the rights of property far more securely than the rights of man. Within this fundamental law capitalism had long been entrenching itself. Its stronghold could not be taken by frontal attack and its flanks were protected by the courts that had assumed the high prerogative of voiding statutory enactments by judicial decree. As a result in no other country was capitalism so safeguarded from hostile attack; it plowed its fields and gathered its harvests secure from disturbance.

Unfortunately the political state did not realize that it was not in reality the democracy it professed to be. The most intelligent liberalism of the times, failing to take into account the economic basis of politics, was satisfied to spend its energy in Civil Service Reform and similar tinkering with the political machinery, convinced that it was only necessary to recover the old aristocratic sense of responsibility in political agents to perfect a democratic government. Not till another generation did liberalism come to understand that the democratic program was still largely unfulfilled, and set about in all earnestness to complete it; but that did not happen till the philosophy of democracy had been far more adequately explored and the simple faith of Jacksonianism had been instructed by the experience of other lands. Popular discontent with the drift toward plutocracy was intensified by the successive economic crises that marked the transition from agrarianism to capitalism. The gospel of progress, it seems, had not taken due account of the price that must be paid in social disturbances, and the breakdowns of 1873–1879 and 1887–1896 with their harsh dislocations aroused a spirit of revolt that issued in broad popular movements. Those movements spun the thread of liberalism that runs through the years from the Gilded Age to the World War—a thread woven of the earlier liberalism that came from the frontier, and the new collectivistic theories that came from Europe. In the eighties and nineties it was still largely native agrarian, but in the early years of the new century it drew heavily on the proletarian philosophies of Europe—seeking to apply old-world experience to American problems. Through it all runs increasingly a note of sobering realism. After a hundred years political romanticism was slowly dying in America.

CHAPTER I

THE PLIGHT OF THE FARMER

I

DEMOCRATIC REACTIONS TO PLUTOCRACY

THE Middle Border was the first to recover from the heady romanticisms of Whiggery. The malady of preëmption and exploitation quickly ran its course there and after the first enthusiasm of settlement had subsided—the staking of claims, the scramble over townsites, the bidding for railway lines—the farmer settled down amidst his corn and wheat and cattle and hogs to learn what sort of living the prairies might provide. With his feet on the sobering earth he was no middle-class adventurer, no buccaneer lying in wait for the golden argosies of Spain, but a sober realist kept sane by wind and weather and kept honest by his daily occupation of tilling and reaping.

As the first wave of settlers spread over the prairies a mood of buoyant hopefulness colored their dreams. The earlier conquest of the Inland Empire had entailed exhausting labor in preliminary clearings, and the stumpage from great forests remained for years to obstruct clean tillage; but here in the Middle Border were treeless fields of black soil, level, uncluttered by stones, inviting the plow. For ages the prairie grass had been growing there, tall as a horseman in the bottoms and plentiful on the uplands; and as the unmarked seasons passed, the potash from the decaying vegetation added a richer fertility to the soil. In natural productiveness it was the fairest portion of America, and as the land-hungry settlers made their pitch there, filing on broad homesteads and building their cabins, a mood of buoyant expectation filled the land. It was not the flamboyant spirit of the Gilded Age, but the hopefulness of those who within a few short years were to transform a wilderness into the world's granary. In his wistful account of the glamour that lay upon the prairies in those first pioneer years—a glamour that soon passed like the morning dews—Hamlin Garland was no frontier romantic but a sober historian.

But as the seventies gave place to the eighties a subtle change came over the mood of the Middle Border. Disappointment and disillusion settled upon a land that before had smiled in the spring sunshine. The harvest was not fulfilling the expectations of the seedtime. The changed mood came in part from the harsh toil and meager living that were the necessary price the frontiersman must pay for his small winnings. It is no holiday job to subdue an untamed land and wrest abundance and comfort from a virgin soil. Only for the young who can project their hopes into the future is it endurable; for the middle-aged and the old it is a heart-breaking task. The history of the western frontier is a long drab story of hardship and privation and thwarted hopes, of men and women broken by the endless toil, the windows of their dreams shuttered by poverty and the doors to an abundant life closed and barred by narrow opportunity. It is true that the prairies took no such toll as the forests had taken; the mean and squalid poverty through which Lincoln passed was not so common in the Middle Border as it had been along the earlier frontier. Nevertheless a fierce climate and a depressing isolation added their discomforts to a bleak existence. The winds were restless on the flat plains, and the flimsy wooden houses, stark and mean, unprotected by trees and unrelieved by shrubbery, were an ill defense against their prying fingers. In winter the blizzards swept out of the North to overmaster the land, and in summer the hot winds came up from the Southwest to sear the countrysides that were rustling with great fields of corn. Other enemies appeared, as it were, out of a void. Endless flights of grasshoppers descended like a plague of locusts, and when they passed the earth was bare and brown where the young wheat had stood. Armies of chinch-bugs came from nobody knew where, and swarming up the tender corn-stalks left them sucked dry and yellow. It is nature's way, to destroy with one hand what it creates with the other; and for years the western farmers were fighting plagues that had possessed the prairies before the settlers came.

The disillusion of the Middle Border deepened into gloom as the widespread economic depression of the times added its discouragements. A period of falling prices was curtailing industry and forcing down the market values of all produce. From such depressions a debtor community always suffers most severely, for falling produce-prices mean rising money-values and a shifting standard of value for deferred payments. The farms of the Middle Border were heavily encumbered to provide tools and livestock and buildings, and the earnings were consumed by the interest that went East to the mortgage-holders. Debt was a luxury the farmer could ill afford, and when the debt was silently augmenting by the rising value of the dollar he was forced to consider his situation. The plight into which he had fallen was graphically summed up in the phrase "ten-cent corn and ten per cent interest"—a phrase that was to become a spark to all the tinder that was gathering from frontier hardships and disappointments. Falling market-values were at the bottom of his troubles. The prices of his staples were sinking below the cost of production. With four-cent eggs, five-cent butter, ten-cent corn, and fifty-cent wheat, with more hogs and cattle than the stockyards would take, and with debts contracted at interest-rates fixed by a higher scale of values, the economic position of the Middle Border was becoming desperate, and in the later eighties a sullen bitterness took possession of the land. As the farmer sat by the kitchen stove and stoked the fire with great ears of corn that were cheaper than coal, he had ample time to contemplate his lot. Ungathered crops for which there was no market would not pay interest. There was coming to be "too much hog in the dollar," as one commentator remarked quaintly. The Middle Border, all too clearly, was strangling from its own productiveness.

It was easy for newspaper critics, armed with the wisdom of the Board of Trade, to point out that overproduction was the trouble with the western farmer, and that so vast a development of staple crops resulting from sowing the prairie states to corn and wheat was certain to bring on disastrous market slumps. It was true. Production had outrun consumption; quantity output had brought on a glut. But it was also true—as the armchair critics were not so careful to point out—that other causes contributed equally to the deflation of the western farmer, the result of which was to despoil him of the last moiety of his earnings. He was in the grip of a complex middleman organization that gouged him at every turn. The gap between producer and consumer was widening to a chasm. The railways charged twenty cents a bushel cartage for wheat from the Mississippi to Chicago, and fifty-two and a half cents to the Atlantic seaboard. The elevator companies fixed monopoly tolls, swindled the farmer in their grain-gradings, and combined to force down the market price at harvest time and raise it after the crop came under their control. The "Livestock Ring," managed by the railways, controlled the Union Stock Yards at Chicago and squeezed the marginal profits from the farmer's cattle and hogs.[1] When on the other hand he bought implements or groceries or household goods he was at the mercy of a non-competitive market, protected by patent-rights and tariffs, to which were added extortionate transportation and middleman charges.

It was his own fault, of course. Due to his own political slackness the farmer had allowed himself to become the common drudge of society. All the exploiting classes had their hands in his pockets. His was the only considerable economic group that exerted no organized pressure to control the price he sold for or the price he paid. While capitalism had been perfecting its machinery of exploitation he had remained indifferent to the fact that he himself was the fattest goose that capitalism was to pluck. He had helped indeed to provide the rope for his own hanging. He had voted away the public domain to railways that were now fleecing him; he took pride in the county-seat towns that lived off his earnings; he sent city lawyers to represent him in legislatures and in Congress; he read middle-class newspapers and listened to bankers and politicians and cast his votes for the policy of Whiggery that could have no other outcome than his own despoiling. And now in the middle eighties he began to feel the rope about his neck, and realized the predicament he was in. It was not alone the local middlemen, or even the railways—he had come to believe—that were to blame. It was the money-power of the East, the grip of Wall Street, that was strangling him—a power that controlled the government at Washington, that manipulated the currency system, and that was engaged in a scheme to augment its holdings by forcing up the value of the dollar and automatically increasing the value of the indebtedness it had gathered in its vaults. Clearly it was high time for the deflated farmer to get into politics on his own account if he were to save himself from beggary, and so during the Gilded Age began a great agrarian revolt against capitalism that was to turmoil the next quarter of a century—a revolt that was to mark the last effective organization of the farmers to combat the new order, the last flare-up of an old-fashioned agrarian America before it was submerged by the middle class.

[1] See Nevins, *The Emergence of Modern America*, pp. 163–164

II

THE FARMER CONSIDERS POLITICS

By the early seventies it was becoming clear to the Middle Border that the policy of Whiggery took no account of the needs of the farmer. Government was indifferent to him, whether at the capital of his state or at Washington, and governmental programs —whether in the matter of protective tariffs and land-grants, in its unconcern at monopoly extortion, or in the contraction of the currency with a view to the resumption of specie payments—ran so counter to his interests that the dullest began to question the fairness of the state. It had ceased to concern itself with the welfare of the whole. The combination of paternalism and *laissez faire* that marked the Whiggery of the times could be interpreted by the suspicious farmer, indeed, only as a surrender of government to capitalism. It had lost all pretense of fairness in the distribution of governmental favors, and withheld or granted aid with the single objective of furthering the interests of powerful groups. It sanctioned the use of the state by business interests for purposes of exploitation, and declined to exercise its power in the interests of the consumer. It granted tariffs and subsidies, yet refused to regulate the monopoly power it had created. It was no longer a government of the people but a government of business, concerned for the interests of exploitation, and if the farmer were to gain a hearing he must first make himself feared.

Of necessity, therefore, the agrarian program entailed a political struggle of great bitterness. There would be no adequate relief granted until the farmers had wrested control of government from the class that was exploiting them. The battle between agrarianism and capitalism, in consequence, from the outset was a struggle for control of the political state, that beginning in single commonwealths was eventually carried to the federal government. Hope of effective aid from state governments quickly proved illusory, for when the Illinois farmers passed a law to curb the railways the federal courts set aside their enactment and bade the farmers—to use a later phrase—go home and slop the hogs. They must not meddle with matters beyond their comprehension. In consequence of such slaps in the face the farmers fell to perfecting their organizations and arousing class consciousness until there issued from the long debates of the Grange and the Farmers' Alliance the great movement of Populism that proposed to reach as far as Washington, install there the representatives of the producing classes, and refashion the political state in accordance with the democratic needs of the plain people.

So ambitious a program needed time, not only for the farmers to organize but to clarify their policy. They were ill equipped for a serious struggle. With the rise of capitalism agriculture had been steadily falling in social prestige. As a result of the decline of the landed squirearchy in the North and the overthrow of the plantation economy in the South, agriculture had lost its traditional leaders who had furnished the brains and supplied the spokesmen in earlier political struggles. In the seventies agriculture was no longer reckoned a pursuit peculiarly suitable to gentlemen. The business man had risen in social prestige as the farmer declined, and instead of being recruited from the natural leaders of society agriculture suffered a draining-off of the more energetic and capable to the cities, leaving the farms in the hands of the less ambitious, who were supplemented in the seventies and eighties by European peasants who settled great portions of the Middle Border. With this loss of social prestige came a new urban contempt for farm life that expressed itself in "Hayseed" cartoons, and in the heedlessness of politicians who were quick to transfer allegiance from a decaying to a rising order.

The farmers of the Middle Border, drawn from many commonwealths and with a high percentage of aliens, were far from a homogeneous class-conscious group like the southern planters. Race, language, and cultural antecedents held them apart, intensifying the aloofness that was a common characteristic of the frontier. Week-days they stuck to their plows and Sundays, unlike the New England farmer, they were little given to churchgoing. The landholdings were commonly a homestead of a hundred and sixty acres, often running to an entire section of six hundred and forty acres. Much land was held idle by speculators, with the result that the isolation of the farmer—dwelling convenient to his fields rather than to neighbors—deepened the suspicious individualism that was an obsession of the agrarian mind, and unfitted him for effective coöperative effort. No political or social philosophy answerable to his needs was at hand, no intellectual leaders like Jefferson or John Taylor to adapt old-world theory to the conditions of the Middle Border, no commanding figure like Old Hickory to marshal the scattered hosts. The Physiocratic theory with its prestige of distinguished advocates and its elaborate social economics had never taken root in the Middle Border; although certain of its prejudices—that the farmer is the sole producer and the sterile middleman must somehow be got rid of—had taken possession of the western mind and largely influenced the ultimate program. But if the western farmer inherited no ready-made philosophy he was daily prodded by harsh reality. He got up and went to bed under the prick of economic necessity, and this made of him a realist and an opportunist, eager to apply homely remedies to homely ills. With the discipline got from hard times he was not easily gulled by bright young city lawyers with their handbooks of capitalistic economics. The new agrarianism of the prairies, in consequence, was a hard-headed, homespun theory, fashioned on the farms, intended to serve the producer rather than the middleman. It had behind it none of the high authority of the schools, and naturally it was mocked and scoffed at by all the spokesmen—editors, lawyers, bankers, scholars, intellectuals—of the prosperous middle class. The farmer had to make his way against the embattled prejudices and contempt of the rest of America.

But before he could become a power in political councils he must organize and use his voting strength as a unit; and as early as the late sixties the work of organization was got under way. It began as a social movement with the Grange that spread widely through the South and Middle West and even gained foothold in the East, bringing together in social groups the farmer families of the neighborhood. It professed to stand outside politics and strove to awaken an interest in coöperative buying and selling, but the community gatherings were certain to find politics waiting for them at the schoolhouse door, and after the program of coöperation had been discussed the talk ran easily into political debate. From the Grange issued in the eighties the Farmers' Alliance, more consciously political in its objective, active in arousing the farmers to political action; and with the hard times that came with the turn of the decade the different groups merged in the broad movement of Populism—a militant political uprising with a definite party program and organization. The flare-up came swiftly and in the first years of the nineties the prairies were aflame and even the cotton-fields of the South were fired. Populism swept from township to township, a militant agrarian movement, providing its own leaders—Tom Watson in Georgia, General Weaver in Iowa, Ignatius Donnelly in Minnesota, sockless Jerry Simpson in Kansas, with Hamlin Garland, and B. O. Flower, and other intellectuals rallying to the farmers' standard. It set up the banner of agrarian democracy, summoned its followers and drilled them for the battles that lay ahead. Huge meetings gathered of the farmers of a county and day-long they listened to speeches that came straight from the hay-fields and the corn-rows, speeches that were an echo of the daily experience of the farmer and the farmer's wife.

It was Mary Ellen Lease of Kansas who struck from the common bitterness a phrase that embodied the militant spirit of Populism. Week after week she traveled the prairie country urging the farmers to "raise less corn and more hell," and at her call the sunburned faces settled into grim purpose. The farmers had become class-conscious. They were enlisted in a class struggle. They used the vocabulary of realism, and the unctuous political platitudes and sophistries of county-seat politicians rolled off their minds like water from a duck's back. They were fighting a great battle—they believed—against Wall Street and the eastern money-power; they were bent on saving America from the plutocracy; and they swept over the county-seat towns, burying the old machine politicians under an avalanche of votes, capturing state legislatures, electing Congressmen and Senators, and looking forward to greater power. In 1896 Populism gained control of the Democratic party and entered on its great campaign to establish the principle of democracy at Washington. It was the last mortal struggle between agrarianism and capitalism, and to understand it one must turn back to the long agitation over the money question.

III

THE GREENBACK MOVEMENT

If in the early nineties the currency question had come to overshadow the questions of the tariff and railway regulation, it was because that problem lay at the heart of the struggle between the rival agrarian and capitalistic economies. The control of the national monetary system by the bankers was vital to the smooth functioning of a capitalistic order, and to assure such control it was desirable that monetary standards and emissions of currency be removed from the sphere of political action and lodged in the hands of business. The problem was difficult, for the right to "coin money and to regulate the value thereof" were functions of sovereignty specifically recognized in the Constitution; and it was a series of moves designed to transfer such functions to private groups that brought on a long political debate over systems of currency.

The intellectual background against which the struggle was set may be sketched briefly. Despite the long battle over the Bank in Jackson's time, little serious thinking on the principles of money and currency had been done in America. Financiers and economists alike followed the current English school, and since the appearance of the famous Bullion Report of 1811 that school had adhered to the intrinsic-value theory of money. While accepting banknotes as a useful medium of exchange, the English classical economists held that only coin is real money, and that the issue of notes must bear a definite ratio to the amount of coin and bullion in the vaults. Money is not a creature of the law. Government cannot create it. Rather it is a convenient token of labor done, and the stamp of the mint is only a certification of weight and fineness. There are but two ways, indeed, in which government can acquire money— through taxation and by borrowing. The "natural operation of the specie standard" was reckoned one of the fundamental "laws of trade," and for government to tamper with it—setting aside the intrinsic-value principle by the emission of irredeemable paper money—was to violate the sanctity of contracts, cheat creditors, increase prices, and disorder business. The law of supply and demand answered all the needs of money regulation.

This was no more than the application of the current theory of *laissez faire* to the problem of currency. But between the Bullion Report of 1811 and the Parliamentary Bank Act of 1844, English theory and practice had undergone two important modifications: the vast development of credit had suggested a free use of bank-notes based on securities other than coin or bullion, and the bime-tallic standard had been superseded by the gold standard. By the terms of the Act of 1844 all banknotes were to be issued against securities and gold and silver coin and bullion in the bank vaults. The margin of issue was fixed at fourteen million pounds sterling. The total amount of banknotes thus "issued on the Credit of such Securities, Coin and Bullion," might not be increased, but within the limits set the Bank was free to increase or decrease issues at will. The Act further provided that "whereas it is necessary to limit the Amount of Silver Bullion on which it shall be lawful . . . to issue Bank of England notes," it should "not be lawful for the Bank of England to retain in . . . said Bank at any time an Amount of Silver Bullion exceeding One Fourth Part of the Gold Coin and Bullion." . . . [2] That gold should eventually have thrust silver aside was natural. In addition to its convenience as a commodity for international shipment, it was less in quantity, not widely dispersed or popularly held, and therefore more easily controlled by the money-brokers. With the function of government restricted to coining such gold as came to the mint, the whole business of currency emissions, with the attendant power of inflation and deflation of credit, would lie in the hands of the bankers who became the custodians of the national monetary system.

During the bitter discussions of currency policies that followed the dislocations of the Civil War, the two most authoritative spokesmen in America on the subject were Senator John Sherman of Ohio, for years Chairman of the Senate Committee on Finance, and David A. Wells, statistician, special Commissioner of the Revenue Bureau, and a scholar deservedly distinguished as an economist. In their views on the currency question both were followers of the classical English school. In two speeches in the Senate, of January 27, 1869, and January 24, 1870, the former stated his position definitely. "Let us," he said, "recognize as an axiom that nothing but coin is real money before we undertake to deal with the currency"; and in another place, narrowing his definition in terms of the English Bank Act, he asserted, "We must . . . recognize the immutable law of currency; and that is, there is but one true standard, and that standard is gold." [3] The weakness of paper money, he believed, was its instability; the ratio of exchange with gold fluctuates too greatly to make it a safe or convenient medium of business. "Last year the fluctuation in paper money amounted to forty-five per cent. Gold, however, remained as stable as the eternal hills, because it was not only the product of labor, but it was labor and value itself." [4] One may make of such an assertion what one will, but it is clear that John Sherman thought ill of the greenbacks, and wanted substituted for them a system of banknotes.

[2] *The Statutes at Large: 7 & 8 Victoriae*, Vol. 84, pp. 188–189.
[3] *Speeches and Reports on Finance and Taxation*, pp. 188, 190.
[4] *Ibid.*, p. 233.

It is impossible [he argued] to give a currency issued by a Government the flexibility to meet the movement of the exchanges. . . . It must have a flexibility which will enable it to be increased in certain periods of the year, and to flow back again into the vaults of the bank at others. I am convinced . . . that in time it will be wise to retire our United States notes and all forms of Government circulation, and depend upon notes issued by private corporations.[5]

Brief as these passages are, they suffice to make clear Sherman's position. He accepted without question the English theory and practice, and he wished to shape American legislation in conformity with them. The experience of the Civil War, and—shall we add— his intimate connections with Wall Street,[6] had confirmed him in his preference for a *laissez-faire* policy in currency matters. He would establish the gold standard, encourage the issue of bank-notes, and turn over the custodianship of the national currency to private interests.

The position of David A. Wells was essentially similar. Wells wrote much and skillfully and he seems to have been the chief authority on whom such intellectuals as Godkin and Dana relied for materials for their editorials on the currency question. Indirectly, therefore, through the medium of editors and newspaper writers his opinions came to have wide influence. During the discussion of resumption of specie payments in the seventies his pen was particularly active. Amongst other things he then wrote *The Cremation Theory of Specie Resumption*, in which he advocated a policy of progressive contraction by the expedient of burning annually a fixed sum in greenbacks; *Robinson Crusoe's Money*, an exposition of the bullion theory of money for popular reading, illustrated by Nast and containing some witty thrusts at such well-known expansionists as Ben Butler, Wendell Phillips, Henry C. Carey, and Senator O. P. Morton; *Contraction*, in which he defended the thesis, "He who is not in favor of contracting the currency is not in favor of paying it, and he who is not in favor of paying it is a repudiator"; and certain other papers later gathered into his *Practical Economics* (1885).

Wells was an uncompromising bullionist and his theory of money is as simple as the doctrine of *laissez faire* on which it rests. Honest money represents labor and therefore possesses intrinsic value. The

[5] "Speech of January 24, 1870," *ibid.*, pp. 225–226.
[6] This laid him open to frequent and often bitter attack. See, among many, Mrs. Marion Todd, *Pizzaro and John Sherman* Chicago, 1891.

experience of the ages has demonstrated that of all commodities gold and silver are the most convenient for the purpose and in consequence they have come to be accepted universally as real money. Every dollar's worth of gold represents a dollar's worth of labor, always and everywhere, measured by the test of the world's needs. It is foolish for politicians and theorists to worry their poor heads over the supply of money, or attempt to predetermine the quantity best suited to the needs of business. The amount of money in circulation will always be regulated by the law of supply and demand. There is limitless gold locked up in the treasure-house of nature, and just so much is unlocked by human labor as the immediate needs of the world require. Gold can neither be inflated nor deflated, for, "There is one and the same law governing alike the supply of gold and of wheelbarrows. They are both tools or commodities, and the country will have and use all of either that it can use profitably." [7] Let government keep its hands off and money will regulate itself. "The value of the gold dollar is fixed and cannot be altered. The value of the paper dollar is constantly fluctuating." [8] That business conditions would be seriously affected by the withdrawal of the greenbacks, or that injustice would be done to debtors, Wells refused to believe. When the poison is withdrawn from the system a state of health reëstablishes itself. "I also count as an absurdity the idea that the business of the country is likely to be unfavorably affected by a deficiency of currency consequent upon contraction in the manner proposed." [9] The gold to take its place would be provided automatically by the infallible law of supply and demand. Thus triply armed with the logic of economic theory Wells pronounced for deflation, immediate and drastic:

I desire the federal government to get out of and abandon forever and as soon as possible this whole business of creating and issuing paper money, be it redeemable or irredeemable, for I believe as long as the federal government continues to recognize anything as money except hard matter-of-fact "labor representing" gold and silver, just so long the country will not have [a] stable and unfluctuating currency. . . .[10]

Such neat logic was out of date on the day that Wells penned it. The needs of business had outgrown the bullion theory of money

[7] *Practical Economics*, p. 54.
[8] *The Cremation Theory of Specie Resumption*, p. 10.
[9] *Ibid.*, p. 10.
[10] *Ibid.*, p. 13.

and credit was taking the place of a metallic currency. The fiction of a gold standard would be adhered to till another seismic dislocation proved its utter inadequacy to a world in confusion and it would be unofficially abandoned. Yet it was such logic that prevailed in America in post-war days, bringing acute distress upon the country as a whole and particular hardship to the Middle Border; and it prevailed because the banking interests followed a selfish and narrow policy marked out for them by the English theory and practice.

The financing of the war had been wasteful and slovenly beyond all precedent, and it had been fiercely criticized by the agrarians. It was a system, said the militant Greenbacker, Thaddeus Stevens, the like of which "no human folly had ever before witnessed." [11] When the war was over and the reorganization of the public finances was up for settlement, the bankers were shrewd enough to make the confusion serve their interests. Their great objective was to get back once more the control of the national credit that the war had taken from them. The National Bank Act of 1863—foolishly opposed by shortsighted state-bank advocates who were jealous of local rights—had been the first great step. By the provisions of the act the national banks were permitted to issue currency on the security of government bonds, in such quantities as they chose, on highly favorable terms, and the result was to drive out of circulation the wild-cat issues of state banks. But the crux of the problem was the question of the greenbacks that the necessities of the war had forced upon the government. The greenbacks were reckoned political money, the control of issues of which lay wholly with Congress. At any moment, responding to popular demand, Congress might deflate the bankers by the emission of new bills. At the time of first issue the financial interests had succeeded in vitiating the greenbacks by writing into the bill a repudiation of the issue by the government itself, and no sooner was the war over than they set about the business of retiring them. Their objective was the same end that English bankers had reached in 1844.

In the reorganization three broad policies were insisted upon by the banking interests: the speedy retirement of the greenbacks, in order to take government out of the credit market, the refunding of all debts on a gold basis, and an immediate return to specie payments. The result was a drastic policy of deflation that brought

[11] J. A. Woodburn, *The Life of Thaddeus Stevens*, p. 573

further turmoil to the country. In ten years the money in circulation was reduced from somewhat over $2,100,000,000 to a little over a billion, or from fifty-eight dollars per capita in 1865 to seventeen dollars per capita in 1876.[12] The inevitable results followed, a swift appreciation in the value of the dollar and the automatic increase in the debt of the country, both public and private, with the fall of commodity prices. Within a decade, measured in commodity values, the liabilities of the American people were nearly doubled by the simple device of changing the standard of deferred payments. Gold might remain as stable as the eternal hills, but somehow all other commodities were shrinking daily. "Them steers," Solon Chase indeed said aptly, "while they grew well, shrank in value as fast as they grew." This remarkable result was brought about, it is well to remember, by the plea for honest money and the plighted faith of the nation. Keeping the public faith, it would seem, meant permitting the creditors to change the terms of their payments after the contract was made. "Who are these reasoners," cried Thaddeus Stevens, in disgust, "who talk so learnedly of the laws of finance and the morality of human dealings, whose consciences are so raw and stick out so far from their excited coverings that no pharmaceutist can heal their inward wound?"[13]

As a debtor community the Middle Border felt the pinch of deflation acutely, and in consequence the money question was thrust sternly upon agrarian attention. On this issue it came finally to fight its great battle, pitting its homespun experience against the authority of the bankers and the teaching of the schools. To the bankers' argument that note issues should be taken out of politics and lodged in the hands of business men, it replied that the issue of currency was a function of sovereignty, and to surrender it to private corporations, as was done by the National Bank Act, was undemocratic. The monetary system of the nation must not become the football of class interests. To the argument of the bullionists that gold was the only fixed and stable standard for deferred payments, it replied that the gold standard was too narrow a base on which to erect a monetary system for an expanding country, that it was notoriously susceptible to manipulation, and that it had been devised by Lombard Street in the interests of capitalism. Since the days of the great struggle over the Bank a remarkable

[12] *Ibid.*, p. 573.   [13] *Ibid.*, pp. 573–574.

change had come over the agrarian mind in its thinking on monetary affairs. In their distrust of all banks and bank-issues Jackson
and Benton had swung sharply back to the bullion theory of money.
They were militant hard-money men. But in the intervening years
a new and revolutionary conception had been slowly making its
way to recognition. In the minds of obscure economists the quantitative theory of money had risen to challenge the bullion theory.
In unorthodox pamphlets and newspaper discussion it was being
pointed out that the value of money is dependent on the amount
in circulation, that gold and silver are commodities fluctuating in
value like other commodities, and that it is the plain duty of the
state to regulate the per capita circulation in accordance with
business needs. To allow the bankers to erect a monetary system on
gold is to subject the producer to the money-broker and measure
deferred payments by a yardstick that lengthens or shortens
from year to year. The only safe and rational currency is a national currency based on the national credit, sponsored by the
state, flexible, and controlled in the interests of the people as a
whole.[14]

By far the most suggestive of these obscure pamphleteers was
Eleazar Lord, a New York banker, who for thirty-five years was a
propagandist for a new currency system and who watched the
bungling of the war finance with acute concern.[15] With the undemocratic nature of banknotes he was not concerned. As a banker
he accepted them as desirable and wished to establish them on a
sound national basis. He was in ardent sympathy with the patriotic nationalism of Henry C. Carey. The loose system of state-bank
issues seemed to him chaotic and he was earnest in espousal of a
common national system. Lord was an acute and stimulating
thinker on monetary matters. He was one of the first Americans to
understand the significance of credit, and he was realist enough to
foresee that the system of the future would be a credit system.
This was the clue to his dissatisfaction with the bullion theory of
money, which he attacked with vigor, and to his acceptance of the

[14] See, amongst many, *Homo's Letters on a National Currency*, Washington, 1817;
Currency Explosions, their Cause and Cure, New York, 1858; *Our Currency: Some of
Its Evils, and the Remedies for them*, by a Citizen of North Carolina, Raleigh,
1861.
[15] His titles are: *Credit, Currency and Banking*, New York, 1828; *A Letter on the
National Currency*, New York, 1861; *Six Letters on the Necessity and Practicability of
a National Currency, etc.*, New York, 1862; and *National Currency: A Review of the
National Banking Law*, New York, 1863.

quantitative theory.[16] He had the scantest respect for Sherman's dogma that gold is as stable as the eternal hills because it is "labor and value itself," or for Wells's belief that the law of supply and demand automatically produces gold enough to meet the needs of business. He would treat gold and silver as commodities varying in price with supply and demand, and make no attempt to relate the money scale to their fluctuations. For years, he said, America accepted the English "standard of currency, their aristocratic definition of wealth, and their distinction between capital and credit," to its disaster.

The so-called specie basis, whenever there is a foreign demand for coin, proves to be a mere fiction, a practical humbug; and whenever, by an excess of imports, this pretended basis is exported to pay foreign debts, the bank-notes are withdrawn from circulation or become worthless, the currency for the time is annihilated, prices fall, business is suspended, debts remain unpaid, panic and distress ensue, men in active business fail, bankruptcy, ruin, and disgrace reign.[17]

To provide a safe, flexible, and convenient currency, Lord proposed a system of national banknotes, based on the wealth of the country and responsive to the needs of a business world founded on credit.

Necessity must teach us whether we can and must have a currency of purely representative value, wholly disconnected from the precious metals, as a basis and standard, or prolong the conflict between coin and paper, commerce and exchange. The existing theory on the subject is too firmly fixed by education, prescription, prejudice and interest, to be overthrown. . . . Such words as *safe, secured, national, uniform, economical, inalienable*, when predicated of any thing but gold as currency, are to the specie-paying theorist mere sounds devoid of significance. . . . Credit must triumph. Can any one blame the well-meaning theorist if he manifests some degree of doubt and alarm in view of the extent to which the actual use of credit, and of the confidence in the use of credit, has already attained? [18]

In the writings of these obscure economists are to be found the seeds of the later agrarian program. Some of them were clearheaded and able men, but they underestimated the power of the banking group. They failed to realize that in a capitalistic society

[16] From what source Lord, and the other amateur economists, derived their theory is not clear. It is possible, of course, to assume that it was from Ricardo and the English economists. For an analysis and rejection of the quantity theory, see J. Lawrence Laughlin, *The Principles of Money*, Chapter VIII.

[17] *A Review of the National Banking Law*, p. 8.

[18] *Ibid.*, p. 34.

no monetary system would be tolerated that was not to the bankers'
liking, and that if it were to their liking they would easily convince
the public that it was the only honest and just system. It was this
lesson that the Greenbackers and Free Silver men were to learn.
No sooner was the issue joined between paper money and the gold
standard than a scurrilous hue and cry was raised by the "sound-
money" men. The bitter dispute that marked American politics
for more than a score of years is a classic example of the distortion
of fact for partisan ends that seems to be an inevitable consequence
of referring a matter of policy to a democratic electorate. Denunciation took the place of exposition, and hysteria of argument; and
in this revel of demagoguery the so-called educated classes—lawyers and editors and business men—were perhaps the most shameless purveyors of humbuggery. Stripped of all hypocrisy the main
issue was this: Should the control of currency issues—with the delegated power of inflation and deflation—lie in the hands of private
citizens or with the elected representatives of the people? It is a
question on which wide disagreement may well exist, for it involves
important differences of social and political theory. But the significant thing is that throughout the years when the subject was debated in every newspaper and on every stump the real issue was
rarely presented for consideration. The bankers did not dare to
present it, for too much was at stake and once it was clearly understood by a suspicious electorate their case was lost. Hence the
strategy of the money group was to obscure the issue, an end they
achieved by dwelling on the single point of inflation and charging
the agrarians with a dishonest policy of repudiation.

Certainly in the minds of many conscientious men the fear of
repudiation was very real and acute, and their fears made timid
souls panicky. The newspapers took their cue from this bogey and
beat the drums so loudly in the cause of "honest money" that all
hope of calm discussion was lost. The issue became so distorted
from class feeling that later historians find it difficult to view the
question dispassionately. So late as 1916 Joseph Gilpin Pyle in his
Life of James J. Hill could still speak of the Greenback movement
as a vicious scheme of "inflation, the boon of the demagogue and
the dream of the great debtor class in this new country," who "increased . . . by the opening up of the West on borrowed capital,
welcomed any measure that might give them a specious justification for discharging their obligations with something worth less

than what they had promised to pay." Describing the genesis of
the free silver movement, he said:

Hence grew up a formidable coalition between mine owners, debtors
unable or unwilling to pay, ambitious politicians, honest theorists led
captive by barren and unpractical abstractions, and a host of men too ignorant to inform themselves, too impassioned by what they heard to wish
to know the truth.[19]

Obviously it was not so simple—or so wicked—as that. To
determine the justice of the charge of repudiation certain facts
must be borne in mind. The gist of the money problem pressing so
heavily on the Middle Border was the question of stabilizing the
currency with a view to stabilizing prices. Under the prick of war-
necessities a sharp inflation of prices had taken place. With the
drastic contraction of the currency following the war, prices fell as
sharply. From 1873 to 1896 a world-wide appreciation in the value
of gold, aggravated by recurrent economic crises, further depressed the market values of commodities, rendering the question
of the solvency of the Middle Border increasingly doubtful. Falling
prices are only the obverse of rising money-values, and to stop the
one it was proposed to cheapen the other, either through the issue
of greenbacks as proposed by the Greenback party, or through the
free coinage of silver as proposed in the plank of the Democratic
platform of 1896. It was not a question of repudiation in favor
of debtors, but a question of correcting an unjust deflation that
favored the creditor class.

IV

GREENBACKISM AND PETER COOPER

The opposition to the program and methods of the rising
plutocracy was not confined to the farmers of the Middle Border.
It was nourished by a widespread distrust of banks and bank-
currencies that was a heritage of the Jacksonian struggle. Amongst
the leaders of the Greenback movement were many eastern men,
some of wide industrial experience, whose economic views and
prejudices were a hold-over from the days of John Taylor, and
who discovered in the post-war finances the same class manipulations of public credit that marked the funding operations of Washington's administration. Men as dissimilar as Horace Greeley,
Thaddeus Stevens, Wendell Phillips, Henry C. Carey, and Peter

[19] Vol. I, p. 485.

Cooper, made common cause with the western farmers in seeking to wrest control of government from the bankers, and establish what they conceived to be a just democratic economy. Picturesque militants grown old in warfare, they were of an earlier generation, inheritors of the ideals of simpler times before production for consumption had been superseded by consumption for profit, ardent equalitarians who would not see their hopes frustrated and America become a plutocracy without a struggle. Greeley, Carey, and Phillips have been considered elsewhere; Stevens was the last of the rugged equalitarians who followed their principles to the bitter end; and Peter Cooper was an unregenerate Jeffersonian who dedicated his last years to combating Wall Street, accepting in 1876, at the age of 85, nomination for the presidency by the National Independent Party, commonly called the Greenback Party.

Like Thaddeus Stevens an ironmaster, grown wealthy by a long life of useful and adventurous industry, builder of the first American locomotive that made possible the success of the Baltimore and Ohio railway, Peter Cooper was the most picturesque figure in New York City in the seventies. With Bryant he shared the distinction of being the patriarch of Broadway. Bred up amidst stern and harsh conditions, at a period when, he said, within his "own recollection unmarried white men could be sold for debt in the State of Connecticut," [20] he was not hardened by the struggle for subsistence. A tender social conscience mellowed an old-fashioned probity and gave character and dignity to a simple rugged nature. Transparently honest, with a certain innate austerity softened by a homely courtesy, he was not a reed to sway in every vagrant breeze, but a great oak with fibers toughened by the storms of years. Like Horace Greeley, whom he much resembled in honest kindliness, he carried the burdens of his country on his heart, and in the midst of abundant prosperity still reckoned himself his brother's keeper. By "nature and temperament a radical reformer," his strongest instinct was a quick sense of justice. He was oppressed by the poverty and misery he saw about him, and he gave so generously to all good causes that he was known to his generation as "the greatest philanthropist in the world." His chief accomplishment was the founding of Cooper Union for free instruction in "practical art and science," on which he expended a fortune.[21] But

---

[20] *Ideas for a Science of Good Government*, p. iii.
[21] *Political and Financial Opinions of Peter Cooper*, p. 23.

he was not one to salve his conscience with a gift of superfluous wealth. His heart was as open as his pocketbook, and he must explore to its hidden sources the infection that was breeding social injustice in the new world. His private interests never blinded him to his larger duties, but he gave his time and strength as readily as his money to whatever cause he espoused.

Such a man was morally incapable of the buccaneering exploitation that marked the Gilded Age. Between Peter Cooper and Jim Fisk was an impassable gulf; they were products of different worlds and different economies. The speculative middleman who thrust himself between the producer and the consumer, with no sense of responsibility to either, but concerned only with immediate profit, was a figure to excite the wrath of an older-fashioned industrialist who had been taught that the only just reward is the reward that comes from productive labor; and in the days of the great barbecue Peter Cooper became deeply concerned for the future of America. It was the new breed of bankers with their control of the money system that were to blame, he came to believe, and he would have reckoned himself false to the obligations of citizenship if he failed to protest against their selfish manipulation of the public credit. He had watched the callous juggling of the national finances by the money-lenders during the Civil War, and had seen a debt of some three billions nearly doubled in the decade after Appomattox by the bond-holders. The new system of National Banks that issued from the emergencies of war had come to control the financial policy of the country, and to Peter Cooper it seemed that their purpose was to perpetuate a debt that enabled them to tax the productive labor of America and to squeeze wealth from a calculating expansion and contraction of the currency. To surrender to such mercenaries the sovereign power of issuing and regulating money seemed to him the abdication of sovereignty, and in so far as he could he felt called in honor to prevent it.

It needed rare courage and complete self-sacrifice to take up the gage of battle and in his old age to renew the war that Andrew Jackson had engaged in forty years before. His good name and his honorable career could not save him from the gibes of politicians or the caustic criticism of honest men. It was a losing fight at best. The struggle had been venomous in Jackson's day when the money-power was in its infancy; and now that the banking interests had grown mighty it was as hopeless as the charge of the Light Brigade

The cause had been lost on the day when Congress wrote into the bill establishing a legal tender for war purposes the single word "except," thereby invalidating the greenback for interest payments on bonds and duties on imports—an act that "drew tears from the eyes of Thaddeus Stevens"; and the bankers who could assert their control in war times had no intention a dozen years later of suffering that control to pass from hands that had grown enormously stronger.

Yet Peter Cooper refused to consider the outlook hopeless. With all the resources he could command he threw himself into the struggle. He scattered "more than a million of documents" broadcast—most of the matter of which he wrote; he appealed to Congress and the President, he challenged candidates, he cited the opinions of the Fathers, and when he was buried under an avalanche of votes—as Horace Greeley had been four years before—he preserved his faith in the "people's cause" and to the last day of his life kept up the great battle. "I always have been, am, and ever shall be with the poor toilers and producers; therefore I desire Congress to legislate for the poor as well as for the rich, who can take care of themselves," [22] he wrote in his ninety-second year, and the spirit that stirred in his old veins appears from such a comment as this:

I consider the persistent class legislation of Congress since the war, a worse despotism than that of Great Britain before the Revolution; because it reduces the laboring classes to periodic distress and starvation, that are worse than any despotism ever was; for monopolizing corporations, whether in the shape of banks or railroads, have no soul. [23]

Peter Cooper's political philosophy was simple and transparent. His teachers were Albert Gallatin, Henry C. Carey, and George William Curtis, and from them he drew three major ideas that had emerged from three generations of American experience: the need for a national monetary system based on legal tender; the necessity for a protective tariff; and the need for an effective civil service. The first was an adaptation of the old agrarian dislike of banknotes; the second came out of Clay's American System as it had been elaborated by Henry C. Carey in the fifties; and the third issued from the Civil Service Reform movement of the seventies. The exigencies of the political situation, however, thrust into the

[22] *Ideas for a Science of Good Government*, p. 272.   [23] *Ibid.*, p. 271.

foreground the money question, and nine-tenths of his writings deal
with that pregnant issue. As an ardent Jacksonian he was deeply
suspicious of the rising money-power, with its corporations and
monopolies, its land-grants and railways and banks, for behind
them he saw the specter of aristocracy. "In America," he said in
1882, "we have no aristocrats except those who have sprung up in
a night—as toad-stools do in a dung-hill." [24] But class legislation
must end in creating classes, and at another time he said, "There
is fast forming in this country an aristocracy of wealth—the worst
form of aristocracy that can curse the prosperity of any country.
. . . Such an aristocracy is without soul and without patriotism.
Let us save our country from this, its most potent, and, as I hope,
its last enemy." [25]

His deep interest in political measures was quickened by an
anxious concern at the hard times that resulted from the policy of
drastic currency deflation. That matters were going ill in America
during the middle seventies every fool knew, and Peter Cooper was
only giving expression to the common knowledge in describing to
President Hayes, in a letter dated August 6, 1876, the "appalling"
economic situation. That it was equally bad in England he did not
point out.

More than two hundred thousand men, within the last few weeks, have
joined in "strikes" on the various railroad lines, the workshops and the
mines of the country, on account of the further reduction in their wages,
already reduced to the living point. That some of these strikes have been
attended with lawless and unjustifiable violence, only shows the intensity
of the evils complained of, and the despair of the sufferers. For four years
past, since the "panic of 1873," millions of men and women, in this hitherto
rich and prosperous country, have been thrown out of employment, or
living on precarious and inadequate wages, have felt embittered with a lot,
in which neither economy nor industry, nor a cheerful willingness to work
hard, can bring any alleviation. Is it to be wondered at, that *enforced
idleness* has made tramps of so many of our laboring population, or induced
them to join the criminal and dangerous classes? [26]

After pointing out the disastrous effects of such hard times on
mining, railways, real estate, and the western farmers, he asserted
that the bankers, although they also were embarrassed, were "very
patient with their troubles. . . for they know, that *money is
appreciating in value all the time.*" He then uncovers the kernel of

[24] *Ibid.*, p. 261.   [25] *Ibid.*, p. 123.   [26] *Ibid.*, pp. 117-118.

his thought—that it is a sovereign duty of government to provide an adequate national currency.

> This bondage has its manifold centre and its secret force in more than two thousand banks, that are scattered through the country. All these banks, are organized expressly to loan out their own money and the money of all those, who will entrust them with deposits. These loans are made to men, whose business-lives will soon become dependent on money, borrowed from corporations, that have a special interest of their own. Such a power of wealth, under the control of the selfish instincts of mankind, will always be able to control the action of our Government, unless that Government is directed by strict principles of justice and of the public welfare. The banks will favor a course of special and partial legislation, in order to increase their power . . . they will never cease to ask for more, as long as there is more, that can be wrung from the toiling masses of the American people.
>
> Such a power should never be allowed to go out from the entire and complete control of the people's Government. The struggle with this money-power, intrenched in the special privileges of banks, has been going on from the beginning of the history of this country. It has engaged the attention of our wisest and most patriotic statesmen. Franklin, Jefferson, Webster, Calhoun, Jackson, have all spoken of the danger of such a power and the necessity of guarding against it.[27]

The solution he offered for the vexing monetary problem accorded with that of the Greenback Party,[28] namely, refusal to recharter those banks *"deceitfully styled national"* and the retirement of all bank currency; the abandonment of the policy of currency contraction; the issue of legal-tender notes to the amount last found necessary for the functions of industry and business; the rejection of a specie basis, the notes to be interconvertible with government bonds bearing interest at 3.65 per cent; issued on demand in any amount in exchange for legal-tender notes; and the establishment of a Postal Savings Bank. No man ever believed more ardently in the sufficiency of his program than Peter Cooper. It was a suggestive proposal, that only a knave would call the visionary scheme of a fool. He was tireless in explanation and argument, the quality of which may be judged from the following passage from a letter to Hayes and Tilden written during the campaign of 1877:

> The worth or exchangeable value of gold is as uncertain as other products of human labor, such as wheat or cotton. The exchangeable value of anything depends on its *convertibility into something else* that has value *at the*

---

[27] *Ibid.*, pp. 109–110.   [28] See *Ibid.*, pp. 59–60.

option of the individual. This rule applies to paper money as to anything else. But how shall Government give an exchangeable value to a paper currency? Can it be done by a standard which is beyond its control and which naturally fluctuates, while the sign of exchange indicated by the paper remains the same? . . .

. . . we must trust our Government with this *whole function* of providing the standards and measures of exchange, as we trust it with the weights and measures of trade. . . . We must require the Government to make this currency, at all times, and, at the option of the individual, *convertible.* But the currency must be convertible into something over which the Government has entire control, and to which it can give a definite as well as a permanent value. This is its own *interest-bearing bonds.* These are, in fact, a mortgage upon the embodied wealth of the whole country. The reality of their value is as sound and as permanent as the Government itself, and the degree of their value can be determined exactly by the rate of interest the Government may think proper to fix.[29]

The Jeffersonianism of Peter Cooper, like the Jeffersonianism of the Middle Border, had taken a bias from the confident nationalism that during the fifties so deeply colored American thought. To assure an adequate national economy, superior in its self-sufficiency to European—and especially English—policies, was a persuasive program that Henry C. Carey devoted his later life to formulating, and that men like Horace Greeley and Peter Cooper disseminated amongst their wide agrarian following. That such a program implied a paternalistic government did not trouble them. Peter Cooper accepted paternalism as a necessary governmental function. He would have the state build and own the great western railway systems; he would use the national domain for the benefit of the settler; he would not tuin over the state to plunderers nor the resources of the nation to speculators. An honest man with a sensitive social conscience, he would have no hand in the great barbecue that wasted more than it consumed; but the times were heedless of the counsels of honest men, and he was loved and laughed at and ignored. Like Franklin in the Constitutional Convention, he had outlived his generation and was thrust aside by the new economy that was taking over the custodianship of America.*

[29] *The Political and Financial Opinions of Peter Cooper*, pp. 22–23.
* In his original plan Professor Parrington included here a discussion entitled "Bimetallism: A heritage of Jacksonian democracy; Ignatius Donnelly, 'Coin' Harvey," but from the references in the next chapter it seems evident that as he worked out his plan he decided to omit this.—*Publisher*.

CHAPTER II

THE DEMOCRACY OF THE AGE OF INNOCENCE

CAPITALISTIC ENCROACHMENTS

I

WITH its heritage of Jacksonianism it was natural for the agrarian movement to attempt to carry further the exploration of the democratic principle, seeking to complete the program that had been left unfulfilled by the Fathers. There were few as yet who questioned the finality of democracy as a political system or its adequacy to all social needs. The growing evils of American life were traced unhesitatingly to an imperfect democratic control of the forces of exploitation. If the plutocracy were making gains at the expense of the plain people it was due to defective governmental machinery, and the immediate problem was the readjustment of that machinery. There must be an extension of democratic control over the economics of society. The great principle of *laissez faire*, that had proved so useful in the earlier struggle against aristocratic paternalisms, was become a shield and buckler for the plutocracy that was rising from the freedoms of a let-alone policy. To curb the ambitions of that plutocracy and preserve the democratic bequest for the common benefit of all, was therefore the immediate problem of the times.

To this end two things remained to be achieved: to wrest possession of the government from the hands of the plutocracy that was befouling it, and to use it for democratic rather than plutocratic ends. The difficulties in the way were many. Entrenched behind the checks and balances of a complex constitution the plutocracy could not easily be dislodged from power; even if it were driven out of the legislative and executive branches of government it would find aid and succor in the judiciary, where a masterful corporation law was interpreted by a bench tender toward all property rights, and jealous of its sovereign prerogative of reviewing all legislative enactments. A surprising change had come over the attitude of the governing class towards democracy. Having gained control of the machinery of government the plutocracy found no cause to quarrel with a situation wholly to its liking. It had mastered the gentle art of guiding the majority will, and secure—as it believed—in its control of the political state, it counted on an indefinite continuation of the policy of preëmption and exploitation. From such a group, whether in Wall Street or at Washington, no new theories of government were to be expected. Business men wanted to be let alone. They clung to the anarchism of the Enlightenment and were stout in defense of the principle of individual initiative. So late as 1916 a group of confirmed individualists reissued Spencer's *Man Versus the State*, with an introduction by Elihu Root, to combat the rising spirit of governmental control. They regarded the American system of government as adequate and final, and wanted no subversive changes. The Constitution had been completed by the post-war enactments that fixed the status of the negro, and for a generation thereafter—except for the silent changes wrought by the judiciary —it remained static. East of the Allegheny Mountains popular interest in political theory had come to an end. A group of academic thinkers like John W. Burgess and Woodrow Wilson, an occasional intellectual like Brooks Adams, isolated radicals like Johann Most and small Marxian groups in Chicago and New York, and leaders of the new proletarian movement like Terence V. Powderly, were still acutely concerned about political theory; but these men and their theories counted for little in the stodgy mass of capitalistic America. The political phase had passed over into the economic; politics was wholly divorced from reality.

But throughout the Middle Border and on to the Pacific Coast the spirit of political democracy was alive and vigorous. There the older frontier Jacksonianism still lingered. For upwards of a half a century creative political thinking in America was largely western agrarian, and from this source came those democratic ideas that were to provide the staple of a later liberalism. The conscious objective of this great movement was to complete the work begun by Jacksonianism, and create a political machinery that should enable the democracy to withstand the shock of the Industrial Revolution. Many thinkers contributed to the work—U'Ren of Oregon, Jerry Simpson of Kansas, Tom Watson of Georgia, "Coin" Harvey of Arkansas, General Weaver of Iowa, Ignatius Donnelly of Minnesota, Henry D. Lloyd of Chicago, to name a handful out of the mass—homespun realists who have been forgotten by a later generation, but whose labors were given to the necessary work of refashioning the political machinery of America, and whose program provided the materials for the later Progressive party. They were commoners, men of the people, unversed in the dogmas of the schools, idealists who drew their inspiration from the Declaration of Independence; they spoke for an older America that feared the rising plutocracy, and they were casting about for ways and means to cut its claws. From their labors came the Greenback Movement, the Farmers' Alliance, Populism; and from them came in turn the Progressive Movement that reaped what they had sown.

II

THIRD-PARTY MOVEMENTS

It is, perhaps, not extreme to interpret the political history of America since 1790 as largely a struggle between the spirit of the Declaration of Independence and the spirit of the Constitution, the one primarily concerned with the rights of man, the other more practically concerned with the rights of property. The humanitarian idealism of the Declaration has always echoed as a battle-cry in the hearts of those who dream of an America dedicated to democratic ends. It cannot be long ignored or repudiated, for sooner or later it returns to plague the councils of practical politics. It is constantly breaking out in fresh revolt. When the major parties have grown callous and indifferent to the wishes of the common people, it has reformulated its principles in third-party platforms. Without its freshening influence our political history would have been much more sordid and materialistic. With the exception of such sporadic outbursts as Antimasonry and Know-nothingism, the third-party movements of the nineteenth century were democratic movements, inspired by a sense of social justice, founded on the Declaration of Independence, and promulgated to recall the American people to their heritage of idealism. The Locofoco party, the Freesoil party, the early Republican party, the Greenback party, the Populist party, the Progressive party, however they differed in immediate programs, have had a common objective, namely, to set man above property as the great object of governmental concern, and preserve in America the democratic principle of equal opportunity.

Despite the fact that they failed in their immediate objectives they served the larger purpose of reminding the major parties that America professes to be a democratic country, and that party platforms must be brought to square with that fact. Thus interpreted the history of party struggle since 1790 falls into three broad phases: the Jeffersonian movement that established the ideal of political democracy; the Jacksonian movement that established equalitarianism crudely in practice; and the successive third-party movements that attempted, in successive reactions, to regain such ground as had been lost, to extend the field, and to perfect the machinery of democratic government. Since the rise of the slavery controversy the major parties, allied with masterful economic groups, have persistently ignored the Declaration of Independence, and repudiated in practice the spirit of democracy. To prevent if possible so grave a treason to our traditional ideals, to assert the rights of the common man against the encroachments of a class, has been therefore the common mission of the third-party movements. The significance of their somewhat scanty success is something the thoughtful American may interpret as he will.

Since Civil War days, discontent has been endemic in the Middle Border, and it has broken out in three great political upheavals: the Greenback movement of the seventies; the Populist movement of the eighties and nineties; and the Non-Partisan League movement of the second decade of the present century. Issuing from a profound resentment at the exploitation from which the farmer suffered, they mark a persistent drift away from the old Jacksonian individualism and an advance toward a socialized conception of the political state. Disciplined by hard times the farmers were learning a lesson from capitalistic Whiggery; if the political state had proved serviceable to business why should it not prove serviceable to agriculture? Why should not a democratic state consider the producers as well as the middleman? Why should it not provide a national currency, a national system of transportation, a democratic banking system, a standard system of grain-grading, public elevators, crop insurance, and the like? Why should the farmer be squeezed at every turn by private companies who did badly what the state could do well? By 1917, in short, the Middle Border had got far from the simple individualism of earlier days and was well advanced toward state socialism; and it was only the ruthless opposition of the business interests, that had no wish to see their private preserves thus rudely invaded, that put a stop to the movement.

Back of all these agrarian programs was the greater problem of the popular control of the political state. How could the undisciplined majority hold in check the disciplined minority? How could poverty meet wealth on an equal footing? The control of politics had fallen into the hands of the machine, and the machine served property interests. Legislatures were bought and sold like corner lots; senatorships went to the highest bidder; judges were more responsive to the wishes of bankers than to those of farmers. To break the power of the machine there must be an extension of democratic control, and to that end new machinery must be provided. Hence the vast agrarian concern with political machinery. From the agrarian agitation—supplemented by proletarian and middle-class recruits—has come the Australian ballot, the Initiative and the Referendum, the Recall, the Direct Primary, and popular election of Senators. The only important agrarian principle that has not been adopted is the principle of proportional representation. If agrarianism lost its great battle over the currency, it won the battle over the income tax. Nullified by a scandalous court decision after it had been long accepted, the income tax was finally established by the tedious method of constitutional amendment—an outcome that owed much to the Middle Border. In casting up the accounts of American democracy, the largest sums must be credited to the Middle Border, as in earlier years they were credited to the Jacksonian frontier. Whether the new machinery is useful or merely cumbersome, there is much disagreement, but it is agrarian in origin and it came from an honest attempt to democratize American politics.*

* The Contents here calls for a third section on the "Populistic Program" (see p. xxxiv for details) and a fourth on "William Jennings Bryan."—*Publisher.*

CHAPTER III

LITERATURE AND THE MIDDLE BORDER*

III

HAMLIN GARLAND AND THE MIDDLE BORDER

IT was not till the end of the eighties that the bitterness of the frontier began to creep into literature. Its slackness and drab poverty had got into the pages of *The Hoosier Schoolmaster*, as its neighborliness had got into Riley; but in these earlier studies there was no brooding sense of social injustice, of the wrongs done the Middle Border by unjust laws, of the hardships that are increased by the favoritism of government. In the year 1887, however, came a significant change of temper. Three very different writers— Harold Frederic, Joseph Kirkland, and Hamlin Garland—turned to the theme of farm life, and dealt with it in a mordantly realistic vein. It was the first conscious literary reaction to the subjection of agriculture to capitalistic exploitation and it was marked by the bitterness of a decaying order.

Seth's Brother's Wife, by Harold Frederic, is a drab tale of farm life in upper York State, as bitter as any tale of the western border. It is a story of defeat, of flight from country to town. The blight of failure is upon the farming community—a blight that embitters old and young; and the sketches of country louts, of soured lives, of broken men and women, do not make pleasant reading. No gentle idyllic light rests on the landscape such as Sarah Orne Jewett discovers on the fields and villages of New England. Sabrina Fairchild, an old maid embittered by the family failure, yet cling- ing to the family pride and hopeful that the family prestige will be restored, is a pathetic and desolate figure, gaunt and sharp-tongued; at mortal feud with another pathetic old woman, who with her husband had emigrated from Massachusetts years before, and held herself proudly above the mean and vulgar neighborhood in which

---

* In Professor Parrington's plan the section given here was to be preceded by a first section on "Edward Eggleston and Frontier Realism," and a second on "Whit- comb Riley and Folk Romance."—*Publisher.*

they had settled. The slack servants, gossipy and impudent, the petty lives, the grasping ways unrelieved by any grace or beauty, and set in a world of petty machine politics, make a drab and unattractive picture. Harold Frederic quite evidently hates this countryside that bred him. He will not, like Hamlin Garland, take up the battle for it against the town. He sees no hope in political programs; he is no Populistic agrarian fighting for justice; he wants only to escape from it to the city, where life may be lived more generously. The "trail of the serpent is over it all," he remarks, "rich and poor, big and little. The nineteenth century is a century of cities; they have given their own twist to the progress of the age —and the farmer is almost as far out of it as if he lived in Alaska. Perhaps there may have been a time when a man could live in what the poet calls daily communion with Nature and not starve his mind and dwarf his soul, but this isn't the century . . . get out of it as soon as you can."[1]

Much less bitter and hopeless is *Zury: The Meanest Man in Spring County* (1887), by Joseph Kirkland, son of Matilda Kirkland, who a generation before had written sketches of the Michigan frontier. In the preface the author points out that his study is "a palpable imitation of Thomas Hardy's 'Far from the Madding Crowd,'" an "attempt to reproduce, on American soil, the unflinching realism . . . of life down in actual contact with the soil itself." It is a tale of pioneer days in Illinois, in the second quarter of the nineteenth century, and it draws a full-length portrait of the son of a Pennsylvania immigrant who struggles up from mean beginnings to prosperity. The niggardliness of frontier life is drawn unsparingly—the harsh struggle for subsistence—but there is no outcry against governmental favoritisms or the law's injustice. It is nature that must be fought and conquered, and the battle needs strong men who must subdue their finer natures and more generous impulses to the work of acquisition. Zury Prouder is a masterful fellow who bends every energy to the business of accumulation. He makes one hand wash the other, and by dint of saving and squeezing and trading and foreclosing he slowly amasses wealth and power. He is a thrifty farmer as well as a shrewd trader, but his soul is seared by the frontier meanness—squeezed into land and stock and mortgages, consumed with the passion for grabbing. It was a reaction from the skimpiness of his youth. The bitterness of

[1] Chapter IV, pp. 26–27.

poverty had entered his heart as a boy, and his life took shape from the youthful resolve—

"Dad, I'm goin' t'own a mortgage 'fore I die; mind what I say."

"Hope ye will, Zury," his father replies. "Yew'll have a holt of the right eend of the poker then; 'n' t'other feller he'll have a holt o' the hot part, same's we've got naow."

"You bet! An' it'll sizzle his hands, tew, afore I'll ever let up on him."

But Kirkland will not let Zury remain a crabbed and hard-fisted son of the frontier. As the frontier hardships grow less the soul that has been seared by poverty is awakened to more generous impulses. Late in life Zury is taken in hand by a Boston woman who had come out as a schoolteacher years before, and whom Zury had given up for a bride with a rich farm, but to whom he eventually returns. Under her care the plates of mail are stripped from his heart, his better nature expands, and the meanest man in Spring County ripens into a kindly and lovable old age. What poverty and hardship had warped and twisted, love straightens out and ennobles; the meanness of the frontier is washed away as the rich soil yields a more abundant life. It is not a great book, but it is vigorous and honest, and its earlier chapters contain some admirable bits of realism. As one of the first stories of the western farmer it is secure of a place in the history of our American fiction.

It was this same year, 1887, that Hamlin Garland, alone and brooding over his studies at the Boston Public Library, wrote his first sketches of life in the Middle Border. The romance was fading from the prairies when he took up his pen. The Golden West of Mark Twain and the bucolic West of Whitcomb Riley had both slipped into the past and the day that was rising was to bring its discouragements that seared men's hopes as the hot winds seared the fields of rustling corn. The burdens of the western farmer were heavy on his shoulders and he could foresee no time when they would be lighter. Depression had settled on the Middle Border, and Hamlin Garland returning to the familiar fields from his Boston studies felt the depression in every fiber of his being. This was his land and his people. The blight laid upon men and women and children by the drab pioneer life was a familiar fact to him. The Garlands and the McClintocks had suffered from it as their neighbors suffered, and a rebellious wrath filled his heart as he contemplated the Middle Border—the barnyards where tired men did the evening chores, the ungainly houses where tired women stood over hot stoves, the fertile acres that produced more than the markets consumed. It was a life without grace or beauty or homely charm—a treadmill existence that got nowhere. If this were the Valley of Democracy then the democracy was a mean thing and hopeless, and having himself escaped from it he would do what he could to help others escape. In the completeness of his disillusion the glamour of romance was swept away and he proposed to set down in honest plain words the manner of life lived by these Middle Border folk, and the sort of earnings won by their toil. He would speak frankly out of the common bitter experience. The way to truth was the way of realism.

To a later generation that never knew the pioneer hardships of the Middle Border, Hamlin Garland seems strangely remote and old-fashioned; yet his intellectual antecedents are both ancient and honorable. At bottom he is an idealist of the old Jeffersonian breed, an earnest soul devoid of humor, who loves beauty and is mightily concerned about justice, and who, discovering little beauty and finding scant justice in the world where fate first set him, turned rebel and threw in his lot with the poor and the exploited. As a young man, consumed with a desire to speak for his people, he espoused a somber realism, for only by and through the truth could he hope to dislodge from men's minds the misconceptions that stood in the way of justice. The Middle Border had no spokesman at the court of letters and if he could gain a hearing there he must not betray his father's household by glossing ungainly reality; he must depict the life of the western farmer as it was lived under the summer sun and the winter cold, what harvests were brought to crib and what sort of wealth was finally gathered.

And yet in the light of his total work one hesitates to call Garland a realist. Perhaps more justly he might be called a thwarted romantic, and his early rebellious realism be traced to its source in a passionate refusal to be denied the beauty that should be a portion of any rational way of living; for when later he found himself in a land of nobler horizons, unsoiled as yet by crude frontier exploitation, when he looked out upon vast mountain ranges and felt the warm sun on the gray plains, he discovered there the romance of his dreams and fell to describing the strange splendors with the gusto of a naïve romantic. *Main-Travelled Roads* and *Prairie Folks* are the protest of one oppressed with the meanness of a world that takes such heavy toll of human happiness; *Her Mountain Lover* is the expression of a frank romantic who glories in the nobility of nature's noblemen; and *The Captain of the Gray-Horse Troop* is a tale in which romance is justified by ethics and the hero discovers in the protection of a weaker race the deepest satisfactions of life. Beauty is excellent, but beauty should walk hand in hand with service—not art for art's sake, but art subdued to the higher good of humanity.

Between these extremes of a stark realism and an ethical romanticism, stand two books, separated by many years and great changes, that embody in more finished form the theme which after all was the master passion of Garland's life—the Middle Border and the rebellions it bred. *Rose of Dutcher's Coolly* is a full-length portrait of an idealist in revolt against the narrowness of farm life, and *A Son of the Middle Border* is an idyll of the past, autobiography done in mellower years when the passions of youth have been subdued to less exigent demands. These books, together with the sketches of *Main-Travelled Roads* and the militant critical theory of *Crumbling Idols*, contain pretty much the whole of Hamlin Garland that after years have cared to remember—the saga of the Middle Border in the days of its great rebellion when the earlier hopes of boundless prosperity were turning to ashes in the mouth.

The striking originality of Garland's work, that sets it apart from other studies of the local-color school, sprang from the sincerity of his reaction to environment. His intellectual development followed the needs of his ardent, inquisitive nature. After quitting the little Academy at Osage, Iowa, he went forth in quest of an education that should explain to him the meaning of life as he had known it. In this search he was singularly fortunate. He was his own mentor and he took what he needed. Boston had long been the Mecca of his dreams and when he found himself there—having made a pious pilgrimage as Howells had done a generation earlier—he threw himself upon his studies with ascetic zeal. Fortunately he enrolled in the Boston Public Library instead of at Harvard, and his formless radicalisms there found food in plenty. Though he lived in Boston some ten years and made friends, he never penetrated the inner literary sanctuary. A somewhat forlorn outsider, unknown and unvouched for, he found no welcome as Howells and Twain had found, and he never entered the pleasant circles where Holmes and Lowell and Fields and Norton and Aldrich and Howells held sway.

Perhaps that fact unconsciously determined his scornful rejection of the Boston genteel in literature; at any rate his denial of the sovereignty of the New England literary rulers left him free to follow other masters who seemed to him more significant. In his bleak little room his ear had caught the greater voices then sounding in Europe and America. His masters were men of intellectual horizons unbounded by Beacon Street and Harvard Square: Taine and Ibsen and Björnson, Turgenev and Tolstoi, Zola and Millet, Darwin and Spencer and Fiske, Walt Whitman and Henry George, and the later Howells with his deeper sociological concern and graver realism. His three great masters came finally to be Whitman, Spencer, and Henry George. To these greater names should be added that of Edward Eggleston, who had been his boyhood idol, and that of Joseph Kirkland, who did much to stimulate and guide his earliest sketches. He did not absorb all these men had to give. He could not stretch his provincial mind suddenly to compass the intellectual realm of his masters. But something he got and that something, woven into the fabric of his thinking, was to make him free. It was the best school of the times, and from his studies Hamlin Garland emerged an uncompromising radical, one of a group of eager young men who gathered about B. O. Flower, and in the sympathetic pages of the *Arena* published their divers radicalisms to a hostile world. He was ready to proclaim new social and literary creeds, ready to go forth to do battle for democratic justice and a democratic art.

The gist of Garland's new literary creed is set forth in *Crumbling Idols*, written in the earliest years of the nineties, when Chicago was preparing the setting for the World's Fair, and gathered into book form in 1894. It is realism modified by the local-color school, by French impressionism, and by Whitman—intensely individualistic, ardently social, and militantly democratic. It would sweep away every fetish of great reputations and authoritative schools, and insist that the artist confront the life that he knows and tell of it truthfully. Following the French example he calls this iconoclastic realism, Veritism. "The *theory* of the veritist," he says, "is, after all, a statement of his passion for truth and for individual expression," and he then goes on:

Art, I must insist, is an individual thing,—the question of one man facing certain facts and telling his individual relations to them. His first care must be to present his own concept. This is, I believe, the essence of veritism. "Write of those things of which you know most, and for which you care most. By so doing you will be true to yourself, true to your locality, and true to your time." [2]

But Veritism in the hands of a disciple of Taine, Whitman, Henry George, and Herbert Spencer must take on ethical values and serve the common well-being. All art, he insists, is "sociologic," and realism is harsh because it is hopeful.

Because the fictionist of to-day sees a more beautiful and peaceful future social life, and, in consequence, a more beautiful and peaceful literary life, therefore he is encouraged to deal truthfully and at close grapple with the facts of his immediate present. His comment virtually amounts to satire or prophesy, or both. Because he is sustained by love and faith in the future, he can be mercilessly true. He strikes at thistles, because he knows the unrotted seed of loveliness and peace needs but sun and the air of freedom to rise to flower and fragrance.

The realist or veritist is really an optimist, a dreamer. He sees life in terms of what it might be, as well as in terms of what it is; but he writes of what is, and, at his best, suggests what is to be, by contrast. . . . He aims to hasten the age of beauty and peace by delineating the ugliness and warfare of the present; but ever the converse of his picture rises in the mind of the reader. He sighs for a lovelier life. He is tired of warfare and diseased sexualism, and Poverty the mother of Envy. He is haggard with sympathetic hunger, and weary with the struggle to maintain his standing place on this planet, which he conceives was given to all as the abode of peace. With his hate in his heart and this ideal in his brain the modern man writes his stories of life. They are not always pleasant, but they are generally true, and always they provoke thought. [3]

It is an excellent self-portrait of the young realist of that early time when all the rebellions of his blood cried out for expression— the troubled years between 1887 and 1893 when the Border was rising and the son of the Border found the flames of his discontent fanned by many winds. From such roots came the most acrid tales that had as yet fruited in American fiction. Few as were the stories of *Main-Travelled Roads* and *Prairie Folks*, they constitute a landmark in our literary history, for they were the first authentic expression and protest of an agrarian America then being submerged by the industrial revolution. No other man in our literature had known so intimately the Middle Border as Hamlin Garland— its restless swarmings from the old hive, never pausing long enough to gather the honey of the new fields, its heedless venturings for the reputed gold that lay beyond the farthest sunsets. He had re-

[2] Chapter III, p. 35.   [3] Chapter IV, pp. 51–53.

sponded to the spell that kept the pioneer moving West; the allurement of the untamed prairie, the poetry of dawn and twilight. But
the poignant spell had been broken for him by the drab realities
that lay between the dawn and the twilight—the crushing round
of toil that took such heavy toll of men's development and wom-
en's happiness. He was familiar with the blight as well as the
bloom of the frontier. He had seen his uncle David McClintock
broken by the Border—the great wistful man with the soul of a
musician; he had seen his mother fail under the burden—the
cheerful, uncomplaining wife, joining with her rich voice in the
pioneer's song of "O'er the hills in legions, Boys!" And after the
disillusion of his final defeat on the bleak Dakota plains—by 1883
woodland and meadow were pretty much alienated from the public
domains and only plains and deserts and mountain valleys and
forests remained—his eyes were opened at last. "I clearly perceived," he said afterwards, "that our Song of Emigration had
been, in effect, the hymn of fugitives!" So he turned his face to the
East to seek the land of desire in Boston.

That chapter of his life was ended. He had learned that the old
romantic tales of the Border were lies to him, whatever they may
have been to earlier generations; but he had yet to naturalize himself in the realm of ideas, and analyze the experiences of his youth
in the light of current social liberalisms. He had begun that work in
1883 on his raw Dakota claim where his leisure hours were given to
Taine's theory of literary determinism, and Henry George's new
gospel of single-tax; and he carried it rapidly forward during three
years of eager reading. During those quiet months in Boston when
he was making himself at home in the world of contemporary
thought, he sketched the first of the stories of western life which
later he gathered together in *Main-Travelled Roads* and *Prairie
Folks*. "You're the first actual farmer in American fiction," said
his friend Kirkland, "now tell the truth about it." This handful of
short stories, fierce in the repressed passion of the writer's heart, was
Garland's reply to the old romantic myths of the West. In these
acrid pages life is not bucolic, it does not chew the cud of contentment "knee-deep in June," but it is stained with dust and
sweat, lacerated by raw nerves, depressed by a sense of economic
failure.

Of the lives of these labor-burdened men and women he intended
to tell the whole truth. But, as he confessed later, he could not.

"Even my youthful zeal faltered in the midst of a revelation of the lives led by the women on the farms of the middle border. Before the tragic futility of their suffering, my pen refused to shed its ink. Over the hidden chamber of their maternal agonies I drew the veil." It was hard for him to view it all with the calm detachment of the objective realist; the Border life was too deeply and intimately personal to him, it had marked him too harshly. And yet in the sense of conveying the spirit of reality he succeeded greatly, and these earliest tales remain notable work which later years have not forgotten. The subdued words of the Prologue offer the fittest of commentaries on the spirit in which they were done.

The Main-travelled road in the West (as everywhere) is hot and dusty in summer, and desolate and drear with mud in fall and spring, and in winter the winds sweep across it; but it does sometimes cross a rich meadow where the songs of the larks and bobolinks and blackbirds are tangled. Follow it far enough, it may lead past a bend in the river where the water laughs eternally over its shallows. Mainly it is long and weariful, and has a dull little town at one end and a home of toil at the other. Like the main-travelled road of life it is traversed by many classes of people, but the poor and the weary predominate.

Main-Travelled Roads, in its harsh objectivity, belonged to the earlier eighties, to the time when the spirit of unrest was still obscurely fermenting in the western mind, before it had clarified in definite agrarian movements and measures. It is clouded by doubt and harassed by uncertainty. No hope offers a way out of the weary tangle. Its psychology is that of the first mood of dejection that came with the failure of western agriculture with its virgin fields, its new machinery, and its specialized crops, to adjust itself to the new capitalistic order. The simple agrarian mind had not learned to play the new game. The sons of the Middle Border were children of the Gilded Age as truly as Colonel Sellers or Commodore Vanderbilt; they were plungers and speculators in land and crops; but they were no match for the Main Street plungers and speculators; and when bankruptcy instead of riches rewarded their hardships, they were embittered. Out of that very natural bitterness sprang the movement of Populism that proposed to take government out of the hands of Main Street and make it serve agriculture. It was the understanding of this fact that made Howells so sympathetic a critic of Garland. But he would encourage the artist rather than the reformer.

. . . these stories are full of the bitter and burning dust, the foul and trampled slush, of the common avenues of life, the life of the men who hopelessly and cheerlessly make the wealth that enriches the alien and the idler, and impoverishes the producer.

If any one is still at a loss to account for that uprising of the farmers of the West which is the translation of the Peasants' War into modern and republican terms, let him read *Main-Travelled Roads*, and he will begin to understand. . . . The stories are full of those gaunt, grim, sordid, pathetic, ferocious figures, whom our satirists find so easy to caricature as Hayseeds, and whose blind groping for fairer conditions is so grotesque to the newspapers and so menacing to the politicians. They feel that something is wrong, and they know that the wrong is not theirs. The type caught in Mr. Garland's book is not pretty; it is ugly and often ridiculous; but it is heart-breaking in its rude despair.[4]

Too soon, however, the will to remain objective weakened and his work took on a different note. "Obscurely forming in my mind," he says of the year 1889, "were two great literary concepts —that truth was a higher quality than beauty, and that to spread the reign of justice should everywhere be the design and intent of the artist. The merely beautiful in art seemed petty, and success at the cost of the happiness of others a monstrous egotism." [5] With this ethical conception of art he returned in 1889 to the old home, after a six years' absence, to experience a poignant reaction to the change that had come over the Border. "Another dry year was upon the land and the settlers were deeply disheartened," he wrote later. "The holiday spirit of eight years before had entirely vanished. In its place was a sullen rebellion against government and against God." [6]

Every house I visited had its individual message of sordid struggle and half-hidden despair. . . . All the gilding of farm life melted away. The hard and bitter realities came back upon me in a flood. Nature was as beautiful as ever. The soaring sky was filled with shining clouds, the tinkle of the bobolink's fairy bells rose from the meadow, a mystical sheen was on the odorous grass and waving grain, but no splendor of cloud, no grace of sunset, could conceal the poverty of these people; on the contrary, they brought out, with a more intolerable poignancy, the gracelessness of these homes, and the sordid quality of the mechanical routine of these lives. I perceived beautiful youth becoming bowed and bent. I saw lovely girlhood wasting away into thin and hopeless age. Some of the women I had known had withered into querulous and complaining spinsterhood,

---

[4] Introduction to *Main-Travelled Roads*.
[5] *A Son of the Middle Border*, Chapter XXVIII, p. 374.
[6] *Ibid.*, Chapter XXIX.

and I heard ambitious youth cursing the bondage of the farm. "Of such pain and futility are the lives of the average man and woman of both city and country composed," I acknowledged to myself with candor, "Why lie about it?" [7]

In such a mood the call of social justice was too insistent to be denied. "With William Morris and Henry George I exclaimed, 'Nature is not to blame. Man's laws are to blame'!" And so the young man of twenty-nine threw himself into the agrarian cause. He took the platform with Mary Ellen Lease and was glad of the farmers' approval of the new doctrine of less corn and more hell. Under the urging of his friend Flower he planned to put the Populist movement into fiction and wrote *A Spoil of Office*. The familiar Iowa backgrounds are in the story—the harsh lives and bent weary figures of men and women—but there is also an idealized heroine who suggests what life may become when injustice is done away with and the blighting toil is lessened—a figure who, as Grange lecturer and Farmers' Alliance speaker, may have been suggested by Mary Ellen Lease. Much inferior as it is to *Main-Travelled Roads*—a social tract rather than a work of art—we cannot well spare it from our Middle Border literature, for it has captured and preserves for later times the spirit of the passionate uprising of the farmers, and it recalls the vast hopes that fermented in that revolt —not well grounded, perhaps, but warm and human. "The heart and center of this movement," says Ida Wilbur, "is a demand for justice, not for ourselves alone, but for the toiling poor wherever found. . . . It is no longer a question of legislating for the farmer; it is a question of the abolition of industrial slavery." [8] There are echoes of an older and simpler America in these pages, of discontents that were put down but not removed—Jacksonianisms, Greenbackisms, anti-monopolistic crusades. Yet they look forward to a time when beauty and well-being shall be the common portion of those who do the work of the world. The way, alas, is "long and weary, and thousands and millions of us must die on the road, I am afraid," says the heroine; but go forward they must, along other paths than the path of capitalism.

Less significant is *Jason Edwards: An Average Man* (1891), that is an elaboration of the note, "The air is full of revolt against things as they are." It is a single-tax reply to the question of a young girl, "Are there any happy people in the world—any working people, I

---

[7] *Ibid.*, Chapter XXVIII, pp. 364-365.   [8] *Ibid.*, p. 245.

mean? Are they all cross and tired and worried and full of care, as we are here?" The story is two chapters in the life of a working-man—his struggle in Boston as a mechanic, and his struggle in Minnesota, whither he flees for a refuge on a homestead. Defeat awaits him in the end, and the conclusion is an illustration of Henry George's thesis that poverty is the entail of land rent. In this and in other studies done under the influence of B. O. Flower, whose appetite for reform literature was insatiable, Hamlin Garland had ceased to be an objective realist and turned propagandist, bringing down on his head the criticisms of conservative readers. One of his friends went so far as to expostulate over the folly of his course. "It is a mistake for you to be associated with cranks like Henry George and writers like Whitman," he said. "It is a mistake to be published in the *Arena*. Your book should have been brought out by one of the old established firms. If you will fling away your radical notions and consent to amuse the governing classes, you will succeed." [9]

It is the agrarian background of Garland's mind that makes him seem old-fashioned to a generation that has forgotten the agrarian roots of our past growth. He was so deeply colored by this earlier native America that he never outgrew it; and when the Populistic revolt had died down, when this last organized agrarian rebellion against the exploiting middle class had become only an episode in our history, he had outlived his day. He was too deeply stirred by Whitman's romantic faith in democracy, too narrowly a disciple of Henry George's Jeffersonian economics, to fit into an industrializing America. Despite his discipleship to European realism he refused to go with the group of young left-wing naturalists who were boldly venturing on new ways of fiction. He would not follow the path of naturalism. Of Norris's *McTeague* he said, "What avail is this study of sad lives? for it does not even lead to a notion of social betterment." [10] He could not bring himself to accept the major criteria of naturalism as they were exemplified in the work of Zola and Strindberg and Hauptmann. A native Jeffersonian, inspired by Whitman and instructed by Henry George and Herbert Spencer, would reject the somber, mechanistic background of naturalist thought. He had learned his science of the Victorian evolutionists, with their grandiose conception of a far-flung benefi-

[9] *A Son of the Middle Border*, Chapter XXXI, p. 417.
[10] *Critic*, Vol. 42, pp. 216–218.

cent progress from the homogeneous to the heterogeneous, and the backgrounds of his mind were radiant with promise. Neither a mechanistic science nor a regimented industrialism had risen in his outlook to bank the fires of his hope. No impersonal determinism had chilled his belief in man as a free-will agent in a moral universe. The vast bleak chemical cosmos that bewildered Theodore Dreiser did not rise before him to dwarf the individual nor overwhelm his aspirations. Like a French romantic of a hundred years before, he remained a confirmed optimist who believed that the future will correct the mistakes of the past, and the peace and beauty for which the human race longs lie immediately ahead. The art of the young man was becoming old-fashioned in the world of Stephen Crane; his ideals were Victorian in the days of Mark Hanna. And so after the agrarian revolt had failed and America lay fat and contented in the lap of McKinley prosperity, he found himself a man without a country, an alien in an industrializing order, and he turned away to the newer West and the romance he had always sought. While America was driving towards regimentation he traveled backward in time to recover a vanishing world of individualism, and the distance rapidly widened between them.

In those romantic wanderings through Colorado and California and into the far Northwest he found a new interest in the frontiersman's exploitation of the Indian, and in *The Captain of the Gray-Horse Troop* and *The Eagle Heart* he has wedded his social ethics to French romanticism, and endowed man in a state of nature with exalted social responsibilities. The old theme is dressed in new clothes and Captain Curtis of the Gray-Horse Troop becomes an Indian agent fighting the lawless and cruel encroachment of the frontiersmen upon the Indian rights; but the theme remains. Garland hated the frontier as fiercely as Cooper hated it, and like him he loved the clean free spaces; but when after his long and somewhat futile rambles he returned to the Middle Border, he found there a new light upon the familiar fields and in that light he wrote his saga of the Garlands and the McClintocks. This was to be his great bequest to American letters. To have sought the spirit of the Middle Border in its hopes and its defeat, to have written the history of the generation that swept across the western prairies, is to compress within covers a great movement and a great experience—one of the significant chapters in our total American history.

CHAPTER III

THE QUEST OF UTOPIA

FROM the welter of unrest of the later years of the century, with its labor struggles, its agrarian bitterness, its concern over the exhaustion of the public lands and a pinching monetary system, its acute distrust of monopolies and corporate power, sprang a very natural eagerness to forecast the future and blaze new roads that might lead to the democratic Canaan. Whither the main-traveled road would lead, discerning idealists knew only too well. To bog down in a mire of plutocracy would be a sorry ending to the great experiment; yet the mud was deepening with every mile of advance and unless another highway appeared the situation was unpromising. The crux of the problem seemed to reside in an extension of the powers of the political state, converting to social ends powers that hitherto had been serving private gain. The plutocracy was pointing the way. If the political state were fairly dedicated to democratic ends, why should not society go forward toward a true commonwealth, founded on a social economy and dedicated to common justice and the common well-being? There was need only to subordinate private interests to collective interests, and substitute coöperation for the present mad scramble of selfish individualism.

In elaboration of this pregnant thought a surprising number of social romances appeared during the last quarter of the century, that were native counterparts of the greater studies in collectivism by European thinkers. A recent study lists forty-eight titles of Utopian romances written between 1884 and 1900.[1] Of these several are communistic, and the rest are socialistic; yet in keeping with the American temper none openly makes use of the terms, and few apply the Marxian doctrine of the class war. Their appeal was directed primarily to the middle class of small business and profes-

---

* The first chapter of this section was to have been "Plutocracy and the Workingman," the second "The Rise of the Left." For the contents see p. xxxv.—*Publisher.*
[1] Allyn B. Forbes, *The Literary Quest for Utopia, 1880–1900.* "Social Forces," Vol. VI, No. 2, December, 1927.

siɔnal men, and they were content to rely on political means to achieve economic ends. Troubled as was the American mind by the rise of a cutthroat exploitation, it was not yet ready to entertain ideas of direct action or trust the proletariat to enforce its will by mass strength. In one story, to be sure—Ignatius Donnelly's *Cæsar's Column* (1890)—there is a gloomy picture of the downfall of civilization caused by the class struggles; but the temper of Donnelly had lost its genial optimism through his long immersion in under-dog contests and had grown mordant and gloomy.

I

EDWARD BELLAMY AND "LOOKING BACKWARD"

When in 1888 Edward Bellamy published *Looking Backward* he gave a huge impetus to the Utopian romance. Third in the list of titles collected by Mr. Forbes, it was to have a wide influence on the thought of the times. It made instant appeal and successive editions were issued to meet the popular demand. Not since *Uncle Tom's Cabin* had an American novel reached so many readers, and Bellamy became at once a national figure, the prophet of a new industrial order. There is abundant evidence to the effect produced upon thoughtful readers. E. C. Stedman, the first critic of the times, spoke of it as a "remarkable and fascinating novel"; Frances E. Willard called it "a revelation and an evangel"; and Howells remarked on "the extraordinary effect which Mr. Bellamy's romance has had with the public." More significant still, *Looking Backward* speedily became the source and inspiration for a series of social organizations that beginning at Boston soon spread over the country. *The Nationalist* was established as the organ of the movement and thousands of eager men and women threw themselves into the work of reshaping American society to conform to the new social ideal. No doubt the enthusiasm was naïve, no doubt it sprang from a social inexperience that underestimated the complexity of the problem, yet the sources, clearly, were a sharp distrust of private capitalism and an idealistic faith in coöperation. In a pronouncement of the Boston "Nationalist Club," January 9, 1889, the cause was rested on two fundamental truths—"The principle of competition is . . . the application of the brutal law of the survival of the strongest and most cunning"; and, "The principle of the Brotherhood of Humanity is one of the eternal truths that govern the world's progress on lines which distinguish human nature from brute nature." [2]

It is not easy to trace the origins of Bellamy's interest in collectivism or the sources of his thought. A journalist and lawyer, he had studied in Germany, where presumably he had come in contact with Marxian socialism. Writing in the *Nationalist* for May, 1889, he commented thus on the origins of *Looking Backward:*

> I never had, previous to the publication of the work, any affiliations with any class or sect of industrial or social reformers nor, to make my confession complete, any particular sympathy with undertakings of the sort. It is only just to myself to say, however, that this should not be taken to indicate any indifference to the miserable condition of the mass of humanity, seeing that it resulted rather from a perception all too clear of the depth and breadth of the social problem and a consequent skepticism as to the effectiveness of the proposed solutions which had come to my notice.
>
> In undertaking to write *Looking Backward* I had, at the outset, no idea of attempting a serious contribution to the movement of social reform. The idea was of a mere literary fantasy, a fairy tale of social felicity. There was no thought of contriving a house which practical men might live in, but merely of hanging in mid-air, far out of the reach of the sordid and material world of the present, a cloud-palace for an ideal humanity. [3]

That the impulse did not come from the Marxians is sufficiently clear from his explanation of the idea of an industrial army. "The idea of committing the duty of maintaining the community to an industrial army, precisely as the duty of protecting it is entrusted to a military army," came to him, he said, from the object-lesson of European militarism. But however little he owed to the Marxians it is clear that Bellamy—the literary amateur who had dabbled in Hawthornesque fantasies—possessed a warm social conscience and a vigorous inquiring mind; and once his attention had been drawn to the evils of industrialism he would respond with the same direct competence that marked the thinking of Henry George. Nine years before *Looking Backward* he had dealt with a sociological theme. In 1879 he wrote *The Duke of Stockbridge, A Romance of Shay's Rebellion,* for the *Berkshire Courier,* which was reissued in book form in 1900. It was a hasty piece of work that falls off greatly in the latter part; yet in its sympathy for the agrarian rebels and its probing of the economic sources of the post-Revolutionary unrest, it was far removed from the temper of Federalist historians. It is an account of the tyranny of property rule—of the exploitation of the debtor farmer by the creditor gentleman made possible by the economic maladjustments resulting from the war. A bitter discontent is in the hearts of the common people. Hatred of lawyers and courts and process-servers, has taken the place of hatred of Tories. Soldiers who had conquered Cornwallis were returning home only to be conquered by writs and imprisoned by sheriffs. The exactions of a brutal law fell upon helpless victims; taxes outran incomes and there was no money to pay. Economic injustice was daily whetting the edge of class bitterness. The animus of Shays's Rebellion is compressed into a few paragraphs that suggest how clearly Bellamy had analyzed the social struggle.

"I use ter think ez there wuzn't no sech varmint ez a tory; but I didn't know nothin' 'bout lawyers and sheriffs them times. I calc'late ye could cut five tories aout o' one lawyer an' make a dozen skunks aout o' what wuz left over."

"I hearn as haow Squire Woodbridge says taxes is ten times what they wuz afore the war, an' its sartin that there ain't one shillin' inter folks' pockets ter pay 'em with where there wuz ten on 'em in them days. . . . It seems darn curis, bein' as we fit ag'in the red coats jest ter git rid o' taxes." [4]

So felt the agrarian. Now for the gentleman:

"That is the trouble nowadays, . . . these numskulls must needs have matters of government explained to them, and pass their own judgment on public affairs. And when they cannot understand them, then, forsooth, comes a rebellion. I think none can deny seeing in these late troubles the first fruits of those pestilent notions of equality, whereof we heard so much from certain quarters, during the late war of independence. I would that Mr. Jefferson and some of the other writers of disturbing democratic rhetoric might have been here in the State the past winter, to see the outcome of their preaching." [5]

Nine years after *Looking Backward* Bellamy published *Equality*, a critical examination of economic history with a view to creating an adequate social economics. The earlier work had drawn the outlines of the democratic society of the future, the later supplied a justification and a commentary. The great theme involved a twofold problem: an analysis of the failure of social justice under private capitalism, and a defense of the working of social capitalism. The two threads are closely interwoven, and the effect is heightened by the contrasts resulting from setting the two social

[4] *The Duke of Stockbridge*, Chapter II, pp. 22, 28.
[5] *Ibid.*, Chapter XXVI, p. 349.

orders over against each other. Innumerable questions, touching diverse phases, are propounded and answered. The apologist of private capitalism is pursued into every stronghold of his logic; he is assailed by a hundred vivid analogies which seek to lay bare the folly of a social system that breeds waste only to breed poverty, that puts a premium upon greed and yet takes away the security of possession, that bids the workers fight each other instead of uniting for the common welfare. But men must see a better before they will leave a worse, and so there is drawn the picture of another commonwealth that must arise when men shall put off the ass's head from their shoulders, and set intelligently to work. America is moving towards such a commonwealth, Bellamy is persuaded, and yet how slow it is to grasp the meaning of democracy! It holds back from its own good, loath to probe the depths of the revolutionary philosophy of liberty, equality, fraternity. Julian West awakes in this new world; his eyes are opened; the ass's head is gone; he knows for the first time the goodness of life in a rational society. And when in a hideous nightmare he returned to the old Boston he had lived in before he fell asleep, he tasted for the first time the full iniquity of the old pigsty arrangement. "I have been in Golgotha," he cried, "I have seen Humanity hanging on a cross!" It is knowledge of the good that must destroy the evil.

It was as a political economist that Bellamy attacked the problems of a democratic society, and his radicalism begins and ends with the interpretation he puts on the phrase. He was far from being a political economist of the schools. His contempt for the older classical dogmas was measureless. Manchesterism with its fetish of *laissez faire* he reckoned no better than a pseudo-science. " 'There were no political economists before the Revolution,' " remarks one of the scholars of the later age.[6] Such books as the *Wealth of Nations*, properly speaking, should be called "Examinations into the Economic and Social Consequences of trying to get along without any Political Economy." Before we shall get forward we must examine our terms.

Economy . . . means the wise husbanding of wealth in production and distribution. Individual economy is the science of this husbandry when conducted in the interest of the individual without regard to any others. Family economy is this husbandry carried on for the advantage of a family group without regard to other groups. Political economy, however, can only mean the husbandry of wealth for the greatest advantage of the political or social body, the whole number of the citizens constituting the political organization. This sort of husbandry necessarily implies a public or political regulation of economic affairs for the general interest. But before the Revolution there was no conception of such an economy, nor any organization to carry it out. All systems and doctrines of economy previous to that time were distinctly and exclusively private and individual in their whole theory and practice. While in other respects our forefathers did in various ways and degrees recognize a social solidarity and a political unity with proportionate rights and duties, their theory and practice as to all matters touching the getting and sharing of wealth were aggressively and brutally individualistic, antisocial, and unpolitical.[7]

A social arrangement based on an individual economy must necessarily result in such monstrosities as the system of private capitalism with its cash nexus. It is no other than an organized system of social warfare, with all the appalling waste of war. Habit has blinded our eyes or we should see the utter bankruptcy of individual competition, that prides itself on its "famous process for beggaring a nation." "Were these serious men I saw about me," cried Julian West as he watched the folly of Washington Street, with its thousand shops madly bidding against each other, its vulgar advertising and cheating and swindling, "or children, who did their business on such a plan? Could they be reasoning beings, who did not see the folly which, when the product is made and ready for use, wastes so much of it in getting it to the user? If people eat with a spoon that leaks half its contents between bowl and lip, are they not likely to go hungry?"[8] What is it but such folly which prevents society from doing the thousand things which cry aloud to be done? So long as men must fight each other for individual subsistence how shall they be able to join forces to fight the common enemies, cold, hunger, disease? Our individualism keeps us poverty-stricken; we are too poor to destroy the social squalor, too poor to save our own lives.

If competition entails irretrievable waste, he points out, the system of competitive profit involves economic suicide. It is a pistol which private industrialism points at its own head. The struggle for profit is the hidden cancer that is eating out the heart of modern society, and Bellamy examines it searchingly in the chapter, "Economic Suicide of the Profit System."[9] Under private

---

[7] *Ibid*, p. 189.
[8] *Looking Backward*, Chapter XXVIII, p. 314.
[9] *Equality*, Chapter XXII.

industrialism profits are the oil to the wheels of industry, which turn in response to the market. By the market is meant those who have money to buy with; and demand is brisk or slack according to the diffusion of economic means. When the buyers are satisfied and abstain from further purchases, the market becomes glutted and the wheels of production cease to turn "though starving and naked mobs might riot in the streets." Profits, however, must come out of somebody's pocket; and the greater they are the more the pocket that pays is emptied; unless replenished by other profits, taken from still other pockets, it ceases to be able to buy in like proportion. In consequence the market slacks off and the wheels of industry run slower. The manufacturer takes his profits out of his workmen, the merchant takes his out of the public—which is another term for the workman; he who takes most grows rich fastest and is most successful. Obviously, however, such riches are acquired at the expense of the public capacity to buy; and such lessening capacity is ominous of gluts and crises to ensue, with losses which must be made good by greater profits when the wheels turn again. It is only too clear that society is suffering from a chronic dyspepsia of its industrial system; it cannot digest its food. The current maxim that a fair exchange is no robbery—so confidently urged—cannot apply to the profit system, for if the exchange is fair there is no profit, and if there is no profit there will be no exchange. The further maxim that demand governs supply and supply keeps pace with demand, refers only to the profit-market, and quite overlooks the important detail of social need.

The stupidity of such a system Bellamy never tires of pointing out. His striking analogy of the stage-coach has become a classic; the less known parable of the water-tank [10] is equally vivid; a hundred other shafts are directed at the profit-theory which underlies our individual economy. Until the sway of such anarchy is broken, until society learns to regulate its industrialism on the principles of a wise political economy, there can be no hope of betterment. To create and apply this wise political economy is the urgent business of democracy if it is not to perish. It must be such an economy as shall satisfy both our ethical ideals and our material needs. It must embody the spirit of democratic solidarity and it must look beyond the demands of the profit-market to the well-being of all. It must substitute coöperation for competitive war-

---

[10] *Equality*, Chapter XXIII, p. 195.

fare. The criminal waste which keeps the gray wolves forever snarl-
ing at the threshold of society, must cease; the specter of poverty
which disorders the lives of men and distempers their hopes, must
be banished by the united strength of all. If democracy cannot
achieve such a democratic political economy it must flounder
through deepening bogs until finally it sinks in the morass of plutocracy.

The fatal mistake of democracy heretofore has been the insufficiency of its program. It is incredible how limited has been its
vision and how few and how minor have been its greatest revolutions. To overthrow monarchy was excellent, but it did not bring
in democracy; rather, the unchecked sway of plutocracy. "'The
people, indeed, nominally were sovereigns; but as these sovereigns
were individually and as a class the economic serfs of the rich, and
lived at their mercy, the so-called popular government became the
mere stalking-horse of the capitalists.'"[11] Political revolutions have
proved heretofore to be mere flashes in the pan; not until the economic revolution has been effected will the old tyranny be blown
to pieces:

The second phase in the evolution of the democratic idea began with
the awakening of the people to the perception that the deposing of kings,
instead of being the main end and mission of democracy, was merely preliminary to its real programme, which was the use of the collective social machinery for the indefinite promotion of the welfare of the people at
large. . . .

Which amounts to saying . . . that there never was a democratic government properly so called before the twentieth century. . . . The so-
called republics of the first phase we class as pseudo-republics or negative
democracies. . . .

Regarded as necessary steps in the evolution of society from pure monarchy to pure democracy, these republics of the negative phase mark a
stage of progress; but if regarded as finalities they were a type far less
admirable on the whole than decent monarchies. In respect especially to
their susceptibility to corruption and plutocratic subversion they were the
worst kind of government possible. . . . How could intelligent men delude themselves with the notion that the most portentous and revolutionary idea of all time had exhausted its influence and fulfilled its mission in
changing the title of the executive of a nation from king to President, and
the name of the national Legislature from Parliament to Congress? . . .
The American people fancied that they had set up a popular government
when they separated from England, but they were deluded. In conquering
the political power formerly exercised by the king, the people had but

[11] *Equality*, Chapter II, p. 21.

taken the outworks of the fortress of tyranny. The economic system which was the citadel and commanded every part of the social structure remained in possession of private and irresponsible rulers, and so long as it was held, the possession of the outworks was of no use to the people, and only retained by the sufferance of the garrison of the citadel. The Revolution came when the people saw that they must either take the citadel or evacuate the outworks.[12]

The significance of the title of Bellamy's supplementary volume should now be clear. The problem of democracy always and everywhere is the problem of achieving economic equality. Without that all talk of liberty and fraternity, all equality before the law, is empty and sinister mockery. How can a man call himself citizen who must beg a fellow citizen to become his master? How shall the wage-taker treat his boss as a brother? Of what worth is equality before the law to one without a job? Democracy and servitude cannot lie down together. Wage-slavery debases the dignity of man; it puts upon him the greatest of indignities, servitude to things; it cheats him of his right to life, liberty, and happiness; it is the evil thing which degrades human society to the level of the pigsty, and puts a premium upon the hoggish instincts of men. It sows suspicion and hate between equals, changes the unsuccessful into cringing sycophants, sets its heel upon the weak and the helpless. The thing were too monstrous to be conceivable were it not the everyday fact of life—more than that, were it not the ideal of a supposedly democratic society, apologized for by our plutocratic culture, defended by all that accounts itself respectable, buttressed by the formidable turrets of the law, written down as a major premise in our treatises on political science: and all in the sacred name of individual enterprise. It is familiarity that blinds us to its evils, and makes its victims only callous or sullen. And it endures because men are deceived by its half-truths, seduced by its specious freedoms, led astray by its fatuous promises. Being taught to set the privilege of fighting above the privilege of helping, how should they not account their egoism more sacred than their altruism?

When men shall leave off bounding their democratic horizons by the old political economy and the old law, Bellamy was persuaded, they will see more clearly. The political science of private property conceived of government as a police power to safeguard the stake of

---

[12] *Ibid.*, Chapter II, pp. 19, 20, 21, 22.

the individual in society. Very well, democracy needs only to re-define the terms "stake-in-society" and "police power" to arrive at a competent philosophy. The definition of the former is ready to hand in the familiar words of the Declaration of Independence—the stake of every man in society is no less than his life, his liberty, and his happiness. To secure him in this stake is the primary function of government. The property interpretation of the stake-in-society principle was sound in its assumption of the economic as the determining basis; we need only to democratize the interpretation to arrive at our end.

"The primal principle of democracy is the worth and dignity of the in-dividual. That dignity, consisting in the quality of human nature, is essen-tially the same in all individuals, and therefore equality is the vital prin-ciple of democracy. To this intrinsic and equal dignity of the individual all material conditions must be made subservient, and personal accidents and attributes subordinated. The raising up of the human being without respect of persons is the constant and only rational motive of the demo-cratic policy. Contrast with this conception that precious notion of your contemporaries as to restricting suffrage. Recognizing the material dis-parities in the circumstances of individuals, they proposed to conform the rights and dignities of the individual to his material circumstances instead of conforming the material circumstances to the essential and equal dig-nity of man."

"In short . . . while under our system we conformed men to things, you think it more reasonable to conform things to men?"

"That is, indeed," replied the doctor, "the vital difference between the old and the new orders." [13]

As a preliminary to this necessary end of conforming things to men there must be a reinterpretation of the functions of the state. Here again Bellamy's political economy gives a surprising twist to the current police theory of government.

"In my day . . . it was considered that the proper functions of govern-ment, strictly speaking, were limited to keeping the peace and defending the people against the public enemy, that is to the military and police powers."

"And in heaven's name, who are the public enemies?" exclaimed Dr. Leete. "Are they France, England, Germany, or hunger, cold, and naked-ness?" [14]

The plutocratic interpretation of the police power signifies no other than the protection of the individual in the enjoyment of the

[13] *Ibid.*, Chapter III, p. 26.
[14] *Looking Backward*, Chapter VI, p. 59.

fruits of his exploitation—that his right to keep and use what he has got must be held more sacred than the welfare of society; that the law, the military, the police, shall defend him in his right to do with his winnings as he will. The democratic interpretation of the police power, on the other hand, holds that the state must intervene to the end that property shall serve a social and not a private interest; that the weak shall not be exploited by individual enterprise; that all shall be protected in their right to life, liberty, and happiness. It demands an ethical basis for the social economy. The legal maxim that a man may do as he will with his own, is open to question. The matter of ownership ceases to be a legal question of title, and becomes a moral question of right and justice. Land, the machinery of production, the profits of organized industry, coal, ores, oil, lumber—are such things justly subject to private preemption? Shall the complex structure of society be bottomed on the law of contract, or on the ethics of social justice? Substitute one for the other and a revolution is accomplished.

Our ethics of wealth is . . . extremely simple. It consists merely in the law of self-preservation, asserted in the name of all against the encroachments of any. It rests upon a principle which a child can understand as well as a philosopher, and which no philosopher ever attempted to refute—namely, the supreme right of all to live, and consequently to insist that society shall be so organized as to secure that right.[15]

Thus in the political science of democracy the old police theory of government merges in an all-embracing trustee theory. To a paternal state is entrusted the protection of the interests of society. That the welfare of all shall be faithfully served, it is essential that the common will control and direct the machinery for the production and distribution of wealth. The anarchy of individualism must give place to an ordered regimentation, under a centralized authority. The social meaning of property must be probed to the bottom and the exact line between public and private rights be marked off. This brings Bellamy to his fundamental principle—the collectivistic organization of industry as the *sine qua non* of a democratic society. How effectively such a centralized state must wage war upon poverty, how adequately it must protect the citizen against the common enemies of cold, hunger, and nakedness, it was the purpose of *Looking Backward* and *Equality* to picture. "A hor-

[15] *Equality*, Chapter XI, p. 74.

rible cockney dream," William Morris called *Looking Backward*, and by way of answer sketched his *News from Nowhere*, loveliest of Utopias with its anarchistic freedom set in country fields. Morris was an artist with an ample share of Ruskinian prejudice against the machinery that Bellamy so greatly developed; nevertheless Bellamy was far more modern and realistic in his understanding of the part the machine will play in the society of the future. To socialize the machine—to put upon it the slave-work of society, surely means much to human freedom.

Looking Backward is a brief for no particular school of socialism, although it inclines somewhat to Fabianism. Not through strikes, boycotts and lockouts, was the great change brought about, but in consequence of the spread of social intelligence and social ethics. Unionism was not the father of the Revolution, nor agrarianism its mother. Direct action and violence in any form rather hindered than helped. Class propaganda was too narrow and too selfish. The anarchists with their "red flag and talk about burning, sacking, and blowing people up," retarded the Revolution by frightening the timid and making "a thousand enemies of their professed cause to one friend." "The labor parties, as such, never could have accomplished anything on a large or permanent scale."

It was not till a rearrangement of the industrial and social system on a higher ethical basis, and for the more efficient production of wealth, was recognized as the interest, not of one class, but equally of all classes, of rich and poor, cultured and ignorant, old and young, weak and strong, men and women, that there was any prospect that it would be achieved. Then the national party arose to carry it out by political methods.[16]

To wait for the consent of all would seem to the impatient a long postponement of the millennium; yet the postponement, Bellamy argued, need not be long. The overreaching greed of private capitalism was daily hastening it. The new order must come about speedily as a necessary consequence of two forces; the compulsion of economic fact, and the stimulus of ideas. As the monopolistic tendencies of private capitalism open the eyes of the dullest to the growth of a plutocratic power beyond the control of the majority, a quick fear of the impending tyranny must lead men to question the larger scope and ultimate significance of the whole system. Under the lash of this fear their minds will open to ideas which have

[16] *Looking Backward*, Chapter XXIV.

long been knocking in vain for admission. The sources of monopolistic power will be examined, and the successive steps by which the few have gained control of the machinery of production will become clear. Already the fertile idea of the unearned increment which the land-taxers have got hold of and are spreading widely, has prepared the way for the revolutionary doctrine of the social fund. Let the common man once understand how small a portion of wealth is produced by his private effort, and how large a portion by the agency of social organization with its heritage of experience and invention, and he will understand how unjustly private capitalism appropriates what it has not earned. The conclusion that wealth should belong to him who produces it, is a deduction of the most elementary ethics; and since the production of wealth in quantity is a consequence of the social organization and social heritage, the conviction becomes irresistible that such wealth belongs to society and cannot justly be appropriated by the individual.[17] Let such an idea spread widely and the way is prepared for the taking over by the state of the machinery of production, and the assumption by it of the obligation of universal trusteeship. Then will come the Revolution. Coöperation will take the place of competition; production and distribution for the common well-being will destroy the malevolent trinity of rent, interest, and profit, which have so long held the world in poverty; the intelligent strength of all will stand between the individual and cold, hunger, and nakedness. The noble words of the Declaration of Independence will no longer be a catch-vote and a mockery to the exploited multitude, but a reality. The democratic ideal, with its social philosophy summarized in the phrase, "the only wealth is life," will destroy the last vestiges of ancient tyranny and men will be free. Rooted in economic equality the fine flower of individualism will expand as it cannot now in unfertile soil; a generous and unstinted culture will spread the spirit of kindliness through society, and a new and nobler art and religion will go hand in hand with the new fellowship.

Only too clearly Edward Bellamy was an incorrigible idealist. He looked into the future with more confident eyes than most of us; he saw in the East the quickening of a new day where we see only darkness. A child of the Enlightenment, he put his trust in the natural goodness of men. They are not inherently base and ignoble, but the victims of an evil system that breeds what is base and ig-

[17] See *Equality*, Chapter XIII—"Private Capital Stolen from the Social Fund."

noble. "The folly of men, not their hard-heartedness, was the great cause of the world's poverty. It was not the crime of man, nor of any class of men, that made the race so miserable, but a hideous, ghastly mistake, a colossal world-darkening blunder." [18] In an arid land shall we waste the little store of water, or shall we regulate it strictly, that the desert may be brought to bloom as a garden?

The labor of men, I explained, was the fertilizing stream which alone rendered earth habitable. It was but a scanty stream at best, and its use required to be regulated by a system which expended every drop to the best advantage, if the world were to be supported in abundance. But how far from any system was the actual practice! Every man wasted the precious fluid as he wished, animated only by the equal motives of saving his own crop and spoiling his neighbor's, that his might sell the better. What with greed and what with spite, some fields were flooded while others were parched, and half the water ran wholly to waste. In such a land, though a few by strength or cunning might win the means of luxury, the lot of the great mass must be poverty, and of the weak and ignorant bitter want and perennial famine.

Let but the famine-stricken nation assume the function it had neglected, and regulate for the common good the course of the life-giving stream, and the earth would bloom like one garden, and none of its children lack any good thing. I described the physical felicity, mental enlightenment, and moral elevation which would then attend the lives of all men. With fervency I spoke of that new world, blessed with plenty, purified by justice and sweetened by brotherly kindness, the world of which I had indeed but dreamed, but which might so easily be made real. But when I had expected now surely the faces around me to light up with emotions akin to mine, they grew ever more dark, angry, and scornful. Instead of enthusiasm, the ladies showed only aversion and dread, while the men interrupted me with shouts of reprobation and contempt. "Madman!" "Pestilent fellow!" "Fanatic!" "Enemy of society!" were some of their cries, and the one who had before taken his eyeglass to me exclaimed, "He says we are to have no more poor. Ha! ha!"

"Put the fellow out!" exclaimed the father of my betrothed, and at the signal the men sprang from their chairs and advanced upon me." [19]

Like Henry George's noble study of social poverty, *Looking Backward* is a suggestive document of a generation that saw its finer spirits repelled by the vulgar individualism of the Gilded Age. In the long run, no doubt, its influence was slight and the hopes of the Bellamy Nationalists, like the hopes of the Single-taxers, were

[18] *Looking Backward*, Chapter XXVIII, p. 328.
[19] *Ibid*, pp. 328-9.

doomed to disappointment. Nevertheless it remains as a testimony to the fact that in a blatant world of preëmption, exploitation, and progress, were some who were concerned for a juster social order than the Gilded Age dreamed of—a true commonwealth that free men might build if they would.*

* At this point was to come a second section entitled "After Bellamy; 'Natural-ism'; Tourgée's *Murvale Eastman*."—*Publisher.*

CHAPTER IV

THE DARKENING SKIES OF LETTERS

So late as 1893, in spite of the stark ugliness of Hamlin Garland's pictures of the Middle Border, American realism was still unlike in temper those somber etchings, burnt into dark patterns by the caustic acids of European experience, that came from the hands of Russian and German and French naturalists—sketches that in their bitter gloom seemed tragically untrue to the homelier experience of America. In appraising such difference in temper Howells ascribed it to the gulf that separated American well-being from the poverty and injustice of European societies. American realism was hopeful because American life was hopeful. The novelist in this singularly favored land must reflect the temper of a people made kindly by an abundant prosperity and democratic justice, and in the sincerity of his realism he will necessarily concern himself with the "more smiling aspects of life, which are the more American." Whoever should strike a "note so profoundly tragic in American fiction" as was struck in Dostoevsky's *Crime and Punishment*, he asserted in 1891, "would do a false and mistaken thing." [1] And in a later work he spoke casually of our "gay American horizons"— surely the most romantic phrase ever applied to a sad and joyless people by a professed realist.

But while Howells was thus summing up the achievements of American realism and somewhat overconfidently forecasting its future temper, he was in fact writing the history of a past phase. Already the clouds were gathering upon our "gay" horizons, and the current optimisms were finding less food to feed on. The economics of this happy America were coming to be regarded by vast numbers as a class economics, forecasting a less democratic future. Young men born in the early seventies, when Mr. Howells was entering upon his new realistic studies, were coming to intellectual maturity in a very different age; a new science and a consolidating economics were creating a somber temper that was eventually to produce in *An American Tragedy*, a story not greatly unlike that

[1] *Criticism and Fiction*, p. 128.

Russian tale which Mr. Howells, a short generation before, had pronounced impossible to American experience. Stephen Crane and Frank Norris and Theodore Dreiser were the intellectual children of the nineties, and their art was a reflection of that sober period of American disillusion.

The artist, of course, in his creative work is only mediately influenced by the current science and philosophy; yet even in his aloofness from the specific problems of the laboratory and the study he can scarcely escape the pervasive influence of the *Zeitgeist*. And so, after Hamlin Garland, the realistic novel again took a new course from the shifting winds of scientific doctrine. The generation that succeeded the rebellious son of the Middle Border came too late to maturity to share his faith in the benevolent universe of Herbert Spencer, and got little comfort from a promised Utopia that only awaited the enactment of certain statutory laws—laws that would assure economic justice to all—to lay open its hospitable realm. Far-reaching changes were coming over the temper of scientific thought. The conclusions of the physical sciences were ravaging the orderly preserves of biological evolution, with its cardinal doctrine of organic growth and historical continuity; the hurrying march of scientific investigation was leaving far behind the benevolent universe conceived of by Victorian thinkers and was coming out upon higher and bleaker tablelands of speculation. The universe that unfolded itself to chemistry and physics was vaster and colder than biological evolution with its doctrine of the conservation of energy, had imagined—a vibrating mechanism shot through with energy, that revealed itself in action and reaction, impersonal, amoral, dwarfing all the gods dreamed of hitherto; a universe in which the generations of men have shrunk to a pin-point in limitless space and all teleological hopes and fears become the emptiest of futilities. It was the conception of determinism that after long denial was at last coming to wide acceptance—a conception that underlay the thinking of such diverse men as Comte and Spencer and Marx, a conception implicit in the doctrine of continuity, in the law of causality, in the Marxian law of concentration; and now disencumbered of its teleological wrappings, disillusioned with the doctrine of progress, it was to shape the new intellectual attitude towards life.

In presence of such an extraordinary intellectual revolution the old anthropomorphisms of metaphysics and ethics were doomed, and from the revelations of physics and chemistry and psychology must come an endeavor after a fresh evaluation of man's duty and destiny in a universe of immeasurable energy. An ethics that should square with the new data of science must take its departure from the bleak fact of a depersonalized universe, wherein man is but a single form of imprisoned energy, localized for a brief instant and rising to momentary consciousness in the eternal flux, about and through whom flows the energy of an unprobed universe. As this mechanistic conception found lodgment in minds prepared by a mechanical economics, the last remaining vestiges of the old French romanticism were swept away; a benevolent, egocentric universe was become unthinkable; progress was no longer the inherent law of matter and of life; but instead, everywhere change, disintegration and reintegration, a ceaseless and purposeless flux to what final end the human mind could not forecast. Thus at a stroke the benevolent cosmos of the fathers, wherein for generations men had been providing themselves with sure refuges, was swept away; and with its passing passed the old faiths—faith in freedom of the will, in a purposive providence, in a universe that had been long in travail to bring forth man, its last and dearest offspring for whom all things work together for good. And with the decay of the traditional faiths the younger generation was left to wander as best it might upon the bleak tablelands of impersonal energy. Spencer's "ultimate of ultimates," the Permanence of Force, that follows the law of evolution and dissolution, had given way to Faraday's electro-energy that is indifferent to purpose.

The intellectual backgrounds were thus preparing for a gloomier realism than Howells's or Garland's, a realism that took its departure from two postulates: that men are physical beings who can do no other than obey the laws of a physical universe; and that in the vast indifferentism of nature they are inconsequential pawns in a game that to human reason has no meaning or rules. To assume that fate which rules human destiny is malignant, is to assume a cosmic interest in man which finds no justification in science; Man at best is only an inconsequential atom in a mechanical flux, or at worst, as Jurgen puts it picturesquely, only a bubble in fermenting swill. Such a conception, of course, made slow headway against the traditional order of thought; and if it had not been aided by a changing economics it would have found few to follow a line of reasoning that led to such unpleasant conclusions. The mind of the artist is more susceptible to concrete social fact than to abstract physical principle, and the swift centralizing of economics in the eighties and the nineties provided the stimulus for the extraordinary reversal of thought marked by the contrast between Emerson and Theodore Dreiser. Emerson was the apotheosis of two centuries of decentralization that destroyed the pessimism brought to the new world by refugees from the old, and found its inevitable expression in the exaltation of the individual, free and excellent, the child of a beneficent order; whereas Dreiser was the first spokesman of a later America once more falling within the shadow of the pessimism that springs from every centralized society shut up within the portals of a static economics; that dwarfs the individual and nullifies his will, reducing him from a child of God to a serf.

Oddly enough it was in the West that the new spirit first expressed itself most adequately; amidst a society that was taking its first steps away from the traditional philosophy of the dispersion. Frank Norris in California, Dreiser in Indiana, Sherwood Anderson in Ohio, Masters and Sandburg and Vachel Lindsay in Illinois, were the spokesmen of the resentment welling up in the American heart at the loss of the older freedom and individual dignity.*

* The manuscript ends here. The first section of this chapter was to be "Edwin Markham and 'The Man with the Hoe.'" The second was to be on "The Rise of Naturalism: Stephen Crane; Frank Norris." The first item of the addenda gives material on this subject and on the two authors. The third would have been "Fiction Discovers the City."—*Publisher.*

ADDENDA

THE material given here comes from various sources, as indicated by the notes. The syllabus referred to is that for Professor Parrington's lectures at the University of Washington, *The American Novel Since 1890* (1925). The order here follows that of the contents of this book.

ADDENDA

NATURALISM IN AMERICAN FICTION *

Naturalism originated in France. Term first used by Zola. Chief example—Flaubert's *Mme. Bovary*. Contrast between Zola and Flaubert reveals two diverse tendencies of the movement—a sociological study of background, with a multitude of characters dwarfed by the *milieu;* and psychological study of individual character.

Naturalism a child of nineteenth-century thought—offspring of Darwin, Marx, Comte, Taine. The scientific movement created a scientific attitude of mind and emphasized the law of causation. From this emerged two fruitful ideas: (1) biological determinism, (2) economic determinism. So Zola and Flaubert. Influence of Claude Bernard—"We take men from the hands of the physiologist solely . . . to solve scientifically the question of how men behave in society."

The criteria of naturalism are:

1. Objectivity. Seek the truth in the spirit of the scientist. "We naturalists, we men of science," Zola says, accepting Bernard's position, "we must admit of nothing occult; men are but phenomena and the conditions of phenomena."

2. Frankness. A rejection of Victorian reticence. The total man and woman must be studied —the deeper instincts, the endless impulses. The three strongest instincts are fear, hunger, sex. In the life of the ordinary person, the third is most critical, hence the naturalist makes much of it.

3. An amoral attitude toward material. The naturalist is not a judge, he holds no brief for any ethical standards. He records what happens. He "must possess a knowledge of the mechanisms inherent in man, show the machinery of his intellectual and sensory manifestations, under the influence of heredity and environment, such as physiology shall give them to us, and then finally, to exhibit man living in social conditions, produced by himself, which he modifies daily and in the heart of which he is undergoing constant transformation." (Zola.) This is difficult to accept. Puritanism.

* Notes for a lecture delivered at the University of California in 1922.—*Publisher*

323

4. A philosophy of determinism. This is the vital principle of naturalism, setting it off from realism. The scientist has turned philosopher. It is the residuum of much pondering over life and its meaning, and may result from:

    a. Sociological emphasis—study of heredity and environment.

    b. A broader mechanistic philosophy—Flaubert, Dreiser.

    c. Fatalism: a world of malignant chance—Hardy.

5. A bias toward pessimism in selecting details. A reaction from the romantic conception of a purposive will.

Romance springs from the longings of a baffled and thwarted will, creating a world as we should like it wherein to find refuge. But the naturalist will tolerate no such refuge. He will envisage the truth, and the truth that he sees is that the individual is impotent in the face of things. Hence it is as the victim, the individual defeated by the world, and made a sardonic jest of, that the naturalist chooses to portray man. Always that conception creeps in. It is seen and felt throughout the texture of the story—a fate lurking in the background and visible to the reader—and at some dramatic moment the conviction comes home to the victim and is crystallized in bitter words wrenched from his baffled will. The business of the story is to lead him up to this crystallization.

There are two main forms—(1) Life is a trap. (2) Life is mean. So Strindberg's Countess Julie: "Everything is wreckage, that drifts over the water until it sinks, sinks." So Ray Pearson in Sherwood Anderson's *Winesburg, Ohio:* "Tricked, by Gad, tricked by life and made a fool of." So D. H. Lawrence: "We are prostituted, oh, prostituted by life." To Ma Westcott "Life is duty. It is a lie." This pressure may come from without—*milieu*—or from within—imperious desires—but the outcome is usually hopeless sorrow—sometimes stolid resignation, sometimes fierce protest, but with no other end than annihilation. An exception is Maugham's *Of Human Bondage.*

6. A bias in selection of characters. The naturalist commonly chooses one of three types:

    a. Characters of marked physique and small intellectual activity —persons of strong animal drives. They range all the way from morons like Norris's McTeague, Zola's Nana, and Dreiser's Jennie Gerhardt to natures like Hardy's Tess, and Sallie in *Of Human Bondage.*

    b. Characters of excited, neurotic temperament, at the mercy of moods, driven by forces that they do not stop to analyze. Such are Strindberg's Countess Julie, Sue, Emma Bovary, and the hero in *Of Human Bondage.* Sometimes this is aggravated by some physical defect, like a club-foot.

   c. An occasional use of a strong character whose will is broken. Thus Hardy's Jude and the doctor in Strindberg's *By the Open Sea.* But such are comparatively infrequent.

Naturalism is pessimistic realism, with a philosophy that sets man in a mechanical world and conceives of him as victimized by that world. *Certain unconscious exaggerations of naturalism.* Since men are victimized either by outer forces—the *milieu*—or by inner drives—impulses and instincts—the naturalist from much brooding is subject to certain temptations:

   1. From concern over a devastating *milieu* he may end in desiring to change that *milieu* to the end that men may achieve happiness. Hence he tends to lose his objectivity and scientific detachment, and becomes a partisan to a cause. Such was the fate of Zola. The philosopher of naturalism, in practice he abandoned his principles and became a reformer, attacking the church, the capitalistic order, etc. His *J'accuse* letter is characteristic of this. *Nana,* almost alone, preserves the naturalistic attitude. This was the failure of the first group of American naturalists—Frank Norris, Robert Herrick, Jack London.

   2. From much study of inner drives of low-grade characters the naturalist is in danger of creating grotesques. Behavioristic psychology may prove to be a further temptation, in creating a "sex complex." So Masters's *Spoon River Anthology,* Sherwood Anderson, D. H. Lawrence, Frank Norris. Most common in the later American naturalists. So Brander Matthews.

   3. From much emphasis on animal impulses the naturalist may turn man into an animal. Men are more than sex-driven creatures —the city is more than the slums. There are sewers, but why not accept the sewer without messing over its contents as they flow to disintegration? This is the commonest objection to naturalism. So Meredith: "The naturalist sees the hog in nature, and takes nature for the hog." It is certainly an overcorrection—a reaction against the complacent optimism of romanticism—against too much shutting of the eyes to slums and filth and sewers. To a mechanist like Dreiser, who traces life and conduct back to chemistry, or to the behaviorist, who traces it to ducts and glands, it is

rational. The charge may be true of Zola, of De Maupassant, of Anderson, of Lawrence, but it is not true of Hardy, of Maugham.

Naturalism and the Conception of Tragedy. Naturalistic books are almost inevitably tragedies, but the philosophy of naturalism that underlies them has played havoc with the Aristotelian conception of tragedy. As Ludwig Lewisohn says, it has "rendered the traditional principle of tragedy wholly archaic." According to the Aristotelian tradition, tragedy results when an essentially noble character of heroic proportions transgresses an immutable moral law by a self-originating will and suffers the punishment dealt by poetic justice. So Macbeth, Othello, Lear, Hamlet. But this assumes two thing: (1) an eternally changeless moral law; (2) the existence of a purposive will. Both of these the naturalist refuses to accept. Compare Hardy.

It became clear that the self-originating element in human action is small. The individual acts in harmony with his character, which is largely the result of complex and uncontrollable causes. It became even clearer that among the totality of moral values an absolute validity can be assigned to a few only. Hence the basic conception of tragic guilt was undermined from within and from without. The transgression of an immutable moral law by a self-originating will was seen to be an essentially meaningless conception, since neither eternally changeless moral law nor an uncaused volition is to be found in the universe that we perceive.[1]

The tragedy of naturalism lies in the disintegration and the pity or irony with which we contemplate man and his fate in the world.

Naturalism and the Traditional American Temper. The two most characteristic qualities of the American temper are Puritanism and optimism—the belief in the supremacy of the moral law, and the conviction that this is a good world that man shapes to his will. This is to be explained historically: the former is traditionally English, the latter a product of new-world economics—a decentralized society. Pessimistic determinism results inevitably from the sense of social pressure on the individual. Social complexity entails a feeling of coercive regimentation by forces too strong to contend against. These forces are both internal and external: environment or the social machine; heredity or the physical machine. The most complete dwarfing of the individual will and significance takes place in the most crowded societies, producing a corresponding philosophy and psychology. So the fatalism of the Orient and the dream of

[1] Ludwig Lewisohn, *Modern Drama*, New York, 1915, p. 3.

Nirvana. The first widespread philosophy of determinism among English people was spread by Calvinism. Predestination was an alien thought, the last expression of a world depressed by Roman regimentation and degeneration. Augustine preached that men are evil, and men are doomed. This old-world dogma was brought to America, where regimentation was impossible. A free economics created a free-will philosophy and psychology. The will to succeed. This flowered in Emerson. Philosophical optimism. The world is good, man is good: let him stand upon his instincts and there abide and the whole world will come round to him. "Trust thyself." Since Emerson's time a new world has been emerging. The old shadow is falling across the American mind. Determinism is in the air.

Complexity and American Determinism. Complexity springs from:

1. Machine industrialism. The bigness of the economic machine dwarfs the individual and creates a sense of impotency.

2. The great city reduces the individual to a unit. By machine methods of transportation and quantity output individual differences are worn away. We dress, live, think, work, play, alike. The *Saturday Evening Post* is fast regimenting the American mind. Standardization.

3. Centralization of wealth is creating a caste regimentation.

4. A mechanistic psychology. Behaviorism: stimulus and response; ducts and glands. The individual conceived as a mechanism driven by instincts and habits.

America today is the greatest, most complex machine the world has ever known. Individualism is giving way to regimentation, caste, standardization. Optimism is gone; pessimism is on the horizon. The psychology of naturalism is being prepared.

Three American writers began an experiment in naturalism in the middle nineties—Stephen Crane, Frank Norris, and Harold Frederic. The early death of all three stopped the movement, which was speedily overwhelmed by the romantic deluge and the muckraking zeal. Crane was tubercular and died at twenty-nine; Norris was cut down in the early thirties; Harold Frederic removed to England, where he died.

I

STEPHEN CRANE *

Stephen Crane was the genius of his generation. His work began with *Maggie: A Girl of the Streets* (1893). "It was the first bit of naturalism in American letters . . . an episodic bit of slum fiction ending with the tragic quality of Greek drama." "The first ironical novel ever written by an American." It was privately printed at first, and not published until 1896. It is detached, objective, amoral, dealing with a world without virtues but tyrannized by taboos. It is a bit of life, beginning and ending casually. Here is the end:

> In a room a woman sat at a table, eating like a fat monk in a picture. A soiled, unshaven man pushed open the door and entered.
> "Well," said he, "Mag's dead." [2]

It is a world without virtue and yet one that uses the social taboo to condemn Mag—the only pure one of the lot. The story was an attack on everything that was respectable in American literature—a notable achievement in a world of shoddy romanticism. It was an affront to every instinct of the genteel tradition, and was rejected by a public steeped in that same shoddy romanticism.

Crane's next novel was the first great American war story— *The Red Badge of Courage* (1894). It was a *tour de force*, inspired by Zola's *Le débâcle*, but more by Tolstoi—*War and Peace* and perhaps *Sebastopol*. The individual is caught between the external war machine and the inner instinct machine. There is a conflict of impulses—fear, pride, the instinct of self-preservation, chiefly the fear of fear. The hero is at the mercy of the crowd psychology and blind chance. Crane follows Tolstoi in assuming that victories are accidents, the outcome of a blind clash of unintelligent forces, rather than due to strategy and generalship. The study is psychological—that of the fear of the recruit, his feeling that he alone is marked as the target of the enemy. The impression of helplessness is the same as in *Maggie*—both are atoms among a host of other atoms.

Short Stories. The best are "The Blue Hotel," "The Experiment in Misery," "The Open Boat." The first is a story of social responsibility and social guilt. The murder of the Swede is just part

* From lecture notes and the syllabus.—*Publisher.*
[2] Stephen Crane, *Works*, New York, 1926, Vol. 10, p. 216.

of the backwash of a topsy-turvy life: the victim of things. "Every sin is the result of a collaboration." The second is a story of a "hobo"—down-and-outer, who hears "the war of the city in his ear." "The protest of the wretch who feels the touch of the imperturbable granite wheels, and who then cries with an impersonal eloquence, with a strength not from him, giving voice to the wail of a whole section, a class, a people." [3]

2

FRANK NORRIS [*]

The most stimulating and militant of our early naturalists—the only one who wrote consciously with a definite creed. He had thought out a naturalistic philosophy under the inspiration of Zola. "He was never without a yellow paper-covered novel of Zola in his hand," wrote his brother of him. His two chief novels reveal the twin tendencies as revealed in *Nana* and *Le débâcle:* The study of the individual in his reaction to environment, and the study of social forces and their impact upon a group of related individuals.

His Work. Falls into three groups: (1) Romance—*Blix, Moran of the Lady Letty*; (2) Naturalism—*McTeague, Vandover and the Brute;* (3) *The Pit* and *A Deal in Wheat.* Between the two latter groups stands *The Octopus.* The dates of the earlier works uncertain. Commonly believed that Norris began as a romantic and worked out of it slowly. Another view that he wrote romances as a means of arriving, side by side with his serious work. Thus he seems to have begun *McTeague* about 1894—although it was not published till 1899.

Theory. His passion for truth more ardent—or more noisy—than Crane's: his objectivity less. The strong conviction of a deterministic universe was on him, but he never quite attained the scientific detachment. His nature large and eager. Like Zola he loved large canvases. This induced him rather to the sociological than to the individualistic study. *The Octopus* more representative of his genius than *McTeague.* Man in society, his theme: not mere men and women as ends in themselves. This grew on him—the second phase. The novelist must deal "with elemental forces, motives that stir whole nations. These cannot be handled as abstractions in fiction. . . . The social tendencies must be ex-

[3] *Ibid.*, Vol. II, p. 21.   [*] Lecture notes.—*Publisher.*

pressed by means of an analysis of the characters of the men and
women who compose that society, and the two must be combined
and manipulated to evolve the purpose—to find the value of x."[4]
Above all, avoid propaganda.

Unskillfully treated, the story may dwindle down and degenerate into
mere special pleading, and the novelist becomes a polemicist, a pamphleteer, forgetting that although his first consideration is to prove his case,
his *means* must be living human beings, not statistics, and that his tools
are not figures, but pictures of life as he sees it. . . .
Consider the reverse—*Fécondité*, for instance. The purpose for which
Zola wrote the book ran away with him. He really did care more for the
depopulation of France than he did for his work. Result—sermons on the
fruitfulness of women, special pleading, a farrago of dry, dull incidents,
overburdened and collapsing under the weight of a theme that should have
intruded only indirectly.[5]

He never quite arrives at the amoral attitude. Ethical values
persist in intruding themselves, sometimes quite incidentally, as in
McTeague, but increasingly, as in *The Octopus* and *The Pit*.

"McTEAGUE"

Dedicated to Gates. The first considerable contribution to
naturalism by an American writer. His carefully written work over
which he labored five years.

Theme. A study in character disintegration that follows upon
economic pressure. The unmaking of a man and woman by the
caprice of events. The characters are simple. McTeague is heavy
and stupid, slow in his movements but a blind bull when aroused.
Trina neat and pretty but with unhappy potentialities in her
thrift. In neither is there a will-to-power strong enough to give
strength of character.

The Note of Determinism. A world of chance that victimizes
them. The note struck by the lottery and the $5,000. By chance
McTeague became a dentist, met Trina, proposed. But the chance
that was making a man of him and a woman of Trina was preparing
their downfall through Marcus Schouler. The wrestling-match was
the turning-point. The two disintegrate together, each aggravating
the weakness of the other. As Trina's neatness was pulling Mac
up and making him self-respecting, so her thrift grew into miserli-

[4] *The Responsibilities of the Novelist*, "The Novel with a 'Purpose,'" Garden
City, N. Y., 1928, Vol. 7, p. 22.
[5] *Ibid.*, p. 22.

ness under pressure of his failure to provide, and this embittered the essentially fair and generous nature of Mac.

Inner Drives. Little sex in the book after the first complication. Both Mac and Trina caught unexpectedly, yet handled differently. The latter pure naturalism. "The Woman is awakened, and, starting from her sleep, catches blindly at what first the newly awakened eyes light upon. It is a spell, a witchery, ruled by chance alone, inexplicable—a fairy queen enamored of a clown with ass's ears." [6] But in McTeague, oddly enough, the same instinct is judged and pronounced evil. Norris abandons the amoral attitude and argues that heritage from the lower life is evil. It is the weeds that spring up and stifle, as in Sherwood Anderson's "Seeds."

Below the fine fabric of all that was good in him ran the foul stream of hereditary evil, like a sewer. The vices and sins of his father and his father's father, to the third and fourth and five hundredth generation, tainted him. The evil of an entire race flowed in his veins. Why should it be? He did not desire it. Was he to blame? [7]

The entire handling of sex in Trina, from the first frightened yielding to the later docile submission to Mac's brutality, his sadism, is admirably handled from the point of view of modern psychology. Norris was not a psychologist but in this he succeeded surprisingly.

Romantic Elements. Yet even in this severe study Norris has yielded to his romantic tendencies.

1. His patent effort to give dramatic unity to the whole through the symbol of gold. An exaggeration that is almost Dickens-like, with its warping singleness. The gold tooth, the $5,000, Trina's twenty-dollar gold pieces, the imaginary gold plate of Maria Macapa, the absurd canary in the gilt cage, the discovery of the gold mine. The wonder is that he didn't give Trina gold hair instead of black.

2. The use of a minor action: Maria Macapa and old Zerkow. The same pursuit of a phantom and the same outcome in murder. McTeague and Trina are real; Maria and Zerkow are grotesques.

3. The use of foils: Old Grannis and Miss Baker. Justified in romantic literature by contrast. The self-effacing, timid drawing together contrasted with the brute directness of McTeague. They do not marry, and preserve their dream world.

[6] Frank Norris, *Complete Works*, New York, n. d., Vol. III, p. 58.
[7] *Ibid.*, p. 22.

4. The use of the revenge motive: Marcus Schouler—the dramatic pursuit into Death Valley and the end.

"VANDOVER AND THE BRUTE"

An unfinished work—but a huge and terrible torso.

Theme. Revealed in the title. The two natures of man and the sloughing-off of the higher till the wolf is left. Done with a terrible directness, till the naked man is on all fours, padding up and down in his room. A grim and sordid theme but not quite achieved. The thing got away from him. If he had chiseled it as he chiseled *McTeague*, holding it off objective and amoral, it would have been a tremendous piece. But it is insufficiently motivated.

Determinism. A study in will. Vandover set over against Charlie Geary and Dolly Haight. The latter a victim of momentary weakness; the former a victim of constitutional pliability. A sensuous egotism that grows and consumes. Geary alone survives—the egoist who drives forward ruthlessly. A study of the slow, long descent—a chain of circumstances that finally binds him hand and foot. His props knocked away one by one—partly by fate, partly by himself: his father, the girl whom he loves, his concern for respectable opinion, his art, his money. The conclusion intensely dramatic—more so than the romance of *McTeague*.

The comment of Garland on *McTeague* applies equally to *Vandover:* "What avail is this study of sad lives? for it does not even lead to a notion of social betterment." His interest is "not that of the ethical teacher."

"THE OCTOPUS"

McTeague and *Vandover* are of the city and its sordid evil ways. They are studies in psychology. *The Octopus* is of the great California valleys and the evils that have come into the farm life with the railroad. It is a study in economics—the first of a long series of such studies. One can easily see how the theme caught the imagination of Norris, how his mind felt the relief from the narrow world and sordid wretchedness of *Vandover*. A certain magnificence in Norris responded to the epic breadth of the valleys—they fired his imagination—the vast sweep and power of nature: the rich soil, the brilliant sun that lays its palpitating heat upon the land, the quick response in flowers and fruit. The land is eager to produce; its fruitfulness is overpowering. There is an epic sweep of life and reproduction here; and this epic of the soil is linked with the tragedy wrought by the Southern Pacific—the economic machinery of man's making. The facts were well known and they took hold of Norris's imagination. His sympathy is aroused and yet instead of attacking the railroad he weaves it into his deterministic philosophy.

Theme. Ostensibly the wheat. Norris planned a huge trilogy of its growing (*The Octopus*), marketing (*The Pit*), consumption (*The Wolf*—never written). In reality, the impotence of unimportant individuals in the struggle with things as they are. In *The Octopus* the individual is dwarfed by the vast spaces, he is crumpled and despoiled by the railroad. The flock of sheep destroyed by the train is only a symbol of the men and women of the valley, under the wheels of modern industrialism.

Action. A huge canvas with crowding figures and abundant action. "The canvas swarms with actualities—plowing, planting, harvesting, sheep-herding, merry-making, rabbit-killing, love, labor, birth, death"—all keyed high and swept into a palpitating background. A "strongly interwrought group of episodes," that fall into certain series of developments too:

1. The atrophy of Magnus Derrick, which might well be a story in itself.

2. The development of Annixter, "out of an absolute, yet not gross, materiality," through the love of Hilma Tree; and then their final annihilation.

3. A host of background characters—supernumeraries—that give a sense of epic sweep.

The Note of Romance. The riot of color, of life, arouse the latent romance of his nature. He cannot remain detached but projects himself into the story in the person of Vanamee. He returns to the use of the symbol as in *McTeague*—the wheat. He allows his villain to perish melodramatically. How much more convincing is the figure of Charlie Geary setting Vandover to work than S. Behrman in the hold of the vessel.

In the end he abandons the amoral attitude. After proclaiming the doctrine of determinism—that the railroads are the masters—not the puppets of men—he takes refuge in a moral order. In the large balance, the wheat remains, rectifying wrong—saving other lives to make good what it here destroys. "The larger view always and through all shams, all wickednesses, discovers the Truth that

will, in the end, prevail, and all things, surely, inevitably, resist-
lessly, work together for good." [8] Nevertheless in contemplating
the injustice done by the railroads, Norris neither demands nor
expects relief.

The Octopus exemplifies Norris' theory of broad-scale work. It
"draws conclusions from a whole congeries of forces, social development, race impulses." It "devotes itself not to the study of men
but of man."

SIDNEY LANIER *

An original nature. Rejects both the genteel tradition and the
ideals of the rising middle class. An artist to whom life means
beauty.

He revivifies nature—is almost pagan in his adoration of the
beauty of the sun and water. A half-personification of the sun-
myth. He is essentially religious. To Longfellow and Tennyson
nature is pretty embroidery; to Emerson it is a dwelling-place of
the oversoul; to Lanier it is an object of adoration. See "The
Marshes of Glynn."

He attacks industrialism—the first of the poets to cry out against
it as a deadly blight on life and civilization. See "Corn," "The
Symphony," "The Jacquerie."

He seeks a new religion, recognizing a quantitative element.

[8] Frank Norris, *The Octopus*, New York, 1906, p. 652.
* Lecture notes.—*Publisher.*

THE INCOMPARABLE MR. CABELL *

The successive volumes of James Branch Cabell have provided the tribe of critical Jeffries with a rich vein of diversion. They have recognized no closed season in their full-lunged pursuit of the strange heirs of Mr. Cabell's invention, and such Homeric absurdities of comment have been flung at him, that he is in a fair way to become our classic example of the fatuousness of contemporary estimates. As whimsical as Bernard Shaw, as provocative as Chesterton, he is more incomprehensible than either to all readers who do not choose to like what they have not always liked. Professing to be a romancer, and defending the glory of romance with inimitable witchery of phrase, he writes no romance that lovers of convention can understand. The lovely fabrics of his tales of Poictesme are all shimmer and sheen, woven of magic and veiling mysteries, instead of the correct taffeta and grosgrain; and the brilliant stuff of his tales of gallantry is fashioned of wit and poetry, instead of the customary wigs and sword play. Those to whom romance suggests *When Knighthood Was in Flower*, will find only obscurities and coarseness in *Figures of Earth* (1921) and *Jurgen* (1919, *enl.* ed. 1921); and those who delight in the stage rufflings of *Monsieur Beaucaire*, will discover only a libertine in *The Cords of Vanity* (1909, rev. ed. 1920). And if the reader boggles at such tales what can he hope to make of that strange, ironical whimsy, *The Cream of the Jest* (1917, rev. ed. 1922)? One needs to walk warily in dealing with Mr. Cabell, or the jest of which he is such a master will turn sardonically upon the critic. In all his thinking vague hinterlands lie behind the commonplace, cryptic meanings lurk behind the obvious; and the credulous, easy-going reader finds himself puzzled, and at last floundering quite hopelessly in a land of bogs and marsh-lights. And yet was ever another writer born to us Americans so insistent upon being understood? He has elaborated his views of life and art at length, and repeated them in successive volumes over nearly a score of years; and finally in what may have been a mood of sheer disgust at the stupidity of those who buy books, he reëlaborated his philosophy and wrote it out in good

* Reprinted by permission from *The Pacific Review*, December, 1921.—*Publisher*

set terms within the covers of a single volume. *Beyond Life* is an essay altogether remarkable for its haunting beauty of phrase, its honest agnosticism, its brooding irony. It is enough to turn one cynic to consider that so noble a book should have called forth from a reputable gentleman, presumably of good taste and sound judgment, the comment that it "contains cheap and shallow pessimistic observations on human limitations."

That *Beyond Life* (1919), with other of Mr. Cabell's books, contains "observations on the limitations of human nature," is quite obvious; for Mr. Cabell deals in comedy, and what is to become of comedy if it shall not observe those limitations and laugh at them? That it is even pessimistic may likewise be argued with some plausibility; but to assert that it is cheap and shallow is preposterous. An inquisitive mind, deeply concerned with ultimate values, cannot be cheap and shallow. And yet the fault of such widespread misinterpretation may lie in part at Mr. Cabell's own doorstep. An inveterate jester, his sallies often carry implications far beyond the obvious; his strange whimsies spring from depths of thought and emotion beyond the understanding of the careless. His attitude towards life is an odd mixture of the modern and the medieval: there is a medieval simplicity and frankness, a naïve wonder at the mystery that underlies the common, an incorrigible idealism; and this medieval attitude is drenched in modern agnosticism. He passes easily from a broad Chaucerian humor that laughs frankly at the relations of men and women, to a mystical idealization of those relations; and the problem of reconciling the humor and the ideal becomes a serious business with him. He hates the cant and dishonesty of our *bourgeois* existence, and he refuses to take seriously the host of petty concerns that most of us are very serious about. If he were less the artist he would join the disaffected and turn to rend this foolish world; but the spirit of comedy saves him and he contents himself with a jest. But the Cabellian jest uncovers depths of meditation that reveal the philosopher and the poet. In his own large meaning of the word Mr. Cabell is an economist. He is greatly dissatisfied with the "futile body-wasting," which under the "dynamic illusion known as common sense" passes for life, and is concerned to discover what abiding increment a man may get from his body during its brief existence as an entity. His mind is haunted with a sense of realities that lie beneath the surface appearances, and that insist on trickling from his pen in strange comments. It is a careless reader who is deceived or put off the scent by his whimsical vocabulary, who insists on conventional meanings for words which Mr. Cabell chooses to use otherwise than conventional persons use them. Romance and realism—words with which he plays constantly and upon which he hangs his philosophy—do not signify the spurious romance of childish minds, or the shoddy realism of practical minds. If one must insist upon translating his vocabulary into ordinary terms, let us understand that to Mr. Cabell romance and realism mean idealism and conventionalism; and to the profound distinction between these two attitudes towards life, he dedicates his work.

I have called Mr. Cabell a poet, and the justification lies in his persistent idealization of life in terms of beauty. At his birth he was endowed by an unkind fate with imagination. Now imagination may be a very pretty and amiable gift, highly useful for gilding one's egoism, putting honey in thistles, proving itself practical by arraying life in gay robes in order that it may seem an altogether lovely and desirable mistress; or it may prove a decidedly parlous faculty to play with. It can summon bogies, and terrors that are vaster and more real than bogies. A brooding imagination can work havoc with one's complacency. When Carlyle was in a mood to enjoy his nerves he would let his imagination range beyond the comfortable confines of convention, to consider the universe and the position of man therein—the black flow of time and the terrifying immensity of background against which man is set; and he would come back to dinner with Jane Welsh Carlyle with a sick stomach and an ill temper. It was not very gallant, but it was very natural to a man unnerved by what he had contemplated. Considered with open eyes reality is too overpowering for weak man, and because he could not relieve the tension with a jest, Carlyle's imagination inflicted chronic dyspepsia upon him. To conventional persons the dyspepsia and Jane Welsh Carlyle's sharp replies to her husband's ill humor, seem the important reality, and the overpowering visions of time and space that were at the root of the family discord, seem no other than romance. In this curious world of convention all things are topsy-turvy, and it needs a tremendous effort of will to set them only a little right.

To this effort Mr. Cabell's life work has been dedicated with unruffled urbanity. Like Carlyle he chooses to roam far in his philosophic quests, and like Thoreau he comes home at nightfall

with little more than a handful of stardust in his wallet. He loves
to sally forth on the greatest of adventures—the pursuit of reality
where it lies broadcast, hidden from practical eyes that refuse to
see. He is impelled by the old wonder that has haunted men from
the beginning of their long upward climb; the wonder and the fear
of life. Now to anyone but a fool or a poet, only too plainly life is
petty and gross and inconsequential, from the moment when with
superfluous blood and pain we are brought into the world, to the
time when we return by an unlovely process to chemical elements.
It is compounded of vanity, as the old poet long ago observed.
The practical, about which we make so much pother and over which
we chatter so foolishly, is only an illusion which men hug because
it keeps them in self-conceit. Mr. Cabell refuses to accept any such
illusions at their face value. He will not be humbugged by foolish
persons who pretend to talk wisely. What is man? he insists on
asking: A parasite on the thin rind of a planet that swings silently
through interstellar space—"an ape who chatters to himself of
kinship with the archangels while filthily he digs for groundnuts."
If this is the reality to which the philosopher must come finally—
and like Hamlet Mr. Cabell does not shirk the contemplation of
graveyard facts—then must the thoughtful man accept logically
a frank pessimism, and on this foundation build such a hut as may
best shelter him for the few days of his unintelligible life. Over this
sorry conclusion Mr. Cabell broods much, and because he is a
human being with a will to enjoy life and think well of himself, he
uses every faculty to scramble out of the pit and find a pleasanter
refuge for the brief time of his existence. The idealist in him
engages the pessimist, and like so many other moderns he goes out
in quest of that which may keep him sane. It is true that man is an
ape reft of his tail and grown rusty at climbing, but is that the
whole story? It is evident that men in all times have refused to
believe that they are not something other than apes—their very
dreams seem to belie a conclusion so mean and ignoble. Is there not
some deeper *élan vital,* some hidden impulse that drives man forward and upward even while his mind is on groundnuts? "Yet
more clearly do I perceive," argues the idealist, "that this same
man is a maimed god. . . . He is under penalty condemned to
compute eternity with false weights and to estimate infinity with a
yardstick; and he very often does it. . . . There lies the choice
which every man must make—or rationally to accept his own

limitations? or stupendously to play the fool and swear that he is at will omnipotent."

This would seem to be a hard choice, but Mr. Cabell does not hesitate. He patches up his agnosticism with the will to believe, on the pragmatic grounds that it seems to work. For man "rationally to accept his own limitations," is to defeat everything worth while in life; it is to yield the battle to a black pessimism. Whereas "stupendously to play the fool and swear that he is at will omnipotent," may end in creating the will to omnipotence, and the fool in some preposterous fashion may prove that he is indeed divine. Let man but accept his logical limitations and he returns to the ape reft of more than his tail, fallen to gibbering in the mud, refusing to take hold of that rope of sand by which miraculously he has drawn himself forward hitherto. For accepting his limitations means contenting himself with material fact, and "the trouble with facts seems to be, that if one treats them out of relation to the rest of life, they become lies." In the "stupefying mist of common sense" men walk blindly. The practical, the conventional, are alien to the deeper reality which is shadowed forth by emotions and dreams; which refuses to disclose itself nakedly, but hides behind symbols, haunting the mind even while one is pottering among inconsequentials. This deeper reality itself may be but a dream, but nevertheless it possesses the power of creating a will to believe, upon which hangs man's destiny. Hence the tales which we tell ourselves are significant because through some occult process they foreshadow the thing that may be; they prod the foolish will to omnipotence to believe that we shall outgrow the ape. For grown rusty at climbing, the ape-man "however dimly, feels himself to be a symbol, and the frail representative of Omnipotence in a place that is not home; and so strives blunderingly, from mystery to mystery, with pathetic makeshifts, not understanding anything, greedy in all desires, and honeycombed with poltroonery, and yet ready to give all, and to die fighting, for the sake of that undemonstrable idea."

It is because he is terrified at the meanness of what practical men call reality, that Mr. Cabell turns away from it to find the true life in dreams. Not only are they pleasanter, they are more useful; they are all that man has to aid him in the appalling task of getting himself out of the slime, that he may walk in green fields. We need to turn Prospero's words around—our dreams are such

stuff as we are made on. They alone are real and salutary, foι
amid all their ramblings they seem dimly to suggest some end;
amidst their rank egoisms they seem to foreshadow a purpose: and
may not that end and purpose be the eventual creation of a life for
man that shall be worthy of his dreams? It is illogical to assume
that man can pull himself up by his own bootstraps, but how else
shall he pull himself up? Is not man the inveterate romancer somehow blindly creating a noble romance of man? "To what does the
whole business tend?" he asks at the conclusion of *Beyond Life*,
"—why, how in heaven's name should I know? We can but be
content to note that all goes forward, toward something. . . . It
may be that we are nocturnal creatures perturbed by rumors of a
dawn which comes inevitably, as prologue to a day wherein we and
our children have no part whatever. It may be that when our
arboreal propositus descended from his palm tree and began to walk
upright about the earth, his progeny were forthwith committed
to a journey in which today is only a way-station. Yet I prefer
to take it that we are components of an unfinished world, and
that we are but as seething atoms which ferment toward its making, if merely because man as he now exists can hardly be the
finished product of any Creator whom one could very heartily
revere. We are being made into something quite unpredictable, I
imagine: and through the purging and the smelting, we are sustained by an instinctive knowledge that we are being made into
something better. For this we know, quite incommunicably, and
yet as surely as we know that we will have it thus. And it is this
will that stirs in us to have the creatures of earth and the affairs of
earth, not as they are, but 'as they ought to be,' which we call
romance. But when we note how visibly it sways all life we perceive that we are talking about God."

From this persistent will to romance—the incorrigible propensity
to follow the dynamic illusion of dreams that is so deep an instinct
of human nature—Mr. Cabell deduces a conception of art that to
careless readers seems whimsically perverse; and from it likewise
emerges the lambent irony that plays like diffused lightning about
the horizons of his thought. The function of art in society, he
insists, is to comfort and inspire man with its divine beauty.
Without the artist this is but a grim and forbidding place where
men live; and unless every man is somewhat the artist, and seeks
his compensations in the lure of romance, it must remain grim and

forbidding. It is therefore the privilege and the duty of the artist "to prevaricate tenderly about the universe"; to create for life a meaning that is not apparent, by clothing it in beauty and adducing for it a noble significance. It is his mission to lure men away from the contemplation of facts which terrify or debase, from all ignoble and depressing realism, to pursue the ideal and entice the imagination to enter and dwell in a world as it ought to be. The artist, therefore, is a Moses in the wilderness, pointing men to the Promised Land, and even enabling them to go forward and taste its fruits while they still dwell in the wilderness.

Now of all the dreams which lure men, the one universal and potent dream, Mr. Cabell asserts with Freudian understanding, is the woman dream. Its roots are deep in the ape-animal; it drives men inexorably, for upon it depends the very existence of the race. And therefore, a shrewd mother-nature has somehow transmuted its base materials into the very stuff of romance, commingling with it all high and generous impulses, making of it the loveliest dream that visits man's weak head. In consequence of which ironic transmutation this lovely dream "hoodwinks humanity through the dynamic illusion known as love, in order that humanity may endure, and the groans of a lover be perpetuated in the wails of an infant." Considered in one light this is the very "cream of the jest" that nature perpetrates upon man; but considered in another light, does it not turn out to be the supreme jest which man has perpetrated upon nature? For once he has been taught the alphabet of romance, through the crude necessity of race preservation, he has gone far in his studies, and turned romancer on a great scale. From this raw material of biological sex-love he has woven the fabrics of his religion, of his art, of his idealism; he has dipped it in gleaming dyes, twisted it to quaint patterns, fashioned from it lovely robes to cover what is ugly. It is the wellspring and source of all romance.

Through this open door of woman-worship Mr. Cabell chooses to enter his world of deeper realities. "There is in every human being that which demands communion with something more fine and potent than itself," and this something more fine and potent he seeks in the woman of his dreams. It was so when the world was young, and it will be so as long as there is youth left in the world. In early times this object of adoration was the witch-woman, the Circes and Calypsos of ancient tales; later it became the lady-mistress of chivalric ideals; today it is the dream maiden whom the young man woos but never finds in marriage, and not finding her is impelled to turn to the ever-young and ever-lovely Helens and Ettarres of old romance. A good half of Mr. Cabell's work is given over to this curious celebration of woman-worship. It is elaborated in *Domnei* (1920), in *Jurgen*, in *Figures of Earth*. In the strange tales of the land of Poictesme the drama flows from the balking and thwarting of this woman quest by the Dame Niafers and Dame Lisas of the commonplace world, to man's undoing. Nevertheless "the long, high, fruitless questing does not ever end, but, rather, is temporarily remitted for the society of Dame Niafer and of Dame Lisa. For . . . one perceives that, even in remote Poictesme, those aging nympholepts, Dom Manuel and Jurgen—they also—were heartened to endure the privileges of happily married persons by a sure faith, discreetly left unvoiced, that these hard-won, fond, wearisome, and implacable wives were, after all, just temporary makeshifts. By and by would Freydis and Helen return, at their own season."—For the dream persists in the very face of present fact, and in this lies man's hope. "In youth all men that live have been converts if but in transitory allegiance, to that religion of the world's youth—to the creed of *domnei*, or woman-worship." Now it is "the very essence of *domnei*, that the woman one loves is providentially set between the lover's apprehension and God, as the mobile and vital image and corporeal reminder of Heaven, as a quick symbol of beauty and holiness, of purity and perfection. In her the lover views all qualities which can be comprehended by merely human faculties." "If but in honor, his heart stays bound to his first and only real love, that woman of whom he never tires. Her coming is not yet. He can but wait, sustained by his sure faith . . . that some day her glory will be apparent, and he will enter gladly into her secret kingdom, and will find her kisses all that in youth he foreknew to be not impossible. . . . And meanwhile this prescience, somehow, informs all art . . . and makes it to him a vital thing. . . . And there seems to be no beauty in the world save those stray hints of her, whose ultimate revealment is not yet. . . . And it is very often through desire to express his faith in this withheld perfection, of which he has been conscious in broken glimpses from afar, that he turns artist. . . . For every art is a confession of faith in that which is not yet."

But however adroitly man has turned the jest against nature, and erected a noble palace from base materials, the jest remains, mixed with the mortar, and the structure cannot endure for long. It is insubstantial, and at any moment the cloud-capped towers may disintegrate and the dream palace disappear, leaving not a rack behind. There remains only the jest. This unhappy ending Mr. Cabell foresees, and hence emerges the profound irony that under-lies all his writing. To such disillusionment must all things come. Life is no more than a comedy, played by puppets; bitter, with more tears than laughter in it; yet because tears are futile and un-nerving, what remains for the gallant gentleman but to confront life with a jest? Mr. Cabell does not wholly forego his chivalric ideal even while he is contemplating the vanity of all endings in the light of their beginnings. As Horvendile the clerk, he clings to it, even though he is doomed to walk the streets of Lichfield, Virginia, in the form of Felix Kennaston, who passes—to his own incredu-lous amusement—as a personage of some importance, with two automobiles and money in four banks. He possesses the magic sigil of Scoteia, by the potency of which he can send forth his soul to meet Ettarre, and recover the raptures that Felix Kennaston no longer knows. But the sigil of Scoteia turns out to be the half-top of a pomade glass from his wife's dressing-table; the potency is gone; and he remains at last no more than a respectable citizen with his automobiles and money in four banks. *The Cream of the Jest* reduces the chivalric ideal to pure irony.

By a transition more natural, perhaps, to a Virginian than to another American, Mr. Cabell turns from the contemplation of chivalry to the study of gallantry; and shifts the theme of his ro-mances from the ecstatic adoration of the Woman, whom to possess is to lose, to the gay pursuit and enjoyment of women. In "The Rivet in Grandfather's Neck" he chooses to set a decidedly shabby and roué gallantry over against a somewhat futile and antiquated southern chivalry. He loves both the gallant and the gentleman, and he spares neither; they are equally the descendants of that Cavalier ideal which flourished so rankly in the soil of the old planter society; nevertheless the quaint and lovable Rudolph Musgrave with his gentle heroics comes off distinctly better than his brilliant half-brother, the novelist John Charteris. One might, indeed, wonder at Mr. Cabell's treatment of the artist Charteris, were it not so distinctly Shavian. It is odd how similar is his con-ception of the artist to the definition of Shaw—one who wriggles into the confidence of women to learn their secrets only to betray them. Nevertheless Jack Charteris, the brilliant thinker and talker of *Beyond Life*, mouthpiece of the Cabellian philosophy, deserves better treatment than he gets in the story of this sorry escapade; he comes quite too near the likeness of the mountebank Sheridan. In *The Cords of Vanity* gallantry reveals itself more attractively; it is gilded with youth and wit and poetry. It is Congreve at his best, scintillating, brilliant, with a delightful affectation of pose and gesture; and it is Marlowe also, with its galloping wit steeped in pure poetry. There is the true Elizabethan rapture of fine words and lovely images and quaint conceits. "Meantime," says young Robert Townsend, "being in love, I refined upon the notions of love with the ingenuity of an Elizabethan." There you have the spirit of the book. It is more than a pretty piece of paganism; it is the brightest tale of gallantry in our literature, masterly in the restrained irony of its inimitable conclusion.

It is obvious, however, that the mood which finally will receive dramatization from Mr. Cabell cannot be summed up in the ideal of gallantry. What that mood is one finds revealed at length by John Charteris in *Beyond Life*. It is the quintessence of irony distilled from long observation of human life, but it is not Congreve, much less is it Sheridan. Those shameless and selfish roués began as artists but they ended as mountebanks; life taught them cynicism and not tenderness; it sharpened their wit and dulled their sympathy. The higher irony lay quite beyond their natures. But with Mr. Cabell tenderness, sympathy, an ardent concern for the inevitable failure that lies in wait upon aspiration, are so strong and urgent that under the governance of a mind less intellectual, they must inevitably run into sentimentality. But there is in Mr. Cabell something of the intellectual austerity of Matthew Arnold, and it conducts him to the same ends. Consider such a passage as this: "Through a merciful dispensation, we are one and all of us created very vain and very dull. . . . Vanity it is that pricks us indefatigably to play the ape to every dream romance induces; yet vanity is but the stirrup-cup: and urgent need arises that human dullness retain us (as it does) securely blinded, lest we observe the wayside horrors of our journey and go mad. One moment of clear vision as to man's plight in the universe would be quite sufficient to set the most philosophic gibbering. Meanwhile with bandaged eyes we advance: and human sanity is guided by the brave and pitiable and tireless dullness of mankind. . . . Yet how varied are the amiable activities of human dullness, which tend alike to protect and to enliven human progress! Dullness it is, of course, that brews and quaffs Dutch courage; . . . that fosters salutary optimism as to the destiny of mankind, in flat defiance of everything mankind can do, and does unblushingly. . . . And finally dullness it is that lifts up heart and voice alike, to view a parasite infesting the epidermis of a midge among the planets, and cries, *Behold, this is the child of God, All-mighty and All-worshipful, made in the likeness of his Father!* . . . These and how many other wholesome miracles are daily brought about by our dullness, by our brave and pitiable and tireless dullness, by our really majestic dullness, in firm alliance with the demiurgic spirit of romance. . . . For that to which romance conducts, in all the affairs of life . . . is plain enough— distinction and clarity, and beauty and symmetry, and tenderness and truth and urbanity."

Here then is the note that still awaits adequate dramatization in a comedy greater than he has yet written—a cosmic irony suffused with tenderness and truth and urbanity. Above all, urbanity. Mr. Cabell has played too long with the ideal of gallantry; he has devoted too much precious time to creating Millamants to fall in love with; he has listened too credulously to the voice of Congreve. "I have read," says Charteris, out of Congreve, "that the secret of gallantry is to accept the pleasures of life leisurely, and its inconveniences with a shrug; as well as that, among other requisites, the gallant person will always consider the world with a smile of toleration, and his own doings with a smile of honest amusement, and Heaven with a smile which is not distrustful—being thoroughly persuaded that God is kindlier than the genteel would regard as rational." Surely the cosmic irony that loves men's dullness because it alone can preserve them from madness, and retorts upon the cosmic terrors with a jest, is higher than gallantry and more enduring. It arrives at tolerance for all human shortcomings; it embraces high and low in its sympathies; it achieves urbanity as a final goal. It is the stuff of which great literature is made. And Mr. Cabell is creating great literature. A self-reliant intellectual, rich in the spoils of all literatures, one of the great masters of English prose, the supreme comic spirit thus far granted us, he stands apart from the throng of lesser American novelists, as Mark Twain stood apart, individual and incomparable.

THE PROBLEM NOVEL AND THE DIVERSION FROM NATURALISM *

No sooner was naturalism fairly under way than it was well-nigh submerged under a wave of social speculation and inquiry. The years 1903–1917 were a distinctive period—a time of extraordinary ferment, when America was seeking to readjust her ideals and institutions to a revolutionary economic order that had come upon her. The popular phase was revealed in the muckraking movement, a movement which instructed the American middle class in certain elements of economics—particularly the close connection between economics and politics. But underneath, an intellectual revolution was in progress, setting steadily towards a new social philosophy. The old America had been intensely conservative, naïvely provincial and self-satisfied, compassed by a complacence founded on optimism—the gospel of the business man. The new America was eager and hopeful, impatient to square institutions to the new conditions. The total movement was profoundly democratic—a new Jacksonianism rising in protest against a menacing plutocracy.

1. *The Movement of Criticism.* The work of a vigorous social idealism. Passed through three broad phases:

a. Political. The movement of Progressivism, 1903–1912. An attempt to democratize the machinery of government to the end that the will of the majority shall prevail. Its impulse and much of its program came from Populism; and it resulted in a clarification of the issue between republicanism and democracy. An attack on the representative system and the checks and balances of the Fathers. It gave rise to a critical examination of the spirit and purpose of the Constitution.[1]

b. Economic. A growing conviction that talk of political democracy is futile except in so far as it leads to economic democracy. That power is economic in origin and that those who control the economics will control the government. The gospel of economic determinism. Certain conclusions emerged:

* Lecture notes.—*Publisher.*
[1] See J. Allen Smith, *The Spirit of American Government;* W. A. White, *The Old Order Changeth.*

1. That capitalism is no longer competitive but monopolistic.

2. That *laissez-faire*ism no longer suffices.

3. That centralization has submerged the individual citizen; that he is impotent before the leviathan corporation; and that henceforth the struggle is to be between organized groups for the control of the state.[2]

c. Literary. An examination and rejection of traditional literary and cultural ideas. An attack upon:

1. Puritan reticence and smug respectability.

2. Middle-class optimism and sentimentality.

Led by H. L. Mencken, Ludwig Lewisohn, and the younger intellectuals. The bias aristocratic.

2. *The Incoming of Old-World Thought.* The breaking-down of the older provincialism and the reception of new ideas.

a. The philosophy of collectivism. Derived chiefly from Germany and England; largely Marxian and Fabian. The conviction that the state must absorb the trust. Later the appearance of syndicalism and guild socialism, based on a distrust of the bureaucratic, omnicompetent state. Anarchism has remained alien in spirit.[3]

b. The new aristocracy. A reversion from an easy-going Jacksonianism based on the doctrine of equalitarianism. A direct denial of that doctrine and the theory of leadership. In business the doctrine of the expert and the rule of efficiency. In philosophy the doctrine of the intellectual aristocrat—a suggestion of Nietzsche and the will to power. Thus Mencken joins hands with Judge Gary in upholding the ethics of the strong. The total result an effective denial of our traditional ideal of democracy.

c. The problem novel. All this ferment entered into literature, tyrannizing in its insistence. Old forms became old-fashioned overnight. The novel was so useful that it was drafted by the new crusading enthusiasm. Romance and naturalism alike were swept away; the political novel and the economic novel took their place to arouse public opinion to action. It was the glorification of propaganda. Except for James Branch Cabell and Edith Wharton not a writer escaped. There is something pathetic in the way the

---

[2] Representative books are: C. A. Beard, *An Economic Interpretation of the Constitution* (1913) and *The Economic Basis of Politics* (1922); Walter Lippman, *Public Opinion* (1922).

[3] See Bertrand Russell, *Proposed Roads to Freedom* (1919); Richard Roberts, *The Unfinished Programme of Democracy* (1920).

harmless bleating romantics were dragged at the chariot wheels of social problems. Booth Tarkington, Mary Johnston, Winston Churchill, William Allen White, were sacrificed equally with potential naturalists like Robert Herrick, Upton Sinclair, and Ernest Poole. Their careers may be seen from Churchill, Poole, and Herrick.

1. Winston Churchill. [The most representative of the spirit of Progressivism.] A conscientious middle-class romantic. Churchill was a faithful reflector of middle-class movements. His work falls into three phases:

[a. *Romantic historical tales.* *Richard Carvel* (1899) the type of Cavalier romance. A blend of Thackeray's *Henry Esmond* and *The Virginians*, John Paul Jones added for extra historical flavor. A double background: (1) the old South of the Revolution with a Loyalist villain and a patriot hero; (2) the London of Brooks Club and a gaming aristocracy, with Charles Fox. The heroine another edition of Beatrix Esmond the hero another Henry Esmond. *The Crisis* (1910) a romance of the borderland of the Civil War: a fire-eating Southern heroine and a sober Yankee-Puritan hero. *The Crossing* (1904) a romance of the settlement of the Inland Empire. A theme not yet adequately dealt with in American fiction. The story breaks in two: the first half Churchill's best work in romance; the last half his worst.*]

b. *Political novels.* Coincided with the rise of the Progressive movement. *Coniston* (1906) a study of the legislative boss in New Hampshire. A reflection of his experience in the state legislature. How the "interests," and in particular the railroads, manage to put their bills through. Jethro Bass sells political control to the highest bidder.

Mr. Crewe's Career (1908): the same theme a generation later. Consolidation of the railroads has brought about absentee dictatorship of state politics. The boss has removed to New York and manages the legislature through his local lawyer. The philosophy of big-business prosperity rests on property rights, held in trusteeship by the corporations that fill the empty dinner pails, make and unmake business confidence. The revolt of the younger generation —Austen Vane and Victoria Flint, in whom stirs a new social conscience.

* From the syllabus.—*Publisher.*

c. *Economic novels.* Began with *The Inside of the Cup* (1913), a venture in higher criticism and social interpretation. So compare *Robert Elsmere* (1888). An attack on old dogmas and an attempt to discover the democratic springs of Christianity. The clash between the reborn Son of God and an unregenerate society, and the need to establish the Kingdom of God in this world. The church today controlled by business subscriptions. The solution to be sought in a free pulpit, supported by the common people, preaching a new social Christianity.

A Far Country (1915), a study in the emptiness of the profit motive. A background of banking—J. P. Morgan and Company. The dissatisfaction of the prodigal son who has wasted his intellectual and moral patrimony—the lawyer who sells his brain to rise and loses the things that make life worth while. His conversion brings the call to self-education.

The Dwelling Place of Light (1917), a study of the blighting effect of industrialism on the native Yankee stock that has failed to rise into the exploiting class. The restlessness of modern life due to the failure of normal instincts to find satisfaction in daily existence—an emptiness due to loss of beauty, freedom, creative craftsmanship. The search for compensation brings death and not life. A background of the Lawrence strike and syndicalism.

2. Robert Herrick. The most promising of the potential naturalists. An intellectual fascinated by the crude materialism of Chicago in the late nineties. Suffered from the inhibitions of a Puritan idealism; the problems of this raw world cried aloud for solution—the woman question, the labor question, the problem of the professions—and warped him away from naturalism, making him an easy victim of the new social enthusiasm. The key to his thought—economic determinism.

The Memoirs of an American Citizen (1905). His best work and the nearest approach to naturalism. A detailed study of the American business man—the captain of industry who rises in a competitive society by his own will. The competitive order, he perceives, requires an ethics different from the Christian ideal. The survival of the fittest means the survival of the strongest, the most cunning and unscrupulous. The realist who deals with facts discovers that he lives in a world of pigs—little pigs of the village, larger hogs of the city. To get in the trough a man must have fingers and toes and use them. The world belongs to the strong.

That which gives dignity is bigness: the larger the hog, the more imposing. Little business is dirty and petty, but big business may become poetic. To grind a mess of sausages is messy, but to provide sausages for every breakfast table in America is grandiose. To realize his ambition Van Harrington plays fast and loose with conventional ethics, but unlike Frank Cowperwood he seeks a new ethics. As a superman his work will be justified by its creativeness, by its service to humanity.

A Life for a Life (1910). In certain other of his work Herrick betrays naturalistic tendencies, notably in *The Web of Life* (1900), where he considers the problem of social complexity and how it binds the life of men and women and determines their fate. But in *A Life for a Life* he surrenders wholly to the problem. His theme is how the predatory egoism of the profit-struggle may be cured, and he presents alternative solutions: syndicalism and Christianity. The cure lies in individual self-conquest—breaking through the web of "things as they are" and choosing life instead of power.

Herrick was on the threshold of naturalism. He felt the complexity of life and the determining force of that complexity; but he failed to achieve the attitude of objectivity.

3. Ernest Poole. *The Harbor* (1915). The culmination of the novel of naturalistic propaganda and the most widely read. A dramatic record of a changing industrial order, traced through three stages: (1) The old world of small competitive business that is dead; (2) The present world of corporation control; (3) The world of syndicalistic control that struggles to be born.

Against this changing world stands the young idealist troubled in his loyalties, who sets up different gods to worship: (1) The idol of art—aloofness from the mass struggle; (2) The idol of efficiency by the supermen who rule in trusteeship; (3) The idol of mass solidarity and workers' control—the conclusion that is on the dawn of realization: "The world for all the workers." *Conclusion*. The ferment of social thought, shot through with Marxianism, familiarized the American novelists with one doctrine important for the naturalist—the doctrine of economic determinism. In none of them did it pass over into a larger conception of philosophical determinism, and this sets the limitation to their naturalism. The common zeal for reform or revolution, moreover, kept them from objectivity. In none is there the calm detachment and the amoral presentation of material without which naturalism sinks into propaganda. Their position presupposes a large confidence in individual initiative—a confidence in the power of men to alter the world they live in. It is admirable, but it is not the way of the naturalists, who do not seek to change what they regard as an essentially unresponsive world that changes only after its own way.

THE PROBLEM NOVEL

JACK LONDON: THE NOVELIST OF THE PROLETARIAT*

Experienced the harsh contacts of a seasonal worker and tramp. Became a Marxian socialist and revolutionist, preaching the war of the classes in *The Iron Heel* (1908), *The Revolution* (1910), and other works. A man of strong vital energy with a philosophy shaped by Darwin, Spencer, and Nietzsche. Emphasizes a passionate will-to-power, a superman of swift and violent action.

The Call of the Wild (1903); a study in atavism, brilliant, poetic, set against a wild Alaska background. The resurgence of the primitive wolf-instincts in a domesticated dog.

The Sea Wolf (1904); the frankest statement in American literature of the unbridled will-to-power, egoistic, amoral. A malignant ferocity in a philosophical, herculean sea captain, whose body is destroyed by paresis, but whose malignancy is unconquered.

Martin Eden (1909); autobiographical. So compare *John Barleycorn* (1913). The former deals with his struggle to educate himself, to write, and to gain recognition. A background of his experience at the University of California. A profound contempt for *bourgeois* standards of life and thought. The note of revolution and the lapsing of the will-to-live.

London carries to the extreme the "elemental" of Norris, translating it into the primitive and abysmal. A potential naturalist in his amoral attitude and his underlying pessimism, but carried away by zeal of revolution. Lacks restraint and finish.

* From the syllabus.—*Publisher.*

UPTON SINCLAIR *

The most insistent and outspoken of the muckrakers. Began as a novelist, but his art submerged by propaganda—a profound suspicion of capitalism and all its ways.

The Jungle (1906); a story of the packing houses and the immigrant: the technique of "speeding up" and the labor scrap-heap. The social consequences of the profit principle—saving everything but the squeal of the hog and the health of the laborer.

King Coal (1917); a story of the Rockefeller coal fields in Colorado and the miners' union. Probably his most skillful story.

Numerous other titles, among them: *The Brass Check*, an examination of the American newspaper—the charge that these are the tools of plutocracy; *The Goose Step*, an examination of the American university—the charge that these serve wealth; *The Goslings*, an attack upon the public school as an agent of capitalism.

* From the syllabus.—*Publisher.*

THEODORE DREISER: CHIEF OF AMERICAN NATURALISTS *

Against this background of eager ferment and various propaganda stands Theodore Dreiser, who is of this changing world and yet apart from it: the most detached and keenly observant of all our writers, a huge figure of ungainly proportions—a heavy-footed peasant with unslaked curiosity and a boundless pity, who is determined to examine critically "this animal called man" and portray him truthfully. He tramps across fields straight to his objective, messing sadly the neat little beds of American convention, peering into the secret places that are marked "Not Open To The Public," keeping nothing hidden, ashamed of nothing, apologizing for nothing. Not since Walt Whitman has there been another such frank and detached projection of reality, such insistence that the world shall stop and consider those facts which convention has politely agreed to ignore. Naturally a great hue and cry of the Pharisees has been raised against him. The respectable middle class will have none of this peasant directness and brutal truth. He has entered our *bourgeois* society "murmurous of morality" with an alien philosophy, which he must defend. At every moment he feels under the necessity of assisting the truth as he sees it, and instead of suffering his portrayal to stand on its own feet he props it up with argument and interminable debate. The artist suffers at the hands of the disputant.

The Man and his Philosophy. Marked by an immense and open-eyed curiosity that ends in agnosticism. His anthropocentric conceptions:

I have lived now to my fortieth year and have seen a good deal of life. . . . But I am one of those curious persons who cannot make up their minds about anything. I read and read. . . . But I find that one history contradicts another, one philosopher drives out another. Essayists, in the main, point out flaws and paradoxes in the current conception of things, novelists, dramatists and biographers spread tales of endless disasters, or silly illusions concerning life, duty, opportunity and the like. And I sit here and read and read, when I have time, wondering.[1]

* Lecture notes.—*Publisher.*   [1] *Hey Rub-a-Dub-Dub*, New York, 1920, p. I.

"Nothing is proved, all is permitted," he says in *The Titan*. Men will do what they think they can get away with. In briefest terms his philosophy may be phrased thus:

1. The world is without reason or meaning to us. Why we are here and to what end is unknowable.

2. Men are chemical compounds, existing in a world where they play about like water-flies, skipping restlessly and unintelligently as their legs drive them, whom the universe in its vast indifference suffers for a time.

3. Men divide into the strong and the weak; not the good and the bad. The will to power, the desire for pleasure, drive men on their courses. What restrains? Moral codes and social conventions, often useful, often harmful.

A metaphysical idealism will always tell him that it is better to preserve a cleanly balance, and the storms of circumstance will teach him a noble stoicism. Beyond this there is nothing which can reasonably be imposed upon the conscience of man.[2]

4. Hence the profound need of sympathy and mercy.

Let no one underestimate the need of pity. We live in a stony universe whose hard, brilliant forces rage fiercely. From the prowling hunger of the Hyrcan tiger to the concentric grip of Arcturus and Canopus there is the same ruthless, sightless disregard of the individual and the minor thing. Life moves in an ordered hierarchy of forces of which the lesser is as nothing to the greater . . . And in the midst of the rip of desperate things—in odd crannies and chance flaws between forces—there spring and blossom these small flowers of sentiment. Tenderness! Mercy! Affection! Sorrow! The Hindus worship an image of pain. And well they may. It is a classic amid the painless, the indifferent—Nirvana. Blessed are the merciful, for they shall receive mercy! No, no. Blessed are the merciful, for they create mercy. Of such is the kingdom of the ideal.[3]

His Attitude toward his Material. Dreiser possesses a vast and terrifying imagination. Like James Branch Cabell he broods over the plight of man in the universe. But he does not seek refuge in the ideal. He will confront things as they are. The very chemistry of decaying flesh fascinates him. It is a phenomenon of this impersonal and relentless universe. Compared with the realities of time and space and force—what is man and what are his puny efforts and ideals?

The damnable scheme of things which we call existence brings about conditions whereby whole masses suffer who have no cause to suffer, and

[2] *The Financier*, New York, c. 1912, p. 250.   [3] *Ibid.*, p. 409.

. . . whole masses joy who have no cause for joy. . . . We suffer for our temperaments, which we did not make, and for our weaknesses and lacks, which are no part of our willing or doing.[4]

His Objectivity. The larger view of life gives detachment. Only one who has emerged from the jungle can see the whole in broad perspective. In no other American writer, except Whitman, is such complete detachment achieved. His life is a long process of stripping away group illusions, of casting off group conventions. And for this the mass cannot forgive him, for the mass live in the strait-jacket of custom, thinking in no other terms than group or tribal terms, worshiping the communal idols, clinging to the tribal taboos. They cannot achieve individuality themselves and they hate Dreiser. It puts him outside the tribe, for the first law of the tribe is tribal-mindedness. Whoever is not of us is against us. Whoever questions the validity of the tribal sanctions is an enemy and must be destroyed. It is in vain that Dreiser asserts vehemently that he is telling the truth. Another version of the truth than the tribal version is not wanted.

The significance of Dreiser lies in the fact that he is an individual apart—one who has broken with the group and sits in judgment on the group sanctions. He is an anarchist who will be partisan to no taboos. This is a rare and perilous thing to do. He stands outside.

His Amoral Attitude. It is on this score that Dreiser stands condemned by our *bourgeois* censors. His amoral attitude is strangely metamorphosed into immorality. His indifference to the common preachments, his inability to accept Christian maxims, his refusal to do lip service to creeds—this is set down as evidence of viciousness, for *ipso facto* there can be no other moral standards than the tribal standards. What is Dreiser's justification? This, that in the physical universe he can discover no morality—no justice, mercy, pity, but everywhere great and indifferent force. And in society—in the instincts of men and in their hidden desires and secret acts—a disregard of conventional morality. Society is steeped in hypocrisy.

He saw no morals anywhere—nothing but moods, emotions, needs, greeds. People talked and talked, but they acted according to their necessities and desires.[5]

But in frankly revealing the hypocrisy of men Dreiser is no cynic. There is in him a profound morality—the morality of truth and pity

---

[4] *Ibid.*, p. 479.   [5] *The Financier*, p. 432.

and mercy. Let us not stone men for their sins but deal generously and kindly with them. What he protests against is superimposed codes. There is, for him, "in Nature, no such thing as the right to do, or the right not to do." [6]

But is there not social expediency? To which the individual for his own good should conform? Experience has taught men some excellent things.

His Work. Dreiser has given us full-length portraits of two women—Sister Carrie and Jennie Gerhardt—and of two men— Eugene Witla and Frank Cowperwood. These constitute his major contribution and on them his reputation rests.* In addition there is *Hey Rub-a-Dub-Dub*, a book of essays in which his philosophy is set forth, a naturalistic play, *The Hand of the Potter*—a study in pathology where the hand of the potter slipped—a book of travel, and some short stories. Of his four major characters the two women are passive and pliable, easily made victims of circumstance. Of the two men one—Eugene Witla—is weak, and the other—Frank Cowperwood—is the supreme example in American literature of the will to power.

The Financier and *The Titan.* A colossal study of the American business man, in two volumes of a total of 1332 pages. Compared with this all other studies are crude and unconvincing. Here the thing has been done once for all.

"These crude and greedy captains of finance had to be given some kind of literary embodiment, and Dreiser has hammered a raw epic out of their lives." [7]

Where did Dreiser get his intimate and detailed information concerning high finance? Where his knowledge of such a character? Out of his own powerful mind. Cowperwood a portrait of Charles Yerkes. Two periods: his Philadelphia life to 1873; his Chicago life to 1898. In both he molds circumstance to his advantage; in both he is caught by chance and fails.

The Man. Driven by three impulses: love of power, love of women, love of art. There is in him a unity of character and an inevitability of development that are overwhelming. Dreiser does not judge, apologize, praise, or condemn; he is content to permit the

---

[6] *Hey Rub-a-Dub-Dub*, p. 87.

* When this was written of course *The American Tragedy, A Book about Myself,* Dreiser's poems, *Moods Cadenced and Declaimed,* and his further books of travel had not been published.—*Publisher.*

[7] Randolph Bourne, *History of a Literary Radical,* p. 203.

character to develop. From first to last he is detached and objective. He presents Cowperwood as a magnificent physical and mental machine: a born fighter and leader, strong, alert, with a cool resourceful mind. A pronounced hardness that goes with strength —contempt for the weakling, impatience with the inefficient. In his sex passages there is no glamour of romance. They are direct and brutal—but more moral than glamorous. Nevertheless great personal charm—the magnetism of a virile mind and indomitable will. To men he is an inspiration, to women a fascination. And yet a frank egoist, self-centered, imperturbable.

The fate of the individualist: in pitting his will against life Cowperwood feared chance, which undid him in Philadelphia. But his very prevision, which carried him to triumph, brought his downfall. The many are stronger than the superman. And in the end, failure. Strength endures for so short a time and is so weak. Age, weakness, social forces—these undermine the strong. A vast irony. Cowperwood is punished not because he is evil but because he is a man.

Cowperwood's Philosophy. From his youth up life was a puzzle to him. Nothing was certain, for beyond and above all was a blind, irrational chance. Nevertheless within reasonable limits it was plain enough that strength and intelligence prevail. This lesson he first learned from the squib and the lobster, and it became his guiding principle. When chance had brought him within the shadow of the penitentiary, he summed it up:

It is a grim, bitter world we are all born into. . . . Who was to straighten out the matter of the unjust equipment with which most people began? Who was to give them strong minds in place of feeble ones, able bodies instead of wretched ones? Where were they to get pure-tendencies instead of impure ones, as the world looked on these things? . . . Some were sent into the world with a great lust and great ability for wealth like himself, a mind swift to see, a body strong to endure; and some were sent half equipped, almost shapeless and formless. . . . Strength and weakness—there lay the key, the answer.[8]

Stuart Sherman on Dreiser:

By eliminating distinctively human motives and making animal instincts the supreme factors in human life, Mr. Dreiser reduces the problem of the novelist to the lowest possible terms. . . . His philosophy quite excludes him from the field in which the great realist must work. He has deliberately rejected the novelist's supreme task—understanding and

[8] *The Financier,* p. 660.

presenting the development of character; he has chosen only to illustrate the unrestricted flow of temperament. He has evaded the enterprise of representing human conduct; he has confined himself to representation of animal behavior.[9]

And the two novels he says are "like a club sandwich composed of slices of business, alternating with erotic episodes." It is true, but the failure is one of art that does not merge them. What would Sherman have? Shall these impulses be eliminated from literature, or from human nature itself?

[9] Stuart P. Sherman, *On Contemporary Literature*, New York, 1923, p. 94. In the syllabus Professor Parrington says: "The most intelligent estimates of Dreiser are in Randolph Bourne, *History of a Literary Radical;* H. L. Mencken, *Prefaces;* and Carl Van Doren, *Contemporary American Novelists.* All other commentators are stupid."

SINCLAIR LEWIS: OUR OWN DIOGENES *

As the row of his pudgy orange-backed volumes lengthens on
the shelf, it becomes evident that Sinclair Lewis is the bad boy of
American letters whose thoughts are on bent-pins while the deacon
is laboring in prayer. His irrepressible satire belongs to a new and
irritatingly effective school. He has studied the technique of the
realists, and under the beguiling pretense of telling the truth
objectively and dispassionately, he insists on revealing to us un-
accommodated man as a poor, bare, forked animal, who like
Jurgen persists in thinking himself a monstrous clever fellow. He
is maliciously severe on all respectable dignities. In his hands the
noble *homo sapiens* of common repute is translated into an ignoble
homo libidinus et ventosissimus—an unattractive animal that runs
in herds, serves its belly, and has a taking way with the dams.
The free-born American citizen, master of the earth and its destiny,
is little flattered by the portrait he draws, and Mr. Lewis finds
himself, in consequence, *persona non grata* in any convention of
Elks or Rotarians.

The method he has chosen to adopt is a clever advance over the
technique of the eighteenth century, when pricking balloons was
the business of every wit. Those older satirists—nagging souls like
Pope and bold bad fellows like Churchill—were mainly concerned
to annoy their victims with pin-pricks. They were too completely
the gentleman to grow chummy with base fellows whom they
frankly despised; and in consequence they never discovered half
the possibilities of the gentle art of satire. Sinclair Lewis is wiser
than they were. He has learned that before one can effectively impale one's victim, one must know all his weaknesses and take him
off his guard. So he ingratiatingly makes up to George F. Babbitt
of Zenith, drinks chummily with him, swaps greasy jokes, learns
all the hidden vanities and secret obscenities that slip out in the
confidences of the cups, beguiles him into painting his own portrait in the manly midnight hours; and when the last garment that
covers his nakedness is stripped off, the flashlight explodes and the

* Published as Number Five of *University of Washington Chapbooks*, 1927.—
Publisher.

360

camera has caught the victim in every feature of his mean and vacuous reality.

No doubt it is an ungentlemanly thing to do—a calculating betrayal of trusting human nature done in the sacred name of art; and it is certain that the unhappy victim will hate the artist when he sees the developed print next morning. Yet the picture is extraordinarily lifelike. All the unlovely details of fat stomach and flabby muscles are sharply revealed. It is too late to put on one's clothes, and *homo sapiens* in the person of George F. Babbitt is revealed as a shambling, two-legged animal, for the world to laugh at. The method is immensely clever; it is the last word in the technique of despoiling one's victim of adventitious dignity, without which life becomes a mean, bleak affair; but it is scarcely charitable. To think well of oneself and to wish to impose that good opinion upon others, are common human weaknesses that every tailor blesses. Without clothes man is only a caricature of the godlike, and the artist who betrays our nakedness to our enemies is very far from a gentleman. The confidences of the cups must be held sacred, for if we cannot drink without fear of our babbling being reported, what becomes of goodfellowship?

But the charge of betraying goodfellowship leaves Sinclair Lewis unconcerned. His satire knows no compunctions. An irreverent soul, he dares the wrath not only of George F. Babbitt, but of the innumerable clubs to which Babbitt belongs. A buoyant scoffer, he does not permit even the organized wrath of the Chamber of Commerce to disturb his equanimity. He provokes respectable people on principle, and he has laid a devilish plan to work systematically through our sacred American decalogue, smashing one commandment after another. Already behind him is strewn a sorry wreckage of established creeds and authoritative slogans—a wreckage that delights the wicked and gives aid and comfort to all evilwishers in our comfortable and excellent society. Not even a banker is sacred to him. Rotarians and Kiwanians, Billy Sundays and Billy Bryans, voluble Congressmen and silent Presidents, even our venerable Constitution itself, he scoffs at and makes merry over. And to add insult to injury, he prospers in his sins. His calculating wickedness returns him a fattening bank account. His impudent satires sell like bargain-counter silk stockings. We pay handsomely to see ourselves most unhandsomely depicted. If we would only take a lesson from the strategy of the heathen Chinese, we might boycott Mr. Lewis's wares and reduce him to the beggary that is more becoming to wickedness than a wanton prosperity. But a Christian people will not go to school to the heathen, and so Mr. Lewis prospers in his wickedness and waxes vulgarly rich.

Now what is the tremendous discovery that Sinclair Lewis makes so much of, and that we pay so great a price to learn? It is no other than this: that the goodly United States of America are peopled by a mighty herd, which like those earlier herds that rumbled about the plains, drives foolishly in whatever direction their noses point— a herd endowed with tremendous blind power, with big bull leaders, but with minds rarely above their bellies and their dams. In the mass and at their own romantic rating they are distinctly imposing —big-necked, red-blooded, lusty, with glossy coats got from rich feeding-grounds, and with a herd power that sweeps majestically onward in a cloud of dust of its own raising, veritable lords and masters of a continent. But considered more critically and resolved into individual members, they appear to the realist somewhat stupid, feeble in brain and will, stuffed with conceit of their own excellence, esteeming themselves the great end for which creation has been in travail, the finest handiwork of the Most High who spread the plains for their feeding-grounds: with a vast respect for totems and fetishes; purveyors and victims of the mysterious thing called Bunk, who valiantly horn to death any audacious heretic who may suggest that rumbling about the plains, filling their bellies, bellowing sacred slogans, and cornering the lushest grass, are scarcely adequate objectives for such immense power: a vast middleman herd, that dominates the continent, but cannot reduce it to order or decency.

Consider, suggests Mr. Lewis, what this rumbling herd signifies in the light of rational and humane ideals. What sort of custodians of civilization are these lumbering mobsters with their back-slappings and bellowings? What becomes of the good life in a society that flowers in Rotarian conventions? The banker has reduced America to the level of a banker's Utopia, and now bids us admire his handiwork. Other societies, aristocratic and feudal, honored the priest and knight and artist above the usurer and tradesman; other generations professed to serve truth and beauty and godliness in their daily lives; but the great American herd cares nothing for such things. In the name of democracy priest and knight and artist are turned lackeys to merchants and realtors, to men who would not recognize faith or chivalry or imagination if they met them on the golf course, and who understand democracy as little as they understand Christianity. In this land of material abundance the good life is reduced to being measured in commissions and percentages; civilization comes to flower in the broker; the mahogany desk is the altar at which we sacrifice in a land of triumphant materialism. "God help the country," said Fenimore Cooper, years ago when the herd was small, "that has only commercial towns for its capitals." "Such a country is past helping," retorts Sinclair Lewis. "God cannot help it, or the Devil. In the name of George F. Babbitt and Dr. Almus Pickerbaugh and the Reverend Elmer Gantry, what can be expected of such a country? A people that worships the great god Bunk shall have its reward!"

To prove his amiable thesis Mr. Lewis has been at enormous pains to gather his materials at their sources. He has taken upon himself to become a specialist in depicting the *genus Americanus*. He has loafed along Main Street, played poker in back rooms with wicked young men, drunk in respectable clubs, and exchanged hearty back-slappings with the sons of Rotary. He has devoted days to the smoking-compartments of Pullmans, garnering the ripest wisdom and choicest stories of traveling salesmen. He has listened to philosophic brokers discourse on ethics, studied political and constitutional theory with realtors, learned all about Bolshevism from presidents of Chambers of Commerce, been instructed in the elements of economics by Republican Congressmen, discovered the fallacies in Darwinian evolution from clerical fundamentalists and the superiority of Fascism over democracy from the greatest captains of industry. No field of American experience has escaped his minute investigation, no authority has eluded his catechizing. In the course of his studies he has come to master the lusty American language in its subtlest shades and manliest *nuances*, from the comic supplement to Dunn and Bradstreet, and he talks easily with Main Street in its own vernacular. His rich and copious vocabulary fills a commonplace scholar with envy, and his ebullient slang, his easy slovenliness of enunciation, inflict on the simple-minded user of the King's English a hopeless inferiority complex.

Thus amply equipped with all the resources of scholarship, he has written four learned treatises in exemplification of the thesis that the *genus Americanus* is cousin-german to the scoffing Mr. Mencken's lately discovered *boobus Americanus*. The introductory study, *Main Street*, provided a comprehensive background and setting for the full-length portraits he was to draw later. Gopher Prairie, situated in the heart of agricultural America—in Meredith Nicholson's Valley of Democracy where the old-fashioned, kindly, neighborly, wholesome, democratic virtues are presumed to thrive in a congenial habitat—becomes in his unsympathetic analysis a place that William Allen White would not recognize as his home town. Here, he tells us, is respectability made sluggish and sterile. Here is "slavery self-sought and self-defended." Here is "dullness made God." Here, diluted and spread over a vast territory, the spirit of Babbitt has erupted in cheap and pretentious county-seats, parasites on the producing hinterland over whose politics and credit and morals Main Street tradesmen have set up a strict custodian-ship—futile and complacent and drab, mere echoes of the greater cities that lie on the horizon and to which the sons of Main Street turn for light and guidance.

It is these greater cities that constitute the true capitals of our red-blooded Americans who proclaim themselves "the greatest race in the world"—fruitful centers from which radiates the phi-losophy of pep, punch, and progress for the upbuilding and en-lightenment of the world. Of these centers the hustling and mighty Zenith is the wonder and admiration of all right-minded citizens; it is the brightest and bloomiest sunflower of the great American garden. And in Zenith dwells George F. Babbitt, realtor, Sinclair Lewis's full-length portrait of a hero sprung from the loins of America, the completest embodiment of the triumphant American genius that is conquering the earth. Babbitt as an upstanding he-member of the great herd is a marvel, the apotheosis of the reg-nant middle class, the finished product of our snappy civilization. Other lands, no doubt, have produced men accounted great. Plato and Saul of Tarsus, St. Francis and Leonardo, Pascal and Galileo and Hegel, were no doubt esteemed in their own times and by their own cities; but Zenith does not go in for out-of-date merchandise; it is up-to-the-minute and it specialized in George F. Babbitts. And so when the Reverend Elmer Gantry rises to influence in Gopher Prairie, he is called to Zenith as its spiritual counselor, and becomes the custodian of the Zenith moralities, the apostle of Zenith Bunk, the devotee of the Zenith Mumbo Jumbo. And through Zenith passes also Martin Arrowsmith the rebel, the perverse outlandish scientist who refuses to worship Mumbo

Jumbo, on his solitary way to discover reality in a world of Zenith chicanery. Babbitt, Gantry, Arrowsmith—these are the figures that Sinclair Lewis comes upon in his exploration of the land of the free and the home of the brave. A somewhat curious showing at the best.

So slashing an attack upon our common creed and practice has naturally aroused vigorous protest. Human nature does not like to have its idols assailed; even the devotees of Mumbo Jumbo will defend their god against the heretics; and Sinclair Lewis has become the target for many a shaft. The critics have pressed home their counter attack with ardor. They insist that he is suffering from an aggravated case of astigmatism, and that in consequence he does not see eye to eye with those of normal vision. The world is out of focus to him—askew in all its structural lines; and this distorted vision prompts those jaundiced opinions and malicious judgments in regard to the ideals cherished by our best citizens. He has deliberately cultivated a spleen that makes him dislike his neighbors because they are comfortable and contented. Diogenes railing at mankind gained a vast reputation, but it is a nice question if Diogenes was a useful citizen. What did he do to further the well-being of his community? How much time and money did he give to charity and the upbuilding of his city? For all his talking Mr. Lewis does not seem to know what the good life is. He rails at Babbitt for not being Plato, but does he understand the A B C of service? To take a homely figure: the family cow, standing knee-deep in June and chewing the cud of contentment, would excite his Diogenic scorn. As a fault-finder and knocker, Brindle is not the equal of Diogenes; but to criticize her mentality and manners, forgetful of the fact that from the contented chewing of a plentiful cud will come a plentiful supply of milk and cream and butter to sweeten the bread of life, is a somewhat sorry business. In her modest, democratic sphere she is devoted to service, and if there is a nobler function, Rotary humbly confesses it had not discovered it. One must not, of course, press too far the analogy between Brindle and Babbitt; the figure is useful only to suggest that even in the lowliest spheres Mr. Lewis completely fails to understand the fine ethical values that underlie and animate the common American life at which he rails. How, then, shall he understand them in the higher? Comfort and service are excellent things in themselves, and if they can be merged in everyday experience, surely the good life is in the way of achievement.

The point is of vast importance, for it is here that Diogenes Lewis, his critics assert, has totally misread the meaning and faith of America. Here in this prosperous land the union between comfort and service—or to put it in more dignified phrase, the synthesis of Hellenism and Hebraism—has been achieved in practice. A rich and abundant life, motivated by a fine sense of ethical responsibility and disciplined by a democratic public school, is, in sober fact, the distinguishing characteristic of America that sets our country apart from all other lands in western civilization. Call it a Babbitt warren if you will, nevertheless where else has the industrial revolution been brought so completely and happily under dominion to the democratic ideal, or been so ennobled by ethical values? Here it has scattered its wealth amongst the plain people with a bountiful hand, until the poorest family enjoys its nickel-plated plumbing, its flivver, its telephone, its radio, its movies, its funnies, and all the thousand aids to comfort and intelligence which a few generations ago were denied kings—the result of all which is a standard of living that our forefathers would have envied. Our Hellenism is, happily, not Greek. That, as every school-boy in America knows, was established in slavery; whereas our modern Hellenism is established in democracy and ennobled by a sensitive social conscience. Here the master serves. The richest and greatest amongst us—our Judge Garys and Andrew Mellons— are servants of the nameless public, and dedicate their creative genius to the common democratic prosperity. Our Hellenism, in short, is engrafted on a sturdy Hebraic root and flowers in righteousness—in charity, in education, in free clinics and hospitals, in scientific foundations, in great public libraries, in all the vast gifts that wealth freely offers to the cause of social amelioration. The Puritan strain is fortunately still the American strain, and we owe much to those excellent origins that Mr. Lewis scoffs at without understanding. Comfort and service—Hellenism and Hebraism: if this is not the good life, where shall one find it? In Bolshevik Russia? After all Diogenes Lewis is no more important—or useful —than the gad-fly that Brindle brushes from her glossy sides as she chews her cud. What gad-fly ever produced butter?

If Sinclair Lewis is unimpressed by such arguments it is because he is quite disillusioned with the current ideal of material progress. His dreams do not find their satisfaction in good roads and cheap gasoline. He would seem to be an incorrigible idealist who has been bred up on the vigorous Utopianisms of the late nineteenth century. In the golden days before the deluge he had gone blithely to school to all the current idealisms that flourished in the land—to Jeffersonian democracy and to Marxian socialism; and in the well-stocked pharmacopoeias of hopeful young liberals he professed to discover specifics for all our social ills. But the war destroyed his faith in nostrums and removed his Utopia to a dim and foggy future. He has not yet traveled so far in disillusion as Mr. Cabell, who has seen fit to dwarf man to the compass of a flea on the epidermis of earth; nor has he achieved the irony—or the technique—of Clarence Darrow, who suggests casually: "Of course I know that Confucius was as great a philosopher as Billy Sunday, and that as a thinker Buddha was the equal of Billy Bryan. But still all orthodox people know that Confucius and Buddha were spurious and the Billy brothers genuine." He has not even achieved the smug satisfaction of the psychologists who impose their preposterous intelligence tests on simple folk and triumphantly discover morons in respectable neighbors. Some lingering faith in our poor human nature he still clings to. In the great American mass that human nature is certainly foolish and unlovely enough. It is too often blown up with flatulence, corroded with lust, on familiar terms with chicanery and lying; it openly delights in hocus-pocus and discovers its miracle-workers in its Comstocks and Aimee Semple McPhersons. But for all its pitiful flabbiness human nature is not wholly bad, nor is man so helpless a creature of circumstance as the cynics would have us believe. There are other and greater gods than Mumbo Jumbo worshiped in America, worthier things than hocus-pocus; and in rare moments even Babbitt dimly perceives that the feet of his idol are clay. There are Martin Arrowsmiths as well as Elmer Gantrys, and human nature, if it will, can pull itself out of the trap. Bad social machinery makes bad men. Put the banker in the scullery instead of the drawing-room; exalt the test-tube and deflate the cash register; rid society of the dictatorship of the middle class; and the artist and the scientist will erect in America a civilization that may become what civilization was in earlier days, a thing to be respected. For all his modernity and the disillusion learned from Pullman-car philosophers, Sinclair Lewis is still an echo of Jean Jacques and the golden hopes of the Enlightenment—thin and far off, no doubt, but still an authentic echo.

Whether we like Mr. Lewis's technique or not, whether we agree with his indictment of middle-class ideals or dissent from it, his writings are suggestive documents symptomatic of a dissatisfied generation given over to disillusion. The optimistic dreams of middle-class capitalism are not so golden as they seemed to us before the war; and these pudgy novels are slashing attacks on a world that in mouthing empty shibboleths is only whistling to keep up its courage. The faith of America is dead. These brisk pages are filled with the doings of automata—not living men but the simulacra of men, done with astonishing verisimilitude, speaking an amazingly realistic language, professing a surprising lifelikeness; yet nevertheless only shells from which the life has departed, without faith or hope or creative energy, not even aware that they are dead.

It is this consciousness of sketching in a morgue that differentiates Mr. Lewis from the earlier satirists of middle-class America, who in the hopeful years before the war were busily engaged in rebuilding the American temple. The preceding generation—earnest souls like Robert Herrick and Jack London and Upton Sinclair—were as well aware of the shortcomings of our industrial order as Sinclair Lewis, and hated them as vigorously. From the days of Emerson and George Ripley, of Carlyle and Ruskin, capitalistic society had been persistently subjected to sharp and devastating analysis; its drabness and regimentation, its sterility and emptiness and joylessness, had been pointed out by many pens. The Victorians long ago discovered that no generous or humane civilization was to be expected from the hands of Plugson of Undershot—that the banker conceiving of human felicity in terms of eight per cent. is a mean and shabby fellow in comparison with St. Francis or Michelangelo. Long before Sherwood Anderson, William Morris had observed that the workman no longer sings in the factory as in other days he sang over his tool, and concluded that the creation of beauty is more important for human happiness than figuring profits from mass production.

But those earlier analysts were dealing with causes of which they could only forecast the ultimate consequences, whereas Sinclair Lewis is dealing with effects. Plugson of Undershot is now the universal dictator. Before the war there was still life and hope in western civilization; it was not yet reduced to being a common Babbitt warren, with its Billy Sundays and Almus Pickerbaughs, its artists and editors and scientists, on the Plugson pay-roll. What emerges from the drab pages of Sinclair Lewis that is suggestive is the authoritative pronouncement that the effects forecast by the earlier critics have become in our day the regnant order of things. Babbitt is the son of Plugson of Undershot, and Babbitt is a walking corpse who refuses to be put decently away to make room for living men. An empty soul, he is the symbol of our common emptiness. Historically he marks the final passing in America of the civilization that came from the fruitful loins of the eighteenth century. For a hundred and fifty years western civilization had sustained its hopes on the rich nourishment provided by the great age of the Enlightenment. Faith in the excellence of man, in the law of progress, in the ultimate reign of justice, in the conquest of nature, in the finality and sufficiency of democracy, faith in short in the excellence of life, was the great driving force in those earlier, simpler days. It was a noble dream—that dream of the Enlightenment —but it was slowly dissipated by an encompassing materialism that came likewise out of the eighteenth century. Faith in machinery came to supersede faith in man; the Industrial Revolution submerged the hopes of the French Revolution. And now we have fallen so low that our faith in justice, progress, the potentialities of human nature, the excellence of democracy, is stricken with pernicious anemia, and even faith in the machine is dying. Only science remains to take the place of the old romantic creed, and science with its psychology and physics is fast reducing man to a complex bundle of glands, at the mercy of a mechanistic universe. Babbitt, to be sure, has not yet discovered the predicament he is in, but Martin Arrowsmith knows; and while Babbitt is whistling somewhat futilely, Arrowsmith is hard at work in the laboratory seeking a new philosophy to take the place of the old. The outlook is not promising, but until a new faith emerges from the test-tube Sinclair Lewis will wander in the fogs of disillusion.

But enough of such crape-hanging at a time when our best minds are engaged in the great work of stabilizing prosperity. What are test-tubes in comparison with the infallible statistics patriotically disseminated by the National City Bank? To parade such heresies in the face of the progressive American public is enough to damn any man, genius or not. We want no carpers or cynics in our congenial membership. We must all get together to put across the drive for a bigger and richer and better America; and so, reluctantly, despite the fact that in many ways he is a good fellow, we blackball Sinclair Lewis.

SHERWOOD ANDERSON: A PSYCHOLOGICAL NATURALIST *

Unlike our earlier naturalists in handling of material and dramatic interests. Concerned with inner life rather than outer, with hidden drives rather than environment. Accepts the main criteria of naturalism: determinism, distortion, pessimism. A lean and sparing writer whose symbolisms are obscure and puzzling. A single theme: the disastrous effect of frustrations and repressions that create grotesques. Due to (1) Crude, narrow environment that drives to strange aberrations; (2) Repressed instincts that break forth in abnormal action. The consequence a black loneliness—the hunger of fellowship and its denial. Limited in scope to episodic crises—hence his better stories short. Many failures: *Marching Men; Windy McPherson's Son; Poor White* (1920); *Many Marriages* (1923)—a clumsy account of a Babbitt gone on a psychological spree; *Horses and Men* (1923)—some more Grotesques; see in particular "A Chicago Hamlet."

Winesburg, Ohio (1918). A prose *Spoon River Anthology*, with an excellent collection of grotesques. Sharp vignettes; lonely, thwarted lives, "confused and disconcerted by the facts of life." A background of earlier America, crude and ugly, that drives to religious fanaticism in Steve Bentley; to passionate rebellion in Kate Swift; to bitter irony in Ray Pearson. Note the deterministic conclusion of "The Untold Lie"—"Tricked, by Gad, that's what I was; tricked by life and made a fool of"; and the pessimism: . . . "he shouted a protest against his life, against all life, against everything that makes life ugly."

The Triumph of the Egg (1921). A strange and difficult book with its subtle symbolisms. The theme is the common hunger for romance and fellowship that confuses itself with sex and is unsatisfied. Suggested in prefatory poem: "I have a wonderful story to tell but know no way to tell it."

1. *The Egg.* An epitome of his philosophy of grotesques. The egg breeds life that is futile, and life reproduces the egg. A morbid disgust that would bottle the egg, and the failure.

* The notes that follow are from the syllabus.—*Publisher.*

370

2. *Out of Nowhere Into Nothing.* Theme is the "white wonder of life"—what it is and the part it plays in shaping life; a sex illusion that in its mystic appeal to youth guarantees the perpetuation of the race. To age there is no "white wonder," but the life processes are dirty, and lead to final imprisonment in a common trap. Hence the "white wonder" is the supreme jest of nature, sardonic, beguiling, gathering its victims who eagerly run their predetermined course.

3. *Brothers.* A suggestion of the true "white wonder of life"— the brotherhood of man in a lonely world—"beyond words, beyond passion—the fellowship in living, the fellowship in life." But men cannot break through the walls of themselves to grasp it, and the dirt of the world destroys its beauty. "The whole story of mankind's loneliness, of the effort to reach out to unattainable beauty, tried to get itself expressed from the lips of a mumbling old man, crazed with loneliness." "We have different names but we are brothers." "Already I have written three hundred, four hundred thousand words. Are there no words that lead into life?" See conclusion of "The Man in the Brown Coat."

A Story Teller's Story (1924). An attempt to lay bare the emotional life of one seeking to be an artist in America; to plumb his own consciousness, to escape from a world he hates. Such escape comes from reaching down "through all the broken surface distractions of modern life to that old craft out of which culture springs." He must pull himself free from a deadening and devastating routine of an industrial society with its empty ambitions. And having found his craft he finds a recompense in life. "I sang as I worked, as in my boyhood I had often seen old craftsmen sing and as I had never heard men sing in factories. And for what I had written at such times I had been called unclean by men and women who had never known me, could have no personal reasons for thinking me unclean. Was I unclean? Were the hands that, for such brief periods of my life, had really served me, had they been unclean at such moments of service?" A stimulating and suggestive document of modern life.

The note of determinism in Anderson expressed in two images, the wall and escape—running to get away from what holds us fast. But in running away from the old self to find a new, we carry the old self with us. Anderson one of the three or four most important men now writing fiction in America. Compare with D. H. Lawrence.

A NEW ROMANCE

The new romance and the new naturalism both spring from a common root—hatred of the meanness and ugliness of modern life; but romance seeks to evade and forget what naturalism examines curiously. It is a defense mechanism against things as they are and springs from:

1. Disgust at the verisimilitude of naturalism that parades the crude ugliness of life as if it were the reality. The dream more important than the fact, for our real existence is within the imagination, removed from material futilities, where we may satisfy our hunger for beauty, for far-ranging adventure, for ideal existence.

2. The impulse to free creation. Real life overshadowed and darkened by a sense of impotence; men are flies caught in the web of circumstance. But in romance the will is unshackled and the free imagination plays with time and space, shaping fate to its liking in terms of beauty, dwelling in a world as we should like it to be. Romance hence is the ideal cosmos of the ego.

3. The spirit of youth that has brooded over life and refuses to abandon its dreams. The inevitable outcome irony, an undertone of sadness, a recognition of the pessimism against which it desires to be a defense. This the final note. So compare the *Eros et mors* of old romance. . . .*

* Cabell omitted, as there is a fuller discussion of him given.—*Publisher.*

1917–1924 *

Introduction: With the entry of America into the war came a sharp change in literary development. Regimentation due to war psychology destroyed the movement of social criticism which dominated fiction between 1903 and 1917. The liberal movement in economics and politics came to an abrupt end, and the problem novel ceased to be written. Almost overnight it became old-fashioned. The year 1918 sterile.[1] With the year 1919 began a new literary period. Three major movements:

1. A resurgence of naturalism, inspired by psychology rather than by economics, with a tendency to impressionism in handling: represented by Sherwood Anderson.

2. A new romanticism, seeking ideal beauty as a defense against reality and emerging in irony: represented by James Branch Cabell.

3. A new criticism: A revolt of the young intellectuals against the dominant middle class—its Puritanism, its Victorianism, its acquisitive ideals: represented by Sinclair Lewis.

I

THE SMALL TOWN IN FICTION

The first expression of the new literature. Chiefly a middle-western development—and a late phase of the literature of the local. A reaction from the "economic city," with its centralizing economics, which dominated the problem novel. Two antagonistic interpretations: (1) The romantic small town, or the theory of a kindly, democratic world; (2) The realistic small town, or the theory of a petty, competitive world.

I. *The Romantic Interpretation of the Small Town.* A hold-over from an earlier period. Derives from Riley; elaborated and defended by Meredith Nicholson, *The Valley of Democracy* (1918). According to this theory the middle-western village is: (1) A land of economic well-being, uncursed by poverty and unspoiled by wealth; (2) A land of "folksiness"—the village a great family in its

---

* From the syllabus.—*Publisher.*

[1] For a statement of the reaction of a young intellectual to the war, see Randolph Bourne, *Untimely Papers*, 1919.

373

neighborliness, friendliness, sympathy; (3) Primarily middle-class, and therefore characteristically American, wholesome, and human in spite of its prosaic shortcomings; (4) The home of American democracy, dominated by the spirit of equality, where men are measured by their native qualities.[2]

WILLIAM ALLEN WHITE: A SON OF THE MIDDLE BORDER

Product of middle-class, Puritan Kansas. Dominated by sentiment, believes in the essential fairness of men. Two major ideas: (1) Belief in the excellence of western village life; (2) Fear lest this life be submerged by industrialism. A romantic and political Progressive. Formulated his political theory in *The Old Order Changeth* (1910)—thesis, that America is changing from representative republicanism to democracy. The problem is to make business honest. Not an intellectual. His plots resemble Thackeray's—leisurely, gossipy, confidential asides, a large canvas, many figures, a long period of time. His attitude admirably expressed in *Emporia and New York* (1906).

At the Court of Boyville (1899). The romance of youth set against the background of the small town. A world of dreams and loveliness: adventures that await beyond the horizon; the glory of pigtails and overalls. The democracy of the vacant lot: rivalry in marbles and hand-springs—the leadership of the capable. Sincerer work than Tarkington's *Penrod*. Contrast with Garland's *Son of the Middle Border*, and Mark Twain's *Tom Sawyer*.

A Certain Rich Man (1909). His plunge into the problem novel. Theme: fear of the economic city that draws the villager into its web. A contrast between the two worlds and two social ideals—the friendly democracy of the older America threatened by economic centralization.

In the Heart of a Fool (1918). One of the last of the problem novels. Theme—the invasion of the small town by industrialism and the disintegration of village virtues. The story of an idealist who opposes the ends of Main Street and his destruction by the herd. A suggestion of Sinclair Lewis. The conclusion—the excellence of love and the foolishness of selfishness. The background characters, studies in the reaction of the older ideal to the new egoism.

[2] For a criticism of Nicholson, see Randolph Bourne, *The History of a Literary Radical*, p. 128.

BOOTH TARKINGTON: THE DEAN OF AMERICAN MIDDLE-CLASS LETTERS

Possesses the virtues of cleverness, optimism, humor, respectability. Honors all the Victorian taboos. Life is an agreeable experience—to the successful, hence it is well to rise. His chief theme, middle-class romance as exemplified in the "valley of democracy": courtship of nice young people through the agencies of parties and picnics. A skillful writer, with a light touch, but his art destroyed by love of popularity—a novel ends well that ends happily. A perennial sophomore, purveyor of comfortable literature to middle-class America.[3]

The Gentleman from Indiana (1899). A dramatization of the "good, dear people" theme. The college man who goes back to his people to live and work with them. A satisfying life results from merging individual life in the common village life. A flabby and somewhat saccharine philosophy.

Alice Adams (1921). The story of an instinctive actress and her competitive struggle for social position and a man. A clever, attractive, lovable girl defeated by her background—led into foolish little deceits to keep up appearances—victim of middle-class conventionality. Shabby parlors versus conservatories as settings for proposals. The Adams family has fallen behind their acquaintances in the business of rising in the world, and Alice sinks to a lower social scale. An overrated book.

The Midlander (1923). A contribution to booster literature and an unconscious satire on the emptiness of the middle-class mind. A real-estate venture and what came of it. The conception that "man is a wealth-and-comfort-producing machine." Supposed to be tragedy, but the tragedy lies in preferring the imported to the domestic article—choosing a New York girl instead of a local one. The suburb thrives, the automobile business goes forward, and the gods of getting on smile in the end.[4]

The other numerous titles of Tarkington signify nothing except to lovers of comfortable literature. The clever Hoosier has ceased to be an artist—the great failure in contemporary American fiction.

DOROTHY CANFIELD (FISHER)

A clever dramatizer of the obvious: believes in the Woman Triumphant, and discovers in the right education of children—particularly girls—the solution of all problems. Two main themes

---

[3] See Mr. Cabell's criticism in *Beyond Life*, pp. 301–307.
[4] For a review see the *Nation*, March 19, 1924.

1. A protest against the demands of "social life." *The Squirrel Cage* (1912). A contribution to the problem novel. A William Morris suggestion of the sufficiency of handicraft as an escape from social demands. An arraignment of the American home where the father scarcely knows the children and the mother is shut away from the outside world.

The Bent Twig (1915). A study of university community life— the struggle between plain living and high thinking—of social pleasure and no thinking.

2. The defense of the village. The belief that community fellowship—a gathering to watch a century plant bloom—breeds an artistic spirit finer than old-world art and culture can offer. Especially a Vermont town is ideal for the proper bringing up of children. *The Brimming Cup* (1920). A story of the right bringing up of children. *Rough Hewn* (1922). The love of art and travel which leads inevitably to a Vermont town and marriage. *Raw Material* (1923). Sketches. The point of view given in "Paul Meyer"—the folly of thinking that a normal girl should prefer philology to matrimony.

II
THE REALISTIC SMALL TOWN AND THE NEW NATURALISM

The work of the younger intellectuals, more disciplined than the muckrakers, with wider culture and severer standards. Concerned for civilization, the things of the spirit, a free creative individualism, rather than political liberalism. A searching criticism of the triumphant middle class, its ideals and its habitat, the town and city; the repressive tyrannies of its herd mind; the futility of its materialism. Back of the novelists is a group of essayists, young critics of established ways: Van Wyck Brooks, Ludwig Lewisohn, Randolph Bourne, H. L. Mencken. They embody a reaction from: (1) The acquisitive ideal of a machine civilization. (2) "The great illusion of American civilization, the illusion of optimism"—the staple of middle-class business morale. (3) The sentimentalism of "comfortable literature," that evades reality and weakens the intellectual fiber. (4) The inhibitions of a Puritanism that has lost its sanctions. (5) The White-Tarkington doctrine of the "beautiful people" and "folksy village."

The movement began with Masters's *Spoon River Anthology*

(1915). An earlier work is E. W. Howe's *Story of a Country Town* (1883):—stark, grim, unrelieved, revealing the "smoldering discontent of an inarticulate frontier."

ZONA GALE—THE TRANSITION FROM ROMANCE TO REALISM

I. Friendship Village romance. *The Loves of Pelleas and Etarre* (1907). Everyone is helpful, everyone loves, or wants to, or is unhappy for lack of it. *Friendship Village* (1908). A world where there is no sorrow, or sickness, and where brotherly love rules. Of the "folksy" school.

II. The shift to realism. *Miss Lulu Bett* (1920). A homely village tragedy of the repressed soul that rebels under the irritation of domestic pin-pricks. Plebeian characters, thin, cheap, tiresome; set in a shoddy world and rubbing each other's nerves. Deacon Dwight a sadist; Miss Lulu a grotesque. Treated from the outside in contrast with Sherwood Anderson's method. *Faint Perfume* (1923). A glorification of martyrdom. The conviction that life is hard, and the excellence of the economy of pain. A partial return to the *Friendship Village* note, but like *Miss Lulu Bett* in the picture of a self-worshiping family.*

.   .   .   .

DONN BYRNE †

American born but Irish bred. His early work, *The Stranger's Banquet* (1919), half problem novel—industrialism—which offered little scope for the Celtic wistfulness in which he conceives romance to lie.

Messer Marco Polo (1921). The romance of distant times and places, of unfamiliar backgrounds and lovely worlds: medieval Venice and its pageantry; a far quest over burning sands; the loveliness of little Golden Bells at the court of Kubla Khan; the ardor of love that tangles itself in religion. A wistfulness and beauty of phrase that remind one of Synge's *Riders to the Sea.* The loveliest romance of recent years.[5]

The Wind That Bloweth (1922). A rich fabric—Gaelic folk; the woman of the boulevard; the white sun-baked road to Damascus;

* Sinclair Lewis omitted, as fuller material has been given.—*Publisher.*
† From the third section in the syllabus, which deals with "A New Romance."—*Publisher.*
[5] See Cabell's review of *Messer Marco Polo* in *Straws and Prayer-Books*, pp. 52–59 The writer's full name is Brian Oswald Donn-Byrne.

the fire of revolution; the crack of cordage as the ship rounds the Horn—a saga of the unquiet heart.

The Changeling (1923). Short stories of quaint places, forgotten people; the Bible and love of Ireland. Done with excellent craftsmanship.

Blind Raftery (1924). A tale of a blind harpist in Dean Swift's Ireland and of his wife, Hilaria, who sings the song of the women of the streets in Cadiz. Life teaches them a philosophy expressed by the harpist in these words: "We sit a little while by ourselves in an apart, dark place, and we learn truths, of how certain things one believes to be good are but vulgar selfish things, and how certain things the small think evil are but futile accidents. And we learn to be kind; such wisdom comes when we are dead. And those who have never died in life . . . are pleasant shallow people, soulless as seals."

ROBERT NATHAN

Began like Donn Byrne with a problem study—*Peter Kindred* (1919). A dual personality cut asunder and embodied in two characters: David the romantic fades out of the story, and Peter becomes a modern, absorbed in eugenics. A background of Phillips Exeter and Harvard.

Autumn (1921). An idyll of loneliness, with a commentary on materialism, done in simple, wistful language.

1. Mr. Jeminy, a village philosopher, disciple of Boëthius and St. Francis, half pagan and yet Christian. Troubled over the poverty of the world that does not amass "love, peace, the quiet of the heart, the work of one's hand."

2. A village background. Mr. Jeminy wished to teach the children the secret of happiness instead of the folly of plus and minus, and was turned out of his school. An echo of *Main Street* in its commentary on village narrowness, hardness, gossip. A frigid Puritanism that disapproves Mr. Jeminy for speaking disrespectfully of God and denies happiness to Mrs. Wicket who is under God's sentence of unhappiness.

3. A note of determinism. A world of grotesques—all are hemmed in and cramped, longing for fresh experience and strange adventures, all are unhappy. So Aaron Bade with his flute and his "awkward thoughts and clumsy feelings." Margaret Bade with her conviction, "Life is so much spilt milk"; Farmer Barly with his

commentary, "Folks are queer crotchets"; Anna Barly with her yearning for the "white wonder of life" and the trap. An indictment of New England for its destruction of natural happiness and the simple joy of life.

4. A profound irony. The end of Mr. Jeminy's hopefulness is disillusion. "Here within this circle of hills, is to be found faith, virtue, passion, and good sense. In this valley youth is not without courage, or age without wisdom." The outcome disproves this faith. Of his many pupils, "Not one is tidy of mind, or humble of heart. Not one has learned to be happy in poverty, or gentle in good fortune." Life as a whole is futile. The dead alone can ask God the meaning of life. "But for us, who remain, it has no meaning." The tale is Robert Frost done in prose—compare "Mending Wall."

The Puppet Master (1923). The most graceful fantasy in American literature. Papa Jonas, the puppet creator and master, watches the love of Annabelle Lee, a rag doll with shoe-button eyes, and Mr. Aristotle, a red-nosed, philosopher-clown puppet; and of Mary Holly and Christopher Lane, the poet. The theme is love—"Love is a man's soul: it does not grow like his hopes, it does not break like his heart. . . . But love goes by after a while." Papa Jonas is Mr. Jeminy, converted to the Stoic philosophy but lacking love. The note of determinism persists, but the Stoic attitude overcomes. "Yes," he said slowly, "one must make the best of what one has."

JOSEPH HERGESHEIMER: A SOPHISTICATED ROMANTIC

Began as a painter. After fourteen years' apprenticeship was accepted by the *Saturday Evening Post*, and began a career in popularity that rivals Tarkington's. Possesses the virtues and vices of the *Post* school. In earlier work a colorist, painting statuesques against artfully arranged backgrounds; a connoisseur of fabrics and poses and nature settings—nearly as "much concerned with the stuffs as with the stuff of life." In *Cytherea* the setting a sophisticated manipulation of the theme, as the hot Cuban night in *Cobra* with its naked primitive passions. A dabbler in psychology that develops into a crude Freudianism, particularly in *Cytherea*. Always a hint of artistic insincerity; something of a poseur yet a sensuous artist nature. His gorgeous prose style spotty and streaked by amazing crudeness.

The Three Black Pennys (1917). A study in the breaking out of willfulness in successive generations, set against a background of the history of iron-making in Pennsylvania. An elaboration of *Tubal Cain*. An anticlimax arranged for dramatic significance, suggesting the decay of romance in a hundred and fifty years of American industrial development. The first episode is Hergesheimer at his best. Howat Penny a study in moods that make him "angry at life"; but swept on by the will to possess. Ludowica Winscomb embodies a favorite theme—the suggestion of an older culture contrasted with the crude American reality. So compare Taou Yuen.

Linda Condon (1919). A study in the decay of surface beauty— an empty form caught in the web of a shallow mother and the demands of stronger natures, but preserved by lack of emotional concern. Handled skillfully, with a somewhat forced unity symbolized by Linda's straight black bang; but the story leaves one with a sense of unconcern for Linda and her fate. The ending melodramatic. Note Van Doren's curious comment—"nearly the most beautiful American novel since Hawthorne and Henry James."

Java Head (1919). The story of an exotic that languishes in an uncongenial habitat. A contrast in backgrounds: the romance of old Salem in the days of the clipper ship; the romance of a far older East that makes Salem seem raw and crude. Taou Yuen a decorative lay figure, with aristocratic suggestions beyond anything the West knows. The dramatic significance of opium, that hangs like a pall over the East and brings degeneration and death to Puritan Salem. The end with its cheap love adventure, a conscious satire on western life. Hergesheimer's best work. A romantic atmosphere got without archaic trappings of speech and manners; nevertheless makes much of costume.

Balisand (1924). A romance of a Virginia Federalist in the days of the Revolution and after. A rich background of plantation life, with a touch of somewhat cheap mysticism. Of the school of Washington rather than Jefferson. A better work than *The Bright Shawl* or *Cytherea*.

His other titles signify little. Yet see the *Saturday Evening Post* for a series of furniture stories. Characteristic of his concern for the "stuffs of life." See in particular, "Mahogany" (Vol. 195, no.

53, January, 1923); "Pewter" (Vol. 196, no. 23, January, 1924);
"Oak" (Vol. 196, no. 3, July, 1923).[6]

IV

CERTAIN OTHER WRITERS

EDITH WHARTON—THE GENTEEL TRADITION AND THE NEW PLUTOCRACY

A temperamental aristocrat, endowed with keen intelligence and ripe culture. Observes the ways of a wealthy society without culture and unconcerned with standards. A protest against the domination of the middle class. Mrs. Wharton isolated in America by her native aristocratic tastes. The older New York society without real distinction, bound by convention and with middle-class concern for respectability; the new society a vulgar plutocracy; outside both a pushing *nouveau-riche* class eager to climb. Hence she turns to the authentic aristocracy of Europe for satisfaction of her genteel tastes. In spirit she belongs to the *ancien régime*. The highest law of society is convention, but it must be noble, not vulgar.

The House of Mirth (1905). A story of New York's gilded society, and how it served one of its daughters. Lily Bart, trained for social leadership in a plutocracy, a finished and costly parasite, seeking a market for her beauty, yet restrained by instinctive refinement from seeing the game through. Lacking money she is caught in a web of convention and destroyed. In her world convention is the social law, and the tragedy flows from her inability to rise above it or to keep it wholly. The contrast between Selden and Trenor—the aristocrat and the plutocrat—characteristic of Mrs. Wharton.

Ethan Frome (1911). A dramatization of the "narrow house" theme—life held relentlessly in the grip of poverty and duty. A bleak and joyless existence that seeks escape and suffers lingering tragedy. Thereafter a stern isolation and iron repression. Mrs. Wharton's finest work.

The Custom of the Country (1915). A study of the social climber. The best of a series of novels satirizing the encroachments on New York exclusiveness by the rising plutocracy and its daughters. The western plutocracy of pork presumably more vulgar than the

[6] For a striking characterization of Hergesheimer, see *The Bookman*, May, 1922 For an appreciation, see Cabell, *Straws and Prayer-Books*, pp. 195-221.

eastern plutocracy of Wall Street, yet between them the older
gentry crushed.   So compare Boyesen, *Social Strugglers* (1893);
Robert Grant, *Unleavened Bread* (1900).   Undine Spragg, like
Selma White, pushing, heartless, vulgar, showy, is set over against
Ralph Marvell, a refined "dabbler with life"; Peter Van Degen,
the "plunger"; and Elmer Moffatt, the self-made man.   She embodies all that Mrs. Wharton most hates; all climbers are vulgar,
she believes, both men and women.

The Age of Innocence (1920).   A study of the older world of the
eighteen-seventies.   A loving yet satirical picture of a Pharisaic
society, "wholly absorbed in barricading self against the un
pleasant"; that lives secluded, protected by its taboos, and f ars
reality.   A sterile world of clan conventions and negations; a
decadent Victorianism.   The Van der Luydens of Skuytercliff are
of the same stuff as the Dagonets in *The Custom of the Country;*
and the dilettante Newland Archer is another Ralph Marvell.   Into
this dead world enters Ellen Olenska with her vivid old-world
experiences, who threatens to rebel, yet finally yields to the clan
taboos.   The book fades out like the lives of the Van der Luydens.
An admirable work.

Old New York (1924).   Four carefully done tales that sketch
New York in the forties, fifties, sixties, and seventies.   A return to
her best manner, with the finish of *The Age of Innocence.*

Her other later work not important.   *Glimpses of the Moon* (1922)
inconsequential; and *A Son at the Front* (1923)—an attempt to
document the reactions of an artist with a son in the army—only
half successful.

Mrs. Wharton a finished artist who grasps her material firmly;
an intellectual attitude, delighting in irony.   Unaffected by the
problem novel, and schools of naturalism or romanticism.   Not a
thinker like Cabell, whose irony springs from an imagination that
contemplates man in his relation to cosmic forces, but an observer
whose irony springs from noting the clash between men and social
convention.   The last of our literary aristocrats of the genteel
tradition.   Her attitude expressed in the words, "*Je suis venue trop
tard dans un monde trop vulgaire.*"

WILLA CATHER: EPICS OF WOMEN

The Middle Border of Hamlin Garland seen through different
eyes.   She looks back lovingly to a pioneer West, as the cradle of

heroic lives. An epic breadth of prairie spaces and industrious years, with a note of regret—*Optima dies prima fugit.* Against this background she sets her immigrant women, with their vigor and wealth of life, and considers how the West has dealt with them. Peasant heroines, with their strong natures hidden under queer speech and garb, set in a waste of wild red grass, bitter winters, burning summers, virgin soil and great loneliness. A long-ignored theme—the lot of the immigrant who has come on a desperate adventure—the struggle of their children with the soil. Compare *The Jungle*, for the industrial exploitation of the immigrant.

Has matured slowly. *The Troll Garden* (1905), and *Alexander's Bridge* (1910), are inconsequential. Her real work done late. Belongs to no school. Is neither naturalistic nor romantic. Is unconcerned with problems. Except for a single attack on the ugliness of the small western town—"The Sculptor's Funeral" in *The Troll Garden*—she ignores middle-class America and its Main Streets. An individual artist, sincere, capable; an excellent craftsman.

O Pioneers (1913). The story of Alexandra Bergson, a daughter of the Middle Border; calm, tenacious, capable; loving the soil and bringing it to abundant productiveness. The new world had brought out diverse qualities in the Swedish peasant family; the older brothers common, dull, vulgarized by Americanization; the younger brother suggestive of the better side of American opportunity. Alexandra the directing mind and controlling will. Over against her is set the Bohemian Marie Tovesky, childlike in her spontaneous enthusiasm. The tragic ending handled with great skill. Thrown about the whole, a harsh Nebraska countryside through changing periods. One who had not lived through similar experiences and loved the memory could not write so.

The Song of the Lark (1915). The story of Thea Kronberg, who by virtue of fierce energy and iron strength rises to triumph as an artist. There are no romantic stage-effects, only the passionate struggle of a tenacious will. Thea a peasant nature of vast solidity. The most convincing story of artist life written by an American. A changing background: the mean little Colorado town, the loneliness of Chicago, Europe, the great spaces of the Southwest.

My Ántonia (1918). The story of Ántonia Shimerda: an opulent peasant nature with strong mother instinct, thwarted by meager opportunities and vulgar environment. Her life runs a narrow round: the early pioneer experience with its loneliness and black tragedy; the town experience of the hired girl, who lives eagerly; the later life of a hard-working mother on a lonely farm. Ántonia "a rich mine of life like the founder of early races," loving, generous, eager, yet belonging to the soil. To vulgarize such natures by cramming them into a conventional mold, passes for Americanization—this the implied thesis.

One of Ours (1922). The story of Claude Wheeler, with strength imprisoned by a society that opens its opportunities to Main Street natures like Bayliss Wheeler. A suggestion of naturalism in the handling of the theme: Claude caught by the negative character Enid Royse because he fails to appreciate the complementary strength of Gladys Farmer—a true Cather woman, enmeshed in Gopher Prairie. A futile, ironical ending: better to die in battle than be destroyed by the pettiness of Gopher Prairie. The war atmosphere seems curiously old-fashioned.

The Lost Lady (1923). A change of theme. The story of Mrs. Forester, an embodiment of traditional feminine charm, quite superior to such incidents as age or loyalty—a type of woman outside Miss Cather's experience and understanding.*

V

SOME WAR BOOKS

The late war the first in our history that has produced an aftermath of searching criticism in fiction or drama. The romantic note dominant in all earlier accounts, particularly of the Revolution and the Rebellion. Such stories written by men who took no part in them. The Civil War produced only one book of realistic criticism, that was mutilated by the publisher to temper its cynicism, and that enjoyed no popularity—*The Recollections of a Private*, by Warren Goss. The late war is producing a considerable group, all realistic and critical; the romantic note has not yet appeared.

JOHN DOS PASSOS

Three Soldiers (1921). A naturalistic handling of war that serves as a commentary on *One of Ours*. The most notable American work on the theme since Stephen Crane's *The Red Badge of Courage.*

* See remarks on Miss Cather in the introduction to the text edition of Ole Rölvaag's *Giants in the Earth*, which follows these syllabus notes.—*Publisher.*

Similar in temper to Henri Barbusse, *Under Fire*, but dealing with the barracks and the drill field. Compare with Andreas Latzko, *Men in War*—impressionistic in handling. Dos Passos a young artist from the university, an idealist who enlists and is disillusioned. A study of the war machine and the effect of regimentation on different types of men—the contrast between army discipline and a lax individualism, and the disasters that may ensue from sudden change. Fuselli a low-grade character who wants to rise; Chrisfield a solid animal who becomes sullen; Andrews a highly nervous organism, to whom routine is killing. Coarse episodes set in a brilliant background: the glamour of militarism gone.

E. E. CUMMINGS

The Enormous Room (1922). A brilliant revelation of the tortures endured by an artist unjustly imprisoned in a French military prison. Supplements *Three Soldiers* in destroying the appeal of military glamour. An attack particularly on the common notion of heroic, chivalrous France.

THOMAS BOYD

Through the Wheat (1923). An impressionistic handling of the reactions of a normal American soldier, Private Hicks, to the war. The keynote is numbness—a deadly numbness which offers the sole defense of the normal mind against the horrors it confronts. Its matter-of-factness, detached point of view, and the ordinariness of the hero, set it apart from *Three Soldiers* and *The Enormous Room*. An excellent bit of impressionism.

LAURENCE STALLINGS

Plumes (1924). A story of war by one who has suffered mutilation from it. The theme—"If you are smashed badly . . . and if you have any intelligence you must remake a world to live in." A study of post-war disillusionment, naturalistically handled. So compare the play in which he collaborated—*What Price Glory?*

VI

YOUTH IN REVOLT—CERTAIN PURVEYORS OF THE HECTIC

A group of youthful poseurs at the mercy of undigested reactions to Nietzsche, Butler, Dadaism, Vorticism, Socialism; overbalanced by changes in American critical and creative standards, and in love with copious vocabularies and callow emotions. Given to satirizing the educational methods of *alma mater;* quick to espouse new causes; enthusiastic for revolt as a profession. A prolific movement which as yet has accomplished nothing seriously creative.

F. SCOTT FITZGERALD

This Side of Paradise (1921); *The Beautiful and the Damned* (1922). A bad boy who loves to smash things to show how naughty he is; a bright boy who loves to say smart things to show how clever he is. Precocious, ignorant—a short candle already burnt out.

STEPHEN VINCENT BENÉT AND FLOYD DELL

Benét: *Heavens and Earth* (1920); *The Beginning of Wisdom* (1921); *Young People's Pride* (1923); *Jean Hugenot* (1923). Floyd Dell: *Moon Calf* (1921); *Briary Bush* (1922); *Janet March* (1923).
Luminaries of the school which holds that the sufficient tests of intellectual emancipation are rolled hose, midnight discussions, black coffee, and the discarding of wedding rings. Floyd Dell the most serious and ablest of the group.

BEN HECHT

Eric Dorn (1921); *Gargoyles* (1922). An almost naturalistic distrust of formal education, love, and government, and an unsubstantiated belief in the efficacy of revolt in general and the romance of city streets in particular. A burnt-out rocket. His last books— *1001 Afternoons in Chicago* (1923) and *Florentine Dagger* (1924) worse than inconsequential.

OLE RÖLVAAG'S "GIANTS IN THE EARTH" *

THE dramatic contrast between Per Hansa, type of the natural pioneer who sees the golden light of promise flooding the wind-swept plains, and Beret, child of an old folk civilization who hungers for the home ways and in whose heart the terror of lone-liness gathers, penetrates to the deeper reality of life as it was lived for three hundred years on the American frontier. It is not a late or rare phenomenon; it is only late and rare in literature. We have been used to viewing the frontier in broad and generous perspective and have responded most sympathetically to the epic note that runs through the tale of the conquest of the continent. It is the great American romance that gives life and drama to our history. It was this epic quality that de Tocqueville felt when he discovered the poetry of America in the silent march of a race toward the far-off Pacific, hewing its way triumphantly through forests and mountains to arrive at its objective. But the emo-tional side, the final ledger of human values, we have too little considered—the men and women broken by the frontier, the great army of derelicts who failed and were laid away, like the Norse immigrant lad, in forgotten graves. The cost of it all in human happiness—the loneliness, the disappointments, the renunciations, the severing of old ties and quitting of familiar places, the appalling lack of those intangible cushions for the nerves that could not be transported on horseback or in prairie schooners: these imponder-ables too often have been left out of the reckoning in our tradi-tional romantic interpretation. But with the growth of a maturer realism we are beginning to understand how great was the price exacted by the frontier; and it is because *Giants in the Earth*, for the first time in our fiction, evaluates adequately the settlement in terms of emotion, because it penetrates to the secret inner life of men and women who undertook the heavy work of subduing the wilderness, that it is—quite apart from all artistic values—a great historical document.

* Introduction to the text edition of Rölvaag's *Giants in the Earth*. Copyright 1929 by Harper and Brothers, by whose permission it is reprinted here.—*Publisher.*

If in one sense the conquest of the continent is the great American epic, in another sense it is the great American tragedy. The vastness of the unexplored reaches, the inhospitality of the wilderness, the want of human aid and comfort when disaster came, these were terrifying things to gentle souls whom fate had not roughhewn for pioneering. Fear must have been a familiar visitor to the heart of the pioneer woman, and for a hundred and fifty years this fear of the dark wilderness was one reason why the settlements clung to the more hospitable seaboard. There, at least, was an outlook toward the old home. But with the crossing of the Allegheny Mountains, following the Revolutionary War, the frontier spirit came into its own. A spirit of restlessness took possession of men, and the thin line of settlements advanced swiftly, overrunning the Inland Empire with its interminable forests and malarial swamps, sprawling rudely from the Great Lakes to the Gulf of Mexico. To subdue the land was no easy task. Upon the old and the weak the wilderness laid a ruthless hand, and even of the strength of the young it took heavy toll. Tragedy was always lurking at the door of the backwoods cabin. In Beveridge's *Life of Lincoln* there is a grim story of the hardships suffered by the Lincoln family in Indiana that leaves no room for romance—husband, wife, two children, and later an old couple, were forced to pig together all winter in a brush camp open on one side to the weather, with only a fire in front for cooking and heating—a mode of life below that of the Indian in his skin teepee. And then a mysterious disease fell upon them, virulent and fateful, and the old couple were taken from their cots on the ground and put away beneath the soil to find what rest they might there. That men should break and women go mad under such strain is no more than may be expected of human nature. Beret, the wife of Per Hansa, brooding in her sod-hut in Dakota, afraid of life and of her own thoughts, and turning for comfort to a dark religion, is a type of thousands of frontier women who—as the historian Ridpath said of his parents—"toiled and suffered and died that their children might inherit the promise."

Very likely we should have felt the tragedy of the frontier long ago if we had been as much concerned with inner experience as with outward act, if we had been psychologists as well as chroniclers. But we have been too prone to romanticize the objective reality and disguise slatternly ways with the garb of backwoods independence. The realistic eighteenth century made no such mistake. Such infrequent glimpses of the first frontier as we catch in our early literature suggest a swift descent into grossness as the settlements were left behind. In the *Journal of Madam Sarah Knight*, which dates from the opening years of the eighteenth century, are brief notes of what fell under her sharp eyes on a horseback trip from Boston to New York. The sketches she has penciled are far from bucolic. Certain of the figures that emerge casually from her pages are no other than decivilized grotesques—animal-like creatures for whom returning to a state of nature meant living filthily in mean huts, traveling back centuries toward the primitive ways of the cavemen. Of the emotional reactions of these early children of the wilderness Madam Knight tells us nothing; so casual an observer would have no opportunity to penetrate beneath the unlovely surface.

A quarter century later Colonel William Byrd, the first gentleman of Virginia, wrote his graphic *History of the Dividing Line*, an account of a boundary survey run between the colonies of Virginia and South Carolina. As the survey leaves the seacoast behind and approaches the frontier, the same characteristics appear that Madam Knight noted—a rough and surly independence, a dislike of established law and order, and a shiftless way of life that is content to subsist off the country. "Lubberland," Colonel Byrd called the Carolina backwoods where a new race of poor whites was springing up—a rude decivilized existence that bore heavily on the women and was heedless of the common amenities of social life. In *Letters from an American Farmer* (1773) written by St. John de Crèvecœur, a cultivated Norman who established himself in the colonies after serving in the French army under Montcalm, the same sharp judgment is passed on the frontier. Crèvecœur was of the romantic school of Rousseau and eloquent in praise of life lived close to nature, yet even he discovers the frontier to be a blot on colonial civilization, the abode of rude and lawless figures who precede by a decade the sober army of occupation.

In the eighteenth century the testimony is clear that the frontiersmen—or "borderers," as they were commonly called—were rough bumptious fellows who fled the settlements partly because of a dislike of ordered and seemly ways. The colonial gentry, men like the Rev. Timothy Dwight, held them in deep contempt and rejoiced when they quitted the settlements and plunged deep into the wilderness beyond the jurisdiction of church and state. Lawlessness, shiftlessness, a passion like Jurgen's to follow after their own wishes and their own desires, seem to have been the characteristics of these rude men and slatternly women, as the aristocratic eighteenth century judged them. That is very far from the whole story, to be sure. Our later historians have made clear that from this same leveling frontier issued the spirit of American democracy, and that from these rough individualists came the great movement of Jacksonianism that swept away the class distinctions of an earlier century. Accepting so much, and recognizing the part played by the frontier in shaping the institutions and the psychology of America, it remains true, nevertheless, that the lot of the backwoodsman was hard and the price he paid in civilization for his freedom was great. The sod house of the Dakota plains was only a late adaptation of the primitive huts that were strung along the earlier frontier. What loneliness filled the hearts of the drab women who made hoecakes and dressed deer skins, what rebellions at their lot stirred dumbly within them, no record remains to tell and no literature has cared to concern itself about.

It was not till the nineteenth century that authentic accounts of the frontier, written by men who had come out of it, began to appear, yet even then in too scant volume. In Longstreet's *Georgia Scenes*, Joseph G. Baldwin's *Flush Times of Alabama and Mississippi*, and Davy Crockett's *Autobiography*, the frontier is painted in homely colors that time cannot fade. Their brisk pages seem to have been dipped in the butternut dye-pot of the backwoods cabin. By far the most significant of them is the braggart but naïvely truthful narrative of the life of Cane-brake Davy who in his several removals followed the advancing frontier the length of the State of Tennessee. Davy would seem to have been the authentic backwoodsman, and the life of the individual may be taken as a description of the genus. Restless, assertive, unsocial, buoyantly optimistic and obsessed with the faith that better land lay farther west, cultivating a bumptious wit that was a defense mechanism against the meanness of daily life, he was only an improvident child who fled instinctively from civilization. As a full-length portrait of the Jacksonian leveler, in the days when the great social revolution was establishing the principles of an equalitarian democracy, the picture is of vast significance. But it is incomplete. Concerning the wife and daughters who were dragged at his heels in the successive removals, the narrative is silent. It is a man's tale, unenriched by the emotional experiences of a woman, and as such it tells only half the story of the frontier.

The *Autobiography* was the last pungent note of realism before the romantic revolution swept over American literature; and it was not till two generations later, when the war was over and the glories of the Gilded Age were fading, that the frontier came to realistic expression again in the works of Hamlin Garland. *Main-Travelled Roads*, the first chapter in the tale of the Middle Border, is a prologue to *Giants in the Earth*, telling the story of the prairie settlement in the idiom of the generation that undertook the great adventure. In these brief tales is compressed the harsh temper of the eighties, when the spirit of revolt was running like wildfire across the prairies and the Middle Border was arming for battle. For a decade or more the farmers' affairs had been out of kilter, and a note of discontent had begun to appear in fiction. Before Garland, western life had been dealt with by Edward Eggleston in *The Hoosier Schoolmaster* and *The Circuit Rider*, and more searchingly by Ed Howe in *The Story of a Country Town*—a drab commentary on life in Atchison, Kansas, in the early eighties. But it is in Joseph Kirkland's *Zury, The Meanest Man in Spring County* (1887), that a deep sense of the meanness of frontier life is first adequately felt. The harsh constrictions of pioneer existence tightened about Zury as a boy when his father was struggling with debt, turning a naturally generous nature into a skinflint mortgage grabber. He early learned that he must fight to survive, and as a result his life was shut up in a narrow round of sordid accumulation. It was the poverty of the frontier, in Kirkland's eyes, that was the great hardship.

Hamlin Garland's more adequate story of the Middle Border, beginning militantly with *Main-Travelled Roads* (1887-92) and flowering in the idyllic saga of the Garlands and McClintocks (1914), is a chronicle that grows more significant as the times it deals with draw further into the past. Throughout his interpretation run two dominant notes: the promise of future fulfillment when the prairies have been brought under the plow—the Per Hansa note of pioneer optimism; and then later, rising slowly into a ground swell, a note of discouragement suggesting the utter futility of a laborious existence. Underlying *Main-Travelled Roads* is a mood of bitterness that springs from a deep sense of failure— a mood that grew harsher with the economic depression of the Middle Border in the eighties. The harvest was not fulfilling the expectations of seed time, and the bow of promise was gone from the prairie fields. The figures of bitter men and despondent women fill his pages and darken the colors of his realism. It is the cost of it all that depresses him—the toll exacted of human happiness. These early studies of Garland's strike the first note of the tragedy of the frontier. Starkly objective, they are sociological sketches, the militant expression of a rebellious mood that had been deepening since the panic of 1873 burst the romantic bubble of frontier hopes. The history of two decades of economic maladjustment, with their Granger Populism, their passionate resentment at the favoritisms of government, their blind striking out at the plutocracy that was visibly rising amid the American democracy, is compressed within a few acrid tales that proposed to tell the plain truth about life on the Middle Border farm. *Main-Travelled Roads* is as complete an expression of the mood of the last years of the century—the outlook upon life, the economic and political problems, the objective treatment of materials —as *Giants in the Earth* is an expression of the vastly different outlook and mood of our own day.

For a generation before 1917, when the movement was brought to a sudden stop, the mind of America was deeply concerned with problems of sociology. The growing spirit of realism was absorbed in politics and economics and concerned itself little with subjective analysis. The intellectuals were busily examining the Constitution in the light of its economic origins and interpreting American history in the light of frontier experience. The novelists, reflecting the current interests, were fascinated by the phenomena of industrialism and were studying curiously the new race of captains of industry who were weaving a strange pattern of life for America. The city had already come to dwarf the country. Chicago bestrode the Middle Border like a colossus, and the novelists found material for their realism in the cut-throat ways of business men. Their stories—harsh and strident as the grinding wheels on the overhead "Loop"—were set against a background of sprawling cities hastening to grow big, where the battles of giants were fought and where the *milieu*—a vast network of impersonal forces—was more significant than the individual men and women who were borne onward in the stream of tendency to submerge or rise as chance determined. A note of stark determinism runs through much of the work; but it was a determinism of environing forces— the objective world of the machine—rather than of character, and in consequence the deeper concern of fiction was sociological, the understanding of this impersonal machine order and the subduing of it to democratic ends. In such a world the farmer and the problems of the Middle Border were become as old-fashioned as ox-carts.

Ten years later, when *Giants in the Earth* was published, such objective treatment of materials was no longer the vogue. Since the war a revolutionary shift of interest has taken place, a shift from the sociological to the psychological. It is no longer the world of objective fact that obtrudes as the significant reality, but the subtler world of emotional experience, the furtive inner life of impulse and desire that Sherwood Anderson probes so curiously. The change of theme was first marked, perhaps, by *Spoon River Anthology*, with its mordant sketches of stunted and thwarted lives that Mr. Masters professes to regard as the natural harvest of a sterile village life. *Spoon River Anthology* is bitter in its sardonic rebellion against the genial optimisms of the "Valley of Democracy." From the epic thrust of expansion issued, as its natural progeny, a race of abortive grotesques, starved figures which suggest to Mr. Masters the cost in human values of severing the ties of kin and kind and throwing aside like an old shoe the creative wealth of social experience. The soil of the frontier village is too thin for men and women to strike deep root and grow to generous stature.

Since the publication of *Spoon River Anthology*, concern for psychological values has pretty much taken possession of our literature. In the lovely pages of Willa Cather's *O Pioneers!* and *My Ántonia* there is revealed a warm sympathy with the emotional life of pioneer women and a poignant understanding of their bleak lot. But the analysis—as in Hamlin Garland's work—draws back from the threshold of final tragedy, pausing before it has penetrated to the hidden core of futility. The waste of all finer values exacted by the prairies is suggested by the queer figures of lonely immigrants who fade in the uncongenial environment, but it is not thrust into the foreground to dominate the scene. The vast stretches of the prairies are there—stern, inhospitable, breeding a dumb homesickness in alien hearts—where the red grass bends before the restless winds and the forces of nature are not easily tamed; but in the end the prairie is subdued and the scars it has laid on men's lives are forgotten. Since Willa Cather, others have dealt with the West—Ruth Suckow, Margaret Wilson, and Herbert Quick, to name a few—yet in none of their work is there the profound insight and imaginative grasp of the theme that gives to *Giants in the Earth* so great a sense of tragic reality.

In this creative return to the theme of the great American adventure the causes of human failure lie deeper than politics or economics. They are to be found in the impersonal forces of nature that are too powerful for the human will to cope with; and in the hidden weakness of fearful souls that cannot live when their roots have been pulled up from the congenial home soil. For all his titanic labors, Per Hansa, the viking, is struck down at last. There are few nobler passages in our fiction—the more telling for its restraint—than the final scene where, driven inexorably by circumstance, Per Hansa sets forth into the February blizzard to fetch a minister to the bedside of his stricken comrade. The note of determinism is there, subtle, pervasive. The Norns of his fathers had decreed that it should be so—in the urgings of the mystical Beret, in the dumb pleadings of the dying Hans Olsa and his broken-hearted wife. Per Hansa the strong, the capable one who never failed, who was cunning enough to outwit fate itself—Per Hansa would go out into the storm and return with the minister who would point the way to heaven to the troubled Hans Olsa. And so, driven by all the imperatives of fate, he sets out, skis on his feet and others at his back, to face the last great adventure. The blinding snow quickly wraps him about, the cold grips his heart, and Per Hansa is seen no more until on a soft May day, when the wheat is green in his fields and the corn is ready for planting, he is found seated by a haystack, his skis beside him and his face turned to the untrodden West. For all the heroic labors of Per Hansa, for all the tragic loneliness of Beret, the end is futility.

And Beret, the sick one, likewise is in the hands of the Norns. She had sinned through love of Per Hansa, and in the long brooding hours on the Dakota plains her mind gives way. She cannot rise to Per Hansa's delight in the newborn son. Peder Victorious—symbol of Per Hansa's buoyant faith—for her is only another evidence of sin. This dark land of Dakota is marked by God's displeasure, and life for her becomes a silent struggle of renunciation and atonement. A primitive Norse Calvinist, victimized by a brooding imagination that sees more devils than vast hell can hold, she dwells "on the border of utter darkness" where the forces of good and evil struggle for the human soul. Across the gloomy Puritanism of her nature fall the shadows of an older and darker faith, and in her nostalgia the old Northland superstitions merge with the somber Northland religion to her undoing. The tragedy of Beret works itself out in the tender corridors of her own heart and, as Professor Commager has suggested, it is as universal as the tragedy of Goethe's Margarethe. In his portrayal of the "sick soul" of Beret hungering for the far homeland the Norse artist has achieved a triumph. The epic conquest of the continent must be read in the light of women's sufferings as well as in that of men's endurance. In whichever light it is read, it becomes something far more suggestive than a drab tale of frontier poverty or a sordid tale of frontier exploitation; it becomes vital and significant as life itself.

Giants in the Earth is a great and beautiful book that suggests the wealth of human potentialities brought to America year after year by the peasant immigrants who pass through Ellis Island and scatter the length and breadth of the land. Written in Norwegian, and stemming from a rich old-world literary tradition, it is at the same time deeply and vitally American. The very atmosphere of the Dakota plains is in its pages, and it could have been written only by one to whom the background was a familiar scene. The artist has lived with these peasant folk; he is one of them, and he penetrates sympathetically to the simple kindly hearts hidden to alien eyes by the unfamiliar folk ways. To gather up and preserve in letters these diverse folk strains before they are submerged and lost in the common American *mores*, would seem to be a business that our fiction might undertake with profit.

Ole Edvart Rölvaag is himself a viking of the Per Hansa strain. Born of fisher folk, 22 April, 1876, on the island of Donna at the very edge of the Arctic circle, he took his name, following a common Norwegian custom, from the name of a cove on the shores of which he was brought up. It is a land barren except for the gorse and heather, and the long winter nights and the restless sea were certain to bring the imagination under their somber spell. At the age of fourteen, discouraged from further schooling by the family that contrasted him unfavorably with a brilliant brother, he turned fisherman, and for five years went off to the Lofoten Islands some two hundred miles away for the winter catches. Distrustful of the future, he made his great decision to come to America, landing in New York in 1896 with only a railway ticket to South Dakota. In the great West, still turmoiled by the agrarian upheaval of the nineties, he joined an uncle who had provided him transportation money, tried his hand at farming, worked at other jobs, and at the age of twenty-three, not having found himself, he turned once more to the formal business of schooling. In the fall of 1899 he entered Augustana College, a preparatory school in Canton, South Dakota. From there he went to St. Olaf College, Northfield, Minnesota, graduating in 1905 at the age of twenty-eight. After a year at the University of Oslo in Norway, he joined the staff of St. Olaf College, where he is now Professor of Norwegian Literature. In the larger sense, however, his education has been got from life, which he seems to have lived with a rich and daring intensity; and it is his own venturesome experience, certainly, that finds expression in the creative realism and brooding imagination of his work. Intellectually and artistically he is of the excellent old-world culture. How greatly his professional studies determined his literary technique only a competent Norwegian critic can judge; yet it is worth while comparing *Giants in the Earth* with Johan Bojer's *The Emigrants*—a work which, when announced as being in preparation, dramatically influenced his own novel.

THE SHORT STORY *

Introduction. With the ferment of the seventies and eighties a new school of literature, that was effectively a denial of the genteel tradition: it was effectively a popularization—a taking it out of the severe realm of the *Atlantic Monthly*. It was an appeal to the middle class. From Henry James to Hamlin Garland a steady shift from right to left. This implied:

1. A shift from genteel to homely material.
2. A shift to realism from the earlier sentimentality. This genteel tradition constantly cropping out anew—in Margaret Deland, in a changed form in Zona Gale. It has been strongest in New England—from Rose Terry Cooke through Sarah Orne Jewett to Mary Wilkins.

The short story commonly believed to be peculiarly representative of our genius—the stripping-away of the superfluous and the love of technical refinement. Derived from Poe and Hawthorne: both artists yet far removed from the tendencies which have controlled the development of the short story since.

Theme. The American short story has dealt largely with the two great themes of all romance, love and adventure. The form constitutes the great staple—is largely provided by women for women. The handling of this love theme reveals the inevitable shift from the genteel tradition to middle-class efficiency, and the spirit of the change is revealed in the changing dress of the heroine. In the seventies, crinoline, innumerable flounces of white muslin, lace parasols—no tan, no freckles, but a gentle pallor. Such dress and such heroines will exude sentiment. It will concern itself with atmosphere. Action brisk and efficient will appear unladylike, almost vulgar. What a change when the heroine clothes herself in a silk flour-sack—showing silk stockings, bare arms and neck—cultivating tan and freckles, bobbing her hair, going in for automobiles and golf and tennis! The older heroine dwelt in a world of sentiment without sex; the present-day heroine lives in a world of sex interest without sentiment. The more flounces in life and literature, the

---

* Lecture notes. This subject was not included in the contents, but contains some matter of interest.—*Publisher.*

less the animal is exposed. Hence action has superseded sentiment
—plot has superseded atmosphere. The hero becomes a Hart,
Schaffner and Marx young business man and the middle-class note
is struck loudly in the honk of the motor-car. The genteel tradition
is laid away with the flowers.

Major Influences during the Sixties. Through the fifties and
sixties literature uncertain and halting. The style largely set by
old-world fashions. Three in particular:

1. Influence of Charlotte and Emily Brontë. A sort of sentimental and mawkish passion. Stilted style, as in Harriet Beecher
Stowe. This fell in with the Irving note of the picturesque and was
exploited in *Godey's Lady's Book.*

2. Influence of Dickens. At its height in the fifties: an emphasis
upon the vulgar—plain and homely characters. Exploited in the
Atlantic by Lowell. So Rose Terry Cooke in *Miss Lucinda* (1861).

3. Influence of the French realistic movement: Balzac, Flaubert.
Only a faint beginning. Still a lot of romance stuff but given a local
color and garnished with humor.

Counter Tendencies. The inevitable development of the middle-
class city and the middle-class magazine, persistently affected by
certain throw-backs to an older American tradition. America is of
the city today, but day before yesterday it was still country, and in
the backgrounds of our minds is a country setting and love of simple people. Three main tendencies:

1. The discovery of the local. The picturesqueness of the strange
and remote in character, manners, speech. The charm of dialect
and interest in out-of-the-way places. This a reaction from too
much pavement and the rubbing-down of individual differences
from city contact. "Characters" are bred in isolated places. This
the dominant note in the short story from 1870 to 1900: to follow
it from Bret Harte on is almost to write a history of the short
story. It does not dominate the longer story. Constance Fenimore
Woolson.

2. The discovery of "human interest." The feeling that men in
the rough—with the bark on—may prove more interesting than
the products of an artificial civilization. This had been spread by
Dickens and by certain of the *Atlantic* writers.

3. The growing interest in realism. At first confused with the
commonplace—so Pattee in his comment on Rose Terry Cooke's
Miss Lucinda. A good deal of this earlier work is only another form

of romance—little affected by the rising French movement. Realism was to come slowly and late. All three of these made against the genteel tradition.

Henry James. His position peculiar. From his youth *déraciné*—his father hated American vulgarity, American journalism, and would not permit his son to take root. He grew up with an aristocratic conception of civilization—his sole interest lay in such civilization, and the manners of the polite society of that civilization. No other American has so hated and feared contamination from the vulgar. He was thus the last flower of the Genteel Tradition, transplanted to an environment more congenial. As the middle-class became more clamorous, he withdrew to the Continent, to England, where the older ideas still lingered. There in the spirit of the realist he wrote with refined art and persistent detachment—even to a punctilious and princely refinement. As Mr. Howells says, "To enjoy his work, to feel its rare excellence, both in conception and expression, is a brevet of intellectual good form."

His World. Always that of the spender, of assured position. His main interest lies in women; their refinement appeals to his refinement—no flappers or vulgarians but elegantly gowned women who never did the family washing. He is concerned with that which is dearest to the heart of aristocracy—standards of excellence. And in this he was true to his conception of civilization, for civilization begins after a competence has been assured. Those who are struggling to acquire have not the leisure, the inclination, for civilization. Hence *Daisy Miller* is a type of much of his work—the contrast between civilized Europe and uncivilized America, the one with standards of culture and manners and the other vulgarian. And his interest in American women results from the fact that they alone in America care for civilization and are painfully seeking to achieve it.

His Realism. The beginnings of the movement which has been called psychological realism, concerning itself with motives and processes of thought—the inner life. Developed by Bourget and far more fully by Dorothy Richardson in such a book as *Pilgrimage*, the inner life of Miriam Henderson in many volumes. Far removed from later psychological fiction founded on Freudian theory—as in D. H. Lawrence, Sherwood Anderson. Again the genteel tradition dealing with people who in the main have genteel impulses only. James held in horror this later naturalism—it was merely vulgarian

The Spirit of the Local. Into this prim world with its incipient realism came the note of the Far West: Mark Twain and Bret Harte, who set a new style—the romantic, picturesque, human-interest story. This is a part of the Pike County idea of literature—a native rogue-tale but with touches of sentiment and shortened to effective form. This followed by Eggleston's *Hoosier Schoolmaster* (1871) and this in turn by the flood of local work of the eighties. The most notable the work of Charles Egbert Craddock, Joel Chandler Harris, Sarah Orne Jewett, and Mary Wilkins. The first discovered the hill people, the second discovered the Negro—his primitive folk-poetry. In the work of the last, a struggle between the genteel tradition and realism—and the final triumph of the latter.

A CHAPTER IN AMERICAN LIBERALISM *

Liberals whose hair is growing thin and the lines of whose figures are no longer what they were, are likely to find themselves today in the unhappy predicament of being treated as mourners at their own funerals. When they pluck up heart to assert that they are not yet authentic corpses, but living men with brains in their heads, they are pretty certain to be gently chided and led back to the comfortable armchair that befits senility. Their counsel is smiled at as the chatter of a belated post-Victorian generation that knew not Freud, and if they must go abroad they are bidden take the air in the garden where other old-fashioned plants—mostly of the family *Democratici*—are still preserved. It is not pleasant for them. It is hard to be dispossessed by one's own heirs, and especially hard when those heirs, in the cheerful ignorance of youth, forget to acknowledge any obligations to a hard-working generation that laid by a very substantial body of intellectual wealth, the income from which the heirs are spending without even a "Thank you." If therefore the middle-aged liberal occasionally grows irritable and indulges in caustic comment on the wisdom of talkative young men it may be set down as the prerogative of the armchair age and lightly forgiven.

Yet in sober fact there are the solidest reasons for such irritation. The younger liberals who love to tweak the nose of democracy are too much enamored of what they find in their own mirrors. They are indisputably clever, they are spouting geysers of smart and cynical talk, they have far outrun their fathers in the free handling of ancient tribal totems—but they are afflicted with the short perspective of youth that finds a vanishing-point at the end of its own nose. There is no past for them beyond yesterday. They are having so good a time playing with ideas that it does not occur to them to question the validity of their intellectual processes or to inquire into the origins of the ideas they have adopted so blithely. Gaily engaged in smashing *bourgeois* idols, the young intellectuals are too busy to realize that it was the older generation that pro-

* This was apparently not intended as the introduction to Part I of Book Three, but covers much of the ground indicated there.—*Publisher*.

401

vided them with a hammer and pointed out the idols to be smashed.
It is the way of youth.

Middle-aged liberals—let it be said by way of defense—at least
know their history. They were brought up in a great age of liberalism—an age worthy to stand beside the golden forties of last century—and they went to school to excellent teachers. Darwin,
Spencer, Mill, Karl Marx, Haeckel, Taine, William James, Henry
George, were masters of which no school in any age need feel
ashamed; nor were such tutors and undermasters as Ruskin,
William Morris, Matthew Arnold, Lester Ward, Walt Whitman,
Henry Adams, to be dismissed as incompetent. To the solution of
the vexing problems entailed by industrialism—in America as well
as in Europe—was brought all the knowledge that had been accumulating for a century. It was a time of reëvaluations when
much substantial thinking was done; when the flood of light that
came with the doctrine of biological evolution lay brilliant on the
intellectual landscape and the dullest mind caught some of the reflection. Few of the young scholars attended the lectures of
Friedrich Nietzsche, and behavioristic psychology had not yet got
into the curriculum; but Ladd and James were inquiring curiously
into the mechanism of the brain, and animal psychology was preparing the way for the later Freudians. It was the end of an age
perhaps, the rich afterglow of the Enlightenment, but the going
down of the sun was marked by sunset skies that gave promise of
other and greater dawns.

To have spent one's youth in such a school was a liberal education. The mind opened of its own will. Intellectual horizons were
daily widening and the new perspectives ran out into cosmic spaces.
The cold from those outer spaces had not yet chilled the enthusiasms that were a heritage from the Enlightenment, and the social
idealism begotten by the democratic nature school still looked confidently to the future. They were ardent democrats—the young
liberals of the nineties—and none doubted the finality or sufficiency
of the democratic principle, any more than Mill or Spencer had
doubted it. All their history and all their biology justified it, and
the business of the times was to make it prevail in the sphere of
economics as it prevailed in the realm of the political. The cure
for the evils of democracy was held to be more democracy, and
when industrialism had been brought under its sway—when America had become an economic democracy—a just and humane civ-

ilization would be on the threshold of possibility. To the achievement of that great purpose the young liberals devoted themselves and the accomplishments of the next score of years were the work of their hands. Certain intellectuals had been democrats—Paine and Jefferson and Emerson and Thoreau and Whitman and Melville—but they were few in comparison with the skeptical Whigs who professed democracy only to bind its hands. The Republican party had not been democratic since former days — and as Henry Adams said in 1880, it was accounted foolishness to believe in it in 1880. Autocracy was a toy to distract the voting man from the business of money-getting.

It was from such a school—richer in intellectual content, one might argue, than any the younger liberals have frequented—that the ferment of twenty years ago issued; a school dedicated to the ideals of the Enlightenment and bent on carrying through the unfulfilled program of democracy. Democratic aspirations had been thwarted hitherto by the uncontrolled play of the acquisitive instinct; the immediate problem of democracy was the control of that instinct in the common interest. Economics had controlled the political state to its narrow and selfish advantage; it was for the political state to resume its sovereignty and extend its control over economics. So in the spirit of the Enlightenment the current liberalism dedicated itself to history and sociology, accepting as its immediate and particular business a reëxamination of the American past in order to forcast an ampler democratic future. It must trace the rise of political power in America in order to understand how that power had fallen into the unsocial hands of economics. The problem was difficult. American political history had been grossly distorted by partisan interpretation and political theory had been dissipated by an arid constitutionalism. The speculative thinker had long been dispossessed by the eulogist and the lawyer, both of whom had subsisted on a thin gruel of patriotic myths. Even the social historians, though dealing in materials rich in suggestion, had been diffident in the matter of interpretation, without which history is no more than the dry bones of chronicle. Inheriting no adequate philosophy of historical evolution, the young school of historians must first provide themselves with one, in the light of which the American past should take on meaning, and the partisan struggles, hitherto meaningless, should fall into comprehensible patterns.

That necessary work was to engage them for years, but in the meanwhile, as critical realists, their immediate business was with facts and the interpretation of facts. John Fiske a few years before had essayed to interpret the rise of democracy in America by analogy from biological evolution, tracing the source of American democracy to the New England town meeting, which he explained as a resurgence of ancient Teutonic folk-ways. The theory was tenuous and it was not till Professor Turner drew attention to the creative influence of the frontier on American life that the historians were provided with a suggestive working hypothesis. Before that hypothesis could be adequately explored, however, and brought into just relations to a comprehensive philosophy of history, the rise of liberalism was well under way, marked by a rich ferment of thought that made the early years of the new century singularly stimulating. That ferment resulted from pouring into the vial of native experience the reagent of European theory—examining the ways of American industrialism in the light of continental socialism; and the result was an awakening of popular interest in social control of economics, a widespread desire to bring an expanding industrialism into subjection to a rational democratic program, that was to provide abundant fuel to the social unrest that had burst forth in sporadic flames for a generation. The great movement of liberalism that took possession of the American mind after the turn of the century—a movement not unworthy to be compared with the ferment of the eighteen forties—was the spontaneous reaction of an America still only half urbanized, still clinging to ideals and ways of an older simpler America, to an industrialism that was driving its plowshare through the length and breadth of the familiar scene, turning under the rude furrows what before had been growing familiarly there. It was the first reaction of America to the revolutionary change that followed upon the exhaustion of the frontier—an attempt to secure through the political state the freedoms that before had come from unpreempted opportunity.

For a quarter of a century following the great westward expansion of the late sixties America had been drifting heedlessly towards a different social order. The shambling frontier democracy that had sufficed an earlier time was visibly breaking down in presence of the imperious power of a centralizing capitalism. The railways were a dramatic embodiment of the new machine civilization that

was running head on into a primitive social organism fashioned by
the old domestic economy, and the disruptions and confusions were
a warning that the country was in for vast changes. New masters,
new ways. The rule of the captain of industry had come. The
farmers had long been in ugly mood, but their great rebellion was
put down in 1896, and never again could they hope to wrest
sovereignty from capitalism. The formal adoption of the gold
standard in 1900 served notice to the world that America had put
away its democratic agrarianism, that a shambling Jacksonian
individualism had had its day, and that henceforth the destiny of
the country lay in the hands of its business men. Capitalism was
master of the country and though for the present it was content to
use the political machinery of democracy it was driving towards an
objective that was the negation of democracy.

The immediate reaction to so broad a shift in the course of
manifest destiny was a growing uneasiness amongst the middle
class—small business and professional men—who looked with fear
upon the program of the captains of industry. Industrialization
brought its jars and upsets. The little fish did not enjoy being
swallowed by the big, and as they watched the movement of
economic centralization encroaching on the field of competition
they saw the doors of opportunity closing to them. It was to this
great body of *petite bourgeoisie* that members of the lesser intellectuals—journalists, sociologists, reformers—were to make appeal.
The work was begun dramatically with the spectacularly advertised
Frenzied Finance, written by Thomas W. Lawson, and appearing as
a series in *McClure's Magazine* in 1903. The immense popular
success of the venture proved that the fire was ready for the fat,
and at once a host of volunteer writers fell to feeding the flames.
The new ten-cent magazines provided the necessary vehicle of
publicity, and enterprising editors were soon increasing their cir-
culations with every issue. As it became evident how popular was
the chord that had been struck, more competent workmen joined
themselves to the group of journalists: novelists—a growing army
of them—essayists, historians, political scientists, philosophers, a
host of heavy-armed troops that moved forward in a frontal
attack on the strongholds of the new plutocracy. Few writers in the
years between 1903 and 1917 escaped being drawn into the movement—an incorrigible romantic perhaps, like the young James
Branch Cabell, or a cool patrician like Edith Wharton; and with

such popular novelists as Winston Churchill, Robert Herrick, Ernest Poole, David Graham Phillips, Upton Sinclair, and Jack London embellishing the rising liberalism with dramatic heroes and villains, and dressing their salads with the wickedness of Big Business; with such political leaders as Bob La Follette and Theodore Roosevelt and Woodrow Wilson beating up the remotest villages for recruits; with such scholars as Thorstein Veblen, Charles A. Beard, and John Dewey, and such lawyers as Louis Brandeis, Frank P. Walsh, and Samuel Untermyer, the movement gathered such momentum and quickened such a ferment as had not been known before in the lands since the days of the Abolition controversy. The mind and conscience of America were stirred to their lowest sluggish stratum, and a democratic renaissance was all aglow on the eastern horizon.

At the core it was a critical realistic movement that spread quietly amongst intellectuals, but the nebulous tail of the comet blazed across the sky for all to wonder at: and it was the tail rather than the core that aroused the greatest immediate interest. Lincoln Steffens, Charles Edward Russell, Ida Tarbell, Gustavus Myers, and Upton Sinclair were read eagerly because they dealt with themes that many were interested in—the political machine, watered stock, Standard Oil, the making of great fortunes, and the like—and they invested their exposures with the dramatic interest of a detective story. Up to 1910 it was largely a muckraking movement—to borrow President Roosevelt's picturesque phrase; a time of brisk housecleaning that searched out old cobwebs and disturbed the dust that lay thick on the antiquated furniture. The Gilded Age had been slovenly and such a housecleaning was long overdue. There was a vast amount of nosing about to discover bad smells, and to sensitive noses the bad smells seemed to be everywhere. Evidently some hidden cesspool was fouling American life, and as the inquisitive plumbers tested the household drains they came upon the source of infection—not one cesspool but many, under every city hall and beneath every state capitol—dug secretly by politicians in the pay of respectable business men. It was these cesspools that were poisoning the national household, and there would be no health in America till they were filled in and no others dug.

It was a dramatic discovery and when the corruption of American politics was laid on the threshold of business—like a bastard on the doorsteps of the father—a tremendous disturbance resulted. There was a great fluttering and clamor amongst the bats and owls, an ominous creaking of the machine as the wrenches were thrown into the well-oiled wheels, and a fierce sullen anger at the hue and cry set up. To many honest Americans the years between 1903 and 1910 were abusive and scurrilous beyond decency, years when no man and no business, however honorable, was safe from the pillory; when wholesale exposure had grown profitable to sensation-mongers, and great reputations were lynched by vigilantes and reputable corporations laid under indictment at the bar of public opinion. Respectable citizens did not like to have their goodly city held up to the world as "corrupt and contented"; they did not like to have their municipal housekeeping brought into public disrepute no matter how sluttish it might be. It was not pleasant for members of great families to read a cynical history of the origins of their fortunes, or for railway presidents seeking political favors to find on the newsstand a realistic account of the bad scandals that had smirched their roads. It was worse than unpleasant, it was hurtful to business. And so quietly, and as speedily as could be done decently, the movement was brought to a stop by pressure put on the magazines that lent themselves to such harmful disclosures. Then followed a campaign of education. Responding to judicious instruction, conducted in the columns of the most respectable newspapers, the American public was soon brought to understand that it was not the muck that was harmful, but the indiscretion of those who commented in print on the bad smells. It was reckoned a notable triumph for sober and patriotic good sense.

So after a few years of amazing activity the muckraking movement came to a stop. But not before it had done its work; not before the American middle class had been indoctrinated in the elementary principles of political realism and had rediscovered the social conscience lost since the days of the Civil War. Many a totem had been thrown down by the irreverent hands of the muckrakers, and many a fetish held up to ridicule, and plutocracy in America would not recover its peace of mind until at great cost the totems should be set up again and the fetishes reanointed with the oil of sanctity. The substantial result of the movement was the instruction it afforded in the close kinship between business and politics—a lesson greatly needed by a people long fed on romantic unrealities. It did not crystallize for the popular mind in the broad principle of economic determinism; that remained for certain of the intellectuals to apply to American experience. But with its sordid object—service—it punished the flabby optimism of the Gilded Age, with its object-lessons in business politics; it revealed the hidden hand that was pulling the strings of the political puppets; it tarnished the gilding that had been carefully laid on our callous exploitation, and it brought under common suspicion the captain of industry who had risen as a national hero from the muck of individualism. It was a sharp guerilla attack on the sacred American System, but behind the thin skirmish-line lay a volunteer army that was making ready to deploy for a general engagement with plutocracy.

With the flood of light thrown upon the fundamental law by the historians, the movement of liberalism passed quickly through successive phases of thought. After the first startled surprise it set about the necessary business of acquainting the American people with its findings in the confident belief that a democratic electorate would speedily democratize the instrument. Of this first stage the late Professor J. Allen Smith's *The Spirit of American Government* (1907) was the most adequate expression, a work that greatly influenced the program of the rising Progressive Party. But changes came swiftly and within half a dozen years the movement had passed from political programs to economic, concerned not so greatly with political democracy as with economic democracy. Of this second phase Professor Beard's notable study, *An Economic Interpretation of the Constitution* (1913), was the greatest intellectual achievement. Underlying this significant work was a philosophy of politics that set it sharply apart from preceding studies—a philosophy that unsympathetic readers were quick to attribute to Karl Marx, but that in reality derived from sources far earlier and for Americans at least far more respectable. The current conception of the political state as determined in its form and activities by economic groups is no modern Marxian perversion of political theory; it goes back to Aristotle, it underlay the thinking of Harrington and Locke and the seventeenth-century English school, it shaped the conclusions of Madison and Hamilton and John Adams, it ran through all the discussions of the Constitutional Convention, and it reappeared in the arguments of Webster and Calhoun. It was the main-traveled road of political thought until a new highway was laid out by French engineers, who, disliking the bog of eco nomics, surveyed another route by way of romantic equalitarianism. The logic of the engineers was excellent, but the drift of politics is little influenced by logic, and abstract equalitarianism proved to be poor material for highway construction. In divorcing political theory from contact with sobering reality it gave it over to a treacherous romanticism. In seeking to avoid the bog of economics it ran into an arid desert.

To get back once more on the main-traveled road, to put away all profitless romanticisms and turn realist, taking up again the method of economic interpretation unused in America since the days of Webster and Calhoun, became therefore the business of the second phase of liberalism to which Professor Beard applied himself. The earlier group of liberals were ill equipped to wage successful war against plutocracy. Immersed in the traditional equalitarian philosophy, they underestimated the strength of the enemies of democracy. They did not realize what legions of Swiss Guards property can summon to its defense. They were still romantic idealists tilting at windmills, and it was to bring them to a sobering sense of reality that *The Economic Interpretation of the Constitution* was written. If property is the master force in every society one cannot understand American institutional development until one has come to understand the part property played in shaping the fundamental law. Interpreted thus the myths that had gathered about the Constitution fell away of themselves and the document was revealed as English rather than French, the judicious expression of substantial eighteenth-century realism that accepted the property basis of political action, was skeptical of romantic idealisms, and was more careful to protect title-deeds to legal holdings than to claim unsurveyed principalities in Utopia. If therefore liberalism were to accomplish any substantial results it must approach its problems in the same realistic spirit, recognizing the masterful ambitions of property, recruiting democratic forces to overmaster the Swiss Guards, leveling the strongholds that property had erected within the organic law, and taking care that no new strongholds should rise. The problem confronting liberalism was the problem of the subjection of property to social justice.

Yet interesting as was the muckraking tail of the comet, far more significant was the core—the substantial body of knowledge gathered by the scholars and flung into the scale of public opinion. The realities of the American past had been covered deep with layers of patriotic myths, provided in simpler days when the young Republic, suffering from a natural inferiority complex, was building up a defense against the acrid criticism of Tory Europe. Those myths had long since served their purpose and had become a convenient refuge for the bats and owls of the night; it was time to strip them away and apply to the past objective standards of scholarship, and to interpret it in the light of an adequate philosophy of history. To this work, so essential to any intelligent understanding of the American experiment, a group of historians and political scientists turned with competent skill, and the solid results of their labor remained after the popular ferment subsided, as a foundation for later liberals to build on.

The journalistic muckrakers had demonstrated that America was not in fact the equalitarian democracy it professed to be, and the scholars supplemented their work by tracing to its historical source the weakness of the democratic principle in governmental practice. America had never been a democracy for the sufficient reason that too many handicaps had been imposed upon the majority will. The democratic principle had been bound with withes like Samson and had become a plaything for the Philistines. From the beginning—the scholars discovered—democracy and property had been at bitter odds; the struggle invaded the Constitutional Convention, it gave form to the party alignment between Hamilton and Jefferson, Jackson and Clay, and then during the slavery struggle, sinking underground like a lost river, it nevertheless had determined party conflicts down to the present. In this ceaseless conflict between the man and the dollar, between democracy and property, the reasons for persistent triumph of property were sought in the provisions of the organic law, and from a critical study of the Constitution came a discovery that struck home like a submarine torpedo—the discovery that the drift toward plutocracy was not a drift away from the spirit of the Constitution, but an inevitable unfolding from its premises; that instead of having been conceived by the fathers as a democratic instrument, it had been conceived in a spirit designedly hostile to democracy; that it was, in fact, a carefully formulated expression of eighteenth-century property consciousness, erected as a defense against the democratic spirit that had got out of hand during the Revolution, and that the much-praised system of checks and balances was designed and intended for no other end than a check on the political power of the majority—a power acutely feared by the property consciousness of the times.

It was a startling discovery that profoundly stirred the liberal mind of the early years of the century; yet the really surprising thing is that it should have come as a surprise. It is not easy to understand today why since Civil War days intelligent Americans should so strangely have confused the Declaration of Independence and the Constitution, and have come to accept them as complementary statements of the democratic purpose of America. Their unlikeness is unmistakable: the one a classical statement of French humanitarian democracy, the other an organic law designed to safeguard the minority under republican rule. The confusion must be charged in part to the lawyers who had taken over the custodianship of the Constitution, and in part to the florid romantic temper of the middle nineteenth century. When the fierce slavery struggle fell into the past, whatever honest realism had risen from the passions of the times was buried with the dead issue. The militant attacks on the Constitution so common in Abolitionist circles after 1835, and the criticism of the Declaration that was a part of the southern argument, were both forgotten, and with the Union reestablished by force of arms, the idealistic cult of the fundamental law entered on a second youth. In the blowsy Gilded Age the old myths walked the land again, wrapped in battle-torn flags and appealing to the blood shed on southern battlefields. It was not till the advent of a generation unblinded by the passions of civil war that the Constitution again was examined critically, and the earlier charge of the Abolitionists that it was designed to serve property rather than men, was heard once more. But this time with far greater weight of evidence behind it. As the historians dug amongst the contemporary records they came upon a mass of fact the Abolitionists had been unaware of. The evidence was written so plainly, in such explicit and incontrovertible words— not only in *Elliott's Debates*, but in the minutes of the several State Conventions, in contemporary letters and memoirs, in newspapers and pamphlets and polite literature—that it seemed incredible that honest men could have erred so greatly in confusing the Constitution with the Declaration.

With the clarification of its philosophy the inflowing waters of liberalism reached flood-tide; the movement would either recede or pass over into radicalism. On the whole it followed the latter course, and the years immediately preceding 1917 were years when American intellectuals were immersing themselves in European collectivistic philosophies—in Marxianism, Fabianism, Syndicalism, Guild Socialism. New leaders were rising, philosophical analysts like Thorstein Veblen who were mordant critics of American economics. The influence of socialism was fast sweeping away the last shreds of political and social romanticism that so long had confused American thinking. The doctrine of economic determinism was spreading widely, and in the light of that doctrine the deep significance of the industrial revolution was revealing itself for the first time to thoughtful Americans. In its reaction to industrialism America had reached the point Chartist England had reached in the eighteen-forties and Marxian Germany in the eighteen-seventies. That was before a mechanistic science had laid its heavy discouragements on the drafters of democratic programs. Accepting the principle of economic determinism, liberalism still clung to its older democratic teleology, convinced that somehow economic determinism would turn out to be a fairy godmother to the proletariat and that from the imperious drift of industrial expansion must eventually issue social justice. Armed with this faith liberalism threw itself into the work of cleaning the Augean stables, and its reward came in the achievements of President Wilson's first administration.

Then the war intervened and the green fields shriveled in an afternoon. With the cynicism that came with post-war days the democratic liberalism of 1917 was thrown away like an empty whiskey-flask. Clever young men began to make merry over democracy. It was preposterous, they said, to concern oneself about social justice; nobody wants social justice. The first want of every man, as John Adams remarked a hundred years ago, is his dinner, and the second his girl. Out of the muck of the war had come a great discovery—so it was reported—the discovery that psychology as well as economics has its word to say on politics. From the army intelligence tests the moron emerged as a singular commentary on our American democracy, and with the discovery of the moron the democratic principle was in for a slashing attack. Almost overnight an army of enemies was marshaled against it. The eugenist with his isolated germ theory flouted the perfectional psychology of John Locke, with its emphasis on environment as the determining factor in social evolution—a psychology on which the whole idealistic interpretation was founded; the beardless philosopher discovered Nietzsche and in his pages found the fit master of the moron—the biological aristocrat who is the flower that every civilization struggles to produce; the satirist discovered the flatulent reality that is middle-class America and was eager to thrust his jibes at the complacent denizens of the Valley of Democracy. Only the behaviorist, with his insistence on the plasticity of the new-born child, offers some shreds of comfort to the democrat; but he quickly takes them away again with his simplification of conduct to imperious drives that stamp men as primitive animals. If the mass—the raw materials of democracy—never rises much above sex appeals and belly needs, surely it is poor stuff to try to work up into an excellent civilization, and the dreams of the social idealist who forecasts a glorious democratic future are about as substantial as moonshine. It is a discouraging essay. Yet it is perhaps conceivable that our current philosophy—the brilliant coruscations of our younger intelligentsia—may indeed not prove to be the last word in social philosophy. Perhaps—is this lèse-majesté—when our youngest liberals have themselves come to the armchair age they will be smiled at in turn by sons who are still cleverer and who will find their wisdom as foolish as the wisdom of 1917 seems to them today. But that lies on the knees of the gods.

BIBLIOGRAPHY

[Professor Parrington left no bibliography apart from the works mentioned in the text. It has been possible to formulate one with some certainty by reference to his personal library, theses written under his supervision, and the record of the books he borrowed from the University of Washington Library. In the two earlier volumes the bibliography is rigidly selective. Needless to say, I have not presumed such knowledge of his intentions. All the pertinent material which it is known that he used is included.—E. H. EBY.]

BOOK I: PART I

I. THE AMERICAN SCENE. For history of the period see Allan Nevins, *The Emergence of Modern America, 1865–1878* (in the series *A History of American Life*, Vol. VIII, New York, 1927); E. P. Oberholtzer, *History of the United States since the Civil War* (3 vols., New York, 1917–1926); Frederick L. Paxson, *Recent History of the United States* (Boston and New York, c. 1921).

For economic backgrounds see Harold Underwood Faulkner, *American Economic History* (New York and London, 1924); Gustavus Meyers, *History of Great American Fortunes* (3 vols., Chicago, 1910); Robert Irving Warshaw, *Jay Gould: The Story of a Fortune* (New York, 1928); and for the part played by railroads see John P. Davis, *The Union Pacific Railway* (New York, 1894); C. E. Russell, *Stories of Great Railroads* (Chicago, 1912); and Charles Francis Adams, Jr., and Henry Adams, *Chapters of Erie and Other Essays* (Boston, 1871).

For political corruption see Don Carlos Seitz, *The Dreadful Decade* (Indianapolis, 1926); and Denis Tilden Lynch, *"Boss" Tweed: The Story of a Grim Generation* (New York, 1927).

For journalism see Allan Nevins, *The Evening Post: A Century of Journalism* (New York, c. 1922); and Frank M. O'Brien, *The Story of the Sun* (New York, c. 1918).

General Ulysses S. Grant, *Personal Memoirs* (2 vols., New York, 1885–1886). For biography see W. E. Woodward, *Meet General Grant* (New York, 1928).

Jay Cooke. See E. P. Oberholtzer, *Jay Cooke, Financier of the Civil War* (2 vols. Philadelphia, c. 1907).

Charles A. Dana, *Recollections of the Civil War* (New York, 1902); J. H. Wilson, *Life of Charles A. Dana* (New York, 1907).

II. THE CULTURE OF THE SEVENTIES. For valuable sidelights on culture in the decade see Constance Mayfield Rourke, *Trumpets of Jubilee* (New York, c. 1927); Paxton Hibben, *Henry Ward Beecher: An American Portrait* (New York, c. 1927); Horace Greeley, *Recollections of a Busy Life* (New York, 1868); James Parton, *The Life of Horace Greeley* (Boston, c. 1896); Lewis Mumford, *The Golden Day: A Study in American Experience and Culture* (New York, 1926); and his *Sticks and Stones, A Study of American Architecture and Civilization* (New York, c. 1924).

For history of literature see Fred Lewis Pattee, *A History of American Literature since 1870* (New York, 1915); his *Sidelights on American Literature*

(New York, 1922); his *The Development of the American Short Story* (New York and London, 1923); and Carl Van Doren, *The American Novel* (New York, 1921).

Thomas Bailey Aldrich, *Prose Works* (7 vols., Boston, 1897); *The Poems of Thomas Bailey Aldrich* (2 vols., Boston, c. 1907). For his life see Ferris Greenslet, *The Life of Thomas Bailey Aldrich* (Boston and New York, 1908).

Mrs. Elizabeth Stuart Ward (Phelps), *The Silent Partner* (Boston, c. 1899); *A Singular Life* (Boston and New York, 1899); *Chapters from a Life* (Boston and New York, 1896).

Sarah Orne Jewett, *A Country Doctor* (Boston and New York, c. 1884); *A Native of Winby and Other Tales* (Boston and New York, c. 1893); *Deephaven* (Boston and New York, 1894). *Tales of New England* (Boston and New York, 1894); *The Life of Nancy* (Boston and New York, 1895); *The Queen's Twin and Other Stories* (Boston and New York, 1899); *The Country of Pointed Firs* (Boston and New York, c. 1910). For her life see *The Letters of Sarah Orne Jewett* (Boston and New York, 1911).

Mrs. Mary E. (Wilkins) Freeman, *A Humble Romance, and Other Stories* (New York, 1887); *The New England Nun, and Other Stories* (New York, 1891); *The Pot of Gold, and Other Stories* (Boston, c. 1892); *Pembroke; a Novel* (New York, c. 1894); *People of Our Neighborhood* (New York, 1901); *The Portion of Labor* (New York, c. 1901). *Young Lucretia, and Other Stories* (New York, 1903); *By the Light of the Soul* (New York and London, 1907).

Walt Whitman, *Leaves of Grass* (Inclusive edition edited by Emory Holloway, Garden City, New York, 1927); *The Complete Prose Works of Walt Whitman* (New York, 1898); *The Half-breed and Other Stories* (New York, 1927); *Autobiographia: or, the Story of a Life* (New York, 1892); *The Gathering of Forces* (New York and London, 1920); and *The Uncollected Poetry and Prose of Walt Whitman* (2 vols., Garden City, New York, 1921). For Whitman's life see Horace Traubel, *With Walt Whitman in Camden* (3 vols., New York, 1908–1914); Emory Holloway, *Whitman* (New York, 1926); John Addington Symonds, *Walt Whitman: a Study* (London, 1893); Léon Bazalgette, *Walt Whitman, the Man and his Work* (Garden City, New York, 1920); John Burroughs, *Whitman: a Study* (Boston and New York, c. 1924); Bliss Perry, *Walt Whitman: his Life and Work* (Boston and New York, 1906); and J. Johnston, M. D., and J. W. Wallace, *Visits to Walt Whitman* (New York, 1918).

For critical studies of his work see Norman Foerster, *American Criticism*, pp. 157–222 (New York, 1928); Basil De Selincourt, *Walt Whitman; a Critical Study* (London, 1914); Horace Traubel (ed.), *In re Walt Whitman* (Philadelphia, 1893).

Samuel Langhorne Clemens (Mark Twain), *The Writings of Mark Twain* (25 vols., New York and London, c. 1910–1911); *The Mysterious Stranger, and Other Stories* (New York and London, 1922); *What is Man?* (New York, 1917).

For his life see *Mark Twain's Autobiography* (New York and London, 1924); Albert Bigelow Paine, *Mark Twain, a Biography* (3 vols. New York, c. 1912); Van Wyck Brooks, *The Ordeal of Mark Twain* (New York, c. 1920); W. D. Howells, *My Mark Twain* (New York, c. 1910).

III. CHANGING THEORY. For a general history of economic theory see, Charles Gide and Charles Rist, *A History of Economic Doctrines from the Time of the Physiocrats to the Present Day* (Authorized translation from the second revised and augmented edition of 1913, Boston, New York, Chicago,

1913); *The Trend of Economics* (Edited by R. G. Tugwell, New York, 1924).

For material covered in this section see Francis Wayland, *Elements of Political Economy* (New York, 1837); Henry Charles Carey, *Principles of Social Science* (3 vols., Philadelphia, 1858–1860); his *The Harmony of Interests: Agricultural, Manufacturing, and Commercial* (2nd ed., New York, 1852); and his *Miscellaneous Works* (Philadelphia, 1875). Francis A. Walker, *The Wages Question, a Treatise on Wages and the Wages Class* (New York, 1891); his *Land and Its Rent* (Boston, 1891); and his *Political Economy* (New York, 1888).

For a general treatment of political theories see William A. Dunning, *A History of Political Theories from Rousseau to Spencer* (New York, 1920); Charles E. Merriam, *History of American Political Theories* (New York, 1920); and his *American Political Ideas: Studies in the Development of American Political Thought, 1865–1917* (New York, 1920).

Theodore Dwight Woolsey, *Political Science: or, the State Theoretically and Practically Considered* (New York, 1900); and his *Communism and Socialism in Their History and Theory* (New York, 1894).

John W. Burgess. *Political Science and Comparative Constitutional Law* (2 vols., Boston and London, 1896–1898); and his *The Sanctity of the Law: Wherein Does It Consist?* (Boston and New York, c. 1927).

J. Allen Smith, *The Growth and Decadence of Constitutional Government* (New York, 1930) is an invaluable aid to those wishing to get Parrington's viewpoint in political theory.

Henry George, *The Writings of Henry George* (Memorial edition, 10 vols., New York, 1898–1900). See particularly *Progress and Poverty* (Vols. I and II), and Henry George, Jr., *The Life of Henry George* (Vol. X).

Henry D. Lloyd, *Wealth Against Commonwealth* (New York, c. 1894); *Lords of Industry* (New York and London, 1910); *Man the Social Creator* (New York, 1906); *Strike of Millionaires Against Miners, or the Story of Spring Valley, with an Open Letter to Millionaires* (Chicago, 1890). For his life see Caroline Augusta Lloyd, *Henry Demarest Lloyd, 1847–1903* (2 vols., New York and London, 1912). (Parrington had intended to discuss Lloyd.)

IV. THE BEGINNINGS OF CRITICISM. Wendell Phillips, *Speeches, Lectures, and Letters* (2 vols., Boston, 1891–1892). For his life see Carlos Martyn, *Wendell Phillips, the Agitator* (Revised ed., New York, 1890); and Charles Edward Russell, *The Story of Wendell Phillips* (Chicago, c. 1914).

George William Curtis, *Nile Notes of a Howadji* (New York, 1851); *Trumps* (New York, 1861); *Potiphar Papers* (New York, 1854); *Prue and I* (New York, n. d.); *Orations and Addresses* (3 vols., New York, 1894); *From the Easy Chair* (3 vols., New York, 1894–1902); *Early Letters of George William Curtis to John S. Dwight; Brook Farm and Concord* (New York and London, 1898). For his life see Edward Cary, *George William Curtis* (Boston and New York, 1894).

Edwin Lawrence Godkin, *Reflections and Comments, 1865–1895* (New York, 1895); *Unforseen Tendencies of Democracy* (Boston, 1893); *Problems of Modern Democracy; Political and Economic Essays* (Third ed., New York, 1898). For his life see, *The Life and Letters of Edwin Lawrence Godkin* (Ed. by Rollo Ogden, 2 vols., New York and London, 1907). See also Gustav Pollak, *The Nation, Fifty Years of American Idealism: the New York Nation, 1865–1915* (New York, 1915).

The political novel: Mark Twain and Charles Dudley Warner, *The Gilded Age* (2 vols., New York, 1873); Henry Adams, *Democracy* (New York,

1880); F. Marion Crawford, *An American Politician* (New York, 1884).
See also Albion W. Tourgee, *A Fool's Errand* (New York, 1880).

The economic novel: John Hay, *The Bread-Winners* (New York, 1883); H. F.
Keenan, *The Moneymakers* (New York, 1885).

The sociological novel: Hjalmar Hjorth Boyessen, *The Mammon of Unright-
eousness* (New York, 1891); his *The Golden Calf* (New York, 1892); and his
Social Strugglers (New York, 1893); Robert Grant, *Unleavened Bread* (New
York, 1900); Samuel Merwin and H. K. Webster, *Calumet K* (New York,
1901); and their *Short Line War* (New York, 1899). Francis Churchill
Williams, *J. Develin-Boss* (New York, 1901); Elliot Flower, *The Spoilsman*
(Boston, 1903); Winston Churchill, *Coniston* (New York, 1907); and his
Mr. Crewe's Career (New York, 1908); Will Payne, *Mr. Salt* (Boston and
New York, 1903); and his *The Money Captain* (New York, 1898).

For general accounts see Carl Van Doren, *The American Novel* (New York,
1921); Fred Lewis Pattee, *A History of American Literature since 1870*
(New York, 1915); John Curtis Underwood, *Literature and Insurgency*
(New York, 1914); and W. D. Howells, *Criticism and Fiction* (New
York, 1891).

For material dealing with Henry Adams and John Hay see William Roscoe
Thayer, *The Life and Letters of John Hay* (2 vols., Boston and New York,
c. 1915). See also the bibliography on Henry Adams, Part II, section II.

BOOK I: PART II

I. DISINTEGRATION AND REINTEGRATION. For a general survey of philosophical
thought during the period see W. H. Hudson, *Philosophies Ancient and
Modern* (London, 1908); Woodbridge Riley, *American Thought from Puritanism to Pragmatism* (New York, 1915); William Archibald Dunning,
A History of Political Theories from Rousseau to Spencer (New York, 1920).

Condorcet, Isidore, August Marie François Xavier, *Ouvres* (Paris, 1847).
See also *A General View of Positivism* (Translated by H. J. Bridges, London,
c. 1908).

Herbert Spencer, *Works* (18 vols., New York, 1915); see also his *Illustrations
of Universal Progress; a Series of Discussions* (New York, 1890).

Ernst Heinrich Haeckel, *The Riddle of the Universe at the Close of the Nineteenth Century* (New York and London, 1900); and his *History of Creation*
(2 vols., New York, 1914).

John Fiske, *American Political Ideas, Viewed from the Standpoint of Universal History* (New York, 1899); *Darwinism and Other Essays* (New ed.
rev. and enl., Boston, 1892); *The Destiny of Man, Viewed in the Light of his
Origin* (18 ed., Boston and New York, 1892); *Essays Historical and Literary*
(2 vols., New York and London, 1902); *Excursions of an Evolutionist*
(Boston and New York, 1892); *The Idea of God as Affected by Modern Knowledge* (Boston and New York, 1892); *Life Everlasting* (Boston and New York,
1902); *Outlines of Cosmic Philosophy, Based on the Doctrine of Evolution,
with Criticisms of the Positive Philosophy* (4 vols., Boston and New York,
c. 1903); *Through Nature to God* (Boston and New York, 1899); *Unseen
World and Other Essays* (11th ed., Boston, 1876). For his life see J. S.
Clark, *Life and Letters of John Fiske* (2 vols., Boston, 1917); and Henry
Holt, *Garrulities of an Octogenarian Editor, with Other Essays Somewhat
Biographical and Autobiographical* (Boston and New York, 1923).

II. THE SKEPTICISMS OF THE HOUSE OF ADAMS. Henry Adams, *The Degredation
of the Democratic Dogma* (New York, 1020); *Democracy, a Novel* (New

York, 1880); *The Education of Henry Adams* (New York, 1918); *History of the United States during the Administration of Jefferson and Madison* (9 vols., New York, 1890–1898); *John Randolph* (Boston, 1895); *Letters to a Niece and Prayer to the Virgin of Chartres; with a Niece's Memoirs by Mabel La Farge* (Boston and New York, 1920); *Life of Albert Gallatin* (Philadelphia, 1880); *Mont-Saint-Michel and Chartres* (Boston and New York, 1913).

Brooks Adams, *America's Economic Supremacy* (New York, 1900); *Law of Civilization and Decay: an Essay on History* (New York, 1895); *The New Empire* (New York, London, 1902); *The Theory of Social Revolutions* (New York, 1913).

Charles Francis Adams, Jr., and Henry Adams, *Chapters of Erie and Other Essays* (Boston, 1871); Charles Francis Adams, Jr., *Charles Francis Adams 1835–1915; an Autobiography* (Boston and New York, 1916). See also W. C. Ford, *A Cycle of Adams Letters, 1861–1865* (2 vols., Boston and New York, 1920).

III. VICTORIAN REALISM. For material in Parrington's introduction to Chapter III see Francis Marion Crawford, *The Novel: What It Is* (New York, 1908); and H. H. Boyessen, *Literary and Social Silhouettes* (New York, 1894).

Henry James, *The Novels and Tales of Henry James* (24 vols., New York, 1907–1909); *Views and Reviews* (Boston, 1908); *The Letters of Henry James* (2 vols., New York, 1920). For criticism and biography see Pelham Edgar, *Henry James, Man and Author* (Boston and New York, 1927); Rebecca West, *Henry James* (New York, c. 1916); Van Wyck Brooks, *The Pilgrimage of Henry James* (New York, 1925).

William Dean Howells, *A Hazard of New Fortunes* (New York, 1891); *A Modern Instance* (Boston and New York, 1881); *Through the Eye of the Needle* (New York and London, 1907); *A Traveler from Altruria* (New York, 1908); *The Rise of Silas Lapham* (Boston, c. 1912); *April Hopes* (New York, 1888); *Certain Delightful English Towns; with Glimpses of the Pleasant Country Between* (New York and London, 1906); *Indian Summer* (Boston, c. 1914); *Venetian Life* (19th ed., new and enl., Boston, c. 1907); *Criticism and Fiction* (New York, 1891); *Literary Friends and Acquaintance* (New York and London, 1901); *Literature and Life* (New York and London, 1902); *My Literary Passions* (New York, c. 1895). For his life see *Life in Letters of William Dean Howells* (2 vols., Garden City, N. Y., 1928); *Years of My Youth* (New York, c. 1916). For critical estimates see Delmar Gross Cooke, *William Dean Howells; a Critical Study* (New York, c. 1922); Oscar W. Firkins, *William Dean Howells* (Cambridge, Mass., 1924); Alexander Harvey, *William Dean Howells; a Study of the Achievement of a Literary Artist* (New York, 1917).

BOOK II: PART I

I. THE PLIGHT OF THE FARMER. For general surveys of the Agrarian movement see Solon Justus Buck, *The Granger Movement* (In *Harvard Historical Studies*, Vol. XIX, Cambridge, 1913); and his *The Agrarian Crusade* (New Haven, c. 1920); F. E. Haynes, *Third Party Movements since the Civil War* (Iowa City, Iowa, c. 1916); F. J. Turner, *The Frontier in American History* (New York, 1920).

For discussions of the currency see *Homo's Letters on a National Currency* (Washington, 1817); *Currency Explosions, their Cause and Cure* (New York, 1858); *Our Currency: Some of Its Evils, and the Remedies for Them* (By a Citizen of North Carolina, Raleigh, N. C., 1861); D. H. Robertson, *Money*

(New York, c. 1922); J. Lawrence Laughlin, *The Principles of Money*, (New York, 1911).

David Ames Wells, *Practical Economics; a Collection of Essays Respecting Certain of the Recent Economic Experiences of the United States* (New York, 1885); *Robinson Crusoe's Money* (New ed. New York, 1896); *The Cremation Theory of Specie Resumption* (New York, 1875); *Contraction of Legal Tender Notes vs. Repudiation and Disloyalty* (New York, 1876).

Eleazar Lord, *Credit, Currency and Banking* (New York, 1828); *A Letter on the National Currency* (New York, 1861); *Six Letters on the Necessity and Practicability of the National Currency, etc.* (New York, 1862); *National Currency: A Review of the National Banking Law* (New York, 1863).

Peter Cooper, *Ideas for a Science of Good Government* (New York, 1883); *The Political and Financial Opinions of Peter Cooper* (New York, 1877).

William Hope Harvey, *Coin's Financial School* (Chicago, c. 1894); and J. A. Woodburn, *The Life of Thaddeus Stevens* (Indianapolis, c. 1913.)

III. HAMLIN GARLAND AND THE MIDDLE BORDER. For studies of the Middle Border see D. A. Dondore, *The Prairie and the Making of Middle America: Four Centuries of Description* (Cedar Rapids, Iowa, 1926); Lucy Lockwood Hazard, *The Frontier in American Literature* (New York, 1927).

For early realism of the Middle Border see Harold Frederick, *Seth's Brother's Wife* (London, 1898); and Joseph Kirkland, *Zury: The Meanest Man in Spring County* (Boston and New York, 1887).

Hamlin Garland, *Back-Trailers from the Middle Border* (New York, 1928); *Boy Life on the Prairie* (Revised ed., New York and London, c. 1899); *The Captain of the Gray Horse Troop: a Novel* (New York, c. 1902); *Crumbling Idols* (Chicago, 1894); *A Daughter of the Middle Border* (New York, 1921); *The Eagle's Heart* (New York, 1900); *Jason Edwards, An Average Man* (New York, 1897); *Main-Travelled Roads* (New York, c. 1891); *Her Mountain Lover* (New York, 1901); *Prairie Folk* (New and rev. ed., New York, 1899); *Rose of Dutcher's Cooly* (New York, c. 1899); *A Son of the Middle Border* (New York, 1917); *A Spoil of Office* (New York, 1897); *Trailmakers of the Middle Border* (New York, 1926).

BOOK II: PART II

II. THE QUEST OF UTOPIA. Edward Bellamy, *The Duke of Stockbridge; a Romance of Shay's Rebellion* (New York and Boston, 1901); *Equality* (3d ed., New York, 1897); *Looking Backward, 2000–1887* (Boston, c. 1889); see also *The Nationalist, a Monthly Magazine* (Vols. 1–3, May, 1889, to April, 1891. Edited by H. W. Austin).

For general material see Allyn B. Forbes, *The Literary Quest for Utopia, 1880–1900* (*Social Forces*, Vol. VII, 1927, pp. 179–189). Lewis Mumford, *The Story of Utopias* (New York, c. 1922); J. O. Hertzler, *The History of Utopian Thought* (New York, 1923).

INDEX

421

Q
R 5
S 6
T 7
U 8
V 9
W 0
X 1